DRUGS AND SOCIETY

ELEVENTH EDITION

Glen R. Hanson

Professor, Department of Pharmacology and Toxicology
Director, Utah Addiction Center
University of Utah
Salt Lake City, Utah
Senior Advisor, National Institute on Drug Abuse

Peter J. Venturelli

Chair and Associate Professor, Department of Sociology and Criminology
Valparaiso University
Valparaiso, Indiana

Annette E. Fleckenstein

Professor, Department of Pharmacology and Toxicology
University of Utah
Salt Lake City, Utah

JONES & BARTLETT
LEARNING

World Headquarters
Jones & Bartlett Learning
5 Wall Street
Burlington, MA 01803
978-443-5000
info@jblearning.com
www.jblearning.com

Jones & Bartlett Learning books and products are available through most bookstores and online booksellers. To contact Jones & Bartlett Learning directly, call 800-832-0034, fax 978-443-8000, or visit our website, www.jblearning.com.

Substantial discounts on bulk quantities of Jones & Bartlett Learning publications are available to corporations, professional associations, and other qualified organizations. For details and specific discount information, contact the special sales department at Jones & Bartlett Learning via the above contact information or send an email to specialsales@jblearning.com.

Some images in this book feature models. These models do not necessarily endorse, represent, or participate in the activities represented in the images.

Production Credits

Chief Executive Officer: Ty Field
President: James Homer
SVP, Chief Operating Officer: Don Jones, Jr.
SVP, Chief Technology Officer: Dean Fossella
SVP, Chief Marketing Officer: Alison M. Pendergast
SVP, Chief Financial Officer: Ruth Siporin
Publisher, Higher Education: Cathleen Sether
Senior Acquisitions Editor: Shoshanna Goldberg
Senior Associate Editor: Amy L. Bloom
Editorial Assistant: Prima Bartlett
Production Manager: Julie Champagne Bolduc
Production Editor: Jessica Steele Newfell
Associate Marketing Manager: Jody Sullivan
VP, Manufacturing and Inventory Control: Therese Connell
Composition: Circle Graphics
Cover Design: Scott Moden
Photo Researcher: Sarah Cebulski
Cover Image: © DENKOU Images GMBH/age fotostock
Printing and Binding: Courier Kendallville
Cover Printing: Courier Kendallville

Library of Congress Cataloging-in-Publication Data

Hanson, Glen (Glen R.)
    Drugs and society / Glen R. Hanson, Peter J. Venturelli, Annette E. Fleckenstein. — 11th ed.
       p. ; cm.
    Includes bibliographical references and index.
    ISBN 978-1-4496-1369-3 (pbk. : alk. paper)
  1. Drugs. 2. Drugs—Toxicology. 3. Drug abuse. I. Venturelli, Peter J. II. Fleckenstein, Annette E.
III. Title.
    [DNLM: 1. Substance-Related Disorders. WM 270]
    RM301.W58 2012
    362.29—dc22

                                    2011008302

6048

Printed in the United States of America
15 14 13 12   10 9 8 7 6 5 4

BRIEF CONTENTS

CONTENTS

CHAPTER 9

CHAPTER 10

CHAPTER 11

FEATURE CONTENTS

SPECIAL FEATURES

PREFACE

The *Eleventh Edition* of *Drugs and Society* is intended to convey to students the impact of drug use and/or abuse on the lives of ordinary people. The authors have combined their expertise in the fields of drug abuse, pharmacology, and sociology with their extensive experiences in research, treatment, teaching, drug policy-making, and drug policy implementation to create an edition that reflects the most current information and understanding relative to drug abuse issues available in a textbook.

Drugs and Society, Eleventh Edition, is an exceptionally comprehensive text on drug use and drug-related problems. This book is written on a personal level and directly addresses college students by incorporating individual drug use and abuse experiences as well as personal and institutional perspectives. Many chapters include excerpts from personal experiences with recreational drug users, habitual (often addicted) drug users, and former drug users. Students will find these personal accounts both insightful and interesting. This approach—implemented in response to suggestions from readers, students, and instructors—makes *Drugs and Society* truly unique. In addition, this revised edition includes special discussions on the genetics of drug abuse and addiction and up-to-date information on the reasons for and consequences of the recent surge in prescription abuse.

Drugs and Society instructs university students studying a range of disciplines to gain a realistic perspective of drug-related problems in our society. Students in nursing, physical education and other health sciences, psychology, social work, and sociology will find that our text provides useful current information and perspectives to help them understand these critical issues:

- Social, psychological, and biological reasons why drug use and abuse occurs
- The results of drug use and abuse
- How to prevent and treat drug use and abuse
- How drugs/medications can be used effectively for therapeutic purposes

To achieve this goal, we have presented the most current and authoritative views on drug abuse in an objective and easily understood manner. Approximately one-third of the references are updated to reflect the new information. To help students appreciate the multifaceted nature of drug-related problems, the *Eleventh Edition* exposes the issues from pharmacological, neurobiological, psychological, and sociological perspectives. Besides including the most current information concerning drug use and abuse topics, each chapter includes updated and helpful learning aids for students:

- **Holding the Line**: Vignettes that help readers assess governmental efforts to deal with drug-related problems.
- **Case in Point**: Examples of relevant clinical issues that arise from the use of each major group of drugs.
- **Here and Now**: Current events that illustrate the personal and social consequences of drug abuse.
- **Family Matters**: Examples of how genetics and heredity contribute to drug abuse and its issues.
- **Prescription for Abuse**: Current stories that illustrate the problems of prescription abuse and its consequences.
- **Point/Counterpoint**: Features that expose students to different perspectives on drug-related issues and encourage them to draw their own conclusions.
- **Highlighted definitions**: Definitions of new terminology are conveniently located on the same page as their discussion in the text.
- **Learning objectives**: Goals for learning are listed at the beginning of each chapter to help students identify the principal concepts being taught.
- **Summary statements**: Concise summaries found at the end of each chapter correlate with the learning objectives.
- **Chapter questions**: Provocative questions at the end of each chapter encourage students to discuss, ponder, and critically analyze their own feelings and biases about the information presented in the book.
- **Concise and well-organized tables and figures**: Updated features found throughout the book present the latest information in an easy to understand format.
- **Color photographs and illustrations**: These additions graphically illustrate important concepts

and facilitate comprehension as well as retention of information.

Because of these updated features, we believe that this edition of *Drugs and Society* is much more "user friendly" than previous editions, has the most current and accurate information available in a textbook, and will encourage student motivation and learning.

Drugs and Society, Eleventh Edition, includes updated statistics and current examples of the key principles being taught in this text. The new topical coverage includes discussion of:

- The current status of prescription abuse, including opiate painkillers, stimulants (e.g., performance-enhancers), and the CNS sedative/hypnotics
- Details on public advertising of prescription products and the resulting consumer controversy
- The most recent information on the personal and social consequences of methamphetamine and narcotic analgesics problems
- The latest status of over-the-counter (OTC) stimulants and decongestants as well as abuse of other OTC products
- Updated data on abuse levels in young people
- Current topics such as steroids in baseball, OxyContin, restrictions on pain pills, and heroin potency
- The latest information on HIV/AIDS impact, especially in drug abusers
- Risk factors and protective factors for drug abuse
- The most recent information on alcohol problems in young people and college students
- Survey data from the "National Household Survey" (National Survey on Drug Use and Health) and "Monitoring the Future"

Chapter Breakdown

The material in the text encompasses biomedical, sociological, and social-psychological views. **Chapter 1** provides a helpful overview: the current dimensions of drug use (statistics and trends) and the most common currently abused drugs. **Chapter 2** comprehensively explains addiction and drug use and abuse from multidisciplinary and theoretical standpoints, and the latest biological, psychological, social-psychological, and sociological perspectives are explained. **Chapter 3** discusses how the law deals with drug use and abuse of both licit (alcohol, over-the-counter, and prescription) and illicit (marijuana, hallucinogens, and cocaine) drugs.

Chapter 4 helps students understand the basic biochemical operations of the nervous and endocrine systems and explains how psychoactive drugs and anabolic steroids alter such functions. **Chapter 5** instructs students about the factors that determine how drugs affect the body. This chapter also details the physiological and psychological variables that determine how and why people respond to drugs used for therapeutic and recreational purposes.

Chapters 6 through 14 focus on specific drug groups that are commonly abused in the United States. Those drugs that depress brain activity are discussed in **Chapter 6** (sedative-hypnotic agents), **Chapters 7 and 8** (alcohol), and **Chapter 9** (opioid narcotics). Drugs that stimulate brain activity are covered in **Chapter 10** (amphetamines, cocaine, and caffeine) and **Chapter 11** (tobacco and nicotine). The last major category of substances of abuse is hallucinogens, which are psychedelics that can alter the senses and create hallucinatory and/or distorted experiences. These substances are discussed in **Chapter 12** (hallucinogens such as LSD, mescaline, Ecstasy, and PCP) and **Chapter 13** (marijuana). **Chapter 14** discusses inhalants, substances that are particularly popular among youth.

Although most drugs that are abused cause more than one effect (for example, cocaine can be a stimulant and have some hallucinatory properties), the classification we have chosen for this text is frequently used by experts and pharmacologists in the drug abuse field and is based on the most likely drug effect. All of the chapters in this section are similarly organized. They discuss:

- The historical origins and evolution of the agents so students can better understand society's attitudes toward, and regulation of, these drugs
- Previous and current clinical uses of these drugs to help students appreciate distinctions between therapeutic use and abuse
- Patterns of abuse and distinctive features that contribute to each drug's abuse potential
- Nonmedicinal and medicinal therapies for drug-related dependence, withdrawal, and abstinence

Chapter 15 explores the topic of drugs and therapy. Like illicit drugs, nonprescription, prescription, and herbal drugs can be misused if not understood. This chapter helps students to appreciate the uses and benefits of proper drug use as well as to recognize that licit (legalized) drugs also can be problematic. This chapter also discusses the recent surge in abuse of prescription drugs such as opioid painkillers, stimulants and CNS depressants and how to mitigate this problem.

Chapter 16 explores drug use in several major subcultures of special populations: sports/athletics, women, adolescents, college students, HIV-positive people, and entertainment. Included in this chapter is a discussion of new media "electronic" drug subcultures that have recently arisen.

Chapter 17 acquaints students with drug abuse prevention. This chapter focuses on the following topics: (1) the most prominent factors affecting an individual's use of drugs, (2) major types of drug prevention programs, (3) major types of drug users that must be recognized before creating a prevention program, (4) the four levels of comprehensive drug prevention programs for drug use and abuse, (5) major family factors that can affect the use of drugs, (6) primary prevention programs in higher education, (7) four recent large-scale prevention programs, and (8) two additional prevention measures that may substitute for the attraction to drug use. **Chapter 18** focuses on assessing addiction and the principles and types of drug dependence treatment.

Instructor's Aids

The ancillary package for the *Eleventh Edition* includes the most contemporary technology. For instructors who adopt this edition, an Instructor's ToolKit CD-ROM (ISBN 978-1-4496-4161-0) is available. Designed for classroom use, this CD contains PowerPoint presentations, a Test Bank, an Image and Table Bank, and Lecture Outlines. Other instructor resources, such as answers to the Student Study Guide, are available electronically. For distance learning options or additional information, call your Jones & Bartlett Learning Representative at 800-832-0034.

Student's Aids

For students using *Drugs and Society, Eleventh Edition,* a Student Study Guide is available as a print option (ISBN 978-1-4496-3437-7) and as an electronic option (ISBN 978-1-4496-3824-5), both which can be packaged with the text or purchased separately. This study guide helps students to master key concepts, new terms, and critical issues.

A companion website, **http://go.jblearning.com/hanson11/**, offers students practical learning and studying tools, including Web links, practice quizzes, animated flashcards, crossword puzzles, and an interactive glossary.

ACKNOWLEDGMENTS

The many improvements that make this the best edition of the *Drugs and Society* series yet could not have occurred without the hard work and dedication of numerous people.

We are indebted to the many reviewers who evaluated the manuscript at different stages of development. Much of the manuscript was reviewed and greatly improved by comments from:

- **R. Todd Coy, PhD**, Colby-Sawyer College
- **Maureen P. Edwards, PhD, CHES**, Montgomery College
- **Ethel Elkins, MHA, MA, LCSW, LMFT, LMHC**, University of Southern Indiana
- **Amanda S. Eymard, MSN, RN**, Nicholls State University
- **Donna E. Fletcher, PhD, LCAS, CSI**, Lenoir-Rhyne University
- **Susan A. Lyman, PhD, CHES**, University of Louisiana at Lafayette
- **Dr. Susan Milstein, CHES, CSE**, Montgomery College
- **William J. Schoen Jr., MA**, University of Colorado Denver
- **Caren L. Steinmiller, PhD**, The University of Toledo
- **John Stogner, MS**, University of Florida

The authors would like to express, once again, their gratitude for the comments and suggestions of users and reviewers of previous editions of *Drugs and Society*. They would also like to acknowledge Peter Myers for his contributions to previous editions of the text.

At their respective institutions, each of the authors would like to thank a multitude of people too numerous to list individually but who have given them invaluable assistance.

Dr. Fleckenstein acknowledges the support of her family in her participation in the preparation of this revised text. She also thanks Dr. Barbara Sullivan, University of Utah, for her expert and thoughtful suggestions for this revision.

At Valparaiso University, Professor Venturelli is very grateful to Nancy Young, associate administrator, School of Law at Valparaiso University; Linda Matera, administrative associate in the College of Arts and Sciences; and Jason Kresich, the department's student aide. Nancy and Jason continuously assisted in revising this new edition. They performed many tasks at various times throughout the revision process, including creating a number of tables and figures, searching the Web for information on drug topics, filing drug articles, and completing the other necessary "chores" for producing the latest information contained in these chapters. Professor Venturelli also thanks Jason for providing a much-needed student's perspective on the ancillary materials accompanying this *Eleventh Edition*. Jason's hard work and humor were not only appreciated but also needed, especially when deadlines had to be met. Professor Venturelli would also like to gratefully acknowledge the other students and working people who were interviewed for hours on end regarding their information, opinions, and personal use and/or experiences with drugs. Even though the final copy of revised chapters remains the author's responsibility, this edition has been *substantially* enhanced by all their efforts, loyalties, and the dedicated assistance of others, which at Jones & Bartlett Learning includes Amy Bloom, Prima Bartlett, Shoshanna Goldberg, Jess Newfell, and Sarah Cebulski. Working with these people on this edition has been productive, instructive, and rewarding.

Dr. Hanson is particularly indebted to his wife, Margaret, for her loving encouragement. Without her patience and support this endeavor would not have been possible. She reminds him that what is truly important in this world is service to our family and to each other. Also appreciated is the support of his children.

ABOUT THE AUTHORS

Dr. Glen R. Hanson, a professor in the Department of Pharmacology and Toxicology at the University of Utah and the director of the Utah Addiction Center, has researched the neurobiology of drug abuse for over 30 years and authored more than 200 scientific papers and book chapters on the subject. Dr. Hanson has lectured on drug abuse topics throughout the world. He served as the Director of the Division of Neuroscience and Behavioral Research at the National Institute on Drug Abuse (NIDA), after which he became NIDA's acting director from 2001 to 2003. He continues to serve as a NIDA senior advisor. As a component of the National Institutes of Health, NIDA is the federal agency recognized as the world's premier science organization dealing with drug abuse issues, and the agency funds 85% of the drug abuse–related research in the world. Dr. Hanson also is the Director of the Utah Addiction Center at the University of Utah, and he works with scientists, public officials, policy makers, and the general public to more effectively deal with problems of drug abuse addiction.

Dr. Peter J. Venturelli has been the coauthor of this text since the Second Edition of *Drugs and Society* in 1988. In addition to revising this text every three years, Dr. Venturelli's experiences and qualifications in academia and professional life include publishing research in drug and ethnic anthologies, other drug texts, and scholarly journals; authoring more than 43 conference papers at national professional sociological meetings; serving in elected and administrative positions in professional drug research associations; receiving several research grants involving drug use and ethnicity; authoring the latest drug research in sociological encyclopedias; and teaching of undergraduate and graduate students full-time for the past 25 years.

Dr. Annette E. Fleckenstein is a professor in the Department of Pharmacology and Toxicology at the University of Utah. She has researched the neurobiology of substance abuse for over 15 years, lectured on drug abuse topics throughout the United States and abroad, and authored more than 90 scientific papers and book chapters on the subject. She continues to lecture to undergraduate, graduate, and professional students.

CHAPTER 1

Introduction to Drugs and Society

Learning ◎bjectives

On completing this chapter you will be able to:

◎ Explain how drug use is affected by biological, genetic, and pharmacological factors as well as cultural, social, and contextual factors.

◎ Develop a basic understanding of drug use and abuse.

◎ Explain when drugs were first used and under what circumstances.

◎ Indicate how widespread drug use is and who the potential drug abusers are.

◎ List four reasons why drugs are used.

◎ Rank in descending order, from most common to least, the most commonly used licit and illicit drugs.

◎ Name three types of drug users, and explain how they differ.

◎ Describe how the mass media promote drug use.

◎ Explain when drug use leads to abuse.

◎ List and explain the stages of drug dependence.

◎ List the major findings regarding drugs and crime.

◎ Define employee assistance programs and explain their role in resolving productivity problems.

◎ Explain the holistic self-awareness approach.

Drugs and Society Online is a great source for additional drugs and society information for both students and instructors. Visit **go.jblearning.com/hanson11** to find a variety of useful tools for learning, thinking, and teaching.

Did You Know?

○ The popular use of legal drugs, particularly alcohol and tobacco, has caused far more deaths, sickness, violent crimes, economic loss, and other social problems than the use of all illegal drugs combined.

○ The effect a drug has depends on multiple factors: (1) the ingredients of the drug and its effect on the body, (2) the traditional use of the drug, (3) individual motivation, and (4) the social and physical surroundings in which the drug is taken.

○ Attempts to regulate drug use were first made as long ago as 2240 BC.

○ After marijuana, illicit prescription drugs are now the second leading drug of abuse.

○ Drug abuse is an "equal-opportunity affliction." This means that drug consumption is found across all income levels, social classes, genders, races, ethnicities, lifestyles, and age groups.

○ Regarding race and ethnicity, the highest percentage of past-month users of illicit drugs reported two or more racial backgrounds.

○ Approximately 73% of drug users in the United States are employed either full- or part-time, and 63% of full-time employees drink alcohol.

○ In industry categories, the heaviest use of alcohol was found in construction; arts, entertainment, and recreation; and mining. The highest amount of illicit drug use was found in food services and construction types of industries.

○ In 2008, nearly a third of state and a quarter of federal prisoners committed their offense under the influence of drugs.

Introduction

Each year, at an accelerating rate, social change driven by technology not only affects us individually but also our family, community, city, nation, and the world. These technological advancements affect our everyday lives. It is no exaggeration to say that today, more than ever before, technology is one of the primary forces driving social change at unprecedented and relentless speed, which is affecting our everyday lives. As an example, let us look at the transformation of the telephone into cellular phone technology. In all likelihood, your great-grandparents had a black stationary rotary type of landline phone at home to communicate with friends and neighbors living at a distance. Your grandparents experienced newer and more stylized versions of the same telephone with perhaps one other telephone installed in another part of their home. While growing up, your parent(s) had the same landline type of telephone, but it came in an array of colors and was even more stylized, and there were several phones throughout their home. Today, your available technology may still include a landline phone with additional accessories, such as a separate phone line for Internet access, an answering machine, and built-in voicemail capability.

An outgrowth of the landline phone and the radiophone, which was used in the military, is a gadget that most of us carry today without any sense of technological awe. The mobile phone or cell phone and its more recent cousin, the smartphone, are portable warehouses of technological services that connect to a cellular network. Current cell phones can include an array of accessories and services beyond making phone calls, including caller identification, voice messaging, voice memos, an alarm clock, a stopwatch, calendars, appointment scheduling, current times in different regions of the world, a calculator, video games, text messaging (or SMS), a camera with photo albums, Internet service, e-mail, infrared, Bluetooth, an MP3 player, storage for downloaded music and/or podcasts, GPS, a radio, and iTunes. The completely portable cellular phone with its keypad and touchscreen was never imagined 25 years ago. Further, newer generations of cellular phones will include unimaginable new applications, accessories, and services.

Consider another example. More than likely, your great-grandparents wrote letters on manual typewriters. Your grandparents wrote letters on electric typewriters, whereas your parents started writing letters on electric typewriters and then had to change to computers. Today, you often communicate with family members and friends by e-mail, instant messaging, Facebook, Twitter, Skype, and MySpace. Although you may perceive many of the electronic devices surrounding your life as normal, a visit to a science and technology museum can offer many surprises and, more than likely, an appreciation for how things were and how much they have changed.

These examples illustrate how technology is in a continuous state of development and how it affects our day-to-day lives. In a sense, the technology we use today will be replaced tomorrow as newer and more advanced forms of innovation gives birth to advanced new technology and software.

What does this have to do with drug use and/or abuse? Just as electronics continually evolve, drugs follow similar paths of evolution. Today, there are thousands of new drugs available that are used either legally or illegally. These drugs are used for medicinal purposes, recreational purposes, or to achieve effects that do not include maintaining health. Other people in society use drugs to cope with pressures emanating from social change. Some people use and eventually abuse drugs to cope with, delay, or even avoid social change.

Despite the extensive amount of available information regarding the dangers of drug use and an increased number of laws prohibiting drug use, more people today continue to abuse legal and illegal types of drugs without medical approval.

Drug Use

Anyone can become dependent on and addicted to a drug. The desire to use a drug before drug dependence (addiction) sets in is both seductive and indiscriminate of its users. Most people do not realize that drug use causes at least three major simultaneous changes:

1. The social and psychological basis of the attraction to a particular drug can be explained as feeling rewarded or satisfied because social pressures can appear to have become postponed, momentarily rectified, or neutralized and defined as nonproblematic.
2. Pharmacologically, the nonmedical use of most drugs alters body chemistry largely by interfering with its proper (homeostatic) functioning. Drugs enhance, slow down, accelerate, or distort the reception and transmission of reality.
3. The desire may satisfy an inborn or genetically programmed need or desire.

(More detail regarding this issue is presented later in this chapter and in Chapter 2.)

Many argue that our "reality" would become perilous and unpredictable if people were legally free to dabble in their drugs of choice. Many do not realize, however, that if abused, even legal drugs can alter our perception of reality, become severely addicting, and destroy our social relationships with loved ones. Before delving into more specific information, which forms the basis of the other chapters in this book, we begin by posing some key questions related to drug use that will be discussed in this chapter:

- What constitutes a drug?
- What are the most commonly abused drugs?
- What are designer drugs?
- How widespread is drug abuse?
- What is the extent and frequency of drug use in our society?
- What are the current statistics on and trends in drug use?
- What types of drug users exist?
- How do the media influence drug use?
- What attracts people to drug use?
- When does drug use lead to drug dependence?
- When does drug addiction occur?
- What are the costs of drug addiction to society?
- What can be gained by learning about the complexity of drug use and abuse?

Dimensions of Drug Use

To determine the perception of drug use in our country, we asked several of the many people we interviewed for this book, "What do you think of the extent and the amount of drug use in our society?" The following are three of the more typical responses:

I think it is a huge problem, especially when you think about the fact that there are so many people doing drugs. Even in my own family, my sister's kids have had drug problems. My niece became addicted to cocaine, nearly died one night from overdosing, had to leave college for a year and go into rehab. I cannot emphasize enough how this was one of the most beautiful (physically and mentally sharp) and polite nieces I ever had. The rest of the family had no idea why she left school last year. Then, just last week, my sister tearfully announced during a Christmas gathering that Cindee was heavily into drugs while attending her second year of college. We were all shocked by this informa-tion. Now, just think how many other kids are addicted to such junk while the people who really care and love them do not have a clue. If the kids are having to deal with this, just stop and think how many other people in other jobs and professions are battling or have caved into their drugs of choice.

How many workers are there on a daily basis doing jobs that require safety and are "high" on drugs? This is a scary thought. Just think of a surgeon on drugs, or an airline pilot. Yes, we have big monster problems with controlling drug use. *(From Venturelli's research files, female dietician in Chicago, age 43, February 9, 2003)*

A second response to the same question:

I use drugs, mainly weed and alcohol, and at least once a month I have a night of enjoying coke with several friends. As long as I am not a burden on my family, I think drug use is a personal choice. Locking up people for their drug use is a violation of my rights as a human being. For many years now, our government has not been able to stop recreational drug use, this is despite the millions that have been arrested, and countless numbers of other drug users incarcerated. What's the point of all this? If after so many years of trying to enforce drug laws has met with failure, we need to take a long hard look at the small percentage of people like me who are fully employed, have families, pay our taxes regularly and outside of drug use, are fully functioning adults. The funny thing is that the two drugs [referring to alcohol and tobacco] that are legalized are far worse or at least as debilitating as the drugs that are legally prohibitive. Drug use is a personal choice and unless you are causing problems for other people, it should remain a personal choice. If I am using drugs on a particular night at home either by myself or with friends and we are not outside causing problems, we should not be in violation of any drug law or laws. Substances to get high have been around for hundreds and probably thousands of years, these substances that some of us like should not be any concern to others. Even my pet cat loves his catnip and appears to get a high from it; should I prohibit this little pleasure? I let him occasionally have it even if, for example, my neighbor thinks catnip is affecting the normal nature of my cat. How about if I get a rise from snorting or smoking one of the herbs in my kitchen cabinet? Whose business is it if I like to use herbs in this manner? Maybe we should also outlaw catnip and herbs? Again, drug use for whatever purpose is a personal decision and all the laws against the use of drugs are not going to stop me from using drugs. *(From Venturelli's research files, male residing in a Midwestern town, age 27, May 6, 2010)*

A third response to the same question:

My drug use? Whose business is it anyway? As long as I don't affect your life when I do drugs, what business is it but my own? We come into the world alone and leave this world alone. I don't bother anyone else about whether or not so and so uses drugs, unless of course, their drug use puts me in jeopardy (like a bus driver or pilot high on drugs). On certain days when things are slow, I even get a little high on cocaine while trading stocks. These are the same clients who I have had for years and who really trust my advice. Ask my clients whether they are happy with my investment advice. I handle accounts with millions of dollars for corporations and even the board of education! Never was my judgment impaired or adversely affected because of too much coke. In fact, I know that I work even better under a little buzz. Now, I know this stuff has the potential to become addictive, but I don't let it. I know how to use it and when to lay off for a few weeks. *(From Venturelli's research files, male investment broker working in a major metropolitan city in California, age 48, June 2, 2000)*

These three interviews reflect contrasting views and attitudes about drug use. The first interview shows the most contrast from the second and third interviews. Both the second and third interview show a similarity of views about drug use, largely from an insider's (the user's) perspective, indicative of a strong determination and belief that drug use should not be legally controlled and should be left to the discretion of users. Although much about these viewpoints can certainly be debated, an interesting finding is that such vastly different views about drug use are not only evident, but more importantly

often divide drug users and non–drug users. Drug users and/or sympathizers of drug use are often considered **insiders** with regard to their drug use, whereas nonusers and/or those who are against drug use are **outsiders**. These two classifications result in very different sets of values and attitudes about drug usage. Such great differences of opinion and views about drugs and drug use often result from the following sources: (1) prior socialization experiences, such as family upbringing, relations with siblings, and types of peer group associations; (2) the amount of exposure to drug use and drug users; (3) the age of initial exposure to drug use; and (4) whether an attitude change has occurred regarding the acceptance or rejection of using drugs. (Most of these influencing factors are discussed further in Chapter 2.) Keep in mind that this book views the following four principal factors as affecting how a drug user experiences a drug:

- *Biological, genetic, and pharmacological factors:* Substance abuse and addiction involve biological and genetic factors. The pharmacology of drug use focuses on how the ingredients of a particular drug affect the body and the nervous system and in turn a person's experience with a particular drug.
- *Cultural factors:* Society's views of drug use, as determined by custom and tradition, affect our initial approach to and use of a particular drug.
- *Social factors:* The motivation for taking a particular drug is affected by needs such as diminishing physical pain; curing an illness; providing relaxation; relieving stress or anxiety; trying to escape reality; self-medicating; heightening awareness; wanting to distort and change visual, auditory, or sensory inputs; or strengthening confidence. Included in the category of social factors is the belief that attitudes about drug use develop from the values and attitudes of other drug users; the norms in their communities, subcultures, peer groups, and families; and the drug user's personal experiences with using drugs. These are also known as influencing social factors.
- *Contextual factors:* Specific contexts define and determine personal dispositions toward drug use, as demonstrated by moods and attitudes about such activity. Specifically, these factors encompass the drug-taking social behavior that develops from the physical surroundings where the drug is used. For example, drug use may be perceived as more acceptable at fraternity parties, while socializing with drug-using friends,

KEY TERMS

insiders
people on the inside; those who approve of and/or use drugs

outsiders
people on the outside; those who do not approve of and/or use drugs

Examples of licit drugs that can be easily abused.

Examples of illicit drugs that can become costly once drug dependence occurs.

outdoors in a secluded area with other drug users, in private homes, secretly at work, or at music concerts.

Paying attention to the cultural, social, and contextual factors of drug use leads us to explore the sociology and psychology of drug use. Equally important are the biological, genetic, and pharmacological factors and consequences that directly focus on why and how drugs may be appealing and how they affect the body—primarily the central nervous system (CNS) and brain functions.

Although substances that affect both mind and body functioning are commonly called **drugs**, researchers in the field of drug or substance abuse use a more precise term: **psychoactive drugs (substances)**. Why the preference for using this term as opposed to *drugs*? Because the term *psychoactive drugs* is more precise in referring to how drugs affect the body. This term focuses on the particular effects these substances have on the CNS and emphasizes how they alter mood, consciousness, perception, and/or behavior. Because of their effects on the brain, psychoactive drugs can be used to treat physical, psychological, or mental illness. Because the body can tolerate increasingly larger doses of them, many psychoactive drugs are used in progressively greater and more uncontrollable amounts to achieve the same level of effect. For many substances, a user is at risk of moving from occasional to regular use or from moderate use to heavy and then chronic use. A chronic user may then risk **addiction** (a mostly psychological attachment) and experience **withdrawal symptoms** that are physical and/or psychological in nature whenever the drug is not supplied.

Generally speaking, any substance that modifies the nervous system and states of consciousness is a drug. Such modification includes one or more of the following: enhancement, inhibition, or dis-

tortion of the body, affecting patterns of behavior and social functioning. Psychoactive drugs are classified as either **licit** (legal) or **illicit** (illegal). (See **Table 1.1** for a list of slang terms used by drug users.) For example, coffee, tea, cocoa, alcohol, tobacco, and **over-the-counter (OTC)** drugs are licit. When licit drugs are used in moderation, they often go unnoticed and are often socially acceptable. Marijuana, cocaine, crack, and all of the hallucinogenic-

KEY TERMS

drug(s)
any substances that modify (either by enhancing, inhibiting, or distorting) mind and/or body functioning

psychoactive drugs (substances)
drug compounds (substances) that affect the central nervous system and alter consciousness and/or perceptions

addiction
generally refers to the psychological attachment to a drug(s); addiction to "harder" drugs such as heroin results in both psychological and physical attachment to the chemical properties of the drug, with the resulting satisfaction (reward) derived from using the drug in question

withdrawal symptoms
psychological and physical symptoms that result when a drug is absent from the body; physical symptoms are generally present in cases of drug dependence to more addictive drugs such as heroin; physical and psychological symptoms of withdrawal include perspiration, nausea, boredom, anxiety, and muscle spasms

licit drugs
legalized drugs such as coffee, alcohol, and tobacco

illicit drugs
illegal drugs such as marijuana, cocaine, and LSD

over-the-counter (OTC)
legalized drugs sold without a prescription

Table 1.1 **A Sampling of Slang Terms Relating to Drugs and Drug Use**

SLANG TERM	WHAT IT MEANS	SLANG TERM	WHAT IT MEANS
007s	Methylenedioxymethamphetamine (MDMA)	Bin Laden	Heroin (after 9/11)
24-7	Crack cocaine	Black beauties	Amphetamines, depressants
51	Crack + marijuana or tobacco	Blasted	Under the influence
80	Oxycontin pill	Blow your mind	Getting high on hallucinogens
Abolic	Veterinary steroids	Blunt	Marijuana inside a cigar
A-bomb	Marijuana cigarette with heroin or opium	Boost and shoot	Steal to support a drug habit
AC/DC	Codeine cough syrup	Brain ticklers	Amphetamines
Acid, acid cube	LSD, sugar cube with LSD	Brown bombers	LSD
Acid freak, head	Heavy user of LSD	Brown sugar	Heroin
Adam	Methylenedioxymethamphetamine (MDMA)	Buda	Marijuana joint and crack
Air blast	Inhalants	Buddha	Potent marijuana spiked with opium
All star	User of multiple drugs	Bundle	Heroin
Amped	High on amphetamines	Ditch weed	Inferior marijuana
Angel dust	PCP	Dr. Feelgood	Heroin
Author	Doctor who writes illegal prescriptions	Easy lay	Gamma hydroxybutyrate (GHB)
Babysit	Guide someone through their first drug experience	Fantasy	GHB
Balloon	A penny balloon with heroin	Flower tippling	Ecstasy (MDMA) mixed with mushrooms
Banano	Cigarette laced with cocaine	Forget-me-drug	Rohypnol
Barbies	Depressants	Fries	Crack cocaine
Battery acid	LSD	Garbage rock	Crack cocaine
Batu	Smokable methamphetamine	Hillbilly heroin	Methamphetamine
Beam me up, Scotty	PCP and crack	Hippie crack	Inhalants
Beanies	Methamphetamine	Hot ice	Smokable methamphetamine
Beast	Heroin plus LSD	Huff, huffing	Inhalants, to sniff an inhalant
Belladonna	PCP	Ice cream habit	Occasional use of drugs
Bender	Drug party	Idiot pills	Depressants
Biker's coffee	Methamphetamine + coffee	Kiddie dope	Prescription drugs

Table 1.1 (*continued*)

SLANG TERM	WHAT IT MEANS	SLANG TERM	WHAT IT MEANS
Lemonade	Poor quality drugs	Special K	Ketamine
Lunch money drug	Rohypnol	Stacking	Use of steroids without a prescription
Magic mushroom	Psilocybin	Strawberry	LSD; female who trades sex for crack or money to buy crack
Monkey dust	PCP	The devil	Crack cocaine
Moon gas	Inhalants	Tornado	Crack cocaine
Mother's little helper	Depressants	Totally spent	Hangover after MDMA
Nose candy	Cocaine	Water-water	Marijuana cigarettes dipped in embalming fluid
Parachute	Smokable crack + heroin	West Coast	Ritalin (ADHD drug)
Pepsi habit	Occasional use of drugs	Working man's cocaine	Methamphetamine
Poor man's coke	Methamphetamine	Zig Zag man	Marijuana rolling papers
Ringer	Good hit of crack; hear bells	Zombie	PCP, heavy user of drugs
Shot	To inject a drug	Zoom	Marijuana laced with PCP

Source: Office of National Drug Control Policy. *Drug Facts: Street Terms.* Washington, DC: Author, 2010. Available at: http://www.whitehousedrugpolicy.gov/streetterms. Accessed March 15, 2011.

types of drugs are examples of illicit drugs. With the exception of marijuana—which some states allow for medical use and small amounts for personal use—federal law continues to prohibit the possession and use of all of these drugs.

Researchers have made some interesting findings about legal and illegal drug use:

- The use of such legal substances as alcohol and tobacco is much more common than the use of illegal drugs such as marijuana, cocaine, heroin, and hallucinogens (psychedelics). Other legal drugs, such as depressants and stimulants, although less popular than alcohol and tobacco, are still more widely used than heroin and LSD. (See **Figure 1.1** for illustrated comparisons.)
- The popular use of licit drugs, particularly alcohol and tobacco, has caused far more deaths, sickness, violent crimes, economic loss, and other social problems than the combined use of all illicit drugs.
- Societal reaction to various drugs changes with time and place. Today, opium is an illegal drug

and widely condemned as a pan-pathogen (a cause of all ills). In the 18th and 19th centuries, however, it was a legal drug and was popularly praised as a panacea (a cure for all ills). Alcohol use was widespread in the United States in the early 1800s, became illegal during the 1920s, and then was legalized a second time and has been widely used since the 1930s. Cigarette smoking is legal in all countries today. In the 17th century, it was illegal in most countries, and smokers were sometimes harshly punished. For example, in Russia, smokers could lose their noses; in Hindustan (India), they could lose their lips; and in China, they could lose their heads (Thio 1983, 1995, 2000). Today, new emphasis in the United States on the public health hazards from cigarettes again is leading some people to consider new measures to restrict or even outlaw tobacco smoking.

Table 1.2 introduces some of the terminology that you will encounter throughout this text. It is important that you understand how the definitions vary.

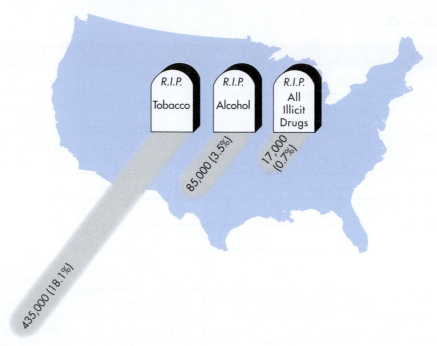

FIGURE 1.1

Annual U.S. deaths and likelihoods of dying from tobacco, alcohol, and illicit drug use.

The average American is 25 times more likely to die from tobacco-related illnesses (cardiovascular disease, respiratory disease, and cancer) than die from illicit drug-related illnesses. He or she is five times more likely to die from alcohol-related illnesses than illicit drug use.

Source: Data from Mokdad, A. H., J. S. Marks, D. F. Stroup, and J. L. Gerberding. "Actual Causes of Death in the United States, 2000." *Journal of the American Medical Association* 291 (10 March 2004):1238–1245.

■ Major Types of Commonly Abused Drugs

There are six types of major drugs in use: (1) prescription drugs, (2) over-the-counter drugs, (3) recreational drugs (coffee, tea, alcohol, tobacco, and chocolate), (4) illicit drugs, (5) herbal preparations (generally derived from plants), and (6) commercial drugs (paints, glues, pesticides, and household cleaning products).

In looking at drug use, this book examines the following topics: (1) OTC drugs; (2) prescription drugs; (3) other drugs and compounds not taken for a medical need or necessity but for pleasure or relief from boredom, stress, or anxiety; and (4) some of the most important information regarding drug use (for example, theories of why drugs are used, legality of drugs, addiction, bodily effects of drug use, lifestyles of drug users, use of drugs within specific subcultures [special populations or subpopulations] that share similar characteristics, and drug abuse treatment and prevention).

To begin, we now briefly examine the major drugs of use and often abuse. The drugs examined next are prescription drugs, performance-enhancing drugs, stimulants, hallucinogens (psychedelics) and other similar compounds, depressants, alcohol, nicotine, cannabis (marijuana and hashish), anabolic steroids, inhalants/organic solvents, narcotics/opiates, and designer drugs. A brief overview is provided here, and these same drugs are discussed in much more detail in separate chapters throughout this book.

Prescription and Performance-Enhancing Drugs

In the United States, young people frequently abuse prescription drugs; the only illicit drug that is abused more frequently is marijuana (Substance Abuse and Mental Health Services Administration [SAMHSA] 2009). In 2009, 2.5% of illicit drug users, over 6.2 million persons age 12 or older, used prescription-type psychotherapeutic drugs nonmedically. For example, according to the National Survey on Drug Use and Health (NSDUH), published in 2009, from 2002 through 2008, 2.9% of 12- to 17-year-olds reported past-year nonmedical prescription pain reliever use and abuse of marijuana was at 6.7%. "A number of national studies and published reports indicate that the intentional abuse of prescription drugs,

Table 1.2 Commonly Used Terms

TERM	DESCRIPTION
Gateway drugs	The word *gateway* suggests a path or entryway leading to an entrance. Gateway is a theory that the early use of alcohol, tobacco products, and marijuana (the most heavily used illicit types of drugs) lead to the use of more powerfully addictive drugs like cocaine, heroin, and highly addictive prescription medicines.
Medicines	Compounds generally prescribed by a physician that treat, prevent, or alleviate the symptoms of disease. (Can also include over-the-counter [OTC] drugs purchased at pharmacies.)
Prescription medicines	Drugs that are prescribed by a physician. Common examples include antibiotics, antidepressants, and drugs prescribed to relieve pain, induce stimulation, or induce relaxation. These drugs are taken under a physician's recommendation because they are more potent than OTC drugs. On a yearly basis, physicians write approximately 3.8 billion prescriptions (Fischer et al. 2010), with sales totaling $234.1 billion in 2008 (Lundy 2010, p. 1).
Over-the-counter (OTC)	OTC drugs can be purchased at will without seeking medical advice or a prescription. Examples include aspirin, laxatives, diet pills, cough suppressants, and sore throat medicines. There are approximately 1000 active ingredients used in the more than 100,000 OTC products available in the marketplace today (Consumer Healthcare Products Association [CHPA] 2001). In 2009, $16.9 billion was spent in the United States on OTC medicines.*
Drug misuse	The unintentional or inappropriate use of prescribed and OTC drugs. Misuse includes, but is not limited to, (1) taking more drugs than prescribed; (2) using OTC or psychoactive drugs in excess without medical supervision; (3) mixing drugs with alcohol or other drugs, often to accentuate euphoric effects or simply not caring about the effects of mixing drugs; (4) using old medicines to self-treat new symptoms of an illness or ailment; (5) discontinuing certain prescribed drugs at will or against a physician's recommendation; and (6) administering prescription drugs to family members or friends without medical approval and supervision.
Drug abuse	Also known as *chemical or substance abuse.* The willful misuse of either licit or illicit drugs for recreation, perceived necessity, or convenience. Drug abuse differs from drug use in that *drug use* is taking or using drugs, whereas *drug abuse* is a more intense and often willful misuse of drugs, often to the point of becoming addicted.
Drug addiction	Drug addiction involves noncasual or nonrecreational drug use. A frequent symptom is intense psychological preoccupation with obtaining and consuming drugs. Most often psychological and—in some cases, depending on the drug—physiological symptoms of withdrawal are manifested when the craving for the drug is not satisfied. Today, more emphasis is placed on the psychological craving (mental attachment) to the drug than on the more physiologically based withdrawal symptoms of addiction. (See Chapter 2 for more detailed information regarding addiction and the addiction process.)

*This amount excludes OTC sales by Wal-Mart and does not include vitamins/minerals/nutritional supplements.

Sources: Fischer, M. A., M. R. Stedman, J. Lii, et al. "Primary Medication Non-Adherence: Analysis of 195,930 Electronic Prescriptions." *Journal of General Internal Medicine* 25 (2010 April):284–290, Epub 4 February 2010; The Henry J. Kaiser Family Foundation. "Prescription Drug Trends." 2010. Available at: http://www.kff.org/rxdrugs/3057.cfm. Accessed February 7, 2011; and Consumer Healthcare Protection Association (CHPA). *OTC Retail Sales—1964–2009.* Available at: http://www.chpa-info.org/pressroom/Retail_Sales.aspx. Accessed February 7, 2011.

such as pain relievers, tranquilizers, stimulants and sedatives, to get high is a growing concern—particularly among teens—in the United States. In fact, among young people ages 12–17, prescription drugs have become the second most abused illegal drug, behind marijuana" (Office of National Drug Control Policy [ONDCP] 2007). In 2008, 15.2 million Americans age 12 or older had taken a prescription pain reliever, tranquilizer, stimulant, or sedative for nonmedical purposes at least once in the year prior to being surveyed (National Institute on Drug Abuse [NIDA] 2010). The Centers for Disease Control and Prevention (CDC 2010) reports that its national survey found that 20.2% of high school students said they had taken a drug such as Ritalin, Xanax, or OxyContin without having a doctor's prescription.

Three categories of prescription drugs that are currently abused are narcotics, depressants, and stimulants. Narcotics (e.g., OxyContin, Vicodin, Percocet) include analgesics or **opioids** that are generally prescribed for physical pain. Abuse occurs when they are used nonmedically because of their euphoric and numbing effects. Depressants (e.g., Xanax, Valium, Librium) are generally used to treat anxiety and sleep disorders. These drugs are abused because of their sedating properties. Stimulants (e.g., Ritalin, Dexedrine, Meridia) are used to treat attention deficit disorder (ADD), attention deficit hyperactivity disorder (ADHD), and asthma. These drugs are abused because of their euphoric effects and energizing potential (Publishers Group 2004).

The two drugs in the stimulants category that are most often abused are Ritalin (methylphenidate hydrochloride) and Adderall (amphetamine). These prescription drugs are legitimately prescribed for ADHD, ADD, and narcolepsy (a sleep disorder) (Center for Substance Abuse Research [CESAR] 2003). When used nonmedically, they are taken orally as tablets or the tablets are crushed into a powder and snorted (a far more popular method). Students often illegally purchase these tablets for $5 each from other students who have a legal prescription for the medication.

> I feel like Dr. Pill. All these brothers [fraternity brothers] are always looking for me at parties so that I can sell them a few tabs. What the heck, I make extra money selling Ritalin, enough to buy essentials like beer and cigarettes. *(From Venturelli's research files, male undergraduate student at a Midwestern university, age 20, December 9, 2004)*

And,

> Funny how when I go back to the frat house during homecoming there are other under-

grads who have taken over my business and continue to sell their prescribed Ritalin mostly for partying. *(A second interview with the same former student quoted at age 26, now employed in real estate, October 2, 2010)*

These drugs often are used in conjunction with alcohol or marijuana to enhance the "high" or for staying awake to increase comprehension and remain focused while reading or studying for an exam (CESAR 2003). Both prescription drugs (Ritalin and Adderall) are readily available and can be easily obtained by teenagers, who may abuse these drugs to experience a variety of desired effects. Increasingly, younger adolescents are obtaining prescription drugs from classmates, friends, and family members or are stealing the drugs from school medicine dispensaries and from other people for whom the drug has been legitimately prescribed.

Ritalin, Adderall, and other stimulant abusers tend to be late junior high school, high school. and college students. "A 2009 national survey found that 5.8% used amphetamines with 2.6% of students in grades 8, 10, and 12 reporting using Ritalin without medical supervision at least once in the past year" (National Survey on Drug Use and Health [NSDUH] 2009). Further, in 2008 it was reported that approximately 16% of college students used *or* had tried Ritalin for recreational purposes and/or felt it necessary to use this drug to study for longer hours (SAMHSA 2009).

Stimulants

Some stimulants can be considered to be **gateway drugs** (see definition in Table 1.2), and these substances act on the central nervous system (CNS) by increasing alertness, excitation, euphoria, pulse rate, and blood pressure. Insomnia and loss of appetite are common outcomes. The user initially experiences pleasant effects, such as a sense of increased energy and a state of euphoria, or "high." In addition, users feel restless and talkative and have trouble sleeping. High doses used over the long term can produce personality changes. Some of the psychological risks associated with chronic stimulant use include violent, erratic, or paranoid behavior. Other effects can include confusion, anxiety and depression, and loss of interest in sex or food. Major stimulants include amphetamines, cocaine and crack, methamphetamine ("meth"), and methylphenidate. Minor stimulants include caffeine, tea, chocolate, and nicotine (the most addictive minor stimulant).

KEY TERMS

opioids
drugs derived from opium

gateway drugs
alcohol, tobacco, and marijuana—types of drugs that when used excessively may lead to using other and more addictive drugs such as cocaine, heroin, or "crack"

Hallucinogens/Psychedelics and Other Similar Drugs

Either synthetic or grown naturally, these drugs produce a very intense alteration of perceptions, thoughts, and feelings. They most certainly influence the complex inner workings of the human mind, causing users to refer to these drugs as psychedelics (because they cause hallucinations or distortion of reality and thinking). In addition to amplifying states of mind, hallucinogenic types of drugs induce a reality that is reported to be qualitatively different from those of ordinary consciousness. For example, while the user is under their influence, these drugs can affect the sense of taste, smell, hearing, and vision. Tolerance to hallucinogens builds very rapidly, which means that increasing amounts of this drug are needed for similar effects. Hallucinogens include LSD, mescaline, **MDMA** (Ecstasy), phencyclidine (PCP), psilocybin or "magic mushrooms," ketamine, and the more potent (hybrid) varieties of marijuana, hashish, and opium that are smoked.

Depressants

These drugs depress the CNS. If taken in a high enough quantity, they produce insensibility or stupor. Depressants are also taken for some of the same reasons as hallucinogens, such as to relieve boredom, stress, and anxiety. In addition, the effects of both opioids (drugs that are derived from opium) and morphine derivatives appeal to many people who are struggling with emotional problems and looking for physical and emotional relief, and in some cases to induce sleep. Depressants include alcohol (ethanol), barbiturates, benzodiazepines (such as diazepam [Valium]), and methaqualone (Quaaludes).

Alcohol

Known as a gateway drug, **ethanol** is a colorless, volatile, and pungent liquid resulting from fermented grains, berries, and other fruits and vegetables. Alcohol is a depressant that mainly affects the CNS. Excessive amounts of alcohol often cause a progressive loss of inhibitions, flushing and dizziness, loss of coordination, impaired motor skills, blurred vision, slurred speech, sudden mood swings, vomiting, irregular pulse, and memory impairment. Chronic heavy use may lead to high blood pressure, arrhythmia (irregular heartbeat), and cirrhosis (severe liver deterioration).

Nicotine

Nicotine is also considered a gateway drug. It is a very addictive, colorless, highly volatile liquid alkaloid found in all tobacco products, including cigarettes, chewing tobacco, pipe tobacco, and cigars. Because nicotine is highly addictive and tobacco use is still socially acceptable under certain circumstances, smokers often start young and have a very difficult time quitting. Long-term use of tobacco products can lead to several different chronic respiratory ailments and cancers.

Cannabis (Marijuana and Hashish)

Cannabis is the most widely used illicit drug in the United States. Marijuana consists of the dried and crushed leaves, flowers, and seeds of the *Cannabis sativa* plant, which readily grows in many parts of the world. Delta 9-tetrahydrocannabinol (THC) is the primary psychoactive, mind-altering ingredient in marijuana that produces euphoria (often referred to as a "high"). Plant parts (mainly the leaves and buds of the plant) are usually dried, crushed, and smoked much like tobacco products. Other ways of ingesting marijuana include crushing and mixing finely crushed leaves into the butter or oil that goes into cookie or brownie batter and baking the batter. Hashish is a cannabis derivative that contains the purest form of resin and the highest amount of THC.

Synthetic Cannabis: Spice and K2

"A package of K2, a synthetic marijuana, is a concoction of dried herbs sprayed with chemicals, used in the herbal blends that are sold in head shops on the Internet to a growing number of teens and young adults" (Caldwell 2010, p. 30). A retired organic chemistry researcher from Clemson University reports such medical problems from synthetic cannabis use as "overdoses, cases of addiction and even suicide" (Caldwell 2010, p. 30).

K2 and Spice are genericized trademarks that first went on sale in 2000, initially as legal herbs. Several years later, it was discovered that this drug contained synthetic cannabinoids that affected the body in similar fashion as marijuana (cannabis). This drug is

KEY TERMS

MDMA
a type of illicit drug known as "Ecstasy" or "Adam" and having stimulant and hallucinogenic properties

ethanol
the pharmacological term for alcohol; a consumable type of alcohol that is the psychoactive ingredient in alcoholic beverages; often called grain alcohol

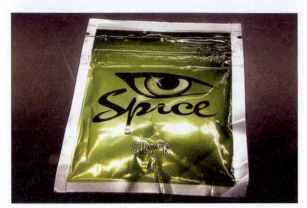

K2 contains synthetic cannabinoids that affect the body in similar fashion as marijuana.

most often smoked like marijuana. Herbs listed on packages of Spice include *Nuymphaea caerulea, Lonotis leonurus, Zornia latifolia, Canavalia maritime, Scutellaria nana, Pedicularis densiflora, Nelumbo nucifera*, and *Leonurus sibiricus*. Examination for the presence of these ingredients was not found by laboratories in Germany. Another finding was that Spice is a product line sold as a legal herb-based alternative to cannabis. The ingredients list contains only herbs and no cannabinoid constituents. Since it began being sold in 2006, the listed ingredients have seemed suspiciously unlikely to produce its reported effects. Numerous organizations have now tested the material, and three chemicals have been identified in various Spice products, including JWH-018, HU-210, and a homologue of CP-47,497 (Erowid 2008). Another study indicated that the following has been found in samples of Spice (USDOJ 2011):

- CP-47,497—a synthetic cannabinoid agonist without the classical cannabinoid chemical structure. Although CP-47,497 is likely to have similar effects in humans as Δ9-tetrahydrocannabinol (Δ9-THC), the main active ingredient of marijuana, CP-47,497, and its homologues are not controlled substances in the United States.
- HU-210 and HU-211 are structurally and pharmacologically similar to Δ9-tetrahydrocannabinol (Δ9-THC), the main active ingredient of marijuana, and it was synthesized around 1988. It was recently purported to be found in the herbal mixture Spice, sold in European countries mainly via Internet shops. HU-210 is a Schedule I controlled substance in the United States, and HU-211 is not a controlled substance in the United States.

- JWH-018, JWH-073, and JWH-074 are synthetic cannabinoid agonists without the classical cannabinoid chemical structure. The substances have been identified in the herbal products such as Spice, K2, and others sold via the Internet and head shops. Although JWH-018, JWH-073, and JWH-074 are likely to have the same effects in humans as Δ9-tetrahydrocannabinol (Δ9-THC), the main active ingredient of marijuana, they are not controlled in the United States. (USDOJ 2011).

To date, the U.S. Army, U.S. Marines, and U.S. Navy have banned this drug, and violators risk immediate expulsion. The U.S. Air Force prohibits it at Nellis Air force base in Las Vegas, Nevada. Currently, states in the United States have already banned the use and sale of this drug or are legislating fines for sale and possession. As of 2011, most states have outlawed or are moving to control and ban spice-type products.

Anabolic Steroids

Steroids are a synthetic form of the male hormone testosterone. They are often used to increase muscle size and strength. Medically, steroids are used to increase body tissue, treat allergies, or reduce swelling. Steroids are available in either liquid or pill form. Athletes have a tendency to use and abuse these drugs because dramatic results can occur with regard to increased body mass and muscle tissue. Some side effects include heart disease, liver cancer, high blood pressure, septic shock, impotence, genital atrophy, manic episodes, depression, violence, and mood swings.

Inhalants/Organic Solvents

Inhalants and organic solvents also are often considered gateway drugs and are very attractive to and popular among preteens and younger teenagers. Products used include gasoline, model airplane glue, and paint thinner. When inhaled, the vapors from these solvents can produce euphoric effects. Organic solvents can also refer to certain foods, herbs, and vitamins, such as "herbal Ecstasy."

Narcotics/Opiates

These drugs also depress the CNS and, if taken in a high enough quantity, produce insensibility or stupor. Narcotics or opiates are highly addictive. Narcotics include heroin, opium, morphine, codeine, meperidine (often a substitute for morphine, also known as Demerol), Darvon, and Percodan.

Inhalants are volatile chemicals, which include many common household substances, that are often the most dangerous drugs, per dose, a person can take. In addition, inhalants are most often used by preteens and younger teens.

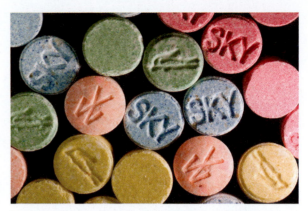

Designer pills containing the illicit drug Ecstasy. This drug has some stimulant properties like amphetamines as well as hallucinogenic properties like LSD.

Designer Drugs/Synthetic Drugs or Synthetic Opioids

In addition to the most commonly abused illicit drug categories just described, innovations in technology have produced new categories known as **designer drugs/synthetic drugs or synthetic opioids**. These relatively new types of drugs are developed by people who seek to circumvent the illegality of a drug by modifying the drug into a new compound. Ecstasy is an example of a designer drug/synthetic drug or synthetic opioid. Such drugs are created as **structural analogs** of substances already scheduled and legally prohibited under the Controlled Substances Act (CSA). Structural analogs are the drugs that result from altered chemical structures of already existing illicit drugs. Generally, these drugs are created by an underground chemist whose goal is to make a profit by creating compounds that mimic, change, or intensify the psychoactive effects of controlled substances. The number of designer drugs that are created and sold illegally is very large.

Anyone with knowledge of college-level chemistry can alter the chemical ingredients and produce new designer drugs, although it may be nearly impossible to predict their properties or effects except by trial and error. Currently, three major types of synthetic analog drugs are available through the illicit drug market: analogs of PCP; analogs of fentanyl and meperidine (both synthetic narcotic analgesics) such as Demerol or MPPP (also called MPTP or PEPAP); and analogs of amphetamine and methamphetamine (which have stimulant and hallucinogenic properties) such as MDMA, known as "Ecstasy" or "Adam," which is widely used on college campuses as a euphoriant.

The production of these high-technology psychoactive substances is a sign of the new levels of risk and additional challenge to the criminal justice system. As the production and risk associated with the use of such substances increase, the need for a broader, better-informed view of drug use becomes even more important than in the past. Appendix B lists, among other information, (1) the most commonly abused drugs in society, (2) their more common street names/terms, (3) medical uses, (4) routes of administration, (5) Controlled Substances Act [CSA] schedules, and (6) duration of detection in the body.

An Overview of Drugs in Society

Many people think that problems with drugs are unique to this era. In reality, drug use and abuse have always been part of nearly all—past and present—human societies. For example, the Grecian oracles of Delphi used drugs, Homer's Cup of Helen induced sleep and provided freedom from care, and the mandrake root mentioned in

KEY TERMS

designer drugs/synthetic drugs or synthetic opioids
new drugs that are developed by people intending to circumvent the illegality of a drug by modifying a drug into a new compound; Ecstasy is an example

structural analogs
a new molecular species created by modifying the basic molecular skeleton of a compound; structural analogs are structurally related to the parent compound

the first book of the Bible, Genesis, produced a hallucinogenic effect. In Genesis 30:14–16, the mandrake is mentioned in association with bartering for lovemaking:

> In the time of wheat harvest Reuben went out, found some mandrakes in the open country, and brought them to his mother Leah. Then Rachel asked Leah for some of her son's mandrakes, but Leah said, "Is it so small a thing to have taken away my husband, that you should take my son's mandrakes as well?" However, Rachel said, "Very well, let him sleep with you tonight in exchange for your son's mandrakes." So when Jacob came in from the country in the evening, Leah went out to meet him and said, "You are to sleep with me tonight; I have hired you with my son's mandrakes." That night he slept with her.

Ancient literature is filled with references to the use of mushrooms, datura, hemp, marijuana, opium poppies, and so on. Under the influence of some of these drugs, many people experienced extreme ecstasy or sheer terror. Some old pictures of demons and devils look very much like those described by modern drug users during so-called bummers, or bad trips. The belief that witches could fly may also have been drug-induced because many natural preparations used in so-called witches' brews induced the sensation of disassociation from the body, as in flying or floating.

As far back as 2240 BC, attempts were made to regulate drug use. For instance, in that year, problem drinking was addressed in the Code of Hammurabi, where it was described as "a problem of men with too much leisure time and lazy dispositions." Nearly every culture has experienced drug abuse, and as found in the historical record, laws were enacted to control the use of certain types of drugs.

■ How Widespread Is Drug Abuse?

As mentioned earlier, drug abuse today is more acute and widespread than in any previous age (see "Here and Now: Persistence of Illicit Drug Use in

the United States, Rural–Urban Comparisons, and a New Drug 'Making the Scene'"). The evidence for this development is how often large quantities of illicit drugs are seized in the United States as well as throughout the world (see "Here and Now: Current Global Status of Illicit Drug Use in Selected Countries" on page 17). Media exposure about illicit drug use is more likely to occur today than in the past. On any given day, you can scan most major national and international newspapers and run across stories about illegal drug manufacture, storage and distribution, use and/or abuse, and convictions. Drug use is an "**equal-opportunity affliction**." This means that no one is immune from the use and/or abuse of both licit and illicit drugs. Research shows that drug consumption is found across the many different income, education, social class, occupation, race and ethnic, lifestyle, and age groups. To date, no one has proved to be immune from drug use and/or abuse.

Many of us, for example, are dismayed or surprised when we discover that certain individuals we admire—our family members (a mother, father, aunt, uncle, cousin, grandparent), close friends, workmates, celebrities, politicians, athletes, clergy, law enforcement personnel, physicians, academics, and even the seemingly upstanding man or woman next door—either admit to, are accused of, need treatment for, or are arrested for licit and/or illicit drug use.

We are also taken aback when we hear that cigarettes, alcohol, and marijuana abuse are commonplace in many public and private middle schools. Furthermore, most of us know of at least one (and many times more than one) close friend or family member who appears to secretly or not so secretly use drugs.

An example of a situation that requires clear thinking without the use of mind-altering drugs.

Here and Now

"Despite tough anti-drug laws, a new survey shows the U.S. has the highest level of illegal drug use in the world" and ". . . Americans report the highest level of cocaine and marijuana use" (WebMD, Warner, and CBS News 2009).

In the 1990s, a variety of factors came together in the United States to extend drug abuse beyond just the very rich or the urban poor. The ease of brewing cheaper, more potent strains of speed (methamphetamine, or "meth") and heroin, coupled with the fact that enforcement officials tended to focus on drug abuse and traffic in urban areas on the East and West Coasts, left middle-class and rural populations throughout the country largely overlooked. Suddenly, the illicit drug market was booming where no one had been looking.

By the late 1990s, speed—which had gained popularity in the 1970s among outlaw bikers, college students facing exams, all-night partygoers, and long-haul truckers—was more sought after than ever. Teenagers, middle-class workers, and suburbanites joined the ranks of methamphetamine users. "We've been fighting it really strongly for nearly seven years," Edward Synicky, a special agent with California's Bureau of Narcotics Enforcement, told *Time* magazine in early 1996. "But cocaine gets all the publicity because it's glamorous. And law enforcement in general doesn't put the resources into meth that it should" (Toufonio et al. 1990).

Increasingly, the illegal substance was produced in clandestine labs set up by both major drug dealers and individual users. By January 1996, John Coonce, head of the U.S. Drug Enforcement Administration's (DEA's) meth-lab task force, said methamphetamine use was "absolutely epidemic." The surge was attributed largely to powerful Mexican drug syndicates and motorcycle gangs that sold their goods on street corners. Speed acquired the nickname "crank" because it was frequently concealed in motorcycle crankcases.

Clandestine manufacture and use of speed were especially high in the West and Southwest. Speed kitchens flourished in California because it was relatively easy for the Mexican syndicates to smuggle in ephedrine, a key ingredient that is tightly controlled in the United States. From the mid-1980s to the mid-1990s, methamphetamine-related hospitalizations in California rose approximately 366%. In Arizona's Maricopa County, methamphetamine-linked crimes jumped nearly 400% over a 3-year period in the early 1990s. (See the sections "The Costs of Drug Use to Society" and "Drugs, Crime, and Violence" later in this chapter.)

Soon this easy-access drug began spreading across the United States. In 1994, DEA field offices in Houston, Denver, Los Angeles, New Orleans, Phoenix, St. Louis, San Diego, and San Francisco were responsible for approximately 86% of the methamphetamine laboratory seizures in the country. By 1996, however, officials were seizing huge shipments of methamphetamine that originated in Mississippi and Tennessee.

Update: Recent information regarding this drug is very positive. The number of past-month methamphetamine users decreased by over half between 2006 and 2008. The numbers were 731,000 in 2006, 529,000 in 2007, and 314,000 in 2008. Further, the number of past-year initiates of methamphetamine among persons age 12 or older was 95,000 in 2008. This estimate was significantly lower than the estimates in 2007 (157,000) and was less than one-third of the number estimated in 2004 (318,000) (SAMHSA 2009).

Although the recent drop in methamphetamine use is very encouraging, news about other types of illicit drug use is not. Some of the more alarming findings indicate that:

- Almost half (49.2%) of youths ages 12 to 17 reported in 2008 that it would be "fairly easy" or "very easy" for them to obtain marijuana if they wanted some. Around one-fifth (22.1%) reported it would be easy to get cocaine. About one in seven (13.8%) indicated that LSD would be "fairly" or "very" easily available, and 13% reported easy availability for heroin (SAMHSA 2009).

- In 2007 and 2008 the rate of illicit drug use among persons age 12 or older held steady at 8% current (past-month), 14.2% in the past year, and 47% during their lifetime (SAMHSA 2009).

- Among those ages 50 to 59 (baby boom cohort), the rate of past-month illicit drug use increased from 2.7% in 2002 to 4.6% in 2008 (SAMHSA 2009).

- Use of most of the several classes of psychotherapeutic drugs—sedatives (barbiturates), tranquilizers, and narcotics other than heroin—has become a larger part of the nation's drug abuse problem. During much of the 1990s and into the 2000s, there was a virtually uninterrupted increase among 12th graders, college students, and young adults in the use of all these drugs (Johnston et al. 2009).

(continued)

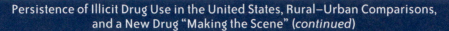

Persistence of Illicit Drug Use in the United States, Rural–Urban Comparisons, and a New Drug "Making the Scene" (*continued*)

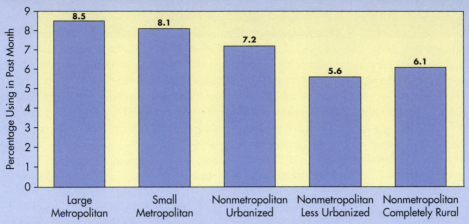

Past-month illicit drug use among persons age 12 or older, by county type: 2008.

Source: Substance Abuse and Mental Health Services Administration (SAMHSA). *Results from the 2008 National Survey on Drug Use and Health: National Findings.* Office of Applied Studies, NSDUH Series H-36, DHHS Publication No. SMA 09-4435. Rockville, MD, 2009.

Metropolitan vs. Nonmetropolitan Illicit Drug Use

- In comparing illicit drug use among persons age 12 or older by type of county in 2008, 8.5% admitted to past-month usage in large metropolitan areas, 8.1% in small metropolitan areas, 7.2% in nonmetropolitan urbanized areas, 5.6% in nonmetropolitan less urbanized areas, and 6.1% in nonmetropolitan completely rural areas.
- Rural teens have a greater risk of using drugs in general than both suburban and urban teens. "Five of the 13 measures of drug use show a significantly higher prevalence rate among rural teens: chewing tobacco (11.5%), chewing tobacco at school (7.6%), smoking cigarettes at school (14.8%), using crack/cocaine (5.9%), and using steroids (7.4%). Only one measure showed a significantly higher prevalence rate among urban teens (smoking marijuana at school, at 6.8%). The remaining seven measures in the study showed no differences by residence" (Mink et al. 2005).
- "The proportion of rural teens who reported ever using crystal meth (15.5%) was almost double the proportion of urban (8.8%) and suburban teens (9.5%)" (Mink et al. 2005).
- Crystal meth was the fourth most commonly used drug among rural teens after alcohol, cigarettes, and marijuana, making it more popular among rural teens than chewing tobacco (Mink et al. 2005).

New Drug Making the Scene

"[I]ncreasing numbers of youths are turning to an herb-based product to get high, and unlike marijuana, it's perfectly legal" (Aathun, 2010). Known as K2, Spice, or fake weed, it is synthetic and marketed as an herbal incense. It mimics THC, the chemical producing the high in marijuana. "Side effects include heart palpitations, respiratory issues, panic attacks, [and] hallucinations" (Aathun, 2010). "K2 may be a mixture of herbal and spice plant products, but it is sprayed with a potent psychotropic drug and likely contaminated with an unknown toxic substance that is causing many adverse effects . . ." (Bryner 2010).

Sources: Aathun, S. "Synthetic Marijuana a Growing Trend Among Teens, Authorities Say." CNN.com. 2010. Available at: http://www.cnn.com/2010/HEALTH/03/23/synthetic.marijuana/index.html?iref=allsearch. Accessed February 25, 2011; Associated Press. "Survey: Drug Use Pervading New Bedford Fleet." *Maine Sunday Telegram* (21 July 1996):1–2; Johnston, L. D., P. M. O'Malley, J. G. Bachman, and J. E. Schulenberg. *Monitoring the Future: National Survey Results on Drug Use, 1975–2008. Volume 1, Secondary School Students.* Bethesda, MD: National Institute on Drug Abuse (NIDA), 2009; Mink, M. D., C. G. Moore, A. O. Johnson, J. C. Probst, and A. B. Martin. *Violence and Rural Teens: Violence, Drug Use, and School-Based Prevention Services in Rural America.* Rockville, MD: South Carolina Rural Health Research Center, Office of Rural Health Policy, U.S. Department of Health and Human Services (USDHHS), U.S. Government Printing Office, 2005; National Narcotics Intelligence Consumers Committee. *The NNICC Report, 1994.* Washington, DC: U.S. Drug Enforcement Agency, 1994:70; National Public Radio (NPR). "All Things Considered." PM News (18 September 1996); SAMHSA, Office of Applied Studies (OAS). *Results from the 2008 National Survey on Drug Use and Health: National Findings.* Rockville, MD: Office of Applied Studies, 2009; Toufonio, A., et al. "There Is No Safe Speed." *Time* (8 January 1990); Warner, J. "U.S. Leads the World in Illegal Drug Use." CBS News (1 July 2009):1. Available at: http://www.cbsnews.com/stories/2008/07/01/health/webmd/main4222322.shtml. Accessed February 25, 2011; and Wilkie, C. "Crack Cocaine Moves South." *Boston Globe* (23 June 1996):19.

■ Extent and Frequency of Drug Use in Society

Erich Goode (2008), a much-respected sociologist, lists four types of drug use:

1. *Legal instrumental use:* Taking prescribed drugs and OTC drugs to relieve or treat mental or physical symptoms.
2. *Legal recreational use:* Using such licit drugs as tobacco, alcohol, and caffeine to achieve a certain mental or psychic state.
3. *Illegal instrumental use:* Taking drugs without a prescription to accomplish a task or goal, such as taking nonprescription amphetamines to drive through the night or relying excessively on barbiturates to get through the day.
4. *Illegal recreational use:* Taking illicit drugs for fun or pleasure to experience euphoria, such as abusing prescribed methylphenidate (Ritalin) as a substitute for cocaine.

Why has the prevalence of licit and illicit drug use remained consistent since 1988? Why has this

Here and Now

Current Global Status of Illicit Drug Use in Selected Countries

Afghanistan

World's largest producer of opium; poppy cultivation decreased 22% to 157,000 hectares in 2008 but remains at a historically high level. Less favorable growing conditions in 2008 reduced potential opium production to 5500 metric tons, down 31% from 2007. If the entire opium crop were processed, 648 metric tons of pure heroin potentially could be produced. The Taliban and other antigovernment groups participate in and profit from the opiate trade, which is a key source of revenue for the Taliban inside Afghanistan. Widespread corruption and instability impede counterdrug efforts. Most of the heroin consumed in Europe and Eurasia is derived from Afghan opium. It is vulnerable to drug money laundering through informal financial networks. Also a regional source of hashish.

Argentina

A transshipment country for cocaine headed for Europe, heroin headed for the United States, and ephedrine and pseudoephedrine headed for Mexico. There is some money-laundering activity, especially in the Tri-Border Area. Law enforcement corruption, a source for precursor chemicals, and increasing domestic consumption of drugs in urban centers, especially cocaine base and synthetic drugs (2008).

Aruba

Transit point for U.S.- and Europe-bound narcotics with some accompanying money-laundering activity. A relatively high percentage of its population consumes cocaine.

Australia

Tasmania is one of the world's major suppliers of licit opiate products. The government maintains strict controls over areas of opium poppy cultivation and the output of poppy straw concentrate. It is a major consumer of cocaine and amphetamines.

Bahamas

Transshipment point for cocaine and marijuana bound for the United States and Europe; also an offshore financial center.

Belgium

Growing producer of synthetic drugs and cannabis. A transit point for U.S.-bound Ecstasy and a source of precursor chemicals for South American cocaine processors. It is a transshipment point for cocaine, heroin, hashish, and marijuana entering Western Europe. Despite a strengthening of legislation, the country remains vulnerable to money laundering related to narcotics, automobiles, alcohol, and tobacco. There is also significant domestic consumption of Ecstasy.

Bolivia

World's third-largest cultivator of coca (after Colombia and Peru) with an estimated 29,500 hectares under cultivation in 2007, a slight increase compared to 2006. It is also the third largest producer of cocaine, estimated at 120 metric tons potential pure cocaine in 2007, and a transit country for Peruvian and Colombian cocaine destined for Brazil, Argentina, Chile, Paraguay, and Europe. Cultivation generally has been increasing since 2000, despite eradication and alternative crop programs. It has weak border controls and some money-laundering activity related to the narcotics trade. It also is a major cocaine consumer (2008).

Brazil

Second-largest consumer of cocaine in the world; it is an important market for Colombian, Bolivian, and Peruvian

(*continued*)

Current Global Status of Illicit Drug Use in Selected Countries (*continued*)

cocaine. It is an illicit producer of cannabis and trace amounts of coca cultivation in the Amazon region, used for domestic consumption. The government has a large-scale eradication program to control cannabis. It is an important transshipment country for Bolivian, Colombian, and Peruvian cocaine headed for Europe, and is also used by traffickers as a way station for narcotics air transshipments between Peru and Colombia. There has been an upsurge in drug-related violence and weapons smuggling. Illicit narcotics proceeds are often laundered through the financial system. There is significant illicit financial activity in the Tri-Border Area (2008).

Burma

Remains the world's second largest producer of illicit opium with an estimated production in 2008 of 340 metric tons, an increase of 26%; poppy cultivation in 2008 totaled 22,500 hectares (a hectare is equivalent to 2.471 acres of surface or land), a 4% increase from 2007. Production in south and east Shan state, the Army's areas of greatest control, remains low. Shan state is the source of 94% of Burma's poppy cultivation. Lack of government will to take on major narcotrafficking groups and lack of serious commitment against money laundering continue to hinder the overall antidrug effort. It is a major source of methamphetamine and heroin for regional consumption (2008).

Canada

Illicit producer of cannabis for the domestic drug market and export to the United States. Use of hydroponics technology permits growers to plant large quantities of high-quality marijuana indoors. Ecstasy production is increasing, some of which is destined for the United States. It is vulnerable to narcotics money laundering because of its mature financial services sector.

China

Major transshipment point for heroin produced in the Golden Triangle region of Southeast Asia. There is growing domestic consumption of synthetic drugs and heroin from Southeast and Southwest Asia. It is a source country for methamphetamine and heroin chemical precursors, despite new regulations on its large chemical industry (2008).

Colombia

Illicit producer of coca, opium poppy, and cannabis. It is the world's leading coca cultivator with 167,000 hectares in coca cultivation in 2007, a 6% increase over 2006, producing a potential of 535 metric tons of pure cocaine. It is also the world's largest producer of coca derivatives. It supplies cocaine to nearly all of the U.S. market and the great majority of other international drug markets. In 2005, aerial eradication dispensed herbicide to treat over 130,000 hectares, but aggressive replanting on the part of coca growers means Colombia remains a key producer. A significant portion of narcotics proceeds are either laundered or invested in Colombia through the black market peso exchange. It is also an important supplier of heroin to the U.S. market, though opium poppy cultivation is estimated to have fallen 25% between 2006 and 2007. Most Colombian heroin is destined for the U.S. market (2008).

Germany

Source of precursor chemicals for South American cocaine processors. It is a transshipment point for and consumer of Southwest Asian heroin, Latin American cocaine, and European-produced synthetic drugs; also a major financial center.

Guatemala

Major transit country for cocaine and heroin. In 2005, it cultivated 100 hectares of opium poppy after reemerging as a potential source of opium in 2004, with potential production of less than 1 metric ton of pure heroin. Marijuana cultivation is for mostly domestic consumption. Its proximity to Mexico makes Guatemala a major staging area for drugs (particularly for cocaine). Money laundering is a serious problem, as is corruption.

Haiti

Caribbean transshipment point for cocaine en route to the United States and Europe; substantial bulk cash smuggling activity; Colombian narcotics traffickers favor Haiti for illicit financial transactions; pervasive corruption; significant consumer of cannabis.

Iran

Despite substantial interdiction efforts and considerable control measures along the border with Afghanistan, Iran remains one of the primary transshipment routes for Southwest Asian heroin to Europe. It also suffers one of the highest opiate addiction rates in the world and has an increasing problem with synthetic drugs. It lacks anti-money laundering laws. Iran has reached out to neighboring countries to share counter-drug intelligence.

Italy

Important gateway for and consumer of Latin American cocaine and Southwest Asian heroin entering the European market. There is money laundering by organized crime and from smuggling.

Current Global Status of Illicit Drug Use in Selected Countries (*continued*)

Mexico

Major drug-producing nation. Cultivation of opium poppy in 2007 rose to 6900 hectares, yielding a potential production of 18 metric tons of pure heroin, or 50 metric tons of "black tar" heroin, the dominant form of Mexican heroin in the western United States. Marijuana cultivation increased to 8900 hectares in 2007 and yielded a potential production of 15,800 metric tons. The government conducts the largest independent illicit-crop eradication program in the world. Mexico continues to be the primary transshipment country for U.S.-bound cocaine from South America, with an estimated 90% of annual cocaine movements toward the United States stopping in Mexico. Major drug syndicates control the majority of drug trafficking throughout the country. It is a producer and distributor of Ecstasy and a significant money-laundering center. It is also a major supplier of heroin and the largest foreign supplier of marijuana and methamphetamine to the U.S. market (2007).

Morocco

One of the world's largest producers of illicit hashish. Shipments of hashish are mostly directed to Western Europe. It is also a transit point for cocaine from South America destined for Western Europe. Morocco is a significant consumer of cannabis.

Netherlands

Major European producer of synthetic drugs, including Ecstasy, and a cannabis cultivator. It is an important gateway for cocaine, heroin, and hashish entering Europe and a major source of U.S.-bound Ecstasy. Its large financial sector is vulnerable to money laundering. The Netherlands is also a significant consumer of Ecstasy.

North Korea

For years, from the 1970s into the 2000s, citizens of the Democratic People's Republic of (North) Korea (DPRK), many of them diplomatic employees of the government, were apprehended abroad while trafficking in narcotics, including two in Turkey in December 2004. Police investigations in Taiwan and Japan in recent years have linked North Korea to large illicit shipments of heroin and methamphetamine, including an attempt by the North Korean merchant ship *Pong Su* to deliver 150 kilograms of heroin to Australia in April 2003.

Pakistan

Significant transit area for Afghan drugs, including heroin, opium, morphine, and hashish, bound for Iran, Western markets, the Gulf States, Africa, and Asia. Financial crimes related to drug trafficking, terrorism, corruption, and smuggling remain problems. Opium poppy cultivation was estimated to be 2300 hectares in 2007, with 600 of those hectares eradicated. Federal and provincial authorities continue to conduct anti-poppy campaigns that utilize forced eradication, fines, and arrests.

Panama

Major cocaine transshipment point and primary money-laundering center for narcotics revenue. Money-laundering activity is especially heavy in the Colón Free Zone. It is an offshore financial center. There are negligible signs of coca cultivation. Monitoring of financial transactions is improving, but official corruption remains a major problem.

Peru

Until 1996 the world's largest coca leaf producer, Peru is now the world's second largest producer of coca leaf, though it lags far behind Colombia. Cultivation of coca in Peru declined to 36,000 hectares in 2007. It is also second largest producer of cocaine, estimated at 210 metric tons of potential pure cocaine in 2007. Finished cocaine is shipped out from Pacific ports to the international drug market. Increasing amounts of base and finished cocaine, however, are being moved to Brazil, Chile, Argentina, and Bolivia for use in the Southern Cone or transshipment to Europe and Africa. There is increasing domestic drug consumption.

Poland

Despite diligent counternarcotics measures and international information sharing on cross-border crimes, it is a major illicit producer of synthetic drugs for the international market as well as a minor transshipment point for Southwest Asian heroin and Latin American cocaine to Western Europe.

South Africa

A transshipment center for heroin, hashish, and cocaine, as well as a major cultivator of marijuana in its own right. Cocaine and heroin consumption in South Africa is on the rise. It is the world's largest market for illicit methaqualone, usually imported illegally from India through various east African countries, but it is increasingly producing its own synthetic drugs for domestic consumption. It is an attractive venue for money launderers given the increasing level of organized criminal and narcotics activity in the region and the size of the South African economy.

United States

World's largest consumer of cocaine (shipped from Colombia through Mexico and the Caribbean), Colombian

(*continued*)

Current Global Status of Illicit Drug Use in Selected Countries (*continued*)

heroin, and Mexican heroin and marijuana. A major consumer of Ecstasy and Mexican methamphetamine and a minor consumer of high-quality Southeast Asian heroin. An illicit producer of cannabis, depressants, stimulants, hallucinogens, and methamphetamine; also a money-laundering center.

Worldwide Facts

Cocaine

Worldwide coca leaf cultivation in 2007 amounted to 232,500 hectares; Colombia produced slightly more than two-thirds of the worldwide crop, followed by Peru and Bolivia. Potential pure cocaine production decreased 7% to 865 metric tons in 2007. Colombia conducts an aggressive coca eradication campaign, but both the Peruvian and Bolivian governments are hesitant to eradicate coca in key growing areas. About 551 metric tons of export-quality cocaine (85% pure) is documented to have been seized or destroyed in 2005. U.S. consumption of export-quality cocaine is estimated to have been in excess of 380 metric tons.

Opiates

Worldwide illicit opium poppy cultivation continued to increase in 2007, with a potential opium production of 8400 metric tons, reaching the highest levels recorded since estimates began in the mid-1980s. Afghanistan is the world's primary opium producer, accounting for 95% of the global supply. Southeast Asia—responsible for 9% of global opium—saw marginal increases in production. Latin America produced 1% of global opium, but most was refined into heroin destined for the U.S. market. If all potential opium was processed into pure heroin, the potential global production in 2007 would have been 1000 metric tons of heroin.

Source: Central Intelligence Agency. *The World Factbook 2009.* Washington, DC: U.S. Government Printing Office, 2009. Available at: https://www.cia.gov/library/publications/the-world-factbook/fields/print_2086.html. Accessed March 15, 2011.

---

trend occurred, when federal, state, and local government expenditures for fighting the drug war have been increasing at the same time? There are several possible answers, none of which, by itself, offers a satisfactory response. One perspective notes that practically all of us use drugs in some form, with what constitutes "drug use" being merely a matter of degree. A second explanation is that more varieties of both licit and illicit drugs are available today. One source estimated that approximately 80% of all currently marketed drugs were either unknown or unavailable 30 years ago (Critser 1996). Regarding prescriptions, Critser (2005, p. 23) states that "the average number of prescriptions per person, annually, in 1993 was seven, and in 2005 it was twelve." Another source stated, "The retail sales of OTC drugs (aspirin, Tylenol, No-Doz, and so on) totaled $16.9 billion in 2009" (Consumer Healthcare Products Association [CHPA] 2010) and yet another source stated "$234.1 billion worth of pharmaceutical prescription drugs were sold in 2008" (Lundy 2010, p. 1). In the United States alone, the rate of yearly prescription growth was estimated between 5.5% and 6% in 2010 (World Pharmaceutical Market Summary 2010). In 2009, the total global prescription pharmaceutical market was $837 billion in sales. Reuters reports, "[G]lobal pharmaceutical sales are expected to reach $1.1 trillion in 2014 . . ." (Berkrot 2010, p. 1). Such figures indicate that it may be more difficult to find people who do not use psychoactive drugs compared to individuals who do.

Further, a third category of drug sales has joined OTC and prescription drugs: herbal medicines, vitamins, minerals, enzymes, and other natural potions. "Out-of-pocket spending on herbal supplements, chiropractic visits, meditation, and other forms of complementary and alternative medicines (CAM) was estimated at $34 billion in a single year" (Boyles 2009). "Americans spend almost a third as much money out-of-pocket on herbal supplements and other alternative medicines as they do on prescription drugs . . ." (Boyles 2009). Drug use is so common that the average household in the United States owns about five drugs, of which two are prescription drugs and the other three are OTC drugs. Of the many prescriptions written by physicians, approximately one-third modify moods and behaviors in one way or another. A National Institute on Drug Abuse (NIDA) study and other research indicates that more than 60% of adults in the United States have, at some time in their lives, taken a psychoactive drug (one that affects mood or consciousness). More than one-third of adults have used or are using depressants or sedatives.

A third explanation is that "... in the modern age, increased sophistication has brought with it techniques of drug production and distribution that have resulted in a worldwide epidemic of drug use" (Kusinitz 1988, p. 149). In the 1980s and 1990s, for example, illicit drug cartels proliferated, and varieties of marijuana with ever-increasing potency infiltrated all urban and rural areas in the United States as well as the world. Many of these varieties are crossbred with ultra-sophisticated techniques and equipment available everywhere.

Finally, even coffee (as discussed in Chapter 10, "Here and Now") has undergone a technological revolution. Higher levels of caffeine content has become available worldwide. This trend has led to the phenomenal growth of the following: (1) franchise duplication of gourmet coffee bars in the United States (e.g., Starbucks, Peet's, Three Brothers Coffee); (2) sales of espresso and cappuccino coffee makers for home use, with accompanying coffee grinders or coffee pods; and (3) sales of specialized coffees and teas through a multitude of e-mail coffee/tea clubs.

Approximately 25 years ago, it was difficult to purchase a cup of espresso or cappuccino in a typical restaurant; today, availability of such types of coffees is commonplace. Even at university unions and libraries, airports, shopping malls, and inner-city coffee shops, it is not unusual to see people lined up waiting to order and purchase their specially made and specially flavored coffee or tea. This is just one example of how caffeine (often seen as a benign drug) has evolved, with many new varieties of coffee beans from exotic islands and countries coming together with more sophisticated electronic equipment, with the result that the idea of simple brewing has been relegated to the past. The standard American "cup of coffee in the morning" has

Often the consumption of drugs (such as caffeine) complements social interaction.

spilled into including coffee during the afternoon and evening. This is a small example of a much-tolerated drug maintaining its own impressive history of development, increased use, complexity in developing many more varieties, and added sophistication.

Drug Use: Statistics, Trends, and Demographics

An incredible amount of money is spent each year for licit (legal) and illicit (illegal) chemicals that alter consciousness, awareness, or mood. Five classes of legal chemicals exist:

1. *Social drugs:* Approximately $90 billion is spent on alcohol each year. Another $51.9 billion goes toward tobacco products, of which 95% comes from cigarette sales. The other 5% accounts for the $2 billion or so spent on cigars, chewing tobacco, pipe tobacco, roll-your-own tobacco, and snuff tobacco. In addition, $5.7 billion is spent on coffee, tea, and cocoa.
2. *Prescription drugs:* As mentioned earlier, $837 billion in worldwide sales was racked up for prescription pharmaceuticals in 2009. The United States is the world's largest pharmaceutical market. In 2008, $234.1 billion of pharmaceutical prescription drugs were sold (Lundy 2010, p. 1). Other figures "... [f]rom 1997 to 2004 indicate that total purchases of outpatient Rx medicines increased approximately 2 billion to nearly 3 billion scripts" (*Pharmacy Times* 2007, p. 2).
3. *Over-the-counter (patent) drugs:* These products, including cough and cold items, external and internal analgesics, antacids, laxatives, antidiarrhea products, sleep aids, sedatives, and so on, account for $23.5 billion in sales.
4. *Nonmedical use of prescription-type drugs:* In recent years, an alarming statistic related to abuse is the growth of the nonmedical use of prescription-type drugs. In 2008, 51.9 million Americans (20.8% of persons age 12 or older) had used prescription-type drugs nonmedically at least once in their lifetime. Even the very young are not immune to significant nonmedical use of prescription-type drugs. For example, 2.5% of 8th graders, 5.1% of 10th graders, and 7.2% of 12th graders used narcotics, specifically OxyContin and Vicodin (Johnston et al. 2009) (see "Here and Now: Sources of Prescription Drugs Misused by Youths"). In addition, when looking at 12th graders alone, in 2007–2008, 8.2% had

Here and Now

Sources of Prescription Drugs Misused by Youth

Friends and family are the most common source of prescription drugs misused* by youths in the United States, according to an analysis of data from the National Survey on Drug Use and Health (NSDUH). Around one-half of youths who reported misusing prescription stimulants (50%), tranquilizers (47%), or sedatives (47%) in the past year said that they most recently obtained the medication free from friends or family, as did one-third of those who reported the misuse of prescription opioids. The second most common source for obtaining stimulants, tranquilizers, and sedatives was purchasing from a friend/ relative, drug dealer/stranger, or the Internet, and the second most common source for obtaining prescription opioids was acquiring them from a physician. Youths who obtained the medication by buying it were more likely to have concurrent substance use and to have 10 or more misuse episodes as compared to those who obtained the medications other ways (data not shown). According to the authors, "these results may help identify subgroups of adolescent prescription misusers who are most vulnerable to consequences from misuse or other substance use" (p. 828).

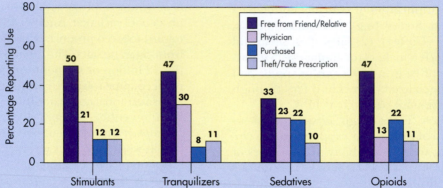

Most recent source of prescription medicines misused in the past year among youths (ages 12 to 17): 2005 and 2006.

*Misuse was defined as "any intentional use of a medication with intoxicating properties outside of a physician's prescription for a bona fide medical condition, excluding accidental misuse."

Note: Respondents also reported that prescription medicines were obtained "some other way" (stimulants, 5%; tranquilizers, 4%; sedatives, 12%; opioids, 7%). Data are from 36,992 adolescents ages 12 to 17 participating in the 2005 and/or 2006 National Survey on Drug Use and Health. Of these youths, 8.3% reported *any* prescription drug misuse in the past year; 7% reported opioid misuse; 2% reported tranquilizer misuse; 2% reported stimulant misuse; and 0.4% reported sedative misuse.

Source: University of Maryland, Center for Substance Abuse Research (CESAR). "Friends and Family Are Most Common Source of Prescription Drugs Misused by Youths." *CESAR FAX* 18(32), 2009, using data from Schepis, T. S., and S. Krishnan-Sarin. "Sources of Prescriptions for Misuse by Adolescents: Differences in Sex, Ethnicity, and Severity of Misuse in a Population-Based Study." *Journal of the American Academy of Child and Adolescent Psychiatry* 48(8):828–836, 2009.

other types of stimulant and depressant-type prescription pills nonmedically within the past year. If we add up 12th graders' nonmedical use of prescription pills, the total annual abuse is 15.4%, which is a significant percentage of younger youths taking prescription pills on an annual basis. Finally, the amount spent on inhalants and other miscellaneous drugs, such as nutmeg and morning glory seeds, cannot be estimated.

How much money goes to purchase illicit drugs? The Office of National Drug Control Policy (ONDCP) estimates what Americans spent on illicit drugs. It found that in the 2000s, Americans spent $64 billion on illicit drugs: $36 billion on cocaine, $10 billion on heroin, $11 billion on marijuana, and $2.7 billion on other illegal drugs and on legal drugs that were misused (ONDCP 2001).

Further, regarding the extent of drug use, studies carried out by the Social Research Group of George Washington University, the Institute for Research in Social Behavior in Berkeley, California, and others provide detailed, in-depth data showing that drug use is universal. A major purpose of their studies was to determine the level of psychoactive drug use among people ages 18 through 74, excluding those people hospitalized or in the armed forces. Data were collected to identify people who used specific categories of drugs (that is, caffeine, sleeping pills, nicotine, alcohol, and other psychoactive drugs). Other studies have shown that people in the 18- to 25-year-old age group are by far the heaviest users and experimenters in terms of past-month and past-year usage (see **Table 1.3**).

Table 1.4 supports the findings of the Social Research Group of George Washington University. In looking at past-month usage, an estimated 13.6 million Americans, or 51.6%, and 128.9 million of the total U.S. population age 12 and older, were drinkers. Statistics also reveal that with regard to

past-month usage of cigarettes, approximately 59.7 million or 23.9% of Americans smoked cigarettes in 2008 (see Table 1.4).

■ Current Patterns of Licit and Illicit Drug Use

Table 1.4 shows that illicit drug use remains an alarming problem. In looking at lifetime use of licit and illicit types of drugs, it is estimated that approximately 20 million Americans age 12 years or older were current illicit drug users in 2008. This number represents 8% of the population age 12 years or older (SAMHSA 2009). The leading types of illicit drugs (see **Figure 1.2**) were marijuana (41%), co-

Table 1.3 Trend Data on the Prevalence of Illicit Drug Use: 2003–2008

USED IN PAST MONTH	2003	2004	2005	2006	2007	2008
Used in Past Month						
All ages 12+	8.2	7.9	8.1	8.1	8	8
12–17	11.2	10.6	9.9	9.6	9.4	9
18–25	20.3	19.4	20.1	19.7	19.6	19.5
26–34	11.1	11.3	11.3	12	11.1	11.3
35+	4.4	4.3	4.7	4.8	4.8	5
Used in Past Year						
All ages 12+	14.7	14.5	14.4	14.5	14.3	14.2
12–17	21.8	21	19.9	19.3	18.5	18.6
18–25	34.6	33.9	34	34.2	33	33.3
26–34	20.1	19.6	20.2	21.1	19.9	19.9
35+	8.1	8.2	8.2	8.3	8.9	8.7
Used in Lifetime (Ever Used)						
All ages 12+	46.4	45.8	46.1	45.4	46.1	47
12–17	30.5	30	27.7	27.3	25.9	25.6
18–25	60.5	59.3	59.3	59.1	57.7	56.9
26–34	57.4	57.3	57	57.8	56.6	58.2
35+	44.8	44.7	46.1	45	47.4	48.9

Source: Substance Abuse and Mental Health Services Administration (SAMHSA). *Results from the 2005 National Survey on Drug Use and Health: National Findings.* Office of Applied Studies, NSDUH Series H-36, DHHS Publication No. SMA 09-4435. Rockville, MD, 2008.

Table 1.4 **National Household Survey on Drug Abuse: 2008**
Percentage of population and estimated number of alcohol, tobacco, and illicit drug users in the United States among persons aged 12 or older.

	LIFETIME*		PAST MONTH	
	PERCENTAGE	**NUMBER OF USERS (IN THOUSANDS)**	**PERCENTAGE**	**NUMBER OF USERS (IN THOUSANDS)**
Alcohol	82.2	205,404	51.6	128,974
Cigarettes	69.6	162,551	23.9	59,781
Marijuana/hashish	41.0	102,404	6.1	15,203
Nonmedical use of any psychotherapeutics[†]	20.8	51,970	2.5	6224
Smokeless tobacco	18.4	45,889	3.5	8670
Cocaine	14.7	36,773	0.7	1855
Crack	3.4	8554	0.1	359
Hallucinogens	14.4	35,963	0.4	1060
LSD	9.4	23,547	0.1	154
Ecstasy	5.2	12,924	0.3	555
PCP	2.7	6631	0.2	24
Pain Relievers	14.0	34,861	1.9	4747
Oxycontin	1.9	4842	0.2	435
Inhalants	8.9	2274	0.3	640
Tranquilizers	8.6	21,476	0.7	1800
Stimulants	8.5	21,206	0.4	904
Methamphetamine	5.0	12,598	0.1	314
Sedatives	3.6	8882	0.1	234
Heroin	1.5	3788	0.1	213
Any illicit drug[§]	47.0	117,325	8.0	20,077

Notes: The results obtained from this national survey were completed at 142,938 addresses, and 68,736 completed interviews were obtained. The survey was conducted from January 2008 through December 2008. Weighted response rates for household screening and for interviewing were 89.0% and 74.4%, respectively.

* Lifetime refers to ever used. This column shows the use of drugs from highest to lowest percentages as well as the number of persons using.

[†] Nonmedical use of prescription-type psychotherapeutics includes the nonmedical use of pain relievers, tranquilizers, stimulants, or sedatives but does *not* include over-the-counter drugs.

[§] Illicit drugs include marijuana/hashish, cocaine (including crack), heroin, hallucinogens, inhalants, or prescription-type psychotherapeutics used nonmedically.

Source: Substance Abuse and Mental Health Services Administration (SAMHSA). *Results from the 2008 National Survey on Drug Use and Health: National Findings.* Office of Applied Studies, NSDUH Series H-36, DHHS Publication No. SMA 09-4435. Rockville, MD, 2009.

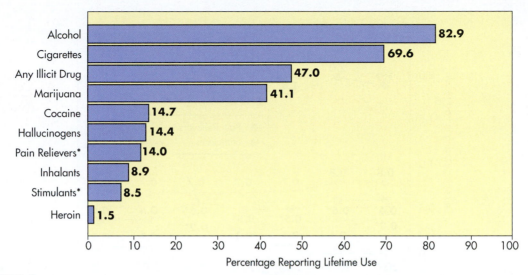

FIGURE 1.2

Percentage of U.S. residents (age 12 or older) reporting lifetime use of alcohol, tobacco, and illicit drugs: 2008.

*Does not include over-the-counter drugs.

Source: Substance Abuse and Mental Health Services Administration (SAMHSA). *Results from the 2008 National Survey on Drug Use and Health: National Findings.* Office of Applied Studies, NSDUH Series H-36, DHHS Publication No. SMA 09-4435. Rockville, MD, 2009.

caine (14.7%), hallucinogens (mainly LSD and Ecstasy, 14.4%), pain relievers (14%), and inhalants (8.9%). Regarding the licit types of drugs used (lifetime use), from highest to lowest the most popular drugs were alcohol (82.2%), cigarettes (69.6%), and nonmedical use of psychotherapeutics (20.8%), which includes pain relievers (14%) and stimulants (8.5%); see Table 1.4.

Figure 1.3 shows the past-month use of illicit drugs among persons age 12 or older. Again, the category "illicit drugs" shows the highest use (20.1 million), followed by use of marijuana (15.2 million), psychotherapeutics (6.2 million), cocaine (1.9 million), hallucinogens (1.1 million), inhalants (0.6 million), and heroin (0.2 million).

Nonmedical Use of Psychotherapeutics (Pain Relievers)

Figure 1.4 shows the number of past-month nonmedical users of different types of psychotherapeutic drugs among persons age 12 or older from 2002–2008. For each of the four drug categories (pain relievers, tranquilizers, stimulants, and sedatives), there is a line showing use over the years from 2002–2008. The rates of past-month use of pain relievers is highest in 2008, with 1.9 million users, followed by tranquilizers (0.7 million), stimulants (0.4 million), and sedatives (0.1 million). **Figure 1.5** looks at the nonmedical use of pain-

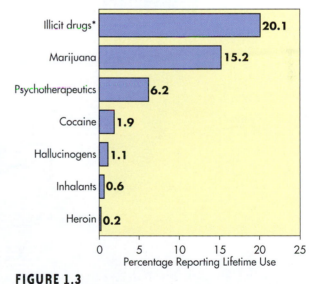

FIGURE 1.3

Past-month use of selected drugs among persons age 12 or older: 2008.

*Illicit drugs include marijuana/hashish, cocaine (including crack), heroin, hallucinogens, inhalants, or prescription-type psychotherapeutics used nonmedically.

Source: Substance Abuse and Mental Health Services Administration (SAMHSA). *Results from the 2008 National Survey on Drug Use and Health: National Findings.* Office of Applied Studies, NSDUH Series H-36, DHHS Publication No. SMA 09-4435. Rockville, MD, 2009.

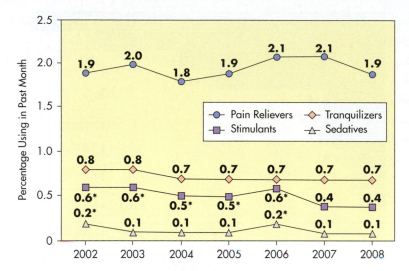

FIGURE 1.4

Past-month nonmedical use of various types of psychotherapeutic drugs among persons age 12 or older: 2002–2008.

*Difference between this estimate and the 2008 estimate is statistically significant at the 0.05 level.

Source: Substance Abuse and Mental Health Services Administration (SAMHSA). *Results from the 2008 National Survey on Drug Use and Health: National Findings.* Office of Applied Studies, NSDUH Series H-36, DHHS Publication No. SMA 09-4435. Rockville, MD, 2009.

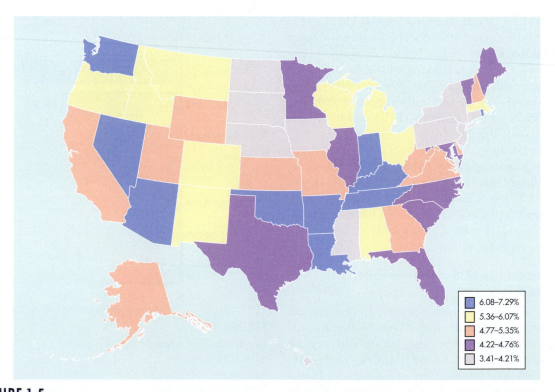

FIGURE 1.5

Annual averages of nonmedical use of pain relievers in the past year among persons age 12 or older, by state: 2006 and 2007.

Source: Hughes, A., Sathe, N., and Spagnola, K. *State Estimates of Substance Use from the 2006-2007 National Surveys on Drug Use and Health.* Office of Applied Studies, Substance Abuse and Mental Health Services Administration, NSDUH Series H-35, DHHS Publication No. 09-4362, Rockville, MD, 2009.

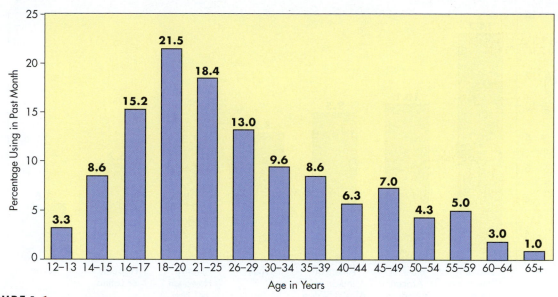

FIGURE 1.6

Past-month illicit drug use among persons age 12 or older, by age: 2008.

···

Source: Substance Abuse and Mental Health Services Administration (SAMHSA). *Results from the 2008 National Survey on Drug Use and Health: National Findings.* Office of Applied Studies, NSDUH Series H-36, DHHS Publication No. SMA 09-4435. Rockville, MD, 2009.

relieving prescription drugs that are being used throughout the United States without a prescription, often taken for the experience or the euphoric effects. In 2006–2007, 5.1% of all persons age 12 or older reported having used pain relievers nonmedically in the past year, a percentage that remained relatively unchanged from 2005–2006. Although not specifically listed in this figure, Arkansas had the highest percentage (7.3%) of persons age 12 or older using pain relievers for nonmedical purposes in the past year; South Dakota had the lowest rate in the nation (3.4%). Arkansas Kentucky, Oklahoma, and Tennessee ranked the top fifth of states for this measure across all age groups and for the total population age 12 or older. Nine states showed significant changes in the nonmedical use of pain relievers in the past year between 2005–2006 and 2006–2007: Connecticut, Florida, Iowa, Nebraska, and Utah had *declines,* and Arkansas, Arizona, Ohio, and Wisconsin had *increases.*

Figure 1.6 shows the past-month use of illicit drugs by age in 2008. With regard to age patterns, the following trends are apparent:

- Rates of drug use showed substantial variation by age. For example, 3.3% of youths ages 12 or 13 reported current illicit drug use in 2008. As in other years, illicit drug use tended to increase for each age category (12–13, 14–15, 16–17, 18–20) until 20, and then beginning at 21 years of age through 65+ illicit drug use showed continual decreases.

- The 18–25 age category showed the highest amount of illicit drug use (21.5%).

- Though not shown on any of the figures, among 18- to 25-year-olds, 19.6% used illicit drugs, 16.5% used marijuana, 1.7% used cocaine, and 1.5% used hallucinogens in 2008 during the past month before being surveyed (SAMHSA 2009).

- An estimated 70% of all psychoactive prescription drugs used by people under 30 years old were obtained without the user having a prescription (SAMHSA 2004).

Racial and Ethnic Differences

Figure 1.7 shows average past-month illicit drug use among persons age 12 or older by racial and ethnic differences in 2008. The figures in this chart reveal the following trends:

- In 2008, from highest to lowest, racial/ethnic groups had the following rates of illicit drug use: Two or more races (14.7%), black or African American (10.1%), American Indian or Alaska native (9.5%), white (8.2%), Native Hawaiian

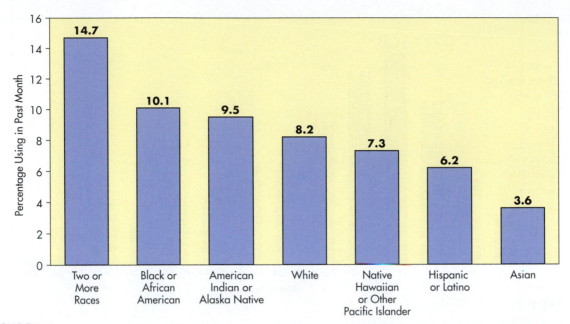

FIGURE 1.7

Past-month illicit drug use among persons age 12 or older, by race/ethnicity: 2008.

Source: Substance Abuse and Mental Health Services Administration (SAMHSA). *Results from the 2008 National Survey on Drug Use and Health: National Findings.* Office of Applied Studies, NSDUH Series H-36, DHHS Publication No. SMA 09-4435. Rockville, MD, 2009.

or other Pacific Islander (7.3%), Hispanic or Latino (6.2%), and Asian (3.6%).

- As in past years when this research was conducted, Asians continue to have the lowest percentage of current illicit drug use, just as many other racial and ethnic group studies on drug use had found previously.
- Although not shown in this figure, among youths ages 12 to 17 in 2008, the rate of current past-month illicit drug use was as follows: Native Hawaiian or other Pacific Islander (18.2%), two or more races (13.5%), white (9.8%), Hispanic or Latino (8.9%), black or African American (8.2%), and Asian (2.7%).
- Among Hispanic groups, Puerto Ricans were the heaviest users of illicit drugs, followed by Mexican Americans and Cuban Americans. Central and South Americans had the lowest amount of current illicit drug use (SAMHSA 2007a).

Gender

In 2008, the following were major findings regarding illicit drug use by gender (SAMHSA 2009):

- As in prior years, in 2008 males were more likely than females among persons age 12 or older to be current illicit drug users (9.9% vs. 6.3%, respectively). The rate of past-month marijuana usage was about twice as high for males as for females. Males were more likely than females to be past-month users of marijuana (7.9% vs. 4.4%). However, males and females had similar rates of past-month nonmedical use of psychotherapeutic drugs (2.6% vs. 2.4%), pain relievers (2.0% vs. 1.8%), tranquilizers (0.7% vs. 0.8%), stimulants (0.4% for both), methamphetamine (0.1% for both), and sedatives (0.1% for both).
- The rate of current illicit drug use among females age 12 or older increased from 5.8% in 2007 to 6.3% in 2008. However, the rate did not change significantly for males from 2007 to 2008 (10.4% and 9.9%, respectively). Current marijuana use also increased among females (from 3.8% to 4.4%), but for males there was no significant change (8% and 7.9%, respectively).
- Among youths ages 12 to 17 in 2008, males and females had similar rates of current use of an illicit drug (9.5% for males and 9.1% for females), cocaine (0.5% and 0.3%), hallucinogens (1.1% and 0.8%), and inhalants (1.1% for both).
- Generally, gender and licit/illicit drug use behavior correlate with specific age periods. Men have a tendency to prefer stimulants in their 30s, depressants in their 40s and 50s, and sedatives from age 60 on. In comparison to men, women are most likely to use stimulants from ages 21 through 39 and depressants more fre-

quently in their 30s. Women's use of sedatives shows a pattern similar to men's use, with the frequency of use increasing with age. Generally, women tend to take pills to cope with problems, whereas men tend to use alcohol and marijuana for the same purpose.

- People older than 35 are more likely to take pills, whereas younger people prefer alcohol and other licit and illicit types of drugs. Among those using pills, younger people and men are more likely to use stimulants than older people and women, who more frequently take sedatives. (The actual usage rates for all psychoactive drugs are probably 35% higher than the reported data.)

- Among younger people (ages 18 through 32 years), use of stimulants and depressants for nonmedical reasons often results from drug misuse or dependency. Methods for obtaining psychoactive drugs for nonmedical purposes include (1) getting drugs from friends and relatives who have legitimate prescriptions, (2) resorting to drug dealers, and (3) purchasing or shoplifting OTC medications.

Pregnant Women

Among pregnant women ages 15 to 44 years, 5.1% used illicit drugs in the past month, based on data averaged for 2007 and 2008 (SAMHSA 2009). This rate was significantly lower than the rate among women in this age group who were not pregnant (9.8%). Among pregnant women, the average rate of current illicit drug use in 2007–2008 (5.1%) did not change significantly from 2005–2006 (4.0%) and was similar to the rate observed in 2003–2004 (4.6%). The rate of current illicit drug use in the combined 2007–2008 data was lower for pregnant women than for nonpregnant women among those ages 18 to 25 (7.1% vs. 16.2%, respectively) and among those ages 26 to 44 (3.0% vs. 6.7%). Among women ages 15 to 17, however, those who were pregnant had a higher rate of use than those who were not pregnant (21.6% vs. 12.9%). With exception of the 15–17 age group, we can generally conclude that pregnant women are less likely to use drugs than similar aged women who are not pregnant.

Education

Illicit drug use rates in 2008 were correlated with educational status (SAMHSA 2009). Among adults age 18 or older, the rate of current illicit drug use was lower for college graduates (5.7%) than for those who did not graduate from high school (8.1%), high school graduates (8.6%), and those with some college (9.4%). However, adults who had graduated from college were more likely to have tried illicit drugs in their lifetime when compared with adults who had not completed high school (51.8% vs. 37.7%). The rate of current illicit drug use declined from 9.3% in 2007 to 8.1% in 2008 among adults who had not completed high school.

College Students

The most significant findings regarding college students and illicit drug use are as follows:

- In the college-age population (persons ages 18 to 22 years), the rate of current illicit drug use was the same among full-time undergraduate college students (20.2%) as for other persons ages 18 to 22 years, including part-time students, students in other grades, and nonstudents (21.9%).

- The rate of current illicit drug use among college students and other 18- to 22-year-olds did not change between 2007 and 2008 (SAMHSA 2009).

- Among full-time college students ages 18 to 22, there were increases from 2007 to 2008 in the current rate of use of hallucinogens (from 1.0% to 2.1%), including Ecstasy (from 0.5% to 1.2%) and LSD (from 0.3% to 0.6%). There were no significant changes in the rates of current use for any drugs among persons ages 18 to 22 who were not full-time college students.

Geographic Area

Several of the more significant findings related to illicit drug use in specific geographic areas follow:

- The rate of illicit drug use in metropolitan areas is higher than the rate in nonmetropolitan counties. Rates were 8.5% in large metropolitan counties, 8.1% in small metropolitan counties, and 6.3% in nonmetropolitan counties.

- Within nonmetropolitan areas, counties that were urbanized had an illicit drug use rate of 7.2%, whereas completely rural counties had a lower rate (6.1%).

- Among persons age 12 or older, the rates of current illicit drug use in the United States were: 9.8% in the West, 8.2% in the Northeast, 7.6% in the Midwest, and 7.1% in the South (SAMHSA 2009).

Criminal Justice Populations/Arrestees

Certain significant findings and correlations are unique to criminal justice populations:

- In 2008, an estimated 1.6 million adults age 18 or older were on parole or other supervised release from prison at some time during the past year. Almost one-fifth of these (18.3%) were current illicit drug users, which was higher than the rate of 7.8% among adults not on parole or supervised release.

- Among the 5.2 million adults on probation at some time in the past year, 23.9% reported current illicit drug use in 2008. This was higher than the rate of 7.5% among adults not on probation in 2008 (SAMHSA 2009).
- In 2008, an estimated 333,000 prisoners were arrested for drug law violations—20% of state inmates and 52% of federal inmates (Sabol, West, and Cooper 2009).
- In 2008, nearly a third of state and a quarter of federal prisoners committed their offense under the influence of drugs, which was unchanged since 2004.
- Among federal inmates, men (50%) were slightly more likely than women (48%) to report drug use in the month before the offense in 2004 (Bureau of Justice Statistics [BJS] 2004).
- Among federal inmates in 2008, 56% of whites, 53% of blacks, and 39% of Hispanics reported using drugs in the month before the offense.
- One in three property offenders in state prisons report drug money as a motive in their crimes.
- Arrestee Drug Abuse Monitoring (ADAM) reports that at the time of arrest, 40% of arrestees tested positive for the presence of multiple drug substances. Approximately 40% tested positive for marijuana, 30% tested positive for cocaine, and 20% tested positive for crack (National Institute of Justice [NIJ] 2009). These three drugs are the most prevalent drugs testing positive for use at the time of arrest. (Very similar percentages were found in the 2004 estimates.) (BJS 2004).

KEY TERMS

experimenters
first category of drug users, typified as being in the initial stages of drug use; these people often use drugs for recreational purposes

compulsive users
second category of drug users, typified by an insatiable attraction followed by a psychological dependence on drugs

floaters or chippers
third category of drug users; these users vacillate between the need for pleasure seeking and the desire to relieve moderate to serious psychological problems; this category of drug user has two major characteristics: (1) a general focus mostly on using other people's drugs (often without maintaining a personal supply of the drug), and (2) vacillation between the characteristics of chronic drug users and experimenter types

■ Types of Drug Users

Just as a diverse set of personality traits (for example, introverts, extroverts, type A, obsessive-compulsive, and so on) exists, so drug users vary according to their general approach or orientation, frequency of use, and types and amounts of the drugs they consume. Some are occasional or moderate users, whereas others display a much stronger attachment to drug use. In fact, some display such obsessive-compulsive behavior that they cannot let a morning, afternoon, or evening pass without using drugs. Some researchers have classified such variability in the frequency and extent of usage as fitting into three basic patterns: experimenters, compulsive users, and "floaters" or "chippers" (members of the last category drift between experimentation and compulsive use).

Experimenters begin using drugs largely because of peer pressure and curiosity, and they confine their use to recreational settings. Generally, they more often enjoy being with peers who also use drugs recreationally. Alcohol, tobacco, marijuana, prescription drugs, hallucinogens, and many of the major stimulants are the drugs they are most likely to use. They are usually able to set limits on when these drugs are taken (often preferred in social settings), and they are more likely to know the difference between light, moderate, and chronic use.

Compulsive users, in contrast, ". . . devote considerable time and energy to getting high, talk incessantly (sometimes exclusively) about drug use . . . [and 'funny' or 'weird' experiences] . . . and become connoisseurs of street drugs" (Beschner 1986, p. 7). For compulsive users, recreational fun is impossible without getting high. Other characteristics of these users include the need to escape or postpone personal problems, to avoid stress and anxiety, and to enjoy the sensation of the drug's euphoric effects. Often, they have difficulty assuming personal responsibility and suffer from low self-esteem. Many compulsive users are from dysfunctional families, have persistent problems with the law, and/or have serious psychological problems underlying their drug-taking behavior. Problems with personal and public identity, excessive confusion about their sexual orientation, boredom, family discord, childhood sexual and/or mental abuse, academic pressure, and chronic depression all contribute to the inability to cope with issues without drugs (see "Case in Point: Ignoring the Signs of Drug Abuse").

Floaters or chippers focus more on using other people's drugs without maintaining a steady supply of drugs. Nonetheless, floaters or chippers,

►Case in Point Ignoring the Signs of Drug Abuse: A Hard Lesson Learned

Michael Alig missed all of the warning signs of the dangers of drug abuse and addiction. He states, "There is no excuse for killing someone, no reason to justify being wholly or even partly responsible for the death of another human being. I have never been a violent person. I don't even like sports." Now in prison for the accidental death of a friend, Michael recalls the following warning signs he refused to note:

1. Michael was living without any real boundaries. Now that he looks back at his life, he says it was out of control, and his friends were out of control.

2. Michael overdosed many times on many different drugs and would often wake up unaware of where he was, where he had been, who he was with, what he was doing with whomever he was with, what took place while he was on drugs, and so on.

3. One time Michael regained consciousness and was in the presence of "...an entire dinner of cocaine on the floor!" which he admits was too tempting to pass up.

4. People around Michael were constantly warning him to stop using drugs, and these were the same people with whom he was annoyed.

5. Just before his arrest, Michael had overdosed numerous times with naloxone, barely escaping death several times.

6. Michael used heroin with the false sense of euphoric security that all was good.

Now Michael, who was called the King of the Club Kids, believes he has finally learned to accept responsibilities as an adult. After solitary confinement for several months to stop using heroin in prison, he says that his approach to life has completely changed. Michael says, "A smile or a laugh isn't just a reaction to the most extreme situations anymore, but to my average daily experiences like eating a piece of sour candy, or seeing a fat boy in the prison yard with the crack of his butt exposed for everyone to see." Michael believes it will take a lot of time for his brain to rewire itself toward enjoying the simple pleasures of life. He states, "Now it will be the small, subtle life experiences that will be my reinforcements...[besides] parties in jail are dangerous." Today, Michael is over 50 years old.

Adapted from Michiana Point of View/Michael Alig. "Alig Missed Signs Along the Road to Tragedy." *The South Bend Tribune* (10 January 1999):B-3.

like experimenters, are generally light to moderate consumers of drugs. Chippers vacillate between the need for pleasure seeking and the desire to relieve moderate to serious psychological problems. As a result, although most are on the path to drug dependence, at this stage they drift between experimental drug-taking peers and chronic drug-using peers. In a sense, these drug users are marginal individuals who do not strongly identify with experimenters or compulsive users. (An example of how the various types of drug users are often adversely affected by peers is discussed in more detail in Chapters 2 and 16.)

■ Drug Use: Mass Media and Family Influences

Studies continually show that the majority of young drug users come from homes in which drugs are liberally used (Goode 1999; National Association for Children of Alcoholics 2005; SAMHSA 1996). Often on a daily basis, children from these homes constantly witness drug use at home. For instance, parents may consume large quantities of coffee to wake up in the morning and other forms of medication throughout the day: cigarettes with morning coffee, pills for either treating or relieving an upset stomach, vitamins for added nutrition, or aspirin for a headache. Finally, before going to bed, the grown-ups may take a few "nightcaps" or a sleeping pill to relax. The following is an interview related to the overuse of drugs:

Yeah, I always saw my mom smoking early in the morning while reading the newspaper and slowly sipping nearly a full pot of coffee. She took prescription drugs for asthma, used an inhaler, and took aspirin for headaches. When she accused me of using drugs at concerts, I would pick up her pack of cigarettes and several prescription bottles and while she was raging on me, I would quietly wave all her drugs close up in front of her face. She would stop nagging within seconds and actually one time I think she wanted to laugh but turned away toward the sink and just started washing cups and saucers. The way I figure it, she has her drugs, and I have mine. She may not agree with my use of my drugs but then she is not better either. It's great to have a drug-using family ain't it? *(From Venturelli's research files, male college student, age 20, June 12, 2000)*

This next interview is an example of how "pill-pilfering" can easily occur:

Yes, I came from a home with dozens of pharmacy prescriptions and with medicine cabinets crammed with over-the-counter drugs. In fact, my mom noticed that certain friends of mine were helping themselves to our medicine cabinet. At first, she told my dad that I was taking the pills. Finally, she had to remove most of the prescription medicines from the guest bathroom and hide them in her bedroom bathroom. This was about four years ago when I was in high school. She was right, several of my friends had a knack of lifting tabs from other homes when visiting friends. I know that one of my friends was into this when he told another friend of mine that our home had a nice variety of great drugs in the bathroom. Now, I know why my friends always had to go to the bathroom whenever they would stop by to see me. *(From Venturelli's research files, male attending a mid-size university in the Midwest, age 20, June 6, 2010)*

Some social scientists believe that everyday consumption of legal drugs—caffeine, prescription and OTC drugs, and alcohol—is fueled by the pace of modern lifestyles and greatly accelerated by the influence of today's increasingly sophisticated mass media.

If you look around your classroom building, the dormitories at your college, your college library, or your own home, evidence of mass media and electronic equipment can be found everywhere. Cultural knowledge and information are transmitted via media through electronic gadgets we simply "can't live without," to the point that they help us define and shape our everyday reality.

In regard to drug advertising, television remains the most influential medium. Most homes today have more than one television. "New findings from Nielsen's Television Audience Report show that in 2009 the average American home had 2.86 TV sets, which is roughly 18% higher than in 2000 (2.43 sets per home) and 43% higher than in 1990 (2.0 sets)" (Nielsenwire 2009, p. 1). Just as the number of televisions in the average home has been increasing over the last 30 years, "Drug firms . . . [have been increasing] . . . their spending on television advertis-

ing to consumers seven-fold from 1996 to 2000 . . ." (CBS News 2002). "Overall advertising spending aimed at ordinary people tripled between 1996 and 2000 to nearly $2.5 billion a year. Drug companies spent $1.6 billion in 2000 on television advertisements for Viagra, Claritin, Allegra, and other brand-name drugs that have become household names . . ." (CBS News 2002). As another example, "Each year, the alcohol industry spends more than a billion dollars on 'measured media' advertising, that is television, radio, print, and outdoor ads" (Federal Trade Commission [FTC] 2007). "The advertising budget for one beer—Budweiser—is more than the entire budget for research on alcoholism and alcohol abusers" (Kilbourne 1989, p. 13). More recent findings indicate that "Alcohol companies spent $4.9 billion on television advertising between 2001 and 2005. They spent 2.1% of this amount ($104 million) on 'responsibility advertisements' " (Center on Alcohol Marketing and Youth [CAMY] 2007).

Radio, newspapers, and magazines are also saturated with advertisements for OTC drugs that constantly offer relief from whatever illness you may have. There are pills for inducing sleep and those for staying awake, as well as others for treating indigestion, headache, backache, tension, constipation, and the like. Using these medicinal compounds can significantly alter mood, level of consciousness, and physical discomfort. Experts warn that such drug advertising is likely to increase.

In the early 1990s, the Food and Drug Administration (FDA) lifted a 2-year ban on consumer advertising of prescription drugs; since then, there has been an onslaught of new sales pitches. In their attempts to sell drugs, product advertisers use the authority of a physician or health expert or the seemingly sincere testimony of a product user. Adults are strongly affected by testimonial advertising because these drug commercials can appear authentic and convincing to large numbers of viewers, listeners, or readers.

The constant barrage of commercials, including many for OTC drugs, relays the message that, if you are experiencing restlessness or uncomfortable symptoms, taking drugs is an acceptable and normal response. As a result, television viewers, newspaper and magazine readers, and radio listeners are led to believe or unconsciously select the particular brand advertised when confronted with dozens upon dozens of drug choices for a particular ailment. In effect, this advertising reaffirms the belief that drugs are necessary when taken for a real or an imagined symptom.

Here and Now

Are the Elderly Abusing Drugs?

As the number of addicted drug abusers addicted to medically prescribed drugs is rapidly growing, "[a]n even more startling fact is that among those abusing prescription medication are the elderly" (Meyer 2005, p. 1). Another recent finding shows that "[d]rug abuse among our senior citizens in America may be rising faster than our younger generation, at least at the moment" (Mstywrl 2005, p. 1). Reported findings include:

- Alcohol is abused most, followed by prescription medications and marijuana. The list also includes some cocaine and heroin use.
- "[I]t is estimated that drug abuse among older adults has increased by 106% for men and 119% for women between 1995 and 2002" (Mstywrl 2005, p. 1).
- Drug addictions among those in this population are rapidly rising.

Other recent findings show that, in regard to the prevalence of substance use among older adults, an estimated 4.3 million adults aged 50 or older—4.7% of adults in this age range—had used an illicit drug in the past year. The illicit drugs most commonly used by older adults were marijuana (2.8%) and prescription-type drugs used nonmedically (2.1%). These percentages translate to 2.5 million past year marijuana users and 1.9 million past year nonmedical users of prescription-type drugs. Only 664,000 older adults (0.7%) reported use of illicit drugs other than marijuana or psychotherapeutics, including 0.5% for co-

caine, 0.1% for hallucinogens, and 0.1% for heroin. By age group, among older adults, the rates of any illicit drug use, marijuana use, and nonmedical use of prescription-type drugs in the past year were highest for those aged 50 to 54 and declined dramatically with increasing age. Marijuana use was more common than nonmedical use of prescription-type drugs for adults aged 50 to 54 and those aged 55 to 59 (6.1% vs. 3.4% and 4.1% vs. 3.2%, respectively). However, among adults aged 65 or older, nonmedical use of prescription-type drugs was more common than marijuana use (0.8% vs. 0.4%) (SAMHSA 2009).

One report showed that "the population of older adults ages 50 to 59 who reported using at least on illicit drug* in the past year—primarily marijuana and nonmedical use of prescription drugs—increased from 5.1% in 2002 to 9.4% in 2007. Additional analyses show that this trend was driven by the aging of the baby boom generation, those born between 1946 and 1964" (CESAR 2009). SAMHSA estimates the current number of substance abusers over the age of 55 is approximately 62 million, with this number growing to 75 million by 2010 (SAMSHA 2009). If the number of users continues to increase, the number of adults over the age of 50 with substance abuse issues will double from 2.5 million in 1999 to 5 million in 2020" (Mstywrl 2005, p. 3). From these findings, it can be said that the extensive drug use the baby boomers experienced in the 60s, 70s, and early 80s follows this generation as they move into their senior years.

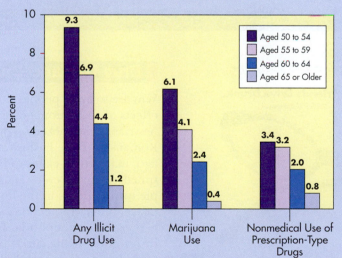

Past year illicit drug use among adults aged 50 or older, by age group: 2006 to 2008.

Source: Substance Abuse and Mental Health Services Administration (SAMHSA), Office of Applied Studies (OAS). *The NSDUH Report: Illicit Drug Used Among Older Adults.* Rockville, MD, 2009.

(continued)

Are the Elderly Abusing Drugs? (*continued*)

An example of elderly drug abuse include the following:

Oh, I started with cigarettes when I was fourteen. Then came the alcohol when I was sixteen, and now I am now 62-years-old and still playing around with drugs. I have several friends who still smoke weed, but not too many around who continue like I do. I generally smoke cigarettes, weed (as they call it today), sometimes buy a little bag of coke and smoke that, too, and drink alcohol. I don't do the coke much because I like to smoke it, and it is tough on the heart. My drug using friends who are around my age don't really know about the coke use; they think I stopped this years ago. I still have days when I long for it, but I have enough of a hard time with the weed and the drinking. My children do not know how much I drink since I live alone, and they even think I have nothing to do with weed. So, I guess I am a closet user. At times I am sorry to continue with these unnecessary drugs, and it's even darn right embarrassing if anyone finds out. Even the cigarettes are a pain in the butt. I just need to get high every now and then, and I don't know why. I think it is something genetic since I want to quit all these drugs but simply do not do it. You asked if I think a lot of the elderly use drugs unnecessarily [drugs used without medical purposes]. Yes, there are many of us, especially the baby boomers who still smoke weed, but we kind of keep it secret. So, if the number of users my age are increasing, I would double the number of users. As I said, many of us just keep it secret because we still work, have good jobs with a lot of responsibilities, and our kids would look down on us if they knew. You asked if I feel addicted to these drugs. Yes, I am addicted since I really don't want to quit everything, yet it is not good for my health and still keep using these drugs. Isn't this a classic example of addiction, which is to keep using drugs even though you know they are not good for you? If it's not addiction, what else would it be? (*From Venturelli's research files, male, age 62, April 22, 2011*)

* Illicit drug use: Any use of marijuana, cocaine, heroin, hallucinogens, inhalants, or nonmedical use of pain relievers, tranquillizers, stimulants, or sedatives.

Sources: Meyer, C. "Prescription Drug Abuse in the Elderly." Associated Content from Yahoo! (15 July 2005). Available at: http://www.associate content.com/article/5731/prescription_drug_abuse_in_the_elderly.html?cat=5. Accessed April 25, 2011; Mstywrl. "Drug Abuse Among Seniors in America: An Ageless Predator." Associated Content from Yahoo! (21 July 2005). Available at: http://www.associatedcontent.com/article/5556/drug_abuse_among_seniors_in_america.html?cat=71. Accessed April 25, 2011; Substance Abuse and Mental Health Services Administration (SAMHSA), Office of Applied Studies (OAS). "Illicit Drug Use among Older Adults." *The NSDUH Report* (29 December 2009): 1–4; and Center for Substance Abuse and Research (CESAR). "Illicit Drug Use Increases Among Adults Ages 50 to 59: Trend Driven by Aging Baby Boom Generation." *CESAR FAX* 18 (7 September 2009).

Amanda Geiger never saw the drunk driver.

Friends Don't Let Friends Drive Drunk.

Photo by Michael Mazzeo

U.S. Department of Transportation

Ad Council

Although the media is often credited with glamorizing dangerous drug use, many successful prevention campaigns have used television, radio, and print media as outlets. Since the Advertising Council began its "Friends Don't Let Friends Drive Drunk" campaign, 79% of Americans have stopped an intoxicated friend from getting behind the wheel.

Drug Use and Drug Dependence

Why are so many people attracted to drugs and the effects of recreational drug use? Like the ancient Assyrians, who sucked on opium lozenges, and the Romans, who ate hashish sweets some 2000 years ago, many users claim to be bored, in pain, frustrated, unable to enjoy life, or alienated. Such people turn to drugs in the hope of finding oblivion, peace, inner connections, outer connections (togetherness), or euphoria. The fact that many OTC drugs never really cure the ailment, especially if taken for social and psychological reasons, and the fact that frequent use of most drugs increases the risk of addiction do not seem to be deterrents. People continue to take drugs for many reasons, including the following:

• Searching for pleasure and using drugs to heighten good feelings.

- Taking drugs to temporarily relieve stress or tension or provide a temporary escape for people with anxiety.
- Taking drugs to temporarily forget one's problems and avoid or postpone worries.
- Viewing certain drugs (such as alcohol, marijuana, and tobacco) as necessary to relax after a tension-filled day at work.
- Taking drugs to fit in with peers, especially when peer pressure is strong during early and late adolescence; seeing drugs as a rite of passage.
- Taking drugs to enhance religious or mystical experiences. (Very few cultures teach children how to use specific drugs for this purpose.)
- Taking drugs to relieve pain and some symptoms of illness.

It is important to understand why historically many people have been unsuccessful in eliminating the fascination with drugs. To reach such an understanding, we must address questions dealing with (1) why people are attracted to drugs, (2) how experiences with the different types of drugs vary (here, many attitudes are conveyed from the "inside"—the users themselves), (3) how each of the major drugs affects the body and the mind, (4) how patterns of use vary among different groups, and (5) what forms of treatment are available for the addicted. In Chapter 2, explanations and responses to such questions are addressed from a more theoretical (explanatory) level. In Chapters 8 through 15, each of the major types of drugs is examined separately.

■ When Does Use Lead to Abuse?

Views about the use of drugs depend on one's perspective. For example, from a pharmacological perspective, if a patient is suffering severe pain because of injuries sustained from an automobile accident, high doses of a narcotic such as morphine or Demerol should be given to control discomfort. While someone is in pain, no reason exists not to take the drug. From a medical standpoint, once healing has occurred and pain has been relieved, drug use should cease. If the patient continues using the narcotic because it provides a sense of well-being or he or she has become dependent to the point of addiction, the pattern of drug intake is then considered abuse. Thus, the amount of drug(s) taken or the frequency of dosing does not

necessarily determine abuse (even though individuals who abuse drugs usually consume increasingly higher doses). Most important is the motive for taking the drug, which is the principal factor in determining the presence of abuse.

Initial drug abuse symptoms include: (1) excessive use, (2) constant preoccupation about the availability and supply of the drug, (3) denial in admitting the excessive use, and (4) reliance on the drug. All of these four factors frequently result in producing the initial symptoms of withdrawal whenever the user attempts to stop taking the drug. As a result, the user often begins to neglect other responsibilities or ambitions in favor of using the drug.

Even the legitimate use of a drug can be controversial. Often, physicians cannot decide even among themselves what constitutes legitimate use of a drug. For example, MDMA ("Ecstasy") is currently prohibited for therapeutic use, but in 1985, when the **Drug Enforcement Administration (DEA)** was deciding MDMA's status, some 35 to 200 physicians (mostly psychiatrists) were using the drug in their practice. These clinicians claimed that MDMA relaxed inhibitions and enhanced communication and was useful as a psychotherapeutic adjunct to assist in dealing with psychiatric patients (Levinthal 1996; Schecter 1989). From the perspective of these physicians, Ecstasy was a useful medicinal tool. However, the DEA did not agree and made Ecstasy a Schedule I drug (see Chapter 3). In a legal sense, Schedule I excludes any legitimate use of the drug in therapeutics; consequently, according to this ruling, anyone taking Ecstasy is guilty of drug abuse (Goode 1999) and is violating drug laws.

If the problem of drug abuse is to be understood and solutions are to be found, identifying the causes of the abuse is most important. When a drug is being abused, it is not legitimately therapeutic; that is, it does not improve the user's physical or mental health. When drug use is not used for therapeutic purposes, what is the motive for taking the drug?

There are many possible answers to this question. Initially, most drug abusers perceive some psychological advantage when using these compounds. For many, the psychological lift is significant enough that they are willing to risk social exclusion, health

KEY TERMS

Drug Enforcement Administration (DEA)
the principle federal agency responsible for enforcing U.S. drug laws

problems, and dramatic changes in personality, arrest, incarceration, and fines to have their drug. The psychological effects that these drugs cause may entail an array of diverse feelings. Different types of drugs have different psychological effects. The type of drug an individual selects to abuse may ultimately reflect his or her own mental state.

For example, people who experience chronic depression, feel intense job pressures, are unable to focus on accomplishing goals, or have a sense of inferiority may find that a stimulant such as cocaine or an amphetamine type of drug appears to provide immediate relief—a solution to a set of psychological frustrations. These drugs cause a spurt of energy, a feeling of euphoria, a sense of superiority, and imagined self-confidence. In contrast, people who experience nervousness and anxiety and want instant relief from the pressures of life may choose a depressant such as alcohol or barbiturates. These agents sedate, relax, provide relief, and even have some amnesiac properties, allowing users to suspend or forget their immediate pressing concerns or problems. People who perceive themselves as creative or who have artistic talents may select hallucinogenic types of drugs to "expand" their minds, heighten their senses, and distort what appears to be a confining and sometimes monotonous nature of reality. As individuals come to rely more on drugs to inhibit, deny, accelerate, or distort their realities, they run the risk of becoming psychologically dependent on drugs—a process described in more detail in Chapters 2, 4, and 5.

Some have argued that taking a particular drug to meet a psychological need, especially if a person is over 21 years of age, is not very different from taking a drug to cure an ailment. The belief here is that physical needs and psychological needs are really indistinguishable. In fact, several drug researchers and writers, including Szasz (1992) and Lenson (1995), believe that drug taking is a citizen's right and a personal matter involving individual decision making. They see drug taking as simply a personal choice to depart from or alter consciousness. Lenson states that taking drugs for recreational purposes is simply an additional form of diversity, a type of mental diversity that should exist with many other acceptable forms of diversity, such as cultural, racial, religious, gender, and sexual orientation diversity. (For additional elaboration on these views, see Venturelli 2000.) Obviously, this is a very different and often extremely controversial point of view that can easily cause polemic and very debatable perspectives!

■ Drug Dependence

Although Chapters 2, 5, and 18 discuss addiction and drug dependence in detail, here we introduce some underlying factors that lead to drug dependence. Our discussion emphasizes drug dependence instead of addiction because the term *addiction* is both controversial and relative, as evidenced with rock and movie stars and their "escapades" with drug dependence. Stars such as Charlie Sheen, Mel Gibson, and Ben Affleck (alcoholism); John Belushi, Lindsay Lohan, and Robin Williams (alcoholism and cocaine); Robert Downey, Jr. (cocaine and heroin); Michael Jackson, Winona Ryder, and Eminem (analgesic prescription drugs) are just a few examples.

Even when drug dependence becomes full-fledged, addiction remains debatable, with many experts unable to agree on one set of characteristics that constitutes addiction. Furthermore, the term *addiction* is viewed by some as a pejorative that adds to the labeling process (see labeling theory in Chapter 2).

The main characteristics necessary for drug dependence are as follows:

- Both physical and psychological factors precipitate drug dependence. Recently, closer attention has been focused on the mental (psychological) attachments than on the physical addiction to drug use as principally indicative of addiction—mostly, the craving aspect of wanting the drug for consumption.
- More specifically, psychological dependence refers to the need that a user may feel for continued use of a drug to experience its effects. Physical dependence refers to the need to continue taking the drug to avoid withdrawal symptoms that often include feelings of discomfort and illness.
- With repeated use there is a tendency to become dependent and addicted to most psychoactive drugs.
- Addiction to a drug sets in when the drug user has advanced within the dependence phase. (Having an addiction to a drug is simply an advanced stage of dependence.)
- Generally, the addiction process involves mental (psychological) and physical (physiological/biophysiological) dependence.

Figure 1.8 shows the process of addiction involves five separate phases: relief, increased use, preoccupation, dependency, and withdrawal. Initially,

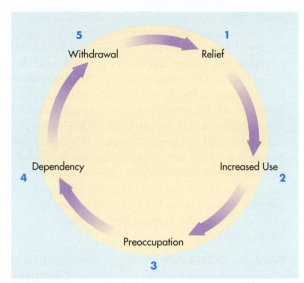

FIGURE 1.8
Stages of drug dependence.

the **relief phase** refers to the relief experienced by using a drug, which allows a potential addict to escape one or more of the following feelings: boredom, loneliness, tension, fatigue, anger, and anxiety. The **increased use phase** involves taking greater quantities of the drug. The **preoccupation phase** consists of a continuous interest with and concern for the substance—that is, always having a supply of the drug and taking the drug is perceived as "normal" behavior. The **dependency phase** is synonymous with addiction. In this phase, more of the drug is sought without regard for the presence of negative physical symptoms, such as congested coughing and/or shortness of breath in cases of cigarette and marijuana addiction, blackouts from advanced alcohol abuse, and moderate to acute soreness and inflammation of nasal passages from snorting cocaine. The **withdrawal phase** involves such symptoms as itching, chills, tension, stomach pain, or depression from the nonuse of the addictive drug and/or an entire set of psychological concerns mainly involving an insatiable craving for the drug (Monroe 1996).

The Costs of Drug Use to Society

Many of the costs of drug addiction go beyond the user. Society pays a high price for drug addiction. Consider, for example, the loss of an addicted person's connection with reality and the loss of responsible dedication to careers and professions, illnesses experienced by the addicted individual, marital strife, shortened lives, and so on. Additionally, the dollar costs of addiction are also enormous.

The **National Institute on Drug Abuse (NIDA)** has estimated that the typical narcotic habit costs the user approximately $150 a day to support his or her addiction. The precise dollar amount spent to support a narcotic addiction largely depends on the geographic location where the drug is procured and used, availability of the drug affecting the price, and numerous other factors. For example, if a heroin addict has a $150-a-day habit, he or she needs about $54,750 per year just to maintain the drug supply. It is impossible for most addicts to get this amount of money legally; therefore, many support their habits by resorting to criminal activity or working as or for drug dealers.

Most crimes related to drugs involve theft of personal property—primarily, burglary and shoplifting—and, less commonly, assault and robbery (often mugging). Estimates are that a heroin addict must steal three to five times the actual cost of the drugs to maintain the habit, or roughly $200,000 per year. Especially with crack and heroin use, a large number of addicts resort to pimping and prostitution. No accurate figures are available regarding the cost of drug-related prostitution, although some law enforcement officials have estimated that prostitutes take in a total of $10 to $20 billion per year. It has also been estimated that nearly three out of every four prostitutes in major cities have a serious drug dependency.

Even though when looking at illicit drug users, yearly methamphetamine (meth) use has been steadily decreasing—from a high of 0.7% users in

KEY TERMS

relief phase
satisfaction derived from escaping negative feelings in using the drug

increased use phase
taking increasing quantities of the drug

preoccupation phase
constant concern with the supply of the drug

dependency phase
synonym for addiction

withdrawal phase
physical and/or psychological effects derived from not using the drug

National Institute on Drug Abuse (NIDA)
the principle federal agency responsible for directing drug use– and abuse–related research

2002 (1.7 million) to 0.5% users (1.3 million) in 2007, to 0.3% users (850,000) in 2008 it is worth noting its past history. In the late 1990s there was a significant concern regarding the increase throughout the country in clandestine laboratories involved in synthesizing or processing this type of illicit drug. Such laboratories produced amphetamine-type drugs, heroin-type drugs, designer drugs, LSD, and processed other drugs of abuse such as cocaine and crack. Back then, the DEA reported that 390 laboratories were seized in 1993, a figure that increased to 967 in 1995. Another example of the phenomenal growth of methamphetamine laboratories was found in Missouri. From 1995 to 1997, seizures of such labs in Missouri increased by 535% (Steward and Sitarmiah 1997). "In Dawson County in western Nebraska . . . 'The percentage of meth-related crimes is through the roof' . . . as reiterated by an investigator with the county sheriff's office. . . . In the state as a whole, officials discovered 38 methamphetamine laboratories in 1999; last year [2001] they discovered 179" (Butterfield 2002, p. A23).

The reasons for such dramatic increases related to the enormous profits and relatively low risk associated with these operations. As a rule, clandestine laboratories are fairly mobile and relatively crude (often operating in a kitchen, basement, or garage) and are run by individuals with only elementary chemical skills.

Another interesting discovery was that these laboratories were not always stationary in locations such as garages, barns, homes, apartments, and so on. Though these stationary labs predominated, especially in the production of methamphetamine, more recently mobile labs have made an appearance:

> Cooking in cars and trucks helped producers in two ways: It eludes identification by law enforcement and motion helps the chemical reaction [of methamphetamine production]. Motels are a new production setting. . . . [though fewer in number today]. Clandestine labs are also set up in federal parklands, where toxic byproducts pose a danger to hikers and campers (ONDCP 2002, p. 58).

To demonstrate how a drug such as methamphetamine affects society, in 2003, the following was reported:

> With portable meth labs popping up everywhere from motel bathrooms to the back seat of a Chevy, it was only a matter of time before they made their way onto campus. Last November, a custodian notified campus police at [uni-

versity in Texas] about what appeared to be a lab set up in a music practice room in the [university's] Fine Arts Center. "We found beakers of red liquid, papers and other residue, and the room had this horrible odor. . . ." Students were on vacation, so the practice room, which had its windows blackened out, would have afforded the occupant a few days to cook. [One campus police official] . . . speculates that this is just the beginning: "Labs are popping up on campuses all over the country. It's just too easy now. You can get the recipe on the Internet. Still, how could someone be so brazen as to set up an operation next to the French horn section? (Jellinek 2003, p. 54)

Because of a lack of training, inexperience, and the danger of experiencing the effects of methamphetamine while making the drug, the chemical "cooking" procedures are performed crudely, sometimes resulting in adulterants and impure products. Such contaminants can be very toxic, causing severe harm or even death to the unsuspecting user as well as a greater likelihood of sudden explosion (Drug Strategies 1995). Fortunately, when looking at all the illicit drugs produced by such underground laboratories, such outbreaks of physically harmful drugs do not occur very often. Partial proof of this is found in the small number of news stories of deaths or poisonings from illicit drugs. Nevertheless, because profit drives these clandestine labs, which obviously have no government supervision, impurities or "cheap fillers" are always possible so that greater profits can be made. Here, caution is very advisable in that drug purchasers do not have any guarantees when purchasing powerful illicit drugs.

Society continues paying a large sum even after users, addicts, and drug dealers are caught and sentenced because it takes from $75 to $1500 per day to keep one person incarcerated. Supporting programs such as methadone maintenance costs much less. New York officials estimate that methadone maintenance costs about $3000 per year per patient. Some outpatient programs, such as those in Washington, DC, claim a cost as low as $8 to $12 per day (not counting cost of staff and facilities), which is much less than the cost of incarceration. A more long-term effect of drug abuse that has substantial impact on society is the medical and psychological care often required by addicts due to disease resulting from their drug habit. Particularly noteworthy are the communicable diseases spread because of needle sharing within the drug-abusing population, such as hepatitis and HIV. (See Chapter 16 for extensive coverage of HIV/AIDS and injection drug use.)

In the United States, at the end of 2006, an estimated 1.1 million Americans were living with HIV—and one in four of them did not know it (CDC 2009b). (AIDS has a tendency to develop within 10 years of the onset of HIV.) Worldwide, approximately 33.4 million people are living with HIV/AIDS (CDC 2009a). This number includes people living in sub-Saharan Africa, Asia, Latin America and the Caribbean, Eastern Europe, Central Asia, North America, Western and Central Europe, North Africa and the Middle East, and Oceania (Clinton 2006). (See Chapter 16 for more detailed information on HIV and AIDS.)

In the United States, HIV is spread primarily through unprotected sexual intercourse and sharing of previously used needles to inject drugs. HIV in the injecting-drug-user subpopulation is transmitted in the small (minuscule) amount of contaminated blood remaining in the used needles. The likelihood of a member of the drug-abusing population contracting HIV directly correlates with the frequency of injections and the extent of needle sharing. Care for AIDS patients lasts a lifetime, and many of these medical expenses come from federal- and state-funded programs. Many cities throughout the United States have publicly funded programs that distribute new, uncontaminated needles to drug addicts. The needles are free of charge in exchange for used injection needles in order to prevent the spread of HIV and hepatitis B and C from contaminated needles. These programs are often referred to as **needle-exchange programs**.

Also of great concern is drug abuse by women during pregnancy. Some psychoactive drugs can have profound, permanent effects on a developing fetus. The best documented is fetal alcohol syndrome (FAS), which can affect the offspring of alcoholic mothers (see Chapter 7). Cocaine and amphetamine-related drugs can also cause irreversible congenital changes when used during pregnancy (see Chapter 10). All too often, the affected offspring of addicted mothers become the responsibility of welfare organizations. In addition to the costs to society just mentioned, other costs of drug abuse include drug-related deaths, emergency room visits and hospital stays, and automobile fatalities.

■ Drugs, Crime, and Violence

There is a long-established close association between drug abuse and criminality. The beliefs (hypotheses) for this association range along a continuum between two opposing views: (1) criminal behavior develops as a means to support addiction, and (2) criminality is inherently linked to the user's personality and occurs independently of drug use (Bureau of Justice Statistics [BJS] 2006; Drug Strategies 1995; McBride and McCoy 2003). In other words, does drug addiction cause a person to engage in criminal behavior such as burglary, theft, and larceny to pay for the drug habit? On the other hand, does criminal behavior stem from an already existing criminal personality such that drugs are used as an adjunct to commit such acts? In other words, are drugs used in conjunction with crime to sedate and give the added confidence needed to commit daring law violations?

The answers to these questions have never been clear because findings that contradict one view in favor of the other continue to mount on both sides. Part of the reason for the controversy about the relationship between criminal activity and drug abuse is that studies have been conducted in different settings and cultures, employing different research methods, and focusing on different addictive drugs. As a result, too many factors are involved to allow us to distinguish the cause from the result. We know that each type of drug has unique addictive potential and that interpretation of exactly when a deviant act is an offense (violation of law) varies. Furthermore, we know that people think differently while under the influence of drugs. Whether criminalistic behavior is *directly* caused by the drug use or whether prior socialization and peer influence work in concert to cause criminal behavior remains unclear. Certainly, we think it would be safe to believe that prior socialization, law-violating peers, and drugs are strong contributing factors for causing criminal behavior.

Although this controversy about the connection between drugs and crime continues to challenge our thinking, the following findings are also noteworthy:

- "The United States leads the world in the number of people incarcerated in federal and state correctional facilities. There are currently

KEY TERMS

needle-exchange programs
publically funded programs that distribute new, uncontaminated needles to drug addicts in exchange for used injection needles in order to prevent the spread of HIV and hepatitis B and C

more than 2 million people in American prisons or jails. Approximately one-quarter of those people held in U.S. prisons or jails have been convicted of a drug offense" (Natarajan et al. 2008, p. 1).

- "The United States incarcerates more people for drug offenses than any other country" (Natarajan et al. 2008, p. 1).
- With an estimated 6.8 million Americans struggling with drug abuse or dependence, the growth of the prison population continues to be driven largely by incarceration for drug offenses (Natarajan et al. 2008, p. 1).
- In 2004, "17% of State and 18% of Federal prisoners committed their crime to obtain money for drugs" (Mumola and Karberg 2007, p. 1). Approximately one out of every six major crimes is committed because of the offender's need to obtain money for drugs.
- In 2006, "[o]f the estimated 265,800 prisoners under state jurisdiction sentenced for drug offenses in 2006, 72,100 were white (27.1%), 117,600 were black (44.2%), and 55,700 were Hispanic (21%)" (Sabol et al. 2009, p. 37).
- In 2008, more than two-thirds of jail inmates were found to be dependent on or to abuse alcohol or drugs.
- Two in five inmates were dependent on alcohol or drugs, and nearly one in four abused alcohol or drugs but were not dependent on them. Jail inmates who met the criteria for substance dependence or abuse (70%) were more likely than other inmates (46%) to have a criminal record.
- Fifty-two percent of female jail inmates were found to be dependent on alcohol or drugs, compared to 44% of male inmates.
- Half of all convicted jail inmates were under the influence of drugs or alcohol at the time of their offense.
- Jail inmates between ages 25 and 44 had the highest rate of substance dependence or abuse (7 in 10 inmates). Those age 55 or older had the lowest rate (nearly 5 in 10 inmates).
- More than 50% of drug or property offenders were dependent on or had abused a substance, compared to over 60% of violent and public-order offenders.
- Women and white inmates are more likely to have used drugs at the time of their offense (Karberg and James 2002).
- Thirty-two percent of state and 26.4% of federal prison inmates reported being under the influence of drugs at the time of their offense in

2004 (see **Table 1.5**). Approximately 44% were incarcerated for drug offenses in state prisons and 32% were incarcerated in federal prisons. Of these, 46% were arrested for possession in state prisons and 21% were arrested in federal prisons. Forty-two percent were serving time in state prisons and 34% were serving time in federal prisons for trafficking in drugs. One outcome of these findings is that one out of every four major crimes committed—violent, property, and drug offenses—involves an offender

Table 1.5 **Percentage of State and Federal Prison Inmates Who Reported Being Under the Influence of Drugs at the Time of Their Offense: 2004**

	STATE	FEDERAL
Total[a]	32.1%	26.4%
Violent Offenses	27.7%	24.0%
Homicide	27.3%	16.8%
Sexual Assault[b]	17.4%	13.8%
Robbery	40.7%	29.4%
Assault	24.1%	20.1%
Property Offenses	38.5%	13.6%
Burglary	41.1%	—
Larceny/theft	40.1%	—
Motor vehicle theft	38.7%	—
Fraud	34.1%	9.3%
Drug Offenses	43.6%	32.3%
Possession	46.0%	20.9%
Trafficking	42.3%	33.8%
Public Order Offenses[c]	25.4%	18.7%
Weapons	27.6%	27.8%
Other public order offenses	24.6%	8.0%

[a] Includes offenses not shown
[b] Includes rape and other sexual assault
[c] Excluding DWI/DUI
— Not calculated; too few cases to permit calculation

Source: Mumola, C., and J. Karberg. *Drug Use and Dependence, State and Federal Prisoners, 2004.* Washington, DC: U.S. Department of Justice, Office of Justice Programs.

who is under the influence of drugs (Mumola and Karberg 2007).

- Another study also shows a dramatic increase in the correlation between drug use and crime. This study by the Robert Wood Johnson Foundation (2001) reported that with regard to homicide, theft, and assault, at least half of the adults arrested for such major crimes tested positive for drugs at the time of their arrest. "Among those convicted of violent crimes, approximately half of state prison inmates and 40% of federal prisoners had been drinking or taking drugs at the time of their offense" (p. 45).

In regard to the connection between drug use and crime, the following findings can be summarized: (1) drug users in comparison to non-drug users are more likely to commit crimes, (2) a high percentage of arrestees are often under the influence of a drug while committing crimes, and (3) a high percentage of drug users arrested for drug use and violence are more likely to be under the influence of alcohol and/or stimulant-types of drugs such as cocaine, crack, and methamphetamines.

Drug-related crimes are undoubtedly overwhelming the U.S. judicial system. Table 1.5 shows the percentage of state and federal inmates reporting being under the influence of drugs at the time of their offenses in 2004. Approximately 29% of state and federal prisoners were under the influence of drugs for violent offenses (e.g., homicide, sexual assault, robbery, assault), 26% for property offenses (e.g., burglary, larceny/theft, motor vehicle theft, fraud), 38% for drug offenses (possession, trafficking), and 22% for public order offenses (e.g., weapons, other public-order offenses) (Mumola and Karberg 2007). Furthermore, nearly 40% of the young people (often younger than 21 years of age) in adult correctional facilities reported drinking before committing a crime.

Drug Cartels

Drug cartels are defined as large, highly sophisticated organizations composed of multiple drug trafficking organizations (DTOs) and **drug cells** with specific assignments such as drug transportation, security/enforcement, or money laundering. (A drug cell is similar to a terrorist cell, consisting of three to five members insuring operational security. Members of adjacent drug cells usually do not know each other or the identity of their leadership.) Drug cartel command-and-control structures are based outside the United States; however, they produce, transport, and distribute illicit drugs domestically with the assistance of DTOs that are either a part of or in an alliance with the cartel. Here are some reports of incidents in the world of drugs, violence, and crime:

> In Mexico, President Felipe Calderon may be the constitutionally elected leader of the nation, but in reality, drug cartels and warlords exercise de facto authority over much of the area. . . . Drug trafficking overwhelmingly is the prevailing social malady throughout the country, particularly along the border with the United States. In spite of lengthy declarations by government officials in Mexico City and Washington, and their insistence that important battles are being won against drug trafficking, criminal organizations like the Tijuana cartel continue to thrive, ruling over whole sections of the Mexican countryside like sectoral feudal lords. . . . The governor of the state of Nuevo Leon (bordering the United States), Natividad Gonzalez Paras, has declared that: "Unfortunately, the drug problem has escalated significantly in the past six to seven years. It is a national problem affecting most of the country's states. It is a dispute between cartels or organizations to control locations, cities, and routes." (Birns and Sánchez 2007)

In another news report:

> Once known merely as "mules" for Colombia's powerful cocaine cartels, today Mexico's narcotics traffickers are the kingpins of this hemisphere's drug trade, and the front line of the war on drugs has shifted from Colombia to America's back door.
>
> In August 2005, the *Christian Science Monitor* reported that according to senior U.S. officials, in the biggest reorganization since the 1980s, Mexican cartels had leveraged the profits from

KEY TERMS

drug cartels
large, highly sophisticated organizations composed of multiple drug trafficking organizations (DTOs) and cells with specific assignments such as drug transportation, security/enforcement, or money laundering

drug cells
are similar to a terrorist cells, consisting of three to five members and ensuring operational security; members of adjacent drug cells usually do not know each other or the identity of their leadership

their delivery routes to wrest control from the Colombian producers. As a result, Mexican drug lords are in control of what the U.N. estimates is a $142 billion a year business in cocaine, heroin, marijuana, methamphetamine, and other illicit drugs.

The new dominance of Mexican cartels has caused a spike in violence along the 2000-mile U.S.–Mexico border where rival cartels are warring against Mexican and U.S. authorities. Drugs are either flown from Colombia to Mexico in small planes, or, in the case of marijuana and methamphetamine, produced locally. Then, they're shipped into the U.S. by boat, private vehicles, or in commercial trucks crossing the border. . . .

The Sept. 26 edition of the *San Antonio Express-News* reported that a new method of intimidation is being utilized by Mexican drug cartels— beheadings. So far this year, at least 26 people have been decapitated in Mexico, with heads stuck on fences, dumped in trash piles, and even tossed onto a nightclub dance floor. In the latter act of violence, which took place in early morning hours of Wednesday, Sept. 6, five heads were scattered on the dance floor of a bar in the state of Michoacan, notorious for drug trafficking. No arrests for the killings have been announced. (Worldpress.org 2006)

And, in another news report:

The dead policeman is found propped against a tree off a dirt road on the outskirts of the city. He is dressed like a cartoon version of a Mexican cowboy wearing a blanket. The murder and symbolic mutilation of *policìa* has become almost routine in Caliacán, capital of the Mexican state of Sinaloa: Pablo Aispuro Ramìrez is one of 90 cops to be killed here this year. There is a note pinned to the body, a warning to anyone who dares to oppose the powerful drug lord who ordered the execution "I'm a copy-cowboy!" the note reads. "Ahoo-ya! There are going to be more soon." (Lawson 2008, p. 76)

And finally,

The Tijuana-based Felix drug cartel and the Juarez-based Fuentes cartel began buying legitimate businesses in small towns in Los Angeles County in the early 1990s. . . . They purchased restaurants, used-car lots, auto-body shops and other small businesses. One of their purposes was to use these businesses for money-laundering operations. Once established in their commu-nity, these cartel-financed business owners ran for city council and other local offices. (Farah 2006, quoting an excerpt from *In Mortal Danger* by Tom Tancredo, a former U.S. Congressman, Colorado)

These news briefs are just a very small sampling of the types of crimes and violence perpetrated by drug dealers. It is clear that production, merchandising, and distribution of illicit drugs have developed into a worldwide operation worth hundreds of billions of dollars (Goldstein 2001); one publication states that the United Nations (UN) estimates that the global world drug trade is worth $320 billion annually (Stopthedrugwar.org 2005). These enormous profits have attracted organized crime, both in the United States and abroad, and all too frequently even corrupt law enforcement agencies (McShane 1994). For the participants in such operations, drugs can mean incredible wealth and power. For example, dating back to 1992, Pablo Escobar was recognized as a drug kingpin and leader of the cocaine cartel in Colombia, and he was acknowledged as one of the world's richest men and Colombia's most powerful man (Wire Services 1992). With his drug-related wealth, Escobar financed a private army to conduct a personal war against the government of Colombia (Associated Press 1992); until his death in 1993, he was a serious threat to his country's stability.

In December 1999, the notorious Juarez drug cartel was believed to be responsible for burying more than 100 bodies (22 Americans) in a mass grave at a ranch in Mexico. All of the deaths were believed to be drug-related. According to a news story on this gruesome discovery, the alleged perpetrator, Vincente Carrillo Fuentes, is one among dozens of drug lords and lieutenants wanted by U.S. law enforcement agents (Associated Press 1999). A more current drug lord, Zambada, age 62, is ". . . one of Mexico's most wanted drug lords, who has never been arrested despite a $5 million reward offered in the United States" (Campbell 2010, p. 1). This same news release indicated that the drug trade would not end until drug cartels are eliminated. Such occurrences, which are often reported by the mass media, indicate the existence of powerful and dangerous drug cartels that are responsible for the availability of illicit drugs around the world.

Drug-related violence takes its toll at all levels, as rival gangs fight to control their "turf" and associated drug operations. Innocent bystanders often become unsuspecting victims of the indiscriminate violence. For example, a Roman Catholic cardinal was killed on May 24, 1993, when a car he was a passenger in was inadvertently driven into the middle of a drug-related shoot-out between traffickers at the international airport in Guadalajara, Mexico. Five other innocent bystanders were killed in the incident (Associated Press 1993). Finally, it was recently reported that when spotted, the Mexican army engages in shooting at cartel members and likewise armed cartel members shoot back. When this occurs, mostly in border towns and cities in Mexico, innocent bystanders, many of them children, are often caught in the cross-fire and are routinely killed (Del Bosque 2010, 1). On April 13, 2010, one report cites just such an incident. In Acapulco, Mexico, 24 people died, half of whom were innocent bystanders. "[T]he shootout broke out in the middle of the day in the center of the town as it was full of bystanders" (Associated Press 2010, p. 38). In many other incidents, unsuspecting people have been injured or killed by drug users who, while under the influence of drugs, commit violent criminal acts.

■ Drugs in the Workplace: A Costly Affliction

"He was a good, solid worker, always on the job—until he suddenly backed his truck over a 4-inch gas line." If the line had ruptured, there would have been a serious explosion, according to the driver's employer. The accident raised a red flag: ". . . under the company's standard policy, the employee was tested for drugs and alcohol. He was positive for both" (Edelson 2000, p. 3). Most adults spend the majority of their hours each day in some type of family environment. For most adults employed full time, the second greatest number of hours is spent in the workplace. Generally, once drug use becomes habitual, it often continues. The National Household Surveys, for example, found evidence of significant drug use among full time workers, with approximately 7% to 9% drinking while working. In the surveys, 65.6% of full-time workers reported alcohol use within the past month. Some 6.4% of full-time workers reported marijuana use within the past month. Part-time employees did not differ much in their use of alcohol and marijuana (SAMHSA 2007b).

Worker Substance Abuse in Different Industries

Substance use in the workplace negatively affects U.S. industry through lost productivity, workplace accidents and injuries, employee absenteeism, low morale, and increased illness. The loss to U.S. companies due to employees' alcohol and drug use and related problems is estimated at billions of dollars a year. Research shows that the rate of substance use varies by occupation and industry (Larson et al. 2007). Studies also have indicated that employers vary in their treatment of substance use issues and that workplace-based employee assistance programs (EAPs) can be a valuable resource for obtaining help for substance-using workers (Delaney, Grube, and Ames 1998; Reynolds and Lehman 2003).

Regarding employment, highlights from SAMHSA (2009) indicate the following:

Illicit Drug Use

- Current illicit drug use differed by employment status in 2008. Among adults age 18 or older, the rate of illicit drug use was higher for unemployed persons (19.6%) than for those who were employed full time (8%) or part time (10.2%). These rates were all similar to the corresponding rates in 2007; see **Figure 1.9**.
- Although the rate of past-month illicit drug use was higher among unemployed persons compared with those from other employment groups, most drug users in 2008 were employed. Of the estimated 17.8 million current illicit drug users age 18 or older in 2008, 12.9 million (72.7%) were employed either full or part time.
- The number of unemployed illicit drug users increased from 1.3 million in 2007 to 1.8 million in 2008, primarily because of an overall increase in the number of unemployed persons between 2007 and 2008.

Alcohol Use

- The rate of current alcohol use was 63% for full-time employed adults age 18 or older in 2008, higher than the rate for unemployed adults (55.5%); however, the rate of heavy use for unemployed persons was 12.8%, which was higher than the rate of 8.8% for full-time employed persons. There was no significant difference in binge alcohol use rates between full-time employed adults (30.3%) and unemployed adults (33.4%).
- Among full-time workers ages 18 to 64, the highest rates of past-month heavy alcohol use were found in construction (15.9%); arts, entertainment, and recreation (13.6%); and mining (13.3%). The industry categories with the lowest rates of heavy alcohol use were edu-

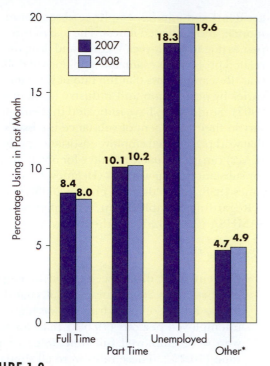

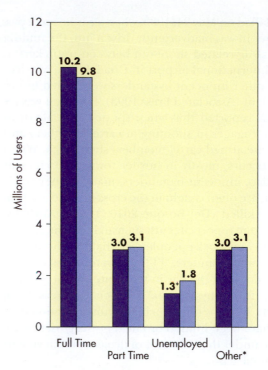

FIGURE 1.9

Past-month illicit drug use among persons age 18 or older, by employment status: 2007 and 2008.

···

*The "Other" employment category includes retired persons, disabled persons, homemakers, students, or other persons not in the labor force.
⁺Difference between this estimate and the 2008 estimate is statistically significant at the 0.05 level.

Source: Substance Abuse and Mental Health Services Administration (SAMHSA). *Results from the 2008 National Survey on Drug Use and Health: National Findings.* Office of Applied Studies, NSDUH Series H-36, DHHS Publication No. SMA 09-4435. Rockville, MD, 2009.

cational services (4.0%) and health care and social assistance (4.3%).

- Most binge and heavy alcohol users were employed in 2008. Among 55.9 million adult binge drinkers, 44.6 million (79.7%) were employed either full or part time. Among 16.8 million heavy drinkers, 13.1 million (78.0%) were employed.

- Rates of binge and heavy alcohol use did not change significantly between 2007 and 2008 for full-time employed or unemployed adults. However, the number of unemployed binge and heavy drinkers did increase (from 2.3 million to 3.0 million for binge use and from 851,000 to 1.2 million for heavy use).

Substance Dependence

- Rates of substance dependence or abuse were associated with current employment status in 2008. A higher percentage of unemployed adults age 18 or older were classified with dependence or abuse (19.0%) than were full-time employed adults (10.2%) or part-time employed adults (11.0%).

- Most adults age 18 or older with substance dependence or abuse were employed full time in 2008. Of the 20.3 million adults classified with dependence or abuse, 12.5 million (61.5%) were employed full time.

Highlights from SAMHSA (2007) indicate the following (see **Figure 1.10**):

- Among the 19 major industry categories, the highest rates of past-month illicit drug use among full-time workers ages 18 to 64 were found in accommodations and food services (16.9%) and construction (13.7%).

- The industry categories with the lowest rates of past-month illicit drug use were utilities (3.8%), educational services (4%), and public administration (4.1%).

- From 2002 to 2004, over half of all past-month illicit drug users (57.5%) and past-month heavy alcohol users (67.3%) ages 18 to 64 were employed full time.

- Approximately 70% of large companies test for drug use. Approximately 50% of medium companies and 22% of small companies per-

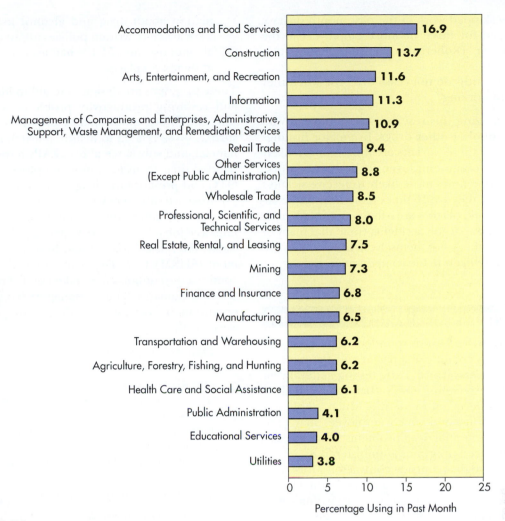

FIGURE 1.10

Past-month illicit drug use among full-time workers ages 18 to 64, by industry categories: 2002–2004 combined.

Source: Substance Abuse and Mental Health Services Administration (SAMHSA). *The National Survey on Drug Use and Health (NSDUH) Report: Worker Substance Use, by Industry Category.* Rockville, MD: Office of Applied Studies, 23 August 2007.

form such testing. Of those companies that drug test, more than 90% use urine analysis, less than 20% use blood analysis, and less than 6% use hair analysis.

- Most companies that administer drug tests test for marijuana, cocaine, opiates, amphetamines, and PCP.
- Age is the most significant predictor of marijuana and cocaine use. Younger employees (18 to 24 years old) are more likely to report drug use than older employees are (25 years or older).
- In general, unmarried workers report roughly twice as much illicit drug and heavy alcohol use as married workers. Among food preparation workers, transportation drivers, and me-

chanics, and in industries such as construction and machinery (not electrical), the discrepancy between married and unmarried workers is especially notable.

- Workers who report having three or more jobs in the previous 5 years are twice as likely to be current or past-year illicit drug users as those who held two or fewer jobs over the same period.
- Workers in occupations that affect public safety, including truck drivers, firefighters, and police officers, report the highest rate of participation in drug testing.
- "Among full-time workers, heavy drinkers and illicit drug users are more likely than those who do not drink heavily or use illicit drugs to

have skipped work in the past month or have worked for three or more employers in the past year" (Robert Wood Johnson Foundation 2001, p. 45).

- Most youths do not cease drug use when they begin working.

In summarizing this research on employees who abuse alcohol or other drugs, five major findings emerge: (1) these workers are 3 times more likely than the average employee to be late to work; (2) they are 3 times more likely to receive sickness benefits; (3) they are 16 times more likely to be absent from work; (4) they are 5 times more likely to be involved in on-the-job accidents (note that many of these hurt others, not themselves); and (5) they are 5 times more likely to file compensation claims.

Employee Assistance Programs

Many industries have responded to drugs in the workplace by creating **drug testing** and **employee assistance programs (EAPs)**. Drug testing generally involves urine screening and/or hair follicle analysis that are undertaken to identify which employees are using drugs and which employees may have current or potential drug problems. EAPs are employer-financed programs administered by a company or through an outside contractor. More than 400,000 EAPs have been established in the United States. The most recent findings regarding workplace substance use policies and programs among full-time workers are (SAMHSA 2007b):

- Of employees ages 18 to 64 who had used an illicit drug in the past month, 32.1% worked for an employer who offered educational information about alcohol and drug use, 71% were aware of a written policy about drug and alcohol use in the workplace, and 45.4% worked for an employer who maintained an EAP or other type of counseling program for employees who have an alcohol- or drug-related problem.
- Among full-time workers who used alcohol heavily in the past month, 37.2% worked for an employer who provided educational infor-

mation about drug and alcohol use, 73.7% were aware of written policies about drug and alcohol use, and 51.1% had access to an EAP at their workplace.

These programs are designed to aid in identifying and resolving productivity problems associated with employees' emotional or physical concerns, such as those related to health, marital, family, financial, and substance abuse. EAPs have also expanded their focus to combat employee abuse of OTC and prescription drugs in addition to illicit psychoactive substances. Overall, the programs attempt to formally reduce problems associated with impaired job performance. Regarding drug testing today, the Society for Human Resource Management (SHRM) (U.S. Department of Labor 2009) conducted an online survey taken by 454 randomly selected human resource managers from diverse organizations. The following drug testing practices were in effect:

- Eighty-four percent of employers required new hires to pass drug screenings.
- Seventy-four percent used drug screening when reasonable suspicion of drug use was believed.
- Fifty-eight percent of organizations used post-accident drug screening.
- Thirty-nine percent used random drug screening.
- Fourteen percent used scheduled drug testing.

Further, 70% of those responding to this survey indicated that their organization has a written policy that addresses drug testing. From these survey results, we can see that the future for employee drug testing has a very bright future. In all probability, if you have not already experienced such a screening, you will experience these screenings throughout your working life.

Venturing to a Higher Form of Consciousness: The Holistic Self-Awareness Approach to Drug Use

Throughout this book, we continually approach drug use from a multidisciplinary perspective, blending pharmacological, psychological, and sociological perspectives and interpretations of the most commonly used licit and illicit drugs. Most chapters discuss the major drugs and their common usage and abuse patterns and emphasize this multi-

KEY TERMS

drug testing
urine, blood screening, or hair analysis used to identify those who may be using drugs

employee assistance programs (EAPs)
drug assistance programs for drug-dependent employees

level approach in an effort to better comprehend how drugs affect both the mind and the body.

As you proceed through this book, it will become apparent that whenever drug use leads to abuse, it rarely results from a single, isolated cause. Instead, it is often caused or preceded by multiple factors, which may include combinations of the following:

- Hereditary (genetic) factors
- Psychological conditioning
- Peer group pressures
- Inability to cope with stress and anxiety of daily living
- Quality of role models
- Degree of attachment to a family structure
- Level of security with gender identity and sexual orientation
- Personality traits
- Perceived ethnic and racial compatibility with larger society and socioeconomic status (social class)

Gaining knowledge of the reasons for drug use, the effects of drugs, and their addictive potential is the purpose of this text. As authors, we strongly endorse and advocate a **holistic self-awareness approach** that emphasizes a healthy balance among mind, body, and spirit. Health and wellness can be achieved only when these three domains of existence are free from any unnecessary use of psychoactive substances. The holistic philosophy is based on the idea that the mind has a powerful influence on maintaining health. All three—mind, body, and spirit—work as a unified whole to promote health and wellness. Similarly, we are in agreement with holistic health advocates who emphasize the following viewpoint:

> Holistic Health is based on the law of nature that a whole is made up of interdependent parts. The earth is made up of systems, such as air, land, water, plants and animals. If life is to be sustained, they cannot be separated, for what is happening to one is also felt by all the other systems. In the same way, an individual is a whole made up of interdependent parts, which are the physical, mental, emotional, and spiritual. While one part is not working at its best, it

impacts all the other parts of that person. . . . A common explanation is to view wellness as a continuum along a line. The line represents all possible degrees of health. The far left end of the line represents premature death. On the far right end is the highest possible level of wellness or maximum well-being. The center point of the line represents a lack of apparent disease. This places all levels of illness on the left half of the wellness continuum. The right half shows that even when no illness seems to be present, there is still a lot of room for improvement. . . . Holistic Health is an ongoing process. As a lifestyle, it includes a personal commitment to be moving toward the right end of the wellness continuum. No matter what their current status of health, people can improve their level of well-being. Even when there are temporary setbacks, movement is always headed toward wellness. (Walter 1999, pp. 1–2)[1]

The passage above embodies the essence of achieving a holistic self-awareness perspective by presenting a unified blend of different perspectives that can add to our awareness of what is at stake when the goal of drug use is for nonmedical purposes, such as using drugs for the sole purpose of achieving a "high." Knowing about the holistic self-awareness perspective should expand people's often limited and narrow values and attitudes about drug use so that the information about and the use of drugs are viewed and understood from pharmacological, psychological, and sociological perspectives.

As mentioned earlier, understanding drug use is important not only for comprehending our own health, but also for understanding the following:

- Why and how others can become attracted to drugs
- How to detect drug use and abuse in others
- What to do (remedies and solutions) when family members and/or friends abuse drugs
- How to help and advise drug abusers about the pitfalls of substance use
- What the best available educational, preventive, and treatment options are for victims of drug abuse
- What danger signals can arise when others you care about exceed normal and/or necessary drug usage

---

KEY TERMS

holistic self-awareness approach
emphasizes that nonmedical and often recreational drug use interferes with the healthy balance among the mind, the body, and the spirit

---

[1]From Walter, Susan. *The Illustrated Encyclopedia of Body-Mind Disciplines.* New York: Rosen Publishing Group, 1999. Used with permission.

Awareness and knowledge about drug use and/or abuse coupled with holistic health awareness can result in self-awareness, and self-awareness leads to self-understanding and self-assurance. Maintaining at least some belief in holistic self-awareness, either as a humanistic philosophy or adding this philosophy into a religious orientation you may already have, should increase an understanding of your own drug use practices as well as those of family members and close friends. By including at least some aspect of holistic self-awareness into the use of psychoactive substances, you will be better equipped to understand not only yourself, but also others who may be in need of advice and role modeling.

Discussion Questions

1. Give an example of a drug-using friend and describe how he or she may be affected by biological, genetic, pharmacological, cultural, social, and contextual factors.

2. Discuss and debate whether the often considered "benign" drug known as marijuana is or is not addictive. In your discussion/debate, consider the finding by the Substance Abuse and Mental Health Services Administration (SAMHSA) that in 2008 for persons age 12 or older, 41% (102.4 million) of illicit drug users used marijuana during their lifetime, and past-month users of this drug accounted for 6.1% (14.2 million) of all illicit drug users. Do you think this often-considered "benign" drug is harmless to society?

3. What is the future of prescription drug abuse? For example, how much will it increase in the years to come? Do you think prescription drugs will ever become *the* drug of choice? Will prescription drug abuse ever surpass the use of marijuana? Should parents be prosecuted for not guarding their legally prescribed drugs, if their children are caught using their parents' prescription pills?

4. In reviewing the ancient historical uses of drugs, how do you think drug use today is different from back then? Explain your answer.

5. Why do Americans use so many legal drugs (for example, alcohol, tobacco, and OTC drugs)? What aspects of our society could possibly cause such extensive drug use?

6. Table 1.3 shows that the amount of drug use remained stable (showing little change in usage rates) from 2003 to 2008. Cite two reasons why you think this trend has occurred despite the media campaigns against drug use promoted by private organizations, state and nationally sponsored media campaigns, and all the efforts of law enforcement organizations.

7. Because many casual and experimental drug users do not gravitate toward excessive drug use, should these two groups be left alone or perhaps be given legal warnings or fines? How should recreational drug users be treated by society?

8. Do the mass media promote drug use, or do they merely reflect our extensive use of drugs? Provide some evidence for your position.

9. At exactly what point do you think drug use leads to abuse? When do you think drug use does not lead to abuse?

10. What do you believe is the relationship between drug use and crime? Does drug use cause crime or is crime simply a manifestation of personality?

11. What principal factors are involved in the relationship between drugs and crime?

12. Should all employees be randomly tested for drug use? If not, which types of employees or occupations should randomly drug test?

13. List and rank order at least three things you found very interesting regarding drug use in this chapter.

14. Should all students and faculty be randomly drug tested at their schools and universities? Why or why not?

15. Do you think the approach advocated by the authors regarding a holistic self-awareness approach toward drug use is a viable one that can be used successfully for stopping drug use? Why or why not? What, if any, additional improvements can be made to strengthen this approach?

Summary

1 Biological issues, genetic issues, pharmacological issues, and cultural, social, and contextual issues are the four principal factors responsible for

determining how a drug user experiences drug use. Biological, genetic, and pharmacological factors take into account how a particular drug affects the body. Cultural factors examine how society's views, determined by custom and tradition, affect the use of a particular drug. Social factors include the specific reasons why a drug is taken and how drug use develops from social factors, such as family upbringing, peer group alliances, subcultures, and communities. Contextual factors account for how drug use behavior develops from the physical surroundings in which the drug is taken.

2 Initial understanding of drug use includes the following key terms: drug, gateway drugs, medicines and prescription medicines, over-the-counter (OTC), drug misuse, drug abuse, and drug addiction.

3 Mentions of drug use date back to biblical times and ancient literature that goes back to 2240 BC. Under the influence of drugs, many people experienced feelings ranging from extreme ecstasy to sheer terror. At times, drugs were used to induce sleep and provide freedom from care.

4 Drug users are found in all occupations and professions, at all income and social class levels, and in all age groups. No one is immune to drug use. Thus, drug use is an equal-opportunity affliction.

5 According to sociologist Erich Goode (1999), drugs are used for four reasons: (a) legal instrumental use, (b) legal recreational use, (c) illegal instrumental use, and (d) illegal recreational use.

6 The most commonly used licit and illicit lifetime drug use (rated from highest to lowest in the frequency of use) are alcohol, cigarettes, marijuana/hashish, nonmedical use of any psychotherapeutic, smokeless tobacco, cocaine, hallucinogens, pain relievers, inhalants, tranquilizers, stimulants, sedatives, and heroin.

7 The three types of drug users are experimenters, compulsive users, and floaters. Experimenters try drugs because of curiosity and peer pressure. Compulsive users use drugs on a full-time basis and seriously desire to escape from or alter reality. Floaters or chippers vacillate between experimental drug use and chronic drug use.

8 The mass media tend to promote drug use through advertising. The constant barrage of OTC drug commercials relays the message that, if you are experiencing some symptom, taking drugs is an acceptable option.

9 Drug use leads to abuse when the following occurs: (a) excessive use, (b) constant concern and preoccupation about the availability and supply of the drug, (c) refusal to admit excessive use, and (d) reliance on the drug.

10 The stages of drug dependence are *relief* from using the drug, *increased use* of the drug, *preoccupation* with the supply of the drug, *dependency* or addiction to the drug, and experiencing (either or both) physical and/or psychological *withdrawal* effects from not using the drug.

11 The following are the major findings of the connection between drugs and crime: (a) drug users are more likely to commit crimes, (b) arrestees are often under the influence of drugs while committing their crimes, and (c) drugs and violence often go hand in hand, especially when alcohol, cocaine, crack, methamphetamine, or other stimulant-types of drugs are used.

12 Employee assistance programs (EAPs) are employer-financed programs administered by a company or through an outside contractor. They are designed to aid in identifying and resolving productivity problems associated with employees' emotional or physical concerns, such as those related to health, marriage, family, finances, and substance abuse. Recently, EAPs have expanded their focus to combat employee abuse of OTC and prescription drugs as well as illicit psychoactive substances.

13 The holistic self-awareness philosophy is based on the idea that the mind, body, and spirit have a powerful influence on maintaining health. These three domains—mind, body, and spirit—work best when unobstructed by unnecessary drug use, and when all three domains work in a unified manner to promote health and wellness.

References

Associated Press. "Program to Fight Drug Smuggling Costs U.S. a Lot, Produces Little." *Salt Lake Tribune* 244 (17 August 1992):A-1.

Associated Press. "Mexican Cardinal, Six Others Killed in Cross-Fire as Drug Battles Erupt in Guadalajara." *Salt Lake Tribune* 246 (25 May 1993):A-1.

Associated Press. "Survey: Drug Use Pervading New Bedford Fleet." *Maine Sunday Telegram* (21 July 1996).

Associated Press. "Discovery of Mexican Graves Unlikely to Slow Flow of Drugs." *The Times* (5 December 1999):A-13.

Associated Press. "Mexico: Drug War Death Toll Worsens, 11 Die in One Shootout, 24 in a Day in Small-Town Gun Battles." *Post Tribune* (Northwest Indiana) 100 (14 March 2010):38.

Berkrot, B. "Global Drug Sales to Top $1 Trillion." Thomson Reuters. 20 April 2010. Available http://www.reuters.com/article/idUKTRE63J0Y520100420

Beschner, G. "Understanding Teenage Drug Use." In *Teen Drug Use,* edited by G. Beschner and A. Friedman, 1–18. Lexington, MA: D.C. Heath, 1986.

Birns, L. and A. Sánchez. "The Government and Mexico: Who Rules Mexico?" Worldpress.org. 23 April 2007:1–5. Available http://www.worldpress.org/Americas/2763.cfmorldpress.org

Boyles, S. "Americans Spend $34 Billion on Alternative Medicines." WebMD. 2009. Available http://www.rxlist.com/script/main/art.asp?articlekey=104255#

Bryner, J. "Fake Weed, Real Drug: K2 Causing Hallucinations in Teens." LiveScience. 3 March 2010. Available http://www.livescience.com/health/fake-marijuana-k2-hallucinations-100303.html

Bureau of Justice Statistics (BJS). *Prisoners: Drugs and Crime Facts.* Washington, DC: U.S. Department of Justice, Office of Justice Programs (OJP), 2004. Available http://bjs.ojp.usdoj.gov/index.cfm?ty=gsearch

Bureau of Justice Statistics (BJS). *Drug Use and Dependence, State and Federal Prisoners.* Washington, DC: U.S. Department of Justice, Office of Justice Programs, 2006a. Available http://bjs.ojp.usdoj.gov/index.cfm?ty=pbdetail&iid=778

Bureau of Justice Statistics (BJS). *Drugs and Crime Facts: Drug Law Violations.* Washington, DC: U.S. Department of Justice, Office of Justice Programs, 2006b.

Butterfield, F. "As Drug Use Drops in Big Cities, Small Towns Confront Upsurge." *New York Times* (11 February 2002): A23. Available http://www.nytimes.com/2002/02/11/us/as-drug-use-drops-in-big-cities-small-towns-confront-upsurge.html?scp=1&sq=As%20Drug%20Use%20Drops%20in%20Big%20Cities,%20Amall%20Towns%20Confront%20Upsurge,%20Butterfield,%20Fox&st=cse

Campbell, R. "Mexican Cartels Cannot be Defeated, Drug Lord Says." Thomson Reuters. 4 April 2010:1. Available http://www.reuters.com/article/idUSTRE6331DZ20100404

CBS News. "Drug Advertising Skyrockets." CBS Worldwide. 13 February 2002. Available http://www.cbsnews.com/stories/2002/02/13/health/main329293.shtml

Center for Substance Abuse Research (CESAR). "First Time Users of Pain Relievers Continue to Surpass All Other Drugs; Number of New Ecstasy and Stimulant Users Increases." *CESAR FAX* (17 September 2007). Available http://www.cesar.umd.edu

Center for Substance Abuse Research (CESAR). "Ritalin and Adderall Abused by Students as Party Drugs and Study Aids." *CESAR FAX* (1 December 2003). Available http://www.cesar.umd.edu

Center for Substance Abuse Research (CESAR). "Friends and Family Are Most Common Source of Prescription Drugs Misused by Youths," *CESAR FAX* 18 (17 August 2009):18.

Center on Alcohol Marketing and Youth (CAMY). "Drowned Out: Alcohol Industry's Responsibility: Advertising on Television, 2001–2005." Washington, DC: Center on Alcohol Marketing and Youth (2007):1–4. Available http://www.camy.org/bin/a/t/responsibility2007execsum.pdf

Centers for Disease Control and Prevention (CDC). *CDC Responds to HIV/AIDS.* Atlanta, GA: U.S. Department of Health and Human Services, CDC, 24 July 2009a:1.

Centers for Disease Control and Prevention (CDC). *HIV/AIDS in the United States.* Atlanta, GA: U.S. Department of Health and Human Services, CDC, 21 August 2009b:1.

Centers for Disease Control and Prevention (CDC). "Youth Risk Behavior Surveillance—United States, 2009. Surveillance Summaries." *Morbidity and Mortality Weekly Report (MMWR)* 59, 4 June 2010:76.

Central Intelligence Agency. *The World Factbook 2009.* Washington, DC: U.S. Government Printing Office, 2009. Available https://www.cia.gov/library/publications/the-world-factbook/fields/print_2086.html

Clinton, Bill. "My Quest to Improve Care." *Newsweek* CXLVII (15 May 2006):50–53.

CNN.com. "Synthetic Marijuana a Growing Trend Among Teens, Authorities Say." 2010. Available http://www.cnn.com/2010/HEALTH/03/23/synthetic.marijuana/index.html?iref=allsearch

Consumer Healthcare Products Association (CHPA). "OTC Retail Sales—1964–2009." 2009. Available http://www.chpa-info.org/aboutchpal/contact_Us.aspx

Critser, G. "Oh, How Happy We Will Be: Pills, Paradise, and the Profits of the Drug Companies." *Harper's Magazine* (June 1996):39–48.

Critser, G. *Generation RX: How Prescription Drugs Are Altering American Lives, Minds and Bodies.* Boston, MA: Houghton-Mifflin, 2005.

Delaney, W., J. W. Grube, and G. M. Ames. "Predicting Likelihood of Seeking Help Through the Employee Assistance Program Among Salaried and Union Hourly Employees." *Addiction* 93 (1998):399–410.

Del Bosque, M. "Mexico's Future in 2010, Calderon's Failed Drug War." *Texas Observer* (5 January 2010):1–2. Available http://www.texasobserver.org/lalinea/calderons-war-on-drugs-is-a-failure

Drug Strategies. *Keeping Score: What We Are Getting for Our Federal Drug Control Dollars 1995.* Washington, DC: Drug Strategies, 1995.

Edelson, E. "Drug Use in the Workplace Plummets." APB News. 7 February 2000:3. Available http://www.cannabisnews.com/news/4/thread4627.shtml

Farah, J. "Invasion USA: Mexican Drug Cartels Take Over U.S. Cities." WorldNet Daily. 18 June 2006. Available http://www.worldnetdaily.com/news/article.asp?article_id=50518

Federal Trade Commission. *Appendix B: Alcohol Advertising Expenditures.* Washington, DC: U.S. Government Printing Office, 2007.

Fischer M. A., M. R. Stedman, L. J. C. Vogeli, W. H. Shrank, M. A. Brookhart, and J. S. Weissman. "Primary Medication Non-Adherence: Analysis of 195,930 Electronic Prescriptions." *Journal of General Internal Medicine.* 25 (2010 April):284–290, Epub 4 February 2010.

Goldstein, A. *Addiction: From Biology to Drug Policy.* New York: Oxford University Press, 2001.

Goode, E. *Drugs in American Society,* 5th ed. Boston, MA: Mc-Graw-Hill, 1999.

Goode, E. *Drugs in American Society,* 7th ed. New York: Mc-Graw-Hill, 2008.

Hughes, A., N. Sathe, and K. Spagnola. *State Estimates of Substance Use from the 2006–2007 National Surveys on Drug Use and Health.* NSDUH Series H-35, HHS Publication No. 09-4362. Rockville, MD: Office of Applied Studies (OAS), Substance Abuse and Mental Health Services Administration (SAMHSA), 2009.

Jellinek, J. "Musical Meth Lab Uncovered." *Rolling Stone.* 20 February 2003:54.

Johnston, L. D., P. M. O'Malley, J. G. Bachman, and J. E. Schulenberg. *Monitoring the Future: National Survey Results on Drug Use, 1975–2008, Volume I: Secondary School Students,* Bethesda, MD: National Institute on Drug Abuse, 2009.

Karberg, J. C., and D. J. James. *Special Report, Substance Dependence, Abuse, and Treatment of Jail Inmates, 2002.* Bureau of Justice Statistics (BJS). Washington, DC: U.S. Department of Justice, Office of Justice Programs, 2002.

Kilbourne, J. "Advertising Addiction: The Alcohol Industry's Hard Sell." *Multinational Monitor* (June 1989):13–16.

Kusinitz, M. "Drug Use Around the World." In *Encyclopedia of Psychoactive Drugs,* edited by S. Snyder. Series 2. New York: Chelsea House, 1988.

Larson, S. L., J. Eyeman, M. S. Foster, and J. C. Gfoerer. *Worker Substance Use and Workplace Policies and Programs.* DHHS Publication No. SMA 07-4273, Analytic Series A-29. Rockville, MD: Substance Abuse and Mental Health Services Administration, Office of Applied Studies, 2007.

Lawson, G. "The War Next Door: As Drug Cartels Battle the Government, Mexico Descends Into Chaos." *Rolling Stone* 1065 (13 November 2008):74–81, 108–111.

Lenson, D. *On Drugs.* Minneapolis, MN: University of Minnesota Press, 1995.

Levinthal, C. F. *Drugs, Behavior, and Modern Society.* Boston, MA: Allyn and Bacon, 1996.

Lundy, J. "Prescription Drug Trends." The Henry J. Kaiser Family Foundation. 2010. Available http://www.kff.org/rxdrugs/3057.cfm

McBride, D. C., and C. B. McCoy. "The Drugs–Crime Relationship: An Analytical Framework." In *Drugs, Crime, and Justice,* edited by L. K. Gaines and B. Kraska, 100–119. Prospect Heights, IL: Waveland Press, 2003.

McShane, L. "Cops Are Crooks in N.Y.'s 30th Precinct." *Salt Lake Tribune* 238 (18 April 1994):A-5.

Mink, M. D., C. G. Moore, A. O. Johnson, J. C. Probst, and A. B. Martin. *Violence and Rural Teens: Violence, Drug Use, and School-Based Prevention Services in Rural America.* Rockville, MD: South Carolina Rural Health Research Center, Office of Rural Health Policy, U.S. Department of Health and Human Services, U.S. Government Printing Office, 2005.

Monroe, J. "What Is Addiction?" *Current Health* 2 (January 1996):16–19.

Mumola, C. J., and J. C. Karberg. "Drug Use and Dependence, State and Federal Prisoners, 2004." Washington, DC: U.S. Department of Justice, 19 January 2007: 1. Available http://bjs.ojp.usdoj.gov/content/pub/pdf/dudsfp04.pdf

Natarajan, N., A. Petteruti, N. Walsh, and J. Ziedenberg. "Substance Abuse Treatment and Public Safety (A Policy Brief)." Justice Policy Institute. January 2008:1. Available http://www.justicepolicy.org/images/upload/08_01_REP_DrugTx_AC-PS.pdf

National Association for Children of Alcoholics. "Children of Addicted Parents: Important Facts." Rockville, MD: HopeNetworks, 2005. Available http://www.hopenetworks.org/addiction/Children%20of%20Addicts.htm

National Institute of Justice (NIJ). *ADAM II, 2008 Annual Report.* Arrestee Drug Abuse (ADAM). U.S. Department of Justice (DOJ), Office of National Drug Control Policy (ONDCP). Washington, DC: U.S. Government Printing Office, 2009.

National Institute on Drug Abuse (NIDA). *Prescription Medications.* Bethesda, MD: U.S. Government Printing Office, 2010.

National Narcotics Intelligence Consumers Committee. *The NNICC Report, 1994.* Washington, DC: U.S. Drug Enforcement Agency, 1994:70.

National Public Radio (NPR). "All Things Considered." PM News (18 September 1996).

National Survey on Drug Use and Health (NSDUH). *The NSDUH Report: Patterns and Trends in Nonmedical Prescription Pain Reliever Use: 2002 to 2005.* Rockville, MD: Substance Abuse and Mental Health Services Administration, Office of Applied Studies, 2007.

Nielsenwire. "More Than Half the Homes in U.S. Have Three or More TVs." The Nielsen Company. 20 July 2009: 1–2. Available http://blog.nielsen.com/nielsenwire/media_entertainment/more-than-half-the-homes-in-us-have-three-or-more-tvs/print

Office of National Drug Control Policy (ONDCP). *What America's Users Spend on Illegal Drugs 1988–2000.* Cambridge, MA: Abt Associates, 2001.

Office of National Drug Control Policy (ONDCP). *Pulse Check: Trends in Drug Abuse.* Washington, DC: Executive Office of the President, Office of National Drug Control Policy, 2002.

Office of National Drug Control Policy (ONDCP). *Teens and Prescription Drugs: An Analysis of Recent Trends on the Emerging Drug Threat.* Washington, DC: Executive Office of the President, Office of National Drug Control Policy, 2007.

Office of National Drug Control Policy (ONDCP). *Drug Facts: Street Terms.* Rockville, MD: Drug Policy Information Clearinghouse, 2010. Available www.whitehousedrugpolicy.gov/streetterms

Pharmacy Times. "Drug Spending Increases Dramatically in 8 Years." 73 (July 2007):2.

Publishers Group. *Prescription Drugs.* Plymouth, MN: 2004. Available http://www.streetdrugs.org/prescription.htm

Reynolds, G. S., and W. E. Lehman. "Levels of Substance Use and Willingness to Use the Employee Assistance Program." *Journal of Behavioral Health Services and Research* 30 (2003):238–248.

Robert Wood Johnson Foundation. *Substance Abuse: The Nation's Number One Health Problem.* Prepared by the Schneider Institute for Health Policy for the Robert Wood Johnson Foundation, Brandeis University. Princeton, NJ: Robert Wood Johnson Foundation, February 2001.

Sabol, W. J., H. C. West, and M. Cooper. *Prisoners in 2008.* Washington, DC: U.S. Bureau of Justice Statistics, U.S. Department of Justice, Office of Justice Programs, December 2009:1–45.

Schecter, M. "Serotonergic-Dopaminergic Mediation of 3,4-Methylenedioxy-Methamphetamine (MDMA, Ecstasy)." *Pharmacology, Biochemistry and Behavior* 31 (1989):817–824.

Steward, P., and G. Sitarmiah. "America's Heartland Grapples with Rise of Dangerous Drug." *Christian Science Monitor* (13 November 1997):1, 18.

Stopthedrugwar.org. "Global: World Drug Trade Worth $320 Billion Annually, UN Says." 1 July 2005:1–2. Available http://stopthedrugwar.org/chronicle-old/393/320billion.shtml

Substance Abuse and Mental Health Services Administration (SAMHSA). *Overview of Findings from the 2003 National Survey on Drug Use and Health.* NSDUH Series H-24, DHHS Publication No. SMA 04-3963. Rockville, MD: Office of Applied Studies, 2004.

Substance Abuse and Mental Health Services Administration (SAMHSA). *Results from the 2005 National Survey on Drug Use and Health: National Findings.* Rockville, MD: Office of Applied Studies, 2006a.

Substance Abuse and Mental Health Services Administration (SAMHSA). *National Survey on Drug Use and Health (NSDUH) Report. Substance Use Disorder and Serious Psychological Distress by Employment Status.* Rockville, MD: Substance Abuse and Mental Health Services Administration, Office of Applied Studies, 2006b.

Substance Abuse and Mental Health Services Administration (SAMHSA). *Results from the 2006 National Survey on Drug Use and Health: National Findings.* Rockville, MD: Substance Abuse and Mental Health Services Administration, 2007.

Substance Abuse and Mental Health Services Administration (SAMHSA), Office of Applied Studies (OAS). *The Relationship Between Family Structure and Adolescent Substance Use.* Rockville, MD: U.S. Department of Health and Human Services, July 1996.

Substance Abuse and Mental Health Services Administration (SAMHSA), Office of Applied Studies. *The National Survey on Drug Use and Health (NSDUH) Report. Worker Substance Use, by Industry Category.* Rockville, MD: Substance Abuse and Mental Health Services Administration, 2007.

Substance Abuse and Mental Health Services Administration (SAMHSA), Office of Applied Studies. *Results from the 2008 National Survey on Drug Use and Health: National Findings.* NSDUH Series H-36, DHHS Publication No. SMA 09-4435. Rockville, MD: Office of Applied Studies, 2009.

Szasz, T. *Our Right to Drugs: The Case for a Free Market.* Westport, CT: Praeger, 1992.

Thio, A. *Deviant Behavior,* 2nd ed. Boston: Houghton Mifflin, 1983:332–333.

Thio, A. *Deviant Behavior,* 4th ed. New York: Harper-Collins College, 1995.

Thio, A. *Deviant Behavior,* 6th ed. New York: Pearson Education, 2000.

Toufonio, A., et al. "There Is No Safe Speed." *Time* (8 January 1990).

U.S. Department of Justice. *Information Brief: Prescription Drug Abuse and Youth.* Johnstown, PA: National Drug Intelligence Center, 2004. Available http://www.usdoj.gov/ndic/pubs/1765

U.S. Department of Labor. *SHRM Survey Reveals Majority of HR Professionals' Organizations Drug Test.* Washington, DC: U.S. Government Printing Office, Department of Labor, 2009.

Venturelli, P. J. "Drugs in Schools: Myths and Reality." In *Annals of the American Academy of Political and Social Science,* 567, edited by W. Hinkle and S. Henry. Thousand Oaks, CA: Sage, 2000.

Walter, S. "Holistic Health." In the *Illustrated Encyclopedia of Body–Mind Disciplines,* edited by N. Alison, 1–2. New York: The Rosen Publishing Group, 1999. Available http://ahha.org/rosen.htm

Warner, J. "U.S. Leads the World in Illegal Drug Use." CBS News. 1 July 2009: 1. Available http://www.cbsnews.com/stories/2008/07/01/health/webmd/main4222322.shtml

Wilkie, C. "Crack Cocaine Moves South." *Boston Globe* (23 June 1996).

Wire Services. "Cocaine Kingpin Escapes After Bloody Shootout." *Salt Lake Tribune* 244 (23 July 1992):A-1.

World Pharmaceutical Market Summary. "Sales Through Retail Pharmacies." Plymouth Meeting, PA: IMS Health, May 2010.

Worldpress.org. "Mexico: Drug Cartels a Growing Threat." 2 November 2006:1–4. Available http://www.worldpress.org/Americas/2549.cfm#down

CHAPTER 2

Explaining Drug Use and Abuse

Did You Know?

- O Contrary to public perception, addiction is a complex disease.

- O Most drugs of abuse include both physical and psychological addictions.

- O Every culture has experienced problems with drug use or abuse. As far back as 2240 BC, Hammurabi, the Babylonian king and lawgiver, addressed the problems associated with excessive use of alcohol.

- O Today, there are many more varieties of drugs and many of these drugs are more potent than they were years ago.

- O According to biological theories, drug abuse has an innate physical beginning stemming from physical characteristics that cause certain individuals either to experiment with or to crave drugs to the point of abuse.

- O Abuse of drugs by some people may represent an attempt to relieve underlying psychiatric disorders.

- O No single theory can explain why most people use drugs.

- O People who perceive themselves as drug users are more likely to develop serious drug abuse problems.

 Drugs and Society Online is a great source for additional drugs and society information for both students and instructors. Visit **go.jblearning.com/hanson11** to find a variety of useful tools for learning, thinking, and teaching.

Learning ◎bjectives

On completing this chapter you will be able to:

- ◎ List three to five major contributing factors responsible for addiction.
- ◎ List and briefly explain three models used to describe addiction.
- ◎ List six reasons why drug use or abuse is a more serious problem today than it was in the past.
- ◎ List and briefly describe the genetic and biophysiological theories that explain how drug use often leads to abuse.
- ◎ Explain how drugs of abuse act as positive reinforcers.
- ◎ Explain the relationships between addiction and other mental disorders and the possible effects of certain drugs.
- ◎ Briefly define and explain reinforcement or learning theory and some of its applications to drug use and abuse.
- ◎ Briefly explain sensation-seeking individuals and drug use.
- ◎ List and briefly describe the four sociological theories broadly known as social influence theories.
- ◎ Explain the link between drug use and other types of devious behaviors.
- ◎ List and describe three factors in the learning process that Howard Becker believes first-time users go through before they become attached to using illicit psychoactive drugs.
- ◎ Define the following concepts as they relate to drug use: primary and secondary deviance, master status, and retrospective interpretation.
- ◎ Explain how Reckless's containment theory accounts for the roles of both internal and external controls regarding the attraction to drug use.
- ◎ Understand how making low-risk and high-risk drug choices directly affects drug use.

Introduction

Chapter 1 provided an overview of drug use. In this chapter, we focus on the major explanations of drug use and/or abuse. The questions we explore are these: Why would anyone voluntarily consume drugs when they are not medically needed or required? Why are some people attracted to altering their minds? Why are others uneasy and uncomfortable with the euphoric effects of recreational drug use? Why do people subject their bodies and minds to the harmful effects of repetitive drug use, eventual addiction, and relapse back into drug use? What logical reasons could explain such apparently irrational behavior?

Following are four perspectives regarding drug use:

First perspective:

Yes, I use a lot of drugs. I like the high from weed [marijuana], the buzz from coke [cocaine], and liquor also. I like psychedelic drugs but can't do them often because one, they are harder to get, and two, I work all the time and go to school at night. Psychedelics require big-time commitment and I just don't have that amount of time anymore to play around with intense mind trips. I think I am biologically attracted to drugs. What else would explain the desire to get high all the time? Some of my friends are worse than me. They don't just hang with the desire to continually want to get high, they just do it. One friend of mine does not accomplish much; my other two friends are coke addicts but they say they are not addicted, they claim to just like it. I don't think a day goes by, unless I am sick with the flu or something, that I don't get at least a little buzzed on some drug. My wife does not do any drugs, but hey, she's cool with my drug use as long as I keep working every day. *(From Venturelli's research files, graduate student and full-time insurance claims adjuster, age 28, July 12, 2000)*

Second perspective:

I grew up in a home with no alcohol present. I never saw my mom or dad drink alcohol. I think when they got married both of them had alcoholic parents. I never knew my grandparents since they died before I was born. My older brother remembers my grandfather since he lived until my brother was seven. He remembers that my grandfather would come over to visit and he was usually acting "weird." Later in life, he realized that my grandfather was probably drinking a lot and was probably under the influence. Anyway, before I was born my grandfather died of a stroke and my mom tells me that it was from drinking too much. He also had liver problems and my dad just recently told me his liver was shot from too much drinking. I tried bringing home a bottle of wine once and my mom and dad just watched me sip a glass without saying a word. They refused to have a drink with me and I recall how odd I felt doing this that when I look back on it, I was probably hurting their feelings. Anyway, I went away to college and during my first year, I started drinking a lot, got into all kinds of trouble with my college friends, law enforcement, my RA in a dorm I was living in, and the Dean of Students, and nearly flunked out of college that first year. After experiencing all these newfound problems, I decided that drinking alcohol was not for me. Besides, I was hurting my parents real bad when I was having these problems. Today at 31, I probably have a few drinks several times a year, but I am not really a drinker. One drink and I feel it right away. I can drink a sweet drink like a margarita, but many of my real close friends do not drink alcohol. I am just not around people who drink and actually, except for some college friends when I was attending Ball State who drank, I hardly ever had friends who drank. I had a girlfriend a few years ago but our relationship ended when I got tired of watching her drink while I waited to leave the bars at the end of the night. How drinkers want to keep drinking is very noticeable to a nondrinker. I also had an acquaintance at work who would call me several nights a week, and I had to listen to his incoherent conversations while he was drinking at home. I got tired of this, and one night I said that I prefer not to talk to him when he was drinking at home. Shortly after that conversation, he and his girlfriend moved away and I never heard from him again. What attracts people to drinking baffles me, and why they continue drinking when they have had plenty already is even more puzzling. I don't think they realize how stupid they act when intoxicated. Fuzzy thinking, uncoordinated, and loud they become are other things I notice. Today, I am dealing with a stepson who is not only drinking at 16 but has also used other types of drugs and I can say that from dealing with his drug use, I am very much against the use of any drugs that are not necessary. *(From Venturelli's research files, male, age 31, May 18, 2010)*

Third perspective:

> When you ask about drug use, I literally draw a blank. This topic is really unknown to me. In my family, my grandparents on my dad's side were big-time drinkers. I think . . . my dad's experiences and especially . . . the car crash that killed my grandparents when they were in their 50s while coming home from a wedding after drinking heavily affected my dad very much. My mom comes from a Mormon family, so obviously she also does not drink any alcohol. My parents raised me and my three brothers without any examples or experiences regarding drug use. In my family, my wife and I hardly ever use any types of drugs—not even much of over-the-counter drugs. Occasionally, I will have a half a glass of wine several times a year, but I have to admit, I would rather be drinking water or freshly made fruit juice. I just do not like the taste and the mild effect that such a small amount of alcohol has on me. As you can imagine, I am very much against the use of any types of drugs, especially the illicit types of drugs. Drugs are addictive and people should not be doing or taking drugs. Taking drugs for fun does not have any real positive outcomes, and in the end, causes a lot of misery to families, and medical problems. I am quite certain that all of our family friends are nondrinkers and I know for certain that our best friends do not use any of the recreational types of drugs. You could say our lives are really drug free. Everything we do as a family is in the absence of drug use. *(From Venturelli's research files, male graduate university student, age 36, May 19, 2007)*

Fourth perspective:

> Yes, I have friends who try to tell me to slow down when we are smoking weed and drinking. I just like to get high until I am about to pass out. If I could, I would be high all day without any time out. Never think about quitting or slowing down when it comes to drugs. The only time I am happy is when I am completely zonked out. I guess I am a little attached to these drugs— I am addicted to them! *(From Venturelli's research files, male high school student in a small Midwestern city, age 15, September 9, 1996)*

The preceding excerpts show extensive variations in values and attitudes regarding drug use. The perspective of the first interviewee represents a type of drug user who is powerfully attracted to drug use. He appears to believe that his attraction to drugs has a biological basis and he wants to feel the effects of drugs on a daily basis. The second interview shows how alcohol use in a previous generation can affect a family's perspective on drug use (primarily agreement on the negative effects of alcohol) and how this prohibitive view of drug use is transmitted and lingers in future generations. After having some preliminary experiences with drug use, the interviewee in the third excerpt matures into a person shunning any recreational chemical alteration of his reality. The perspective of the third interviewee shows that if a person's early environment is drug free, then drug use is not an option. Finally, the perspective of the fourth interviewee represents a type of drug user who is unaware of the pitfalls of drug addiction and is recklessly involved with substance abuse. These four views represent a limited range of reasons and motivations that push people to either use or not use drugs.

Why the differences in drug use? In this chapter, we offer plausible explanations regarding why people use drugs recreationally and examine the motivations underlying drug use. We offer different major theoretical explanations about what causes people to initially use and often eventually abuse drugs.

To accomplish these goals, this chapter frames these and literally dozens of other perspectives *within* the major biological, psychological, and sociological perspectives. Similar to the United States, nearly all other countries are experiencing increasing amounts of drug use within certain subcultures. Moreover, as we attempt to offer major scientific and theoretical explanations for drug use, we should be able to develop a much more comprehensive understanding of why drugs are so seductive, and why so many people succumb, become addicted, and inflict damage to themselves and others as they become "hijacked" by the nonmedical use of drugs. Not only does this hold true for members of U.S. society, but also for countless numbers of others throughout the world.

Drug Use: A Timeless Affliction

Historical records document drug use as far back as 2240 BC, when Hammurabi, the Babylonian king and lawgiver, addressed the problems associated with drinking alcohol. Even before then, the Sumerian people of Asia Minor, who created the cuneiform (wedge-shaped) alphabet, included references to a "joy plant" that dates from about 5000 BC. Experts indicate that the plant was an opium poppy used as a sedative (O'Brien et al. 1992).

As noted in Chapter 1, virtually every culture has experienced problems with drug use or abuse. Today's drug use problems are part of a very long and rich tradition.

> These [intoxicating] substances have formed a bond of union between men of opposite hemispheres, the uncivilized and the civilized; they have forced passages which, once open, proved of use for other purposes; they produced in ancient races characteristics which have endured to the present day, evidencing the marvelous degree of intercourse that existed between different peoples just as certainly and exactly as a chemist can judge the relations of two substances by their reactions. (Louis Lewin, *Phantasica*, in Rudgley 1993, p. 3)

The quest for explaining drug use is more important than ever as the problem continues to evolve. There are many reasons why drug use and abuse are even more serious issues now than they were in the past:

- From 1960 to the present, drug use has become a widespread phenomenon.
- Today, drugs are much more potent than they were years ago. The drug content of marijuana in 1960 was 1% to 2%; today, due to new cultivation techniques, it varies from 4% to nearly 10%. "... [S]amples seized by law enforcement agencies from 1975 through 2007 ... found that the average amount of THC reached 9.6% in 2007, compared with 8.75% the previous years" (*USA Today* 2008).
- Whether they are legal or not, drugs are extremely popular. Their sale is a multibillion dollar a year business, with a major influence on many national economies.
- More so today than years ago, both licit and illicit drugs are introduced and experimented with by youth at a younger age. These drugs often are supplied by older siblings, friends, and acquaintances.
- Through the media, people in today's society are more affected by direct television and radio advertising, especially by drug companies that are "pushing" their newest drugs. Similarly, advertisements and sales promotions (coupons) for alcohol, coffee, tea, and vitamins are targeted to receptive consumer audiences, as identified through sophisticated market research.

- Today, there is greater availability and wider dissemination of drug information. Literally thousands of web sites provide information on drug usage, chat rooms devoted to drug enthusiasts, and instructions on how to make drugs or purchase them on the Internet. On a daily basis, hundreds of thousands of "spam" e-mails are automatically sent regarding information on purchasing OTC drugs and prescription drugs without medical authorization (medical prescription). "The percentage of spam in email traffic averaged 85.2% in 2009" (Kaspersky Lab 2010).
- Crack and other manufactured drugs offer potent effects at low cost, vastly multiplying the damage potential of drug abuse (Clatts et al. 2008; Inciardi, Lockwood, and Pottieger 1993; Office of National Drug Control Policy [ONDCP] 2003).
- Drug use endangers the future of a society by harming its youth and potentially destroying the lives of many young men and women. When gateway drugs, such as alcohol and tobacco, are used at an early age, a strong probability exists that the use will progress to other drugs, such as marijuana, cocaine, and amphetamines. Early drug use will likely lead to a lifelong habit, which usually has serious implications for the future.
- Drug use and especially drug dealing are becoming major factors in the growth of crime rates among the young. Membership in violent delinquent gangs is growing at an alarming rate. Violent shootings, drive-by killings, carjacking, and "wilding" occur frequently in cities (and increasingly in small towns).
- Seven in 10 drug users work full time (*The Capitol Times* 1999). More recent findings also indicate that of 2.9 million adults ages 18 to 64 employed full time who had co-occurring substance use disorder and serious psychological distress, nearly 60% were not treated for either problem, and less than 5% were treated for both problems (Substance Abuse and Mental Health Services Administration [SAMHSA] 2008). Such startling findings regarding employment and drug use lead to not only decreased productivity, absenteeism, job turnover, and medical costs but also near or serious accidents and mistakes caused by workers.
- Another related problem is that drug use is especially serious today because we have become highly dependent on the expertise of others and highly dependent on technology.

For example, the operation of sophisticated machines and electronic equipment requires that workers and professionals be free of the intoxicating effects of mind-altering drugs. Imagine the chilling fact that on a daily basis, a certain percentage of pilots, surgeons, and heavy-equipment operators are under the influence of mind-altering drugs while working, or that a certain percentage of school-bus drivers are under the effects of, say, marijuana and/or cocaine.

With remarkable and unsurpassed excellence in scientific, technological, and electronic accomplishments, one might think that in the United States, drug use and abuse would be considered irrational behavior. One might also think that the allure of drugs would diminish on the basis of the statistically high proportions of accidents, crimes, domestic violence and other relationship problems, and early deaths that result from the use and abuse of both licit and illicit drugs. Yet, as the latest drug use figures show (see Chapter 1), knowledge of these effects is often not a deterrent to drug use.

Considering these costs, what explains the continuing use and abuse of drugs? What could possibly sustain and feed the attraction to use mind-altering drugs? Why are drugs used when the consequences are so well documented and predictable?

In answering these questions, we need to recall from Chapter 1 some basic reasons why people take drugs:

- People may be searching for pleasure.
- Drugs may relieve stress or tension or provide a temporary escape for people with excessive anxieties or severe depression.
- Peer pressure is a strong influence, especially for young people.
- In some cases, drugs may enhance religious or mystical experiences.
- Drugs are used to enhance recreational pursuits, such as the popular use of Ecstasy at raves and music festivals.
- Some believe that illicit use of drugs can enhance work performance, such as the use of cocaine by stockbrokers, office workers, and lawyers.
- Drugs (primarily performance-enhancing drugs) can be used to improve athletic performance.
- Drugs can relieve pain and the symptoms of an illness.

Although these reasons may indicate some underlying causes of excessive or abusive drug use, they also suggest that the variety and complexity of explanations and motivations are almost infinite. For any one individual, it is seldom clear when the drug use shifts from nondestructive use to abuse and addiction. When we consider the wide use of such licit drugs as alcohol, nicotine, and caffeine, we make the following discoveries: (1) More than 88% of the U.S. population use different types of drugs on a daily basis (National Institute on Drug Abuse [NIDA] 2007; SAMHSA 2009); (2) more than half (54%) have tried an illicit drug by the time they finish high school; and (3) three out of four students (75%) have consumed alcohol (more than just a few sips) by the end of high school, and nearly half (47%) had done so by 8th grade (Johnston et al. 2009).

Further, as we will see in later chapters, some drugs can mimic many of the hundreds of moods people can experience. We can, therefore, begin to understand why the explanations for drug use and abuse are multiple and depend on both socialization experiences and biological differences. As a result of these two factors, which imply hundreds of variations, explanations for drug use cannot be forced into one or two theories.

Researchers have tackled the drug use and abuse question from three major theoretical positions: biological, psychological, and sociological perspectives. Although the remainder of this chapter discusses these three major types of theoretical explanations, before delving into them, we begin with a discussion of the motivation or "engine" responsible for the consistent attraction to recreational and/or nonmedical use of drugs—namely, addiction.

The Origin and Nature of Addiction

Humans can develop a very intense relationship with chemicals. Most people have chemically altered their mood at some point in their lives, if only by consuming a cup of coffee or a glass of white wine, and a majority do so occasionally. Yet for some individuals, chemicals become the center of their lives, driving their behavior and determining their priorities, even to the point at which catastrophic consequences to their health and social well-being ensue. Although the word *addiction* is an agreed-upon term referring to such behavior, little agreement exists as to the origin, nature, or boundaries of the concept of addiction. It has been classified as a very bad habit, a failure of will or morality, a symptom of other problems, or a chronic disease in its own right.

Although public perception of drug abuse and addiction as a major social problem has waxed and waned over the past 20 years, the social costs of addiction have not: The total criminal justice, health, insurance, and other costs in the United States are roughly estimated at $90 to $185 billion annually, depending on the source. Despite numerous prevention efforts, the "War on Drugs," and a decline in the heavy drug use of the 1960s and 1970s, lessons learned in one decade seem to quickly pass out of awareness.

For example, the rate of lifetime use of marijuana among 12th graders in 1991 was approximately 36%; in 2008, it had increased to approximately 42.6% (Johnston et al. 2009). Alcohol, which is legal for adults but illegal for youths, also creates problems when used by the very young.

> Alcohol has been tried by 39% of current 8th graders, 58% of 10th graders, 72% of 12th graders, and 85% of college students; active use is also widespread. Most important, perhaps, is the prevalence of occasions of heavy drinking—five or more drinks in a row at least once in the prior two-week period [before surveys were taken] . . . which was reported by 8% of 8th graders, 16% of 10th graders, 25% of 12 graders, and 40% of college students surveyed in 2008. (Johnston et al. 2009, p. 26)

As the previous quote shows, alcohol use remains very widespread among today's teenagers. Among 8th graders in 2008, 39% report having tried alcohol (more than just a few sips), and nearly one in five (18%) say they have already been drunk at least once (Johnston et al. 2009). Further, the very large number of 8th graders who have already begun using the so-called "gateway drugs" (tobacco, alcohol, inhalants, and marijuana) suggest that a substantial number are also at risk of proceeding further to such drugs as LSD, cocaine, amphetamines, and heroin. Government officials and researchers believe that decreases in perceived harmfulness of using a drug are often leading indicators of future increases in actual use of that drug. "The authors of this study suggest that these trends may reflect 'generational forgetting' of the dangers of these drugs, leaving the newer cohorts vulnerable to a resurgence of use" (Center for Substance Abuse Research [CESAR] 2007, p. 7). From these major studies, it is apparent that both licit and illicit types of drugs continue to penetrate into increasingly younger age groups.

■ Defining Addiction

Addiction can be described as a complex disease. In 1964, the World Health Organization (WHO) of the United Nations defined it as "a state of periodic or chronic intoxication detrimental to the individual and society, which is characterized by an overwhelming desire to continue taking the drug and to obtain it by any means" (pp. 9–10). Accordingly, addiction is characterized as compulsive, at times uncontrollable, drug craving, seeking, and use that persist even in the face of extremely negative consequences (NIDA 1999). This relentless pursuit of a drug of choice occurs despite the fact that the drug is usually harmful and injurious to bodily and mental functions.

The word *addiction*, derived from the Latin verb *addicere,* refers to the process of binding to things. Today, the word largely refers to a chronic adherence to drugs. This can include both physical and psychological dependence. *Physical dependence* is the body's need to constantly have the drug or drugs; *psychological dependence* is the mental inability to stop using the drug or drugs.

The *Diagnostic and Statistical Manual of Mental Disorders,* 4th edition, text revision (*DSM-IV-TR*), published by the American Psychiatric Association (2000), differentiates among intoxication by, abuse of, and addiction to drugs. Although *substance abuse* is considered maladaptive, leading to recurrent adverse consequences or impairment, it is carefully differentiated from true addiction, called *substance dependence,* the essential feature of which is continued use despite significant substance-related problems known to the user. Many of the following features are usually present:

- *Tolerance:* The need for increased amounts or diminished effect of same amount
- *Withdrawal:* The experience of a characteristic withdrawal syndrome for the specific substance, which can be avoided by taking closely related substances; unsuccessful attempts to cut down
- *Compulsive behavior:* An increasing amount of time spent in substance-related activities, such as obtaining, using, and recovering from the substance's effects

An additional final definition of addiction is also noteworthy. The National Institute on Drug Abuse

(NIDA) defines addiction as "... a chronic, relapsing brain disease that is characterized by compulsive drug-seeking and use, despite harmful consequences. It is considered a brain disease because drugs change the brain—they change its structure and how it works. These brain changes can be long lasting and can lead to the harmful behaviors seen in people who abuse drugs" (NIDA 2008a, p. 5).

■ Models of Addiction

Various models attempt to describe the essential nature of drug addiction. Newspaper accounts of "inebriety" in the 19th and early 20th centuries contain an editorializing undertone that looks askance at the poor morals and lifestyle choices followed by the inebriate. This view has been termed the **moral model**, and although it may seem outdated from a modern scientific standpoint, it still characterizes an attitude among many traditional North Americans and members of many ethnic groups.

The prevailing concept or model of addiction in the United States is the **disease model**. Most proponents of this concept specify addiction to be a chronic and progressive disease, over which the sufferer has no control. This model originated in part from research among members of Alcoholics Anonymous (AA) performed by Jellinek, one of the founders of addiction studies (1960). He observed a seemingly inevitable progression in his subjects, which they made many failed attempts to stop drinking. This philosophy is currently espoused by the recovery fellowships of AA and Narcotics Anonymous (NA), and the treatment field in general. It has even permeated the psychiatric and medical establishments' standard definitions of addiction. There are many variations within the broad rubric of the disease model. This model has been bitterly debated: viewpoints range from fierce adherence to equally fierce opposition, with intermediate views casting the disease concept as a convenient myth (Smith, Milkman, and Sunderworth 1985).

Those who view addiction as another manifestation of something gone awry with the personality system adhere to the **characterological or personality predisposition model**. Every school of psychoanalytic, neopsychoanalytic, and psychodynamic psychotherapy has its specific "take" on the subject of addiction (Frosch 1985). Tangentially, many addicts are also diagnosed with **personality disorders**

(formerly known as "character disorders"), such as impulse control disorders and sociopathy. Although few addicts are treated by **psychoanalysis** or psychoanalytic psychotherapy, a characterological type of model was a formative influence on the drug-free, addict-run, "therapeutic community" model, which uses harsh confrontation and time-extended, sleep-depriving group encounters. People who follow the therapeutic community model conclude that addicts must have withdrawn behind a **"double wall" of encapsulation**, where they failed to grow, making such techniques necessary.

Others view addiction as a "career," a series of steps or phases with distinguishable characteristics. One career pattern of addiction includes six phases (Clinard and Meier 1992; Waldorf 1983):

1. Experimentation or initiation
2. Escalation (increasing use)
3. Maintenance or "taking care of business" (optimistic use of drugs coupled with successful job performance)
4. Dysfunction or "going through changes" (problems with constant use and unsuccessful attempts to quit)

KEY TERMS

moral model
the belief that people abuse alcohol because they choose to do so

disease model
the belief that people abuse alcohol because of some biologically caused condition

characterological or personality predisposition model
the view of chemical dependency as a symptom of problems in the development or operation of the system of needs, motives, and attitudes within the individual

personality disorders
a broad category of psychiatric disorders, formerly called "character disorders," that includes the antisocial personality disorder, borderline personality disorder, schizoid personality disorder, and others; these serious, ongoing impairments are difficult to treat

psychoanalysis
a theory of personality and method of psychotherapy originated by Sigmund Freud, focused on unconscious forces and conflicts and a series of psychosexual stages

"double wall" of encapsulation
an adaptation to pain and avoidance of reality, in which the individual withdraws emotionally and further anesthetizes himself or herself by chemical means

5. Recovery or "getting out of the life" (arriving at a successful view about quitting and receiving drug treatment)
6. Ex-addict (having successfully quit)

Finally, after examining countless theories that attempt to list and/or predict the stages of addiction to alcohol, tobacco, and/or illicit drug use, the following set of stages appears to be the most salient regarding addiction to drug use: (1) initial initiation and use of the drug, (2) patterned continuation into using the drug, (3) transition to drug abuse, (4) attempts at cessation (stopping the use), and (5) relapse (a return to abusive usage).

■ Factors Contributing to Addiction

Many, perhaps millions, of individuals use or even occasionally abuse drugs without compromising their basic health, legal, and occupational status and social relationships. Why do a significant minority become caught up in abuse and addictive behavior? The answer stems from the fact that many (i.e., not a single) factors generally contribute to an individual becoming addicted (Syvertsen 2008). **Table 2.1** represents a compilation of factors identified as complicit in the origin or "etiology" of addiction, taken from the fields of psychology, sociology, and addiction studies.

In addition to the social and cultural factors listed in Table 2.1, other "cultural" risk factors for development of abuse include the following:

- Drinking at times other than at meals
- Drinking alone
- Drinking defined as an antistress and antianxiety potion
- Patterns of solitary drinking (immediately drinking, smoking marijuana, or using other drugs after work; weekend drinking; late night drinking)
- Drinking defined as a rite of passage into an adult role
- Recent introduction of a chemical into a social group with insufficient time to develop informal social control over its use (Marshall 1979)

It is important to recall that the "mix" of risk factors differs for each person. It varies according to social, cultural, age, individual, and family idiosyncrasies. Most addiction treatment professionals believe that it is difficult, if not impossible, to tease out these factors before treatment, when the user is still "talking to a chemical," or during

early treatment, when the brain and body are still recuperating from the effects of long-term abuse. Once a stable sobriety is established, one can begin to address any underlying problems. An exception is the mentally ill chemical abuser, whose treatment requires special considerations from the outset.

In addition to the factors just listed, a number of age-dependent stressors and conflicts sometimes promote drug misuse. Risk factors that apply especially to adolescents include the following:

- Peer norms favoring use
- Misperception of peer norms (users set the tone)
- Power of age group (peer norms versus other social influences)
- Conflicts that generate anxiety or guilt, such as dependence versus independence, adult maturational tasks versus fear, new types of roles versus familiar safe roles
- Teenage risk taking, sense of omnipotence or invulnerability
- Use defined as a rite of passage into adulthood
- Use perceived as glamorous, sexy, facilitating intimacy, fun, and so on

Risk factors that apply especially to middle-aged individuals include the following:

- Loss of meaningful role or occupational identity due to retirement
- Loss, grief, or isolation due to loss of parents, divorce, or departure of children ("empty nest syndrome")
- Loss of positive body image
- Dealing with a newly diagnosed illness (e.g., diabetes, heart problems, cancer)
- Disappointment when life's expectations are not met

Even in each of these age groups, a mix of factors is at play. The adolescent abuser might have risk factors that were primarily neurological vulnerabilities, such as undiagnosed attention deficit hyperactivity disorder. Alternatively, he or she may experience failure and rejection at school, disappoint his or her parents, or be labeled odd, lazy, or unintelligent (Kelly and Ramundo 2006).

In response to the information presented in Table 2.1, a student who was a recovering alcoholic commented: "You're an alcoholic because you drink!" He had a good point: The mere presence of one, two, or more risk factors does not create addiction. Drugs must be available, they must be used, and they must become a pattern of adaptation to

Table 2.1 **Risk Factors for Addiction**

RISK FACTOR	LEADING TO THIS EFFECT
Biologically Based Factors (genetic, neurological, biochemical, and so on)	
A less subjective feeling of intoxication	More use to achieve intoxication (warning signs of abuse absent)
Easier development of tolerance; liver enzymes adapt to increased use	Easier to reach the addictive level
Lack of resilience or fragility of higher (cerebral) brain functions	Easy deterioration of cerebral functioning, impaired judgment, and social deterioration
Difficulty in screening out unwanted or bothersome outside stimuli (low stimulus barrier)	Feeling overwhelmed or stressed
Tendency to amplify outside or internal stimuli (stimulus augmentation)	Feeling attacked or panicked; need to avoid emotion
Attention deficit hyperactivity disorder and other learning disabilities	Failure, low self-esteem, or isolation
Biologically based mood disorders (depression and bipolar disorders)	Need to self-medicate against loss of control or pain of depression; inability to calm down when manic or to sleep when agitated
Psychosocial/Developmental "Personality" Factors	
Low self-esteem	Need to block out pain; gravitation to outsider groups
Depression rooted in learned helplessness and passivity	Use of a stimulant as an antidepressant
Conflicts	Anxiety and guilt
Repressed and unresolved grief and rage	Chronic depression, anxiety, or pain
Posttraumatic stress syndrome (as in veterans and abuse victims)	Nightmares or panic attacks
Social and Cultural Environment	
Availability of drugs	Easy frequent use
Chemical-abusing parental model	Sanction; no conflict over use
Abusive, neglectful parents; other dysfunctional family patterns	Pervasive sense of abandonment, distrust, and pain; difficulty in maintaining attachments
Group norms favoring heavy use and abuse	Reinforced, hidden abusive behavior that can progress without interference
Misperception of peer norms	Belief that most people use or favor use or think it's "cool" to use
Severe or chronic stressors, as from noise, poverty, racism, or occupational stress	Need to alleviate or escape from stress via chemical means
"Alienation" factors: isolation, emptiness	Painful sense of aloneness, normlessness, rootlessness, boredom, monotony, or hopelessness
Difficult migration/acculturation with social disorganization, gender/generation gaps, or loss of role	Stress without buffering support system

any of the many painful, threatening, uncomfortable, or unwanted sensations or stimuli that occur in the presence of genetic, psychosocial, or environmental risk factors. Prevention workers often note the presence of multiple messages encouraging use: the medical use of minor tranquilizers to offset any type of psychic discomfort; the marketing of alcohol as sexy, glamorous, adult, and facilitative of social interaction; and so forth.

The Vicious Cycle of Addiction

> First, the man takes a drink, then the drink takes a drink, then the drink takes the man.
> *(Traditional Chinese proverb)*

Drug addiction develops as a process, and it is not a sudden occurrence. The body makes simple physiological adaptations to the presence of alcohol and other drugs. For instance, brain cell tolerance and increased metabolic efficiency of the liver can develop, necessitating consumption of more of the chemical to achieve the desired effect. Physical dependence can also develop, in which cell adaptations cause withdrawal syndromes to occur in the absence of the chemical.

Other factors can promote the cycle of addiction. For instance, drug abuse impairs cerebral functioning, including memory, judgment, behavioral organization, ability to plan, ability to solve problems, and motor coordination. Thus, poor decision making, impaired and deviant behavior, and overall dysfunction result in adverse social consequences, such as accidents, loss of earning power and relationships, and impaired health. Such adverse social and health consequences cause pain, depression, and lowered self-esteem, which may result in further use of the drug as an emotional and physical anesthetic. The addict often adapts to this chronically painful situation by erecting a defense system of denial, minimization, and rationalization; the chemical blunting of reality may exacerbate this denial of reality. It is unlikely, at this point, that the addict or developing addict will feel compelled to cease or cut back on drug use on his or her own (Tarter, Alterman, and Edwards 1983).

Family, friends, and colleagues often unwittingly "enable" the maintenance and progression of addiction. Examples include making excuses for addicts, literally and figuratively bailing them out, taking up the slack, denying and minimizing their problems, and otherwise making it possible for addicts to avoid facing the reality and consequences of what they are doing to themselves and others. Although these friends may be motivated by simple naïveté, embarrassment, or misguided protectiveness, there are often hidden gains in taking up this role, known popularly as "codependency" (Beattie 1987; Mental Health America [MHA] 2010). Varieties of cultural and organizational factors also operate in the workplace or school that allow denial of the existence or severity of abuse or dependency. This triad of personal denial, peer and kin denial and codependency, and institutional denial represents a formidable impediment to successful intervention and recovery (Miller 1995; Myers 1990).

■ Nondrug Addictions?

The addictive disease model and the 12-step recovery model followed by AA and NA have seemed so successful for both addicts and their families and friends that other unwanted syndromes have been added to the list of "addictions." The degree to which the concept of addiction fits these syndromes varies. Gambling, for example, shows progressive worsening, loss of control, relief of tension from the activity, and continuance despite negative (often disastrous) consequences experienced by the addicted gambler. Some recovering gamblers even claim to have experienced a form of withdrawal. Gamblers Anonymous is a fellowship that has formed to assist its members. Clearly, gambling as an activity has much in common with chemical addictions, but it is debatable whether it belongs in the category of addiction (for example, the *DSM-IV-TR* does not include it).

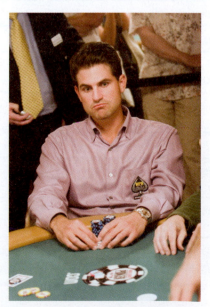

Like drug use, gambling can become addictive.

Many other groups have followed in the footsteps of Gamblers Anonymous, including those related to eating (Overeaters Anonymous) and sexual relationships (The Augustine Fellowship, Sex and Love Addicts Anonymous). In recent years, any excessive or unwanted behaviors, including excess shopping, chocolate consumption, and even Internet use, have been labeled "addictions," which has led to satirical reporting in the press. Addiction professionals lament the overdefinition, which they believe trivializes the seriousness and suffering of rigorously defined addictions.

Major Theoretical Explanations: Biological

As noted in Chapter 1, biological explanations have tended to use genetic theories and the disease model to explain drug addiction. The view that alcoholism is a sickness dates back approximately 200 years (Conrad and Schneider 1980; Heitzeg 1996). The disease perspective is upheld by Jellinek's (1960) view that alcoholism largely involves a loss of control over drinking and that the drinker experiences clearly distinguishable phases in his or her drinking patterns. For example, concerning alcoholism, the illness affects the abuser to the point of loss of control. Thus, the disease model views drug abuse as an illness in need of treatment or therapy.

According to biological theories, drug abuse has a beginning stemming from physical characteristics that cause certain individuals either to experiment with or to crave drugs to the point of abusive use. **Genetic and biophysiological theories** explain addiction in terms of genetics, brain dysfunction, and biochemical patterns.

Biological explanations emphasize that the central nervous system (CNS) reward sensors in some people are more sensitive to drugs, making the drug experience more pleasant and more rewarding for these individuals (Khantzian 1998; Mathias 1995). In contrast, others find the effects of drugs of abuse very unpleasant; such people are not likely to be attracted to these drugs (Farrar and Kearns 1989).

Most experts acknowledge that biological factors play an essential role in drug abuse. These factors likely determine how the brain responds to these drugs and why such substances are addictive. It is thought that by identifying the nature of the biological systems that contribute to drug abuse problems, improved prevention and treatment methods can be developed (Koob 2000; Kuehn 2010; NIDA 2008b).

All the major biological explanations related to drug abuse assume that these substances exert their **psychoactive effects** by altering brain chemistry or neuronal (basic functional cell of the brain) activity. Specifically, the drugs of abuse interfere with the functioning of **neurotransmitters**, chemical messengers used for communication between brain regions (see Chapter 4 for details).

The following sections detail three principal biological theories that help explain why some drugs are abused and why certain people are more likely to become addicted when using these substances.

Abused Drugs as Positive Reinforcers

Biological research has shown that stimulating some brain regions with an electrode causes very pleasurable sensations. In fact, laboratory animals would rather self-administer stimulation to these brain areas than eat or engage in sex. It has been demonstrated that drugs of abuse also activate these same pleasure centers of the brain (NIDA 2008b, p. 15; Weiss 1999).

It is generally believed that most drugs with abuse potential enhance pleasure centers by causing the release of specific brain neurotransmitters such as **dopamine** (Bespalov et al. 1999; NIDA 2008b, p. 17). How do drugs work in the brain?

All drugs of abuse directly or indirectly target the brain's reward system by flooding the circuit with dopamine. Dopamine is a neurotransmitter present in regions of the brain that regulates movement, emotion, cognition, motivation, and

KEY TERMS

genetic and biophysiological theories
explanations of addiction in terms of genetic brain dysfunction and biochemical patterns

psychoactive effects
how drug substances alter and affect the brain's mental functions

neurotransmitters
the chemical messengers released by nervous (nerve) cells for communication with other cells

dopamine
a neurotransmitter present in regions of the brain that regulates movement, emotion, cognition, motivation, and feelings of pleasure; it mediates the rewarding aspects of most drugs of abuse

feelings of pleasure. The overstimulation of this system, which rewards our natural behavior, produces the euphoric effects sought by people who abuse drug and teaches them to repeat the behavior. (NIDA 2008b, p. 17)

Brain cells become accustomed to the presence of these neurotransmitters and crave them when they are absent, leading the person to seek more drugs (NIDA 2008b; Spanagel and Weiss 1999). In addition, it has been proposed that overstimulation of these brain regions by continual drug use "exhausts" these dopamine systems and leads to depression and an inability to experience normal pleasure (Volkow 1999).

■ Drug Abuse and Psychiatric Disorders

Biological explanations are thought to be responsible for the substantial overlap that exists between drug addiction and mental illness (NIDA 2007) (see "Do Genes Matter?").

Do Genes Matter?

What Is the Relationship Between Addiction and Other Mental Disorders?

Because of the similarities, severe drug dependence itself is classified as a form of psychiatric disorder by the American Psychiatric Association (see the discussion of the *DSM-IV-TR* classifications later in this chapter). For example, abuse of drugs can, in and of itself, cause mental conditions that mimic major psychiatric illness, such as schizophrenia, severe anxiety disorders, and suicidal depression (APA 2000). It is believed that these similarities occur as a result of common chemical factors that are altered both by drugs of abuse and during episodes of psychiatric illness (NIDA 1993). Several important potential consequences of this relationship may help you understand the nature of drug abuse problems.

- *Psychiatric disorders and drug addiction sometimes occur simultaneously.* This conclusion is supported by the fact that substance abuse–related problems often coexist with other mental diseases such as conduct disorder, schizophrenia, and mood disorders (APA 2000). Due to the common mechanisms, drug abuse is likely to expose or worsen psychiatric illnesses, making management of these problems considerably more difficult (APA 2000).

- *Therapies that are successful in treating psychiatric disorders may be useful in treating mental problems caused by drugs of abuse.* It is likely that many of the therapeutic lessons we learn about dealing with psychiatric illnesses can be useful in drug abuse treatment, and vice versa.

- *Abuse of drugs by some people may represent an attempt to relieve underlying psychiatric disorders.* Such people commonly use CNS depressants such as alcohol to relieve anxiety, whereas CNS stimulants such as cocaine are frequently used by patients with depression disorders (Grinspoon 1993). In such cases, if the underlying psychiatric problem is relieved, the likelihood of successfully treating the drug abuse disorder improves substantially.

There is some good evidence that a comorbid relationship exists between addiction and other mental disorders (NIDA 2008a, 2009).

What Is Comorbidity?

Comorbidity is a term used to describe two or more disorders or illnesses occurring in the same person. They can occur at the same time or one after the other. Comorbidity also implies interactions between the illnesses that can worsen the course of both.

Is Drug Addiction a Mental Illness?

Yes, addiction changes the brain in fundamental ways, disturbing a person's normal hierarchy of needs and desires and substituting new priorities connected with procuring and using the drug. The resulting compulsive

KEY TERMS

comorbidity
two or more disorders or illnesses occurring in the same person; they can occur either simultaneously or one after the other; also implies interactions between the illnesses that can worsen the course of both

Do Genes Matter? *(continued)*

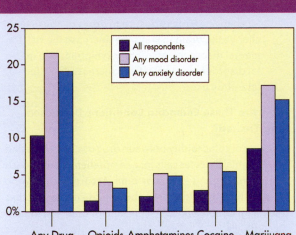

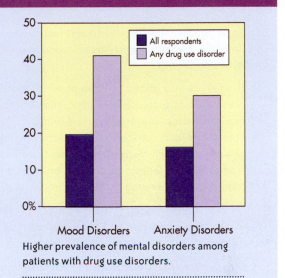

High prevalence of drug abuse and dependence among individuals with mood and anxiety disorders.

Reprinted from U.S. Department of Health and Human Services, National Institutes of Health, National Institute on Drug Abuse. (2010). Comorbidity: Addiction and Other Mental Illnesses. *Research Report Series*. (NIH Publication Number 10-5771).

Higher prevalence of mental disorders among patients with drug use disorders.

Reprinted from U.S. Department of Health and Human Services, National Institutes of Health, National Institute on Drug Abuse. (2010). Comorbidity: Addiction and Other Mental Illnesses. *Research Report Series*. (NIH Publication Number 10-5771).

behaviors that weaken the ability to control impulses, despite the consequences, are similar to hallmarks of other mental illnesses.

How Common Are Comorbid Drug Addiction and Other Mental Illnesses?

Many people who are addicted to drugs are also diagnosed with other mental disorders and vice versa. For example,

compared with the general population, people addicted to drugs are roughly twice as likely to suffer from mood and anxiety disorders, with the reverse also true.*

Why Do These Disorders Often Co-Occur?

Although drug use disorders commonly occur with other mental illnesses, this does not mean that one caused the

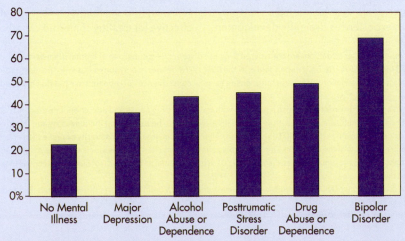

Higher prevalence of smoking among patients with mental disorders.

Reprinted from U.S. Department of Health and Human Services, National Institutes of Health, National Institute on Drug Abuse. (2010). Comorbidity: Addiction and Other Mental Illnesses. *Research Report Series*. (NIH Publication Number 10-5771).

(continued)

Do Genes Matter? (continued)

other, even if one appeared first. In fact, establishing causality or even directionality (i.e., which came first) can be difficult. However, research suggests the following possibilities for their co-occurrence:

- Drug abuse may bring about symptoms of another mental illness. Increased risk of psychosis in some marijuana users suggests this possibility.
- Mental disorders can lead to drug abuse, possibly as a means of "self-medication." Patients suffering from anxiety or depression may rely on alcohol, tobacco, and other drugs to temporarily alleviate their symptoms.

These disorders could also be caused by common risk factors, such as:

- *Overlapping genetic vulnerabilities:* Common genetic factors may make a person susceptible to both addiction and other mental disorders or to having a greater risk of a second disorder once the first appears.
- *Overlapping environmental triggers:* Stress, trauma (such as physical or sexual abuse), and early exposure to drugs are common factors that can lead to addiction and other mental illnesses.
- *Involvement of similar brain regions:* Brain systems that respond to reward and stress, for example, are affected by drugs of abuse and may show abnormalities in patients who have certain mental disorders.
- *Drug use disorders and other mental illnesses are developmental disorders:* That means they often begin in the teen years or even younger—periods when the brain experiences dramatic developmen-

tal changes. Early exposure to drugs of abuse may change the brain in ways that increase the risk for mental disorders. Also, early symptoms of a mental disorder may indicate an increased risk for later drug use.

How Are These Comorbid Conditions Diagnosed and Treated?

The rate of comorbidity between drug use disorders and other mental illnesses calls for a comprehensive approach that identifies and evaluates both. Accordingly, anyone seeking help for either drug abuse/addiction or another mental disorder should be checked for both and treated accordingly.

Several behavioral therapies have shown promise for treating comorbid conditions. These approaches can be designed to target patients according to specific factors such as age or marital status: some therapies have proved more effective for adolescents, whereas others have shown greater effectiveness for adults; some therapies are designed for families and groups, others for individuals.

Although several medications exist for treating addiction and other mental illnesses, most have not been studied in patients with comorbidities. For example, individuals addicted to heroin, prescription pain medications, cigarettes, or alcohol can be treated with appropriate medications to ease withdrawal symptoms and drug craving; similarly, separate medications are available to help improve the symptoms of depression and anxiety. More research is needed, however, to better understand how such medications act when combined in individuals with comorbidities, or whether such medications can be dually effective for treating comorbid conditions.

*Drug abuse and drug dependence, or addiction, are considered drug use disorders—a subgroup of mental disorders—when they meet the diagnostic criteria delineated in the *DSM-IV-TR*. Drug dependence, as the *DSM-IV-TR* defines it, is synonymous with the term *addiction,* which will be used preferentially in this book. Criteria for drug abuse hinge on the harmful consequences of repeated use but do not include compulsive use, tolerance, or withdrawal.

Disorders (also known as mood disorders) increase a person's vulnerability to drug abuse and addiction. The diagnosis and treatment of the mood disorder can reduce the risk of future drug use. Note that the inverse may also be true, in that the diagnosis and treatment of drug use disorders may reduce the risk of developing other mental illnesses and, if they do occur, lessen their severity or make them more amenable to effective treatment. Finally, more than 40% of the cigarettes smoked in this country are smoked by individuals with a psychiatric disorder, such as major depressive disorder, alcoholism, posttraumatic stress disorder (PTSD), schizophrenia, or bipolar disorder, which contributes greatly to their increased morbidity and mortality.

Source: National Institute on Drug Abuse (NIDA). "Comorbidity: Addiction and Other Mental Disorders." *NIDA InfoFacts.* Bethesda, MD: U.S. Department of Health and Human Services, 2011:1–2.

Genetic Explanations

Why does one person become dependent on drugs while another, exposed to the same environment and experiences, does not? (Schaffer Library of Drug Policy 1994, p. 1)

One biological theory receiving scrutiny suggests that inherited traits can predispose some individuals to drug addiction (Lemonick with Park 2007; Mac Pherson 2002, p. 1). Such theories have been supported by the observation that increased frequency of alcoholism and drug abuse exists among children of alcoholics and drug abusers (APA 2000; Uhl et al. 1993). Using adoption records of some 3000 individuals from Sweden, researchers Cloninger, Gohman, and Sigvardsson conducted one of the most extensive research studies examining genetics and alcoholism. They found that ". . . children of alcoholic parents were likely to grow up to be alcoholics themselves, even in cases where the children were reared by nonalcoholic adoptive parents almost from birth" (Doweiko 2009). Such studies estimate that drug vulnerability due to genetic influences accounts for approximately 38% of all cases, whereas environmental and social factors account for the balance (Uhl et al. 1993).

Other studies attempting to identify the specific genes that may predispose the carrier to drug abuse problems have suggested that a brain target site (called a receptor—see Chapter 4 for details) for dopamine is altered in a manner that increases the drug abuse vulnerability (Radowitz 2003; Wyman 1997). Studies that test for genetic factors in complex behaviors such as drug abuse are very difficult to conduct and interpret. It is sometimes impossible to design experiments that distinguish among genetic, social, environmental, and psychological influences in human populations. For example, inherited traits are known to be major contributors to psychiatric disorders, such as schizophrenia and depression. Many people with one of these illnesses also have a substance abuse disorder (APA 2000). A high incidence of an abnormal gene in a cocaine-abusing population, for example, not only may be linked to drug abuse behavior but also may be associated with depression or another psychiatric disorder (Uhl, Persico, and Smith 1992).

Theoretically, genetic factors can directly or indirectly contribute to drug abuse vulnerability in several ways:

- Psychiatric disorders that are genetically determined may be relieved by taking drugs of abuse, thus encouraging their use.

- In some people, reward centers of the brain may be genetically determined to be especially sensitive to addictive drugs; thus, the use of drugs by these people would be particularly pleasurable and would lead to a high rate of addiction.

- Volkow states that "addiction is a medical condition" and that "[i]n the brains of addicts, there is reduced activity in the prefrontal cortex where rational thought can override impulsive behavior" (Kuehn 2010; Lemonick with Park 2007).

- Character traits, such as insecurity and vulnerability, that often lead to drug abuse behavior may be genetically determined, causing a high rate of addiction in people with those traits (Kuehn 2010).

- Factors that determine how difficult it is to break away from drug addiction may be genetically determined, causing severe craving or very unpleasant withdrawal effects in some individuals. People with this predisposition are less likely to abandon their drug of abuse.

The genetic theories for explaining drug abuse may help us to understand the reasons that drug addiction occurs in some individuals but not in others. In addition, if genetic factors play a major role in drug abuse, it might be possible to use genetic screening to identify those people who are especially vulnerable to drug abuse problems and to help such individuals avoid exposure to these substances.

Major Theoretical Explanations: Psychological

Psychological theories mostly deal with mental or emotional states, which are often associated with or exacerbated by social and environmental factors. Psychological explanations of addiction include one or more of the following: escape from reality, boredom (Burns 1997), inability to cope with anxiety, destructive self-indulgence to the point of constantly desiring intoxicants, blind compliance with drug-abusing peers, self-destructiveness, and conscious and unconscious ignorance regarding the harmful effects of abusing drugs. Another author writes the following:

. . . psychological theory explains that drug use and abuse begins because of the unconscious motivations within all of us. We are not aware of these motivations, not even when they manifest themselves. So, there are unconscious conflicts and motivations that reside within us as well as our reactions to early events in our lives that move a person toward drug use and abuse. The motivations for drug use are within us, and we are not aware of them, nor are we aware that those are the reasons we have chosen to turn to drugs. In this case, the person may be weak or without self-esteem or even see themselves in the opposite manner, as all-important. Drug use then becomes a sort of crutch to make up for all that is wrong with their lives and wrong with their selves." (Moore 2008, p. 1)

Freud established early psychological theories. He linked "primal addictions" with masturbation and postulated that all later addictions, including those involving alcohol and other drugs, were caused by ego impairments. Freud said that drugs compensate for insecurities that stem from parental inadequacies, which themselves may cause difficulty in adequately forming bonds of friendships. He claimed that alcoholism (see Chapter 8) is an expression of the death instinct, as are self-destruction, narcissism, and oral fixations. Although Freud's views represent interesting intuitive insights often not depicted in other theories, his theoretical concerns are difficult to observe and test, and they do not generate enough concrete data for verification.

■ Distinguishing Between Substance Abuse and Mental Disorders

The American Psychiatric Association has established widely accepted categories of diagnosis for behavioral disorders, including substance abuse. As standardized diagnostic categories, the characteristics of mental disorders have been analyzed by professional committees over many years and today are summarized in the *DSM-IV-TR*. In addition to categories for severe psychotic disorders and more common neurotic disorders, experts in the field of psychiatry have established specific diagnostic criteria for various forms of substance abuse. All patterns of drug abuse that are described in this text have a counterpart description in the *DSM-IV-TR* for medical professionals. For example, the *DSM-IV-TR* discusses the mental disorders resulting from the use or abuse of sedatives, hypnotics, or antianxiety drugs; alcohol; narcotics; amphetamine-like drugs; cocaine; caffeine; nicotine (tobacco); hallucinogens; phencyclidine (PCP); inhalants; and cannabis (marijuana). This manual of

psychiatric diagnoses discusses in detail the mental disorders related to the drug use, the side effects of medications, and the consequences of toxic exposure to these substances (APA 2000).

Because of the similarities between, and the coexistence of, substance-related mental disorders and primary psychiatric disorders, it is sometimes difficult to distinguish between the two problems. However, for proper treatment to be rendered, the cause of psychological symptoms must be determined. According to *DSM-IV-TR* criteria, substance use (or abuse) disorders can be identified by the occurrence and consequence of dependence, abuse, intoxication, and withdrawal. These important distinguishing features of substance abuse disorders are discussed in detail in Chapter 5 and in conjunction with each drug group.

According to the *DSM-IV-TR*, the following information can also help distinguish between substance-induced and primary mental disorders: (1) personal and family medical, psychiatric, and drug histories; (2) physical examinations; and (3) laboratory tests to assess physiological functions and determine the presence or absence of drugs. However, the possibility of a primary mental disorder should not be excluded just because the patient is using drugs—remember, many drug users use drugs to self-medicate their primary psychiatric problems (NIDA 2008a). The coexistence of underlying psychiatric problems in a drug user is suggested by the following circumstances: (1) The psychiatric problems do not match the usual drug effects (e.g., use of marijuana usually does not cause severe psychotic behavior); (2) the psychiatric disorder was present before the patient began abusing substances; and (3) the mental disorder persists for more than 4 weeks after substance use ends. The *DSM-IV-TR* makes it clear that elucidating the relationship between mental disorders and substances of abuse is important for proper diagnosis, treatment, and understanding (APA 2000).

■ The Relationship Between Personality and Drug Use

Since medieval times, personality theories of increasing sophistication have been used to classify long-term behavioral tendencies or traits that appear in individuals, and these traits have long been considered to be influenced by biological or chemical factors. Although such classification systems have varied widely, nearly all have shared two commonly observed dimensions of personality: introversion and extroversion. Individuals who show a predominant tendency to turn their thoughts and feelings inward rather than to direct attention outward have been considered to show the trait of *introversion*. At the opposite extreme, a tendency to seek outward activity and share feelings with others has been called *extroversion*. Of course, every individual shows a mix of such traits in varying degrees and circumstances.

In some research studies, introversion and extroversion patterns have been associated with levels of neural arousal in brainstem circuits (Apostolides 1996; Carlson 1990; Gray 1987), and these forms of arousal are closely associated with effects caused by drug stimulants or depressants.

Drugs like cocaine, alcohol, or Prozac all affect these processes and an individual's degree of extroversion. They can artificially correct an ineffective dopamine system and make someone feel more sociable or motivated to pursue a goal. Low levels of serotonin, correlated with depression, may make people more responsive to dopamine and more susceptible to dopamine-stimulating drug use such as the use of cocaine, alcohol, amphetamine, opiates, and nicotine (Lang 1996).

Such research hypothesizes that people whose systems produce high levels of sensitivity to neural arousal may find high-intensity external stimuli to be painful and may react by turning inward. With these extremely high levels of sensitivity, such people may experience neurotic levels of anxiety or panic disorders. At the other extreme, individuals whose systems provide them with very low levels of sensitivity to neural arousal may find that moderate stimuli are inadequate to produce responses. To reach moderate levels of arousal, they may turn outward to seek high-intensity external sources of stimulation (Eysenck and Eysenck 1985; Gray 1987; Rousar et al. 1995).

Because high- and low-arousal symptoms are easy to create by using stimulants, depressants, or hallucinogens, it is possible that these personality patterns of introversion or extroversion affect how a person reacts to substances. For people whose experience is predominantly introverted or extroverted, extremes of high or low sensitivity may lead them to seek counteracting substances that become important methods of bringing experience to a level that seems bearable.

■ Theories Based on Learning Processes

How are drug use patterns learned? Research on learning and conditioning explains how human beings acquire new patterns of behavior by the close association or pairing of one significant reinforcing stimulus with another less significant or neutral stimulus. Also known as **social learning theory** (Bandura 1977; explained more fully in the "Social Learning Theory" section later in this chapter), this theory emphasizes that learned associations occur in the presence of other people using drugs coupled with other, often preconceived associations with the attitudes of society and friends about drug use (Gray 1999). In this method of learning, people form expectations and become used to certain behavior patterns. This specific process of learning is known as conditioning, and it explains why pleasurable activities may become intimately connected with other activities that are also pleasurable, neutral, or even unpleasant. In addition, people can turn any new behavior into a recurrent and permanent one by the process of **habituation**—repeating certain patterns of behavior until they become established or habitual.

The basic process by which learning mechanisms can lead a person into drug use is also described in Bejerot's **addiction to pleasure theory** (Bejerot 1965, 1972, 1975; NIDA 1980). This theory assumes that it is biologically normal to continue a pleasure stimulus once started. Several research findings support this theory, indicating that "a strong, biologically based need for stimulation appears to make sensation-seeking young adults more vulnerable to drug abuse" (Mathias 1995, p. 1; also supporting this view is Khantzian 1998). A second research finding complementing this theory states, "Certain areas of the brain, when stimulated, produce pleasurable feelings. Psychoactive substances are capable of acting on these brain mechanisms to produce these sensations. These pleasurable feelings become reinforcers that drive the continued use of the substances" (Gardner 1992, p. 43). People at highest risk for drug use and addiction are those who maintain a constant preoccupation with getting high,

KEY TERMS

social learning theory
a theory that places emphasis on how an individual learns patterns of behavior from the attitudes of others, society, and peers

habituation
repeating certain patterns of behavior until they become established or habitual

addiction to pleasure theory
a theory assuming that it is biologically normal to continue a pleasure stimulus once begun

seek new or novel thrills in their experiences, and are known to have a relentless desire to pursue physical stimulation or dangerous behaviors and are classified as **sensation-seeking individuals** (Zuckerman 2000).

Drug use may also be reinforced when it is associated with receiving affection or approval in a social setting, such as within a peer group relationship. Initially, the use of drugs may not be very important or pleasurable to the individual. However, eventually the affection and social rewards experienced when drugs are used become associated with the drug. Drug use and intimacy may then become perceived as very worthwhile.

I don't know how to explain why but an attractive part of cocaine use is the instant feeling of intimacy with others who are also snorting this drug. You just don't want to leave the scene when the lines are cut on the glass surface and people are taking turns snorting coke. Even after I have had four or five lines and the conversation is very friendly and engaging, leaving the scene because someone is waiting for you at home or even if you have to meet with someone that night does not matter. Usually, everyone is feeling high, a lot of feelings of togetherness, and open to intimate conversation. I never saw anyone getting violent or anything like that, but I hear that it can happen especially if you have a grudge against someone before doing the coke. I think that coke just makes you more open and if you are an angry person then it will just bring it out in you. My experiences have been that everyone is just so friendly and everyone just pretends not to be overly anxious to do the next line. Actually, everyone is kind of pretending, because what they really want is more powder up their nose and an unending amount of time for talking the night away. *(From Venturelli's research files, male graduate student, residing in Chicago, age 26, May 18, 2000)*

It is important to keep in mind that the amount of a drug taken can affect the extent of sociability, as the interview below indicates:

Yes, I did read that quote [referring to the preceding quote] about how friendly everyone is while snorting lines. Well, I bet that person does not do too much coke—maybe it is like a weekend thing. What I am trying to say is that everyone is friendly at the beginning when snorting lines, but after doing a lot of snorting, people get real quiet—they sort of geek out. You see, too much of it at any one time makes you feel overloaded. It's like an amphetamine bombardment. In the beginning, it is like a "dusting" and people can become real friendly and talkative, but after doing it for an hour or so, it gets to you. Whenever I overdo it, and it is easy to do so, I become real quiet and several times even when I tried to change my mood by having sex, I could not even "get it up" so-to-speak. I usually do very well when I just have a little, but too much certainly can cause the sexual desire to peak, but the follow through is an entirely different matter. Too much just geeks you out after a while. *(From Venturelli's research files, male construction working in Indiana, age 28, June 9, 2007)*

By the conditioning process, a pleasurable experience such as drug taking may become associated with a comforting or soothing environment. When this happens, two different outcomes may result. First, the user may feel uncomfortable taking the drug in any other environment. Second, the user may become very accustomed or habituated to the familiar environment as part of the drug experience. The user may not experience the same level of rush or high in this environment and in response may take more drugs or seek a different environment.

Finally, through this process of conditioning and habituation, a drug user becomes accustomed to unpleasant effects of drug use such as withdrawal symptoms. Such unpleasant effects and experiences may become habituated—neutralized or less severe in their impact—so that the user can continue taking drugs without feeling or experiencing the negative effects of the drug.

■ Social Psychological Learning Theories

Other extensions of reinforcement or learning theory focus on how positive social influences by drug-using peers reinforce the attraction to drugs. Social interaction, peer camaraderie, social approval, and drug use work together as positive reinforcers to sustain drug use (Akers 1992). Thus, if the effects of drug use become personally reward-ing "or become reinforcing through conditioning, the chances of continuing to use are greater than for stopping" (Akers 1992, p. 86). It is through learned expectations or association with others who reinforce drug use that individuals learn the pleasures of drug taking (Becker 1963, 1967). Sim-ilarly, if drug use leads to poor and disruptive so-cial interactions, drug use may cease.

Note that positive reinforcers, such as peers, other friends and acquaintances, family members, and drug advertisements, do not act alone in incit-ing and sustaining drug use. Learning theory as de-fined here also relies on some variable amounts of imitation and trial-and-error learning methods.

Finally, **differential reinforcement**—defined as the ratio between reinforcers favorable and disfavorable for sustaining drug use behavior—must be consid-ered. The use and eventual abuse of drugs can vary with certain favorable or unfavorable reinforcing experiences. The primary determining conditions are listed here:

- The amount of exposure to drug-using peers versus non-drug-using peers
- The general preference for drug use in a par-ticular neighborhood or community
- The age of initial use (younger adolescents are more greatly affected than older adolescents)
- The frequency of drug use among peers

Major Theoretical Explanations: Sociological

Sociological explanations for drug use share impor-tant commonalities with psychological explanations under social learning theories. The main features distinguishing psychological and sociological expla-nations are that psychological explanations focus more on how the internal states of the drug user are affected by social relationships within families, peers, and other close and more distant relation-ships, whereas sociological explanations focus on how factors external to the drug user affect drug use. Such outside forces include the types of fami-lies, adopted lifestyles of peer groups, and types of neighborhoods and communities in which avid drug users reside. The sociological perspective views the motivation for drug use as largely determined by the types and quality of bonds (attachment versus detachment) that the drug user or potential drug user has with significant others and with the social environment in general. The degree of influence and involvement with external factors affecting the individual compared with the influence exerted by internal states distinguishes sociological from psychological analyses.

As previously stated, no one biological and psy-chological theory can adequately explain why most people use drugs. People differ from one another in terms of personality, motivational factors, up-bringing, learned priority of values and attitudes, and problems faced. Because of these differences, many responses and reasons exist why people take drugs, which results in a plurality of theoretical ex-planations. Furthermore, the diverse perspectives of biology, psychology, and sociology offer their own explanations for drug use and abuse.

There are two sets of sociological theories: social influence and social structural. **Social influence theo-ries** focus on microscopic explanations that concen-trate on the roles played by significant others and their impact on an individual. **Structural influence theories** focus on macroscopic explanations of drug use and the assumption that the organizational structure of society has a major independent impact on an individual's use of drugs. The next sections examine these theories.

Social Influence Theories

The theories presented in this section are (1) social learning, (2) role of significant others in socializa-tion, (3) labeling, and (4) subculture theories. These theories share a common theme: An individual's motivation to seek drugs is caused by social influ-ences or social pressures.

Social Learning Theory

Social learning theory explains drug use as learned behavior. Conventional learning occurs through

KEY TERMS

differential reinforcement
ratio between reinforcers, both favorable and disfavorable, for sustaining drug use behavior

social influence theories
sociological theories that view a person's day-to-day social relations as a primary cause for drug use

structural influence theories
theories that view the structural organization of a society, peer group, or subculture as directly responsible for drug use

imitation, trial and error, improvisation, rewarded behavior, and cognitive mental associations and processes (Liska and Messner 1999; Ritzer and Goodman 2010). Social learning theory focuses directly on how drug use and abuse are learned through interaction with other drug users.

This theory emphasizes the pervasive influence of *primary groups*—that is, groups that share a high amount of intimacy and spontaneity and whose members are emotionally bonded. Families and long-term friends are examples of primary groups. In contrast, secondary groups share segmented relationships in which interaction is based on prescribed role patterns. An example of a secondary group is the relationship between you and a sales-clerk in a grocery store or relationships between employees scattered throughout a corporation. Social learning theory addresses a type of interaction that is highly specific. This type of interaction involves learning specific motives, techniques, and appropriate meanings that are commonly attached to a particular type of drug.

The following are examples of first-time users learning drug-using techniques from their social circles:

The first time I tried smoking weed, nothing much happened. I always thought it was like smoking a cigarette. When the joint came around the first time, I refused it. The next time it came around, I noticed everyone was looking at me. So, I took the joint and started to inhale, then exhale. My friend sitting next to me said something to the effect, "Dude, hold it in; don't waste it. This is good weed and we don't have that much between us." Right after that, we did some "shotguns." This is where someone exhales directly into your mouth— lips to lips. My friend filled my lungs with his exhaled weed breath. After the first comment about holding it in, I started to watch how everyone was inhaling and realized that you really don't smoke weed like an ordinary cigarette; you have to hold in the smoke. *(From Venturelli's research files, male high school student in a small Midwestern town, age 16, February 15, 1997)*

I first started using drugs, mostly alcohol and pot, because my best friend in high school was using drugs. My best friend Tim [a pseudo-nym] learned from his older sister. Before I actually tried pot, Tim kept telling me how great

it was to be high on dope; he said it was much better than beer. I was really nervous the first time I tried pot with Tim and another friend, even though I heard so much detail about it from Tim. The first time I tried it, it was a complete letdown. The second time (the next day, I think it was), I remember I was talking about a teacher we had and in the middle of the conversation, I remember how everything appeared different. I started feeling happy and while listening to Tim as he poked jokes about the teacher, I started to hear the background music more clearly than ever before. By the time the music ended and a new CD started, I knew I was high. *(From Venturelli's research files, male student at a private liberal arts college in the Midwest, age 22, February 15, 1997)*

First time I tried acid [LSD], I didn't know what to expect. Schwa [a pseudonym] told me it was a very different high from grass [marijuana]. After munching on one "square" [one dose of LSD]—after about 20 minutes— I looked at Schwa and he started laughing and said, "Feelin' the effects, Ki-ki?" I said, "Is this it? Is this what it feels like? I feel weird." With a devious grin . . . Schwa said, "Yep. We are now on the runway, ready to take off. Just wait a little while longer, it's going to get better and better. Fasten your seat belts!" *(From Venturelli's research files, male, age 33, May 6, 1996)*

Learning to perceive the effects of the drug is the second major outcome in the process of becoming a regular user. Here, the ability to feel the authentic effects of the drug is being learned. The more experienced drug users in the group impart their knowledge to naive first-time users. The coaching information they provide describes how to recognize the euphoric effects of the drug.

I was just curious after watching my roommate with his friends frequently passing around a joint and remember always saying "I'll pass on that" many times. One night I just tried it with my roommate late at night. I really did not know how to even smoke it, but my roommate made more coaching comments as I was taking hits. The first few puffs nothing happened, but after I took in two huge hits, and coughing as it nearly choked me, I started to feel different. I had kind of a mellow feeling. I was talking about something and in the middle of the conversation I started to focus on everything around me like I was in some kind of trance, not heavy, but my mind was in several places as I spoke. After a few moments, I said, "I feel different not like I drank alcohol but just feel different." My roommate smiled and said, "You like the feeling?" I said I did not know but there was nothing bad in my feelings about what I had just done. It was like a change in the way I was processing input coming in. I remember saying that I felt kind of like light-headed and relaxed. My roommate said something like "Welcome to the world of marijuana, Mr. Schaffer (pseudonym)!" We just both laughed. *(From Venturelli's research files, male attending a small, private liberal arts college in the Midwest, age 18, May 21, 2010)*

Another example of learning to perceive the effects:

I just sat there waiting for something to happen, but I really didn't know what to expect. After the fifth "hit," I was just about ready to give up ever getting high. Then suddenly, my best buddy looked deeply into my eyes and said, "Aren't you high yet?" Instead of just answering the question, I immediately repeated the same words the exact way he asked me. In a flash, we both simultaneously burst out laughing. This uncontrollable laughter went on for what appeared to be over 5 minutes. Then he said, "You silly ass, it's not like an alcohol high, it's a 'high high.' Don't you feel it? It's a totally different kind of high." At that very moment, I knew I was definitely high on the stuff. If this friend would not have said this to me, I probably would have continued thinking that getting high on the hash was impossible for me. *(From Venturelli's research files, male attending a small, private liberal arts college in the Southeast, age 17, May 15, 1984)*

Once drug use has begun, continuing the behavior involves learning the following sequence: (1) identifying where and from whom the drug can be purchased, (2) maintaining steady contact with drug dealers, (3) developing a preoccupation with maintaining the secrecy of use from authority figures and casual non–drug-using acquaintances, (4) reassuring yourself that the drug use is pleasurable,

(5) using with more frequency, and (6) replacing non–drug-using friends with drug-using friends.

Role of Significant Others

After a pattern of drug use has been established, the learning process plays a role in sustaining drug-taking behavior. Edwin Sutherland (1947; Akers 2009; Liska and Messner 1999), a pioneering criminologist in sociology, believed that the mastery of criminal behavior depended on the frequency, duration, priority, and intensity of contact with others who are involved in similar behavior (Heitzeg 1996). This theory can also be applied to drug-taking behavior.

In applying Sutherland's principles of social learning to drug use, which he called differential association theory, the focus is on how other members of social groups reward criminal behavior and under what conditions this deviance is perceived as important and pleasurable.

Becker's and Sutherland's theories explain why adolescents may use psychoactive drugs. Essentially, both theories say that the use of drugs is learned during intimate interaction with others who serve as a primary group. (See "Here and Now: Symptoms of Drug and Alcohol Abuse" for information on how the role of significant others can determine a child's disposition toward or away from illicit drug use.)

Learning theory also explains how adults and the elderly are taught the motivation for using a particular type of drug. This learning occurs through influences such as drug advertising, with its emphasis on testimonials by avid users, by medical experts, and by actors and actresses portraying physicians

This child is role-playing largely by imitating the habits of a significant other.

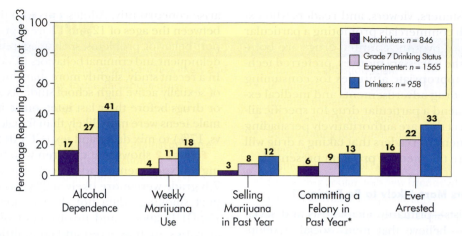

FIGURE 2.2

Percentage of grade 7 nondrinkers, experimenters, and drinkers exhibiting problem behaviors at age 23.

....

*Felonies were defined as buying, selling, or holding stolen goods, taking a joy ride without the vehicle owner's permission, breaking into property, arson, or attempted arson.

Note: Nondrinkers never had a drink, not even a few sips. Experimenters drank less than three times in the past year and none in the past month. Drinkers drank three or more times in the past year or drank in the past month. Subjects were assessed in grade 7, again in grade 12, and again at age 23.

Source: University of Maryland, Center for Substance Abuse Research (CESAR). "Ten-Year Prospective Study of Public Health Problems Associated with Early Drinking." *CESAR FAX* 12(36), 2003, using data from Ellickson, P. L., J. S. Tucker, and D. J. Klein. "Ten-Year Prospective Study of Public Health Problems Associated with Early Drinking." *Pediatrics* 111(5):949–955, 2003.

to peer influence, increased delinquency, and lower achievement in school. In general, drug abusers have 14 characteristics in common:

1. Their drug use usually follows clear-cut developmental steps and sequences. Use of legal drugs, such as alcohol and cigarettes, almost always precedes use of illegal drugs.
2. Use of certain drugs, particularly habitual use of marijuana, is linked to amotivational syndrome, which some researchers believe is a general change in personality.[1] This change is characterized by apathy, lack of interest, and inability or difficulty accomplishing goals. Past research also clearly shows that marijuana use is often responsible for attention and short-term memory impairment and confusion (NIDA 1996a).
3. Immaturity, maladjustment, or insecurity usually precede the use of marijuana and other illicit drugs.

4. Those more likely to try illicit drugs, especially before age 12, usually have a history of poor school performance and classroom disobedience.
5. Delinquent or repetitive deviant types of behavior usually precede involvement with illicit drugs.
6. A set of values and attitudes that facilitates the development of deviant behavior exists before the person tries illicit drugs.
7. A social setting in which drug use is common, such as communities and neighborhoods in which peers use drugs indiscriminately, is likely to reinforce and increase the predisposition to drug use.
8. Drug-induced behaviors and drug-related attitudes of peers are usually among the strongest predictors of subsequent drug involvement.
9. Children who feel their parents are distant from their emotional needs are more likely to become drug addicted (see "Here and Now: Does Divorce Affect Adolescent Drug Use?").
10. The younger people are when they begin using drugs, the higher the probability of continued and accelerated drug use. Likewise, the older people are when they start using drugs, the lower the probability of accelerated use and addiction. The period of greatest risk of initiation

---

[1]Some argue that perhaps a general lack of ambition (*lethargic behavior*) may *precede* rather than *result from* marijuana use or that amotivational syndrome is present in some heavy marijuana users *before* the initial use of this drug, and when the drug is used, the syndrome becomes more pronounced. In any case, some drug researchers believe that when used steadily, marijuana and the amotivational syndrome occur together.

Here and Now

Does Divorce Affect Adolescent Drug Use?

"When parents make a decision to divorce . . . , children are expected to cope with the decision. Except in cases involving abuse, it is rare that children will thrive during a divorce. The impact of divorce is that children will have problems and experience symptoms" (Conner 2009). One of the major symptoms listed by Conner (among others), a clinical psychologist, is drug or alcohol abuse. Further, as an example of how drug users may be affected by socialization, a study conducted by Needle (Conner 2009; Needle, Su, and Doherty 1990; NIDA 1990; Siegel and Senna 1994) found higher drug use among adolescents whose parents divorced. According to the study, children who are adolescents when their parents divorce exhibit more extensive drug use and experience more drug-related health, legal, and other problems than their peers. This study linked the extent of teens' drug use to their age at the time of their parents' divorce. Teenagers whose parents divorce were found to use more drugs and experience more drug-related problems than two other groups of adolescents: those who were age 10 or younger when their parents divorced, and those whose parents remained married.

This study has important implications for drug abuse prevention efforts. Basically, it says that not everyone is at the same risk for drug use. People at greater risk can be identified, and programs should be developed to meet their special needs.

In this research project, drug use among all adolescents increased over time. However, drug use was higher among adolescents whose parents had divorced when their children were either preteens or teenagers. Drug use was highest for those teens whose parents divorced during their children's adolescent years. Such families also reported more physical problems, family disputes, and arrests.

The research results showed that distinct gender differences existed in the way that divorce affected adolescent drug use, whether the divorce occurred during the offspring's childhood or adolescent years. Males whose parents divorced reported more drug use and drug-related problems than females. Females whose caretaking parents remarried experienced increased drug use after the remarriage. By contrast, males whose caretaking parents remarried reported a decrease in drug-related problems following the remarriage.

The researchers caution that these findings may have limited applicability, because most of the families studied were white and had middle to high income levels. Needle also notes that the results should not be interpreted as an argument in favor of the nuclear family. Overall, divorce affects adolescents in complex ways and remarriage can influence drug-using behavior; particularly when disruptions occur during adolescence, such turmoil can "trigger" a desire for extensive recreational licit and illicit drug use, often leading to drug abuse.

---

and habitual use of illicit drugs is usually over by the early twenties.

11. The family structure has changed, with substantially more than half, 72 million, or 59.2% (U.S. Department of Labor 2010) of all women in the United States now working outside the home. A higher divorce rate has led to many children being raised in single-parent households. How the lack of a stay-at-home parent or how membership in a single-family household affects the quality of child care and nurturing is difficult to assess.

12. Mobility obstructs a sense of permanency, and it contributes to a lack of self-esteem. Often, when children are repeatedly moved from one location to another, their community becomes nothing more than a group of strangers. They may have little pride in their home or community and have no commitment to society.

13. Among minority members, a major factor involved in drug dependence is a feeling of powerlessness due to discrimination based on race, social standing, or other attributes. Groups subject to discrimination have a disproportionately high rate of unemployment and below-average incomes. In the United States, approximately 15.6 million children (21%) are reared in poverty (Landau 2010). The adults they have as role models may be unemployed and experience feelings of powerlessness. Higher rates of delinquency and drug addiction occur in such settings.

14. Abusers who become highly involved in selling drugs begin by witnessing that drug trafficking

is a lucrative business, especially in rundown neighborhoods. In some communities, selling drugs seems to be the only available route to real economic success (Jones 1996; Shelden, Tracy, and Brown 2001).

Labeling Theory

Although controversy continues over whether labeling is a theory or a perspective (Akers 1968, 1992; Heitzeg 1996; Plummer 1979), this text takes the position that labeling is a theory (Cheron 2001; Hewitt 1994; Liska and Messner 1999), primarily because it explains something very important with respect to drug use. Although labeling theory does not fully explain why initial drug use occurs, it does detail the processes by which many people come to view themselves as socially deviant from others. Note that the terms *deviant* (in cases of individuals) and *deviance* (in cases of behavior) are sociologically defined as involving the violation of significant social norms held by conventional society. The terms are not used in a judgmental manner, nor are the individuals judged to be immoral or "sick"; instead, the terms refer to an absence of the patterns of behavior expected by conventional society.

Labeling theory says that other people whose opinions we value have a determining influence over our self-image (Best and Luckenbill 1994; Goode 1997; Liska and Messner 1999). (For an example of how labeling theory applies to real-life situations, see "Case in Point.")

Implied in this theory is the idea that we exert only a small amount of control over the image we portray. In contrast, members of society, especially those we consider to be significant others, have much greater influence and power in defining or redefining our self-image. The image we have of ourselves is vested in the people we admire and look to for guidance and advice. If these people come to define our actions as deviant, then their definition becomes incorporated as a "fact" of our reality.

We can summarize labeling theory by saying that the labels we use to describe people have a profound influence on their self-perceptions. For example, imagine a fictitious individual named Billy. Initially, Billy does not see himself as a compulsive drug user but as an occasional recreational drug user. Let us also assume that Billy is very humorous, unpretentious, and very outspoken about his drug use and likes to exaggerate the amount of marijuana he smokes on a daily basis. Slowly, Billy's friends begin to perceive him as a "real stoner." According to labeling theory, what happens to Billy? Because of being noticed when "high," his self-presentation, and the comments he makes about the pleasures of drug use, his friends may begin to reinforce the exaggerated drug use image. At first, Billy may enjoy the reflected image of a "big-time" drug user, but after nearly all of his peers maintain a constant exaggerated image, his projected image may turn negative, especially when his friends show disrespect for his opinions. In this example, labeling theory predicts that Billy's perception of himself will begin to mirror the consistent perception expressed by his accusers. If he is unsuccessful in eradicating the addict image or, in this example, the "stoner" image, Billy will reluctantly concur with the label that has been thrust on him. Or, to strive for a self-image as an occasional marijuana user, Billy may abandon his peers so that he can become acceptable once more in the eyes of other people.

An important originator of labeling theory is Edwin Lemert (Lemert 1951; Liska and Messner 1999; Williams and McShane 1999), who distinguished between two types of deviance: primary and secondary deviance. Primary deviance is inconsequential deviance, which occurs without having a lasting impression on the perpetrator. Generally, most first-time violations of law, for example, are primary deviations. Whether the suspected or accused individual has committed the deviant act does not matter. What matters is whether the individual identifies with the deviant behavior.

Secondary deviance develops when the individual begins to identify and perceive himself or herself as deviant. The moment this transition occurs, deviance shifts from being primary to secondary. Many adolescents casually experiment with drugs. If, however, they begin to perceive themselves as drug users, then this behavior is virtually impossible to eradicate. The same holds true with OTC

KEY TERMS

labeling theory
the theory emphasizing that other people's perceptions directly influence one's self-image

primary deviance
any type of initial deviant behavior in which the perpetrator does not identify with the deviance

secondary deviance
any type of deviant behavior in which the perpetrator identifies with the deviance

▶ Case in Point Specific Signs of Marijuana Use

This excerpt, from the author's files, illustrates labeling theory.

After my mom found out, she never brought it up again. I thought the incident was over—dead, gone, and buried. Well . . . it wasn't over at all. My mom and dad must have agreed that I couldn't be trusted anymore. I'm sure she was regularly going through my stuff in my room to see if I was still smoking dope. Even my grandparents acted strangely whenever the news on television would report about the latest drug bust in Chicago. Several times that I can't ever forget were when we were together and I could hear the news broadcast on TV from my room about some drug bust. There they all were whispering about me. My grandma asking if I "quitta the dope." One night, I overheard my mother reassure my dad and grandmother that I no longer was using dope. You can't believe how embarrassed I was that my own family was still thinking that I was a dope fiend. They thought I was addicted to pot like a junkie is addicted to heroin! I can tell you that I would never lay such a guilt trip on my kids if I ever have kids. I remember that for 2 years after the time I was honest enough to tell my mom that I had tried pot, they would always whisper about me, give me the third degree whenever I returned late from a date, and go through my room looking for dope. They acted as if I was hooked on drugs. I remember that for a while

back then I would always think that if they think of me as a drug addict, I might as well get high whenever my friends "toke up." They should have taken me at my word instead of sneaking around my personal belongings. I should have left syringes lying around my room!

Approximately 17 years after this interview was conducted, this author was able to revisit the same interviewee, who at the time of this second interview was 37 years of age. After showing him the same excerpt I had written he commented:

You know Professor, while today marijuana use is no longer such a big deal, I can still tell you that it took years to finally convince my family that I was not a "big time drug user." Though my grandma is now dead, I can still remember how she would look at me when I would tell her that I just smoke it once in a while. I knew she never believed that I was just an occasional user by the look on her face, when she would ask ". . . and last night when you went out, did you smoke the dope again?" My mom, who is now living with her sister, still mentions how I went wild those days when I was drugging it up! Yes, I have to say it had a big impact on me when my own family believed I was a drug addict back then. I will never forget those looks from my family every time I would walk into the house on weekends when I would return from a night out with my friends.

Sources: Interview with a 20-year-old male college student at a private university in the Midwest, conducted by Peter Venturelli on November 19, 1993. Second interview with same interviewee, 37 years of age, June 2010.

drug abuse. The moment an individual believes that he or she feels better after using a particular drug, the greater the likelihood that he or she will consistently use the drug.

Howard Becker (1963) believed that certain negative status positions (such as alcoholic, mental patient, ex-felon, criminal, drug addict, and so on) are so powerful that they dominate others (Pontell 1996; Williams and McShane 1999). In the earlier example, if people who are important to Billy call him a "druggie," this name becomes a powerful label that takes precedence over any other status positions Billy may occupy. This label becomes Billy's **master status**—that he is a mindless "stoner." Even if Billy is also an above-average biology major,

an excellent musician, and a dependable and caring person, such factors become secondary because his primary status has been recast as a "druggie." Furthermore, once a powerful label is attached, it becomes much easier for the individual to uphold the image dictated by members of society and simply to act out the role expected by significant others. Master status labels distort an individual's

KEY TERMS

master status

major status position in the eyes of others that clearly identifies an individual; for example, doctor, professor, alcoholic, heroin addict public image because other people expect consistency in role performance.

Once a negative master status has been attached to an individual's public image, labeling theorist Edwin Schur asserted that retrospective interpretation occurs. **Retrospective interpretation** is a form of "reconstitution of individual character or identity" (Schur 1971, p. 52). It largely involves *redefining* a person's image within a particular social stereotype, category, or group (see cartoon as an illustration). In the eyes of his peers, Billy is now an emotional, intelligent, yet weird or "freaky" stoner.

Finally, William I. Thomas's (1923) contribution to labeling theory can be summarized in the following theorem: "If men define situations as real, they are real in their consequences" (p. 19). Thus, according to this dictum, when someone is perceived as a drug user, the perception functions as the reality of that person's character and in turn shapes his or her self-perception.

Subculture Theory

Subculture theory speaks to the role of peer pressure and the behavior resulting from peer group influences. In all groups, there are certain members who are more popular and respected and, as a result, exert more social influence than other peer members. Often, these more socially endowed members are group leaders, task leaders, or emotional leaders who possess greater ability to influence others. Drug use that results from peer pressure demonstrates the extent to which these more popular and respected leaders can influence and pressure others to initially use or abuse drugs. These four excerpts from interviews illustrate subculture theory:

> When I was 9 or 10, three of my best friends would all take turns sneaking alcohol out of our parents' houses. Then in one of our garages, we would drink the liquor and smoke

cigarettes. It was like a street corner thing but it was in a garage. In high school, we would look for the "party-people" and hang out with them. Usually on a Friday or some other school day, we would cut classes and drink and get high at someone's house that would be available. We were a tight-ass group—the goal would be to find a party somewhere. In high school we just hung out together and were known on campus as "the party animals." *(From Venturelli's research files, male college student in a small town in the Midwest, age 21, November 23, 2000)*

A second account:

> I first started messing around with alcohol in high school. In order to be part of the crowd, we would sneak out during lunchtime at school and get "high." About 6 months after we started drinking, we moved on to other drugs. . . . Everyone in high school belongs to a clique, and my clique was heavy into drugs. We had a lot of fun being high throughout the day. We would party constantly. Basically, in college, it's the same thing. *(From Venturelli's research files, male student at a small, religiously affiliated private liberal arts college in the Southeast, age 19, February 9, 1985)*

A third account:

> I remember Henri was from Holland, and he never tried coke. One night all three of us were at Joe's apartment and Joe had a hefty amount of coke that he brought out from his bedroom. We started snorting it and when it was Henri's turn he said, "I never did this and maybe I shouldn't do it now." Paul, who was also a good friend of Henri, said "Come on Henri, it won't do that much to you." Henri looked at each of us and shot back with "Okay, I will try it once." Well, that night Henri had about as much coke as the two of us had. It was all okay until Henri suddenly got sick and vomited a good number of times. We spent a good part of the night taking care of Henri making sure he did not pass out and made sure to get him back to his apartment and call it a night. Henri was just not used to the coke and we probably let him have too much being his first time. *(From Venturelli's research files, all three mentioned were seniors in college at a liberal arts college in Chicago, August 18, 2009)*

KEY TERMS

retrospective interpretation
social psychological process of redefining a person in light of a major status position; for example, homosexual, physician, professor, alcoholic, convicted felon, or mental patient

subculture theory
explains drug use as a peer-generated activity

The fourth interview illustrates how friendship, coupled with subtle and not-so-subtle peer pressure, influences the novice drug enthusiast:

> There I was on the couch with three of my friends, and as the joint was being passed around, everyone was staring at me. I felt they were saying, "Are you going to smoke with us or will you be a holdout again?" *(From Venturelli's research files, male university student, age 20, April 10, 1996)*

In sociology, charismatic leaders are viewed as possessing status and power, defined as distinction in the eyes of others. In drug-using peer groups, such leaders have power over inexperienced drug users. Members of peer groups are often persuaded to experiment with drugs if the more popular members say, "Come on, try some, it's great" or "Trust me, you'll really get off on this, come on, just try it." In groups where drugs are consumed, the extent of peer influence coupled with the art of persuasion and camaraderie are powerfully persuasive and cause the spread of drug use.

A further extension of subculture theory is the *social and cultural support perspective*. This perspective explains drug use and abuse in peer groups as resulting from an attempt by peers to solve problems collectively. In the neoclassic book *Delinquent Boys: The Culture of the Gang* (1955), Cohen pioneered a study that showed for the first time that delinquent behavior is a collective attempt to gain social status and prestige within the peer group (Liska and Messner 1999; Siegel and Senna 1994; Williams and McShane 1999). Members of certain peer groups are unable to achieve respect within the larger society. Such status-conscious youths find that being able to commit delinquent acts and yet evade law enforcement officials is admirable in the eyes of their delinquent peers. In effect, Cohen believed, delinquent behavior is a subcultural solution for overcoming feelings of status frustration and low self-esteem largely determined by lower class status.

Although Cohen's emphasis is on explaining juvenile delinquency, his notion that delinquent behavior is a subcultural solution can easily be applied to drug use and abuse primarily in members of lower-class peer groups. Underlying drug use and abuse in delinquent gangs, for example, results from sharing common feelings of alienation and low self-esteem and a collective feeling of escaping from a society that appears noncaring, noninclusive, distant, and hostile.

Consider the current upsurge in violent gang memberships (see Chapter 16 for more details on adolescents and gangs). In such groups, not only is drug dealing a profitable venture, but drug use also serves as a collective response to alienation and estrangement from conventional middle-class society. The hope of sudden monetary gain from drug dealing is perceived as a quick ticket into the middle class. In cases of violent minority gang members, the alienation results from racism, poverty, effects of migration and acculturation, and effects of minority status in a white, male-dominated society such as the United States (Glick and Moore 1990; Moore 1978, 1993; Sanders 1994; Thornberry 2001).

◾ Structural Influence Theories

Structural influence theories focus on how elements in the *organization* of a society, group, or subculture affect the motivation and resulting drug use behavior that is for nonmedical—most often recreational—use. The belief is that no single factor in the society, the group, or the subculture produces the attraction to drug use, but rather that the organization itself or the lack of organization largely causes this behavior to occur.

Social disorganization and social strain theories (Liska and Messner 1999; Werner and Henry 1995) identify the different kinds of social change that are disruptive and explain how, in a general

This cartoon illustrates the reflective process in retrospective interpretation that often occurs in daily conversations when we think that our unspoken thoughts are undetectable and hidden. In reality, however, these innermost thoughts are clearly conveyed through body language and nonverbal gestures.

Courtesy of Alex Silvestri.

sense, people are adversely affected by the change. Social disorganization theory asks, "What in the structure and organization of the social order (the larger social structure) causes people to deviate?" Social strain theory attempts to answer the question, "What in the structure and organization of the family, the peer, and employee social structure causes someone to deviate?" This theory suggests that frustration results from being unable to secure the means to achieve sought-after goals, such as the goal of securing good income without much education, a well-paying job without prior training, and so on. Such perceived shortcomings compel an individual to deviate to achieve desired goals.

Overall, social disorganization theory describes a situation in which, because of rapid social change, previously affiliated individuals no longer find themselves integrated into a community's social, commercial, religious, and economic institutions. When this type of alienation occurs, community members whose parents were perhaps more affiliated find themselves more disconnected and feel a lack of effective attachment to the social order. As a result, these disconnected or "disaffiliated" people find deviant behavior to be an attractive alternative.

An essential factor for proper socialization includes trusting relationships within a relatively stable environment. As will be discussed later in this chapter, when major identity development and personality transformations occur during the

teen years, some stability and trusting relationships in the immediate environment are crucial. Today, however, most Westernized societies (including the United States) are experiencing rapid technological development and social changes, which result in more destabilizing and disorienting factors that affect us (Gergen 2000; Ritzer 1999, 2011).

Although on the surface most people appear to have little or no difficulty adapting to rapid technological social change, many people find themselves forced to maintain a frantic pace merely to "keep up" on a daily basis. The drive to keep up with social and technological innovation is more demanding today than ever before (Gergen 2000). The constant need to keep pace with change and the increasing multiplicity of realities, and ever more contradictory realities, produced by such change often appears barely controllable and somewhat chaotic. Some individuals who are unable to cope with the constant demand for change and the required adjustment to all this change have difficulty securing a stable self-identity. For example, consider the large number of people who need psychological counseling and therapy because they find themselves unable to cope with personal, family, and work-related problems and conflicts. In a recent study, "an estimated 26.2% of Americans ages 18 and older—about one in four adults—suffer from a diagnosable mental disorder in a given year" (Kessler et al. 2005, p. 617). The following interview shows how such confusion and lack of control can easily lead to drug use:

Interviewee: The world is all messed up.

Interviewer: Why? In what way?

Interviewee: Nobody gives a damn anymore about anyone else.

Interviewer: Why do you think this is so?

Interviewee: It seems like life just seems to go on and on. . . . I know that when I am under the influence, life is more mellow. I feel great! When I am high, I feel relaxed and can take things in better. Before I came to Chalmers College [a pseudonym], I felt home life was one great big mess; now that I am here, this college is also a big pile of crap. I guess this is why I like smoking dope. When I am high, I can forget my problems. My surroundings are friendlier; I am even more pleasant! Do you know what I mean? *(From Venturelli's research*

An example of feeling stressed and experiencing strain from an overly demanding society.

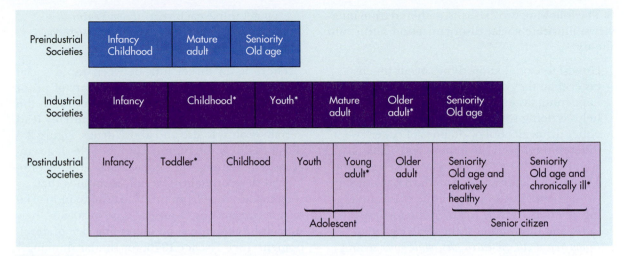

FIGURE 2.3

Levels of technological development and resulting subcultures.

*Represents a newly developed and separate stage of identification and expression from the prior era.

files, male marijuana user attending a small, private liberal arts college in the Southeast, age 19, February 12, 1984)

Similarly, an interview illustrates how a work environment can affect drug use:

I had one summer job once where it was so busy and crazy that a group of us workers would go out on breaks just to get high. We worked the night shift and our "high breaks" were between 2:00 and 5:00 in the morning. *(From Venturelli's research files, female first-year college student, age 20, July 28, 1996)*

Current Social Change in Most Societies

Does social change per se cause people to use and abuse drugs? In response to this question, social change—defined as any measurable change caused by technological advancement that disrupts cultural values and attitudes about everyday life—does not by itself cause widespread drug use. In most cases, social change materialistically advances a culture by profoundly affecting the manner of how things are accomplished. At the same time, rapid social change disrupts day-to-day behavior anchored by tradition, which has a tendency to fragment such conventional social groups as families, neighborhoods, and communities. By **conventional behavior**, we mean behavior that is largely

dictated by custom and tradition and that evaporates or goes into a state of flux because of the speed of social change.

Examples of social change include the number of youth subcultures that proliferated during the 1960s (Yinger 1982) and other more recent lifestyles and subcultures, such as rappers, punk rockers, metalheads, grunge rockers, taggers, skinheads, Satanists, new wavers, rave enthusiasts (Wooden 1995), gangstas, and Goths. Furthermore, two other subcultures, teenagers and the elderly, both have become increasingly independent and, in some subgroups, alienated from other age groups in society (see **Figure 2.3**).

Simply stated, today's social, religious, and political institutions no longer embrace, influence, and lead people as they did in the past. Consequently, people are free to explore different means of expression and types of recreation. For many, this liberating experience leads to new and exciting outcomes; for others, this freedom from conventional societal norms and attitudes creates a type of alienation that can lead to drug use and abuse.

KEY TERMS

conventional behavior
behavior largely dictated by custom and tradition, which is often disrupted by the forces of rapid technological change

The following two excerpts, gathered from interviews, illustrate social disorganization and strain theory:

> Honest to God, I know things occur much faster than they did 20 years ago. Change is happening faster and occurs more often. What helps is doing some drugs at night at home. I either drink alcohol or do lines of coke. Two different highs but I like them both. This is about the only recreation I have except for the TV at night, after working all darn day nonstop writing letters, answering phone calls, attending meetings, having to go on-site for inspections, and many other things I do each day. *(From Venturelli's research files, male home security systems manager, age 29, Chicago, Illinois, June 23, 2000)*

Second interview:

> Just as CNN flashes one news item after another at rapid speed, my life is similar. Most work days are so crammed with trying to constantly keep up, maintain my house and all that property upkeep demands, take care of the kids when my wife works nights, help clean the house, cook meals for all of us (since I am better at cooking than my wife), and dozens of other demands, that when the kids are finally asleep my wife and I try to relax with some combination of alcohol and weed. (We had to give up the coke because the kids are getting older and we don't mind if they find out we drink and smoke dope but the other stuff is out of the question. We don't want them to ever know we did coke.) Plus, those nights of staying up late when doing coke is too much for me now at this age. Really, the only time we can relax is when the kids are asleep and we can have a few drinks before going to bed. I keep hoping things will slow down, but it seems to either remain at the same frenzy pace or

> even get worse each year. *(From Venturelli's research files, male residing in a Midwestern town, age 31, February 10, 2010)*

There is no direct link between rapid social change and drug use. However, plenty of proof exists that certain dramatic changes occur in the organization of society, and may eventually lead certain groups to use and abuse drugs. Figure 2.3 illustrates how the number of life-cycle stages increases depending on a society's level of technological development. Overall, it implies that, as societies advance from preindustrial to industrial to our current postindustrial type of society, new subcultures emerge at an increasing rate of development. (See Fischer 1976, for similar thinking.) In contrast to industrial and postindustrial societies, preindustrial societies do not have as many separate and distinct periods and cycles of social development. What is shown in Figure 2.3 and implied here is that the greater the number of distinct life cycles, the greater the fragmentation between the members of different stages of development. Generation gaps (conflicting sets of values and attitudes between age cohorts) cause much ignorance and lack of insight between age-group subcultures. This often leads to separation and fragmentation across age groups who develop and live within distinct lifestyle patterns, increasing the likelihood of conflict.

Control Theory

The final major structural influence theory, control theory, emphasizes influences outside the self as the primary cause for deviating to drug use and/or abuse. **Control theory** places importance on positive socialization. **Socialization** is the process by which individuals learn to internalize the attitudes, values, and behaviors needed to become participating members of conventional society. Generally, control theorists believe that human beings can easily become deviant if left without the social controls provided by family, social groups, and organizations. Thus, control theory theorists emphasize the necessity of maintaining bonds to family, school, peer groups, and other social, political, and religious organizations (Liska and Messner 1999; Thio 2010). In the 1950s and 1960s, criminologist Walter C. Reckless (1961; Liska and Messner 1999; Siegel and Senna 1994) developed the containment theory. According to this theory, the socialization process results in the creation of strong or weak internal and external control systems. The degree of self-control, high or low frus-

KEY TERMS

control theory
theory that emphasizes when people are left without bonds to other groups (peers, family, social groups), they generally have a tendency to deviate from upheld values and attitudes

socialization
the growth and development process responsible for learning how to become a responsible, functioning human being

tration tolerance, positive or negative self-perception, successful or unsuccessful goal achievement, and either resistance or adherence to deviant behavior determine internal control. Environmental pressures, such as social conditions, may limit the accomplishment of goal-striving behavior; such conditions include poverty, minority group status, inferior education, and lack of employment.

The external, or outer, control system consists of effective or ineffective supervision and discipline, consistent or inconsistent moral training, and positive or negative acceptance, identity, and self-worth. Many believe that latchkey or unsupervised children have a higher risk of becoming delinquent due to nonexistent and/or sporadic supervision and the uneven levels of attention they receive. Drug-addicted parents are often at risk for raising children with delinquent tendencies because these parents are more apt to be inconsistent with discipline as a result of their drug addiction(s).

In applying this theory to the use or abuse of drugs, we could say that if an individual has a weak external social control system, the internal control system must take over to manage the external pressure. Similarly, if an individual's external social control system is strong, his or her internal control system will not be seriously challenged. If, however, either the internal or external control system is contradictory (weak internal versus strong external), or the worst-case scenario in which both internal and external controls are weak, drug abuse is much more likely to occur.

Table 2.2 shows the likelihood of drug use resulting from either strong or weak internal and external control systems. It indicates that if both internal and external controls are strong, the use and abuse of drugs are much less likely to occur.

Table 2.2 Likelihood of Drug Use

INDIVIDUAL INTERNAL CONTROL	EXTERNAL SOCIAL CONTROL	
	Strong	**Weak or Nonexistent**
Strong	Least likely (almost never)	Less likely (probably never)
Weak	More likely (probably will)	Most likely (almost certain)

Travis Hirschi (1971; Liska and Messner 1999; Thio 2010), a much-respected sociologist and social control theorist, believes that delinquent behavior tends to occur when people lack (1) attachment to others, (2) commitment to goals, (3) involvement in conventional activity, and (4) belief in a common value system. If a child or adolescent is unable to become circumscribed and attached to a family setting, school curriculum, and nondelinquent peers, then the drift to delinquent behavior is most likely inevitable.

We can apply Hirschi's theories to drug use as follows:

- Drug users are less likely than nonusers to be closely tied to their parents.
- Good students are less likely to use drugs.
- Drug users are less likely to participate in social clubs and organizations and engage in team sport activities.
- Drug users are very likely to have friends whose activities are congruent with their own attitudes. (Drug users "hang with" other drug users and delinquents "hang with" other delinquents.) Similarly, non–drug-using adolescents are often closest with other non-drug-using adolescents.

The following excerpt illustrates how control theory works:

I was 15 when my mother confronted me with drug use. I nearly died. We have always been very close and she really cried when she found my "dugout" [paraphernalia that holds a quantity of marijuana] and a "one hitter" [a tubular device for smoking very small quantities of this drug] in her car. My fear was that she would inquire about my drug use with our next-door neighbors, whose children were my best friends. The neighbor residing on the left of our house was one of my high school teachers who knew me from the day I was born. The neighbor on the right side of our house was our church pastor. For a while after she confronted me, I just sneaked around more whenever I wanted to get high. After a few months, I became so paranoid of how my mother kept looking at me when I would come in at night that I eventually stopped smoking weed. Our family is very close and the town I live in (at that time the population was 400) was filled with gossip. I could not handle the pressure, so I quit. (*From Venturelli's research files, female postal worker residing in a small Midwestern town, age 22, February 9, 1997*)

In conclusion, control theory depicts how conformity with supportive groups may prevent deviance. It suggests that control is either internally or externally enforced by family, school, and peer group expectations. In addition, individuals who are not equipped with an internal system of self-control reflecting the values and beliefs of conventional society or who feel personally alienated from major social institutions may deviate without feeling guilty for their actions, often because peer pressure results in a suspension or modification of internal beliefs.

Danger Signals of Drug Abuse

How does one know when the use of drugs moves beyond normal use? Many people are prescribed drugs that affect their moods. Using these drugs wisely can be important for both physical and emotional health. Sometimes, however, it may be difficult to decide when use of drugs to handle stress or anxiety becomes inappropriate. It is important that your use of drugs does not result in either dependency or addiction. The following are some danger signals that can help you evaluate your drug use behavior:

1. Do people who are close to you often ask about your drug use? Have they noticed any changes in your moods or behavior?
2. Do you become defensive when a friend or relative mentions your drug or alcohol use?
3. Do you believe you cannot have fun without alcohol or other drugs?
4. Do you frequently get into trouble with the law, school officials, family, friends, or significant others because of your alcohol or other drug use?
5. Are you sometimes embarrassed or frightened by your behavior under the influence of drugs or alcohol?
6. Have you ever switched to a new doctor because your regular physician would not prescribe the drug you wanted?

7. When you are under pressure or feel anxious, do you automatically take a sedative, a drink, or both?
8. Do you turn to drugs after becoming upset, after confrontations or arguments, or to relieve uncomfortable feelings?
9. Do you take drugs more often or for purposes other than those recommended by your doctor?
10. Do you often mix drugs and alcohol?
11. Do you drink or take drugs regularly to help you sleep or even to relax?
12. Do you take a drug to get going in the morning?
13. Do you find it necessary or nearly impossible to not use alcohol and/or other drugs to have sex?
14. Do you find yourself not wanting to be around friends who do not use drugs or drink on a regular basis?
15. Have you ever seriously thought that you may have a drug addiction problem?
16. Do you make promises to yourself or others that you will stop getting drunk or using drugs?
17. Do you drink and/or use drugs alone, often secretly?

A higher number of "yes" answers indicates a greater likelihood that you are abusing alcohol and/or drugs. Many places offer help at the local level, such as programs in your community listed in the phone book under "Drug Abuse" or "Drug Counseling." Other resources include community crisis centers, telephone hotlines, and the National Mental Health Association.

■ Low-Risk and High-Risk Drug Choices

As will become readily apparent throughout this text, some very real risks are associated with recreational drug use. Low-risk and high-risk drug choices refer to two major levels of alcohol and other drug use. **Low-risk drug choices** refer to values and attitudes that keep the use of alcohol and other drugs in control. **High-risk drug choices** refer to values and attitudes that lead to using drugs habitually and addictively, resulting in emotional, psychological, and physical health problems. Low-risk choices include abstinence from all drugs or remaining in true control of the quantity and frequency of drugs taken.

Low-risk choices require self-monitoring your consumption of alcohol and other drugs to reduce your risk of an alcohol and other drug-related problem. Both "low-risk" and "high-risk" are ap-

KEY TERMS

low-risk drug choices
developing values and attitudes that lead to controlling the use of alcohol and drugs

high-risk drug choices
developing values and attitudes that lead to using drugs both habitually and addictively

propriate descriptive concepts that allow us to focus on the health and safety issues involved in drug use and refer to developing and maintaining completely different values and attitudes in your approach to alcohol and other drugs.

This chapter described numerous factors influencing drug use, theoretical explanations, and reasons why people start using or abusing drugs. A good number of theories were covered that attempt to explain initial and habitual use. Some people can easily become addicted to alcohol and other drugs because of inherited characteristics, personality, mental instability or illness, and vulnerability to present situations. Others who have more resistance to alcohol and drug addiction may have stronger convictions and abilities to cope with different situations.

Maintaining a Low-Risk Approach

To minimize the risk of alcohol and drug-related problems, we suggest you remain aware of the following:

- Investigate your family drug history. Does anyone in your family have a history of alcohol or drug abuse? How many members of your family who have alcohol or drug problems are blood relatives? In other words, are you more likely to become dependent on alcohol or drugs because of the possibility of inherited genes or because of the values and attitudes to which you are exposed?
- Do you particularly enjoy the effects of alcohol and other drugs? Do you spend a lot of time thinking about how "good" it feels to be high?
- Does it seem as if the only time you really have fun is when you are using alcohol and other drugs?
- Keep in mind the following accepted findings, which are also covered throughout this text:
  - *Body size:* A small person typically becomes more impaired by drug use than a larger person.
  - *Gender:* Women typically become more impaired than men of the same size, especially with regard to alcohol use, but with other types of drugs as well.
  - *Other drugs:* Taking a combination of drugs generally increases the risk of impairment and, in some combinations, accidental death.
  - *Fatigue or illness:* Fatigue and illness increase impairment from alcohol and increase the risk for impairment.
  - *Mind-set:* As you set out to drink or use other drugs, are you expecting heavy use of alcohol or heavy involvement with drugs to the point of inebriation or severe distortion of reality as the evening's outcome? More importantly, what view do you have regarding moderate versus heavy use of drugs?
  - *Empty stomach:* Taking drugs on an empty stomach increases drug effects.

Also keep in mind that most excessive drug use comes with the following risks:

- It is against all school policies.
- It is unlawful behavior (risky with the law).
- Excessive alcohol and other drug use usually leads not only to public attention, but also to criminal justice attention (police and the courts). Jail time or prison, fines, costly forced rehabilitation programs, and community service work are possible outcomes.
- The defense costs involved in even simple drug possession charges are often $3000 to $8000 (often beyond an individual's ability to pay for such legal services).
- A criminal record is a public record and can be acquired or suddenly come to the attention of school officials (especially loan officers and/or government loan personnel), credit bureaus, as well as any other community members.

We leave you with this question: *Are excessive drug use and the resulting drug dependence still worth such risks?* This question is critical, especially when we know that the more often drugs are consumed, the greater the potential not only for drug dependence and addiction, but also for damage to health, personal well-being, family and interpersonal relationships, and community respect.

Discussion Questions

1. Define the terms *addiction, tolerance, dependence,* and *withdrawal.*

2. Describe and contrast the disease and characterological (personality predisposition) models of addiction.

3. List several biological, social, and cultural factors that may be responsible for addiction to drugs.

4. In addition to better cultivation techniques, cite several other possible reasons why the potency

of the average marijuana joint has increased since 1960.

5. Given that more than approximately 88% of the U.S. population are daily drug users in some form, do you think we need to reexamine our strict drug laws, which may be punishing a sizable number of drug users in our society who stubbornly want to use their drugs of choice?

6. Is there any way to combine the biological and sociological explanations for why people use drugs so that the two perspectives do not conflict? (Sketch out a synthesis between these two sets of theoretical explanations.)

7. What do you understand is the relationship between mental illness and drug abuse? Why is this relationship important?

8. Do you accept the behavioristic view that one school of psychology offers for explaining why people come to abuse drugs? (In a general sense, this view primarily states that when behavior is reinforced people repeat behaviors that are rewarded.) Explain your answer in terms of drug use and/or abuse.

9. In reviewing the psychological and sociological theories, which best explain drug use? Defend your answer.

10. Does differential association theory take into account non–drug-using individuals whose socialization environment was drug-infested? Explain your answer.

11. Do you really believe drug users are socialized differently and that these alleged differences account for drug use? Defend your answer.

12. Can divorce be blamed for adolescent drug use? Why or why not? If so, to what extent?

13. To what extent do you think rapid social change is a major cause of drug use and abuse? Cite three examples of how the speed of change in today's society may explain current drug use.

14. Is making low-risk choices regarding drug use a more realistic approach for drug moderation than advocating "Just say no" to drug use? Why or why not?

Summary

1 Chemical dependence has been a major social problem throughout U.S. history.

2 People define chemical addiction in many ways. The essential feature is a chronic adherence to drugs despite significant negative consequences.

3 The major models of addiction are the moral model, the disease model, and the characterological or personality predisposition model.

4 Transitional periods, such as adolescence and middle age, are associated with unique sets of risk factors.

5 Addiction is a gradual process during which a minority of drug users become caught up in vicious cycles that worsen their situation, cause psychological and biological abnormalities, and increase their drug use. Although not inevitable, addiction has a tendency to progress.

6 Drug use is more serious today than in the past because (a) it has increased dramatically since 1960; (b) today's illicit drugs are more potent than in the past; (c) the media present drug use as rewarding; (d) drug use physically harms members of society; and (e) drug use and drug dealing by violent gangs are increasing at alarming rates.

7 Genetic and biophysiological theories explain addiction in terms of genes, psychiatric disorders, reward centers in the brain, character traits, brain dysfunction, and biochemical patterns.

8 Drugs of abuse interfere with the functioning of neurotransmitters, chemical messengers used for communication between brain regions. Drugs with abuse potential enhance the pleasure centers by causing the release of a specific brain neurotransmitter such as dopamine, which acts as a positive reinforcer.

9 The American Psychiatric Association classifies severe drug dependence as a form of psychiatric disorder. Drug abuse can cause mental conditions that mimic major psychiatric illnesses, such as schizophrenia, severe anxiety disorders, and suicidal depression.

10 Four genetic factors can contribute to drug abuse: (a) Many genetically determined psychiatric disorders are relieved by drugs of abuse, which in turn encourages their use; (b) high rates of addiction result from people who are genetically sensitive to addictive drugs; (c) such character traits as insecurity and vulnerability, which often have a biological basis, can lead to drug abuse behavior; and (d) the inability to break away from a particular type of drug addiction may in part be genetically

determined, especially when severe craving or very unpleasant withdrawal effects dominate.

11 Introversion and extroversion patterns have been associated with levels of neural arousal in brain stem circuits. These forms of arousal are closely associated with effects caused by drug stimulants or depressants.

12 Reinforcement or learning theory says that the motivation to use or abuse drugs stems from how the "highs" from alcohol and other drugs reduce anxiety, tension, and stress. Positive social rewards and influences by drug-using peers also promote drug use.

13 Social influence theories include social learning, the role of significant others, labeling, and subculture theories. Social learning theory explains drug use as a form of learned behavior. Significant others play a role in the learning process involved in drug use and/or abuse. Labeling theory says that other people we consider important can influence whether drug use becomes an option for us. If key people we admire or fear come to define our actions as deviant, then the definition becomes a "fact" in our reality. Subculture theories trace original drug experimentation, use, and/or abuse to peer pressure and influence.

14 A number of consistencies in socialization patterns are found among drug abusers, ranging from immaturity, maladjustment, and insecurity to exposure and belief that a life with drug use is appealing and that selling drugs is a very lucrative business.

15 Sociologist Howard Becker believes that first-time drug users become attached to drugs because of three factors: (a) they learn the techniques of how to use drug; (b) they learn to perceive the pleasurable effects of drugs; and (c) they learn to enjoy the drug experience.

16 Primary deviance is when deviant behavior is initially tried, yet the perpetrator does not identify with the deviant behavior; hence, it is inconsequential deviant behavior. Secondary deviance is when the perpetrator begins to identify with the deviant behavior (i.e., "Yes, I am a drug user, so what if I am?").

17 Both internal and external social control should prevail concerning drug use. Internal control deals with internal psychic and internalized social attitudes. External social control is exemplified by living in a neighborhood and community in which drug use and abuse are severely criticized or not tolerated as a means to seek pleasure or avoid stress and anxiety.

18 Low-risk and high-risk drug use choices refer to the process of developing values and attitudes toward alcohol and other drugs. Low-risk drug choices encompass values and attitudes leading to a controlled use of alcohol and drugs—from total abstinence to very moderate use. High-risk choices encompass values and attitudes leading to using drugs both habitually and addictively.

References

Akers, R. L. "Problems in the Sociology of Deviance: Social Definition and Behavior." *Social Forces* 6 (June 1968): 455–465.

Akers, R. L. *Drugs, Alcohol, and Society: Social Structure, Process, and Policy.* Belmont, CA: Wadsworth, 1992.

Akers, R. L. *Social Learning and Social Structure: A General Theory of Crime and Deviance.* Brunswick, NJ: Transaction, 2009.

American Psychiatric Association (APA). "Substance-Related Disorders." In *Diagnostic and Statistical Manual of Mental Disorders (DSM-IV-TR),* 4th ed. revised. A. Francis, Chair, 191–295. Washington, DC: American Psychiatric Association, 2000.

Apostolides, M. "Special Report: The Addiction Revolution: Old Habits Get New Choices." *Psychology Today* 29 (September/October 1996):33–43, 75–76.

Bandura, A. *Social Learning Theory.* Englewood Cliffs, NJ: Prentice Hall, 1977.

Beattie, M. *Codependent No More.* San Francisco: Harper, 1987.

Becker, H. S. *Outsiders: Studies in the Sociology of Deviance.* New York: Free Press, 1963.

Becker, H. S. "History, Culture, and Subjective Experience: An Exploration of the Social Basis of Drug-Induced Experiences." *Journal of Health and Social Behavior* 8 (1967): 163–176.

Bejerot, N. "Current Problems of Drug Addiction." *Lakartidingen* (Sweden) 62, 50 (1965):4231–4238.

Bejerot, N. *Addiction: An Artificially Induced Drive.* Springfield, IL: Thomas, 1972.

Bejerot, N. "The Biological and Social Character of Drug Dependence." In *Psychiatrie der Gegenwart, Forschung und Praxis,* 2nd ed., edited by K. P. Kisker, J. E. Meyer, C. Muller, and E. Stromogrew, Vol. 3, 488–518. Berlin: Springer-Verlag, 1975.

Bespalov, A., A. Lebedev, G. Panchenko, and E. Zvartau. "Effects of Abused Drugs on Thresholds and Breaking Points of Intracranial Self-Stimulation in Rats." *European Neuropsychopharmacology: The Journal of the European College of Neuropharmacology* 9 (1999):377–383.

Best, J., and D. F. Luckenbill. *Organizing Deviance,* 2nd ed. Englewood Cliffs, NJ: Prentice-Hall, 1994.

Burns, D. B. "The Web of Caring: An Approach to Accountability in Alcohol Policy." In *Designing Alcohol and Other Drug Prevention Programs in Higher Education.* Newton, MA: Higher Education Center for Alcohol and Other Drug Prevention, 1997. Available http://www.edc.org/hec/pubs/theorybook/burns.html

Carlson, N. *Psychology: The Science of Behavior,* 3rd ed. Boston: Allyn and Bacon, 1990.

Center for Substance Abuse Research (CESAR). "Early Alcohol Users More Likely to Report Substance Use and Criminal Activity as Young Adults." September 2003. Available http://www.cesar.umd.edu

Center for Substance Abuse Research (CESAR). "Eighth Graders' Perceived Harmfulness of Ecstasy, LSD, and Inhalant Use Continues to Decrease; Suggests Vulnerability to Resurgence of Use." 23 April 2007. Available http://www.cesar.umd.edu

Center for Substance Abuse Research (CESAR). "Slightly More Than One-Fifth of Sexually Active High School Students Used Alcohol or Drugs Before Their Last Intercourse in 2009; Males More Likely than Females to Mix Drugs and Sex." *CESAR FAX* 19 (28 June 2010). Available http://www.cesar.umd.edu

Cheron, J. M. *Symbolic Interactionism: An Introduction, an Interpretation, an Integration,* 7th ed. Englewood Cliffs, NJ: Prentice-Hall, 2001.

Clatts, M., D. L. Welle, L. A. Goldsamt, and S. E. Lankenau. "An Ethno-Epidemiological Model for the Study of Trends in Illicit Drug Use." In *The American Drug Scene: An Anthology,* edited by J. A. Inciardi and K. McElrath, 225–249. New York: Oxford University Press, 2008.

Clinard, M. B., and R. F. Meier. *Sociology of Deviant Behavior,* 8th ed. Fort Worth, TX: Harcourt Brace Jovanovich, 1992.

Cohen, A. K. *Delinquent Boys: The Culture of the Gang.* Glencoe, IL: Free Press, 1955.

Conner, M. G. "Children During Divorce." *Crisis Counseling,* 29 January 2009. Available http://www.crisiscounseling.com/TraumaLoss/DivorceChildren.htm

Conrad, P., and J. W. Schneider. *Deviance and Medicalization.* St. Louis, MO: Mosby, 1980.

Conway, K. P., W. M. Compton, F. S. Stinson, and B. F. Grant. "Lifetime Comorbidity of DSM-IV Mood and Anxiety Disorders: Results from the National Epidemiological Survey on Alcohol and Related Conditions." *Journal of Clinical Psychiatry* 67 (2006):247–257.

Doweiko, H. E. *Concepts of Chemical Dependency,* 7th ed. Belmont, CA: Brooks/Cole Cengage Learning, 2009.

Ellickson, P. L., J. S. Tucker, and D. J. Klein. "Ten-Year Prospective Study of Public Health Problems Associated with Early Drinking." *Pediatrics* 111, 5 (2003):949–955.

Eysenck, H. J., and M. W. Eysenck. *Personality and Individual Differences: A Natural Science Approach.* New York: Plenum Press, 1985.

Farrar, H., and G. Kearns. "Cocaine: Clinical Pharmacology and Toxicology." *Journal of Pediatrics* 115 (1989):665–675.

Fischer, C. S. *The Urban Experience.* New York: Harcourt Brace Jovanovich, 1976.

Frosch, W. A. "An Analytic Overview of the Addictions." In *The Addictions: Multidisciplinary Perspectives and Treatments,* edited by H. Milman and H. Shaffer, pp. 160–173. Lexington, MA: Lexington Books/D.C. Heath, 1985.

Gardner, E. L. "Brain Reward Mechanisms." In *Substance Abuse: A Comprehensive Textbook,* 2nd ed., edited by J. H. Lowinson, P. Ruiz, R. B. Millman, and J. G. Langrod, 60–69. Baltimore: Williams & Wilkins, 1992.

Gergen, K. *The Saturated Self: Dilemmas of Identity in Contemporary Life.* New York: Basic Books, 2000.

Glick, R., and J. Moore, eds. *Drugs in Hispanic Communities.* New Brunswick, NJ: Rutgers University Press, 1990.

Goode, E. *Deviant Behavior,* 5th ed. Upper Saddle River, NJ: Prentice Hall, 1997.

Gray, J. A. *The Psychology of Fear and Stress,* 2nd ed. Cambridge, UK: Cambridge University Press, 1987.

Gray, P. *Psychology,* 3rd ed. New York: Worth, 1999.

Grinspoon, L. "Update on Cocaine." *Harvard Mental Health Letter* 10 (September 1993):1–4.

Heitzeg, N. A. *Deviance: Rulemakers and Rulebreakers.* Minneapolis, MN: West, 1996.

Hewitt, J. P. *Self and Society: A Symbolic Interactionist Social Psychology,* 6th ed. Boston: Allyn and Bacon, 1994.

Hirschi, T. *Causes of Delinquency,* 2nd ed. Los Angeles: University of California Press, 1971.

Inciardi, J. A., D. Lockwood, and A. E. Pottieger. *Women and Crack Cocaine.* New York: Macmillan, 1993.

Jellinek, E. M. *The Disease Concept of Alcoholism.* Highland Park, NJ: Hillhouse Press, 1960.

Johnston, L. D., P. M. O'Malley, J. G. Bachman, and J. E. Schulenberg. *Monitoring the Future: National Survey Results on Drug Use, 1975–2008, Volume I: Secondary School Students.* Bethesda, MD: National Institute on Drug Abuse, 2009.

Jones, J. *Hep-Cats, Narcs, and Pipe Dreams: A History of America's Romance with Illegal Drugs.* Baltimore, MD: Johns Hopkins University Press, 1996.

Kaspersky Lab. "Kaspersky Security Bulletin: Spam Evolution 2009." Available http://www.securelist.com/en/analysis/204792102/Kaspersky_Security_Bulletin_Spam_Evolution_2009

Kelly, K., and P. Ramundo. *You Mean I'm Not Lazy, Stupid, and Crazy?!* New York: Scribner, 2006.

Kessler, R. C., W. T. Chiu, O. Demler, and E. E. Walters. "Prevalence, Severity, and Comorbidity of Twelve-Month DSM-IV Disorders in the National Comorbidity Survey Replication (NCS-R)." *Archives of General Psychiatry* 62 (2005):617–627.

Khantzian, E. J. "Addiction as a Brain Disease." *American Journal of Psychiatry* 155 (June 1998):711–713.

Koob, G. "Drug Addiction." *Neurobiology of Disease* 7, 5 (October 2000):543–545.

Kuehn, B. M. "Integrated Care Key for Patients with Both Addiction and Mental Illness." *Journal of the American Medical Association* 303 (19 May 2010):1905–1907.

Landau, E. "Children's Quality of Life Declining, Says Report." CNN.com. 2010. Available http://www.cnn.com/2010/HEALTH/06/08/children.wellbeing/index.html

Lang, S. "Cornell Psychologist Finds Chemical Evidence for a Personality Trait and Happiness." *Cornell University Science News* (11 October 1996). Available http://www.news.cornell.edu/releases/Oct96/chem.personality.ssl.html

Lasser K., J. W. Boyd, S. Woolhandler, D. U. Himmelstein, D. McCormick, and D. H. Bor. "Smoking and Mental Illness: A Population-Based Prevalence Study." *Journal of the American Medical Association* 284 (2000):2606–2610.

L.A.W. Publications. *Let's All Work to Fight Drug Abuse.* Addison, TX: C&L Printing, 1985:38.

Lemert, E. M. *Social Psychology: A Systematic Approach to the Theory of Sociopathic Behavior.* New York: McGraw-Hill, 1951.

Lemonick, M. D., with A. Park. "The Science of Addiction." *Time* (14 July 2007):42–48.

Liddle, H. "AAMFT Consumer Update: Adolescent Substance Abuse." American Association for Marriage and Family Therapy (AAMFT). Available http://www.aamft.org/families/Consumer_Updates/AdolescentSubstanceAbuse.asp

Liska, A. E., and S. F. Messner. *Perspectives on Crime and Deviance.* Upper Saddle River, NJ: Prentice Hall, 1999.

MacPherson, K. "It Takes a Rat to Show How Drugs Alter Brains." *The Star Ledger,* 28 August 2010:1–2. Available http://www.nj.com/specialprojects/index.ssf?/specialprojects/addicts/addicts0826.html

Marshall, M. "Conclusions." In *Beliefs, Behavior, and Alcoholic Beverages: A Cross-Cultural Survey,* edited by M. Marshall, 451–457. Ann Arbor, MI: University of Michigan Press, 1979.

Mathias, R. "Novelty Seekers and Drug Abusers Tap Same Brain Reward System, Animal Studies Show." *NIDA Notes* 10, 4 (July/August1995):1–5.

Mental Health America (MHA). "Factsheet: Co-dependency." 2010. Available http://www.nmha.org/go/codependency

Miller, N. S. *Addiction Psychiatry: Current Diagnosis and Treatment.* New York: Wiley, 1995.

Moore, J. *Homeboys: Gangs, Drugs and Prison in the Barrios of Los Angeles.* Philadelphia: Temple University Press, 1978.

Moore, J. "Gangs, Drugs, and Violence." In *Gangs: The Origins and Impact of Contemporary Youth Gangs in the United States,* edited by S. Cummings and D. J. Monti, 27–46. Albany: State University of New York Press, 1993.

Moore, J. "Psychological Theory of Drug Abuse." *Yahoo Health.* (22 October 2008):1–2. Available http://www.associatedcontent.com/article/1117664/psychological_theory_of_drug_abuse.html?cat=5

Myers, P. L. "Sources and Configurations of Institutional Denial." *Employee Assistance Quarterly* 5(B) (1990):43–54.

National Institute on Drug Abuse (NIDA). *Theories on Drug Abuse: Selected Contemporary Perspectives.* NIDA Research Monograph Series. U.S. Department of Health and Human Services. Rockville, MD: U.S. Government Printing Office, 1980.

National Institute on Drug Abuse (NIDA). "Study Finds Higher Use Among Adolescents Whose Parents Divorce." *NIDA Notes* 5 (Summer 1990):10.

National Institute on Drug Abuse (NIDA). "Double Trouble: Substance Abuse and Psychiatric Disorders." *NIDA Notes* 8 (November/December 1993):20.

National Institute on Drug Abuse (NIDA). "Attention and Memory Impaired in Heavy Users of Marijuana." Rockville, MD: Office of the National Institute on Drug Abuse, 20 February 1996a.

National Institute on Drug Abuse (NIDA). *Principles of Drug Addiction Treatment.* New York: The Lindesmith Center, 1996b.

National Institute on Drug Abuse (NIDA). *Principles of Drug Addiction Treatment.* National Institutes of Health Publication No. 99-4180, October 1999.

National Institute on Drug Abuse (NIDA). "Addiction and Co-Occurring Mental Disorders." *NIDA Notes* 21 (February 2007):3.

National Institute on Drug Abuse (NIDA). *Comorbidity: Addiction and Other Mental Illnesses.* Research Report Series. Bethesda, MD: U.S. Department of Health and Human Services, 2008a.

National Institute on Drug Abuse (NIDA). *Drugs, Brains, and Behavior: The Science of Addiction.* Bethesda, MD: National Institutes of Health, U.S. Department of Health and Human Services, 2008b.

National Institute on Drug Abuse (NIDA). "Comorbidity: Addiction and Other Mental Disorders." *NIDA InfoFacts.* Bethesda, MD: U.S. Department of Health and Human Services, 2009:1–2.

National Survey on Drug Use and Health (NSDUH) Report. *Marijuana Use and Delinquent Behaviors among Youths.* Research Triangle Park, NC: Office of Applied Studies, Substance Abuse and Mental Health Services Administration, 16 May 2008:1–5.

Needle, R. H., S. S. Su, and W. J. Doherty. "Divorce, Remarriage, and Adolescent Substance Use: A Prospective Longitudinal Study." *Journal of Marriage and the Family* 52 (1990):157–159.

O'Brien, R., S. Cohen, G. Evans, and J. Fine. *The Encyclopedia of Drug Abuse,* 2nd ed. New York: Facts on File, 1992.

Office of National Drug Control Policy (ONDCP). *Drug Facts: Cocaine.* Rockville, MD: White House Drug Policy Clearing House, November 2003.

Plummer, K. "Misunderstanding Labelling Perspectives." In *Deviant Interpretations,* edited by D. Downes and P. Rock, 85–121. London: Robertson, 1979.

Pontell, H. N. *Social Deviance,* 2nd ed. Upper Saddle River, NJ: Prentice Hall, 1996.

Radowitz, J. V. "Smoking and Drug Abuse Traits Linked to Genes." *The Independent,* 18 June 2003, Independent Digital (UK) Ltd.

Reckless, W. C. "A New Theory of Delinquency." *Federal Probation* 25 (1961):42–46.

Ritzer, G. *Enchanting a Disenchanted World: Revolutionizing the Means of Consumption.* Thousand Oaks, CA: Pine Forge Press, 1999.

Ritzer, G. *The McDonaldization of Society,* 6th ed. Thousand Oaks, CA: Pine Forge Press, 2011.

Ritzer, G., and D. Goodman. *Sociological Theory,* 8th ed. New York: McGraw Hill Higher Education, 2010.

Rousar, E., K. Brooner, M. W. Regier, and G. E. Bigelow. "Psychiatric Distress in Antisocial Drug Abusers: Relation to Other Personality Disorders." *Drug and Alcohol Dependence* 34 (1995):149–154.

Rudgley, R. *Essential Substances: A Cultural History of Intoxicants in Society.* New York: Kodansha International, 1993.

Sanders, W. B. *Gangbangs and Drive-bys: Grounded Culture and Juvenile Gang Violence.* New York: Aldine De Gruyter, 1994.

Schaffer Library of Drug Policy. *Technologies for Understanding and Preventing Substance Abuse and Addition. Chapter 3: Biology and Pharmacology.* 18 October 1994. Available http://www.druglibrary.org/schaffer/library/studies/ota/ch3.htm

Schur, E. M. *Labeling Deviant Behavior.* New York: Harper & Row, 1971.

Shelden, R. G., S. K. Tracy, and W. B. Brown. *Youth Gangs in American Society,* 2nd ed. Belmont, CA: Wadsworth/Thomson Learning, 2001.

Siegel, L. J., and J. J. Senna. *Juvenile Delinquency: Theory, Practice and Law.* St. Paul, MN: West, 1994.

Smith, D., E. Milkman, and S. Sunderwirth. "Addictive Disease: Concept and Controversy." In *Addictions: Multidisciplinary Perspectives and Treatments,* pp. 145–159, edited by H. Milkman and H. J. Shaffer. Lexington, MA: Lexington Books/D.C. Heath, 1985.

Spanagel, R., and F. Weiss. "The Dopamine Hypothesis of Reward: Past and Current Status." *Trends in Neuroscience* 22 (1999):521–527.

Substance Abuse and Mental Health Services Administration (SAMHSA). *Study Shows Strong Relationship Between Adolescent Behavior Problems and Alcohol Use.* Press Release. Rockville, MD: U.S. Department of Health and Human Services, 1 March 2000.

Substance Abuse and Mental Health Services Administration (SAMHSA). *National Survey on Drug Use and Health (NSDUH) Report. Substance Use Disorder and Serious Psychological Distress by Employment Status.* Rockville, MD: Substance Abuse and Mental Health Services Administration, Office of Applied Studies, 2008.

Substance Abuse and Mental Health Services Administration (SAMHSA), Office of Applied Studies (OAS). *Results from the 2008 National Survey on Drug Use and Health: National Findings.* Rockville, MD: Office of Applied Studies, 2009.

Sutherland, E. *Principles of Criminology,* 4th ed. Philadelphia: Lippincott, 1947.

Syvertsen, J. L. "Some Considerations on the Disease Concept of Addiction." In *The American Drug Scene: An Anthology,* edited by J. Inciardi and K. McElrath, 16–26. New York: Oxford University Press, 2008.

Tarter, R. E., A. Alterman, and K. L. Edwards. "Alcoholic Denial: A Biopsychosociological Interpretation." *Journal of Studies on Alcohol* 45 (1983):214–218.

The Capitol Times. "Seven in 10 Drug Users Work Full-Time." 1999. Available http://www.mapinc.org/drugnews/v99/n983/a01.html

Thio, A. *Deviant Behavior,* 10th ed. Boston, MA: Allyn and Bacon, 2010.

Thomas, W. I., with D. S. Thomas. *The Child in America.* New York: Knopf, 1923.

Thornberry, T. P. "Risk Factors for Gang Membership." In *The Modern Gang Reader,* 2nd ed., edited by J. Miller, C. L. Maxson, and M. W. Klein, 32–42. Los Angeles: Roxbury, 2001.

Uhl, G., K. Blum, E. Noble, and S. Smith. "Substance Abuse Vulnerability and D-2 Receptor Genes." *Trends in Neurological Sciences* 16 (1993):83–88.

Uhl, G., A. Persico, and S. Smith. "Current Excitement with D-2 Dopamine Receptor Gene Alleles in Substance Abuse." *Archives of General Psychiatry* 49 (February 1992): 157–160.

U.S. Department of Labor. "Quick Stats on Women Workers, 2009." Washington, DC, 2010. Available http://www.dol.gov/wb/stats/main.htm

USA Today. "Report: Marijuana Potency Rises." 2008. Available http://www.usatoday.com/news/health/2008-06-12-marijuana_N.htm

Volkow, N. *Cocaine and the Changing Brain: Changes in Human Brain Systems After Longterm Cocaine Use* (1 February 1999). Available http://www.drugabuse.gov/meetsum/ccb/volkow.html

Waldorf, D. "Natural Recovery from Opiate Addiction: Some Social Psychological Processes of Untreated Recovery." *Journal of Drug Issues* 13 (1983):237–280.

Weiss, F. "Cocaine and the Changing Brain: Cocaine Dependence and Withdrawal—Neuroadaptive Changes in Brain Reward and Stress Systems." 1999. Available http://archives.drugabuse.gov/meetings/ccb/weiss.html

Werner, E., and S. Henry. *Criminological Theory: An Analysis of Its Underlying Assumptions.* Fort Worth, TX: Harcourt Brace College, 1995.

Williams III, F. P., and M. D. McShane. *Criminological Theory,* 3rd ed. Upper Saddle River, NJ: Prentice Hall, 1999.

Witmer, D. "Warning Signs of Teenage Drug Abuse." About.com, 2010. Available http://parentingteens.about.com/cs/drugsofabuse/a/driug_abuse20.htm

Wooden, W. S. *Renegade Kids, Suburban Outlaws: From Youth Culture to Delinquency.* Belmont, CA: Wadsworth/Thomson Learning, 1995.

World Health Organization Expert Committee on Addiction-Producing Drugs. *World Health Organization Technical Report* 273 (1964):9–10.

Wyman, J. "Promising Advances Toward Understanding the Genetic Roots of Addiction." *NIDA Notes* 12 (July/August 1997):1–5.

Yinger, M. J. *Countercultures: The Promise and the Peril of a World Turned Upside Down.* New York: Free Press, 1982.

Zuckerman, M. "Are You a Risk Taker? What Causes People to Take Risks? It's Not Just a Behavior. It's a Personality." *Psychology Today* (1 November 2000). Available http://www.psychologytoday.com/articles/200011/are-you-risk-taker

CHAPTER 3

Drug Use, Regulation, and the Law

Learning ◎bjectives

On completing this chapter you will be able to:

◎ Identify the major criteria that determine how society regulates drugs.

◎ Explain the significance of the Pure Food and Drug Act of 1906 and why it was important in regulating drugs of abuse.

◎ Describe the changes in drug regulation that occurred because of the Kefauver-Harris Amendment of 1962.

◎ Identify and explain the stages of testing for an investigational new drug.

◎ Discuss the special provisions (exceptions) made by the Food and Drug Administration (FDA) for drug marketing.

◎ Outline the procedures used by the FDA to regulate nonprescription drugs.

◎ Outline the major approaches used to reduce substance abuse.

◎ Explain the main arguments for and against legalizing drugs.

◎ List the most common types of drug testing.

◎ Describe four major factors required for workable drug policies (pragmatic drug policies).

Did You Know?

○ Some patent medicines sold at the turn of the twentieth century contained opium and cocaine and were highly addictive.

○ Before World War II, all drugs, except those classified as narcotics, were available without prescription.

○ Enforcement of drug use policies and drug laws differs across different countries.

○ In 2009, an estimated 21.8 million Americans age 12 or older were current (past-month) illicit drug users.

○ The United States spends approximately $3.83 billion per year on drug interdiction.

 Drugs and Society Online is a great source for additional drugs and society information for both students and instructors. Visit **go.jblearning.com/hanson11** to find a variety of useful tools for learning, thinking, and teaching.

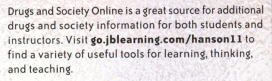

Introduction

Society mandates that it maintain control over which drugs are permissible and which drugs are prohibited. Through legislation, we decide which drugs are licit and illicit. We decide which licit drugs are readily available "over-the-counter" (OTC) and which can be obtained by prescription only. Thus, drug laws prohibit indiscriminate use of what society defines as a drug. As we saw in Chapter 1, licit and illicit drugs can produce vastly different effects on both mental and bodily functions. Chapters 4 and 5 focus on how and why different types of drugs affect our bodies. In this chapter, you will come to better understand how society attempts to control drug use and abuse. In particular, this chapter examines the development of drug regulations in the United States that apply to both the manufacture of drugs and the control of their use. Although many think that the regulation of drug manufacturing and drug abuse lie at the opposite ends of the spectrum, regulation of drug manufacturing and abuse of drugs actually evolved from the same process.

Cultural Attitudes About Drug Use

Currently, cultural attitudes in the United States regarding the use of drugs blend beliefs in individuals' rights to live their lives as they desire with society's obligation to protect its members from the burdens imposed by uncontrolled behavior. The history of drug regulation consists of regulatory swings in response to attempts by government to balance these two factors while responding to public pressures and perceived public needs. For example, 100 years ago most people expected the government to protect citizens' rights to produce and market new foods and substances; they did not expect or desire the government to regulate product quality or claims. Instead, the public relied on private morals and common sense to obtain quality and protection in an era of simple technology. Unfortunately, U.S. society had to learn by tragic experience that its trust was not well placed; many unscrupulous entrepreneurs were willing to risk the safety and welfare of the public in an effort to maximize profits and acquire wealth. In fact, many medicines of these earlier times were not merely ineffective but often dangerous.

Because of the advent of high technology and the rapid advancements society has made, we now rely on highly trained experts and government "watchdog" agencies for consumer information and protection. Out of this changing environment have evolved two major guidelines for controlling drug development and marketing:

1. Society has the right to protect itself from the damaging effects of drug use. This concept not only is closely aligned with the emotional and highly visible issues of drug abuse, but also includes protection from other drug side effects. Thus, although we expect the government to protect society from drugs that can cause addiction, we also expect it to protect us from drugs that cause cancer, cardiovascular disease, or other threatening medical conditions.
2. Society has the right to demand that drugs approved for marketing be safe and effective to the general public. If drug manufacturers promise that their products will relieve pain, those drugs should be analgesics; if they promise that their products will relieve depression, those drugs should be antidepressants; if they promise that their products will relieve stuffy noses, those drugs should be decongestants.

The public, through the activities of regulatory agencies and statutory enactments, has attempted to require that drug manufacturers produce safe and effective pharmaceutical products. Closely linked to these efforts is the fact that society uses similar strategies to protect itself from the problems associated with the specific drug side effect of dependence or addiction, which is associated with drug abuse.

The Road to Regulation and the FDA

In the late 1800s and early 1900s, sales of uncontrolled medicines flourished and became widespread. Many of these products were called patent medicines, which signified that the ingredients were secret, not that they were patented. The decline of patent medicines began with the 1906 Pure Food and Drug Act, which required manufacturers to indicate the amounts of alcohol, morphine, opium, cocaine, heroin, and marijuana extract on the label of each product. It became obvious at this time that many medicinal products on the market labeled "nonaddictive" were, in fact, potent drugs "in sheep's labeling" and could cause severe dependence. However, most government interest at the time centered on regulation of the food industry, not drugs.

Even though federal drug regulation was based on the free-market philosophy that consumers could make choices for themselves, it was decided that the public should have information about possible dependence-producing drugs to ensure that they understood the risks associated with using these products. The Pure Food and Drug Act made misrepresentation illegal, so that a potentially addicting patent drug could not be advertised as "non–habit forming." This step marked the beginning of new involvement by governmental agencies in drug manufacturing.

Shortcomings in the Pure Food and Drug Act quickly became obvious. For example, the law did not allow the government to stop the distribution of dangerous preparations designed to reduce weight. One such product contained dinitrophenol, a compound that purportedly increased metabolic rate and was responsible for many deaths (FDA 2010c).

The Pure Food and Drug Act was modified, albeit not in a consumer-protective manner, by the Sherley Amendment in 1912. The distributor of a cancer "remedy" was indicted for falsely claiming on the label that the contents were effective. The case was decided in the U.S. Supreme Court in 1911. Justice Holmes, writing for the majority opinion, said that, based on the 1906 act, the company had not violated any law because legally all it was required to do was accurately state the contents and their strength and quality. The accuracy of the therapeutic claims made by drug manufacturers was not controlled. Congress took the hint and passed the Sherley Amendment to add to the existing law the requirement that labels should not contain "any statement . . . regarding the curative or therapeutic effect . . . which is false and fraudulent." However, the law required that the government prove fraud, which turned out to be difficult (and is still problematic). This amendment did not improve drug products but merely encouraged pharmaceutical companies to be more vague in their advertisements (Temin 1980).

Prescription Versus OTC Drugs

The distinction between prescription and OTC drugs is relatively new to the pharmaceutical industry. All non-narcotic drugs were available OTC before World War II. It was not until a drug company unwittingly produced a toxic product that killed 107 people that the FDA was given control over drug safety in the 1938 Federal Food, Drug,

and Cosmetic Act (Hunter, Rosen, and DeChristoforo 1993). The bill had been debated for several years in Congress and showed no promise of passage. Then, a pharmaceutical company decided to sell a liquid form of a sulfa drug (one of the first antibiotics) and found that the drug would dissolve well in a chemical solvent, diethylene glycol (presently used in antifreeze products). The company marketed the antibiotic as Elixir Sulfanilamide without testing the solvent for toxicity. Under the 1906 Pure Food and Drug Act, the company could not be prosecuted for the toxicity of this form of drug or for not testing the formulation of the drug on animals first. It could only be prosecuted for mislabeling the product on the technicality that elixir refers to a solution in alcohol, not a solution in diethylene glycol. Again, it was apparent that the laws in place provided woefully inadequate protection for the public.

The 1938 act differed from the 1906 law in several ways. It defined *drugs* to include products that affected bodily structure or function even in the absence of disease. Companies had to file applications with the government for all new drugs showing that they were safe (not effective—just safe) for use as described. The drug label had to list all ingredients and include the quantity of each, as well as provide instructions regarding correct use of the drug and warnings about its dangers. In addition, the act eliminated a Sherley Amendment requirement to prove intent to defraud in drug misbranding cases (FDA 2010d).

Before passage of the 1938 act, you could go to a doctor and obtain a prescription for any non-narcotic drug or go to the pharmacy directly if you had already decided what was needed. The labeling requirement in the 1938 act allowed drug companies to create a class of drugs that could not be sold legally without a prescription. It has been suggested that the actions by the FDA were motivated by the frequent public misuse of two classes of drugs developed before passage of the 1938 law: sulfa antibiotics and barbiturates. People often took too little of the antibiotics to cure an infection and too much of the barbiturates and became addicted.

The 1938 Food, Drug, and Cosmetic Act allowed the manufacturer to determine whether a drug was to be labeled prescription or nonprescription. The same product could be sold as prescription by one company and as OTC by another. After the Durham-Humphrey Amendment was passed in 1951, almost all new drugs were placed in the prescription-only class. The drugs that were patented and marketed after World War II included potent new antibiotics and phenothiazine tranquilizers such as Thorazine. Both the FDA and the drug firms thought these products were potentially too dangerous to sell OTC. The Durham-Humphrey Amendment established the criteria, which are still used today, for determining whether a drug should be classified as prescription or nonprescription. Basically, if a drug does not fall into one of the following three categories, it is considered nonprescription:

1. The drug is habit-forming.
2. The drug is not safe for self-medication because of its toxicity.
3. The drug is a new compound that has not been shown to be completely safe.

In 1959, Senator Estes Kefauver initiated hearings concerned with the enormous profit margins earned by drug companies due to the lack of competition in the market for new, patented drugs. Testimony by physicians revealed that an average doctor in clinical practice often was not able to evaluate accurately the efficacy of the drugs he or she prescribed. The 1938 law did not give the FDA authority to supervise clinical testing of drugs; consequently, the effectiveness of drugs being sold to the public was not being determined. Both the Kefauver and Harris Amendments put forth in Congress were intended to deal with this problem but showed no likely signs of becoming law until the thalidomide tragedy occurred.

During the Kefauver hearings, the FDA received an approval request for Kevadon, a brand of thalidomide that the William Merrell Company hoped to market in the United States. **Thalidomide** had been used in Europe as a sedative for pregnant women. Despite ongoing pressure, medical officer Frances Kelsey refused to allow the request to be approved (FDA 2010e) because of insufficient safety data. By 1962, the horrifying effects of thalidomide on developing fetuses became known. There are two approximately 24-hour intervals early in pregnancy when thalidomide can alter the development of the arms and legs of an embryo. If a woman takes thalidomide on one or both of these days, the infant could be born with abnormally developed arms and/or legs (called **phocomelia**, from the Greek words for flippers, or "seal-shaped limbs"). Even though Kevadon was never approved for marketing in this country, Merrell had distributed more than 2 million tablets in the United States for investigational use—use that the law and regulations left mostly unchecked. Once thalidomide's deleterious effects became known, the FDA moved quickly to recover the supply from physicians, pharmacists, and patients. For her efforts, Kelsey received the President's Distinguished Federal Civilian Service Award in 1962, the highest civilian honor available to government employees (FDA 2010e).

Although standard testing probably would not have detected the congenital effect of thalidomide and the tragedy would likely have occurred anyway, these debilitated infants stimulated passage of the 1962 Kefauver and Harris Amendments. They strengthened the government's regulation of both the introduction of new drugs and the production and sale of existing drugs. The amendments required, for the first time, that drug manufacturers demonstrate the efficacy as well as the safety of their drug products. The FDA was empowered to retract approval of a drug that was already being marketed. In addition, the agency was permitted to regulate and evaluate drug testing by pharmaceutical companies and mandate standards of good drug-manufacturing policy.

Characteristic limb deformities caused by thalidomide.

KEY TERMS

thalidomide
a sedative drug that, when used during pregnancy, can cause severe developmental damage to a fetus

phocomelia
a birth defect; impaired development of the arms, legs, or both

The Rising Demand for Effectiveness in Medicinal Drugs

To evaluate the effectiveness of the more than 4000 drug products that were introduced between 1938 and 1962, the FDA contracted with the National Research Council to perform the Drug Efficacy Study. This investigation started in 1966 and ran for 3 years. The council was asked to rate drugs as either effective or ineffective. Although the study was supposed to be based on scientific evidence, this information often was not available, which meant that conclusions sometimes relied on the clinical experience of the physicians on each panel; these judgments were not always based on reliable information.

A legal challenge resulted when the FDA took an "ineffective" drug off the market and the manufacturer sued. This action finally forced the FDA to define what constituted an adequate and well-controlled investigation. Adequate, documented clinical experience was no longer satisfactory proof that a drug was safe and effective. Each new drug application now had to include information about the drug's performance in patients compared with the experiences of a carefully defined control group. The drug could be compared with (1) a placebo, (2) another drug known to be active based on previous studies, (3) the established results of no treatment, or (4) historical data about the course of the illness without the use of the drug in question. In addition, a drug marketed before 1962 could no longer be grandfathered in. If the company could not prove the drug had the qualifications to pass the post-1962 tests for a new drug, it was considered a new, unapproved drug and could not legally be sold.

Regulating the Development of New Drugs

The amended Federal Food, Drug, and Cosmetic Act in force today requires that all new drugs be registered with and approved by the FDA. The FDA is mandated by Congress to (1) ensure the rights and safety of human subjects during clinical testing of experimental drugs, (2) evaluate the safety and efficacy of new treatments based on test results and information from the sponsors (often health-related companies), and (3) compare potential benefits and risks to determine whether a new drug should be approved and marketed. Because of FDA regulations, all pharmaceutical companies must follow a series of steps when seeking permission to market a new drug (see **Figure 3.1**).

Regulatory Steps for New Prescription Drugs

Step 1: Preclinical Research and Development

A chemical must be identified as having potential value in the treatment of a particular condition or disease. The company interested in marketing the chemical as a drug must run a series of tests on at least two or more animal species. Careful records must be kept of side effects, absorption, distribution,

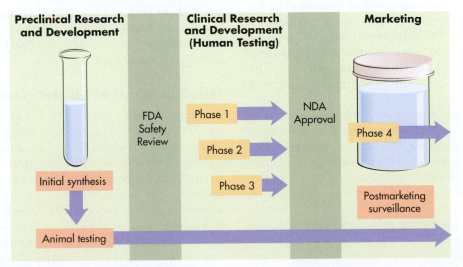

FIGURE 3.1

Steps required by the FDA for reviewing a new drug.

metabolism, excretion, and the dosages of the drug necessary to produce the various effects. Carcinogenic, mutagenic, and teratogenic variables are tested. The dose–response curve must be determined along with potency, and then the risk and benefit of the substance must be calculated (see Chapter 5). If the company still believes there is a market for the substance, it forwards the data to the FDA to obtain an investigational new drug (IND) number for further tests.

Step 2: Clinical Research and Development

Animal tests provide some information, but ultimately tests must be done on the species for which the potential drug is intended—that is, humans. These tests usually follow three phases.

Phase 1 is called *the initial clinical stage*. Small numbers of volunteers (usually 20–100), typically healthy people but sometimes patients, are recruited to establish drug safety and dosage ranges for effective treatment and to examine side effects. Formerly, much of this research was done on prison inmates, but because of bad publicity and the possibility of coercion, fewer prisoners are used today. Medical students, paid college student volunteers, and volunteers being treated at free clinics are more often used after obtaining informed consent. The data from Phase 1 clinical trials are collected, analyzed, and sent to the FDA for approval before beginning the next phase of human subject testing.

Phase 2 testing is called the *clinical pharmacological evaluation stage*. The effects of the drug are tested to eliminate investigator bias and to determine side effects and the effectiveness of the treatment. Because the safety of the new drug has not been thoroughly established, a few patients (perhaps 100–300 volunteers) with the medical problem the drug is intended to treat participate in these studies. Statistical evaluation of this information is carried out before proceeding with Phase 3 testing.

Phase 3 is the *extended clinical evaluation stage*. By this time, the pharmaceutical company has a good idea of both drug effectiveness and dangers. The drug can be offered safely to a wider group of participating clinics and physicians, who cooperate in the administration of the potential drug—when medically appropriate—to thousands of volunteer patients who have given informed consent.

This stage makes the drug available on a wide experimental basis. Sometimes, by this point, there has been publicity about the new drug, and people with the particular disease for which the drug was developed may actively seek out physicians licensed to experiment with it.

During Phase 3 testing, safety checks are made and any side effects that might show up as more people are exposed to the drug are noted. After the testing program concludes, careful analysis is made of the effectiveness, side effects, and recommended dosage. If there are sufficient data to demonstrate that the drug is safe and effective, the company submits a new drug application (NDA) as a formal request that the FDA consider approving the drug for marketing. The application usually comprises many thousands of pages of data and analysis, and the FDA must sift through it and decide whether the risks of using the drug justify its potential benefits. The FDA usually calls for additional tests before the drug is determined to be safe and effective and before granting permission to market it.

Step 3: Permission to Market

At this point, the FDA can allow the drug to be marketed under its patented name. In 2001, the average cost of developing a new drug was over $1 billion (Adams and Brantner 2010). The situation is similar elsewhere, although in some countries the clinical evaluations are less stringent and require less time.

Once the drug is marketed, it continues to be closely scrutinized for adverse effects. This postmarketing surveillance is often referred to as Phase 4 and is important because, in some cases, negative effects may not show up for a long time. For example, it was determined in 1970 that diethylstilbestrol (DES), when given to pregnant women to prevent miscarriage, causes an increased risk of a rare type of vaginal cancer in their daughters when these children enter their teens and young adult years. The FDA subsequently removed from the market the form of DES that had been used to treat pregnant women.

Exceptions: Special Drug-Marketing Laws

There is continual concern that the process used by the FDA to evaluate prospective drugs is laborious and excessively lengthy. Hence, an amendment was passed to accelerate the evaluation of urgently needed drugs. The so-called fast-track rule has been applied to the testing of certain drugs used for the treatment of rare cancers, AIDS, and some other diseases. As a result, these drugs have reached the market after a much-reduced testing program. For example, the FDA reviewed Gleevac, a treatment for chronic myeloid leukemia, in 4 months. Pegasys, a combination product for the treatment of hepatitis C, was approved in 3.5 months (FDA 2010b).

A second amendment, the Orphan Drug Law, allows drug companies to receive tax advantages if they develop drugs that are not very profitable because they are useful in treating only small numbers of patients, such as those who suffer from rare diseases. A rare disease is defined as one that affects fewer than 200,000 people in the United States or one for which the cost of development is not likely to be recovered by marketing.

The federal government and the FDA are continually refining the system for evaluating new drugs to ensure that new effective therapeutic substances can be made available for clinical use as soon as it is safely possible. Some of these modifications reflect the fact that patients with life-threatening diseases are willing to accept greater drug risks to gain faster access to potentially useful medications. Attempts to accelerate the drug review are exemplified by the Prescription Drug User Fee Act of 1992. This law required drug manufacturers to pay fees to the FDA for the evaluation of NDAs. Congress required the FDA to use these fees to hire more reviewers so as to expedite the reviews.

The Regulation of Nonprescription Drugs

The Durham-Humphrey Amendment to the Food, Drug, and Cosmetic Act made a distinction between prescription and nonprescription (OTC) drugs and required the FDA to regulate OTC drug marketing. In 1972, the FDA initiated a program to evaluate the effectiveness and safety of the nonprescription drugs on the market and to ensure that they included appropriate labeling (for more details, see Chapter 15). A panel of drug experts including physicians, pharmacologists, and pharmacists reviewed each so-called active ingredient in the OTC medications. Based on the recommendations of these panels, the ingredients were placed in one of the following three categories:

I. Generally recognized as safe and effective for the claimed therapeutic indication
II. Not generally recognized as safe and effective or unacceptable indications
III. Insufficient data available to permit final classification

By 1981, the panels had made initial determinations about over 700 ingredients in more than 300,000 OTC drug products and submitted more than 60 reports to the FDA.

In the second phase of the OTC drug review, the FDA evaluated the panels' findings and submitted a tentative adoption of the panels' recommendations (after revision, if necessary), following public comment and scrutiny. After some time and careful consideration of new information, the agency issued a final ruling and classification of the ingredients under consideration.

Here and Now

Secure and Responsible Drug Disposal Act

In October 2010, President Barack Obama signed into law the Secure and Responsible Drug Disposal Act. The act addresses the problem that patients were not allowed to return drugs to a Drug Enforcement Agency registrant because this type of return would be outside the "closed chain of distribution" that was a consequence of the Controlled Substances Act. As a result of this restriction, persons seeking to reduce the amount of expired or unwanted prescription drugs in their homes previously had few disposal options.

Up to 17% of prescribed medication is never used. If improperly disposed, these medications can contribute to drug diversion, accidental poisonings, and potentially environmental problems. The bill allows consumers to give controlled substances to specially designated individuals, such as law enforcement officials, for disposal. It also allows long-term care facilities to dispose of certain prescription drugs on behalf of their residents.

Sources: Gilbert, J. A., and W. T. Koustas. "Secure and Responsible Drug Disposal Act Passes Congress." 3 October 2010. Available at: http://www.fdalawblog.net/fda_law_blog_hyman_phelps/2010/10/secure-and-responsible-drug-disposal-act-passes-congress.html. Accessed March 4, 2011; Utah.gov. "Proper Medication Disposal." 2010. Available at: http://www.medicationdisposal.utah.gov. Accessed March 4, 2011; and Govtrack.us. "S. 3397: Secure and Responsible Drug Disposal Act of 2010." 2010. Available at: http://www.govtrack.us/congress/bill.xpd?bill=s111-3397. Accessed March 4, 2011.

■ The Effects of the OTC Review on Today's Medications

The review process for OTC ingredients has had a significant impact on the public's attitude about OTC products and their use (both good and bad) in self-medication. It was apparent from the review process that many OTC drug ingredients did not satisfy the requirements for safety and effectiveness. Consequently, it is almost certain that, in the future, there will be fewer active ingredients in OTC medicines, but these drugs will be safer and more effective than ever before.

In addition, with heightened public awareness, greater demand has been brought to bear on the FDA to make better drugs available to the public for self-medication. In response to these pressures, the FDA has adopted a **switching policy**, which allows the agency to review prescription drugs and evaluate their suitability as OTC products. The following criteria must be satisfied if a drug is to be switched to OTC status:

- The drug must have been marketed by prescription for at least 3 years.
- Use of the drug must have been relatively high during the time it was available as a prescription drug.
- Adverse drug reactions must not be alarming, and the frequency of side effects must not have increased during the time the drug was available to the public.

In general, this switching policy has been well received by the public. The medical community and the FDA are generally positive about OTC switches as well. There are some concerns, however, that the wider access to more effective drug products will lead to increased abuse or misuse of OTC products. Hence, emphasis is placed on adequate labeling and education to ensure that consumers have sufficient information to use OTC products safely and effectively.

The Regulation of Drug Advertising

Much of the public's knowledge and impressions about drugs come from advertisements. It is difficult to ascertain the amount of money currently spent by the pharmaceutical industry to promote its products. One study estimated that total spending on promotion increased from $11.4 billion in 1996 to $29.9 billion in 2005. The same study reported that the percentage of sales spent on promotion grew from 14.2% to 18.2% during that same period (Donahue, Cevasco, and Rosenthal 2007).

There is no doubt that these promotional efforts by pharmaceutical manufacturers have a tremendous impact on the drug-purchasing habits of the general public and health professionals.

The economics of prescription drugs are unique because a second party, the health professional, dictates what the consumer, the patient, will purchase. As a general rule, the FDA oversees most issues related to advertising of prescription drugs. In contrast, the Federal Trade Commission (FTC) regulates OTC advertising (FDA 2010a).

According to the FDA (2009b), physicians indicate that, for the most part, the advertisements for prescription drugs on television and radio have had both positive and negative effects on their patients and practices. The FDA has conducted surveys directed toward physicians to better understand how direct-to-consumer (DTC) prescription drug promotion affects the patient–doctor relationship, with the intent of informing the agency if advertising rules need to be changed in order to ensure better consumer understanding of the risks and benefits of prescription drugs. Highlights of the surveys include:

- Most physicians surveyed agreed that because their patient saw a DTC advertisement, he or she asked thoughtful questions during the visit. Approximately the same percentage of physicians thought the advertisements made their patients more aware of possible treatments.
- The physicians surveyed indicated that the advertisements did not convey information about risks and benefits equally well. In fact, 78% of physicians responded that their patients understand the possible benefits of the drug very well or somewhat, compared to 40% of physicians who indicated that their patients understand the possible risks.
- Approximately 75% of physicians surveyed indicated that DTC ads cause patients to think that the drug works better than it does, and many physicians felt some pressure to prescribe something when patients mentioned DTC ads.
- The physicians surveyed reported that patients understand that they need to consult a health-care provider concerning appropriate treatments. Eighty-two percent responded either

KEY TERMS

switching policy
an FDA policy allowing the change of suitable prescription drugs to over-the-counter status

"very well" or "somewhat" when asked if they believe that their patients understand that only a physician can decide if a drug is appropriate for them.

A significant amount of prescription drug promotion is directed at health professionals. The approaches employed by manufacturers to encourage health professionals to prescribe their products include advertising in prestigious medical journals, direct mail advertising, and some radio and television advertising. Government advertising regulations control all printed and audio materials distributed by drug salespeople. Perhaps the most effective sales approach is for drug representatives to personally visit health professionals; this tactic is harder to regulate.

Many health professionals rely on drug company salespeople for the so-called latest scientific information concerning drugs and their effects. Although these representatives of the drug industry can provide an important informational service, it is essential that health professionals remember that these people make a living by selling these products, and often their information may be biased accordingly.

Many people in and out of the medical community have questioned the ethics of drug advertising and marketing in the United States and are concerned about the negative impact that deceptive promotion has on target populations. One of the biggest problems in dealing with misleading or false advertising is defining such deception. Probably the best guideline for such a definition is summarized in the Wheeler-Lea Amendment to the FTC Act:

> The term *false advertisement* means an advertisement, other than labeling, which is misleading in a material respect; and in determining whether any advertisement is misleading, there shall be taken into account not only representations . . . but the extent to which the advertisement fails to reveal facts.

Tough questions are being asked as to how much control should be exerted over the pharmaceutical industry to protect the public without excessively infringing on the rights of these companies to promote their goods. The solutions to these problems will not be simple. Nevertheless, efforts to keep drug advertisements accurate, in good taste, and informative are worthwhile and are necessary if the public is expected to make rational decisions about drug use (see "Here and Now: What's in an Ad?").

■ Federal Regulation and Quality Assurance

No matter what policy is adopted by the FDA and other drug-regulating agencies, there will always be those who criticize their efforts and complain that they do not do enough or that they do too much. On the one hand, the FDA has been blamed for being excessively careful and requiring too much testing before new drugs are approved for marketing. On the other hand, when new drugs are

Here and Now

What's in an Ad?

The Federal Food, Drug, and Cosmetic Act requires that all drug advertisements contain brief summary relating to side effects, contraindications, and effectiveness. The current regulations specify that this information disclosure must include all the risk information in a product's approved labeling. Typically, print advertisements include a reprinting of the risk-related sections of the approved labeling, although sponsors can write this risk information in language appropriate for the targeted audience.

In addition to the specific disclosure requirements, advertisements cannot be misleading or false or omit material facts. They also must present a fair balance between effectiveness and risk information.

In addition, all prescription drug broadcast advertisements must abide by two specific requirements. First, these must include the product's most important risk-related information in the audio or audio and visual parts of the advertisement. Second, these must contain either a brief summary of the advertised product's risk information or make adequate provision for disseminating the product's approved labeling in association with the advertisement.

Source: U.S. Food and Drug Administration (FDA), Division of Drug Marketing, Advertising, and Communications (DDMAC). "DDMAC Frequently Asked Questions (FAQs)." 2009. Available at: http://www.fda.gov/AboutFDA/CentersOffices/CDER/ucm090308.htm. Accessed February 16, 2011.

released and cause serious side effects, the FDA is condemned for being sloppy in its control of drug marketing.

What is the proper balance, and what do we, as consumers, have the right to expect from the government? These are questions each of us should ask, and we have a right to share our answers with government representatives.

Regardless of our individual feelings, it is important to understand that the current (and likely future) federal regulations do not ensure drug safety or effectiveness for everyone. Too many individual variables alter the way each of us responds to drugs, making such universal assurances impossible. Federal agencies can only deal with general policies and make general decisions. For example, what if the FDA determines that a given drug is reasonably safe in 95% of the population and effective in 70%? Are these acceptable figures, or should a drug be safe in 99% and effective in 90% before it is deemed suitable for general marketing? What of the 5% or 1% of the population who will be adversely affected by this drug? What rights do they have to be protected?

There are no simple answers to these questions. Federal policies are inevitably compromises that assume that the clinician who prescribes the drug and/or the patient who buys and consumes it will be able to identify when use of that drug is inappropriate or threatening. Unfortunately, sometimes drug prescribing and drug consuming are done carelessly and unnecessary side effects occur or the drug does not work. Then the questions surface again: Are federal drug agencies doing all they can to protect the public? Should the laws be changed?

It is always difficult to predict the future, especially when it depends on sometimes-fickle politicians and erratic public opinion. Nevertheless, with the dramatic increase in new and better drugs becoming available to the public, it is not likely that federal or state agencies will diminish their role in regulating drug use. Now more than ever, the public demands safer and more effective drugs. This public attitude will likely translate into even greater involvement by regulatory agencies in issues of drug development, assessment, and marketing.

Another reason for increased regulation in the future is that many of the larger pharmaceutical companies have become incredibly wealthy. Several of the most profitable companies have become subsidiaries of large corporations, and there is concern that some may be driven more by profit margins than by philanthropic interests. In such an environment, governmental agencies are essential to ensure that the rights of the public are protected.

Drug Abuse and the Law

The laws that govern the development, distribution, and use of drugs in general and drugs of abuse in particular are interrelated. There are, however, some unique features concerning the manner in which federal agencies deal with the drugs of abuse that warrant special consideration. A summary of drug abuse laws in the United States is shown in **Table 3.1**.

Coffee, tea, tobacco, alcohol, marijuana, hallucinogens, depressants (such as barbiturates), and narcotics have been subject to a wide range of controls, varying from none to rigid restrictions. A few countries historically have instituted severe penalties, such as strangulation for smoking tobacco or opium, and strict bans on alcohol. In other countries, these substances have been deemed either legal or prohibited, depending on the political situation and the desires of the population. Historically, laws have been changed when so many people demanded access to a specific drug of abuse that it would have been impossible to enforce a ban (as in the revocation of Prohibition) or when the government needed tax revenues that could be raised by selling the drug (one argument for legalizing drugs of abuse today). A current example is the controversy over decriminalization or legalization of marijuana (see Chapter 13).

The negative experiences that Americans had at the turn of the 20th century with addicting substances such as opium led to the **Harrison Act of 1914**. It marked the first legitimate effort by the federal government to regulate and control the production, importation, sale, purchase, and distribution of addicting substances. The Harrison Act served as the foundation and reference for subsequent laws directed at regulating drug abuse issues.

Today, the Comprehensive Drug Abuse Prevention and Control Act of 1970 largely determines the ways in which law enforcement agencies deal with substance abuse. This act divided substances with abuse potential into categories based on the

KEY TERMS

Harrison Act of 1914
the first legitimate effort by the U.S. government to regulate addicting substances

Table 3.1 **Federal Laws Associated with the Control of Narcotics and Other Abused Drugs**

DATE	NAME OF LEGISLATION	SUMMARY OF COVERAGE AND INTENT OF LEGISLATION
1914	Harrison Act	First federal legislation to regulate and control the production, importation, sale, purchase, and free distribution of opium or drugs derived from opium.
1924	Heroin Act	Made it illegal to manufacture heroin.
1956	Narcotics Control Act	Intended to impose very severe penalties for those convicted of narcotics or marijuana charges.
1965	Drug Abuse Control Amendments (DACA)	Adopted strict controls over amphetamines, barbiturates, LSD, and similar substances, with provisions to add new substances as the need arises.
1970	Comprehensive Drug Abuse Prevention and Control Act	Replaced previous laws and categorized drugs based on abuse and addiction potential as well as therapeutic value.
1973	Methadone Control Act	Placed controls on methadone licensing.
1973	U.S. Drug Enforcement Administration (DEA)	Remodeled the Bureau of Narcotics and Dangerous Drugs to become the DEA.
1986	Analogue (Designer Drug) Act	Made illegal the use of substances similar in effects and structure to substances already scheduled.
2000	Drug Addiction Treatment Act	Allowed qualified physicians to dispense or prescribe specially approved Schedule III, IV, and V narcotics for the treatment of opioid addiction in medical treatment settings, rather than limiting it to specialized drug treatment clinics.
2010	Secure and Responsible Drug Disposal Act	Allowed consumers to give controlled substances to specially designated individuals, such as law enforcement officials, for disposal.

degree of their abuse potential and their clinical usefulness. The classifications, which are referred to as *schedules,* range from I to V. *Schedule I* substances have high abuse potential and no currently approved medicinal use; health professionals cannot prescribe them. *Schedule II* drugs also have high abuse potential but are approved for medical purposes and can be prescribed with restrictions. The distinctions between *Schedule II through V* substances reflect the likelihood of abuse occurring and the degree to which the drugs are controlled by governmental agencies. The least addictive and least regulated of the substances of abuse are classified as Schedule V drugs (see "Here and Now: Controlled Substance Schedules").

In determining into which schedule a drug or other substance should be placed, or whether a substance should be decontrolled or rescheduled, several factors are considered (U.S. Drug Enforcement Administration [DEA] 2010). Specific findings are not required for each factor. The factors include:

1. The actual or relative potential for abuse of the drug.
2. Scientific evidence of the pharmacological effects of the drug.
3. The state of current scientific knowledge regarding the substance. (Criteria 2 and 3 are closely related. However, the second is primarily concerned with pharmacological effects whereas the third deals with all scientific knowledge with respect to the drug.)
4. Its history and current pattern of abuse.
5. What, if any, risk there is to the public health.
6. The psychological or physiological dependence liability of the drug.
7. The scope, duration, and significance of abuse.
8. Whether the substance is an immediate precursor of a substance already controlled. The Controlled Substance Act allows inclusion of immediate precursors on this basis alone into the appropriate schedule and thus safeguards against possibilities of clandestine manufacture.

Here and Now

Controlled Substance Schedules

Controlled substances classified as Schedule I, II, III, IV, or V drugs are described here.

Schedule I

- The drug or other substance has a high potential for abuse.
- The drug or other substance has no currently accepted medical use in treatment in the United States.
- There is a lack of accepted safety for use of the drug or other substance under medical supervision.

Schedule II

- The drug or other substance has a high potential for abuse.
- The drug or other substance has a currently accepted medical use in treatment in the United States or a currently accepted medical use with severe restrictions.
- Abuse of the drug or other substance may lead to severe psychological or physical dependence.

Schedule III

- The drug or other substance has less potential for abuse than the drugs or other substances in Schedules I and II.
- The drug or other substance has a currently accepted medical use in treatment in the United States.
- Abuse of the drug or other substance may lead to moderate or low physical dependence or high psychological dependence.

Schedule IV

- The drug or other substance has a low potential for abuse relative to the drugs or other substances in Schedule III.
- The drug or other substance has a currently accepted medical use in treatment in the United States.
- Abuse of the drug or other substance may lead to limited physical dependence or psychological dependence relative to the drugs or other substances in Schedule III.

Schedule V

- The drug or other substance has a low potential for abuse relative to the drugs or other substances in Schedule IV.
- The drug or other substance has a currently accepted medical use in treatment in the United States.
- Abuse of the drug or other substance may lead to limited physical dependence or psychological dependence relative to the drugs or other substances in Schedule IV.

Source: U.S. Department of Justice, U.S. Drug Enforcement Administration (DEA). "Drugs of Abuse." 2005. Available at: http://www.justice.gov/dea/pubs/abuse/doa-p.pdf. Accessed March 4, 2011.

Penalties for illegal use and/or trafficking of these agents vary according to the agent's schedule, amount possessed, and number of previous drug-associated offenses (see **Table 3.2**).

■ Drug Laws and Deterrence

As previously indicated, drug laws often do not serve as a satisfactory deterrent against the use of illicit drugs. People have used and abused drugs for thousands of years despite governmental restrictions. It is very likely they will continue to do so despite stricter laws and greater support for law enforcement.

As the amount of addiction increased during the mid-1960s, many ill-conceived programs and laws were instituted as knee-jerk reactions, with little understanding about the underlying reasons for the rise in drug abuse. Unpopular, restrictive laws rarely work to reduce the use of illicit drugs. Even as laws become more restrictive, they usually have little impact on the level of addiction; in fact, in some cases addiction problems actually have increased. For example, during the restrictive years of the 1960s and 1980s, drugs were sold everywhere to everyone—in high schools, colleges, and probably every community. In the 1980s especially, increasingly large volumes of drugs were sold throughout the United States. Billions of dollars were paid for those drugs. Although no one knows precisely how much was exchanged, the amount likely approached $80 to $100 billion per year for

Table 3.2 **Federal Trafficking Penalties**

DRUG/SCHEDULE	QUANTITY	PENALTIES	QUANTITY	PENALTIES
Cocaine (Schedule II)	500–4999 g mixture	**First Offense:** Not less than 5 years, and not more than 40 years. If death or serious injury, not less than 20 years or more than life. Fine of not more than $5 million if an individual, $25 million if non individual.	5 kg or more mixture	**First Offense:** Not less than 10 years, and not more than life. If death or serious injury, not less than 20 years or more than life. Fine of not more than $10 million if an individual, $40 million if not an individual.
Cocaine base (Schedule II)	28–279 g mixture		280 g or more mixture	
Fentanyl (Schedule II)	40–399 g mixture		400 g or more mixture	
Fentanyl analogue (Schedule I)	10–99 g mixture		100 g or more mixture	
Heroin (Schedule I)	100–999 g mixture	**Second Offense:** Not less than 10 years, and not more than life. If death or serious injury, life imprisonment. Fine of not more than $8 million if an individual, $50 million if not an individual.	1 kg or more mixture	**Second Offense:** Not less than 20 years, and not more than life. If death or serious injury, life imprisonment. Fine of not more than $20 million if an individual, $75 million if not an individual.
LSD (Schedule I)	1–9 g mixture		10 g or more mixture	
Methamphetamine (Schedule II)	5–49 g pure or 50–499 g mixture		50 g or more pure or 500 g or more mixture	
PCP (Schedule II)	10–99 g pure or 100–999 g mixture		100 g or more pure or 1 kg or more mixture	**Two or More Prior Offenses:** Life imprisonment.

DRUG/SCHEDULE	QUANTITY	PENALTIES
Other Schedule I and II drugs (and any drug product containing gamma hydroxybutyric acid)	Any amount	**First Offense:** Not more than 20 years. If death or serious injury, not less than 20 years or more than life. Fine $1 million if an individual, $5 million if not an individual. **Second Offense:** Not more than 30 years. If death or serious injury, not less than life. Fine $2 million if an individual, $10 million if not an individual.
Other Schedule III drugs	Any amount	**First Offense:** Not more than 10 years. Fine $500,000 if an individual, $2.5 million if not an individual. **Second Offense:** Not more than 20 years. If death or serious injury, not more than 30 years. Fine $1.5 million if an individual, $5 million if not an individual.
All other Schedule IV drugs	Any amount	**First Offense:** Not more than 5 years. Fine $250,000 if an individual, $1 million if not an individual.
Flunitrazepam (Schedule IV)	Less than 1 mg	**Second Offense:** Not more than 10 years. Fine $500,000 if an individual, $2 million if not an individual.
All Schedule V drugs	Any amount	**First Offense:** Not more than 1 year. Fine $100,000 if an individual, $250,000 if not an individual. **Second Offense:** Not more than 4 years. Fine $200,000 if an individual, $500,000 if not an individual.

(continued)

Table 3.2 (continued)

DRUG	QUANTITY	FIRST OFFENSE	SECOND OFFENSE
Marijuana (Schedule 1)	1000 kg or more mixture; or 1000 or more plants	• Not less than 10 years, not more than life • If death or serious injury, not less than 20 years, not more than life • Fine of not more than $4 million if an individual, $10 million if other than an individual	• Not less than 20 years, not more than life • If death or serious injury, mandatory life • Fine of not more than $8 million if an individual, $20 million if other than an individual
Marijuana (Schedule 1)	100–999 kg mixture; or 100–999 plants	• Not less than 5 years, not more than 40 years • If death or serious injury, not less than 20 years, not more than life • Fine of not more than $2 million if an individual, $5 million if other than an individual	• Not less than 10 years, not more than life • If death or serious injury, mandatory life • Fine of not more than $4 million if an individual, $10 million if other than an individual
Marijuana (Schedule 1)	More than 10 kg hashish; 50–99 kg mixture More than 1 kg of hashish oil; 50–99 plants	• Not more than 20 years • If death or serious injury, not less than 20 years, not more than life • Fine of $1 million if an individual, $5 million if other than an individual	• Not more than 30 years • If death or serious injury, mandatory life • Fine of $2 million if an individual, $10 million if other than an individual
Marijuana (Schedule 1)	1–49 plants; less than 50 kg mixture	• Not more than 5 years • Fine of not more than $250,000 if an individual, $1 million if other than an individual	• Not more than 10 years • Fine of $500,000 if an individual, $2 million if other than an individual
Hashish (Schedule 1)	10 kg or less		
Hashish oil (Schedule 1)	1 kg or less		

Source: U.S. Drug Enforcement Administration (DEA). "Federal Trafficking Penalties and Federal Trafficking Penalties—Marijuana." Available at: http://www.usdoj.gov/dea/agency/penalties.htm. Accessed February 16, 2011.

all illegal drugs, of which the two biggest subcategories were an estimated $30 billion for cocaine and $24 billion for marijuana.

Because of the large sums of money involved, drugs have brought corruption to all levels of society. Other problems associated with the implementation of drug laws are an insufficient number of law enforcement personnel and inadequate detention facilities; consequently, much drug traffic goes unchecked. In addition, the judiciary system sometimes gets so backlogged that many cases never reach court. Plea-bargaining is often used to clear the court docket. Many dealers and traffickers are back in business on the same day they are arrested. This apparent lack of punishment seriously damages the morale of law enforcers, legislators, and average citizens.

It is estimated that in 2007, over 1.6 million adults and over 195,000 juveniles were arrested in the United States for drug-abuse violations (U.S. Department of Justice [USDOJ] 2010b). This problem represents a tremendous cost to society in terms of damaged lives and family relationships; being arrested for a drug-related crime seriously jeopardizes a person's opportunity to pursue a normal life. Drug taking is closely tied to societal problems, and it will remain a problem unless society provides more meaningful experiences to those who are most susceptible to drug abuse. Improved education and increased support should be given to preteens because that is the age when deviant behavior starts. In cases in which drug education programs have been successful in involving students, the amount of drug taking and illegal activity seems to have decreased (see Chapter 17).

Factors in Controlling Drug Abuse

Three principal issues influence laws regarding drug abuse:

1. If a person abuses a drug, should he or she be treated as a criminal or as a sick person afflicted with a disease?
2. How is the user (supposedly the victim) distinguished from the pusher (supposedly the criminal) of an illicit drug, and who should be more harshly punished—the person who creates the demand for the drug or the person who satisfies the demand?
3. Are the laws and associated penalties effective deterrents against drug use or abuse, and how is effectiveness determined?

In regard to the first issue, drug abuse may be considered both an illness and a crime. It can be a psychiatric disorder, an abnormal functional state in which a person is compelled (either physically or psychologically) to continue using the drug. It becomes a crime when the law, reflecting social opinion, makes abuse of the drug illegal. Health issues are clearly involved because uncontrolled abuse of almost any drug can lead to physical and psychological damage. Because the public must pay for healthcare costs or societal damage, laws are created and penalties are implemented to prevent or correct drug abuse problems (see Table 3.2 on federal trafficking penalties).

Concerning the second issue, drug laws have always been more lenient on the user than the seller of a drug of abuse. Actually, it is often hard to separate user from pusher because many drug abusers engage in both activities. Because huge profits are often involved, some people may not use the drugs they peddle and are only pushers; the law tries to deter use of drugs by concentrating on these persons but has questionable success. Organized crime is involved in major drug sales, and these "drug rings" have proven hard to destroy.

In regard to the third issue, considerable evidence indicates that, in the United States, criminal law has only limited success in deterring drug abuse. During 2009, approximately 36.5% of 12th graders used an illicit drug during the prior 12 months; marijuana was used by 32.8%, LSD by 1.9%, and cocaine by 3.4% (Johnston et al. 2010). It is clear that the drug abuse problem is far from being resolved, and many feel that some changes should be made in how we deal with this problem.

Strategies for Preventing Drug Abuse

The U.S. government and the public became concerned about the increasing prevalence of drug use during the 1960s, when demonstrations and nationwide protests against the Vietnam War proliferated as youth (mostly college students) rebelled against what they viewed as an unnecessary and unjust war. During the 1960s and early 1970s, for the first time, large numbers of middle- and upper–middle-class youth began using licit and illicit gateway drugs on a massive scale. In response, the government developed strategies for combating drug use and abuse. Important strategies it employed were **supply reduction**, **demand reduction**, and **inoculation**. More recently, the use of **drug courts** has become a major strategy.

Supply Reduction Strategy

Early attempts at drug abuse prevention included both the Harrison Narcotic Act of 1914 and the 18th Amendment (Prohibition) to the U.S. Constitution. Both laws were intended to control the manufacture and distribution of classified drugs, with legislators anticipating that these restrictions would compel people to stop using drugs. The laws enforced supply reduction, which involves a lessening, restriction, or elimination of available drugs.

KEY TERMS

supply reduction
a drug reduction policy aimed at reducing the supply of illegal drugs and controlling other therapeutic drugs

demand reduction
attempts to decrease individuals' tendencies to use drugs, often aimed at youth, with emphasis on reformulating values and behaviors

inoculation
a method of abuse prevention that protects drug users by teaching them responsibility

drug courts
a process that integrates substance abuse treatment, incentives, and sanctions and places nonviolent, drug-involved defendants in judicially supervised rehabilitation programs

Supply reduction drug prevention policy attempts to curtail the supply of illegal drugs or their precursors and exert greater control over other, more therapeutic drugs. Part of the supply reduction policy includes **interdiction**, which is defined as decreasing the amounts of these agents that are carried across U.S. borders by using foreign crop eradication measures and agreements, by imposing stiff penalties for drug trafficking, and by controlling alcoholic beverages through licensing.

The United States dedicates enormous resources to interdiction programs. For fiscal year 2009, the federal drug control budget for interdiction was $3.83 billion (White House 2008). Although seizures of large caches of illicit drugs are reported routinely in the national press, there is relatively little indication that the availability of drugs has diminished substantially. For example, according to the National Threat Assessment, cocaine availability has decreased but heroin, marijuana, methamphetamine, and methylenedioxymethamphetamine remain widely available (USDOJ 2010a). One can argue that as long as a strong demand for these psychoactive agents exists, demand will be satisfied if the price is right. Even if interdiction successfully reduces the supply of one drug of abuse, if demand persists, that drug is usually replaced by another drug with similar abuse potential (for example, substitution of amphetamines for cocaine; see Chapter 10).

■ Demand Reduction Strategy

The demand reduction approach attempts to minimize the actual demand for drugs. Through programs and activities often aimed at youth, emphasis is placed on reformulating values, attitudes, skills, and behaviors conducive to resisting drug use. (Chapter 17 provides extensive information about methods and techniques for reducing drug use.) As part of this strategy, support for medical and group drug treatment programs for abusers is encouraged. Although this approach does not address drug supply, it does attempt to curb and eventually eliminate the need to purchase drugs by reducing the buyer's demand.

Drug abuse is a complex and very individual problem, with many causes and aggravating factors. Even so, experience has shown that prevention and treatment are better strategies and, in the long run, less costly than interdiction or incarceration (Kreit 2009). The following are some suggestions and strategies for how to reduce demand for drugs:

- The top priority of any prevention program, if it is to provide a long-term solution, must be reduction of drug demand by youth. Children must be the primary focus in any substance abuse program. Achieving success requires stabilizing defective family structures, implementing school programs that create an antidrug attitude, establishing a drug-free environment, and promoting resistance training to help youth avoid drug involvement. In addition, children should be encouraged to become involved in alternative activities that can substitute for drug-abusing activity. Potential drug abusers need to be convinced that substance abuse is personally and socially damaging and unacceptable.

- Education about drug abuse must be carefully designed and customized for the target population or group. For example, education based on scare tactics is not likely to dissuade adolescents from experimenting with drugs. Adolescents are at a point in their lives when they feel invincible, and graphically depicting the potential health consequences of drug and alcohol abuse has little impact. A discussion about the nature of addiction and the addiction process is more likely to influence their attitudes. Adolescents need to understand why people use drugs to appreciate the behavior patterns in themselves. Other important topics that should be discussed are how drug abuse works and why it leads to dependence. To complement drug education, adolescents also should be taught coping strategies that include effective decision-making and problem-solving skills.

- Attitudes toward drug abuse and its consequence must be changed. The drug use patterns of many people, both young and old, are strongly influenced by their peers. If individuals believe that drug abuse is glamorous and contributes to acceptance by friends and associates, the incidence of drug abuse will remain high. In contrast, if the prevailing message in society is that drug abuse is unhealthy and not socially acceptable, the incidence will be much lower.

KEY TERMS

interdiction
the policy of cutting off or destroying supplies of illicit drugs

- Replacement therapy has been shown to be a useful approach to weaning the individual off of drugs of abuse. A common example of this strategy is the use of the narcotic methadone to treat the heroin addict (see Chapter 9). Use of methadone prevents the cravings and severe effects of withdrawal routinely associated with breaking the heroin habit. Unfortunately, many heroin addicts must be maintained on methadone indefinitely. Even though methadone is easier to control and is less disruptive than heroin, one drug addiction has been substituted for another, which draws criticism. Replacement therapy certainly is not the entire answer to all drug abuse problems, but it often can provide a window of opportunity for behavioral modification so that a long-term solution to the abuse problem is possible.

■ Inoculation Strategy

The inoculation method of abuse prevention aims to protect drug users by teaching them responsibility. The emphasis is on being accountable, rational, and responsible about drug use, and informing users about the effects of drugs on both mind and bodily function. Nonalcohol parties and responsible drinkers who use designated drivers are outcomes of applying inoculation strategy.

■ Drug Courts

Drug courts are designed to deal with nonviolent, drug-abusing offenders. As of July 2009, there were 2038 fully operational drug courts in the United States and 226 that were in the planning stages (National Criminal Justice Referral Service [NCJRS] 2009). Drug courts integrate mandatory drug testing, substance abuse treatment, sanctions, and incentives in a judicially supervised setting. These courts hold offenders accountable for their actions and provide them with the support and tools necessary to rebuild their lives and become productive members of the community.

Current and Future Drug Use

During the administrations of former Presidents Ronald Reagan and George H. W. Bush (1980–1992), the official policy of the U.S. federal government included a "get tough" attitude about drug abuse. Slogans such as "Just Say No" and "War on Drugs" reflected the frustration of a public that had been victimized by escalating crime (many incidents were drug related); personally touched by drug tragedies in families, at work, or with associates and friends; and economically strained by dealing with the cost of the problem.

Much remains to be accomplished in the fight against substance abuse. For example, and as summarized by the USDOJ (2010a):

- National Survey on Drug Use and Health (NSDUH) data indicate that in 2008, 14.2% of individuals 12 years of age or older had used illicit drugs during the past year.
- In 2008, the NSDUH estimated that 7 million individuals age 12 or older had abused or were dependent on illicit drugs in the past year, compared with 6.9 million in 2007.
- According to the Substance Abuse and Mental Health Services Administration (SAMHSA), combined 2002–2007 data indicate that during the prior year, an estimated 2.1 million children (3%) in the United States lived with at least one parent who abused or was dependent on illicit drugs, and 1 in 10 children under age 18 lived with a substance-addicted or substance-abusing parent.
- The approximately one-quarter of offenders in state and local correctional facilities and the more than half of offenders in federal facilities incarcerated on drug-related charges represent an estimated 620,000 individuals who are not in the workforce.

Fighting the "War on Drugs" is clearly difficult and complex. Despite substantial efforts, significant problems still exist and require the attention of politicians, clinicians, law enforcement agencies, families, counselors, and all concerned citizens.

An example of the many public awareness advertisement cautions against drinking and driving.

■ Drug Legalization Debate

The persistence of the drug abuse problem and the high cost in dollars and frustration of waging the "War on Drugs" have energized the ongoing debate regarding legalizing the use of drugs of abuse. Proponents of legalization are no longer limited to libertarians and so-called academic intellectuals. Increasingly, this group includes representatives of a distressed law enforcement system. For example, some discontented judges whose courts are swamped with drug cases and police officers who spend much of their on-duty time trying to trap and arrest every drug dealer and user on the street are publicly declaring that the drug laws are wasteful and futile.

Individuals and groups promoting the legalization of all substances of abuse commonly cite several arguments. For instance, proponents often contend that if drugs were legalized, violence and crime would become less frequent. These individuals point out that users often commit crimes to pay for illicit drugs. If these drugs were legal, then the tremendous profits associated with drugs because of their illegal status would disappear and, once gone, the black market and criminal activity associated with drugs would be eliminated. Furthermore, legalization would decrease law enforcement costs by eliminating the backlog of drug-related court cases and reduce populations in overcrowded prisons.

Conversely, opponents of drug legalization believe that legalization would lead to increased availability of drugs, which would in turn lead to increased use. They point out that the use of drugs, especially methamphetamine, phencyclidine (PCP), and cocaine, is often associated with violent criminal behavior. Numerous studies demonstrate the links among drugs, violence, and crime; the link between alcohol, a legal substance, and crime is also well documented. According to legalization opponents, drug use would merely increase the incidence of crime, even if the drugs were legally purchased. Accordingly, the economic (as well as social) cost to society would increase.

Legalization proponents claim that making illicit drugs licit would not cause more of these substances to be consumed, nor would addiction increase. They note correctly that many people use drugs in moderation. Furthermore, many would choose not to use drugs, just as many abstain currently from tobacco and alcohol. Opponents contend that if drugs were made licit and more widely available, usage and addiction rates would increase.

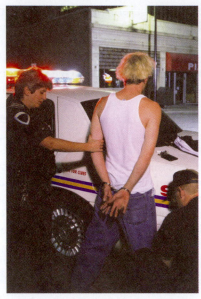

Substance abuse can lead to serious legal problems.

These individuals contend that legalizing drugs sends a message that drug use (like tobacco and alcohol) is acceptable and encourages drug use among people who currently do not use drugs.

Proponents claim that drug legalization would allow users the right to practice a diversity of consciousness. Just as diversity of race, ethnicity, sexual orientation, religion, and other varied lifestyles are allowed, legalization of drugs would permit citizens in our society to alter their consciousness without legal repercussions as long as they do not harm or threaten the safety and security of others. Moreover, proponents argue that education, health care, road building, and a wide array of other worthwhile causes would benefit from the taxes that could be raised by legalizing and then taxing drugs. They argue that the United States has spent billions of dollars to control drug production, trafficking, and use with few, if any, positive results. They contend that the money spent on drug control should be shifted to other, more productive endeavors.

Opponents believe that health and societal costs would increase with drug legalization. It has been predicted that drug treatment costs; hospitalization for long-term, drug-related diseases; and treatment of the consequences of drug-associated family violence would further burden our already strapped healthcare system. Such a policy would increase costs to society due to greater medical and social problems resulting from greater availability and increased use of drugs. Two of the most frequently abused substances, alcohol and tobacco, are both legal and readily available today. These two substances cause more medical, social, and personal problems than all the illicit drugs of abuse combined. Many question whether society really wants to legalize additional drugs with abuse potential.

Although arguments for both sides warrant consideration, extreme policies are not likely to be implemented; instead, a compromise will most probably be adopted. For example, areas potentially ripe for compromise include the following (Kalant 1992):

- *Selective legalization:* Eliminate harsh penalties for those drugs of abuse that are the safest and least likely to cause addiction, such as marijuana.
- *Control of substances of abuse by prescription or through specially approved outlets:* Have the availability of the illegal drugs controlled by physicians and trained clinicians, rather than by law enforcement agencies.
- *Discretionary enforcement of drug laws:* Allow greater discretion by judicial systems for prosecution and sentencing of those who violate drug laws. Such decisions would be based on perceived criminal intent.

In conclusion, drug legalization remains a highly divisive issue in the United States. Although legalization would lessen the number of drug violators involved in the criminal justice system, the problems associated with legalizing current illicit drugs cause many members in our society to view this idea with disfavor. As stated earlier, opponents of legalization argue that we already have massive problems with licit drugs such as tobacco and alcohol. According to them, legalizing additional types of drugs would produce a substantial increase in the rate of addiction and in the social and psychological problems associated with drug use. Proponents favoring legalization assert that, despite the current drug laws and severe penalties for drug use, people continue to use illicit drugs.

▪ Drug Testing

In response to the demand by society to stop the spread of drug abuse and its adverse consequences, drug testing has been implemented in some situations to detect drug users. The most common types of drug testing use Breathalyzers and laboratory studies of urine, blood, and hair specimens. Urine and blood testing are preferred for detecting drug use. Hair specimen testing must overcome technical problems before hair can be used as a definitive proof of drug use, including complications from hair treatment (e.g., hair coloring) and environmental absorption.

The drugs of abuse most frequently tested for are marijuana, cocaine, amphetamines, narcotics, sedatives, and anabolic steroids. Drug testing is often mandatory in some professions in which public safety is a concern (such as airline pilots, railroad workers, law enforcement employees, and medical personnel) and for employees of some organizations and companies as part of general policy (such as the military, many federal agencies, and some private companies). Drug testing also often is mandatory for participants in sports at all levels—whether in high school, college, international, or professional competition—to prevent unfair advantages that might result from the pharmacological effects of these drugs and to discourage the spread of drug abuse among athletes. Likewise, drug testing is used routinely by law enforcement agencies to assist in the prosecution of those believed to violate drug abuse laws. Finally, drug testing is used by health professionals to assess the success of drug abuse treatment—that is, to determine whether a dependent patient is diminishing his or her drug use or has experienced a relapse in drug abuse habits.

Drug testing to identify drug offenders is usually accomplished by analyzing body fluids (in particular urine), although other approaches (such as analysis of expired air for alcohol) are also used. To understand the accuracy of these tests, several factors should be considered.

- *Testing must be standardized and conducted efficiently.* To interpret testing results reliably, it is essential that fluid samples be collected, processed, and tested using standard procedures. Guidelines for proper testing procedures have been established by federal regulatory agencies as well as scientific organizations. Deviations from established protocols can result in false positives (tests that indicate a drug is present when none was used), false negatives (tests that are unable to detect a drug that is present), or inaccurate assessments of drug levels.
- *Sample collection and processing must be done accurately and confidentially.* In many cases, drug testing can have punitive consequences (for example, athletes cannot compete or employees are fired if results are positive). Consequently, drug users often attempt to outsmart

the system. Some individuals have attempted to avoid submitting their own drug-containing urine for testing by filling specimen bottles with "clean" urine from artificial bladders hidden under clothing or in the vagina or by introducing "clean" urine into their own bladders just before collection. To confirm the legitimacy of the specimen, it often is necessary to have the urine collection witnessed directly by a trustworthy observer. To ensure that the fluid specimens are not tampered with and that confidentiality is maintained, samples should be immediately coded and movement of each sample from site to site during analysis should be documented and confirmed.

Just as it is important that testing identify individuals who are using drugs, it is also important that those who have not used drugs not be wrongfully accused. To avoid false positives, all samples that test positive in screening (usually via fast and inexpensive procedures) should be analyzed again using more accurate, sensitive, and sophisticated analytical procedures to confirm the results.

- *Confounding factors that interfere with the accuracy of the testing can be inadvertently or deliberately present.* For example, dietary consumption of pastries containing poppy seeds can be sufficient to cause a positive urine test for narcotic opioids in some cases. Excessive intake of fluid or use of diuretics increases the volume of urine formed and decreases the concentration of drugs, making them more difficult to detect.

The dramatic increase in drug testing since 1985 has caused experts to question its value in dealing with drug abuse problems. Unfortunately, drug testing often is linked exclusively to punitive consequences, such as disqualification from athletic competition, loss of job, or even fines and imprisonment. Use of drug testing in such negative ways does little to diminish the number of drug abusers or deal with their personal problems. However, drug-testing programs can have positive consequences by identifying drug users who require professional care. After being referred for drug rehabilitation, the offender can be monitored using drug testing to confirm the desired response to therapy. In addition, tests can identify individuals who put others in jeopardy because of their drug abuse habits when they perform tasks that are dangerously impaired by the effects of these drugs (for example, airline pilots, train engineers, and truck drivers).

The widespread application of drug testing to control the illicit use of drugs in the general population would be extremely expensive, difficult to enforce, and almost certainly ineffective. In addition, such indiscriminate testing would likely be viewed as an unwarranted infringement on individual privacy and declared unconstitutional. However, the use of drug testing to discourage inappropriate drug use in selected crucial professions that directly impact public welfare appears to be publicly tolerated. Even so, it is probably worthwhile to periodically revisit the issue of drug testing and analyze its benefits and liabilities relative to public safety and individual privacy issues.

■ Pragmatic Drug Policies

Several principles for a pragmatic drug policy emerge from a review of past drug policies and an understanding of the drug-related frustrations of today. To create drug policies that work, the following suggestions are offered:

- It is important that the government develop programs that are consistent with the desires of the majority of the population.
- Given the difficulties and high cost of efforts to prevent illicit drugs from reaching the market, it is logical to deemphasize interdiction and instead stress programs that reduce demand. To reduce demand, drug education and drug treatment must be top priorities.
- Government and society need to better understand the role played by law in their efforts to reduce drug addiction. Antidrug laws by themselves do not eliminate drug problems; indeed, they may even create significant social difficulties (for example, as did the Prohibition laws banning all alcohol use). Used properly and selectively, however, laws can reinforce and communicate expected social behavior and values (for example, laws against public drunkenness or against driving a vehicle under the influence of alcohol).
- Programs that employ "public consensus" should be implemented more effectively to campaign against drug abuse. For example, antismoking campaigns demonstrate the potential success that could be achieved by programs that alter drug abuse behavior. Similar approaches can be used to change public attitudes about drugs through education without making moral judgments and employing cru-

sading tactics. Our society needs to engage in more collaborative programs in which drug-using individuals and their families, communities, and helping agencies work together.

Discussion Questions

1. Describe the FDA approval process for assessing the safety and efficacy of a newly developed drug. What are its advantages and disadvantages?

2. Name the principal legislative initiatives that mandate that drugs be proven safe or effective.

3. What are the principal advantages and disadvantages of switching products from prescription to OTC status?

4. What could account for the vast differences in attitudes and opinions regarding drug use and the law voiced by drug users/abusers and nonusers of drugs?

5. Would decriminalization of illicit drug use increase or decrease drug-related social problems? Justify your answer.

6. Compare and contrast supply reduction, demand reduction, and inoculation strategies for dealing with drug abuse.

7. List the principal arguments for and against legalizing drugs of abuse such as marijuana and cocaine.

Summary

1 Societies have evolved to believe that they have the right to protect themselves from the damaging impact of drug use and abuse. Consequently, governments, including that of the United States, have passed laws and implemented programs to prevent social damage from inappropriate drug use. In addition, such societies have come to expect that drugs are effective.

2 The 1906 Pure Food and Drug Act was not a strong law, but it required manufacturers to include on labels the amounts of alcohol, morphine, opium, cocaine, heroin, and marijuana extract in each product. It represented the first real attempt to make consumers aware of the active contents in the drug products they were consuming.

3 The 1938 Federal Food, Drug, and Cosmetic Act gave the FDA control over drug safety.

4 The 1951 Durham-Humphrey Amendment to the Food, Drug, and Cosmetic Act made a formal distinction between prescription and nonprescription drugs.

5 The Kefauver-Harris Amendment of 1962 required manufacturers to demonstrate both the efficacy and the safety of their products.

6 All drugs to be considered for marketing must first be tested for safety in animals. Following these initial tests, if the FDA favorably reviews the drug, it is given IND status. It then generally undergoes three phases of human clinical testing before receiving final FDA approval.

7 In 1972, the FDA initiated a program to ensure that all OTC drugs were safe and effective. Specific panels were selected to evaluate the safety and effectiveness of OTC drug ingredients. Each of the ingredients was classified into a particular category: I, II, or III.

8 The switching policy of the FDA allows the agency to review prescription drugs and evaluate their suitability as OTC products.

9 Controversy exists as to how to best reduce substance abuse. A principal strategy used by governmental agencies to achieve this objective is interdiction; the majority of money used to fight drug abuse is spent on trying to stop and confiscate drug supplies. Experience has proved that interdiction is often ineffective. To reduce drug abuse, demand for these substances must be diminished. Youth must be a top priority in any substance abuse program. Treatment that enables drug addicts to stop their habits with minimal discomfort should be provided. Finally, education should be used to change attitudes toward drug abuse and its consequences. Potential drug abusers need to be convinced that substance abuse is personally and socially damaging and is unacceptable.

10 Major strategies for combating drug use and abuse are supply reduction, demand reduction, and inoculation. Supply reduction involves using drug laws to control the manufacturing and distribution of classified drugs. Demand reduction aims to reduce the actual demand for drugs by working mainly with youth and teaching them to resist drugs. Inoculation aims to protect potential drug users by teaching them responsibility and explaining the effects of drugs on bodily and mental functioning.

11 Drug courts are designed to deal with nonviolent, drug-abusing offenders. They require substance abuse treatment and implement sanctions in a judicially supervised program. This emerging strategy has had positive social and economic impacts.

12 In response to the demand by society to stop the spread of drug abuse and its adverse consequences, drug testing has been implemented in some situations to detect drug users. Common drug testing uses Breathalyzers and analysis of urine, blood, and hair specimens. Urine and blood testing are the preferred methods of testing for drug use. Hair specimen testing must overcome a number of technical problems before it can be used as a definitive proof of drug use, including complications caused by hair treatment and environmental absorption.

References

Adams, C. P., and V. V. Brantner. "Spending on New Drug Development." *Health Economics* 19 (2010): 130–141.

Donahue, J. M., M. Cevasco, and M. B. Rosenthal. "A Decade of Direct to Consumer Advertising of Prescription Drugs." *New England Journal of Medicine* 357 (2007): 673–681.

Food and Drug Administration (FDA). "DDMAC Frequently Asked Questions (FAQs)." 2009a. Available http://www.fda.gov/AboutFDA/CentersOffices/CDER/ucm090308.htm

Food and Drug Administration (FDA). "The Impact of Direct to Consumer Advertising." 2009b. Available http://www.fda.gov/Drugs/ResourcesForYou/Consumers/ucm143562.htm

Food and Drug Administration (FDA). "Basics of Drug Ads." 2010a. Available http://www.fda.gov/Drugs/ResourcesForYou/Consumers/PrescriptionDrugAdvertising/ucm072077.htm

Food and Drug Administration (FDA). "Fast Track, Accelerated Approval and Priority Review." 2010b. Available http://www.fda.gov/forconsumers/byaudience/forpatientadvocates/speedingaccesstoimportantnewtherapies/ucm128291/htm

Food and Drug Administration (FDA). "Request for Comments on First Amendment Issues." 2010c. Available http://www.fda.gov/ohrms/dockets/dailys/02/Sep02/091802/80027f41.pdf

Food and Drug Administration (FDA). "Significant Dates in U.S. Food and Drug Law History." 2010d. Available http://www.fda.gov/AboutFDA/WhatWeDo/History/Milestones/ucm128305.htm.

Food and Drug Administration (FDA). "This Week in FDA History—July 15, 1962." 2010e. Available http://www.fda.gov/AboutFDA/WhatWeDo/History/ThisWeek/ucm117836.htm

Gilbert, J. A., and W. T. Koustas. "Secure and Responsible Drug Disposal Act Passes Congress." 3 October 2010. Available http://www.fdalawblog.net/fda_law_blog_hyman_phelps/2010/10/secure-and-responsible-drug-disposal-act-passes-congress.html

Govtrack.us. "S. 3397: Secure and Responsible Drug Disposal Act of 2010." 2010. Available http://www.govtrack.us/congress/bill.xpd?bill=s111-3397

Hunter, J. R., D. L. Rosen, and R. DeChristoforo. "How FDA Expedites Evaluation of Drugs." *Welcome Trends in Pharmacy* (January 1993): 2–9.

Johnston, L. D., P. M. O'Malley, J. G. Bachman, and J. E. Schulenberg. *Monitoring the Future: National Survey Results on Drug Use, 1975–2009. Volume I: Secondary School Students* (NIH Publication No. 10-7584). Bethesda, MD: NIH, 2010.

Kalant, H. "Formulating Policies on the Non-medical Use of Cocaine." In *Cocaine: Scientific and Social Dimensions. Ciba Foundation Symposium* 166, 261–276. New York: Wiley, 1992.

Kreit, A. *Toward a Public Health Approach to Drug Policy.* Washington, DC: American Constitutional Society for Law and Policy, March 2009.

National Criminal Justice Referral Service (NCJRS). "Drug Courts—Facts and Figures." 2009. Available http://www.ncjrs.gov/spotlight/drug_courts/facts.html

Temin, P. *Taking Your Medicine: Drug Regulation in the United States.* Cambridge, MA: Harvard University Press, 1980.

U.S. Department of Justice (USDOJ). *National Drug Threat Assessment.* 2010a. Document 2010-Q0317-001.

U.S. Department of Justice (USDOJ), Bureau of Justice Statistics. "Key Facts at a Glance." 2010b. Available http://bjs.ojp.usdoj.gov/content/glance/tables/drugtab.cfm

U.S. Drug Enforcement Administration (DEA). The Controlled Substances Act, 2010. Available http://www.justice.gov/dea/pubs/abuse/doa-p.pdf

U.S. Drug Enforcement Administration (DEA). "Federal Trafficking Penalties and Federal Trafficking Penalties—Marijuana." n.d. Available http://www.usdoj.gov/dea/agency/penalties.htm

Utah.gov. "Proper Medication Disposal." 2010. Available http://www.medicationdisposal.utah.gov

White House. *National Drug Control Strategy: FY 2009 Budget Summary.* February 2008. Available http://www.whitehousedrugpolicy.gov/publications/policy/09budget/index.html

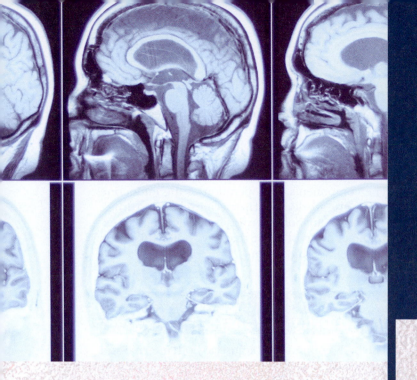

CHAPTER 4

Homeostatic Systems and Drugs

Did You Know?

- The brain is composed of approximately 100 billion neurons that communicate with one another by releasing chemical messengers called neurotransmitters.

- Many drugs exert their effects by interacting with specialized protein regions in cell membranes called receptors.

- Some natural chemicals produced by the body have the same effect as narcotic drugs; these chemicals are called endorphins.

- The body produces a natural substance called anandamide that has effects similar to those produced by marijuana and drugs that are related to THC (tetrahydrocannabinol).

- Drugs that affect the neurotransmitter dopamine usually alter perception of pleasure, mental state, and motor activity, and can cause addiction behavior.

- The hypothalamus is the principal brain region for control of endocrine systems.

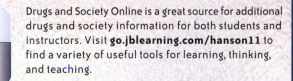

Drugs and Society Online is a great source for additional drugs and society information for both students and instructors. Visit **go.jblearning.com/hanson11** to find a variety of useful tools for learning, thinking, and teaching.

Learning ◎bjectives

On completing this chapter you will be able to:

- ◎ Explain the similarities and differences between the nervous and endocrine systems.
- ◎ Describe how a neuron functions.
- ◎ Describe the role of receptors in mediating the effects of hormones, neurotransmitters, and drugs.
- ◎ Distinguish between receptor agonists and antagonists, and describe how their effects relate to those of neurotransmitters.
- ◎ Describe the different features of the principal neurotransmitters associated with drug addiction.
- ◎ Outline the principal components of the central nervous system, and explain their general functions.
- ◎ Identify which brain areas are most likely to be affected by drugs of abuse.
- ◎ Be familiar with the endorphin and cannabinoid nervous systems and their role in substance abuse.
- ◎ Distinguish between the sympathetic and parasympathetic nervous systems.
- ◎ Identify the principal components of the endocrine system.
- ◎ Explain how and why anabolic steroids are abused and the health impact attributed to abuse.

Introduction

Why is your body susceptible to the influence of drugs, some natural products (e.g., herbs), and other substances? Part of the answer is that your body is constantly adjusting and responding to its environment in an effort to maintain internal stability and balance. This delicate process of dynamic adjustments—**homeostasis**—is necessary to optimize bodily functions and is essential for survival. These continual adjustments help to maintain physiological and psychological balances and are mediated by the release of endogenous regulatory chemicals (such as neurotransmitters from neurons and **hormones** from glands). Many drugs, including substances that are abused, exert intended or unintended effects by altering the activity of these regulatory substances, which changes the status and function of the **nervous system** and/or **endocrine system**. For example, all drugs of abuse profoundly influence mental states by altering the chemical messages of the neurotransmitters in the brain, and some alter endocrine function by affecting the release and activity of hormones. By understanding the mechanisms of how drugs alter these body processes, we are able to distinguish drug benefits and risks and devise therapeutic strategies to deal with related biomedical problems.

This chapter is divided into two sections. The first is a brief overview that introduces the basic concept of how the body is controlled by nervous systems and explains why drugs influence the elements of these systems. The second section is intended for readers who desire a more in-depth understanding of the anatomical, physiological, and biochemical

KEY TERMS

homeostasis
maintenance of internal stability; often biochemical in nature

hormones
chemical messengers released into the blood by glands

nervous system
relating to the brain, spinal cord, neurons, and their associated elements

endocrine system
relating to hormones, their functions, and sources

neurons
specialized nerve cells that make up the nervous system and release neurotransmitters

glia
supporting cells that are critical for protecting and providing sustenance to the neurons

basis of homeostatic functions. In this second section, the elements of the nervous system are discussed in greater detail, followed by an examination of its major divisions: the central, peripheral, and autonomic nervous systems (CNS, PNS, and ANS). The components and operation of the endocrine system also are discussed in specific relation to drugs. The use of anabolic steroids is presented as an example of drugs of abuse that have powerful effects on the endocrine system.

Overview of Homeostasis and Drug Actions

The body continuously adjusts to both internal and external changes in the environment. To cope with these adjustments, the body systems include elaborate self-regulating mechanisms. The name given to this compensatory action is homeostasis, which refers to the maintenance of internal stability or equilibrium of the body and its functions. For example, homeostatic mechanisms control the response of the brain to changes in the physical, social, and psychological environments, as well as regulate physiological factors such as body temperature, metabolism, nutrient utilization, and organ functions. The two principal systems that help human beings maintain homeostasis are the nervous system and the endocrine system (described in Section 2). They are independent yet work together in a coordinated manner, and often both are influenced by common factors, such as drugs.

1: Introduction to Nervous Systems

All nervous systems consist of specialized cells called **neurons** and **glia** (or non-neuronal cells). The glia are supporting cells and are critical for protecting and providing sustenance to the neurons. Although the glia are necessary for survival of the neurons and proper functioning of the nervous systems, because they do not appear to be direct targets of the drugs of abuse this cell population will not be discussed in detail. Neurons are responsible for conducting the homeostatic functions of the brain and other parts of the nervous system by receiving and sending information. The transfer of messages by neurons includes electrochemical processes that involve the following elements (see **Figure 4.1**):

- Glia surround the neuron and its processes to support its ability to send chemical messages and provide nutrients for the neurons.

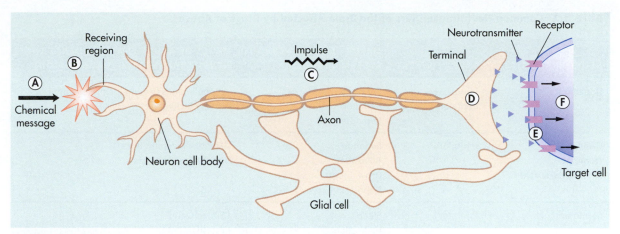

FIGURE 4.1

The process of sending messages by neurons. The receiving region (**B**) of the neuron is activated by an incoming message (**A**) near the neuronal cell body. The neuron sends an electricity-like chemical impulse (**C**) down the axon to its terminal (**D**). The impulse causes the release of neurotransmitters from the terminal to transmit the message to the target. This is done when the neurotransmitter molecules activate the receptors on the membranes of the target cell (**E**). The activated receptors then cause a change to occur in intracellular functions (**F**). Glial cells (glia) surround the neurons and their axons to enhance their abilities to send impulses and to support their other cellular functions.

- The receiving region of the neuron (B) is affected by a chemical message (A) that either excited it (causing the neuron to send its own message) or inhibits it (preventing the neuron from sending a message).

- If the message is excitatory, a chemical impulse (C) (much like electricity) moves from the receiving region of the neuron, down its wirelike processes (called **axons**) to the sending region (called the terminal) (D). When the electrochemical impulse reaches the terminal, chemical messengers called neurotransmitters are released (for examples see **Table 4.1**).

- The neurotransmitters travel very short distances and bind to specialized and specific receiving proteins called **receptors** on the outer membranes of their target cells (E).

- Activation of receptors by their associated neurotransmitters causes a change in the activity of the target cell (F). The target cells can be other neurons or cells that make up organs (such as the heart, lungs, kidneys, and so on), muscles, or glands.

Neurons are highly versatile and, depending on their functions, can send discrete excitatory or inhibitory messages to their target cells or organs. Neurons are distinguished by the types of chemical substances they release as neurotransmitters to send their messages. The neurotransmitters represent a wide variety of molecules that are classified according to their functional association as well as their ability to stimulate or inhibit the activity of target neurons, organs, muscles, and glands. They are discussed in greater detail in Section 2.

An example of a common neurotransmitter used by neurons in the brain to send messages is the substance dopamine. When released from neurons associated with the pleasure center in the brain, dopamine causes substantial euphoria by activating its receptor on target neurons (Deadwyler 2010; O'Brien 2006). This effect is relevant to drugs of abuse because the addictive properties of these substances relate to their ability to stimulate dopamine release from these neurons (for example, amphetamine or cocaine) and thus cause pleasant euphoric effects in the user (O'Brien 2006).

It is important to understand that many of the desired and undesired effects of psychoactive drugs (which alter the mental functions of the brain), such as the drugs of abuse, are due to their ability to alter the neurotransmitters associated with neurons.

KEY TERMS

axons

an extension of the neuronal cell body along which electrochemical signals travel

receptors

special proteins in a membrane that are activated by natural substances or drugs to alter cell function

Table 4.1 **Common Neurotransmitters of the Brain Affected by Drugs of Abuse**

NEUROTRANSMITTER	TYPE OF EFFECT	MAJOR CENTRAL NERVOUS SYSTEM CHANGES	DRUGS OF ABUSE THAT INFLUENCE THE NEUROTRANSMITTER (DRUG ACTION)
Dopamine	Inhibitory–excitatory	Euphoria Agitation Paranoia	Amphetamines (e.g., methamphetamine), cocaine (activate)
GABA (gamma-aminobutyric acid)	Inhibitory	Sedation Relaxation Drowsiness Depression	Alcohol, diazepam-type, barbiturates (activate)
Serotonin	Inhibitory	Sleep Relaxation Sedation	LSD (activate), Ecstasy (MDMA)
Acetylcholine	Excitatory–inhibitory	Mild euphoria Excitation Insomnia	Tobacco, nicotine (stimulate)
Endorphins	Inhibitory	Mild euphoria Blockage of pain Slow respiration	Narcotics (activate)
Anandamide	Inhibitory	Relaxation Increased sense of well-being	Tetrahydrocannabinol (marijuana) (stimulates)

Some of the transmitter messenger systems most likely to be affected by drugs of abuse are listed in Table 4.1 and are discussed in greater detail in Section 2.

2: Comprehensive Explanation of Homeostatic Systems

For those desiring a more complete understanding of the consequences of drug effects on the homeostatic systems of the body, this section provides an in-depth discussion of the anatomical and physiological nature and biological arrangements of the nervous and endocrine systems. Because drugs of abuse are most likely to exert their psychoactive effects on neurons and their receptor targets, the nervous system is presented first and

in greater depth, followed by a briefer description of endocrine function.

The Building Blocks of the Nervous System

The nervous system is composed of the brain, spinal cord, and all the neurons that connect to other organs and tissues of the body. Nervous systems enable an organism to receive information about the internal and external environment and to make the appropriate responses essential to survival. Considerable money and scientific effort are currently being dedicated to exploring the mechanisms whereby the nervous system functions and processes information, resulting in frequent exciting discoveries. Much of the exciting new knowledge about this system comes from the study of **genetics** (e.g., the study of cellular DNA and its functions) and **molecular biology** (i.e., the study of cellular functions and their regulation). These disciplines include research tools that help us to understand how genes regulate factors such as inheritability and the role of gene expression in determining risk factors for drug addiction that are

KEY TERMS

genetics
study of cellular DNA and its functions

molecular biology
study of cellular functions and their regulation

Family Matters: What About Genes?

Research strongly suggests that at least 50% of our susceptibility to experiencing drug addiction (and maybe more for nicotine and alcohol) is determined by genes we receive from our parents. In other words, addiction vulnerabilities are often inherited and genes at least partially explain why problems with drug abuse are much more abundant in some families. Although this is an evolving science, approximately 100 genes have already been linked to issues related to drug dependence (Drgon et al. 2010). Although these genetic findings are very exciting to scientists and have helped us understand why drug addiction occurs, the clinical value of such discoveries is controversial. For example, the public is often skeptical about testing for, and using, genetic information in the clinical management of diseases, especially those with negative overtones such as drug addiction. In addition, physicians and other clinicians are not sure how they can use genetic information in their everyday practices. However, despite the reluctance by both patients and practitioners, genetics is likely to play a critical role in the future development of more effective management of drug abuse problems. For example, once the genetic factors that cause addiction vulnerabilities are identified and mapped it will be possible to do genetic screening to identify individuals who are at greatest risk for developing drug abuse disorders. Such genetic screens will not only identify a high-risk person but also provide information as to what the vulnerability is and how to best prevent or treat the problems. It is likely that such analysis will be part of a more comprehensive and integrated genetic screen that tests for vulnerability to hundreds of common psychiatric and physical diseases and will provide a general readout of a person's potential for physical and emotional health (Price 2008).

passed from parents to offspring (Conway et al. 2010; Learn.Genetics 2010) (see "Family Matters: What About Genes?").

■ The Neuron: The Basic Structural Unit of the Nervous System

The fundamental building block of the nervous system is the nerve cell, or neuron. Each neuron in the CNS (brain and spinal cord) is in close proximity with other neurons, forming a complex network. The human brain contains about 100 billion neurons, each of which is composed of similar components but with different shapes, sizes, and distinguishing neurochemistry. Neurons do not form a continuous cellular network. They always remain separate, never actually touching, although they are in close proximity. The typical point of communication between one neuron and another is called a

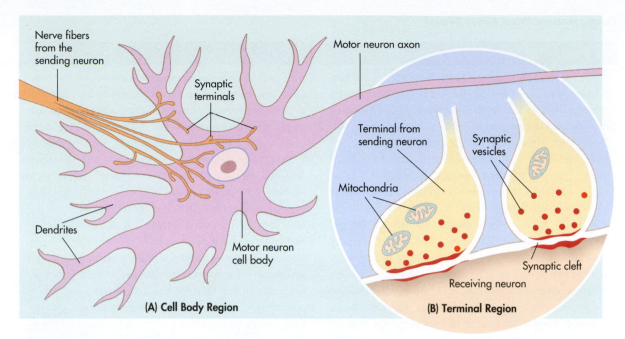

FIGURE 4.2

(A) Each neuron may have many synaptic connections. They are designed to deliver short bursts of a chemical transmitter substance into the synaptic cleft, where the substance can act on the surface of the receiving nerve cell membrane. Before release, molecules of the chemical neurotransmitter are stored in numerous vesicles, or sacs. **(B)** A close-up of the synaptic terminals, showing the synaptic vesicles and mitochondria. Mitochondria are specialized structures that help supply the cell with energy. The gap between the synaptic terminal and the target membrane is the synaptic cleft.

synapse. The gap (called the **synaptic cleft**) between neurons at a synapse may be only 0.00002 millimeter wide, but it is essential for proper functioning of the nervous system (see **Figure 4.2**).

The neuron has a cell body with a nucleus and receiving regions called **dendrites**, which are short, treelike branches that are influenced by information from the environment and surrounding neurons such as released neurotransmitters.

The axon of a neuron is a threadlike extension that receives information from the dendrites near the cell body, in the form of an electrochemical impulse; then, like an electrical wire, it transmits the impulse to the cell's terminal. Although most axons

are less than 1 inch in length, some may be quite long; for example, some axons extend from the spinal cord to the toes.

At the synapse, information is transmitted chemically to the next neuron, as shown in Figure 4.1. A similar synaptic arrangement also exists at sites of communication between neurons and target cells in organs, muscles, and glands; that is, neurotransmitters are released from the message-sending neurons and activate receptors located in the membranes of message-receiving target cells.

There are two types of synapses: excitatory and inhibitory. The *excitatory synapse* initiates an impulse in the receiving neuron when stimulated, thereby causing release of neurotransmitters or increasing activity in the target cell. The *inhibitory synapse* diminishes the likelihood of an impulse in the receiving neuron or reduces the activity in other target cells. A receiving neuron or target cell may have thousands of synapses connecting it to other neurons and their excitatory or inhibitory information (see Figure 4.2A). The final cellular activity is a summation of these many excitatory and inhibitory synaptic signals and underscores the connectivity and complexity of these systems.

KEY TERMS

synapse
site of communication between a message-sending neuron and its message-receiving target cell

synaptic cleft
a minute gap between the neuron and target cell, across which neurotransmitters travel

dendrites
short branches of neurons that receive transmitter signals

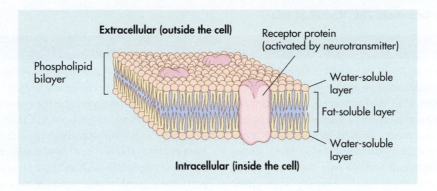

FIGURE 4.3

Cell membranes consist of a double layer of phospholipids. The water-soluble layers are pointed outward and the fat-soluble layers are pointed toward each other. Large proteins, including receptors, float in the membrane. Some of these receptors are activated by neurotransmitters to alter the activity of the cell.

The Nature of Drug Receptors

Receptors are special proteins located in the membranes of receiving neurons and other target cells (see **Figure 4.3**). They help regulate the activity of cells in the nervous system and throughout the body. These selective protein sites on specific cells act as transducers to communicate the messages caused by endogenous messenger substances (chemicals produced and released within the body), such as neurotransmitters and hormones. The receptors process the complex information each cell receives as it attempts to maintain metabolic stability, or homeostasis, and fulfill its functional role (Kandel and Siegelbaum 2000; Luscher and Slesinger 2010). Many drugs used therapeutically and almost all drugs of abuse exert their effects on the body by directly or indirectly interacting (either to activate or antagonize) with these receptors.

Understanding how receptors interact with specific drugs has led to some interesting results. For example, **opiate receptors** (sites of action by narcotic drugs, such as heroin and morphine) are naturally present in animal and human brains (Fattore et al. 2004; Walsh, Unterwald, and Izenwasser 2010). Why would human and animal brains have receptors for opiate narcotics, which are plant chemicals? Discovery of the opiate receptors suggested the existence of internal (endogenous) neurotransmitter substances in the body that normally act at these receptor sites and have effects like narcotic drugs, such as codeine and morphine. This finding led to the identification of the body's own opiates, the **endorphins** (Sabatowski et al. 2004). Another endogenous system that has been discovered because of specific receptor targets in the brain is the **cannabinoid system**. This is an example of novel CNS pathways identified and characterized because of our ability to study and understand genetics (Matsuda 1997). These include pathways that are characterized by proteins activated by THC (tetrahydrocannibinol), the active ingredient in marijuana. These cannabinoid receptors are linked to functions associated with mood, reward, motivation, pain perception, decision making, and appetite (Bosier et al. 2010). Because of their involvement in such critical CNS functions, the cannabinoid systems are more than just targets for marijuana (see "Prescription for Addiction: The 'Spice' of Life"), but likely can also be manipulated medically for legitimate therapeutic purposes. As with the endorphins, natural neurotransmitter substances have been discovered in the brain that selectively activate the cannabinoid receptors. These substances have a fatty acid nature and include the substance **anandamide** (Shim 2010). Specific receptors have also been found for the CNS depressant diazepam (Valium), which activates benzodiazepine receptors (Bateson 2004). Although less is known about the natural benzodiazepine system, it is likely that natural substances are also produced in the brain that mimic the effects of Valium and cause natural sedation and relaxation; however, as of yet

KEY TERMS

opiate receptors
receptors activated by opioid narcotic drugs such as heroin and morphine

endorphins
neurotransmitters that have narcotic-like effects

cannabinoid system
biological target of tetrahydrocannabinol in marijuana

anandamide
a naturally occurring fatty acid neurotransmitter that selectively activates cannabinoid receptors

Prescription for Addiction: The "Spice" of Life

"Of course, banning it will make criminals out of all the teens that use it. That's what we want, right?" This is a quote from a teenager who has used a recent drug phenomenon called *Spice* or *K2* and is concerned Spice will soon be outlawed by the government, making it unavailable. Its growing popularity is causing considerable concerns among healthcare professionals and law enforcement agencies. Spice consists of herbs that are technically legal in most parts of the country, and it is marketed as an herbal incense. However, these herbs are sprayed with synthetic chemicals that mimic THC and, when smoked, cause a marijuana experience. Because Spice-like products have only become available relatively recently in smoke shops and head shops in the United States, little is known about their adverse effects, but the similarity with THC suggests that the pharmacological actions are likely to resemble marijuana. Therein lies the dilemma: because it has not been declared illegal in many parts of the country and is not regulated by government agencies, it has enjoyed dramatic popularity with teenage and young adult consumers who have come to refer to it as a "legal marijuana high." Needless to say agencies such as the DEA and other federal and local law enforcement groups are concerned about the adverse effects of Spice and its likelihood to cause dependence, and recommend its tight control or even elimination. In contrast, many young consumers and so-called "personal freedom advocates" believe that until there is reliable proof that Spice causes serious adverse and addicting effects that they should not be deprived of using and "enjoying" this product.

Source: Aarthun, S. "Synthetic Marijuana a Growing Trend Among Teens, Authorities Say." CNNHealth. 2010. Available at: http://www.cnn.com/2010/HEALTH/03/23/synthetic.marijuana/index.html. Accessed February 15, 2011.

the identity of these Valium-like natural transmitters remain a mystery. The natural benzodiazepine, opioid, and cannabinoid systems are discussed in greater detail in Chapters 6, 9, and 13, respectively.

Much remains unknown about how receptors respond to or interact with drugs. Using molecular biology techniques, many of these receptors have been found to initiate a cascade of linked chemical reactions, which can change intracellular environments to produce either activation or inactivation of cellular functions and metabolism (Ferguson 2007).

Receptors that have been isolated and identified are protein molecules; it is believed that the shape of the protein is essential in regulating a drug's interaction with a cell. If the drug is the proper shape and size and has a compatible electrical charge, it may substitute for the endogenous messenger substance and activate the receptor protein by causing it to change its shape, or conform. These molecular events have given us insight into why drug abuse occurs and how to prevent and treat addiction (Koob and Volkow 2010).

KEY TERMS

agonistic
a type of substance that activates a receptor

antagonistic
a type of substance that blocks a receptor

■ Agonistic and Antagonistic Effects on Drug Receptors

A drug may have two different effects on a receptor when interaction occurs: **agonistic** or **antagonistic**.

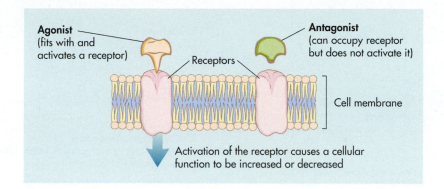

FIGURE 4.4

Interaction of agonist and antagonist with membrane receptor. When this receptor is occupied and activated by an agonist, it can cause cellular changes.

As shown in **Figure 4.4**, an agonistic drug interacts with the receptor and produces some type of cellular response, whereas an antagonistic drug interacts with the receptor but prevents that response.

An agonistic drug mimics the effect of a messenger substance (such as a neurotransmitter) that is naturally produced by the body and interacts with the receptor to cause some cellular change. For example, narcotic drugs are agonists that mimic the naturally occurring endorphins and activate opiate receptors; the THC in marijuana is an agonist that activates cannabinoid receptors. An antagonist has the opposite effect: It inhibits the sequence of metabolic events that a natural substance or an agonist drug can stimulate, usually without initiating an effect itself. Thus, the drug naloxone (created to treat heroin overdoses) is an antagonist at the opiate receptors and blocks the effects of narcotic drugs, such as heroin, as well as the effects of the naturally occurring endorphins. In contrast, as of yet in the United States, there is no FDA-approved antagonist for the cannabinoid receptors; however, in some European countries the drug Rimonabant has been available to treat obesity by suppressing appetite, an effect caused by blockade of the cannabinoid receptors; however, due to significant psychiatric side effects this drug is no longer available in most countries. Other cannabinoid antagonists are being developed to replace it (Giraldo 2010).

Neurotransmitters: The Messengers

Many drugs affect the activity of neurotransmitters by altering their synthesis, storage, release, or deactivation (e.g., metabolism). By changing these processes, a drug may modify or block information transmitted by these neurochemical messengers. Thus, by altering the amount of neurotransmitters, such drugs can act indirectly, like agonists and an-

tagonists, even though they do not directly change neurotransmitter receptors. They do influence the activity of these receptors by altering the amount of neurotransmitters available to naturally influence receptor function.

Experimental evidence shows that many different neurotransmitters exist, although much remains to be learned about their specific functions. These biochemical messengers are selectively released from specific neurons. Transmitters frequently altered by drugs of abuse include acetylcholine (ACh), norepinephrine, epinephrine, dopamine, serotonin, gamma-aminobutyric acid (GABA), the endorphins (peptides), and cannabinoids such as anandamide (fatty acids). Because of the unique shapes and chemical features, each neurotransmitter affects only its specific receptors (Bloom 1995; Churdler 2010). Drugs can also affect these receptors if they are sufficiently similar in shape to the neurotransmitters. **Figure 4.5** summarizes some of the important features of the common neurotransmitters.

Neurotransmitters are inactivated after they have done their job by diffusion away from their receptor target or metabolism (by enzymes), or they are taken back up into the neuron by selective transporter proteins. If a deactivating enzyme or the reuptake is blocked by a drug, the effect of the transmitter may be prolonged or intensified.

Acetylcholine

Large quantities of acetylcholine (ACh) are found in the brain. ACh is one of the major neurotransmitters in the autonomic portion of the PNS, which is discussed later in the chapter.

Neurons that respond to ACh are distributed throughout the brain. Depending on the region, ACh can have either excitatory or inhibitory effects. The receptors activated by ACh have been divided into two main subtypes based on the response to two

Acetylcholine
Chemical type: Choline product
Location: CNS—Basal ganglia, cortex, reticular activating system
PNS—Neuromuscular junction, parasympathetic system
Action: Excitatory (nicotine receptor) and inhibitory (muscarinic receptor)

Anandamide
Chemical type: Fatty acid
Location: CNS—Cortex, cerebellum, limbic system
Other—Immune system, pain regions, reproductive system
Action: Relaxation, analgesia, hunger

Dopamine
Chemical type: Catecholamine
Location: CNS—Basal ganglia, limbic system, hypothalamus
Action: Usually inhibitory

Endorphins
Chemical type: Peptide (small protein)
Location: CNS—Basal ganglia, hypothalamus, brain stem, spinal cord
Other—Gut, cardiovascular system
Action: Inhibitory (narcotic-like effects)

Epinephrine
Chemical type: Catecholamine
Location: CNS—Minor
PNS—Adrenal glands
Action: Usually excitatory

GABA
Chemical type: Amino acid
Location: CNS—Basal ganglia, limbic system, cortex
Action: Usually inhibitory

Norepinephrine
Chemical type: Catecholamine
Location: CNS—Limbic system, cortex, hypothalamus, reticular activating system, brain stem, spinal cord
PNS—Sympathetic nervous system
Action: Usually inhibitory; some excitation

Serotonin (5HT)
Chemical type: Tryptophan-derivative
Location: CNS—Basal ganglia, limbic system, brain stem, spinal cord, cortex
Other—Gut, platelets, cardiovascular
Action: Usually inhibitory

FIGURE 4.5

Features of common neurotransmitters.

CNS, central nervous system; PNS, peripheral nervous system.

drugs derived from plants: muscarine and nicotine. Muscarine (a substance in mushrooms that causes mushroom poisoning) and similarly acting drugs activate **muscarinic** receptors. Nicotine, whether experimentally administered or inhaled by smoking tobacco, stimulates **nicotinic** receptors.

Catecholamines

Catecholamines include the neurotransmitter compounds norepinephrine, epinephrine, and dopamine, all of which have similar chemical structures. Neurons that synthesize catecholamines convert the amino acids (building blocks of proteins) pheny-

lalanine or tyrosine to dopamine. In some neurons, dopamine is further converted to norepinephrine, and finally to epinephrine (see **Figure 4.6**).

After release, most of the catecholamines are taken back up into the neurons that released them, to be used over again; this process is called *reuptake*. An enzymatic breakdown system also metabolizes the catecholamines to inactive compounds. The reuptake process and the activity of metabolizing enzymes, especially monoamine oxidase (MAO), can be greatly affected by some of the drugs of abuse. If these deactivating enzymes or reuptake systems are blocked, the concentration of norepinephrine and dopamine may build up in the brain, significantly increasing the effect. Cocaine, for example, prevents the reuptake of norepinephrine and dopamine in the brain, resulting in continual stimulation of neuron catecholamine receptors.

Norepinephrine and Epinephrine

Although norepinephrine and epinephrine are structurally very similar, their receptors are selective and do not respond with the same intensity to either

KEY TERMS

muscarinic
a receptor type activated by ACh; usually inhibitory

nicotinic
a receptor type activated by ACh; usually excitatory

catecholamines
a class of biochemical compounds including the transmitters norepinephrine, epinephrine, and dopamine

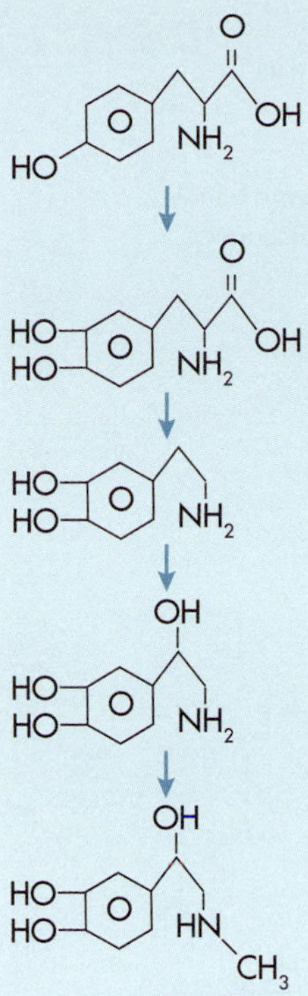

FIGURE 4.6

Synthetic pathway for catecholamine neurotransmitters. The starting material is the amino acid tyrosine. By enzymatic action the tyrosine becomes L-DOPA and is then converted to dopamine, followed by norepinephrine and finally epinephrine.

transmitter or to **sympathomimetic** drugs. Just as the receptors to ACh can be separated into muscarinic and nicotinic types, the norepinephrine and epinephrine receptors are classified into alpha and beta categories. Receiving cells may have alpha- or beta-type receptors, or both. Norepinephrine acts predominantly on alpha receptors and with less action on beta receptors.

The antagonistic (blocking) action of many drugs that act on these catecholamine receptors can be selective for alpha receptors, whereas others block only beta receptors. This distinction can be therapeutically useful. For example, beta receptors tend to stimulate the heart, whereas alpha receptors constrict blood vessels; thus, a drug that selectively affects beta receptors can be used to treat heart ailments without directly altering the state of the blood vessels (Westfall and Westfall 2006).

Dopamine

Dopamine is a catecholamine transmitter that is particularly influenced by drugs of abuse (Deadwyler

2010; O'Brien 2006). Most, if not all, drugs that elevate mood have abuse potential or cause psychotic behaviors and alter the activity of dopamine in some way, particularly in brain regions associated with regulating mental states and reward systems. In addition, dopamine is an important transmitter in controlling movement and fine muscle activity as well as endocrine functions. Thus, because many drugs of abuse affect dopamine neurons, they can also alter all of these functions.

Serotonin

Serotonin (5-hydroxytryptamine, or 5HT) is synthesized in neurons and elsewhere (for example, in the gastrointestinal tract and platelet-type blood cells) from the dietary source of tryptophan. Tryptophan is an essential amino acid, meaning that human beings do not have the ability to synthesize it and must obtain it through diet. Like the catecholamines, serotonin is degraded by the enzyme MAO; thus, drugs that alter this enzyme affect levels of not only catecholamines but also serotonin.

Serotonin is also found in the upper brain stem, which connects the brain and the spinal cord (see **Figure 4.7**). Axons from serotonergic neurons are distributed throughout the entire CNS. Serotonin generally inhibits action of its target neurons. One important role of the serotonergic neurons is to prevent overreaction to various stimuli. Consequently, a change in serotonergic systems can cause aggressiveness, excessive motor activity, exaggerated mood swings, insomnia, and abnormal sexual behavior. Serotonergic neurons also help regulate the release of hormones from the hypothalamus. Because many drugs of abuse affect serotonin systems, use of these drugs can interfere with these systems.

Alterations in serotonergic neurons, serotonin synthesis, and degradation have been proposed to be factors in mental illness and to contribute to the side effects of many drugs of abuse. In support of this hypothesis is the fact that drugs such as psilocybin and lysergic acid diethylamide (LSD), which have serotonin-like chemical structures, are frequently abused because of their hallucinogenic properties and can cause psychotic effects (see Chapter 12).

KEY TERMS

sympathomimetic
agents that mimic the effects of norepinephrine or epinephrine

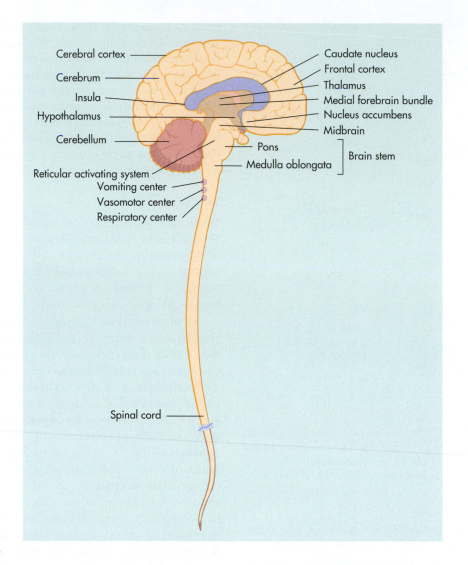

FIGURE 4.7

Functional components of the central nervous system. The caudate nucleus is part of the basal ganglia and important for behavior selection and motor activity. Limbic structures include the hypothalamus, nucleus accumbens, thalamus, medial forebrain bundle, and frontal cortex of the cerebrum. They are important for controlling emotions, reward perception, and other mental states and are critical for appropriate decision making. The insula has been identified as important for motivation.

Major Divisions of the Nervous System

The nervous system can be divided into two major components: the **central nervous system (CNS)** and the **peripheral nervous system (PNS)**. The CNS consists of the brain and spinal cord (see Figure 4.7), which re-

KEY TERMS

central nervous system (CNS)
one of the major divisions of the nervous system, composed of the brain and spinal cord

peripheral nervous system (PNS)
includes the neurons outside the CNS

ceive information through the input nerves of the PNS. This sensory information allows the CNS to evaluate the specific status of all organs and the general status of the body. After receiving and processing this information, the CNS reacts by regulating muscle and organ activity through the output nerves of the PNS (Lefkowitz, Hoffman, and Taylor 1995).

The PNS is composed of neurons whose cell bodies or axons are located outside the brain or spinal cord. It consists of input and output nerves to the CNS. The PNS input to the brain and spinal cord conveys sensory information such as pain, pressure, and temperature, whereas its output activities are separated into somatic types (control of voluntary muscles) and autonomic types (control of unconscious functions, such as essential organ [e.g., heart] and gland activity [e.g., adrenal gland]).

The Central Nervous System

The human brain is an integrating (information processing) and storage device with abilities unequaled by the most complex computers. It can handle not only a great deal of information simultaneously from the senses but also can evaluate and modify the response to the information rapidly. Although the brain weighs only 3 pounds, its 100 billion neurons give it the potential to perform a multitude of functions, often simultaneously. The following are some important brain regions particularly influenced by drugs of abuse.

The Reticular Activating System

The reticular activating system (RAS) is an area of the brain that receives input from all of the sensory systems as well as from the cerebral cortex. The RAS is found at the junction of the spinal cord and the brain (see Figure 4.7). One of its major functions is to control the brain's state of arousal (sleep versus awake).

Because of its complex, diffuse network structure, the RAS is very susceptible to the effects of drugs. It is sensitive to the effects of LSD, potent stimulants such as cocaine and amphetamines, and CNS depressants such as alcohol and benzodiazepines (e.g., Valium). Norepinephrine and ACh are important neurotransmitters in the RAS. High levels of epinephrine, norepinephrine, or stimulant drugs, such as amphetamines, activate the RAS. In contrast, drugs that block the actions of another transmitter, ACh, called **anticholinergic** drugs (for example, antihistamines), suppress RAS activity, causing sleepiness.

The Basal Ganglia

The basal ganglia include the caudate nucleus and are the primary centers for involuntary and finely tuned motor functions involving, for example, posture and muscle tone. In addition, these structures are involved in establishing and maintaining behaviors. Two important neurotransmitters in the basal ganglia are dopamine and ACh. Damage to neurons in this area may cause Parkinson's disease, the progressive yet selective degeneration of the main dopaminergic neurons in the basal ganglia. The structures of the basal ganglia are especially important for developing addictions and affecting decision making.

A close association exists between control of motor abilities and control of mental states. Both functions rely heavily on the activity of dopamine-releasing neurons. Consequently, drugs that affect dopamine activity usually alter both systems, resulting in undesired side effects. For example, heavy use of tranquilizers (drugs that block dopamine receptors such as chlorpromazine [Thorazine]) in the treatment of psychotic patients can produce Parkinson-like symptoms. If such drugs are administered daily over several years, problems with motor functioning may become permanent. Drugs of abuse, such as stimulants, increase dopamine activity, causing enhanced motor activity as well as psychotic behavior.

The Limbic System

The limbic system includes an assortment of linked brain regions located near to and including the hypothalamus (see Figure 4.7). Besides the hypothalamus, the limbic structures include the thalamus, medial forebrain bundle, **nucleus accumbens**, and front portion of the cerebral cortex. Functions of the limbic and basal ganglia structures are inseparably linked; drugs that affect one system often affect the other as well.

The primary roles of limbic brain regions include regulating emotional activities (such as fear, rage, and anxiety), memory, modulation of basic hypothalamic functions (such as endocrine activity), and activities such as mating, procreation, and caring for the young. In addition, reward centers are also believed to be associated with limbic structures, particularly in the nucleus accumbens. For this reason, it is almost certain that the mood-elevating effects of drugs of abuse are mediated by these limbic systems of the brain.

For example, studies have shown that, when given the option, laboratory animals will self-administer most stimulant drugs of abuse (such as amphetamines and cocaine) through a cannula surgically placed into limbic structures (such as the medial forebrain bundle, nucleus accumbens, or frontal cerebral cortex). This self-administration is achieved by linking injection of the drug into the cannula with

KEY TERMS

anticholinergic
agents that antagonize the effects of acetylcholine

nucleus accumbens
part of the CNS limbic system and a critical brain region for reward systems

a lever press or other activity by the animal (Porrino et al. 2004). It is thought that the euphoria or intense "highs" associated with these drugs result from their effects on these brain regions. Some of the limbic system's principal transmitters include dopamine, norepinephrine, and serotonin; dopamine activation especially appears to be the primary reinforcement that accounts for the abuse liability of most drugs (DiChiara et al. 2004).

The Cerebral Cortex

The unique features of the human cerebral cortex give human beings a special place among animals. The cortex is a layer of gray matter made up of nerves and supporting cells that almost completely surrounds the rest of the brain and lies immediately under the skull (see Figure 4.7). It is responsible for receiving sensory input, interpreting incoming information, and initiating voluntary motor behavior. Many psychoactive drugs, such as psychedelics, dramatically alter the perception of sensory information by the cortex and cause hallucinations that result in strange behavior.

A particularly critical part of the cortex is called the **frontal cortex**. This and associated cortical areas store memories, control complex behaviors, help process information, and help make decisions. Some psychoactive drugs disrupt the normal functioning of these areas, thereby interfering with an individual's ability to deal effectively and rationally with complex issues. Consequently, the behavior of persons addicted to drugs often appears bizarre and inappropriate, and in extreme cases can even lead to violence and criminal behavior (Valliant and Clark 2009).

Insula

The insula is a structure recently implicated in drug addiction. It is located deep in the brain, connected with the pleasure pathways, and appears to be important for motivation. A recent finding determined that smokers who sustain an injury to their insula lose interest in using tobacco (Vorel et al. 2007). This region has been associated with other addiction behaviors as well (Koob and Volkow 2010).

KEY TERMS

frontal cortex
cortical region essential for information processing and decision making

autonomic nervous system (ANS)
controls the unconscious functions of the body

The Hypothalamus

The hypothalamus (see **Figure 4.8**) is located near the base of the brain. It integrates information from many sources and serves as the CNS control center for the ANS and many vital support functions such as cardiovascular activity, hormone release, and temperature and appetite regulation (Kyrou and Tsigos 2009). It also serves as the primary point of contact between the nervous and endocrine systems. Because the hypothalamus helps control the ANS, it is responsible for maintaining homeostasis in the body; thus, drugs that alter its function can have a major impact on systems that control homeostasis. The catecholamine transmitters are particularly important in regulating the function of the hypothalamus, and most drugs of abuse that alter the activity of norepinephrine and dopamine are likely to alter the activity of this brain structure as well.

The Autonomic Nervous System

Although the cell bodies of the neurons of the **autonomic nervous system (ANS)** are located within the brain or spinal cord, their axons project outside of the CNS to involuntary muscles, organs, and glands; thus, the ANS is considered part of the PNS. The ANS is an integrative, or regulatory, system that does not require conscious control (that is, you do not have to think about it to make it function). It is usually considered primarily a motor or output system. A number of drugs that cannot enter the CNS because of the blood–brain barrier are able to affect the ANS only. The ANS is divided into two functional components: the sympathetic and the parasympathetic nervous systems (Westfall and Westfall 2006). Both systems include neurons that project to most visceral organs and to smooth muscles, glands, and blood vessels (see Figure 4.8).

The two components of the ANS generally have opposite effects on an organ or its function. The working of the heart is a good example of sympathetic and parasympathetic control. Stimulation of the parasympathetic nervous system slows the heart rate, whereas stimulation of the sympathetic nerves accelerates it. These actions constitute a constant biological check-and-balance, or regulatory system. Because the two parts of the ANS work in opposite ways much of the time, they are considered physiological antagonists. These two systems control most of the internal organs, the circulatory system, and the secretory (glandular) system. The sympathetic

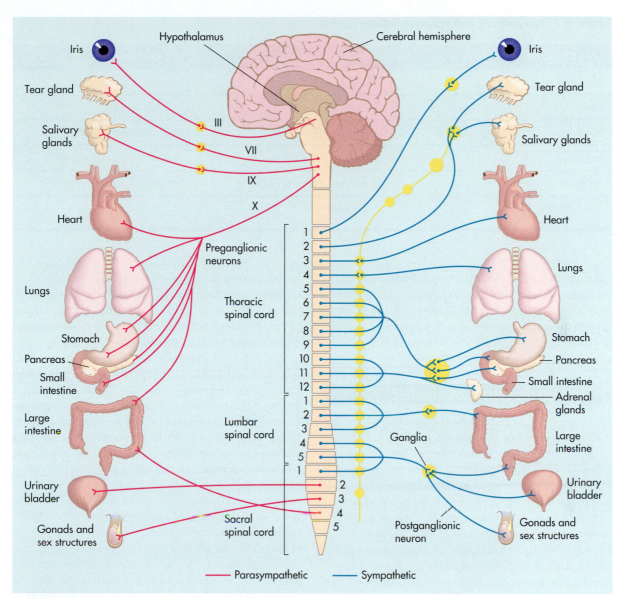

FIGURE 4.8

Autonomic pathways of the parasympathetic and sympathetic nervous systems and the organs affected.

system is normally active at all times; the degree of activity varies from moment to moment and from organ to organ. The parasympathetic nervous system is organized mainly for limited, focused activity and usually conserves and restores energy rather than expends it. For example, it slows the heart rate, lowers blood pressure, aids in absorption of nutrients, and is involved in emptying the urinary bladder. **Table 4.2** lists the structures and/or functions of the sympathetic and parasympathetic nervous systems and their effects on one another.

The two branches of the ANS use two different neurotransmitters. The parasympathetic branch releases ACh at its synapses, whereas the sympathetic

neurons release norepinephrine. An increase in epinephrine in the blood released from the adrenal glands (see the next section) or the administration of drugs that enhance norepinephrine activity causes the body to respond as if the sympathetic nervous system had been activated. As previously mentioned, such drugs are referred to as *sympathomimetics*. Thus, taking amphetamines (which enhance the sympathetic nervous system by releasing norepinephrine and epinephrine) raises blood pressure, speeds up heart rate, slows down motility of the stomach walls, and may cause the pupils of the eyes to enlarge; other so-called "uppers," such as cocaine, have similar effects.

Table 4.2 **Sympathetic and Parasympathetic Control**

STRUCTURE OR FUNCTION	SYMPATHETIC	PARASYMPATHETIC
Heart rate	Speeds up	Slows
Breathing rate	Speeds up	Slows
Stomach wall	Slows motility	Increases motility
Skin blood vessels	Constricts	Dilates (vasomotor function)
Iris of eye	Constricts (pupil enlarges)	Dilates
Vomiting center	Stimulates	—

Drugs that affect ACh release, metabolism, or interaction with its respective receptor are referred to as *cholinergic* drugs. They can either mimic or antagonize the parasympathetic nervous system, according to their pharmacological action.

The Endocrine System

The endocrine system consists of glands, which are ductless (meaning that they secrete their chemical messengers, called hormones, directly into the bloodstream) (see **Figure 4.9**). These hormones are essential in regulating many vital functions, including metabolism, growth, tissue repair, and sexual behavior, to mention just a few. In contrast to neurotransmitters, hormones tend to have a slower onset, a longer duration of action, and a more generalized target. Although a number of tissues are capable of producing and releasing hormones, three of the principal sources of these chemical messengers are the pituitary gland, the adrenal glands, and the sex glands.

Endocrine Glands and Regulation

The pituitary gland is often referred to as the *master gland*. It controls many of the other glands that make up the endocrine system by releasing regu-

lating factors and growth hormone. Besides controlling the brain functions already mentioned, the hypothalamus helps control the activity of the pituitary gland and thereby has a very prominent effect on the endocrine system.

The adrenal glands are located near the kidneys and are divided into two parts: the outer surface, called the *cortex*, and the inner part, called the *medulla*. The adrenal medulla is actually a component of the sympathetic nervous system and releases adrenaline (another name for *epinephrine*) during sympathetic stimulation. Other important hormones released by the adrenal cortex are called *corticosteroids* or just **steroids**. Steroids help the body respond appropriately to crises and stress. In addition, small amounts of male sex hormones (chemically related to the steroids), called **androgens**, are released by the adrenal cortex. The androgens produce anabolic effects that increase the retention and synthesis of proteins, causing growth in the mass of tissues such as muscles and bones (Snyder 2006).

Sex glands are responsible for the secretion of male and female sex hormones that help regulate the development and activity of the respective reproductive systems. The organs known as gonads include the female ovaries and the male testes. The activity of the gonads is regulated by hormones released from the pituitary gland (see Figure 4.9) and, for the most part, remains suppressed until puberty. After activation, estrogens and progesterones are released from the ovaries, and androgens (principally testosterone) are released from the testes. These hormones are responsible for the development and maintenance of the secondary sex characteristics. They influence not only sex-related body features but also emotional states, suggesting that these sex hormones enter the brain and significantly affect the functioning of the limbic systems.

KEY TERMS

steroids
hormones related to the corticosteroids released from the adrenal cortex

androgens
male sex hormones

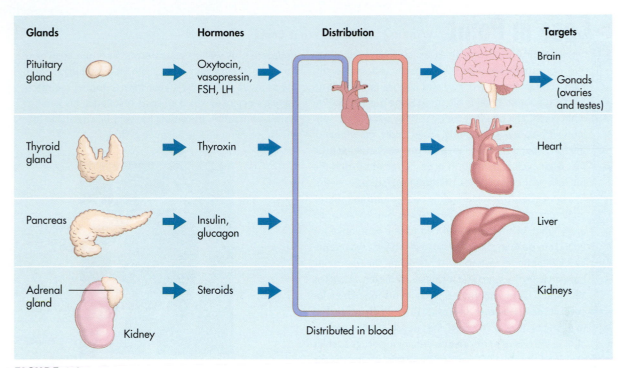

Glands	Hormones	Distribution	Targets
Pituitary gland	Oxytocin, vasopressin, FSH, LH		Brain → Gonads (ovaries and testes)
Thyroid gland	Thyroxin		Heart
Pancreas	Insulin, glucagon		Liver
Adrenal gland / Kidney	Steroids	Distributed in blood	Kidneys

FIGURE 4.9

Examples of some glands in the endocrine system.

FSH, follicle-stimulating hormone; LH, luteinizing hormone.

For the most part, drugs prescribed to treat endocrine problems are intended as replacement therapy. For example, diabetic patients suffer from a shortage of insulin produced by the pancreas, so therapy consists of insulin injections. Patients who suffer from dwarfism receive insufficient growth hormone from the pituitary gland; thus, growth hormone is administered to stimulate normal growth. Because some hormones can affect growth, muscle development, and behavior, they are sometimes abused to enhance athletic performance or bodybuilding.

The Abuse of Hormones: Anabolic Steroids

Androgens are the hormones most likely to be abused in the United States. In 2009, these drugs were self-administered by 1.5% of high school seniors in this country (Johnston 2010). Testosterone, the primary natural androgen, is produced by the testes. Naturally produced androgens are essential for normal growth and development of male sex organs as well as secondary sex characteristics such as male hair patterns, voice changes, muscular development, and fat distribution. The androgens are also necessary for appropriate growth spurts during adolescence (Snyder 2006). Accepted therapeutic use of the androgens is usually for replacement in males with abnormally functioning testes.

Androgens clearly have an impressive effect on development of tissue (Kolata 2002). In particular, they cause pronounced growth of muscle mass and a substantial increase in body weight in young men with deficient testes function. Because of these effects, androgens are classified as anabolic (able to stimulate the conversion of nutrients into tissue mass) steroids (they are chemically similar to the steroids).

In addition, many athletes and trainers know that, when taken in very high doses, androgens can enhance muscle growth and increase strength above that achieved by normal testicular function, thereby improving athletic performance (Snyder 2006). Because of this effect, male and female athletes, as well as nonathletes who are into body building and sports, have been attracted to these drugs in hopes

▶ Case in Point   Winning . . . But at What Cost?

The ability of drugs such as steroids and other "performance-enhancing" substances to make athletes run faster, be stronger, and endure longer are no longer disputed. What is disputed is the question of "At what cost?" The message being sent by today's star athletes all too often is unsettling. For example, the winner of the 2006 Tour de France, Floyd Landis, was heralded to be just what cycling needed in order to move beyond the multiple scandals of drugs. His apparent "squeaky clean" image was based on a Mennonite background and charismatic personality. But this façade was quickly stripped away when arbitrators ruled two to one to remove his 2006 Tour de France title because of lab tests that identified synthetic testosterone in his urine. Despite being banned from the sport and losing all credibility as well as $2 million, Landis continued to claim his innocence for several years. However, in May 2010 he finally confessed to a long history of "doping" that began in 2002 and included the use of performance-enhancing drugs such as the blood-booster EPO and blood transfusions to increase endurance, as well as testosterone and human growth hormone (HGH) to elevate strength. He admitted to spending as much as $90,000 a year for his doping regimens. Landis's desire to win at all costs resulted in his winning nothing but rather becoming the very first cyclist to lose his Tour de France title because of drugs.

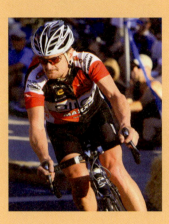

Source: Times Topics. "Floyd Landis." *New York Times* (May 2010). Available at: http://topics.nytimes.com/top/reference/timestopics/people/l/floyd_landis/index.htm. Accessed February 15, 2011.

of enlarging muscle size, improving their athletic performances, and enhancing their physiques (see Chapter 16) despite their risks to both body and careers (see "Case in Point: Winning . . . But at What Cost?").

Several studies have suggested that anabolic hormones can have especially substantial negative effects. Athletic trainers and managers claim to see increases in severe injuries such as tears of muscles and ligaments due to aggravated trauma in over-muscled bodies exposed to these steroids (Verducci 2002). These drugs can also affect the limbic structures of the brain. Consequently, they may cause excitation and a sense of superior strength and performance in some users. These effects, coupled with increased aggressiveness, could encourage continual use of these drugs. Other CNS effects, however, may be disturbing to the user. Symptoms that may occur with very high doses include uncontrolled rage (referred to as "roid rage"), headaches, anxiety, insomnia, and perhaps paranoia (Drug Facts and Comparisons 2005; Talih, Fattal, and Malone 2007). Because of concern about the abuse potential and side effect profile of the anabolic steroids, these drugs are controlled as Schedule III substances.

■ Designer Steroids

In an attempt to circumvent the restriction on steroid use, some athletes have used the "designer" steroid known as tetrahydrogestrinone (THG). The Food and Drug Administration (FDA) banned THG

Anabolic steroids can cause pronounced growth of muscle mass.

in products classified as nutritional supplements. Because of concerns that athletes were using THG to enhance performance, professional athletic organizations and the International Olympic Committee test athletes for this drug (Gardner 2003) and disqualify them from competition if it is detected.

Conclusion

All psychoactive drugs affect brain activity by altering the ability of neurons to send and receive chemical messages. Consequently, drugs of abuse exert their addicting effects by stimulating or blocking the activity of CNS neurotransmitters or their receptors. Thus, to appreciate why these drugs are abused and the nature of their dependence, how neurons and their neurotransmitter systems function must be understood. In addition, many scientists believe that elucidating how substances of abuse affect nervous systems will help identify why some persons are at greater risk for abuse problems and will lead to new and more effective methods for preventing and treating drug addiction.

Discussion Questions

1. What are the similarities and differences between neurotransmitters and hormones?

2. Why is it important for the body to have chemical messengers that can be quickly released and rapidly inactivated?

3. Why are receptors so important in understanding the effects of drugs of abuse?

4. What role do the opioid and cannabinoid systems play in drug abuse, and how can these neurosystems be used therapeutically?

5. Why is it not surprising that drugs that affect the catecholamine transmitters also affect the endocrine system?

6. What are some mechanisms whereby a drug of abuse can increase the activity of dopamine transmitter systems in the brain?

7. How can knowing that the insula of the brain is important for motivation be used to treat tobacco addiction?

8. Why might a drug of abuse that damages the associative cortex make the user especially vulnerable to addiction?

9. Was classifying anabolic steroids as Schedule III drugs justified? What do you think will be the long-term consequence of this action?

Summary

1 The nervous and endocrine systems help mediate internal and external responses to the body's surroundings. Both systems release chemical messengers to achieve their homeostatic functions. These messenger substances are called neurotransmitters and hormones, and they carry out their functions by binding to specific receptors. Many drugs exert their effects by influencing these chemical messengers.

2 The neuron is the principal cell type in the nervous system. This specialized cell consists of dendrites, a cell body, and an axon. It communicates with other neurons and organs by releasing neurotransmitters, which can cause either excitation or inhibition at their target sites.

3 The chemical messengers from glands and neurons exert their effects by interacting with special protein regions in membranes called receptors. Because of their unique construction, receptors interact only with molecules that have specific shapes. Activation of receptors can alter the functions of the target system.

4 Endorphin (opioid) and cannabinoid systems were discovered due to drugs of abuse such as the opioid narcotics and marijuana, respectively. Besides being the target of drugs of abuse, these systems also have the potential to be pharmacologically manipulated to achieve therapeutic outcomes.

5 Agonists are substances or drugs that stimulate receptors. Antagonists are substances or drugs that bind to receptors and prevent them from being activated.

6 A variety of substances are used as neurotransmitters by neurons in the body. The classes of transmitters include the catecholamines, serotonin, acetylcholine, GABA, peptides, and cannabinoids. These transmitters are excitatory, inhibitory, or sometimes both, depending on which receptor is being activated. Many drugs selectively act to either enhance or antagonize these neurotransmitters and their activities.

7 The central nervous system consists of the brain and spinal cord. Regions within the brain help to regulate specific functions. The hypothalamus controls endocrine and basic body functions. The basal ganglia include the caudate nucleus and are primarily responsible for controlling motor activity and learned behaviors. The limbic system regulates mood and mental states and establishing behaviors. The cerebral cortex helps interpret, process information, make decisions, and respond to input information.

8 The limbic system and its associated transmitters, especially dopamine and serotonin, are major sites of action for the drugs of abuse. Substances that increase the activity of dopamine cause a sense of well-being and euphoria, which encourages psychological dependence.

9 The autonomic nervous system is composed of the sympathetic and parasympathetic systems; neurons associated with these systems release noradrenaline and acetylcholine as their transmitters, respectively. These systems work in an antagonistic fashion to control unconscious, visceral functions such as breathing and cardiovascular activity. The parasympathetic nervous system usually helps conserve and restore energy in the body, whereas the sympathetic nervous system is continually active.

10 The endocrine system consists of glands that synthesize and release hormones into the blood. Distribution via blood circulation carries these chemical messengers throughout the body, where they act on specific receptors. Some of the principal structures include the pituitary, adrenals, and gonads (testes and ovaries).

11 Anabolic steroids are structurally related to the male hormone testosterone. They are often abused by both male and female athletes trying to build muscle mass, and are referred to as "performance enhancers." The continual use of high doses of anabolic steroids can cause annoying and dangerous side effects. The long-term effects of low, intermittent doses of these drugs have not been determined. Because of concerns voiced by most medical authorities, anabolic steroids are controlled substances and have been classified as Schedule III substances.

References

Aarthun, S. "Synthetic Marijuana a Growing Trend Among Teens, Authorities Say." CNNHealth. 2010. Available http://www.cnn.com/2010/HEALTH/03/23/synthetic.marijuana/index.html

Bateson, A. "The Benzodiazepine Site of the GABA A Receptor: An Old Target with a New Potential." *Sleep Medicine* 5 (2004):S9–S59.

Bloom, F. "Neurotransmission and the Central Nervous System." In *The Pharmacological Basis of Therapeutics*, 9th ed., edited by J. Harman and T. Limbird, 267–293. New York: McGraw-Hill, 1995.

Bosier, B., G. Muccioli, E. Hermans, and D. Lambert. "Functionally Selective Cannabinoid Receptor Signaling: Therapeutic Implications and Opportunities." *Biochemical Pharmacology* 80 (2010):1–12.

Churdler, E. "Neuroscience for Kids." 2010. Available http://faculty.Washington.edu/chudler/chnt1.html

Conway, K., J. Levy, M. Vanyukov, et al. "Measuring Addiction Propensity and Severity: The Need for a New Instrument." *Drug and Alcohol Dependence* (May 2010):4–12.

Deadwyler, S. "Electrophysiological Correlates of Abused Drugs: Relation to Natural Rewards." *Annals of the New York Academy of Science* 1187 (2010):140–147.

DiChiara, G., V. Bassareo, S. Fenu, et al. "Dopamine and Drug Addiction: The Nucleus Accumbens Shell Connections." *Neuropharmacology* 47 Suppl. 1 (2004):227–241.

Drgon, T., P. Zhang, C. Johnson, et al. "Genome Wide Association for Addiction: Replicated Results and Comparisons of Two Analytic Approaches." *PLoS One* 5 (2010):e8832.

Drug Facts and Comparisons. 59th ed. St. Louis: Wolters Kluwar Health, 2005:322–336.

Fattore, L., G. Cossu, M. Spano, et al. "Cannabinoids and Rewards: Interactions with Opioid Systems." *Critical Reviews in Neurobiology* 16 (2004):147–158.

Ferguson, S. "Phosphorylation-Independent Attenuation of GPCR Signaling." *Trends in Pharmacological Science* 28 (2007):173–179.

Gardner, A. "Controversy Grows Over Designer Steroid. Feds Ban THG: Grand Jury Subpoenas Top Athletes." *Healthscout* (30 October 2003):10F2.

Giraldo, J. "How Much Inverse Agonist a Neutral Antagonist Can Be. Questions After the Rimonabant Issue." *Drug Discovery Today* (4 May 2010).

Johnston, L. "Monitoring the Future 2009." 2010. Available http://monitoringthefuture.org/data/09data.html

Kandel, E., and S. A. Siegelbaum. "Overview of Synaptic Transmission." In *Principles of Neural Science*, 4th ed., edited by E. Kandel, J. Schwartz, and T. Jessell, 175–186. New York: McGraw-Hill, 2000.

Kolata, G. "With No Answers on Risks: Steroid Users Still Say 'Yes.'" *New York Times* (2 December 2002). Available http://www.nytimes.com

Koob, G. F., and N. Volkow. "Neurocircuitry of Addiction." *Neuropsychopharmacology* 35 (2010):217–238.

Kyrou, I., and C. Tsigos. "Stress Hormones: Physiological Stress and Regulation of Metabolism." *Current Opinions in Pharmacology* 9 (2009):787–793.

Learn.Genetics. "Genetics Is an Important Factor in Addiction." University of Utah, Genetic Science Learning Center. 2010. Available http://learn.genetics.utah.edu/content/addiction/genetics

Lefkowitz, R., B. Hoffman, and P. Taylor. "Neurotransmission, the Autonomic and Somatic Motor Nervous Systems." In *The Pharmacological Basis of Therapeutics,* 9th ed., edited by J. Hardman and T. Limbird, 361–396. New York: McGraw-Hill, 1995.

Luscher, C., and P. Slesinger. "Emerging Roles for G-Protein-Gated Inwardly Rectifying Potassium (GIRK) Channels in Health and Disease." *Nature Reviews Neuroscience* 11 (2010): 301–315.

Matsuda, L. "Molecular Aspects of Cannabinoid Receptors." *Critical Reviews in Neurobiology* 11 (1997):143–166.

O'Brien, C. "Drug Addiction and Drug Abuse." In *The Pharmacological Basis of Therapeutics,* 11th ed., edited by L. Brunton, J. Lazo, and K. Parker, 607–627. New York: McGraw-Hill, 2006.

Porrino, L., J. Daunais, H. Smith, and M. Nadar. "The Expanding Effects of Cocaine: Studies in Nonhuman Primate Model of Cocaine Self-Administration." *Neuroscience Biobehavioral Reviews* 27 (2004):893–920.

Price, M. "Genes Matter in Addiction." *Monitor* 39 (2008):14.

Sabatowski, R., D. Shafer, S. Kasper, H. Brunsch, and L. Radbruh. "Pain Treatment: A Historical Overview." *Current Pharmaceutical Design* 10 (2004):701–716.

Shim, J. Y. "Understanding Functional Residuals of the Cannabinoid CB1 Receptor for Drug Discovery." *Current Topics in Medicinal Chemistry* (6 April 2010):779–798.

Snyder, P. "Androgens." In *The Pharmacological Basis of Therapeutics,* 11th ed., edited by L. Brunton, J. Lazo, and K. Parker, 1573–1585. New York: McGraw-Hill, 2006.

Talih, F., O. Fattal, and D. Malone. "Anabolic Steroid Abuse: Psychiatric and Physical Costs." *Cleveland Clinical Journal of Medicine* 74 (2007):341–344.

Times Topics. "Floyd Landis." *New York Times.* May 2010. Available http://topics.nytimes.com/top/reference/times topics/people/l/floyd_landis/index.html

Valliant, P., and L. Clark. "An Evaluation of Nonassaultive and Assaultive, and Sexually Assaultive Adolescents at Pretrial Sentencing: A Comparison on Cognition, Personality, Aggression, and Criminal Sentiments." *Psychological Reports* 105 (2009):1077–1091.

Verducci, T. "The Injury Toll." (2002 May 28). Available http://www.CNNSI.com

Vorel, S., A. Bisaga, G. McKhann, and H. Kleber. "Insula Damage and Quitting Smoking." *Science* 317 (2007):318–319.

Walsh, S., E. Unterwald, and S. Izenwasser. "Contemporary Advances in Opioid Neuropharmacology." *Drug and Alcohol Dependence* 108 (2010):153–155.

Westfall, T., and D. Westfall. "Neurotransmission. The Autonomic and Somatic Motor Nervous Systems." In *The Pharmacological Basis of Therapeutics,* 11th ed., edited by L. Brunton, J. Lazo, and K. Parker, 137–181. New York: McGraw-Hill, 2006.

CHAPTER 5

How and Why Drugs Work

Did You Know?

- Twenty percent of the total hospital costs in the United States are due to medical care for health damage caused by substances of abuse.
- The same dose of a drug does not have the same effect on everyone.
- In excessive doses, almost any drug or substance can be toxic.
- Sixty-five percent of the strokes among young Americans are related to cigarette, cocaine, or amphetamine use.
- Many people who abuse cocaine also abuse alcohol to counter unpleasant side effects.
- Many of the overdose deaths caused by prescription drugs are due to unanticipated drug interactions.
- Many drugs are unable to pass from the blood into the brain.
- Gender affects responses to alcohol and tobacco.
- Hereditary factors may predispose some individuals to becoming psychologically dependent on drugs with abuse potential.

Drugs and Society Online is a great source for additional drugs and society information for both students and instructors. Visit **go.jblearning.com/hanson11** to find a variety of useful tools for learning, thinking, and teaching.

Learning Objectives

On completing this chapter you will be able to:

- Describe some of the common unintended drug effects.
- Explain why the same dose of a drug may affect individuals differently.
- Explain the difference between potency and toxicity.
- Describe the concept of a drug's "margin of safety."
- Identify and give examples of additive, antagonistic, and potentiative (synergistic) drug interactions.
- Identify the pharmacokinetic factors that can influence the effects caused by drugs.
- Cite the physiological and pathological factors that influence drug effects.
- Explain the significance of the blood–brain barrier to psychoactive drugs.
- Define threshold dose, plateau effect, and cumulative effect.
- Discuss the role of the liver in drug metabolism and the consequences of this process.
- Define biotransformation.
- Describe the relationships among tolerance, withdrawal, rebound, physical dependence, and psychological dependence.
- Discuss the significance of placebos in drug therapy and drug abuse.
- Describe drug craving, and explain how it can cause relapse to a drug addiction.

Introduction

A common belief is that drugs can solve most of life's serious physical, emotional, and medical problems. Although medications are essential to treatment for many diseases, excessive reliance on drugs causes unrealistic expectations that may lead to dangerous—even fatal—consequences. For example, drug addiction and dependence often follow from such unrealistic drug expectations. Obviously, not every person who uses drugs inappropriately becomes a drug addict, nor are patients who use drugs as prescribed by the doctor immune from becoming physically and mentally dependent on their prescribed medications. In fact, because of individual variability, it is difficult to predict accurately which drug users will or will not have drug problems such as addiction and dependence.

In this chapter, we consider the factors that account for the variability of drug responses—that is, what determines how the body responds to drugs and why some drugs work but others do not. First, we review the general effects of drugs, both intended and unintended. The correlation between the dose and response to a drug is addressed next, followed by a discussion of how drugs interact with one another. The section on pharmacokinetic factors considers how drugs are introduced into, distributed throughout, and eliminated from the body, along with physiological and pathological variables that modify how drugs affect the body. The final sections in the chapter consider concepts important to understanding drug abuse, such as tolerance, physical versus psychological dependence, and addiction.

The Intended and Unintended Effects of Drugs

When physicians prescribe drugs, their objective is usually to cure or relieve symptoms of a disease. Frequently, however, drugs cause unintended effects that neither the physician nor the patient expected. These are called **side effects**.

A response that is considered a side effect in one situation may, in fact, be the therapeutic objective in another. For example, the antihistamines found in many over-the-counter (OTC) drugs have an intended main effect of relieving allergy symptoms, but they often cause annoying drowsiness as a side effect; in fact, for this reason their labels include warnings that they should not be used while driving a car. These antihistamines are also included in OTC sleep aids, in which their sedating action is the desired main effect.

Side effects can influence many body functions and occur in any organ (see **Figure 5.1**), and they send more than 700,000 people to U.S. hospitals every year, according to the Centers for Disease Control and Prevention (CDC) and the Food and Drug Administration (FDA). The following are basic kinds of side effects that can result from drug use:

- Nausea or vomiting
- Changes in mental alertness such as sedation or nervousness
- Dependence, which compels people to continue using a drug because they want to achieve a desired effect or because they fear unpleasant reactions, called **withdrawal**, that occur when use of the drug is discontinued
- Allergic reactions (hypersensitive reactions or sensitization), often experienced as rashes or breathing difficulty
- Changes in cardiovascular activity altering the activity of the heart or blood pressure

This short list of side effects demonstrates the types of risks involved whenever any drug (prescription, nonprescription, illicit, and even some herbal products) is used. Consequently, before taking a drug, whether for therapeutic or recreational use, you should understand its potential problems and determine whether the benefits justify the risks. For example, it is important to know that morphine is effective for relieving severe pain, but it also depresses breathing and retards intestinal activity, causing constipation. Likewise, amphetamines can be used to suppress appetite for losing weight, but they also increase blood pressure and stimulate the heart, and may even cause hemorrhaging. Cocaine is a good local anesthetic, but it can be extremely addicting and can cause tremors or even seizures. The greater the danger associated with using a drug, the less likely that the benefits will warrant its use.

Adverse effects of drugs of abuse are particularly troublesome in the United States. Studies have suggested that tens of billions of dollars are spent each year in the United States because of medical care and premature deaths related to the use of addicting substances (Cartwright 2008; Rice 1999).

KEY TERMS

side effects
unintended drug responses

withdrawal
unpleasant effects that occur when use of a drug is stopped

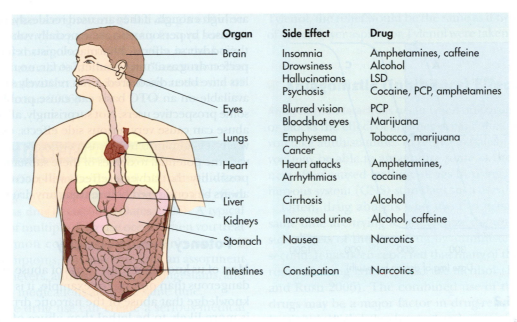

Organ	Side Effect	Drug
Brain	Insomnia	Amphetamines, caffeine
	Drowsiness	Alcohol
	Hallucinations	LSD
	Psychosis	Cocaine, PCP, amphetamines
Eyes	Blurred vision	PCP
	Bloodshot eyes	Marijuana
Lungs	Emphysema	Tobacco, marijuana
	Cancer	
Heart	Heart attacks	Amphetamines,
	Arrhythmias	cocaine
Liver	Cirrhosis	Alcohol
Kidneys	Increased urine	Alcohol, caffeine
Stomach	Nausea	Narcotics
Intestines	Constipation	Narcotics

FIGURE 5.1

Common side effects with drugs of abuse. Almost every organ or system in the body can be negatively affected by the substances of abuse.

The Dose–Response Relationship of Therapeutics and Toxicity

All effects—both desired and unwanted—are related to the amount of drug administered. A small concentration of drug may have one effect, whereas a larger dose may create a greater effect or a different effect entirely. Because some correlation exists between the response to a drug and the quantity of the drug dose, it is possible to calculate **dose–response** curves (see **Figure 5.2**).

Once a dose–response curve for a drug has been determined in an individual, it can be used to predict how that person will respond to different doses of the drug. For example, the dose–response curve for user B in Figure 5.2 shows that 600 mg of aspirin will relieve only 50% of his or her headache. It is important to understand that not everyone responds the same way to a given dose of drug. Thus, in Figure 5.2, although 600 mg of aspirin gives 50% relief from a headache for user B, it relieves 100% of the headache for user A and none of the headache for user C. This variability in response can make it difficult to predict the precise drug effect from a given dose.

Many factors can contribute to the variability in drug responses (Buxton 2006). One of the most important is **tolerance**, or reduced response over time to the same dosage, an effect that is examined carefully in a later section of this chapter. Other factors include the size of the individual, stomach contents if the drug is taken by mouth, different levels of enzymatic activity in the liver (which changes the drug via metabolic action), acidity of the urine (which affects the rate of drug elimination), time of day, and state of the person's health. Such multiple interacting factors make it difficult to calculate accurately the final drug effect for any given individual at any given time.

■ Margin of Safety

An important concept for developing new drugs for therapy, as well as for assessing the probability of serious side effects for drugs of abuse, is called

KEY TERMS

dose–response
correlation between the amount of a drug given and its effects

tolerance
changes in the body that decrease response to a drug even though the dose remains the same

and the person becomes groggy. A person in this state may forget that he or she has taken the pills and repeat the dose. The combination of these two depressants (or other depressants, such as antihistamines) can interfere with the CNS to the point where vital functions such as breathing and heartbeat are severely impaired.

Although the mechanisms of interaction among CNS depressants are not entirely clear, these drugs likely enhance one another's direct effects on inhibitory chemical messengers in the brain (see Chapter 4). In addition, interference by alcohol with liver-metabolizing enzymes contributes to the synergism that arises with the combination of alcohol and some depressants, such as barbiturates (Fleming, Mihic, and Harris 2006; Hobbs, Rall, and Verdoorn 1995; National Institute on Alcohol Abuse and Alcoholism 2010).

■ Dealing with Drug Interactions

Although many drug effects and interactions are not very well understood, it is important to be aware of them. A growing body of evidence indicates that many of the drugs and substances we deliberately consume will interact and produce un-expected and sometimes dangerous effects (see **Table 5.1**). It is alarming to know that many of the foods we eat and some chemical pollutants also interfere with and modify drug actions. Pesticides, traces of hormones in meat and poultry, traces of metals in fish, nitrites and nitrates from fertilizers, and a wide range of chemicals—some of which are used as food additives—have been shown, under certain conditions, to interact with some drugs (Meckling 2006).

It is essential that the public be educated about the interactions most likely to occur with drugs that are prescribed, self-administered legitimately (for example, OTC drugs and herbal products), or taken recreationally (for example, drugs of abuse) (see "Prescription for Abuse: Deadly Drug Mix"). People need to be aware that OTC and herbal drugs are as likely to cause interaction problems as prescription drugs. For example, an OTC or herbal decongestant that contains mild CNS stimulants (e.g., pseudoephedrine) taken with potent CNS stimulants, such as cocaine and amphetamines, can cause interactions that fatally affect the heart and brain. If any question arises concerning the possibility of drug interaction, individuals should talk to their physician, pharmacist, or other healthcare providers.

Prescription for Abuse: A Loaded Weapon

April Rovero was in complete shock when she learned that Joey, her son, was dead from a deadly mixture of prescription drugs. "You just can't believe your son is gone. . . . Your mind goes numb," she said. Because drugs are prescribed, many young people mistakenly think they can't be dangerous and use the drugs in ways for which they never were intended. For example, users sometimes crush the prescription pills and then place the powder in their nose for snorting or smoke or inject the drugs. Such methods accelerate the rate at which these drugs enter the body and increase the likelihood of their interacting with other drugs and the potential for causing dangerous side effects. This was the case with Joey. He and his friends went to visit a "dirty doctor" (a doctor who flagrantly and excessively prescribes drugs to patients for abuse purposes) to buy prescription drugs for "recreational" purposes. The doctor gave Joey 90 tablets of the painkiller Percocet, 90 doses of the muscle relaxant Soma, and 30 tablets of the anti-anxiety medication Xanax. This drug combination plus some alcohol was enough to stop Joey's breathing and resulted in his death—sudden, unexpected, and terribly tragic.

Source: Mills, D. "A Loaded Weapon: Concern Over Prescription Pill Abuse in Teens." Patch Blog. (28 May 2010.) Available at: http://Danville.patch.com/articles/a-loaded-weapon-concern-over-prescription-pill-abuse-in-teens. Accessed March 2, 2011.

Table 5.1 Common Interactions with Substances of Abuse

DRUG	COMBINED WITH	CONSEQUENCE OF INTERACTION
Sedatives		
Diazepam (Valium), triazolam (Halcion)	Alcohol, barbiturates	Increase sedation
Stimulants		
Amphetamines, cocaine	Insulin	Decrease insulin effect
	Antidepressants	Cause hypertension
Narcotics		
Heroin, morphine	Barbiturates, Valium	Increase sedation
	Anticoagulant	Increase bleeding
	Antidepressants	Cause sedation
	Amphetamines	Increase euphoria
Tobacco		
Nicotine	Blood pressure medication	Elevate blood pressure
	Amphetamines, cocaine	Increase cardiovascular effects
Alcohol		
	Cocaine	Produces cocaethylene, which enhances euphoria and toxicity

Prescription for Abuse: Deadly Drug Mix

His real name was Adam Goldstein, but as a popular rock musician he was better known by his stage name, DJ AM. Although he had openly discussed his problems with substance addictions, he continued to struggle with drug problems until they eventually led to his overdose death in August 2009. The toxicology examination determined that DJ AM had in his system a combination of CNS depressants that included prescription drugs such as narcotic painkillers (OxyContin and Vicodin), antianxiety drugs (Xanax, Ativan, and Klonopin), and an antihistamine (Benadryl). Six pills were found in his stomach and an OxyContin capsule was lodged in his throat, suggesting his death was sudden. After breaking down his apartment door, paramedics found DJ AM dead in his New York City apartment shirtless and wearing sweatpants, a victim of addiction and apparently ignorant about the deadly interactions of the prescription CNS depressants that killed him.

Source: Associated Press. "DJ AM's Death Ruled Accidental Drug Overdose." 2009. Available at: http://today.msnbc.msn.com/id/33072533. Accessed March 2, 2011.

Many drug abusers are multiple drug (polydrug) users with little concern for the dangerous interactions that might occur. It is common, for example, for drug abusers to combine multiple CNS depressants to enhance their effects, to combine a depressant with a stimulant to titrate a CNS effect (to determine the smallest amount that can be taken to achieve the desired "high"), or to experiment with a combination of stimulants, depressants, and hallucinogens just to see what happens. The effects of such haphazard drug mixing are impossible to predict, difficult to treat in emergency situations, and all too frequently fatal.

Pharmacokinetic Factors that Influence Drug Effects

Although it is difficult to predict precisely how any single individual will be affected by drug use, the following major factors represent different aspects of the body's response that should be considered when attempting to anticipate a drug's effects (Buxton 2006):

- How does the drug enter the body? (administration)
- How does the drug move from the site of administration into the body's system? (absorption)
- How does the drug move to various areas in the body? (distribution)
- How and where does the drug produce its effects? (activation)
- How is the drug inactivated, metabolized, and/or excreted from the body? (biotransformation and elimination)

These issues relate to the **pharmacokinetics** of a drug and are important considerations when predicting the body's response. They can impact the drug levels that are detected in the body when a drug test is conducted.

■ Forms and Methods of Taking Drugs

Drugs come in many forms. How a drug is formulated—solution, powder, capsule, or pill—

influences the rate of passage into the bloodstream and consequently its efficacy. The means of introducing the drug into the body will also affect how quickly the drug enters the bloodstream and how it is distributed to the site of action, as well as how much will ultimately reach its target and exert an effect (Buxton 2006) (see **Figure 5.3**). The principal forms of drug administration are *oral ingestion, inhalation, injection,* and *topical application.*

Oral Ingestion

One of the most common and convenient ways of taking a drug is orally. This type of administration usually introduces the drug into the body by way of the stomach or intestines. Following oral administration, it is difficult to control the amount of drug that reaches the site of action, for three reasons:

1. The drug must enter the bloodstream after passing through the wall of the stomach or intestines without being destroyed or changed to an inactive form. From the blood, the drug must diffuse to the target area and remain there in sufficient concentration to have an effect.

2. Materials in the stomach or intestines, such as food, may interfere with the passage of some drugs through the gut lining and thus prevent drug action. For example, food in your stomach will diminish the effects of alcohol by altering its absorption.

3. The liver might metabolize orally ingested drugs too rapidly, before they are able to exert an effect. The liver is the major detoxifying organ in the body, which means it removes chemicals and toxins from the blood and usually changes them into an inactive form that is easy for the body to excrete. This function is essential to survival, but it creates a problem for the pharmacologist in developing effective drugs or the physician prescribing the correct dose of a drug to treat a serious disease. The liver is especially problematic to oral administration because the substances absorbed from the digestive tract usually go to the liver before being distributed to other parts of the body and their site of action. For this reason, cocaine taken orally is not very effective.

Inhalation

Some drugs are administered by inhalation into the lungs through the mouth or nose. The lungs include large beds of capillaries, so chemicals capable of crossing membranes can enter the blood as rapidly as they can via intravenous (IV) injection and can be

Method of Administration	Onset	Duration	Effect
Smoking			
Cocaine	Fast (~15 seconds)	Brief (10–15 minutes)	Potent and strong
Heroin	Fast (~20 seconds)	Short (1–2 hours)	Potent and strong
Intravenous			
Cocaine	Fast (20 seconds)	Short (30 minutes)	Potent and strong
Heroin	Fast (1–2 minutes)	Short (1–2 hours)	Potent and strong
Snorting			
Cocaine	Moderate (~10 minutes)	Short (45 minutes)	Less potent
Heroin	Moderate (~15 minutes)	Short (1–2 hours)	Less potent
Oral			
Cocaine (coca leaf)	Slow (30 minutes)	Moderate (~2–4 hours)	Minor
Methadone	Slow (30–60 minutes)	Long (24 hours)	Less euphoria/ used for treatment

FIGURE 5.3

Relationship between the method of drug administration and drug effects.

equally as dangerous (Meng et al. 1999). Ether, chloroform, and nitrous oxide anesthetics are examples of drugs that are therapeutically administered by inhalation. Nicotine, cocaine, methamphetamine, THC in marijuana, and heroin are drugs of abuse that can be inhaled as smoke (Mathias 1997). One serious problem with inhalation is the potential for irritation to the mucous membrane lining of the lungs; another is that the drug may have to be continually inhaled to maintain the concentration necessary for an effect. Inhalation of illicit drugs of abuse is common to prevent contracting AIDS, which can be transmitted by IV injection with contaminated needles (Meng et al. 1999; National Institute on Drug Abuse [NIDA] 1999; Wood 2009).

Injection

Some drugs are given by **intravenous (IV)**, **intramuscular (IM)**, or **subcutaneous (SC)** injection. A major advantage of administering drugs by IV is the speed of action; the dosage is delivered rapidly and directly, and often less drug is needed because it reaches the site of action quickly. This method can be very dangerous if the dosage is calculated incorrectly, the drug effects are unknown, or the user is especially sensitive to the drug's adverse effects. In addition, impurities in injected materials may irritate the vein; this issue is a particular problem in the drug-abusing population, in which needle sharing frequently occurs. The injection itself injures the vein by leaving a tiny point of scar tissue where the vein is punctured. If repeated injections are administered into the same area, the elasticity of

Drugs can be introduced into the body using various mechanisms such as pills, capsules, oral liquids, topicals, or injections.

KEY TERMS

intravenous (IV)
drug injection into a vein

intramuscular (IM)
drug injection into a muscle

subcutaneous (SC)
drug injection beneath the skin

the vein is gradually reduced, causing the vessel to collapse.

Intramuscular injection can damage the muscle directly if the drug preparation irritates the tissue or indirectly if the nerve controlling the muscle is damaged. If the nerve is destroyed, the muscle will degenerate (atrophy). A subcutaneous injection may damage the skin at the point of injection if a particularly irritating drug is administered. Another danger of drug injections arises when contaminated needles are shared by drug users. This danger has become a serious problem in the spread of infectious diseases such as AIDS and hepatitis (NIDA, 2007).

Topical Application

Those drugs that readily pass through surface tissue such as the skin, the lining of the nose, and under the tongue can be applied topically, for systemic (whole-body) effects. Although many drugs do not appreciably diffuse across these tissue barriers into the circulation, there are notable exceptions. For example, a product to help quit smoking, a nicotine transdermal patch (Nicoderm), is placed on the skin; the drug passes through the skin and enters the body to prevent tobacco craving and withdrawal. In addition, several drugs of abuse, such as heroin and cocaine, can be "snorted" into the nose and rapidly absorbed into the body through the nasal lining.

■ Distribution of Drugs in the Body and Time-Response Relationships

Following administration (regardless of the mode), most drugs are distributed throughout the body in the blood. The circulatory system consists of many miles of arteries, veins, and capillaries and includes 5 to 6 liters of blood. Once a drug enters the bloodstream by passing through thin capillary walls, it is rapidly diluted and carried to organs and other body structures. It requires approximately 1 minute for the blood, and consequently the drugs it contains, to circulate completely throughout the body.

KEY TERMS

blood–brain barrier
selective filtering between the cerebral blood vessels and the brain

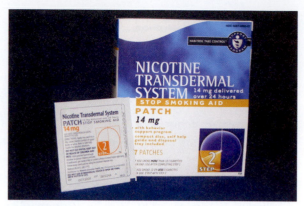

Transdermal nicotine patches are popular smoking cessation aids.

Factors Affecting Distribution

Drugs have different patterns of distribution depending on the following chemical properties (Buxton 2006):

- Their ability to pass across membranes and through tissues
- Their molecular size (large versus small molecules)
- Their solubility properties (do they dissolve in water or in fatty [oily] solutions?)
- Their tendency to attach to proteins and tissues throughout the body

These distribution-related factors are very important because they determine whether a drug can pass across tissue barriers in the body and reach its site of action. By preventing the movement of drugs into organs or across tissues, these barriers may interfere with drug activity and limit the therapeutic usefulness of a drug if they do not allow it to reach its site of action. Such barriers may also offer protection by preventing entry of a drug into a body structure where it can cause problems.

Blood is carried to the nerve cells of the brain in a vast network of thin-walled capillaries. Drugs that are soluble in fatty (oily) solutions are most likely to pass across these capillary membranes (known as the **blood–brain barrier**) into the brain tissue. Most psychoactive drugs, such as the drugs of abuse, are able to pass across the blood–brain barrier with little difficulty. However, many water-soluble drugs cannot pass through the fatty capillary wall; such drugs are not likely to cross this biological barrier and affect the brain. An interesting practical application of this pharmacokinetic principal is the use of "vaccines" to treat nicotine (Erb 2010) or cocaine (Martell et al. 2009) dependence. Like other vaccines, this approach stimulates the body to produce antibodies against a chemical target that is introduced into the body (often injected under the skin). Consequently, when specially formulated nicotine or cocaine (a chemical form that causes an immuno-reaction) is injected into the body, it stimulates the production of reactive antibodies in the patient. These antibodies will then bind to nicotine or cocaine that is later consumed and has entered into the bloodstream. With the attached antibody, the drug is too large to get across biological barriers such as the blood–brain barrier, and often becomes pharmacologically inactive. This means that the antibodies prevent nicotine or cocaine from being rewarding or from having effects on the brain in general and help the addict to stop using the substance (Martell et al. 2009).

A second biological barrier, the placenta, prevents the transfer of certain molecules from the mother to the fetus. A principal factor that determines passage of substances across the placental barrier is molecule size. Large molecules do not usually cross the placental barrier, whereas small molecules do. Because most drugs are relatively small molecules, they usually cross from the maternal circulation into the fetal circulation; thus, most drugs (including drugs of abuse) taken by a woman during pregnancy enter and affect the fetus. This can cause a baby of a heroin-using mother, for example, to experience severe withdrawal symptoms after birth (Keegan et al. 2010).

Required Doses for Effects

Most drugs do not take effect until a certain amount has been administered and a crucial concentration has reached the site of action in the body. The smallest amount of a drug needed to elicit a response is called its **threshold dose**.

The effectiveness of some drugs may be calculated in a *linear* (straight-line) fashion—that is, the more drug that is taken, the more drug that is distributed throughout the body and the greater the effect. However, many drugs have a maximum possible effect, regardless of dose; this is called the **plateau effect**. OTC medications, in particular, have a limit on their effects. For example, use of the non-prescription analgesic aspirin can effectively relieve your mild to moderate pain, but aspirin will not effectively treat your severe pains, regardless of the dose taken. Other drugs may cause distinct or opposite effects, depending on the dose. For example, low doses of alcohol may appear to act like a stimulant, causing the drinker to be talkative and

social, whereas high doses usually cause sedation resulting in drowsiness and eventually sleep or in extreme cases even coma.

Time-Response Factors

An important factor that determines responses is the time that has elapsed between when a drug was administered and the onset of its effects. The delay in effect after administering a drug often relates to the time required for the drug to disseminate from the site of administration to the site of action. Consequently, the closer a drug is placed to the target area, the faster the onset of action.

The drug response is often classified as immediate, short-term, or **acute**, referring to the response after a single dose. The response can also be **chronic**, or long-term—a characteristic usually associated with repeated doses. The intensity and quality of a drug's acute effect may change considerably within a short period of time. For example, the main intoxicating effects of a large dose of alcohol generally peak in less than 1 hour and then gradually taper off. In addition, an initial stimulating effect by alcohol may later change to sedation and depression.

The effects of long-term, or chronic, use of some drugs can differ dramatically from the effects noted with their short-term, or acute, use. The administration of small doses may not produce any immediately apparent detrimental effect, but chronic use of the same drug (frequent use over a long time) may yield prolonged effects that do not become apparent until years later. Although for most people there is little evidence to show any immediate damage or detrimental response to short-term use of small doses of tobacco, its chronic use has damaging effects on heart and lung functions (Westmaas and Brandon 2004). Because of these long-term consequences, research on tobacco and its effects often continues for years, making it difficult to unequivocally prove a correlation between specific diseases or health problems and use of this

KEY TERMS

threshold dose
minimum drug dose necessary to cause an effect

plateau effect
maximum drug effect, regardless of dose

acute
immediate or short-term effects after taking a single drug dose

chronic
long-term effects, usually after taking multiple drug doses

substance. Thus, the results of tobacco research are often disputed by tobacco manufacturers with vested financial interests in the substance and its public acceptance.

Another important time factor that influences drug responses is the interval between multiple administrations. If sufficient time for drug metabolism and elimination does not separate doses, a drug can accumulate within the body. This drug buildup due to relatively short dosing intervals is referred to as a **cumulative effect**. Because of the resulting high concentrations of drug in the body, unexpected prolonged drug effects or toxicity can occur when multiple doses are given within short intervals. This situation occurs with cocaine or methamphetamine addicts who repeatedly administer these stimulants during "binges" or "runs," increasing the likelihood of dangerous effects.

■ Inactivation and Elimination of Drugs from the Body

Immediately after drug administration, the body begins to eliminate the substance in various ways. The time required to remove half of the original amount of drug administered is called the **half-life** of the drug. The body eliminates the drug either directly without altering it chemically or (in most instances) after it has been metabolized (chemically altered) or modified. The process of changing the chemical or pharmacological properties of a drug by metabolism is called **biotransformation** (Buxton 2006). **Metabolism** usually makes it possible for the body to inactivate, detoxify, and excrete drugs and other chemicals, although metabolism can sometimes actually cause a drug such as heroin to become *more* active.

KEY TERMS

cumulative effect
buildup of a drug in the body after multiple doses taken at short intervals

half-life
time required for the body to eliminate and/or metabolize half of a drug dose

biotransformation
process of changing the chemical properties of a drug, usually by metabolism

metabolism
chemical alteration of drugs by body processes

metabolites
chemical products of metabolism

The liver is the primary organ that metabolizes drugs in the body. This complex biochemical laboratory contains hundreds of enzymes that continuously synthesize, modify, and deactivate biochemical substances such as drugs. The healthy liver is also capable of metabolizing many of the chemicals that occur naturally in the body (such as hormones). These metabolizing enzymes are highly regulateable. Genetic variations in their structures can account for a wide variation in their activity, influencing onset, duration, and potency of drug effects, thereby affecting vulnerability to developing dependence and addiction (see "Family Matters: Genetics of Metabolic Enzymes and Alcoholism"). After the liver enzymes metabolize a drug (the resulting chemicals are called **metabolites**), the products usually pass into the urine or feces for final elimination. Drugs and their metabolites can appear in other places as well, such as sweat, saliva, or expired air (Buxton 2006).

The kidneys are probably the next most important organs for drug elimination because they remove metabolites and foreign substances from the body. The kidneys constantly eliminate substances from the blood. The rate of excretion of some drugs by the kidneys can be altered by making the urine more acidic or more alkaline. For example, nicotine and amphetamines can be cleared faster from the body by making the urine slightly more acidic, and salicylates and barbiturates can be cleared more rapidly by making it more alkaline. Such techniques are used in emergency rooms and can be useful in the treatment of drug overdosing. Changing urine acidity is also a technique used by drug abusers to accelerate elimination of substances from their body that would be identified by drug tests and result in disqualification from sports competition, loss of a job, or even termination of parole and a return to incarceration (Andersen 2010).

The body may eliminate small portions of drugs through perspiration and exhalation. Approximately 1% of consumed alcohol is eliminated in the breath and thus may be measured with a Breathalyzer; this apparatus is used by police officers in evaluating suspected drunk drivers. Most people are aware that consumption of garlic will change body odor because garlic is excreted through perspiration. Some drugs are handled in the same way. The mammary glands are modified sweat glands, so it is not surprising that many drugs are concentrated and excreted in milk during lactation, including antibiotics, nicotine, barbiturates, caffeine, and alcohol. Excretion of drugs in a mother's milk can pose a particular concern during nursing because the excreted drugs can be consumed by and affect the infant.

Family Matters: Genetics of Metabolic Enzymes and Alcoholism

It has been known for a long time that alcoholism frequently clusters in some families and even to some extent in some races, suggesting that its expression is strongly influenced by heritability and gene expression. However, only lately, because of sophisticated molecular biology techniques, have we finally been able to identify some of the specific genes involved and how their expression influences the development of alcoholism. A particularly compelling discovery is the finding that liver enzymes known as alcohol dehydrogenases exist in several variant forms that are determined by a person's genetics. One variant of this enzyme is unique to people of African descent and some Native American tribes. This form of alcohol dehydrogenase is unique because of its ability to rapidly break down alcohol and produce a very unpleasant metabolite known as acetaldehyde. Consequently, persons and races with this variant enzyme are much less likely to have family histories of alcoholism because they experience a less rewarding subjective response when consuming alcoholic beverages. In addition, children of mothers with this enzyme variant are less likely to have alcohol-related birth defects because it is less likely that their mothers will consume alcohol during pregnancy.

Source: Scott, M., and R. Taylor. "Health-Related Effects of Genetic Variations of Alcohol-Metabolizing Enzymes in African Americans." *Alcohol Research and Health.* 2007. Available at: http://findarticles.com/p/articles/mi_m0CXH/is_1_30/ai_n21041753. Accessed March 2, 2011.

■ Physiological Variables that Modify Drug Effects

As previously mentioned, individuals' responses to drugs vary greatly, even when the same doses are administered in the same manner. This variability can be especially troublesome when dealing with drugs that have a narrow margin of safety. Many of these variables reflect differences in the pharmacokinetic factors just discussed and are associated with diversity in body size, composition, or functions. They include the following factors (Buxton 2006):

- *Age:* Changes in body size and makeup occur throughout the aging process, from infancy to old age. Changes in the rates of drug absorption, biotransformation, and elimination also arise as a consequence of aging. As a general rule, young children and elderly people should be administered smaller drug doses (calculated as drug quantity per unit of body weight) due to their immature or compromised body processes.

- *Gender:* Variations in drug responses due to gender usually relate to differences in body size, composition, or hormones (male versus female types—for example, androgens versus estrogens). Most clinicians find many more similarities than differences between males and females relative to their responses to drugs, although there are clinically relevant differences in the effects of alcohol and tobacco on males and females.

- *Pregnancy:* During the course of pregnancy, unique factors must be considered when administering drugs. For example, the physiology of the mother changes as the fetus develops and puts additional stress on organ systems, such as the heart, liver, and kidneys. This increased demand can make the woman more susceptible to the toxicity of some drugs. In addition, as the fetus develops, it can be very vulnerable to drugs with **teratogenic** properties (which cause abnormal development). Consequently, it is usually advisable to avoid taking any drugs during pregnancy, if possible.

The Breathalyzer takes advantage of the fact that alcohol is partially eliminated from the body in the breath.

KEY TERMS

teratogenic
something that causes physical defects in a fetus

■ Pathological Variables that Modify Drug Effects

Individuals with diseases or compromised organ systems need to be particularly careful when taking drugs. Some diseases can damage or impair organs that are vital for appropriate and safe responses to drugs. For example, hepatitis (inflammation of and damage to the liver caused by a viral infection) interferes with the metabolism and disposal of many drugs, resulting in a longer duration of drug action and increased likelihood of side effects. Similar concerns are associated with kidney disease, which compromises renal activity and diminishes excretion capacity. Because many drugs affect the cardiovascular system (especially drugs of abuse, such as stimulants, tobacco, and alcohol), patients with a history of cardiovascular disease (heart attack, stroke, hypertension, or abnormal heart rhythm) should be particularly cautious when using drugs. They should be aware of medicines that stimulate the cardiovascular system, especially those that are self-administered, such as OTC decongestants and diet aids. These drugs should be either avoided or used only under the supervision of a physician.

■ Pharmacokinetics and Drug Testing

As discussed in Chapter 3, drug testing has become an important part of the prevention, detection, and treatment of drug abuse. Many of the pharmacokinetic elements discussed in this section have important implications on drug testing and its ability to reliably determine which, how much, and when drugs have been abused. For example, how rapidly a drug gets into the blood or the urine after it is consumed, how long it stays in the body, and what its metabolites are can all profoundly influence drug testing outcomes. However, even though we have come to rely a great deal on drug testing to evaluate employees, discourage athletes from cheating, and determine compliance in persons with a history of drug abuse problems, we should appreciate that this technology has significant drawbacks that should be considered if we are

to accurately interpret its outcomes. To illustrate this point, see "Here and Now: Drug Test Results Can Be Flawed."

Adaptive Processes and Drug Abuse

Your body systems are constantly changing so they can establish and maintain balance in their physiological and mental functions; such balance is necessary for optimal functioning of all organ systems, including the brain, heart, lungs, gastrointestinal tract, liver, and kidneys. Sometimes, drugs interfere with the activity of the body's systems and compromise their normal workings. These drug-induced disruptions can be so severe that they can even cause death. For example, stimulants can dangerously increase the heart rate and blood pressure and cause heart attacks, whereas CNS depressants can diminish brain activity, resulting in unconsciousness and a loss of breathing reflexes.

To protect against potential harm, the organ systems of the body can adjust to disruption. Of particular relevance to drugs of abuse are the adaptive processes known as *tolerance* and **dependence** (both psychological and physical types) and the related phenomenon of *withdrawal* (see **Figure 5.4**).

Tolerance and dependence are closely linked, most likely to result from multiple drug exposures, and thought to be caused by similar mechanisms. Tolerance occurs when the response to the same dose of a drug decreases with repeated use (O'Brien 2006). Increasing the dose can sometimes compensate for tolerance to a drug of abuse. For the most part, the adaptations that cause the tolerance phenomenon are also associated with altered physical and psychological states that lead to dependence. The user develops dependence in the sense that if the drug is no longer taken, the systems of the body become overcompensated and unbalanced, causing withdrawal. In general, withdrawal symptoms are opposite in nature to the direct effects of the drug that caused the dependence (O'Brien 2006).

Although tolerance, dependence, and withdrawal are all consequences of adaptation by the body and its systems, they are not inseparable processes. It is possible to become tolerant to a drug without developing dependence, and vice versa (see **Table 5.2**). The following sections provide greater detail about these adaptive drug responses, which are very important for many therapeutic drugs and almost all drugs of abuse (O'Brien 2006).

KEY TERMS

dependence
physiological and psychological changes or adaptations that occur in response to the frequent administration of a drug

Here and Now

Drug Test Results Can Be Flawed

We often rely on the outcomes of drug testing to make critical decisions about whom we should hire or fire, who has violated conditions of their parole and should go back to jail, which athlete has cheated and should be disqualified from competition, or how well a patient is responding to drug treatment. However, although results from drug testing can be an important tool, drug testing is far from perfect and its flaws should be considered when basing important decisions upon its outcomes. For example, the following are facts and myths about this technology that should be remembered:

- *Fact:* The poppy seeds on a single bagel are sufficient to test positive for opioid narcotics such as Lortab or Vicodin.
- *Fiction:* Most standard drug tests screen for the opioid drug oxycodone (active ingredient in OxyContin), methadone, and the very potent opioid drug, fentanyl. (Explanation: This is false because if these are drugs of interest, they must be specially requested to be included in the screening.)
- *Fact:* In 2009 about 150 million drug tests were conducted in the United States.
- *Fact:* Most physicians do not know what drugs are included in a "standard" drug test.
- *Fact:* About 5–10% of tested patients will have inaccurate results.

- *Fiction:* Passive inhalation of marijuana or cocaine accounts for 20% of the positives when testing for these substances. (Explanation: This is false because casual breathing of cocaine or marijuana smoke are insufficient to cause a positive outcome on standard drug tests.)
- *Fiction:* Methods to mask or falsify a drug test never work. (Explanation: Actually, efforts to mask a positive drug test appear to work about 50% of the time. Strategies such as adding bleach or household cleaner such as Drano to urine samples can mask drug detection.)

Source: Fiore, K. "APA: Drug Test Results Often Flawed." MedPage Today. 23 May 2010. Available at: http://www.medpagetoday.com/MeetingCoverage?APA/20253. Accessed March 2, 2011.

■ Tolerance to Drugs

The extent of tolerance and the rate at which it is acquired depend on the drug, the person using the drug, the dosage, and the frequency of administration. Some drug effects may be reduced more rapidly than others when drugs are used frequently. Tolerance to effects that are rewarding or reinforcing often causes users to increase the dosage. Sometimes, abstinence from a drug can reduce tolerance, but with renewed use, the tolerance can return quickly. It is important to remember that the body does not necessarily develop tolerance to all effects of a drug equally.

The exact mechanisms by which the body becomes tolerant to different drug effects are not completely understood, but may be related to those mechanisms that cause dependence (American Psychiatric Association 2000). Several processes have been suggested as candidates. Drugs such as barbiturates stimulate the body's production of metabolic enzymes, primarily in the liver, and cause drugs to be inactivated and eliminated faster. In addition, evidence suggests that a considerable degree of CNS tolerance to some drugs develops independent of changes in the rate of metabolism or excretion. This process reflects the adaptation of drug target sites in nervous tissue, such as neurotransmitter receptors, so that the effect produced by the same concentration of drug decreases over time.

Another type of drug response that can appear to be tolerance, but is actually a learned adjustment, is called behavioral compensation. Drug effects that are troubling may be compensated for or hidden by the drug user. Thus, alcoholics learn to

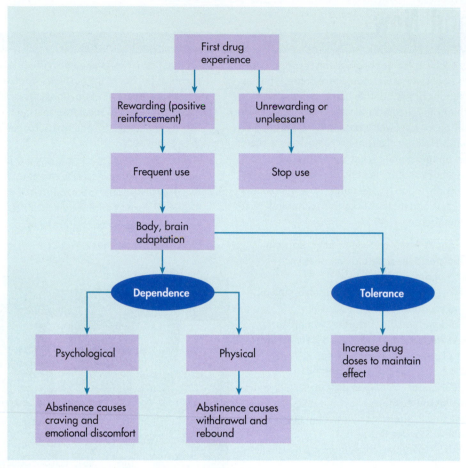

FIGURE 5.4

The relationship and consequences of adaptive processes to drug abuse. The processes discussed in the text are highlighted in the figure.

speak and walk slowly to compensate for the slurred speech and stumbling gait that alcohol consumption usually causes. To an observer, it might appear as though the pharmacological effects of the drug are diminished, but they are actually unchanged. Consequently, this type of adaptation is not a true form of tolerance.

Other Tolerance-Related Factors

The tolerance process can affect drug responses in several ways. We have discussed the effect of tolerance that diminishes the action of drugs and causes the user to compensate by increasing the dose. The following are examples of two other ways

that processes related to tolerance can influence drug responses.

Reverse Tolerance (Sensitization)

Under some conditions, a response to a drug is elicited that is the opposite of tolerance. This effect is known as **reverse tolerance**, or sensitization. If you were sensitized, you would have the same response to a lower dose of a drug as you initially did to the original, higher dose. This condition seems to occur in users of morphine as well as amphetamines and cocaine (McDaid et al. 2005).

Although the causes of reverse tolerance are still unclear, some researchers believe that its development depends on how often, how much, and in which setting the drug is consumed. It has been speculated that this heightened response to drugs of abuse may reflect adaptive changes in the nervous tissues (target site of these drugs). The reverse tolerance that occurs with cocaine use may be re-

KEY TERMS

reverse tolerance
enhanced response to a given drug dose; opposite of tolerance

Table 5.2 **Tolerance, Dependence, and Withdrawal Properties of Common Drugs of Abuse**

DRUG	TOLERANCE	PSYCHOLOGICAL DEPENDENCE	PHYSICAL DEPENDENCE	WITHDRAWAL SYMPTOMS (INCLUDE REBOUND EFFECTS)
Barbiturates	■■ Moderate	■■ Moderate	■■■ Intense	Restlessness, anxiety, vomiting, tremors, seizures
Alcohol	■■ Moderate	■■ Moderate	■■■ Intense	Cramps, delirium, vomiting, sweating, hallucinations, seizures
Benzodiazepines	■ Some	■■ Moderate	■■ Moderate	Insomnia, restlessness, nausea, fatigue, twitching, seizures (rare)
Narcotics (heroin)	■■■ Intense	■■ Moderate	■■■ Intense	Vomiting, sweating, cramps, diarrhea, depression, irritability, gooseflesh
Cocaine, amphetamines	■* Some	■■■ Intense	■■ Moderate	Depression, anxiety, drug craving, need for sleep ("crash"), anhedonia
Nicotine	■ Some	■■ Moderate	■■ Moderate	Highly variable; craving, irritability, headache, increased appetite, abnormal sleep
Caffeine	■ Some	■ Some	■ Some	Anxiety, lethargy, headache, fatigue
Marijuana	■ Some	■ Some	■ Some	Irritability, restlessness, decreased appetite, weight loss, abnormal sleep
LSD (lysergic acid diethylamide)	■■ Moderate	■ Some	— Not significant	Minimal
PCP (phencyclidine)	■ Some	■ Some	■ Some	Fear, tremors, some craving, problems with short-term memory

■■■ Intense   ■■ Moderate   ■ Some   — Not significant
*Can sensitize.

sponsible for the psychotic effects or the seizures caused by its chronic use (O'Brien 2006).

Cross-Tolerance

Development of tolerance to a drug sometimes can produce tolerance to other similar drugs. This phenomenon, known as **cross-tolerance**, may be due to altered metabolism resulting from chronic drug use. For example, a heavy drinker will usually exhibit tolerance to barbiturates, other depressants, and anesthetics because the alcohol has induced (stimulated) his or her liver metabolic enzymes to inactivate these other drugs more rapidly. Cross-tolerance might also occur among drugs that cause similar pharmacological actions. For example, if adaptations have occurred in nervous tissue that cause tolerance to one drug, such changes might produce tolerance to other similar drugs that exert their effects by interacting with that same nervous tissue site. This is common with all of the opioid narcotics including both the prescription (e.g., morphine) and illegal (e.g., heroin) drugs (Houtsmuller et al. 1998).

KEY TERMS

cross-tolerance
development of tolerance to one drug causes tolerance to related drugs

■ Drug Dependence

Drug dependence can be associated with either physiological or psychological adaptations. Physical dependence reflects changes in the way organs and systems in the body respond to a drug, whereas psychological dependence is caused by changes in attitudes and expectations. In both types of dependence, the individual experiences a need (either physical or emotional) for the drug to be present for the body or the mind to function normally.

Physical Dependence

In general, the drugs that cause physical dependence also are associated with a drug withdrawal phenomenon called the **rebound effect**. This condition is sometimes known as the *paradoxical effect* because the symptoms included in rebound phenomena are nearly opposite to the direct effects of the drug. For example, a person regularly consuming alcohol or benzodiazepines will be depressed physically while the drug is in the brain, but during withdrawal may become irritable, hyperexcited, and nervous and generally show symptoms of extreme stimulation of the nervous system, and perhaps even life-threatening seizures. These reactions constitute the rebound effect.

Physical dependence may develop with high-intensity use of such common drugs as alcohol, Xanax, narcotics, and other CNS depressants. However, with moderate, intermittent use of these drugs, most people do not become significantly physically dependent. Those who do become physically dependent often experience damaged social and personal skills and relationships and impaired brain and motor functions.

Withdrawal symptoms resulting from physical dependency can be mitigated by administering a sufficient quantity of the original drug or one with similar pharmacological activity. The latter case, in which different drugs can be used inter-changeably to prevent withdrawal symptoms, is called **cross-dependence**. For example, benzodiazepines and other CNS depressants can be used to treat the abstinence syndrome experienced by the chronic alcoholic. Another example is the use of methadone, a long-acting narcotic, to treat withdrawal from heroin (O'Brien 2006). Such therapeutic strategies allow the substitution of safer and more easily managed drugs for dangerous drugs of abuse and play a major role in treatment of drug dependency.

Psychological Dependence

The World Health Organization states that **psychological dependence** instills a feeling of satisfaction and psychic drive that requires periodic or continuous administration of the drug to produce a desired effect or to avoid psychological discomfort. This sense of dependence usually leads to repeated self-administration of the drug in a fashion described as abuse. Such dependence may be found either independent of or associated with physical dependence. Psychological dependence does not produce the physical discomfort, rebound effects, or life-threatening consequences that can be associated with physical dependence. Even so, it does produce intense cravings and strong urges that frequently draw former drug abusers back to their habits of drug self-administration. In many instances, psychological aspects may be more significant than physical dependence in maintaining chronic drug use. Thus, the major problem with cocaine or nicotine dependence is not so much the physical aspect, because withdrawal can be successfully achieved in a few weeks; rather, strong urges often cause a return to chronic use of these substances because of psychological dependence.

How does psychological dependence develop? If the first drug trial is rewarding, a few more rewarding trials will follow until drug use becomes a conditioned pattern of behavior. Continued positive psychological reinforcement with the drug leads, in time, to primary psychological dependence. Primary psychological dependence, in turn, may produce uncontrollable compulsive abuse of any psychoactive drug in certain susceptible people, leading to physical dependence. The degree of drug dependence is contingent on the nature of the psychoactive substance, the quantity used, the duration of use, and the characteristics of the person and his or her environment.

Even strong psychological dependence on some psychoactive substances does not necessarily result

KEY TERMS

rebound effect
form of withdrawal; paradoxical effects that occur when a drug has been eliminated from the body

cross-dependence
dependence on a drug can be relieved by other similar drugs

psychological dependence
dependence that results because a drug produces pleasant mental effects

in injury or social harm. For example, typical dosages of mild stimulants such as coffee usually do not induce serious physical, social, or emotional harm. Even though the effects on the CNS are barely detectable by a casual observer, strong psychological dependence on stimulants like tobacco and caffeine-containing beverages may develop; however, the fact that their dependence does not typically induce antisocial and destructive behavior distinguishes them from most forms of dependence-producing drugs.

Psychological Factors

The general effect of most drugs is greatly influenced by a variety of psychological and environmental factors. Unique qualities of an individual's personality, his or her past history of drug and social experience, attitudes toward the drug, expectations of its effects, and motivation for use are extremely influential. These factors are often referred to collectively as the person's **mental set**. The setting, or total environment, in which a drug is taken may profoundly modify its effect.

The mental set and setting are particularly important in influencing the responses to psychoactive drugs (drugs that alter the functions of the brain). For example, ingestion of LSD, a commonly abused hallucinogen, can cause pleasant, even spiritual-like experiences in comfortable, congenial surroundings. In contrast, when the same amount of LSD is consumed in hostile, threatening surroundings, the effect can be frightening, taking on a nightmarish quality.

■ The Placebo Effect

The psychological factors that influence responses to drugs, independent of their pharmacological properties, are known as **placebo effects**. The word *placebo* is derived from Latin and means "I shall please." The placebo effect is most likely to occur when an individual's mental set is susceptible to suggestion. A placebo drug is a pharmacologically inactive compound that the user thinks causes some therapeutic or physiological change. In some persons or in particular settings, a placebo substance may have surprisingly powerful consequences (Solomon 2002). For example, a substantial component of most pain is perception. Consequently, placebos administered as pain relievers and promoted properly can provide dramatic relief. There-

fore, in spite of what appears to be a drug effect, the placebo is not considered a pharmacological agent because it does not directly alter any body functions by its chemical nature.

The bulk of medical history may actually be a history of confidence in the cure—a history of placebo medicine—because many effective cures of the past have been shown to be without relevant pharmacological action, suggesting that their effects were psychologically mediated. In fact, even today, some people argue that placebo effects are a significant component of most drug therapy, particularly when using OTC medications or herbal products. It is important when testing new drugs for effectiveness that drug experiments be conducted in a manner that allows a distinction to be drawn between pharmacological and placebo effects. Such studies can usually be done by treating one group with the real drug and another group with a placebo that looks like the drug, and then comparing the responses to both treatments.

Addiction and Abuse: The Significance of Dependence

The term *addiction* has many meanings (see Chapter 2). It often is used interchangeably with *dependence* or *drug abuse* (drug addiction). The traditional model of the addiction-producing drug is based on opiate narcotics and requires the individual to develop tolerance and both physical and psychological dependence. This model often is not satisfactory because only a few commonly abused drugs fit all of these parameters. It is clearly inadequate for many drugs that can cause serious dependency problems but that produce little tolerance, even with extended use (see Table 5.2).

Because it is difficult to assess the contribution of physical and psychological factors to drug dependency, determining whether all psychoactive drugs truly cause drug addiction poses a challenge. To alleviate confusion, it has been suggested that the term *dependence* (either physical or psychological) be used instead of *addiction*. However, because

KEY TERMS

mental set
the collection of psychological and environmental factors that influence an individual's response to drugs

placebo effects
effects caused by suggestion and psychological factors independent of the pharmacological activity of a drug

of its acceptance by the public, the term *addiction* is not likely to disappear from general use. In addition, addiction often implies compulsive behavior (i.e., a need to have and use a drug despite negative consequences), which can be independent of physical dependence. This confusion is likely to continue until some consensus can be reached regarding how to best define this concept.

Some have speculated that the only means by which drug dependence/addiction can be eliminated from society is to prevent exposure to those drugs that have the potential to be abused. Because some drugs are such powerful, immediate reinforcers (i.e., they cause a rapid reward), it is feared that rapid dependence (psychological) will occur when anyone uses them. Although it may be true that most people, under certain conditions, could become dependent on some drug with abuse potential, in reality most people who have used psychoactive drugs do not develop significant psychological or physical dependence or addiction. For example, approximately 87% of those who use alcohol experience minimal personal injury and few negative social consequences. Of those who have used stimulants, depressants, or hallucinogens for illicit recreational purposes, only 10% to 20% become significantly dependent (O'Brien 2006). The following sections discuss some possible reasons for the variability.

■ Hereditary Factors

The reasons why some people readily develop dependence on psychoactive drugs and others do not are not well understood. Of importance may be heredity, which predisposes some people to drug abuse (Kreek at al. 2004), and the interaction of genetic vulnerability with high-risk environments (see "Family Matters: Family Addictions and Genetics"). For example, studies of identical and fraternal twins have revealed a greater similarity in the rate of alcoholism for identical twins than for fraternal twins if alcohol abuse begins before the age of 20 years (McGue, Pickens, and Svikis 1992; Vanyukov and Tarter 2000). Because identical twins have 100% of their genes in common whereas fraternal twins share significantly fewer of their genes, these results suggest that genetic factors can be important in determining the likelihood of alcohol dependence (O'Brien 2006; Scott and Taylor 2007). It is possible that similar genetic factors contribute to other types of drug dependence as well (Kreek et al. 2004).

■ Drug Craving

Frequently, a person who becomes dependent develops a powerful, uncontrollable desire for drugs during or after withdrawal from heroin, cocaine, alcohol, nicotine, or other addicting substances. This desire for drugs is known as craving. Because researchers do not agree as to the nature of craving, there does not exist a universally recognized scientific definition or an accepted method to measure this psychological phenomenon; however, it is thought to be distinct from the phenomenon of withdrawal. Some drug abuse experts claim that craving is the principal cause of drug abuse and re-

Family Matters: Family Addictions and Genetics

Substance abuse, alcoholism, and associated trauma seem to have both genetic and environmental components, the interaction of which can have serious consequences. For example, alcoholism tends to run in families. Thus, children of alcoholics are at high risk to become alcohol users themselves because of their genetic vulnerability as well as because of the traumatic environments to which they are often exposed. Levels of conflict in families characterized by alcoholism are much higher than in families with no alcoholism. The environment to which children with alcoholic parents are exposed may include a lack of communication, emotional and physical violence, isolation, and financial problems. At least half of all cases of child maltreatment are linked to a prevalence of substance abuse and alcoholism in the home. It has also been reported that children who receive prenatal exposure to drugs are two to three times more likely to be neglected or abused.

Sources: Learn.Genetics. "Genetics Is an Important Factor in Addiction." Genetic Science Learning Center. (posted 2010). Available at: http://learn.genetics.utah.edu/content/addiction/genetics. Accessed March 2, 2011; and About.com: Alcoholism. "Genetics of Alcoholism." The Recovery Place (posted 2010). Available at: http://alcoholism.about.com/od/genetics/Genetics_of_Alcoholism.htm. Accessed March 2, 2011.

lapse after treatment; others believe that it is not a cause but a side effect of drugs that produce dependence. Craving is often assessed by (1) questioning patients about the intensity of their drug urges; (2) measuring physiological changes such as increases in heart and breathing rates, sweating, and subtle changes in the tension of facial muscles; and (3) determining patients' tendency to relapse into drug-taking behavior (Hester and Garavan 2004).

Evidence indicates that at least two levels of craving can exist. For example, cocaine users experience an acute craving when using the drug itself, but the ex-cocaine abuser can have chronic cravings that are triggered by familiar environmental cues that elicit positive memories of cocaine's reinforcing effects.

Although it is not likely that craving itself causes drug addiction, it is generally believed that if pharmacological or psychological therapies could be devised that reduced or eliminated drug craving, treatment of drug dependence would be more successful. Thus, many researchers are attempting to identify medications or psychological strategies that interfere with the development and expression of the craving phenomenon.

■ Other Factors

If a drug causes a positive effect in the user's view, it is much more likely to be abused than if it causes an aversive experience (see Figure 5.4). Perhaps genetic factors influence the brain or personality so that some people find taking drugs an enjoyable experience (at least initially), whereas others find the effects very unpleasant and uncomfortable (**dysphoric**) (Vergne and Anton 2010). Other factors that could contribute significantly to drug use patterns include (1) peer pressure (especially in the initial drug experimentation); (2) home, school, and work environments (Swadi 1999); (3) mental state; and (4) excessive stress. It is estimated that 30% to 60% of drug abusers have some underlying psychiatric illness, such as personality disorder, major depression, bipolar disorder, or schizophrenia (Buckley and Brown 2006). In some cases, the drug user may be attempting to relieve symptoms associated with the mental disorder by self-medicating with the substance of abuse (Buckley and Brown 2006).

It is difficult to identify all of the specific factors that influence the risk of drug abuse for each individual. (Some of the possible influences are discussed in Chapter 2.) If such factors could be identified, treatment would be improved and those at greatest risk for drug abuse could be determined and informed of their vulnerability.

1. What is the significance of drug "potency" in the therapeutic use and the abuse of drugs?

2. How can drug interactions be both detrimental and beneficial? Give examples of each.

3. Why would a drug with a relatively narrow "margin of safety" be approved by the Food and Drug Administration for clinical use? Give an example.

4. What are possible explanations for the fact that you (for example) may require twice as much of a drug to get an effect as does your friend?

5. Why might the blood–brain barrier prevent a drug from having abuse potential?

6. Contrary to your advice, a friend is going to spend $20 on methamphetamine. What significance will the pharmacokinetic concepts of threshold, half-life, cumulative effect, and biotransformation have on your friend's drug experience?

7. How would the factors of tolerance, physical dependence, rebound, and psychological dependence affect a chronic heroin user?

8. Why would the lack of physical dependence on LSD for some drug abusers make it less likely to cause addiction than cocaine, which does cause physical dependence?

Summary

1 All drugs have intended and unintended effects. The unintended actions of drugs can include effects such as nausea, altered mental states, dependence, a variety of allergic responses, and changes in the cardiovascular system.

KEY TERMS

dysphoric
characterized by unpleasant mental effects; the opposite of euphoric

2 Many factors can affect the way an individual responds to a drug: dose, inherent toxicity, potency, and pharmacokinetic properties such as the rate of absorption into the body, the way it is distributed throughout the body, and the manner in which and rate at which it is metabolized and eliminated. The form of the drug as well as the manner in which it is administered can also affect the response to a drug.

3 Potency is determined by the amount of a drug necessary to cause a given effect. Toxicity is the ability of the drug to affect the body adversely. A drug that is very toxic is very potent in terms of causing a harmful effect.

4 A drug's margin of safety relates to the difference in the drug doses that cause a therapeutic or a toxic effect. The bigger the difference, the greater the margin of safety.

5 Additive interactions occur when the effects of two drugs are combined; for example, the analgesic effects of aspirin plus acetaminophen are additive. Antagonistic effects occur when the effects of two drugs cancel; for example, the stimulant effects of caffeine tend to antagonize the drowsiness caused by antihistamines. Synergism (potentiation) occurs when one drug enhances the effect of another; for example, alcohol enhances the CNS depression caused by Valium.

6 Pharmacokinetic factors include absorption, distribution, biotransformation, and elimination of drugs. These factors can vary substantially between persons and have a significant impact on the outcome and interpretation of drug testing outcomes.

7 Many physiological and pathological factors can alter the response to drugs. For example, age, gender, and pregnancy are all factors that should be considered when making drug-related decisions. In addition, some diseases can alter the way in which the body responds to drugs. Medical conditions associated with the liver, kidneys, and cardiovascular system are of particular concern.

8 For psychoactive drugs to influence the brain and its actions, they must pass through the blood–brain barrier. Many of these drugs are fat-soluble and able to pass through capillary walls from the blood into the brain.

9 The threshold dose is the minimum amount of a drug necessary to have an effect. The plateau effect is the maximum effect a drug can have, regardless of dose. The cumulative effect is the buildup of the drug in the body due to multiple doses being taken within short intervals.

10 The liver is the primary organ for the metabolizing of drugs and many naturally occurring substances in the body, such as hormones. By altering the molecular structure of drugs, the metabolism usually inactivates drugs and makes them easier to eliminate through the kidneys.

11 Biotransformation is the process that alters the molecular structure of a drug. Metabolism contributes to biotransformation.

12 Drug tolerance causes a decreased response to a given dose of a drug. It can be caused by increasing metabolism and elimination of the drug by the body or by a change in the systems or targets that are affected by the drug.

13 Physical dependence is characterized by the adaptive changes that occur in the body due to the continual presence of a drug. These changes, which are often chemical in nature, reduce the response to the drugs and cause tolerance. If drug use is halted after physical dependence has occurred, the body is overcompensated, causing a rebound response. Rebound effects are similar to the withdrawal that occurs because drug use is stopped for an extended period. Psychological dependence occurs because drug use is rewarding, causing euphoria, increased energy, and relaxation, or because stopping drug use produces craving.

14 Suggestion can have a profound influence on a person's drug response. Health problems with significant psychological aspects are particularly susceptible to the effects of placebos. For example, because the intensity of pain is related to its perception, a placebo can substantially relieve pain discomfort. Other placebo responses may likewise be due to the release of endogenous factors in the body.

15 A powerful, uncontrollable desire (craving) for drugs can occur with chronic use of some drugs of abuse. Although craving by itself may not cause drug addiction, if it can be eliminated, treatment of substance abuse is more likely to be successful.

References

About.com. Alcoholism. "Genetics of Alcoholism." The Recovery Place. 2010. Available http://alcoholism.about.com/od/genetics/Genetics_of_Alcoholism.htm

Aleccia, J. "Toxic Mix of Pills, Alcohol Fuels Spike in Deaths." MSNBC Health. 2008. Available http://www.msnbc.msn.com/id/25886212

American Psychiatric Association. "Substance Related Disorders." In *Diagnostic and Statistical Manual of Mental Disorders,* 4th ed., text revision, 191–295. Washington, DC: APA, 2000.

Andersen, A. "Urine Drug Tests, Lab Drug Screen on Blood, Hair: Understanding Drug Detection Duration." Suite101.com. 2010. Available http://mindbodyfitness.suite101.com/article.cfm/urine-drug-tests-lab-drug-screen-on-blood-hair

Associated Press. "DJ AM's Death Ruled Accidental Drug Overdose." 2009. Available http://today.msnbc.msn.com/id/33072533

Buckley, P., and E. Brown. "Prevalence and Consequences of Dual Diagnosis." *Journal of Clinical Psychiatry* 67 (2006): e01.

Buxton, I. "Pharmacokinetics and Pharmacodynamics." In *The Pharmacological Basis of Therapeutics,* 11th ed., edited by L. Brunton, J. Lazo, and K. Parker, 1–39. New York: McGraw-Hill, 2006.

Cartwright, W. "Economic Costs of Drug Abuse: Financial, Costs of Illness, and Services." *Journal of Substance Abuse Treatment* 34 (2008): 224–233t.

Coffin, P., S. Galea, J. Ahern, A. Leon, D. Vlahov, and K. Tardiff. "Opiates, Cocaine and Alcohol Combinations in Accidental Overdose Deaths in New York City, 1990–1998," *Addiction* 98 (2003): 739–747.

Erb, R. "Shot May Let Smokers Quit." *Detroit Free Press.* 22 May 2010.

Fillmore, M., and C. Rush. "Polydrug Abusers Display Impaired Discrimination-Reversal Training Learning in a Model of Behavioral Control." *Journal of Psychopharmacology* 20 (2006): 24–32.

Fiore, K. "APA: Drug Test Results Often Flawed." MedPage Today. 23 May 2010. Available http://www.medpagetoday.com/MeetingCoverage?APA/20253

Fleming, M., S. Mihic, and A. Harris. "Ethanol." In *The Pharmacological Basis of Therapeutics,* 11th ed., edited by L. Brunton, J. Lazo, and K. Parker, 591–606. New York: McGraw-Hill, 2006.

Hester, R., and H. Garavan. "Executive Dysfunction in Cocaine Addiction: Evidence for Discordant Frontal, Cingulate, and Cerebellar Activity." *Journal of Neuroscience* 24 (2004): 11017–11022.

Hobbs, W. R., T. Rall, and T. Verdoorn. "Hypnotics and Sedatives: Ethanol." In *The Pharmacological Basis of Therapeutics,* 9th ed., edited by J. Hardman and L. Limbird, 386–396. New York: McGraw-Hill, 1995.

Houtsmuller, E., S. Walsh, K. Schuh, R. Johnson, M. Stitzer, and G. Bigelow. "Dose-Response Analysis of Opioid Cross-Tolerance and Withdrawal Suppression During LAAM Maintenance." *Journal of Pharmacology and Experimental Therapeutics* 285 (1998): 387–396.

Keegan, J., M. Parva, M. Finnegan, A. Gerson, and M. Belden. "Addiction in Pregnancy." *Journal of Addictive Disorders* 29 (2010): 175–191.

Kreek, M., S. Schlussman, G. Bart, K. Laforge, and E. Butelman. "Evolving Perspectives on Neurobiological Research on the Addictions: Celebration of the 30th Anniversary of NIDA." *Neuropharmacology* 47 Supplement 1 (2004): 324–344.

Learn.Genetics. "Genetics Is an Important Factor in Addiction." Genetic Science Learning Center. 2010. Available http://learn.genetics.utah.edu/content/addiction/genetics

Martell, B. A., F. M. Orson, J. Poling, E. Mitchell, R. D. Rossen, T. Gardner, and T. R. Kosten. "Cocaine Vaccine for the Treatment of Cocaine Dependence in Methadone-Maintained Patients: A Randomized, Double-Blind, Placebo-Controlled Efficacy Trial." *Archives of General Psychiatry* 66 (2009): 1116–1123.

Mathias, R. "Rate and Duration of Drug Activity Play Major Roles in Drug Abuse, Addiction and Treatment." *NIDA Notes* 12 (March/April 1997): 8–11.

McDaid, J., J. Dallimore, A. Mackie, A. Mickiewicz, and T. Napier. "Cross-Sensitization to Morphine in Cocaine-Sensitized Rats: Rats' Behavioral Assessments Correlate with Enhanced Responding of Ventral Pallidal Neurons to Morphine and Glutamate, with Diminished Effects of GABA." *Journal of Pharmacology and Experimental Therapeutics* 313 (2005): 1182–1193.

McGue, M., R. Pickens, and D. Svikis. "Sex and Age Effects on the Inheritance of Alcohol Problems: A Twin Study." *Journal of Abnormal Psychology* 101 (January 1992): 3–17.

Meckling, K. *Nutrient–Drug Interactions.* Boca Raton, FL: CRC Press, 2006.

Meng, Y., M. Dukat, D. Bridgen, B. R. Martin, and A. H. Lichtman. "Pharmacological Effects of Methamphetamine and Other Stimulants via Inhalation Exposure." *Drugs and Alcohol Dependence* 53 (1999): 111–120.

Merck. The Merck Manuals Online Medical Library. Drug Interactions. 2010. Available http://www.merck.com/mmpe/sec20/ch302/ch302d.html#CHDCEIIF

Mills, D. M. "A Loaded Weapon: Concern Over Prescription Pill Abuse in Teens." Patch Blog. 28 May 2010. Available http://Danville.patch.com/articles/a-loaded-weapon-concern-over-prescription-pill-abuse-in-teens

National Institute on Alcohol Abuse and Alcoholism (NIAAA). "Alcohol–Medication Interactions." About.com Alcoholism. 2010. Available http://alcoholism.about.com/cs/alerts/l/blnaa27.htm

National Institute on Drug Abuse (NIDA). "Infectious Diseases and Drug Addiction." *NIDA Notes* 14 (1999): 15.

National Institute on Drug Abuse (NIDA). "What Are HIV and AIDS?" NIDA for Teens. 2007. Available http://teens.drugabuse.gov/facts/facts_hiv1.asp

Oates, J. "The Science of Drug Therapy." In *The Pharmacological Basis of Therapeutics,* 11th ed., edited by L. Brunton, J. Lazo, and K. Parker, 117–136. New York: McGraw-Hill, 2006.

O'Brien, C. "Drug Addiction and Drug Abuse." In *The Pharmacological Basis of Therapeutics,* 10th ed., edited by

J. Hardman and L. Limbird, 621–644. New York: McGraw-Hill, 2001.

O'Brien, C. "Drug Addiction and Drug Abuse." In *The Pharmacological Basis of Therapeutics,* 11th ed., edited by L. Brunton, J. Lazo, and K. Parker, 607–627. New York; McGraw-Hill, 2006.

Rice, D. P. "Economic Costs of Substances of Abuse, 1995." *Proceedings of the Association of American Physicians* 111 (1999): 119–125.

Santora, M. "Deadly Drug Mix Resurfaces in New York." *New York Times* (2006 August 30): A19.

Scott, M., and R. Taylor. "Health-Related Effects of Genetic Variations of Alcohol-Metabolizing Enzymes in African Americans." *Alcohol Research and Health.* 2007. Available http://findarticles.com/p/articles/mi_m0CXH/is_1_30/ai_n21041753

Solomon, S. "A Review of Mechanisms of Response to Pain Therapy: Why Voodoo Works." *Headache* 42 (2002): 656–662.

Swadi, H. "Individual Risk Factors for Adolescent Substance Use." *Drug and Alcohol Dependence* 55 (1999): 209–224.

University of Michigan. "Selected Herb–Drug Interactions." University of Michigan Health System. 2010. Available http://www.med.umich.edu/1libr/aha/umherb01.htm

Vanyukov, M. M., and R. E. Tarter. "Genetic Studies of Substance Abuse." *Drug and Alcohol Dependence* 59 (2000): 101–123.

Vergne, D. E., and F. Anton. "Aripiprazole: A Drug with a Novel Mechanism of Action and Possible Efficacy for Alcohol Dependence." *CNS and Neurological Disorders—Drug Targets* 9 (2010): 50–54.

Westmaas, J., and T. Brandon. "Reducing Risk in Smokers." *Current Opinions on Pulmonary Medicine* 10 (2004): 284–288.

Wood, E. "Crack Smoking Rooms May Cut HIV Risk: Study." CBC News. 19 October 2009. Available http://www.cbc.ca/canada/windsor/story/2009/10/19/crack-smoking-hiv.html

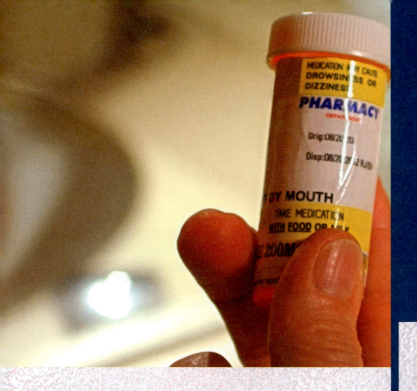

CHAPTER 6

CNS Depressants: Sedative-Hypnotics

Did You Know?

- Alcohol temporarily relieves anxiety and stress because of its central nervous system (CNS) depressant effects.
- Benzodiazepines are by far the most frequently prescribed CNS depressants.
- Most people who are dependent on benzodiazepines obtain their drugs legally by prescription.
- Long-term users of Xanax can experience severe withdrawal symptoms if drug use is stopped abruptly.
- Our bodies probably produce a natural antianxiety substance that functions like drugs such as Valium, triazolam (Halcion), and alprazolam (Xanax).
- The short-acting CNS depressants are the most likely to be abused.
- Inappropriate use of the short-acting general anesthetic Propofol was likely the cause of death for the pop singer Michael Jackson.
- GHB (gamma-hydroxybutyrate) is a Schedule I "club drug" that occurs naturally in the body and can be easily synthesized by using information available on the Internet.

Learning Objectives

On completing this chapter you will be able to:

- Identify the primary drug groups used for CNS depressant effects.
- Explain the principal therapeutic uses of the CNS depressants and their relationship to drug dose.
- Explain why CNS depressant drugs are commonly abused.
- Identify the unique features of benzodiazepines.
- Relate how benzodiazepine dependence usually develops.
- Describe the differences in effects produced by short- versus long-acting CNS depressants.
- Describe the CNS depressant properties of antihistamines, and compare their therapeutic usefulness to that of benzodiazepines.
- List the four principal types of people who abuse CNS depressants.
- Identify the basic principles in treating dependence on CNS depressants.
- Explain the unique properties of Propofol as a potential drug of abuse.
- Explain why GHB is abused and how it relates to its analog compounds.
- Explain the role of detoxification in the treatment of dependency on CNS depressants.

 Drugs and Society Online is a great source for additional drugs and society information for both students and instructors. Visit **go.jblearning.com/hanson11** to find a variety of useful tools for learning, thinking, and teaching.

Introduction

Central nervous system (CNS) depressants are some of the most widely used and abused drugs in the United States. Why? When taken at low doses, they all produce a qualitatively similar "high" by their disinhibitory effects on the brain. In addition, they relieve stress and anxiety and even induce sleep—effects that appeal to many people, particularly those who are struggling with emotional problems and looking for a break, physically and mentally. CNS depressants also can cause a host of serious side effects, including problems with tolerance and dependence. Ironically, many individuals who become dependent on depressants obtain them through legitimate means: a prescription given by a physician. In fact, these drugs are second only to the narcotic medications as the most frequently abused group of prescription medications (Office of National Drug Control Policy [ONDCP] 2010). Depressants also are available on the street, although this illicit source does not account for the bulk of the problem.

In this chapter, we briefly review the history of CNS depressants, in terms of both development and use, and then discuss the positive and negative effects these drugs can produce. Each of the major types of depressant drugs is then reviewed in detail:

benzodiazepines (Xanax- or Valium-like drugs), *barbiturates,* and other minor categories. We move on to an examination of abuse patterns related to depressant drugs, and discuss how drug dependence and withdrawal are treated. Finally, we conclude with a discussion of natural depressants.

An Introduction to CNS Depressants

Why are CNS depressants problematic? First, in contrast to most other substances of abuse, CNS depressants are usually not obtained illicitly and self-administered but rather are prescribed under the direction of a physician. Second, use of CNS depressants can cause very alarming—even dangerous—behavior if not monitored closely; most problems associated with these drugs occur due to inadequate professional supervision and chronic use. Third, several seemingly unrelated drug groups have some ability to cause CNS depression and all too frequently are the cause of death by drug overdoses (see "Case in Point: Heath Ledger"). When these drugs are combined, bizarre and dangerous interactions can result. (See Chapter 5 for a discussion on drug interactions.) Particularly problematic is the combination of alcohol with other CNS de-

►Case in Point   Heath Ledger: He Died Accidently from Taking Too Many Pills

The New York City medical examiner confirmed what most people already suspected: on January 22, 2008, popular movie star Heath Ledger died from taking too many pills. The death was accidental and was declared to be "acute intoxication by the combined effects of oxycodone, hydrocodone, diazepam, temazepam, alprazolam and doxylamine." All of these drugs were legally prescribed CNS depressants, and represented the drug categories of opioid narcotics, benzodiazepines, and antihistamines. It was implied by the examiner that the level of none of these drugs was high enough to cause death by itself, suggesting that the death was not suicide. Death appeared to be due to an accumulative effect of the interactions of all of these depressants and was more the consequence of taking too many pills and ignorance of drug interactions rather than a desire to die.

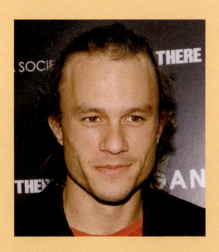

Source: Tyler, J. "Heath Ledger's Cause of Death Made Official." Celebrity Blend. (6 February 2008). Available at: http://www.cinemablend.com/celebrity/Heath-Ledger-s-Cause-Of-Death-Made-Official-8740.html. Accessed March 4, 2011.

pressants. Finally, CNS depressants can cause disruptive personality changes that are unpredictable and sometimes very threatening.

This chapter will help you understand the nature of the CNS depressant effects. In addition, the similarities and differences among the commonly prescribed CNS depressant drugs are discussed.

■ The History of CNS Depressants

Before the era of modern drugs, the most common depressant used to ease tension, cause relaxation, and help forget problems was alcohol. These effects undoubtedly accounted for the immense popularity of alcohol and help explain why this traditional depressant is the most commonly abused drug of all time. (Alcohol is discussed in detail in Chapters 7 and 8.)

Attempts to find CNS depressants other than alcohol that could be used to treat nervousness and anxiety began in the 1800s with the introduction of bromides. These drugs were very popular until their toxicities became known. In the early 1900s, bromides were replaced by **barbiturates**. Like bromides, barbiturates were initially heralded as safe and effective depressants; however, problems with tolerance, dependence, and lethal overdoses soon became evident. It was learned that the doses of barbiturates required to treat anxiety also could cause CNS depression, affecting respiration and impairing mental functions (Charney, Mihic, and Harris 2006). The margin of safety for barbiturates was too narrow, so research for safer CNS depressants began again.

It was not until the 1950s that the first **benzodiazepines** were marketed as substitutes for the dangerous barbiturates. Benzodiazepines were originally viewed as extremely safe and free from the problems of tolerance, dependence, and withdrawal that occurred with the other drugs in this category (Mondanaro 1988). Unfortunately, benzodiazepines have since been found to be less than ideal antianxiety drugs. Although relatively safe when used for short periods, long-term use can cause dependence and withdrawal problems much like those associated with their depressant predecessors (Charney et al. 2006). These problems have become a major concern of the medical community, as is discussed in greater detail later in the chapter.

Many of the people who become dependent on CNS depressants such as benzodiazepines began using the drugs under the supervision of a physician. Some clinicians routinely prescribe CNS depressants for patients with stress, anxiety, or apprehension without trying nonpharmacological approaches, such as psychotherapy or counseling. This practice sends an undesirable and often detrimental message to patients—that is, CNS depressants are a simple solution to their complex, stressful problems. The following quote illustrates the danger of this practice:

> I am still, unfortunately, lost in "'script addiction." . . . I have gone on-line asking for pills. I could really identify with the one posting about doctors who continue to write the 'scripts to increase/continue the patient "flow." This is exactly what is happening with me and my doctor. (*From America Online Alcohol and Drug Dependency and Recovery message board.*)

During the 1970s and 1980s, there was an epidemic of prescriptions written for CNS depressants. For example, in 1973, 100 million prescriptions were written for benzodiazepines alone. Approximately twice as many women as men were taking these drugs at this time; a similar gender pattern continues today. During this period, many homemakers made CNS depressants a part of their household routine, as described in the lyrics of the song "Mother's Little Helper" on the Rolling Stones' album *Flowers*:

> "Kids are different today"
> I hear ev'ry mother say
> Mother needs something today to calm her down
> And though she's not really ill,
> There's a little yellow pill.
> She goes running for the shelter of a mother's little helper
> And it helps her on her way, gets her through her busy day.

As the medical community became more aware of the problem, the use of depressants declined (Latner 2000). Today, efforts are being made by pharmaceutical companies and scientists to find new classes of CNS depressants that can be used to relieve stress and anxiety without causing serious side effects such as dependence and withdrawal.

KEY TERMS

barbiturates
potent CNS depressants, usually not preferred because of their narrow margin of safety

benzodiazepines
the most popular and safest CNS depressants in use today

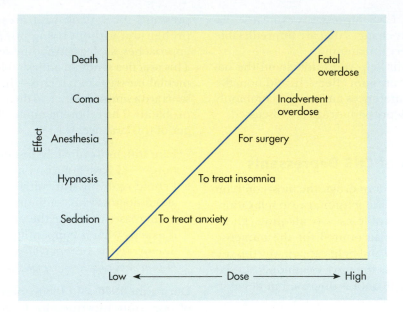

FIGURE 6.1

Dose-dependent effects of CNS depressants. The therapeutic outcome may change according to the dose administered (e.g., a low dose of a CNS depressant can be effective to relieve the anxiety associated with stress whereas a higher dose may cause drowsiness and be effective in the treatment of insomnia).

■ The Effects of CNS Depressants: Benefits and Risks

The CNS depressants are a diverse group of drugs that share an ability to reduce CNS activity and diminish the brain's level of awareness. Besides the benzodiazepines, barbiturate-like drugs, and alcohol, depressant drugs include **antihistamines** and opioid narcotics such as heroin (see Chapter 9).

KEY TERMS

antihistamines
drugs that often cause CNS depression, are used to treat allergies, and are often included in over-the-counter (OTC) sleep aids

sedatives
CNS depressants used to relieve anxiety, fear, and apprehension

anxiolytic
drug that relieves anxiety

hypnotics
CNS depressants used to induce drowsiness and encourage sleep

amnesiac
causing the loss of memory

anesthesia
a state characterized by loss of sensation or consciousness

Depressants are usually classified according to the degree of their medical effects on the body. For instance, **sedatives** cause mild depression of the CNS and relaxation. This drug effect is used to treat extreme anxiety and often is referred to as **anxiolytic**. Many sedatives also have muscle-relaxing properties that enhance their relaxing effects.

Depressants also are used to promote sleep and are frequently prescribed. Approximately 43 million sleeping pills were distributed in the United States in 2005. This represented a 32% increase over 2001 (Payne 2006). **Hypnotics** (from the Greek god of sleep, Hypnos) are CNS depressants that encourage sleep by inducing drowsiness. Often when depressants are used as hypnotics, they produce **amnesiac** effects as well. As already mentioned, the effects produced by depressants can be very enticing and encourage inappropriate use.

The effects of the CNS depressants tend to be dose dependent (see **Figure 6.1**). Thus, if you were to take a larger dose of a sedative, it might have a hypnotic effect. Often, the only difference between a sedative and a hypnotic effect is the dosage; consequently, the same drug may be used for both purposes by varying the dose. By increasing the dose still further, an anesthetic state can be reached. **Anesthesia**, a deep depression of the CNS, is used to achieve a controlled state of unconsciousness so that a patient can be treated, usually by surgery, in relative comfort and without memory of a traumatic experience. With the exception of benzodiazepines, if the dose of most of the depressants is increased much more, coma or death will ensue because the CNS becomes so depressed that vital centers controlling breathing and heart activity cease to function properly (*Drug Facts and Comparisons* 2010b).

As a group, CNS depressant drugs used in a persistent fashion cause tolerance. Because of the diminished effect due to the tolerance, users of these drugs continually escalate their doses. Under such conditions, the depressants alter physical and psychological states, resulting in dependence. The dependence can be so severe that abrupt drug abstinence results in severe withdrawals that include life-threatening seizures (*Drug Facts and Comparisons* 2010b). Because of these dangerous pharmacological features, treatment of dependence on CNS depressants must proceed very carefully (O'Brien 2006). This issue is discussed in greater detail at the end of this chapter and in Chapter 5.

Types of CNS Depressants

All CNS depressants are not created equal. Some have wider margins of safety; others have a greater potential for nonmedicinal abuse. These differences are important when considering the therapeutic advantages of each type of CNS depressant. In addition, unique features of the different types of depressants make them useful for treatment of other medical problems. For example, some barbiturates and benzodiazepines are used to treat forms of epilepsy or acute seizure activity, whereas opioid narcotics are used to treat many types of pain. Some of these unique features will be dealt with in greater detail when the individual drug groups are discussed. The benzodiazepines, barbiturate-like drugs, antihistamines, and the naturally occurring gamma-hydroxybutyrate (GHB) are discussed in this chapter. Other CNS depressants, such as alcohol and opiates, are covered in Chapters 7, 8, and 9.

The unique features of the CNS depressants help determine the likelihood of their abuse. For example, abuse is more likely to occur with the fast-acting depressant agents than with those agents that have long-lasting effects. Currently, nonmedicinal use of the sedatives occurs in approximately 2–4% of the population. This abuse is most likely to be caused by the benzodiazepines such as Xanax and Valium (Substance Abuse and Mental Health Services Administration [SAMHSA] 2007).

CNS depressants can be used as hypnotics to initiate sleep.

Benzodiazepines: Valium-Type Drugs

Benzodiazepines are by far the most frequently prescribed CNS depressants for anxiety and sleep. In fact, in 2008, 85 million prescriptions were filled for the top benzodiazepine (Balestra 2009). Because of their wide margin of safety (death from overdose is rare), benzodiazepines have replaced barbiturate-like drugs for use as sedatives and hypnotics (Balestra 2009). Benzodiazepines were originally referred to as *minor tranquilizers*, but this terminology erroneously implied that they had pharmacological properties similar to those of antipsychotic drugs (*major tranquilizers*), when they are actually very different. Consequently, the term *minor tranquilizer* is usually avoided by clinicians. The first true benzodiazepine, chlordiazepoxide (Librium), was developed for medical use and marketed about 1960. The very popular drug Valium came on the market about the same time. In fact, Valium was so well received that from 1972 to 1978 it was the top-selling prescription drug in the United States. Its popularity has since declined considerably and it has been replaced by benzodiazepines such as alprazolam (Xanax), lorazepam (Ativan), flurazepam (Dalmane), temazepam (Restoril), and triazolam (Halcion) (U.S. Drug Enforcement Administration [DEA] 2010a, 2010b).

Because of dependence problems, the benzodiazepines are now classified as Schedule IV drugs (see Appendix B). In recent years, considerable

Prescription for Abuse: Too Much of A Good Thing

Mr. Starr attends a "12 Steps to Recovery" program filled with recovering alcoholics; however, Mr. Starr's drug problem is not alcohol but another CNS depressant known as Klonopin or clonazepam. Mr. Starr was prescribed this popular benzodiazepine to deal with a very stressful divorce. The antianxiety effects of Klonopin were very settling and stabilizing, at least at first. However, with time the benefits diminished, but he continued to use the drug for 6 years. It was when Mr. Starr went to see a new psychiatrist that he was told he had become extremely dependent on this sedative drug. He resolved to get himself off of Klonopin and began to taper the doses slowly. He described the effects as "ripping me apart." For more than 1½ years Mr. Starr had extreme difficulty sleeping, his heart would race, and he had night sweats. He couldn't tell if he spoke clearly and he completely withdrew from friends and family. It required 2½ years after he stopped taking Klonopin for his sleep patterns to return to normal.

....

Source: Balestra, K. "Anti-Anxiety Drugs Raise New Fears." *Washington Post.* 30 June 2009. Available at: http://www.socialanxietyhelp.com/article.anti.anxiety.drugs.raise.new.fears.htm. Accessed March 4, 2011.

concern has arisen that benzodiazepines are overprescribed because of their perceived safety; it has been said, somewhat facetiously, that the only way a person could die from using benzodiazepines would be to choke on them. Clinicians are concerned about this overconfident attitude toward benzodiazepines and their potential for dependence (Balestra 2009), and warn patients against prolonged and unsupervised administration of these drugs (Charney et al. 2006) (see "Prescription for Abuse: Too Much of a Good Thing").

Medical Uses

Benzodiazepines are used for an array of therapeutic objectives, including the relief of anxiety, treatment of neurosis, relaxation of muscles, alleviation of lower back pain, treatment of some convulsive disorders, induction of sleep (hypnotic), relief from withdrawal symptoms associated with narcotic and alcohol dependence, and induction of amnesia, usually for preoperative administration (administered just before or during surgery or very uncomfortable medical procedures) (Charney et al. 2006; DEA 2010a, 2010b).

Mechanisms of Action

In contrast to barbiturate-type drugs, which cause general depression of most neuronal activity, benzodiazepines selectively affect those neurons that have receptors for the neurotransmitter gamma aminobutyric acid (GABA) (Charney et al. 2006). GABA is a very important inhibitory transmitter in several regions of the brain: the limbic system, the reticular activating system, and the motor cortex (see Chapter 4). In the presence of benzodiazepines, the inhibitory effects of GABA are increased. Depression of activity in these brain regions likely accounts for the ability of benzodiazepines to alter mood (a limbic function), cause drowsiness (a reticular activating system function), and relax muscles (a cortical function). The specific GABA-enhancing effect of these drugs explains the selective CNS depression caused by benzodiazepines.

Of considerable interest is the observation that these Valium-like drugs act on specific receptor sites that are linked to the GABA receptors in the CNS (Balestra 2009). As yet, no endogenous substance has been identified that naturally interacts with this so-called benzodiazepine site. It is very likely, however, that a natural benzodiazepine does exist that activates this same receptor population and serves to reduce stress and anxiety by natural means. Because benzodiazepines have specific target receptors, it has been possible to develop a highly selective antagonist drug, flumazenil (Romazicon). This drug is used to treat benzodiazepine overdoses, but must be used carefully because its administration can precipitate withdrawal in people taking benzodiazepines (Charney et al. 2006).

Types of Benzodiazepines

Because benzodiazepines are so popular and thus profitable, several of these drugs are available by prescription. Currently, approximately 15 benzodiazepine compounds are available in the United States and some 20 additional benzodiazepines are marketed in other countries (DEA 2010b).

Benzodiazepines are distinguished primarily by their duration of action (see **Table 6.1**). As a general rule, the short-acting drugs are used as hypnotics to treat insomnia, thus allowing the user to awake in the morning with few aftereffects (such as a hangover). The long-acting benzodiazepines tend to be prescribed as sedatives, giving prolonged relaxation and relief from persistent anxiety. Some of the long-acting drugs can exert a relaxing effect for as long as 2 to 3 days. One reason for the long action in some benzodiazepines is that they are converted by the liver into metabolites that are as

Table 6.1 Half-Lives of Various Benzodiazepines

DRUG	HALF-LIFE (HOURS)
Alprazolam (Xanax)	12–15
Chlordiazepoxide (Librium)	5–30
Clonazepam (Klonopin)	18–50
Diazepam (Valium)	20–50
Estazolam (ProSom)	10–24
Lorazepam (Ativan)	10–20
Midazolam (Versed)	1–12
Oxazepam (Serax)	5–21
Quazepam (Doral)	25–41
Temazepam (Restoril)	10–17
Triazolam (Halcion)	1.5–5.5
Zolpidem (Ambien; not a true benzodiazepine)	2–5

Source: Charney, D., S. Mihic, and R. Harris. "Hyponotics and Sedatives." In *The Pharmacological Basis of Therapeutics*, 11th ed., edited by L. Brunton, J. Lazo, and K. Parker, 401-427. New York: McGraw-Hill, 2006.

active as the original drug (Charney et al. 2006; DEA 2010b). For example, Valium has a half-life of 20 to 80 hours and is converted by the liver into several active metabolites, including oxazepam (which itself is marketed as a therapeutic benzodiazepine).

Side Effects

Reported side effects of benzodiazepines include drowsiness, lightheadedness, lethargy, impairment of mental and physical activities, skin rashes, nausea, diminished libido, irregularities in the menstrual cycle, blood cell abnormalities, and increased sensitivity to alcohol and other CNS depressants (Charney et al. 2006). In contrast to barbiturate-type drugs, only very high doses of benzodiazepines have a significant impact on respiration. There are few verified instances of death resulting from overdose of benzodiazepines alone (Longo and Johnson 2000). Almost always, serious suppression of vital functions occurs when these drugs are combined with other depressants, most often alcohol (Charney et al. 2006).

Although their long-term effectiveness has been challenged, benzodiazepines are used almost 50%

of the time to treat persistent disorders such as chronic insomnia (Gorman 2003). Benzodiazepines have less effect on **REM sleep** (rapid eye movement, the restive phase) than do barbiturates. Consequently, sleep under the influence of benzodiazepines is more likely to be restful and satisfying. However, prolonged use of hypnotic doses of benzodiazepines may cause rebound (see Chapter 5) increases in REM sleep and insomnia when the drug is stopped, especially if used for long periods of time (Balestra 2009).

On rare occasions, benzodiazepines can have **paradoxical effects**, producing unusual responses, such as nightmares, anxiety, irritability, sweating, and restlessness (*Drug Facts and Comparisons* 2010b). Bizarre, uninhibited behavior—extreme agitation with hostility, paranoia, and rage—may occur as well. One such case was reported in 1988 in Utah. A 63-year-old patient who was taking Halcion (a relatively short-acting benzodiazepine) murdered her 87-year-old mother. The suspect claimed that the murder occurred because of the effects of the drug and that she was innocent of committing a crime. Her defense was successful, and she was acquitted of murder. After her acquittal, the woman initiated a $21 million lawsuit against Upjohn Pharmaceuticals for marketing Halcion, which she claimed was a dangerous drug. The lawsuit was settled out of court for an undisclosed amount. This tragic episode came to a surprising conclusion in 1994 when the daughter committed suicide (Associated Press 1994).

Critics' complaints that Halcion causes unacceptable "amnesia, confusion, paranoia, hostility and seizures" (Associated Press 1994, p. D-3) prompted the Food and Drug Administration (FDA) to closely evaluate this benzodiazepine. Despite the fact that several other countries have banned Halcion, the FDA concluded that its benefits outweigh the reported risks; however, the FDA also concluded that, "In no way should this [the FDA's conclusion] suggest that Halcion is free of side effects. It has long been recognized and emphasized in Halcion's labeling that it is a potent drug that produces the same type of adverse effects as other CNS sedative hypnotic drugs" (*Drug Facts and Comparisons* 2010b, pp. 739–740). Although the FDA did not require

KEY TERMS

REM sleep
the restive phase of sleep associated with dreaming

paradoxical effects
unexpected effects

that Halcion be withdrawn, it did negotiate changes in the labeling and package inserts with Halcion's manufacturer, Upjohn Pharmaceuticals. These changes emphasize appropriate Halcion use in treatment of insomnia and additional information about side effects, warnings, and dosage. As a result of these concerns, sales of Halcion plummeted, causing it to fall from the 18th-largest-selling prescription drug in 1987 to not even being one of the top 200 most-prescribed drugs in 2008 (Drugs.com 2010).

There is no obvious explanation for the strange benzodiazepine-induced behaviors. It is possible that, in some people, the drugs mask inhibitory centers of the brain and allow expression of antisocial behavior that is normally suppressed and controlled. Related concerns have also been made public about another very popular benzodiazepine, alprazolam (Xanax). In 1990, Xanax became the first drug approved for the treatment of panic disorder—repeated, intense attacks of anxiety that can make life unbearable (McEvoy 2003). Reports that long-term use of Xanax can cause severe withdrawal effects and a stubborn dependency on the drug raised public concerns about use of benzodiazepines in general. For example, how many people are severely dependent on these CNS depressants? What is the frequency of side effects such as memory impairment, serious mood swings, and cognitive problems? And how many patients using the benzodiazepines would be better served with nondrug psychotherapy? Clearly, use of the benzodiazepines to relieve acute stress or insomnia can be beneficial, but these drugs should be prescribed at the lowest dose possible and for the shortest time possible or withdrawal problems can result, as illustrated in the following quote:

> I was put on alprazolam (Xanax) two and a half years ago by [my] doctor. Now told by another doctor that it is for short-term use only and I am trying to get off slowly, but having difficulty. [I] have never used other drugs and do not have any information on the withdrawal process. *(From America Online Alcohol and Drug Dependency and Recovery message board.)*

Two relatively new benzodiazepine-like CNS depressants approved for short-term treatment of insomnia are zolpidem (Ambien) and zalephon (Sonata). These both are classified as Schedule IV drugs (DEA 2010a, 2010b; Drugs.com 2010; MedicineNet.com 2007). They have abuse potential, especially when used chronically and when they interact with other CNS depressants such as alcohol and narcotic analgesics (Drugs.com 2010).

Tolerance, Dependence, Withdrawal, and Abuse

As with most CNS depressants, frequent, chronic use of benzodiazepines can cause tolerance, dependence (both physical and psychological), and withdrawal (*Drug Facts and Comparisons* 2010b). Such side effects are usually not as severe as those of most other depressants, and they occur only after using the drugs for prolonged periods (*Drug Facts and Comparisons* 2010b). In addition, for most people, the effects of the benzodiazepines are not viewed as reinforcing; thus, compared with other depressants, such as barbiturates, benzodiazepines are not especially addicting (O'Brien 2006). However, these drugs should be prescribed with caution for patients with a history of drug abuse (O'Brien 2006).

Withdrawal can mimic the condition for which the benzodiazepine is given; for example, withdrawal symptoms can include anxiety or insomnia (Charney et al. 2006; DEA 2010a, 2010b). In such cases, a clinician may be fooled into thinking that the underlying emotional disorder is still present and may resume drug therapy without realizing that the patient has become drug dependent. This can happen after as little as 1 month of treatment. In situations in which users have consumed high doses of benzodiazepine over the long term, more severe, even life-threatening withdrawal symptoms may occur (*Drug Facts and Comparisons* 2010b); depression, panic, paranoia, and convulsions (Charney et al. 2006) have been reported (see **Table 6.2**). Severe withdrawal can often be avoided by gradually weaning the patient from the benzodiazepine (Charney et al. 2006). Long-term use of benzodiazepines (periods exceeding 3 to 4 months) to treat anxiety or sleep disorders has not been shown to be therapeutically useful for most patients (*Drug Facts and Comparisons* 2010b). Even so, this approach is a common indiscriminate practice. As one user explains:

> I went through a trauma 4 years ago, and the doctor prescribed a very high dose of Ativan. Well, I soon became addicted, both emotionally and physically . . . How do I get off? . . . This stuff is very addicting and my body can't really function without it. *(From America Online Alcohol and Drug Dependency and Recovery message board)*

It is very unusual to find nontherapeutic drug-seeking behavior in a patient who has been properly removed from benzodiazepines, unless that individual already has a history of drug abuse (DEA 2010a, 2010b; Longo and Johnson 2000). Research has shown that when benzodiazepines are the

Table 6.2   **Abstinence Symptoms That Occur When Long-Term Users of Benzodiazepines Abruptly Stop Taking the Drug**

DURATION OF ABSTINENCE	SYMPTOMS
1–3 days	Often no noticeable symptoms
3–4 days	Restlessness, agitation, headaches, problems eating, and inability to sleep
4–6 days	The preceding symptoms plus twitching of facial and arm muscles and feeling of intense burning in the skin
6–7 days	The preceding symptoms plus seizures

Source: Hobbs, W., T. Rall, and T. Verdoorn. "Hypnotics and Sedatives." In *The Pharmacological Basis of Therapeutics*, 9th ed., edited by J. Hardman and L. Limbird, 361–396. New York: McGraw-Hill, 1995.

primary drug of abuse, these CNS depressants are usually self-administered to prevent unpleasant withdrawal symptoms in dependent users. If benzodiazepine-dependent users are properly weaned from the drugs and withdrawal has dissipated, there is no evidence that craving for the benzodiazepines occurs because people usually do not consider the benzodiazepines particularly reinforcing (Kosten and Hollister 1998). An exception to this conclusion appears to be former alcoholics. Many people with a history of alcoholism find the effects of benzodiazepines rewarding; consequently, almost one-fourth of prior alcoholics use benzodiazepines chronically (Johansson et al. 2003).

Benzodiazepines are commonly used as a secondary drug of abuse and combined with illicit drugs. For example, it is very common to find heroin users who are dependent on benzodiazepines as well (Backmund et al. 2005; DEA 2010a).

Another frequent combination is the use of benzodiazepines with stimulants such as cocaine (DEA 2010a; DeMaria, Sterling, and Weinstein 2000).

Some addicts claim that this combination enhances the pleasant effects of the stimulant and reduces the "crashing" that occurs after using high doses. (More is said about benzodiazepine abuse later in this chapter.)

It should also be mentioned that benzodiazepines are occasionally used to make people vulnerable to sexual assaults referred to as date rapes (Charney et al. 2006). The use of CNS depressants to commit these acts of violence is discussed in greater detail later in the chapter, but such assaults have sometimes involved the use of the **club drug** Rohypnol. Rohypnol (sometimes called Rophie, Roche, or Forget Me) is the proprietary name for flunitrazepam, a benzodiazepine. Rohypnol, which has been outlawed in the United States, comes as a tablet that can be dissolved in beverages without leaving an odor or taste and impairs short-term memory, making victims unable to recall details of the assault (DEA 2010a, 2010b; National Institute on Drug Abuse 2000; Publishers Group 2002). In 2009, 1.0% of high school seniors claimed to have used this drug (Johnston, O'Malley, Bachman, and Schulenberg 2010).

Barbiturates

Barbiturates are barbituric acid derivatives that are used in medicine as sedatives and hypnotics. Barbituric acid was first synthesized by A. Bayer (of aspirin fame) in Germany in 1864. The reason that he chose the name barbituric acid is not known.

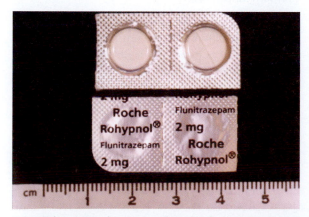

Rohypnol is a benzodiazepine outlawed in the United States.

Some have speculated that the compound was named after a girl named Barbara whom Bayer knew. Others think that Bayer celebrated his discovery on the Day of St. Barbara in a tavern that artillery officers frequented. (St. Barbara is the patron saint of artillery soldiers.)

The first barbiturate, barbital (Veronal), was used medically in 1903. Since then, more than 2500 barbiturates have been synthesized; of these about 50 were actually approved for human use. However, due to serious side effects only a few are still prescribed for medical purposes (DEA 2010b). The names of the barbiturates traditionally end in *-al*, indicating a chemical relationship to barbital, the first one synthesized. Historically, barbiturates have played an important role in therapeutics because of their effectiveness as sedative-hypnotic agents, which allowed them to be routinely used in the treatment of anxiety, agitation, and insomnia. However, because of their narrow margin of safety and their abuse liability, barbiturates have been largely replaced by safer drugs, such as benzodiazepines. Despite the reduced therapeutic use of the barbiturates, in 2009, 5.2% of high school seniors claimed to have recreationally used a barbiturate (Johnston et al. 2010).

Uncontrolled use of barbiturates can cause a state of acute or chronic intoxication. Initially, there may be some loss of inhibition, euphoria, and behavioral stimulation—a pattern often seen with moderate consumption of alcohol. When taken to relieve extreme agitation or mental stress, barbiturates may cause delirium and produce other side effects that can include nausea, nervousness, rash, and diarrhea. The person intoxicated with barbiturates may have difficulty thinking and making judgments, may be emotionally unstable, may be uncoordinated and unsteady when walking, and may slur speech (not unlike the drunken state caused by alcohol).

When used for their hypnotic properties, barbiturates cause an unnatural sleep. The user awakens feeling tired, edgy, and quite unsatisfied, most likely because barbiturates markedly suppress the REM phase of sleep. (REM sleep is necessary for the refreshing renewal that usually accompanies a good sleep experience.) Because benzodiazepines suppress REM sleep (as do all CNS depressants) less severely than barbiturates, use of these agents as sleep aids is generally better tolerated.

Continued misuse of barbiturate drugs has a cumulative toxic effect on the CNS that is more life threatening than misuse of opiates. When taken in large doses or in combination with other CNS depressants, barbiturates may cause death from respiratory or cardiovascular depression. Because of this toxicity, barbiturates have been involved in many drug-related deaths, both accidental and suicidal. Repeated misuse induces severe tolerance of and physical dependence on these drugs. Discontinuing use of short-acting barbiturates in people who are using large doses can cause dangerous withdrawal effects such as life-threatening seizures. "Signs & Symptoms: Effects of Barbiturates and Other Depressants" summarizes the range of effects of barbiturates and other depressants on the mind and body.

Concern about the abuse potential of barbiturates caused the federal government to include some of these depressants in the Controlled Substances Act (DEA 2010b). Consequently, the short-acting barbiturates, such as pentobarbital and secobarbital, are classified as Schedule II drugs, whereas the long-acting barbiturates, such as phenobarbital, are less rigidly controlled as Schedule IV drugs (see Appendix B).

Effects and Medical Uses

Barbiturates have many pharmacological actions. They depress the activity of nerves and skeletal, smooth, and cardiac muscles and affect the CNS in several ways, ranging from mild sedation to coma, depending on the dose. At sedative or hypnotic dosage levels, only the CNS is significantly affected. Higher anesthetic doses cause slight decreases in blood pressure, heart rate, and flow of urine. The metabolizing enzyme systems in the liver are important in inactivating barbiturates; thus, liver damage may result in exaggerated responses to barbiturate use (Charney et al. 2006).

Low doses of barbiturates relieve tension and anxiety, effects that give several barbiturates substantial abuse potential. The drawbacks of barbiturates are extensive and severe:

- They lack selectivity and safety.
- They have a substantial tendency to create tolerance, dependence, withdrawal, and abuse.
- They cause problems with drug interaction.

As a result, barbiturates have been replaced by benzodiazepines in most treatments, and only about a dozen are still in medical use (DEA 2010b). Because of this decreased use, these drugs tend not to be readily available and are becoming less frequently abused in this country (Johnston et al. 2010). The long-acting phenobarbital is still frequently used for its CNS depressant activity to alleviate or prevent convulsions in some epileptic

Signs & Symptoms **Effects of Barbiturates and Other Depressants**

	BODY	MIND
Low dose	Drowsiness	Decreased anxiety, relaxation
	Trouble with coordination	Decreased ability to reason and solve problems
	Slurred speech	
	Dizziness	Difficulty in judging distance and time
	Staggering	
	Double vision	Amnesia
	Sleep	
	Depressed breathing	Brain damage
	Coma (unconscious and cannot be awakened)	
	Depressed blood pressure	
High dose	Death	

patients and seizures caused by strychnine, cocaine, and other stimulant drugs. Thiopental (Pentothal) and other ultrashort- and short-acting barbiturates are used as anesthesia for minor surgery and as preoperative anesthetics in preparation for major surgery.

Mechanism of Action and Elimination

The precise mechanism of action for barbiturates is unclear. Like benzodiazepines, they likely interfere with activity in the reticular activating system, the limbic system, and the motor cortex. However, in contrast to benzodiazepines, barbiturates do not seem to act at a specific receptor site; they probably have a general effect that enhances the activity of the inhibitory transmitter GABA (Charney et al. 2006). Because benzodiazepines also increase GABA activity (albeit in a more selective manner), these two types of drugs have overlapping effects. Because the mechanisms whereby they exert their effects are different, it is not surprising that these two types of depressants also have different pharmacological features.

The fat solubility of barbiturates is another important factor in the duration of their effects (Charney et al. 2006). Barbiturates that are the most fat soluble move in and out of body tissues (such as the brain) rapidly and are likely to be shorter acting. Fat-soluble barbiturates also are more likely to be stored in fatty tissue; consequently, the fat

content of the body can influence the effects on the user. Because women have a higher body–fat ratio than men, their reaction to barbiturates may be slightly different.

Withdrawal from barbiturates after dependence has developed causes hyperexcitability because of the rebound of depressed neural systems. Qualitatively (but not quantitatively), the withdrawal symptoms are similar for all sedative-hypnotics (Trevor and Lay 1998).

Table 6.3 gives details on the barbiturates that are abused most frequently.

■ Other CNS Depressants

Although benzodiazepines and barbiturates are used the most frequently to produce CNS depressant effects, many other agents, representing an array of distinct chemical groups, can similarly reduce brain activity. Although the mechanisms of action might be different for some of these drugs, if any CNS depressants (including alcohol) are combined, they will interact synergistically and can suppress respiration in a life-threatening manner. Thus, it is important to avoid such mixtures if possible. Even some over-the-counter (OTC) products, such as cold and allergy medications, contain drugs with CNS depressant actions.

Table 6.3 **Details on the Most Frequently Abused Barbiturates**

DRUG	NICKNAMES	EFFECTS
Amobarbital (Amytal Sodium)	Blues, blue heavens, blue devils	Moderately rapid action
Pentobarbital (Nembutal Sodium)	Nembies, yellow jackets, yellows	Short-acting
Phenobarbital (Luminal Sodium)	Purple hearts	Long-acting barbiturate particularly well suited for treatment of epilepsy
Secobarbital (Seconal Sodium)	Reds, red devils, red birds, Seccy	Short-acting with a prompt onset of action
50% amobarbital and 50% secobarbital (Tuinal)	Tooeys, double trouble, rainbows	Results in a rapidly effective, moderately long-acting sedative

Nonbarbiturate Drugs with Barbiturate-Like Properties

This category of depressants includes agents that are not barbiturates but have barbiturate-like effects (Charney et al. 2006). All of these drugs cause substantial tolerance, physical and psychological dependence, and withdrawal symptoms. The therapeutic safety of these CNS depressants more closely resembles that of barbiturates than benzodiazepines; consequently, like barbiturates, these agents have been replaced by the safer and easier-to-manage benzodiazepines (Charney et al. 2006).

Because these drugs have significant abuse potential, they are restricted much like other CNS depressants. In this group of depressants, methaqualone is a Schedule II drug; glutethimide and methyprylon are Schedule III drugs; and chloral hydrate is a Schedule IV drug. Each classification is based on the drug's relative potential for physical and psychological dependence. Abuse of Schedule II drugs may lead to severe or moderate physical dependence or high psychological dependence, and abuse of Schedule III drugs may cause moderate physical and psychological dependence. Schedule IV drugs are considered much less likely to cause either type of dependence.

Chloral Hydrate

Chloral hydrate (Noctec), or "knock-out drops," has the unsavory reputation of being a drug that is slipped into a person's drink to cause unconsciousness. In the late 1800s, the combination of chloral hydrate and alcohol was given the name Mickey Finn on the waterfront of the Barbary Coast of San Francisco when sailors were in short supply. An unsuspecting man would have a friendly drink and wake up as a crew member on an outbound freighter to China.

Chloral hydrate is a good hypnotic, but it has a narrow margin of safety. This compound is a stomach irritant, especially if given repeatedly and in fairly large doses. Addicts may take enormous doses of the drug; as with most CNS depressants, chronic, long-term use of high doses will cause tolerance and physical dependence (Charney et al. 2006).

Glutethimide

Glutethimide (Doriden) is another example of a barbiturate-like drug that can be abused and that causes severe withdrawal symptoms. It also induces blood abnormalities in sensitive individuals, such as a type of anemia and abnormally low white cell counts. Nausea, fever, increased heart rate, and convulsions occasionally occur in patients who have been taking this sedative regularly in moderate doses.

Methyprylon

Methyprylon (Noludar) is a short-acting nonbarbiturate that is used as a sedative and hypnotic. Its effects are similar to those of Doriden, and it is capable of causing tolerance, physical dependence, and addiction, much like barbiturates.

Methaqualone

Few drugs have become so popular so quickly as methaqualone. This barbiturate-like sedative-hypnotic was introduced in India in the 1950s as an antimalarial agent. Its sedative properties, however, were soon discovered. It became available in the United States as Quaalude, Mequin, and Parest.

After several years of street abuse, methaqualone was classified as a Schedule II drug. Since 1985, methaqualone has not been manufactured in the United States because of adverse publicity, although in 2009 almost 0.6% of high school seniors in the United States claimed to have used it (Johnston et al. 2010).

Common side effects of methaqualone include fatigue, dizziness, anorexia, nausea, vomiting, diarrhea, sweating, dryness of the mouth, depersonalization, headache, and paresthesia of the extremities (a pins-and-needles feeling in the fingers and toes). Hangover is frequently reported.

Antihistamines

Antihistamines are drugs used in both nonprescription and prescription medicinal products. The most common uses for antihistamines are to relieve the symptoms associated with the common cold, allergies, and motion sickness (see Chapter 15). Although frequently overlooked, many antihistamines cause significant CNS depression and are used as both sedatives and hypnotics (*Drug Facts and Comparisons* 2010a). For example, the agents hydroxyzine (Vistaril) and promethazine (Phenergan) are prescribed for their sedative effects, whereas diphenhydramine is commonly used as an OTC sleep aid (e.g., Compoz Nighttime Sleep Aid).

The exact mechanism of CNS depression caused by these agents is not totally known but appears to relate to their blockage of acetylcholine receptors in the brain (they antagonize the muscarinic

Antihistamines are found in OTC medicines, which are used to relieve cold and allergy symptoms.

receptor types). This anticholinergic activity (see Chapter 4) helps cause relaxation and sedation and can be viewed as a very annoying side effect when these drugs are being used to treat allergies or other problems.

Therapeutic Usefulness and Side Effects

Antihistamines are viewed as relatively safe agents. Compared with other more powerful CNS depressants, antihistamines do not appear to cause significant physical or psychological dependence or addiction problems, although drugs with anticholinergic activity, such as the antihistamines, are sometimes abused, especially by children and teenagers (Scharman et al. 2006). However, tolerance to antihistamine-induced sedation occurs quite rapidly. Reports of significant cases of withdrawal problems when use of antihistamines is stopped are rare. This situation may reflect the fact that these agents are used as antianxiety drugs for only minor problems and for short periods of time (often only for a single dose).

One significant problem with antihistamines is the variability of responses they produce. Different antihistamines work differently on different people. Usually therapeutic doses cause decreased alertness, relaxation, slowed reaction time, and drowsiness. But it is not uncommon for some individuals to be affected in the opposite manner—that is, an antihistamine sometimes causes restlessness, agitation, and insomnia. There are even cases of seizures caused by toxic doses of antihistamine, particularly in children (Scharman et al. 2006). Side effects of antihistamines related to their anticholinergic effects include dry mouth, constipation, and inability to urinate. These factors probably help to discourage high-dose abuse of these drugs. However, OTC antihistamines are still sometimes taken for recreational purposes despite the unpleasant side effects (Hughes et al. 1999).

Even though antihistamines are relatively safe in therapeutic doses, they can contribute to serious problems if combined with other CNS depressants. Many OTC cold, allergy, antimotion, and sleep aid products contain antihistamines and should be avoided by patients using the potent CNS depressants or alcohol.

New Generation of Sleep Aids

In the past few years, several prescription products have been marketed for treating insomnia with the claim that they are less sedating and less likely to cause dependence than the traditional benzodiazepines and barbiturates. These heavily marketed medications include brand names such as Ambien, Lunesta, Rozerem, and Sonata. It is clear that although less sedating than the older sedative/hypnotics, this new generation of sleep aids can cause next-day sedation and have resulted in some dependency, especially when used with other CNS depressants such as alcohol (Payne 2006).

Propofol, An Abused General Anesthetic

Propofol (Diprivan) was initially made available in 1986 and used intravenously for rapid sedation, analgesia, and general anesthesia in hospital or outpatient clinics. Its use for these purposes continues today. It has also been used off-label (i.e., not officially approved by the FDA) to relieve severe chronic or migraine headaches in pain clinics or for sleep induction in patients suffering from insomnia. Initially, propofol was thought to be free of abuse liability. However, although physical dependence is rare, because use of this drug can cause euphoria and relieve stress and pain, it has been abused and even involved in suicides or accidental deaths (Kirby, Colaw, and Douglas 2010), as was found to be the case in the highly publicized death of pop singer Michael Jackson (see "Case in Point: Misuse of Propofol Causes Jackson's Death").

Recent abuse problems have particularly involved medical professionals such as doctors and nurses who have access to this anesthetic. Some doctors claim it has unique features and have referred to their experience with propofol as "dancing with the white rabbit." Part of its attraction is that it is not a scheduled substance, it is easy to obtain, and its effects wear off in a matter of minutes (McKenzie 2009).

GHB (Gamma-Hydroxybutyrate): The Natural Depressant

GHB is a colorless, tasteless, and odorless substance found naturally in the body resulting from the metabolism of the inhibitory neurotransmitter GABA (see Chapter 4; Drasbek, Christensen, and Jensen 2006; Lingenhoehl et al. 1999). It was first synthesized nearly 30 years ago by a French researcher who intended to study the CNS effects of GABA (Poldrugo and Addolorato 1999). It was initially believed that GHB exerted its effects by enhancing CNS GABA systems, although this mechanism has been questioned (Carter et al. 2003). There is some evidence that GHB is itself a neuromodulator with its own receptor targets in the brain (Carter et al. 2003). Because of its central depressant effects, GHB has been used in Europe as an adjunct for general anesthesia, a treatment for insomnia and narcolepsy (a daytime sleep disorder), and a treatment for alcoholism and alcohol withdrawal

---

▶ Case in Point   Misuse of Propofol Causes Jackson's Death ◀

Pop singing star Michael Jackson died from an overdose of the potent general anesthetic propofol in June 2009. Because this drug is routinely administered intravenously it is only available to medical personnel in a clinical setting and almost never sent home with patients. In the case of Jackson, his personal physician had been making the drug available to help Jackson sleep and to deal with his anxiety prior to performances. A member of Jackson's staff called for help when Jackson appeared to have a severe adverse reaction to propofol that caused abnormal hot and cold sensations throughout his body. By the time help arrived, it was too late and Jackson was deceased. The inappropriate manner in which propofol was given to Jackson appears to be the basis for charges of manslaughter that were filed against his personal physician. This tragedy is a reminder that propofol should be used with great caution because if administered inappropriately, even by a physician, its side effects can be deadly.

Source: Kaufman, G. "What Is Propofol and Why Was Michael Jackson Allegedly Using It?" MTV News Top Stories. (1 July 2009). Available at: http://www.mtv.com/news/articles/1615103/20090701/jackson_michael.jhtml. Accessed March 4, 2011.

and narcotic dependence (Nava et al. 2007). During the 1980s, GHB became available without a prescription in health food stores and was used principally by body builders to stimulate the release of growth hormone with the intent to reduce fat and build muscle (Publishers Group 2002; Vendel 2009). More recently, this substance became popular for recreational use due to what was described as a pleasant, alcohol-like, hangover-free high with aphrodisiac properties (Morgenthaler and Joy 1994; VZ-Life 2010), and, because of its potential for abuse, access to GHB was restricted by the DEA in 2000. In 2009, 1.1% of high school seniors were reported to have used GHB (Johnston et al. 2010). Because of its frequent use by young people at nightclubs and bars, GHB became known as a club drug (Sumnall et al. 2008). Some of its common street names include: G, Gamma-OH, Liquid E, Georgia, Home Boy, Liquid X, Scoop, Water, and Everclear (Vendel 2009).

GHB is generally taken orally after being mixed with a liquid or beverage. It has a rapid onset and, when large doses are consumed, can cause unconsciousness and coma in 15 to 40 minutes. These dangerous effects typically require emergency room treatment. Often, the recovery is also rapid with persons regaining consciousness in 2 to 4 hours (Publishers Group 2002).

Due to concerns about GHB abuse and side effects, an advisory warning that this substance is unsafe was first issued by the FDA in 1990. In 1997, the FDA released another warning that GHB was not approved for clinical use in the United States and was a potentially dangerous substance. Finally, due to the

rising illicit use of GHB and resultant problems, this drug was made a Schedule I Controlled Substance by the DEA in March 2000 (DEA 2000).

Despite claims about its benign nature (Dean, Morganthalwer, and Fowkes 1997), evidence is mounting that in high doses, GHB can be dangerous and even deadly (Vendel 2009). A number of documented deaths have been attributed to GHB overdoses as of 2009 (Vendel 2009). It has been reported that GHB use can cause significant side effects, such as hormonal problems, sleep abnormalities, drowsiness, nausea, vomiting, and changes in blood pressure (AddictionSearch 2010; Teter and Guthrie 2001; Vendel 2009). Both users and clinicians seem to agree that GHB is most dangerous when combined with other drugs, especially other CNS depressants such as alcohol (AddictionSearch 2010; DEA 2000).

Because GHB is illegal in the United States, it is currently available only through the underground "gray market" as a "bootleg" product manufactured by kitchen chemists and with suspicious quality and purity. The lack of reliability of these GHB-containing products and the highly variable responses of different people to this substance increase the likelihood of problems when using this depressant.

Instructions on how to make GHB are readily available on multiple Internet sites. It is typically portrayed as a relatively benign substance, but one for which proper dosing is critical for "safe" use (Vendel 2009).

There is some debate as to whether the use of GHB can cause dependence and withdrawal. Some evidence suggests that chronic high-dose use of GHB may lead to prolonged abuse and a withdrawal syndrome consisting of insomnia, anxiety, and tremors that typically resolves in 3 to 12 days (Craig et al. 2000; Galloway et al. 1997; Mioto and Roth 2001). Another major concern with this substance is its use in cases of date rape. Because GHB can be stored as a clear, colorless, odorless liquid, it is easily added undetected to a beverage such as an alcoholic drink (NIDA 2000; Vendel 2009). Its amnesiac and sedative properties disable users and make them vulnerable to sexual assault (Leshner 2000; Vendel 2009). Despite attempts to vigorously prosecute these cases, because the victims frequently are unable to recall details of the attack and the drug disappears so quickly from the bloodstream (its half-life is 2 to 3 hours), rape under the influence of GHB can be difficult to prove.

Other GHB-related drugs have become readily available as substitutes, although they are only legal

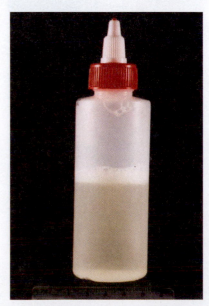

GHB often is stored as a clear, colorless, odorless liquid.

if they are included in products technically not intended for human use. These products are supposedly promoted as chemical solvents and typically make a disclaimer that the products are not for human consumption, even though the label often implies that the product may be ingested. For example, the label on one industrial solvent stated, "Warning! Accidental ingestion . . . will produce GHB in your body. If you ingest some by mistake, don't take alcohol or any other drug" (U.S. Department of Justice [USDOJ] 2002). The most commonly used of these GHB analogs are gamma-butyrolactone (GBL) and 1,4-butanediol (BD) (USDOJ 2003; Vendel 2009). Because these compounds are converted into GHB in the body, they can cause serious side effects.

Patterns of Abuse with CNS Depressants

The American Psychiatric Association (APA) considers dependence on CNS depressants to be a psychiatric disorder. According to its widely used *Diagnostic and Statistical Manual of Mental Disorders,* 4th edition, text revision (DSM-IV-TR) (American Psychiatric Association 2000), a substance dependence disorder can be diagnosed when three of the following criteria are satisfied at any time in a 12-month period:

1. The person needs greatly increased amounts of the substance to achieve the desired effect or experiences a markedly diminished effect with continued use of the substance.
2. Characteristic withdrawal occurs when drug use is stopped, which encourages continued use of the substance to avoid the unpleasant effects.
3. The substance is consumed in larger amounts over a longer period of time than originally intended.
4. The person shows persistent desire or repeated unsuccessful efforts to decrease or control substance use.
5. A great deal of time is spent obtaining and using the substance or recovering from its effects.
6. All daily activities revolve around the substance—important social, occupational, or recreational activities are given up or reduced because of substance use.
7. The person withdraws from family activities and hobbies to use the substance privately or spend more time with substance-using friends.
8. The person continues use of the substance despite recognizing that it causes social, occupational, legal, or medical problems (see "Case in Point: Representative Patrick Kennedy Pleads for Help").

▶Case in Point   Representative Patrick Kennedy Pleads for Help

On May 4, 2006, representative Patrick Kennedy crashed his car into a Capitol barricade late at night. Fortunately, no one was seriously injured, but Kennedy agreed to plead guilty on a charge of driving under the influence of prescription drugs. The congressman has a history of having problems using CNS depressants such as sedative-hypnotics and alcohol. He admits he has difficulty managing his stress levels and sometimes inappropriately uses depressants to cope with the adverse emotions. Because of his experiences with these drugs, Congressman Kennedy has developed an appreciation for the problem of substance dependence in general and prescription abuse in particular. This awareness has motivated Kennedy to work for passage of a congressional bill that would require group health plans to offer benefits for mental health and drug dependence at the same level as for other medical conditions.

Source: Miga, A. "Kennedy Slowly Battles Drug Addiction." *Washington Post.* (2 May 2007). Available at: http://www.washingtonpost.com/wp-dyn/content/article/2007/05/02/AR2007050201758.html. Accessed March 4, 2011.

A review of the previous discussion about the properties of CNS depressants reveals that severe dependence on these drugs can satisfy all these DSM-IV-TR criteria; thus, according to the APA, dependence on CNS depressants is classified as a form of mental illness.

The principal types of people who are most inclined to abuse CNS depressants include the following:

- Those who seek sedative effects to deal with emotional stress, to try to escape from problems they are unable to face. Sometimes, these individuals are able to persuade clinicians to administer depressants for their problems; at other times, they self-medicate with depressants that are obtained illegally.

- Those who seek the excitation that occurs, especially after some tolerance has developed. Instead of depression, they feel exhilaration and euphoria.

- Those who try to counteract the unpleasant effect or withdrawal associated with other drugs of abuse, such as some stimulants, lysergic acid diethylamide (LSD), and other hallucinogens.

- Those who use sedatives in combination with other depressant drugs such as alcohol and heroin. Alcohol plus a sedative gives a faster high but can be dangerous because of the multiple depressant effects and synergistic interaction. Heroin users often resort to barbiturates if their heroin supply is compromised.

As mentioned earlier, depressants are commonly abused in combination with other drugs (*Drug Facts and Comparisons* 2010b). In particular, opioid narcotic users take barbiturates, benzodiazepines, and other depressants to augment the effects of a weak batch of heroin or to counteract a rapidly shrinking supply. Chronic narcotic users also claim that depressants help to offset tolerance to opioids, thereby requiring less narcotic to achieve a satisfactory response by the user. It is not uncommon to see joint dependence on both narcotics and depressants (DEA 2010a, 2010b).

Another common use of depressants is by alcoholics to soften the withdrawal from ethanol or to help create a state of intoxication without the telltale odor of alcohol. Interestingly, similar strategies are also used therapeutically to help detoxify the alcoholic. For example, long-acting barbiturates or benzodiazepines are often used to wean an alcohol-dependent person away from ethanol. Treatment with these depressants helps to reduce the severity of withdrawal symptoms, making it easier and safer for alcoholics to eliminate their drug dependence.

Finally, as already mentioned, CNS depressants are used in conjunction with alcohol to commit sexual assaults. Because these drugs are sedating, remove inhibitions, and can induce a temporary state of amnesia, they are sometimes secretly added to an alcoholic beverage to incapacitate the intended victim of a date rape. Some studies suggest that about 40% of women who are sexually assaulted have alcohol in their blood, 20% have cannabinoids (from marijuana use), 8% have cocaine, 8% have a benzodiazepine, 4% have amphetamines, 4% have GHB, less than 2% have opioid narcotics, and 1% have barbiturates (Elsohly and Salamone 1999).

In general, those who chronically abuse the CNS depressants prefer (1) the short-acting barbiturates, such as pentobarbital and secobarbital; (2) the barbiturate-like depressants, such as glutethimide, methyprylon, and methaqualone; or (3) the faster-acting benzodiazepines, such as diazepam (Valium), alprazolam (Xanax), or lorazepam (Ativan). Dependence on sedative-hypnotic agents can develop insidiously. Often, a long-term patient is treated for persistent insomnia or anxiety with daily exposures to a CNS depressant. When an attempt to withdraw the drug is made, the patient becomes agitated, unable to sleep, and severely anxious; a state of panic may be experienced when deprived of the drug. These signs are frequently mistaken for a resurgence of the medical condition being treated and are not recognized as part of a withdrawal syndrome of the CNS depressant. Consequently, the patient commonly resumes use of the CNS depressant, and the symptoms of withdrawal subside. Such conditions generally lead to a gradual increase in dosage as tolerance to the sedative-hypnotic develops. The patient becomes severely dependent on the depressant, both physically and psychologically, and the drug habit becomes an essential feature in the user's daily routines. Only after severe dependence has developed does the clinician often realize what has taken place. The next stage is the unpleasant task of trying to wean the patient from the drug (**detoxification**) with as little discomfort as possible.

KEY TERMS

detoxification
elimination of a toxic substance, such as a drug, and its effects from the body

Table 6.4 **Lifetime Prevalence of Abuse of CNS Depressants for 12th Graders**

	1992	1995	1998	2001	2004	2007	2009	2010
Any illicit drug	40.7%	48.4%	54.1%	53.9%	51.1%	46.8%	46.7%	48.2%
All depressants (including benzodiazepines)	5.5%	7.4%	8.7%	8.7%	9.9%	9.3%	8.2%	7.5%

Source: Johnston, L. D., P. M. O'Malley, J. G. Bachman, and J. E. Schulenberg. *Monitoring the Future.* "Long-Term Trends in Lifetime Prevalence of Use of Various Drugs in Grade 12 (Table 15)." Ann Arbor, MI: University of Michigan, 2010. Available at: http://www.monitoringthefuture.org/data/ 10data.html#2010data-drugs. Accessed March 4, 2011.

The prevalence of abuse of illicit CNS depressants appeared to peak in the early 1980s for 12th graders. Illegal use of these drugs then decreased dramatically; however, abuse of these drugs has rebounded recently (see **Table 6.4**).

■ Treatment for Withdrawal

All sedative-hypnotics, including alcohol and benzodiazepines, can produce physical dependence and a barbiturate-like withdrawal syndrome if taken in sufficient dosage over a long period. Withdrawal symptoms include anxiety, tremors, nightmares, insomnia, anorexia, nausea, vomiting, seizures, delirium, and maniacal activity.

The duration and severity of withdrawal depend on the particular drug taken. With short-acting depressants, such as pentobarbital, secobarbital, and methaqualone, withdrawal symptoms tend to have a faster onset of action and be more severe. They begin 12 to 24 hours after the last dose and peak in intensity between 24 and 72 hours later. Withdrawal from longer-acting depressants, such as phenobarbital and diazepam, develops more slowly and is less intense; symptoms peak on the fifth to eighth day (Trevor and Lay 1998). Not surprisingly, the approach to detoxifying a person who is dependent on a sedative-hypnotic depends on the nature of the drug itself (that is, to which category of depressants it belongs), the severity of the dependence, and the duration of action of the drug. The general objectives of detoxification are to eliminate drug dependence (both physical and psychological) in a safe manner while minimizing discomfort. Having achieved these objectives, it is hoped that the patient will be able to remain free of dependence on all CNS depressants. However, in reality detoxification is rarely sufficient by itself to assure long-term abstinence from the drug.

Often, the basic approach for treating severe dependence on sedative-hypnotics is substitution with either pentobarbital or the longer-acting phenobarbital for the offending, usually shorter-acting, CNS depressant. Once substitution has occurred, the long-acting barbiturate dose is gradually reduced. Using a substitute is necessary because abrupt withdrawal for a person who is physically dependent can be dangerous, causing life-threatening seizures. This substitution treatment uses the same rationale as the treatment of heroin withdrawal by methadone replacement. Detoxification also includes supportive measures such as vitamins, restoration of electrolyte balance, and prevention of dehydration. The patient must be watched closely during this time because he or she will be apprehensive, confused, and unable to make logical decisions (O'Brien 2006).

If the person is addicted to both alcohol and barbiturates, the phenobarbital dosage must be increased to compensate for the double withdrawal. Many barbiturate addicts who enter a hospital to be treated for withdrawal are also dependent on heroin. In such cases, the barbiturate dependence

Detoxification of patients often is done in groups to provide support during this difficult time.

should be addressed first because the associated withdrawal can be life-threatening. Detoxification from any sedative-hypnotic should take place under close medical supervision, typically in a hospital (O'Brien 2006).

It is important to remember that elimination of physical dependence is not a cure. The problem of psychological dependence can be much more difficult to handle. If an individual is abusing a CNS depressant because of emotional instability, personal problems, or a very stressful environment, eliminating physical dependence alone will not solve the problem and drug dependence is likely to recur. These types of patients require intense psychological counseling and must be trained to deal with their difficulties in a more constructive and positive fashion. Without such psychological support, benefits from detoxification will only be temporary, and therapy will ultimately fail.

Natural Depressants

Some plants that contain naturally occurring CNS depressants are included in herbal products or made into herbal teas for relaxation or as treatment for sleep problems (McQueen and Hume 2006). Probably the best known of this group is the kava kava plant (*Piper methysticum*). This plant belongs to the pepper family and grows on South Pacific islands (Wong 2010). Drinks and bars containing extracts from kava kava root are legally available in many health food stores, are especially popular in Polynesian populations, and are sometimes used in religious ceremonies. The extract is prepared from the part of the kava kava plant beneath the surface of the ground. Small amounts of kava kava can produce euphoria and increased sociability, whereas larger doses cause substantial relaxation, lethargy, relaxed lower limbs, and eventually sleep (Boerner et al. 2003). Some users may experience visual and auditory hallucinations that can last 1 to 2 hours. Some users report that kava kava drinks can make the mouth numb much like topical local anesthetics used by dentists. There have also been rare case reports of liver damage in frequent users (Wong 2010).

A second type of common herb that contains CNS depressants is the *Datura* family of plants. Although these botanicals are typically associated with hallucinogenic effects, in smaller amounts they sometimes can cause sedation and even induce sleep. Examples of these plants include *Datura inoxia* (devil's trumpet) and *Datura stramonium* (jimson

weed or thornapple). The active ingredients in these plants are typically anticholinergic drugs such as atropine or scopolamine. In lower doses, these herbs, especially if they contain scopolamine, have been used to encourage sleep. In fact, the actions of the herbs are somewhat similar to the OTC antihistamine-containing sleep aids, which also work due to their anticholinergic actions. In higher doses, both atropine and scopolamine can cause hallucinogenic effects. The anticholinergic actions of these herbs can be quite annoying and include constipation, dry mouth, and blurred vision, just to mention a few (Mishra 2010).

Discussion Questions

1. Why did benzodiazepine drugs replace barbiturates as the sedative-hypnotic drugs most prescribed by physicians?

2. Which features of CNS depressants give them abuse potential?

3. Why is long-term use of the benzodiazepines more likely than short-term use to cause dependence?

4. Why are some physicians careless when prescribing benzodiazepines for patients suffering from severe anxiety?

5. Currently, sleep aid products are available OTC. Should the FDA also allow sedatives to be sold without a prescription? Support your answer.

6. Are there any real advantages to using barbiturates as sedatives or hypnotics? Should the FDA remove them from the market?

7. What types of people are most likely to abuse CNS depressants? Suggest ways to help these people avoid abusing these drugs.

8. Should propofol be scheduled, and if so, as what category?

9. What is the appeal of using GHB? Why is it used to commit sexual assaults?

10. What dangers are associated with treating individuals who are severely dependent on CNS depressants?

11. Why are CNS depressants often combined with alcohol, and what is the consequence?

12. Why is detoxification by itself usually insufficient to achieve long-term therapeutic success when dealing with severe CNS depressant dependence?

Summary

1 Several unrelated drug groups cause CNS depression, but only a few are actually used clinically for their depressant properties. The most frequently prescribed CNS depressants are benzodiazepines, which include drugs such as Valium, Ambien, and Xanax. Barbiturates once were popular, but, because of their severe side effects, they are no longer prescribed by most clinicians. Much like barbiturates, drugs such as chloral hydrate, glutethimide, and methaqualone are little used today. Finally, some OTC and prescription antihistamines, such as diphenhydramine, hydroxyzine, and promethazine, are used for their CNS depressant effects.

2 The clinical value of CNS depressants is dose dependent. When used at low doses, these drugs relieve anxiety and promote relaxation (sedatives). When prescribed at higher doses, they can cause drowsiness and promote sleep (hypnotics). When administered at even higher doses, some of the depressants cause anesthesia and are used for patient management during surgery.

3 The rapidly acting general anesthetic propofol has become well known because of its role in the accidental death of pop singer Michael Jackson. Although not currently scheduled, its abuse is becoming a problem with physicians and nurses who have access to it at work. Sometimes propofol is also used to relieve pain or help someone sleep.

4 Because CNS depressants can relieve anxiety and reduce stress, they are viewed as desirable by many people. If used frequently over long periods, however, they can cause tolerance that leads to dependence.

5 The principal reason that benzodiazepines have replaced barbiturates in the treatment of stress and insomnia is that benzodiazepines have a greater margin of safety and are less likely to alter sleep patterns. Benzodiazepines enhance the GABA transmitter system in the brain through a specific receptor, whereas the effects of barbiturates are less selective. Even though benzodiazepines are safer than barbiturates, dependence and significant withdrawal problems can result if the former drugs are used indiscriminately.

6 Often, benzodiazepine dependence occurs in patients who suffer stress or anxiety disorders and are under a physician's care. If the physician is not careful and the cause of the stress is not resolved, drug treatment can drag on for weeks or months. After prolonged benzodiazepine therapy, tolerance to the drug develops; when benzodiazepine use is stopped, withdrawal occurs, which itself causes agitation. A rebound response to the drug might resemble the effects of emotional stress (agitation), so use of benzodiazepine is continued. In this way, the patient becomes severely dependent.

7 The short-acting CNS depressants are preferred for treatment of insomnia. These drugs help the patient get to sleep and then are inactivated by the body; when the user awakens the next day, he or she is less likely to experience residual effects than with long-acting drugs. The short-acting depressants are also more likely to be abused because of their relatively rapid onset and intense effects. In contrast, the long-acting depressants are better suited to treating persistent problems such as anxiety and stress. The long-acting depressants are also used to help wean dependent people from their use of short-acting compounds such as alcohol.

8 Many antihistamines cause sedation and drowsiness due to their anticholinergic effects. Several of these agents are useful for short-term relief of anxiety and are available in OTC sleep aids. The effectiveness of these CNS depressants is usually less than that of benzodiazepines. Because of their anticholinergic actions, antihistamines can cause some annoying side effects. These agents are not likely to be used for long periods; thus, dependence or serious abuse usually does not develop.

9 The people most likely to abuse CNS depressants include individuals who (a) use drugs to relieve continual stress; (b) paradoxically feel euphoria and stimulation from depressants; (c) use depressants to counteract the unpleasant effects of other drugs of abuse, such as stimulants; and (d) combine depressants with alcohol and heroin to potentiate the effects.

10 The basic approach for treating dependence on CNS depressants is to detoxify the individual in a safe manner while minimizing his or her discomfort. This state is achieved by substituting a long-acting barbiturate or benzodiazepine, such as phenobarbital or Valium, for the offending CNS depressant. The long-acting drug causes less severe withdrawal symptoms over a longer period of time. The dependent person is gradually weaned from the substitute drug until he or she is depressant-free.

11 GHB is a naturally occurring substance related to the neurotransmitter GABA that has been used for its sedating, euphorigenic, and muscle-building properties. It also has been used to debilitate victims of date rape during sexual assaults. Because of concerns that this substance is frequently abused, GHB was classified as a Schedule I drug in 2000.

12 Some plants such as kava kava that contain naturally occurring CNS depressants are included in herbal teas for relaxation or treatment of insomnia.

References

AddictionSearch. "GHB Addiction, Abuse, Detox and Treatment." 27 May 2010. Available http://www.addiction search.com/treatment_articles/article/ghb-addiction-abuse-detox-and-treatment_27.html

American Psychiatric Association. "Substance Related Disorders." In *Diagnostic and Statistical Manual of Mental Disorders,* 4th ed., text revision, 191–295. Washington, DC: APA, 2000.

Associated Press. "Woman Who Used Halcion Defense Hangs Self." *Salt Lake Tribune* 248 (July 27, 1994): D-3.

Backmund, M., K. Meyer, C. Henkel, M. Soyka, J. Reimer, and C. Schutz. "Co-consumption of Benzodiazepines in Heroin Users, Methadone-Substituted and Codeine-Substituted Patients." *Journal of Addiction Disorder* 24 (2005): 17–29.

Balestra, K. "Anti-Anxiety Drugs Raise New Fears." *Washington Post.* 30 June 2009. Available http://www.socialanxiety help.com/article.anti.anxiety.drugs.raise.new.fears.htm

Boerner, R., H. Sommer, W. Berger, U. Kuhn, U. Schmidt, and M. Manner. "Kava Kava Extract LI 150 Is as Effective as Opipramol and Buspirone in Generalized Anxiety Disorder." *Phytomedicine* 10 Supplement 4 (2003): 38–49.

Carter, L., L. Flores, H. Wu, C. Weibin, A. Unzeitig, A. Coop, and C. France. "The Role of GABA-B Receptors in the Discriminative Stimulus Effects of GHB in Rats: Time Course and Antagonism Studies." *Journal of Pharmacology and Experimental Therapeutics* 305 (2003): 668–674.

Charney, D., S. Mihic, and R. Harris. "Hypnotics and Sedatives." In *The Pharmacological Basis of Therapeutics,* 11th ed., edited by L. Brunton, J. Lazo, and K. Parker, 401–427. New York: McGraw-Hill, 2006.

Craig, K., H. Gomez, J. McMannus, and T. Bania. "Severe Gamma-Hydroxybutyrate Withdrawal: A Case Report and Literature Review." *Journal of Emergency Medicine* 18 (2000): 65–70.

Dean, W., J. Morgenthaler, and S. Fowkes. *GHB: The Natural Mood Enhancer: The Authoritative Guide to Its Responsible Use.* Petaluma, CA: Smart Publications, 1997.

DeMaria, P., R. Sterling, and S. Weinstein. "The Effect of Stimulant and Sedative Use on Treatment Outcome of Patients Admitted to Methadone Maintenance Treatment." *American Journal of Addiction* 9 (2000): 145–153.

Drasbek, K., J. Christenen, and K. Jensen. "Gamma-Hydroxybutyrate—A Drug of Abuse." *Acta Neurologica Scandinavia* 115 (2006): 368.

Drug Facts and Comparisons. "Antihistamines." 2010 Pocket Version, 14th ed., 480–493. St. Louis, MO: Wolters Kluwar Health, 2010a.

Drug Facts and Comparisons. "Sedatives/Hypnotics/Non-barbiturate." 2010 Pocket Version, 14th ed., 732–748. St. Louis, MO: Wolters Kluwar Health, 2010b.

Drugs.com. "Top 200 Drugs for 2009." 2010. Available http://www.drugs.com/top200.html

Elsohly, M., and S. Salamone. "Prevalence of Drugs Used in Cases of Alleged Sexual Assault." *Journal of Analytical Toxicology* 23 (1999): 141–146.

Galloway, G., S. Frederick, F. Staggers, M. Gonzales, S. Stalcup, and D. Smith. "Gamma-Hydroxybutyrate: An Emerging Drug of Abuse That Causes Physical Dependence." *Addiction* 92 (1997): 89–96.

Gorman, J. "Treating Generalized Anxiety Disorder." *Journal of Clinical Psychiatry* 64 (2003): 24–29.

Hobbs, W., T. Rall, and T. Verdoorn. "Hypnotics and Sedatives." In *The Pharmacological Basis of Therapeutics,* 9th ed., edited by J. Hardman and L. Limbird, 361–396. New York: McGraw-Hill, 1995.

Hughes, G., J. McElnay, C. Hughes, and P. McKenna. "Abuse/Misuse of Non-prescription Drugs." *Pharmacy World Science* 21 (1999): 251–255.

Johansson, B., M. Berglund, M. Hanson, C. Pohlen, and I. Persson. "Dependence on Legal Psychotropic Drugs Among Alcoholics." *Alcohol, Alcoholism* 38 (2003): 613–618.

Johnston, L. D., P. M. O'Malley, J. G. Bachman, and J. E. Schulenberg. Monitoring the Future. "Long-Term Trends in Lifetime Prevalence of Use of Various Drugs in Grade 12 (Table 15)." Lansing, MI: University of Michigan, 2010. Available http://www.monitoringthefuture.org/data/10data.html#2010data-drugs

Kaufman, G. "What Is Propofol and Why Was Michael Jackson Allegedly Using It?" TV News Top Stories. 1 July 2009. Available www.mtv.com/news/articles/1615103/20090701/jackson_michael.jhtml

Kirby, R., J. Colaw, and M. Douglas. "Death from Propofol: Accident, Suicide, or Murder." *Anesthesia and Analgesia* 108 (2010): 1182–1184.

Kosten, T., and L. Hollister. "Drugs of Abuse." In *Basic and Clinical Pharmacology,* 7th ed., edited by B. Katzung, 516–531. Stamford, CT: Appleton & Lange, 1998.

Latner, A. "The Top 200 Drugs of 1999." *Pharmacy Times* 66 (2000): 16–32.

Leshner, A. E. "Club Drug Alert." *NIDA Notes* 14 (2000): 3. Available http://archives.drugabuse.gov/NIDA_Notes/NNVol14N6/DirRepVol14N6.html

Lingenhoehl, K., R. Brom, J. Heid, P. Beck, W. Froestl, K. Kaupman, et al. "Gamma-Hydroxybutyrate Is a Weak Agonist Against Recombinant GABA (B) Receptors." *Neuropharmacology* 38 (1999): 1667–1673.

Longo, L., and B. Johnson. "Addiction: Part I. Benzodiazepines, Side Effects, Abuse Risks and Alternatives." *American Family Physician* 61 (2000): 2121–2128.

McEvoy, G., ed. *American Hospital Formulary Service Drug Information.* Bethesda, MD: American Society of Hospital Pharmacists, 2003.

McKenzie, J. "More Medical Professionals Abuse Propofol." ABC News. 21 August 2009. Available http://abcnews.go.com/Health/drug-propofol-abused-medical-professionals/story?id=8375255

McQueen, C., and A. Hume. "Introduction to Botanical and Nonbotanical Natural Medicines." In *Handbook of Nonprescription Drugs,* 15th ed., edited by R. Berardi, 1095–1136. Washington, DC: American Pharmacists Association, 2006.

MedicineNet.com. "Zolpidem, Ambien, Ambien CR, Zolpimist, Edluar, Tovalt ODT (discontinued)." 2007. Available http://www.medicinenet.com/zolpidem/article.htm

Miga, A. "Kennedy Slowly Battles Drug Addiction." *Washington Post.* 2 May 2007. Available http://www.washingtonpost.com/wp-dyn/content/article/2007/05/02/AR2007050201758.html

Mioto, K., and B. Roth. *GHB Withdrawal.* Austin, TX: Texas Commission on Alcohol and Drug Abuse, March 2001.

Mishra, M. P. "Ranchers, Conservation Groups Split on Grazing Ruling Impact—Center for Biological Diversity." Ecosensorium.org. 2010. Available http://www.ecosensorium.org

Mondanaro, J. *Chemically Dependent Women.* Lexington, MA: Lexington Books/D.C. Heath, 1988.

Morgenthaler, J., and D. Joy. *Special Report on GHB.* Petaluma, CA: Smart Publication, 1994.

National Institute on Drug Abuse. "What Are Club Drugs?" *NIDA Notes* 14 (22 May 2000). Available http://www.drugabuse.gov/NIDA_Notes/NNVol14N6/WhatAre.html

Nava, F., S. Premi, E. Manzato, W. Campagnola, W. Luccini, and L. Gessa. "Gamma-Hydroxybutyrate Reduces Both Withdrawal Symptoms and Hypercortisolism in Severe Abstinent Alcoholics: An Open Study vs. Diazepam." *American Journal of Drug and Alcohol Abuse* 33 (2007): 379–392.

O'Brien, C. "Drug Addiction and Drug Abuse." In *The Pharmacological Basis of Therapeutics,* 11th ed., edited by L. Brunton, J. Lazo, and K. Parker, 607–627. New York: McGraw-Hill, 2006.

Office of National Drug Control Policy. "Prescription Drugs." 2010. Available http://www.whitehousedrugpolicy.gov/drugfact/prescrptn_drgs/index.html

Payne, J. "Report: Go Easy on Sleeping Pills." *Washington Post.* 15 August 2006. Available http://www.washingtonpost.com/wp-dyn/content/article/2006/08/14/AR2006081400875.html

Poldrugo, F., and G. Addolorato. "The Role of Gamma-Hydroxybutyrate Acid in the Treatment of Alcoholism: From Animal to Clinical Studies." *Alcohol, Alcoholism* 34 (1999): 15–34.

Publishers Group. "Street Drugs." 2002. Available http://www.Streetdrugs.org

Scharman, E., A. Erdman, P. Wax, P. Chyka, E. Caravati, et al. "Diphenhydramine and Dimenhydrinate Poisoning: An Evidence-Based Consensus Guideline for Out-of-Hospital Management." *Clinical Toxicology* (Philadelphia) 44 (2006): 205–233.

Substance Abuse and Mental Health Services Administration (SAMHSA). "2006 National Survey on Drug Use and Health." Office of Applied Studies. 2007. Available http://www.oas.samhsa.gov/nsduhlatest.htm

Sumnall, H., K. Woolfall, S. Edwards, J. Cole, and C. Beynon. "Use, Function, and Subjective Experiences of Gamma-Hydroxybutyrate (GHB)." *Drugs and Alcohol Dependency* 92 (2008): 286–290.

Teter, C., and S. Guthrie. "A Comprehensive Review of MDMA and GHB: Two Common Club Drugs." *Pharmacotherapy* 21 (2001): 1486–1513.

Trevor, A., and W. Lay. "Sedative-Hypnotic Drugs." In *Basic and Clinical Pharmacology,* 7th ed., edited by B. Katzung, 354–371. Stamford, CT: Appleton & Lange, 1998.

Tyler, J. "Heath Ledger's Cause of Death Made Official." Celebrity Blend. 6 February 2008. Available http://www.cinemablend.com/celebrity/Heath-Ledger-s-Cause-Of-Death-Made-Official-8740.html

U.S. Department of Justice (USDOJ). "Information Bulletin. GHB Analogs." Product No. 2002-L0424-0034, 2002.

U.S. Department of Justice (USDOJ). "National Drug Threat Assessment 2003." National Drug Intelligence Center, Product No. 2003-Q0317-001 (January 2003).

U.S. Drug Enforcement Administration. "Gamma Hydroxybutyric Acid (GHB, Liquid X, Goop, Georgia Home Boy)." DEA Bulletin DEA/ODE #000612 (12 June 2000).

U.S. Drug Enforcement Administration. "Benzodiazepines." DEA Briefs and Background, Drugs and Drug Abuse. 2010a. Available http://www.justice.gov/dea/concern/benzodiazepines.html

U.S. Drug Enforcement Administration. "Drug Information: B." 2010b. Available http://www.justice.gov/dea/concern/b.html

Vendel, C. "The Drug GHB Is Deceptive, Deadly and Often Overlooked." Prospectus News. 2 September 2009. Available http://media.www.prospectusnews.com/media/storage/paper1305/news/2009/09/02/News/Ghb-Deceptive.Deadly.And.Often.Overlooked-3762901.shtml#5

VZ-Life. "GHB: Signs and Symptoms of Use." VZ-Life, Life Initiatives for Employees. 29 March 2010. Available https://www.achievesolutions.net/achievesolutions/en/Content.do?contentId=4107

Wong, C. "Kava—What Is Kava?" About.com: Alternative Medicine. 2010. Available http://altmedicine.about.com/od/kava/p/kava.htm

CHAPTER 7

Alcohol: Pharmacological Effects

Did You Know?

- Alcohol is the most consumed drug in the world.
- Ethanol leads all other substances of abuse in treatment admissions.
- Ethanol is the only alcohol used for human consumption; most of the other common alcohols are poisonous.
- Some wild animals and insects become drunk after seeking out and consuming alcohol-containing fermented fruit.
- Alcohol-related deaths outnumber deaths related to other drugs of abuse (except tobacco) by a four to one margin.
- Women who abuse alcohol are more likely to suffer depression than male abusers.
- The lethal level of alcohol is between 0.4% and 0.6% by volume in the blood.
- Consumption of alcohol by adolescents can cause persistent damage to their brain development.
- Among alcoholics, liver disorders account for approximately 10–15% of deaths.
- There are medications approved by the FDA for the treatment of alcohol dependence, although they are not universally effective.
- Fetal alcohol syndrome (FAS) is characterized by facial deformities, growth deficiencies, and mental retardation.
- Addictions such as alcoholism are among the most inherited of the mental illnesses.

Learning Objectives

On completing this chapter you will be able to:

- Explain how common alcohol (ethanol) is a drug.
- Explain the pharmacokinetic properties of alcohol and describe how they influence the effects of the drug.
- Explain the role of alcohol in "polydrug" abuse.
- Identify the possible physical effects of prolonged heavy ethanol consumption.
- Explain what alcohol dependence is and how it is treated.
- Explain the potential cardiovascular benefits and problems of moderate alcohol use and the dose-dependent nature of these effects.
- Describe fetal alcohol syndrome (FAS) and its effects.
- Explain how prolonged consumption of alcohol affects the brain and nervous system, liver, digestive system, blood, cardiovascular system, sexual organs, endocrine systems, and kidneys, and how it leads to mental disorders and damage to fetuses.
- Describe why use of alcohol by adolescents is particularly problematic and why this should influence the discussion about underage drinking.
- Explain why there is concern about how college students use alcohol.
- Explain why malnutrition is so common among alcoholics.

Drugs and Society Online is a great source for additional drugs and society information for both students and instructors. Visit **go.jblearning.com/hanson11** to find a variety of useful tools for learning, thinking, and teaching.

Introduction

In Chapters 7 and 8, we examine several aspects of alcohol use. This chapter focuses on how alcohol affects the body from a pharmacological perspective. Chapter 8 discusses the social aspects of this drug—mainly the effects and consequences of alcohol on an individual's personal and social life.

Alcohol is the most widely consumed drug in the world, and for many it is as much a part of daily life as eating. Even so, most of those who use it don't understand how it works or why it can change their personalities and behavior in bizarre and unpredictable ways, causing respectable and dependable people to engage in foolish and even dangerous behaviors (Gowin 2010). As a licit drug, alcohol is extensively promoted socially through advertising. Alcoholic beverage companies spent almost $5 billion on television advertising of their products from 2001 to 2005 (Center on Alcohol Marketing and Youth 2007; see "Here and Now: Alcohol Ads Affect Kids"). But more important, drinking is perceived as acceptable. The popularity of this drug is clear; in 2009, 56.5% of high school seniors said they had been drunk sometime during their life (Johnston 2009). Binge drinking among teens is thought to be at epidemic levels with about 25% of the teenagers in this country participating in episodes of very heavy alcohol use (CBS News 2007). College youth also consume large quantities of alcohol, and many authorities believe alcohol is the leading drug problem among this population (Califano 2010).

This chapter focuses on the many adverse effects of alcohol on the human body. Overall, it provides

Because of frequent advertising, use of alcohol is perceived as normal and acceptable.

you with a foundation to understand the pharmacological nature of alcohol. We hope that such an understanding of how this drug affects the various organ systems of the body will lead to more responsible use and less abuse of alcohol. Because of its widespread consumption, alcohol leads all other addicting substances as a reason for treatment admissions. In 2008, of the approximately 2 million people admitted for treatment of substance dependence, 64% received treatment for alcoholism (Substance Abuse and Mental Health Services Administration [SAMSHA] 2009).

Here and Now

Alcohol Ads Affect Kids

Alcohol advertisers spend about $2 billion per year on promoting their products to consumers in the United States. A report from the Center on Alcohol Marketing and Youth at Georgetown University revealed that underage youth were more likely to hear radio ads promoting beer and other alcoholic beverages than were people of legal drinking age. This is partially due to the fact that the alcohol radio advertising most often was placed on radio stations with "youth" music formats that routinely have a disproportionately large listening audience of 12- to 20-year-olds. These data suggest that the alcohol industry targets the underage population for its alcoholic products. In addition, recent studies have observed that advertising substantially impacts the decision of youth to drink as well as what and how they will drink. These findings suggest that one effective approach for discouraging underage drinking is to restrict advertising of alcoholic products.

Sources: Center on Alcohol Marketing and Youth. "Radio Daze: Alcohol Ads Tune in Underage Youth." Georgetown University (2 April 2003): 1, 2; and The Center on Alcohol Marketing and Youth. "Alcohol Advertising and Youth." 2010. Available at: http://www.camy.org/factsheets/sheets/Alcohol_Advertising_and_Youth.html. Accessed March 4, 2011.

The Nature and History of Alcohol

Alcohol has been part of human culture since the beginning of recorded history. The technology for alcohol production is ancient. Several basic ingredients and conditions are needed to produce this substance: sugar, water, yeast, and warm temperatures.

The process of making alcohol, called **fermentation**, is a natural one. It occurs in ripe fruit and berries and even in honey that bees leave in trees. These substances contain sugar and water and are found in warm climates, where yeast spores are transported through the air. Animals such as elephants, baboons, birds, wild pigs, and bees will seek out and eat fermented fruit. Elephants under the influence of alcohol have been observed bumping into one another and stumbling around. Intoxicated bees fly an unsteady beeline toward their hives. Birds eating fermented fruit become so uncoordinated that they cannot fly or, if they do, crash into windows or branches. In fact, fermented honey, called **mead**, may have been the first alcoholic beverage.

The Egyptians had breweries 6000 years ago; they credited the god Osiris with introducing wine to humans. The ancient Greeks used large quantities of wine and credited a god, Bacchus (Dionysus), with introducing the drink. Today, we use the words *bacchanalia* and *dionysian* to refer to revelry and drunken events. The Hebrews were also heavy users of wine. The Bible mentions that Noah, just nine generations removed from Adam, made wine and became drunk.

Alcohol is produced by a single-celled microscopic organism, one of the yeasts, that breaks down sugar by a metabolic form of combustion, thereby releasing carbon dioxide and forming water and ethyl alcohol as waste products. Carbon dioxide creates the foam on a glass of beer and the fizz in champagne. Fermentation continues until the sugar supply is exhausted or the concentration of alcohol reaches the point at which it kills the yeast (12–14%). Thus, 12–14% is the natural limit of alcohol found in fermented wines or beers.

The **distillation** device, or still, was developed by the Arabs around 800 AD and was introduced into medieval Europe around 1250 AD. By boiling the fermented drink and gathering the condensed vapor in a pipe, a still increases the concentration of alcohol, potentially to 50% or higher. Because distillation made it easier for people to get drunk, it greatly intensified the problem of alcohol abuse. However, even before the invention of the still, alcoholic beverages had been known to cause problems in heavy users that resulted in severe physical and psychological dependence. But not until the past century did the concept of alcoholism as a disease develop (Mann, Herman, and Hienz 2000) (see "Here and Now: A Century of Alcohol").

Alcohol as a Drug

Alcohol (more precisely designated as ethanol) is a natural product of fermentation and considered by many as the number one abused drug (Alcoholism and Drug Addiction Help 2010). Its impact on college students has been particularly disturbing, with reports stating that binge drinking among such individuals is commonplace (Mullins 2009). This psychoactive substance depresses the central nervous system (CNS) while influencing almost all major organ systems of the body (Gowin 2010). Alcohol is also an addictive drug in that it may produce a physical and behavioral dependence (National Institute on Alcohol Abuse and Alcoholism 2007). Although tradition and attitude are important factors in determining the use patterns of this substance, the typical consumer rarely appreciates the diversity of pharmacological effects caused by alcohol, the drug. The pharmacological action of alcohol accounts for both its pleasurable and CNS effects as well as its hazards to health and public safety.

Alcohol as a Social Drug

Why is alcohol often perceived as an acceptable adjunct to such celebrations as parties, birthdays, weddings, and anniversaries, and as a way of relieving stress and anxiety? Social psychologists refer to the perception of alcohol as a **social lubricant**. This term implies that drinking is misconceived as safely promoting conviviality and social interaction, and

KEY TERMS

fermentation
biochemical process through which yeast converts sugar to alcohol

mead
fermented honey often made into an alcoholic beverage

distillation
heating fermented mixtures of cereal grains or fruits in a still to evaporate and be trapped as purified alcohol

social lubricant
belief that drinking (misconceived as safe) represses inhibitions, strengthens extroversion, and leads to increased sociability

Here and Now

A Century of Alcohol

An overwhelming need to consume alcohol (known today as alcoholism) was first described in the literature by Benjamin Rush in 1784, but the concept that excessive use of alcohol is a disease didn't really evolve until the past 100 or so years. This perspective was encouraged by the "temperance movement" of the late 19th century. Because of the ill effects of alcohol, temperance legally became "Prohibition" in 1919. Prohibition (which made alcohol illegal) was initially successful in reducing consumption, but consumption began to rebound in the late 1920s. However, it has been suggested that Prohibition was repealed in 1933 not because it failed to reduce alcohol use but because of shifting policy during the Great Depression that argued liquor manufacturing would create jobs and provide taxes on alcoholic beverages that could fund government programs.

The second half of the 20th century saw the emergence of the belief that genetics plays a major role in alcoholism. This concept suggests that because of inherited traits, some families and individuals are more vulnerable to alcohol addiction than others. Researchers today are energetically moving forward to identify which genes might contribute to the development and expression of the addiction in an effort to improve prevention and treatment for alcoholism.

Source: Quindien, A. "America's Most Pervasive Drug Problem Is the Drug That Pretends It Isn't." *Salt Lake Tribune* (20 April 2000): A-11.

---

as an activity that bolsters confidence by repressing inhibitions and strengthening extroversion. Why do many people have to be reminded that alcohol is a drug like marijuana or cocaine and may have serious consequences for some people? Four reasons explain this misconception:

1. The use of alcohol is legal.
2. Through widespread advertising, the media promote the notion that alcohol consumption is as normal and safe as drinking fruit juices and soft drinks.
3. The distribution, advertisement, and sale of alcoholic beverages are widely practiced.
4. Alcohol use has a long tradition, dating back to 4000 BC (Bachelor 2010).

■ Impact of Alcohol

Although many consider the effects of alcohol enjoyable and reassuring, the adverse pharmacological impacts of this drug are extensive. Its use causes approximately 14 million cases of alcoholism (severe alcohol dependence), and its effects are associated with more than 100,000 deaths each year in the United States (Fleming, Mihic, and Harris 2006). It is estimated that at some time during their lives, almost 50% of all Americans will be involved in an alcohol-related traffic accident and over 2% of night-time drivers have a blood-alcohol content that exceeds legal amounts (0.08%) (Kerlikowske 2010).

The pharmacological effects of alcohol abuse cause severe dependence, which is classified as a psychiatric disorder according to the *Diagnostic and Statistical Manual of Mental Disorders,* 4th edition, text revision (DSM-IV-TR) (National Institutes of Health 2010) criteria. These effects also disrupt personal, family, social, and professional functioning and frequently result in multiple illnesses and accidents, violence, and crime (Hanson and Li 2003). Alcohol consumed during pregnancy can lead to devastating damage to offspring and is a principal cause of mental retardation in newborns (Hanson and Li 2003). After tobacco, alcohol is the leading cause of premature death in America. In the United States, approximately $176 billion is spent annually dealing with the social and health problems resulting from the pharmacological effects of alcohol (Marin Institute 2007). Of course, such estimates fall short in assessing the emotional upheaval and human suffering caused by this drug.

Despite all of the problems that alcohol causes, our free society has demanded access to this drug. At the same time, it is unthinkable to ignore the tremendous negative social impact of this drug. There are no simple answers to this dichotomy, yet clearly governmental and educational institutions could do more to protect members of society from the dangers associated with alcohol. The best weapons we have against the problems caused by alcohol are education, prevention, and treatment (see Chapter 17).

Drinking and College Students

Alcohol consumption by college students and its negative consequences are arguably on the rise, leading to almost 2000 drinking-related deaths per year. About 45% of students have binged on alcohol in the previous month, and about 29% of students have ever driven under the influence of alcohol. Each year about 100,000 sexual assaults are linked to college student drinking, and about 700,000 assaults in total are committed by drinking students (Mozes 2010; Reinberg 2009a). These findings suggest the college student population is vulnerable to alcohol-related problems. These types of troubling statistics have been interpreted by some observers to be evidence that attempts by college presidents and chancellors to lower the minimum legal drinking age from 21 to 18 should not be encouraged. However, there is a confusing observation that the higher legal age of 21 years reduced binge drinking in noncollege 18- to 20-year-olds, but had little effect on college students of the same age. One possible explanation is that most of the noncollege participants in the study were still living at home and somewhat under parental supervision, whereas most of the college students lived away from home, on their own, and often had older friends who could legally buy alcoholic products for the under-age students (*New York Times* 2009). Although there is some controversy as to the severity of college drinking, everyone agrees that greater efforts should be made by colleges, government, and businesses to prevent alcohol-related deaths, injuries, and crimes (Epstein 2010).

Under-Age Drinking

Youth who start drinking alcohol at an early age have a much greater likelihood of developing alcohol dependence when they become adults. Possible explanations for this effect include: (1) an altered expression of genes, which affects vulnerability to alcoholism (Agrawal 2009) and (2) interference with normal development of critical brain systems important for learning, memory, attention, information processing, and proper decision making (Reinberg 2009b; Trudeau 2010). In addition, early drinkers are at increased vulnerability to the effects of other drugs as an adult, such as nicotine in tobacco (American Public University 2010). Findings such as these are especially disturbing in light of the facts that nearly 75% of students consume alcohol and 50% of them have been drunk before

they graduate from high school (Moyer 2010). It is becoming apparent that heavy exposure to the toxic effects of alcohol during adolescence may have long-lasting and profound effects on young people, leading to mental health problems throughout their lives (Moyer 2010). For this reason, the American Academy of Pediatrics recommends that physicians discourage underage drinking by: (1) screening their adolescent patients for alcohol use; (2) discussing the hazards of alcohol use with their teenage patients; (3) encouraging parents to be good role models for their children; and (4) supporting the continuation of 21 as the minimum legal drinking age (American Academy of Pediatrics 2010). Many experts believe that parents are key to preventing alcohol use by their children. They suggest that parents who send ambiguous messages to their kids about drinking or through their words and actions encourage teen alcohol consumption are enabling this toxic behavior (Califano 2010) (see "Case in Point: Parents Must Say No").

The Properties of Alcohol

Technically, alcohol is a chemical structure that has a hydroxyl group (OH, for one oxygen and one hydrogen atom) attached to a carbon atom. Of the many types of alcohol, several are important for the purposes of this book. The first is **methyl alcohol** (*methanol* or *wood alcohol*), which is made from wood products. Its metabolites are poisonous. Small amounts (4 mL) cause blindness by affecting the retina, and larger amounts (80–150 mL) are usually fatal. Methyl alcohol is added to ethyl alcohol (*ethanol* or *grain alcohol*, the drinking type) that is intended for industrial use so people will not drink it. A similar mixture also is sometimes added to illegally manufactured ("bootleg") liquor.

Another type of poisonous alcohol, **ethylene glycol**, is used in antifreeze. A third type, **isopropyl alcohol**, is commonly used as rubbing alcohol and as an antiseptic (a solution for preventing the growth of microorganisms). These two types of alcohol are also poisonous if consumed.

KEY TERMS

methyl alcohol
wood alcohol

ethylene glycol
alcohol used as antifreeze

isopropyl alcohol
rubbing alcohol, sometimes used as an antiseptic

►Case in Point   Parents Must Say No

Mike and Molly threw a graduation summer beer bash for their 18-year-old son and invited other varsity football players. Although all the young men were expected to check their car keys at the door, the beer flowed freely as the teens socialized, shouted over the loud music, and gave hugs and high-fives to the "cool parents." If you were to ask the young party participants, they likely would have nominated Mike and Molly for the "Parents of the Year Award." The parents were eager to be part of their son's life and wanted to be viewed as young-at-heart and progressive. In fact, they likely would have argued that they were wiser and better parents than those who prohibited alcohol use by their children because they "related to their son and his friends." Mike and Molly are part of the 20–25% of parents who supply alcohol to their teens, claiming that their teenagers are going to drink anyway, so they might as well drink at home under parental supervision. Other parents claim that drinking by adolescents is part of growing up and

becoming an adult. "After all," they often say, "I drank when I was a teenager and it didn't hurt me any." Research has overwhelmingly demonstrated that underage drinking actually is a very dangerous rite of passage for many teens. Taking the car keys away provides minimal protection to a drunk adolescent. Consider the drunken kid who falls down the stairs; or wanders into the backyard and falls into the pool and drowns; or walks home after the party but staggers into the street and is hit by a car; or vomits and chokes to death; and of course, what about the teen who finds his or her keys and drives the car anyway. Such tragic alcohol-related accidents result in about 5000 deaths in people under the age of 21 each year. These types of circumstances are why experts say the solution to underage drinking is not for parents to be indulgent and enable the practice but for parents to never provide alcohol or condone drinking. Parents must send a clear "don't use" message because being a "cool parent" doesn't substitute for being a good parent.

Sources: Cooke, B. "Parents, Teens, and Alcohol: A Dangerous Mix." FamilyEducation.com. 1 July 2010. Available at: http://life.familyeducation.com/teen/drugs-and-alcohol/29591.html. Accessed March 4, 2011; English, B. "On Drinking, Parents Need to Just Say No." *Boston Globe.* 16 May 2010. Available http://www.boston.com/yourtown/milton/articles/2010/05/16/on_drinking_parents_need_to_just_say_no_to_kids. Accessed March 4, 2011; and WTOP. "ER Visits for Underage Drinkers Soar." WTOP.com (radio). 1 July 2010. Available at: http://www.wtop.com/?nid=25&sid=1993373. Accessed March 4, 2011.

Pure ethyl alcohol (ethanol) is recognized as an official drug in the U.S. Pharmacopoeia, although the various alcoholic beverages are not listed for medical use. Alcohol can be used as a solvent for other drugs or as a preservative. It is used to cleanse, disinfect, and harden the skin and to reduce sweating. A 70% alcohol solution is an effective bactericide. However, it should not be used on open wounds because it will dehydrate the injured tissue and worsen the damage. Alcohol may be deliberately injected in or near nerves to treat severe pain;

it causes local anesthesia and deterioration of the nerve. In all alcoholic beverages—beer, wine, liqueurs or cordials, and distilled spirits—the psychoactive agent is the same, but the amount of ethanol varies (see **Table 7.1**). The amount of alcohol is expressed either as a percentage by volume or, in the older proof system, as a measurement based on the military assay method. To make certain that they were getting a high alcohol content in the liquor, the British military would place a sample on gunpowder and touch a spark to it. If the

Table 7.1 The Concentration of Ethanol in Common Alcoholic Beverages

TYPE OF BEVERAGE	CONCENTRATION OF ETHANOL
U.S. beers	4–6%
Wine coolers	4–10%
Cocktails and dessert wines	17–20%
Liqueurs	22–50%
Distilled spirits	40% and higher

alcohol content exceeded 50%, it would burn and ignite the gunpowder. This test was "proof" that the sample was at least 50% alcohol. If the distilled spirits were "under proof," the water content would prevent the gunpowder from igniting. The percentage of alcohol volume is one-half the proof number. For example, 100-proof whiskey has a 50% alcohol content.

The Physical Effects of Alcohol

How does alcohol affect the body? **Figure 7.1** illustrates how alcohol is absorbed into the body. After a drink, alcohol has direct contact with the mouth, esophagus, stomach, and intestines, acting as an irritant and an **anesthetic** (blocking sensitivity to pain). In addition, alcohol influences almost every organ system in the body after entering the bloodstream. Alcohol diffuses into the blood rapidly after consumption by passing through gastric and intestinal walls (the absorption process). Once the alcohol is in the small intestine, its absorption is

Different alcoholic beverages have a wide range of alcohol content.

largely independent of the presence of food, unlike in the stomach, where food retards absorption.

The effects of alcohol on the human body depend on the amount of alcohol in the blood, known as the **blood alcohol concentration (BAC)**. This concentration largely determines behavioral and physical responses to alcoholic beverages. Relative to behavior, circumstances in which the drinking occurs, the drinker's mood, and his or her attitude and previous experience with alcohol all contribute to the reaction to drinking. People demonstrate individual patterns of psychological functioning that may affect their reactions to alcohol as well. For instance, the time it takes to empty the stomach may be either reduced or accelerated as a result of anger, fear, stress, nausea, and the condition of the stomach tissues.

The blood alcohol level produced depends on the presence of food in the stomach, the rate of alcohol consumption, the concentration of the alcohol, and the drinker's body composition. Fatty foods, meat, and milk slow the absorption of alcohol, allowing more time for its metabolism and reducing the peak concentration in the blood. When alcoholic beverages are taken with a substantial meal, peak BACs may be as much as 50% lower than they would have been had the alcohol been consumed by itself. When large amounts of alcohol are consumed in a short period, the brain and other organs are exposed to higher peak concentrations. Generally, the more alcohol in the stomach, the greater the absorption rate. There is, however, a modifying effect of very strong drinks on the absorption rate. The absorption of drinks stronger than 100 proof is inhibited. This effect may be due to blocked passage into the small intestine or irritation of the lining of the stomach, causing mucus secretion, or both. (See "Here and Now: Half-Truths About Alcohol.")

Diluting an alcoholic beverage with water helps to slow down absorption, but mixing with carbonated beverages increases the absorption rate. The carbonation causes the stomach to empty its contents into the small intestine more rapidly, causing a more rapid "high." The carbonation in champagne has the same effect.

KEY TERMS

anesthetic
a drug that blocks sensitivity to pain

blood alcohol concentration (BAC)
concentration of alcohol found in the blood, often expressed as a percentage

1. **Mouth**—Alcohol is consumed orally.

2. **Stomach**—Alcohol goes right into the stomach. A little of the alcohol passes through the wall of the stomach and into the bloodstream. Most of the alcohol continues down into the small intestine.

3. **Small intestine**—Alcohol goes from the stomach into the small intestine. Most of the alcohol is absorbed through the walls of the intestine and into the bloodstream.

4. **Bloodstream**—The bloodstream carries the alcohol to all parts of the body, such as the brain, heart, and liver.

5. **Liver**—As the bloodstream carries the alcohol around the body, it passes through the liver. The liver changes the alcohol to water, carbon dioxide, and energy. The process is called *oxidation*. The liver can oxidize only about one-half ounce of alcohol per hour. Thus, until the liver has time to oxidize all of the alcohol, the alcohol continues passing through all parts of the body, including the brain.

6. **Brain**—Alcohol goes to the brain almost as soon as it is consumed. It continues passing through the brain until the liver oxidizes all the alcohol into carbon dioxide, water, and energy.

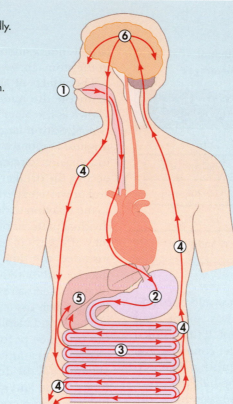

FIGURE 7.1

How alcohol is absorbed in the body.

Source: National Institute on Alcohol Abuse and Alcoholism. *Alcohol Health and Research World.* Washington, DC: U.S. Department of Health and Human Services, 1988.

Here and Now

Half-Truths About Alcohol

Much is known about alcohol, but much more needs to be learned to effectively and safely manage its use. There are several half-truths that are commonly believed by the general public that should be clarified.

- *Belief:* Alcohol, if used in moderation, is healthy for everyone.
- *Fact:* Moderate drinking benefits only men older than 50 years of age and women who are post-menopausal. Even for these populations, the benefits appear to be minimal in persons who already have healthy lifestyles.
- *Belief:* Pound for pound, women hold their liquor as well as men.
- *Fact:* Because women have proportionally less body water and tend to metabolize alcohol more slowly than men, women become more intoxicated with comparable dose consumption per body weight.
- *Belief:* A drink before bed induces sleep.
- *Fact:* After moderate drinking, onset of sleep may be faster, but the sleep itself becomes restless, marked by frequent wakings and inability to get back to sleep.
- *Belief:* If you don't feel drunk, it is okay to drive.
- *Fact:* People are typically unable to determine accurately how much alcohol is in their system. For most states in the United States, 0.08–0.1% alcohol in the blood is the legal threshold for driving (i.e., it is against the law to drive with this blood alcohol content or higher), but studies have shown that driving performance is significantly impaired at half this concentration.

Sources: "Your Health: Alcohol: The Whole Truth, Seven Half-Truths About Drinking, Exposed." *Consumer Reports* 64 (December 1999): 60–61; National Institute on Alcohol Abuse and Alcoholism (NIAAA). "FAQs for the General Public." 2007. Available at: http://www.niaaa.nih.gov/FAQs/General-English. Accessed March 4, 2011; and Greenfield, S. "Women and Alcohol Use Disorders." *Harvard Review Psychiatry* 10 (2002): 76–85.

Once in the blood, distribution occurs as the alcohol uniformly diffuses throughout all tissues and fluids, including fetal circulation in pregnant women or the milk of a nursing mother (BabyCenter 2010). Because the brain has a large blood supply, its activity is quickly affected by a high alcohol concentration in the blood. Body composition—the amount of water available for the alcohol to be dissolved in—is a key factor in BAC and distribution. The greater the muscle mass, the lower the BAC that will result from a given amount of alcohol. This relationship arises because muscle has more fluid volume than does fat. For example, if two men each weigh 180 pounds but one man has substantially more lean mass than the other man, the former will have a lower blood alcohol level after consuming 4 ounces of whiskey. The leaner man will show fewer effects. A woman of a weight equivalent to a man will have a higher blood alcohol level because women generally have a higher percentage of fat. Thus, they are affected more by identical drinks.

Alcoholic beverages contain almost no vitamins, minerals, protein, or fat—just large amounts of carbohydrates (Kovacs 2010). Alcohol cannot be used by most cells; it must be metabolized by an enzyme, **alcohol dehydrogenase**, which is found almost exclusively in the liver. Alcohol provides more calories per gram than does carbohydrate or protein and only slightly less than does pure fat. Because it can provide many calories, the drinker's appetite may be satisfied; as a result, he or she may not eat properly, causing malnutrition (Kovacs 2010). The tolerance that develops to alcohol is comparable to that observed with barbiturates (see Chapter 6). Some people have a higher tolerance for alcohol and can more easily disguise intoxication.

Alcohol and Tolerance

Repeated use of alcohol results in tolerance and reduces many of alcohol's pharmacological effects. As with other psychoactive drugs, tolerance to alcohol encourages increased consumption to regain its effects and can lead to severe physical and psychological dependence (Fleming et al. 2006). Tolerance to alcohol is similar to that seen with CNS depressants, such as the benzodiazepines. It consists of both an increase in the rate of alcohol metabolism (due to stimulation of metabolizing enzymes in the liver; see Chapter 5) and a reduced response by neurons and transmitter systems (particularly by increasing the activity of the inhibitory neurotransmitter, gamma-aminobutyric acid [GABA]) to this drug. Development of tolerance to alcohol is extremely variable; some users can consume large quantities of this drug with minor pharmacological effects. The tolerance-inducing changes caused by alcohol can also alter the body's response to other drugs (referred to as cross-tolerance; see Chapter 5) and can specifically reduce the effects of some other CNS depressants (Fleming et al. 2006; NIAAA 2007b).

Many chronic alcohol users learn to compensate for the motor impairments of this drug by modifying their patterns of behavior. These adjustments are referred to as **behavioral tolerance**. Examples of this adjustment include individuals altering and slowing their speech, walking more deliberately, or moving more cautiously to hide the fact that they have consumed debilitating quantities of alcohol.

Alcohol Metabolism

Alcohol is principally inactivated by liver metabolism (Fleming et al. 2006). The liver metabolizes alcohol at a slow and constant rate and is unaffected by the amount ingested. Thus, if one can of beer is consumed each hour, the BAC will remain constant without resulting in intoxication. If more alcohol is consumed per hour, the BAC will rise proportionately because large amounts of alcohol that cannot be metabolized spill over into the bloodstream.

Polydrug Use

It is a common practice to take alcohol with other drugs, such as tobacco (Hanson 2010), prescription drugs (NIAAA 2010), and even illegal substances (Hedden et al. 2010); this mode of consumption is known as **polydrug use** (NIAAA 2010), and it occurs in about 64% of alcoholics (Hedden et al. 2010). Mixing alcohol with other types of drugs can intensify intoxication. This probably helps explain why

KEY TERMS

alcohol dehydrogenase
principal enzyme that metabolizes ethanol

behavioral tolerance
compensation for motor impairments through behavioral pattern modification by chronic alcohol users

polydrug use
the concurrent use of multiple drugs

marijuana users are more likely to combine their marijuana use with alcohol than with other drugs (Liquori, Gatto, and Jarrett 2002; Peters and Hughes 2010). In a recent report, approximately 64% of those seeking treatment for alcoholism also were diagnosed with another drug dependence (Hedden et al. 2010).

The reasons why individuals combine alcohol with other drugs of abuse are not always apparent. The following explanations have been proposed (Hettema, Corey, and Kendler 1999):

- Alcohol enhances the reinforcing properties of other CNS depressants.
- It decreases the amount of an expensive and difficult-to-get drug required to achieve the desired effect.
- It helps to diminish unpleasant side effects of other drugs of abuse, such as the withdrawal caused by CNS stimulants (NIAAA 1993).
- There is a common predisposition to use alcohol and other substances of abuse.

Clearly, coadministration of alcohol with other substances of abuse is a common practice that can be very problematic and result in dangerous interactions.

■ Short-Term Effects

The impact of alcohol on the CNS is most similar to that of sedative-hypnotic agents such as barbiturates. Alcohol depresses CNS activity at all doses (Meehan 2008), producing definable results.

At low to moderate doses, **disinhibition** occurs; this loss of conditioned reflexes reflects a depression of inhibitory centers of the brain. The effects on behavior are variable and somewhat unpredictable. To a large extent, the social setting and mental state determine the individual's response to such alcohol consumption. For example, alcohol can cause one person to become euphoric, friendly, and talkative but can prompt another to become aggressive and hostile. Low to moderate doses also interfere with motor activity, reflexes, and coordination. Often this impairment is not apparent to the affected person (Centers for Dis-

ease Control and Prevention [CDC] 2008; "Your Health" 1999).

In moderate quantities, alcohol slightly increases the heart rate; slightly dilates blood vessels in the arms, legs, and skin; and moderately lowers blood pressure. It stimulates appetite, increases production of gastric secretions, and markedly stimulates urine output. At higher doses, the social setting has little influence on the expression of depressive actions of the alcohol. The CNS depression incapacitates the individual, causing difficulty in walking, talking, and thinking. These doses tend to induce drowsiness and cause sleep. If large amounts of alcohol are consumed rapidly, severe depression of the brain system and motor control area of the brain occurs, producing incoordination, confusion, disorientation, stupor, anesthesia, coma, and even death (CDC 2008).

The lethal level of alcohol is between 0.4% and 0.6% by volume in the blood (Fleming et al. 2006). Death is caused by severe depression of the respiration center in the brain stem, although the person usually passes out before drinking an amount capable of producing this effect. Although an alcoholic may metabolize the drug more rapidly than a light drinker, the toxicity level of alcohol stays about the same. In other words, it takes approximately the same concentration of alcohol in the body to kill a nondrinker as to kill someone who drinks on a regular basis. The amount of alcohol required for anesthesia is very close to the toxic level, which is why it would not be a useful anesthetic. See "Signs & Symptoms: Psychological and Physical Effects of Various Blood Alcohol Concentration Levels" for a summary of the psychological and physical effects of various BAC levels.

As a general rule, it takes as many hours as the number of drinks consumed to sober up completely. Despite widely held beliefs, drinking black coffee, taking a cold shower, breathing pure oxygen, and so forth will not hasten the sobering process. Stimulants such as coffee may help keep the drunk person awake but will not improve judgment or motor reflexes to any significant extent.

The Hangover

A familiar consequence of overindulgence is fatigue combined with nausea, upset stomach, headache, sensitivity to sounds, and ill temper—the hangover (Athlete.org 2010; Wiese, Shlipak, and Browner 2000). These symptoms are usually most severe many hours after drinking, when little or no alcohol remains in the body. No simple explanation exists

KEY TERMS

disinhibition
loss of conditioned reflexes due to depression of inhibitory centers of the brain

Signs & Symptoms

Psychological and Physical Effects of Various Blood Alcohol Concentration Levels

NUMBER OF DRINKS*	BLOOD ALCOHOL CONCENTRATION	PSYCHOLOGICAL AND PHYSICAL EFFECTS
1	0.02–0.03%	No overt effects, slight mood elevation
2	0.05–0.06%	Feeling of relaxation, warmth; slight decrease in reaction time and in fine muscle coordination
3	0.08–0.09%	Balance, speech, vision, hearing slightly impaired; feelings of euphoria, increased confidence; loss of motor coordination
3–4	0.08%	Legal intoxication
4	0.11–0.12%	Coordination and balance becoming difficult; distinct impairment of mental faculties, judgment
5	0.14–0.15%	Major impairment of mental and physical control; slurred speech, blurred vision, lack of motor skills
7	0.20%	Loss of motor control—must have assistance in moving about; mental confusion
10	0.30%	Severe intoxication; minimum conscious control of mind and body
14	0.40%	Unconsciousness, threshold of coma
17	0.50%	Deep coma
20	0.60%	Death from respiratory failure

Note: For each hour elapsed since the last drink, subtract 0.015% blood alcohol concentration, or approximately one drink.

*One drink = one beer (4% alcohol, 12 oz) or one highball (1 oz whiskey).

Source: Modified from data given in Ohio State Police Driver Information Seminars and the National Clearinghouse for Alcohol and Alcoholism Information, 5600 Fishers Lane, Rockville, MD 85206.

for what causes the hangover. Theories include accumulation of acetaldehyde (a metabolite of ethanol), dehydration of the tissues, poisoning due to tissue deterioration, depletion of important enzyme systems needed to maintain routine functioning, an acute withdrawal (or rebound) response, and metabolism of the impurities in alcoholic beverages.

The body loses fluid in two ways through alcohol's **diuretic** action, which sometimes results in dehydration: (1) the water content, such as in beer, increases the volume of urine, and (2) the alcohol depresses the center in the hypothalamus of the brain that controls release of a water conservation hormone (antidiuretic hormone). With less of this hormone, urine volume is further increased. Thus, after drinking heavily, especially the highly concentrated forms of alcohol, the person is thirsty. However, this effect by itself does not explain the symptoms of hangover.

The type of alcoholic beverage one drinks may influence the hangover that results. Some people are more sensitive to particular alcohol impurities than others. For example, some drinkers have no problem with white wine but an equal amount of some red wines gives them a hangover. Whiskey, scotch, and rum may cause worse hangovers than vodka or gin, given equal amounts of alcohol, because vodka and gin have fewer impurities. There is little evidence that mixing different types of drinks per se produces a more severe hangover. It is more likely that more than the usual amount of alcohol is consumed when various drinks are sampled.

A common treatment for a hangover is to take a drink of the same alcoholic beverage that caused the hangover. This practice is called "taking the hair of the dog that bit you" (from the old notion that the burnt hair of a dog is an antidote to its bite). This treatment might help the person who is physically dependent, in the same way that giving heroin

KEY TERMS

diuretic
a drug or substance that increases the production of urine

to a heroin addict eases the withdrawal symptoms. The "hair of the dog" method may work by depressing the centers of the brain that interpret pain or by relieving a withdrawal response. In addition, it may affect the psychological factors involved in having a hangover; distraction or focusing attention on something else may ease the effects.

Another remedy is to take an analgesic compound such as an aspirin–caffeine combination after drinking. This treatment is based on the belief that aspirin helps control headache; the caffeine may help counteract the depressant effect of the alcohol. In reality, these ingredients have no effect on the actual sobering-up process. In fact, products such as aspirin, caffeine, and Alka-Seltzer can irritate the stomach lining to the point where the person feels worse.

■ Dependence

According to the World Health Organization, approximately 140 million people around the world are afflicted with alcohol-related disorders. It is estimated that in the United States 12.5 million men and women suffer from alcoholism. In this group, men are three times more likely than women to develop significant dependence on this drug (Alcohol Abuse Essentials 2010).

In 2009, 47% of high school seniors drank enough alcohol to get drunk (Johnston 2009). Unfortunately, many people become so dependent on the psychological influences of alcohol that they become compulsive, continually consuming it. These individuals can be severely handicapped because of their alcohol dependence and often become unable to function normally in society. People who have become addicted to this drug are called alcoholics and likely include many of the 27% of high school seniors who get drunk at least monthly (Johnston 2009). Because of the disinhibition, relaxation, and sense of well-being mediated by alcohol, some degree of psychological dependence often develops even in routine users, and the availability of alcoholic beverages at social gatherings becomes required.

Because of the physiological effects, physical dependence also results from the regular consumption of large quantities of alcohol. This consequence becomes apparent when ethanol use is abruptly interrupted and withdrawal symptoms result. The severity of the withdrawal can vary according to the length and intensity of the alcohol habit. The pro-

totypic withdrawal patterns are as follows (Fleming et al. 2006):

- *Stage 1 (minor):* Restlessness, anxiousness, sleeping problems, agitation, tremors, and rapid heartbeat
- *Stage 2 (major):* "Minor" symptoms plus hallucinations, whole-body tremors, increased blood pressure, and vomiting
- *Stage 3 (delirium tremens):* Fever, disorientation, confusion, seizures, and fatality in 3% to 5% of cases

Recovery from alcohol dependence is a long-term process. Because of the severe withdrawal and the need for behavioral adjustments, most people relapse several times before long-term abstinence is achieved. Even people who have not used alcohol for years may relapse under very stressful circumstances (Bressert 2006). The behavioral and emotional treatment of alcoholism is discussed in more detail in Chapter 8.

Medications for Dependence

Although alcohol dependence afflicts about 4% of the adult population, only 10% to 15% of these patients receive appropriate treatment. This is partially due to the misconception that alcoholism is best dealt with by "willpower" and medicine has no role. However, as we have discussed in this chapter, there are numerous neurobiological consequences of chronic alcohol use; thus, it makes sense that biological strategies based on medications can be helpful in treating persons severely dependent on alcohol. There are currently three medications approved by the FDA for adjunctive intervention (i.e., they should be used in combination with behavioral therapy). These include the following (Miller 2008):

- The oldest drug approved for alcoholism treatment, disulfiram (Antabuse), has become less popular with many doctors because it makes users very sick and nauseous when they consume alcohol. It works by interfering with the metabolism of alcohol. It is easily avoided if the patient is anticipating drinking and is typically only helpful in the treatment of highly motivated alcoholics.
- Naltrexone (an opiate antagonist; see Chapter 9) relieves alcohol craving and helps to reduce the relapse rates in alcohol-dependent patients. Although about 20% of this population have a positive response to naltrexone treatment, the other 80% are for the most part

nonresponsive. One possible explanation for this finding is the existence of an opioid receptor variant in the responsive group that makes people vulnerable to the addicting effects of alcohol, which can be suppressed by naltrexone treatment. Thus, the lack of such a variant opioid gene in the majority of alcoholics could explain their lack of response to naltrexone (Falloon 2010).

- The third drug, acamprosate (Campral) blocks the release of the exciting neurotransmitter glutamate, which reduces withdrawal in abstinent alcoholics.

Although these FDA-approved medications have significantly influenced strategies used to treat alcoholism, they are far from being universally effective. There continues to be considerable research as we try to discover even more effective medications for treating the problems of alcoholism. For optimal benefit, alcoholics need to be carefully subtyped (including features such as age, gender, duration of dependence, mental status, and even genetic makeup) and matched to the appropriate medication and behavioral therapy (Johnson 2010).

■ Alcohol and Genetics

Large scale studies of twins suggest that addictions such as alcoholism are among the most inherited types of mental illnesses. Consequently, because of our unique gene patterns some of us get hooked on alcohol whereas others can party hard, but afterwards walk away without any need or desire to consume more alcohol (Wallis 2009). Research has demonstrated that the specific genes that contribute to these inherited vulnerabilities can influence elements of alcohol drinking such as excessive consumption, dampen neuronal feedback that warns a person that he or she has consumed too much alcohol, or enhance the sense of pleasure after drinking alcohol (Bowman 2009).

Differences in the intensity of a hangover or the negative effects of drinking such as nausea or dizziness can also be influenced by genetics (see "Family Matters: Asian Glow") and are likely to affect frequency of use and the development of addiction to alcohol. Despite the prominent role of heritability in the expression of alcohol dependence, the environment is equally as important; if it is supportive and healthy it can diminish the genetic influence and reduce the likelihood that alcoholism will be expressed even when a person's genetics increase the risk (Wallis 2009).

Family Matters: Asian Glow

The way people are affected by the after effects of drinking has a significant influence on the likelihood of addiction. For example, if drinking causes nausea, vomiting, and a very unpleasant reaction, then repeated heavy use is not likely and alcoholism probably won't occur. Two variant genes found in about 36% of Asian populations such as Chinese, Japanese, and Koreans cause the build-up of a very annoying and unpleasant metabolite of alcohol known as acetaldehyde, which in turn causes side effects such as nausea, vomiting, sweating, chest pains, and flushing of the face known as *Asian glow*. Such reactions are typically unpleasant enough to encourage those with these genes to avoid alcohol and protects them against becoming alcoholics. Interestingly, the accumulation of acetaldehyde and its effects also can be promoted independent of genetics by using the medication Antabuse. Because of its ability to block the elimination of acetaldehyde after drinking, Antabuse is given to discourage alcohol-dependent people from abusing this drug.

Sources: Buddy, T. "Antabuse Treatment for Alcoholism." About.com. 30 July 2009. Available at: http://alcoholism.about.com/od/meds/a/antabuse.htm. Accessed March 4, 2011; and Wallis, C. "The Genetics of Addiction: Research Shows How Genes and the Childhood Experience Pave the Road to Substance Abuse." CNNMoney.com. 16 October 2009. Available at: http://money.cnn.com/2009/10/16/news/genes_addiction.fortune/index.htm. Accessed March 4, 2011.

The Effects of Alcohol on Organ Systems and Bodily Functions

As mentioned earlier, BAC depends on the size of the person, presence of food in the stomach, rate of drinking, amount of carbonation, and ratio of muscle mass to body fat. Furthermore, alcohol has pervasive effects on the major organs and fluids of the body (Rethinking Drinking 2010). In fact, the effects of this substance on body functions potentially can be so profound and destructive that alcoholism (severe addiction) is now considered a disease (NIAAA 2010). The pervasive effects of alcohol on bodily organs are discussed in greater detail in the following sections.

■ Brain and Nervous System

Every part of the brain and nervous system is affected—and in extreme cases can be damaged—

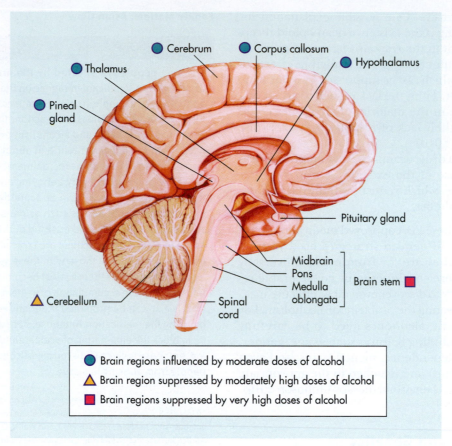

Brain regions influenced by moderate doses of alcohol

Brain region suppressed by moderately high doses of alcohol

Brain regions suppressed by very high doses of alcohol

FIGURE 7.2

The principal control centers of the brain affected by alcohol consumption. Note that all areas of the brain are interconnected.

by alcohol (see **Figure 7.2**). A relatively recent study demonstrated that even moderate consumption of alcohol can cause shrinkage of brain size. People who routinely drink more than 14 drinks per week lose approximately 1.6% of brain size compared to nondrinkers. The greatest effect was observed in female heavy drinkers over 70 years of age (Reinberg 2007). In low to moderate doses, alcohol suppresses subcortical inhibitions of the cortical control centers, resulting in disinhibition. It also increases the release of endorphins (see Chapter 4), which likely contributes to the rewarding properties of alcohol and explains why naltrexone, an opioid receptor antagonist, is an effective treatment for some alcoholics (Science Daily 2009). In higher doses, it depresses the cerebellum, causing slurred speech and staggering gait. These doses also impair a person's ability to do tasks that require vigilance and rapid decision making. Often these people are unaware that their performance is impaired, making them potentially dangerous when engaging in activities such as driving a car (Bankhead 2009).

Very high doses depress the respiratory centers of the medulla, resulting in death (Fleming et al. 2001). Furthermore, alcohol alters the production and functioning of transmitters such as dopamine, serotonin, GABA, and brain endorphins (Ratsma, van der Stelt, and Gunning 2002). A recent report suggests that even cannabinoid receptors (see Chapter 13)—the targets of the active ingredients in marijuana—are affected by alcohol (Basavarajappa 2007). These neurochemical effects contribute to the fact that alcohol consumption can aggravate underlying psychiatric disorders such as depression and schizophrenia (Bertolote et al. 2004) and may suggest novel ways to develop more effective therapies (Basavarajappa 2007).

Heavy drinking over many years may result in serious mental disorders and irreversible damage to the brain and peripheral nervous system, leading to permanently compromised mental function and memory and alterations in other brain systems (Baxamusa 2010). In addition, abrupt cessation of alcohol consumption in the alcoholic can result in

▶Case in Point Mickey Mantle Dies from Complications of Alcoholism

Mickey Mantle, the legendary center fielder for the New York Yankees, died August 14, 1995, at the age of 63, from complications of alcoholism. During his heyday as a baseball star, his heavy drinking was discreetly hidden from adoring fans. It wasn't until well after his retirement from baseball that Mantle checked himself into a treatment clinic and admitted publicly that he had been severely dependent on alcohol for most of his life. He sought professional treatment only after doctors warned Mantle that his drinking habits had almost destroyed his liver. Despite heroic attempts to save Mantle's life with a liver transplant in June of the same year, a cancer from the diseased liver spread rapidly, resulting in death only 2 months later.

Sources: Knight-Ridder/Tribune News Service, 14 August 1995, pp. 814–829; and "Mickey Mantle." 24 April 2004. Available at: http://fixedreference.org/en/20040424/wikipedia/Mickey_Mantle. Accessed February 16, 2011.

serious withdrawal effects such as life-threatening seizures, and require intensive emergency care (Physorg 2009).

▪ Liver

Among alcoholics, liver disorders are responsible for 10% to 15% of deaths (Fairbanks 2009; Worman 2000). There are three stages of alcohol-induced liver disease (Kirby 2009; Worman 2000). In the first stage, known as alcoholic fatty liver, liver cells increase the production of fat, resulting in an enlarged liver. This direct toxic effect on liver tissue is known as the **hepatotoxic effect**. This effect is reversible and can disappear if alcohol use is stopped. Several days of drinking five or six alcoholic beverages each day produces fatty liver in males. For females, as few as two drinks of hard liquor per day several days in a row can produce the same condition. After several days of abstaining from alcohol, the liver returns to normal.

The second stage develops as the fat cells continue to multiply. Generally, irritation and swelling that result from continued alcohol intake cause **alcoholic hepatitis**. At this stage, chronic inflammation sets in and can be fatal. This second stage also is reversible if the intake of alcohol ceases.

Unlike stages 1 and 2, stage 3 is not reversible. Scars begin to form on the liver tissue during this stage. These scars are fibrous, and they cause hard-

ening of the liver as functional tissue shrinks and deteriorates. This condition of the liver is known as **cirrhosis** and often is fatal. (See "Case in Point: Mickey Mantle Dies from Complications of Alcoholism.")

The liver damage caused by heavy alcohol consumption can cause problems when taking drugs that affect liver function. For example, the over-the-counter analgesic acetaminophen (Tylenol) can have a deleterious effect on the liver, especially when the function of this organ has already been compromised by alcohol (Ramack 2004).

▪ Digestive System

The digestive system consists of gastrointestinal structures involved in processing and digesting food and liquids; it includes the mouth, pharynx,

KEY TERMS

hepatotoxic effect
a situation in which liver cells increase the production of fat, resulting in an enlarged liver

alcoholic hepatitis
the second stage of alcohol-induced liver disease in which chronic inflammation occurs; reversible if alcoholic consumption ceases

cirrhosis
scarring of the liver and formation of fibrous tissues; results from alcohol abuse; irreversible

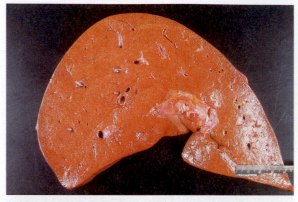

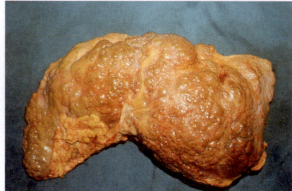

A normal liver (top) as it would be found in a healthy human body. An abnormal liver (bottom) that exhibits the effects of moderate to heavy alcohol consumption.

esophagus, stomach, and small and large intestines. As alcohol travels through the digestive system, it irritates tissue and can even damage the tissue lining as it causes acid imbalances, inflammation, and acute gastric distress. Often, the result is gastritis (an inflamed stomach) and heartburn. The more frequently consumption takes place, the greater the irritation. One out of three heavy drinkers suffers from chronic gastritis. Furthermore, the heavy drinker has double the probability of developing cancer of the mouth and esophagus because alcohol passes these two organs on the way to the stomach.

Prolonged heavy use of alcohol may cause ulcers, hiatal hernia, and cancers throughout the digestive tract. The likelihood of cancers in the mouth, throat, and stomach dramatically increases (15 times) if the person is also a heavy smoker (Lee et al. 2005). The pancreas is another organ associated with the digestive system that can be damaged by heavy alcohol consumption. Alcohol can cause pancreatitis, pancreatic cirrhosis, and alcoholic diabetes (Fleming et al. 2006).

■ Blood

High concentrations of alcohol diminish the effective functioning of the hematopoietic (blood-building) system. They decrease production of red blood cells, white blood cells, and platelets. Problems with clotting and immunity to infection are not uncommon among alcohol abusers. Often, the result is lowered resistance to disease. Heavy drinking appears to affect the bone marrow, where various blood cells are formed. The suppression of the bone marrow can contribute to anemia, in which red blood cell production cannot keep pace with the need for those cells. Heavy drinkers are also likely to develop alcoholic bleeding disorders because they have too few platelets to form clots (Fleming et al. 2006).

■ Cardiovascular System

The effects of ethanol on the cardiovascular system have been extensively studied, but much remains unknown. Ethanol causes dilation of blood vessels, especially in the skin. This effect accounts for the flushing and sensation of warmth associated with alcohol consumption.

The long-term effects of alcohol on the cardiovascular system are dose dependent. Some studies have suggested that regular light to moderate drinking (two or fewer glasses of wine per day) actually reduces the incidence of heart diseases such as heart attacks, strokes, and high blood pressure by 20% to 40% in some populations (Thompson 2009). The type of alcoholic beverage consumed does not appear to be important as long as the quantity of alcohol consumed is moderate (1–2.5 ounces per day; Huget 2009; "Your Health" 1999). Although the precise explanation for this coronary benefit is not known, it has been suggested to be related to the effects of moderate alcohol doses in relieving stress and increasing the blood concentration of high-density lipoproteins (HDL) (Bakalar 2006). HDL is a molecular complex used to transport fat through the bloodstream, and its levels are negatively correlated with cardiovascular disease. In addition, moderate levels of alcohol decrease the formation of blood clots that can plug arteries and deprive tissues of essential oxygen and nutrients. The populations most likely to benefit from the protective properties of moderate levels of alcohol appear to be men older than 50 years of age and postmenopausal women. Moderate drinking on a daily average is approximately one drink (e.g., a glass of wine) for women and two drinks for men. However, it should be noted that some scientists argue that it is not the alcohol itself that protects against cardiovascular disease but the fact that moderate drinkers tend to live healthier lifestyles such as not smoking, eating good diets, and engaging in regular exercise (Rabin 2009). These confounds need further study to determine if moderate consumption of alcohol is as healthy as suggested by earlier studies. Regardless of whether or not moderate drinking is healthy, it is clear that drinking more than moderate amounts of alcohol can result in increased health risks that more than offset the benefits (Biotech Week 2004).

Some of the confusion about alcohol's health influences may be due to the fact that the cardiovascular protective effect of moderate drinking is at least partially race specific. A report suggests that alcohol use that prevents cardiovascular disease in white men may actually increase heart disease in black men (Fuchs 2004).

Because of the potential for developing addiction to alcohol and the increased health risk with heavy drinking, most health providers and researchers would not encourage a nondrinker to start to consume alcohol in an attempt to gain a health benefit. In addition, even in those populations most likely to benefit from moderate alcohol consumption, the benefit is likely to disappear in persons who already have healthy lifestyles that include low-fat diets, stress and weight management techniques, and regular exercise ("Your Health" 1999). In general, most clinicians believe that alcohol use kills more people (approximately 100,000/year) than it saves, and those it kills tend to be younger (Hanson and Li 2003; Special Report 1997; Thompson 2009).

Chronic intense use of alcohol changes the composition of heart muscle by replacing it with fat and fiber, resulting in a heart muscle that becomes enlarged and flabby. Congestive heart failure from **alcoholic cardiomyopathy** often occurs when heart muscle is replaced by fat and fiber. Other results of alcohol abuse that affect the heart are irregular heartbeat or arrhythmia, high blood pressure, and stroke. A common example of damage is "holiday heart," so called because people drinking heavily over a weekend turn up in the emergency room with a dangerously irregular heartbeat. Chronic excessive use of alcohol by people with arrhythmia causes congestive heart failure. Malnutrition and vitamin deficiencies associated with prolonged heavy drinking also con-

tribute to cardiac abnormalities (Fairfield and Fletcher 2002).

Sexual Organs

Although alcohol lowers social inhibition, its use interferes with sexual functioning. As Shakespeare said in *Macbeth*, alcohol "provokes desire, but it takes away the performance." Continued alcohol use causes prostatitis, which is an inflammation of the prostate gland. This condition directly interferes with a man's ability to maintain an adequate erection during sexual stimulation. Another frequent symptom of alcohol abuse is atrophy of the testicles, which results in lowered sperm count and diminished hormones in the blood (Dhawan and Sharma 2002; Emanuele and Emanuele 2010).

Endocrine System

As mentioned in Chapter 4, endocrine glands release hormones into the bloodstream. The hormones function as messengers that directly affect cell and tissue function throughout the body. Alcohol abuse alters endocrine functions by influencing the production and release of hormones, and affects endocrine regulating systems in the hypothalamus, pituitary, and gonads. Because of alcohol abuse, levels of testosterone (the male sex hormone) may decline, resulting in sexual impotence, breast enlargement, and loss of body hair in men. Women experience menstrual delays, ovarian abnormalities, and infertility (Fleming et al. 2006).

Kidneys

Frequent abuse of alcohol can severely damage the kidneys. The resulting decrease in kidney function diminishes this organ's ability to process blood and properly form urine and can result in serious metabolic problems. Another consequence of impaired kidney function in alcoholics is that they tend to experience more urinary tract infections than do nondrinkers or moderate drinkers (Fleming et al. 2006; NIAAA 1997).

KEY TERMS

alcoholic cardiomyopathy
congestive heart failure due to the replacement of heart muscle with fat and fiber

■ Mental Disorders and Damage to the Brain

Persons with mental disorders are significantly more likely to have an alcohol problem (Fitzpatrick 2010). This may be in part because heavy alcohol consumption compromises the functions of those parts of the brain that control emotions and social behavior (Healy 2009). For example, long-term heavy drinking can severely affect memory, judgment, and learning ability (Fleming et al. 2006). **Wernicke-Korsakoff's syndrome** is a characteristic psychotic condition caused by alcohol use and the associated nutritional and vitamin deficiencies. Patients who are brain-damaged cannot remember recent events, and compensate for their memory loss with confabulation (making up fictitious events that even the patient accepts as fact).

■ The Fetus

In pregnant women, alcohol easily crosses the placenta, and often damages the fetus in cases of moderate to excessive drinking. It can also cause spontaneous abortion due to its toxic actions. Another tragic consequence of high alcohol consumption during pregnancy is **fetal alcohol syndrome (FAS)**, which is characterized by facial deformities, growth deficiency, mental retardation, and joint and limb abnormalities (Fleming et al. 2006; Vorvick 2009). The growth deficiency occurs in embryonic development, and the child usually does not catch up after birth. The mild to moderate mental retardation does not appear to lessen with time, apparently because the growth impairment affects the functional development of the brain as well.

The severity of FAS appears to be dose related: The more the mother drinks, the more severe the fetal damage. A safe lower level of alcohol consumption has not been established for pregnant women (Vorvick 2009). Birthweight decrements have been found at levels corresponding to about two drinks per day, on average. Clinical studies have

Fetal alcohol syndrome is characterized by facial deformities as well as growth deficiency and mental retardation.

established that alcohol itself clearly causes the syndrome; it is not related to the effects of smoking, maternal age, parity (number of children a woman has borne), social class, or poor nutrition. One study reports that 30–45% of women who are moderate to heavy alcohol consumers will give birth to a child with FAS (Life Science Weekly 2004). In addition, a recent study demonstrated that just a few episodes of heavy drinking by a pregnant woman increases the likelihood that the offspring will also abuse alcohol later in life (Psychology Today 2007).

■ Gender Differences

Research has demonstrated that there are important pharmacological differences in how males and females respond to the consumption of alcohol. For example, in women heavy alcohol use will cause accelerated damage to the brain, liver, heart, and muscles compared to male users (Leigh 2007). These differences persist even after adjusting for the quantity of alcohol according to the differences in gender size. It is thought that at least part of the greater sensitivity of women to the effects of this drug is due to their tendency to metabolize alcohol more slowly than their male counterparts (Baraona et al. 2001), or it may be due to a higher percentage of body fat in females, leading to greater retention of the drug (Leigh 2007). In addition, problems associated with alcohol abuse might express differently in men and women, with females more likely to experience depression whereas men are more likely to binge drink and engage in fighting (Norton 2007). Other differences relate to their response to treatment. Gender differences in treatment outcomes likely reflect factors such as women's tendency to have a later onset of alcohol use and associated problems, a more positive family history, more marital disruption (Gomberg 2003), and more associated psychiatric disorders, such as depression, anxiety, and stress (Women's Health Weekly 2003). Although the reasons for these differences are unclear, they must be considered as researchers and clinicians try to elucidate the causes, consequences, and most effective treatments for alcoholism.

■ Malnutrition

As previously mentioned, malnutrition is a frequent and extremely serious consequence of severe alcoholism that tends to occur most often in less affluent alcoholics. It has been suggested that malnutrition exaggerates the damage that alcohol causes to the body's organs, especially the liver (Alcohol Alert 2005; Lieberman 2003). Malnutrition apparently expresses so frequently in this population because many alcoholics find it difficult to eat a balanced diet with adequate caloric intake. For example, heavy alcohol consumption often is associated with diets low in fruits and vegetables and high in calories from alcoholic beverages, added sugars, and unhealthy fats (WIVB-TV 2010). Many alcoholics consume between 300 and 1000 kilocalories per day (2000 kilocalories per day is considered normal for an average man). In addition, most of the calories consumed by alcoholics come from alcohol, which contains 7 kilocalories/gram (less than fat, which contains 9 kilocalories/gram). The malnutrition problem is aggravated because alcohol's calories are empty—that is, alcohol does not contain other nutrients such as vitamins, minerals, protein, or fat. Because alcoholics may be deriving 50% or more of their usual caloric intake from alcoholic beverages, profound deficiencies in important nutrients result, leading to serious degeneration of health. In addition, the malnutrition problems may be further aggravated because of the damage done to the gastrointestinal tract by chronic exposure to the irritating effects of high doses of alcohol. This can damage the linings of both the stomach and intestines, thereby interfering with the proper absorption of essential nutrients from food (Roberts 2009).

Discussion Questions

1. What evidence indicates that alcohol is a drug like marijuana, cocaine, or heroin?

2. Explain how alcohol is manufactured.

3. In the Western world, alcohol use has a long history. List and discuss some of these historical events, and describe how they affect present attitudes.

4. Explain how the effect of alcohol on brain function compares to that caused by other CNS depressants.

5. Explain how alcohol affects the mouth, stomach, small intestine, brain, liver, and bloodstream.

6. List at least five factors that affect the absorption rate of alcohol in the bloodstream.

7. Explain why alcohol is commonly consumed together with other drugs.

8. List three short-term effects of alcohol abuse.

9. Explain why moderate use of ethanol may prevent heart attacks.

10. Describe the symptoms and causes of a hangover.

11. What characterizes FAS?

12. How does gender affect responses to alcohol?

13. Why is malnutrition a common occurrence in alcoholics, and what are its consequences?

Summary

1 Alcohol is considered a drug because it is a CNS depressant, and it affects both mental and physiological functioning.

2 Three types of poisonous alcohols are methyl alcohol, made from wood products; ethylene glycol, used as antifreeze; and isopropyl alcohol, used as an antiseptic. A fourth type, ethanol, is the alcohol used for drinking purposes.

3 The blood alcohol level produced depends on the presence of food in the stomach, the rate of alcohol consumption, the concentration of alcohol, and the drinker's body composition.

4 Alcohol depresses CNS activity at all doses. Low to moderate doses of alcohol interfere with motor activities, reflexes, and coordination. In moderate quantities, alcohol slightly increases heart rate; slightly dilates blood vessels in the arms, legs, and skin; and moderately lowers blood pressure. It stimulates appetite, increases production of gastric secretions, and at higher doses markedly stimulates

urine output. The CNS depression incapacitates the individual, causing difficulty in walking, talking, and thinking.

5 Alcohol is commonly used in combination with other drugs (a) to enhance reinforcing properties; (b) to reduce the amount of expensive or hard-to-get drug required for an effect; (c) to reduce unpleasant side effects; or (d) because a predisposition for use of alcohol and other drugs exists.

6 According to the World Health Organization, approximately 140 million people around the world are afflicted with alcohol-related disorders. It is estimated that in the United States, 12.5 million men and women suffer from alcoholism. These persons can be so severely handicapped that they are unable to function normally in society. In the United States only 10–12% of alcoholics receive appropriate treatment. In addition to important behavioral therapy, there are three medications approved by the FDA for adjunctive intervention for alcoholism: (a) disulfiram (Antabuse), which interferes with alcohol metabolism; (b) naltrexone (an opiate antagonist); and (c) acamprosate (Campral), which blocks the release of glutamate. Although these medications are very useful in managing alcoholics, they are not universally effective.

7 Moderate daily alcohol use can reduce cardiovascular diseases in men older than 50 years of age and in postmenopausal women.

8 Long-term heavy alcohol use directly causes serious damage to nearly every organ and function of the body.

9 Prolonged heavy drinking causes various types of muscle disease and tremors. Heavy alcohol consumption causes irregular heartbeat. Heavy drinking over many years results in serious mental disorders and permanent, irreversible damage to the brain and peripheral nervous system. Memory, judgment, and learning ability can deteriorate severely.

10 Women who are alcoholics or who drink heavily during pregnancy have a higher rate of spontaneous abortions. Infants born to drinking mothers have a high probability of being afflicted with FAS. These children have characteristic patterns of facial deformities, growth deficiency, joint and limb irregularities, and mental retardation.

11 Alcohol has pervasive effects on the major organs and fluids of the body. Every part of the brain and nervous system is affected and can be damaged by alcohol. Among alcoholics, liver disorders include alcoholic fatty liver, alcoholic hepatitis, and cirrhosis. Alcohol also irritates tissue and damages the digestive system. Heavy use of alcohol seriously affects the blood, heart, sexual organs, endocrine system, and kidneys.

12 Malnutrition is a common occurrence in severe alcoholism. It is the result of decreased caloric intake by alcoholics and the diminished consumption of essential nutrients due to the nutritional deficiency of alcoholic beverages.

References

Achord, J. L. "Alcohol and the Liver." *Scientific American Medicine* 2 (1995): 16–25.

Agrawal, A. "Young Age at First Drink May Affect Genes and Risk for Alcoholism." Science News. 19 September 2009. Available http://www.sciencedaily.com/releases/2009/09/090918181458.htm

Alcohol Abuse Essentials. "What Is Alcohol Abuse?" 2010. Available http://www.alcohol-abuse-essentials.com

Alcoholism and Drug Addiction Help. "Understanding Alcoholism and Understanding Drug Addiction: Because Understanding Breeds Power to Facilitate Change." 2010. Available http://www.alcoholism-and-drug-addiction-help.com/understanding-alcoholism.html

American Academy of Pediatrics. "Policy Statement—Alcohol Use by Youth and Adolescents: A Pediatric Concern." 1 July 2010. Available http://pediatrics.aappublications.org/cgi/reprint/peds.2010-0438v1

American Psychiatric Association (APA). *Diagnostic and Statistical Manual of Mental Disorders,* 4th ed., text revision (DSM-IV-TR). Washington, DC: American Psychiatric Association, 2000.

American Public University. "Teenage Smoking 'Leads to Increased Susceptibility to Alcohol Withdrawal in Adulthood.'" 7 March 2010. Available http://www.thaindian.com/newsportal/health/teenage-smoking-leads-to-increased-susceptibility-to-alcohol-withdrawal-in-adulthood_100330972.html

Athlete.org. "The Athlete. Drug Abuse, Alcoholic Effects." 2010. Available http://www.theathlete.org/anti-depression

BabyCenter. "Alcohol and Nursing Moms." BabyCenter Medical Advisory Board. April 2010. Available http://www.babycenter.com/0_alcohol-and-nursing-moms_3547.bc

Bachelor, R. "Historic Relationship Between Religion and Alcohol." Suite101.com. 30 January 2010. Available http://archaeology.suite101.com/article.cfm/historic-relationship-between-religion—alcohol

Bakalar, N. "For Heart Health, Liquor Is Quicker for Women and Slower for Men." *New York Times* (6 June 2006): D-5.

Bankhead, C. "Booze Baffles Brain After Binge." MedPage Today. 22 December 2009. Available http://www.medpagetoday.com/psychiatry/addictions/17656

Baraona, E., C. Abittan, K. Dohmen, M. Moretti, G. Pazzote, Z. Chayes, et al. "Gender Differences in Pharmacokinetics of Alcohol." *Alcohol Clinical Experimental Research* 25 (2001): 502–507.

Basavarajappa, B. "The Endocannabinoid Signaling System: A Potential Target for Next Generation Therapeutics for Alcoholism." *Minireview of Medicinal Chemistry* 7 (2007): 769–779.

Baxamusa, B. "Alcohol Dementia Prognosis." Buzzle.com. 2010. Available http://www.buzzle.com/articles/alcohol-dementia-prognosis.html

Bertolote, J., A. Fleishmann, D. DeLeo, and D. Wasserman. "Psychiatric Diagnoses and Suicide: Revisiting the Evidence." *Crisis* 25 (2004): 147–155.

Biotech Week. "Excess Drinking Shortens Life by 30 Years." *Morbidity and Mortality Weekly Report.* 53 (20 October 2004): 866–870.

Bowman, L. "Medical Journal: Alcoholism vs. Drinking Too Much." Scripps Howard News Science. 30 December 2009. Available http://scrippsnews.com/content/medical-journal-alcoholism-vs-drinking-too-much

Bressert, S. "Stress and Drinking." PsychCentral. 2006. Available http://psychcentral.com/lib/2006/stress-and-drinking

Buddy, T. "Antabuse Treatment for Alcoholism." About.com: Alcoholism. 30 July 2009. Available http://alcoholism.about.com/od/meds/a/antabuse.htm

Califano, J. "Statement of Joseph A. Califano, Jr. on Teens and Parents." National Center on Addiction and Substance Abuse at Columbia University. 1 July 2010. Available http://www.casacolumbia.org/templates/Chairman Statements.aspx?articleid=602&zoneid=31

CBS News. "More Teens Are Binge Drinking." CBS Evening News. 2 January 2007. Available http://www.cbsnews.com/stories/2007/01/02/eveningnews/main2324726.shtml

Center on Alcohol Marketing and Youth. "Drops in the Bucket: Alcohol Industry Responsibility, Advertising on Television in 2001." Georgetown University (3 February 2003a): 1, 2.

Center on Alcohol Marketing and Youth. "Radio Daze: Alcohol Ads Tune in Underage Youth." Georgetown University (2 April 2003b): 1, 2.

Center on Alcohol Marketing and Youth. "Drowned Out." Georgetown University (25 September 2007).

Center on Alcohol Marketing and Youth "Alcohol Advertising and Youth." Georgetown University. 2010. Available http://www.camy.org/factsheets/sheets/Alcohol_Advertising_and_Youth.html

"Centerpiece: Alcohol in Perspective." *Wellness Letter* 9 (February 1993): 4–6.

Centers for Disease Control and Prevention (CDC). "Frequently Asked Questions. Introduction to Alcohol." 2008. Available http://www.cdc.gov/alcohol/faqs.htm

Cooke, B. "Parents, Teens, and Alcohol: A Dangerous Mix." FamilyEducation.com. 1 July 2010. Available http://life.familyeducation.com/teen/drugs-and-alcohol/29591.html

Dhawan, K., and A. Sharma. "Prevention of Chronic Alcohol and Nicotine-Induced Azospermia, Sterility and Decreased Libido, by a Novel Tri-substituted Benzoflavone Moiety." *Life Science* 71 (2002): 3059–3069.

Emanuele, M., and N. Emanuele. "Alcohol and the Male Reproductive System." NIAAA. 2010. Available http://pubs.niaaa.nih.gov/publications/arh25-4/282-287.htm

English, B. "On Drinking, Parents Need to Just Say No." *Boston Globe.* 16 May 2010. Available http://www. boston.com/yourtown/milton/articles/2010/05/16/on_drinking_parents_need_to_just_say_no_to_kids

Epstein, J. "Students Aren't the Only Boozers." Inside HigherEd. 4 June 2010. Available http://www.inside highered.com/news/2010/06/04/acha

Fairbanks, K. "Alcoholic Liver Disease." Cleveland Clinic, Center for Continuing Education. 2009. Available http://www.clevelandclinicmeded.com/medicalpubs/disease management/hepatology/alcoholic-liver-disease

Fairfield, K., and R. Fletcher. "Vitamins for Chronic Disease Prevention in Adults: Scientific Review." *Journal of the American Medical Association* 288 (2002): 1720.

Falloon, K. "Naltrexone Has Mixed Effects in Alcoholics." Post-Gazette.com News/Health. 30 June 2010. Available http://post-gazette.com/pg/10181/1069113-114.stm

Fitzpatrick, M. "Treat Mental-Health, Addiction Issues Together: Report." *Vancouver Sun.* 9 April 2010. Available http://www.vancouversun.com/health/Treat+mental+health+addiction+issues +together+report/2782390/story.html

Fleming, M., S. Mihic, and R. Harris. "Ethanol." In *The Pharmacological Basis of Therapeutics,* 10th ed., edited by J. Hardman and L. Limbird, 429–446. New York: McGraw-Hill, 2001.

Fleming, M., S. Mihic, and R. Harris. "Ethanol." In *The Pharmacological Basis of Therapeutics,* 11th ed., edited by L. Brunton, J. Lazo, and K. Parker, 591–606. New York: McGraw-Hill, 2006.

Fuchs, F. "Association Between Alcoholic Beverage Consumption and Incidence of Coronary Heart Disease in Whites and Blacks—The Atherosclerosis Risk in Communities Studies." *American Journal of Epidemiology* 160 (2004): 466–474.

Gomberg, E. "Treatment for Alcohol-Related Problems: Special Populations: Research Opportunities." *Recent Developments in Alcoholism* 16 (2003): 313–333.

Gowin, J. "Your Brain on Alcohol: Is the Conventional Wisdom Wrong About Booze?" *Psychology Today.* 10 June 2010. Available http://www.psychologytoday.com/blog/you-illuminated/201006/your-brain-alcohol

Greenfield, S. "Women and Alcohol Use Disorders." *Harvard Review Psychiatry* 10 (2002): 76–85.

Hanson, D. "Triple Play for Addicts". Addiction Inbox, The Science of Substance Abuse. 2 June 2010. Available http://addiction-dirkh.blogspot.com/2010/06/triple-play-for-addicts.html

Hanson, G. R., and T. K. Li. "Public Health Implications of Excessive Alcohol Consumption." *Journal of the American Medical Association* 289 (2003): 1031, 1032.

Healy, M. "Alcoholism Disrupts Ability to Read Emotions, Conduct Relationships." *Los Angeles Times.* 12 August 2009. Available http://latimesblogs.latimes.com/booster_shots/2009/08/alcoholism-disrupts-ability-to-read-emotions-conduct-relationships-heres-how.html

Hedden, S. L., S. S. Martins, R. J. Malcolm, L. Floyd, C. E. Cavanaugh, and W. W. Latimer. "Patterns of Illegal Drug Use Among an Adult Alcohol Dependent Population: Results from the National Survey on Drug Use and Health." *Drug and Alcohol Dependence* 106 (2010): 119–125.

Hettema, J., L. Corey, and K. Kendler. "A Multivariate Genetic Analysis of the Use of Tobacco, Alcohol and Caffeine in a Population Sample of Male and Female Twins." *Drug and Alcohol Dependency* 57 (1999): 9–78.

Hitti, M. "Does Smoking Make You Drink More?" WebMD. 2006 July 24. Available http://www.webmd.com/smoking-cessation/news/20060724/smoking-drinking

Huget, J. "Eat, Drink and Be Healthy; The Pros and Cons of Drinking; Weighing Alcohol's Effects on the Body." *Washington Post.* 31 December 2009. Available http://www.washingtonpost.com/wp-dyn/content/linkset/2008/10/14/LI2008101401092.html

Johnson, B. "Medication Treatment of Different Types of Alcoholism." *American Journal of Psychiatry* 167 (2010): 630–639.

Johnston, L. "Monitoring the Future 2009." 2009. Available http://monitoringthefuture.org/data/09data.html#2009data-drugs

Kerlikowske, G. "Drug Czar Says More People Drive Under Influence of Drugs Than Alcohol." PolitiFact. 5 April 2010. Available http://www.politifact.com/truth-o-meter/statements/2010/apr/05/gil-kerlikowske/drug-czar-says-more-people-drive-under-influence-d

Kirby, S. "Four Stages of Alcoholic Liver Disease." Suite101.com. 2009. Available http://www.suite101.com/content/four-stages-of-alcoholic-liver-disease-a129360

Kovacs, B. "Alcohol and Nutrition." MedicineNet.com. 2010. Available http://www.medicinenet.com/alcohol_and_nutrition/article.htm

Larroque, B., and M. Kaminski. "Prenatal Alcohol Exposure and Development at Preschool Age: Main Results of a French Study." *Alcoholism: Clinical and Experimental Research* 22 (1998): 295–303.

Lee, C., J. Lee, D. Wu, H. Hsu, E. Kao, H. Huang, et al. "Independent and Combined Effects of Alcohol Intake, Tobacco Smoking and Betel Quid Chewing on the Risk of Esophageal Cancer in Taiwan." *International Journal of Cancer* 113 (2005): 475–482.

Leigh, S. "A Woman's Brain Hit Harder by Alcohol Abuse; Damage Occurs Faster and with Fewer Drinks, Study Finds." Health Day (April 27, 2007). Available http://abcnews.go.com/Health/Healthday/story?id=4506743&page=1

Lieberman, C. "Relationship Between Nutrition, Alcohol Use, and Liver Disease." *Alcohol Research and Health* 27 (2003): 220–231.

Life Science Weekly. "Fetal Alcohol Syndrome Is Still a Threat, Says Publication." 28 September 2004. Available http://www.highbeam.com/doc/1G1-122472653.html

Liquori, A., C. Gatto, and D. Jarrett. "Separate and Combined Effects of Marijuana and Alcohol on Mood, Equilibrium and Simulated Driving." *Psychopharmacology* 163 (2002): 399–405.

Mann, K., D. Herman, and A. Heinz. "One Hundred Years of Alcoholism: The Twentieth Century." *Alcohol and Alcoholism* 35 (2000): 10–15.

Marin Institute. "Health Care Costs of Alcohol." 2007. Available http://www.marininstitute.org/alcohol_policy/health_care_costs.htm

Meehan, R. "Alcohol and Health." Biology Reference. 2008. Available http://www.biologyreference.com/A-Ar/Alcohol-and-Health.html

Miller, G. "Psychopharmacology: Tackling Alcoholism with Drugs." Science.com. 11 April 2008. Available http://www.sciencemag.org/cgi/content/short/320/5873/168

Moyer, C. "Teen Alcohol Use Interferes with Brain Development." American Medical News. 10 May 2010. Available http://www.ama-assn.org/amednews/2010/05/10/prsb0510.htm

Mozes, A. "1 in 5 College Students Admitted to Drunk Driving, Study Found." HealthDay. 2 June 2010. Available http://www.businessweek.com/lifestyle/content/healthday/639483.html

Mullins, K. "Binge Drinking and College Students." Digital Journal. 3 June 2009. Available http://www.digitaljournal.com/article/273572

National Center on Addiction and Substance Abuse at Columbia University. "Wasting the Best and the Brightest." CASA Press Release. 15 March 2007. Available http:// www.casacolumbia.org/absolutenm/templates/Press Releases.aspx?articleid= 477&zoneid=65

National Institute on Alcohol Abuse and Alcoholism (NIAAA). *8th Special Report to Congress on Alcohol and Health.* September 1993: 121.

National Institute on Alcohol Abuse and Alcoholism (NIAAA). "Alcohol's Effect on Organ Function." *Alcohol Health and Research World.* 1997. Available http://pubs.niaaa.nih.gov/publications/arh21-1/toc21-1.htm

National Institute on Alcohol Abuse and Alcoholism (NIAAA). "Alcohol Alert: Alcoholic Liver Disease." 2005. Available http://pubs.niaaa.nih.gov/publications/aa64/aa64.htm

National Institute on Alcohol Abuse and Alcoholism (NIAAA). "FAQs for the General Public." 2007a. Available http://www.niaaa.nih.gov/FAQs/General-English

National Institute on Alcohol Abuse and Alcoholism (NIAAA). "Harmful Interactions: Mixing Alcohol with Medicines." 2007b. Available http://pubs.niaaa.nih.gov/publications/medicine/medicine.htm

National Institute on Alcohol Abuse and Alcoholism (NIAAA). "Rethinking Drinking: Alcohol and Your Health." 2010. Available http://pubs.niaaa.nih.gov/publications/RethinkingDrinking/Rethinking_Drinking.pdf

New York Times. "Binge Drinking on Campus." 30 June 2009. Available http://www.nytimes.com/2009/07/01/opinion/01wed3.html

Norton, A. "Men and Women Show Alcohol Problems Differently." Reuters Health. 24 April 2007. Available http://www.reuters.com/article/healthNews/idUSLAU37677020070423

Office of Applied Studies. "2006 National Survey on Drug Use and Health: National Results." SAMHSA. 2007. Available http://www.oas.samhsa.gov/p0000016.htm

Peters, E. and J. Hughes. "Daily Marijuana Users with Past Alcohol Problems Increase Alcohol Consumption During Marijuana Abstinence." *Drug and Alcohol Dependence* 106 (2010): 111–118.

Physorg. "A New Understanding of Why Seizures Occur with Alcohol Withdrawal." Physorg.com. 17 October 2009. Available http://www.physorg.com/news175017259.html

Psychology Today. "Pregnant and Under the Influence." 1 May 2007. Available http://psychologytoday.com/articles/pto-2691.html

Quindien, A. "America's Most Pervasive Drug Problem Is the Drug That Pretends It Isn't." *Salt Lake Tribune* (20 April 2000): A11.

Rabin, R. "Alcohol's Good for You? Some Scientists Doubt It." *New York Times* (16 June 2009). Available http://www.nytimes.com/2009/06/16/health/16alco.html

Ramack, B. "Acetaminophen Misconceptions." *Hepatology* 40 (2004): 10–15.

Ratsma, J., O. van der Stelt, and W. Gunning. "Neurochemical Markers of Alcoholism Vulnerability." *Alcohol and Alcoholism* 37 (2002): 522–533.

Reinberg, S. "Drinking Shrinks the Brain." HealthScout. 2 May 2007. Available http://www.healthscout.com/template.asp?page=newsdetail&ap=1&id=604213

Reinberg, S. "At U.S. Colleges, Binge Drinking Is on the Rise. Efforts Similar to Campaign Against Smoking Are Needed, Expert Suggests." ABC News/Health. 16 June 2009a. Available http://abcnews.go.com/Health/Healthday/story?id=7846733&page=1

Reinberg, S. "Binge Drinking May Damage Teens' Brains." ABC News/Health. 22 April 2009b. Available http://abcnews.go.com/Health/Healthday/story?id=7406188&page=1

Roberts, K. "The Nutritional Impact the Body Endures During Alcohol Abuse and Alcoholism." Brighthub Health. 2009. Available http://www.brighthub.com/health/diet-nutrition/articles/28922.aspx

Science Daily. "Low to Moderate, Not Heavy, Drinking Releases 'Feel-Good' Endorphins in the Brain." 20 March 2009. Available http://www.sciencedaily.com/releases/2009/03/090319161503.htm

"Special Report: Alcohol: Weighing the Benefits and Risks for You." *U.C. Berkeley Wellness Letter* 13 (August 1997): 4–5.

Substance Abuse and Mental Health Services Administration. "Treatment Episode Data Set (TEDS)." 2009. Available http://wwwdasis.samhsa.gov/teds08/teds2k8natweb.pdf

Thompson, D. "Drinking Your Way to Health? Perhaps Not." Healthfinder.gov. 21 October 2009. Available http://vedicviews-worldnews.blogspot.com/2009/10/expert-say-recent-studies-touting.html

Trudeau, M. "Teen Drinking May Cause Irreversible Brain Damage." NPR. 30 June 2010. Available http://www.npr.org/templates/story/story.php?storyId=122765890

U.S. National Library of Medicine. "Fetal Alcohol Syndrome." MedlinePlus. 2010. Available http://www.nlm.nih.gov/medlineplus/fetalalcoholsyndrome.html

Vorvick, L. "Fetal Alcohol Syndrome." MedlinePlus. 2009. Available http://www.nlm.nih.gov/medlineplus/ency/article/000911.htm

Wallis, C. "The Genetics of Addiction Research Shows How Genes and the Childhood Experience Pave the Road to Substance Abuse." CNNMoney.Com, Fortune. 16 October 2009. Available http://money.cnn.com/2009/10/16/news/genes_addiction.fortune/index.htm

Wiese, J., M. Shlipak, and W. Browner. "The Alcohol Hangover." *Annals of Internal Medicine* 134 (2000): 533, 534.

Williams, S. "Medications for Treating Alcohol Dependence." *American Family Physician* 2 (2005): 1775–1780.

WIVB-TV. "Alcohol Intake Linked to Diet Quality." 27 March 2010. Available http://www.wivb.com/dpps/health/healthy_living/alcohol-intake-linked-to-diet-quality_3291906

Women's Health Weekly. "Female Drinkers and Drug Users Tend to Have More Depressive Disorders." 20 March 2003: 1.

Worman, H. "Alcoholic Liver Disease." Columbia University. 2000. Available http://cpmcnet.columbia.edu/dept/gi/alcohol.html

WTOP. "ER Visits for Underage Drinkers Soar." WTOP.com (radio). 1 July 2010. Available http://www.wtop.com/?nid=25&sid=1993373

"Your Health: Alcohol: The Whole Truth, Seven Half-Truths About Drinking, Exposed." *Consumer Reports* 64 (December 1999): 60–61.

CHAPTER 8

Alcohol: Behavioral Effects

Did You Know?

- Seventy-seven percent of the U.S. population believes that alcohol creates the most problems in our society.
- A relatively recent Gallup Poll reports that 64% of the adult population drinks alcohol and 26% reported excessive alcohol consumption (Jones 2006).
- Americans consumed twice as much alcohol in 1830 as they do now.
- Of all U.S. adult minority groups, Asian Americans have the highest rate of abstinence, the lowest rate of heavy drinking, and the lowest level of drinking-related problems.
- People have complained about fraternity drinking since 1840.
- Most of the economic costs of alcohol and drug problems fall on taxpayers, most of whom do not abuse alcohol and drugs.
- From 8th to 12th grades, the percentage of students using alcohol doubled to approximately 60%.
- Approximately 18% of 8th graders, 37% of 10th graders, and 55% of 12th graders said they have been drunk at least once in their lifetime.
- On weekend nights throughout the United States, 70% of all fatal single-vehicle crashes involve a driver who is legally intoxicated.
- Less affluent people drink less than more affluent individuals.

Learning Objectives

On completing this chapter you will be able to:

- Cite some of the latest statistics on the use of alcohol.
- Cite the countries with the highest and lowest rates of alcohol consumption.
- Discuss major ways alcohol is costly to our society.
- Discuss the main events of the temperance movement and the Prohibition era.
- Define alcoholism and identify the general characteristics of an alcoholic.
- Cite some of the cultural differences for defining problem drinkers.
- Explain how culture influences the views about alcohol.
- List four cultural factors that affect our views about consuming alcohol.
- List four findings about alcohol consumption and college students.
- Provide at least three reasons why the effects of alcohol consumption differ in women and men.
- Understand the differences between codependency and enabling behaviors.
- List two major factors that alcohol treatment must consider.

Drugs and Society Online is a great source for additional drugs and society information for both students and instructors. Visit **go.jblearning.com/hanson11** to find a variety of useful tools for learning, thinking, and teaching.

Introduction

First interview:

As a clerk here at this store, I see all kinds of people buying alcohol. Sometimes, you can tell who more than likely have big problems with alcohol by just looking at them. One man comes in about three times a week, usually at night. He buys fifths, half gallons, and pints of vodka. He is usually well dressed and works at some office job somewhere here in town. I know someone who knows him, and a lady friend of his says that if you call him up after 10 at night, his speech is slurred, and she knows for a fact that he keeps pints under his car seat while driving during the day. This lady friend lives right next door to him and she sees him going to and from work and taking swigs from his stash so-to-speak. *(From Venturelli's research files, female liquor store clerk in a small Midwestern town, age 50, August 9, 1999)*

Second interview:

I even knew a professor who would buy pints of whiskey as soon as we would open in the morning. He would drive off and go to your university [referring to the author's university] to teach. He was a heck of a nice fella, always ready with a joke and very pleasant to talk to, but I knew he had a problem with this stuff. *(From Venturelli's research files, female liquor store clerk in a small Midwestern town, age 50, August 9, 1999)* [Update: This professor with an alleged drinking problem has changed jobs and is no longer at this university.]

Third interview:

I vividly recall at age 10 seeing at least three or four middle-aged men arrive at my father's tavern as soon as the doors were opened at 8:00 A.M. on most mornings, desperately looking for the morning's first drink of alcohol. I recall my dad would crack a raw egg into an 8-ounce glass. Draft beer and the raw egg filled the glass half full. The reason for the raw egg was to get some breakfast protein and the reason for the half-full glass of beer was because their hands were very shaky and they had to steady the drink to their mouths. Immediately following what my dad referred to as a "full" breakfast were at least several double shots of Jim Beam whiskey. These alcoholic customers had to have the drinks so that they could feel

"normal" for the rest of the day. Some would even be dressed in formal attire ready to go off to their office jobs. *(Venturelli, personal observation, May 18, 2000)*

Fourth interview:

I have this friend who works as a restaurant manager and has a big drinking problem. On most evenings, he calls as soon as he reaches home from work late at night. Each time, and as he is talking to me on the phone, I can hear the jingling of the ice cubes in his glass. Sometimes he already had a few cocktails before he calls so as soon as he starts talking I can immediately distinguish by the way he speaks that he is already half-drunk. As he continues drinking and contradicting himself, in mostly a one way conversation—him talking to me, I have to listen to a lot of nonsensical talk that makes me feel like he is using me as someone to call so he can unload all the problems that went on with his job for the day. After 10–15 minutes of listening, I often try to end the conversation by saying, "I have to get up real early tomorrow morning so I need to get to bed." This usually ends the conversation. I realize he is lonely (living by himself), but why do I have to endure this nearly every night? I guess I feel sorry for him, but it is unfair to be used this way. He often claims he is an alcoholic and says at least he is a functioning alcoholic. I know he puts in many hours at work and probably because he sees so many of his customers drinking all day long, maybe he develops some kind of thirst for alcohol when he is off work. How many times he asks me to take him to the liquor store to buy vodka, and the funny thing is that I hardly drink anymore. Each time I take him to buy liquor on days when he is off work, he always comes out with a half-gallon bottle of vodka that is usually consumed within a week. He cannot drive since his driving record is abominable with 4 DUIs to date. He says in 10 years he will be able to drive again—God help us when he does! At a very young age when he received his first DUI, he went off the road completely drunk and hit a barn, actually went through a barn, and killed a steer with his car! I sometimes laugh about this when I picture the accident but it is not funny. Just imagine if it were a pedestrian or another car? I know he has a big alcohol problem but it appears he also knows it without either desiring or seeking help for his alcoholism. I keep imagining what hell it must be if I had to live with him as his roommate. *(From Venturelli's research files, male high school teacher in a small Midwestern town, age 53, July 4, 2010)*

Alcohol Consumption in the United States

Similar to nearly all societies past and present, alcohol has always been a part of American society. The preceding quotes illustrate how an individual can consume an excessive amount of a psychoactive and addictive substance without necessarily coming to the attention of anyone except perhaps a neighbor or friend, a lone liquor store employee, or even a bar owner and his young son. Furthermore, this same depressant chemical is often not perceived as a drug by many Americans. It is considered more of a social substance, something that is "always" found at social gatherings and is even expected at such gatherings.

Consider these findings from the National Household Survey on Drug Abuse in 2008 (Substance Abuse and Mental Health Services Administration [SAMHSA] 2009):

- Slightly more than half of Americans age 12 or older reported being **current drinkers** of alcohol in the 2008 survey (51.6%). This translates to an estimated 129 million people, which is similar to the 2007 estimate of 126.8 million people (51.1%).
- More than one-fifth (23.3%) of persons age 12 or older participated in **binge drinking** at least once in the 30 days prior to the survey in 2008. This translates to about 58.1 million people. (This is the same percentage reported in 2007 [23.3%].)
- In 2008, heavy drinking (**heavy use**) was reported by 6.9% of the population age 12 or older, or 17.3 million people. This percentage is similar to the rate of heavy drinking in 2007 (6.9%) and 2003 (6.8%).
- In 2008, rates of current alcohol use were 3.4% among persons ages 12 or 13, 13.1% of persons ages 14 or 15, 26.2% of 16- or 17-year-olds, 48.7% of those ages 18 to 20, and 69.5% of 21- to 25-year-olds (see **Figure 8.1**). These estimates showed significant declines from 2007 for the 14- or 15-year-olds (from 14.7% to 13.1%) and for the 16- or 17-year-olds (from 29% to 26.2%).

- Among older age groups, the prevalence of current alcohol use decreased with increasing age, from 67.4% among 26- to 29-year-olds to 50.3% among 60- to 64-year-olds and 39.7% among people age 65 or older.
- Rates of binge alcohol use in 2008 were 1.5% among 12- or 13-year-olds, 6.9% among 14- or 15-year-olds, 17.2% among 16- or 17-year-olds, 33.7% among persons ages 18 to 20, and peaked among those ages 21 to 25 at 46%. The 2008 binge drinking rate for 16- or 17-year-olds showed a decrease from 2007, when it was 19.4%.
- The binge drinking rate decreased beyond young adulthood from 36.4% of 26- to 34-year-olds to 18.8% of persons age 35 or older.
- The rate of binge drinking was 41% for young adults ages 18 to 25. Heavy alcohol use was reported by 14.5% of persons ages 18 to 25. These rates are similar to the rates in 2007 (41.8% and 14.7%, respectively).
- Persons age 65 or older had lower rates of binge drinking (8.2%) than adults in other age groups. The rate of heavy drinking among persons age 65 or older was 2.2%.

Encouraging findings also indicate that the rate of current alcohol use among youth ages 12 to 17 declined from 15.9% in 2007 to 14.6% in 2008. Youth binge and heavy drinking rates were 8.8% and 2.0%, respectively. The 2008 rate for youth binge drinking was also lower than the 2007 rate, which was 9.7%. However, these trends indicate that despite all the laws, increased campaigns and advertisements against drug and alcohol abuse, and continually increasing enforcement expenditures since 1994, the number of underage drinkers has not changed much (SAMHSA 2008).

KEY TERMS

current alcohol use (current drinkers)
at least one drink in the past 30 days; can include binge and heavy use

binge use (binge drinking)
a pattern of drinking five or more drinks for men and four or more drinks for women on a single occasion, such as the same time or within two hours of each other, on at least 1 day in the past 30 days; includes heavy use

heavy use (heavy drinkers)
five or more drinks on the same occasion on each of 5 or more days in the past 30 days

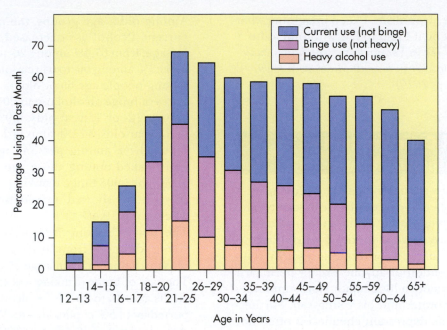

FIGURE 8.1

Current, binge, and heavy alcohol use among persons aged 12 or older, by age: 2008.

Source: Substance Abuse and Mental Health Services Administration (SAMHSA). *Results from the 2008 National Survey on Drug Use and Health: National Findings.* Office of Applied Studies, NSDUH Series H-36, DHHS Publication No. SMA 09-4435. Rockville, MD, 2009.

Current Statistics and Trends in Alcohol Consumption

A Gallup Poll indicated that 64% of the adult population drinks alcohol, whereas 26% reported excessive alcohol consumption patterns (Gallup Poll 2007). In an earlier Gallup Poll, 29% of the population reported that drinking alcohol has caused family problems, and 77% of those questioned indicated that in comparison to all other drug problems, alcohol creates the most family problems in our society (Jones 2007; Newport 2000).

In looking at more detailed figures about consumption patterns, we find the following (summarized largely from Newport 2000, unless otherwise designated):

- Gallup has not found much change in drinking patterns among the public. Currently 64% report themselves as being current drinkers. (In 1939, the average was 63%.) In regard to regular drinking, Gallop reports it to be 4.8 alcoholic beverages in the past week. In 2001, the average was below four drinks (Jones 2007).

- Of the 64% who report drinking alcohol in the United States, 40% of men prefer to drink beer, whereas women prefer wine.
- As men age, their preference for beer steadily decreases.
- Overall, as both men and women age, they say wine is their favorite alcoholic beverage.
- Lower-income drinkers prefer beer, whereas higher-income drinkers prefer wine.
- The highest rate of family drinking problems is among 18- to 29-year-olds.
- Currently, 42% of the population report family disputes caused by excessive drinking; 17% reported this problem in 1996.
- Sixty-four percent claim they drink and 36% report that they abstain. In 1999, 61% drank and 39% abstained.
- Gallup also reports that of the 64% of Americans who claim they consume alcohol, 40% prefer beer, 34% prefer wine, and 22% prefer harder forms of liquor (e.g., vodka, gin, scotch; Jones 2007).
- Of the total number of drinkers, 26% reported that they drink more than they should.
- Estimated yearly spending for healthcare services was $18.8 billion for alcohol prob-

lems and medical consequences of alcohol consumption and $9.9 billion for other types of drug problems.

- Yearly, an estimated $82 billion was lost in potential productivity due to both alcohol and other drug abuse.

- Worldwide, adults (age 21 or older) consume on average 5 liters of pure alcohol from beer, wine, and spirits per year. The average alcohol consumption is highest in Europe, followed by the Americas, and Africa. Alcohol consumption tends to increase with economic development; however, consumption remains low in some regions where the majority of the population is Muslim (GreenFacts 2009).

- Throughout the world, the highest per capita consumptions[1] in 2006 were Romania (10.5 liters), Austria (10.5 liters), Hungary (10.4 liters), and Russia (10.3 liters). The lowest consumption was in Norway (8.3 liters) while the United Kingdom (8.3 liters) was mid-range in European consumption. Alcohol consumption in most European countries was stable in 2006. Furthermore, in some European countries, consumption fell substantially. For example, France fell from 17.2 liters in 1970 to 10.0 liters in 2006 and Italy fell from 16.0 liters in 1970 to 8.1 liters in 2006 (Coghill et al. 2009, p. 13).

- In contrast to common assumptions, the higher the level of education attained, the higher the likelihood of current alcohol use. College graduates registered an average of 93% alcohol use, those with some college 91%, high school graduates 86%, and those with less than a high school degree 76% (SAMHSA 1999b).

- Drinking is commonly believed to be associated with poverty, yet according to a Gallup Poll, the people most likely to drink have higher incomes, are younger than age 65, do not attend church, live in regions of the United States other than the South, and are more likely to identify themselves as liberals.

- Research shows that much of the economic burden of alcohol and drug problems falls on the population of taxpayers who do not abuse alcohol and drugs. Government, private insurance, and other members of households bear most of these costs (Office of Applied Studies [OAS] 2001).

■ Percentages of the Drinking Population: A Pyramid Model

What percentage of our society drinks alcohol? A pyramid can be constructed based on the amount of alcohol consumed, the pattern of drinking, or the "problem" or "illness" dimension (e.g., by attempting to calculate what proportion of Americans are "abusers" or "dependent"; the criteria for each were discussed in Chapter 7). For example, at the beginning of this chapter, the first two interviews discussed people who bought and consumed liquor and are prime examples of alcohol drinkers who probably imbibe approximately 1 quart per day. This, by most definitions, is a clear diagnostic criterion for a diagnosis of alcoholism. Interestingly, all four of the chapter's opening examples indicate that the alcohol drinkers are apparently functional, or at least they manage to create this impression.

The pyramid shown in **Figure 8.2** has a base of 35% who are **teetotalers**, then a layer of about 13% who occasionally drink, and a top 52% who drink regularly. Some 11 million Americans, or 5.5% of Americans age 12 or older, had five or more drinks on the same occasion at least five different days in the past month, which is one possible definition of heavy drinking. Different definitions of what constitutes heavy drinking exist. Thus, if we define heavy drinking differently—for example, as more than two drinks per day—we come up with a much larger slice of the pyramid—three times as large.

Another recent study from the Centers for Disease Control and Prevention for 2005 to 2007 (Center for Substance Abuse Research [CESAR] 2010b) indicated that nearly two-thirds (61%) of U.S. adults are current drinkers. The majority of these current drinkers were infrequent drinkers (11 drinks or less in the past year) or light drinkers

---

[1]Consumption includes beer, wine, and spirits but not ciders and wine coolers.

KEY TERMS

teetotalers
individuals who drink no alcoholic beverages whatsoever; a term in common usage in decades past

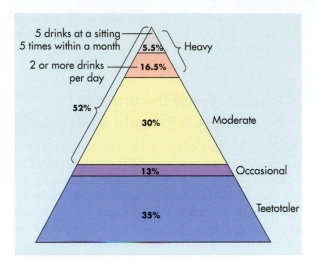

FIGURE 8.2

Broad distribution of drinking behaviors.

(3 drinks or less per week). Around one-fourth were moderate drinkers and 8% were heavier drinkers.

■ Dual Problems: Underage and Adult Drinking

As we saw in Figure 8.1, concerning age, alcohol consumption does not have any boundaries. Although all states have had a legal drinking age of 21 since 1988, a high percentage of the underage population drinks alcohol. Overall, in looking at a larger and more detailed picture of the percentages and types of groups reporting alcohol use in 2008, the following findings are reported (SAMHSA 2009):

Underage Alcohol Use

1. In 2008, about 10.1 million persons ages 12 to 20 (26.4% of this age group) reported drinking alcohol in the past month. Approximately 6.6 million (17.4%) were binge drinkers, and 2.1 million (5.5%) were heavy drinkers.
2. In 2008, rates of current, binge, and heavy alcohol use among underage persons declined between 2002 and 2008. Current use dropped from 28.8% to 26.4%, binge use declined from 19.3% to 17.4%, and heavy use declined from 6.2% to 5.5%.
3. Past-month underage alcohol use rates declined between 2002 and 2008.
4. Students may be more likely to drink and drive on prom and graduation nights, according to

a survey of 11th- and 12th-grade students across the country. Nearly all of the students surveyed (90%) said that their peers are more likely to drink and drive on prom night, and 79% report the same for graduation night. Despite this belief, students do not seem to think that driving on these nights is dangerous. Less than one-third (29%) reported that they believe that driving on prom night comes with a high degree of danger, and 25% said the same for graduation night. These findings suggest that there is a need to provide high school students with prevention messages that paint an accurate picture of the risks and consequences for drinking and driving during prom and graduation season (CESAR 2010a).

Alcohol Use: Age 12 or Older by Ethnicity and Race

5. **Figure 8.3A** shows that among persons age 12 or older in 2008, whites were more likely than other racial/ethnic groups to report current use of alcohol (56.2%). The rates were 47.5% for persons reporting two or more races, 43.3% for American Indians or Alaska natives, 43.2% for Hispanics, 41.9% for blacks, and 37% for Asians.
6. Among youths ages 12 to 17 in 2008, Asians had lower overall rates of current alcohol use than any other racial/ethnic group (5.7%); 10.1% of black youths, 13.6% of those reporting two or more races, 14.8% of Hispanic youths, and 16.3% of white youths were current drinkers.
7. Figure 8.3A also shows that the rate of binge alcohol use was lowest among Asians (11.9%). Rates for other racial/ethnic groups were 20.4% for blacks, 22.0% for persons reporting two or more races, 24% for whites, 24.4% for American Indians or Alaska Natives, and 25.6% for Hispanics.

Driving Under the Influence of Alcohol

8. **Figure 8.3B** shows that in 2008, driving under the influence of alcohol was associated with age. An estimated 7.2% of 16- or 17-year-olds, 16.7% of 18- to 20-year-olds, and 26.1% of 21- to 25-year-olds reported driving under the influence of alcohol in the past year. Beyond age 25, these rates showed a general decline with increasing age.
9. **Figure 8.3C** shows that in 2008, an estimated 12.4% of persons age 12 or older drove under

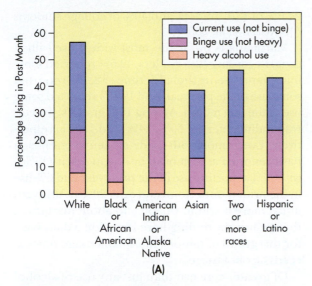

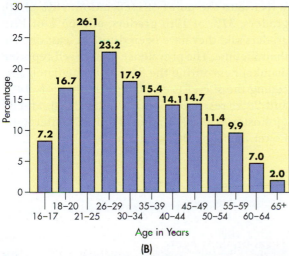

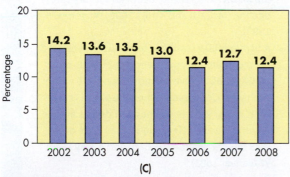

FIGURE 8.3

(**A**) Current, binge, and heavy alcohol use among persons by race/ethnicity, 2008. (**B**) Driving under the influence of alcohol in the past year among persons age 16 or older, by age, 2008. (**C**) Driving under the influence of alcohol in the past year among persons age 12 or older, 2008.

Source: Substance Abuse and Mental Health Services Administration (SAMHSA). *Results from the 2008 National Survey on Drug Use and Health: National Findings.* Office of Applied Studies, NSDUH Series H-36, DHHS Publication No. SMA 09-4435. Rockville, MD, 2009.

the influence of alcohol at least once in the past year. This percentage has dropped since 2002, when it was 14.2%. The 2008 estimate corresponds to 30.9 million persons.

10. Though not shown in any of the three figures in Figure 8.3, among persons age 12 or older, males were more likely than females (16.0% vs. 9.0%) to drive under the influence of alcohol in the past year.

Education and Alcohol Use

11. Among adults age 18 or older, the rate of past-month alcohol use increased with increasing levels of education. Among adults with less than a high school education, 36.8% were current drinkers in 2008, significantly lower than the 67.9% of college graduates who were current drinkers. However, among adults age 26 or older, binge and heavy alcohol use rates were lower among college graduates (19.5% and 4.6%, respectively) than among those who had not completed college (23.2% and 7.0%, respectively).

College Students and Alcohol Use

12. Young adults ages 18 to 22 enrolled full time in college were more likely than their peers not enrolled full time (i.e., part-time college students and persons not currently enrolled in college) to use alcohol in the past month, binge drink, and drink heavily. Among full-time college students in 2008, 61.0% were current drinkers, 40.5% binge drank, and 16.3% were heavy drinkers. Among those not enrolled full time in college, these rates were 54.2%, 38.1%, and 13.0%, respectively. Rates of current alcohol use and binge use for full-time college students decreased from 2007, when they were 63.7% and 43.6%, respectively.

13. The pattern of higher rates of current alcohol use, binge alcohol use, and heavy alcohol use among full-time college students compared with rates for others ages 18 to 22 has remained consistent since 2002.

Employment Status and Alcohol Use

14. The rate of current alcohol use was 63% for full-time employed adults age 18 or older in 2008, higher than the rate for unemployed adults (55.5%). However, the rate of heavy use for unemployed persons was 12.8%, which was higher than the rate of 8.8% for full-time employed persons. There was no significant difference in binge drinking between full-time

employed adults (30.3%) and unemployed adults (33.4%).

15. Most binge and heavy alcohol users were employed in 2008. Among 55.9 million adult binge drinkers, 44.6 million (79.7%) were employed either full or part time. Among 16.8 million heavy drinkers, 13.1 million (78.0%) were employed.

16. Rates of binge and heavy alcohol use did not change significantly between 2007 and 2008 for full-time employed or unemployed adults. However, the number of unemployed binge and heavy drinkers did increase (from 2.3 million to 3.0 million for binge use and from 851,000 to 1.2 million for heavy use).

Alcohol and the Very Young

Use of either of the two major licit drugs, alcohol and cigarettes, remains more widespread than use of any of the illicit drugs. Alcohol has been tried by 38.9% of current 8th graders, 58.3% of 10th graders, 78.9% of 12th graders, and 85.3% of college students; active use is also widespread. Most important is the prevalence of occasions of heavy drinking—five or more drinks in a row at least once in the prior 2-week period—which was reported by 8.1% of 8th graders, 16% of 10th graders,

24.6% of 12th graders, and 40% of college students (Johnston et al. 2009).

Marijuana is by far the most widely used illicit drug. Regarding 12th graders, 42.6% reported some marijuana use in their lifetime, 32.4% reported some use in the past year, and 19.4% reported some use in the past month. Among 10th graders, the corresponding rates are 30%, 24%, and 13.8%, respectively. Even among 8th-grade students, marijuana has been used at least once by one in seven (15%), with 11% reporting use in the prior year and 6% use in the prior month (Johnston et al. 2009). Although much more is said in Chapter 13 about marijuana, the noteworthy finding here is that on a daily basis for this group of minors, marijuana usage now exceeds alcohol usage.

Of greater concern than just any use of alcohol is its use to the point of inebriation: 18% of 8th graders, 37% of 10th graders, and 55% of 12th graders said they have been drunk at least once in their lifetime. The prevalence rates of self-reported drunkenness during the 30 days immediately preceding the survey are strikingly high—5%, 14%, and 28%, respectively, for grades 8, 10, and 12 (Johnston et al. 2009). (See "Point/Counterpoint: Lower the Legal Drinking Age?")

▶ Point/Counterpoint Lower the Legal Drinking Age?

The United States, Pakistan, Palau, and Sri Lanka are the only four countries throughout the world that set the minimum legal drinking age at 21 (see Table 8.1). A clear majority of countries, 82 of them, such as Argentina, Australia, China, Denmark, France, Ireland, Israel, and the United Kingdom, to name a few, specify a minimum age of 18. Thirteen other countries, such as Belgium, Germany, Greece, Italy, Luxemburg, Norway, Poland, and Portugal, set the legal drinking age to 16. Sixteen countries, such as Albania, Fiji, Ghana, Jamaica, Morocco, and Vietnam, do not specify any legal age for alcohol consumption (Hanson 2009a).

Arguments against lowering the legal limit for consuming alcohol are as follows:

- A higher minimum legal drinking age (MLDA) is effective in preventing alcohol-related deaths and injuries among youth. When the MLDA is lowered, injury and death rates increase; when

the MLDA is increased, death and injury rates decline (McCartt and Kirley 2006; Wagenaar 1993).

- A higher MLDA results in fewer alcohol-related problems among youth, and the 21-year-old MLDA saves the lives of more than 1000 youth each year. Conversely, when the MLDA is lowered, motor vehicle crashes and deaths among youth increase. At least 50 studies have evaluated this correlation (McCartt and Kirley 2006; Wagenaar 1993).

- Research shows that when the MLDA is 21, people younger than age 21 drink less overall and continue to do so through their early twenties (O'Malley and Wagenaar 1991).

- Higher MLDAs reduce traffic fatalities involving drivers 18 to 20 years old by saving approximately 1000 lives each year (American Medical Association 2011).

Lower the Legal Drinking Age? (*continued*)

- "Young drivers are less likely than adults to drive after drinking alcohol, but their crash risk is substantially higher when they do" (McCartt and Kirley 2006).
- "...a preponderance of evidence shows that MLDA is an effective deterrent to underage drinking and driving and has reduced alcohol-related crashes among young drivers" (McCartt and Kirley 2006).

Arguments for lowering the legal limit for consuming alcohol are as follows:

- The United States has the strictest youth drinking laws in western civilization and yet has the most drinking-related problems among its young. And there seems to be a connection between these two facts (Hanson 2009b)
- A study of a large sample of young people between the ages of 16 and 19 in Massachusetts and New York after Massachusetts raised its drinking age revealed that the average, self-reported daily alcohol consumption in Massachusetts did not decline in comparison with New York (Hanson 1999).
- Comparison of college students attending schools in states that had maintained, for at least 10 years, a minimum drinking age of 21 with those in states that had similarly maintained minimum drinking ages below 21 revealed few differences in drinking problems (Hanson 1999).
- A study of all 50 states and the District of Columbia found "a positive relationship between the purchase age and single-vehicle fatalities." Thus, single-vehicle fatalities were found to be more frequent in those states with high purchase ages (Hanson 1999).
- Comparison of drinking before and after the passage of raised minimum age legislation has generally revealed little impact on behavior. For example, a study that examined college students' drinking behavior before and after an increase in the minimum legal drinking age from 18 to 19 in New York found the law had no impact on underage students' consumption rates, intoxication rates, drinking attitudes, or drinking problems. These studies were corroborated by other researchers at a different college in the same state (Hanson 1999).

- An examination of East Carolina University students' intentions regarding their behavior following passage of the age-21 drinking law revealed that only 6% intended to stop drinking, 70% planned to change their drinking location, 21% expected to use a false or borrowed identification to obtain alcohol, and 22% intended to use other drugs. Anecdotal statements by students indicated the belief by some that it "might be easier to hide a little pot in my room than a six pack of beer" (Hanson 1999).

Research and the information from sources in this chapter indicate that with regard to under-21 alcohol violations, the United States continues to have serious problems. Thus, we are not any better than most countries regarding the percentage of minors consuming alcohol, despite our unique minimum age-21 requirement for alcohol consumption. What about the idea that instead of prohibiting alcohol consumption to those under age 21 (which to date continues to be ineffective), we need to teach moderation at an early age so that the percentage of youth who decide to consume alcohol can learn to do so responsibly? Because the age-21 requirement has not deterred our nation's youth from consuming alcohol and in light of younger and younger age groups consuming alcohol, do you think it is time to reconsider lowering the age limit of alcohol consumption so that:

1. We are more in alignment with the majority of countries. Eighty-two countries at present allow alcohol consumption at 18 years of age and older.
2. We can eliminate costly, burdensome, and unnecessary underage drinking violations. These infractions with the law include fines, legal costs, imprisonment, court time, legal expenses, and introducing our nation's youth into the criminal justice system (which many believe should remain "lean and mean" so it can effectively prohibit and prosecute serious law violators).
3. We can teach responsible drinking and drinking in moderation, and alcohol consumption can be promoted and taught to be a "normal" part of behavior when eating or socializing with friends (like consuming coffee or fruit juice). Such prevention measures can clearly emphasize that excessive alcohol consumption is a sign of immaturity and lack of self-respect.

(*continued*)

Lower the Legal Drinking Age? (continued)

How successful do you think a campaign calling for lowering the legal drinking age would be with (1) family members, (2) your school, (3) your community, (4) your city/town, and (5) American society in general? Would it be successful? If yes, why? If no, why not? Have you had any experiences in foreign countries where alcohol consumption was not severely restricted? If so, what did you observe?

In essence, do you think we should try to change the current drinking laws, in light of the fact that the current laws continue to be ineffective? Why are we not like other nations with regard to age limits on the use of alcohol? How important is it for the United States to be like other nations?

Sources: American Medical Association (AMA). "Facts About Youth and Alcohol." Chicago, IL: AMA Newsletter, 2011; Hanson, D. J. "Binge Drinking." Potsdam, NY: Sociology Department, State University of New York, 2009. Available at: http://www2.potsdam.edu/hansondj/BingeDrinking.html. Accessed March 14, 2011; Hanson, D. J. "Why We Should Lower the Drinking Age to 19." Potsdam, NY: Sociology Department, State University of New York, 2009. Available at: http://www2.potsdam.edu/hansondj/YouthIssues/1046348192.html. Accessed March 14, 2011; McCartt, A. T., and B. B. Kirley. "Minimum Purchase Age Laws: How Effective Are They in Reducing Alcohol-Impaired Driving?" Arlington, VA: Insurance Institute for Highway Safety, 2006. Available at: http://onlinepubs.trb.org/onlinepubs/circulars/ec123.pdf. Accessed March 14, 2011; O'Malley, P. M., and A. C. Wagenaar. "Effects of Minimum Drinking Age Laws on Alcohol Use, Related Behaviors and Traffic Crash Involvement Among American Youth: 1976–1987." *Journal of Studies on Alcohol* 52 (1991): 478–491; and Wagenaar, A. C. "Minimum Drinking Age and Alcohol Availability to Youth: Issues and Research Needs." In *Economics and the Prevention of Alcohol-Related Problems*, edited by M. E. Hilton and B. Bloss, 175–200. National Institute on Alcohol Abuse and Alcoholism (NIAAA) Research Monograph No. 25, NIH Pub. No. 93-3513. Bethesda, MD: NIAAA, 1993.

With regard to the three major types of alcohol (beer, wine coolers, and liquor) used by junior high and high school students, we find that from 9th through 12th grades, alcohol consumption increases dramatically (Johnston et al. 2009; Pride USA Survey 1998). In looking at 12th graders' consumption of alcohol, white underage students are much more likely to binge drink (30%) compared with African American students (11%) and Hispanic students (22%). Finally, boys in 12th grade are more likely to drink alcohol on a daily basis compared with girls of the same grade and age; daily use among boys is reported at 4%, whereas the rate among girls is reported at 1.7%. Boys are more likely than girls to drink large quantities of alcohol in a single sitting; 28% of 12th-grade males reported drinking five or more drinks in a row 2 weeks prior to being surveyed, but only 21% of the 12th-grade females drank the same amount. When reviewing the statistics, keep in mind that females differ from males in terms of their alcohol drinking capacities (see Chapter 7 for more details).

■ Economic Costs of Alcohol Abuse

It important to realize that "Most of the costs of alcohol abuse result from the adverse effects of alcohol consumption on health" (About.com 2010a). In estimating the costs of alcohol abuse as it relates to illnesses, three major categories that have to be included are: ". . . (1) expenditures on medical treatment (a large proportion of which is for the many medical consequences of alcohol consumption; the remainder is for treatment of alcohol abuse and dependence themselves), (2) the lost productivity that results from workers' abuse of alcohol, and (3) the losses to society from premature deaths that are due to alcohol problems" (About.com 2010a).

The economic costs of alcohol abuse to society are staggering. A recent statement by Ting-Kai Li, MD, Director of the National Institute on Alcohol Abuse and Alcoholism (NIAAA), highlighted the following (Li 2008, p. 1):

According to the Centers for Disease Control and Prevention, alcohol is the third leading cause of preventable death in the U.S. Even more importantly from a public health perspective, alcohol misuse negatively affects the quality of life for millions of Americans. The World Health Organization ranks alcohol as one of the top ten causes of Disability Adjusted Life Years (DALYs) in the United States. Alcohol also contributes to a number of the other leading causes of DALYs, e.g., motor vehicle accidents, brain and liver disease, and cancer. Alcohol problems cost the U.S. an estimated $185 billion annually, with almost half the cost resulting from lost productivity due to alcohol-related disabilities. According to NIAAA's National Epidemiologic Survey on Alcohol and Related Conditions, over 18 million people ages 18 and older suffer from alcohol abuse or dependence and only 7 percent of them receive

Table 8.1 **World Minimum Drinking Ages**

The legal drinking age for different countries varies extensively.

NO MINIMUM DRINKING AGE	Norway*	China	Lithuania	Turkey
Albania	Poland	Columbia	Malawi	Turkmenistan
Armenia	Portugal	Congo, Republic of	Mauritius	Uganda
Azerbaijan	Spain (age 16 in Asturias)	Costa Rica	Mexico	Ukraine
Comoros		Croatia	Moldova	United Kingdom (age 5 at home or age 16 out with parents)
Equatorial Guinea	**AGE 17**	Czech Republic	Mongolia	
Fiji	Cyprus	Denmark	Mozambique	
Gabon		Dominican Republic	Namibia	Uruguay
Ghana	**AGE 18**	Ecuador	New Zealand	Vanuatu
Guinea-Bissau	Algeria	Egypt*	Niger	Venezuela
Jamaica	Argentina	El Salvador	Nigeria	Zambia
Kyrgyzstan	Australia	Eritrea	Norway*	Zimbabwe
Morocco	Bahamas	Estonia	Panama	
Solomon Islands*	Barbados	Ethiopia	Papua New Guinea	**AGE 19**
Swaziland*	Belarus	Finland	Peru	Nicaragua
Togo	Belize	France	Philippines	South Korea
Vietnam	Bermuda	Guatemala	Russia	
	Bolivia	Guyana	Samoa	**AGE 20**
AGE 16	Botswana	Hungary	Seychelles	Iceland
Antigua	Brazil	Indonesia	Singapore	Japan
Barbados	British Virgin Islands	Ireland	Slovak Republic	Paraguay
Belgium	Bulgaria	Israel	South Africa	
Georgia	Cameroon	Jamaica	Spain (age 16 in Asturias)	**AGE 21**
Germany	Canada (age 19 in some provinces)	Kazakhstan	St. Maarten	Pakistan (for non-Muslims, prohibited for Muslims)
Greece*	Cape Verde	Kenya	Sweden*	
Italy	Central African Republic	Latvia	Thailand	Palau
Luxemburg		Lesotho	Trinidad and Tobago	Sri Lanka
Malta	Chile			United States

*Various qualifications and/or exception apply.

Source: Hanson, D. J. "Minimum Legal Drinking Ages around the World." Available at: http://www2.potsdam.edu/hansondj/LegalDrinkingAge.html. Accessed March 9, 2011.

any form of treatment. Furthermore, heavy drinkers who do not have dependence but are nevertheless at risk for adverse health and psychosocial outcomes are seldom identified. The consequences of alcohol misuse can affect both drinkers and those around them at all stages of life, from damage due to alcohol exposure of the developing embryo, to injuries, to tissue and organ damage resulting from chronic, heavy alcohol use. Therefore, for NIAAA to achieve its goal of reducing the heavy burden of illness from alcohol misuse, the Institute's research focus must be broader than simply reducing alcohol-related mortality; it must encompass reducing the risk for all of the aforementioned negative alcohol-related outcomes at all stages of life.

From a global perspective, when including illness, accidents, and crimes connected to alcohol, the costs add up to more than $250 billion yearly (Reuters Limited 1999). Another estimate indicates that in the United States, alcohol abuse and addiction are a major burden to society. Estimates of the total overall costs of alcohol abuse in the United States—including health- and crime-related costs as well as losses in productivity—exceed $235 billion (National Institute on Drug Abuse [NIDA] 2011).

The following are some of the current results of alcohol abuse shown in **Figure 8.4** (NIAAA 2000; SAMHSA 2009):

- The estimated cost of alcohol abuse and alcoholism (not including other drugs) to the United States was approximately $184.6 billion in 1998. (This cost rises approximately 12.5% yearly.)
- This estimate amounted to roughly $683 for every man, woman, and child living in the United States in 1998.

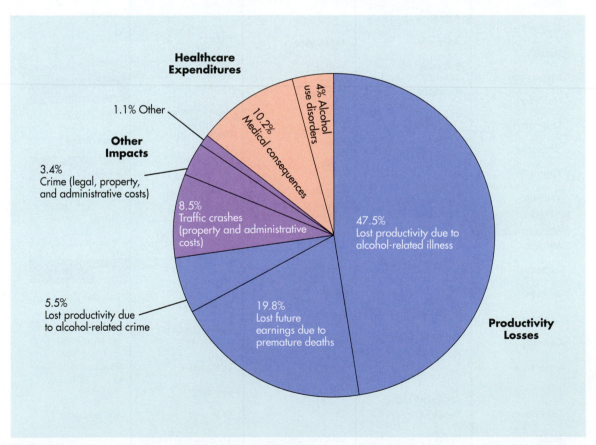

FIGURE 8.4

Economic costs of alcohol abuse, United States, 1998 (total estimated cost: $184.6 billion).

Source: Harwood, H., D. Fountain, and G. Livermore. *The Economic Costs of Alcohol and Drug Abuse in the United States, 1992.* Report prepared for the National Institute on Drug Abuse and the National Institute on Alcohol and Alcoholism, National Institutes of Health, U.S. Department of Health and Human Services. NIH Pub. No. 98-4327. Rockville, MD: National Institute on Drug Abuse, 1998.

- More than 70% of the estimated costs of alcohol abuse were attributed to lost productivity ($134.2 billion), most of which resulted from alcohol-related illness or premature death.
- Most of the remaining estimated costs were expenditures for healthcare services to treat alcohol use disorder and the medical consequences of alcohol consumption ($26.3 billion, or 14.3% of the total), property and administrative costs of alcohol-related motor vehicle crashes ($15.7 billion, or 8.5%), and various criminal justice system costs of alcohol-related crime ($6.3 billion, or 3.4%).

Regarding how the burden of the costs of alcohol abuse is distributed across various segments of society, **Figure 8.5** shows the following (published in NIAAA 2000; reference Harwood 2000; Harwood et al. 1998):

- Much of the economic burden of alcohol abuse falls on segments of the population other than the alcohol abusers themselves.

- Approximately 45% of the estimated total cost is borne by alcohol abusers and their families, almost all of which is due to lost or reduced earnings.
- Approximately 20% of the total estimated cost of alcohol abuse is borne by the federal government and 18% by state and local governments.
- Nearly three-fourths of the costs borne by the federal government take the form of reduced tax revenues resulting from alcohol-related productivity losses, and most of the remaining federal burden relates to healthcare costs. The burden on state and local governments (reductions in tax revenue) resulting from such productivity losses accounts for just over half, while 38% is for criminal justice and motor-vehicle–related costs. Private insurance arrangements (including life, health, auto, fire, and other kinds of insurance) shoulder the burden for 10% of the total estimated cost, primarily in the area of healthcare costs and motor vehicle crashes.

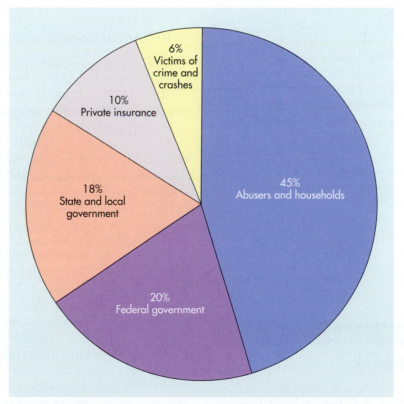

FIGURE 8.5

Distribution of the costs of alcohol abuse.

Source: Harwood, H., D. Fountain, and G. Livermore. *The Economic Costs of Alcohol and Drug Abuse in the United States, 1992.* Report prepared for the National Institute on Drug Abuse and the National Institute on Alcohol and Alcoholism, National Institutes of Health, U.S. Department of Health and Human Services. NIH Pub. No. 98-4327. Rockville, MD: National Institute on Drug Abuse, 1998.

- Six percent of the total costs are borne by victims of alcohol-related crimes (including homicide) and by nondrinking victims of alcohol-related motor vehicle crashes.

Other findings include that the percentage of traffic fatalities that are alcohol related remains at around 40%, according to data from the National Highway Transportation Safety Administration's Fatality Analysis Reporting System (FARS) (CESAR 2005). Another set of findings in a published report by the National Institute on Alcohol Abuse and Alcoholism (NIAAA 2000) discloses the following:

- Each year, more than 107,400 people die because of alcohol-related abuse.
- Productivity losses resulting from alcohol-related illness were estimated at $87.6 billion for 1998.
- Total costs attributed to alcohol-related motor vehicle crashes were estimated to be $24.7 billion.
- Expenditures for alcohol-related crime totaled $6.2 billion, and $17.4 billion for illicit drugs.
- Alcohol abuse is estimated to have contributed to 25% to 30% of violent crime.
- Alcohol is officially linked to at least half of all highway fatalities, and that figure includes only legal intoxication. In all states, the cutoff for the blood alcohol level is 0.08%. In as many as 70% of all single-vehicle fatal crashes on weekend nights, the driver was legally intoxicated, and this proportion holds during most weekends throughout the United States. Interestingly, this single issue has been the only alcohol problem that has inspired very vocal and effective groups to lobby for stricter enforcement of laws against alcohol-impaired automobile driving. Groups such as MADD (Mothers Against Drunk Driving) and SADD (Students Against Drunk Driving) are the largest prevention organizations in the nation.

History of Alcohol in America

Drinking Patterns

From a peak in 1830, when the amount of alcohol ingested by the average American was 7.1 gallons per year, use declined continuously until 1871–1880, when the average was 1.72 gallons. Numbers then rose to a high in 1906–1910 to 2.6 gallons and then fell to 1.96 gallons just before Prohibition, 1916–1919. Under Prohibition, less than a gallon

Current advertisement stressing the need to have a designated non-alcohol–consuming driver if others are consuming alcohol.

of absolute alcohol per person was consumed annually, on average. During the last half of the 20th century, alcohol consumption stayed constant, within the 2- to 3-gallon range. Wine and beer gained in popularity, while the popularity of "spirits" (hard liquor) declined (Hanson 2009b; Lender 1987).

Historical Considerations

Alcoholic beverages have played an important role in the history of the United States as well as in most countries throughout the world. Most likely, fermentation was the first method for making alcohol, dating to 4200 BC. As early as 100 AD, it appears that brandy was the first distilled beverage. In Ireland and Scotland, whiskey was first distilled in the 1400s, and gin began appearing in the 1600s, after being initially distilled by a Flemish physician. Other types of liquor also have distinct origins. For example, rum was first invented in Barbados in the 1650s. Bourbon was first made near Georgetown, Kentucky, in the late 1700s. In the United States, the first distillery was created in the 1600s in the area that is now New York City.

In colonial America, alcohol was viewed very favorably. From an economic standpoint, the manufacturing of rum, ". . . which is the residue left after sugar has been made from sugar cane . . . was introduced to the world, and presumably invented, by the first European settlers in the West Indies (no one knows when it was first produced or by what individual)" (Hanson 2009b). Rum became New England's largest and most profitable industry in the so-called triangle trade. It acquired this name because Yankee traders would sail with a cargo of rum to the West Coast of Africa, where they bargained the "demon" for slaves. From there, they sailed to the West Indies, where they bartered the slaves for molasses. Finally, they took the molasses back to New England, where it was made into rum, thus completing the triangle. For many years, New England distilleries flourished and the slave trade proved highly lucrative (see **Figure 8.6**). "[In] . . . 1657, a rum distillery was operating in Boston. It was highly successful and within a generation the manufacture of rum would become colonial New England's largest and most prosperous industry" (Hanson 2009b; Roueche 1963, p. 178). This slave trade triangle continued until 1807, when an act of Congress prohibited the importation of slaves.

From a social standpoint, the consumption of alcohol was seen as a part of life. The colonial tavern "was a key institution, the center of social and political life" (Levine 1983, p. 66). In the 17th and 18th centuries, alcohol flowed freely at weddings, baptisms, and funerals. Especially in the 18th century, people drank at home, at work, and while traveling. In the 19th century, largely because of the temperance movement, taverns became stigmatized and were viewed as dens where the lower classes, immigrants, and mostly men would congregate. "Any drinking, [Lyman Beecher] argued, was a step toward 'irreclaimable' slavery to liquor" (Lender and Martin 1987). People in the 19th century began to report that they were addicted to alcohol. Here is where the temperance movement had its effects in bringing about a change in attitudes regarding drinking.

FIGURE 8.6
Slave trade triangle.

From the Temperance Movement (1830–1850) to the Prohibition Era (1920–1933)

The time from the temperance movement to the Prohibition era was a very turbulent period in the history of alcohol in America. The period of heaviest drinking in America began during Jefferson's term of office (1800–1808). The nation was going through uneasy times, trying to stay out of the war between Napoleon and the British allies. The transient population had increased, especially in the seaport cities, and the migration westward had begun. Heavy drinking had become a major form of recreation and a "social lubricant" at elections and public gatherings. The temperance movement never began with the intention of stopping alcohol consumption but with the goal of encouraging moderation. In fact, in the 1830s, at the peak of this early campaign, temperance leaders (many of whom drank beer and wine) recommended abstinence only from distilled spirits, not from the other forms of alcohol such as beer or wine. This movement developed from several very vocal spiritual leaders who preached that alcohol harms "the health and physical energies of a nation" and that alcohol interfered with the spreading of the gospel. Later, as is explained shortly in more detail, the temperance movement went against all other forms of alcohol.

Because the temperance movement was closely tied to the abolitionist movement as well as to the African American church, African Americans were preeminent promoters of temperance. Leaders such as Frederick Douglass stated, "it was as well to be a slave to master, as to whisky and rum. When a slave was drunk, the slaveholder had no fear that he would plan an insurrection; no fear that he would escape to the north. It was the sober, thinking slave who was dangerous, and needed the vigilance of his master to keep him a slave" (Douglass 1892, p. 133).

Over the next decades, partly in connection with religious revivals, the meaning of temperance was gradually altered from "moderation" to "total abstinence." All alcoholic beverages were attacked as being unnecessary, harmful to health, and inherently poisonous. Over the course of the 19th century, the demand gradually arose for total prohibition (Austin 1978).

By the late 19th and early 20th centuries, a number of countries either passed legislation or created alcohol restrictions. Most of these laws and restrictions eventually failed. In the United States, attempts to control, restrict, or abolish alcohol were made, but they all met with abysmal failure. From 1907 to

1919, 34 states passed prohibition laws. Finally, on a national scale, the 18th Amendment to the Constitution was ratified in 1919 in an attempt to stop the rapid spread of alcohol addiction. In January 1920, alcohol was outlawed. As soon as such a widely used substance became illegal, criminal activity to satisfy the huge demand for alcohol flourished. Illegal outlets developed for purchasing liquor. Numerous not-so-secret **speakeasies** developed as illegal establishments where people could buy and consume alcoholic beverages, despite the laws of Prohibition. **Bootlegging** was a widely accepted activity. In effect, such "dens of sin" filled the vacuum for many drinkers during Prohibition.

During the temperance movement and Prohibition period, doctors and druggists prescribed whiskey and other alcohol known as **patent medicines** (see "Case in Point: The Great American Fraud").

By 1928, doctors made an estimated $40 million per year writing prescriptions for whiskey. Patent medicines flourished, with alcohol contents as high as 50%. Whisko, a "nonintoxicating stimulant," was 55 proof (or 27.5% alcohol). Another, Kaufman's Sulfur Bitters, was labeled "contains no alcohol" but was 40 proof (20% alcohol) and did not contain sulfur. There were dozens of others, many of which contained other types of drugs, such as opium.

Both Prohibitionists and critics of the law were shocked by the violent gang wars that broke out between rivals seeking to control the lucrative black market in liquor. More important, a general disregard for the law developed. Corruption among law enforcement agents was widespread and organized crime began and grew to be an enormous illegitimate business. In reaction to these developments, political support rallied against Prohibition, resulting in its repeal in 1933 by the 21st Amendment. Early in the 20th century, women suffragettes had been prominent temperance organizers; paradox-

ically, flappers organized against Prohibition and were vital in gathering the signatures for its repeal.

Three main developments occurred because of Prohibition. First, alcohol use continued to diminish for the first 2 or 3 years after Prohibition was in effect. This trend had begun several years before the law was passed. More importantly, after 3 years of steady decline, the use of distilled liquors rose every year afterward. Further, even minors were becoming addicted to alcohol during this period.

Second, enforcement of laws against alcohol use was thwarted by corrupt law enforcement officials, enforcement was uneven (in some areas of the United States, enforcement was lax, whereas in other areas it was very strict), and law enforcement experienced more than 50% turnover in its ranks. Corruption of law enforcement officials stands out as a paramount concern. Reportedly, 10% of law enforcement was "on the take" and had to be continually discharged.

Third, among the Western Europeans who immigrated to the United States en masse during this period, the consumption of alcohol was culturally prescribed. Prohibition against alcohol usage to the Italian, German, French, Polish, Irish, and other European-based immigrants was perceived as unnecessary and an infringement to the right to common existence. One 93-year-old Italian American émigré to Chicago exemplified some of these attitudes:

> Well, when we were not allowed to drink because of the government, I thought it was a stupid law. Many of us here in the neighborhood [a fading Italian American community in Chicago's West Side and the original home of Venturelli] made lots of money as "alki cookers."

Al Capone ("Scarface") (center), the undisputed leader of Chicago's gang scene during Prohibition, made millions of dollars in his bootlegging operations until he was convicted of tax evasion in 1931 and eventually imprisoned in Alcatraz.

KEY TERMS

speakeasies
places where alcoholic beverages were illegally consumed and sold during the Prohibition era from 1920–1933 (in some states, Prohibition was longer than this period of time)

bootlegging
making, distributing, and selling alcoholic beverages during the Prohibition era

patent medicines
the ingredients in these uncontrolled "medicines" were secret, often consisting of large amounts of colored water, alcohol, cocaine, or opiates

▶Case in Point The Great American Fraud: Patent Medicines◀

In the late 1800s and early 1900s, before the days of FDA legislation, the sales of uncontrolled medicines flourished and became widespread. Many of these products were called patent medicines, which signified that the ingredients were secret, not that they were patented. The law of the day seemed to be more concerned with someone's recipe being stolen than with preventing harm to the naive consumer. Some of these patent medicines included toxic ingredients such as acetanilide in Bromo-Seltzer and Orangeine and prussic (hydrocyanic) acid in Shiloh's Consumption Cure.

Most patent medicines appear to have been composed largely of either colored water or alcohol, with an occasional added ingredient such as opium or cocaine. Hostetter's Stomach Bitters with 44% alcohol could easily have been classified as liquor. Sale of Peruna (28% alcohol) was prohibited to Native Americans because of its high alcoholic content. Birney's Catarrh Cure contained 4% cocaine. Wistar's Balsam of Wild Cherry, Dr. King's Discovery for Consumption, Mrs. Winslow's Soothing Syrup, and several others contained opiates as well as alcohol.

The medical profession of the mid- and late 19th century was ill prepared to do battle with the ever-present manufacturers and distributors of patent medicines. Qualified physicians during this time were rare. Much more common were medical practitioners with poor training and little scientific understanding. In fact, many of these early physicians practiced a brand of medicine that was generally useless and frequently more life-threatening than the patent medicines themselves.

In 1905, *Collier's Magazine* ran a series of articles called the "Great American Fraud," which warned of the abuse of patent medicines. This brought the problem to the public's attention (Adams 1906). *Collier's* coined the phrase "dope fiend" from "dope," an African word meaning "intoxicating substance." The American Medical Association (AMA) joined in and widely distributed reprints of the *Collier's* story to inform the public about the dangers of these medicines, even though the AMA itself accepted advertisements for patent medicines that physicians knew were addicting. The publicity created mounting pressure on Congress and President Theodore Roosevelt to do something about these fraudulent products. In 1905, Roosevelt proposed that a law be enacted to regulate interstate commerce of misbranded and adulterated foods, drinks, and drugs. This movement received further impetus when Upton Sinclair's book *The Jungle* was published in 1906—this nauseatingly realistic exposé detailed how immigrant laborers worked under appalling conditions of filth, disease, putrefaction, and other extreme exploitations at Chicago's stockyards.

Two substances used in patent medicines helped shape attitudes that would form the basis of regulatory policies for years to come: the opium derivatives (narcotic drugs, such as heroin and morphine) and cocaine (see Chapter 3).

This poster advertises one of the patent medicines that contained liberal doses of opium and a high concentration of alcohol. This medicine was widely used to treat tuberculosis ("consumption") around the turn of the century, when more than 25% of all adult deaths were attributable to this disease. The U.S. government finally forced the remedy off the market by 1920.

We would make the alcohol in our bathtubs and sell to other people or even to those mafia types. Oh, it was horrible cheap and crappy alcohol; if you drank too much the night before, it gave you headaches sometimes for days. On Sunday afternoons, if you walked through this neighborhood in the hot summer days, you could smell the alcohol oozing from people's windows. Nearly everyone my mother's and father's age and older at the time made extra money as alki cookers. It was actually a good law [referring to Prohibition] for making a few bucks to help out the family expenses. No one around here gave a damn about the law, because too many were "on the take" so-to-say . . . and it was not just us [referring to the local Italian Americans]. At least for us when we meet together and eat for fun, alcohol is like the air we breathe. Who the hell is going to change that, especially something so deep? *(From Venturelli's research files, male neighborhood resident, age 93, May 26, 2000)*

Defining Alcoholics

As discussed in Chapter 7 and at the beginning of this chapter, creating absolute definitions or categories of behavior that represent an alcoholic type is very difficult because all behaviors vary enormously from one person to the next; thus most behaviors range along a continuum. Adding to this confusion is the fact that some disagreement exists among experts on what the exact criteria should be regarding the definition of an alcoholic. In other words, when can a person be defined as an alcoholic? Is it the daily drinker or the inebriated weekend drinker? What if the excessive drinking only involves one type of liquor, such as beer, which is often considered less potent than hard liquor? What if the person is able to maintain a job and provide for his or her family? How does this type of alcoholic compare with an unemployed resident of skid row? In the minds of many Americans, an alcoholic is a derelict who frequents skid rows, train stations, and bus terminals; panders for money; and sleeps on a park bench at night. Yet, this stereotypical image of an alcoholic represents only a very small percentage of the millions of Americans who qualify as alcoholic by any of the accepted medical definitions. The more typical alcoholic, in fact, is similar to the example of the professor or businessman purchasing alcohol at a liquor store (described at the opening of this chapter). In effect, most functioning alcoholics are secret or closeted drinkers who look very much like everyday working people.

■ Cultural Differences

Although more will be presented later in this chapter about the pervasive role that culture plays in

drinking behavior, we begin with a quote highlighting cultural differences in interpreting alcohol consumption:

> Even definitions of a "problem drinker" differ from one culture to the next. In Poland, loss of productivity tends to demonstrate a drinking problem, while Californians emphasize drunk driving as an important and sometimes key indicator . . . [Among Italian Americans, an inability to provide for one's family because of heavy drinking qualifies a person as an alcoholic.] . . . Some methods of assessing problem drinking look to behavior that leads to a brush with the law. However, drunkenness may or may not lead to disruptive behavior. In the Netherlands, alcoholic beverage consumption is similar to that in Finland and Poland, but there is much less disruptive or public drinking. In these nations, the actual amount of alcohol consumed is not indicated by the arrest figures, the actual amount consumed (as a separate category), and the number of physical ailments caused by excessive alcohol consumption. Secondly, the social response to drunkenness may not be arrest and conviction. Ireland, for example, has traditionally used psychiatric institutions to control drunkenness. (Osterberg 1986, p. 83)

Estimates vary, but it is believed that approximately three-fourths of problem drinkers are men and one-fourth are women. The proportion of women has risen in recent years. This increase occurred for two reasons: (1) Women as problem drinkers are more visible and numerous because they now make up about half of the workforce, and (2) women are more likely to acknowledge the problem and seek treatment, especially if they are in white-collar occupations. Thus, female problem drinkers may now be more visible and more self-assured as well as more numerous.

Next, in attempting to define alcoholism, we turn to models that speak of the state of addiction. **Alcoholism** is a state of physical and psychological addiction to ethanol, a psychoactive substance (see also Chapter 7). It was once viewed as a vice and dismissed as sinful, but over the years, there has been a shift from this perspective to one that views alcoholism as a disease. The sinfulness perspective failed to focus on the fact that alcoholism is an addiction—an illness—and not the result of a lack of personal discipline and morality.

Attempts to expand the basic definition of alcoholism to include symptoms of the condition and psychological and sociological factors have been difficult; no one definition satisfies everyone. The World Health Organization defines alcohol dependence syndrome as a syndrome characterized by a state, mental and usually also physical, resulting from drinking alcohol. This state is characterized by behavioral and other responses that include a compulsion to drink alcohol (like an unquenchable thirst) on a continuous or periodic basis to experience its psychic effects and sometimes to avoid the discomfort of its absence; tolerance may or may not be present (NIAAA 1980).

Another more classic explanation of alcoholism that remains popular is, "Alcoholism is a chronic behavioral disorder manifested by repeated drinking of alcoholic beverages in excess of the dietary and social uses of the community, to an extent that interferes with the drinker's health or his social or economic functioning" (Keller 1958, p. 78). Another definition emphasizes, "Alcoholism is a chronic, primary, hereditary disease that progresses from an early, physiological susceptibility into an addiction characterized by tolerance changes, physiological dependence, and loss of control over drinking. [In this definition], [P]sychological symptoms are secondary to the physiological disease and not relevant to its onset" (Gold 1991, p. 99).

A final definition from Royce and Scratchley (1996, p. 3) defines ". . . alcoholism as a chronic primary illness or disorder characterized by some loss of control over drinking, with habituation or addiction to the drug alcohol, or causing interference in any major life function, for example: health, job, family, friends, legal or spiritual." In their working definition of alcoholism, Royce and Scratchley (1996) list three major factors: "(1) Some loss of control, but it need not be total . . . (2) Dependence or need can be psychological or physiological . . . and (3) Interference with normal functioning" (p. 3).

In summary, the preceding definitions either list or hint at the following major components of alcoholism (NIAAA 2007):

- *Craving:* An overwhelming compulsion to drink even when not feasible, such as at work, driving a car, mowing a lawn, and so on.
- *Very impaired or loss of control:* An inability to limit one's drinking once drinking has begun; for example, one drink only before going to bed is impossible to control.
- *Physical dependence:* The presence of withdrawal symptoms when attempting to abstain from usage. Such symptoms as nausea, sweating, shakiness, and anxiety about the availability of alcohol are common

- *Tolerance:* A need to continually increase the amount of alcohol consumed to maintain its effects (or to maintain the "buzz").

■ Alcohol Abuse and Alcoholism

When attempting to understand the meaning of chronic drinking, one additional clarification that should be made is to distinguish between **alcohol abuse** and alcoholism. The two explanations of drinking behavior differ as a matter of degree. When speaking of alcohol abuse, the craving, loss of control, and physical dependence just listed as primary manifestations are less prominent and not as pronounced as in alcoholism. There is diminished ability to fulfill obligations and goals; more occasions of drinking at the wrong time, such as while driving; legal problems such as driving under the influence; and relationship problems. Note that many of these problems that result from alcohol abuse are also experienced by alcoholics, but not all manifestations of alcoholics are experienced by alcohol abusers. For example, an alcoholic may repeatedly argue with family members two or three times per week, whereas an alcohol abuser may have fewer occurrences of the same type of alcohol-inspired arguments with a family member. Thus, even though the alcohol abuser has fewer occasions of uncontrollable drinking than the alcoholic, the drinking remains largely uncontrollable when it occurs. For many years, people with drinking problems were lumped together under the label alcoholic, and alcohol abusers were assumed to be suffering from the same illness. Today, because of greater understanding about addiction and addictive behaviors, the distinction between the two terms leads to a more precise understanding of excessive alcohol abuse (see "Here and Now: Are You 'On the Road' to Alcoholism?").

■ Types of Alcoholics

Although written more than 5 decades ago, Jellinek's (1960) original personality typology (characterizations) differentiating the types of alcoholics

KEY TERMS

alcohol abuse
uncontrollable drinking that leads to alcohol craving, loss of control, and physical dependence but with less prominent characteristics than found in alcoholism

Here and Now

Are You "On the Road" to Alcoholism?

Answer the following questions with either a simple "yes" or "no."

1. Do you frequently drink because you have problems or need to relax?
2. When out with friends, do you become irritated or bored when the evening does not lead to the use of alcohol and/or drugs?
3. Do you drink when you get mad at other people, such as your friends or parents?
4. Do you find yourself careless of your loved ones when you're drinking alcohol?
5. Do you often prefer to drink alone?
6. Are your grades suffering because of the time you spend drinking?
7. Do you stop drinking "for good" and then start again?
8. Have you begun to drink in the morning, before school or work?
9. Do you often gulp your drinks?
10. Do you have loss of memory because of your drinking?
11. Do you lie about the amount you drink?
12. Do you ever get into trouble when you are drinking?
13. Do you drink to forget about problems and/or trouble?
14. Do you get drunk when you drink, even when you do not plan to?
15. Do you think you are cool when you can hold your liquor?

If you answered more than one as "yes," you may have a drinking problem that will become increasingly problematic, moving in the direction of alcoholism.

---

remains very important for adding more preciseness in understanding alcohol abuse and its outcomes. Jellinek's categories are as follows:

- *Alpha alcoholism:* Mostly a psychological dependence on alcohol to bolster an inability to cope with life. The alpha type constantly needs alcohol and becomes irritable and anxious when it is not available.
- *Beta alcoholism:* Mostly a social dependence on alcohol. Often, although not exclusively, this type is a heavy beer drinker who continues to meet social and economic obligations. Some nutritional deficiencies can occur, including organic damage such as gastritis and cirrhosis.
- *Gamma alcoholism:* The most severe form of alcoholism. This type of alcoholic suffers from emotional and psychological impairment. Jellinek believed this type of alcoholic suffered from a true disease and progresses from a psychological dependence to physical dependence. Loss of control over when alcohol is consumed and how much is taken characterizes the latter phase of this type of alcoholism.
- *Delta alcoholic:* Called the maintenance drinker (Royce 1989). The person loses control over drinking and cannot abstain for even a day or two. Many wine-drinking countries such as France and Italy contain delta-type alcoholics who sip wine throughout most

of their waking hours. Being "tipsy" but never completely inebriated is typical of the delta alcoholic.
- *Epsilon alcoholic:* This type of alcoholic is characterized as a binge drinker. The epsilon-type drinker drinks excessively for a certain period (for days and sometimes weeks) but then abstains completely from alcohol until the next binge period. The dependence on alcohol is both physical and psychological. Loss of control over the amount consumed is another characteristic of this type of alcoholic.
- *Zeta alcoholic:* This category was added to Jellinek's types to describe the moderate drinker who becomes abusive and violent. Although this type also is referred to as a "pathological drinker" or "mad drunk," zeta types may not be addicted to alcohol.

Another, much more recent classification of alcoholism subtypes includes five alcohol-dependent subtypes created by Dr. Moss and colleagues (National Institutes of Health [NIH] and NIAAA 2007). Quoted extensively, the five types are:

- *Young adult subtype:* 31.5% of U.S. alcoholics. Young adult drinkers, with relatively low rates of co-occurring substance abuse and other mental disorders, a low rate of family alcoholism, and who rarely seek any kind of help for their drinking.

- *Young antisocial subtype:* 21% of U.S. alcoholics. Tend to be in their mid-twenties, and had early onset of regular drinking and alcohol problems. More than half come from families with alcoholism, and about half have a psychiatric diagnosis of antisocial personality disorder. Many have major depression, bipolar disorder, and anxiety problems. More than 75% smoke cigarettes and marijuana, and many have cocaine and opiate addictions. More than one-third of these alcoholics seek help for their drinking.
- *Functional subtype:* 19.5% of U.S. alcoholics. Typically middle-aged, well-educated, with stable jobs and families. About one-third have a multigenerational family history of alcoholism, about one-quarter have major depressive illness sometime in their lives, and nearly 50% are smokers.
- *Intermediate familial subtype:* 19% of U.S. alcoholics. Middle-aged, with about 50% from families with multigenerational alcoholism. Almost half have had clinical depression, and 20% have had bipolar disorder. Most of these individuals smoke cigarettes, and nearly one in five have had problems with cocaine and marijuana use. Only 25% ever seek treatment for their problem drinking.
- *Chronic severe subtype:* 9% of U.S. alcoholics. Composed mostly of middle-aged individuals who had early onset of drinking and alcohol problems, with high rates of antisocial personality disorder and criminality. Almost 80% come from families with multigenerational alcoholism. They have the highest rates of other psychiatric disorders including depression, bipolar disorder, and anxiety disorders as well as high rates of smoking, and marijuana, cocaine, and opiate dependence. Two-thirds of these alcoholics seek help for their drinking problems, making them the most prevalent type of alcoholic in treatment.

Other classifications differentiate alcoholics by their reaction to the drug as quiet, sullen, friendly, or angry types. Another method is to classify alcoholics according to drinking patterns: people with occupational, social, escape, and emotional disorders.

■ Major Traditional Distinctions Between "Wet" and "Dry" Cultures

Before delving into the next section regarding how culture defines and views the use of alcohol, it is interesting to note that traditionally alcohol re-

Many cultural social interactions demand drinking together.

searchers distinguished countries as either wet or dry. In wet cultures, alcohol is integrated into daily life and activities (e.g., is consumed with meals) and is widely available and accessible. In these cultures, abstinence rates are low, and wine is largely the beverage of preference. European countries bordering the Mediterranean have traditionally exemplified wet cultures.

In dry cultures, alcohol consumption is not as common during everyday activities (e.g., it is less frequently a part of meals) and access to alcohol is more restricted. Abstinence is more common, but when drinking occurs, it is more likely to result in intoxication; moreover, wine consumption is less common. Examples of traditionally dry cultures include the Scandinavian countries, the United States, and Canada (Bloomfield et al. 2003b). Although Bloomfied et al. indicate that the wet/dry distinction is less applicable today because of cross-cultural influences resulting in cultural homogenization, past research used the wet/dry distinction for many centuries. Today, the wet/dry distinction is less evident and is not as clear-cut for reasons cited here.

Recent comparative research, however, has found that, especially in Europe, the wet/dry distinction seems to be disappearing and a homogenization of consumption rates and beverage preferences is increasingly evident. Room and Mäkelä (2000) have reconsidered the simple wet/dry dichotomy and have instead proposed a new typology that considers a variety of drinking behaviors, such as the regularity of drinking and the extent of drunkenness. Such a typology may better fit the distinctions in drinking cultures that are emerging today. Nevertheless, the wet/dry dichotomy has represented a scale of extremes on which to measure drinking cultures and around which a fair amount of past research literature has been organized (Bloomfield et al. 2003b).

Cultural Influences

This section explains how views of alcohol are culturally determined—that is, how culture encodes the thoughts, attitudes, values, and beliefs about alcohol, and how it influences our behavior regarding the use and abuse of alcohol.

> I was just drinking beer a lot and hardly ever drank the hard stuff. I was drinking about a six-pack after work each night. My wife never said anything much about my drinking. Then as time went on, I remember that I would start drinking beer earlier and earlier after work. Then came the six-pack and an extra quart of beer each night while sitting home trying to relax after a pressure-filled day at the office. Well, little did I realize then, I was having a drinking problem and it was only beer! I could not believe that I was sort of a beer alcoholic. Back then, I never thought that silly ole' beer could get a person hooked. *(From Venturelli's research files, male member of Alcoholics Anonymous, age 32, April 12, 2000)*

Or,

> Q: Do you consider yourself a heavy drinker?
> A: No, I only drink beer.
> Q: But, you are often drunk at night?
> A: Yeah, but it's only beer.

These two interviews illustrate a belief shared by many Americans, which is that the milder alcohols such as beer, wine, and wine coolers are often placed outside the domain of potentially addictive types of beverages. Some may even believe that the distilled spirits such as vodka, gin, and whiskey are the only types of addictive alcoholic beverages. Finally, the comment that "I don't use and never would use drugs; I only drink" can easily be heard being espoused by a large portion of Americans (probably a majority), who place alcohol in a completely separate category from drugs. However, each 12-ounce bottle of beer is equal to 1 ounce of liquor. Thus, two beers equal a double shot of bourbon or vodka.

■ Culture and Drinking Behavior

Another way of looking at how culture influences us is to stand outside of our culture and see how people behave when intoxicated in our culture and in a variety of other cultures in an effort to understand the real relationship among culture, alcohol, and human beings. A major contribution to our knowledge of intoxicated behavior from an outside perspective comes from the field of cultural anthropology.

As we saw earlier in the distinction between wet and dry cultures, how alcohol is used varies culturally. Does culture also affect how or in what way we view alcohol? Why would our culture differ from other cultures in the use and abuse of alcoholic beverages? We focus on these two questions in this section.

Throughout the world, cultures create a climate for the development of attitudes toward most behaviors. Like other behaviors, the use of alcohol is embedded within our culture. Culture does more than contain the attitudes and feelings that people have toward alcohol use: It dictates the variety, the attachment, and the intensity of attitudes that are held toward other people's behavior. For example, in the 1930s, American college students acquired a "reverence for strong drink" (Room 1984, p. 8). Although for decades many people believed that college students "majored in drinking," during the 1930s, students grew to consider heavy use as romantic and adult, resonating with the romantic, heavy-drinking expatriate community of writers in Paris, such as Ernest Hemingway.

American culture in general views ethanol-containing beverages as sexy, mature, sophisticated, facilitating socializing, and enhancing status. Today, many of these beliefs are communicated through the mass media, and advertising is a key medium of communication. Advertising uses positive images to persuade observers to purchase a particular brand of alcohol. For example, what messages are found in newspapers and especially magazines about drinking certain types of wine, bourbon, gin, scotch, and the numerous types of domestic and imported beers? What attitudes are generally conveyed when a sexy, glamorous woman is dressed in formal evening attire standing next to her man in front of a perfectly glowing fireplace, smiling confidently as he stares into her eyes and sips his special-label cognac?

■ Culture and Disinhibited Behavior

The concept of **drunken comportment** was first formulated by MacAndrew and Edgerton (1969). Drunken comportment refers to the behavior demonstrated while under the influence of alcohol within the norms and expectations of a particular culture. Instead of simply labeling drinking behavior as "drunken behavior," this concept sensitizes us to how drinking behavior is influenced by cultural norms and expectations. For example, in the United States, drinking is comported to mean time out away from duties and obligations. "The symbolism of alcohol in American culture contains this motif of release and remission, as in the emergence of TGIF [Thank God It's Friday]" (Gusfield 1986, p. 203). Another example is that in some cultures, drinking occurs during celebrations and festivities, and as part of religious ceremony. In France and Italy, drinking alcohol occurs while eating with family members.

Alcohol is a **disinhibitor**, which refers to depression of the cerebral cortex functions. When this occurs, it results in a suspension of rational or thoughtful constraints on impulsive behavior. Inhibitions (inner raw feelings and attitudes) are normally controlled through rationality and logical thought processes. The popular image of office Christmas parties at which too much alcohol is consumed and parties that get out of control because of overconsumption of alcohol are examples. People at such events can easily become uncontrollable, loud, impulsive, and just plain irrational. In such situations, outbreaks of arguing and physical and verbal abuse are more likely to occur. Such behavior is disinhibited behavior.

Although all of us know that the alcohol content that is usually measured in terms of alcohol proof (see Chapter 7 for more details) has an independent effect on the user, two additional factors contribute to the effects of alcohol: **set and setting** (Goode 1999; Zinberg 1984; Zinberg and Robertson 1972). Set is the individual's expectation of what a drug will do to his or her personality. Setting is both the physical environment and the social environment in which the drug is consumed. How important are these two distinctions? Some psychologists contend that both set and setting can overshadow the pharmacological effects of most drugs. In fact, set and setting are far more influential in determining a drug user's experience even when less addictive drugs, such as alcohol and marijuana, are used, in contrast to more potent addictive drugs, such as cocaine and heroin. Good examples of this are when people who drink alcohol say "I felt that drink right away" or "I drank a lot last night but I had something on my mind and dude, I was just not in the partying mood."

A review of various ethnographic studies (Marshall 1983) reveals **pseudointoxicated** behavior among Tahitians, Rarotongans, Chippewa, Dakota, Pine Ridge and Teton Sioux, Aleuts, Baffin Island Inuits, and Potawatomi—that is, people acting drunk before or seconds after the bottle is opened, or as the drink is consumed. The frequency of use or the amount consumed has less effect on how drinkers comport themselves; instead, the cultural values, beliefs, mental maps, and norms cause a particular behavioral outcome. Using the terminology of psychology, we would say that it is not the biochemical effects on the brain alone that account for disinhibitory behavior but rather the belief that one has been drinking a substance that has a disinhibitory effect; that is, the mental (cognitive) appraisal of the physiological state allows disinhibited behavior. In using the terminology of sociology and revising a famous sociological axiom, we could say, "what we believe to be (or personally define as true) is true in its consequences or in the obtained results." Thus, if you believe you are drunk and you act drunk, then you are drunk.

Cultures vary in how they evaluate alcohol consumption. Some religions in the United States view drinking as evil, whereas other religions view alcohol as a gift from God and use it in religious ceremonies. In some subcultures, excessive use of alcohol is an indication of manhood, strength, and virility; in other subcultures, excessive alcohol use in public is disgusting and embarrassing. Even drug education has different perspectives. Do we emphasize total abstinence or teach people how to drink in moderation? Why such vastly different approaches? Because our culture includes contradictory practices on this front.

Similarly, the views we maintain about alcohol abuse and addiction vary. For example, is alcoholism a disease? Is it prescribed by certain customs within ethnic groups? Does it result from some type

KEY TERMS

disinhibitor
a psychoactive chemical that depresses thought and judgment functions in the cerebral cortex, which has the effect of allowing relatively unrestrained behavior (as in alcohol inebriation)

set and setting
set refers to the individual's expectation of what a drug will do to his or her personality; setting is the physical and social environments where the drug is consumed

pseudointoxicated
acting drunk even before alcohol has had a chance to cause its effects

of personality flaw? The three concepts discussed in this section—drunken comportment, set and setting, and pseudointoxication—demonstrate that social and cultural contexts exert their influences independently of the effects of alcohol consumption.

Culture Provides Rules for Drinking Behavior

Many cultures, such as traditional Italian and Jewish cultures, permit moderate drinking within the family, especially at meals, but disapprove of drunken behaviors. Note that many differences separate these groups. For example, Italians use wine as a food item, whereas it has only ritual value among Orthodox Jews. In one study of Scandinavian nations, by contrast, drinking was considered separated from work. Where drinking at work was permitted, however, it was allowed to go on to the point of intoxication (Makela 1986). Finnish, Polish, and Russian cultures are associated with binge drinking whereas French culture is linked with sipping. In the United States, we encounter a vast variety of subgroups; some heavy drinkers may live in a community in which it is not considered excessive to drink with their friends out of paper bags on the street in the morning. In other communities, all outdoor drinking is done in either parks, restaurants, bars, or outdoor cafes. Some people may belong to a "workplace culture of drinking" at a particular country club, construction site, or law firm where "three-martini lunches" are not unheard of. Perhaps this type of drinking is not much different from the habits of teenage peer groups. To be "treated" for this behavior might seem as strange as going into rehab for acting "normal."

Culture Provides Ceremonial Meaning for Alcohol Use

The first notable work on ceremonial use and ethnic drinking practices was undertaken by Bales (1946), who attempted to explain the different rates of drinking between Jews (low) and Irish (high) in terms of symbolic and ceremonial meanings. For Jews, drinking had familial and sacramental significance, whereas for the Irish it represented male convivial bonding.

A high rate of heavy drinking was observed among the Irish in the 1800s. It was said that these individuals drank because they were Irish. Today, some descendants of the Irish continue to live the stereotype; for them, it represents "Irishness"—they drink because they are Irish. A button displayed on St. Patrick's Day proclaimed, "Today I'm Irish, Tomorrow I'm Hung Over," and a *New York Post* supplement declared this event to be "Three Days of Drinking and Revelry." With regard to Hasidic Jews, the belief is that they can ". . . drink alcohol, [and] it is considered a 'mitzvah' (good deed) when done so on the Sabbath and on holidays" (Answers.com 2011). Further, Rabbi Daniel Siegel writes,

> [O]verall, the approach of the Jewish rabbinic tradition is to encourage the moderate use of alcohol, particularly wine, within the frameworks provided by existing commandments which require one to be happy in their fulfillment. Wine is an important part of Sabbath and holiday observances, life cycle celebrations, and the holiday of Purim. In the Hassidic world, a small amount of vodka is a legitimate preparation for listening to the teachings of the rabbi and, in oral traditions, a measured amount of alcohol on a regular basis is considered good for one's health. (Dartmouth Center on Addiction, Recovery and Education 2008, p. 3)

Culture Provides Models of Alcoholism

Chapter 2 discussed models of addiction, such as the disease model. U.S. citizens define alcoholism as a disease far more often than French Canadians or French people, for example (Babor et al. 1986). Some South Bronx Hispanics have ascribed alcoholism to "spells," spirits (Garrison and Podell 1981), the evil eye (*mal ojo*), or witchcraft (*brujeria*). The entire addiction also may be ignored or bypassed; ulcers, divorce, or car accidents that an alcohol counselor may recognize as alcoholism-based may instead be traced directly to supernatural influence. One way or another, if it is attributed to a supernatural cause, a supernatural solution may be called upon to cure this problem. Thus, many seek the help of a folk curer (e.g., *espiritista, santero*). Some African Americans interpret their problems as a punishment from God, and they may subscribe to a moral model that conflicts with a disease or other psychiatric or addictive model.

■ Cultural Stereotypes of Drinking May Be Misleading

African American drinking patterns run the gamut from middle-class cocktail lounges (as seen in liquor ads in *Ebony*), to blue-collar wakes and birthday parties, to the "bottle-gang" of homeless poor. By class, middle-class African American women drinkers are not dramatically different from middle-class white women drinkers; they are typically moderate drinkers, with few nondrinkers and heavy drinkers. Poorer African American female groups have a larger proportion of nondrinkers; among those who do drink, more are heavy drinkers. Breaking it down further, being married, older, and church affiliated has been associated with nonacceptance of heavy drinking (Gary and Gary 1985; Kinney 2000). At historically black colleges and universities, blacks have lower levels of alcohol and other types of drug consumption than are observed at colleges and universities with a majority of white students. At all colleges and universities, white students drink significantly more than African American students (Kinney 2000).

Gordon, who studied a Connecticut city in 1981, examined three Hispanic groups, all new to the United States and all blue collars. In this group, Dominicans drank less after migration. They emphasized suave or sophisticated drinking, and they saw drunkenness as indecent (without respect). Alcoholics were seen as "sick," perhaps from some tragic experience. Guatemalans drank substantially more after migration: One-third of males were often drunk and binged most weekends. Being drunk was considered glamorous and sentimentalized—like Humphrey Bogart under the hanging light bulb, alone in a hotel room. These individuals boasted of hangovers, even when they did not have one. The Guatemalan Alcoholics Anonymous (AA) group was alien to Puerto Ricans. Puerto Ricans broke down into middle-class American-style moderate drinkers, depressed and wife-abusing alcoholic welfare recipients, and various sorts of polydrug abusers, including those who entered into the mainland "druggie" youth culture (Gordon 1981). Among Hispanics in general, men were twice as likely to be involved in heavy drinking as both white and African American males (Kinney 2000). In fact, African American students have the lowest lifetime, annual, and 30-day prevalence rates for alcohol use; they also tend to have the lowest rates for daily drinking (NIDA 1999).

Even when looking at physiological responses to alcohol, ethnicity appears to matter. The long-term effects of alcohol dependence are reported to cause more damage to the immune systems of African Americans than other ethnic groups. The greater sensitivity to alcohol and its damaging effects puts this group at an increased risk for infection and, in many cases, at a greater likelihood of death (About.com 2003).

In regard to the international frequency of drinking, Bloomfield et al. (2003a) report the following:

- Spain had the highest frequency of drinking for men, Italy had the highest frequency for women, and Ireland had the lowest frequency for both genders.
- Among nine European countries, France had the highest and Finland had the lowest frequency of drinking (i.e., number of drinking occasions within a month).
- Wilsnack and colleagues (2000), with their sample of 10 countries, found the highest frequencies of drinking (i.e., number of drinking occasions in a month) among Dutch women and Czech men and the lowest frequencies among Estonian women and men.
- In two studies, Italy had the highest and Finland the lowest rates of daily drinking.
- In a two-country comparison of drinking and nondrinking respondents, Germany reported almost twice as many drinking days as did U.S. respondents.
- All of these studies suggest that the main wine-consuming (and wine-producing) countries of Europe have the highest frequencies of drinking.
- The frequency of consumption was highest in the United Kingdom, followed by the European countries and Canada; the United States ranked third.
- A 2005 study of 45 countries, listed the total liters of pure alcohol consumed per drinking-age person (which includes beer, wine, and spirits). This study found that the lowest ranking countries (bottom 10 countries, highest to lowest) were Sweden, South Africa, Venezuela, Norway, Thailand, Brazil, China, Colombia, Taiwan, and Mexico (Institute of Alcohol Studies 2005).

As information on cultural differences in alcohol use and abuse has become known throughout the alcohol abuse field, administrative agencies have attempted to incorporate these insights into professional standards of practice, under the rubric of "cultural competence." Prevention and treatment programs are to be evaluated from the standpoint of their competence in providing services to the cultural populations they serve. To avoid stereotyping, these considerations include understanding of such variables as ethnic acculturation and skills at eliciting information on the cultural background of clients (Office for Substance Abuse Prevention [OSAP] 1992). Prevention issues such as consumption of gateway drugs and media advocacy have been refined to target ethnic at-risk populations. For example, urban African American youth are bombarded with aggressive marketing of 40-ounce malt liquors, known as "40s." Consumption of 40s is celebrated in rap lyrics such as "Tap the Bottle." The alcohol content of malt liquors ranges from 5.6% to 8%, compared with 3.5% for regular beers. This large, inexpensive bottle of potent brew offers a cheap high, often leading to alcohol abuse. Moreover, in the mid-1990s, 40s drinking increasingly became associated with marijuana smoking, going together like cookies and milk, and used before school or at "hooky parties."

■ Culture Provides Attitudes Regarding Alcohol Consumption

Although cultures often maintain generalized (normative) attitudes regarding alcohol use and abuse, significant differences in attitudes also exist within cultures (Arkin and Funkhouser 1992; Inciardi 1992). The United States is characterized as culturally ambivalent regarding alcohol use (Kinney 2000); that is, alcohol consumption varies enormously across our culture. Different geographic regions, diverse religious beliefs, and racial and ethnic differences result in confusing attitudes about drinking alcohol. Other factors that contribute to diversity in attitudes include social upbringing, peer group dynamics, social class, income, education, and occupational differences.

What specific impact do such attitudes have on drinking? As just mentioned, attitudes are responsible for making alcohol consumption acceptable or unacceptable—or even relished as a form of behavior. For example, in one segment of impoverished African American groups, alcohol use and abuse are so common that they have become accepted behavior. The following excerpt describes an accepted use of alcohol consumption:

A party without liquor or a street rap without a bottle is often perceived as unimaginable. These attitudes about drinking are shaped as youth grow up seeing liquor stores in their communities next to schools, churches, and homes. Liquor stores and bootleg dealers frequently permeate the black residential community, where in traditionally white communities they are generally restricted to commercial or business zones. With liquor stores throughout the fabric of black residential life, black youth grow up seeing men drinking in the streets and relatives drinking at home. (Harper 1986)

Contrast this attitude with orthodox religious and fundamentalist communities in which the use of alcohol and other drugs is strictly prohibited:

I was raised in a very religious, Seventh-Day Adventist family. My father was a pretty strong figure in our little church of 18 members. My mother stayed home most of the time, living in a way like an Old Testament kind of biblical life, so-to-speak. We were strict vegetarians, and all of us in the family had to be very involved with church life. The first time I ever saw alcohol outside of always hearing how corrupting it was to the mind and the body, was when I was 7. One day the father of a friend of mine—the only non-Adventist family friend I was allowed to play with—was drinking a beer in the kitchen when we walked in. I asked, "What's that?" The father's reply was "This is beer, dear John." I looked strangely at him and pretended to be amused at the father's answer. Actually, inside I remember being very surprised and scared at the same time for I was always told that people who drink alcohol were not doing what God wanted them to do in life. *(From Venturelli's research files, male university student, age 18, May 21, 1993)*

From these contrasting examples, we can see that the values expressed through group and family attitudes regarding drug use are very significant in determining the extent of alcohol consumption.

College and University Students and Alcohol Use

Over the years, alcohol use and consumption rates among college students have remained largely stable, although rates for other drugs show a lot more variance. For example, marijuana use has dramatically risen, fallen, and then risen again. In looking at alcohol consumption and college students, some interesting findings exist. The following statistics provided by Hingston et al. in College Drinking—Changing the Culture (NIAAA 2010) are especially noteworthy:

- *Death:* 1825 college students between the ages of 18 and 24 die from alcohol-related unintentional injuries, including motor vehicle crashes, each year.
- *Injury:* 599,000 students between the ages of 18 and 24 are unintentionally injured under the influence of alcohol.
- *Assault:* 696,000 students between the ages of 18 and 24 are assaulted by another student who has been drinking.
- *Sexual abuse:* 97,000 students between the ages of 18 and 24 are victims of alcohol-related sexual assault or date rape.
- *Unsafe sex:* 400,000 students between the ages of 18 and 24 had unprotected sex and more than 100,000 students between the ages of 18 and 24 report having been too intoxicated to know if they consented to having sex.
- *Academic problems:* About 25% of college students report academic consequences of their drinking including missing class, falling behind, doing poorly on exams or papers, and receiving lower grades overall (NIAAA 2010).
- *Health problems/suicide attempts:* More than 150,000 students develop an alcohol-related health problem and between 1.2% and 1.5% of students indicate that they tried to commit suicide within the past year due to drinking or drug use (NIAAA 2010).
- *Drunk driving:* 3,360,000 students between the ages of 18 and 24 drive under the influence of alcohol (NIAAA 2010).
- *Vandalism:* About 11% of college student drinkers report that they have damaged property while under the influence of alcohol (NIAAA 2010).
- *Property damage:* More than 25% of administrators from schools with relatively low drinking levels and over 50% from schools with high drinking levels say their campuses have a "moderate" or "major" problem with alcohol-related property damage (NIAAA 2010).
- *Police involvement:* About 5% of 4-year college students are involved with the police or campus security as a result of their drinking, and 110,000 students between the ages of 18 and 24 are arrested for an alcohol-related violation such as public drunkenness or driving under the influence (NIAAA 2010).
- *Alcohol abuse and dependence:* 31% of college students met criteria for a diagnosis of alcohol abuse and 6% for a diagnosis of alcohol dependence in the past 12 months, according to questionnaire-based self-reports about their drinking (NIAAA 2010).

Additional findings:

- College students drink an estimated 4 billion cans of beer annually.
- Total amount of alcohol consumed by college students each year is 430 million gallons, enough for every college and university in the United States to fill an Olympic-size swimming pool.
- As many as 360,000 of the nation's 12 million undergraduates will die from alcohol-related causes while in school. This is more than the number who will receive master's and doctorate degrees.
- Nearly half of all college students are binge drinkers.
- The number of college women who drink to get drunk has more than tripled in the past 10 years, rising from 10% to 35%.
- On America's college campuses, alcohol is often responsible for 28% of all students who drop out of college before completing their bachelor's degree.
- Seventy-five percent of male students and 55% of female students involved in acquaintance rape had been drinking or using drugs at the time.
- For college men, alcohol consumption is inversely related to the size of the institution; that is, male students at smaller institutions consume far more than those at larger institutions. (Lack of social activities could be a precipitating factor.)
- Nearly one-quarter of students report failing a test or project because of the aftereffects of drinking or doing drugs.
- Although only 2 in 20 college students are arrested for driving under the influence, ". . . 27% of students said they drove while under the influence of alcohol . . . [and this] . . . translates to 2.1 million students" (Boyd et al. 2003).
- A related consequence of alcohol abuse is motor vehicle accidents. For young people under the age of 25, motor vehicle accidents rate as the number one cause of death (Presley, Meilman, and Lyerla 1996).

- Findings from the CORE Institute survey (see the discussion following this list) indicate that 300,000 of today's college students will die of alcohol-related causes, such as drunk driving accidents, liver disorders, sexually transmitted infections from improper sexual protection (lack of condoms leading to HIV), cancers from alcohol abuse, and severely damaged organs from chronic drinking (Phoenix House 2009)

- Although the average cost for book purchases for classes is about $800 per year (Allison 2004), the average student spends about $900 on alcohol each year

- On the positive side, there is a small but very significant downward trend in alcohol use on America's campuses. In 1985, the percentage of college students who had consumed alcohol in the previous 30 days was approximately 80%. By 1990, that number had declined to 74.5% and it continues to decline each year. However, counterbalancing this positive trend, the use of other illegitimate-type drugs continues to increase. Further, past and more current studies show that although overall alcohol consumption is slowly decreasing, binge drinking remains high on most campuses throughout the United States (Wechsler et al. 2000a; English et al. 2009).

Other recent findings (Johnston et al. 2009) indicate that:

- Since 1980, college students have generally had *daily drinking* rates that were slightly lower than their age peers, suggesting that they were more likely to confine their drinking to weekends, when they tend to drink a lot.

- The rate of daily drinking among the noncollege group fell from 8.3% in 1980 to 3.2% in 1994, rose to 5.8% by 2000, and dropped to 3.7% in 2008. Daily drinking by the college group also dropped in approximately the same time period, from 6.5% in 1980 to 3.0% in 1995, then increased to 5.0% in 2002; since then it has remained at 4–5%.

- College males report considerably higher rates of daily drinking than college females (5.1% versus 3.3% in 2008). This gender difference also exists in the noncollege group (5.0% versus 2.7% in 2008). Given that the physiological impacts of five drinks are considerably greater for the typical young female versus the typical young male, it is not surprising that we find substantial gender differences in the prevalence of having five or more drinks in a row.

Alcohol consumption is routine at many social activities for college students.

Among college students and young adults generally, there also are substantial gender differences in alcohol use, with college males drinking the most. In 2008, for example, half (49%) of all college males reported having five or more drinks in a row over the previous 2 weeks versus one-third (34%) of college females. Throughout the years, this gender difference has narrowed gradually, with the rate declining somewhat for males and increasing somewhat for females.

The CORE Institute survey is a validated survey instrument that has been administered to more than 1 million students—by far the largest sample of college students surveyed. The available figures from this survey (Core Institute 2008) indicate that on average, approximately 84% of college students consumed alcohol within the year this survey was given and 72% consumed alcohol within the 30 days prior to when the survey was administered. The average number of drinks that students consumed was 5.4 per week (Core Institute 2008). Approximately 55% engaged in binge drinking within 30 days before the CORE survey was administered. Of all the drugs reported, alcohol was the most heavily abused on college campuses, followed by tobacco (44%) and marijuana (31%).

■ Binge Drinking

A recent Swedish study defines a binge as the consumption of half a bottle of spirits or two bottles of wine on the same occasion. Similarly, a study in Italy found that consuming an average of eight drinks a day was considered normal drinking—clearly not bingeing. In the United Kingdom, bingeing is commonly defined as consuming 11 or more drinks on an occasion. However, in the United States, some researchers have defined bingeing as consuming five or more drinks on an occasion (an "occasion" can refer to an entire day). [Recently] . . . , some have even expanded the definition to include consuming four or more drinks on an occasion by a woman. (Hanson 2009a, p. 1)

The widely reported study by Wechsler and colleagues (1994 and 2000b) brought the issue of binge drinking to the public's attention. One report, which surveyed 17,592 students at 140 campuses, revealed that 44% engaged in binge drinking, which impacted on many areas of students' lives—both their own and those of others whose lives were disrupted by this behavior (giving rise to the term *secondhand drinking*).

As mentioned in the previous section, 42% to 55% of all college students often binge drink.[2] This type of alcohol consumption remains very worrisome to anyone supporting, nurturing, protecting, caring for, and responsible for the behavior of young people in this subculture. In addition, health professionals see this as a serious form of alcohol abuse.

One may question whether all five-drink episodes qualify as binge drinking, a term that calls to mind a weekend of drinking, or Jellinek's epsilon alcoholism. However, 11.1% of males and 7.4% of females reported three or more episodes of memory loss during the past year due to drug or alcohol use, of which the overwhelming majority were alcohol-related, both because alcohol is the major drug consumed by students and because it produces amnesiac episodes. Amnesiac episodes are accepted as symptoms of problem drinking behavior.

In one national survey of 17,600 students at 140 4-year colleges and universities, which is regularly conducted by the Harvard School of Public Health (Wechsler et al. 2000a, p. 1), the findings were as follows:

- "Overall, 44% of the students were binge drinkers. Among men, 50% were binge drinkers; among women, the figure was 39%."
- "The main reason given for binge drinking was 'to get drunk.'"

- "Being white, involved in athletics, or a resident of a fraternity or sorority made it more likely that a student would be a binge drinker."
- "White students were over twice as likely to be binge drinkers compared to other racial/ethnic groups."
- "Students who said that religious participation is not very important to them were more than twice as likely to be binge drinkers compared to other students."
- "Students who said that athletic participation was very important or important to them were also one-and-a-half times more likely to be binge drinkers."
- "Residents of fraternities or sororities were four times as likely to be binge drinkers compared to other students."

Another study revealed the following:

- Community college students were less likely to engage in binge drinking; 29.9% had binged in the previous 2 weeks compared with 40.4% of their peers at 4-year schools.
- Approximately one-fourth of all males enrolled at 4-year colleges reported three or more binge episodes during the previous 2 weeks.
- Students who lived on campus were more likely to binge drink than those who lived off campus. Furthermore, older, working, off-campus students were less likely to engage in such behavior, lowering their scores in this regard relative to the standard college student.
- American Indian/Alaska Native students had the highest frequency of drinking episodes, binge drinking, and memory loss, followed (in order) by white, Hispanic, African American, and Asian students (NIAAA 2008).

It is not unusual for college students to overconsume alcohol when they are partying.

---

[2]The variation depends on the methodology of testing (self-report versus survey) and type of campuses (private versus public institutions, alcohol policies and extent of police enforcement, size of campuses, urban versus rural campuses, commuter versus dormitory, and college versus university).

■ Gender and Collegiate Alcohol Use

The findings from the CORE survey consistently indicate greater frequency of male drinking, frequency of male binge drinking, and consequences of drinking. In a review of the literature addressing gender and student drinking patterns, Berkowitz and Perkins (1987) found a historical pattern of male-dominated college drinking patterns. The transition into college is associated with a doubling of the percentages of those who drink for both genders. Both men and women drink to enhance sociability or social interaction, to escape negative emotions or release otherwise unacceptable ones, and to simply get drunk. "Drinking to get drunk" is generally considered more of a male pursuit. Indeed, males are more frequently associated with binge drinking and negative public consequences than female drinkers. Severe drunkenness and a customary rowdiness or drunken comportment are normative for male drinkers who binge, with the results including fighting, property damage, and troubles with authorities. The latter were twice as likely to be male problems.

Unsurprisingly, drinking is inversely related to academic achievement. With heavier drinkers, grades suffered for both male and female students. According to the studies cited by Berkowitz and Perkins (1987) for binge drinkers, the impact on impaired academic performance is just as great for women drinkers. More recent information (Core Institute 2008; De Jong 1995; Presley et al. 1996; Wechsler 2000a, 2000b) corroborates this finding and shows similar consequences among male and female binge drinkers in terms of health problems, personal injury, and unplanned sexual activity. Over the past few decades, drinking behaviors (amount and percentage of drinking) have been becoming more similar between males and females.

Alcohol Consumption Patterns of Women

Women are affected by alcohol differently than are men. Women possess greater sensitivity to alcohol, have a greater likelihood of addiction, and develop alcohol-related health problems sooner than men.[3]

___
[3]Even currently accepted definitions of binge drinking differ by gender. For men, binge drinking consists of five or more drinks in one sitting; for women, binge drinking consists of four or more drinks in one sitting.

Why do women respond differently than men to alcohol? Three reasons are (1) women have a smaller body size (men are generally larger than women); (2) women absorb alcohol sooner than men because on average they possess more body fat and body fat does not dilute alcohol as well as water (male bodies contain more water); and (3) women possess less of a metabolizing enzyme that functions to get rid of (process out) alcohol.

In Great Britain, the proportion of women drinking has risen steadily since 1984. This increase in drinking still holds true for all age groups with the exception of women older than 65 (Alcohol Concern 2000). Other notable facts regarding women and drinking can be summarized as follows (About.com 1998a, 1998b):

- Although men begin drinking earlier in life, women are more likely than men to start drinking heavily later in life.
- Women are more easily affected by alcohol consumption, both its effects and diseases related to alcoholism—cirrhosis of the liver, stomach cancer, and so on.
- Women's alcohol consumption is often similar to that of people they are close to, such as a lover or husband.
- Full-time working, professionally oriented women drink at the end of their working day, whereas women who stay at home drink alcohol throughout the day.
- More women in alcohol treatment come from sexually abusive homes (70%), in comparison to men (12%).
- Today, women are more visible and their behavior, especially alcohol consumption, is more observable (e.g., drinking in bars, purchasing alcohol).

Figure 8.7 shows the prevalence of binge drinking among childbearing-age women (18–44) by state (Centers for Disease Control and Prevention [CDC] 2010). The U.S. average of all the states and territories for any use of alcohol by women is approximately 50%, and binge drinking is 14.7% for all childbearing-age women. When looking at binge drinking, the state of Wisconsin has the highest percentage (23.9%) and the Virgin Islands has the lowest percentage (6.1%).

Figure 8.7 also shows that:

- The highest consumption (first tier of states), with 23.9%–19.5% of childbearing women binging on alcohol, is in the following states: Wisconsin, North Dakota, Iowa, Washington, DC, and Massachusetts.

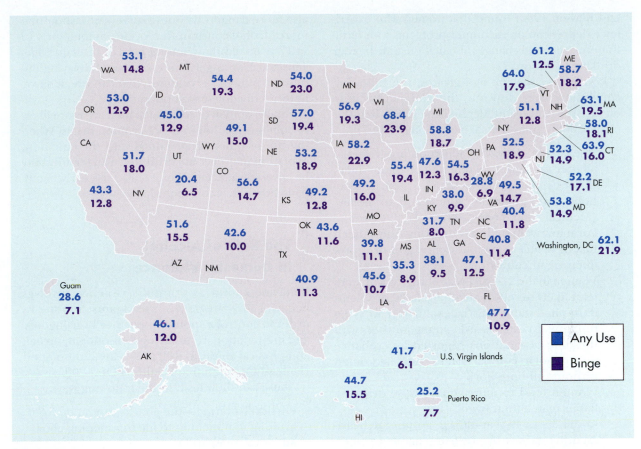

FIGURE 8.7

Prevalence of any use and binge drinking* among childbearing-age women (18–44 years), United States, Behavioral Risk Factor Surveillance System (BRFSS): 2008.

....

*Consumption of an average of seven or more drinks per week or five or more drinks on at least one occasion during the preceding month.

Source: Centers for Disease Control and Prevention (CDC). "Fetal Alcohol Spectrum Disorders (FASDs): State-Specific Weighted Prevalence Estimates of Alcohol Use (Percentage of Any Use/Binge Drinking) Among Women Aged 18–44 Years—BRFSS, 2008." Atlanta, GA: Centers for Disease Control and Prevention. Available at: http://www.cdc.gov/ncbddd/fasd/data.html. Accessed February 16, 2011.

- The second highest states (second tier), ranging from 19.4% to 15% of childbearing women binging on alcohol, are the following: Illinois, South Dakota, Minnesota, Montana, Nebraska, Pennsylvania, Michigan, Maine, Rhode Island, Nevada, Vermont, Delaware, Ohio, Connecticut, Missouri, Arizona, Hawaii, and Wyoming.
- The third highest states (third tier), with 14.9%–10.4% of childbearing women binging on alcohol, are the following: Maryland, New Jersey, Washington, Colorado, Virginia, Idaho, Oregon, California, Kansas, New York, Georgia, New Hampshire, Indiana, Alaska, North Carolina, Oklahoma, South Carolina, Texas, Arkansas, Florida, and Louisiana.
- The fourth highest states/territories (fourth tier), with 10.3%–6.1% of childbearing women

binging on alcohol, are the following: Alabama, New Mexico, Kentucky, Mississippi, Tennessee, Puerto Rico, Guam, West Virginia, Utah, and Virgin Islands.

As a group, alcohol-abusing women are more likely to drink alone at home. A high incidence of alcohol abuse is found in women who are unemployed and looking for work, whereas less alcohol abuse is likely in women who are employed part-time. Divorced or separated women, women who never marry, and those who are unmarried and living with a partner are more likely to use and abuse alcohol than married women. Other high-risk groups are women in their twenties and early thirties and women with heavy-drinking husbands or partners. Other researchers (Williams et al. 1997; Wilsnack, Wilsnak, and Klassen 1986) found that women who experience depression or encounter problems with fertility or menopausal changes also demonstrate heavier drinking behavior.

Looking at specific age groups, the following conclusions were drawn by the National Institute on Alcohol Abuse and Alcoholism (1990), Register et al. (2002), and Medical News Today (2007):

- The course of alcohol addiction progresses at a faster rate among women than among men. Recent research shows that ". . . female alcoholics are generally younger than males" (Medical News Today 2007, p. 1).
- For many women, heavy drinking came after a health problem such as depression or reproductive difficulties.
- Women in the 21- to 34-year-old age group were least likely to report alcohol-related problems if they had stable marriages and were working full time. In other words, young mothers with full-time occupations reported less reliance on alcohol in comparison to childless women without full-time work.
- Women tend to marry men whose drinking habits match their own.
- In the 35- to 49-year-old age group, the heaviest drinkers were divorced or separated women without children in the home.
- In the 50- to 64-year-old age group, the heaviest drinkers were women whose husbands or partners drank heavily.
- Women 65 years or older constitute less than 10% of drinkers with drinking problems.

More alcohol consumption is also found in women who closely work in traditionally so-called masculine occupations and levels of management, such as executives and traditional blue-collar occupations. In April 1995, former First Lady Betty Ford made the following statement:

Today, we know that when a woman abuses alcohol or other drugs, the risk to her health is much greater than it is for a man. Yet there is not enough prevention, intervention, and treatment targeting women. It is still much harder for women to get help. That needs to change. (SAMHSA 1995, p. 14)

In fact, women risk serious health consequences when they choose to use alcohol and other drugs. Alcohol, in particular, can often be devastating to women's health.

Not only does alcohol have a greater immediate effect on women, but its long-term risks are also more dangerous. Some surveys now show that more alcohol consumption occurs among girls 12 to 17 years old than among boys of the same age. This places young women at a risk of delaying the onset of puberty, a condition that can wreak havoc in terms of adolescent maturation.

Finally, women in contrast to men are more likely to combine alcohol with prescription drugs. When the use of other drugs enters into the equation, ovulation may become inhibited and fertility may be adversely affected. Women also risk early menopause when they consume alcohol.

■ The Role of Alcohol in Domestic Violence

Behavior known as domestic violence involves behavior that one person uses against another in order to control a spouse or partner by using fear and intimidation. It can involve emotional, sexual, and physical abuse, as well as threats and isolation (Federal Occupational Health [FOH] 2005).

Abuse can show itself in the following ways:

Physical battering—the attacks can range from bruising to punching to life-threatening choking or use of weapons.

Sexual abuse—a person is forced to have sexual intercourse with the abuser or take part in unwanted sexual activity

Psychological battering—psychological violence can include constant verbal abuse, harassment, excessive possessiveness, isolating the victim from friends and family, withholding money and destruction of personal property. (FOH 2005, p. 3)

Much attention became focused on domestic violence in the mid-1990s through high-profile criminal cases such as those involving the Menendez brothers and O. J. Simpson. The increased emphasis on decreasing domestic violence has inspired much research into its causes and effects as well as into common traits of abusers. Recent studies have found a significant relationship between the incidence of battering and the abuse of alcohol; furthermore, the abuse of alcohol overwhelmingly emerges as a primary predictor of marital violence (De Jong 1995; Drug Strategies 1999). A study of 2000 American couples conducted in 1993 showed that rates of domestic violence were as much as 15 times higher in households in which the husband was described as "often" being drunk as opposed to "never" drunk (About.com 2010b; Collins and Messerschmidt 1993). The same study found that alcohol was present in more than half of all reported incidences of domestic abuse. Further, "[a]nother study . . . [showed] . . . that the percentage of batterers who are under the influence of alcohol when they assault their partners ranges from 48 percent to 87 percent, with most research indicating a 60 to 70 percent rate of alcohol abuse and a 13 to 20 percent rate of drug abuse" (About.com 2010b).

Domestic violence also creates significant problems for its victims later in life. A study of 472 women by the Research Institute on Addictions found that 87% of female alcoholics had been physically or sexually abused as children (Drug Strategies 1999; Miller and Downs 1993). The insidiousness of domestic violence may exist because of the consistent abuse of alcohol that is associated with both abusers and victims. Given these disturbing statistics, more research and counseling programs focused on the prevention of alcoholism and subsequent domestic violence are necessary before the very foundations of identity, security, and happiness are forever destroyed. As one reformed alcoholic explains:

> It was really terrible. I would drink by myself in the living room and fight with my wife in other parts of the house. I knew I needed help when I shoved her around on the night of her birthday and threw a wet kitchen washcloth and hit her in the face. Before that night, I never would have done this, but her nagging about my drinking that night got to me more than on other nights and it caused me to lose control. *(From Venturelli's research files, male, age 48, July 2010)*

■ Alcohol and Sex

Alcohol use is linked to an overwhelming proportion of unwanted sexual behaviors, including **acquaintance and date rape**, unplanned pregnancies, and sexually transmitted infections, including HIV infections (Abbey 1990; World Health Organization [WHO] 1998). Factors that immediately come to mind include disinhibition concerning restraints on sexuality, poor judgment, and unconsciousness or helplessness on the part of victims. The links between unwanted sex and substance abuse are subtler than many imagine, however. Although disinhibition, impulsivity, and helplessness are certainly major considerations, other elements come into play, as illustrated in the following paragraphs.

Recall the drunken comportment thesis that was introduced in the section on culture and drinking behavior. Some nonreligious ceremonial drinking settings incorporate expectations of disinhibited behaviors, such as at holiday office parties. Drinking is a signal or cue that it is acceptable to be amorous, even sexually aggressive, and that the intoxicated object of one's affections will not object and is disinhibited.

Intoxicated people are not as capable of attending to multiple cues. When cues are ambiguous, drunken men are more likely to miss the ambiguity and to interpret cues as meaning that sex will occur and should be initiated. (Men are generally more likely to interpret friendly cues as sexual signals, but intoxication makes this misunderstanding more likely.) In addition, possible dangers implicit in a private setting, on a date, with a drunken male will not be picked up as often or as easily by the intoxicated and potentially victimized female (Abbey 1990).

Alcohol and the Family: Destructive Types of Social Support and Organizations for Victims of Alcoholics

■ Codependency and Enabling

Codependency and enabling generally occur together. **Codependency** (which some call co-alcoholism) refers to a relationship pattern, and enabling refers to a set of specific behaviors (Doweiko 2009). Codependency is defined as the behavior displayed by either addicted or nonaddicted family members (codependents) who identify with the alcohol addict and cover up the excessive drinking behavior. An example of codependency is when a family member remains silent

KEY TERMS

acquaintance and date rape
unplanned and unwanted forced sexual attack from a friend or a date partner

codependency
behavior displayed by either addicted or nonaddicted family members (codependents) who identify with the alcohol addict and cover up the excessive drinking behavior, allowing it to continue and letting it affect the codependent's life

when empty bottles of vodka (for example) are discovered under a bed or in the garage.

Enablers are those close to the alcohol addict who deny or make excuses for enabling the excessive drinking. Often, both codependency and enabling are done by the same person. An example is the husband who calmly conspires and phones his wife's place of employment and reports that his wife has the stomach flu when the reality is that she is too drunk or hung over to realize it is time to go to work.

Such a husband is both codependent and an enabler. He lies to cover up his wife's addiction and enables her not to face her irresponsible drinking behavior. In this example, the husband is responsible for perpetuating the spouse's addiction. Even quiet toleration of the alcoholic's addiction enables the drinker to continue the drinking behavior.

Children of Alcoholics and Adult Children of Alcoholics

Alcoholism is a disease of the family. Not only is there a significant genetic component that is passed from generation to generation, but the drinking problems of a single family member affect all other family members. The family environment and genetics can perpetuate a vicious and destructive cycle. (George Washington University Medical Center 2002)

Children of alcoholics are at high risk for developing problems with alcohol and other drugs; they often do poorly at school, live with pervasive tension and stress, have high levels of anxiety and depression, and experience coping problems (George Washington University Medical Center 2002, pp. 1–2).

It is estimated that out of 260 million Americans, 14 million Americans—7.4% of the population—meet the diagnostic criteria for alcohol abuse or alcoholism (Grant et al. 1997).

Approximately 9.7 million children age 17 or younger were living in households with one or more adults who were classified as having a diagnosis of alcohol abuse or dependence within the past year, according to data from the National Longitudinal Alcohol Epidemiologic Survey (NLAES). Approximately 70 percent of these children were bio-

logical, foster, adopted, or stepchildren. Therefore, 6.8 million children, or about 15 percent of children age 17 or younger, meet the formal definition of children of alcoholics (COAs) (Zucker et al. 2009, pp. 23–24).

Children of alcoholics are at high risk of developing the same attachment to alcohol as their parents. Alcoholics are more likely than nonalcoholics to have an alcoholic parent, sibling, or other relative.

Within the last decade, both COAs and adult children of alcoholics (ACOAs) have been studied extensively. Here are some findings concerning these two groups:

- COAs have an increased risk of alcohol involvement because "Genetically transmitted differences in response to alcohol . . . make drinking more pleasurable and/or less aversive" (Zucker et al. 2009, p. 24).
- "Higher transmission of risky temperamental and behavioral traits . . . lead the COAs into greater contact with earlier and heavier drinking peers" (Zucker et al. 2009, p. 24).
- COAs are two to four times more likely to develop alcoholism. In addition, both COAs and ACOAs are more likely to marry into families in which alcoholism is prevalent.
- Approximately one-third of alcoholics come from families in which one parent was or is an alcoholic.
- Both physiological and environmental factors appear to place COAs and ACOAs at greater risk of becoming alcoholics.
- COAs and ACOAs exhibit more symptoms of depression and anxiety than do children of nonalcoholic parents.
- Young children of alcoholics exhibit an excessive amount of crying, bed-wetting, and sleep problems, such as nightmares.
- Teenagers display excessive perfectionism, hoarding, staying by themselves (loners), and excessive self-consciousness.
- Phobias develop, and difficulty with school performance is not uncommon.

Treatment of Alcoholism

Chapter 18 provides an overview of treatment and rehabilitation of addicts. Although treatment of alcoholism and treatment of other addictions have somewhat separate historical roots and consequently gave rise to separate therapy systems, governmental authorities, and counselor certifi-

KEY TERMS

enablers
those close to the alcohol addict who deny or make excuses for enabling his or her excessive drinking

cations, they have now merged in most states in the United States. In addition to recognizing that alcohol is a drug addiction, epidemiologically few "pure" alcoholics and drug addicts exist anymore. Most addicts drink in addition to their other drug addictions (making them polydrug users); many alcoholics abuse other drugs; and some move through stages of heroin, methadone, and alcohol use, in that order. Alcoholism and its treatment have a few special features:

- While addicts remain in denial, the socially acceptable nature of drinking, or even of heavy drinking, makes it easier to maintain denial as a psychological defense. As an example, it is more difficult to remain in denial of crack addiction.
- Although all addictions could result in **relapsing syndrome** and most addicts have a tendency to relapse, the social environment that permits or even encourages drinking and the ready availability of alcohol make it easy to relapse without a radical shift in lifestyle. Again, the alcoholic is buffered within a subcultural (social and cultural) cloud of use. Alcoholics Anonymous remains particularly vigilant in looking for signs of relapse, advising the alcoholic to "keep the memory regarding the misery of addiction green," to HALT (which stands for do not get too hungry, angry, lonely, or thirsty/ tired because these are possible relapse triggers), and not to become isolated from others but to stay in the support system, making phone calls and attending "90 meetings in 90 days."
- Alcohol rehabilitation differs from other addiction treatments mainly in its medical ramifications. Alcoholism is devastating to the liver, muscles, nutritional system, gastrointestinal system, and brain. Alcoholics who have become "dry" only recently may still suffer from pancreatitis, weakness, impaired cognitive capacities, and so forth. The fact that treatment is so structured, simplified, and made into a slogan ("Don't drink and go to meetings," "Keep coming: It works") makes it possible for the bleary and confused, recently dried-out alcoholic to follow. (An AA term for this condition is *mokus*.) Although the cognitive impairment tends to clear up somewhat over a period of 6 months (unless clear cortical wasting has occurred, a condition known as "wet brain"), the alcoholic is often physically ravaged to an extent that requires years to mend the damage, if it is ever possible.
- The alcoholic is typically more emotionally fragile than other addicts in treatment.

- The other major medical ramification is withdrawal. Withdrawal from alcohol and withdrawal from barbiturates are the two most severe withdrawal syndromes. Before modern medical management techniques, many individuals succumbed to **acute alcohol withdrawal syndrome**.

Getting Through Withdrawal

An alcoholic who is well nourished and in good physical condition can go through withdrawal as an outpatient with reasonable safety. However, an acutely ill alcoholic needs medically supervised care. A general hospital ward is best for preliminary treatment. The alcohol withdrawal syndrome is quite similar to that described in Chapter 6 for barbiturates and other sedative hypnotics. Symptoms typically appear within 12 to 72 hours after total cessation of drinking but can appear whenever the blood alcohol level drops below a certain point. The alcoholic experiences severe muscle tremors, nausea, and anxiety. In extremely acute alcohol syndromes, a condition known as **delirium tremens (DTs)** occurs, in which the individual hallucinates, is delirious, and suffers from a high fever and rapid heartbeat. Delirium tremens, commonly called DTs, is an uncommon but life-threatening condition.

Alcohol withdrawal syndrome reaches its peak intensity within 24 to 48 hours. About 5% of the alcoholics in hospitals and perhaps 20% to 25% who suffer the DTs without treatment die. Phenobarbital, chlordiazepoxide (Librium), and diazepam (Valium) are commonly prescribed to prevent withdrawal symptoms. Simultaneously, the alcoholic may need treatment for malnutrition and vitamin deficiencies (especially the B vitamins). Pneumonia is also a frequent complication. After the alcoholic patient is over the acute stages of intoxication and withdrawal, administration of CNS depressants may be continued for a few weeks, with care taken

KEY TERMS

relapsing syndrome
returning to the use of alcohol after quitting

acute alcohol withdrawal syndrome
symptoms that occur when an individual who is addicted to alcohol does not maintain his or her usual blood alcohol level

delirium tremens (DTs)
the most severe, even life-threatening form of alcohol withdrawal, involving hallucinations, delirium, and fever

definitions include chronic behavioral disorders, repeated drinking to the point of loss of control, health disorders, and difficulty functioning socially and economically.

7 The definition of who is a problem drinker varies from one culture to the next. In Poland, a person becomes a problem drinker when there is a loss of productivity. Californians find that drunken driving violations are a key indication. For Italian Americans, an inability to provide for one's family because of heavy drinking qualifies a person as a problem drinker.

8 Culture influences our view of alcohol and alcohol consumption. Culture dictates the self-definition, attachment, and intensity of our behavior. For example, with regard to drinking, much of how we feel after ingesting alcohol is determined by social and psychological experiences. In addition to the amount consumed, drunken comportment refers to society's expectations regarding drinking behavior. Set and setting refer to the expectation and the environment where alcohol is consumed. Pseudointoxication refers to the psychological belief regarding how one feels under the effects of alcohol—that is, how inebriated the drinker imagines he or she is due to the effect of the consumed alcohol.

9 The broader ways in which culture influences the consumption of alcohol are the following: (a) culture provides rules for drinking behavior; (b) culture provides ceremonial meaning for alcohol use; (c) culture provides models of alcoholism; and (d) culture provides attitudes regarding alcohol consumption.

10 Use of alcohol by college students results in a significant increase in the numbers of incidences of death, injury, assault, sexual abuse, unsafe sex, academic problems, health problems, suicide attempts, drunk driving, vandalism, property damage, police involvement, and alcohol abuse and dependence. Additional noteworthy findings include: (a) college students consume an estimated 4 billion cans of beer annually; (b) nearly half of all college students are binge drinkers; (c) one consequence of alcohol abuse is motor vehicle accidents (the number one cause of death in people younger than age 25 is motor vehicle accidents); and (d) 75% of male students and 55% of female students involved in acquaintance rape had been drinking or using drugs at the time.

11 In comparison to men, women possess greater sensitivity to alcohol, are more likely to become addicted, and are more likely to develop health problems earlier in life than men. Three main reasons why women are more sensitive and are more easily affected by alcohol use are (a) men have larger bodies than women; (b) women absorb alcohol sooner than men because women have more body fat (fat does not dilute alcohol) and men's bodies contain more water; and (c) women possess less of a metabolizing enzyme that functions to get rid of (process out) alcohol.

12 Codependency and enabling generally occur together. Codependency is the behavior that a family member or close friend displays to cover up the excessive drinking. Enabling refers to anyone who helps the excessive drinker deny or makes excuses for the excessive drinking.

13 Alcoholism treatment must take into consideration physical withdrawal and denial.

References

Abbey, A. "Sex and Substance Abuse: What Are the Links?" *Eta Sigma Gamman* 22 (Fall 1990): 16–18.

About.com. "Alcoholism: Are Women More Vulnerable to Alcohol's Effects?" 1998a. Available http://alcoholism.about.com/cs/alerts/l/blnaa46.htm

About.com. "Alcoholism: Greater Risks for Women." 4 November 1998b. Available http://alcoholism.about.com/cs/women/a/aa981104.htm

About.com. "African-American Drinking Patterns More Deadly." 23 November 2003. Available http://alcoholism.about.com/cs/heal/a/blarg030312.htm

About.com. "Alcoholism: Domestic Abuse and Alcohol." 9 July 2010a. Available http://alcoholism.about.com/cs/abuse/a/aa990331.htm?p=1

About.com. "Alcoholism: Estimating the Costs of Alcohol Abuse." 2010b. Available http://alcoholism.about.com/cs/alerts/l/blnaa11.htm

About.com. "Alcoholism: Nalmefene." 2010c. Available http://alcoholism.about.com/od/nalmefene/Nalmefene.htm

About.com. "Alcoholism: Naltrexone." 2010d. Available http://alcoholism.about.com/od/naltrexone/Naltrexone.htm

Adams, S. H. "The Great American Fraud." *Collier's* 36, 5 (1905): 17–18; 10 (1905): 16–18; 16 (1906): 18–20.

Allison, C. "Sticker Shock—The Average Price of a College Textbook is $61.66 and Rising: Why Are Books So Expensive?" WD Communications, 2004. Available http://www.back2college.com/shock.htm

American Medical Association (AMA). "Facts About Youth and Alcohol." Chicago, IL: AMA Newsletter, 2011.

Answers.com. "Can Hasidic Jews Drink Alcohol?" Answers Corporation, 2011. Available http://wiki.answers.com/Q/Can_Hasidic_Jews_drink_alcohol

Arkin, E. B., and J. E. Funkhouser, eds. *Communicating About Alcohol and Other Drugs: Strategies for Reaching Populations at Risk,* OSAP Prevention Monograph No. 5. Rockville, MD: Office of Substance Abuse Prevention, U.S. Department of Health and Human Services, 1992.

Austin, G. A. "Perspectives on the History of Psychoactive Substance Use." *National Institute on Drug Abuse Research Issues* 23. Washington, DC: U.S. Department of Health, Education, and Welfare, 1978.

Babor, T. F., M. Hesselbrock, S. Radouce-Thomas, L. Feguer, J. P. Ferrant, and K. Choquette. "Concepts of Alcoholism Among American, French-Canadian, and French Alcoholics." In *Alcohol and Culture: Comparative Perspectives from Europe and America,* edited by T. F. Babor, 98–109. New York: Academy of Sciences, 1986.

Bales, R. F. "Cultural Differences in Rates of Alcoholism." *Quarterly Journal of Studies on Alcohol* 6 (1946): 489–499.

Berkowitz, A. D., and H. W. Perkins. "Recent Research on Gender Differences in Collegiate Alcohol Use." *Journal of American College Health* 36 (September 1987): 12–15.

Bloomfield, K., T. Stockwell, G. Gmel, and N. Rehn. "International Comparisons of Alcohol Consumption." *Alcohol Research and Health* 27, 11 (2003a): 95–109.

Bloomfield, K., T. Stockwell, G. Gmel, and N. Rehn. *International Comparisons of Alcohol Consumption.* Bethesda, MD: National Institute on Alcohol Abuse and Alcoholism (NIAAA) of the National Institutes of Health (NIH), 2003b.

Boyd, C. J., S. E. McCabe; and H. d'Arcy. "A Modified Version of the Cage as an Indicator of Alcohol Abuse and Its Consequences Among Undergraduate Drinkers." *Substance Abuse* 24 (December 2003): 221–232.

Brisbane, F. L. "A Self-Help Model for Working with Black Women of Alcoholic Parents." *Alcoholism Treatment Quarterly* 2 (Fall 1985a/Winter 1986): 47–53.

Brisbane, F. L. "Understanding the Female Child Role of Family Hero in Black Alcoholic Families." *Bulletin of the New York State Chapter of the National Black Alcoholism Council* 4 (April 1985b).

Center for Substance Abuse Research (CESAR). "Alcohol-Related Traffic Fatalities Remain Steady at Around 40%." 10 October 2005. Available http://www.cesar.umd.edu/cesar/cesarfax/vol14/14-41.pdf

Center for Substance Abuse Research (CESAR). "Nearly All 11th and 12th Graders Believe Their Peers Are More Likely to Drink and Drive on Prom and Graduation Nights; Less Than One-Third Think Driving on These Nights Is Dangerous." 26 April 2010a. Available http://www.cesar.umd.edu

Center for Substance Abuse Research (CESAR). "Nearly Two-Thirds of U.S. Adults Are Current Drinkers; Majority Are Infrequent or Light Drinkers." 29 March 2010b. Available http://www.cesar.umd.edu

Centers for Disease Control and Prevention (CDC). "Alcohol Consumption among Women Who Are Pregnant or Who Might Become Pregnant—United States, 2002." *Morbidity and Mortality Weekly Report* 53 (24 December 2004): 1178–1181.

Centers for Disease Control and Prevention (CDC). "Fetal Alcohol Spectrum Disorders (FASDs)—State-Specific Weighted Prevalence Estimates of Alcohol Use (Percentage of Any Use/Binge Drinking) Among Women Aged 18–44 Years—BRFSS, 2008." Atlanta, GA: Centers for Disease Control and Prevention. 19 May 2010. Available http://www.cdc.gov/ncbddd/fasd/data.html

Coghill, N., P. Miller, and M. Plant. "Future Proof: Can We Afford the Cost of Drinking Too Much?" London, England: Alcohol Concern, October 2009.

Collins, J. J., and M. A. Messerschmidt. "Epidemiology of Alcohol-Related Violence." *Alcohol, Health, and Research World* 17 (1993): 93–100.

Core Institute. "Core Alcohol and Drug Survey Results for 2006." Carbondale, IL: Core Institute, Southern Illinois University, Carbondale, 2008. Available http://www.core.siuc.edu

Dartmouth Center on Addiction, Recovery and Education (DCARE). "Jewish Tradition: Alcohol and Judaism: One View." September 17, 2008. Available at http://www.dartmouth.edu/~dcare/topics/jewish.html

Davis, L. "Acting Out Your Issues Through Psychodrama." Tucson, AZ: Sierra Tucson. Available http://www.sierratucson.com/sierratucson_articles/acting-out-your-issues-through-psychodrama.php

De Jong, J. "Scope of the Problem: Gender and Drinking." *Catalyst (Higher Education Center for Alcohol and Other Drug Prevention)* 1 (Spring 1995): 1.

Douglass, F. *Life and Times of Frederick Douglass.* New York: Collier Books, 1892 (1967): 147–148.

Doweiko, H. E. *Concepts of Chemical Dependency,* 4th ed. Monterey, CA: Brooks/Cole, 1999.

Doweiko, H. E. *Concepts of Chemical Dependency,* 7th ed. Monterey, CA: Brooks/Cole, 2009.

Drug Strategies. "Alcohol and Crime." *Millennium Hangover: Keeping Score on Alcohol.* Washington, DC (1999): 5. Available http://www.drugstrategies.com/pdf/Score99.pdf

English, E. M., M. D. Shutt, and S. B. Oswalt. "Decreasing Use of Alcohol, Tobacco, and Other Drugs on a College Campus: Exploring Potential Factors Related to Change." *Journal of Student Affairs Research and Practice* 46, 2009. Available http://journals.naspa.org/jsarp/vol46/iss2/art3

Federal Occupational Health. "Let's Talk: Close the Door on Domestic Violence." U.S. Public Health Service Program Support Center, Department of Health and Human Services. Health Ink Communications. 2005. Available http://www.hhs.gov/ohr/eap/newsletter/fall05.pdf

Gallup Poll. "Alcohol and Drinking." 2007. Available http://www.galluppoll.com/poll/1582/alcohol-drinking.aspx

Garrison, V., and J. Podell. "Community Support Systems Assessment for Use in Clinical Interviews." *Schizophrenia Bulletin* 7 (1981): 1.

Gary, L. E., and R. B. Gary. "Treatment Needs of Black Alcoholic Women." *Alcoholism Treatment Quarterly* 2 (1985): 97–113.

George Washington University Medical Center. "Ensuring Solutions to Alcohol Problems: Alcohol and the Family." Washington, DC: George Washington University Medical

Center, 2002. Available http://www.ensuringsolutions. org/resources/resources_show.htm?doc_id=339037

Gold, M. S. *The Good News About Drugs and Alcohol.* New York: Villard Books, 1991.

Goode, E. *Drugs in American Society.* Boston: McGraw-Hill, 1999.

Gordon, A. J. "The Cultural Context of Drinking and Indigenous Therapy for Alcohol Problems in Three Migrant Hispanic Cultures." *Journal of Studies on Alcohol* supplement 9 (1981): 217–240.

Grant, B. F., T. C. Harford, P. Chou, R. Pickering, D. A. Dawson, E. S. Stinson, and J. Noble. "Prevalence of DSM-IV Alcohol Abuse and Dependence: United States." *Alcohol Health Research World* 18 (1997): 243–248.

GreenFacts. "Scientific Facts on Alcohol." GreenFacts Scientific Board. 10 May 2009. Available http://www.greenfacts. org/en/alcohol/index.htm

Gusfield, J. R. *Symbolic Crusade: Status Politics and the American Temperance Movement,* 2nd ed. Chicago: University of Illinois, 1986.

Hanson, D. J. "Binge Drinking." Sociology Department, State University of New York, Potsdam. 2009a. Available http:// www2.potsdam.edu/hansondj/BingeDrinking.html

Hanson, D. J. "History of Alcohol and Drinking Around the World." Sociology Department, State University of New York, Potsdam. 2009b. Available http://www2.potsdam. edu/hansondj/Controversies/1114796842.html

Hanson, D. J. "Why We Should Lower the Drinking Age to 19." Sociology Department, State University of New York, Potsdam. 2009c. Available http://www2.potsdam.edu/ hansondj/YouthIssues/1046348192.html

Harper, F. D. *The Black Family and Substance Abuse.* Detroit, MI: Detroit Urban League, 1986.

Harwood, H. *Updating Estimates of the Economic Costs of Alcohol Abuse in the United States: Estimates, Update Methods and Data.* Report prepared by The Lewin Group for the National Institute on Alcohol Abuse and Alcoholism, 2000.

Harwood, H., D. Fountain, and G. Livermore. *The Economic Costs of Alcohol and Drug Abuse in the United States, 1992.* NIH Pub. No. 98-4327. Rockville, MD: National Institute on Drug Abuse, 1998.

Hingson, R. W., W. Zha, and E. R. Weitzman. "Magnitude of and Trends in Alcohol-Related Mortality and Morbidity Among U.S. College Students Ages 18–24, 1998–2005." *Journal of Studies on Alcohol and Drugs* 16 (July 2009): 12–20.

Inciardi, J. A. *The War on Drugs II.* Mountain View, CA: Mayfield, 1992.

Institute of Alcohol Studies. "World Drink Trends." Available http://www.ias.org.uk/resources/publications/ warc/worlddrinks_2005.html

Jellinek, E. M. *The Disease Concept of Alcoholism.* New Haven, CT: College and University Press, 1960.

Johnston, L. D., P. M. O'Malley, and J. G. Bachman. *Monitoring the Future: National Results on Adolescent Drug Use: Overview of Key Findings.* NIH Pub. No. 06-5882. Bethesda, MD: National Institute on Drug Abuse, 2005.

Johnston, L. D., P. M. O'Malley, J. G. Bachman, and J. E. Schuelenberg. *Monitoring the Future: National Survey Results on Drug Use, 1975–2008, Volume I: Secondary School Students,* Bethesda, MD: National Institute on Drug Abuse, 2009.

Jones, J. M. "U.S. Drinkers Consuming Alcohol More Regularly." The Gallup Poll. 31 July 2006. Available http:// www.gallup.com/poll/23935/US-Drinkers-Consuming-Alcohol-More-Regularly.aspx

Jones, J. M. "Beer Again Edges Out Wine as Americans' Drink of Choice." The Gallup Poll. 12 July 2007. Available http://www.gallup.com/poll/28234/Beer-Again_Edges_ Wine-Americans_Drink_Choice.aspx

Keller, M. "Alcoholism: Nature and Extent of the Problem: Understanding Alcoholism." *Annals of the American Academy of Political and Social Science* 315 (1958): 1–11.

Kinney, J. *Loosening the Grip,* 6th ed. Boston: McGraw-Hill, 2000.

Kolevzon, M. S., and R. G. Green. *Family Therapy Models.* New York: Springer, 1985.

Lender, M. E., and J. K. Martin. *Drinking in America,* rev. ed. New York: Free Press, 1987.

Levine, H. G. "The Good Creature of God and the Demon Rum." In *Research Monograph No. 12: Alcohol and Disinhibition: Nature and Meaning of the Link,* 111–161. Rockville, MD: National Institute on Alcohol Abuse and Alcoholism, 1983.

Li, T-K. *FY 2009 President's Budget Request for NIAAA—Director's Statement before the House Subcommittee on Labor-HHS Appropriations.* Bethesda, MD: National Institute on Alcohol Abuse and Alcoholism (NIAAA), 5 March 2008: 1.

MacAndrew, C., and R. B. Edgerton. *Drunken Comportment: A Social Explanation.* Chicago, IL: Aldine, 1969.

Makela, K. "Attitudes Towards Drinking and Drunkenness in Four Scandinavian Countries." In *Alcohol and Culture: Comparative Perspectives from Europe and America. Annals of the New York Academy of Science* 472, edited by T. F. Babor. New York: New York Academy of Sciences, 1986.

Marshall, M. "Four Hundred Rabbits: An Anthropological View of Ethanol as a Disinhibitor." In *Alcohol and Disinhibition: Nature and Meaning of the Link,* NIAAA Research Monograph No. 12. Washington, DC: U.S. Department of Health and Human Services, 1983.

McCartt, A. T., and B. B. Kirley. *Minimum Purchase Age Laws: How Effective Are They in Reducing Alcohol-Impaired Driving?* Arlington, VA: Insurance Institute for Highway Safety, 2006. Available http://onlinepubs.trb.org/onlinepubs/ circulars/ec123.pdf.

Medical News Today. "Alcohol Consumption More Detrimental to Women." Research Triangle Park, NC: RTI International, 7 May 2007. Available http://www.medical newstoday.com/articles/70062.php

Miller, B. A., and W. R. Downs, "The Impact of Family Violence on the Use of Alcohol by Women." *Alcohol, Health, and Research World* 17 (1993): 137–143.

National Clearinghouse for Alcohol and Drug Information (NCADI). *The Fact Is . . . Alcoholism Tends to Run in Families.* OSAP Prevention Resource Guide. Rockville, MD: NCADI, 1992.

National Institute on Alcohol Abuse and Alcoholism (NIAAA). *Facts About Alcohol and Alcoholism.* Washington, DC: U.S. Government Printing Office, 1980.

National Institute on Alcohol Abuse and Alcoholism (NIAAA). *Seventh Special Report to the U.S. Congress on Alcohol and Health.* Washington, DC: U.S. Government Printing Office, 1990.

National Institute on Alcohol Abuse and Alcoholism (NIAAA). *Tenth Special Report to the U.S. Congress on Alcohol and Health.* NIH Pub. No. 97-5017. Bethesda, MD: National Institute on Alcohol Abuse and Alcoholism, 1997.

National Institute on Alcohol Abuse and Alcoholism (NIAAA). *10th Special Report to the U.S. Congress on Alcohol and Health: Highlights from Current Research.* Washington, DC: U.S. Government Printing Office, June 2000.

National Institute on Alcohol Abuse and Alcoholism (NIAAA). "Frequently Asked Questions on Alcohol Abuse and Alcoholism." 2007. Available http://www.niaaa.nih.gov/faqs/general-english

National Institute on Alcohol Abuse and Alcoholism (NIAAA). *Alcohol Research—A Lifespan Perspective.* Alcohol Alert 74. Rockville, MD: National Institute on Alcohol Abuse and Alcoholism Publication Distribution Center, January 2008.

National Institute on Alcohol Abuse and Alcoholism (NIAAA). "College Drinking—Changing Culture. A Snapshot of Annual High-Risk College Drinking Consequences." 21 July 2010. Available http://www.collegedrinkingprevention.gov/StatsSummaries/snapshot.aspx

National Institute on Drug Abuse (NIDA). *National Survey Results on Drug Use from the Monitoring the Future Study, 1975–1998. Volume 1: Secondary School Students.* Washington, DC: U.S. Government Printing Office, 1999.

National Institute on Drug Abuse (NIDA). "NIDA Info Facts: Understanding Drug Abuse and Addiction." National Institutes of Health (NIH), U.S. Department of Health and Human Services (USDHHS). February 2011. Available http://www.drugabuse.gov/infofacts/understand.html

National Institutes of Health (NIH), the National Institute on Alcohol Abuse and Alcoholism (NIAAA), U.S. Department of Health and Human Services (USDHHS). *Researchers Identify Alcoholism Subtypes.* Bethesda, MD: Government Printing Office, 2007. Available http://www.nih.gov/news/pr/jun2007/niaaa-28.htm

Newport, F. "Alcohol and Drinking." The Gallup Organization. 13–15 November 2000. Available http://www.gallup.com/poll/1582/alcohol-drinking.aspx

Office for Substance Abuse Prevention (OSAP). *Cultural Competence for Evaluators.* DHHS Pub. No. (ADM) 92-1884. Washington, DC: Office for Substance Abuse Prevention, U.S. Department of Health and Human Services, 1992.

Office of Applied Studies (OAS), Substance Abuse and Mental Health Services Administration (SAMHSA). *The NHSDA Report: Alcohol Use.* Rockville, MD: Substance Abuse and Mental Health Services Administration, 2001. Available http://www.drugabusestatistics.samhsa.gov

Office of Applied Studies (OAS), Substance Abuse and Mental Health Services Administration (SAMHSA). "Driving Under the Influence (DUI) Among Young Persons." National Survey on Drug Use and Health (NSDUH). Rockville, MD: SAMHSA, 2004.

O'Malley, P. M., and A. C. Wagenaar. "Effects of Minimum Drinking Age Laws on Alcohol Use, Related Behaviors and Traffic Crash Involvement Among American Youth: 1976–1987." *Journal of Studies on Alcohol* 52 (1991): 478–491.

Osterberg, E. "Alcohol-Related Problems in Cross-National Perspective. Alcohol and Culture: Comparative Perspectives from Europe and America." *Annals of the New York Academy of Sciences* 472 (1986): 10–21.

Phoenix House. "School Daze?" 2009. Available http://www.factsontap.org/factsontap/alcohol_and_student_life/school_daze.htm

Presley, C., P. Meilman, and R. Lyerla. *Recent Statistics on Alcohol and Other Drug Use on American College Campuses: 1995–1996.* Carbondale, IL: CORE Institute, Southern Illinois University at Carbondale, 1996.

Pride USA Survey. Surveys for 1994–1995, 1995–1996, and 1996–1997. 1998. Available http://www.pridesurveys.com/supportfiles/9899drug.html

Register, T. C., J. M. Cline, and C. A. Shively. "Minority Women and Alcohol Use." *Alcohol Research and Health* (2002): 243–244.

Reuters Limited. "Global Costs of Alcohol Abuse Top $250 Billion." Yahoo News: Health Headlines. 27 December 1999: 1–2.

Room, R. "A Reverence for Strong Drink: The Lost Generation and the Elevation of Alcohol in American Culture." *Journal of Studies on Alcohol* 43 (1984): 540–545.

Room, R., and K. Mäkelä. "Typologies of the Cultural Position of Drinking." *Journal of Studies on Alcohol* 61 (2000): 475–483.

Roueche, B. "Alcohol in Human Culture." In *Alcohol and Civilization,* edited by L. P. Salvatore, 167–182. New York: McGraw-Hill, 1963.

Royce, J. E. *Alcohol Problems and Alcoholism,* rev. ed. New York: Free Press, 1989.

Royce, J. E., and D. Scratchley. "Definition of Alcoholism." eNotAlone.com, excerpted from *Alcoholism and Other Drug Problems,* 1996. Available http://www.enotalone.com/article/5538.html

Satir, V. *Conjoint Family Therapy.* Palo Alto, CA: Science and Behavior Books, 1964.

Substance Abuse and Mental Health Services Administration (SAMHSA). *Making the Link: Alcohol, Tobacco, and Other Drugs and Women's Health.* Pub. No. ML011. Rockville, MD: U.S. Department of Health and Human Services, Spring 1995.

Substance Abuse and Mental Health Services Administration (SAMHSA). *1998 Fact Sheet, National Household Survey on Drug Abuse.* Rockville, MD: Office of Applied Studies, U.S. Department of Health and Human Services, August 1999a.

Substance Abuse and Mental Health Services Administration (SAMHSA). *National Household Survey on Drug Abuse: Main Findings, 1997.* Rockville, MD: Office of Applied Studies, U.S. Department of Health and Human Services, August 1999b.

Substance Abuse and Mental Health Services Administration (SAMHSA). *Overview of Findings from the 2003*

National Survey on Drug Use and Health. Rockville, MD: Office of Applied Studies, U.S. Department of Health and Human Services, 2004a.

Substance Abuse and Mental Health Services Administration (SAMHSA). *Results from the 2003 National Survey on Drug Use and Health: National Findings.* Rockville, MD: Office of Applied Studies, 2004b.

Substance Abuse and Mental Health Services Administration (SAMHSA). "SAMHSA Unveils Guide to Introduce Substance Abuse Treatment Providers to Family Therapy." Rockville, MD: U.S. Department of Health and Human Services, 2004c. Available http://www.samhsa.gov/news/newsreleases/040929nr_tip39.htm

Substance Abuse and Mental Health Services Administration (SAMHSA). *Results from the 2005 National Survey on Drug Use and Health: National Findings.* Rockville, MD: Office of Applied Studies, 2006.

Substance Abuse and Mental Health Services Administration (SAMHSA). *Results from the 2008 National Survey on Drug Use and Health: National Findings.* Rockville, MD: Office of Applied Studies, 2009.

Substance Abuse and Mental Health Services Administration (SAMHSA), Office of Applied Studies. *National Household Survey on Drug Abuse, The NHSDA Report. Alcohol Use by Persons Under the Legal Drinking Age of 21.* Rockville, MD: Office of Applied Studies, 9 May 2003.

Wagenaar, A. C. "Minimum Drinking Age and Alcohol Availability to Youth: Issues and Research Needs." In *Economics and the Prevention of Alcohol-Related Problems,* edited by M. E. Hilton and B. Bloss, 175–200. National Institute on Alcohol Abuse and Alcoholism (NIAAA) Research Monograph No. 25, NIH Pub. No. 93-3513. Bethesda, MD: NIAAA, 1993.

Wechsler, H., A. Davenport, G. Dowdall, B. Moeykens, and S. Castillo. "Health and Behavioral Consequences of Binge Drinking in College. A National Survey of Students at 140 Campuses." *Journal of the American Medical Association* 272 (7 December 1994): 1672–1677.

Wechsler, H, G. W. Dowdall, A. Davenport, and W. DeJong. *Binge Drinking on Campus: Results of a National Study.* Harvard School of Public Health, Higher Education Center for Alcohol and Other Drug Prevention. Washington, DC: U.S. Department of Education, 2000a.

Wechsler, H., J. Eun Lee, M. Kuo, and H. Lee. "College Binge Drinking in the 1990s: A Continuing Problem: Results of the Harvard School of Public Health 1999 College Alcohol Study." 1999 College Alcohol Study (CAS) Binge Drinking Survey. Boston, MA: Harvard School of Public Health, 2000b.

Wegscheider, S. *Another Chance.* Palo Alto, CA: Science and Behavior Books, 1991.

Williams, G. D., F. S. Stinson, D. A. Parker, T. C. Harford, and V. Noble. "Demographic Trends, Alcohol Abuse and Alcoholism, 1985–1995." Epidemiologic Bulletin No. 15. *Alcohol, Health, and Research World* 11 (1997): 80–83.

Wilsnack, R. W., N. D. Vogeltanz, and S. C. Wilsnack. "Gender Differences in Alcohol Consumption and Adverse Drinking Consequences: Cross-Cultural Patterns." *Addiction* 95 (2000): 251–265.

Wilsnack, S. C., R. W. Wilsnack, and A. D. Klassen. "Epidemiological Research on Women's Drinking, 1978–1984." In *Women and Alcohol: Health-Related Issues.* Research Monograph No. 16. Washington, DC: U.S. Government Printing Office, 1986.

World Health Organization (WHO). "Trends in Substance Use and Associated Health Problems." *Trends in Substance Use.* Fact Sheet No. 127 (1998). Available http://www.who.int/inffs/en/fact127.html

Zinberg, N. E. *Drug, Set, and Setting: The Basis for Controlled Intoxicant Use.* New Haven, CT: Yale University Press, 1984.

Zinberg, N. E., and J. A. Robertson. *Drugs and the Public.* New York: Simon & Schuster, 1972.

Zucker, R. A., J. E. Donovan, A. S. Masten, M. E. Mattson, and H. B. Moss. "Developmental Processes and Mechanisms—Ages 0–10." *Alcohol Research and Health* 32 (2009): 16–29.

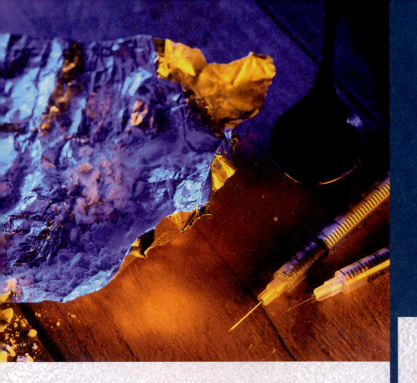

CHAPTER 9

Narcotics (Opioids)

Did You Know?

- The release of natural substances called endorphins activate opioid receptors and can mimic the effects of narcotics such as heroin.
- By the end of the 19th century, almost 1 million Americans were addicted to opiates, primarily due to the use of patent medicines that contained opium products.
- Narcotics are among the most potent analgesics available today.
- In the past decade, treatment for nonmedical use of prescription pain relievers has increased more than four-fold and currently accounts for two-thirds of prescription abuse in the United States.
- Because of concern about abusing prescription narcotic analgesics, many clinicians are hesitant to prescribe sufficient quantities of these drugs to adequately manage severe, long-term pain.
- Addiction to prescription narcotic analgesics rarely happens when these medications are used properly to treat pain.
- There is evidence that acupuncture reduces pain by activating a natural opioid system.
- Many heroin addicts have been exposed to the AIDS virus.
- Heroin supplies today are more potent, cheaper, and more readily available than a decade ago.
- One designer drug, made from the narcotic fentanyl, is 6000 times more potent than heroin.
- Some heroin addicts have to be treated with the narcotic methadone for the rest of their lives to keep them from abusing heroin.
- Dextromethorphan (a common over-the-counter cough medicine chemically related to codeine), when taken in high doses, can cause phencyclidine (PCP)-like hallucinations.

Learning Objectives

On completing this chapter you will be able to:

- Describe the principal pharmacological effects of narcotics, their biological targets, and their main therapeutic uses.
- Identify the major side effects of narcotics, in particular their abuse potential.
- Distinguish between narcotic physical dependence and addiction.
- Identify the abuse patterns for heroin.
- Outline the stages of heroin dependence.
- List the withdrawal symptoms that result from narcotic dependence, list potential treatments, and discuss the significance of tolerance.
- Describe and compare the use of methadone and buprenorphine in treating narcotic addiction.
- Identify the unique features of fentanyl that make it appealing to illicit drug dealers but dangerous to narcotic addicts.
- Describe how "designer" drugs have been associated with narcotics and Parkinson's disease.
- Describe why dextromethorphan in cough medicines is abused.
- Identify the opioid features of tramadol and its potential for abuse.

 Drugs and Society Online is a great source for additional drugs and society information for both students and instructors. Visit **go.jblearning.com/hanson11** to find a variety of useful tools for learning, thinking, and teaching.

Introduction

The proportion of persons admitted for substance abuse treatment whose principal problem was nonmedical use of prescription pain medication (i.e., narcotic analgesics) has gone from 2.2% to almost 10% in the past decade. This startling escalation has made abuse of these drugs the second most prevalent form of illegal drug use in the United States (Bloomberg BusinessWeek 2010). What are these drugs, where do they come from, and how do they work?

The term *narcotic* in general means a central nervous system (CNS) depressant that produces insensibility or stupor. The term has also come to designate those drugs and substances with pharmacological properties related to opium ingredients and their drug derivatives. All opioid narcotics activate opioid receptors and have abuse potential. Narcotics are frequently prescribed for pain relief (**analgesics**), to reduce coughing (**antitussive**), and to reduce diarrhea.

In this chapter, we introduce the opioid narcotics with a brief historical account. The pharmacological properties and therapeutic uses of these drugs are discussed, followed by a description of, and distinction between, their side effects and problems with tolerance, withdrawal, dependence, and addiction. Narcotic abuse, its risks and outcomes, is presented in detail, with special emphasis on heroin. In addition, treatment approaches for narcotic addiction, dependence, and withdrawal are included. This chapter concludes with descriptions of other commonly used opioid narcotics and related drugs.

What Are Narcotics?

The word *narcotic* has been used to label many substances, from opium to marijuana to cocaine. The translation of the Greek word *narkoticos* is "benumbing or deadening." The term *narcotic* is sometimes used to refer to a CNS depressant, producing insensibility or stupor, and at other times to refer to an addicting drug. Most people would not consider marijuana among the narcotics today, although for many years it was included in this category. Although pharmacologically cocaine is not a narcotic either, it is still legally classified as such. Perhaps part of this confusion is due to the fact that cocaine, as a local anesthetic, can cause a numbing effect.

For purposes of the present discussion, the term *narcotic* is used to refer to those naturally occurring substances derived from the opium poppy and their synthetic substitutes. These drugs are referred to as the **opioid** (or opiate) narcotics because of their association with opium. They have similar pharmacological features, including abuse potential, pain-relieving effects (referred to as analgesics), cough suppression, and reduction of intestinal movement, often causing constipation, but useful in reducing severe diarrhea. Some of the most commonly used opioid narcotics are listed in **Table 9.1**.

The History of Narcotics

The opium poppy, *Papaver somniferum,* from which opium and its naturally occurring narcotic derivatives are obtained, has been cultivated for millennia. A 6000-year-old Sumerian tablet has an ideograph for the poppy shown as "joy" plus "plant," suggesting that the addicting properties of this substance have been appreciated for millennia. The Egyptians listed opium along with approximately 700 other medicinal compounds in the famous Ebers Papyrus (circa 1500 BC).

The Greek god of sleep, Hypnos, and the Roman god of sleep, Somnus, were portrayed as carrying containers of opium pods, and the Minoan goddess of sleep wore a crown of opium pods. During the so-called Dark Ages that followed the collapse of the Roman Empire, Arab traders actively engaged in traveling the overland caravan routes to China and to India, where they introduced opium. Eventually, both China and India grew their own poppies.

■ Opium in China

The opium poppy had a dramatic impact in China, causing widespread addiction (Karch 1996). Initially, the seeds were used medically, as was opium later. However, by the late 1690s, opium was being smoked and used for diversion. The Chinese government, fearful of the weakening of national vital-

Table 9.1 Commonly Used Opioid Narcotic Drugs and Products

NARCOTIC DRUGS	COMMON NAMES	MOST COMMON USES
Heroin	Horse, smack, junk (street names)	Abuse
Morphine	Several	Analgesia
Methadone	Dolophine	Treat narcotic dependence
Meperidine	Demerol	Analgesia
Oxycodone	Percodan, OxyContin	Analgesia
Propoxyphene	Darvon	Analgesia
Codeine	Several	Analgesia, antitussive
Loperamide	Imodium A-D	Antidiarrheal
Diphenoxylate	Lomotil	Antidiarrheal
Opium tincture	Paregoric	Antidiarrheal
Buprenorphine	Suboxone	Treat narcotic dependence

ity by the potent opiate narcotic, outlawed the sale of opium in 1729. The penalty for disobedience was death by strangulation or decapitation. Despite these laws and threats, the habit of opium smoking became so widespread that the Chinese government went a step further and forbade its importation from India, where most of the opium poppy was grown. In contrast, the British East India Company (and later the British government in India) encouraged cultivation of opium. British companies were the principal shippers to the Chinese port of Canton, which was the only port open to Western merchants. During the next 120 years, a complex network of opium smuggling routes developed in China with the help of local merchants, who received substantial profits, and local officials, who pocketed bribes to ignore the smugglers.

Everyone involved in the opium trade, but particularly the British, continued to profit until the Chinese government ordered the strict enforcement of the edict against importation. Such actions by the Chinese caused conflict with the British government and helped trigger the Opium War of 1839 to 1842. Great Britain sent in an army, and by 1842, 10,000 British soldiers had won a victory over 350 million Chinese. Because of the war, the island of Hong Kong was ceded to the British, and an indemnity of $6 million was imposed on China to cover the value of the destroyed opium and the cost of the war. In 1856, a second Opium War broke out. Peking was occupied by British and French troops, and China was compelled to make further concessions to Britain. The importation of opium continued to increase until 1908, when Britain and China made an agreement to limit the importation of opium from India (Austin 1978).

■ American Opium Use

Meanwhile, in 1803, a young German named Frederick Serturner extracted and partially purified the active ingredients in opium. The result was 10 times more potent than opium itself and was named

Famous cartoon, showing a British sailor shoving opium down the throat of a Chinese man, which dates back to the Opium War of 1839–1842.

morphine after Morpheus, the Greek god of dreams. This discovery increased worldwide interest in opium. By 1832, a second compound had been purified and named *codeine,* after the Greek word for "poppy capsule" (Maurer and Vogel 1967).

The opium problem was aggravated further in 1853, when Alexander Wood perfected the hypodermic syringe and introduced it first in Europe and then in America. Christopher Wren and others had worked with the idea of injecting drugs directly into the body by means of hollow quills and straws, but the approach was never successful or well received. Wood perfected the syringe technique with the intent of preventing morphine addiction by injecting the drug directly into the veins rather than by oral administration (Golding 1993). Unfortunately, just the opposite happened; injection of morphine increased the potency and the likelihood of dependence (Maurer and Vogel 1967).

The hypodermic syringe was used extensively during the Civil War to administer morphine to treat pain, dysentery, and fatigue (Kosten and Hollister 1998). A large percentage of the soldiers who returned home from the war were addicted to morphine. Opiate addiction became known as the "soldier's disease" or "army disease."

By 1900, an estimated 1 million Americans were dependent on opiates (Abel 1980). This drug problem was made worse because of (1) Chinese laborers, who brought with them to the United States opium to smoke (it was legal to smoke opium in the United States at that time); (2) the availability of purified morphine and the hypodermic syringe; and (3) the lack of controls on the large number of patent medicines that contained opium derivatives (Karch 1996). Until 1914, when the Harrison Narcotic Act was passed (regulating opium, coca leaves, and their products), the average opiate addict was a middle-aged, Southern, white woman who functioned well and was adjusted to her role as a wife and mother. She bought opium or morphine legally by mail order from Sears and Roebuck or at the local store, used it orally, and caused very few problems. A number of physicians were addicted as well. One of the best-known morphine addicts was William Holsted, a founder of Johns Hopkins Medical School. Holsted was a very productive surgeon and innovator, although secretly an addict for most of his career. He became dependent on morphine as a substitute for his cocaine dependence (Brecher 1972).

Looking for better medicines, chemists found that modification of the morphine molecule resulted in a more potent compound. In 1898, diacetylmorphine was placed on the market as a cough suppressant by Bayer. It was to be a "heroic" drug, without the addictive potential of morphine—it thus received the name *heroin.*

Heroin was first used in the United States as a cough suppressant and to combat addiction to other substances (Hubbard 1998). However, its inherent abuse potential was quickly discovered. When injected, heroin is more addictive than most of the other narcotics because of its ability to enter the brain rapidly and cause a euphoric surge (DiChiara and North 1992). Heroin was banned from U.S. medical practice in 1924, although it is still prescribed legally as an analgesic in other countries (Bammer 2005).

The Vietnam War was an important landmark for heroin use in the United States (Hubbard 1998). It has been estimated that as many as 40% of the

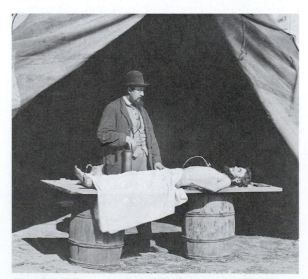

With the development of the hypodermic needle and its use during the Civil War, heroin addiction became more likely and more severe.

Chinese laborers often smoked heroin at the turn of the 20th century.

Heroin use by soldiers fighting in Afghanistan is a great concern.

U.S. soldiers serving in Southeast Asia at this time used heroin to combat the frustrations and stress associated with this unpopular military action. Although only 7% of the soldiers continued to use heroin after returning home, those who were addicted to this potent narcotic became a major component of the heroin-abusing population in this country (Golding 1993).

Heroin smoking became popular in the mid-1980s in response to the AIDS epidemic. This was due to a fear of HIV infection when using infected needles to administer the drug intravenously (Hubbard 1998). The effect resulting from inhalation is as intense as that caused by injection, although a very pure drug is required for smoking. Smoking continues to be a favorite form of heroin administration today.

As experience has shown, problems with the opiate drugs such as heroin are closely linked with war and its associated miseries and pains. As our country again finds itself in the middle of an extended and increasingly less popular military engagement in the Middle East, problems with heroin are becoming more and more apparent (Edwards 2010). As during previous wars, soldiers turn to drugs like heroin to cope and even to survive emotionally in a war zone. This is reflected in comments such as: "Life is unbearable. You don't know whether you're going to be alive in 10 minutes' time or not." "Life has few pleasures; you're uncomfortable . . . the food is pretty awful, the ever-present smell of death and you see some of your closest buddies die before your very eyes." "So life is really unbearable and heroin is cheap" (Edwards 2010).

Pharmacological Effects

Even though opioid narcotics have a history of being abused, they continue to be important therapeutic agents.

Narcotic Analgesics

The most common clinical use of the opioid narcotics is as analgesics to relieve pain. These drugs are effective against most varieties of pain, including *visceral* (associated with internal organs of the body) and *somatic* (associated with skeletal muscles, bones, skin, and teeth) types. Used in sufficiently high doses, narcotics can even relieve the intense pain associated with some types of cancer (Gutstein and Akil 2006).

The opioid narcotics relieve pain by activating the same group of receptors that are controlled by the endogenous substances called *endorphins* (Trigo et al. 2010). As discussed in Chapter 4, the endorphins are a family of peptides (small proteins) that are released in the brain, in the spinal cord, and from the adrenal glands in response to stress and painful experiences. When released, the endorphins serve as transmitters and stimulate receptors designated as opioid types. Activation of opioid receptors by either the naturally released endorphins or administration of the narcotic analgesic drugs blocks the transmission of pain through the spinal cord or brain stem and alters the perception of pain in the "pain center" of the brain. Because the narcotics work at multiple levels of pain transmission, they are potent analgesics against almost all types of pain.

Interestingly, the endorphin system appears to be influenced by psychological factors as well. Thus, natural activation of opioid receptors also contributes to the regulation of emotional behaviors such as stress, learning, and memory as well as the regulation of the brain's reward circuits (Trigo et al. 2010). It is possible that pain relief caused by administration of placebos or nonmedicinal manipulation such as acupuncture is due in part to the natural release of endorphins (Eshkevari and Heath 2005). This relationship suggests that physiological, psychological, and pharmacological factors are intertwined in pain management through the opioid system, which makes it impossible to deal with one without considering the others.

Although the narcotics are very effective analgesics, they do cause some side effects that are particularly alarming; thus, their clinical use usually is limited to the treatment of moderate to severe pain (*Drug Facts and Comparisons* 2010). Other, safer drugs, such as the aspirin-type analgesics (see Chapter 15), are preferred for pain management when possible. Often, the amount of narcotic required for pain relief can be reduced by combining a narcotic, such as codeine, with aspirin or acetaminophen (the active ingredient in Tylenol). Such combinations reduce the chance of significant narcotic side effects while providing adequate pain relief (*Drug Facts and Comparisons* 2010).

Morphine is a particularly potent pain reliever and often is used as the analgesic standard by which other narcotics are compared (Gutstein and Akil 2006). With continual use, tolerance develops to the analgesic effects of morphine and other narcotics, sometimes requiring a dramatic escalation of doses to maintain adequate pain control (*Drug Facts and Comparisons* 2010).

Because pain is expressed in different forms with many different diseases, narcotic treatment can vary considerably. Usually, the convenience of oral narcotic therapy is preferred but often is inadequate for severe pain. For short-term relief from intense pain, narcotics are effective when injected subcutaneously or intramuscularly. Narcotics can also be given intravenously for persistent and potent analgesia or administered by transdermal patches for sustained chronic pain (*Drug Facts and Comparisons* 2010). Despite the fact that most pain can be relieved if enough narcotic analgesic is properly administered, physicians frequently underprescribe narcotics or are not well trained in proper pain management or how to use the opioid narcotics responsibly (Meier 2010; Young 2007). Because of fear of causing narcotic addiction or creating legal problems with federal agencies such as the Drug Enforcement Administration (DEA) (see "Here and Now: Are Restrictions on Pain Pills Too Painful?"), many patients in the United States are often inadequately treated for their pain (Jointogether.org 2010). An important rule of narcotic use is that adequate

pain relief should not be denied because of concern about the abuse potential of these drugs (Hall and Sykes 2004). Indeed, addiction to narcotics is rare in patients receiving these drugs for therapy unless they have a history of drug abuse or have an underlying psychiatric disorder (Gutstein and Akil 2006; O'Brien 2006).

Occasionally, there are outbreaks of abuse of commonly prescribed narcotic products such as OxyContin (Brady 2010; "'Oxy' Kids Crisis" 2007). This product includes the opiate oxycodone, which has the approximate narcotic potency of morphine and can be obtained with relative ease. Authorities claim that the illegal pills come from doctors' offices, from dealers who fake illness to get legal prescriptions or who are writing phony orders, and from others who steal the supplies from pharmacies. OxyContin has been called *oxys*, *O.C.*, and *killers* on the street and is popular with narcotic abusers because of its rapid and potent effect. However, many, if not most, of those who use prescriptions drugs for nonmedical purposes obtain their painkillers from the medicine cabinets of a family member or a friend (*Alcoholism and Drug Abuse Weekly* 2010a). On the street, the drug can cost 10 times its prescription price. Because of its potent ability to suppress respiration, OxyContin appears to have been involved in overdose deaths throughout the country, although there is some evidence that other drugs were also involved in many of these cases. Critics claim that part of the abuse problem with OxyContin stems from overuse in situations that should be managed by a less potent and less addicting opioid analgesic.

Here and Now

Are Restrictions on Pain Pills Too Painful?

Because of a spiraling increase in the abuse of prescription "painkillers," the DEA has warned doctors who specialize in pain management that they risk special investigation if they do not comply with DEA guidelines. For example, the DEA recommends avoiding the use of opioid analgesics for the treatment of pain in patients who have a history of abusing these drugs. In addition, the DEA frowns upon the practice of doctors writing prescriptions for these pain drugs that can be filled on a future date. These and other restrictive DEA policies are viewed by some pain doctors as overregulation. Some are concerned that physicians will hesitate to prescribe even needed pain medication for fear of being investigated and charged with breaking the law. They worry that the DEA's actions are sending a chilling message that could result in withholding opioid narcotics from millions of patients who cannot be adequately treated by other drugs.

Sources: Kaufman, M. "New DEA Statement Has Pain Doctors More Fearful." *Washington Post* (30 November 2004): A-17; and Borigini, M. "Prescribing Narcotics: A Doctor's Point of View." Health Central, Chronic Pain Connection. 27 October 2008. Available at: http://www.healthcentral.com/chronic-pain/c/91/46424/prescribing-view. Accessed March 14, 2011.

■ Other Therapeutic Uses

Opioid narcotics are also used to treat conditions not related to pain. For example, these drugs suppress the coughing center of the brain, so they are effective antitussives. Codeine, a natural opioid narcotic, is commonly included in cough medicine. In addition, opioid narcotics slow the movement of materials through the intestines, a property that can be used to relieve diarrhea or can cause the side effect of constipation (*Drug Facts and Comparisons* 2010). Paregoric contains an opioid narcotic substance and is commonly used to treat severe diarrhea.

When used carefully by the clinician, opioid narcotics are very effective therapeutic tools. Guidelines for avoiding unnecessary problems with these drugs include the following (Rolfs 2008):

- Opioid pain relievers should only be used for pain when severity warrants and after consideration of other nonopioid pain medications such as aspirin or ibuprofen.
- Doses and duration of use should be limited as much as possible while permitting adequate therapeutic care.
- The patient should be counseled to store the medications securely, not share with others, and dispose of drugs properly when the pain has subsided and the medication is no longer needed.
- Long-duration opioid drugs should not be used to treat acute pain, except in situations where adequate monitoring can be conducted.
- The use of opioids should be reevaluated if pain persists beyond the anticipated time period for acute pain management.
- A comprehensive evaluation should be conducted before initiating opioid treatment.
- The provider should consider conducting a screen for risk of abuse or addiction before initiating opioid treatment.
- A treatment plan should be established between the doctor and patient that includes measurable goals for reduction of pain and improvement of function.
- The patient, and if appropriate, family members, should be informed of the risks and benefits of the opioid treatment. Sometimes a written contract identifying these elements should be prepared and signed.
- Opioid treatment should be discontinued if the terms of the contract are not being met by the patient.

- If significant abuse is suspected, the clinician should discuss the concerns with the patient and help the patient find appropriate treatment.

■ Abuse of Prescription Opioid Painkillers

As already mentioned, the abuse of prescription opioid painkillers has become a major problem in the United States and has been described by the American Drug Czar (i.e., director of the Office of National Drug Control Policy [ONDCP]), R. Gil Kerlikowske, as the "nation's fastest-growing drug problem" (*USA Today* 2010). An example of what has become all too common is the tragic narcotic overdose death of Leslie Cooper near Portsmouth, Ohio. She was never known to wander the streets or dark alleys to get her opioid narcotics. She received her drugs "legally" from multiple doctors and "pain-management clinics." Her problem with these prescription analgesics started when doctors prescribed potent painkillers to deal with the severe discomfort after a difficult surgery. More surgeries were necessary, which meant continual demand for, and access to, the opioid pain relievers. Something went terribly wrong and Leslie paid the price with her life. In her system was found a deadly combination of depressant drugs prescribed for muscle relaxation and depression, and two very potent narcotic analgesics. Leslie fell asleep and did not wake up. This is an example of why the misuse of these pain killers has led to a doubling of emergency room visits since 2004 (*USA Today* 2010), and also has caused some critics to question whether many doctors who prescribe such drugs are sufficiently trained in either proper pain or substance abuse management (Meier 2010).

Abuse problems with these drugs are partially due to the facts that these narcotic analgesics are very popular and account for about 7% of all prescribed drugs and that the number of patients who are taking the long-lasting versions of the agents (e.g., OxyContin) has increased 30% during the past decade (Meier 2010). This means that these drugs are more readily available and their use more widely accepted than ever before. However, it is important to appreciate that when used properly (i.e., as prescribed), the likelihood of becoming addicted to these narcotics for most people is very small (likely less than 1%; O'Brien 2006). But there are risk factors that make some patients more likely to have problems with these drugs; for those with these

Prescription for Addiction: What Makes People Vulnerable?

For most patients, the responsible use of prescription opioid analgesics is very helpful in the management of moderate to severe pain; however, a relatively small population has factors that can increase the danger of becoming addicted to these drugs as much as 25-fold. The risks that lead to this vulnerability include:

- Family history of substance abuse problems, which suggests the likelihood of genetic vulnerability (Levran et al. 2009)

- Dependence on nicotine, alcohol, or sleeping pills
- Depression
- Use of psychiatric medications
- Younger than 65 years of age

The value of identifying these risks is they may help warn which patients require special consideration and caution when prescribing narcotics to treat their pain.

Sources: Sify News. "Risk Factors for Painkiller Addiction Identified." 28 August 2010. Available at: http://sify.com/news/risk-factors-for-painkiller-addiction-identified-news-scitech-ki3pEjahbic.html. Accessed March 14, 2011; Reuters. "Do Smokers Use More Prescription Painkillers?" 17 June 2010. Available at: http://www.reuters.com/article/idUSTRE65G5RQ20100617. Accessed March 14, 2011; Medical News Today. "Study Identifies Risk Factors for Painkiller Addiction and Links the Addiction to Genetics." 28 August 2010. Available at: http://www.medicalnewstoday.com/articles/199263.php. Accessed March 14, 2011; and American Academy of Pain Medicine. "Psychiatric Factors Linked to Increased Risk for Misuse of Opioid Medications." 23rd Annual Meeting. Abstract 151. 7 February 2007.

risk factors the rate of addiction jumps to 25% (see "Prescription for Addiction: What Makes People Vulnerable?") (Sify News 2010).

Abuse of prescription opioid narcotics such as OxyContin and illicit narcotics such as heroin might seem to some people very different because one comes from a doctor and the other from drug dealers in the street. But in reality, because both types of drugs are opiates, they both can cause similar addiction, overdoses, and even death. In fact, a surprising rise in heroin abuse is occurring across the United States, which is likely in part the result of people who become addicted to the prescription opioid painkillers and switch to heroin because it is more accessible and easier to obtain. Heroin also can cost as little as one-fifth the price of prescription medications. All too often cases of heroin overdose deaths appear to have their origins from the victim first being exposed to the opioid narcotics during a chronic treatment for pain often associated with sports-related injuries (Valenzuela 2010; Willis 2008).

■ Mechanisms of Action

As mentioned earlier, the opioid receptors are the site of action of the naturally occurring endorphin peptide transmitters and are found throughout the nervous system, intestines, and other internal organs. Because narcotic drugs such as morphine and heroin enhance the endorphin system by directly stimulating opioid receptors, these drugs have widespread influences throughout the body.

For example, the opioid receptors are present in high concentration within the limbic structures of the brain. Stimulation of these receptors by narcotics causes release of the transmitter dopamine in limbic brain regions. This effect contributes to the rewarding actions of these drugs and leads to dependence and abuse (see "Signs & Symptoms: Narcotics") (Trigo et al. 2010; Zocchi et al. 2003).

■ Side Effects

One of the most common side effects of the opioid narcotics is constipation. Other side effects include

Signs & Symptoms Narcotics

POSSIBLE SIGNS OF USE	POSSIBLE SIGNS OF OVERDOSE
Euphoria	Low and shallow breathing
Drowsiness	Clammy skin
Respiratory depression	Convulsions
Constricted pupils	Coma
Nausea	Possible death

drowsiness, mental clouding, respiratory depression (suppressed breathing is usually the cause of death from overdose), nausea and vomiting, itching, inability to urinate, a drop in blood pressure, and constricted pupils (*Drug Facts and Comparisons* 2010). This array of seemingly unrelated side effects is due to widespread distribution of the opioid receptors throughout the body and their involvement in many physiological functions (Gourlay 2004; Trigo et al. 2010). With continual use, tolerance usually develops to some of these undesirable narcotic responses.

Drugs that selectively antagonize the opioid receptors can block the effects of natural opioid systems in the body and reverse the effects of narcotic opiate drugs (*Drug Facts and Comparisons* 2010). When an opioid antagonist such as the drug naloxone is administered alone, it has little noticeable effect. The antiopioid actions of naloxone become more apparent when the antagonist is injected into someone who has taken a narcotic opioid drug. For example, naloxone will cause (1) a recurrence of pain in the patient using a narcotic for pain relief, (2) the restoration of consciousness and normal breathing in the addict who has overdosed on heroin, and (3) severe withdrawal effects in the opioid abuser who has become dependent on narcotics (*Drug Facts and Comparisons* 2010; Szalavitz 2005). Because of the ability of these antagonists to block the effects of opioid drugs, they are also used as treatment for some opioid-dependent patient (Laino 2010).

An interesting recent use of opioid antagonists is to treat alcohol dependence. The Food and Drug Administration (FDA) has approved the use of naltrexone (a narcotic antagonist) in a regular and extended-release formulation to relieve the craving of alcoholics for excessive alcohol consumption (*Drug Facts and Comparisons* 2010; Laino 2010).

Abuse, Tolerance, Dependence, and Withdrawal

All the opioid narcotic agents that activate opioid receptors have abuse potential and are classified as scheduled drugs (see **Table 9.2**). Their patterns of abuse are determined by the ability of these drugs to cause tolerance, dependence, withdrawal effects, and eventually addiction. However, it is important to recognize that because a patient treated by these drugs for pain develops physical dependence and

Table 9.2 Schedule Classification of Some Common Narcotics

NARCOTIC	SCHEDULE
Heroin	I
Morphine	II, III
Methadone	II
Fentanyl	II
Hydromorphone	II
Meperidine	II
Codeine	II, III, V
Buprenorphine	III
Pentazocine	IV
Tramadol	Unscheduled
Narcotics combined with nonsteroidal anti-inflammatory drugs	III

Source: Drug Enforcement Administration (DEA). Controlled Substances Act. 1 February 2010. Available at: http://uscode.house.gov/download/pls/21C13.txt. Accessed March 16, 2011.

experiences significant withdrawal when the drug is abruptly removed, they are not necessarily addicted (Hitti 2010). In fact, relatively few patients properly receiving the opioid narcotics for pain relief will go on to become truly addicted, even though they may develop physical dependence and are temporarily uncomfortable when the narcotic treatment is discontinued. This distinction between physical dependence and the compulsive need to use the opioid narcotics despite very negative consequences (e.g., addiction) is very important and needs to be appreciated in order to provide proper pain management, especially for severe long-term pain conditions (Get the Facts 2010).

The process of tolerance literally begins with the first dose of a narcotic, but tolerance does not become clinically evident until after 2 to 3 weeks of frequent use (either therapeutic- or abuse-related). Tolerance occurs most rapidly with high doses given in short intervals and is a common result of the extended clinical use of prescription opioid painkillers. It also is caused by abuse of these narcotics in addicted persons. The result of tolerance is that doses of these drugs must be increased (sometimes several-fold) to retain or regain the therapeutic or nonmedicinal narcotic effects. Physical dependence invariably accompanies severe tolerance (Reisine and Pasternak 1995). Psychological dependence can also develop with continual narcotic use because these drugs can cause euphoria and relieve stress. Such psychological dependence leads to compulsive use (Gutstein and Akil 2006; O'Brien 2006). Because all narcotics affect the same opioid systems in the body, developing tolerance to one narcotic drug means the person has cross-tolerance to all drugs in this group.

The development of psychological and physical dependence makes stopping the drug uncomfortable due to resulting unpleasant withdrawals. Someone who has used potent narcotics for a long time, like a major long-term addict, will experience severe withdrawal effects such as exaggerated pain responses, agitation, anxiety, stomach cramps and vomiting, joint and muscle aches, runny nose, and an overall flu-like feeling. Although these withdrawal symptoms are not fatal, they are extremely aversive and encourage continuation of the narcotic habit (McEvoy 2003). Overall, the narcotics have similar actions; there are differences, however, in their potencies, severity of side effects, likelihood of being abused, and clinical usefulness.

■ Heroin Abuse

"My parents had no idea. My mom thought I was smoking a lot of weed and taking diet pills, because who would've thought that such a bad drug (heroin) could be so easily accessible to me. Growing up, everything is pushed on you. You're trying to be the smartest, trying to compete with everyone. Heroin was an escape."

"It hits you hard, but it's so smooth and enticing at the same time. It hits you like a train of false love."

"Believe it or not, as a high school teenager, it is easier for us to get than alcohol." *(Quotes from three young people in rehabilitation in New York; Buckley 2009)*

These quotes from three young people illustrate the powerful attraction of heroin and help explain why it is so frequently abused. They also illustrate that the use of heroin, especially by teenagers and young adults, appears to be increasing. The likely explanations for this recent rise in popularity include the facts that high-grade heroin has become very cheap and readily available (Schneider 2009). In addition, it appears that elevated heroin use is an indirect consequence of the increase in the abuse of prescription opioid painkillers. Thus, as more people abuse the prescribed narcotics they increase their consumption because they develop tolerance. This makes their habit more expensive and makes it more difficult to obtain enough of the prescription drugs to satisfy their nonmedical (addiction) needs. Consequently, these people frequently switch to street heroin, which is a fraction of the cost while being reasonably pure and potent (Cole 2010; Schneider 2009). Of course, this switch to heroin increases the risk of getting a bad batch of drug that is much more potent than expected or contains other drugs that are more dangerous. The unintended outcomes can be, at the least, very dangerous and result in a trip to the emergency room, or in the extreme, can cause an accidental overdose fatality (Bernstein 2010; Caldwell and Salter 2010).

Heroin is currently classified as a Schedule I drug by the DEA (see Table 9.2). It is not approved for any clinical use in the United States, is one of the most widely abused illegal drugs in the world, and is reported to account for more than $120 billion in global sales each year (Chossudovsky 2006; GlobalSecurity.org 2010). It is also thought to be associated with some of the highest mortality rates and most emergency room visits of any of the illegal drugs of abuse in the United States (National Institute on Drug Abuse [NIDA] 2005). Heroin was illicitly used more than any other drug of abuse in the United States (except for marijuana) until 20 years ago, when it was unseated by cocaine (DiChiara and North 1992). In 2009, 0.7% of high school seniors reported having used heroin during the previous year, and 1.2% indicated that they had used this drug sometime during their life (Johnston 2010).

From 1970 through 1976, most of the heroin reaching the United States originated from the Golden Triangle region of Southeast Asia, which includes parts of Burma, Thailand, and Laos. During that period, the United States and other nations purchased much of the legal opium crop from Turkey in an effort to stop opium from being converted into heroin. From 1975 until 1980, the major heroin supply came from opium poppies grown in Mexico. The U.S. government furnished the Mexican government with helicopters, herbicide sprays, and financial assistance to destroy the poppy crop. Changes in political climates have shifted the source of supply back to the Golden Triangle and Latin American countries (e.g., Colombia; Seper 2003) and more recently to Afghanistan where 92% of the world's heroin is currently produced (Christensen 2010), accounting for approximately $3 billion in revenue for local farmers (AFP 2010). Heroin produced in Afghanistan has taken a heavy toll on the Afghan people (Christenson 2010) (see "Here and Now: Afghans' Drug War"). It has been speculated that heroin trafficked from Afghanistan has killed more than a million people worldwide in the past decade (AFP 2010), and as previously discussed, is a substantial problem for U.S. and NATO soldiers fighting in the Afghanistan war (Edwards 2010). Despite these disturbing effects, the United States has stopped its previous policy of crop eradication because it alienated the poorest Afghan populations who rely on this crop to survive and support

their families and tended to turn them against the efforts by the American/European-supported government to eliminate insurgent groups such as the Taliban. More recently, the U.S. government and military have been trying to convince farmers to replace their opium poppies with other profitable crops (AFP 2010; Starikov 2010). Despite these efforts to be more "compassionate and understanding," many experts question the effectiveness of these strategies (Starikov 2010).

Heroin Combinations

Heroin is typically smuggled into the United States from one of four foreign sources: Mexico, South America, Southeast Asia (e.g., Burma), or Southwest Asia (e.g., Afghanistan). It is carried into the United States hidden in commercial and private vehicles driven from Mexico or Canada or carried by couriers traveling on commercial flights. Pure heroin is a white powder. Other colors, such as brown Mexican heroin, result from unsatisfactory

Here and Now

Afghans' Drug War

How goes the "war" in Afghanistan? The answer may be quite different depending on whether you are referring to the military war being fought against the Taliban with guns, explosives, and military maneuvers or the drug war being fought against poor opium farmers trying to survive on meager earnings that come from the few acres they are able to cultivate. Opium crops are particularly well suited to this land and historically brought good prices. Consequently, it is difficult to convince the poor farmers that crops that allow them to feed their families are evil and should be stopped. Despite the fact that efforts by both the Afghan and U.S. governments to educate opium farmers and help them develop profitable alternative crops reduced poppy cultivation by 22% in 2009, production of Afghan opium has risen dramatically during the Afghan War and currently is thought to provide 92% of the world's heroin. Just because they produce the opium, the Afghan people are not immune to its problems. It is speculated that 1 in 25 Afghans is an addict, and there are very few resources to

provide adequate treatment or initiate effective prevention programs. Statistics such as these are powerful evidence that the Afghans' drug war goes very badly indeed.

Sources: Constable, P. "A Poor Yield for Afghans' 'War on Drugs.'" *Washington Post* (19 September 2006): 14A; and Christenson, S. "Heroin Addiction Takes Brutal Toll on Afghanistan." *San Antonio Express-News.* 24 May 2010. Available at: http://www.mysanantonio.com/news/local_news/in_kabul_regrets_rehab_and_redemption_94714589.html?showFullArticle=y. Accessed March 14, 2011.

processing of morphine or from adulterants. Heroin is usually "cut" (diluted) with lactose (milk sugar) to give it bulk and thus increase profits. When heroin first enters the United States, it can be up to 95% pure; by the time it is sold to users, its purity can be as low as 3% or (recently) as high as 70% (Epstein and Gfroerer 1998; Schneider 2009; Stockman 2003). If users are unaware of the variance in purity and do not adjust doses accordingly, the results can be extremely dangerous and occasionally fatal (Bernstein 2010; NIDA 2005).

Heroin has a bitter taste, so sometimes it is cut with quinine, a bitter substance, to disguise the fact that the heroin content has been reduced. Quinine can be a deadly adulterant. Part of the "flash," or immediate rush, from direct injection of heroin may be caused by this contaminant. Quinine is an irritant, and it causes vascular damage, acute and potentially lethal disturbances in heartbeat, depressed respiration, coma, and death from respiratory arrest. Opiate poisoning causes acute pulmonary edema as well as respiratory depression. To counteract the constipation caused by heroin, sometimes mannitol is added for its laxative effect.

Another potentially lethal combination emerges when heroin is laced with the much more potent artificial narcotic fentanyl. This adulterated heroin can be extremely dangerous due to its unexpected potency (NIDA 2004).

Frequently, heroin is deliberately combined with other drugs when self-administered by addicts (Hickman et al. 2007). According to the National Institute on Drug Abuse (NIDA)–sponsored Drug Abuse Warning Network (DAWN) survey of emergency rooms in the United States, 41% of the reported heroin abuse cases involved other drugs of abuse in combination with this narcotic. Heroin is most frequently used with alcohol, but it is often combined with CNS stimulants, such as cocaine (Hickman et al. 2007). Some crack cocaine smokers turn to heroin to ease the jitters caused by the CNS stimulant (Leland 1996). It also has been reported that heroin addicts use cocaine to withdraw or detoxify themselves from heroin by gradually decreasing amounts of heroin while increasing

Crude heroin is dark and sometimes referred to as black tar heroin, whereas purified heroin is a white powder.

amounts of cocaine. This drug combination is called **speedballing**, and addicts claim the cocaine provides relief from the unpleasant withdrawal effects that accompany heroin abstinence in a dependent user (Rowlett et al. 2010).

Profile of Heroin Addicts

An estimated 600,000 to 1 million active heroin addicts live in the United States, a figure that has remained relatively stable despite changes in the number of infrequent and moderate users. Heroin addicts often search for a better and purer drug; however, if they do find an unusually potent batch of heroin, there is a good chance they will get more than they bargained for. Addicts are sometimes found dead with the needle still in the vein after injecting a particularly potent batch of heroin (Caldwell and Salter 2010). More than 3000 deaths occur annually in the United States from heroin overdoses (Caldwell 2010). Death associated with heroin injection is usually due to concurrent use of alcohol or barbiturates—not the heroin alone—and frequently occurs after an addict has gone weeks or months without the drug and injects the same amount of heroin he or she used before, not realizing that tolerance has worn off (Rombey 2003b).

Hard-core addicts often share a common place where they can stash supplies and equipment for their heroin encounters. These locations, called *shooting galleries,* serve as gathering places for addicts (Cowan and Carvel 2006). Shooting galleries can be set up in homes, but are usually located in less established locations such as abandoned cars, cardboard lean-tos, and weed-infested vacant lots. An entrance charge often is required of the patrons. Conditions in shooting galleries are notoriously filthy, and these places are frequented by intravenous heroin users with bloodborne infections that can cause AIDS or hepatitis. Because of needle sharing and other unsanitary practices, shooting galleries have become a place where serious communicative diseases are spread to a wide range of people of different ages, races, genders, and socioeconomic statuses (Bearak 1992; Nakamura 2008). In some countries such as the United Kingdom, there are controversial efforts to develop government-regulated shooting galleries in order to assure sanitary conditions and clean needles for the heroin addicts to prevent their exposure to the dangers of contracting devastating and potentially deadly diseases (Leach 2009).

The heroin in shooting galleries is typically prepared by adding several drops of water to the white powder in an improvised container (such as a metal bottle cap), and lightly shaking the container while heating it over a small flame to dissolve the powder. The fluid is then drawn through a tiny wad of cotton to filter out the gross contaminants into an all-too-often used syringe where it is ready for injection (Bearak 1992).

Some addicts become fixated on the drug's paraphernalia, especially the needle. They can get a psychological "high" from playing with the needle and syringe. The injection process and syringe plunger action appear to have sexual overtones for them. As one reformed user explained, "I think what I miss more than heroin sometimes is just the ritual of shooting up." A current user concurred, explaining, "You get addicted to the needle . . . Just the process of sticking something into your vein, having such a direct involvement with your body . . ." ("Mary" 1996, p. 42; Winkler et al. 2010).

Heroin and Crime

In 1971, the Select Committee on Crime in the United States released a report on methods used to combat the heroin crisis that arose in the 1950s and 1960s. This report was a turning point in setting up treatment programs for narcotic addicts. The report stated that drug arrests for heroin use had increased 700% since 1961, and that the cost of heroin-related crimes to U.S. society was estimated to exceed $3 billion per year. Other studies since that time have linked heroin addiction with crime (McMurran 2007).

Although many young heroin addicts come from affluent or middle-class families (Weiss 1995), research shows heavy users (usually addicts who inject

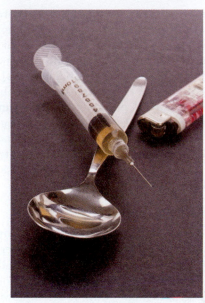

Heroin paraphernalia is usually simple and crude but effective: a spoon on which to dissolve the narcotic and a makeshift syringe with which to inject it.

their heroin) are frequently poorly educated with minimal social integration and live in neighborhoods surrounded by poverty (Nandi et al. 2010). Because of these disadvantages, these heroin addicts often have a low level of employment, exist in unstable living conditions, and socialize with other illicit drug users. Clearly, such undesirable living conditions encourage criminal activity. However, three other factors also likely contribute to the association between heroin use and crime:

1. The use of heroin and its pharmacological effects encourage antisocial behavior that is crime related. Depressants such as heroin diminish inhibition and cause people to engage in activities they normally would not. The effects of heroin and its withdrawal make addicts self-centered, demanding, impulsive, and governed by their "need" for the drug.
2. Because heroin addiction is expensive, the user is forced to resort to crime to support the drug habit (McMurran 2007).
3. A similar personality is driven to engage in both criminal behavior and heroin use. Often, heroin addicts start heroin use about the same time they begin to become actively involved in criminal activity. In most cases, the heroin user has been taking other illicit drugs, especially marijuana, years before trying heroin (Reid, Elifson, and Sterk 2007).

These findings suggest that for many heroin addicts, the antisocial behavior causes the criminal behavior rather than the criminal behavior resulting from the heroin use. Thus, the more a drug such as heroin is perceived as being illegal, desirable, and addictive, the more likely it will be used by deviant criminal populations. However, typically heroin users are not violent, although they may participate in criminal activity to fund their drug habit. Violence is more likely associated with heroin trafficking and distribution because of the criminal groups involved in this activity.

Patterns of Heroin Abuse

It has become apparent that problems with narcotics are no longer confined to the inner cities, but have infiltrated suburban areas and small towns and afflict both rich and poor (see "Here and Now: Heroin Use in a Small Town"). The following are recent heroin trends (see **Table 9.3**):

- Heroin use among adolescents and young adults, after holding steady through much of the first decade in 2000, is thought to be rising due to a decrease in cost, and increases in purity and availability (Cole 2010; Schneider 2009).
- Heroin has become purer (60–70% purity) and cheaper ($10/bag[~100mg]) (Schneider 2009).
- Thanks to the greater purity, new users are able to administer heroin in less efficient ways, such as smoking and snorting, and avoid the dangers of intravenous use (Cole 2010). Many youths believe that heroin can be used safely if it is not injected.

- Because of its association with popular fashions and entertainment, heroin has been viewed as glamorous and chic, especially by many young people, despite its highly publicized lethal consequences. The look of being "wasted" and unkempt has been referred to as "heroin chic" (Urban Dictionary 2005). However, this "druggy look" and malnourished appearance has fallen out of fashion within the glamour business because of its very negative implications and health consequences (Quinion 2005).
- Approximately 190,000 emergency room visits each year are due to heroin overdoses (My Addiction.com 2010).

Stages of Dependence

Initially, the early effects of heroin are often unpleasant, especially after the first injection (Gutstein and Akil 2006). It is not uncommon to experience nausea and vomiting after administration; gradually, however, the euphoria overwhelms the aversive effects (Quinion 2005). There are two major stages in the development of a psychological dependence on heroin or other opioid narcotics:

1. In the rewarding stage, euphoria and positive effects occur in at least 50% of users. These positive feelings and sensations increase with continued administration and encourage use.
2. Eventually, the heroin or narcotic user must take the drug to avoid withdrawal symptoms that start about 6 to 12 hours after the last dose. At this stage, it is said that "the monkey is on his

Here and Now

Heroin Use in a Small Town

Heroin is supposed to be a "big town" drug, but is gaining popularity in smaller towns. This is very disturbing to those who have chosen to live the rural life with the belief that such an environment will somehow protect them from the ugliness, fear, and pain of typical metropolitan drug problems. They are finding out that drugs such as heroin can be anywhere and used by anybody. Stories like that of Sandi Daost are tragic: her 19-year-old son Robby died from a heroin overdose after months of going in and out of rehab centers trying to stay clean. He grew up in the typical small town—Springville, Utah. The family believed that Robby finally had kicked the habit. He had been clean

for 7 months and laughed and joked with the family again. He had a job and a cute girlfriend and was attending church with his family. One Sunday, he told his mother he was going to play golf with a friend. Robby didn't go golfing, but made his last trip to meet his heroin connection. He was found in his bed the next morning, dead from a heroin overdose. The citizens of Springville were bewildered and shocked because within a relatively short time, five other heroin overdose deaths occurred to young men also in their late teens or early 20s. We expect this type of thing in Los Angeles or New York, but no one seems to have an answer to "why in Springville?"

Sources: Rombey, D. "Heroin Is Silent Scourge of Sheltered Springville." *Deseret News* (9 June 2003): A-1; Rombey, D. "Heroin Takes Toll on Families." *Deseret News* (10 June 2003): A-1; and Van Hollen, J. "Heroin Abuse Now a Rural Threat Too." *The Cap Times.* 3 October 2010. Available at: http://host.madison.com/ct/news/opinion/mailbag/article_c47ae879-6bf7-5bf3-a2e5-87c2bebf92a0.html. Accessed March 14, 2011.

Table 9.3 **Prevalence of Heroin and Other Opioid Abuse Among High School Seniors**

YEAR	ANNUAL USE		LIFETIME USE	
	HEROIN	OTHER OPIOIDS	HEROIN	OTHER OPIOIDS
1989	0.6%	4.4%	1.3%	8.3%
1995	1.1%	4.7%	1.6%	7.2%
1999	1.1%	6.7%	2.0%	10.2%
2002	1.0%	9.4%*	1.7%	13.5%*
2007	0.9%	9.2%	1.5%	13.1%
2009	0.7%	9.2%	1.2%	13.2%

* In 2002, the question text was changed in half of the questionnaire forms. The list of examples of narcotics other than heroin was updated: Talwin, laudanum, and paregoric—all of which had negligible rates of use by 2001—were replaced with Vicodin, OxyContin, and Percocet. The 2002 data presented here are based on the changed forms only; N is one half of N indicated. In 2003, the remaining forms were changed to the new wording. Data based on all forms beginning in 2003.

Sources: Johnston, L. D., P. M. O'Malley, J. G. Bachman, and J. E. Schulenberg. Monitoring the Future. "Trends in Lifetime Prevalence of Use of Various Drugs in Grades 8, 10, and 12 (Table 1)." Ann Arbor, MI: University of Michigan, 2010. Available at http://monitoringthe future.org/data/10data/pr10t1.pdf. Accessed April 22, 2011; and Johnston, L. D., P. M. O'Malley, J. G. Bachman, and J. E. Schulenberg. Monitoring the Future. "Trends in Annual Prevalence of Use of Various Drugs in Grades 8, 10, and 12 (Table 2)." Ann Arbor, MI: University of Michigan, 2010. Available at http://monitoringthe future.org/data/10data/pr10t2.pdf. Accessed April 22, 2011.

back." This stage is psychological dependence. If 1 grain of heroin (about 65 milligrams) is taken over a 2-week period on a daily basis, the user becomes physically dependent on the drug.

Methods of Administration

Many heroin users start by sniffing the powder or injecting it into a muscle (intramuscular) or under the skin ("skin popping"). Because of the increased purity and decreased cost, many of today's heroin users are administering their drug by smoking and snorting (Caldwell and Salter 2010; Schneider 2010).

Most established heroin addicts still prefer to **mainline** the drug (intravenous injection) (Community Epidemiology Work Group [CEWG] 2002). The injection device can be made from an eyedropper bulb, part of a syringe, and a hypodermic needle. Mainlining drugs causes the thin-walled veins to become scarred and, if done frequently, the veins will collapse. Once a vein is collapsed, it can no longer be used to introduce the drug into the blood. Addicts become expert in locating new veins to use: in the feet, the legs, the neck, even the temples. When addicts do not want "needle tracks" (scars) to show, they inject under the tongue or in the groin ("Opioids" 1996).

Heroin Addicts and AIDS

As noted previously, because needle sharing is common among heavy heroin users, the transmission of deadly communicable diseases such as AIDS is a major problem (see Chapter 17). The Centers for Disease Control and Prevention (CDC) reports that more than 250,000 AIDS patients in the United States contracted the HIV virus through drug injection; most were heroin users (DrugWarFacts 2010). Fear of contracting this deadly disease has contributed to the increase of administering this drug by smoking and snorting (Healthtree 2010); however, many heroin users who start by smoking and snorting eventually progress to intravenous administration due to its more intense effects (Leland 1996).

Heroin and Pregnancy

Devin acts like any normal two-year-old. He particularly enjoys the fast-food Chick-fil-A restaurant and playing with the barbecue sauce containers. Looking at Devin gives no clue that his mother had become addicted to prescription painkillers when she discovered her pregnancy. She was urged by her sister to seek professional help immediately. Devin was born on time and was undersized at 5 pounds and 5 ounces. Devin was able to avoid the worst withdrawal symptoms after birth because he was immediately placed on methadone and gradually weaned to allow his small body to adjust to not having the painkillers that his mother had been using throughout her pregnancy. Devin was lucky: other babies under

KEY TERMS

mainline
to inject a drug of abuse intravenously

similar circumstances who do not receive proper medical care suffer through severe feeding problems, vomiting, diarrhea, muscle stiffness, and severe tremors. These babies cry constantly as they experience severe narcotic withdrawal and in extreme cases they may even suffer seizures. (Colon 2011)

Many women use heroin during their pregnancy. In the United States, as many as 7000 infants are born each year to women who chronically used either heroin or other opioid drugs during their pregnancies (Bhuveneswar et al. 2008). There is no evidence that prenatal exposure to opioid drugs causes overt structural damage, although incidents of smaller birth weights or even reduced head size have been reported in infants born to mothers using opioid drugs (Wang 2010). The most devastating consequence of heroin or opioid use during pregnancy appears to be physical dependence in the newborn, resulting in withdrawal symptoms usually immediately after birth. These symptoms are characterized by high-pitched crying, inconsolability, tightened muscle tone, tremors, vomiting, and even seizures. Elements of this withdrawal persist for weeks (Wang 2010). Treatment for such withdrawal problems generally includes low doses of a long-lasting opioid narcotic to reduce the intensity of the symptoms and then a gradual tapering of the dose to eventually wean the infant from the drug. For heroin, this typically takes up to 2 weeks (Pain and Central Nervous System 2005; Wang 2010). In addition, there is some evidence that the use of heroin during pregnancy increases the likelihood of sudden infant death syndrome (SIDS) in offspring (American SIDS Institute 2005).

Withdrawal Symptoms

After the effects of heroin wear off, the addict usually has only a few hours in which to find the next dose before severe withdrawal symptoms begin. A single "shot" of heroin lasts only 4 to 6 hours. It is enough to help addicts "get straight" or relieve the severe withdrawal symptoms called dope sickness but is not enough to give a desired "high" (Bearak 1992). Withdrawal symptoms start with a runny nose, tears, and minor stomach cramps. The addict may feel as if he or she is coming down with a bad cold (Galanter and Kleber 2008). Between 12 and 48 hours after the last dose, the addict loses all of his or her appetite, vomits, has diarrhea and abdominal cramps, feels alternating chills and fever, and develops goose pimples all over (going "cold turkey"). Between 2 and 4 days later, the addict continues to experience some of the symptoms just described, as well as aching bones and muscles and powerful muscle spasms that cause violent kicking motions ("kicking the habit"). After 4 to 5 days, symptoms start to subside, and the person may get his or her appetite back. However, attempts to move on in life will be challenging because compulsion to keep using the drug remains strong.

The severity of the withdrawal varies according to the purity and strength of the drug used and the personality of the user. The symptoms of withdrawal from heroin, morphine, and methadone are summarized in **Table 9.4**. Withdrawal symptoms from opioids such as morphine, codeine, meperidine, and others are similar, although the time frame and intensity vary (Galanter and Kleber 2008; Gutstein and Akil 2006).

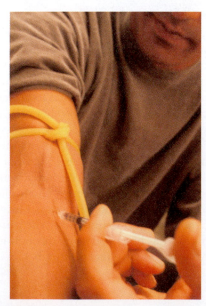

A heroin addict "mainlining" his drug.

■ Treatment of Heroin and Other Narcotic Dependence

The ideal result of treatment for dependency on heroin or other narcotics is to help the addict live a normal, productive, and satisfying life without drugs (Galanter and Kleber 2008). Unfortunately, the minority of heroin addicts receive adequate treatment for their addiction. Of those who are treated, relatively few heroin users become absolutely "clean" from drug use; thus, therapeutic compromise often is necessary (see **Figure 9.1**). In the real world, treatment of heroin dependency is considered successful if the addict does the following:

Table 9.4 Symptoms of Withdrawal from Heroin, Morphine, and Methadone

SYMPTOMS	HEROIN	TIME IN HOURS MORPHINE	METHADONE
Craving for drugs; anxiety	4	6	24–48
Yawning, perspiration, runny nose, tears	8	14	34–48
Pupil dilation, goose bumps, muscle twitches, aching bones and muscles, hot and cold flashes, loss of appetite	12	16	48–72
Increased intensity of preceding symptoms, insomnia, raised blood pressure, fever, faster pulse, nausea	18–24	24–36	≥72
Increased intensity of preceding symptoms, curled-up position, vomiting, diarrhea, increased blood sugar, foot kicking ("kicking the habit")	26–36	36–48	—

1. Stops using heroin
2. No longer associates with dealers or users of heroin
3. Avoids dangerous activities often associated with heroin use (such as needle sharing, injecting unknown drugs, and frequenting shooting galleries) (Tur 2010)
4. Improves employment status
5. Refrains from criminal activity
6. Is able to enjoy normal family and social relationships

For more than 30 years, many heroin addicts have achieved these goals by substituting a long-lasting synthetic narcotic, such as methadone, for the short-acting heroin (Galanter and Kleber 2008; O'Brien 2006; Zickler 1999). The maintenance ("substitute") narcotic is made available to heroin-dependent people through drug treatment centers under the direction of trained medical personnel. The dispensing of the substitute narcotic is tightly regulated by governmental agencies. The rationale for the substitution is that a long-acting drug such as methadone can conveniently be taken once a day (Galanter and Kleber 2008; O'Brien 2006) to prevent the unpleasant withdrawal symptoms that occur within 4 hours after each heroin use (see Table 9.4). Although the substitute narcotic may also have abuse potential and be scheduled by the DEA (see Table 9.2), it is given to the addict in its oral form; thus, its onset of action is too slow to cause a rush like that associated with heroin use, which means that its abuse potential is substantially less (Galanter and Kleber 2008). In addition, the cost to society is dramatically reduced. According to one study, an untreated heroin addict costs the community $21,000 for 6 months, but the cost of methadone maintenance for a person dependent on heroin is only about $1000 for the same period (Hubbard 1998; Substance Abuse and Mental Health Services Administration [SAMHSA] 2008).

Currently, methadone is approved by the FDA for "opiate maintenance therapy" in the treatment of heroin (or other narcotic) dependency (Galanter and Kleber 2008). It has been used in heroin treatment for more than 30 years. Although it is not the best treatment for every person dependent on an opiate drug, it is an effective tool for managing many heroin addicts (Benfield 2010). Proper use

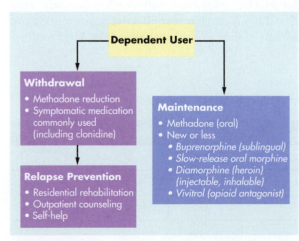

FIGURE 9.1

The principal aspects of treating heroin addiction include minimizing the very aversive withdrawal effect (usually with drug adjuncts); preventing relapse (usually with behavioral modification); and, if necessary, providing maintenance support with other opioid-like drugs that have longer action than heroin.

of methadone has been shown to effectively decrease illicit use of narcotics and other undesirable behavior related to drug dependence (Galanter and Kleber 2008). Although methadone does not tend to make users high, it helps heroin addicts by reducing their drug craving (Benfield 2010). Often methadone-assisted therapy will be long-term and even for the rest of the addict's life (Miller 2010). The methadone is typically well tolerated, although if misused it can be problematic and has been associated with a startling number of overdose deaths across the country (Colberg 2010; Miller 2010).

A second narcotic, buprenorphine, which is used as an analgesic, also has been approved for treatment of narcotic dependence (Hanson 2003). Because buprenorphine is both an opioid agonist and antagonist, it has minimal potential for dependence and is easy to manage, which makes this drug a desirable substitute for heroin (*Drug Facts and Comparisons* 2010). Efforts are being made to provide education and training to primary care physicians so they will be able to use buprenorphine to treat patients addicted to narcotics in their own offices (SAMHSA 2010). This novel strategy opens the door to physicians heretofore not involved in the treatment of drug addiction to become familiar with substance abuse management and hopefully increase the opportunities to diagnose and treat these patients. There is considerable discussion as to how buprenorphine products compare to methadone in treatment of dependence on, and addiction to, opioids in general and heroin in particular. Although the issues clearly require further study, there is some evidence that buprenorphine is usually the better and safer strategy for

detoxification (i.e., treatment of withdrawal) and treatment for infants of opiate-addicted mothers (Boughton 2010; Meader 2010; ACOG 2010). However, such claims are disputed by some experts in the field (Bates 2010; More 2008).

A third, and very different drug approved in 2010 by the FDA to treat heroin and other opioid addictions is Vivitrol, an extended-release form of naltrexone, an opioid antagonist (National Center for Biotechnology Information [NCBI] 2010; Rubin 2010). In 2006, Vivitrol was originally approved as a treatment for alcoholism because of its ability to reduce alcohol craving and its consumption (Drugs.com 2010a; Rubin 2010). Vivitrol has been found to also reduce craving for narcotic drugs such as heroin. Its administration consists of a monthly deep muscle injection. Some of the potential side effects of using Vivitrol include: (1) interference with thinking or reactions, (2) wheezing, (3) enhanced pain, and (4) mood changes (Drugs.com 2010a).

Table 9.5 compares the opioids that have been used for maintenance therapy. Other drugs used less frequently for similar maintenance therapy of heroin addicts include slow-release oral morphine and even heroin itself for addicts who do not respond to the other maintenance opioid drugs (Bammer et al. 1999).

Some people, including some professionals involved in drug abuse therapy, view heroin or narcotic addiction as a "failure of the will" and see methadone treatment as substituting one addiction for another. However, evidence has demonstrated that this approach is very effective in preventing the spread of infectious diseases such as AIDS and he-

Table 9.5 **Comparison of Narcotic Substitutes Used in Opiate Maintenance Therapy**

PROPERTIES	METHADONE	BUPRENORPHINE
Administration	Oral	Oral or sublingual
Frequency of doses	Daily	Daily
Other uses	Analgesic	Analgesic
Physical dependence	Yes	Little
Causes positive subjective effects	Yes	Yes
Abuse potential	Yes	Limited

Source: Swan, N. "Two NIDA-Tested Heroin Treatment Medications Move Toward FDA Approval." *NIDA Notes* (March/April 1993): 45.

patitis and helps the heroin addict to return to a normal productive life (McClure 2009). Unrealistic treatment expectations are sometimes imposed on heroin addicts, leading to high failure rates. For example, some methadone treatment programs distribute inadequate methadone doses to maintain heroin or narcotic abstinence (Recovery Helpdesk 2010); alternatively, narcotic-dependent patients may be told their methadone will be terminated within 6 months regardless of their progress in the program. Such ill-advised policies often drive clients back to their heroin habits and demonstrate that many professionals who treat heroin and narcotic dependency do not understand that methadone is not a cure for heroin addiction but is a means to achieve a healthier, more normal lifestyle (McClure 2009).

It also is essential to understand that even proper treatment does not guarantee resolution of heroin or narcotic addiction (see "Case in Point: Heroin Addiction"). To maximize the possibility of successful treatment, clients must also participate in regular counseling sessions to help modify the drug-seeking behavior and receive on-site care from professionals, including job training, career development, education, general medical care, and family counseling. These supplemental services dramatically improve the success rate of narcotic dependence treatment (Grinspoon 1995; Heroin Detox 2010; McLellan et al. 1993).

Other Narcotics

A large number of nonheroin narcotics are used for medical purposes. However, many are also distributed in the streets, such as morphine, methadone, codeine, hydromorphone (Dilaudid), meperidine (Demerol), and other synthetics (hydrocodone [Vicodin] and oxycodone [OxyContin]). A few of the most commonly abused opioids are discussed briefly in the following sections. Except where noted, they are all Schedule II or III drugs.

◼ Morphine

As noted earlier, morphine is the standard by which other narcotic analgesic agents are measured (Way, Fields, and Way 1998). It has been used to relieve pain since it was first isolated in 1803. Morphine has about half the analgesic potency of heroin but 12 times the potency of codeine. It is commonly used to relieve moderate to intense pain that cannot be controlled by less potent and less dangerous narcotics. Because of its potential for serious side effects, morphine is generally used in a hospital setting where emergency care can be rendered, if necessary. Most pain can be relieved by morphine if high enough doses are used (Reisine and Pasternak 1995; Way et al. 1998); however, morphine is most effective against continuous dull pain.

▶ Case in Point   Heroin Addiction: Not a Funny Matter

Artie Lange, a regular "funnyman" on "The Howard Stern Show," was discovered by his mother bleeding on his Hoboken apartment floor. According to paramedics, Lange had been stabbed nine times with a kitchen knife. Police investigators concluded the wounds were self-inflicted and called it a suicide attempt. Lange had experienced multiple bouts of serious depression associated with a heroin addiction. Despite treatment, Lange manifested self-destructive tendencies that apparently led to this attempt to take his own life. His behavior had been compared to other self-destructive comics such as Chris Farley and John Belushi, who both experienced untimely deaths apparently by accidental causes linked to their drug/heroin use.

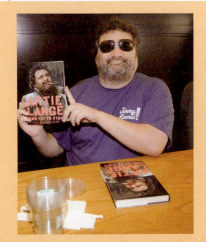

Source: Relative, S. "Artie Lange Stabbed Himself Nine Times, Attempted Suicide Confirmed." Associated Content, Arts and Entertainment. 8 January 2010. Available at: http://www.associatedcontent.com/article/2568063/artie_lange_stabbed_himself_nine_times.html. Accessed February 16, 2011.

The side effects that occur when using therapeutic doses of morphine include drowsiness, changes in mood, and inability to think straight. In addition, therapeutic doses depress respiratory activity; thus, morphine decreases the rate and depth of breathing and produces irregular breathing patterns. Like the other narcotics, it can create an array of seemingly unrelated effects throughout the body, including nausea and vomiting, constipation, blurred vision, constricted pupils, and flushed skin (*Drug Facts and Comparisons* 2010; Way et al. 1998).

The initial response to morphine is varied. In normal people who are not suffering pain, the first exposure can be unpleasant, with nausea and vomiting being the prominent reactions. However, continual use often leads to a euphoric response and encourages dependence. When injected subcutaneously, the effects of heroin and morphine are almost identical; this situation occurs because heroin is rapidly metabolized in the body into morphine. After intravenous administration, the onset of heroin's effects is more rapid and more intense than that of morphine because heroin is more lipid-soluble and enters the brain faster. Because heroin is easier to manufacture and is more potent, it is more popular in illicit trade than morphine. Even so, morphine also has substantial abuse potential and is classified as a Schedule II substance (McEvoy 2003).

Tolerance to the effects of morphine can develop very quickly if the drug is used continuously. For example, an addict who is repeatedly administering the morphine to get a "kick" or maintain a "high" must constantly increase the dose. Such users can build up to incredible doses. One addict reported using 5 grams of morphine daily; the normal analgesic dose of morphine is 50 to 80 milligrams per day (Jaffe and Martin 1990). Such high doses are lethal in a person without tolerance to narcotics.

■ Methadone

Methadone was first synthesized in Germany in 1943, when natural opiate analgesics were not available because opium could not be obtained from the Far East during World War II. Methadone was first called *Dolophine,* after Adolf Hitler; one company still uses that trade name. (On the street, methadone pills have been called dollies.) As previously described, methadone is often substituted for heroin in the treatment of narcotic-dependent people (*Drug Facts and Comparisons* 2010). It is an effective analgesic, equal to morphine if injected and more potent if taken orally (*Drug Facts and Comparisons* 2010; Way et al. 1998).

The physiological effects of methadone are the same as those of morphine and heroin. As a narcotic, methadone produces psychological dependence, tolerance, and then physical dependence and addiction if repeated doses are taken (Belluck 2003; *Drug Facts and Comparisons* 2010). It is effective for about 24 to 36 hours; therefore, the addict must take methadone daily to avoid narcotic withdrawal. It is often considered as addictive as heroin if injected; consequently, because methadone is soluble in water, it is formulated with insoluble, inert ingredients to prevent it from being injected by narcotic addicts.

Among methadone's most useful properties are cross-tolerance with other narcotic drugs and a less intense withdrawal response (Recovery Helpdesk 2010). If it reaches a sufficiently high level in the blood, methadone blocks heroin euphoria. In addition, withdrawal symptoms of patients physically dependent on heroin or morphine and the postaddiction craving can be suppressed by oral administration of methadone (Meader 2010). The effective dose for methadone maintenance is 50 to 100 milligrams per day to treat severe withdrawal symptoms (*Drug Facts and Comparisons* 2010; Way et al. 1998; Zickler 1999).

The value of substituting methadone for heroin lies in its longer action. Because addicts no longer need heroin to prevent withdrawal, they often can be persuaded to leave their undesirable associates, drug sources, and dangerous lifestyles. The potential side effects from methadone are the same as those from morphine and heroin, including constipation and sedation; yet if properly used, methadone is a safe drug (*Drug Facts and Comparisons* 2010).

When injecting methadone, some people feel the same kind of euphoria that can be obtained from heroin. Methadone addicts receiving maintenance treatment sometimes become euphoric if the dose is increased too rapidly. There are cases of people who injected crushed methadone pills and developed serious lung conditions from particles that lodged in the tissue, creating a condition somewhat like emphysema. The number of deaths from methadone overdose have increased substantially. Data from the CDC demonstrate methadone-related deaths in the United States increased more than five-fold in the past decade. The reasons for this startling increase include the following (Zielinski 2010):

- Large quantities of methadone are being stolen from legitimate businesses such as hospitals and pharmacies for personal use or to sell.
- Excessive amounts of methadone are being accumulated and abused by doctor-shopping, prescription fraud, or illegal Internet pharmacy web sites.
- It is being misused by patients who received their methadone by legitimate prescriptions for pain.
- Because of increases in pain management clinics, it has become easier to obtain methadone.

Like heroin, methadone overdoses can be reversed by the antagonist naloxone if the person is treated in time.

Fentanyls

The fentanyls belong to a family of very potent narcotic analgesics (more than 200 times the potency of morphine) that are often administered intravenously for general anesthesia. These synthetic opioid narcotics include drugs such as sufentanil and alfentanil (Gutstein and Akil 2007). Fentanyls are also used in transdermal systems (patches on the skin) and as lollipops in the treatment of chronic pain (Adams 2010). Occasionally, reports surface of individuals abusing a fentanyl patch by licking, swallowing, or even smoking it (Hull et al. 2007).

It is estimated that some 100 different active forms of fentanyl could be synthesized; up to now, about 10 derivatives have appeared on the street. They are considered to be "designer" drugs (see Chapter 1). Because of their great potency, ease of production, and low costs, the fentanyls have sometimes been used to replace heroin (Fodale 2006). Fentanyl-type drugs can appear in the same forms and colors as heroin, so there is nothing to alert users that they have been sold a heroin substitute (NIDA 2007). Due to their powerful effects, these drugs are especially dangerous, and incredibly small doses can cause fatal respiratory depression in an unsuspecting heroin user (Adams 2010; Fodale 2006). It is likely that hundreds have died from overdosing with heroin laced with fentanyl. Because of an enhanced "high," addicts are tempted to use these lethal combinations (Boddigger 2006). Because these drugs are sometimes very difficult to detect in the blood owing to the small quantities used, there is no reliable information regarding the extent of fentanyl abuse. Fentanyl is so potent that abusing the patch has caused overdoses and even death (AboutLawsuits 2010; Douglas 2006).

Hydromorphone

Hydromorphone (Dilaudid) is prepared from morphine and used as an analgesic and cough suppressant. It is a stronger analgesic than morphine and is used to treat moderate to severe pain. Nausea, vomiting, constipation, and euphoria may be less marked with hydromorphone than with morphine (Karch 1996; Way et al. 1998). It is becoming more popular with opiate addicts due to its potency; however, combination with other CNS depressants can be fatal (Marsh 2009). On the street, it is taken in tablet form or injected.

Oxycodone

Oxycodone (OxyContin) is a moderate narcotic analgesic that in the past decade has been increasingly abused as the proprietary product OxyContin and has created considerable controversy (see "Here and Now: OxyContin Controversy Rages"). OxyContin is a long-lasting version of oxycodone and is considered to be an important and effective therapy for the treatment of severe pain from cancer or other lingering diseases (DrugLib 2010; *Drug Facts and Comparisons* 2010). A dramatic rise in the abuse of OxyContin has been a considerable cause for alarm by officials. Street names for OxyContin include *OC, kicker, OxyCotton*, and *hillbilly heroin* (CBS News 2007). This drug is easily abused by simply crushing the tablet, which the abuser can then ingest, inject, inhale, or place rectally. The drug can have particularly serious side effects when injected because it has a prolonged extended action (AddictionSearch 2010).

The problems with OxyContin are underscored by the report that in 2009, 4.9% and 5.1% of high school seniors and 10th graders, respectively, abused this drug (Johnston 2010). Interestingly, the abuse rate by this population for the less potent Vicodin was almost double that for OxyContin, likely due to easier access (Johnston 2010). Concern has been further heightened with reports of drug rings, including physicians illegally distributing OxyContin (McCartney and Risling 2010). Deaths and trips to the emergency room caused by OxyContin

Here and Now

OxyContin Controversy Rages

Controversy surrounds the drug OxyContin, with some hailing its painkilling abilities even as others emphasize its potentially deadly effects. At a 3-day conference on drug abuse prevention, protesters held up signs referring to friends and family members who they claimed had died as a result of OxyContin overdose, in the hopes of raising awareness about the potential problems associated with the drug. One protester described a young man who had gone through withdrawal and depression after being prescribed the drug as a painkiller, and who eventually died from an accidental overdose. Others recognized the beneficial effects of the drug, noting that OxyContin had relieved pain that other drugs could not alleviate in their loved ones. Most individuals attending the conference felt that the problem was not OxyContin or prescriptions, but rather persuading communities to work together to create solutions to the abuse of this drug.

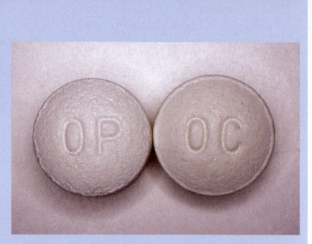

Source: Bloodsworth, D. "Crowd Protests." 20 November 2003. Available at: http://www.oxyabusekills.com/crowdprotests.html. Accessed February 16, 2011.

are becoming more and more common and are concerning to both medical and law enforcement organizations (DEA 2010). However, these reports of adverse events associated with OxyContin use must be put into perspective by the knowledge that the vast majority of these emergency events are associated with drug abuse or physical causes (e.g., cancer) in addition to the effects of OxyContin (*Biotech Week* 2003). As a result, the FDA and DEA control OxyContin at the same level as morphine.

■ Meperidine

Meperidine (Demerol) is a synthetic drug that frequently is used as an analgesic for treatment of moderate pain; it can be taken in tablet form or injected. Meperidine is about one-tenth as powerful as morphine, and its use can lead to dependence (Gutstein and Akil 2006). This drug is sometimes given too freely by some physicians because tolerance develops, requiring larger doses to maintain its therapeutic action. With continual use, it causes physical dependence. Meperidine addicts may use large daily doses (3–4 grams per day). Repeated use of high doses of meperidine can cause seizures (Gutstein and Akil 2006; *Drug Facts and Comparisons* 2010).

■ Buprenorphine

Buprenorphine, a mild-to-moderate narcotic analgesic, was available as a Schedule V pain reliever for years. As discussed earlier, after extensive research, this drug was approved in 2002 as an effective medication for the treatment of narcotic abuse and dependence (Hanson 2003). Buprenorphine has been shown to be effective in relieving the cravings for narcotic pain relievers with minimal tendency to cause addiction itself (Bates 2010a). Although buprenorphine has been reported to have a minimal high (Leinweind 2006) when used properly, there have been isolated reports of occasional deaths, especially when combined with other CNS depressant drugs (Williams 2009). Despite buprenorphine's significant safety record and its minimal propensity for abuse, its new FDA-approved indication would cause it to be dispensed to patients with drug abuse histories, so the DEA revised it classification to a Schedule III drug. Of particular importance is the fact that buprenorphine (in the form of Subutex and Suboxone, a combination of buprenorphine and the opioid antagonist, naloxone) has been approved for the treatment of opiate dependence in an office setting. Trained physicians are allowed to treat up to 100 narcotic-dependent patients with buprenorphine in their medical offices

(Curley 2007). This means opioid addictions and dependence can now be treated with a prescribed medication by trained primary care physicians, in the offices of private doctors. This is an important step in what may become a revolution in addiction treatment, allowing patients to discreetly receive help from a family doctor for their substance abuse problem (Bates 2010a). Since buprenorphine was approved in 2002 as the first office-based treatment for opiate addiction, only about 300,000 patients have received prescriptions for this drug (Bates 2010a). Currently, almost 20,000 physicians are certified to prescribe it for treatment of opioid drug dependence (Kuehn 2010). With time, it is hoped that use of buprenorphine by primary care physicians will become rather routine (Anderson 2007).

MPTP: A "Designer" Tragedy

Attempts to synthesize illicit designer versions of meperidine by street chemists have proved tragic for some unsuspecting drug addicts. In 1976, a young drug addict with elementary laboratory skills attempted to make a meperidine-like drug by using shortcuts in the chemical synthesis. Three days after self-administering his untested drug product, the drug user developed a severe case of tremors and motor problems identical to Parkinson's disease, a neurological disorder generally occurring in the elderly. Even more surprising to attending neurologists was that this young drug addict improved dramatically after treatment with levodopa, a drug that is very effective in treating the symptoms of traditional Parkinson's disease. After 18 months of treatment, the despondent addict committed suicide. An autopsy revealed he had severe brain damage that was almost identical to that occurring in classical Parkinson's patients. It was concluded that a by-product resulting from the sloppy synthesis of the meperidine-like designer narcotic was responsible for the irreversible brain damage.

This hypothesis was confirmed by a separate and independent event on the West Coast in 1981, when a cluster of relatively young heroin addicts (ages 22–42) in the San Francisco area also developed symptoms of Parkinson's disease. All of these patients had consumed a new "synthetic heroin" obtained on the streets, which was produced by attempting to synthesize meperidine-like drugs (Aminoff 1998; Langston et al. 1983). Common to both incidents was the presence of the compound MPTP, which was a contaminant resulting from the careless synthesis. MPTP is metabolized to a very reactive molecule in the brain that selectively destroys neurons containing the transmitter dopamine in the motor regions of the basal ganglia (see Chapter 4). Similar neuronal damage occurs in classical Parkinson's disease over the course of 50 to 70 years, whereas ingestion of MPTP dramatically accelerates the degeneration to a matter of days (Goldstein 1994). As tragic as the MPTP incident was, it was heralded as an important scientific breakthrough—MPTP is now used by researchers as a tool to study why Parkinson's disease occurs and how to treat it effectively (Lane and Dunnett 2008).

Codeine

Codeine is a naturally occurring constituent of opium and the most frequently prescribed of the narcotic analgesics. It is used principally as a treatment for minor to moderate pain and as a cough suppressant. Maximum pain relief from codeine occurs with 30 to 50 milligrams. Usually, when prescribed for pain, codeine is combined with either a salicylate (such as aspirin) or acetaminophen (Tylenol). Aspirin-like drugs and opioid narcotics interact in a synergistic fashion to give an analgesic equivalence greater than what can be achieved by aspirin or codeine alone.

Although not especially powerful, codeine may still be abused. Codeine-containing cough syrup is currently classified as a Schedule V drug. Because the abuse potential is considered minor, the FDA has ruled that codeine cough products can be sold without a prescription; however, the pharmacist is required to keep them behind the counter and must be asked in order to provide codeine-containing cough medications. Despite the FDA ruling, many states have more restrictive regulations and require that codeine-containing cough products be available only by prescription (Way et al. 1998).

Although codeine dependence is possible, it is not very common; most people who abuse codeine developed narcotic dependence previously with one of the more potent opioids. In general, large quantities of codeine are needed to satisfy a narcotic addiction; therefore, it is not commonly marketed on the street.

Pentazocine

Pentazocine (Talwin) was first developed in the 1960s in an effort to create an effective analgesic with low abuse potential. When taken orally, its analgesic effect is slightly greater than that of codeine.

Its effects on respiration and sedation are similar to those of the other opioids, but it does not prevent withdrawal symptoms in a narcotic addict. In fact, pentazocine will precipitate withdrawal symptoms if given to a person on methadone maintenance (Gutstein and Akil 2006). Pentazocine is not commonly abused because its effects can be unpleasant, resulting in dysphoria. It is classified as a Schedule IV drug.

■ Propoxyphene

Propoxyphene (Darvon, Dolene) is structurally related to methadone, but it is a much weaker analgesic, about half as potent as codeine (Gutstein and Akil 2006). Like codeine, propoxyphene is frequently given in combination with aspirin or acetaminophen. Although it was once an extremely popular analgesic, the use of propoxyphene declined as its potency was questioned. Research suggested that this narcotic was no more effective in relieving pain than aspirin (Gutstein and Akil 2006). To a large extent, new, more effective nonnarcotic analgesics replaced propoxyphene. In very high doses, it caused delusions, hallucinations, and convulsions and even fatal heart problems. Alone, propoxyphene caused little respiratory depression; however, when combined with alcohol or other CNS depressants, this drug could depress respiration. Due to these negative properties, the FDA requested the removal of this controversial painkiller, and it was removed from the market in 2010 (Stein 2010).

■ Tramadol

Tramadol (Ultram) was first introduced into the U.S. market in 1994 as a synthetic, moderately effective analgesic sometimes used as a substitute for opioid painkillers (Smith 2010). Although tramadol itself causes some activation of opioid receptors in the brain, it appears that its analgesic properties are related to more than just its opioid actions. For example, tramadol alters GABA, noradrenaline, and serotonin transmitter systems as well, in a manner that might contribute to its atypical analgesic properties. For this reason, tramadol may have some antidepressant effects that augment its analgesic abilities (Medic8 2010).

Tramadol is frequently prescribed for patients who either do not respond well or have difficulty with the opioid painkillers. Despite the fact that opioid action likely is not the sole basis of its analgesia, it is significant enough to cause some dependence issues. For example, there is an illegal street market for this substance, where it is known by names such as *chill pills* or *ultra*. There are clinicians who claim that for some patients tramadol can cause a serious opioid-like dependence (Smith 2010). Such conclusions are based on findings such as: (1) from 1998 to 2006 there was a six-fold increase in admissions for treatment of tramadol-related dependence; (2) for teens, tramadol is easier to get than alcohol and easy to sell on the streets; (3) emergency room visits nationwide that included tramadol as a significant component went from about 5000 in 2004 to about 13,500 in 2008; and (4) there is evidence that regular daily use of tramadol can cause physical dependence and causes withdrawals when discontinued abruptly (Lanier et al. 2010). These increases in tramadol-related problems correspond to an explosion in its popularity, resulting in about 26 million prescriptions being dispensed by retailers in 2008 (Smith 2010). Tramadol is available as both regular and extended-release tablets (Drugs.com 2010b).

Even though tramadol is marketed as an opioid drug with low risk of dependence and most health authorities consider it to have a relatively low dependence liability, it is clear that some patients can become addicted to this analgesic (Breakthrough Addiction Recovery 2010). Currently, tramadol is available only by prescription, but is not scheduled by the DEA even though the prescribing information typically warns that tramadol "may induce psychological and physical dependence of the morphine-type." In some countries, tramadol is actually available OTC (Breakthrough Addiction Recovery 2010). Because of many clinical complaints across the country, the DEA is reviewing the status of tramadol products in order to determine if scheduling of these drugs would be appropriate.

Narcotic-Related Drugs

Although not classified as narcotics, the following drugs are either structurally similar to narcotics (dextromethorphan) or are used to treat narcotic withdrawal (clonidine) or overdose (naloxone).

■ Dextromethorphan

Dextromethorphan is a synthetic used in cough remedies since the 1960s and can be purchased without prescription. Although its molecular structure resembles that of codeine, this drug does not have analgesic action nor does it cause typical narcotic dependence (Encyclopedia Britannica 2010).

Although dextromethorphan is not traditionally considered a major drug abuse problem, recent studies are cause for concern. They reveal that more than 3 million young people have used OTC products containing dextromethorphan to get high (Buddy 2008). Overdose of dextromethorphan-containing cough medicines has been reported in the United States and other countries, sometimes resulting in deadly consequences (see "Here and Now: Dextromethorphan"). From 1998–2008, 72 cases of dextromethorphan-related deaths were identified. The majority of these cases were suicides, often involving multiple substances (Traynor 2010). Abuse of dextromethorphan typically occurs among adolescents and young adults (Traynor 2010). The relatively few cases of addiction reveal a pattern of high-dose use for months to even years. The principal symptoms of abuse include altered perceptions, sense of floating, hallucinations, visual distortions, and even paranoia and psychotic reactions. Its effects have been described to be similar to those of phencyclidine (PCP) and the general anesthetic ketamine (Morgan, Porritt, and Poling 2006). There is some suggestion that both physical and psychological dependence can occur with dextromethorphan, resulting in withdrawal when its use is discontinued (Mutschler et al. 2010). Dextromethorphan is sometimes mixed with drugs such as alcohol, amphetamines, and cocaine to give unusual psychoactive interactions. As of 2010, the DEA had taken no steps to restrict the use of dextromethorphan in over-the-counter (OTC) products; in fact, advisers to the FDA voted against placing this drug in a schedule of controlled substances, which likely will preclude the DEA from making a change in its category (Traynor 2010).

Young people are becoming aware of dextromethorphan's abuse potential from web sites on the Internet. A growing number of these sites have promoted dextromethorphan as a powerful OTC mind-altering drug. Included on these sites are personal experiences of users as well as directions on how to use the drug, predictions about what to expect, warning signs of adverse reactions, and instructions as to how to extract dextromethorphan from OTC cough medicines (Vaults of Erowid 2007).

Clonidine

Clonidine (Catapres) was created in the late 1970s. It is not a narcotic analgesic and has no direct effect

Here and Now

Dextromethorphan: No Coughing Matter

Dextromethorphan, a key active ingredient in cough suppressants, is the reason why many young people are using OTC cough medicines to get high. The substance—also known as robo, skittles, dxm, dex, and tussin—is found in at least 80 OTC products. Dextromethorphan usually produces a disassociative feeling (roboing, robo rolling, robo tripping) or a feeling of intoxication, but its abuse can also lead to psychotic behavior. When large amounts of dextromethorphan are taken, the drug attaches to receptors in the central nervous system—the same receptors to which PCP attaches. In the long term, this effect can cause depression, memory problems, and suicidal tendencies. Dextromethorphan abuse also can result in death: in 2005, five teenage boys from three different states died after ingesting dextromethorphan powder from an online source that illegally sold the drug in bulk. The company was closed down the next year.

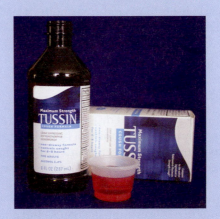

Sources: Magnus, E. "Addicted to Cough Medicine?" MSNBC News. 27 March 2004. Available at: http://www.msnbc.msn.com/id/4608341. Accessed March 14, 2011; and Traynor, K. "Advisers Vote Against Declaring Dextromethorphan a Controlled Substance." American Society of Health Pharmacists. 2010. Available at: http://www.ashp.org/import/news/HealthSystemPharmacyNews/newsarticle. aspx?id=3418. Accessed March 14, 2011.

on the opioid receptors; instead, it stimulates receptors for noradrenaline. Its principal use is as an oral antihypertensive (*Drug Facts and Comparisons* 2010; O'Shea, Law, and Melichar 2010). Clonidine is mentioned here because it is a nonaddictive, noneuphorigenic prescription medication with demonstrated efficacy in relieving some of the physical effects of opiate withdrawal (such as vomiting and diarrhea). However, clonidine does not alter narcotic craving or the generalized aches associated with withdrawal (O'Brien 2006; O'Shea et al. 2010). The dosing regimen is typically a 7- to 14-day inpatient treatment for opiate withdrawal. Length of treatment can be reduced to 7 days for withdrawal from heroin and short-acting opiates; the 14-day treatment is needed for the longer-acting methadone-type opiates. Because tolerance to clonidine may develop, opiates are discontinued abruptly at the start of treatment. In this way, the peak intensity of withdrawal will occur while clonidine is still maximally effective (McEvoy 2003).

One of the most important advantages of clonidine over other treatments for opiate withdrawal detoxification is that it shortens the time for withdrawal to 14 days compared with several weeks or months using standard procedures, such as methadone treatment (O'Shea et al. 2010). The potential disadvantage of taking clonidine is that it can cause serious side effects of its own, the most serious being significantly lowered blood pressure, which can cause fainting and blacking out (*Drug Facts and Comparisons* 2010; O'Shea et al. 2010). Overall, its lack of abuse potential makes clonidine particularly useful in rapid treatment of narcotic dependence; however, the long-term benefit is controversial (Gowing et al. 2003).

■ Naloxone/Naltrexone

Naloxone and the related drug naltrexone are relatively pure narcotic antagonists. These drugs attach to opiate receptors in the brain and throughout the body. They do not activate the receptors, but rather prevent narcotic drugs, such as heroin and morphine, from having an effect. By themselves, these antagonists do not cause much change, but potently block or reverse the effects of all narcotics. Because of its antagonistic properties, naloxone is a useful antidote in the treatment of narcotic overdoses; its administration rapidly reverses life-threatening, narcotic-induced effects on breathing and the cardiovascular system (*Alcoholism and Drug Abuse Weekly* 2010b; O'Brien 2006). However, if not used

carefully, this antagonist will also block the analgesic action of the narcotics and initiate severe withdrawals in narcotic-dependent people (Way et al. 1998). Its use has been proposed to prevent addicts from experiencing the effects of heroin (Mathias 2003); in fact, as discussed earlier in this chapter, an extended form of naloxone (its effect persists for 1 month) called Vivitrol was recently approved by the FDA for the treatment of heroin addiction (Rubin 2010). However, many individuals dependent on heroin are not interested in using this drug because it can precipitate withdrawal symptoms. But a recent study found that of those heroin addicts who received six monthly injections, 70% did not go back to heroin use (this was twice the success rate of heroin addicts given placebo), and they claimed that the Vivitrol reduced their cravings for the opiate drug (Rubin 2010).

An interesting use of naloxone has been to combine it with buprenorphine in small quantities (Suboxone). As long as this product is taken as prescribed, the quantity of naloxone is too small to have an antagonistic effect; however, if Suboxone is consumed in high doses, such as would occur if it were being abused, there would be sufficient naloxone to block the opioid effect (Center for Substance Abuse Research [CESAR] 2003). The FDA also has approved Suboxone to reduce the craving for alcohol in the treatment of chronic alcoholism (*Drug Facts and Comparisons* 2010). There are additional reports suggesting that opioid receptors may contribute to other drug addictions such as those caused by nicotine and psychostimulants. At this time it is not clear if an opioid antagonist like naloxone would be effective in treating these other addictions.

Natural Narcotic Substances

Although many herbal preparations can cause drowsiness or have some analgesic properties, few of these actually contain opioid narcotic drugs. The naturally occurring opioid drugs include morphine, codeine, heroin, papaverine, and thebaine and are found only in the opium poppy, *Papaver somniferum.* Although several varieties of opium-yielding poppies exist, they are typically winter crops in the Southern Hemisphere and do best in climates that have warm days and cool nights. All of the plants thrive in sandy soil. Most of the active drugs are found in the seepage from the seed heads located beneath the flower petals of the poppy flowers, although small amounts of these active ingredients are found in other parts of the plant such as the stem and leaves. Although

Opium poppy containing natural narcotics such as morphine, codeine, and heroin.

this species of plant can survive in the United States if the environment is rigidly controlled, the vast majority of the supplies of the naturally occurring narcotic drugs are brought into the country, either legally and sold as legitimate pharmaceuticals or smuggled across borders and sold as illicit narcotics.

Discussion Questions

1. Why do narcotics have high abuse potential?

2. What are the principal clinical uses of the opioid narcotics?

3. What is the relationship between endorphin systems and the opioid narcotics?

4. Why do the opioid pain relievers account for two-thirds of prescription drug abuse?

5. What effect has the rising abuse of prescription narcotic analgesics had on legitimately prescribing these drug for pain management?

6. What is the difference between opioid addiction and opioid physical dependence?

7. Why was there a substantial increase in heroin abuse in the United States throughout the 1990s?

8. Why does heroin addiction contribute to criminal activity?

9. What are the principal withdrawal effects when heroin use is stopped in addicts?

10. How does methadone maintenance work for the treatment of narcotic dependence? Explain a possible drawback to this approach.

11. How does buprenorphine compare to methadone as treatment for narcotic addictions?

12. How does naloxone (e.g., Vivitrol) compare to methadone maintenance treatment for heroin/opioid addiction?

13. What is considered to be successful treatment for heroin addiction?

14. How does morphine compare with heroin?

15. How does tramadol compare to other opioid analgesics?

16. Why is dextromethorphan potentially addicting, and what should the federal government do to stop its abuse?

17. What does the fact that naloxone is effective in the treatment of alcoholism suggest about the role of endogenous opioid systems in alcohol dependence?

Summary

1 The term *narcotic* refers to naturally occurring substances derived from the opium poppy and their synthetic substitutes. These drugs are referred to as the opioid (or opiate) narcotics because of their association with opium. For the most part, the opioid narcotics possess abuse potential, but they also have important clinical value and are used to relieve all kinds of pain (they are analgesic), suppress coughing (they are antitussive), and stop diarrhea.

2 The principal side effects of the opioid narcotics, besides their abuse potential, include drowsiness, respiratory depression, nausea and vomiting, constipation, inability to urinate, and sometimes a drop in blood pressure. These side effects can be annoying or even life-threatening, so caution is required when using these drugs.

3 Heroin is the most likely of the opioid narcotics to be severely abused; it is easily prepared from opium and has a rapid, intense effect.

4 When narcotics such as heroin are first used by people not experiencing pain, the drugs can cause unpleasant, dysphoric sensations. However,

euphoria gradually overcomes the aversive effects. The positive feelings increase with narcotic use, leading to psychological dependence. After psychological dependence, physical dependence occurs with frequent daily use, which reinforces the narcotic abuse. If the user stops taking the drug after physical dependence has occurred, severe withdrawal symptoms result.

5 Tolerance to narcotics can occur rapidly with intense use of these drugs. This tolerance can result in the use of incredibly large doses of narcotics that would be fatal to a nontolerant person.

6 Methadone and buprenorphine are frequently used to help narcotic addicts stop using heroin or one of the other highly addicting drugs. Oral methadone relieves the withdrawal symptoms that would result from discontinuing narcotics. Methadone can also cause psychological and physical dependence, but it is less addicting than heroin and easier to control. Buprenorphine is distinct from methadone in that it has been approved for use in primary care settings and may be safer for treating women who use opioid narcotics during pregnancy.

7 Fentanyls are very potent synthetic opioid narcotics. They can be easily synthesized and converted into drugs that are as much as 3000 to 6000 times more potent than heroin itself. Detection and regulation of these fentanyl derivatives by law enforcement agencies are very difficult. The fentanyl-type drugs are used as heroin substitutes and have killed narcotic addicts because of their unexpected potency.

8 Attempts to create designer narcotics have led to the synthesis of very potent fentanyl-like drugs that are responsible for a number of overdose deaths. In addition, attempts to synthesize a meperidine (Demerol) designer drug resulted in the inadvertent creation of MPTP, a very reactive compound that causes a dramatic onset of Parkinson's disease in its users.

9 Tramadol is an atypical opioid-like analgesic that has some antidepressant actions that might contribute to its effectiveness as a moderately potent pain killer. It likely has less addicting properties than most of the other opioid narcotics, but its dramatic rise in popularity has revealed a potential for causing dependence and withdrawal in some patients. Although not currently scheduled, the DEA is considering its addition to the list of controlled substances.

10 Dextromethorphan is a codeine-related drug used as an antitussive in OTC cough medicines. In very high doses, dextromethorphan can cause PCP-like hallucinations and sensory distortions. The abuse of this drug has not been substantial enough to result in its removal or special control by federal agencies.

References

Abel, E. L. *Marijuana: The First Twelve Thousand Years.* New York: Plenum, 1980.

AboutLawsuits. "Fentanyl Pain Patch Wrongful Death Lawsuit Results in $13.3 Million Verdict." 28 October 2010. Available http://www.aboutlawsuits.com/fentanyl-pain-patch-wrongful-death-lawsuit-results-in-133-million-verdict-1560

ACOG (American Congress of Obstetricians and Gynecologists). "Donald F. Richardson Memorial Prize Paper Award Winners Present Research." 19 May 2010. Available http://www.acog.org/from_home/publications/press_releases/nr05-18-10.cfm

Adams, K. "Search for Answers in Fentanyl Death Raises More Questions." *Virginian-Pilot.* 18 May 2010. Available http://hamptonroads.com/2010/05/search-answers-fentanyl-death-raises-more-questions

AddictionSearch. "OxyContin Addiction, Abuse and Treatment." 2010. Available http://www.addictionsearch.com/treatment_articles/article/oxycontin-addiction-abuse-and-treatment_16.html

AFP. "Afghan Heroin Took Million Lives Last Decade: Russia." 8 June 2010. Available http://www.google.com/hostednews/afp/article/ALeqM5jJR7-F4pCliXVIW-uLrVyWQAM6GA

Alcoholism and Drug Abuse Weekly. "Marijuana, Prescription Painkiller Abuse Rises in 2009." 20 September 2010a. Available http://onlinelibrary.wiley.com/doi/10.1002/adaw.20250/abstract

Alcoholism and Drug Abuse Weekly. "Naloxone Distribution Saves More Than 400 Lives in SF OD Project." 1 November 2010b. Available http://onlinelibrary.wiley.com/doi/10.1002/adaw.20256/abstract

American Academy of Pain Medicine. "Psychiatric Factors Linked to Increased Risk for Misuse of Opioid Medications." 23rd Annual Meeting, Abstract 151. 7 February 2007.

American SIDS Institute. "Reducing the Risk of SIDS." 2005. Available http://www.sids.org/prevent.htm

Aminoff, M. "Pharmacologic Management of Parkinsonism and Other Movement Disorders." In *Basic and Clinical Pharmacology,* 7th ed., edited by Bertram Katzung, 450–463. Stamford, CT: Appleton and Lange, 1998.

Anderson, L. "A Drug-War Setback. Red Tape, Doctors Say, Cuts Buprenorphine Prescription." *Baltimore Sun.* 20 June 2007. Available http://articles.baltimoresun.com/2007-06-20/news/0706200045_1_buprenorphine-drug-addiction-medicaid

Austin, G. A. *Perspective on the History of Psychoactive Substance Use.* NIDA Research Issues No. 24. Washington, DC: U.S. Department of Health, Education, and Welfare, 1978.

Bammer, G. "Heroin Maintenance Bibliography." March 2005. Available http://www.drugpolicy.org/library/bibliography/heroin

Bammer, G., A. Dobler-Mikola, M. Fleming, J. Strang, and A. Uchtenhagen. "The Heroin Prescribing Debate: Integrating Science and Politics." *Science* 284 (1999): 1277–1278.

Bates, B. "NIDA Seeks Family Physicians to Treat Opioid-Dependent Youth." *Family Practice News* 40 (2010a): 1–51.

Bates, B. "Psychiatrists Still 'Out of Sync' on Buprenorphine." Elsevier Global Medical News. 22 April 2010. Available http://www.thefreelibrary.com/Attitudes+'out+of+sync'+on+buprenorphine-a0228519234

Bearak, B. "Junkies Playing Roulette with Needles." *Salt Lake Tribune* (29 November 1992): A-4.

Belluck, P. "Methadone, Once the Way Out, Suddenly Grows as a Killer Drug." *New York Times* (9 February 2003): 8.

Benfield, P. "Methadone: Is It Really a Proper Treatment For Heroin Addicts." Helium.com. 25 June 2010. Available http://www.helium.com/items/1871881-methadone-for-heroin-withdrawal

Bernstein, M. "Heroin Kills More Oregonians in 2009 Than Cocaine and Meth Combined." *The Oregonian.* 5 April 2010. Available http://www.oregonlive.com/portland/index.ssf/2010/04/heroin_kills_more_oregonians_i.html

Bhuvaneswar, C., G. Chang, L. Epstein, and T. Stern. "Cocaine and Opioid Use During Pregnancy: Prevalence and Management." *Primary Care Companion to the Journal of Clinical Psychiatry* 10 (2008): 59–65.

Biotech Week. "Purdue Pharma: OxyContin Rarely the Sole Cause of Drug Abuse Deaths." (19 March 2003): 1.

Bloomberg BusinessWeek. "More Americans Abusing Prescription Painkillers." 15 July 2010. Available http://www.businessweek.com/lifestyle/content/healthday/641186.html

Boddigger, D. "Fentanyl-Laced Street Drugs Kill Hundreds." *Lancet* 368 (2006): 1237–1238.

Borigini, M. "Prescribing Narcotics: A Doctor's Point of View." Health Central, Chronic Pain Connection. 27 October 2008. Available http://www.healthcentral.com/chronic-pain/c/91/46424/comments

Boughton, B. "Buprenorphine Treatment Safer Than Methadone for Infants of Opiate-Addicted Mothers." Medscape. 21 May 2010. Available http://www.medscape.com/viewarticle/722213

Brady, S. "New Formulation for OxyContin." 8 June 2010. Available http://www.healthnews.com/medical-updates/new-formulation-for-oxycontin-4289.html

Breakthrough Addiction Recovery. "Tramadol." 1 November 2010. Available http://www.breakthroughaddiction-recovery.com/content-page-188-Tramadol.html

Brecher, E. M. *Licit and Illicit Drugs.* Boston: Little, Brown, 1972.

Buckley, C. "Young and Suburban, and Falling for Heroin." *New York Times.* 27 September 2009. Available http://www.nytimes.com/2009/09/27/nyregion/27heroin.html

Buddy, T. "Cough Syrup More Abused by Youth than Meth." About.com: Alcoholism. 29 January 2008. Available http://alcoholism.about.com/b/2008/01/29/cough-syrup-more-abused-by-youth-than-meth.htm

Caldwell, A. "Deadly Ultra-Pure Heroin Arrives in US." Huffington Post. 24 May 2010. Available http://www.huffingtonpost.com/2010/05/24/deadly-ultrapure-heroin-a_n_587648.html

Caldwell, A., and J. Salter. "Cheap, Ultra-Pure Heroin Kills Instantly." Associated Press, Today People. 24 May 2010. Available http://today.msnbc.msn.com/id/37319358/ns/us_news-crime_and_courts

CBS News. "OxyContin: Pain Relief vs. Abuse." 11 June 2007. Available http://www.cbsnews.com/stories/2007/06/19/health/webmd/main2953950.shtml

Center for Substance Abuse and Research (CESAR). "Buprenorphine Now Available for Treating Heroin Dependence in U.S." CESAR FAX. University of Maryland 12 (31 March 2003): 1.

Chossudovsky, M. "Who Benefits from the Afghan Opium Trade?" Global Research. 21 September 2006. Available http://www.globalresearch.ca/index.php?context=va&aid=3294

Christenson, S. "Heroin Addiction Takes Brutal Toll on Afghanistan." *San Antonio Express-News.* 24 May 2010. Available http://www.mysanantonio.com/news/local_news/in_kabul_regrets_rehab_and_redemption_94714589.html?showFullArticle=y

Colberg, S. "Methadone Deaths Climb, Oklahoma Officials Say People Get Drugs from Many Sources." *The Oklahoman.* 27 September 2009. Available http://newsok.com/methadone-deaths-climb-oklahoma-officials-say/article/3404370

Cole, C. "Heroin Back on Streets." *Arizona Daily Sun.* 30 May 2010. Available http://azdailysun.com/news/local/article_729609c8-078e-5b95-b1ca-3c5753b9ce4d.html

Colon, D. "Number of Newborns Addicted to Painkillers Rising." NPR. 16 February 2011. Available http://www.npr.org/2011/02/16/133805289/number-of-newborns-addicted-to-painkillers-rising

Community Epidemiology Work Group (CEWG). Vol. 1. *Highlights and Executive Summary.* NIDA, NIH Publications No. 03-5109A. Bethesda, MD: National Institutes of Health, December 2002.

Constable, P. "A Poor Yield for Afghans' War on Drugs." *Washington Post* (19 September 2006): 14A.

Cowan, R., and J. Carvel. "Heroin Addicts Could Inject Themselves at Supervised Centres in Police-Backed Plans." Guardian Unlimited. 23 May 2006. Available http://www.guardian.co.uk/society/2006/may/23/drugsandalcohol.drugs

Curley, B. "New Law Expands Access to Buprenorphine." Join Together. 2007. Available http://www.jointogether.org/news/features/2007/new-law-expands-access-to.html

DiChiara, G., and A. North. "Neurobiology of Opiate Abuse." *Trends in Pharmacological Sciences* 13 (May 1992): 185–193.

Douglas, J. "Painkiller Patch Abuse Blamed for Deaths." *Los Angeles Times* (15 June 2006).

Drug Enforcement Administration (DEA). "OxyContin." March 2010. Available http://www.justice.gov/dea/concern/oxycontin.html

Drug Facts and Comparisons. St. Louis, MO: Wolters Kluwer, 2010 (Pocket Version): 244–247, 520–590.

DrugLib. "OxyContin (Oxycodone Hydrochloride)—Summary." 2010. Available http://www.druglib.com/druginfo/oxycontin

Drugs.com. "Vivitrol." 22 October 2010. Available http://www.drugs.com/vivitrol.html

Drugs.com. "What's Tramadol?" 1 November 2010. Available http://www.drugs.com/tramadol.html

DrugWarFacts. "HIV/AIDS and Injection Drug Use." 2010. Available http://www.drugwarfacts.org/cms/node/48

Edwards, M. "Soldiers At Risk of Getting Hooked on Heroin." 6 June 2010. Available http://www.abc.net.au/news/stories/2010/06/03/2917713.htm?section=world

Encyclopedia Britannica. "Dextromethorphan." Encyclopedia Britannica Academic Edition 2010. Available http://www.britannica.com/EBchecked/topic/160532/dextromethorphan

Epstein, J., and J. Gfroerer. "Data Point to Increase in Numbers of Young Heroin Users." *Connection* (a semiannual newsletter published by the Association for Health Services Research) (June 1998): 3.

Eshkevari, L., and J. Heath. "Use of Acupuncture for Chronic Pain: Optimizing Clinical Practice." *Holistic Nursing Practice* 19 (2005): 217–221.

Fodale, V. "Killer Fentanyl: A Lesson from Anesthesiology." *Lancet* 368 (2006): 1237–1238.

Forensic Drug Abuse Advisor. "Buprenorphine-Related Deaths." 15 (2 February 2003): 1, 2.

Galanter, M., and H. Kleber. *The American Psychiatric Publishing Textbook of Substance Abuse Treatment*. Arlington VA: American Psychiatric Publishing, 2008.

Get the Facts. "Methadone Maintenance and Buprenorphine Therapy." DrugWarFacts.org. 2009. Available http://www.drugwarfacts.org/cms/node/55

Get the Facts. "Pain Management." DrugWarFacts.org. 2010. Available http://www.drugwarfacts.org/cms/node/59

GlobalSecurity.org. "Afghanistan Drug Market." 2010. Available http://www.globalsecurity.org/military/world/afghanistan/drugs-market.htm

Golding, A. "Two Hundred Years of Drug Abuse." *Journal of the Royal Society of Medicine* 86 (May 1993): 282–286.

Goldstein, A. *Addiction from Biology to Drug Policy*. New York: Freeman, 1994: 137–154.

Gourlay, G. "Advances in Opioid Pharmacology." *Supportive Care for Cancer* (21 December 2004): 153–159.

Gowing, L., M. Farrell, R. Ali, and J. White. "Alpha 2 Adrenergic Agonists for the Management of Opioid Withdrawal." *Cochrane Database Systems Review* 2 (2003).

Grinspoon, L. "Psychotherapy for Methadone Patients—Part II." *Harvard Mental Health Letter* 12 (October 1995): 7.

Gutstein, H., and H. Akil. "Opioid Analgesics." In *The Pharmacological Basis of Therapeutics,* 11th ed. Edited by L. Brunton, J. Lazo, and K. Parker, 547–590. New York: McGraw-Hill, 2006.

Hall, E., and N. Sykes. "Analgesia for Patients with Advanced Disease." *Postgraduate Medical Journal* 80 (2004): 148–154.

Hanson, G. R. "Opening the Door to Mainstream Medical Treatment of Drug Addiction." *NIDA Notes* 17 (January 2003): 3, 4.

Healthtree. "Heroin: One of the Most Dangerous Addictive Drugs." 9 August 2010. Available http://www.healthtree.com/articles/substance-abuse/heroin

Heroin Detox. "Medication with Counseling May Improve Heroin Treatment." 2010. Available http://www.heroin-detox.org/heroin-treatment-improved.htm

Hickman, M., S. Carrivick, S. Paterson, N. Hunt, D. Zador, L. Cusick, and J. Henry. "London Audit of Drug-Related Overdose Deaths: Characteristics and Typology, and Implications for Prevention and Monitoring." *Addiction* 102 (2007): 317–323.

Hitti, M. "Prescription Painkiller Addiction: 7 Myths." WebMD. 2 August 2010. Available http://www.care2.com/c2c/groups/disc.html?gpp=15009&pst=879478

Hubbard, R. "Focus on Heroin: Increase in Users and Changing Treatment System Present New Challenges for Services Researchers." *Connection* (a semiannual newsletter published by the Association for Health Services Research) (June 1998): 1–2.

Hull, M., M. Juhascik, F. Mazur, M. Flomenbaum, and G. Behonick. "Fatalities Associated with Fentanyl and Coadministered Cocaine on Opiates." *Journal of Forensic Science* 52 (2007): 1383–1388.

Jaffe, J., and M. Martin. "Opioid Analgesics and Antagonists." In *The Pharmacological Basis of Therapeutics,* 8th ed., edited by A. Gilman, T. Rall, A. Nies, and P. Taylor, 522–573. New York: Pergamon, 1990.

Johnston, L. "Monitoring the Future 2009." 2010. Available http://www.monitoringthefuture.org/data/09data.html

Jointogether.org. "Moral Judgment Still Plays a Role in Prescribing Pain Meds." 1 March 2010. Available http://www.jointogether.org/news/headlines/inthenews/2010/moral-judgment-still-plays-a.html

Karch, S. "Narcotics." In *The Pathology of Drug Abuse*, 281–408. New York: CRC, 1996.

Kosten, T., and L. Hollister. "Drugs of Abuse." In *Basic and Clinical Pharmacology,* 7th ed., edited by B. Katzun, 516–531. Stamford, CT: Appleton & Lange, 1998.

Kuehn, B. "Buprenorphine May Boost HIV Treatment." *Journal of the American Medical Association* 304 (2010): 261–263.

Laino, C. "Extended-Release Naltrexone Reduces Opioid Use." Medscape Medical News. 3 June 2010. Available http://www.medscape.com/viewarticle/722907

Lane, E., and S. Dunnett. "Animal Models of Parkinson's Disease and L-dopa Induced Dyskinesia. How Close Are We to the Clinic?" *Psychopharmacology* 199 (2008): 303–312.

Langston, J., P. Ballard, J. Tetrud, and I. Irwin. "Chronic Parkinsonism in Humans Due to a Product of Meperidine-Analogue Synthesis." *Science* 219 (1983): 979–980.

Lanier, R., M. Lofwall, M. Mintzer, G. Bigelow, and E. Strain. "Physical Dependence Potential of Daily Tramadol Dosing in Humans." *Psychopharmacology* (Berl) 211 (2010): 457–466.

Leach, B. "Heroin 'Shooting Galleries' Should Be Introduced." Telegraph.co.uk. 14 September 2009. Available http://www.telegraph.co.uk/news/uknews/crime/6185533/Heroin-shooting-galleries-should-be-introduced.html

Leinweind, D. "Baltimore Has New Way to Treat Addict." *USA Today.* 5 October 2006: 5a.

Leland, J. "The Fear of Heroin Is Shooting Up." *Newsweek* (26 August 1996): 55–56.

Levran, O., D. Londono, K. O'Hara, M. Randesi, J. Rotrosen, P. Casasonte, et al. "Heroin Addiction in African Americans: A Hypothesis-Driven Association Study." *Genes Brain and Behavior* 8 (2009): 531–540.

Marsh, J. "Opiate Addiction and Dilaudid." Suite101.com. 4 May 2009. Available http://www.suite101.com/content/opiate-addiction-and-dilaudid-a114964

"Mary." *Rolling Stone* 30 (1996): 42–43.

Mathias, R. "New Approaches Seek to Expand Naltrexone Use in Heroin Treatment." *NIDA Notes* 17 (January 2003): 8.

Maurer, D., and V. Vogel. *Narcotics and Narcotic Addiction,* 3rd ed. Springfield, IL: Thomas, 1967.

McCartney, A., and G. Risling. "Corey Haim's OxyContin Obtained Through Major Drug Ring." Huffington Post. 28 October 2010. Available http://www.huffingtonpost.com/2010/03/13/corey-haims-oxycontin-obt_n_497813.html

McClure, C. "Global Drug Policy and the HIV/IDU Epidemic in Eastern Europe and Central Asia." International AIDS Society. 2009. Available http://www.iasociety.org/Web/WebContent/File/CraigMcClure_SODAK%202009.pdf

McEvoy, G., ed. "Opiate Agonists and Antagonists." In *American Hospital Formulary Service Drug Information,* 2022–2097. Bethesda, MD: American Society of Hospital Pharmacists, 2003.

McLellen, T., O. Arndt, D. Metzger, G. Woody, and C. O'Brien. "The Effects of Psychosocial Services in Substance Abuse Treatment." *Journal of the American Medical Association* 269 (21 April 1993): 1953–1959.

McMurran, M. "What Works in Substance Misuse Treatments for Offenders." *Criminal Behavior and Mental Health* 17 (2007): 225–233.

Meader, N. "A Comparison of Methadone, Buprenorphine and Alpha2 Adrenergic Agonists for Opioid Detoxification: A Mixed Comparison Meta-analysis." *Drug and Alcohol Dependence* 108 (2010): 110–114.

Medic8. "Tramadol-Drug Information." 1 November 2010. Available http://www.medic8.com/medicines/Tramadol.html

Medical News Today. "Study Identifies Risk Factors for Painkiller Addiction and Links the Addiction to Genetics." 28 August 2010. Available http://www.medicalnewstoday.com/articles/199263.php

Meier, B. "Move to Restrict Pain Killers Puts Onus on Doctors." *New York Times.* 28 July 2010. Available http://www.nytimes.com/2010/07/29/business/29pain.html

Miller, D. "Common Ground Emerges in the Methadone vs. Drug-Free Recovery Debate." Behavioral Health Central. 2 February 2010. Available http://behavioralhealthcentral.com/index.php/20100514223479/Special-Features/common-ground-emerges-in-the-methadone-vs-drug-free-recovery-debate.html

More, J. "The Debate Over Drug Abuse Treatment: Methadone vs. Buprenorphine." Treatment Solutions Network. 28 July 2008. Available http://www.treatmentsolutionsnetwork.com/blog/index.php/2008/07/23/the-debate-over-drug-abuse-treatment-methadone-vs-buprenorphine

Morgan, T., M. Porritt, and A. Poling. "Effects of Dextromethorphan on Rats' Acquisition of Responding with Delayed Reinforcement." *Pharmacology and Biochemical Behavior* 85 (2006): 637–642.

Mutschler, J., A. Koopmann, M. Grosshans, D. Hermann, K. Mann, and F. Kiefer. "Dextromethorphan Withdrawal and Dependence Syndrome." *Deutsches Ärzteblatt International* 107 (2010): 537–540.

MyAddiction.com. "Heroin Addiction Stats and Facts." 2010. Available http://www.myaddiction.com/education/articles/heroin_statistics.html

Nakamura, D. "City to Spend $650,000 on Needle Exchange Programs." *Washington Post.* 3 January 2008. Available http://www.washingtonpost.com/wp-dyn/content/article/2008/01/02/AR2008010201905.html

Nandi, A., T. Glass, S. Cole, H. Chu, S. Galea, D. Celentano, et al. "Neighborhood Poverty and Injection Cessation in a Sample of Injection Drug Users." *American Journal of Epidemiology* 171 (2010): 391–398.

National Center for Biotechnology Information (NCBI). "Naltrexone Injection." PubMed Health. 1 May 2010. Available http://www.ncbi.nlm.nih.gov/pubmedhealth/PMH0000486

National Institute on Drug Abuse (NIDA). "Research Report Series—Heroin Abuse and Addiction." December 2004. Available http://www.drugabuse.gov/ResearchReports/heroin/heroin5.html

National Institute on Drug Abuse (NIDA). "NIDA InfoFacts: Heroin." January 2005. Available http://www.drugabuse.gov/Infofax/heroin.html

National Institute on Drug Abuse (NIDA). "Fentanyl." 2007. Available http://www.drugabuse.gov/drugpages/fentanyl.html

O'Brien, C. "Drug Addiction and Drug Abuse." In *The Pharmacological Basis of Therapeutics,* 11th ed. Edited by L. Brunton, J. Lazo, and K. Parker, 607–627. New York: McGraw-Hill, 2006.

"Opioids." *Medical Letter* 38 (10 May 1996).

O'Shea, J., F. Law, and J. Melichar. "Lofexidine/Clonidine for Withdrawal." ClinicalEvidence, Mental Health. 2010. Available http://clinicalevidence.bmj.com/ceweb/conditions/meh/1015/1015_I5.jsp

"'Oxy' Kids Crisis." *New York Post* (18 June 2007). Available http://www.nypost.com/p/news/regional/item_2RyopB29Z8esHu8oe50qkK

Pain and Central Nervous System. "Helping Opiate-Addicted Babies." *Pain and Central Nervous System Week* (5 September 2005). Available http://www.newsrx.com/newsletters/Pain-and-Central-Nervous-System-Week/2005-09-05/09052005333968W.html

Quinion, M. "Heroin Chic." World Wide Words. January 2005. Available http://www.worldwidewords.org/turnsofphrase/tp-her1.htm

Recovery Helpdesk. "10 Things You Should Know About Methadone: A Low Methadone Dose Is Not Necessarily the Best Methadone Dose." 2010. Available http://www.recoveryhelpdesk.com/2010/05/14/series-10-things-you-should-know-about-methadone-number-10

Reid, L., K. Elifson, and C. Sterk. "Ecstasy and Gateway Drugs: Initiating the Use of Ecstasy and Other Drugs." *Annals of Epidemiology* 17 (2007): 74–80.

Reisine, T., and G. Pasternak. "Opioid Analgesics and Antagonists." In *The Pharmacological Basis of Therapeutics,* 9th ed., edited by J. Hardman and L. Limbird, 521–555. New York: McGraw-Hill, 1995.

Relative, S. "Artie Lange Stabbed Himself Nine Times, Attempted Suicide Confirmed." Arts and Entertainment. 8 January 2010. Available http://www.associatedcontent.com/article/2568063/artie_lange_stabbed_himself_nine_times.html

Reuters. "Do Smokers Use More Prescription Painkillers?" 17 June 2010. Available http://www.reuters.com/article/idUSTRE65G5RQ20100617

Rolfs, R. "Utah Clinical Guidelines on Prescribing Opioids." (2008). Available http://health.utah.gov/prescription/pdf/Utah_guidelines_pdfs.pdf

Rombey, D. "Heroin Is Silent Scourge of Sheltered Springville." *Deseret News* (9 June 2003a): A-1.

Rombey, D. "Heroin Takes Toll on Families." *Deseret News* (10 June 2003b): A-1.

Rowlett, J., S. Negus, T. Shippenberg, N. Mello, S. Walsh, and R. Spealman. "Combined Cocaine and Opioid Abuse: From Neurobiology to the Clinic." Harvard Medical School. 2010. Available http://www.opioids.com/speedballs/index.html

Rubin, R. "FDA OKs Vivitrol to Treat Heroin, Narcotic Addictions." *USA Today.* 13 October 2010. Available http://www.usatoday.com/yourlife/health/2010-10-14-opioid14_ST_N.htm

Schneider, E. "The New Suburban Scourge; Heroin Goes In and Out of Fashion, But It's Never Been So Cheap or So Pure." *Newsday.* 27 September 2009. Available http://www.newsday.com/opinion/opinion-heroin-has-never-been-so-cheap-pure-and-easy-to-find-1.1476468

Seper, J. "Colombia Policy Cited for Rise in Heroin Use; Investigators Hit Focus on Cocaine." *Washington Times* (26 May 2003): A-1.

Sify News. "Risk Factors for Painkiller Addiction Identified." 28 August 2010. Available http://sify.com/news/risk-factors-for-painkiller-addiction-identified-news-scitech-ki3pEjahbic.html

Smith, C. "Experts Push for Painkiller Tramadol to Be on Controlled List." *Pittsburgh Tribune-Review.* 28 March 2010. Available http://www.pittsburghlive.com/x/pittsburghtrib/news/pittsburgh/s_673740.html

Starikov, N. "The United States and Afghan Heroin." OrientalReview.org. 23 March 2010. Available http://oriental-review.org/2010/03/23/the-united-states-and-afghan-heroin-2

Stein, R. "Painkiller Is Pulled Off Market at FDA's Request." *Washington Post.* 20 November 2010. Available http://www.washingtonpost.com/wp-dyn/content/article/2010/11/19/AR2010111906786.html

Stockman, F. "Heroin Is Surpassing Cocaine as Users' Choice." *Boston Globe* (26 May 2003): A-1.

Substance Abuse and Mental Health Services Administration (SAMHSA). "The Costs of Alcohol and Drug Treatment." About.com: Alcoholism. 31 December 2008. Available http://alcoholism.about.com/od/pro/a/blsam040527.htm

Substance Abuse and Mental Health Services Administration (SAMHSA). "Physician Waiver Qualifications." 2010. Available http://buprenorphine.samhsa.gov/waiver_qualifications.html

Szalavitz, M. "The Shot That Saves." *New York Times.* 21 August 2005. Available http://www.nytimes.com/2005/08/21/opinion/nyregionopinions/21CIszalavitz.html

Traynor, K. "Advisers Vote Against Declaring Dextromethorphan a Controlled Substance." American Society of Health Pharmacists. 2010. Available http://www.ashp.org/import/news/HealthSystemPharmacyNews/newsarticle.aspx?id=3418

Trigo, J. M., E. Martin-Garcia, F. Berrendero, P. Robledo, and R. Maldonado. "The Endogenous Opioid System: A Common Substrate in Drug Addiction." *Drug and Alcohol Dependence* 108 (2010): 183–194.

Tur, K. "Saving Lives with Heroin Needles." NBC New York. 19 August 2010. Available http://www.nbcnewyork.com/news/local-beat/The-Syringe-Exchange-Saved-My-Life-101112079.html

Urban Dictionary. "Heroin Chic." 5 October 2005. Available http://www.urbandictionary.com/define.php?term=heroin%20chic

USA Today. "Our View on Drug Addiction: Doctors Abet Growing Abuse of Pain Medication." 20 June 2010. Available http://www.usatoday.com/news/opinion/editorials/2010-06-21-editoril21_ST_N.htm?loc=interstitialskip

Valenzuela, B. E. "Heroin Use on the Rise." *Daily Press* (Victorville, CA). 28 August 2010. Available http://www.vvdailypress.com/news/use-21415-rise-heroin.html

Van Hollen, J. "Heroin Abuse Now a Rural Threat Too." The Cap Times. 3 October 2010. Available http://host.

madison.com/ct/news/opinion/mailbag/article_c47a
e879-6bf7-5bf3-a2e5-87c2bebf92a0.html

Vaults of Erowid. "Dextromethorphan." 6 January 2007. Available http://www.erowid.org/chemicals/dxm/dxm.shtml

Wang, M. "Perinatal Drug Abuse and Neonatal Drug Withdrawal." eMedicine from WebMD. 12 April 2010. Available http://emedicine.medscape.com/article/978492-overview

Way, W., H. Fields, and E. L. Way. "Opioid Analgesics and Antagonists." In *Basic and Clinical Pharmacology,* 7th ed., edited by B. Katzung, 496–515. Stamford, CT: Appleton & Lange, 1998.

Weiss, E. "Seattle Scene Represents Nation's Rising Heroin Use." All Things Considered, National Public Radio. 2 January 1995.

Williams, S. "Suboxone Abuse Grows After Outpatient Use Authorized." JSOnline, *Milwaukee-Wisconsin Journal Sentinel.* 2 April 2009. Available http://www.jsonline.com/news/milwaukee/42366057.html

Willis, M. "OxyContin Users Turning to Heroin." Drug-Rehabs. 2008. Available http://www.drug-rehabs.com/HeroinReplacesOxycontin.htm

Winkler, M., P. Weyers, R. Mucha, B. Stippekohl, and P. Pauli. "Conditioned Cues for Smoking Elicit Preparatory Responses in Healthy Smokers." *Psychopharmacology* (Berl.) 213 (February 2011): 781–789.

Young, D. "Scientists Examine Pain Relief and Addiction." *American Society of Health-System Pharmacists* 64 (2007): 796–798.

Zickler, P. "High-Dose Methadone Improves Treatment Outcomes." *NIDA Notes* 14 (1999): 81–82.

Zielinski, N. "Methadone Deaths Increase in the US." Examiner.com. 1 August 2010. Available http://www.examiner.com/public-health-in-grand-rapids/methadone-deaths-increase-the-us

Zocchi, A., E. Girlanda G. Varnier, I. Sartori, L. Zanetti, G. Wildish, et al. "Dopamine Responsiveness to Drugs of Abuse: A Shell-Core Investigation in the Nucleus Accumbens of the Mouse." *Synapse* 50 (2003): 293–302.

Learning ◎bjectives

On completing this chapter you will be able to:

- ◎ Explain how amphetamines work.
- ◎ Identify the FDA-approved uses for amphetamines.
- ◎ Recognize the major side effects of amphetamines on brain and cardiovascular functions.
- ◎ Identify the terms *speed, ice, run, high,* and *tweaking* as they relate to amphetamine use.
- ◎ Explain what "designer" amphetamines are and how Ecstasy compares to methamphetamine.
- ◎ Explain what "club drugs" are.
- ◎ Describe why stimulants are used as "performance enhancers" and why they should be considered dangerous.
- ◎ Explain how methylphenidate (e.g., Ritalin) compares to methamphetamine.
- ◎ Trace the changes in attitude toward cocaine abuse that occurred in the 1980s and explain why they occurred.
- ◎ Compare the effects of cocaine with those of amphetamines.
- ◎ Identify the different stages of cocaine withdrawal.
- ◎ Discuss the different approaches to treating cocaine dependence.
- ◎ Identify and compare the major sources of the caffeine-like xanthine drugs.
- ◎ List the principal physiological effects of caffeine.
- ◎ Compare caffeine dependence and withdrawal to that associated with the major stimulants.
- ◎ Describe the beverages known as "energy drinks" and relate their potential risks.
- ◎ Understand the potential dangers of using herbal stimulants such as ephedra.
- ◎ Identify the role of the FDA in regulating herbal stimulants.

Did You Know?

- ○ The first therapeutic use of amphetamines was in inhalers to treat nasal congestion.
- ○ Illegal methamphetamine can be easily made from drugs found in common over-the-counter (OTC) decongestants and some herbal products.
- ○ Methylphenidate (Ritalin), a drug prescribed to treat hyperactive children (ADHD), is sometimes used illegally by college students to suppress fatigue while studying long hours for exams.
- ○ Ecstasy has both psychedelic and stimulant properties.
- ○ Smoking "freebased" or "crack" cocaine is more dangerous and more addicting than other forms of administration.
- ○ Using high doses of amphetamines or cocaine can cause behavior that resembles schizophrenia.
- ○ Caffeine is the most frequently used stimulant in the world.
- ○ Caffeine is the principal active ingredient in most "energy drinks."
- ○ Herbal stimulants promoted as "natural highs" contain CNS stimulants such as caffeine or guarana.
- ○ Ephedrine found in natural herbal products has caused fatal cardiovascular problems in unsuspecting athletes and was removed from the list of FDA-approved OTC products.

Drugs and Society Online is a great source for additional drugs and society information for both students and instructors. Visit **go.jblearning.com/hanson11** to find a variety of useful tools for learning, thinking, and teaching.

Introduction

Stimulants are substances that cause the user to feel energized and experience a sense of increased energy and a state of euphoria, or "high." This effect is likely due to the ability of these drugs to release dopamine (Deslandes, Pache, and Sewell 2002). When used excessively, the user may also feel restless and talkative and have trouble sleeping. High doses administered over the long term can produce personality changes or even induce violent, dangerous, psychotic behavior. Persons addicted to potent stimulants make notoriously bad decisions that hurt them and their loved ones. The following is a quote from a former stimulant (i.e., methamphetamine) user:

> For 5 months I hung out with a crew who cooked meth. My job was to write bad checks to get ingredients to make it. This was my life. My house was a mess and I couldn't take care of anyone including myself. I weighed 100 pounds and stayed up for weeks at a time because I never ran out of gas. . . . I also picked my eye for no reason, until it would get so swollen and red it would stay shut for days. I had my first son when I was 26 and later gave up my second son for adoption because I was such a mess. . . . My mother called social services and made sure that I was not allowed to take care of my children. (Snider 2007)

Many users self-medicate psychological conditions (for example, depression or attention deficit hyperactivity disorder [ADHD]) with stimulants. Because the initial effects of stimulants are so pleasant, these drugs are repeatedly abused, leading to dependence.

In this chapter, you will learn about two principal classifications of stimulant drugs. Major stimulants, including amphetamines and cocaine, are addressed first, given their prominent role in current illicit and prescription drug abuse problems in the United States. The chapter concludes with a review of minor stimulants—in particular, caffeine. The stimulant properties of over-the-counter (OTC) sympathomimetics and "herbal highs" also are discussed. (Because nicotine has unique stimulant properties, it is covered separately in Chapter 11 on tobacco.)

KEY TERMS

uppers
CNS stimulants

Major Stimulants

All major stimulants increase alertness, excitation, and euphoria; thus, these drugs are referred to as **uppers**. The major stimulants are classified as either Schedule I ("designer" amphetamines) or Schedule II (amphetamine, cocaine, and methylphenidate [Ritalin]) controlled substances because of their abuse potential. Although these drugs have properties in common, they also have unique features that distinguish them from one another. The similarities and differences of the major stimulants are discussed in the following sections.

■ Amphetamines

More than 12 million Americans have abused methamphetamine and 1.5 million of these users are addicted to this potent stimulant (Partnership 2007); in 2009 approximately 500,000 people were using this potent stimulant monthly (Reinberg 2010). This is up from 314,000 monthly users in 2008, and is thought to reflect a growing acceptance of illicit methamphetamine among young people (Reinberg 2010) as well as a resurgence in availability. Amphetamines are potent synthetic central nervous system (CNS) stimulants capable of causing dependence due to their euphorigenic properties and ability to eliminate fatigue. Despite their addicting effects, amphetamines can be legally prescribed by physicians for appetite control in weight-loss programs, narcolepsy, and hyperactivity disorders (eGetgoing 2010). Consequently, amphetamine abuse occurs in people who acquire their drugs by both legitimate and illicit means (eGetgoing 2010).

The History of Amphetamines

The first amphetamine was synthesized by the German pharmacologist L. Edeleano in 1887, but it was not until 1910 that this and several related compounds were tested in laboratory animals. Another 17 years passed before Gordon Alles, a researcher looking for a more potent substitute for ephedrine (used as a decongestant at the time), self-administered amphetamine and gave a firsthand account of its effects. Alles found that when inhaled or taken orally, amphetamine dramatically reduced fatigue, increased alertness, and caused a sense of confident euphoria (Grinspoon and Bakalar 1978).

Because of Alles's impressive findings, the Benzedrine (amphetamine) inhaler became available in 1932 as a nonprescription medication in drugstores across the United States. The Benzedrine inhaler, marketed for nasal congestion, was widely abused for its stimulant action but continued to be available OTC until 1949. Because of a loophole in a law that was passed later, not until 1971 were all potent amphetamine-like compounds in nasal inhalers withdrawn from the market (Grinspoon and Bakalar 1978; McCaffrey 1999).

Owing to the lack of restrictions during this early period, amphetamines were sold to treat a variety of ailments, including obesity, alcoholism, bed-wetting, depression, schizophrenia, morphine and codeine addiction, heart block, head injuries, seasickness, persistent hiccups, and caffeine mania. Today, most of these uses are no longer approved as legitimate therapeutics but would be considered forms of drug abuse.

World War II provided a setting in which both the legal and "black market" use of amphetamines flourished (Grinspoon and Bakalar 1978). Because of their stimulating effects, amphetamines were widely used by the Germans, Japanese, and British in World War II to counteract fatigue. By the end of World War II, large quantities of amphetamines were readily available without prescription in seven types of nasal inhalers (Rich and Jordan 2010).

In spite of warnings about these drugs' addicting properties and serious side effects, the U.S. armed forces issued amphetamines on a regular basis during the Korean War and, in fact, may still make it available to pilots in the Air Force to relieve fatigue (Rich and Jordan 2010). Amphetamine use became widespread among truck drivers making long hauls; it is believed that among the earliest distribution systems for illicit amphetamines were truck stops along major U.S. highways. High achievers under continuous pressure in the fields of entertainment, business, and industry often relied on amphetamines to counteract fatigue. Homemakers used them to control weight and to combat boredom from unfulfilled lives. At the height of the U.S. epidemic in 1967, some 31 million prescriptions were written for **anorexiants** (diet pills) alone.

Today, a variety of related drugs and mixtures exist, including amphetamine substances such as dextroamphetamine (Dexedrine), methamphetamine (Desoxyn), and amphetamine itself. Generally, if doses are adjusted, the psychological effects of these various drugs are similar, so they will be discussed as a group. Other drugs with some of the same pharmacological properties are phenmetrazine (Preludin) and methylphenidate (Ritalin). Not only are illicit stimulants a significant drug abuse problem, but legal stimulants are the second most frequently abused drug on college campuses, with 15–20% of students using these drugs (J. Smith 2010). Common slang terms for amphetamines include *speed, crystal, meth, bennies, dexies, uppers, pep pills, diet pills, jolly beans, copilots, hearts, footballs, white crosses, crank,* and *ice.*

How Amphetamines Work

Amphetamines are synthetic chemicals that are similar to natural neurotransmitters such as norepinephrine (noradrenaline), dopamine, and the stress hormone epinephrine (adrenaline). The amphetamines exert their pharmacological effect by increasing the release and blocking the metabolism of these catecholamine substances as well as serotonin (see Chapter 4), both in the brain and in nerves associated with the sympathetic nervous system. Because amphetamines cause release of norepinephrine from sympathetic nerves, they are classified as sympathomimetic drugs. The amphetamines generally cause an arousal or activating response (also called the *fight-or-flight response*) that is similar to the normal reaction to emergency situations, stress, or crises. Amphetamines also cause alertness so that the individual becomes aroused, hypersensitive to stimuli, and feels "turned on." These effects occur even without external sensory input. This activation may be a very pleasant experience in itself, but a continual high level of activation may convert to anxiety, severe apprehension, or panic.

Amphetamines have potent effects on dopamine in the reward (pleasure) center of the brain (see Chapter 4). This action probably causes the "flash" or sudden feeling of intense pleasure that occurs when amphetamine is taken intravenously. Some users describe the sensation as a "whole-body orgasm," and many associate intravenous methamphetamine use with sexual feelings. The actual effect of these drugs on sexual behavior is quite variable and dependent on dose (McCaffrey 1999).

What Amphetamines Can Do

A curious condition commonly reported with heavy amphetamine use is **behavioral stereotypy**, or getting hung up. This term refers to a simple activity

KEY TERMS

anorexiants
drugs that suppress the activity of the brain's appetite center, causing reduced food intake

behavioral stereotypy
meaningless repetition of a single activity

that is done repeatedly. An individual who is "hung up" will get caught in a repetitious thought or act for hours. For example, he or she may take objects apart, like radios or clocks, and carefully categorize all the parts, or sit in a tub and bathe all day, persistently sing a note, repeat a phrase of music, or repeatedly clean the same object. This phenomenon seems to be peculiar to potent stimulants such as the amphetamines and cocaine. Similar patterns of repetitive behavior also occur in psychotic conditions, which suggests that the intense use of stimulants such as amphetamines or cocaine alters the brain in a manner like that causing psychotic mental disorders (American Psychiatric Association [APA] 2000) and can lead to violent behavior.

Chronic use of high doses of amphetamines causes dramatic decreases in the brain content of the neurotransmitters dopamine and serotonin that persist for months even after drug use is stopped (Gehrke et al. 2003). These decreases have been shown to reflect damage to the CNS neurons that release these transmitters. It is not clear why this neuronal destruction occurs, although there is evidence that the amphetamines can stimulate production of very reactive molecules, called *free radicals*, which in turn damage brain cells (National Institute on Drug Abuse [NIDA] 2010b).

Approved Uses

Until 1970, amphetamines were prescribed for a large number of conditions, including depression, fatigue, and long-term weight reduction. In 1970, the Food and Drug Administration (FDA), acting on the recommendation of the National Academy of Sciences, restricted the legal use of amphetamines to three medical conditions: (1) narcolepsy, (2) attention deficit hyperactivity disorder (ADHD), and (3) short-term weight reduction programs (APA 2000; eGetgoing 2010).

Narcolepsy

Amphetamine treatment of narcolepsy is not widespread because this condition is a relatively rare disorder. The term **narcolepsy** comes from the Greek words for numbness and seizure. A person who has narcolepsy falls asleep as frequently as 50 times a day if he or she stays in one position for very long. Taking low doses of amphetamines helps keep narcoleptic people alert.

Attention Deficit Hyperactivity Disorder

This common behavioral problem in children and adolescents involves an abnormally high level of physical activity, an inability to focus attention, and frequent disruptive behavior. Four to six percent of children and adults have ADHD (Polanczyk and Rohde 2007). The drug commonly used to treat children with ADHD is the amphetamine-related methylphenidate or Ritalin (discussed later in this chapter).

Weight Reduction

The most common use of amphetamines is for the treatment of obesity. Amphetamines and chemically similar compounds are used as anorexiants to help obese or severely overweight people control appetite. Amphetamines are thought to act by affecting the appetite center in the hypothalamus of the brain, which causes the user to decrease food intake. The FDA has approved short-term use of amphetamines for weight loss programs but has warned of their potential for abuse. Many experts believe that the euphoric effect of amphetamines is the primary motivation for their continued use in weight reduction programs. It is possible that many obese people have a need for gratification that can be satisfied by the euphoric feeling this drug produces (Wang et al. 2004). If the drug is taken away, these individuals return to food to satisfy their need and sometimes experience "rebound," causing them to gain back more weight than they lost. Some persons who become addicted to amphetamine-like substances begin illicit use of these drugs by trying to prevent weight gain or to lose weight on their own without the guidance of a physician (APA 2000).

Side Effects of Therapeutic Doses

The two principal side effects of therapeutic doses of amphetamines are (1) abuse, which has already been discussed at length, and (2) cardiovascular toxicities. Many of these effects derive from the amphetamine-induced release of epinephrine from the adrenal glands and norepinephrine from the nerves associated with the sympathetic nervous system. The effects include increased heart rate, elevated blood pressure, and damage to vessels, especially small veins and arteries (Drug War Facts 2004; Drugs.com 2010; Swan 1996). In users with a history of heart attack, coronary arrhythmia, or

KEY TERMS

narcolepsy
a condition causing spontaneous and uncontrolled sleeping episodes

Here and Now

Meth and Crime

Uncontrolled abuse of methamphetamine damages the brain in such a manner that the user becomes impulsive and often reacts to situations in a violent unpredictable way. Such reactions result in tragic consequences, such as a 62-year-old man who was charged with second-degree assault in connection with a stabbing after a fight broke out. Or another man who stabbed an acquaintance with a kitchen knife during an argument. Or two young men who attacked and severely wounded a 17-year-old high school student because of a drug deal that went bad. Police are frustrated because of the frequency of such crimes and the fact that their jails are filled with methamphetamine users. The ultimate solution is clearly not to hire more police and build more jails, but rather to try to provide proper drug treatment to get meth addicts off of this destructive drug, or better still, to develop better proactive strategies that prevent people from abusing methamphetamine in the first place.

Source: Klouda, N., and S. Pearson. "Crimes Rise with Meth Addiction." *Homer Tribune.* 28 July 2010. Available at: http://homertribune.com/2010/07/crimes-rise-with-meth-addiction. Accessed March 16, 2011.

---

hypertension, amphetamine toxicity can be severe or even fatal.

Current Misuse

Because amphetamine drugs can be readily and inexpensively synthesized in makeshift laboratories for illicit sale, can be administered by several routes, and cause a more sustained effect than cocaine, these drugs are more popular than cocaine in many parts of the United States (Johnston 2010). Surveys suggest that there was a decline in the abuse of amphetamines in the late 1980s and early 1990s in parallel with a similar trend in cocaine abuse (Johnston 2010). However, in 1993, the declines were replaced by a rise in the number of persons abusing amphetamines. By 2001, approximately 5.6% of high school seniors used amphetamines at least each month. By 2009 this had declined to approximately 3.0% of high school seniors in the United States who regularly used amphetamines (Johnston 2010). In 2010 there were indications that the demand for illegal methamphetamine was increasing, perhaps due to a shift in attitude of the younger generation (Simmons 2010) or as a consequence of the rise in unemployment associated with the recession of 2008 (Graham 2010). Of those who abuse methamphetamine and become addicted, many end up in the criminal justice system (Klouda and Pearson 2010; see "Here and Now: Meth and Crime"), accounting for about 30% of the court cases in the United States (Leinwand 2007).

Because of the potential for serious side effects, U.S. medical associations have asked all physicians to be more careful about prescribing amphetamines. Presently, use is recommended only for narcolepsy and some cases of hyperactivity in children (*Drug Facts and Comparisons* 2010; Hoffman and Lefkowitz 1995). In spite of FDA approval, most medical associations do not recommend the use of amphetamines for weight loss. Probably less than 1% of all prescriptions now written are for amphetamines, compared with 8% in 1970.

Amphetamine abusers commonly administer a dose of 10 to 30 milligrams. Besides the positive effects of this dose—the "high"—it can cause hyperactive, nervous, or jittery feelings that encourage the use of a depressant such as a benzodiazepine, barbiturate, or alcohol to relieve the discomfort of being "wired" (Hoffman and Lefkowitz 1995; Office of National Drug Control Policy [ONDCP] 2010).

A potent and commonly abused form of amphetamine is **speed**, an illegal methamphetamine available as a white, odorless, bitter-tasting crystalline powder for injection. Methamphetamine is a highly addictive stimulant that is often cheaper and much longer lasting than cocaine (American Council for Drug Education 2007). The profit for the speed manufacturer is substantial enough to make illicit production financially attractive (Ordonez 2008). Because the cost ranges from $10 to $20 a dose, it is sometimes known as the "poor man's cocaine"

KEY TERMS

speed
an injectable methamphetamine used by drug addicts

Here and Now

Agassi Admits Using Meth

In his autobiography, Andre Agassi, the tennis star, admitted to using crystal methamphetamine and lying about it to tennis authorities after failing a drug test. Agassi said that for a moment he was worried about how fans would respond to the revelation that he used drugs, but the concern did not last long. This very popular athlete described his methamphetamine experience as follows: "I snort some. I ease back on the couch and consider the Rubicon I've just crossed. There is a moment of regret, followed by vast sadness. Then comes a tidal wave of euphoria that sweeps away every negative thought in my head. I've never felt so alive, so hopeful—and I've never felt such energy. I'm seized by a desperate desire to clean. I go tearing around my house, cleaning it from top to bottom. I dust the furniture. I scour the tub. I make the beds."

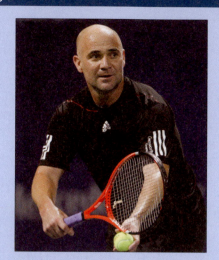

Source: Wyatt, B. "Agassi Admits Using Crystal Meth." CNN.com. 28 October 2009. Available at: http://www.cnn.com/2009/SPORT/10/28/tennis.agassi.crystal.meth/index.html. Accessed February 17, 2011.

(Leinwand 2007). Despite this image of being a particular problem of the working class, there are many examples of rich and famous people who also abuse this potent stimulant (see "Here and Now: Agassi Admits Using Meth").

Methamphetamine is relatively easy and inexpensive to make. The illicit manufacturers are usually individuals without expertise in chemistry. Such people, referred to as "cookers," can produce methamphetamine batches by using cookbook-style recipes (often obtained in jail or over the Internet). The most popular recipe uses common OTC ingredients—ephedrine, pseudoephedrine, and phenylpropanolamine—as **precursor chemicals** for the methamphetamine. To discourage the illicit manufacture of this potent stimulant, the Comprehensive Methamphetamine Control Act was passed in the United States in October 1996. This law increases penalties for trafficking in methamphetamine and in the precursor chemicals used to create this drug and gives the government authority to regulate and seize these substances (Comprehensive Methamphetamine Control Act 2010). Despite the success in shutting down larger neighborhood

operations with this and similar local laws, there has been a very concerning trend for drug users to make their own meth in small batches using simpler and cruder methods that consist of what has become known as "shake and bake" approaches. These scaled down recipes require relatively small numbers of decongestant pills that are crushed and mixed with common household chemicals; the procedure can be done in inconspicuous places such as a bathroom or in a car. Although no flame is required to "cook" the mixture, the procedure sometimes can produce powerful explosions, fires, and toxic waste (Juozapavicius 2009). For example, recently a man in southeast Missouri was seen jumping from his car with his crotch on fire holding a flaming bottle, which he quickly dumped before immediately returning to his car and driving away. Upon closer inspection, the bottle was a "shake and bake" effort to make methamphetamine (ListOwn 2010).

Due to the ease of production and the ready availability of chemicals used to prepare methamphetamine, this drug became particularly problematic in the United States and was declared the number 1 drug problem in the majority of counties across the country in 2006 (Rutledge 2006). Traditional methamphetamine users have been white, male, blue-collar workers over 26 years of age, although a disturbingly high rate of use has

KEY TERMS

precursor chemicals
chemicals used to produce a drug

Here and Now

Innocent Victims of Meth

In many of the meth labs seized, children are found who have been exposed to the toxins used to "cook" the drug as well as the emotional and physical abuse of parents more preoccupied with satisfying their addiction than caring for their children. Burners have been left on next to a baby's crib. Bottles filled with potent acids are stored in the refrigerator. Children have been starved, and 3-year-olds left to care for themselves and also care for a baby brother or sister while their mom or dad binges on meth for days or even weeks and then crashes into a sleeping stupor. Explosive ingredients are abundant with vaporized drugs, contaminating the food, drinking water, clothing, and even the air. Officials must decide what to do with children abused and injured both physically and emotionally by parents who ignore their children's basic needs because they are so preoccupied with obtaining their next meth fix. Reports are that meth addiction has caused foster-care programs across the country to be swamped with young victims.

Source: Tseng, N. "Children Fall by Wayside in Meth-Addicted Homes." *Orlando Sentinel* (11 September 2005): B1.

developed among adolescents (3–5% annual use; Johnston 2010) and young women in the United States. This most recent methamphetamine epidemic appeared to begin in the western states and moved east (NIDA Community Epidemiology Workgroup [CEWG] 2007). Despite pockets of severe problems, in general, methamphetamine abuse is still less common on the East Coast (Leinwand 2007; NIDA CEWG 2007).

When discovered, the so-called meth or speed labs are raided by law enforcement agencies across the country. In 2003, the DEA funded the cleanup of approximately 12,000 illegal methamphetamine labs, most of which were in the western United States. This number decreased to 3866 in 2008 (Doyle 2010) but was increasing again in 2009 (U.S. Department of Justice 2010). The laboratory operators are usually well armed, and the facilities are frequently booby-trapped with explosives. Not surprisingly, these operations pose a serious threat to their neighbors (U.S. Department of Justice 2003a) and to residents, especially children, in the structure that contains the lab (U.S. Department of Justice 2002) (see "Here and Now: Innocent Victims of Meth"). Law enforcement personnel and firefighters are also at risk when dealing with methamphetamine labs owing to ignitable, corrosive, reactive, and toxic chemicals that might explode, start a fire, emit toxic fumes, or cause serious injury at the site. The toxic chemicals can create fumes that contaminate neighboring buildings, the water supply, or soil. These labs are especially dangerous when they are set up in poorly ventilated rooms (Kennedy 1999) (see "Here and Now: Chemical Toxins Associated with Meth Labs").

Although still a problem, as already mentioned, the incidences of "mom and pop" neighborhood methamphetamine labs has dramatically decreased across the nation since 2003. This was mainly due to federal and state laws that limit access to large quantities of precursor drugs found in OTC decongestants. The statutes require these decongestant products be kept behind the pharmacy counter, and the quantity sold to a customer must be minimal in order to limit access (Leinwand 2007) (see "Holding the Line: Cold Restrictions"). Although successful in decreasing the number of small neighborhood meth labs in the United States, this strategy unfortunately appears to have had minimal effect on actual supplies of this drug for illegal sales. Methamphetamine is being smuggled across the U.S. border from Mexico (Berkes 2007) and is being manufactured by criminal organizations from chemicals diverted by the ton from Asian pharmaceutical companies (Huus 2007; Randolph 2007; Savage and Gordon 2010). It is estimated that

Here and Now

Chemical Toxins Associated with Meth Labs

Methamphetamine labs can be set up almost anywhere and pose a serious threat to occupants as well as to law officers and emergency personnel. The following are some of the chemicals often present and their toxic potentials.

Chemicals Toxic Reactions

Sodium hydroxide	Irritant to skin and eyes
Ammonia	Induces vomiting and nausea
Ether, acetone, and alcohol	Flammable
Chloroform	Carcinogen and volatile
Mercuric chloride	Poisonous (used as insecticide)
Cyanide gas	Extremely poisonous if breathed
Acids	Potent irritants
Iodine	Irritant; causes nausea, headaches, and dizziness
Phosphene gas	Poisonous, flammable (used as nerve gas)

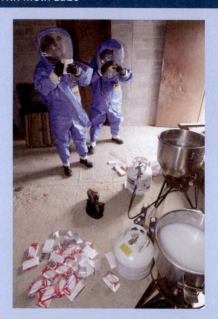

Source: Office of National Drug Control Policy (ONDCP). Synthetic Drug Control Strategy. June 2006. Available at: http://dhs.alabama.gov/pdf/info/synthetic_strategy.pdf. Accessed March 16, 2011.

currently the vast majority of meth is imported, keeping supplies abundant, purity high, and costs low (Leinwand 2007; U.S. Department of Justice 2010). In addition, small neighborhood labs are making a significant comeback, particularly in the Midwest, due to a strategy referred to as "smurfing." Smurfs, who are becoming increasingly organized, enlist the help of many friends and associates to purchase the methamphetamine precursor chemicals such as pseudoephedrine (e.g., in decongestants) in quantities below the legal limits. In this way large amounts of these chemicals can be accumulated and then sold to methamphetamine producers (U.S. Department of Justice 2010). Due to strategies such as "shake-and-bake" or "smurfing," the number of methamphetamine lab seizures and busts skyrocketed to over 2000 in Tennessee alone in 2010 (Salter 2011).

Patterns of High-Dose Use

Amphetamines can be taken orally, intravenously, or by smoking. The intensity and duration of effects vary according to the mode of administration. The methamphetamine addict frequently uses chronic, high doses of amphetamines intravenously and can be infected with HIV (see Chapter 16) (The Body 2010). Another approach to administering amphetamines is smoking **ice**, which can cause effects as potent, but perhaps more prolonged and erratic, than intravenous doses. The initial effect (after 5 to 30 minutes) of these potent stimulants is called the **rush** and includes a racing heartbeat and elevated blood pressure, metabolism, and pulse. During this phase, the user has powerful impressions of pleasure and enthusiasm. The next stage is the **high** (4 to 16 hours after drug use) when the person feels aggressively smarter, energetic, talkative, and powerful and may initiate and complete highly ambitious tasks. The amphetamine addict tries to

Holding the Line Cold Restrictions

As of September 30, 2006, it became somewhat more difficult for a person with a cold, and a lot more difficult for persons desiring to make methamphetamine from decongestant ingredients, to readily obtain adequate OTC cold medicine for their needs. This is due to a federal law to stop the manufacture of methamphetamine in illegal meth labs found in homes, garages, or basements. To achieve this objective, the new restrictions require customers to show a picture ID to purchase cold medicine such as NyQuil Cold & Flu, Actifed Cold & Allergy, and Claritin-D. These and similar decongestant products that contain drugs that can be converted into methamphetamine must be kept behind the store counters in most states. Customers must sign a logbook identifying what they purchased and where they live. The logbook remains on file for 2 years. This law restricts purchase to 3–6 grams of product/day and 9 grams/month. In Oregon and Mississippi these medicines are only available by prescription.

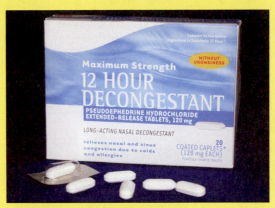

Ingredients to make methamphetamine are found in common OTC decongestants.

maintain the high for as long as possible, with continual drug use leading to extended mental and physical hyperactivity; this is referred to as a **run** or **binge** and can persist from 3 to 15 days. Persistent use of these drugs, such as methamphetamine, to maintain the high for long periods of time is called **tweaking**. The tweaker often has neither slept nor eaten much for 3 to 15 days and can be extremely irritable and paranoid and have an elevated body temperature, a condition known as **hyperpyrexia**. This is a potentially dangerous stage for medical personnel or law enforcement officers because if the tweaker becomes agitated, he or she can respond violently to the efforts of others to help. To relieve some of the side effects of the extensive use of methamphetamine, tweakers often use a depressant such as alcohol, barbiturates, benzodiazepines, or opioid narcotics (O'Brien and Anthony 2009). The consequences of such a drug combination are to intensify negative feelings and worsen the dangers of the drug. Tweakers are frequently involved in domestic violence and frequently injure their children and partners (Transitions 2007). Withdrawal follows for 30 to 90 days, including feelings of depression and lethargy. During this phase, craving can be intense and the abuser may even become suicidal. Because a dose of methamphetamine often relieves these symptoms, many addicts in treatment return to abusing this stimulant (Prevline 1999).

After the first day or so of a run, unpleasant symptoms become prominent as the dosage is increased. Symptoms commonly reported at this stage are teeth grinding, disorganized patterns of thought and behavior, stereotypy, irritability, self-consciousness, suspiciousness, and fear. Hallucinations and delusions that are similar to a paranoid psychosis and indistinguishable from schizophrenia can occur (APA 2000; NIDA 2010b). The person is likely to show aggressive and antisocial behavior for no apparent reason, although recent brain imaging studies have revealed that addictions to the amphetamines can cause long-term damage to the brain's inhibitory control centers (Kuehn 2007; NIDA 2010b). Severe chest pains, abdominal discomfort that mimics appendicitis, and fainting from

KEY TERMS

run
intense use of a stimulant, consisting of multiple administrations over a period of days

binge
similar to a run, but usually of shorter duration

tweaking
repeated administration of methamphetamine to maintain the high

hyperpyrexia
elevated body temperature

Signs & Symptoms Summary of the Effects of Amphetamines on the Body and Mind

	BODY	MIND
Low dose	Increased heartbeat.	Decreased fatigue
	Increased blood pressure	Increased confidence
	Decreased appetite	Increased feeling of alertness
	Increased breathing rate	Restlessness, talkativeness
	Inability to sleep	Increased irritability
	Sweating	Fearfulness, apprehension
	Dry mouth	Distrust of people
	Muscle twitching	Behavioral stereotypy
	Convulsions	Hallucinations
	Fever	Psychosis
	Chest pain	
	Irregular heartbeat	
High dose	Death due to overdose	

overdosage are sometimes reported. "Cocaine bugs" represent one bizarre effect of high doses of potent stimulants such as amphetamines: The user experiences strange feelings, like insects crawling under the skin. The range of physical and mental symptoms experienced from low to high doses is summarized in "Signs and Symptoms: Summary of the Effects of Amphetamines on the Body and Mind."

Toward the end of the run, the adverse symptoms dominate. When the drug is discontinued because the supply is exhausted or the symptoms become too unpleasant, an extreme crash can occur, followed by prolonged sleep, sometimes lasting several days. On awakening, the person is lethargic, hungry, and often severely depressed. The amphetamine user may overcome these unpleasant effects by smoking ice or injecting speed, thereby initiating a new cycle (APA 2000).

Continued use of massive doses of amphetamine often leads to considerable weight loss, sores on the skin, poor oral hygiene and deterioration of the teeth (Rauscher 2006; Shetty et al. 2010), non-healing ulcers, liver disease, hypertensive disorders, cerebral hemorrhage (stroke), heart attack, kidney damage, and seizures (Fox 2010; Hall and Hando 1993; Kinkead and Romboy 2004). For some of these effects, it is impossible to tell if they are caused by the drug, poor eating habits, or other factors associated with the lifestyle of people who inject methamphetamine.

Speed freaks are generally unpopular with the rest of the drug-taking community, especially "acid-heads" (addicts who use lysergic acid diethylamide [LSD]), because of the aggressive, unpredictable behavior associated with use of potent stimulants (Elias 2010). In general, drug abusers who take high doses of these agents, such as amphetamines or cocaine, are more likely to be involved in violent crimes than those who abuse other drugs (Substance Abuse and Mental Health Services Administration [SAMHSA] 2010). Heavy users are generally unable to hold steady jobs because of their drug habits and often have a parasitic relationship with the rest of the illicit drug-using community.

Although claims have been made that amphetamines do not cause physical dependence, it is almost certain that depression (sometimes suicidal), lethargy, muscle pains, abnormal sleep patterns, and, in severe cases, suicide attempts occur after high chronic doses as part of withdrawal (NIDA 2000; Wrong Diagnosis 2010). During withdrawal from amphetamine use, the dependent user often turns to other drugs for relief (Cantwell and McBride 1998). Rebound from the amphetamines is opposite to that experienced with withdrawal from CNS depressants (see Chapter 6).

Although the effects of amphetamines on the unborn fetus are difficult to evaluate and not fully understood (Science Daily 2010a), some human studies suggest that there is a possibility of serious problems in the offspring. This research shows that babies born to methamphetamine-using mothers are much more likely to be preterm and less likely to survive. In addition, almost 40% of the meth-exposed babies are at least temporarily removed from their mothers to be adopted or placed in Child Protective Services or foster care (Harding 2010). Studies on the long-term effects on the offspring of methamphetamine moms have been more difficult to conduct, but suggest that brain structures are altered, particularly if these women are also consuming alcohol. These congenital problems could lead to long-term cognitive or behavioral problems (Science Daily 2010a). The methamphetamine-abusing expectant mothers are also vulnerable to serious pregnancy problems of their own such as uncontrolled high blood pressure and delivery complications (Harding 2010).

There is evidence that repeated high-dose use of amphetamines, such as methamphetamine, by adolescents or adults causes long-term and perhaps permanent damage to both dopamine and serotonin neurotransmitter systems of the brain (Cohen 2006; Hanson, Rau, and Fleckenstein 2004). This brain damage may result in persistent episodes of psychosis (NIDA 2010b; Yui et al. 1997) as well as long-lasting memory, motor impairment, and cognitive deficits (Hanson et al. 2004; Volkow et al. 2001). Abuse of amphetamines often seriously damages personal relationships with friends, associates, and even family members. Particularly disturbing is the increasing methamphetamine use by young

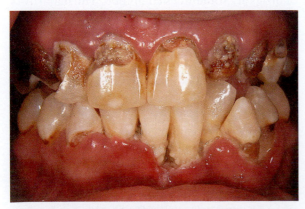

Devastation of oral structures, called "meth mouth," sometimes is associated with methamphetamine addiction.

mothers. Moms on meth have claimed that use of this stimulant makes them feel invincible, and like they can run around the world—and then do it again. They claim to lose weight, but they also can lose their instinct to mother their children as they become obsessed with the drug (Holt 2005). Consequently, children are being exposed to dangerous levels of this drug in many forms (see "Here and Now: Small Town, Big Problems").

Treatment

Admissions for treatment of methamphetamine addiction more than doubled from 2000 to 2005 (Join Together 2006). However, after this time, there was evidence that efforts in both the United States and neighboring Mexico to restrict access to the decongestant drugs used to synthesize methamphetamine significantly reduced the number of methamphetamine addicts who have voluntarily entered treatment (Cunningham et al. 2010). But more recent findings suggest that both domestic and Mexican methamphetamine labs are finding ways to get around the laws and avoid detection, resulting in a significant resurgence in methamphetamine supplies and purity in the United States.

The dependence disorder caused by the amphetamines is very hard, but not impossible, to treat successfully. Many methamphetamine addicts have significant impairment of their decision-making ability and do not self-refer, but are forced into treatment by drug courts and other components of the criminal justice system (Newswise 2007; Science Daily 2009). Presently, the most effective treatments for amphetamine addiction are behavioral interventions to help modify thinking patterns, improve cognitive skills, change expectations, and increase coping with life's stressors. Amphetamine support groups also appear to be successful as adjuncts to behavioral therapies. There currently are no well-established pharmacological treatments for amphetamine dependency (Elkashef et al. 2008). Approaches used for cocaine have been tried with some success. Antidepressant medication may help relieve the depression that occurs during early stages of withdrawal (Raskin 2005; NIDA 2006).

The persistence of the methamphetamine effects makes this addiction especially difficult to address effectively. The word on the street has been that many of the effects of this stimulant are permanent and its cognitive damage might not be reversible. Although there is ample evidence that hard-core use of methamphetamine for extended periods does have devastating effects on decision making, impulsivity, memory, and other functions, evidence

Here and Now

Small Town, Big Problems: The Female Methamphetamine Epidemic

Methamphetamine has caused a drug-related epidemic never before experienced in this country. Its abuse and devastating social effects have taxed public social services in unanticipated ways. One of the most striking aspects of this drug's abuse is its appeal to young adult women, many of whom have children. Typically, the number of women seeking treatment for drug addiction are considerably lower than the number of men in the same situation; however, in many regions roughly equal numbers of men and women seek help for methamphetamine as their primary addiction. Clearly, the destructive influence of methamphetamine abuse is taking an enormous toll on homes and families. Consequently, criminal justice systems for women offenders have been overwhelmed.

Women who are addicted to methamphetamine often do not do well in conventional drug treatment. Because of the potent addicting properties of this drug, they typically struggle with the requirements of probation or parole and often end up back in prison and their children end up in family services and foster care. Although it is not clear why this stimulant is so seductive to young women, women who use methamphetamine typically have:

- A history of chronic unemployment
- A live-in partner who also uses drugs
- A history of physical and sexual abuse
- A history of suicide attempts
- Motivation to use methamphetamine for weight control
- Psychiatric drug-related problems

For female methamphetamine addicts, "this drug is a massive black hole. It's swallowing these people alive and takes a miracle to put these families back together again."

Sources: "Escalation in Methamphetamine Use Also Leads to Escalation in Social Service." *Health & Medicine Week* (14 February 2005); and Rowan-Szal, G., G. Joe, W. Simpson, J. Greener, and J. Vance. "During-Treatment Outcomes Among Female Methamphetamine-Using Offenders in Prison-Based Treatments." *Journal of Offender Rehabilitation* 48 (2009): 388–401.

---

is accumulating that suggests that recovery from these effects is possible. However, effective treatment is not simple or cheap, and typically requires more than a year of intense intervention consisting of drug abstinence; cognitive, emotional, and motivational rehabilitation; and often career and skills development (McManis 2009).

Amphetamine Combinations

As previously mentioned, amphetamines are frequently used in conjunction with a variety of other drugs such as barbiturates, benzodiazepines, alcohol, and heroin (Nuckols and Kane 2003; Science Daily 2010a). Amphetamines intensify, prolong, or otherwise alter the effects of LSD, and the two types of drugs are sometimes combined. The majority of speed users have also had experience with a variety of psychedelics or other drugs. In addition, people dependent on opiate narcotics frequently use amphetamines or cocaine. These combinations are sometimes called **speedballs**.

"Designer" Amphetamines

Underground chemists can synthesize drugs that mimic the psychoactive effects of amphetamines. Although the production of such drugs diminished in the early 1990s, their use by American teens surged in the late 1990s and early 2000s, as reflected in the fact that more than 9% of high school seniors

KEY TERMS

speedballs
combinations of amphetamine or cocaine with an opioid narcotic, often heroin

used the designer amphetamine known as MDMA in 2001. This rate dramatically decreased to 3% in 2005, reflecting a concern about its potential harmful effects. However, the rate of annual use rose modestly to 4.3% in 2009, suggesting that the concerns about the risk of recreational use of the designer amphetamines have been diminishing (Johnston 2010).

Designer amphetamines sometimes differ from the parent compound by only a single element. These "synthetic spinoffs" pose a significant abuse problem because often several different designer amphetamines can be made from the parent compound and still retain the abuse potential and physical risks of the original substance.

For many years, the production and distribution of designer amphetamines were not illegal, even though they were synthesized from controlled substances. In the mid-1980s, however, the DEA actively pursued policies to curb their production and sale. Consequently, many designer amphetamines were outlawed under the Substance Analogue Enforcement Act of 1986, which makes illegal any substance that is similar in structure or psychological effect to any substance already scheduled, if it is manufactured, possessed, or sold with the intention that it be consumed by human beings (Beck 1990).

The principal types of designer amphetamines are:

- Derivatives from amphetamine and methamphetamine that retain the CNS stimulatory effects, such as methcathinone ("cat")
- Derivatives from amphetamine and methamphetamine that have prominent psychedelic effects in addition to their CNS stimulatory action, such as MDMA (Ecstasy)

Because the basic amphetamine molecule can be easily synthesized and readily modified, new amphetamine-like drugs occasionally appear on the streets. Although these designer amphetamines are thought of as new drugs when they first appear, in fact most were originally synthesized from the 1940s to the 1960s by pharmaceutical companies trying to find new decongestant and anorexiant drugs to compete with the other amphetamines. Some of these compounds were found to be too toxic to be marketed but have been rediscovered by "street chemists" and are sold to unsuspecting victims trying to experience a new sensation. **Table 10.1** lists some of these designer amphetamines.

Some designer drugs of abuse that are chemically related to amphetamine include DOM (STP), methcathinone (called cat or bathtub speed), mephedrone (methylmethcathinone, called "Meow Meow" or drone), MDA, and MDMA (or methylenedioxymethamphetamine, called Ecstasy, X, E, XTC, or Adam). As of 2011, all of these drugs, except mephedrone, were classified as Schedule I agents.

MDMA (Ecstasy)

Among the designer amphetamines, MDMA continues to be the most popular. It gained widespread popularity in the United States throughout the 1980s, and its use peaked in 1987 despite its classification as a Schedule I drug in 1985 by the DEA. At the height of its use, 39% of the undergraduates at Stanford University reported having used MDMA at least once (Randall 1992a). In the late 1980s and early 1990s, use of MDMA declined in this country, but about this time it was "reformulated." This reformulation was not in a pharmacological sense but in a cultural context.

Table 10.1 "Designer" Amphetamines

AMPHETAMINE DERIVATIVE	PROPERTIES
Methcathinone ("cat")	Properties like those of methamphetamine and cocaine
Methylenedioxymethamphetamine (MDMA, "Ecstasy")	Stimulant and hallucinogen
Methylenedioxyamphetamine (MDA)	More powerful stimulant and less powerful hallucinogen than MDMA
4-methylaminorex	CNS stimulant like amphetamine
N,N-dimethylamphetamine	One-fifth the potency of amphetamine
4-thiomethyl-2, 5-dimethoxyamphetamine	Hallucinogen
Para-methoxymethamphetamine	Weak stimulant

The "rave" scene in England provided a new showcase for MDMA or Ecstasy (Randall 1992a). Partygoers attired in "Cat in the Hat" hats and psychedelic jumpsuits paid $20 to dance all night to heavy, electronically generated sound mixed with computer-generated video and laser light shows. An Ecstasy tablet could be purchased for the sensory enhancement caused by the drug (Randall 1992b). At one time, it was estimated that as many as 31% of English youth from 16 to 25 years old had used Ecstasy (Grob et al. 1996). The British rave counterculture and its generous use of Ecstasy were exported to the United States in the early 1990s. High-tech music and video trappings were encouraged by low-tech laboratories that illegally manufactured the drug and shipped it into this country. Because of these sensory-enriched environments, Ecstasy became the drug of choice for many young people in the United States (Cloud 2000) and globally (United Nations Office on Drugs and Crime 2009) looking for a novel "chemical" experience. To this day the rave phenomenon continues to be a major attraction to youthful participants and an excuse for heavy MDMA use (*Journal of the American Medical Association* [JAMA] 2010).

The international seizures of MDMA in 2007 almost doubled that reported for 1998, suggesting that the global abuse of Ecstasy continues to escalate (United Nations Office on Drugs and Crime 2009). Currently, more than 90% of these illegal drugs originate in European countries such as the Netherlands and Belgium, which are the principal source for Ecstasy smuggled into the United States (United Nations Office on Drugs and Crime 2009). However, recently there has been an increase in U.S. homegrown labs, which produce MDMA and methamphetamine despite the fact that the process of making MDMA is very hazardous and the chemicals used for synthesis are difficult to obtain (Narconon 2010). Besides sensory enhancement, the association of Ecstasy with raves—where there is intense dancing, crowded conditions and plenty of drugs—all too often results in Ecstasy-related medical emergencies and on rare occasions even death (JAMA 2010).

Because of its frequent association with raves, clubs, and bars, MDMA is known as a club drug. At its peak in 2000, Ecstasy was used by 11% of all U.S. high school seniors. During the next few years, however, the popularity of this drug declined; in 2005, only 3% of high school seniors reported use, but by 2009 the rate of use by this group increased to 4.3% (Johnston 2010). The more recent findings

also suggest that Ecstasy is more likely to be used by females than males (Wu et al. 2010).

Some have compared the rave culture and its use of MDMA to the acid-test parties of the 1960s and the partygoers' use of LSD and amphetamines (Cloud 2000; JAMA 2010; Randall 1992a). Some say this drug is not likely to cause significant dependence for most casual users, but intense use appears to be able to lead to addiction. The incidents of medical emergencies caused by MDMA reported by hospitals from 1999 to 2001 almost doubled, suggesting that during this period more intense use of this drug caused severe dependence in some users (U.S. Department of Justice 2003b). However, part of the explanation for the dramatic reduction in MDMA use in 2005 by young populations was likely a reaction to some highly publicized overdoses of Ecstasy and a perceived increase in the "risk" of this drug (Johnston 2010).

MDMA was first inadvertently discovered in 1912 by chemists at E. Merck in Darmstadt, Germany (Grob et al. 1996). No pharmaceutical company has ever manufactured MDMA for public marketing, and the FDA has never approved it for therapy. MDMA was first found by the DEA on the streets in 1972 in a drug sample bought in Chicago (Beck 1990). The DEA earnestly began gathering data on MDMA abuse a decade later, which led to its classification as a Schedule I substance in 1985, despite the very vocal opposition by a number of psychiatrists who had been giving MDMA to patients since the late 1970s to facilitate communication, acceptance, and fear reduction (Beck 1990). Some health professionals believe that MDMA should be made available to clinicians for the treatment of some psychiatric disorders such as fear and anxiety (Benedetti 2002; Cloud 2000). In fact, with FDA

Ecstasy tablets are often imprinted with cartoon figures.

approval, small trial studies are being conducted to test the safety of this drug and its potential value in treating conditions such as posttraumatic stress disorder (PTSD; Buchen 2010; Drug Monkey 2007). MDMA and related designer amphetamines are somewhat unique from other amphetamines in that, besides causing excitation, they have prominent psychedelic effects (Tancer and Johanson 2007; see Chapter 12). These drugs have been characterized as combining the properties of amphetamine and LSD (Schifano et al. 1998). The psychedelic effects of MDMA are likely caused by release of the neurotransmitter serotonin (Tancer and Johanson 2007). After using hallucinogenic amphetamines, the mind is often flooded with irrelevant and incoherent thoughts and exaggerated sensory experiences and is more receptive to suggestion.

MDMA often is viewed as a "smooth amphetamine" and does not appear to cause the severe depression, "crash," or violent behavior (U.S. Department of Justice 2003b) often associated with frequent high doses of the more traditional amphetamines. As mentioned earlier, MDMA was originally thought to be nonaddictive; however, some reports suggest that addiction does occur when high doses of this drug are used (Everything Addiction 2010; Jansen 1999). Many users tend to be predominantly positive when describing their initial MDMA experiences (Cloud 2000). They claim the drug causes them to dramatically drop their defense mechanisms or fear responses while they feel an increased empathy for others (Benedetti 2002). Combined with its stimulant effects, this action often increases intimate communication and association with others (Cloud 2000; ScienceDaily 2010a). However, heavy users often experience adverse

effects, such as loss of appetite, grinding of teeth, muscle aches and stiffness, sweating, rapid heartbeat, hostility, anxiety, and altered sleep patterns (NIDA 2010a). In addition, fatigue can be experienced for hours or even days after use. In high doses, MDMA can cause panic attacks and severe anxiety (NIDA 2007c, 2010a). There is evidence that these high doses can significantly damage serotonin neurons or other systems in the brain and cause long-term memory deficits and psychological disturbances in some people (Lyles and Cadet 2003; Montgomery et al. 2010; Turillazzi et al. 2010). The duration of these high-dose CNS effects has not been determined and may vary based on the intensity of the bingeing (Kish et al. 2010).

Recreational use of Ecstasy has been linked to physical emergencies and even occasional fatalities that are similar to those caused by amphetamines and cocaine (King and Corkery 2010; Schifano et al. 2010). The leading causes of deaths associated with MDMA use appear to be complications from hyperthermia (related to heatstroke), metabolic problems, or underlying heart problems (DEA 2003; Kaye, Darke, and Duflou 2009; King and Corkery 2010).

Because of its popularity, occasional "spinoff" Ecstasy drugs show up in dance clubs frequented by young people. For example, a substance called "Frenzy" or "Nemesis" has been used in the Detroit area and is thought to be smuggled across the Canadian border. The official name of the drug is n-benzylpiperazine or BZP. It is sold in the shape of cartoon characters and has a chemistry that resembles MDMA (Pardo 2010). BZP is not available in pharmacies, but can be purchased over the Internet and has been used in the club scene since the 1990s. However, the pharmacology of this drug looks more like that of the amphetamines than MDMA in that it has stimulant effects that cause feelings of euphoria, alertness, and increased energy. With high doses, BZP induces states of paranoia and anxiety accompanied by increased heart rate, blood pressure, and body temperature (Pardo 2010).

Methylphenidate: A Special Amphetamine

Methylphenidate (Ritalin) is related to the amphetamines but is a relatively mild CNS stimulant, especially when used orally, that has been used to alleviate depression. Research now casts doubt on its effectiveness for treating depression, but it is effective in treating narcolepsy (a sleep disorder). As explained previously, Ritalin has also been found

Dancers at a "rave" often consume Ecstasy for sensory enhancement.

to help calm children and adults suffering from attention deficit hyperactivity disorder (ADHD). ADHD is characterized by an inability to focus attention and increased impulsivity. These features make it difficult to stay "on-task," impair learning abilities, and can lead to social and personal frustrations (Tye et al. 2009). Like Adderall (amphetamine) and Provigil (Modafinil), Ritalin is routinely used to treat this condition in both children and adults. Use of these drugs can improve scholastic performance in 70% of those with ADHD. Ritalin is frequently the drug of choice for this indication (NIDA 2009). The stimulant potency of Ritalin lies between that of caffeine and amphetamine. Although it is not used much on the street by hardcore drug addicts, there are increasingly more frequent reports of use by high school and college students because of claims that it helps them to "study better," "party harder," and enhance their "performance" in general (Shropshire 2010). However, there is no evidence that when used properly and taken orally this drug will cause serious dependence or addiction (Volkow and Swanson 2008). Recent statistics from the Monitoring the Future Survey suggest that 2.1% of high school seniors used this drug for nonmedical purposes in 2010 (Johnston 2010). Because of its potential for abuse, some critics claim its medical use in the treatment of childhood ADHD may increase the likelihood that patients will later abuse drugs; however, this has not been found to be the case (Volkow and Swanson 2008). High doses of Ritalin can cause tremors, seizures, and strokes. Ritalin has been classified as a Schedule II drug, like the other prescribed amphetamines. Its principal mechanism of action is to block the reuptake of dopamine and noradrenaline into their respective neurons; thus, its pharmacological action is more like cocaine than methamphetamine.

Performance Enhancers

Performance enhancers is a term frequently used to describe stimulants, or other drugs, taken to increase physical or mental endurance to embellish one's performance and achieve a more positive outcome. As illustrated in the following real-life example, some college students have come to rely on these drugs to get through the stressful challenges of school.

KEY TERMS

performance enhancers
drugs taken to increase physical or mental endurance to embellish one's performance

Janell (real name withheld), a college sophomore, is only one of all too many students who pray for a miracle every finals week to help them cram in the studying time to survive this very demanding ritual. The miracle that Janell, and others like her, are hoping for comes from the stimulant effects of drugs such as Ritalin and Adderall. Recognizing the use of these substances comes with significant risk, Janell says, "I am afraid that if I keep taking Adderall during stressful times, I will become addicted." Although these "performance enhancing" drugs can be legally prescribed, the way Janell is using them is not medically sanctioned and can do her great harm. But, despite the potential for very serious consequences for this form of drug abuse, Janell responds, "If you expect me to pass five major tests in one week, you better believe that I am going to take Adderall. I need to get in the zone, Nothing else seems to work for me." (Keenan 2010)

Unfortunately, many students and adults do not appreciate the full adverse potential of this practice, or they choose to ignore the possibility that they might become addicted, experience psychosis, or have a severe cardiovascular reaction if they routinely use the prescription stimulants for illegal nonmedical purposes (Shropshire 2010). If these drugs are not being obtained legally by prescription, how do those who use them as performance enhancers obtain them? Often the supply comes from other students who have ADHD and a legitimate prescription, and are willing to sell, or sometimes give away, their extra pills.

There is no argument that the popularity of these "performance-enhancing" substances has been increasing with many college, and even high school students (Ricker and Nicolino 2010); however, the value and safety of this practice are being debated (see "Prescription for Abuse: Colleges Are Laboratories for Drug Neuroenhancing").

■ Cocaine

In the past, cocaine eradication has been considered to be a top priority. This cocaine policy reflected the fact that from 1978 to 1987 the United States experienced the largest cocaine epidemic in history. Antisocial and criminal activities related to the effects of this potent stimulant were highly visible and widely publicized.

Prescription for Abuse: Colleges Are Laboratories for Drug Neuroenhancing

Although everyone agrees that unsupervised use of stimulants to help with studying or to improve one's performance in other intellectual or physical ways is potentially dangerous, does it actually help improve the likelihood of success in the classroom, on the playing field, or in the workplace? The answer to this question is being debated, but there is good evidence that those who have some degree of ADHD do benefit from stimulant medications like Adderall or Ritalin and will perform better in academic endeavors (Shropshire 2010). What about everyone else? It is said that college campuses have become laboratories for researching pharmacological neuroenhancement. Although evidence is equivocal, a commentary in 2008 in a prestigious journal called the use of cognitive enhancement drugs inevitable and stated that ". . . Society must respond to the growing demand . . . by rejecting the idea that 'enhancement' is a dirty word." The authors of this article went on to clarify that their statement was intended to encourage a rational and realistic approach to what they perceived as an inevitability, that is, that in the future our society will realize that these cognitive enhancing drugs are ". . .

increasingly useful for improved quality of life and extended work productivity" (Sederer 2010). Others counter with the argument that "advocates fail to recognize the severe personal and societal consequences that such availability would generate, looking instead to a pharmaceutical solution that would, in the end, cause more problems than it would solve" (Hessert 2009).

As recently as the early 1980s, cocaine use was not believed to cause dependency because it does not cause gross withdrawal effects, as do alcohol and narcotics (Goldstein 1994). In fact, a 1982 article in *Scientific American* stated that cocaine was "no more habit forming than potato chips" (Van Dyck and Byck 1982). This perception has clearly been proven false; cocaine is so highly addictive that it is readily self-administered not only by human beings but also by laboratory animals (Cumming, Caprioli, and Dalley 2010). Surveys suggest that during 2000, 2.7 million chronic and 3.0 million casual cocaine users lived in the United States (ONDCP 2003). There is no better substance than cocaine to illustrate the "love–hate" relationship that people can have with drugs. Many lessons can be learned by understanding the impact of cocaine and the social struggles that have ensued as people and societies have tried to determine their proper relationship with this substance.

The History of Cocaine Use

Cocaine has been used as a stimulant for thousands of years. Its history can be classified into three eras, based on geographic, social, and thera-

peutic considerations. Learning about these eras can help us understand current attitudes about cocaine (Emedicinehealth 2010).

The First Cocaine Era

The first cocaine era was characterized by an almost harmonious use of this stimulant by South American Indians living in the regions of the Andean Mountains, and dates back to about 2500 BC in Peru. It is believed that the stimulant properties of cocaine played a major role in the advancement of this isolated civilization, providing its people with the energy and motivation to realize dramatic social and architectural achievements while being able to endure tremendous hardships in barren, inhospitable environments. The *Erythroxylon coca* shrub (cocaine is found in its leaves) was held in religious reverence by these people until the time of the Spanish conquistadors (Golding 1993).

The first written description of coca chewing in the New World was by the explorer Amerigo Vespucci in 1499:

They were very brutish in appearance and behavior, and their cheeks bulged with the leaves of a certain green herb, which they chewed like cattle, so that they could hardly speak. Each had around his neck two dried gourds, one full of that herb in their mouth, the other filled with a white flour-like powdered chalk. . . . [This was lime, which was mixed with the coca to enhance its effects.] When I asked . . . why they carried these leaves in their mouth, which they did not eat, . . . they replied it prevents them from feeling hungry, and gives them great vigor and strength. (Aldrich and Barker 1976, p. 3)

It is ironic that there are no indications that these early South American civilizations had any significant social problems with cocaine, considering the difficulty it has caused contemporary civilizations. There are three possible explanations for their lack of significant negative experiences with coca:

1. The Andean Indians maintained control of the use of cocaine. For the Incas, coca could only be used by the conquering aristocracy, chiefs, royalty, and other designated honorables (Aldrich and Barker 1976).
2. These Indians used the unpurified, and less potent, form of cocaine in the coca plant.
3. Chewing the coca leaf was a slow, sustained form of oral drug administration; therefore, the effect was much less potent, and less likely to cause serious dependence, than snorting, intravenous injection, or smoking techniques most often used today.

The Second Cocaine Era

A second major cocaine era began in the 19th century. During this period, scientific techniques were used to determine the pharmacology of cocaine and identify its dangerous effects. It was also during this era that the threat of cocaine to society—both its members and institutions—was first recognized (DiChiara 1993; Musto 1998). At about this time, scientists in North America and Europe began experimenting with a purified, white, powdered extract made from the coca plant.

In the last half of the 19th century, Corsican chemist Angelo Mariani removed the active ingredients from the coca leaf and identified cocaine. This purified cocaine was added into cough drops and into a special Bordeaux wine called Vin Mariani (Musto 1998). The Pope gave Mariani a medal in appreciation for the fine work he had done developing this concoction. The cocaine extract was publicized as a magical drug that would free the body from fatigue, lift the spirits, and cause a sense of well-being, and the cocaine-laced wine became

An Andean chews coca leaves.

widely endorsed throughout the civilized world (Fischman and Johanson 1996). Included in a long list of luminaries who advocated this product for an array of ailments were the Czar and Czarina of Russia; the Prince and Princess of Wales; the Kings of Sweden, Norway, and Cambodia; commanders of the French and English armies; President McKinley of the United States; H. G. Wells; August Bartholdi (sculptor of the Statue of Liberty); and some 8000 physicians.

The astounding success of this wine attracted imitators, all making outlandish claims. One of these cocaine tonics was a nonalcoholic beverage named Coca-Cola, which was made from African kola nuts and advertised as the "intellectual beverage and temperance drink"; it contained 4 to 12 milligrams per bottle of the stimulant (DiChiara 1993). By 1906, Coca-Cola no longer contained detectable amounts of cocaine, but caffeine had been substituted in its place. In 1884, the esteemed Sigmund Freud published his findings on cocaine in a report called "Uber Coca." Freud recommended this "magical drug" for an assortment of medical problems, including depression, hysteria, nervous exhaustion, digestive disorders, hypochondria, "all diseases which involve degeneration of tissue," and drug addiction.

In response to a request by Freud, a young Viennese physician, Karl Köller, studied the ability of cocaine to cause numbing effects. He discovered that it was an effective local anesthetic that could be applied to the surface of the eye and permitted painless minor surgery to be conducted. This discovery of the first local anesthetic had tremendous worldwide impact. Orders for the new local anesthetic, cocaine, overwhelmed pharmaceutical companies.

Soon after the initial jubilation over the virtues of cocaine came the sober realization that with its benefits came severe disadvantages. As more people used cocaine, particularly in tonics and patent medicines, the CNS side effects and abuse liability became painfully evident. By the turn of the 20th century, cocaine was being processed from the coca plant and purified routinely by drug companies. People began to snort or inject the purified form of this popular powder, which increased both its effects and its dangers. The controversy over cocaine exploded before the American public in newspapers and magazines.

As medical and police reports of cocaine abuse and toxicities escalated, public opinion demanded that cocaine be banned. In 1914, the Harrison Act misleadingly classified both cocaine and coca as narcotic substances (cocaine is a stimulant) and outlawed their uncontrolled use.

Although prohibited in patent and nonprescription medicines, prescribed medicinal use of cocaine continued into the 1920s. Medicinal texts included descriptions of therapeutic uses for cocaine to treat fatigue, vomiting, seasickness, melancholia, and gastritis. However, they also included lengthy warnings about excessive cocaine use, "the most insidious of all drug habits" (Aldrich and Barker 1976).

Little of medical or social significance occurred for the next few decades (Fischman and Johanson 1996). The medicinal use of cocaine was replaced mostly by the amphetamines during World War II because cocaine could not be supplied from South America. (Cocaine is not easily synthesized, so even today the supply of cocaine, both legal and illegal, continues to come from the Andean countries of South America.) During this period, cocaine continued to be employed for its local anesthetic action, was available on the "black market," and was used recreationally by musicians, entertainers, and the wealthy. Because of the limited supply, the cost of cocaine was prohibitive for most would-be consumers. Cocaine abuse problems continued as a minor concern until the 1980s.

The Third Cocaine Era

With the 1980s came the third major era of cocaine use. This era started much like the second in that the public and even the medical community were naive and misinformed about the drug. Cocaine was viewed as a glamorous substance and portrayed by the media as the drug of celebrities. Its use by prominent actors, athletes, musicians, and other members of a fast-paced, elite society was common knowledge. By 1982, more than 20 million Americans had tried cocaine in one form or another, compared with only 5 million in 1974 (Green 1985).

The following is an example of a report from a Los Angeles television station in the early 1980s, which was typical of the misleading information being released to the public:

Cocaine may actually be no more harmful to your health than smoking cigarettes or

The "refreshing" element in Vin Mariani was coca extract.

Sigmund Freud was an early advocate of cocaine, which he referred to as a "cure-all."

drinking alcohol; at least that's according to a 6-year study of cocaine use [described in *Scientific American*]. It concludes that the drug is relatively safe and, if not taken in large amounts, it is not addictive. (Byck 1987)

With such visibility, an association with prestige and glamour, and what amounted to an indirect endorsement by medical experts, the stage was set for another epidemic of cocaine use. Initially, the high cost of this imported substance limited its use. With increased demand, however, came increased supply, and prices tumbled from an unaffordable $100 per "fix" to an affordable $10. The epidemic began.

By the mid-1980s, cocaine permeated all elements of society. No group of people or part of the country was immune from its effects. Many tragic stories were told of athletes, entertainers, corporate executives, politicians, fathers and mothers, high school students, and even children using and abusing cocaine. It was no longer the drug of the laborer or even the rich and famous. It was everybody's drug and everybody's problem (Golding 1993). As one user recounted:

> I think I was an addict. I immediately fell in love with cocaine. I noticed right away it was a drug that you had power with, and I wanted more and more. (*From Venturelli's research files, male, age 22*)

Cocaine availability decreased sharply in the United States in 2009 resulting in an increase in price for a pure gram of cocaine from about $95 in 2006 to $175 toward the end of 2009. The purity of cocaine also diminished during this time, from 68% to 46%. The reasons for the shortages of cocaine at this time were thought to relate to several factors including decreased production in Colombia and increased seizures of cocaine destined for Mexico and trafficking into the United States (DEA 2010). However, it is important to appreciate that these trends can reverse very quickly.

Cocaine Production

Because cocaine is derived from the coca plant, which is imported from the Andean countries, the United States' problems with this drug have had a profound effect on several South American countries. With the dramatic rise in U.S. cocaine demand in the early 1980s, coca production in South America increased in tandem. The coca crop is by far the most profitable agricultural venture in some of these countries. In addition, it is easily cultivated and maintained (the coca plant is a perennial and remains productive for decades) and can be harvested several times a year (on average, two to four). The coca harvest has brought many jobs and some prosperity to these struggling economies.

It has been claimed that the U.S. coca eradication program has seriously influenced the fragile economies of poor Latin American countries, such as Bolivia and Peru, causing anti-American sentiment, especially in poor rural communities that depend on money from their coca crops (Caesar 2002). In addition, the spraying of herbicides from U.S.-piloted aircraft to destroy coca harvests is suspected of posing health hazards to the native populations (DeYoung 2003). Because of these problems, there is evidence that the attempts by the U.S. government to control cocaine abuse by eliminating coca crops have not been as successful as hoped and have been extremely costly (P. Smith 2010). Thus, although there are claims that after 10 years of effort, by 2008 cocaine cultivation in Colombia had decreased by about 30%, there were corresponding increases in cocaine production in the neighboring countries of Bolivia and Peru (Just the Facts 2010). In addition, in this region a literal war has been ongoing between government military and law enforcement groups and drug traffickers as well as illegal paramilitary groups. Thousands of people on both sides have been killed during fighting, as have almost 20,000 innocent civilians (P. Smith 2010). Although there has been some progress, government officials are clearly frustrated, as is apparent in the following quote from a highly regarded Latin American analyst:

> We've tried everything. Aggressive aerial spraying of fields, manual eradication, as well as softer measures to entice producers to adopt other crops, and it's all failed. As long as the price of cocaine remains inflated by prohibition, there is big profit and big incentive for producers and traffickers to grow the plant and export the product to the US and elsewhere. . . . I don't see this is a battle that can be won. (P. Smith 2010)

Trafficking of illegal cocaine is very profitable and often very dangerous (see "Here and Now: Bloody 'Drug War' Fought in Streets of Mexico"). Because of the highly addictive nature of cocaine and the profits associated with the illegal purchasing and selling of this drug, criminal groups frequently engage in violent struggles for control of the cocaine market (P. Smith 2010; Weiner 2003). In some

Here and Now

Bloody "Drug War" Fought in Streets of Mexico

Drug cartels ship hundreds of tons of cocaine to the United States. Because of the billions of dollars that can be made from this illegal market, gangs fight each other for control of the production and merchandising of this substance. This competition frequently turns violent. In Mexico during a particularly bloody week in 2010, 15 people were killed in a car wash, 14 were massacred at a teenager's birthday party, 13 were shot dead at a drug rehabilitation center, 7 were mowed down in the street, 4 factory workers were slaughtered on a bus, and 9 police officers died in an ambush. Such blatant violence has become almost a way of life in some parts of Mexico, but perhaps the most shocking aspect of these acts of wanton homicide is that most of the victims had nothing whatsoever to do with the drug cartels or the government forces fighting each other over drug-related issues. These people just happened to be in the wrong place at the wrong time and were inno-cently killed. Such violence has everyone wondering how this can be stopped. Is victory even possible in the war against the drug cartels?

Source: Tuckman, J. "Mexico's Drug Wars: The End of an Exceptionally Bloody Week." Guardian.co.uk. 29 October 2010. Available at: http://www.guardian.co.uk/world/2010/oct/29/mexico-drug-wars-bloody-week. Accessed March 16, 2011.

ways it is like "playing whack-a-mole." As efforts to shut down drug cartels in Mexico intensify, they tend to pop up elsewhere. For example, with increased cocaine seizures in Mexico, the Dominican Republic has developed into a main transit point for shipping this drug into both the United States and Europe. As a result, drug-related crime has been increasing in Caribbean countries. From 2001 to 2009, the Dominican Republic's homicide rate nearly doubled and the country has become overwhelmed with an increase in drug-trafficking violence and organized crime, while the police are making the biggest drug busts in the country's history. A similar increase in drug-related problems is also occurring in Puerto Rico, another affected Caribbean country (Fieser 2010). Solutions are elusive, and it is clear that without a significant reduction in demand the profit for producing, trafficking, and selling cocaine will remain high and attractive to illegal and dangerous groups.

Cocaine Processing

Cocaine is one of several active ingredients from the leaves of *Erythroxylon coca* (its primary source). The leaves are harvested two or four times per year and used to produce coca paste, which contains as much as 80% cocaine. The paste is processed in clandestine laboratories to form a pure, white hydrochloride salt powder (Hatsukami and Fischman 1996). Often, purified cocaine is **adulterated** (or "cut") with substances such as powdered sugar, talc, arsenic, lidocaine, strychnine, and methamphetamine before it is sold on the streets. Adverse responses to street cocaine are sometimes caused by the additives, not the cocaine itself. The resultant purity of the cut material ranges from 10% to 85%.

Cocaine is often sold in the form of little pellets, called *rocks*, or as flakes or powder. If it is in pellet form, it must be crushed before use. Street names used for these cocaine products have included *blow, snow, flake, C, coke, toot, white lady, nuggets, tornado, rock(s),* and *fat bags.*

Current Attitudes and Patterns of Abuse

Given contemporary medical advances, we now have a greater understanding of the effects of cocaine and its toxicities and the dependence

KEY TERMS

adulterated
contaminating substances are mixed in to dilute the drugs

Cocaine is often sold in a form that appears like small rocks.

it produces. The reasons for abusing cocaine are better understood as well. For example, it has been suggested that some chronic cocaine users are self-medicating their psychiatric disorders, such as depression, attention deficit disorders, or anxiety (AddictionInfo 2010). Such knowledge helps in identifying and administering effective treatment. The hope is that society will never again be fooled into thinking that cocaine abuse is glamorous or an acceptable form of entertainment.

Attempts are being made to use this understanding (either recently acquired or merely relearned) to educate people about the true nature of cocaine. Such education was likely responsible for trends of declining cocaine use observed from 1987 to 1991 (see **Figure 10.1**). Decreases occurred in virtually

every age group evaluated during this period. Surveys during this time revealed that, in general, cocaine use became less acceptable; these changes in attitude almost certainly contributed to the dramatic reduction in use. From 1992 to 1999 cocaine use rose, but leveled off during much of the first decade in 2000 and then dropped again in 2010 to 2.9% in high school seniors (Johnston 2010). This was likely due to increased cocaine seizures, a reduction in availability, and an increase in cost (Just the Facts 2010). Despite decreased cocaine use, the United States still leads the world in cocaine consumption and spends $37 billion annually, although the European market of $34 billion is not too far behind (Fieser 2010).

Cocaine Administration

Cocaine can be administered orally, inhaled into the nasal passages, injected intravenously, or smoked. The form of administration is important in determining the intensity of cocaine's effects, its abuse liability, and the likelihood of toxicity (NIDA 2010c).

Oral administration of cocaine produces the least potent effects; most of the drug is destroyed in the gut or liver before it reaches the brain. The result is a slower onset of action with a milder, more sustained stimulation. This form is least likely to cause health problems and dependence. South American Indians still take cocaine orally to increase their strength and for relief from fatigue. Administration usually involves prolonged chewing of the coca leaf, resulting in the consumption of about 20 to 400 milligrams of the drug (Encyclopedia Britan-

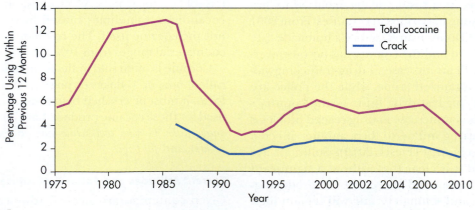

FIGURE 10.1

Trends in cocaine and crack use by high school seniors, 1975–2010. These data represent the percentages of high school seniors surveyed who reported using cocaine during the year.

Note: Crack cocaine did not become widely available until 1986.

Source: Johnston, L. D., P. M. O'Malley, J. G. Bachman, and J. E. Schulenberg. *Monitoring the Future.* "Long-Term Trends in Annual Prevalence of Use of Various Drugs in Grade 12 (Table 16)." Ann Arbor, MI: University of Michigan, 2010. Available at: http://monitoringthefuture.org/data/10data/pr10t16.pdf. Accessed March 4, 2011.

nica 2010). Oral use of cocaine is not common in the United States.

"Snorting" involves inhaling cocaine hydrochloride powder into the nostrils, where deposits form on the lining of the nasal chambers and approximately 100 milligrams of the drug passes through the mucosal tissues into the bloodstream (NIDA 2010c). Substantial CNS stimulation occurs in several minutes, persists for 30 to 40 minutes, and then subsides. The effects occur more rapidly and are shorter-lasting and more intense than those achieved with oral administration because more of the drug enters the brain more quickly. Because concentrations of cocaine in the body are higher after snorting than after oral ingestion, the side effects are more severe. One of the most common consequences of snorting cocaine is rebound depression, or "crash," which is of little consequence after oral consumption. As a general rule, the intensity of the depression correlates with the intensity of the euphoria (A.D.A.M. 2010).

According to studies performed by the National Institute on Drug Abuse, 10% to 15% of those who try intranasal (snorting) cocaine go on to heavier forms of dosing, such as intravenous administration. Intravenous administration of cocaine is a relatively recent phenomenon because the hypodermic needle was not widely available until the late 1800s. This form of administration contributed to many of the cocaine problems that appeared at the turn of the 20th century. Intravenous administration allows large amounts of cocaine to be introduced very rapidly into the body and causes severe side effects and dependence. Within seconds after injection, cocaine users experience an incredible state of euphoria. The "high" is intense but short-lived; within 15 to 20 minutes, the user experiences dysphoria and is heading for a "crash." To prevent these unpleasant rebound effects, cocaine is readministered every 10 to 30 minutes. Readministration continues as long as there is drug available (NIDA 2010c).

This binge activity resembles that seen in the methamphetamine "run," except it is usually shorter in duration. When the cocaine supply is exhausted, the binge is over (Zickler 2001). Several days of abstinence may separate these episodes; the average cocaine addict binges once to several times a week, with each binge lasting 4 to 24 hours. Cocaine addicts claim that all thoughts turn toward cocaine during binges; everything else loses significance. This pattern of intense use is how some people blow all of their money on cocaine.

"Freebasing" paraphernalia. A water pipe is often used to smoke freebased cocaine, or "crack." Cocaine administered by smoking is very potent and fast-acting; the effect lasts for 10 to 15 minutes, after which depression occurs. This is the most addicting form of cocaine.

Freebasing is a method of reducing impurities in cocaine and preparing the drug for smoking. It produces a type of cocaine that is more powerful than normal cocaine hydrochloride. One way to "freebase" is to treat the cocaine hydrochloride with a liquid base such as sodium carbonate or ammonium hydroxide. The cocaine dissolves, along with many of the impurities commonly found in it (such as amphetamines, lidocaine, sugars, and others). A solvent, such as petroleum or ethyl ether, is added to the liquid to extract the cocaine. The solvent containing the cocaine floats to the top and is drawn off with an eyedropper; it is placed in an evaporation dish to dry, and crystalized cocaine residue is then crushed into a fine powder, which can be smoked in a special glass pipe (Enotes 2010).

The effects of smoked cocaine are as intense or more intense than those achieved through intravenous administration (Fischman and Johanson 1996). The onset is very rapid, the euphoria is dramatic, the depression is severe, the side effects are dangerous, and the chances of dependence are high (NIDA 2007c). The reason for these intense reactions to inhaling cocaine into the lungs is that the

KEY TERMS

freebasing
conversion of cocaine into its alkaline form for smoking

drug passes rapidly through the lining of the lungs and into the many blood vessels present; it is then carried almost directly to the brain.

Freebasing became popular in the United States in the 1980s due to the fear of diseases such as AIDS and hepatitis, which are transmitted by sharing contaminated hypodermic needles. But freebasing involves other dangers. Because the volatile solvents required for freebasing are very explosive, careless people have been seriously burned or killed during processing. Street synonyms used for freebased cocaine include *coke, crystal, happy dust, snow, stuff, sugar, white horse*, and *wings* (Thesaurus.com 2010).

Crack Cocaine

Between 1985 and 1986, a special type of freebased cocaine known as **crack** or "rock" appeared on the streets (Hatsukami and Fischman 1996). By 1988, approximately 5% of high school seniors had tried crack. As of 1992 this number had fallen to 2.6%, and was down further by 2010 to 1.4% (Johnston 2010). Crack can be smoked without the dangerous explosive solvents mentioned earlier in the discussion of freebasing. It is made by taking powdered cocaine hydrochloride and adding sodium bicarbonate (baking soda) and water. The paste that forms removes impurities as well as the hydrochloride from the cocaine. The substance is then dried into hard pieces called rocks, which may contain as much as 90% pure cocaine. Other slang terms for crack include *big C, blow, nose candy, snow, Lady*, and *rock* (Partnership 2010). Like freebased cocaine, crack is usually smoked in a glass water pipe. When the fumes are absorbed into the lungs, they act rapidly, reaching the brain within 8 to 10 seconds. An intense "rush" or "high" results, and later a powerful state of depression, or "crash," occurs. The high may last only 3 to 5 minutes, and the depression may persist from 10 to 40 minutes or longer in some cases. As soon as crack is smoked, the nervous system is greatly stimulated by the release of dopamine, which seems to be involved in the rush. Cocaine prevents resupply of this neurotransmitter, which may trigger the crash.

KEY TERMS

crack
already processed and inexpensive "freebased" cocaine, ready for smoking

crack babies
infants born to women who used crack cocaine during pregnancy

Because of the abrupt and intense release of dopamine, smoked crack is viewed as a drug with tremendous potential for addiction and antisocial behavior (NIDA 2010c); some users consider it to be more enjoyable than cocaine administered intravenously. Crack and cocaine marketing and use are often associated with criminal activity (APA 2000) such as robberies and homicides (Swan 1995).

In general, crack use has been more common among African American and Hispanic populations than among white Americans. Of special concern is the use of crack among women during pregnancy. Children born under these circumstances have been referred to as **crack babies**. Even though the effects of crack on fetal development are not fully understood, many clinicians and researchers have predicted that these crack babies will impose an enormous social burden as they grow up. However, other experts have expressed concern that the impact of cocaine on the fetus is grossly overstated and have suggested that behavioral problems seen in these children are more a consequence of social environment than direct pharmacological effects (Vidaeff and Mastrobattista 2003). This issue is discussed in greater detail later in this section.

It is not coincidental that the popularity of crack use paralleled the AIDS epidemic in the mid-1980s. Because crack administration does not require injection, theoretically the risk of contracting HIV from contaminated needles is avoided. Even so, HIV infection still occurs in crack users because many crack smokers also use cocaine intravenously, thereby increasing their chances of becoming infected with HIV (see Chapter 16). Another reason for HIV infection (as well as other sexually transmitted diseases, such as syphilis and gonorrhea) among crack users is the dangerous sexual behavior in which these people engage (ScienceDaily 2010b). Not only is crack commonly used as payment for sex, but its users are also much less inclined to be cautious about their sexual activities while under the influence of this drug (Ladd and Petry 2003).

Major Pharmacological Effects of Cocaine

Cocaine can have profound effects on several vital systems in the body (*Drug Facts and Comparisons* 2010; Emedicinehealth 2010). With the assistance of modern technology, the mechanisms whereby cocaine alters body functions have become better understood. Such knowledge may eventually lead to better treatment of cocaine dependence.

Most of the pharmacological effects of cocaine use stem from enhanced activity of catecholamine (dopamine, noradrenaline, adrenaline) and serotonin transmitters. It is believed that the principal action of the drug is to block the reuptake and inactivation of these substances following their release from neurons. Such action prolongs the activity of these transmitter substances at their receptors and substantially increases their effects. The summation of cocaine's effects on these four transmitters causes CNS stimulation (Woolverton and Johnston 1992). The increase of noradrenaline activity following cocaine administration increases the effects of the sympathetic nervous system and alters cardiovascular activity.

CNS Effects

Because cocaine has stimulant properties, it has antidepressant effects as well. Some users self-administer cocaine to relieve severe depression or the negative symptoms of schizophrenia (Markou and Kenny 2002), but in general its short-term action and abuse liability make cocaine unsatisfactory for the treatment of depression disorders. The effects of stimulation appear to increase both physical and mental performance while masking fatigue. High doses of cocaine cause euphoria (based on the form of administration) and enhance the sense of strength, energy, and performance. Because of these positive effects, cocaine has intense reinforcing properties, which encourage continual use and dependence (Nathan, Bresnick, and Battei 1998).

Cocaine addicts can often distinguish between the two phenomena of the rush and the high associated with cocaine administration. Both the rush and the high peak about 3 minutes after use. The rush seems to be associated with elevated heart rate, sweating, and feelings of "speeding" or "being out of control"; the high includes feelings of euphoria, self-confidence, well-being, and sociability. Drug craving also occurs rapidly and is evident as soon as 12 minutes after administration. Interestingly, brain scans of cocaine users have demonstrated that specific brain regions are associated with these drug effects; thus, the rush and craving are linked with different regions of the limbic system in the brain (see Figure 4.7) (Stocker 1999).

The feeling of exhilaration and confidence caused by cocaine can easily become transformed into irritable restlessness and confused hyperactivity (APA 2000). In addition, high chronic doses alter personality, frequently causing psychotic behavior that resembles paranoid schizophrenia (Leard-Hansson 2006). For example, in an interview with Peter Venturelli, a 17-year-old female explained that a cocaine-abusing friend ". . . was so coked up that he carved the word 'pain' in his arm and poured coke on it. He thought it symbolized something." In addition, cocaine use heightens the risk of suicide, major trauma, and violent crimes (APA 2000; MedlinePlus 2010). In many ways, the CNS effects of cocaine resemble those of amphetamines, although perhaps with a more rapid onset, a more intense high (due partially to the manner in which the drugs are administered), and a shorter duration of action (APA 2000). Besides dependence, other notable CNS toxicities that can be caused by cocaine use include headaches, temporary loss of consciousness, seizures, and death.

Cardiovascular System Effects

Cocaine can initiate pronounced changes in the cardiovascular system by enhancing the sympathetic nervous system, increasing the levels of adrenaline, and causing vasoconstriction (Zickler 2002). The initial effects of cocaine are to increase heart rate and elevate blood pressure. While the heart is being stimulated and working harder, the vasoconstriction effects deprive the cardiac muscle of needed blood (Fischman and Johanson 1996). Such a combination can cause severe heart arrhythmia (an irregular contraction pattern) or heart attack. Other degenerative processes have also been described in the hearts and blood vessels of chronic cocaine users (Kloner and Rezkalla 2003). In addition, the vasoconstrictive action of this sympathomimetic can damage other tissues, leading to stroke, lung damage in those who smoke cocaine, destruction of nasal cartilage in those who snort the drug, and injury to the gastrointestinal tract (Goodger, Wang, and Pogrel 2005).

Local Anesthetic Effects

Cocaine was the first local anesthetic used routinely in modern-day medicine (Musto 1998). There is speculation that in ancient times, Andes Indians of South America used cocaine-filled saliva from chewing coca leaves as a local anesthetic for surgical procedures (Aldrich and Barker 1976); however, this assumption is contested by others (Byck 1987). Even so, cocaine is still used as a local anesthetic for minor pharyngeal (back part of the mouth and upper throat area) surgery due to its good vasoconstriction (reduces bleeding) and topical, local numbing effects. Although relatively safe when applied topically, significant amounts of cocaine can enter the bloodstream and, in sensitive people, cause CNS stimulation, toxic psychosis, or, on rare occasions, death (MayoClinic 2010).

Cocaine Withdrawal

Considerable debate has arisen as to whether cocaine withdrawal actually happens and, if so, what it involves. With the most recent cocaine epidemic and the high incidence of intense, chronic use, it has become apparent that nervous systems do become tolerant to cocaine and that, during abstinence, withdrawal symptoms occur (APA 2000). In fact, because of CNS dependence, the use of cocaine is less likely to be stopped voluntarily than is the use of many other illicit drugs (Sofuoglu et al. 2003). Certainly, if the withdrawal experience is adverse enough, a user will be encouraged to resume the cocaine habit.

The extent of cocaine withdrawal is proportional to the duration and intensity of use. The physical withdrawal symptoms are relatively minor compared with those caused by long-term use of CNS depressants and by themselves are not considered to be life-threatening (MedlinePlus 2007). Short-term withdrawal symptoms include depression (chronic cocaine users are 60 times more likely to commit suicide than nonusers), sleep abnormalities, craving for the drug, agitation, and anhedonia (inability to experience pleasure). Long-term withdrawal effects include a return to normal pleasures, accompanied by mood swings and occasional craving triggered by cues in the surroundings (APA 2000; Mendelson and Mello 1996).

Of particular importance to treatment of chronic cocaine users is that abstinence after bingeing appears to follow three unique stages, each of which must be dealt with in a different manner if relapse is to be prevented. These phases are classified as phase 1, or "crash" (occurs 9 hours to 4 days after drug use is stopped); phase 2, or withdrawal (1 to 10 weeks); and phase 3, or extinction (indefinite). The basic features of these phases are outlined in **Table 10.2** (APA 2000).

Treatment of Cocaine Dependence

Cocaine dependence is classified as a psychiatric disorder by the American Psychiatric Association (APA 2000) and results in many persons seeking treatment for drug addiction (Platt, Rowlett, and Spealman 2002). Treatment of this condition has improved as experience working with these patients has increased. Even so, success rates vary for different programs. The problem with program assessments is that they often do not take into account patients who drop out. Also, no clear-cut criteria for qualifying success have been established. For example, is success considered to be abstaining from cocaine for 1 year, 2 years, 5 years, or forever?

No one treatment technique has been found to be significantly superior to others or universally effective (MedlinePlus 2010; NIDA 2007a), nor is there a particularly effective medication to treat cocaine addiction (Platt et al. 2002). Consequently, substantial disagreement exists as to what is the best strategy for treating cocaine dependency. There is a major ongoing effort by federal agencies and scientists to find effective therapy for cocaine addiction. Most treatments are directed at relieving craving. Major differences in treatment approaches include (1) whether outpatient or inpatient status is deemed appropriate, (2) which drugs and what

Table 10.2 Cocaine Abstinence Phases

PHASE 1: "CRASH"	PHASE 2: WITHDRAWAL	PHASE 3: EXTINCTION
24–48 hours since last binge	1–10 weeks since last binge	Indefinite since last binge
Initial Agitation, depression, anorexia, suicidal thoughts	*Initial* Mood swings, sleep returns, some craving, little anxiety	Normal pleasure, mood swings, occasional craving, cues trigger craving
Middle Fatigue, no craving, insomnia	*Middle and late* Adhendonia, anxiety, intense craving, obsessed with drug seeking	
Late Extreme fatigue, no craving, exhaustion		

Source: Garwin, F. "Cocaine addiction: Psychology and neurophysiolohy." *Science* 251 (1991): 1580–1586.

dosages are used to treat patients during the various stages of abstinence, and (3) what length of time the patient is isolated from cocaine-accessible environments.

It is important to treat each individual patient according to his or her unique needs. Some questions that need to be considered when formulating a therapeutic approach include the following:

- Why did the patient begin using cocaine, and why has dependency occurred?
- What is the severity of abuse?
- How has the cocaine been administered?
- What is the psychiatric status of the patient? Are there underlying or coexisting mental disorders, such as depression or attention deficit disorder?
- What other drugs are being abused along with the cocaine?
- What is the patient's motivation for eliminating cocaine dependence?
- What sort of support system (family, friends, coworkers, and so on) will sustain the patient in the abstinence effort?

Outpatient Versus Inpatient Approaches

The decision as to whether to treat a patient who is dependent on cocaine as an outpatient or an inpatient is based on a number of factors. For example, inpatient techniques allow greater control than outpatient treatment; thus, the environment can be better regulated, the training of the patient can be more closely supervised, and the patient's responses to treatment can be more closely monitored. In contrast, the advantages of the outpatient approach are that supportive family and friends are better able to encourage the patient, the surroundings are more comfortable and natural, and potential problems that might occur when the patient returns to a normal lifestyle are more likely to be identified. In addition, outpatient treatment is less expensive.

Cocaine-dependent patients should be matched to the most appropriate strategy based on their personalities, psychiatric status, and the conditions of their addiction. For instance, a cocaine addict who lives in the inner city, comes from a home with other drug-dependent family members, and has little support probably would do better in the tightly controlled inpatient environment. However, a highly motivated cocaine addict who comes from a supportive home and a neighborhood that is relatively free of drug problems would probably do better on an outpatient basis.

Therapeutic Drug Treatment

Several drugs have been used to treat cocaine abstinence, some of which are themselves active on dopamine systems, but none has been found to be universally effective. Besides relieving acute problems of anxiety, agitation, and psychosis, drugs can diminish cocaine craving; this effect is achieved by giving drugs such as bromocriptine or levodopa, which stimulate the dopamine transmitter system, or the narcotic buprenorphine (TreatmentCenters.net 2010). As mentioned, the pleasant aspects of cocaine likely relate to its ability to increase the activity of dopamine in the limbic system. When cocaine is no longer available, the dopamine system becomes less active, causing depression and anhedonia, which result in a tremendous craving for cocaine. The intent of these cocaine substitutes is to stimulate dopamine activity and relieve the cravings. Although this approach sometimes works initially, it is temporary. In the third phase of cocaine abstinence, antidepressants such as desipramine are effective for many cocaine-dependent patients in relieving underlying mood problems and occasional cravings.

The beneficial effects of these drugs are variable and not well studied. There is some debate over their use. Drugs are, at best, only adjuncts in the treatment of cocaine dependence. Successful treatment of cocaine abuse requires intensive counseling; strong support from family, friends, and coworkers; and a highly motivated patient. It is important to realize that a complete "cure" from cocaine dependence is not likely; ex-addicts cannot return to cocaine and control its use.

Recovery from Cocaine Dependence

Although numerous therapeutic approaches exist for treating cocaine addiction, successful recovery is not likely unless the individual will substantially benefit by giving up the drug. Research has shown that treatment is most likely to succeed in patients who are middle-class, employed, and married; for example, 85% of addicted medical professionals recover from cocaine addiction. These people can usually be convinced that they have too much to lose in their personal and professional lives by continuing their cocaine habit. In contrast, a severely dependent crack addict who has no job, family, home, or hope for the future is not likely to be persuaded that abstinence from cocaine would be advantageous, so therapy is rarely successful. As mentioned earlier, there currently is no uniformly effective pharmacological treatment available to deal with long-term cocaine addiction, although intensive research to identify such therapeutic agents is under way.

Polydrug Use by Cocaine Abusers

Treatment of most cocaine abusers is complicated by the fact that they are *polydrug* (multiple drug) users. It is unusual to find a person who abuses only cocaine. For example, many cocaine abusers also use alcohol (Pennings, Leccese, and Wolff 2002). In general, the more severe the alcoholism, the greater the severity of the cocaine dependence. Alcohol is used to relieve some of the unpleasant cocaine effects, such as anxiety, insomnia, and mood disturbances (Pennings et al. 2002). This drug combination can be dangerous for several reasons (Pennings et al. 2002):

- The presence of both cocaine and alcohol (ethanol) in the liver results in the formation of a unique chemical product called cocaethylene, which is created in the reaction of ethanol with a cocaine metabolite. Cocaethylene often is found in high levels in the blood of victims of fatal drug overdoses and appears to enhance the euphoria as well as the cardiovascular toxicity of cocaine.
- Both cocaine and alcohol can damage the liver; thus, their toxic effects on the liver are likely to add together when the drugs are used in combination.
- The likelihood of damaging a fetus is enhanced when both drugs are used together during pregnancy.
- Cardiovascular stress is increased in the presence of both drugs.

Like users of amphetamines, cocaine abusers frequently coadminister narcotics, such as heroin; this combination is called a speedball and has been associated with a high risk for HIV infection (NIDA 2007b). Cocaine users sometimes combine their drug with other depressants, such as benzodiazepines, or marijuana to help reduce the severity of the crash after their cocaine binges. Codependence on cocaine and a CNS depressant can complicate treatment but must be considered.

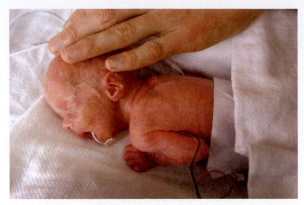

Infants born to crack-using mothers are often premature.

Cocaine and Pregnancy

One of the consequences of widespread cocaine abuse is that since the mid-1980s many babies in the United States have been born to mothers who used cocaine during pregnancy (Winkel 2010). Cocaine use during pregnancy is highest in poor, inner-city regions. Many of these **cocaine babies** have been abandoned by their mothers and left to the welfare system for care. It is still not clear exactly what types of direct effects cocaine has on the developing fetus (Winkel 2010). Some early studies have been criticized because (1) the pregnant populations examined were not well defined and properly matched, (2) use of other drugs (such as alcohol) with cocaine during pregnancy was often ignored, and (3) the effects of poor nutrition, poor living conditions, and a traumatic lifestyle were not considered when analyzing the results. Due to these problems, much of the earlier work examining prenatal effects of cocaine is flawed, and the conclusions are questionable (Vidaeff and Mastrobattista 2003; Women's Health Week 2006).

It is known that cocaine use during pregnancy can cause vasoconstriction of placental vessels, thereby interfering with oxygen and nutrient exchange between mother and child, or contraction of the uterine muscles, resulting in trauma or premature birth. Current data also suggest that infants exposed to cocaine during pregnancy are more likely to suffer a small head (microencephaly), reduced birthweight, increased irritability, and subtle learning and cognitive deficits (March of Dimes 2003; Singer et al. 2004). Other findings also suggest that children who experienced prenatal cocaine exposure have problems with some motor skills, subtle deficits in IQ, and some minor problems with language development, attention span, and ability to gather and use information (March of Dimes 2003).

KEY TERMS

cocaine babies
infants born to women who used cocaine during their pregnancy

Clearly, many individuals exposed to cocaine during fetal development can function normally in society, but they sometimes require special help, especially if they are allowed to be raised by their cocaine-addicted mother (Winkel 2010).

Minor Stimulants

Minor stimulants enjoy widespread use in the United States because of the mild lift in mood provided by their consumption. The most popular of these routinely consumed agents are methyl-xanthines (commonly called *xanthines*), such as caffeine, which are consumed in beverages made from plants and herbs. Other minor stimulants are contained in OTC medications, such as cold and hay fever products; these will be mentioned briefly in this chapter but discussed at greater length in Chapter 15. Because of their frequent use, some dependence on these drugs can occur; however, serious dysfunction due to dependence is infrequent. Consequently, abuse of xanthines such as caffeine is not viewed as a major health problem by most health experts (Medicinenet 2010). However, there has been recent concern that many people, especially adolescents and young adults, do not appreciate that caffeine is a drug and consume it more like food, resulting in side effects and even trips to the emergency room (Hitti 2006).

Caffeine-like Drugs (Xanthines)

Caffeine is the world's most frequently used stimulant and perhaps its most popular drug (Medicinenet 2010). Beverages and foods containing caffeine are consumed by almost all adults and children living in the United States today (see **Table 10.3**). In this country, the average daily intake of caffeine is approximately 289 mg (the equivalent of approximately 2–3 cups of coffee), with as many as 30% of Americans consuming 600 mg or more per day (Medicinenet 2010). Almost 80% of the world's population consumes caffeine daily (Medicinenet 2010). The most common sources of caffeine include coffee beans, tea plants, kola nuts, maté leaves, guaraná paste, yoco bark, and an array of herbal and so-called "natural products."

Although the consumption of caffeine-containing drinks can be found throughout history, the active stimulant caffeine was identified by German and French scientists in the early 1820s. Caffeine was described as a substance with alkaloid (basic) prop-

Table 10.3 Caffeine Content of Beverages and Chocolate

BEVERAGE (MG/CUP)	CAFFEINE CONTENT	AMOUNT
Brewed coffee	90–135	5 oz
Instant coffee	35–164	5 oz
Decaffeinated coffee	1–6	5 oz
Tea	25–70	5 oz
Cocoa	5–25	5 oz
Coca-Cola	45	12 oz
Pepsi-Cola	38	12 oz
Mountain Dew	70	12 oz
Energy drinks	80–160	8–16 oz
Excedrin (OTC medication)	65	
NoDoz (OTC medication)	34	
Vivarin (OTC medication)	200	
Chocolate bar	1–35	1 oz

Source: MedicineNet. "Caffeine." 2010. Available at: http://www.medicinenet.com/caffeine/article.htm. Accessed March 16, 2011.

erties that was extracted from green coffee beans and referred to as *kaffebase* by Ferdinand Runge in 1820 (Gilbert 1984). In the course of the next 40 to 60 years, caffeine was identified in several other genera of plants that were used as sources for common beverages. These included tea leaves (originally the caffeine-like drug was called *thein*); guaraná paste (originally the drug was called *guaranin*); Paraguay tea, or maté; and kola nuts. Certainly, the popularity of these beverages over the centuries attests to the fact that most consumers find the stimulant effects of this drug desirable.

The Chemical Nature of Caffeine

Caffeine belongs to a group of drugs that have similar chemical structures and are known as the **xanthines**. Besides caffeine, other xanthines are

KEY TERMS

xanthines
the family of drugs that includes caffeine

theobromine (which means "divine leaf"), discovered in cacao beans (used to make chocolate) in 1842, and *theophylline* (which means "divine food"), isolated from tea leaves in 1888. These three agents have unique pharmacological properties (which are discussed later), with caffeine being the most potent CNS stimulant.

Beverages Containing Caffeine

To understand the unique role that caffeine plays in U.S. society, it is useful to gain perspective on its most common sources: unfermented beverages.

Coffee

Coffee is derived from the beans of several species of coffea plants. The *Coffea arabica* plant grows as a shrub or small tree and reaches 4 to 6 meters in height when growing wild. Coffee beans are primarily cultivated in South America and East Africa and constitute the major cash crop for exportation in several developing countries.

The name *coffee* was likely derived from the Arabian word *kahwa* or named after the Ethiopian prince Kaffa. From Ethiopia, the coffee tree was carried to Arabia and cultivated (Kihlman 1977); it became an important element in Arabian civilization and is mentioned in writings dating back to 900 AD.

Coffee probably reached Europe through Turkey and was likely used initially as a medicine. By the middle of the 17th century, coffeehouses had sprung up in England and France—places to relax, talk, and learn the news. These coffeehouses turned into the famous "penny universities" of the early 18th century where, for a penny a cup, you could listen to some of the great literary and political figures of the day.

Coffee was originally consumed in the Americas by English colonists, although tea was initially preferred. Tea was replaced by coffee following the Revolutionary War. Because tea had become a symbol of English repression, the switch to coffee was more a political statement than a change in taste. The popularity of coffee grew as U.S. boundaries moved west. In fact, daily coffee intake continued to increase until it peaked in 1986, when annual coffee consumption averaged 10 pounds per person. Although concerns about the side effects associated with caffeine use have since caused some decline in coffee consumption, this beverage still plays a major role in the lifestyles of most Americans (Medicinenet 2010), with approximately 56% of adults in the United States being coffee drinkers in 2006 (Painter 2006).

Tea

Tea is made from the *Camellia sinensis* plant, which is native to China and parts of India, Burma, Thailand, Laos, and Vietnam. Tea contains two xanthines: caffeine and theophylline. As with coffee, the earliest use of tea is not known.

Although apocryphal versions of the origin of tea credit Emperor Shen Nung for its discovery in 2737 BC, the first reliable account of the use of tea as a medicinal plant appears in an early Chinese manuscript written around 350 AD. The popular use of tea slowly grew. The Dutch brought the first tea to Europe in 1610, where it was accepted rather slowly; with time, it was adopted by the British as a favorite beverage and became an integral part of their daily activities. In fact, the tea trade constituted one of the major elements of the English economy. Tea revenues made it possible for England to colonize India and helped to bring on the Opium Wars in the 1800s, which benefited British colonialism (see Chapter 9).

The British were constantly at odds with the Dutch as they attempted to monopolize the tea trade. Even so, the Dutch introduced the first tea into America at New Amsterdam around 1650. Later, the British gained exclusive rights to sell tea to the American colonies. Because of the high taxes levied by the British government on tea being shipped to America, tea became a symbol of British rule.

Soft Drinks

The second most common source of caffeine is soft drinks. In general, the caffeine content per 12-ounce serving ranges from 30 to 60 milligrams (see Table 10.3). Soft drinks account for most of the caffeine consumed by U.S. children and teenagers; for many people, a can of cola has replaced the usual cup of coffee. Recently, because of its general acceptance, caffeine has been added to juices, water, and even combined with alcoholic drinks. Super-caffeinated energy drinks have dramatically increased in popularity, with names like Red Bull, Monster, Full Throttle, Rockstar, and Amp. Approximately one-third of 12- to 24-year-olds regularly consume these beverages, accounting for $3 billion of sales annually in the United States (Parker-Pope 2008a). Although manufacturers of these high-dose caffeine drinks claim they do not specifically target teenagers in their marketing strategies, the reality is that adolescents are heavy consumers of "energy" drinks (Griffith 2008). This is evident from the reports by Poison Control Systems and emergency rooms of dramatic increases in calls and visits by young people complaining of caffeine-related overdose symptoms such as shakiness, tremors, dizziness, nausea, vomiting, agitation, increased heart rate, and elevated blood pressure (Griffith 2008). Another concern relates to observations that consumption of these drinks is associated with what has become known as *toxic jock* behavior: a combination of behaviors that reflect an inclination to engage in dangerous risk-taking such as unprotected sex, substance abuse, and violence (Parker-Pope 2008b). These observations do not mean that the caffeine causes this poor decision making, but it does appear that kids who are heavily involved in consuming these beverages are more likely to ignore basic rules of common sense related to their health and safety (Parker-Pope 2008b).

As mentioned above, caffeine also has been added to alcoholic beverages with names such as Four Loco and Joose. Despite claims by the manufacturers that a combination of caffeine and alcohol was "generally recognized as safe," evidence has been accumulating that especially in under-age consumers these products pose a significant health risk. After a year-long review of evidence, complaints, and claims, the FDA concluded that this drug combination may mask feelings of drunkenness, prompting consumers to engage in dangerous activities such as driving while under the influence of alcohol. As a result of this FDA conclusion, the caffeine–alcohol combination products have been removed from the market (Kesmodel 2010).

Social Consequences of Consuming Caffeine-Based Beverages

It is impossible to accurately assess the social impact of consuming beverages containing caffeine, but certainly the subtle (and sometimes not so subtle) stimulant effects of the caffeine present in these drinks have some social influence. These beverages have become integrated into social customs and ceremonies and recognized as traditional drinks.

Today, drinks containing caffeine are consumed by many people with ritualistic devotion first thing in the morning, following every meal, and at frequent interludes throughout the day known as "coffee breaks" or "tea times." The immense popularity of these products is certainly a consequence of the stimulant actions of caffeine. Both the dependence on the "jump-start" effect of caffeine and the avoidance of unpleasant withdrawal consequences in the frequent user ensure the continual popularity of these products.

Other Natural Caffeine Sources

Although coffee and tea are two of the most common sources of natural caffeine in the United States, other caffeine-containing beverages and food are popular in different parts of the world. Some of the most common include guaraná from Brazil; maté from Argentina, Southern Brazil, and Paraguay; and kola nuts from West Africa, West Indies, and South America (Kihlman 1977).

Chocolate

Although chocolate contains small amounts of caffeine (see Table 10.3), the principal stimulant in chocolate is the alkaloid theobromine, named after the cocoa tree, *Theobroma cacao*. (*Theobroma* is an Aztec word meaning "fruit of the gods.") The Aztecs thought very highly of the fruit and seed pods from the cacao tree, and they used the beans as a medium of exchange in bartering. The Mayan Indians adopted the food and made a warm drink from the beans that they called *chocolatl* (meaning "warm drink"). The original chocolate drink was a very thick concoction that had to be eaten with a spoon. It was unsweetened because the Mayans apparently did not know about sugar cane.

Hernando Cortés, the conqueror of Mexico, took some chocolate cakes back to Spain with him in 1528, but the method of preparing them remained a secret for nearly 100 years. It was not until 1828 that the Dutch worked out a process to remove much of the fat from the kernels to make a chocolate powder that was the forerunner of the cocoa we know today. The cocoa fat, or cocoa butter as it is called, was later mixed with sugar and pressed into bars. In 1847, the first chocolate bars appeared on the market. By 1876, the Swiss had developed milk chocolate, which is highly popular in today's confectioneries.

OTC Drugs Containing Caffeine

Although the consumption of beverages is by far the most common source of xanthines, a number of popular OTC products contain significant quantities of caffeine. For example, many OTC analgesic products (e.g., Anacin and Excedrin) contain approximately 30–60 milligrams of caffeine per tablet. Higher doses of 100–200 milligrams per tablet are included in stay-awake (NoDoz) and "picker-upper" (Vivarin) products (Medicinenet 2010). The use of caffeine in these OTC drugs is highly controversial and has been criticized by clinicians who are unconvinced of caffeine's benefits. Some critics believe that the presence of caffeine in these OTC

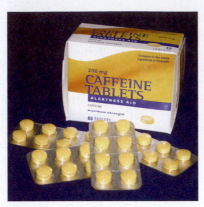

OTC caffeine products frequently contain the equivalent of 2–3 cups of coffee and are used to stay awake.

drugs is nothing more than a psychological gimmick to entice customers through mild euphoric effects provided by this stimulant.

Despite this criticism, it is likely that caffeine has some analgesic (pain-relieving) properties of its own (Dunwiddie and Masino 2001). Studies suggest that 130 milligrams, but not 65 milligrams, of caffeine is superior to a placebo in relieving nonmigraine headaches. In addition, the presence of caffeine has been shown to enhance aspirin-medicated relief from surgical pain (such as tooth extraction). Based on such findings, some clinicians recommend the use of caffeine in the management of some types of headaches and minor to moderate pains (Zhang 2001).

Physiological Effects of the Xanthines

The xanthines significantly influence several important body functions. Although the effects of these drugs are generally viewed as minor and short-term (Goldstein 1994), when used in high doses or by people who have severe medical problems, these drugs can be dangerous. The following sections summarize the responses of the major systems to xanthines.

CNS Effects

Among the common xanthines, caffeine has the most potent effect on the CNS, followed by theophylline; for most people, theobromine has relatively little influence. Although the CNS responses of users can vary considerably, in general 100 to 200 milligrams of caffeine enhances alertness, causes arousal, and diminishes fatigue (Medicinenet 2010). Caffeine is often used to block drowsiness and facilitate mental activity, such as when cramming for examinations into the early hours of the morning.

In addition, caffeine stimulates the formation of thoughts but does not improve learning ability in the wide-awake student. The effects of caffeine are most pronounced in unstimulated, drowsy consumers (Medicinenet 2010). The CNS effects of caffeine also diminish the sense of boredom (Medicinenet 2010). Thus, people engaged in dull, repetitive tasks, such as assembly-line work, or nonstimulating and laborious exercises, such as listening to a boring professor, often consume caffeinated beverages to help compensate for the tedium. Most certainly, xanthine drinks are popular because they cause these effects on brain activity.

Adverse CNS effects usually occur with doses greater than 300 milligrams per day. Some of these include insomnia, increased tension, anxiety, and initiation of muscle twitches. Doses over 500 milligrams can be dysphoric (unpleasant) and can cause panic sensations, chills, nausea, and clumsiness. Extremely high doses of caffeine, from 5 to 10 grams, frequently result in seizures, respiratory failure, and death (APA 2000).

Cardiovascular and Respiratory Effects

Drugs that stimulate the brain usually stimulate the cardiovascular system as well. The response of the heart and blood vessels to xanthines is dependent on dose and previous experience with these mild stimulants. Tolerance to the cardiovascular effects occurs with frequent use (Medicinenet 2010). With low doses (100–200 milligrams), heart activity can either increase, decrease, or do nothing; at higher doses (more than 500 milligrams), the rate of contraction of the heart increases. Xanthines usually cause minor vasodilation in most of the body. In contrast, the cerebral blood vessels are vasoconstricted by the action of caffeine. In fact, cerebral vasoconstriction likely accounts for this drug's effectiveness in relieving some minor vascular headaches caused by vasodilation of the cerebral vessels.

Among the xanthines, theophylline has the greatest effect on the respiratory system, causing air passages to open and facilitate breathing. Because of this effect, tea has often been recommended to relieve breathing difficulties, and theophylline is frequently used to treat asthma-related respiratory problems.

Other Effects

The methylxanthines have noteworthy—albeit mild—effects on other systems in the body. They cause a minor increase in the secretion of digestive juices in the stomach, which can be significant to individuals suffering from stomach ailments such as ulcers. These drugs also increase urine formation (as any heavy tea drinker undoubtedly knows).

Caffeine Intoxication

Consuming occasional low doses of the xanthines (the equivalent of two to three cups of coffee per day) is relatively safe for most users (Kluger 2004). However, frequent use of high doses causes psychological as well as physical problems called **caffeinism**. This condition is found in about 10% of the adults who consume coffee (APA 2000).

The CNS components of caffeine intoxication are recognized as a "psychoactive substance-induced psychiatric disorder" in DSM-IV-TR criteria established by the American Psychiatric Association (2000). The essential features of this disorder are restlessness, nervousness, excitement, insomnia, flushed face, diuresis, muscle twitching, rambling thoughts and speech, and stomach complaints. These symptoms can occur in some sensitive people following a dose as low as 250 milligrams per day. Caffeine doses in excess of 1 gram per day may cause muscle twitching, rambling thoughts and speech, heart arrhythmias, and motor agitation. With higher doses, hearing ringing in the ears and seeing flashes of light can occur. Some researchers suggest consuming large quantities of caffeine is associated with cancers of the bladder, ovaries, colon, and kidneys. These claims have not been reliably substantiated (Medicinenet 2010; Nawrot et al. 2003; Painter 2006).

One problem with many such studies is that they assess the effect of coffee consumption on cancers rather than the effect of caffeine itself. Because coffee contains so many different chemicals, it is impossible to determine specifically the effect of caffeine in such research (Medicinenet 2010). Other reports claim that caffeine promotes cyst formation in women's breasts. Although these conclusions have been challenged, many clinicians advise patients with breast cysts to avoid caffeine (Pruthi 2010). Finally, some reports indicate that very high doses of caffeine given to pregnant laboratory animals can cause stillbirths or offspring with low birthweights or limb deformities. However, studies found that moderate consumption of caffeine (less than 300 milligrams per day) did not significantly affect human fetal development (Medicinenet 2010). Generally, expectant mothers are advised to avoid or at least reduce caffeine use during pregnancy just to be safe (Medicinenet 2010).

Based on the information available, no strong evidence exists to suggest that moderate use of caffeine leads to disease (Medicinenet 2010). In fact, some recent research has suggested that moderate caffeine consumption may even reduce the risk of degenerative diseases of the brain such as Parkinson's disease and Alzheimer's disease (Fackelmann 2006; Painter 2006). There are, however, implications that people with existing severe medical problems—psychiatric disorders (such as severe anxiety, panic attacks, and schizophrenia), cardiovascular disease, and possibly breast cysts—may be at greater risk when consuming caffeine. Realistically, other elements, such as alcohol and fat consumption and smoking, are much more likely to cause serious health problems (Gurin 1994).

Caffeine Dependence

Caffeine causes limited dependence, which, for most people, is relatively minor compared with that of the potent stimulants; thus, the abuse potential of caffeine is much lower and dependence is less likely to interfere with normal daily routines (Kluger 2004; Medicinenet 2010). Despite this, caffeine use is thought to be able to produce a significant addiction in some people (Biotech Week 2004). Consequently, 50% of those consuming one to three cups of coffee each day develop headaches when withdrawing and 10% become significantly depressed, anxious, or fatigued without their coffee. Some people experience elements of withdrawal every morning before their first cup and claim caffeine gives them an edge at work or in school (Shute 2007). However, caffeine is so readily available and socially accepted (almost expected) that the high quantity of consumption has produced many modestly dependent users. In fact, we are seeing younger and younger persons consuming more and more caffeine; from 2004 to 2007 the percentage of 18- to 24-year-olds who consumed caffeine daily went from 16% to 31% (Shute 2007; see "Here and Now: Caffeine Emergencies").

The degree of physical dependence on caffeine is highly variable but related to dose. With typical caffeine withdrawal, adverse effects can persist for several days (see **Table 10.4**). Although these symptoms are unpleasant, they usually are not severe enough to prevent most people from giving up their coffee or cola drinks if motivated. It is noteworthy, however, that many of those patients who are treated

KEY TERMS

caffeinism
symptoms caused by taking high chronic doses of caffeine

Here and Now

Caffeine Emergencies

Because of the increased popularity of caffeine-containing products, especially with teenagers, poison control centers across the country are reporting increased numbers of people presenting at emergency rooms with rapid heart rates and nausea from caffeine overdose. Such was the case when a 14-year-old boy recently showed up at a Minneapolis emergency room having difficulty with breathing after washing down several caffeine pills with so-called "energy drinks" in order to continue playing video games all night. But instead of having a night of video recreation with friends, he spent the evening in an intensive care unit intubated until the caffeine cleared from his system and normal breathing was restored.

Source: Shute, N. "Americans Young and Old Crave High-Octane Fuel, and Doctors Are Jittery." *U.S. News and World Report* (29 April 2007): 58–68.

for caffeinism relapse into their caffeine-consuming habits (Wheeler 2010).

Variability in Responses

Caffeine is eventually absorbed entirely from the gastrointestinal tract after oral consumption. In most users, 90% of the drug reaches the bloodstream within 20 minutes and is distributed into the brain and throughout the body very quickly (Sawynok and Yaksh 1993). The rate of absorption of caffeine from the stomach and intestines differs from person to person by as much as six-fold. Such wide variations in the rate at which caffeine enters the blood from the stomach likely account for much of the variability in responses to this drug.

■ OTC Sympathomimetics

Although often overlooked, the sympathomimetic decongestant drugs included in OTC products such as cold, allergy, and diet aid medications have stimulant properties like those of caffeine (Urban Dictionary 2010). For most people, the CNS impact of these drugs is minor, but for those people who are very sensitive to these drugs, they can cause jitters and interfere with sleep. For such individuals, OTC products containing the sympathomimetics should be avoided before bedtime (Answers.com 2010).

The common OTC sympathomimetics are shown in **Table 10.5** and include ephedrine, pseudoephedrine, and phenylephrine. In the past, these drugs have been referred to as "look-alikes," suggesting they have effects similar to the more potent

Table 10.4 **Caffeine Withdrawal Syndrome**

SYMPTOM	DURATION
Headache	Several days to 1 week
Decreased alertness	2 days
Decreased vigor	2 days
Fatigue and lethargy	2 days
Nervousness	2 days

Source: Based on Holtzman, S. "Caffeine as a model drug of abuse." *Trends in Pharmacological Sciences* 11 (1990): 355–356.

Table 10.5 **Common OTC Sympathomimetics**

DRUG	OTC PRODUCT (FORM)
Ephedrine	Before removed, was used as a decongestant (oral, nasal spray, or nasal drops)
Naphazoline	Decongestant (nasal spray or nasal drops)
Oxymetazoline	Decongestant (nasal spray or nasal drops)
Phenylephrine	Decongestant (oral, nasal spray, nasal drops, or eye drops)
Pseudoephedrine	Decongestant (oral)
Tetrahydrozoline	Decongestant (eye drops)

Source: Scolaro, K. "Disorders Related to Colds and Allergy." In *Handbook of Nonprescription Drugs*, 15th ed., 201–228. Washington, DC: American Pharmaceutical Association, 2004.

stimulants such as amphetamine. Although much less potent than amphetamines (even though they can be used as precursor chemicals to make meth-amphetamine), these minor stimulants can be abused and have caused deaths (Cucchiara and Levine 2010). Attempts to keep these drugs from being promoted as potent stimulants resulted in passage of the federal and state Imitation Controlled Substances Acts. These statutes prohibit the packaging of OTC sympathomimetics to look like amphetamines.

Despite these laws, occasionally other products containing the OTC sympathomimetics are promoted on the street as "harmless speed" and "OTC uppers." It is likely that use of such products can lead to the abuse of more potent stimulants.

As previously mentioned, some of the sympathomimetics that are included in cold medicines can be readily converted into methamphetamine. For this reason, as of 2006 federal statutes require these products be secured in a locked case behind the counter and sold in limited quantities (Baldauf 2006).

■ Herbal Stimulants

Some OTC sympathomimetics occur naturally and are also found in herbal stimulants or dietary supplements sold by mail and in novelty stores, beauty salons, health food stores, online, and sometimes by health professionals, including physicians. (To appreciate this point, complete an Internet search for "herbal stimulant.") These pills have been sold under many names such as "Rave Herbal Stimulant," "Legal Herbal Weed," and "Herbal Ecstasy," and often contain stimulants such as ephedrine, ephedra, or ma huang. These products are promoted as natural highs to be used as diet aids, energy boosters, or performance enhancers for athletics (Legal Herbal Drugs 2007). Excessive use of these products can cause seizures, heart attacks, and strokes (Gugliotta 2000). In fact, several deaths and many cases of severe reactions have been reported in the United States from excessive use of these products (*Washington Times* 2003). The death of a major league baseball player (see "Here and Now: Diet Pills Are Russian Roulette for Athletes")

Here and Now

Diet Pills Are Russian Roulette for Athletes

Steve Bechler, a 23-year-old pitcher for the Baltimore Orioles of the American League, died in 2003 after collapsing on the field during running drills due to "multiple organ failure resulting from heat stroke," says the autopsy report. Ephedrine was found in Bechler's body and likely contributed to his death. He was reported to be using an ephedrine supplement called Xenadrine RFA-1. Although advised not to use it by his trainer, Bechler was taking this ephedrine-containing product to get his weight down after being criticized by coaches for being too heavy and not performing well in preseason drills. A teammate explained that heavy athletes like Bechler are under a lot of pressure to control their weight to make big-league teams. Although at the time of Bechler's death use of ephedrine was not prohibited by Major League Baseball, it was prohibited by the National Football League in 2002. The NFL's ban came after Korey Stringer, a lineman for the Minnesota Vikings who was taking an ephedrine product, died after collapsing during a training camp workout in 2001. Ephedrine in OTC dietary supplements has since been made illegal by the FDA due to serious side effects and death, such as these incidents described above.

Sources: Shipley, A. "Bechler's Diet Pills Draw Scrutiny." *Washington Post* (19 February 2003): D-1; and Mayo Clinic Health. "Ephedra (Ephedra sinica)/ma Huang." Health Information (2010). Available at: http://www.mayoclinic.com/health/ephedra/NS_patient-ephedra. Accessed May 3, 2011.

resulted in particularly strong pressure to ban OTC products, including dietary supplements, containing either the herb ephedra or the active ingredient ephedrine (Shipley 2003). In response to these pressures, the FDA banned the use of ephedrine or ephedra in OTC products; however, it is difficult to actually remove herbal stimulants from the marketplace because of a 1994 federal law that prohibits such action until the FDA conclusively proves the dangers of these substances (Miller and Longtin 2010). Numerous lawsuits have been filed against herbal companies that manufactured products containing ma huang and the drug ephedrine. These legal actions claim that such products have caused serious illness and even death. Several of these lawsuits have been settled out of court, reportedly for millions of dollars. Even before the FDA ban, because ephedrine can be converted into methamphetamine, the Comprehensive Methamphetamine Act passed in 1996 regulated the amount of ephedrine that could be purchased or sold at one time (Sprague, Harrod, and Teconchuk 1998).

Global Stimulant Abuse

Like the United States, other countries have been seriously impacted by the abuse of stimulant drugs, causing governments and law enforcement agencies around the world and international organizations such as the United Nations Office on Drugs and Crime to search for solutions (United Nations Office on Drugs and Crime 2009). For the most part these drugs are referred to as amphetamine-type stimulants (ATS) or cocaine and their various forms. The ATS drugs include amphetamines such as methamphetamine, methcathinone, and MDMA and related substances.

■ Stimulant Production

Because most ATS drugs are synthetics, they can be produced anywhere and are relatively inexpensive. As mentioned before, for this reason these drugs are often perceived as a "poor-man's cocaine." It is estimated that about 650 metric tons of the ATS drugs were manufactured globally in 2007, of which about 130 metric tons were MDMA (United Nations Office on Drugs and Crime 2009). A pattern exists of shifting manufacturing from developed to developing countries to take advantage of these poorer countries' vulnerabilities and less sophisticated law enforcement strategies to fight organized crime organizations and their inability to stop manufacturing and sale of these substances. This is illustrated by the shift from the small neighborhood methamphetamine labs in the United States of 2000–2005 to the more recent large sophisticated meth labs run by organized drug cartels and crime syndicates in Mexico (United Nations Office on Drugs and Crime 2009).

In contrast, because cocaine is a natural substance derived from a plant, its production is limited to those regions that have climate and geographic conditions conducive to coca cultivation. Countries that produce the vast majority of the world's cocaine supply are Bolivia, Peru, and Colombia. The global cocaine supply decreased to 845 metric tons in 2008. These recent declines were largely due to a 28% reduction in cocaine production in Colombia as a result of pressure from the United States (United Nations Office on Drugs and Crime 2009).

■ Stimulant Trafficking

Global seizures of ATS have been increasing since 2000, with amphetamine and methamphetamine leading the way (United Nations Office on Drugs and Crime 2009), accounting for 84% of all seizures. However, 2007 saw a dramatic jump in international seizures of MDMA (16% of all ATS confiscated). Typically, trafficking of ATS drugs is intraregional because they can readily be manufactured locally and usually do not need to be smuggled across international borders. In contrast, the precursor chemicals from which ATS drugs are synthesized

Organizations of the United Nations, such as its Office on Drugs and Crime, work with countries around the world to identify critical drug problems and to develop global solutions that cross international borders.

are typically diverted from legitimate markets for decongestant and cold medicines in Asia (United Nations Office on Drugs and Crime 2007).

Cocaine trafficking patterns are somewhat opposite of those for the ATS drugs. Following several years of expansion, the quantity of cocaine seized in 2006 decreased and remained reduced in 2007 and 2008. This reflects the reduction in cocaine production mentioned earlier and the resultant increases in cocaine prices and purity (United Nations Office on Drugs and Crime 2009).

Global Stimulant Consumption

It is roughly estimated that globally between 72 and 250 million persons annually consume illicit drugs. This figure includes the entire gamut of users from casual abusers to heavy consumers who have become problematic drug addicts (United Nations Office on Drugs and Crime 2009). The intense users are likely very dependent on their drug of choice, cause a serious drain on public health and law enforcement resources, and would benefit from proper treatment. It is estimated that globally there are 13 to 38 million of these problem drug users, ages 15–64 years (United Nations Office on Drugs and Crime 2009).

Different drugs tend to cause problems for different global regions. Marijuana is particularly troubling for Africa and Australia; heroin is especially problematic for Asia and Europe; the ATS drugs are a major problem for Asia, North America, and Australia; and cocaine causes the greatest problem in North and South Americas, with the United States being the largest consumer in absolute numbers (United Nations Office on Drugs and Crime 2009). By comparison, the ATS drugs are consumed by almost two-fold more people around the world (about 40 million annually) than cocaine (about 20 million). For comparison, the global use of MDMA is similar to that for cocaine (United Nations Office on Drugs and Crime 2009).

Global Drug Policy

Like the United States, most countries around the world are looking for solutions to the personal and social consequences of drug abuse in general and the stimulant problems in particular. Lively discussions about demand, production, and trafficking occur between countries to try to stem the tide of drug abuse/addiction and its devastating consequences. The causes are many and the solutions are complex and evasive. There are heated discussions between nations on topics such as (1) who is principally at fault for the problems (i.e., the nations that produce or consume), (2) should these drugs be legalized or at least be decriminalized, and (3) can taxing of such drug products be used to raise needed public revenues. The international discussions resemble those occurring throughout the United States. What has become evident to everyone is that although specific solutions are difficult, all nations are in this together. Drug problems and drug policies to address these problems cross national borders, impacting global efforts to find solutions; thus, to be successful in our attempts to mitigate these drug problems we must have global cooperation and work together.

Discussion Questions

1. Should the FDA continue to approve amphetamines for the treatment of obesity? Why?

2. How are methamphetamine and Ecstasy similar, and how do they differ?

3. Should children be taken from mothers who are addicted to methamphetamine or cocaine?

4. What have past experiences taught us about cocaine? Do you think we have finally learned our lesson concerning this drug?

5. If clinical trials demonstrate that MDMA is effective in the treatment of stress and anxiety, should the FDA approve its use by prescription? What would be the effect on recreational MDMA use by young people if the FDA approved MDMA for treating PTSD?

6. Why does the method of cocaine administration make a difference in how a user is affected by this drug? Use examples to substantiate your conclusions.

7. Why do people use crack cocaine, and what are the major toxicities caused by the use of high doses of this stimulant?

8. How is cocaine dependence treated? What are the rationales for the treatments?

9. How does caffeine compare with cocaine and amphetamine as a CNS stimulant?

10. Because of caffeine's potential for abuse, do you think the FDA should control it more tightly? Defend your answer.

11. Do you feel that herbal stimulants, such as ephedra and ma huang, should have been removed from OTC products?

12. How do global efforts to address stimulant abuse problems affect the people and policies in the United States?

Summary

1 Amphetamines, originally developed as decongestants, are potent stimulants. Some amphetamines have been approved by the FDA as (a) diet aids to treat obesity, (b) treatment for narcolepsy, and (c) treatment for attention deficit hyperactivity disorder in children.

2 In therapeutic doses, amphetamines can cause agitation, anxiety, and panic owing to their effects on the brain; in addition, they can cause an irregular heartbeat, increased blood pressure, heart attack, or stroke. Intense, high-dose abuse of these drugs can cause severe psychotic behavior, stereotypy, and seizures as well as the severe cardiovascular side effects just mentioned.

3 Speed refers to the use of intravenous methamphetamine. Ice is smoked methamphetamine. A run is a pattern of intense, multiple dosing over a period of days that can cause serious neurological, psychiatric, and cardiovascular consequences.

4 Tweakers are individuals who repeatedly self-administer methamphetamine to maintain the high. They often have not slept or eaten for days, are very irritable, and sometimes are paranoid or even violent.

5 "Designer" amphetamines are chemical modifications of original amphetamines. Some designer amphetamines, such as Ecstasy, have some abuse potential and are marketed on the street under exotic and alluring names.

6 Ecstasy has both psychedelic and stimulant properties due to its ability to release serotonin and dopamine in the brain. This combination of pharmacological effects makes this drug particularly attractive to younger populations engaging in sensory-rich activities, such as dances called raves.

7 In the early 1980s, cocaine was commonly viewed by the U.S. public as a relatively safe drug with glamorous connotations. By the mid-1980s, it became apparent that cocaine was a very addicting drug with dangerous side effects.

8 The CNS and cardiovascular effects of both amphetamines and cocaine are similar. However, the effects of cocaine tend to occur more rapidly, be more intense, and wear off more quickly than those of amphetamines.

9 The intensity of the cocaine effect and the likelihood of dependence occurring are directly related to the means of administration. Going from least to most intense effect, the modes of cocaine administration include chewing, snorting, injecting, and smoking (or freebasing).

10 Crack is cocaine that has been converted into its "freebase" form and is intended for smoking.

11 Cocaine withdrawal goes through three main stages: (a) the "crash," the initial abstinence phase consisting of depression, agitation, suicidal thoughts, and fatigue; (b) withdrawal, including mood swings, craving, anhedonia, and obsession with drug seeking; and (c) extinction, when normal pleasure returns and cues trigger craving and mood swings.

12 Treatment of cocaine dependence is highly individualistic and has variable success. The principal strategies include both inpatient and outpatient programs. Drug therapy often is used to relieve short-term cocaine craving and to alleviate mood problems and long-term craving. Psychological counseling and support therapy are essential components of treatment.

13 Caffeine is the most frequently consumed stimulant in the world. It is classified as a xanthine (methylxanthine) and is added to a number of beverages, including water, and has even been added to alcoholic drinks. It is also included in some OTC medicines such as analgesics and "stay-awake" products. Caffeine causes minor stimulation of cardiovascular activity, kidney function (it is a diuretic), and gastric secretion.

14 Dependence on caffeine can occur in people who regularly consume large doses. Withdrawal can cause headaches, agitation, and tremors. Although unpleasant, withdrawal from caffeine dependence is much less severe than that from amphetamine and cocaine dependence.

15 OTC sympathomimetics such as ephedrine have been consumed in high doses and used as "legal" highs. Although not as potent as the major stimulants, the recreational use of these drugs can be dangerous. Because of those potential dangers, the FDA has prohibited the use of ephedrine in OTC products.

16 Stimulant abuse and addiction are problems that are global in nature. Because these drugs are manufactured around the world and trafficked across international borders, it is impossible to find lasting solutions to these problems without working with other countries to help stem the production and smuggling of these illegal substances.

References

A.D.A.M. "Cocaine Withdrawal." *New York Times,* Health Guide. 13 December 2010. Available http://health. nytimes.com/health/guides/disease/cocaine-withdrawal/overview.html

AddictionInfo. "Self Medication Hypothesis, ADHD and Cocaine." AddictionInfo.org News and Views on Substance Abuse. 2010. Available http://www.addictioninfo.org/articles/751/2/Self-Medication-Hypothesis-ADHD—Cocaine/Page2.html

Aldrich, M., and R. Barker. In *Cocaine: Chemical, Biological, Social and Treatment Aspects,* edited by S. J. Mule, 3–10. Cleveland, OH: CRC, 1976.

American Council for Drug Education. "Basic Facts About Drugs: Methamphetamine." 2007. Available http://www.acde.org/common/meth.pdf

American Psychiatric Association. "Substance-Related Disorders." In *Diagnostic and Statistical Manual of Mental Disorders,* 4th ed., text revision, 223–250. Washington, DC: American Psychiatric Association, 2000.

Answers.com. "Decongestant." 2010. Available http://www.answers.com/topic/decongestan

Baldauf, S. "Vanished Behind the Counter." *US News and World Report.* 2 October 2006. Available http://health.usnews.com/usnews/health/articles/060924/2cold.htm

Beck, J. "The Public Health Implications of MDMA Use." In *Ecstasy,* edited by S. Peroutka, 77–103. Norwell, MA: Kluwer, 1990.

Benedetti, W. "Ecstasy Supporters Hope FDA-Approved Study Will Vindicate Drug." *Seattle Post-Intelligencer.* 9 May 2002. Available http://seattlepi.nwsource.com/lifestyle/69629_ecstasystudy.shtml

Berkes, H. "Mexican 'Ice' Replaces Home-Cooked Meth in U.S." National Public Radio (3 April 2007).

Biotech Week. "Caffeine Withdrawal Recognized as a Disorder." 20 October 2004. Available http://www.newsrx.com/newsletters/Biotech-Week/2004-10-20.html.

Buchen, L. "Party Drug Could Ease Trauma Long Term." NatureNews. 16 April 2010. Available http://www.nature.com/news/2010/100416/full/news.2010.188.html

Byck, R. "Cocaine Use and Research: Three Histories." In *Cocaine: Chemical and Behavioral Aspects,* edited by S. Fisher, 3–17. London: Oxford University Press, 1987.

Caesar, M. "US Finds Anger in South America." *Toronto Globe and Mail* (31 August 2002). Available http://www.commondreams.org/headlines02/0831-06.htm

Cantwell, B., and A. McBride. "Self Detoxification by Amphetamine-Dependent Patients: A Pilot Study." *Drug and Alcohol Dependence* 49 (1998): 157–163.

Cloud, J. "The Lure of Ecstasy." *Time* 155 (5 June 2000): 60.

Cohen, G. "A Front-Line Physician's Perspective on the Crystal Meth Epidemic." *Counselor* 7 (October 2006): 51, 52.

Comprehensive Methamphetamine Control Act (MCA). 2010. Available http://designer-drug.com/ptc/12.162.180.114/dcd/chemistry/dojmeth1.txt

Cucchiara, B., and S. Levine. "Stroke Associated with Drug Abuse." MedLink Neurology. 2010. Available http://www.medlink.com/medlinkcontent.asp

Cumming, P., D. Caprioli, and J. W. Dalley. "What Have PET and 'Zippy' Told Us About the Neuropharmacology of Drug Addiction?" *British Journal of Pharmacology* 10 (2010): 1476–5381.

Cunningham, J., L. Bojorquez, O. Campollo, L. Liu, and C. Maxwell. "Mexico's Methamphetamine Precursor Chemical Interventions: Impacts on Drug Treatment Admissions." *Addiction* 105 (2010) 1973–1983.

Deslandes, P., D. Pache, and R. Sewell. "Drug Dependence: Neuropharmacology and Management." *Journal of Pharmacy and Pharmacology* 54 (2002): 885–895.

DeYoung, K. "U.S.: Coca Cultivation Drops in Colombia." *Washington Post* (28 February 2003): A-19.

DiChiara, G. "Cocaine: Scientific and Social Dimensions." *Trends in Neurological Sciences* 16 (1993): 39.

Doyle, M. "Report: 2006 Anti-meth Law Reduced Number of U.S. Labs." McClatchy. 6 July 2010. Available http://www.mcclatchydc.com/2010/07/06/97092/report-2006-anti-meth-law-reduced.html

Drug Addiction Treatment. "Women and Methamphetamine Use." 8 March 2010. Available http://www.drugaddictiontreatment.com/types-of-addiction/street-drug-addiction/women-and-methamphetamine-use

Drug Enforcement Agency (DEA). "Ecstasy Statistics." 19 July 2003. Available http://theDEA.org/statistics.html

Drug Enforcement Agency (DEA). "Drug Availability in the United States." *National Threat Assessment 2010.* 2010. Available http://www.justice.gov/ndic/pubs38/38661/cocaine.htm

Drug Facts and Comparisons. St. Louis, MO: Wolters Kluwar, 2005: 917–941, 2081.

Drug Monkey. "Slate on MDMA Clinical Trials." 8 February 2007. Available http://drugmonkey.wordpress.com/2007/02/08/slate-on-mdma-clinical-trials

Drug War Facts. "Methamphetamine." 2004. Available http://www.drugwarfacts.org/methamph.htm

Drugs.com. "Amphetamine Side Effects." Drug Information Online. 15 November 2010. Available http://www.drugs.com/sfx/amphetamine-side-effects.html

Drugwatch. "Ephedrine." 2010. Available http://www.drugwatch.com/ephedrine

Dunwiddie, T., and S. Masino. "The Role and Regulation of Adenosine in the Central Nervous System." *Annual Review of Neuroscience* 24 (2001): 31–55.

eGetgoing. "Drug and Alcohol Information, Prescription Amphetamines." 13 November 2010. Available http://www.egetgoing.com/drug_rehab/prescription_amphetamines.asp

Elias, P. "One of the 'Speed Freak Killers' to Be Freed." SF-Gate.com. 12 September 2010. Available http://articles .sfgate.com/2010-09-12/news/23999735_1_first-degree-murder-charges-methamphetamine-cyndi-vanderheiden

Elkashef, A., F. Vocci, G. Hanson, J. White, W. Wickes, and J. Tiihonen. "Pharmacotherapy of Methamphetamine Addiction: An Update." *Substance Abuse* 29 (2008): 31–49.

Emedicinehealth. "Cocaine Abuse." 2010. Available http:// www.emedicinehealth.com/cocaine_abuse/article_ em.htm

Encyclopedia Britannica. "Science and Technology: Cocaine." Encyclopedia Britannica Academic Edition. 2010. Available http://www.britannica.com/EBchecked/topic/ 123441/cocaine

Enotes. "Freebasing." Encyclopedia of Drugs, Alcohol, and Addictive Behavior. 2010. Available http://www.enotes. com/drugs-alcohol-encyclopedia/freebasing

Everything Addiction. "MDMA: A Stimulant Drug You Should Avoid." 19 July 2010. Available http://www. everythingaddiction.com/drugs-addiction/club-drugs/ mdma-a-stimulant-drug-you-should-avoid

Fackelmann, K. "Can Caffeine Protect Against Alzheimer's?" *USA Today* (6 November 2006): 4D.

Fieser, E. "Drug Wars in Mexico, Colombia Push Drug Trade to Dominican Republic." *Christian Science Monitor.* 5 November 2010. Available http://www.csmonitor. com/World/Americas/2010/1105/Drug-wars-in-Mexico-Colombia-push-drug-trade-to-Dominican-Republic

Fischman, M., and C. Johanson. "Cocaine." In *Pharmacological Aspects of Drug Dependence: Towards an Integrated Neurobehavior Approach Handbook of Experimental Pharmacology,* edited by C. Schuster and M. Kuhar, 159–195. New York: Springer-Verlag, 1996.

Fox, M. "Amphetamines Could Damage Heart Artery: U.S. Study." *The Post Chronicle.* 18 August 2010. Available http:// promises.com/promisesnews/articles/amphetamines/ amphetamine-abuse-can-cause-serious-damage-to-aorta-in-young-people

Gehrke, B., S. Harrod, W. Cass, and M. Bardo. "The Effect of Neurotoxic Doses of Methamphetamine on Methamphetamine-Conditioned Place Preference in Rats." *Psychopharmacology (Berlin)* 166 (2003): 249–257.

Gilbert, R. "Caffeine Consumption." In *The Methylxanthine Beverages and Foods: Chemistry, Consumption, and Health Effects,* edited by G. Spiller, 185–213. New York: Liss, 1984.

Golding, A. "Two Hundred Years of Drug Abuse." *Journal of the Royal Society of Medicine* 86 (May 1993): 282–286.

Goldstein, A. *Addiction from Biology to Drug Abuse.* New York: Freeman, 1994.

Goodger, N., J. Wang, and M. Pogrel. "Palatal and Nasal Necrosis Resulting from Cocaine Misuse." *British Dental Journal* 198 (2005): 333–334.

Graham, D. "Oregon's Simple Solution to the Meth Epidemic." *Newsweek.* 26 March 2010. Available http:// www.newsweek.com/id/235528

Green, E. "Cocaine, Glamorous Status Symbol of the 'Jet Set,' Is Fast Becoming Many Students' Drug of Choice." *Chronicle of Higher Education* 13 (November 1985): 1, 34.

Griffith, D. "Energy Drinks Implications." *Sacramento Bee.* 11 May 2008. Available http://thesportdigest.com/article/ energy-drinks-implications-student-athletes-and-athletic-departments

Grinspoon, L., and J. Bakalar. "The Amphetamines: Medical Use and Health Hazards." In *Amphetamines: Use, Misuse and Abuse,* edited by D. Smith, 18–33. Boston: Hall, 1978.

Grob, C., R. Poland, L. Chang, and T. Ernst. "Psychobiological Effects of 3,4-Methylenedioxymethamphetamine in Humans: Methodological Considerations and Preliminary Observations." *Behavioral Brain Research* 73 (1996): 103–107.

Gugliotta, G. "Ephedra Lawsuits Show Big Increase." *Washington Post* (23 July 2000): A-1.

Gurin, J. "Coffee and Health." *Consumer Reports* (October 1994): 650–651.

Hall, W., and J. Hando. "Illicit Amphetamine Use Is a Public Health Problem in Australia." *Medical Journal of Australia* 159 (1993): 643–644.

Hanson, G. R., K. Rau, and A. Fleckenstein. "The Methamphetamine Experience: A NIDA Partnership." *Neuropharmacology* 47 (2004): 92–100.

Harding, A. "Meth Use in Pregnancy Endangers Mom and Baby." Reuters Health. 29 July 2010. Available http://www.reuters.com/article/2010/07/29/us-meth-pregnancy-idUSTRE66S5M720100729

Hatsukami, D., and M. Fischman. "Crack Cocaine and Cocaine Hydrochloride." *Journal of the American Medical Association* 276 (1996): 1580–1588.

Hessert, A. "The New Performance Enhancing Drugs." *Neuroanthropology.* 4 June 2009. Available http://neuro anthropology.net/2009/06/04/the-new-performance-enhancing-drugs

Hitti, M. "Caffeine Abuse: Buzz Gone Wrong." WebMD. 16 October 2006. Available http://www.webmd.com/ content/article/128/117124

Hoffman, B., and R. Lefkowitz. "Catecholamines, Sympathomimetic Drugs, and Adrenergic Receptor Antagonists." In *The Pharmacological Basis of Therapeutics,* 9th ed., edited by J. Hardman and L. Limbird, 199–248. New York: McGraw-Hill, 1995.

Holt, L. "Former Meth Addicts Jenny Madonecky and Faye Benner Speak About Crystal Meth Addiction." *Saturday Today Show,* NBC (8 October 2005).

Huus, K. "Crystal Cartels Alter Face of U.S. Meth Epidemic." MSN.com. 2007. Available http://www.msnbc.msn.com/ id/14817871

Jansen, K. "Ecstasy (MDMA)." *Drug and Alcohol Dependence* 53 (1999): 121–124.

Johnston, L. "Monitoring the Future 2009." 2010. Available http://monitoringthefuture.org/data/09data/pr09t3.pdf

Join Together. "Study Says More Seeking Meth Treatment." 6 March 2006. Available http://www.jointogether.org/ news/headlines/inthenews/2006/study-says-more-seeking-meth.html

Journal of the American Medical Association. "Ecstasy Overdoses at a New Year's Eve Rave—Los Angeles, California, 2010." 304 (2010): 629–632.

Juozapavicius, J. "New Meth Formula Avoids Anti-Drug Laws." ABC News (U.S.). 24 August 2009. Available http://www.november.org/stayinfo/breaking09/New_Meth_Formula.html

Just the Facts. "Coca Cultivation and Counter-Drug Efforts in the Andean Region." 2 March 2010. Available http://justf.org/blog/2010/03/02/coca-cultivation-and-counter-drug-efforts-andean-region

Kaye, S., S. Darke, and J. Duflou. "Methylenedioxymethamphetamine (MDMA)-related Fatalities in Australia: Demographics, Circumstances, Toxicology and Major Organ Pathology." *Drug and Alcohol Dependence* 104 (2009): 254–261.

Keenan, B. "Adderall Is 'Secret Miracle' for Illegal Use." The Breeze. 22 April 2010. Available http://www.breezejmu.org/article_8d88baa4-757c-554f-9d36-9e48c47fb35a.html

Kennedy, K. "Meth Mania: Even Cops Duck for Cover." *Salt Lake Tribune* (28 June 1999): B-1.

Kesmodel, D. "FDA Bans Mixing Caffeine, Alcohol." *Wall Street Journal*. 18 November 2010. Available http://online.wsj.com/article/SB100014240527487046486045 75620673854960904.html

Khan, M. "Drugs Used to Enhance Studying Draw Concern." *Miami Herald* (8 July 2003). Available http://www.bio.net/mm/neur-sci/2003-July/054834.html

Kihlman, B. *Caffeine and Chromosomes*. Amsterdam: Elsevier, 1977.

King, L. A., and J. M. Corkery. "An Index of Fatal Toxicity for Drugs of Misuse." *Human Psychopharmacology* 25 (2010): 162–166.

Kinkead, L., and D. Romboy. "Meth Emergency." *Deseret Morning News* 153 (14 November 2004): A1, A15–A17.

Kish, S., J. Lerch, Y. Furukawa, J. Tong, T. McCluskey, and D. Wilkins. "Decreased Cerebral Cortical Serotonin Transporter Binding in Ecstasy Users: A Positron Emission Tomography/[11-C]DASB and Structural Brain Imaging Study." *Brain* 133 (2010): 1779–1797.

Kloner, R., and S. Rezkalla. "Cocaine and the Heart." *New England Journal of Medicine* 348 (2003): 487–488.

Klouda, N., and S. Pearson. "Crimes Rise with Meth Addiction." *Homer Tribune*. 28 July 2010. Available http://homertribune.com/2010/07/crimes-rise-with-meth-addiction

Kluger, J. "The Buzz on Caffeine." *Time* (20 December 2004): 62.

Kuehn, B. "Brain Scans, Genes Provide Addiction Clues." *Journal of the American Medical Association* 297 (2007): 1419–1421.

Ladd, G., and N. Petry. "Antisocial Personality in Treatment-Seeking Cocaine Abusers: Psychosocial Functioning and HIV Risk." *Journal of Substance Abuse Treatment* 24 (2003): 323–330.

Leard-Hansson, J. "Cocaine-Induced Psychosis and Schizophrenia." *Clinical Psychiatry News*. February 2006. Available http://findarticles.com/p/articles/mi_hb4345/is_2_34/ai_n29281255

Legal Herbal Drugs. "Aphrodisiacs, Stimulants, Hallucinogens . . ." 2007. Available http://www.herbalhighs.co.uk/stimulants.htm

Leinwand, D. "Feds Score Against Homegrown Meth." *USA Today* (2 July 2007): A3.

ListOwn. "How to Make Shake and Bake Meth." November 2010. Available http://www.listown.com/group/how-to-make-shake-and-bake-meth-6199

Lyles, J., and J. Cadet. "MDMA Neurotoxicity: Cellular and Molecular Mechanisms." *Brain Research Review* 42 (2003): 155–168.

March of Dimes. "Illicit Drug Use During Pregnancy." July 2003. Available http://www.marchofdimes.com/professionals/14332_1169.asp

Markou, A., and P. Kenny. "Neuroadaptations to Chronic Exposure to Drugs of Abuse: Relevance to Depression Symptomology Even Across Psychiatric Diagnostic Categories." *Neurotoxicology Research* 4 (2002): 297–313.

MayoClinic. "Cocaine (Topical Route)." 15 December 2010. Available http://www.mayoclinic.com/health/drug-information/DR600467

Mayo Clinic Health. "Ephedra (Ephedra sinica)/ma Huang." Health Information (2010). Available http://www.mayoclinic.com/health/ephedra/NS_patient-ephedra

McCaffrey, B. "Methamphetamine." ONDCP, Drug Policy Information Clearinghouse. NCJ-1756677 (May 1999): 1–3.

McKoy, K. "Teens Are Abusing Drugs." Examiner.com—Atlanta. 24 August 2009.

McManis, S. "For Former Meth Users, 'Give It a Year.' " *Sacramento Bee*. 23 August 2009. Available http://www.facesandvoicesofrecovery.org/resources/in_the_news/2009/2009-08-23_former_meth.php

MedicineNet. "Caffeine." 2010. Available http://www.medicinenet.com/caffeine/article.htm

MedlinePlus. "Cocaine Withdrawal." U.S. National Library of Medicine. 2007. Available http://vsearch.nlm.nih.gov/vivisimo/cgi-bin/query-meta?v%3Aproject=medlineplus&query=cocaine+withdrawal+

MedlinePlus. "Cocaine Withdrawal." 15 November 2010. Available http://www.nlm.nih.gov/medlineplus/ency/article/000947.htm

Mendelson, J., and N. Mello. "Management of Cocaine Abuse and Dependence." *New England Journal of Medicine* 334 (1996): 965–972.

Miller, H., and D. Longtin. "Death By Dietary Supplement." Forbes.com. 2010. Available http://www.forbes.com/2010/03/23/dietary-supplemetns-herbal-fda-opinions-contributors-henry-i-miller-david-longtin.html

Montgomery, C., N. P. Hatton, J. E. Fisk, R. S. Ogden, and A. Jansari. "Assessing the Functional Significance of Ecstasy-Related Memory Deficits Using a Virtual Paradigm." *Human Psychopharmacology* 25 (2010): 318–325.

Musto, D. "International Traffic in Coca Through the Early 20th Century." *Drug and Alcohol Dependence* 49 (1998): 145–156.

Narconon. "Ecstasy/MDMA Manufacturing and Statistics." Friends of Narconon. 2010. Available http://www.friendsofnarconon.org/drug_education/news/latest_news/ecstasy%10mdma_manufacturing_and_statistics

Nathan, K., W. Bresnick, and S. Battei. "Cocaine Abuse and Dependence." *CNS Drugs* 10 (1998): 43–59.

National Institute on Drug Abuse (NIDA). "Diagnosis and Treatment of Drug Abuse in Family Practice." May 2000. Available http://www.nida.nih.gov/Diagnosis-Treatment/Diagnosis.html

National Institute on Drug Abuse (NIDA). "Methamphetamine Abuse and Addiction." 2006. Available http://www.nida.nih.gov/researchreports/methamph/Methamph.html

National Institute on Drug Abuse (NIDA). "An Individual Drug Counseling Approach to Treat Cocaine Addiction." 2007a. Available http://www.nida.nih.gov/TXManuals/IDCA/IDCA3.html

National Institute on Drug Abuse (NIDA). "NIDA InfoFacts. Crack and Cocaine." 2007b. Available http://www.nida.nih.gov/infofacts/cocaine.html

National Institute on Drug Abuse (NIDA). "NIDA InfoFacts: MDMA (Ecstasy)." 2007c. Available http://www.nida.nih.gov/infofacts/ecstasy.html

National Institute on Drug Abuse (NIDA). "Stimulant ADHD Medications—Methylphenidate and Amphetamines." NIDA InfoFacts. 2009. Available http://www.drugabuse.gov/Infofacts/ADHD.html

National Institute on Drug Abuse (NIDA). "MDMA (Ecstasy)." March 2010a. Available http://drugabuse.gov/infofacts/ecstasy.html

National Institute on Drug Abuse (NIDA). "Methamphetamine: Abuse and Addiction." NIDA Research Report Series. 13 November 2010b. Available http://drugabuse.gov/researchreports/methamph/methamph3.html

National Institute on Drug Abuse (NIDA). "NIDA InfoFacts: Cocaine." March 2010c. Available http://drugabuse.gov/infofacts/cocaine.html

National Institute on Drug Abuse (NIDA), Community Epidemiology Work Group (NIDA CEWG). "Proceedings of the Epidemiology Work Group on Drug Abuse." January 2007. Available http://www.drugabuse.gov/about/organization/cewg/Reports.html

Nawrot, P., S. Jordan, J. Eastwood, J. Rotstein, A. Hugenholtz, and M. Feeley. "Effects of Caffeine on Human Health." *Food Additives and Contaminants* 20 (2003): 1–30.

Newswise. "Researchers See Trends in Synthetic Stimulant Misuse." 27 March 2007. Available http://www.newswise.com/articles/view/528426/?sc=mwtn

Nuckols, C., and J. Kane. "Methamphetamine Addiction: 'Speed' Still Kills." *Counselor* 4 (2003): 14–18.

O'Brien, M., and J. Anthony. "Extra-medical Stimulant Dependence Among Recent Initiates." *Drug and Alcohol Dependence* 104 (2009): 147–155.

Office of National Drug Control Policy (ONDCP). "Cocaine." ONDCP Drug Policy Information Clearinghouse. 2003. Available http://www.whitehousedrugpolicy.gov/drugfact/cocaine/index.html

Office of National Drug Control Policy (ONDCP). Synthetic Drug Control Strategy. June 2006a. Available http://dhs.alabama.gov/pdf/info/synthetic_strategy.pdf

Office of National Drug Control Policy (ONDCP). "A Focus on Methamphetamine and Prescription Drug Abuse." Synthetic Drug Control Strategy. June 2006b. Available http://www.justice.gov/olp/pdf/synthetic_strat2006.pdf

Office of National Drug Control Policy (ONDCP). "Street Terms: Drugs and the Drug Trade." November 2010. Available http://www.whitehousedrugpolicy.gov/streetterms/ByType.asp?intTypeID=24

Ordonez, F. "Mexican Gangs Provide Most U.S. 'Meth.' " McClatchy Newspapers. 29 April 2008. Available http://www.mcclatchydc.com/2008/04/29/35281/mexican-gangs-provide-most-us.html

Painter, K. "Good News, Coffee Lovers." *USA Today* (6 November 2006): 4D.

Pardo, S. "New Party Drug Hits Clubs." *Detroit News*. 9 March 2010. Available http://www.drugs-forum.com/forum/showthread.php?t=122788

Parker-Pope, T. "Energy Drinks Linked to Risky Behavior Among Teenagers." *New York Times* (27 May 2008a). Available http://www.nytimes.com/2008/05/27/health/27iht-27well.13247828.html

Parker-Pope, T. "New Teen Health Worry-Energy in a Can." *New York Times* (26 May 2008b). Available http://well.blogs.nytimes.com/2008/05/27/new-teen-health-worry-energy-in-a-can

Pennings, E., A. Leccese, and F. Wolff. "Effects of Concurrent Use of Alcohol and Cocaine." *Addiction* 97 (2002): 773–783.

Platt, D., J. Rowlett, and R. Spealman. "Behavioral Effects of Cocaine and Dopaminergic Strategies for Preclinical Medication Development." *Psychopharmacology* 163 (2002): 265–282.

Polanczyk, G., and L. Rohde. "Epidemiology of Attention-Deficit/Hyperactivity Disorder Across the Lifespan." *Current Opinions of Psychiatry* 20 (2007): 386–392.

Prevline. "Methamphetamine." 1999. Available http://ncadistore.samhsa.gov/catalog/facts.aspx?topic=6

Pruthi, S. "Does Caffeine Cause Breast Cysts?" MayoClinic.com. 2010. Available http://www.mayoclinic.com/health/breast-cysts/AN00889

Randall, T. "Ecstasy-Fueled 'Rave' Parties Become Dances of Death for English Youths." *Journal of the American Medical Association* 268 (1992a): 1505–1506.

Randall, T. " 'Rave' Scene, Ecstasy Use, Leap Atlantic." *Journal of the American Medical Association* 268 (1992b): 1506.

Randolph, T. "Hazelden Study Suggests Drop in Meth Use." Minnesota Public Radio. 19 June 2007. Available http://minnesota.publicradio.org/display/web/2007/06/19/methdecline/?dssource=1

Raskin, A. "Study Suggests Antidepressant May Help Treat Meth Addiction." *Los Angeles Times* (23 November 2005). Available http://articles.latimes.com/2005/nov/23/science/sci-meth23

Rauscher, M. "Methamphetamine Hard on the Teeth." Reuters Health. 5 October 2006. Available http://www.medicineonline.com/news/12/6307/methamphetamine-hard-on-the-teeth.html

Reinberg, S. "Use of Marijuana, Ecstasy, Methamphetamine on Rise in U.S." Bloomberg BusinessWeek. 16 September 2010. Available http://www.businessweek.com/lifestyle/content/healthday/643236.html

Rich, T., and M. Jordan. "Mother's Little Helper—The History of Amphetamine and Antidepressant Use in America." Wellcorps. 13 November 2010. Available http://www.wellcorps.com/Mothers-Little-Helper-The-History-of-Amphetamine-and-Anti-Depressant-Use-in-America.html

Ricker, R., and V. Nicolino. "Adderall: The Most Abused Prescription Drug in America." Huffington Post. 21 June 2010. Available http://www.huffingtonpost.com/dr-ronald-ricker-and-dr-venus-nicolino/adderall-the-most-abused_b_619549.html

Rowan-Szal, G., G. Joe, W. Simpson, J. Greener, and J. Vance. "During-Treatment Outcomes Among Female Methamphetamine-Using Offenders in Prison-Based Treatments." *Journal of Offender Rehabilitation* 48 (2009) 388–401.

Rutledge, J. "Counties Call Meth Top Drug Problem." *Washington Times* (19 July 2006). Available http://www.highbeam.com/doc/1G1-148374058.html

Salter, J. "Tenn. Overtakes Mo. In Meth Lab Seizures, Busts." The Associated Press. Nems360.com (3 March 2011). Available http://m.nems360.com/nems360/db_106200/contentdetail.htm;jsessionid=56F473B3DF8AA417B264C5AE9E0528A7?contentguid=lmKWBpqk&detailindex=3&pn=0&ps=4

Savage C., and M. Gordon. "U.S. Delays Release of Report Tying Meth to Mexico." *New York Times.* 8 June 2010. Available http://www.nytimes.com/2010/06/09/world/americas/09mexico.html

Sawynok, J., and T. Yaksh. "Caffeine as an Analgesic Adjuvant: A Review of Pharmacology and Mechanisms of Action." *Pharmacological Reviews* 45 (1993): 43–85.

Schifano, F., J. Corkery, V. Naidoo, A. Oyefeso, and H. Ghodse. "Overview of Amphetamine-Type Stimulant Mortality Data—UK, 1997–2007." *Neuropsychobiology* 61 (2010): 122–130.

Schifano, F., L. Furia, G. Forza, N. Minicuci, and R. Bricolo. "MDMA ('Ecstasy') Consumption in the Context of Polydrug Abuse: A Report on 50 Patients." *Drug and Alcohol Dependence* 52 (1998): 85–90.

Schiller, C., and P. Allen. "Follow-up of Infants Prenatally Exposed to Cocaine." Pediatric Nursing 31 (2005): 427–436.

Science Daily. "Brain Functions That Can Prevent Relapse Improve After a Year of Methamphetamine Abstinence." 29 June 2009. Available http://www.sciencedaily.com/releases/2009/06/090629165114.htm

Science Daily. "Brain Abnormalities Identified That Result from Prenatal Methamphetamine Exposure." 17 March 2010a. Available http://www.sciencedaily.com/releases/2010/03/100316174208.htm

Science Daily. "Crack and Cocaine Use a Significant HIV Risk Factor for Teens." 1 April 2010b. Available http://www.sciencedaily.com/releases/2010/03/100331141006.htm

Science Daily. "MDMA (Ecstasy)-Assisted Psychotherapy Relieves Treatment-Resistant PTSD, Study Suggests." 20 July 2010c. Available http://www.sciencedaily.com/releases/2010/07/100719082927.htm

Sederer, L. "Paying the Piper: Brain Neuroenhancers." Huffington Post. 1 June 2009. Available http://www.huffingtonpost.com/lloyd-i-sederer-md/paying-the-piper-brain-ne_b_209702.html

Shetty, V., L. Moohey, C. Zigler, T. Belin, D. Murphy, and R. Rawson. "The Relationship Between Methamphetamine Use and Increased Dental Disease." *Journal of the American Dental Association* 141 (2010): 307–309.

Shipley, A. "Bechler's Diet Pills Draw Scrutiny." *Washington Post* (19 February 2003): D-1.

Shropshire, J. "College Students Don't See Dangers of ADHD Drug Abuse." BusinessLexington. 13 May 2010. Available http://www.bizlex.com/Articles-c-2010-05-12-92606.113117-College-students-dont-see-dangers-of-ADHD-drug-abuse.html

Shute, N. "Americans Young and Old Crave High-Octane Fuel, and Doctors Are Jittery." *U.S. News and World Report* (29 April 2007): 58–68.

Simmons, A. "Teen Attitudes on Meth Are Surprising." *Atlanta Journal-Constitution.* 10 March 2010. Available http://www.ajc.com/news/teen-attitudes-on-meth-358058.html

Singer, L., S. Minnes, E. Short, R. Arendt, K. Farkas, and B. Lewis. "Cognitive Outcomes of Preschool Children with Prenatal Cocaine Exposure." *Journal of the American Medical Association* 291 (2004): 2448–2456.

Smith, J. "The Two Sides of Prescription Drug Abuse on Campus." Student Stuff.com. 16 February 2010. Available http://www.studentstuff.com/2010/02/16/the-two-sides-of-prescription-drug-abuse-on-campus

Smith, P. "Plan Colombia: Ten Years Later." Stop DrugWar. 15 July 2010. Available http://stopthedrugwar.org/chronicle/2010/jul/15/plan_colombia_ten_years_later

Snider, G. "I Thought This Was My Destiny." Partnership for a Drug-Free America. 2006. Available http://www.askninanow.com/articleofthemonth1.html

Sofuoglu, M., S. Dudish-Poulsen, S. Brown, and D. Hatsukami. "Association of Cocaine Withdrawal Symptoms with More Severe Dependence and Enhanced Subjective Response to Cocaine." *Drug and Alcohol Dependence* 69 (2003): 273–282.

Sprague, J., A. Harrod, and A. Teconchuk. "The Pharmacology and Abuse Potential of Ephedrine." *Pharmacy Times* (May 1998): 72–80.

Stocker, S. "Cocaine Activates Different Brain Regions for Rush Versus Craving." *NIDA Notes* 13 (1999): 7–10.

Substance Abuse and Mental Health Services Administration (SAMHSA). "Medical Aspects of Stimulant Use Disorders." SAMHSA/CSAT Treatment Protocols. 2010. Available http://www.ncbi.nlm.nih.gov/books/NBK26312

Swan, N. "31% of New York Murder Victims Had Cocaine in Their Bodies." *NIDA Notes* 10 (March/April 1995): 4.

Swan, N. "Response to Escalating Methamphetamine Abuse Build on NIDA-Funded Research." *NIDA Notes* 11 (November/December 1996): 1–12.

Tancer, M., and C. Johanson. "The Effects of Fluoxetine on the Subjective and Physiological Effects of 3,4-Methylenedioxymethamphetamine (MDMA) in Humans." *Psychopharmacology (Berlin)* 189 (2007): 565–573.

The Body. "Crystal Methamphetamine and HIV/AIDS: News and Research." The Body, The Complete HIV/AIDS Resource. November 2010. Available http://www.thebody.com/index/whatis/crystal_meth_news.html

Thesaurus.com. "Freebase." 2010. Available http://thesaurus.com/browse/freebase

Transitions Recovery Program. "Methamphetamine." 2007. Available http://www.drug-rehabcenter.com/methamphetamine.htm

Treatment-Centers.net. "Useful New Addiction Treatment News." 2010. Available http://www.treatment-centers.net/articles/useful-new-addiction-treatment-news.html

Tseng, N. "Children Fall By Wayside in Meth-Addicted Homes." *Orlando Sentinel* (11 September 2005): B1.

Tuckman, J. "Mexico's Drug Wars: The End of an Exceptionally Bloody Week." Guardian.co.uk. 29 October 2010. Available http://www.guardian.co.uk/world/2010/oct/29/mexico-drug-wars-bloody-week

Turillazzi, E., I. Riezzo, M. Neri, S. Bello, and V. Fineschi. "MDMA Toxicity and Pathological Consequences: A Review About Experimental Data and Autopsy Findings." *Current Pharmaceutical Biotechnology* 11 (2010): 500–509.

Tye, K., L. Tye, J. Cone, E. Hekkelman, P. Janak, and A. Bonci. "Methylphenidate Facilitates Learning-Induced Amygdala Plasticity." *Nature Neuroscience* 13 (2009): 475–481.

United Nations Office on Drugs and Crime. *World Drug Report 2009*. Vienna: United Nations Office on Drugs and Crime, 2009.

Urban Dictionary. "1. Pseudo-ephedrine." 2010. Available http://www.urbandictionary.com/define.php?term=decongestant

U.S. Department of Justice. "Children at Risk." Information Bulletin (July 2002). Product Number 2002-L0424-001.

U.S. Department of Justice. "Methamphetamine." National Drug Threat Assessment (April 2003a). Product Number 2003-Q0317-001: 13–25.

U.S. Department of Justice. "National Drug Threat Assessment 2003." National Drug Intelligence Center (January 2003b). Product No. 2003-Q0317-001: 51–58.

U.S. Department of Justice. "National Methamphetamine Threat Assessment 2010." National Drug Intelligence Center (2010). Product No. 2010-Q0317-004.

Van Dyck, C., and R. Byck. "Cocaine." *Scientific American* 246 (1982): 128–141.

Vidaeff, A., and J. Mastrobattista. "In Utero Cocaine Exposure: A Thorny Mix of Science and Mythology." *American Journal of Perinatology* 20 (2003): 165–172.

Volkow, N., L. Chang, G. Wong, J. Fowler, and D. Francesch. "Loss of Dopamine Transporters in Methamphetamine Abusers Recovers with Protracted Abstinence." *Journal of Neuroscience* 21 (2001): 9414–9418.

Volkow, N., and J. Swanson. "Does Childhood Treatment of ADHD with Stimulant Medication Affect Substance Abuse in Adulthood?" *American Journal of Psychiatry* 165 (2008): 553–555.

Wang, G., N. Volkow, P. Thanos, and J. Fowler. "Similarity Between Obesity and Drug Addiction As Assessed by Neurofunctional Imaging: A Concept Review." *Journal of Addiction Disease* 23 (2004): 39–53.

Washington Times. "Yet Another Warning Against Ephedra." (5 February 2003): A-5.

WD. "Methamphetamine Withdrawal." Wrong Diagnosis. 17 November 2010. Available http://www.wrongdiagnosis.com/m/methamphetamine_withdrawal/intro.htm

Weiner, T. "9 Linked to Drug War Found Slain Outside Mexican Border City." *New York Times* (3 April 2003): A-5.

Wheeler, R. "Hooked on Caffeine?" Everyday Health. 2010. Available http://www.everydayhealth.com/addiction/hooked-on-caffeine.aspx

Winkel, B. "Real Crack Babies." Treatment Solutions Network, Connections for Recovery. 25 October 2010. Available http://www.treatmentsolutionsnetwork.com/blog/index.php/2010/10/25/real-crack-babies

Women's Health Weekly. "Bad Behavior in Kids Is Not Linked to Prenatal Cocaine Exposure." 22 May 2006. Available http://www.newsrx.com/newsletters/Women's-Health-Weekly12006-05-221/05222006333122ww.html

Woolverton, W., and K. Johnston. "Neurobiology of Cocaine Abuse." *Trends in Pharmacological Sciences* 13 (1992): 193–200.

Wu, P., X. Liu, T. Pham, J. Jin, B. Fan, and Z. Jin. "Ecstasy Use Among US Adolescents from 1999 to 2008." *Drug and Alcohol Dependence* 112 (2010): 33–38.

Wyatt, B. "Agassi Admits Using Crystal Meth." CNN.com. 28 October 2009. Available http://www.cnn.com/2009/SPORT/10/28/tennis.agassi.crystal.meth/index.html

Yui, K., K. Goto, S. Ikemoto, and T. Ishiguro. "Methamphetamine Psychosis: Spontaneous Recurrence of Paranoid-Hallucinating States and Monoamine Neurotransmitter Function." *Journal of Clinical Psychopharmacology* 17 (1997): 34–43.

Zhang, W. "A Benefit–Risk Assessment of Caffeine as an Analgesic Adjuvant." *Drug Safety* 24 (2001): 1127–1142.

Zickler, P. "Methamphetamine, Cocaine Abusers Have Different Patterns of Drug Use, Suffer Different Cognitive Impairments." *NIDA Notes* 16 (December 2001): 11.

Zickler, P. "Cocaine's Effect on Blood Components May Be Linked to Heart Attack and Stroke." *NIDA Notes* 17 (2002): 5.

CHAPTER 11

Tobacco

Did You Know?

- ○ Approximately 27.7% of the U.S. population age 12 or older reports current (past month) use of a tobacco product.
- ○ Tobacco use is the leading preventable cause of death in the United States.
- ○ Tobacco kills approximately 443,000 U.S. citizens each year.
- ○ Nicotine is one of thousands of chemicals found in cigarette smoke.
- ○ Nearly 4000 young people in the United States will begin smoking today.
- ○ Several smoking cessation aids are available, including nicotine gum, patches, nasal spray, and inhalers. In addition, newer prescription drugs are now used to help with smoking cessation.

Learning ◎bjectives

On completing this chapter you will be able to:

- ◎ Describe the social and economic costs of smoking in the United States.
- ◎ Describe the history of tobacco use.
- ◎ Explain how the quality of leaf tobacco has changed since the mid-1950s.
- ◎ Describe the pharmacological effects of nicotine.
- ◎ List several disease states caused by cigarette smoking.
- ◎ Explain the consequences of environmental tobacco smoke on nonsmokers.
- ◎ List several reasons individuals smoke.
- ◎ List several strategies that aid in smoking cessation.

Drugs and Society Online is a great source for additional drugs and society information for both students and instructors. Visit **go.jblearning.com/hanson11** to find a variety of useful tools for learning, thinking, and teaching.

Tobacco Use: Scope of the Problem

Tobacco use is the leading preventable cause of death in the United States, accounting for an estimated 443,000 deaths per year (Centers for Disease Control and Prevention [CDC] 2010c). Another 8.6 million have a serious illness caused by smoking (CDC 2010l, 2010m). The impact of nicotine addiction in terms of morbidity, mortality, and economic costs to society is staggering. Tobacco use results in an annual cost of $96 billion in medical expenditures and another $97 billion from lost productivity (CDC 2010b). The total economic costs (direct medical and lost productivity) associated with cigarette smoking are estimated at $10.47 per pack of cigarettes sold in the United States (CDC 2010b; 2010i). These high costs will likely continue and increase in the future because it is estimated that each day, nearly approximately 3450 people younger than age 18 start smoking, and an estimated 850 become daily smokers (CDC 2010n).

Although much of this chapter deals with tobacco use in the United States, it is noteworthy that tobacco is used throughout the world and that markets for tobacco sales abroad have expanded in recent years. "Tobacco is the single largest cause of preventable death and a risk factor for 6/8 of the leading causes of death" (World Health Organization [WHO] 2010). The World Health Organization (WHO) estimates that tobacco kills 4.9 million people each year. By about 2020, if current smoking trends continue, that number will double.

■ Current Tobacco Use in the United States

In 2009, 69.7 million Americans, or 27.7% of the population age 12 or older, reported current use of a tobacco product. Among these individuals, 2.1 million smoked tobacco in pipes, 8.6 million used smokeless tobacco, 13.3 million smoked cigars, and 58.7 million smoked cigarettes (Substance Abuse and Mental Health Services Administration [SAMHSA] 2010). Approximately 33.5% of males and 22.2% of females age 12 or older were current users of any tobacco product (SAMHSA 2010).

The rate of past-month tobacco use among 12- to 17-year-olds remained steady from 2008 to 2009 (11.4% and 11.6%, respectively). The rate of past-

The WHO estimates that by 2020 tobacco will kill 10 million people per year worldwide. Early exposure increases the chance that young people will become regular adult smokers.

month cigarette use among 12- to 17-year-olds also remained steady between 2008 and 2009 (9.1% and 8.9%, respectively) but declined from 2002 when the rate was 13.0%. However, past-month smokeless tobacco use among youths increased from 2.0% in 2002 to 2.3% in 2009 (SAMHSA 2010).

Past-month tobacco use among individuals age 12 or older by U.S. region is as follows: approximately 25.7% of the population in the Midwest region, 24.5% in the South region, 20.3% in the West region, and 21.9% in the Northeast region. Level of educational attainment was also correlated with tobacco usage: 35.4% of adults age 18 or older who did not complete high school smoked cigarettes, whereas only 13.1% of college graduates smoked (SAMHSA 2010).

More than 345 billion cigarettes were purchased in the United States in 2008, with three companies responsible for 85% of sales: Philip Morris, Reynolds American, Inc., and Lorillard (CDC 2010b).

Several investigators have suggested that tobacco can serve as a gateway drug. In other words, its use may lead to the use of other drugs. Although this possibility remains controversial, it is noteworthy that research indicates that cigarette smokers are more likely to use illicit drugs than are nonsmokers (SAMHSA 2010). For example, in 2009, among persons age 12 or older, 22.4% of past-month cigarette smokers reported concurrent use of an illicit drug, compared with 4.5% of persons who were not current cigarette smokers (SAMHSA 2009). Past-month alcohol use was reported by 67.1% of current cigarette smokers, compared with 47.2% of those who did not use cigarettes in the past month. The association also was found with binge drinking

(44.8% of current cigarette users vs. 17.2% of current nonusers) and heavy drinking (16.4% vs. 3.9%, respectively).

Cigarette Smoking: A Costly Addiction

The past 25 years have been marked by a steady decline in cigarette consumption. Still, an estimated 58.7 million Americans age 12 or older smoke cigarettes (SAMHSA 2010), even though this single behavior will result in death or disability for many of its users.

As noted earlier, tobacco use is responsible for approximately 443,000 deaths each year in the United States (CDC 2010c). This includes approximately 126,000 deaths from ischemic heart disease, 128,900 deaths from lung cancer, 35,300 deaths from other forms of cancer, 92,900 deaths from chronic pulmonary obstructive disease, 15,900 deaths from stroke, and approximately 44,000 deaths from other diagnoses (CDC 2010m) (see **Figure 11.1**). In fact, cigarette smoking is the leading preventable cause of death in the United States (CDC 2010c). More deaths are caused each year by tobacco use than by HIV, illegal drug use, murders, alcohol use, suicides, and motor vehicle injuries combined (CDC 2009c).

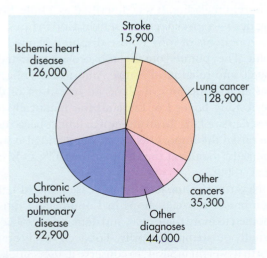

FIGURE 11.1

Annual deaths attributable to cigarette smoking: 2000–2004.

Source: Centers for Disease Control and Prevention (CDC). "Tobacco Use: Targeting the Nation's Leading Killer: At a Glance 2010." 2011. Available at: http://www.cdc.gov/chronicdisease/resources/publications/AAG/osh.htm. Accessed March 16, 2011.

Overall mortality rates decline the longer ex-smokers abstain from smoking. The mortality rate for ex-smokers is related to the number of cigarettes they used to smoke per day and the age at which they started to smoke. People who stop smoking at approximately age 30 reduce their risk of dying from smoking-related diseases by more than 90%. Those who quit at approximately age 50 reduce their risk of dying prematurely by 50% (National Cancer Institute [NCI] 2010a).

The History of Tobacco Use

Like alcohol, tobacco has a long history of use in the Americas and is indigenous to the United States. In fact, tobacco was one of the New World's contributions to the rest of humanity. The word *tobacco* may have come from *tabacco*, which was a two-pronged tube used by the natives of Central America to take snuff. Columbus reported receiving tobacco leaves from the natives of San Salvador in 1492. However, the native peoples had been smoking the leaves for many centuries before Columbus arrived. Practically all native people—from Paraguay to Quebec—used tobacco. The Mayans regarded tobacco smoke as divine incense that would bring rain in the dry season. The oldest known representation of a smoker is a stone carving from a Mayan temple, which shows a priest puffing on a ceremonial pipe. The Aztecs used tobacco in folk medicine and religious ritual.

Indeed, Native Americans used tobacco in every manner known: smoked as cigars and cigarettes (wrapped in corn husks) and in pipes; as a syrup to be swallowed or applied to the gums; chewed and snuffed; and administered rectally as a ceremonial enema (O'Brien et al. 1992; Schultes 1978).

In the 1600s, Turkey, Russia, and China all imposed death penalties for smoking. In Turkey, smoking was introduced in the 1600s, spread in popularity, and instantly created two camps. On the one hand, poets praised tobacco as one of four elements of the world of pleasure that also included opium, coffee, and wine. On the other hand, priests were violently opposed to this substance. They created the legend that tobacco grew from Mohammed's spittle after he was bitten by a viper, sucked out the venom, and spat.

Murad (Amurath) IV, known as Murad the Cruel, who reigned during 1623–1640, executed many of his subjects caught smoking.

Whenever the Sultan went on his travels or on a military expedition, his halting-places were always distinguished by a terrible increase in the number of executions. Even on the battlefield, he was fond of surprising men in the act of smoking . . . he would punish them by beheading, hanging, quartering, or crushing their hands and feet and leaving them helpless between the lines. . . . Nevertheless, in spite of all the horrors of this lust [smoking] that seemed to increase with age, the passion for smoking still persisted. . . . Even the fear of death was of no avail with the passionate devotees of the habit. (Corti 1931)

The Romanov tsars publicly tortured smokers and exiled them to Siberia. The Chinese decapitated anyone caught dealing in tobacco with the "outer barbarians." Yet smoking continued to grow to epidemic proportions. Despite their opposition to anything foreign, the Chinese became the heaviest smokers in Asia, thus facilitating the later spread of opium smoking. Thus, no nation whose population has learned to use tobacco products has been successful in outlawing use or getting people to stop.

Snuffing first became fashionable in France during the reign of Louis XIII and spread throughout the European aristocracy. Snuffing was regarded as daintier and more elegant than constantly exhaling smoke. King Louis XIV, however, detested all forms of tobacco and would not permit its use in his presence. (He would have banned it, but he needed the tax revenue that tobacco brought in.) His sister-in-law, Charlotte of Orleans, was one of the few at court who agreed with him. As she wrote to her sister, "It is better to take no snuff at all than a little; for it is certain that he who takes a little will soon take much, and that is why they call it 'the enchanted herb,' for those who take it are so taken by it that they cannot go without it." Napoleon is said to have used 7 pounds of snuff per month (Corti 1931).

■ Popularity in the Western World

When tobacco reached Europe, it was at first merely a curiosity, but its use spread rapidly. Europeans had no name for the process of inhaling smoke, so they called this "drinking" smoke. Perhaps the first European to inhale tobacco smoke was Rodrig de Jerez, a member of Columbus's crew. He had seen people smoking in Cuba and brought the habit to Portugal. When he smoked in Portugal, his friends, seeing smoke coming from his mouth, believed he was possessed by the devil. As a result, he was placed in jail for several years (Heimann 1960; O'Brien et al. 1992).

In 1559, the French ambassador to Portugal, Jean Nicot, grew interested in this novel plant and sent one as a gift to Catherine de Medici, Queen of France. The plant was named *Nicotiana tabacum* after him.

The next several hundred years saw a remarkable increase in the use of tobacco. Portuguese sailors smoked it and left tobacco seeds scattered around the world. Over the next 150 years, the Portuguese introduced tobacco to trade with India, Brazil, Japan, China, Arabia, and Africa. Many large tobacco plantations around the world were started by the Portuguese at this time.

An early Christian religious leader, Bishop Bartolome de las Casas (1474–1566), reported that Spanish settlers in Hispaniola (Haiti) smoked rolled tobacco leaves in cigar form like the natives. When the bishop asked about this disgusting habit, the settlers replied that they found it impossible to give up.

As the use of tobacco spread, so did the controversy about whether it was bad or good. Tobacco use inspired the first major drug controversy of global dimensions. As a medicine, tobacco was at first almost universally accepted. Nicholas Monardes, in his description of New World plants (dated 1574), recommended tobacco as an infallible cure for 36 different maladies. It was described as a holy, healing herb—a special remedy sent by God to humans.

Opponents of tobacco use disputed its medical value. They pointed out that tobacco was used in the magic and religion of Native Americans. Tobacco was attacked as an evil plant, an invention of the devil. King James I of England was fanatically opposed to smoking. In an attempt to limit tobacco use, he raised the import tax on tobacco and also sold the right to collect the tax (Austin 1978; O'Brien et al. 1992).

Nevertheless, tobacco use increased. By 1614, the number of tobacco shops in London had mushroomed to more than 7000, and demand for tobacco usually outstripped supply. Tobacco was literally worth its weight in silver; to conserve it, users smoked it in pipes with very small bowls. Use of tobacco grew in other areas of the world as well.

In 1642, Pope Urban VIII issued a formal decree forbidding the use of tobacco in church under penalty of immediate excommunication. This decree was in response to the fact that priests and worshippers had been staining church floors with tobacco juice. One priest in Naples sneezed so hard after taking snuff that he vomited on the altar in full sight of the congregation. In response, Pope Innocent X issued another edict against tobacco use in 1650, but the clergy and the laity continued to take snuff and smoke. Finally, in 1725, Pope Benedict XIII, himself a smoker and "snuff-taker," annulled all previous edicts against tobacco (Austin 1978).

History of Tobacco Use in America

Tobacco played a significant role in the successful colonization of the United States (Langton 1991). In 1610, John Rolfe was sent to Virginia to set up a tobacco industry. At first, the tobacco planted in Virginia was a native species, *Nicotiana rustica,* that was harsh and did not sell well. But in 1612, Rolfe managed to obtain some seeds of the Spanish tobacco species *Nicotiana tabacum,* and, by 1613, the success of the tobacco industry and the Virginia colony was ensured.

The history of tobacco smoking in the United States is rich in terms of the tremendous number of laws, rules, regulations, and customs that have arisen around the habit of smoking. Many states have had laws prohibiting the use of tobacco by young people as well as women of any age. In the 1860s, for instance, it was illegal in Florida for anyone younger than the age of 21 to smoke cigarettes. A 20-year-old caught smoking could be taken to court and compelled to reveal his source (the cigarette "pusher"). In Pennsylvania, as in South Carolina, any child not informing on his or her cigarette supplier was a criminal.

Use of spittoons (on floor at ends of table) was considered a preferment in public conduct.

Cigars became popular in the United States in the early 1800s. Cigar manufacturers fought the introduction of cigarettes for many years. They spread rumors that cigarettes contained opium, were made with tobacco from discarded cigar butts, were made with paper made by Chinese lepers, and so on. By about 1920, however, cigarette consumption started to exceed that of cigars. The introduction of the cigarette-rolling machine in 1883 spurred cigarette consumption because cigarettes became cheaper than cigars. By 1885, 1 billion cigarettes per year were being produced. Americans produced more than 709.7 billion cigarettes in 1990 (CDC 2009a). More recent estimates show that the number of cigarettes manufactured in the United States fell to 471.6 billion in 2007 (CDC 2009a).

Tobacco Production

Although there are more than 60 species of plants, *Nicotiana tabacum* is the primary species of tobacco cultivated in the United States. Its mature leaves are 1 to 2.5 feet long. The nicotine content ranges from 0.3% to 7%, depending on the variety, leaf position on the stalk (the higher the position, the more nicotine), and growing conditions.

After harvesting and drying, tobacco leaves are shredded, blown clean of foreign matter and stems, remoisturized with glycerine or other chemical agents, and packed in huge tobacco silos. The tobacco is stored for 1 to 2 years to age, during which time the tobacco becomes darker and loses moisture, nicotine, and other volatile substances. When aging has been completed, moisture is again added and the tobacco is blended with other varieties.

There are many types of tobacco, with varying characteristics of harshness, mildness, and flavor. Bright, also called flue-cured or Virginia, has traditionally been among the most common type used in cigarettes. (Flue-cured tobacco is cured with heat transmitted through a flue without exposure to smoke or fumes.) Developed just before the Civil War, this technique made tobacco smoke more readily inhalable.

The amount of leaf tobacco in a cigarette has declined since 1956. There are at least two reasons for this drop. The first reason is the use of reconstituted sheets of tobacco. Parts of the tobacco leaves and stems that were discarded in earlier years are now ground up, combined with many other ingredients to control factors such as moisture, flavor, and color, and then rolled out as a flat, homogenized sheet of reconstituted tobacco. This sheet is shredded and mixed with regular leaf tobacco, thus reducing production costs. Nearly one-fourth of the tobacco in a cigarette comes from tobacco scraps made into reconstituted sheets. (See "Here and Now: What Is in Tobacco Smoke?")

A second technological advance has further reduced the amount of tobacco needed. This process, called puffing, is based on freeze-drying the tobacco and then blowing air or an inert gas, such as carbon dioxide, into it. The gas expands, or puffs up, the plant cells so they take up more space, are lighter, and can absorb additives better. Additives may include extracts of tobacco, as well as nontobacco flavors such as licorice, cocoa, fruit, spices, and floral compositions. (Licorice was first used in tobacco as a preservative around 1830 and became appreciated only later as a sweetener.) Synthetic flavoring compounds also may be used.

In the 1870s, a "cigarette girl" could roll about four cigarettes per minute by hand. When James Duke leased and improved the first cigarette-rolling machine in 1883, he could make about 200 cigarettes per minute. This advance was the last link in the chain of development leading to the modern American blended cigarette. Today's machines make more than 3600 uniform cigarettes per minute.

Tar and nicotine levels in cigarettes have dropped considerably over the past 40 years (Bartecchi, MacKenzie, and Shrier 1995; Palfai and Jankiewicz 1991). Most cigarettes today are low-tar and low-nicotine types. The filter tip, in which the filter is made of cellulose or in some cases charcoal, has also become common; the vast majority of all cigarettes sold currently in the United States have filter tips. The filter does help remove some of the harmful substances in smoke, but most, such as carbon monoxide, pass through into the mouth and lungs. The health consequences of many more substances found in cigarettes have not been adequately analyzed.

In 2006, domestic cigarette consumption was 372 billion pieces, 4 billion less than the previous year (CDC 2009a). Declines in sales have been attributed to health concerns, aggressive antismoking campaigns, price increases, and decreased social acceptance of smoking. **Figure 11.2** shows the relationship between smoking rates and major smoking and health events.

■ Government Regulation

In the early 1960s, attitudes toward tobacco use began to change in the United States. Before this time, tobacco was perceived as being devoid of any negative consequences. After years of study and hundreds of research reports about the effects of smoking, the Advisory Committee to the U.S. Surgeon General reported in 1964 that cigarette smoking is a cause of lung cancer and laryngeal cancer in men, a probable cause of lung cancer in women, and the most important cause of chronic bronchitis. The committee stated, "cigarette smoking is a health hazard of sufficient importance in the United States to warrant appropriate remedial action." In 1965, Congress passed legislation setting up the National Clearinghouse for Smoking and Health. This organization has the responsibility of monitoring, compiling, and reviewing the world's medical literature on the health consequences of smoking.

This clearinghouse published reports in 1967, 1968, and 1969. The statistical evidence presented in 1969 made it difficult for Congress to avoid warning the public that smoking was dangerous to their health. Since November 1, 1970, all cigarette packages and cartons have had to carry this label: "Warning: The Surgeon General Has Determined That Cigarette Smoking Is Dangerous to Your Health." In 1984, Congress enacted legislation requiring cigarette advertisements and packages to post four distinct warnings (see **Figure 11.3**), which are to be rotated every 3 months.

Further pressure on Congress prompted laws to be passed that prohibited advertising tobacco on

Here and Now

What Is in Tobacco Smoke?

Tobacco smoke contains chemicals that are harmful to smokers and nonsmokers alike. Of the 4000 chemicals in tobacco smoke, at least 250 are known to be harmful, including hydrogen cyanide, ammonia, and carbon monoxide. Among these 250 harmful chemicals, greater than 50 have been found to be carcinogens. These carcinogens include arsenic, benzene, ethylene oxide, and vinyl chloride. Other suspected carcinogens in tobacco include formaldehyde, benzo[α]pyrene, and toluene.

Source: National Cancer Institute (NCI). "Harms of Smoking and Health Benefits of Quitting." 2010. Available at: http://www.cancer.gov/cancertopics/factsheet/Tobacco/cessation. Accessed March 29, 2011.

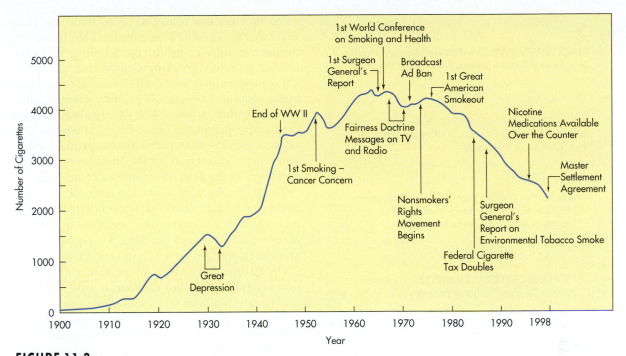

FIGURE 11.2

Annual adult per capita cigarette consumption and major smoking and health events, United States: 1900–1998.

Sources: U.S. Department of Agriculture (USDA), Economic Research Service. "Trends in the Cigarette Industry After the Master Settlement Agreement." 2001. Available at: http://www.ers.usda.gov/Publications/TBS/Oct01/TBS250-01. Accessed March 29, 2011; and Surgeon General's Report. "The Health Consequences of Involuntary Smoking." 1986. Available at: http://profiles.nlm.nih.gov/ps/access/NNBCPM.pdf. Accessed March 29, 2011.

radio and television after January 2, 1971. The intent was to limit the media's ability to make smoking seem glamorous and sophisticated. The loss in revenue to radio and television was enormous.

The 1979 publication *Smoking and Health: A Report of the Surgeon General* gave what was then up-to-date information on research about the effects of tobacco on cardiovascular disease, bronchopulmonary disease, cancer, peptic ulcer, and pregnancy. It also emphasized the increase in smoking by women and girls over the preceding 15 years. The 1981 U.S. Surgeon General's report, *The Changing Cigarette,* gave further information, and the 1985 report, *The Health Consequences of Smoking,* gave research findings showing the relationship of smoking, cancer, and chronic lung disease in the workplace.

Over the years, private insurance companies, as well as state and federal agencies, have paid billions of dollars to cover healthcare costs presumably resulting from diseases caused by tobacco use. A series of lawsuits have forced large tobacco companies to compensate for some of these losses. In a landmark settlement in 1998, 47 states reached an agreement with five major tobacco companies to pay a settlement estimated at exceeding $200 billion. Important features of this "Master Settlement Agreement" include:

- Limitations on advertising
- Ban on cartoon characters in advertising
- Ban on "branded" merchandise
- Limitations on sponsorship of sporting events
- Disbanding of tobacco trade organizations
- Funds designated to support antismoking measures and research to reduce youth smoking (U.S. Department of Agriculture [USDA] 2001)

All 50 states have enacted laws that restrict the purchase, possession, or use of tobacco products by minors. Although no state has completely banned the sale of tobacco products through vending machines, none allow such sales to minors. In fact, many states have created additional restrictions intended to reduce youth access to vending machines. Some have banned the placement of vending machines in areas accessible to young people and allow their placement only in bars, liquor stores, adult clubs, and other adult-oriented establishments.

Since 1985, numerous other reports on smoking and health by the U.S. Surgeon General have been issued; they invariably repeat the assertions about

SURGEON GENERAL'S WARNING: Quitting Smoking Now Greatly Reduces Serious Risks to Your Health.

SURGEON GENERAL'S WARNING: Smoking Causes Lung Cancer, Heart Disease, Emphysema, and May Complicate Pregnancy.

SURGEON GENERAL'S WARNING: Smoking by Pregnant Women May Result in Fetal Injury, Premature Birth, and Low Birth Weight.

SURGEON GENERAL'S WARNING: Cigarette Smoke Contains Carbon Monoxide.

FIGURE 11.3

Warnings on cigarette labels. Four warnings must be rotated on cigarette packages. The messages are based on the report of the U.S. Surgeon General, *The Health Consequences of Smoking* (1985), and they went into effect on October 12, 1985.

the devastating effects of cigarette smoking. For a historical summation of the developments between cigarette consumption and efforts to diminish cigarette use, see Figure 11.2. A summary of federal policy and legislation regarding the regulation of tobacco sales, marketing, and use is provided in **Table 11.1**.

In June 2009, President Barack Obama signed legislation that granted the FDA the authority to regulate tobacco products. This law, the Family Smoking Prevention and Tobacco Control Act (FSPTCA), put special emphasis on youth (CDC 2010d, 2010k; FDA 2010a, 2010b, 2010c, 2010d, 2010e) because research indicates that most tobacco users become addicted at a young age and

when they are too young to understand the risks (FDA 2009). The FSPTCA gave the FDA broad authority over tobacco products, including the ability to: (1) establish good manufacturing practices; (2) set and enforce standards for tobacco product ingredients and design; (3) institute product labeling and health warnings; and (4) regulate the marketing and promotion of tobacco products. The act also requires FDA premarket approval for certain new products and for the industry to provide reporting to the FDA on a number of subjects.

The term *tobacco product* means any product made or derived from tobacco that is intended for human consumption, including any component, part, or accessory of a tobacco product. This includes cigarettes, cigarette tobacco, and smokeless tobacco (FDA 2010c). According to the FDA (2009), the primary goal of regulating tobacco products is "to use the best available science to guide the development and implementation of effective public health strategies to reduce the burden of illness and death caused by tobacco products." As a consequence of its charge to regulate, the FDA has:

- Established the Center for Tobacco Products
- Convened a Tobacco Products Scientific Advisory Committee that has begun to study the impact of the use of menthol in cigarettes on the public health
- Begun to enforce the prohibition described in the act on manufacturing, distributing, or selling certain flavored cigarettes, such as spice-, fruit-, and candy-flavored cigarettes
- Implemented new statutory authorities, under which tobacco product manufacturers have registered their establishments and listed their products with the FDA, and provided detailed information about product ingredients and their own research into the health effects of their products
- Established the tobacco user fee program, which provides funding for FDA tobacco regulation support activities (FDA 2010a, 2010f)

Pharmacology of Nicotine

In 1828, **nicotine** was discovered to be one component of tobacco. This colorless, highly volatile liquid alkaloid is one of more than 4000 chemicals found in the smoke from tobacco products such as cigarettes (National Institute on Drug Abuse [NIDA] 2010). When smoked, nicotine enters the lungs and is then absorbed into the bloodstream. When chewed (**tobacco chewing**) or dipped (**snuff dipping**),

KEY TERMS

nicotine
a colorless, highly volatile liquid alkaloid

tobacco chewing
the absorption of nicotine through the mucous lining of the mouth

snuff dipping
placing a pinch of tobacco between the gums and the cheek

Table 11.1 Federal Policy and Legislation: Selected Actions of the United States

YEAR	ACTION(S)
1967	Federal Communications Commission rules that the Fairness Doctrine (an attempt to ensure that all coverage of controversial issues by a broadcast station be balanced and fair) applies to cigarette advertising. Stations broadcasting cigarette commercials must donate airtime to antismoking messages.
1971	Fairness Doctrine antismoking messages end when cigarette advertising is prohibited on radio and television.
1973	Civil Aeronautics Board requires no-smoking sections on all commercial airline flights.
1975	Cigarettes are discontinued in K-rations and C-rations given to soldiers and sailors.
1987	Department of Health and Human Services establishes a smoke-free environment in its facilities.
1992	Federal Trade Commission takes first enforcement action under the Comprehensive Smokeless Tobacco Health Education Act, alleging that Pinkerton Tobacco Company's Red Man brand name appeared illegally during a televised event.
1993	Environmental Protection Agency releases final risk assessment on environmental tobacco smoke (ETS) and classifies ETS as a Group A (known human) carcinogen.
1994	Occupational Safety and Health Administration announces proposed regulation to prohibit smoking in the workplace, except in separately ventilated smoking rooms. Department of Defense (DOD) bans smoking in DOD workplaces.
1995	Department of Justice reaches a settlement with Philip Morris to remove tobacco advertisements from the line of sight of television cameras in sports stadiums. President Clinton announces the publication of the Food and Drug Administration's proposed regulations that would restrict the sale, distribution, and marketing of cigarettes and smokeless tobacco products to protect children and adolescents.
1996	On August 23, 1996, President Clinton announces the nation's first comprehensive program to prevent children and adolescents from smoking cigarettes or using smokeless tobacco and beginning a lifetime of nicotine addiction. With the August 1996 publication of a final rule on tobacco in the *Federal Register*, the Food and Drug Administration (FDA) will regulate the sale and distribution of cigarettes and smokeless tobacco to children and adolescents. The provisions of the FDA rule are aimed at reducing youth access to tobacco products and the appeal of tobacco advertising to young people. Additionally, the FDA will propose to require the major tobacco companies to educate young people about the real health dangers associated with tobacco use through a multimedia campaign.
1997	President Clinton announces an Executive Order to make all federal workplaces smoke free.
2000	The Supreme Court rules against the Food and Drug Administration, finding that the agency lacks the authority to regulate tobacco.
2009	President Obama signs into law the Family Smoking Prevention and Tobacco Control Act.

Source: Modified from Centers of Disease Control and Prevention (CDC). "Selected Actions of the U.S. Government Regarding the Regulation of Tobacco Sales, Marketing, and Use (excluding laws pertaining to agriculture or excise tax)." 2009. Available at: http://www.cdc.gov/tobacco/data_statistics/by_topic/policy/regulation/index.htm. Accessed March 16, 2011.

nicotine is absorbed through the mucous lining of the mouth.

The amount of nicotine absorbed into the body varies according to several factors:

- The exact composition of the tobacco used
- How densely the tobacco is packed in the cigarette and the length of the cigarette smoked
- Whether a filter is used and the characteristics of the filter
- The volume of smoke inhaled
- The number of cigarettes smoked throughout the day

Depending on how tobacco is taken, the rate at which it enters the bloodstream varies widely. Cigarette smoking results in rapid distribution of nicotine throughout the body; it reaches the brain within 10 seconds of inhalation. A typical smoker will take 10 puffs on a cigarette during the 5 minutes that the cigarette is lit. Thus, a person who smokes 1½ packs (30 cigarettes) each day gets 300 "hits" of nicotine to the brain each day (NIDA 2009). In contrast, cigar and pipe smokers typically do not inhale the smoke; nicotine is absorbed more slowly through the lining of the mouth.

■ Effects of Nicotine on the Central Nervous System

Nicotine produces an intense effect on the central nervous system. Research has demonstrated that nicotine activates the brain circuitry in regions responsible for regulating feelings of pleasure. In particular, nicotine increases the release of the neurotransmitter dopamine in the so-called reward or pleasure pathways of the brain. This effect likely contributes to the abuse potential of the stimulant.

The pharmacokinetic properties of nicotine also enhance its abuse potential. Cigarette smoking allows nicotine to enter the brain rapidly, with drug levels peaking within 10 seconds of inhalation. The acute effects of this rapid increase in brain concentration dissipate within a few minutes, causing the smoker to continue to dose frequently throughout the day in an effort to maintain the pleasurable effects of the drug.

■ Other Effects of Nicotine

In addition to its direct effects in the brain, nicotine increases the respiration rate at low dose levels because it stimulates the receptors in the carotid artery (in the neck) that monitor the brain's need for oxygen. It also stimulates the cardiovascular system by releasing epinephrine, which increases coronary blood flow, heart rate, and blood pressure. The effect is to raise the oxygen requirements of the heart muscle. Initially, nicotine stimulates salivary and bronchial secretions; it then inhibits them.

Nicotine has been used as an insecticide, and at higher concentrations it can be extremely toxic. Symptoms of nicotine poisoning include sweating, vomiting, mental confusion, diarrhea, and breathing difficulty. Respiratory failure from the paralysis of muscles usually brings on death. The fatal dose for adults is 60 milligrams. Most cigarettes in the U.S. market today contain 10 milligrams or more of nicotine; through smoke, the average smoker takes in 1 to 2 milligrams of nicotine from every cigarette (NIDA 2009). It is virtually impossible to overdose, in part because a smoker feels the effects before any lethal amount can accumulate in the body (Schelling 1992).

Cigarette Smoking

Cigarette smokers not only tend to die at an earlier age than nonsmokers, but also have a higher probability of developing certain diseases, including cardiovascular disease, cancer, bronchopulmonary disease, and other illnesses, which are described in the following sections.

■ Cardiovascular Disease

Overwhelming evidence shows that cigarette smoking increases the risk of cardiovascular disease. Smoking causes coronary heart disease, the leading cause of death in the United States. In fact, compared with nonsmokers, smoking increases the risk of coronary heart disease two to four times (CDC 2009c). Cigarette smoking also causes aneurysm (a swelling and/or weakening) of the abdominal aorta (a major artery in the body). Smoking also causes reduced circulation, thus putting smokers at greater risk for developing peripheral artery disease (CDC 2009c). Women who smoke double their risk of developing coronary artery disease (CDC 2009h).

■ Cancer

Cigarette smoking is a major cause of cancers of the lung, bladder, pancreas, cervix, esophagus, stom-

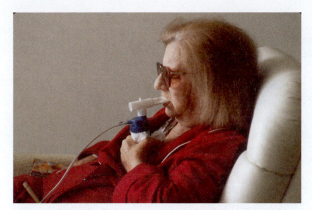

Cigarette smoking is a leading cause of bronchopulmonary disease.

ach, oral cavity, and kidney (CDC 2009c). The risk of cancer increases according to the number of cigarettes smoked each day, the number of years a person has smoked, and the age at which smoking began. For example, the risk of lung cancer in men who smoke two or more packs per day is 23 times greater than the risk for nonsmokers; the risk for women smokers is approximately 13 times greater than for nonsmokers (CDC 2009c).

Bronchopulmonary Disease

Cigarette smoking is the leading cause of bronchopulmonary disease, which includes a host of lung ailments. Cigarette damages the airways and alveoli (small air sacs in the lungs), and causes emphysema and chronic airway obstruction (CDC 2009c). Respiratory infections are more prevalent and more severe among cigarette smokers—particularly heavy smokers—than among nonsmokers.

Effects on Pregnancy

Cigarette smoking has several harmful effects besides those described above, particularly for pregnant women, including increased risk for stillbirth, preterm delivery, low birth weight, and sudden infant death syndrome (CDC 2009c, 2009e). Further, the nicotine found in cigarettes may: (1) reduce the amount of blood in the fetal cardiovascular system and (2) cause constrictions in the blood vessels of the umbilical cord and uterus, thereby decreasing the amount of oxygen available to the fetus (CDC 2004). Of note, approximately 13% of women report having smoked during their final 3 months of pregnancy (CDC 2009f).

"Light" Cigarettes

There is no conclusive evidence of reduced health risks associated with low-tar cigarettes. Filtered cigarettes (i.e., those with small holes or perforations that dilute the smoke with air) reduce levels of tar, nicotine, and carbon monoxide at the mouth end of the filter and should be of some limited benefit. However, many smokers lose this benefit because they often smoke more cigarettes per day, increase puff number and volume, or block the filter holes with their fingers or lips (NCI 2010a) (see "Here and Now: The Truth About Light Cigarettes").

Electronic Cigarettes

Electronic cigarettes (e-cigarettes) are devices designed to deliver nicotine or other substances to a user as a vapor. These products often resemble cigarettes, cigars, or pipes. For individuals who desire to use e-cigarettes without others noticing, some devices are designed to look like pens. E-cigarettes are generally composed of a rechargeable, battery-operated heating element, a replaceable cartridge that may contain nicotine (or other chemicals), and an atomizer that, when heated, converts the cartridge into a vapor. The user can then inhale the vapor (FDA 2010c).

The FDA has not evaluated e-cigarettes for effectiveness or safety. However, in limited laboratory studies of certain samples, the FDA found significant quality issues that indicate that quality control processes used to manufacture these products might be substandard or nonexistent. Experts have also raised concerns that the marketing of products such as e-cigarettes may lead young people to try other tobacco products and may increase nicotine addiction among young people (FDA 2010c).

Tobacco Use and Exposure Without Smoking

Smokeless Tobacco

Although it is customary to associate the effects of tobacco use with smoking, in fact millions of nonsmokers experience tobacco effects through their use of smokeless tobacco products. Approximately 3.3% of adults age 18 or older use smokeless tobacco currently. This represents 6.5% of men and 0.4% of women (CDC 2009d).

Here and Now

The Truth About Light Cigarettes

Many smokers choose low-tar, mild, or light cigarettes because they believe that these cigarettes may be less harmful to their health than regular or full-flavor cigarettes. Unfortunately, light cigarettes do not reduce the health risks of smoking. The only way to reduce risk to oneself and others is to stop smoking completely. Common questions and answers pertaining to low-tar, mild, or light cigarettes follow.

What About the Lower Tar and Nicotine Numbers on Light Cigarette Packs and in Ads for Lights?

These numbers are determined using smoking machines that smoke every brand of cigarettes exactly the same way. These numbers cannot absolutely predict the amount of tar and nicotine a particular smoker may get because people do not smoke cigarettes the same way the machines do, and because no two individuals smoke the same way.

How Do Light Cigarettes Trick the Smoking Machines?

Tobacco companies design light cigarettes with tiny pinholes on the filters. These vents are uncovered when cigarettes are smoked on smoking machines. As a result, these vents dilute cigarette smoke with air when light cigarettes are puffed on by the machines, causing measurements of artificially low tar and nicotine levels. Many smokers do not know that vent holes are on their cigarette filters. Without realizing it and because it is difficult to avoid, many block the tiny vent holes with their fingers or lips—which basically turns the light cigarette into a regular cigarette. Some cigarette makers increased the length of the paper covering the cigarette filter, which decreases the number of puffs that occur during the machine test. The result is that the machine measures less tar and nicotine levels than is available to the smoker.

Because, unlike machines, individuals crave nicotine, they may inhale more deeply; take larger, more rapid, or more frequent puffs; or smoke a few extra cigarettes each day to get enough nicotine to satisfy their craving. This is called compensating, and it results in smokers inhaling more tar, nicotine, and other harmful chemicals than the machine-based numbers suggest.

What Is the Scientific Evidence About the Health Effects of Light Cigarettes?

The National Cancer Institute (NCI) has concluded that light cigarettes provide no benefit to smokers' health. According to its report, those people who switch to light cigarettes from regular cigarettes are likely to inhale the same amount of hazardous chemicals and remain at high risk for developing smoking-related cancers and other diseases.

Have the Tobacco Companies Conducted Research on the Amount of Nicotine and Tar People Actually Inhale While Smoking Light Cigarettes?

The tobacco industry's own documents show that companies were aware that smokers of light cigarettes compensate by taking bigger puffs. Industry documents also show that the companies were aware of the difference between machine-measured yields of tar and nicotine and the amount the smoker actually inhales.

What Is the Bottom Line for Smokers Who Want to Protect Their Health?

There is no such thing as a safe cigarette. The only proven way to reduce your risk of smoking-related disease is to quit smoking completely. Research has shown that people who quit before age 30 eliminate almost all of their risk of developing a tobacco-related disease. Even smokers who quit at age 50 reduce their risk of dying from a tobacco-related disease.

Source: National Cancer Institute (NCI). "'Light' Cigarettes and Cancer Risk." 2010. Available at: http://www.cancer.gov/cancertopics/factsheet/Tobacco/light-cigarettes. Accessed March 16, 2011.

KEY TERMS

chewing tobacco
tobacco leaves shredded and twisted into strands for chewing purposes

snuff
finely ground smokeless tobacco that can be moist or dry

There are two main forms of smokeless tobacco in the United States (CDC 2009d). The first, **chewing tobacco**, comes in the form of loose leaf, a plug, or a twist. The second, **snuff**, is finely ground tobacco that can be moist, dry, or packaged in sachets. Most smokeless tobacco users place the product in their cheek or between their cheek and gum. Users

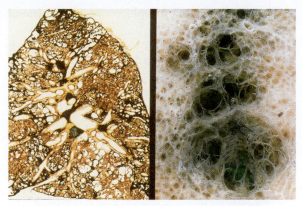

Heavy smoking can severely damage the lungs and cause emphysema. A diseased lung due to smoking (left) and a healthy nonsmoker's lung (right).

suck or chew the tobacco and then spit out the juices. Thus, smokeless tobacco is often called spitting tobacco.

Smokeless tobacco contains powerful chemicals that can injure tissues in the mouth and throat. The following findings have been made regarding smokeless tobacco (CDC 2009d):

- Smokeless tobacco use can lead to nicotine addiction and dependence.
- Adolescents who use smokeless tobacco are more likely to become cigarette smokers.
- Smokeless tobacco contains 28 cancer-causing agents (carcinogens).
- Smokeless tobacco is also strongly associated with leukoplakia—a precancerous lesion of the soft tissue in the mouth that consists of a white patch or plaque that cannot be scraped off.
- Smokeless tobacco increases the risk of developing cancer of the oral cavity and pancreas.
- Smokeless tobacco use during pregnancy increases the risks for preeclampsia (i.e., a condition that may include high blood pressure, fluid retention, and swelling), premature birth, and low birth weight.
- Smokeless tobacco use by men causes reduced sperm count and abnormal sperm cells.
- Smokeless tobacco is associated with recession of the gums, gum disease, and tooth decay.

The popularity of smokeless tobacco is due in part to effective advertising campaigns. During 2006, a record $308 million was spent on moist snuff advertising and promotion (CDC 2010a). Some experts also believe that the increasing popularity of this tobacco product relates to its ability to satisfy the addiction to nicotine where smoking is prohibited. Thus, smokeless tobacco use is perceived as an alternative to smoking in smoke-free environments.

Recently, new smokeless tobacco products have entered the U.S. market. These include snus, a form of moist snuff, and "dissolvable" products such as lozenges, orbs, sticks, and strips. These products can be more appealing than traditional smokeless tobacco products to females and youth because they do not require spitting and can be used discreetly. Further, these products are available in a range of flavors, which research suggests makes products more attractive to youth (CDC 2010a).

Secondhand Smoke

The health of individuals who neither smoke nor chew is also adversely affected by tobacco, specifically, exposure to **secondhand smoke**—also known as **environmental tobacco smoke (ETS)**—that is inhaled by passive nonsmokers. Secondhand smoke includes a mixture of smoke that comes directly from the lighted tip of a cigarette, cigar, or pipe (CDC 2010e). Passive smoking refers to nonsmokers' inhalation of tobacco smoke. Studies of smoking and its effects have directed increased attention to secondhand smoke because smokers and nonsmokers alike breathe in the burning tobacco smoke that pollutes the air. This type of smoke contains at least 250 toxic chemicals, including over 50 carcinogens (CDC 2010e).

Exposure to ETS has serious health consequences. Secondhand smoke exposure causes an estimated 46,000 heart disease deaths annually in the United States (CDC 2009g). Breathing secondhand smoke has immediate harmful effects on the cardiovascular system of nonsmokers that can increase the risk for heart attack. People who currently have heart disease are at especially high risk. Nonsmokers who are exposed to ETS at work or home increase their heart disease risk by 25–30% (CDC 2010e).

In addition to increased risk of cardiovascular disease, secondhand smoke causes significant respiratory problems (CDC 2009g). For example, nonsmokers who are exposed to secondhand smoke at

KEY TERMS

secondhand smoke
smoke released into the air from a lighted cigarette, cigar, or pipe tip and exhaled mainstream smoke

environmental tobacco smoke (ETS)
a term referring to secondhand smoke

work or home increase their lung cancer risk by 20–30%. As a consequence, secondhand smoke exposure causes an estimated 3400 lung cancer deaths annually among adult nonsmokers in the United States (CDC 2010e).

Of note, pregnant women who are exposed to secondhand smoke have a 20% greater chance of giving birth to a low birth weight baby (CDC 2009f). Children who are exposed to secondhand smoke are more likely to develop ear infections, respiratory infections, and more severe and frequent asthma attacks (CDC 2010e).

Reasons for Smoking and the Motivation to Quit

Reasons for Smoking

Nicotine dependency through cigarette smoking is not only one of the most common forms of drug addiction, but also one responsible for numerous deaths. As noted previously, more deaths each year are caused by tobacco use than by HIV, illegal drug use, murders, alcohol use, suicides, and motor vehicle injuries combined (CDC 2009c). Tobacco use continues despite the fact that, since the 1960s, medical research and government assessments have clearly proved that smoking leads to premature death.

If one asks tobacco users why they smoke, their answers are often quite similar:

- It is relaxing.
- It decreases the unpleasant effects of tension, anxiety, and anger.
- It satisfies the craving.
- It is a habit.
- It provides stimulation, increased energy, and arousal.
- It allows the manipulation of objects that have become satisfying habits (the cigarette, pipe, and so on).

In addition,

- Parents and/or siblings smoke.
- A close friend or boyfriend/girlfriend smokes.

Tobacco use fosters dependence for a number of reasons:

- The habit can be rapidly and frequently reinforced by inhaling tobacco smoke.
- The rapid metabolism and clearance of nicotine allows frequent and repeated use, which is

encouraged by the rapid onset of withdrawal symptoms.
- Smoking has complex pharmacological effects—both central and peripheral—that may satisfy a variety of the needs of the smoker.
- Some groups offer psychological and social rewards for use, especially the peer groups of young people.
- Smoking patterns can be generalized; that is, the smoker becomes conditioned to smoke with specific activities. For example, some smokers feel the need to smoke after a meal, when driving, and so on.
- Smoking is reinforced by both pharmacological effects and ritual.
- There is no marked performance impairment. In fact, smoking enhances performance in some cases. (Nicotine produces a state of alertness, prevents deterioration of reaction time, and improves learning.)

These reasons may not only explain why people continue to smoke, but also reveal why it is often difficult for them to stop.

Smokers appear to regulate their intake of nicotine. For example, the smoker of a low-nicotine cigarette often smokes more and inhales more deeply. The average one-pack-a-day smoker is estimated to self-administer thousands of pulses (one pulse per inhalation) of nicotine to nicotinic receptors in the brain per year. This rate greatly surpasses the stimulation rate of any other known form of substance abuse. A habit that is reinforced as frequently and easily as smoking is very hard to break.

Other factors responsible for creating the addiction to nicotine follow:

- Cigarettes are readily available.
- No equipment other than a lighter or match is needed.
- Cigarettes are portable and easy to store.
- Cigarettes are legal for individuals over age 18.
- Other rewarding behaviors can occur while smoking (for example, drinking, socializing, and eating).

Benefits of Cessation

Individuals who stop smoking greatly reduce their risk for disease and premature death. Although the health benefits are greater for people who stop at earlier ages, cessation is beneficial at all ages. For example, smokers who quit at approximately age 30 reduce their risk of premature death from smoking-related diseases by more than 90%. Individuals who quit at approximately age 50 reduce their risk of dying prematurely by 50% compared with those who continue to smoke. Finally, even those who quit at approximately age 60 or older live longer than those who continue to smoke (National Cancer Institute [NCI] 2010a). According to the National Cancer Institute (2010a), immediate health benefits of quitting smoking are significant, and include:

- A return to normalcy of heart rate and blood pressure (which are abnormally high while smoking)
- A decline of carbon monoxide in the blood within hours
- Improved circulation, production of less phlegm, and decreased rate of coughing and sneezing within weeks
- Substantial improvements in lung function within several months

In addition, and according to the CDC (2010g), cessation of smoking is associated with the following health benefits, including reducing:

- The risk for lung and other types of cancer
- The risk for coronary heart disease, stroke, and peripheral vascular disease
- Respiratory symptoms such as coughing, wheezing, and shortness of breath
- The risk of developing chronic obstructive pulmonary disease
- The risk for infertility in women
- The risk of having a low birth weight baby

■ The Motivation to Quit

> Quitting smoking is easy. I've done it a thousand times. —*Mark Twain*

Approximately 70% of adult smokers report that they want to quit smoking, and millions have attempted to do so (CDC 2010g). When habitual smokers stop smoking on their own, without the use of smoking cessation aids, they may experience a variety of unpleasant withdrawal effects, including craving for tobacco, irritability, restlessness, sleep disturbances, gastrointestinal disturbances, anxiety, and impaired concentration, judgment, and psychomotor performance. The onset of nicotine withdrawal symptoms may occur within hours or days after quitting and may persist from a few days to several months. Frustration over these symptoms leads many people to start smoking again. The intensity of withdrawal effects may be mild, moderate, or severe; it is not always correlated with the amount smoked.

The National Cancer Institute (2010b) has several recommendations of alternative activities that ex-smokers might try as aids to handle the cravings associated with quitting and get through the withdrawal period. These include:

- Remind yourself that cravings will pass.
- Avoid situations and activities (like drinking alcohol) that you normally associate with smoking.
- As a substitute for smoking, try chewing on carrots, pickles, sunflower seeds, apples, celery, or sugarless gum or hard candy. Keeping your mouth busy may stop the psychological need to smoke.
- Try this exercise: Take a deep breath through your nose and blow out slowly through your mouth. Repeat 10 times.

Of note, studies in 20 U.S. communities demonstrated that employees who work in environments that implemented smoke-free polices—policies that completely eliminate smoking in indoor public places and work areas (CDC 2010j)—were almost twice as likely to stop smoking that those who worked in settings that permitted smoking everywhere. Further, adolescents who work in smoke-free environments are less likely to become smokers (CDC 2010f).

In addition to behavioral modifications, several pharmacological interventions are available to aid in smoking cessation. These include nicotine replacement therapy (e.g., nicotine gum, patches, lozenges, inhalers, sprays) and agents such as bupropion (Zyban) and varenicline (Chantix).

Nicotine Gum

Nicotine gum can be purchased over the counter without a prescription. Chewing the gum allows the rapid absorption of nicotine through the mucous membranes of the mouth. Users chew the gum until noting a peppery taste, and then hold it against the cheek to permit faster absorption. The user will chew on and off for about 20 to 30 minutes.

Significant advantages afforded by nicotine gum are that it is easy to use and allows the user to control the dose of nicotine by controlling the number of pieces chewed each day. Individuals gradually decrease the number of pieces chewed each day, with a goal of complete abstinence from the drug. Side effects of the gum can include a bad taste, throat irritation, nausea (if the gum is swallowed), jaw discomfort (if chewed too rapidly), and racing heartbeat.

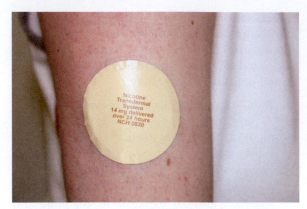

A transdermal patch, an example of a popular therapy for quitting smoking.

Nicotine Patches

Nicotine patches, also known as *transdermal nicotine systems,* are available without a prescription. The patch, which is directly applied and worn on the skin, releases a continuous flow of small doses of nicotine to quell the desire for cigarette-provided nicotine. The method of delivering nicotine to the skin reduces the withdrawal symptoms as the smoker attempts to quit. As the nicotine doses are lowered over a course of weeks, the smoker is weaned away from nicotine. The most common side effects are mild skin irritations such as redness and itching.

Nicotine Nasal Spray, Inhalers, and Lozenges

Nicotine nasal sprays are available by prescription only. This form of administration rapidly delivers nicotine to the bloodstream as it is absorbed through the membranous lining of the nasal passages. It is easy to use and gives immediate relief of withdrawal symptoms. The most common side effects of using the spray include coughing, sinus irritation, runny nose, watery eyes, sneezing, and throat irritation. It is generally not recommended for individuals with asthma, allergies, or other pulmonary problems.

Like nicotine nasal sprays, nicotine inhalers are available only by prescription. The nicotine inhaler is a small plastic tube that contains a nicotine plug. When the user puffs on the inhaler, the plug provides nicotine vapor into the mouth. One advantage to the inhaler is that the action of puffing it mimics some of the behaviors associated with smoking. Side effects associated with its use include coughing and throat irritation. Nicotine lozenges are alternatives to sprays and inhalers. Like nicotine patches and gums, these can be purchased without a prescription.

Varenicline and Bupropion

Varenicline (marketed as Chantix) acts at receptors in the brain affected by nicotine. It provides some nicotine effects to ease withdrawal symptoms and blocks the effects of nicotine from cigarettes if users resume smoking. Its most common side effects include nausea, constipation, flatulence, vomiting, trouble sleeping, and/or vivid, strange dreams. Other serious side effects can include changes in behavior, depressed mood, hostility, and suicidal thoughts or actions. Other symptoms are included in the medication guide for patients.

Bupropion (marketed as Zyban) also helps patients to abstain from smoking; however, the precise means by which it accomplishes this is unknown. Noteworthy, this agent, when marketed as Wellbutrin, is also used as an antidepressant. Its side effects can include dry mouth and insomnia. Other serious potential side effects can include risks of serious psychiatric problems, seizures, high blood pressure, and allergic reactions.

Smoking Prohibition Versus Smokers' Rights

In response to the banning of smoking from certain public facilities throughout the United States, people who want to continue smoking have formed ac-

Here and Now
Taxing Cigarettes

Cigarettes are subject to both federal and state taxes. As of July 1, 2010, the average state cigarette excise tax rate was approximately $1.44 per pack but varied from 17 cents in Missouri to $4.35 in New York.

Proponents of taxing cigarettes claim that increases in cigarette prices lead to significant reductions in cigarette smoking (CDC 2009b). For example, a 10% increase in price has been estimated to reduce overall cigarette consumption among adolescents and young adults by approximately 4%. Increasing cessation among smokers and reducing smoking initiation among potential young smokers as a consequence of price purportedly lead to these reductions.

Source: Centers for Disease Control and Prevention (CDC). "Economic Facts About U.S. Tobacco Production and Use." 2010. Available at: http://www.cdc.gov/tobacco/data_statistics/fact_sheets/economics/econ_facts/index.htm. Accessed March 16, 2011.

tion groups to press their right to smoke. Although these groups have made some modest gains, the trend toward restricting and banning cigarette smoking remains very strong. Antismoking groups have been highly successful in their own efforts, and restrictions on the sale of cigarettes and tobacco products remain very tight (CDC 2009b). Further, approximately 47% of Americans live under state or local laws that make workplaces, restaurants, and bars completely smoke-free (CDC 2010l).

Discussion Questions

1. If smoking is the most preventable cause of disease and premature death in the United States, why do people continue to smoke?

2. How effective are the health warning labels on cigarette packages?

3. List and define the diseases that cigarette smokers are most likely to contract.

4. What effects do cigarettes have on the fetus?

5. Why is smokeless tobacco perceived as safer than other forms of tobacco?

6. Who is most likely to smoke and why?

7. Why do people who smoke become dependent on tobacco?

8. Assess the major methods for quitting smoking. Which methods are most likely to succeed?

9. Do you think smokers should have the right to smoke in public places? Explain.

Summary

1 Nicotine is a highly addictive substance.

2 Approximately 27.7% of the U.S. population age 12 or older reports current use of a tobacco product.

3 Nicotine is the substance in tobacco that causes dependence. This drug initially stimulates and then depresses the nervous system.

4 The amount of tobacco absorbed varies according to five factors: (a) the exact composition of tobacco being used; (b) how densely the tobacco is packed in the cigarette and the length of the cigarette smoked; (c) whether a filter is used and the characteristics of the filter; (d) the volume of the smoke inhaled; and (e) the number of cigarettes smoked throughout the day.

5 Cigarette smoking is an addiction that is costly in several ways. For instance, each year approximately 443,000 deaths in the United States are attributed to cigarette smoking.

6 Chewing tobacco and snuff are types of smokeless tobacco products that are commonly referred to as "spit tobacco." Chewing tobacco consists of tobacco leaves that are shredded and twisted into strands and then either chewed or placed in the cheek between the lower lip and gum.

7 Cigarette smokers tend to die at an earlier age than nonsmokers. They also have a greater probability of contracting various illnesses, including types of cancers, chronic bronchitis and emphysema, diseases of the cardiovascular system, and peptic ulcers. In addition, smoking has adverse effects on pregnancy and may harm the fetus.

References

Austin, G. A. *Perspectives on the History of Psychoactive Substance Use.* Washington, DC: National Institute on Drug Abuse, 1978.

Bartecchi, C. E., T. D. MacKenzie, and R. W. Shrier. "The Global Tobacco Epidemic." *Scientific American* (May 1995): 49.

Centers for Disease Control and Prevention (CDC). "Highlights: Impact on Unborn Babies, Infants, Children, and Adolescents." 2004. Available http://www.cdc.gov/tobacco/data_statistics/sgr/2004/highlights/children/index.htm

Centers for Disease Control and Prevention (CDC). "Cigarette Production, Exports, and Domestic Consumption—United States, 1990–2007." 2009a. Available http://www.cdc.gov/tobacco/data_statistics/tables/economics/expdcom

Centers for Disease Control and Prevention (CDC). "Federal Tax Increase." 2009b. Available http://www.cdc.gov/tobacco/basic_information/tobacco_industry/tax_increase

Centers for Disease Control and Prevention (CDC). "Health Effects of Cigarette Smoking." 2009c. Available http://www.cdc.gov/tobacco/data_statistics/fact_sheets/health_effects/effects_cig_smoking

Centers for Disease Control and Prevention (CDC). "Smokeless Tobacco Facts." 2009d. Available http://www.cdc.gov/tobacco/data_statistics/fact_sheets/smokeless/smokeless_facts/index.htm#use

Centers for Disease Control and Prevention (CDC). "Smoking During Pregnancy." 2009e. Available http://www.cdc.gov/tobacco/basic_information/health_effects/pregnancy/index.htm

Centers for Disease Control and Prevention (CDC). "Tobacco Use and Pregnancy." 2009f. Available http://www.cdc.gov/reproductivehealth/TobaccoUsePregnancy/index.htm

Centers for Disease Control and Prevention (CDC). "Tobacco-Related Mortality." 2009g. Available http://www.cdc.gov/tobacco/data_statistics/fact_sheets/health_effects/tobacco_related_mortality

Centers for Disease Control and Prevention (CDC). "Women and Tobacco." 2009h. Available http://www.cdc.gov/tobacco/data_statistics/fact_sheets/populations/women

Centers for Disease Control and Prevention (CDC). "CDC Congressional Testimony. Smokeless Tobacco: Impact on the Health of Our Nation's Youth and Use in Major League Baseball." 2010a. Available http://www.cdc.gov/washington/testimony/2010/t20100414.htm

Centers for Disease Control and Prevention (CDC). "Economic Facts About U.S. Tobacco Production and Use." 2010b. Available http://www.cdc.gov/tobacco/data_statistics/fact_sheets/economics/econ_facts/index.htm

Centers for Disease Control and Prevention (CDC). "Fast Facts." 2010c. Available http://www.cdc.gov/tobacco/data_statistics/fact_sheets/fast_facts/index.htm

Centers for Disease Control and Prevention (CDC). "New Tobacco Controls Have Public Health Impact." 2010d. Available http://www.cdc.gov/Features/TobaccoControls/?s_cid=tobacco_003

Centers for Disease Control and Prevention (CDC). "Secondhand Smoke (SHS)." 2010e. Available http://www.cdc.gov/tobacco/data_statistics/fact_sheets/secondhand_smoke/general_facts/#estimates

Centers for Disease Control and Prevention (CDC). "Smoke-Free Policies Reduce Smoking." 2010f. Available http://www.cdc.gov/tobacco/data_statistics/fact_sheets/secondhand_smoke/protection/reduce_smoking/index.htm

Centers for Disease Control and Prevention (CDC). "Smoking Cessation." 2010g. Available http://www.cdc.gov/tobacco/data_statistics/fact_sheets/cessation/quitting/index.htm

Centers for Disease Control and Prevention (CDC). "State Cigarette Excise Taxes—United States 2009." 2010h. Available http://www.cdc.gov/mmwr/preview/mmwrhtml/mm5913a1.htm

Centers for Disease Control and Prevention (CDC). "State Cigarette Minimum Price Laws—United States 2009." 2010i. Available http://www.cdc.gov/mmwr/preview/mmwrhtml/mm5913a2.htm

Centers for Disease Control and Prevention (CDC). "State Preemption of Local Smoke-Free Laws in Government Work Sites, Private Work Sites, and Restaurants—United States 2005–2009." 2010j. Available http://www.cdc.gov/mmwr/preview/mmwrhtml/mm5904a4.htm

Centers for Disease Control and Prevention (CDC). "Tobacco Control Act: Resources and FDA Regulations." 2010k. Available http://www.cdc.gov/tobacco/stateandcommunity/fda_regs/index.htm

Centers for Disease Control and Prevention (CDC). "Tobacco Use: Smoking and Secondhand Smoke." 2010l. Available http://www.cdc.gov/VitalSigns/pdf/2010-09-vitalsigns.pdf

Centers for Disease Control and Prevention (CDC). "Tobacco Use: Targeting the Nation's Leading Killer: At a Glance 2010." 2010m. Available http://www.cdc.gov/chronicdisease/resources/publications/AAG/osh.htm

Centers for Disease Control and Prevention (CDC). "Youth and Tobacco Use." 2010n. Available http://www.cdc.gov/tobacco/data_statistics/fact_sheets/youth_data/tobacco_use/index.htm

Corti, E. C. *A History of Smoking.* London: Harrap and Company, 1931.

Food and Drug Administration (FDA). "For Consumers: Q & A with Lawrence Deyton." 2009. Available http://www.fda.gov/ForConsumers/ConsumerUpdates/ucm183919.htm

Food and Drug Administration (FDA). "Frequently Asked Questions on the Passage of the Family Smoking Prevention and Tobacco Control Act (FSPTCA)." 2010a. Available http://www.fda.gov/TobaccoProducts/NewsEvents/ucm173174.htm

Food and Drug Administration (FDA). "FDA Marks First Anniversary of Tobacco Control Act." 2010b. Available http://www.fda.gov/NewsEvents/Newsroom/PressAnnouncements/ucm216406.htm

Food and Drug Administration (FDA). "E-Cigarettes: Questions and Answers." 2010c. Available http://www.fda.gov/ForConsumers/ConsumerUpdates/ucm225210.htm

Food and Drug Administration (FDA). "Signing of the Family Smoking Prevention and Tobacco Control Act" 2010d. Available http://www.fda.gov/TobaccoProducts/NewsEvents/ucm182982.htm

Food and Drug Administration (FDA). "Tobacco Control Act One Year Anniversary." 2010e. Available http://www.fda.gov/TobaccoProducts/NewsEvents/ucm216493.htm

Food and Drug Administration (FDA). "U.S. Food and Drug Administration Center for Tobacco Products 2009–2010: Inaugural Year in Review." 2010f. Available http://www.fda.gov/downloads/TobaccoProducts/NewsEvents/UCM216374.pdf

Heimann, R. K. *Tobacco and Americans.* New York: McGraw-Hill, 1960.

Langton, P. A. *Drug Use and the Alcohol Dilemma.* Boston: Allyn and Bacon, 1991.

National Cancer Institute (NCI). "Harms of Smoking and Health Benefits of Quitting." 2010a. Available http://www.cancer.gov/cancertopics/factsheet/Tobacco/cessation

National Cancer Institute (NCI). "How to Handle Withdrawal Symptoms and Triggers When You Decide to Quit Smoking." 2010b. Available http://www.cancer.gov/cancertopics/factsheet/Tobacco/symptoms-triggers-quitting

National Cancer Institute (NCI). " 'Light' Cigarettes and Cancer Risk." 2010c. Available http://www.cancer.gov/cancertopics/factsheet/Tobacco/light-cigarettes

National Institute on Drug Abuse (NIDA). *NIDA Research Report—Tobacco Addiction, 2009.* NIH Publication No. 09-4342. Available http://www.nida.nih.gov/PDF/TobaccoRRS_v16.pdf

National Institute on Drug Abuse (NIDA). "NIDA for Teens—Tobacco Addiction." 2010. Available http://teens.drugabuse.gov/facts/facts_nicotine1.php

O'Brien, R., S. Cohen, G. Evans, and J. Fine. *The Encyclopedia of Drug Abuse,* 2nd ed. New York: Facts on File and Greenspring, 1992.

Palfai, T., and H. Jankiewicz. *Drugs and Human Behavior.* Dubuque, IA: William C. Brown, 1991.

Schelling, T. C. "Addictive Drugs: The Cigarette Experience." *Science* (24 January 1992): 430–433.

Schultes, R. E. "Ethnopharmacological Significance of Psychotropic Drugs of Vegetal Origin." In *Principles of Psychopharmacology,* 2nd ed., edited by W. G. Clark and J. del Guidice, 41–70. New York: Academic Press, 1978.

Substance Abuse and Mental Health Services Administration (SAMHSA). *Results from the 2009 National Survey on Drug Use and Health: Volume I. Summary of National Findings.* NSDUH Series H-38A, HHS Publication No. SMA 10-4586 Findings. Rockville, MD: Office of Applied Studies, 2010.

Surgeon General's Report. "The Health Consequences of Involuntary Smoking." 1986. Available http://profiles.nlm.nih.gov/ps/access/NNBCPM.pdf

U.S. Department of Agriculture (USDA), Economic Research Service. "Trends in the Cigarette Industry After the Master Settlement Agreement." 2001. Available http://www.ers.usda.gov/Publications/TBS/Oct01/TBS250-01

World Health Organization (WHO). "Q & A Tobacco." 2010. Available http://www.who.int/topics/tobacco/qa/en/index.html

CHAPTER 12

Hallucinogens (Psychedelics)

Learning ◎bjectives

On completing this chapter you will be able to:

◎ Explain why hallucinogens became so popular during the 1960s.

◎ Describe how hallucinogens alter the senses.

◎ Outline how psychedelic, stimulant, and anticholinergic effects are expressed in the three principal types of hallucinogens.

◎ Describe why some psychotherapists believe that using MDMA for their patients may be beneficial.

◎ Explain the reasons for Ecstasy's recent up and down patterns of use.

◎ Explain how hallucinogens differ from other commonly abused drugs in terms of their addicting properties and their ability to cause dependence.

◎ Describe the effects that environment and personality have on the individual's response to hallucinogens.

◎ Explain the term *club drugs* and describe their particular problems.

◎ Characterize how PCP differs from other hallucinogens and why it is so dangerous.

◎ Explain the similarities between PCP and ketamine.

◎ Describe the recreational and legal status of *Salvia divinorum*.

Did You Know?

○ Hallucinogens were abused by relatively few people in the United States until the social upheaval of the 1960s.

○ Some hallucinogens—such as LSD—have been used by psychiatrists to assist in psychotherapy with certain patients.

○ Ecstasy has been tested in FDA-approved clinical trials for its ability to treat PTSD conditions.

○ Hallucinogens such as LSD do not tend to be physically addicting.

○ The senses are grossly exaggerated and distorted under the influence of hallucinogens.

○ Ecstasy abuse increased dramatically from 1996 to 2000 due to its popularity as a "club drug" and its use at "rave" parties. Its use then declined, but it has risen again due to reduced perceived risk by younger populations.

○ For some users, hallucinogens can cause frightening, nightmarish experiences called bad trips.

○ Phencyclidine (PCP) and ketamine were originally developed as general anesthetics, but because of their ability to cause psychosis their use in humans is either prohibited or very limited.

○ Abuse of high doses of OTC cough medicines that contain dextromethorphan is a problem with young populations and can cause a PCP-like hallucinogenic or psychotic effect.

Drugs and Society Online is a great source for additional drugs and society information for both students and instructors. Visit **go.jblearning.com/hanson11** to find a variety of useful tools for learning, thinking, and teaching.

Introduction

A person on LSD who becomes depressed, agitated, or confused may experience these feelings in an overwhelming manner that grows on itself. The best solution is to remove disturbing influences, get him or her to a safe, comforting environment, and reassure the "tripper" that things are alright. It may comfort those who fear that they are losing their minds to be reminded that it will end in several hours. (Honig 2007)

This quote from an experienced user illustrates the sensory and emotional distortions that can be caused by using **hallucinogens** or **psychedelics**. The word *psychedelic* comes from the Greek root meaning "mind-revealing" (*Harvard Mental Health Letter* 2006). In this chapter, we begin with a brief historical review of the use of hallucinogens, tracing the trend in the United States from the 1960s to today. Next, the nature of hallucinogens and the effects they produce are examined. The rest of the chapter addresses the various types of psychedelic agents—LSD types, phenylethylamines (including Ecstasy), anticholinergics, natural products, and other miscellaneous substances.

The History of Hallucinogen Use

People have known and written about drug-related hallucinations for centuries. Throughout the ages, individuals who saw visions or experienced hallucinations were perceived as being holy or sacred, as receiving divine messages, or possibly as being bewitched and controlled by the devil. There are many indications that medicine men, shamans, witches, oracles, and perhaps mystics and priests of various groups were familiar with drugs and herbs

Protests against the Vietnam War in the 1960s and 1970s often included the use of hallucinogens.

that caused such experiences and today are known as hallucinogens (National Institute on Drug Abuse [NIDA] 2001).

Before the 1960s, several psychedelic substances, such as mescaline from the peyote cactus, could be obtained from chemical supply houses with no restriction in the United States. Abuse of hallucinogens did not become a major social problem in this country until this decade of racial struggles, the Vietnam War, and violent demonstrations. Many individuals frustrated with the hypocrisy of "the establishment" tried to "turn on and tune in" by using hallucinogens as pharmacological crutches.

Psychedelic drugs became especially popular when some medical professionals such as then-Harvard psychology professor Timothy Leary reported that these drugs allowed users to get in touch with themselves and achieve a peaceful inner serenity (Associated Press 1999). At the same time, it became well publicized that the natural psychedelics (such as mescaline and peyote) for many years had been used routinely by some religious organizations of Native Americans for enhancing spiritual experiences. This factor contributed to the mystical, supernatural aura associated with hallucinogenic agents and added to their enticement for the so-called dropout generation.

With widespread use of LSD, it was observed that this and similar drugs may induce a form of psychosis-like schizophrenia (American Psychiatric Association [APA] 2000). The term **psychotomimetic** was coined to describe these compounds; this term means "psychosis mimicking" and is still used in medicine today. The basis for the designation is the effects of these drugs that induce mental states that impair an individual's ability to recognize and respond appropriately to reality.

By the mid-1960s, federal regulatory agencies had become concerned with the misuse of hallucinogens and the potential emotional damage caused by these drugs. Access to hallucinogenic agents was restricted, and laws against their distribution were passed. Despite the problems associated with these psychedelics, some groups demanded that responsible use with therapeutic benefits was possible and that trained clinicians be allowed legal access to these substances.

The Native American Church

The hallucinogen peyote plays a central role in the ceremonies of Native Americans who follow a religion that is a combination of Christian doctrine and Native American religious rituals. Members of this church are found as far north as Canada. They believe that God made a special gift of this sacramental plant to them so that they might commune more directly with Him. The first organized peyote church was the First-Born Church of Christ, incorporated in 1914 in Oklahoma. The Native American Church of the United States was chartered in 1918 and is the largest such group at present (approximately 100,000–200,000 members) (2010).

Because of the religious beliefs of the members of the Native American Church concerning the powers of peyote, when Congress legislated against its use in 1965, it allowed room for religious use of this

Peyote is used as a sacramental plant by members of the Native American Church as part of their religious ceremonies.

psychedelic plant. The American Indian Religious Freedom Act of 1978 was an attempt by Congress to allow the members of the Native American Church access to peyote due to constitutional guarantees of religious freedom. Due to controversy inspired by the original piece of legislation, an amendment to the 1978 act was signed in 1994, which specifically protected the use of peyote in Native American Church ceremonies. This amendment also prohibits use of peyote for nonreligious purposes (Native American Church 2008). However, despite these efforts by Congress to resolve this issue, controversies continue to arise (see "Case in Point: Peyote and the Rights of Native Americans").

▶ Case in Point Peyote and the Rights of Native Americans: How Far Should It Go? ◀

Although federal law protects the rights of Native Americans to use peyote for religious purposes if they are members of the Native American Church, issues remain unresolved. For example, Jonathan Fowler, a member of the Grand Traverse Band of Ottawa and Chippewa Indians, requested a judge allow his 4-year-old son to ingest peyote with him, as part of a religious ritual at the Native American Church of the Morning Star. The boy's mother opposed the request, fearing potential neurological damage to the boy. Although the use of peyote in Native American rituals is legal in all 50 states, the judge ruled against Fowler, stating that the boy could use peyote when he becomes old enough

to comprehend its effects and with permission from both parents. Several Native American congregations who use peyote already have age limitations indicating who can take the substance during religious rites. Another issue relates to members of this church who are not of Indian ancestry. Lawsuits have been filed in federal courts that contend all members of the Native Church regardless of their ancestry should be allowed to include peyote use as part of their religious practice. This case has not been resolved, but suggests that in the future other lawsuits are likely to be contested in court that relate to this practice of religious use of hallucinogenic drugs.

Sources: Center for Cognitive Liberty and Ethics. "Court Says No Peyote for Native American Boy." 22 April 2003. Available at: http://www.cognitiveliberty.org/dll/peyote_boy.html. Accessed March 18, 2011; and Dobner, J. "American Indian Church Sues Feds Over Peyote Use." *Native American Times.* 20 September 2010. Available at: http://www.nativetimes.com/index.php?option=com_content&view=article&id=4268:american-indian-church-sues-feds-over-peyote-use&catid=51&Itemid=27. Accessed March 18, 2011.

Timothy Leary advocated legalization of LSD in the 1960s.

■ Timothy Leary and the League of Spiritual Discovery

In 1966, 3 years after being fired by Harvard because of his controversial involvement with hallucinogens (Associated Press 1999), Timothy Leary undertook a constitutional strategy intended to retain legitimate access to another hallucinogen, LSD. He began a religion called the League of Spiritual Discovery; LSD was the sacrament. This unorthodox religious orientation to the LSD experience was presented in a manual called *The Psychedelic Experience* (Leary, Metzner, and Alpert 1964), which was based on the *Tibetan Book of the Dead*. It became the "bible" of the psychedelic drug movement.

The movement grew, but most members used street LSD and did not follow Leary's directions. Leary believed that the hallucinogenic experience was only beneficial under proper control and guidance. But most members of this so-called religion merely used the organization as a front to gain access to an illegal drug. Federal authorities did not agree with Leary's freedom of religion interpretation and in 1969 convicted him for possession of marijuana and LSD and sentenced him to 20 years imprisonment (Stone 1991). Before being incarcerated, Leary escaped to Algeria and wandered for a couple of years before being extradited to the United States. He served several years in jail and was released in 1976.

KEY TERMS

psychotogenics
substances that initiate psychotic behavior

Even in his later years, Leary continued to believe that U.S. citizens should be able to use hallucinogens without government regulation. He died in 1996 at the age of 75 years, revered by some but despised by others (Associated Press 1999; "Many Were Lost" 1996).

Hallucinogen Use Today

Today, the use of hallucinogens (excluding marijuana) is primarily a young-adult phenomenon (Johnston et al. 2010). Although the use rate has not returned to that of the late 1960s and early 1970s (approximately 16%), in high school seniors lifetime use in 2010 was 8.6% (Johnston et al. 2010) (see **Table 12.1**).

The Nature of Hallucinogens

Agreement has not been reached on what constitutes a hallucinogenic agent (O'Brien 2006), for several reasons. First, a variety of seemingly unrelated drug groups can produce hallucinations, delusions, or sensory disturbances under certain conditions. For example, besides the traditional hallucinogens (such as LSD), high doses of anticholinergics, cocaine, amphetamines, and steroids can cause hallucinations.

In addition, responses to even the traditional hallucinogens can vary tremendously from person to person and from experience to experience (see "Signs & Symptoms: Hallucinogens"). Multiple mechanisms are involved in the actions of these drugs, which contribute to the array of responses that they can cause. These drugs most certainly influence the complex inner workings of the human mind and have been described as psychedelic, **psychotogenic**, or psychotomimetic. The features of hallucinogens that distinguish them from other drug groups are their ability to alter perception, thought, and feeling in such a manner that does not normally occur except in dreams or during experiences of extreme religious exaltation (NIDA 2009). We examine these characteristics throughout this chapter.

■ Sensory and Psychological Effects

In general, LSD is considered the prototype agent against which other hallucinogens are measured (NIDA 2001). Typical users experience several

Table 12.1 Trends in the Use of LSD and All Hallucinogens by 8th, 10th, and 12th Graders, 1994–2010

	USED DURING LIFETIME (PERCENTAGE)					USED DURING YEAR (PERCENTAGE)					USED DURING MONTH (PERCENTAGE)				
	1994	1996	2004	2006	2010	1994	1996	2004	2006	2010	1994	1996	2004	2006	2010
8TH GRADERS															
LSD	3.7	5.1	1.8	1.6	1.8	2.4	3.5	1.1	0.9	1.2	1.1	1.5	0.5	0.4	0.6
All hallucinogens	4.3	5.9	3.5	3.4	3.4	2.7	4.1	2.2	2.1	2.2	1.3	1.9	1.0	0.9	1.0
10TH GRADERS															
LSD	7.2	9.4	2.8	2.7	3.0	5.2	6.9	1.6	1.7	1.9	2.0	2.4	0.6	0.7	0.7
All hallucinogens	8.1	10.5	6.4	6.1	6.1	5.8	7.8	4.1	4.1	4.2	2.4	2.8	1.6	1.5	1.6
12TH GRADERS															
LSD	10.5	12.6	4.6	3.3	4.0	6.9	8.8	2.2	1.7	2.6	2.6	2.5	0.7	0.6	0.8
All hallucinogens	11.4	14.0	9.7	8.3	8.6	7.6	10.1	6.2	4.9	5.5	3.1	3.5	1.9	1.5	1.9

Source: Johnston, L. D., P. M. O'Malley, J. G. Bachman, and J. E. Schulenberg. (14 December 2010). "Marijuana use is rising; ecstasy use is beginning to rise; and alcohol use is declining among U.S. teens." 14 December 2010. University of Michigan News Service. Available at: http://monitoringthefuture.org/data/10data.html#2010data-drugs. Accessed March 16, 2011.

Signs & Symptoms Hallucinogens

POSSIBLE SIGNS OF USE	EXTREME REACTIONS
Heightened senses	Increased body temperature (MDMA)
Loss of control	Electrolyte imbalance
Loss of identity	Cardiac arrest
Illusions and hallucinations	A nightmare-like trip (LSD)
Altered perception of time and distance	Unable to direct movement, feel pain, or remember

stages of sensory experiences; they can go through all stages during a single "trip" or, more likely, will pass through only some. These stages are as follows:

1. Heightened, exaggerated senses
2. Loss of control
3. Self-reflection
4. Loss of identity and a sense of cosmic merging

The following illustrations of the stages of the LSD experience are based primarily on an account by Solomon Snyder (1974), a highly regarded neuroscientist (one of the principal discoverers of endorphins; see Chapter 4), who personally experienced the effects of LSD as a young resident in psychiatry.

Altered Senses

In his encounter with LSD, Snyder used a moderate dose of 100 to 200 micrograms and observed few discernible effects for the first 30 minutes except some mild nausea. After this time had elapsed, objects took on a purplish tinge and appeared to be vaguely outlined. Colors, textures, and lines achieved an unexpected richness. Perception was so exaggerated that individual skin pores "stood out and clamored for recognition" (Snyder 1974, p. 42). Objects became distorted; when Snyder focused on his thumb, it began to swell, undulate, and then moved forward in a menacing fashion. Visions filled with distorted imagery occurred when his eyes were closed. The sense of time and distance changed

dramatically; "a minute was like an hour, a week was like an eternity, a foot became a mile" (Snyder 1974, p. 43). The present seemed to drag on forever, and the concept of future lost its meaning. The exaggeration of perceptions and feelings gave the sense of more events occurring in a time period, giving the impression of time slowing.

An associated sensation described by Snyder is called **synesthesia**, a crossover phenomenon between senses. For example, sound develops visual dimensions, and vice versa, enabling the user to see sounds and hear colors. These altered sensory experiences are described as a heightened sensory awareness and relate to the first component of the psychedelic state (NIDA 2009).

Loss of Control

The second feature of LSD also relates to altered sensory experiences and a loss of control (O'Brien 2006). The user cannot determine whether the psychedelic trip will be a pleasant, relaxing experience or a "bad trip," with recollections of hidden fears and suppressed anxieties that can precipitate neurotic or psychotic responses. The frightening reactions may persist for a few minutes or several hours and be mildly agitating or extremely disturbing. Some bad trips can include feelings of panic, confusion, suspicion, helplessness, and a total lack of control. The following example illustrates how terrifying a bad trip can be:

> I was having problems breathing [and] my throat was all screwed up. The things that entered my mind were that I was dead and people were saying good-bye, because they really meant it. I was witnessing my own funeral. I was thinking that I was going to wake either in the back seat of a cop car or in the hospital. *(From Venturelli's files, male, age 19)*

KEY TERMS

synesthesia
a subjective sensation or image of a sense other than the one being stimulated, such as an auditory sensation caused by a visual stimulus

Replays of these frightening experiences can occur at a later time, even though the drug has not been taken again; such recurrences are referred to as **flashbacks** (NIDA 2010a) or hallucinogen persisting perception disorder (Halpern and Pope 2003).

It is not clear what determines the nature of the sensory response. Perhaps it relates to the state of anxiety and personality of the user or the nature of his or her surroundings. It is interesting that Timothy Leary tried to teach his "drug disciples" that "turning on correctly means to understand the many levels that are brought into focus; it takes years of discipline, training and discipleship" ("Celebration #1" 1966). He apparently felt that, with experience and training, you could control the sensory effects of the hallucinogens. This is an interesting possibility but has never been well demonstrated.

Self-Reflection

Snyder (1974) made reference to the third component of the psychedelic response in his LSD experience. During the period when sensory effects predominate, self-reflection also occurs. While in this state, Snyder explained, the user "becomes aware of thoughts and feelings long hidden beneath the surface, forgotten and/or repressed" (p. 44). As a psychiatrist, Snyder claimed that this new perspective can lead to valid insights that are useful psychotherapeutic exercises.

Some psychotherapists have used or advocated the use of psychedelics for this purpose since the 1950s, as described many years before by Sigmund Freud, to "make conscious the unconscious" (Snyder 1974, p. 44). Although a case can be made for the psychotherapeutic use of this group of drugs, the Food and Drug Administration (FDA) has not yet approved any of these agents for psychiatric use; it has, however, approved clinical trials to study the psychedelic/stimulant drug, Ecstasy, to evaluate if it would be useful in the treatment of posttraumatic stress disorder (PTSD) (Vastag 2010). Although considerable caution is still needed due to the somewhat unpredictability of these drugs, more and more small studies are examining the effects of psychedelic drugs such as psilocybin and LSD to treat emotional problems such as depression in cancer patients, obsessive-compulsive disorder, and end-of-life anxiety. Some of the reported results have been encouraging, but they are very preliminary and still small-scale. There is concern that some of the reported benefits have been exaggerated by scientists-turned-evangelists who are anxious to make these drugs routine therapeutics (Tierney 2010). Only time will tell how, or if, the medical/ scientific community will react to the "new science" that is promoted as evidence that psychedelics have an important therapeutic role to play in modern-day medicine. Clearly, this is a controversy that is far from being resolved.

Loss of Identity and Cosmic Merging

The final features that set the psychedelics apart as unique drugs were described by Snyder (1974) as the "mystical-spiritual aspect of the drug experience." He claimed, "It is indescribable. For how can anyone verbalize a merging of his being with the totality of the universe? How do you put into words the feeling that 'all is one,' 'I am of the all,' 'I am no longer.' One's skin ceases to be a boundary between self and others" (p. 45). Because consumption of hallucinogen-containing plants has often been part of religious ceremonies, it is likely that this sense of cosmic merging and union with all humankind correlates to the exhilaratingly spiritual experiences described by many religious mystics.

The loss of identity and personal boundaries caused by hallucinogens is not viewed as being so spiritually enticing by all. In particular, for individuals who have rigid, highly ordered personalities, the dissolution of a well-organized and well-structured world is terrifying because the drug destroys the individual's emotional support. Such an individual finds that the loss of a separate identity can cause extreme panic and anxiety. During these drug-induced panic states, which in some ways are schizophrenic-like, people have committed suicide and homicide. These tragic reactions are part of the risk of using hallucinogenics and explain some of the FDA's hesitancy to legalize or authorize them for psychotherapeutic use.

■ Mechanisms of Action

As with most drugs, hallucinogens represent the proverbial "double-edged sword." These drugs may cause potentially useful psychiatric effects for many people. However, the variability in positive versus negative responses, coupled with lack of understanding as to what factors are responsible for the variables, suggest that these drugs may be dangerous for some patients and difficult to manage.

KEY TERMS

flashbacks
recurrences of earlier drug-induced sensory experiences in the absence of the drug

Some researchers have suggested that all hallucinogens act at a common central nervous system (CNS) site to exert their psychedelic effects. Although this hypothesis has not been totally disproven, there is little evidence to support it. The fact that so many different types of drugs can cause hallucinogenic effects suggests that multiple mechanisms are likely responsible for their actions.

The most predictable and typical psychedelic experiences are caused by LSD or similar agents. Consequently, these agents have been the primary focus of studies intended to elucidate the nature of hallucinogenic mechanisms. Although LSD has effects at several CNS sites, ranging from the spinal cord to the cortex of the brain, its effects on the neurotransmitter serotonin most likely account for its psychedelic properties (Education.com 2010). That LSD and similar drugs alter serotonin activity has been proven; how they affect this transmitter is not so readily apparent.

Although many experts believe changes in serotonin activity are the basis for the psychedelic properties of most hallucinogens, a case can be made for the involvement of norepinephrine, dopamine, acetylcholine, and perhaps other transmitter systems as well (see Chapter 4). Only additional research will be able to sort out this complex but important issue.

Types of Hallucinogenic Agents

Due to recent technological developments, understanding of hallucinogens has advanced; even so, the classification of these drugs remains somewhat arbitrary. Many agents produce some of the pharmacological effects of the traditional psychedelics, such as LSD and mescaline.

A second type of hallucinogen includes those agents that have amphetamine-like molecular structures (referred to as phenylethylamines) and possess some stimulant action; this group includes drugs such as DOM (dimethoxymethylamphetamine), MDA (methylenedioxyamphetamine), MDMA (methylenedioxymethamphetamine or Ecstasy), and likely mephedrone (methyl methcathinone). These agents vary in their hallucinogen or stimulant properties. MDA is more like an amphetamine (stimulant), whereas MDMA is more like LSD

KEY TERMS

ergotism
poisoning by toxic substances from the ergot fungus *Claviceps purpurea*

(hallucinogen). In large doses, however, each of the phenylethylamines causes substantial CNS stimulation.

The third major group of hallucinogens comprises the anticholinergic drugs, which block some of the receptors for the neurotransmitter acetylcholine (see Chapter 4). Almost all drugs that antagonize these receptors cause hallucinations in high doses. Many of these potent anticholinergic hallucinogens are naturally occurring and have been known, used, and abused for millennia.

■ Traditional Hallucinogens: LSD Types

The LSD-like drugs are considered to be the prototypical hallucinogens and are used as the basis of comparison for other types of agents with psychedelic properties. Included in this group are LSD itself and some hallucinogens derived from plants, such as mescaline from the peyote cactus, psilocybin from mushrooms, dimethyltryptamine (DMT) from seeds, and myristicin from nutmeg. Because LSD is the principal hallucinogen, its origin, history, and properties are discussed in detail, providing a basis for understanding the other psychedelic drugs.

Lysergic Acid Diethylamide

Lysergic acid diethylamide (LSD) is a relatively new drug, but similar compounds have existed for a long time. For example, accounts from the Middle Ages tell about a strange affliction that caused pregnant women to abort and others to develop strange burning sensations in their extremities. Today, we call this condition **ergotism** and know it is caused by

Albert Hofmann created LSD in 1938 while trying to synthesize a drug to study psychosis.

eating grains contaminated by the ergot fungus. This fungus produces compounds related to LSD called the *ergot alkaloids* (Goldstein 1994; NIDA 2007b). Besides the sensory effects, the ergot substances can cause hallucinations, delirium, and psychosis (Titi Tudorancea Bulletin 2010).

In 1938, Albert Hofmann, a scientist for Sandoz Pharmaceutical Laboratories of Basel, Switzerland, worked on a series of ergot compounds in a search for active chemicals that might be of medical value. Lysergic acid was similar in structure to a compound called nikethamide, a stimulant, and Hofmann tried to create slight chemical modifications that might merit further testing. The result of this effort was the production of lysergic acid diethylamide, or LSD. Hofmann's experience with this new compound gave insight into the effects of this drug (Smith 2008).

Soon after LSD was discovered, the similarity of experiences with this agent to the symptoms of schizophrenia were noted, which prompted researchers to investigate correlations between the two (Weber 2006). The hope was to use LSD as a tool for producing an artificial psychosis to aid in understanding the biochemistry of psychosis (NIDA 2001). Interest in this use of LSD has declined because it is generally accepted that LSD effects differ from natural psychoses.

The use of LSD in psychotherapy has also been tried in connection with the treatment of alcoholism, autism, paranoia, schizophrenia, and various other mental and emotional disorders (Weber 2006). Even though there continues to be advocates for the therapeutic use of LSD (as discussed earlier in this chapter), the administration of LSD for clinical objectives has not been approved for general use because of its limited proven successes, legal aspects, difficulty in obtaining the pure drug, adverse reactions to the drug ("bad trips" can occur under controlled as well as uncontrolled conditions), and rapid tolerance buildup in some patients. However, there has been a recent resurgence in combining low doses of LSD with psychotherapy to treat depression, compulsive disorders, or chronic pain. Researchers conducting small studies claim that for some patients the drug can be a catalyst to help change perception of problems and make the patient more responsive to the behavioral therapies (Kelland 2010). No one believes that this approach will be a panacea or universally effective, and even the strongest of advocates emphasize that it is important to use only low doses for relatively short periods of time (Kelland 2010; Marsa 2008).

Nonmedical interest in LSD and related drugs began to grow during the 1950s and peaked in the 1960s, when LSD was used by millions of young Americans for chemical escape. On rare occasions, a "bad trip" would cause a user to feel terror and panic; these experiences resulted in well-publicized accidental deaths due to jumping from building tops or running into the pathway of oncoming vehicles (U.S. Department of Justice 1991).

As with other hallucinogens, the use of LSD by teenagers declined somewhat over the 1970s and 1980s but began to rise again in the early 1990s. The reason for this rise was thought to relate to a decline in the perceived dangers of using LSD and an increase in peer approval. However, surveys have demonstrated that recent dramatic drops in LSD use have not been explained (Johnston et al. 2010) (see Table 12.1). Of high school seniors sampled in 1975, 11.3% had used LSD sometime during their life; that number declined to 8.6% in 1992, rebounded to 12.2% in 1999, and tumbled to 4.6% in 2004 and 4.0% in 2010. LSD users are typically college or high school students, white, middle-class, and risk-takers (Johnston et al. 2010).

Synthesis and Administration

LSD is a complex molecule that requires about 1 week to be synthesized. Because of the sophisticated chemistry necessary for its production, LSD is not manufactured by local illicit laboratories but requires the skills of a trained chemist (U.S. Department of Justice 2002, 2003). Because of LSD's potency, it has been difficult to locate illicit LSD labs; small quantities of LSD are sufficient to satisfy the demand and can be easily transported without detection. The last publicized major LSD lab seizure in the United States was in 2000 when a Drug Enforcement Agency (DEA) raid in Kansas resulted in a temporary 95% decrease in LSD supplies (DEA 2010).

The physical properties of LSD are not distinctive. In its purified form, LSD is colorless, odorless, and tasteless. It can be purchased in several forms, including tiny tablets (about one-tenth the size of aspirins, called microdots), capsules, thin squares of gelatin called "window panes," or more commonly dissolved and applied to paper as "blotter acid" and cut up into 0.25-inch squares for individual dosing (Partnership 2010). Each square is swallowed or chewed and represents a single dose. One gram of LSD can provide 10,000 individual doses and be sold on the streets for $50,000. Although LSD usually is taken by mouth, it is sometimes injected. It costs about $1–10/dose (Schaffer Library 2007).

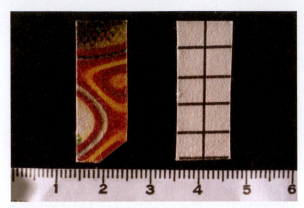

Small quantities of LSD are applied to squares of absorbent blotter paper to be chewed or swallowed.

Physiological Effects

Like many hallucinogens, LSD is remarkably potent. The typical dose today is 20 to 30 micrograms, compared with a typical dose of 150 to 300 micrograms in the 1960s. This difference in dose likely explains why today fewer users of LSD are experiencing severe side effects (NIDA 2007b). In monkeys, the lethal dose has been determined to be about 5 milligrams per kilogram of body weight.

When taken orally, LSD is readily absorbed and diffused into all tissues. It passes through the placenta into the fetus and through the blood–brain barrier. The brain receives about 1% of the total dose.

Within the brain, LSD is particularly concentrated in the hypothalamus, the limbic system, and the auditory and visual reflex areas. Electrodes placed in the limbic system show an "electrical storm," or a massive increase in neural activity, which might correlate with the overwhelming flood of sensations and the phenomenon of synesthesia reported by the user (NIDA 2001). LSD also activates the sympathetic nervous system; shortly after the drug is taken, body temperature, heart rate, and blood pressure rise; the person sweats; and the pupils of the eyes dilate. Its effects on the parasympathetic nervous system increase salivation and nausea (NIDA 2007b). These systemic effects do not appear to be related to the hallucinogenic properties of the drug.

The effect of LSD begins within 30 to 90 minutes after ingestion and can last up to 12 hours. Tolerance to the effects of LSD develops more rapidly and lasts longer than tolerance to other hallucinogens (NIDA 2001). Tolerance develops very quickly to repeated doses, probably because of a change in sensitivity of the target cells in the brain rather than a change in its metabolism. Tolerance wears off within a few days after the drug is discontinued. Because there are no withdrawal symptoms, a person does not become physically dependent, but some psychological dependency on LSD can occur (NIDA 2007b).

Behavioral Effects

Because LSD alters a number of systems in the brain, its behavioral effects are many and variable among individuals (Goldstein 1995; NIDA 2009). The following sections address common CNS responses to this drug.

Creativity and Insight

A question often raised by researchers interested in experimenting with LSD is this: Does LSD help expand the mind, increasing insight and creativity? This question is extremely difficult to answer because no one has ever determined the origin of insight and creativity. Moreover, each of us views these qualities differently.

Subjects under the influence of LSD often express the feeling of being more creative, but creative acts such as drawing and painting are hindered by the motor impairment caused by LSD. The products of artists under the influence of the drug usually prove to be inferior to those produced before the drug experience. Paintings done in LSD creativity studies have been described as reminiscent of "schizophrenic art."

In an often-cited study, creativity, attitude, and anxiety tests on 24 college students found that LSD had no objective effect on creativity, although many of the subjects said they felt they were more creative (McGlothin, Cohen, and McGlothin 1967). This paradox is noted in several studies of LSD use. The subjects believe they have more insight and provide better answers to life's problems, but they do not or cannot demonstrate this increase objectively. Overt behavior is not modified, and these new insights are short-lived unless they are reinforced by modified behavior.

In spite of these results, some researchers still contend that LSD can enhance the creative process. For example, Oscar Janigar, a psychiatrist at the University of California, Los Angeles, claimed to have determined that LSD does not produce a tangible alteration in the way a painter paints; thus, it does not turn a poor painter into a good one. However, Janigar claimed that LSD does alter the way the painter appraises the world and allows the artist to "plunge into areas where access was restricted by confines of perceptions" and consequently becomes more creative (Tucker 1987, p. 16).

Adverse Psychedelic Effects

It is important to remember that there is no typical pattern of response to LSD. The experience varies for each user as a function of the person's set, or expectations, and setting, or environment, during the experience (Publishers Group 2002). Two of the major negative responses are described as follows (NIDA 2009; Pahnke et al. 1970):

1. The psychotic adverse reaction, or "freakout," is an intense, nightmarish experience. The subject may have complete loss of emotional control and experience paranoid delusions, hallucinations, panic attacks, psychosis, and catatonic seizures. In rare instances, some of these reactions are prolonged, lasting days.
2. The nonpsychotic adverse reaction may involve varying degrees of tension, anxiety, fear, depression, and despair but not as intense a response as the "freakout."

A person with deep psychological problems or a strong need to be in conscious control or one who takes the drug in an unfavorable setting is more likely to have an adverse reaction than a person with a well-integrated personality. Severe LSD behavioral toxicity can be treated with tranquilizers or a sedative like a benzodiazepine.

Perceptual Effects

Because the brain's sensory processing is altered by a hallucinogenic dose of LSD, many kinds of unusual illusions can occur. Some users report seeing shifting geometrical patterns mixed with intense color perception; others observe the movement of stationary objects, such that a speck on the wall appears as a large blinking eye or an unfolding flower. Interpretation of sounds can also be scrambled; a dropped ashtray may become a gun fired at the user, for instance. In some cases, LSD alters perceptions to the extent that people feel they can walk on water or fly through the air. The sensation that the body is distorted and even coming apart is another common effect, especially for novice users. Thoughts of suicide and sometimes actual attempts can be caused by use of LSD as well (NIDA 2009).

Many LSD users find their sense of time distorted, such that hours may be perceived as years or an eternity. As discussed earlier, users may also have a distorted perception of their own knowledge or creativity; for instance, they may feel their ideas or work are especially unique, brilliant, or artistic. When analyzed by a person not on LSD or explained after the "trip" is over, however, these ideas or creations are almost always quite ordinary.

This head was sculpted by a university student while under the influence of LSD.

In sum, LSD alters perception such that any sensation can be perceived in the extreme. An experience can be incredibly beautiful and uplifting. However, sometimes the experience can be very unpleasant.

The flashback is an interesting but poorly understood phenomenon of LSD use. Although usually thought of as being adverse, sometimes flashbacks are pleasant and even referred to as "free trips." During a flashback, sensations caused by previous LSD use return, although the subject is not using the drug at the time.

There are three broad categories of negative LSD-related flashbacks:

1. *"Body trip"*: Recurrence of an unpleasant physical sensation
2. *"Bad mind trip"*: Recurrence of a distressing thought or emotion
3. *Altered visual perception:* The most frequent type of recurrence, consisting of seeing dots, flashes, trails of light, halos, false motion in the peripheral field, and other sensations

Flashbacks are most disturbing because they come on unexpectedly. Some have been reported years after use of LSD; for most people, however, flashbacks usually subside within weeks or months after taking LSD. The duration of a flashback is variable, lasting from a few minutes to several hours (NIDA 2009).

Although the precise mechanism of flashbacks is unknown, physical or psychological stresses and some drugs such as marijuana may trigger these experiences (NIDA 2009). It has been proposed that flashbacks are an especially vivid form of memory that becomes seared into the subconscious mind due to the effects of LSD on the brain's transmitters.

Treatment consists of reassurance that the condition will go away and use of a sedative such as diazepam (Valium), if necessary, to treat the anxiety or panic that can accompany the flashback experience.

Genetic Damage and Birth Defects

Experiments conducted in the mid-1960s suggested that LSD could cause birth defects, based on the observation that, when LSD was added to a suspension of human white blood cells in a test tube, the chromosomes of these cells were damaged. From this finding, it was proposed that when LSD was consumed by human beings, it could damage the chromosomes of the male sperm, female egg, or cells of the developing infant. Such damage theoretically could result in congenital defects in offspring (Dishotsky et al. 1971).

Carefully controlled studies conducted after news of LSD's chromosomal effects were made public did not support this hypothesis. Experiments revealed that, in contrast to the test tube findings, there is no chromosomal damage to white blood cells or any other cells when LSD is given to a human being (Dishotsky et al. 1971).

Studies have also shown that there are no carcinogenic or mutagenic effects from using LSD in experimental animals or human beings, with the exception of the fruit fly. (LSD is a mutagen in fruit flies if given in doses that are equivalent to 100,000 times the hallucinogenic dose for people.) Teratogenic effects occur in mice if LSD is given early in pregnancy. LSD may be teratogenic in rhesus monkeys if it is injected in doses (based on body weight) exceeding at least 100 times the usual hallucinogenic dose for humans. In other studies, women who took street LSD but not those given pure LSD had a higher rate of spontaneous abortions and births of malformed infants; this finding suggests that contaminants in adulterated LSD were responsible for the fetal effects and not the hallucinogen itself (Dishotsky et al. 1971).

Early Human Research

In the 1950s, the U.S. government—specifically, the Central Intelligence Agency (CIA) and the army—became interested in reports of the effects of mind-altering drugs, including LSD. Unknown to the public at the time, these agencies conducted tests on human beings to learn more about such compounds and determine their usefulness in conducting military and clandestine missions. These activities became public when a biochemist, Frank Olson, killed himself in 1953 after being given a drink laced with LSD. Olson had a severe psychotic reaction and was being treated for the condition when he jumped out of a 10th-story window. His family was told only that he had committed suicide. The connection to LSD was not uncovered until 1975. The court awarded Olson's family $750,000 in damages in 1976.

In 1976, the extent of these studies was revealed; nearly 585 soldiers and 900 civilians had been given LSD in poorly organized experiments in which participants were coerced into taking this drug or not told that they were receiving it. Powerful hallucinogens such as LSD can cause serious psychological damage in some subjects, especially when they are unaware of what is happening (Remsberg 2010; Willing 2007).

The legal consequences of these LSD studies continued for years. As recently as 1987, a New York judge awarded $700,000 to the family of a mental patient who killed himself after having been given LSD without an explanation of the drug's nature. The judge said that there was a "conspiracy of silence" among the army, the Department of Justice, and the New York State Attorney General to conceal events surrounding the death of the subject, Harold Blauer (Covert America 2010).

Mescaline (Peyote)

Mescaline is one of approximately 30 psychoactive chemicals that have been isolated from the peyote cactus and used for centuries in the Americas (see "Here and Now: Peyote"). One of the first reports on the peyote plant was made by Francisco Hernandez to the court of King Philip II of Spain. King Philip was interested in reports from the earlier Cortés expedition about strange medicines the natives used, and sent Hernandez to collect information about herbs and medicines. Hernandez worked on this project from 1570 to 1575 and reported on the use of more than 1200 plant remedies as well as the existence of many hallucinogenic plants. He was one of the first to record the eating of parts of the peyote cactus and the resulting visions and mental changes.

In the 17th century, Spanish Catholic priests asked their Indian converts to confess to the use of peyote, which they believed was used to conjure up demons. However, nothing stopped its use. By 1760,

Here and Now

Peyote: An Ancient Indian Way

Members of the Native American Church use the buttons of the hallucinogenic peyote cactus to brew a sacramental tea as sacred to them as the bread and wine of the Christian Eucharist. As described by one member, "Peyote is a gift given to the Indians, but its ways cannot be obtained overnight. It has to be done with sincerity. It becomes part of your way of life. One has to walk that walk." Those who accept this form of worship believe that respectful use of peyote can be a gateway to the realm of the spirit, visions, and guidance. The use of peyote as part of the latest New Age craze is very disturbing to members of this church and is viewed almost as a form of sacrilege.

Source: Mims, B. "Peyote: When the Ancient Indian Way Collides with a New Age Craze." *Salt Lake Tribune* 258 (1 July 1999): A-10; and Native American Church. 2008. Available http://www.nativeamericanchurch.com. Accessed February 17, 2011.

use of peyote had spread into what is now the United States. Peyote has been confused with another plant, the mescal shrub, which produces dark red beans that contain an extremely toxic alkaloid called *cytisine*. This alkaloid may cause hallucinations, convulsions, and even death. In addition, a mescal liquor is made from the agave cactus. Partly because of misidentification with the toxic mescal beans, the U.S. government outlawed the use of both peyote and mescaline for everyone except members of the Native American Church (Mims 2000). Mescaline has been used for decades by this group as part of their religious sacrament. A recent study suggested that long-term religious use of peyote does not have significant psychological effects or cause problems with cognitive performance in Native Americans (Halpern et al. 2005).

Mescaline is the most active drug in peyote; it induces intensified perception of colors and euphoria in the user. However, as Aldous Huxley said in *The Doors of Perception* (1954), his book about his experimentation with mescaline, "Along with the happily transfigured majority of mescaline takers there is a minority that finds in the drug only hell and purgatory." After Huxley related his experiences with mescaline, it was used by an increasing number of people.

Physiological Effects

The average dose of mescaline that will cause hallucinations and other physiological effects is from 300 to 600 milligrams. It may take up to 20 peyote (mescal) buttons (ingested orally) to get 600 milligrams of mescaline.

Based on animal studies, scientists estimate that a lethal dosage is 10 to 30 times greater than that which causes behavioral effects in human beings. (About 200 milligrams is the lowest mind-altering dose.) Death in animals results from convulsions and respiratory arrest. Mescaline is perhaps 1000 to 3000 times less potent than LSD and 30 times less potent than another common hallucinogen, psilocybin (Mathias 1993). Psilocybin is discussed later in this chapter.

Mescaline's effects include dilation of the pupils (**mydriasis**), increase in body temperature, anxiety, visual hallucinations, and alteration of body image. The last effect is a type of hallucination in which parts of the body may seem to disappear or to become grossly distorted. Mescaline induces vomiting in many people and some muscular relaxation (sedation). Apparently, there are few aftereffects or

The peyote cactus contains a number of drugs; the best known is mescaline.

KEY TERMS

mydriasis
pupil dilation

drug hangover feelings at low doses. Higher doses of mescaline slow the heart and respiratory rhythm, contract the intestines and the uterus, and cause headache, difficulty in coordination, dry skin with itching, and hypertension (high blood pressure).

Mescaline users report that they lose all awareness of time. As with LSD, the setting for the "trip" influences the user's reactions. Most mescaline users prefer natural settings, most likely due to the historical association of this drug with Native Americans and their nature-related spiritual experiences (often under the influence of this drug). The visual hallucinations achieved depend on the individual. Colors are at first intensified and may be followed by hallucinations of shades, movements, forms, and events. The senses of smell and taste are enhanced. Some people claim (as with LSD) that they can "hear" colors and "see" sounds, such as the wind. Synesthesia occurs naturally in a small percentage of cases. At low to medium doses, a state of euphoria is reported, often followed by a feeling of anxiety and less frequently by depression. Occasionally, users observe themselves as two people and experience the sensation that the mind and the body are separate entities. A number of people have had cosmic experiences that are profound—almost religious—and in which they discover a sense of unity with all creation. People who have this sensation often believe they have discovered the meaning of existence.

Mechanism of Action

Within 30 to 120 minutes after ingestion, mescaline reaches a maximum concentration in the brain. The effects may persist for as long as 9 or 10 hours. Hallucinations may last up to 2 hours and are usually affected by the dose level. About half the dose is excreted unchanged after 6 hours and can be recovered in the urine for reuse (if peyote is in short supply). A slow tolerance builds up after repeated use, and there is cross-tolerance to LSD. As with LSD, mescaline intoxication can be alleviated or stopped by taking a dose of chlorpromazine (Thorazine), a tranquilizer, and to a lesser extent by taking diazepam (Valium). Like LSD, mescaline probably exerts much of its hallucinogenic effects by altering serotonin systems (Aghajanian and Marck 2000; NIDA 2009).

Analysis of street samples of mescaline obtained in a number of U.S. cities over the past decade shows that the chemical sold rarely is authentic. Regardless of color or appearance, these street drugs are usually other hallucinogens, such as LSD, 2,6-dimethoxy-4-methylamphetamine (DOM), or PCP. If a person decides to take hallucinogenic street drugs, "let the buyer beware." Not only is the actual content often different and potentially much more toxic than bargained for (they are frequently contaminated), but the dosage is usually unknown even if the drug is genuine.

Psilocybin

The drug psilocybin has a long and colorful history. Its principal source is the *Psilocybe mexicana* mushroom of the "magic" variety (Goldstein 1994; U.S. Department of Justice 2002). It was first used by some of the early natives of Central America more than 2000 years ago. In Guatemala, statues of mushrooms that date back to 100 B.C. have been found. The Aztecs later used the mushrooms for ceremonial rites. When the Spaniards came into Mexico in the 1500s, the natives were calling the *Psilocybe mexicana* mushroom "God's flesh" (*Harvard Mental Health Letter* 2006). Because of this seeming sacrilege, the natives were harshly treated by the Spanish priests.

Gordon Wasson identified the *Psilocybe mexicana* mushroom in 1955. The active ingredient was extracted in 1958 by Albert Hofmann, who also synthesized LSD. Doing research, Hofmann wanted to make certain he would feel the effects of the mushroom, so he ate 32 of them, weighing 2.4 grams (a medium dose by Native American standards) and then recorded his hallucinogenic reactions (Burger 1968).

Timothy Leary also tried some psilocybin mushrooms in Mexico in 1960; apparently, the experience influenced him greatly. On his return to Harvard, he carried out a series of experiments using psilocybin with student groups. Leary was careless in experimental procedures and did some work in uncontrolled situations. His actions caused a major administrative upheaval, ending in his departure from Harvard.

One of Leary's questionable studies was the "Good Friday" experiment in which 20 theological students were given either a placebo or psilocybin in a double-blind study (that is, neither the researcher nor the subjects know who gets the placebo or the drug), after which all attended the same 2.5-hour Good Friday service. The experimental group reported mystical experiences whereas the control group did not (Pahnke and Richards 1966). Leary believed that the experience was of value and that, under proper control and guidance, the hallucinatory experience could be beneficial.

Psilocybin is not very common on the street. Generally, it is administered orally and is eaten either fresh or dried. Accidental poisonings are common for those who mistakenly consume poisonous mushrooms rather than the hallucinogenic variety.

The dried form of these mushrooms contains from 0.2% to 0.5% psilocybin. The hallucinogenic effects produced are quite similar to those of LSD, and there is a cross-tolerance among psilocybin, LSD, and mescaline, suggesting they have similar mechanisms of action. The effects caused by psilocybin vary with the dosage taken. Up to 4 milligrams cause a pleasant experience, relaxation, and some body sensation. In some subjects, higher doses cause considerable perceptual and body image changes, accompanied by hallucinations.

Although psilocybin has been reported to be helpful in the treatment of depression for some people, in extreme cases, psilocybin can cause mental problems and induce the first stages of schizophrenia-like psychosis (NIDA 2001; Unger 2010; Vollenwelder et al. 1998; The Week 2010). Psilocybin stimulates the autonomic nervous system, dilates the pupils, and increases body temperature. There is some evidence that psilocybin is metabolized into psilocin, which is more potent and may be the principal active ingredient. Psilocin is found in mushrooms, albeit in small amounts. Like the other hallucinogens, psilocybin apparently causes no physical dependence (NIDA 2009).

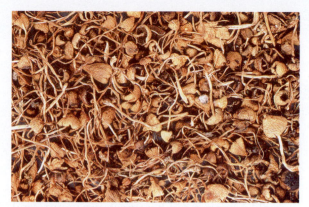

The Psilocybe mushroom is the source of the hallucinogens psilocybin and psilocin.

Tryptamines

Some compounds related to the tryptamine class of drugs (molecules that resemble the neurotransmitter serotonin) have hallucinogenic properties and can exist naturally in herbs, fungi, and animals or can be synthesized in the laboratory. Most of these compounds are Schedule I drugs and illegal (DEA 2002b). Two examples are discussed in this section.

Dimethyltryptamine

Dimethyltryptamine (DMT) is a short-acting hallucinogen found in the seeds of certain leguminous trees native to the West Indies and parts of South America (Schultes 1978) and reported to occur naturally in the human body in low quantities (Horgan 2010). It is also prepared synthetically in illicit laboratories, and is reported to have both beneficial and terrifyingly adverse effects (Horgan 2010). For centuries, the powdered seeds have been used as a snuff called cohoba in pipes and snuffing tubes. Haitian natives claim that, under the influence of the drug, they can communicate with their gods. Its effects occur rapidly and may last less than 1 hour, which has earned it the nickname "the businessman's lunch break" drug (Carollo 2010).

DMT has no effect when taken orally; it is inhaled either as smoke from the burning plant or in vaporized form. DMT is sometimes added to parsley leaves or flakes, tobacco, or marijuana to induce its hallucinogenic effect. The usual dose is 60 to 150 milligrams. In structure and action, it is similar to psilocybin, although it is not as powerful. Like the other hallucinogens discussed, DMT does not cause physical dependence.

Foxy

The synthetic substance chemically named 5-methoxy-N,N-diisopropyltryptamine (Foxy) is a relatively new hallucinogen. This drug has been used at raves and clubs in Arizona, California, New York, and Florida. It was added to the DEA Schedule I category in 2004. At lower doses, Foxy can cause euphoria; at higher doses, its effects are similar to LSD, causing hallucinations and psychedelic experiences (DEA 2002b; enotes 2010).

Nutmeg

High doses of nutmeg can be quite intoxicating, causing symptoms such as drowsiness, stupor, delirium, and sleep. Prison inmates have known about this drug for years, so in most prisons use of spices such as nutmeg is restricted. It is typically young people who experiment with nutmeg to get high, but because of the frequent unpleasant side effects, abusers often end up either in an emergency room or calling a poison control center and usually are not interested in trying nutmeg again. Needless to say, nutmeg is not perceived as a major drug abuse problem by authorities (Conley 2010).

Nutmeg contains 5% to 15% myristica oil, which is responsible for the physical effects. Myristicin (about 4%), which is structurally similar to mescaline, and elemicin are probably the most potent psychoactive ingredients in nutmeg. Myristicin blocks release of serotonin from brain neurons. The exterior covering of the nutmeg seed also contains the hallucinogenic compound myristicin.

Two tablespoons of nutmeg (about 14 grams) taken orally cause a rather unpleasant "trip" with a dreamlike stage; rapid heartbeat, dry mouth, and thirst are experienced as well. Agitation, apprehension, and a sense of impending doom may last about 12 hours, with a sense of unreality persisting for several days (Claus, Tyler, and Brady 1970; Conley 2010).

■ Phenylethylamine Hallucinogens

The phenylethylamine drugs are chemically related to amphetamines. Phenylethylamines have varying degrees of hallucinogenic and CNS stimulant effects, which are likely related to their ability to release serotonin and dopamine, respectively. Consequently, the phenylethylamines that predominantly release serotonin are dominated by their hallucinogenic action and are more LSD-like, whereas those more inclined to release dopamine are dominated by their stimulant effects and are amphetamine-like.

Dimethoxymethylamphetamine

The basic structure of dimethoxymethylamphetamine (DOM or STP) is amphetamine. Nonetheless, it is a fairly powerful hallucinogen that seems to work through mechanisms similar to those found with mescaline and LSD. In fact, the effects of DOM are similar to those caused by a combination of amphetamine and LSD, with the hallucinogenic effects of the drug overpowering the amphetamine-like physiological effects. Like other hallucinogens, DOM is not considered to be particularly addicting, and users experience tolerance with multiple drug exposures (Summit Malibu 2010).

"Designer" Amphetamines

"Designer" amphetamines were discussed in Chapter 10 but are presented again here owing to their hallucinogenic effects. Their hybrid actions as psychedelic stimulants not only make them a particularly fascinating topic for research, but also provide a unique experience described by drug abusers as a "smooth amphetamine" or an **entactogen** (implying that the pleasurable sensation of touch is enhanced). This characterization likely accounts for the popularity of the designer amphetamines (de la Torre et al. 2004).

3,4-Methylenedioxyamphetamine

3,4-Methylenedioxyamphetamine (MDA), first synthesized in 1910, is structurally related to both mescaline and amphetamine. Early research found that MDA is an anorexiant (causing loss of appetite) as well as a mood elevator in some persons. Further research has shown that the mode of action of MDA is similar to that of amphetamines. It causes additional release of the neurotransmitters serotonin, dopamine, and norepinephrine (Baggot et al. 2010).

In the past, MDA was used as an adjunct to psychotherapy. In one study, eight volunteers who had previously experienced the effects of LSD under clinical conditions were given 150 milligrams of MDA. Effects of the drug were noted between 40 and 60 minutes following ingestion by all eight subjects. The subjective effects following administration peaked at the end of 90 minutes and persisted for approximately 8 hours. None of the subjects experienced hallucinations, perceptual distortion, or closed-eye imagery, but they reported that the feelings the drug induced had some relationship to those previously experienced with LSD. The subjects found that both drugs induced an intensification of feelings, increased perceptions of self-insight, and heightened empathy with others during the experience. Most of the subjects also felt an increased sense of aesthetic enjoyment at some point during the intoxication. Seven of the eight subjects said they perceived music as "three-dimensional" (Naranjo, Shulgin, and Sargent 1967).

On the street, MDA has been called the *love drug* because of its effects on the sense of touch and the attitudes of the users. Users often report experiencing a sense of well-being (likely a stimulant effect) and heightened tactile sensations (like a hallucinogenic effect) and thus increased pleasure through sex and expressions of affection. Those under the influence of MDA frequently focus on interpersonal relationships and demonstrate an overwhelming desire or need to be with or talk to people. Some users say they have a very pleasant "body high"—more sensual than cerebral, and more empathetic than introverted. For these reasons, MDA is sometimes used by persons attending raves, much like MDMA or Ecstasy (Baggott et al. 2010).

The unpleasant side effects most often reported are nausea, periodic tensing of muscles in the neck, tightening of the jaw and grinding of the teeth, and dilation of the pupils. Street doses of MDA range from 100 to 150 milligrams. Serious convulsions and death have resulted from larger doses, but in these cases the quantity of MDA was not accurately measured. Ingestion of 500 milligrams of pure MDA has been shown to cause death. The only reported adverse reaction to moderate doses is a marked physical exhaustion, lasting as long as 2 days (Marquardt, DiStefano, and Ling 1978).

An unpleasant MDA experience should be treated the same as a bad trip with any hallucinogen. The person should be "talked down" (reassured) in a friendly and supportive manner. The use of other drugs is rarely needed, although medical attention may be necessary. Under the Comprehensive Drug Abuse Prevention and Control Act of 1970, MDA is classified as a Schedule I substance; illegal possession is a serious offense.

Methylenedioxymethamphetamine

Methylenedioxymethamphetamine (MDMA) is a modification of MDA but is thought to have more psychedelic and less stimulant activity (for example, euphoria) than its predecessor. MDMA is also structurally similar to mescaline. This drug has become known as Ecstasy, XTC, and Adam (Zickler 2000). (Ecstasy also is discussed in Chapter 10.)

MDMA was synthesized in 1912 to suppress appetite, but due to bizarre side effects it was withdrawn from development until it became widely used in the 1980s (Adam 2006). This designer amphetamine can be produced easily, although the process can be hazardous and the chemicals used for the synthesis are difficult to obtain (DEA 2002a; Narconon 2010). Although the synthesis can be done by local illicit laboratories (Hyslop 2000), most of the MDMA supplies in this country are smuggled in from outlaw drug laboratories in European countries such as the Netherlands. The unusual psychological effects it produces are part of the reason for its popularity. The drug causes euphoria, increased energy, increased sensitivity to touch, and lowered inhibitions. Many users claim it intensifies

emotional feelings without sensory distortion and that it increases empathy and awareness both of the user's body and of the aesthetics of the surroundings (Farley 2000). Some consider MDMA to be an aphrodisiac. Because MDMA lowers defense mechanisms and reduces inhibitions, it has even been used during psychoanalysis (Vastag 2010). In fact, recently there have been reports that an initial FDA-approved clinical trial has demonstrated that MDMA was effective in the treatment of 10 or 12 patients suffering from PTSD (Mithoefer et al. 2011). Obviously this represents a very small study, and the results must be confirmed by other much larger clinical trials.

MDMA—popularized in the 1980s by articles in *Newsweek* (Adler 1985), *Time* (Toufexis 1985), and other magazines—recently was again touted on the national newsstands as a drug with euphoric effects, potential therapeutic value, and lack of serious side effects. MDMA is popular with college-age students and young adults (Johnston et al. 2010; Office of National Drug Control Policy [ONDCP] 2008). Because of its effect of enhancing sensations, MDMA has been used as part of a countercultural rave scene, including high-tech music and laser light shows. Observers report that MDMA-linked rave parties are reminiscent of the acid parties of the 1960s and 1970s. The latest cycle of MDMA popularity peaked in 2001 and was being used by 10% of high school seniors (Johnston et al. 2010). However, due to reports of MDMA neurotoxicity and persistent negative side effects, use of this drug decreased dramatically and by 2006 was being used by only 4.1% of high school seniors. But by 2010 the use of Ecstasy by this group increased slightly to 4.5% (Johnston et al. 2010).

Because of the widespread abuse of MDMA, the DEA prohibited its use by formally placing it on the Schedule I list in 1988 (ONDCP 2008). At the time of the ban, it was estimated that as many as 200 physicians were using the drug in psychotherapy (Greer and Tolbert 1990) and an estimated 30,000 doses per month were being taken for recreational purposes. Currently, MDMA is referred to as a "club drug" because of its frequent use at rave dances, clubs, and bars (ONDCP 2008). It costs 25–50 cents to produce a tablet of Ecstasy in Europe, but on the street that same tablet costs $20–30 (essortment 2010). MDMA is usually taken orally, but it is sometimes snorted or even occasionally smoked. After the high starts, it may persist for minutes or even an hour, depending on the person, the purity of the drug, and the environment

Ecstasy is frequently used at raves to increase sensory stimulation and the pleasure of touching.

in which it is taken. When coming down from an MDMA-induced high, people often take small oral doses known as "boosters" to get high again. If they take too many boosters, they become very fatigued the next day. The average dose is about 75 to 150 milligrams; toxic effects have been reported at higher doses. Some statistics suggest that almost 50% of the tablets sold as MDMA actually contain other drugs such as aspirin, caffeine, cocaine, methamphetamine, or pseudoephedrine (Tanner-Smith 2006).

There is disagreement as to the possible harmful side effects of MDMA. Use of high doses can cause psychosis and paranoia (NIDA 2010b). Some negative physiological responses caused by recreational doses include dilated pupils, dry mouth and throat, clenching and grinding of teeth (resulting in the use of baby pacifiers), muscle aches and stiffness (in 28% of users), fatigue (in 80% of users), insomnia (in 38% of users), agitation, and anxiety. Some of these reactions can be intense and unpredictable. Under some conditions, death can be caused by hyperthermia (elevated body temperature), instability of the autonomic nervous system, underlying cardiovascular problems, or kidney failure (Kaye, Darke, and Duflou 2009; King and Cockery 2010).

Several studies have demonstrated long-term damage to serotonin neurons in the brain following a single high dose of either MDMA or MDA, which may result in impaired memory, diminished ability to process information, and heightened impulsivity (Kish et al. 2010). Although the behavioral significance of this damage in people is not clear, at the present time caution using this drug is warranted (see "Here and Now: MDMA's Users").

There has been considerable debate as to the addictive properties of MDMA. Some claim this drug is like LSD with little likelihood of causing physical dependence, whereas others claim its properties are likely to be more amphetamine-like and suggest that up to 40% of those who use MDMA routinely have developed some dependence (NIDA 2010a). Part of the difficulty in sorting out this controversy is that most moderate MDMA users also use other drugs, making it difficult to determine which effects are specifically attributable to the MDMA. The potential of MDMA to cause addiction and dependence is likely somewhere between that of amphetamine and LSD. Because of its ability to cause euphoria and release dopamine in the brain, it is very probable that heavy use or administration by smoking or injection can cause significant dependence.

Here and Now

MDMA's Users

Studies examining regular and novice (first-time) Ecstasy users found that regular users consume, on average, 1.8 MDMA tablets whereas the novice users take 1.4 MDMA tablets. Both groups report positive moods during activities such as a rave dance. However, days later, both Ecstasy groups often feel significantly depressed, unsociable, unpleasant, and ill-tempered. Verbal recall is also diminished in MDMA users, who remembered only 60% to 70% of the words recalled by control groups. Those who use Ecstasy regularly have the most difficulty remembering. The heaviest users also report variable acute negative experiences that can include psychotic thoughts, panic attacks, anxiety, and insomnia.

Sources: Parrott, A., and J. Lasky. "Ecstasy (MDMA) Effects Upon Mood and Cognition: Before, During and After a Saturday Night Dance." *Psychopharmacology* 139 (1998): 261–268; and Karlsen, S., O. Spigset, and L. Slordal. "The Dark Side of Ecstasy: Neuropsychiatric Symptoms After Exposure to 3,4-Methylenedioxymethamphetamine." *Basic and Clinical Pharmacology and Toxicology* 102 (2008): 15–24.

■ Anticholinergic Hallucinogens

The anticholinergic hallucinogens include naturally occurring alkaloid (bitter organic base) substances that are present in plants and herbs found around the world. These drugs are often mentioned in folklore and in early literature as being added to potions. They are thought to have killed the Roman Emperor Claudius and to have poisoned Hamlet's father. Historically, they have been the favorite drugs used to eliminate inconvenient people (Marken, Stoner, and Bunker 1996). Hallucinogens affecting the cholinergic neurons also have been used by South American Indians for religious ceremonies (Schultes and Hofmann 1980) and were probably used in witchcraft to give the illusion of flying, to prepare sacrificial victims, and even to give some types of marijuana ("superpot") its kick.

The potato family of plants (*Solanaceae*) contain most of these mind-altering drugs. The following three potent anticholinergic compounds are commonly found in these plants: (1) scopolamine, or hyoscine; (2) hyoscyamine; and (3) atropine. Scopolamine may produce excitement, hallucinations, and delirium even at therapeutic doses. With atropine, doses bordering on toxic levels are usually required to obtain these effects (Schultes and Hofmann 1973). All of these active alkaloid drugs block some acetylcholine receptors (see Chapter 4).

These alkaloid drugs can be used as ingredients in cold symptom remedies because they have a drying effect and block production of mucus in the nose and throat. They also prevent salivation; therefore, the mouth becomes uncommonly dry and perspiration may stop. Atropine may increase the heart rate by 100% and dilate the pupils markedly, causing inability to focus on nearby objects. Other annoying side effects of these anticholinergic drugs include constipation and difficulty in urinating. These inconveniences tend to discourage excessive abuse of these drugs for their hallucinogenic properties. Usually, people who abuse these anticholinergic compounds are receiving the drugs by prescription (Marken et al. 1996; MayoClinic 2010).

Anticholinergics can cause drowsiness by affecting the sleep centers of the brain. At large doses, a condition occurs that is similar to a psychosis, characterized by delirium, loss of attention, mental confusion, and sleepiness (Carlini 1993). Hallucinations may also occur at higher doses. At very high doses, paralysis of the respiratory system may cause death.

Although hundreds of plant species naturally contain anticholinergic substances and consequently can cause psychedelic experiences, only a few of the principal plants are mentioned here.

Atropa Belladonna: The Deadly Nightshade Plant

Knowledge of *Atropa belladonna* is very old, and its use as a drug is reported in early folklore. The name of the genus, *Atropa*, is the origin for the drug name atropine and indicates the reverence the Greeks had for the plant. Atropos was one of the three Fates in Greek mythology, whose duty it was to cut the thread of life when the time came. This plant has been used for thousands of years by assassins and murderers. In *Tales of the Arabian Nights*, unsuspecting potentates were poisoned with atropine from the deadly nightshade or one of its relatives. Fourteen berries of the deadly nightshade contain enough drug to cause death.

The species name, *belladonna*, means "beautiful woman." In early Rome and Egypt, girls with large pupils were considered attractive and friendly. To create this condition, they would put a few drops of an extract of this plant into their eyes, causing the pupils to dilate (Marken et al. 1996). Belladonna has also enjoyed a reputation as a love potion.

Mandragora Officinarum: The Mandrake

The mandrake contains several active psychedelic alkaloids: hyoscyamine, scopolamine, atropine, and mandragorine. Mandrake has been used as a love potion for centuries but has also been known for its toxic properties. In ancient folk medicine, mandrake was used to treat many ailments in spite of its side effects. It was recommended as a sedative, to relieve nervous conditions, and to relieve pain (Schultes and Hofmann 1980), as portrayed in the 2007 movie, *Pan's Labyrinth*.

The root of the mandrake is forked and, viewed with a little imagination, may resemble the human body (as portrayed in the *Harry Potter and the Chamber of Secrets* movie in 2002). Because of this resemblance, it has been credited with human attributes, which gave rise to many superstitions in the Middle Ages about its magical powers. Shakespeare referred to this plant in *Romeo and Juliet*. In her farewell speech, Juliet says, "And shrieks like mandrakes torn out of the earth, that living mortals hearing them run mad."

Hyoscyamus Niger: Henbane

Henbane is a plant that contains both hyoscyamine and scopolamine. In AD 60, Pliny the Elder spoke of henbane: "For this is certainly known, that if one takes it in drink more than four leaves, it will put him beside himself" (Jones 1956). Henbane was also used in the orgies, or bacchanalias, of the ancient world.

Although rarely used today, henbane has been given medicinally since early times. It was frequently used to cause sleep, although hallucinations often occurred if given in excess. It was likely included in witches' brews and deadly concoctions during the Dark Ages (Schultes and Hofmann 1980).

Datura Stramonium: Jimsonweed

The *Datura* genus of the *Solanaceae* family includes a large number of related plants found worldwide. The principal active drug in this group is scopolamine; there are also several less active alkaloids.

Throughout history, these plants have been used as hallucinogens by many societies. They are mentioned in early Sanskrit and Chinese writings and were revered by the Buddhists. There is also some indication that the priestess (oracle) at the ancient Greek Temple of Apollo at Delphi was under the influence of this type of plant when she made prophecies (Schultes 1970). Before the supposed divine possession, she appeared to have chewed leaves of the sacred laurel. A mystic vapor was also reported to have risen from a fissure in the ground. The sacred laurel may have been one of the *Datura* species, and the vapors may have come from burning these plants.

Jimsonweed gets its name from an incident that took place in 17th-century Jamestown. British soldiers ate this weed while trying to capture Nathaniel Bacon, who had made seditious remarks about the king. Consumption of jimsonweed is still occasionally done by young people who are searching for an inexpensive hallucinogenic experience. Because this wild weed grows in most parts of the United States it is relatively easy to find and is free. This plant has been referred to by names such as angel's trumpet, locoweed, and stinkweed. The hallucinogenic effects from this plant are mainly due to the presence of the two powerful anticholinergic drugs atropine and scopolamine in the roots. Often the person who consumes the jimsonweed in a stew or other brew ends up in the emergency room complaining of hallucinations, confusion, dilated pupils, and rapid heart-

Datura stramonium, or jimsonweed, is a common plant that contains the hallucinogenic drug scopolamine.

beat. Because of the very unpleasant side effects, abuse of jimsonweed is not considered to be a major drug abuse problem, but most emergency rooms will occasionally see an unsuspecting young person who foolishly experiments with jimsonweed for a cheap and natural high and gets much more than expected (MedTox 2010).

■ Other Hallucinogens

Technically, any drug that alters perceptions, thoughts, and feelings in a manner that is not normally experienced except in dreams can be classified as a hallucinogen. Because the brain's sensory input is complex and involves several neurotransmitter systems, drugs with many diverse effects can cause hallucinations (NIDA 2001).

Four agents that do not conveniently fit into the principal categories of hallucinogens are discussed in the following sections.

Phencyclidine

Phencyclidine (PCP) is considered by many experts as the most dangerous of the hallucinogens (APA 2000; Maier 2003). PCP was developed in the late 1950s as an intravenous anesthetic. Although it was found to be effective, it had serious side effects such as precipitating schizophrenia-like symptoms that caused it to be discontinued for human use (Farwell 2010; NIDA 2001). Sometimes when people were recovering from PCP anesthesia, they experienced delirium and manic states of excitation lasting 18 hours (APA 2000). PCP is currently a Schedule II drug, legitimately available only as an anesthetic for animals, but it has even been banned from veterinary practice since 1985 because of its high theft rate. Most, if not all, PCP used in the United States today is produced illegally (National Drug Intelligence Center 2004).

Street PCP is mainly synthesized from readily available chemical precursors in clandestine laboratories. Within 24 hours, cooks (the makers of street PCP) can set up a lab, make several gallons of the drug, and destroy the lab before the police can locate them. Liquid PCP is then poured into containers and ready for shipment (Maier 2003).

PCP first appeared on the street drug scene in 1967 as the *PeaCe Pill*. In 1968, it reappeared in New York as a substance called hog. By 1969, PCP was found under a variety of guises. It was sold as angel dust and sprinkled on parsley for smoking. Today, it is sold on the streets under many different slang names, including *angel dust, supergrass, killerweed, embalming fluid, bobbies, dippies, hydro a,* and *purple haze,* to mention a few (Dewan 2003; Maier 2003).

In the late 1960s, PCP began to find its way into a variety of street drugs sold as psychedelics. By 1970, authorities observed that phencyclidine was used widely as a main ingredient in psychedelic preparations. It has been frequently substituted for and sold as LSD, mescaline, marijuana, and cocaine (Maier 2003; National Drug Intelligence Center 2004).

One difficulty in estimating the effects or use patterns of PCP is caused by variance in drug purity. Also, there are about 30 **analogs** of PCP, some of which have appeared on the street. PCP has so many other street names that people may not know they are using it or they may have been deceived when buying what they thought was LSD or mescaline (Dewan 2003). Users may not question the identity of the substances unless they have a bad reaction.

PCP is available as a pure, white crystalline powder; as tablets; or as capsules. However, because it is usually manufactured in makeshift laboratories, it is frequently discolored by contaminants from a tan to brown with a consistency ranging from powder to a gummy mass (U.S. Department of Justice 1991). PCP can be taken orally, smoked, sniffed, or injected (NIDA 2007c). In the late 1960s through the early 1970s, PCP was mostly taken orally, but it is now commonly snorted or applied to dark brown cigarettes, or leafy materials such as parsley, mint,

oregano, marijuana, or tobacco, and smoked (U.S. Department of Justice 2003). By smoking PCP, the experienced user is better able to limit his or her dosage to a desired level. After smoking, the subjective effects appear within 1 to 5 minutes and peak within the next 5 to 30 minutes. The high lasts about 4 to 6 hours, followed by a 6- to 24-hour "comedown" (APA 2000).

In the 1979 national drug survey performed by the National Institute on Drug Abuse, about 7% of U.S. high school seniors had used PCP in a 12-month period; however, in 2010, that rate had dropped dramatically to 1.0% (Johnston et al. 2010).

Physiological Effects

Although PCP may have hallucinogenic effects, it can cause a host of other physiological actions, including stimulation, depression, anesthesia, and analgesia. The effects of PCP on the CNS vary greatly. At low doses, the most prominent effect is similar to that of alcohol intoxication, with generalized numbness. As the dose of PCP increases, the person becomes even more insensitive and may become fully anesthetized. Large doses can cause coma, convulsions, and death (APA 2000).

The majority of peripheral effects are apparently related to activation of the sympathetic nervous system (see Chapter 5). Flushing, excess sweating, and a blank stare are common, although the size of the pupils is unaffected. The cardiovascular system reacts by increasing blood pressure and heart rate. Other effects include side-to-side eye movements (called nystagmus), muscular incoordination, double vision, dizziness, nausea, and vomiting (National Drug Intelligence Center 2004). These symptoms occur in many people who take medium to high doses.

Psychological Effects

PCP has unpleasant effects most of the time it is used. Why, then, do people use it repeatedly as their drug of choice?

PCP has the ability to markedly alter the person's subjective feelings; this effect may be reinforcing, even though the alteration is not always positive. Some say use of PCP makes them feel godlike and powerful (Maier 2003). There is an element of risk, not knowing how the trip will turn out. PCP may give

KEY TERMS

analogs
drugs with similar structures

the user feelings of strength, power, and invulnerability (NIDA 2007c). Other positive effects include heightened sensitivity to outside stimuli, a sense of stimulation and mood elevation, and dissociation from surroundings. Also, PCP is a social drug; virtually all users report taking it in groups rather than during a solitary experience. PCP also causes serious perceptual distortions. Users cannot accurately interpret the environment and as a result may do what appear to be absurd things such as jump out of a window thinking they can fly (APA 2000).

Chronic users may take PCP in "runs" extending over 2 to 3 days, during which time they do not sleep or eat. In later stages of chronic administration, users may develop outright paranoia, unpredictable violent behavior, and auditory hallucinations (APA 2000; Farwell 2010). Law enforcement officers claim to be more fearful of suspects on PCP than of suspects on other drugs of abuse. Often such people seem to have superhuman strength and are totally irrational and very difficult—even dangerous—to manage (NIDA 2007a, 2007c).

PCP has no equal in its ability to produce brief psychoses similar to schizophrenia (Jentsch and Roth 1999). The psychoses—induced with moderate doses given to normal, healthy volunteers—last about 2 hours and are characterized by changes in body image, thought disorders, estrangement, autism, and occasionally rigid inability to move (**catatonia**, or catalepsy). Subjects report feeling numb, have great difficulty differentiating between themselves and their surroundings, and complain afterward of feeling extremely isolated and apathetic. They are often violently paranoid during the psychosis (APA 2000; Medical Letter 1996). When PCP was given experimentally to hospitalized chronic schizophrenics, it made them much worse not for a few hours but for 6 weeks. PCP is not just another hallucinogen—many authorities view it as much more dangerous than other drugs of abuse (Dewan 2003; Maier 2003).

Medical Management

The diagnosis of a PCP overdose is frequently missed because the symptoms often closely resemble those of an acute schizophrenic episode. Simple, uncomplicated PCP intoxication can be managed with the same techniques used in other psychedelic drug cases. It is important to have a quiet environment, limited contact with an empathic person capable of determining any deterioration in the patient's physical state, protection from self-harm, and the availability of hospital facilities. Talking down is not helpful; the patient is better off isolated from external stimuli as much as possible.

Valium is often used for its sedating effect to prevent injury to self and to staff and also to reduce the chance for severe convulsions. An antipsychotic agent (for example, haloperidol [Haldol]) is frequently administered to make the patient manageable (Jaffe 1990).

The medical management of a comatose or convulsing patient is more difficult. The patient may need external respiratory assistance and external cooling to reduce fever. Blood pressure may have to be reduced to safe levels and convulsions controlled. Restraints and four to five strong hospital aides are often needed to prevent the patient from injuring himself or herself or the medical staff. After the coma lightens, the patient typically becomes delirious, paranoid, and violently assaultive (see "Case in Point: PCP Use Can Mean Violent Trouble").

Effects of Chronic Use

Chronic PCP users may develop a tolerance to the drug; thus, a decrease in behavioral effects and toxicity can occur with frequent administration. Different forms of dependence may occur when tolerance develops. Users may complain of vague cravings after cessation of the drug. In addition, long-term difficulties in memory, speech, and thinking persist for 6 to 12 months in the chronic user (NIDA 2007c). These functional changes are accompanied by personality deficits such as social isolation and states of anxiety, nervousness, and extreme agitation (APA 2000; Farwell 2010).

Ketamine

Ketamine has been considered a club drug (Cloud 2010). Its annual use in 2010 by high school seniors was 1.6% (Johnston et al. 2010). Almost all persons who abuse ketamine have abused at least three other illicit drugs (Center for Substance Abuse Research [CESAR] 2006), and those who abuse it chronically lose cognitive function and experience a deteriorating sense of well-being (Morgan, Muetzelfeldt, and Curran 2010). Ketamine, like PCP, was originally developed for its general anesthetic properties (AddictionSearch 2010; NIDA 2001). Its effects resemble those of PCP except they are more rapid

KEY TERMS

catatonia
a condition of physical rigidity, excitement, and stupor

▶Case in Point   PCP Use Can Mean Violent Trouble

Although PCP use has fallen out of favor in recent years, occasionally a PCP-precipitated tragedy occurs that reminds us why this drug is considered to be one of the most dangerous of the substances of abuse. In July 2010 the son of the Dallas police chief was shot and killed by a police officer after he had gunned down two innocent bystanders. The medical examiner discovered PCP in his system. Witnesses related that before the senseless rampage, while humming to himself, the young man had stripped to his boxers, a frequent behavior of PCP users because they have the sensation that bugs are crawling all over their skin. Before shooting the two men, the chief's son manifested considerable aggression and paranoia, which is consistent with the fact that PCP users often become violent because they think that someone is trying to kill them. Accounts such as this are reminders of the terrible consequences of abusing this powerful hallucinogen.

Source: Farwell, S. "Though PCP Use Has Been Falling, Drug Can Still Lead to Violent Trouble." *Dallas Morning News.* 9 July 2010. Available at: http://www.dallasnews.com/sharedcontent/dws/news/localnews/crime/stories/070910dnmetpcp.1cef8c6.html. Accessed March 16, 2011.

and less potent (NIDA 2001). Depending on the dose, ketamine can have many effects, ranging from feelings of weightlessness to out-of-body or near-death experiences. Ketamine, often referred to as "Special K," has been abused as a "date rape" drug like other CNS depressants, such as Rohypnol or gamma-hydroxybutyrate (GHB) (see Chapter 6; NIDA 2001). Abuse of ketamine has been reported in many cities throughout the United States, and the drug is sometimes snorted as a substitute for cocaine. Several deaths have been linked to ketamine overdoses (NIDA 2007a).

Despite its potential as a drug of abuse, recent studies have suggested that it may have some potential as an antidepressant. When given to severely depressed patients in a small clinical trial it resulted in a "robust and rapid (within minutes)

antidepressant response." However, it should be pointed out that the improvement was temporary and patients were again depressed 2 weeks after the ketamine treatment (Cloud 2010). The explanation for this effect is being investigated.

Dextromethorphan

Dextromethorphan is the active ingredient used in many OTC cough medicines because of its ability to suppress the cough reflex (CESAR 2005). Although harmless in low recommended doses, if consumed in high quantities (approximately 10 times the recommended dose), it can cause some hallucinogenic effects much like PCP and ketamine do as well as other symptoms such as confusion, numbness, disorientation, and stomach pain (Gresser 2010). The effects of dextromethorphan can vary and have been described as ranging from a mild stimulant effect to a complete dissociation from one's body and can last for several hours. Abuse of dextromethorphan is typically done by teenagers and is sometimes referred to as "roboing" (CESAR 2005). Recreational use of cough medicines containing this drug reached 6.6% in high school seniors in 2010 (Johnston et al. 2010). This practice of consuming high doses of cough medicine can be extremely dangerous and on occasions even fatal (see "Prescription for Abuse: Cough Medicine Abuse"). Most young people who abuse cough medicines are abusing other substances such as marijuana, LSD, or Ecstasy. This surprisingly high rate of abuse for cough medicines has caused some to suggest that these products be removed from shelves and placed behind the pharmacy counters or only be sold to consumers over the age of 18. Although the FDA has considered these strategies, as of yet its advisory

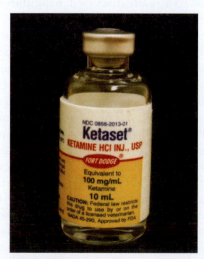

Ketamine is frequently used as a general anesthetic for veterinary procedures.

Prescription for Abuse: Cough Medicine Abuse—Nothing to Be Sneezed At

Although abuse of cough medicine has not been considered serious enough by the FDA or other federal agencies to do anything more than issue warnings, many parents are concerned because cough syrup abuse seems to be on the rise, as it is cheap and readily available to almost anyone, including teenagers. It is generally known by young people that high doses of cough medicines that contain the drug dextromethorphan can cause euphoria, some stimulation, and even hallucinations. However, what is not appreciated by many potential young consumers is that high-dose abuse of these products can have serious negative consequences. For example, some of the cough syrups also contain other ingredients such as the analgesic drug acetaminophen (active ingredient in Tylenol). When consumed in high doses (as would be the case if someone were to ingest 10 times the recommended dose of an acetaminophen-containing cough medicine to achieve a high), the high doses of acetaminophen can do permanent and even fatal damage to the liver. In addition, high doses of dextromethorphan itself cause a dissociative effect (e.g., confusion), loss of motor control, nausea,

dizziness, fever, hypertension, and difficulty breathing. For long-term abusers, dependence on the dextromethorphan can occur, causing significant withdrawal symptoms such as insomnia, dysphoria, and depression. Finally, cough medicine overdoses often are accompanied by alcohol use, resulting in potentially life-threatening interactions such as severe depressed breathing.

Source: Marsh, J. "DXM Addiction: Drug Addiction and Cough Syrup Abuse." Suite101.com. 13 August 2010. Available at: http://www.suite101.com/content/dxm-addiction-drug-addiction-and-cough-syrup-abuse-effects-a273947. Accessed March 16, 2011.

panel of medical experts has advised against them (Gresser 2010).

Marijuana

In high doses, marijuana use can result in image distortions and hallucinations (Nunez and Gurpegui 2002). Some users claim that marijuana can enhance hearing, vision, and skin sensitivity, although these claims have not been confirmed in controlled laboratory studies.

Although typical marijuana use does not appear to cause severe emotional disorders like the other hallucinogens, some experts suggest it can aggravate underlying mental illness such as depression, schizophrenia, or anxiety (NIDA 2010c). Each month, thousands of people seek professional treatment due to marijuana-related problems (Narconon 2007). In contrast to other hallucinogens that have a combination of stimulant and psychedelic effects, high doses of marijuana cause a combination of depression and hallucinations and enhance the appetite (Fleckenstein 2000). Marijuana is discussed thoroughly in Chapter 13.

Natural Substances

Naturally Occurring Hallucinogens

Many plants contain naturally occurring hallucinogens. As already discussed, examples of such substances include mescaline from the peyote cactus, psilocybin from psilocybe mushrooms, and anticholinergic drugs such as atropine from the deadly nightshade plant, mandrake, or jimsonweed. Although some of these plants have been used for medicinal purposes for centuries, typically the therapeutic benefit has not been a consequence of the hallucinogenic effects of the substance. For example, anticholinergic drugs usually cause CNS depression and induce sleep; therefore, herbs that contain these drugs have been used as sleep potions. The hallucinogenic properties of some natural products, such as peyote, are viewed as positive by some cultures. As already mentioned, peyote is employed in a religious context as a sacrament for the Native American Church. In the United States today, the hallucinogen-containing natural substances are generally not viewed as therapeutic and are more likely to be used for their mind-altering properties as recreational drugs by adolescents (see "Case in Point: Jimsonweed Toxicity in Maryland"). In 2006 there were almost 1000 reported incidents of poisonings with these hallucinogenic plants, most frequently by kids trying to get high (Leinwand 2006). Some users claim because these are natural rather than synthetic sources of a hallucinogenic episode, that somehow it makes the experience more rewarding and desirable. There is no evidence that the natural-versus-synthetic features of a hallucinogen are responsible for the quality of a drug-induced hallucination. Frequently, consumption of these seeds and weeds causes severe hallucinations, dry mouth, hyperthermia, seizures, and occasionally death (Leinwand 2006; Russell 2010).

Salvia Divinorum

Occasionally, obscure hallucinogenic herbs make their way into the culture of hallucinogenic substance users. This migration has become easier because of the Internet and specialized web sites that provide information (some accurate and much anecdotal) and the means to acquire these typically natural substances. For example, a relatively recent hallucinogenic fad has been the use of the Mexican herb *Salvia divinorum,* a drug that did not reach the United States until the late 1980s (Allday 2007). In 2010 this plant was abused by 5.5% of high school seniors in the United States, a rate of use little changed from that in 2009 (Johnston et al. 2010). This bright, leafy green plant is usually smoked but can also be chewed, crushed, or mixed in a drink (Fernandez 2008). This relatively unknown plant is referred to as "diviner's mint," and although it is legal in most states, despite its ability to cause intense hallucinations, "out-of-body" experiences, and short-term memory loss, the federal government has been considering legislation to regulate this hallucinogenic plant as a Schedule I substance like marijuana (Melnick 2010). Promotions for these products include advertising claims such as "The Mazatec people have preserved *Salvia divinorum* and the knowledge surrounding its use for hundreds of years. We are privileged to have them share their sacred herb with us" (Jones 2001, p. A14). The dried herb sells for $10–60 a hit depending on the quality and purity of the product (Detrick 2010). The substance typically makes the user introverted while "altering the consciousness in unusual ways" (Vince 2006) (see "Here and Now: A Legal High . . . At Least for Now"). This herb can have dramatic effects on perception similar to LSD (Allday 2007), causing hallucinations when chewed or smoked (Leinwand 2003). It typically is not used in social settings and frequently is used only once because for some people the effects can be quite unpleasant, often triggering a lack of coordination and frightening perceptions (Fernandez 2008). Because of its frequent negative consequences, this herb is not viewed as particularly addicting for most people (Detrick 2010; Pienciak 2003). However, some users describe a pleasant experience that is "almost innocent and quaint," with one teenage user describing the effects of salvia as causing "ferris wheels, flying pigs and fairies wearing a green dress" (Fernandez 2008).

▶ **Case in Point**   **Jimsonweed Toxicity in Maryland**   ◀

Jimsonweed is a natural herb with medicinal purposes that include treatment for asthma, muscle spasms, and whooping cough. It also causes a cluster of very annoying and even dangerous side effects. Because of these toxic effects, intentional and unintentional use of jimsonweed can often result in an unexpected visit to an emergency room. For example, six adults of the same family were admitted to a Maryland hospital emergency room suffering from extreme hallucinations, incoherence, dilated pupils (causing blurred vision), a very rapid heartbeat, and, in one case, unconsciousness. The symptoms lasted several hours and the patients remained in the hospital 2–4 days. Follow-up investigations discovered that all of the patients had consumed a meal of homemade stew that included jimsonweed. The preparer of the stew inadvertently included cuttings from a jimsonweed plant outside the kitchen door without a knowledge of the plant's toxic consequences. Such emergency experiences are all too frequent results of ignorance about this natural, but potent, hallucinogen.

Source: Russell, J. "Jimsonweed Poisoning Associated with a Homemade Stew." *Morbidity and Mortality Weekly Report* 59 (2010): 102–104. Available at: http://www.faqs.org/periodicals/201002/1971642741.html. Accessed March 16, 2011.

Here and Now

A Legal High . . . At Least for Now

One user described smoking *Salvia divinorum* he purchased legally at a local health shop near his home. He related an experience unlike any other that gave him a consciousness-expanding journey. His body felt disconnected, resulting in people and objects taking on a cartoonish, surreal, and marvelous appearance. Abruptly the visions ended and the user found himself back in his room with his "sitter" (a person designated to watch the drug user to prevent accidents or harm—this was recommended on the product's package). The user felt awkward and clumsy when talking or trying to stand. Within a couple of minutes his mind felt clear although his body was damp from sweating. The whole experience lasted approximately 5 minutes. The user admits little is known about the adverse effects of salvia and acknowledges the need for additional study. Intriguing descriptions such as this have attracted interest from both young people curious about the effects of this "mysterious" drug and law enforcement agencies wary that abuse of salvia may escalate into a major drug problem. These reactions have been further enhanced by reports of abuse by celebrities such as the pop singer and former child star, Miley Cyrus, who has been shown in controversial Internet videos smoking a pipe with salvia while laughing uncontrollably with garbled speech. But as of yet, products containing legal hallucinogenic herbs such as salvia are available in shops throughout most of the United States and around the world without regulation. This is because levels of salvia use appear to be somewhat static, supporting observations that use of this hallucinogen does not appear to be particularly addicting and causes an experience many users are not particularly eager to repeat.

Sources: Vince, G. "Legally High." *New Scientist* (30 September 2006): 40–45; Thier, D. "Salvia Takes Center Stage In Miley Cyrus Bong Video Drama." AOLNews. 13 December 2010. Available at: http://www.aolnews.com/2010/12/13/salvia-takes-center-stage-in-miley-cyrus-bong-video-drama. Accessed March 16, 2011; and Detrick, B. "Salvia Takes a Starring Role." *New York Times.* 23 December 2010. Available at: http://www.nytimes.com/2010/12/26/fashion/26noticed.html?_r=1. Accessed March 16, 2011.

More recent reports from some scientists researching the active ingredient salvinorum A suggest that this drug may be useful in the treatment of conditions such as chronic pain, dementias, schizophrenia, bipolar disorders, or even drug addiction itself. Much more research needs to be conducted to determine which, if any, of these claims are clinically significant (Melnick 2010).

Discussion Questions

1. Why were substances with hallucinogenic properties used by ancient religions and cults?

2. Would you expect natural hallucinogens such as peyote to have less adverse effects than other hallucinogens? Why or why not?

3. Why would a drug with both stimulant and hallucinogenic effects have peculiar abuse potential, especially to young people?

4. Why do some users find psychedelic experiences terrifying while others find them desirable?

5. Do you think the federal government is justified in deceiving the public about the dangers of hallucinogens to convince people to stop using these drugs? Defend your answer.

6. How do the side effects of LSD compare with those of the CNS stimulants?

7. Why does MDMA have the potential to be popular?

8. Do you think it is all right to research psychedelic drugs such as LSD and MDMA to deter-

mine if they have medicinal value? What are the advantages and disadvantages of doing this?

9. Why is PCP more dangerous than LSD?

10. How do PCP and ketamine compare?

11. What is the best way to convince people that hallucinogenic drugs of abuse can be harmful?

12. What is a flashback, and how is it caused?

13. Should *salvia divinorum* be more tightly controlled by the government?

Summary

1 Many drugs can exert hallucinogenic effects. The principal hallucinogens include LSD types, phenylethylamines, and anticholinergic agents. The four major effects that occur from administering LSD are (a) heightened senses, (b) loss of sensory control, (c) self-reflection or introspection, and (d) loss of identity or sense of cosmic merging.

2 Hallucinogens exaggerate sensory input and cause vivid and unusual visual and auditory effects.

3 The classic hallucinogens, such as LSD, cause predominantly psychedelic effects. Phenylethylamines are related to amphetamines and cause varying combinations of psychedelic and stimulant effects. Anticholinergic drugs also produce psychedelic effects when taken in high doses.

4 One of the prominent effects of hallucinogens is self-reflection. The user becomes aware of thoughts and feelings that had been forgotten or repressed. It is claimed that some experiences help to clarify motives and relationships and cause periods of greater openness. These effects have been promoted by some psychiatrists as providing valid insights useful in psychotherapy, especially for managing conditions such as PTSD, anxiety disorders, and depression.

5 The classic hallucinogens do not cause physical dependence. Although some tolerance can build up to the hallucinogenic effects of drugs such as LSD, withdrawal effects are usually minor.

6 The environment plays a major role in determining the sensory response to hallucinogens. Environments that are warm, comfortable, and hospitable tend to create a pleasant sensory response to the psychedelic effects of these drugs. Threat-ening, hostile environments are likely to lead to intimidating, frightening "bad trips."

7 In some users, high doses of LSD can cause a terrifying destruction of identity, resulting in panic and severe anxiety that resembles schizophrenia. Another psychological feature commonly associated with LSD is the flashback phenomenon. LSD use can cause recurring, unexpected visual and time distortions that last a few minutes to several hours. Flashbacks can occur months to years after use of the drug.

8 Designer amphetamines such as MDMA (Ecstasy) have been included in the "club drug" phenomenon. MDMA has been used frequently by young people to enhance the sensory experience of raves and the nightclub scene. Although viewed by some as harmless and even therapeutic, evidence of potentially serious negative physiological and neurological consequences suggests that these drugs can be extremely dangerous in high doses and under some conditions.

9 Hallucinogens purchased on the street are often poorly prepared and contaminated with adulterant substances. This practice of cutting the pure drugs with other substances also makes use of street hallucinogens very dangerous.

10 PCP differs from the other traditional hallucinogens in several ways. (a) It is a general anesthetic in high doses. (b) It causes schizophrenia-like psychosis. PCP can produce incredible strength and extreme violent behavior, making users very difficult and dangerous to manage. (c) Management of the severe psychological reactions to PCP requires drug therapy, whereas treatment of other hallucinogens often requires only reassurance, talking down, and supportive therapy. (d) Reactions to overdoses include fever, convulsions, and coma. Ketamine is related to, but less potent than, PCP and shares many of its pharmacological effects.

11 Other substances also abused for their hallucinogenic properties include dextromethorphan, a common OTC anticough medication, and some natural herbs, such as *Salvia divinorum,* that are promoted over the Internet.

References

Adam, D. "Truth About Ecstasy's Unlikely Trip from Lab to Dance Floor." *The Guardian.* 18 August 2006. Available http://guardian.co.uk/uk/2006/aug/18/topstories3.drugsandalcohol

AddictionSearch. "Ketamine Addiction, Abuse and Withdrawal." 2010. Available http://www.addictionsearch.com/treatment_articles/article/ketamine-addiction-abuse-and-withdrawal_23.html

Adler, J. "Getting High on Ecstasy." *Newsweek* (15 April 1985): 15.

Aghajanian, G., and G. Marck. "Serotonin Model of Schizophrenia Emerging Role of Glutamate Mechanisms." *Brain Research Review* 31 (2000): 302–312.

Allday, E. "Legal, Intense Hallucinogen Raises Alarms, Salvia Divinorum Produces Short Dreamlike Experience." *San Francisco Chronicle.* 27 June 2007. Available http://sfgate.com/cgibin/article.cgi?f=/c/a/2007/06/27/MNGDPQMLU31.DTL

American Psychiatric Association (APA). *Diagnostic and Statistical Manual of Mental Disorders,* 4th ed., text revision (DSM-IV-TR). Washington, DC: APA, 2000.

Associated Press. "60s Icon Timothy Leary Cooperated with the FBI." *Salt Lake Tribune* 258 (1 July 1999): A-10.

Baggott, M., J. Siegrist, G. Galloway, L. Robertson, J. Coyle, et al. "Investigating the Mechanisms of Hallucinogen-Induced Visions Using 3,4-Methyleneamphetamine (MDA): A Randomized Controlled Trial in Humans." *PLoS One* 5(12).doi14074.doi10.1371/journal.pone.001407. Available http://www.plosone.org/article/info%3Adoi%2F10.1371%2Fjournal.pone.0014074

Burger, A., ed. "Quotes from Albert Hofmann." *Drugs Affecting the Central Nervous System. Psychotomimetic Agents,* vol. 2. New York: Dekker, 1968.

Carlini, E. "Preliminary Note: Dangerous Use of Anticholinergic Drugs in Brazil." *Drugs and Alcohol Dependence* 32 (1993): 1–7.

Carollo, K. "Georgetown Students Arrested for Manufacturing Illegal Drug in Dorm Room." ABC News. 25 October 2010. Available http://abcnews.go.com/Health/MindmoodNews/georgetown-university-students-busted-illegal-drug-manufacturing/story?id=11963382&tqkw=&tqshow=&page=2

"Celebration #1." *New Yorker* 42 (1966): 43.

Center for Cognitive Liberty and Ethics. "Court Says No Peyote for Native American Boy." 22 April 2003. Available http://www.cognitiveliberty.org/dll/peyote_boy.html

Center for Substance Abuse Research (CESAR). "Dextromethorphan." 2005. Available http://www.cesar.umd.edu/cesar/drugs/dxm.asp

Center for Substance Abuse Research (CESAR). "Majority of U.S. Youths and Young Adults Who Have Used Club Drugs Have Used 3 or More Types of Illicit Drugs." [FAX] (22 May 2006).

Claus, E. P., V. E. Tyler, and L. R. Brady. *Pharmacognosy,* 6th ed. Philadelphia: Lea & Febiger, 1970.

Cloud, J. "Is Ketamine a Quick Fix for Hard-To-Treat Depression?" *Time* (2 August 2010). Available http://www.time.com/time/health/article/0,8599,2008151,00.html

Conley, M. "Nutmeg Treated as Drug for Hallucinogenic High." ABC World News. 9 December 2010. Available http://abcnews.go.com/Health/large-doses-nutmeg-hallucinogenic-high/story?id=12347815&page=1

Covert America. "LSD, the CIA, and Mind Control: The Notorious Project MK Ultra." 17 August 2010. Available http://covertamerica.com/2010/08/17/lsd-the-cia-and-mind-control-the-notorious-project-mk-ultra

de la Torre, R., M. Farré, P. Roset, S. Abanade, M. Segura, and J. Cami. "Human Pharmacology of MDMA: Pharmacokinetics, Metabolism, and Disposition." *Therapeutic Drug Monitor* 26 (2004): 137–144.

Detrick, B. "Salvia Takes a Starring Role." *New York Times.* 23 December 2010. Available http://www.nytimes.com/2010/12/26/fashion/26noticed.html?_r=1

Dewan, S. "A Drug Feared in the '70s Is Tied to Suspect in Killing." *New York Times* (6 April 2003).

Dishotsky, N. I., W. D. Loughman, R. E. Mogar, and W. R. Lipscomb. "LSD and Genetic Damage." *Science* 172 (1971): 431–440.

Dobner, J. "American Indian Church Sues Feds Over Peyote Use." *Native American Times.* 20 September 2010. Available http://www.nativetimes.com/index.php?option=com_content&view=article& id=4268:american-indian-church-sues-feds-over-peyote-use&catid=51&Itemid=27

Drug Enforcement Agency (DEA). "September 2002 Highlight." Domestic Strategy. December 2002a. Publication No. DEA-02060.

Drug Enforcement Agency (DEA). "Trippin on Tryptamine." Intelligence Brief. October 2002b. Document No. DEA-02052.

Drug Enforcement Agency (DEA). "D-Lysergic Acid Diethylamide." DEA Drugs and Chemicals of Concern. 2010. Available http://www.deadiversion.usdoj.gov/drugs_concern/lsd/lsd.htm

Education.com. "NIDA InfoFacts: LSD." 2010. Available http://www.education.com/reference/article/Ref_NIDA_InfoFacts_LSDenotes. "Dimethyltryptamine (DMT)—Effects on the Body." 2010. Available http://www.enotes.com/drugs-substances-encyclopedia/dimethyltryptamine-dmt/effects-body

Essortment. "Ecstasy-MDMA." 2010. Available http://www.essortment.com/articles/ecstasy_100011.htm

Farley, C. "Rave New World." *Time* 15 (5 June 2000): 69.

Farwell, S. "Though PCP Use Has Been Falling, Drug Can Still Lead to Violent Trouble." *Dallas Morning News.* 9 July 2010. Available http://www.dallasnews.com/sharedcontent/dws/news/localnews/crime/stories/070910dnmetpcp.1cef8c6.html

Fernandez, D. "Salvia Becoming 'Drug du Jour' for Some Teens; Hallucinogenic Herb Salvia Divinorum Causes Concern as Young Adults Use It to Get a Cheap High." WebMD. 26 June 2008. Available http://www.salvia.net/articles.php?id=29

Fleckenstein, A. "Pharmacological Aspects of Substance Abuse." In *Remington: The Science and Practice of Pharmacy,* 20th ed., edited by A. Gennaro, 1175–1182. Baltimore, MD: Lippincott Williams & Wilkins, 2000.

Goldstein, A. *Addiction from Biology to Drug Policy.* New York: Freeman, 1994.

Goldstein, F. "Pharmacological Aspects of Substance Abuse." In *Remington's Pharmaceutical Sciences,* 19th ed., edited by A. R. Gennaro, 780–794. Easton, PA: Mack, 1995.

Greer, G., and R. Tolbert. "The Therapeutic Use of MDMA." In *Ecstasy: The Clinical, Pharmacological and Neurotoxicological Effects of the Drug MDMA,* edited by S. J. Peroutka, 28. Boston: Kluwer, 1990.

Gresser, E. "Cough Syrup As Problem Drug?" AOL News. 25 October 2010. Available http://www.aolnews.com/2010/10/25/opinion-cough-syrup-as-problem-drug

Halpern, J., and H. Pope. "Hallocinogen Persisting Perception Disorder: What Do We Know After 50 Years?" *Drug and Alcohol Dependence* 69 (2003): 109–119.

Halpern, J., A. Sherwood, J. Hudson, D. Yurgelun-Todd, and H. Pope. "Psychological and Cognitive Effects of Long-Term Peyote Use Among Native Americans." *Biological Psychiatry* 58 (2005): 624–631.

Harvard Mental Health Letter. "Reviving the Study of Hallucinogens." 1 October 2006. Available http://read.health.harvard.edu/user/user.fas/s=784/fp=3/tp=76?T=open_summary,940482&P=summary

Honig, D. "LSD FAQ" 2007. Available http://www.erowid.org/chemicals/lsd/lsd_faq.shtml#bad%20trips

Horgan, J. "DMT Is in Your Head, But It May Be Too Weird for the Psychedelic Renaissance." *Scientific American.* 16 April 2010. Available http://www.scientificamerican.com/blog/post.cfm?id=dmt-is-in-your-head-but-it-may-too-2010-04-16

Huxley, A. *The Doors of Perception.* New York: Harper, 1954.

Hyslop, M. "Townsend Spearheads Campaign to Curb Rising Use of Ecstasy." *Washington Times* (29 September 2000): C-1.

Jaffe, J. "Drug Addiction and Drug Abuse." In *The Pharmacological Basis of Therapeutics,* 8th ed., edited by A. Gilman, T. Rall, A. Nies, and P. Taylor, 522–573. New York: Pergamon, 1990.

Jentsch, J., and R. Roth. "The Neuropsychopharmacology of Phencyclidine: From NMDA Receptor Hypofunction to the Dopamine Hypothesis of Schizophrenia." *Neuropsychopharmacology* 20 (1999): 201–225.

Johnston, L. D., P. M. O'Malley, J. G. Bachman, and J. E. Schulenberg. "Marijuana Use Is Rising; Ecstasy Use Is Beginning to Rise; and Alcohol Use Is Declining Among U.S. Teens." University of Michigan News Service. 14 December 2010. Available http://monitoringthefuture.org/data/10data.html#2010data-drugs

Jones, R. "New Cautions About an Herb That's Hip, Hallucinogenic and Legal." *New York Times* (9 July 2001): A-14.

Jones, W. H. S. *Natural History.* Cambridge, MA: Harvard University Press, 1956.

Karlsen, S., O. Spigset, and L. Slordal. "The Dark Side of Ecstasy: Neuropsychiatric Symptoms After Exposure to 3,4-Methylenedioxymethamphetamine." *Basic and Clinical Pharmacology and Toxicology* 102 (2008): 15–24.

Kaye, S., S. Darke, and J. Duflou. "Methylenedioxymethamphetamine (MDMA)-Related Fatalities in Australia: Demographics, Circumstances, Toxicology and Major Organ Pathology." *Drug and Alcohol Dependence* 104 (2009): 254–261.

Kelland, K. "Scientists Suggest Fresh Look at Psychedelic Drugs." ABC News. 18 August 2010. Available http://www.commondreams.org/headline/2010/08/18-4

King, L. A., and J. M. Cockery. "An Index of Fatal Toxicity for Drugs of Misuse." *Human Psychopharmacology* 25 (2010): 162–166.

Kish, S., J. Lerch, Y. Furukawa, J. Tong, T. McCluskey, D. Wilkins, S. Houle, et al. "Decreased Cerebral Cortical Serotonin Transporter Binding in Ecstasy Users: A Positron Emission Tomography/[11-C]DASB and Structural Brain Imaging Study." *Brain* 133 (2010): 1779–1797.

Leary, T., R. Metzner, and R. Alpert. *The Psychedelic Experience.* New Hyde Park, NY: University Books, 1964.

Leinwand, D. "Teens, and Now DEA, Are on Trail of Hallucinogenic Herb." *USA Today* (23 June 2003): 1.

Leinwand, D. "Jimson Weed Users Chase High All the Way to the Hospital." *USA Today.* 1 November 2006. Available http://www.usatoday.com/news/nation/2006-11-01-jimson_x.htm

Maier, T. "PCP Is Rearing Its Ugly Head Again." *Insight on the News* (17 February 2003): 4–6.

"Many Were Lost Because of Leary." Letters (to the editor). *USA Today* 14 (3 June 1996): 12-A.

Marken, P., S. Stoner, and M. Bunker. "Anticholinergic Drug Abuse and Misuse." *CNS Drugs* 5 (1996): 190–199.

Marquardt, G. M., V. DiStefano, and L. L. Ling. "Pharmacological Effects of (S)-, and (R)-MDA." In *The Psychopharmacology of Hallucinogens,* edited by R. C. Stillman and R. E. Willette. New York: Pergamon, 1978.

Marsa, L. "Acid Test." *Discover* (June 2008): 52–57.

Marsh, J. "DXM Addiction: Drug Addiction and Cough Syrup Abuse." Suite101.com. 13 August 2010. Available http://www.suite101.com/content/dxm-addiction-drug-addiction-and-cough-syrup-abuse-effects-a273947

Mathias, R. "NIDA Research Takes a New Look at LSD and Other Hallucinogens." *NIDA Notes* 8 (March/April 1993): 6.

MayoClinic. "Anticholinergic (Oral Route, Parenteral Route, Rectal Route, Transdermal Route)." MayoClinic.com. 2010. Available http://www.mayoclinic.com/health/druginformation/DR602315/DSECTION=side-effects

McGlothin, W., S. Cohen, and M. S. McGlothin. "Long-Lasting Effects of LSD on Normals." *Archives of General Psychiatry* 17 (1967): 521–532.

Medical Letter. "Phencyclidine (PCP)." 38 (10 May 1996): 45.

MedTox. "Jimson Weed Poisoning Gives Insight to the Effects Experienced by 'Locoweed' Abusers." *MedTox Journal,* Public Safety Substance Abuse Newsletter. April 2010. Available http://www.medtox.com/Resources/Images/5414.pdf

Melnick, M. "A Mexican Hallucinogen Piques Scientists' and Regulators' Interest." *Time.* 8 December 2010. Available http://healthland.time.com/2010/12/08/a-mexican-hallucinogen-is-piquing-scientists-and-regulators-interest

Mims, B. "Peyote: When the Ancient Indian Way Collides with a New Age Craze." *Salt Lake Tribune* 260 (12 August 2000): C-1.

Mithoefer, M., M. Wagner, A. Mithoefer, I. Jerome, and R. Doblin. "The Safety and Efficacy of [+/−]3,4 Methylenedioxymethamphetamine-Assisted Psychotherapy in Subjects with Chronic, Treatment-Resistant Posttraumatic Stress Disorder: The First Randomized Controlled Pilot Study." *Journal of Psychopharmacology* (2011).

Morgan, C., L. Muetzelfeldt, and H. Curran. "Consequences of Chronic Ketamine Self-Administration Upon Neurocognitive Function and Psychological Wellbeing: A 1-Year Longitudinal Study." *Addiction* 105 (2010): 121–133.

Naranjo, C., A. T. Shulgin, and T. Sargent. "Evaluation of 3,4 Methylenedioxyamphetamine (MDA) as an Adjunct to Psychotherapy." *Medicina et Pharmacologia Experimentalis* 17 (1967): 359–364.

Narconon. "FAQ About Marijuana." Narconon of Southern California. 2007. Available http://www.addictionca.com/FAQ-marijuana.htm

Narconon. "Ecstasy/MDMA Manufacturing and Statistics." Friends of Narconon. 2010. Available http://www.friendsofnarconon.org/drug_education/news/latest_news/ecstasy%10mdma_manufacturing_and_statistics

National Drug Intelligence Center. Intelligence Bulletin. "PCP, Increasing Availability and Abuse." 2004. DOJ Document ID No. 2004-L0424-002.

National Institute on Drug Abuse (NIDA). "Hallucinogens and Dissociative Drugs." NIDA Research Report Series. March 2001. NIH Publication No. 01-4209.

National Institute on Drug Abuse (NIDA). "NIDA Infofacts: Club Drugs (GHB, Ketamine, and Rohypnol)." 2007a. Available http://nida.nih.gov/Infofax/clubdrugs.html

National Institute on Drug Abuse (NIDA). "Infofacts. LSD." 2007b. Available http://nida.nih.gov/Infofax/lsd.html

National Institute on Drug Abuse (NIDA). "Infofacts. PCP (Phencyclidine)." 2007c. Available http://nida.nih.gov/Infofax/pcp.html

National Institute on Drug Abuse (NIDA). "InfoFacts. Hallucinogens—LSD, Peyote, Psyilocybin, and PCP." 2009. Available http://www.drugabuse.gov/Infofacts/hallucinogens.html

National Institute on Drug Abuse (NIDA). "InfoFacts. LSD." Education.com. December 2010a. Available http://www.education.com/reference/article/Ref_NIDA_InfoFacts_LSD

National Institute on Drug Abuse (NIDA). "InfoFacts. MDMA (Ecstasy)." December 2010b. Available http://drugabuse.gov/infofacts/ecstasy.html

National Institute on Drug Abuse (NIDA). "Topics in Brief. Marijuana—An Update from the National Institute on Drug Abuse." December 2010c. Available http://www.nida.nih.gov/pdf/tib/marijuana.pdf

Native American Church. 2008. Available http://www.nativeamericanchurch.com

Nunez, L., and M. Gurpegui. "Cannabis-Induced Psychosis: A Cross-Sectional Comparison with Acute Schizophrenia." *Acta Psychiatrica Scandinavia* 105 (2002): 1173–1178.

O'Brien, C. "Drug Addiction and Drug Abuse." In *The Pharmacological Basis of Therapeutics,* 11th ed., edited by L. Brunton, J. Lazo, and K. Parker, 607–627. New York: McGraw-Hill, 2006.

Office of National Drug Control Policy (ONDCP). "Drug Facts: Club Drugs." January 2008. Available http://whitehousedrugpolicy.gov/drugfact/club/index.html

Pahnke, W. N., A. A. Kurland, S. Unger, C. Savage, and S. Grof. "The Experimental Use of Psychedelic (LSD) Psychotherapy." In *Hallucinogenic Drug Research: Impact on Science and Society,* edited by J. R. Gamage and E. L. Zerkin. Beloit, WI: Stash, 1970.

Pahnke, W. N., and W. A. Richards. "Implications of LSD and Experimental Mysticism." *Journal of Religion and Health* 5 (1966): 175–208.

Parrott, A., and J. Lasky. "Ecstasy (MDMA) Effects Upon Mood and Cognition: Before, During and After a Saturday Night Dance." *Psychopharmacology* 139 (1998): 261–268.

Partnership, The. "The Drug Guide, LSD." The Partnership at DrugFree.org. 2010. Available http://www.drugfree.org/drug-guide/lsd

Pienciak, R. "DEA Issues Warning for Legal Herb Stronger Than LSD." *Daily News* (NY). (25 July 2003).

Publishers Group. "Street Drugs." Plymouth, MN: Publishers Group, 2002.

Remsberg, R. "Found in the Archives: Military LSD Testing." NPR. 1 December 2010. Available http://www.npr.org/blogs/pictureshow/2010/12/01/131724898/lsd-testing

Russell, J. "Jimsonweed Poisoning Associated with a Homemade Stew." *Morbidity and Mortality Weekly Report.* 2010. Available http://www.faqs.org/periodicals/201002/1971642741.html

Schaffer Library. "DEA LSD Field Division Assessments." Schaffer Library of Drug Policy. 2007. Available http://www.druglibrary.org/schaffer/dea/pubs/lsd/LSD-8.htm

Schultes, R. E. "The Plant Kingdom and Hallucinogens (Part III)." *Bulletin on Narcotics* 22 (1970): 25–53.

Schultes, R. E. "Ethnopharmacological Significance of Psychotropic Drugs of Vegetal Origin." In *Principles of Psychopharmacology,* 2nd ed., edited by W. G. Clark and J. del Giudice. New York: Academic Press, 1978.

Schultes, R. E., and A. Hofmann. *The Botany and Chemistry of Hallucinogens.* Springfield, IL: Thomas, 1973.

Schultes, R. E., and A. Hofmann. *The Botany and Chemistry of Hallucinogens,* 2nd ed. Springfield, IL: Thomas, 1980.

Smith, C. "Albert Hofmann, the Father of LSD, Dies at 102." *New York Times.* 30 April 2008. Available http://www.nytimes.com/2008/04/30/world/europe/30hofmann.html

Snyder, S. H. *Madness and the Brain.* New York: McGraw-Hill, 1974.

Stone, J. "Turn On, Tune In, Boot Up." *Discover* 12 (June 1991): 32–33.

Summit Malibu. "Tryptamine Abuse and Addiction." Summit Malibu. 2010. Available http://www.summitmalibu.com/malibu-drug-alcohol-dual-diagnosis-rehab/tag/hallucinogen

Tanner-Smith, E. "Pharmacological Content of Tablets Sold as 'Ecstasy' Results from an Online Testing Service." *Drug and Alcohol Dependence* 83 (2006): 243–254.

Thier, D. "Salvia Takes Center Stage In Miley Cyrus Bong Video Drama." AOLNews. 13 December 2010. Available http://www.aolnews.com/2010/12/13/salvia-takes-center-stage-in-miley-cyrus-bong-video-drama

Tierney, J. "Hallucinogens Have Doctors Tuning in Again." *New York Times.* 11 April 2010. Available http://www.nytimes.com/2010/04/12/science/12psychedelics.html

Titi Tudorancea Bulletin. "Ergotism." 9 October 2010. Available http://www.tititudorancea.com/z/ergotism.htm

Toufexis, A. "A Crackdown on Ecstasy." *Time* (10 June 1985): 64.

Tucker, R. "Acid Test." *Omni* (November 1987): 16.

Unger, S. "Mescaline, LSD, Psilocybin and Personality Change." Bluehoney.org. 10 January 2010. Available http://bluehoney.org/2010/01/10/mescaline-lsd-psilocybin-and-personality-change

U.S. Department of Justice. "Let's All Work to Fight Drug Abuse." Pamphlet from DEA published by L.A.W. Publications and distributed with permission by International Drug Education Association, 1991.

U.S. Department of Justice. "Drugs, Youth, and the Internet." Information Bulletin (October 2002): Product No. 2002-L0424-006.

U.S. Department of Justice. National Drug Threat Assessment 2003. "Other Dangerous Drugs, Hallucinogens." National Drug Intelligence Center. (2003): Product No. 2003-Q0317-001.

Vastag, B. "Can the Peace Drug Help Clean Up the War Mess?" *Scientific American.* 20 April 2010. Available http://www.maps.org/media/view/can_the_peace_drug_help_clean_up_the_war_mess

Vince, G. "Legally High." *New Scientist* (30 September 2006): 40–45.

Vollenwelder, F., M. Vollenwelder-Scherpenhuyzen, A. Baber, N. Vogel, and D. Nell. "Psilocybin Induces Schizophrenia-like Psychosis in Human via a Serotonin-2 Agonist Action." *NeuroReport* 9 (1998): 3897–3902.

Weber, B. "Prairie LSD Studies Coined 'Psychedelic.' " *Toronto Star* (6 October 2006): A8.

Week, The. "Medicinal 'Magic Mushrooms': The New Prozac?" 14 April 2010. Available http://theweek.com/article/index/201851/medicinal-magic-mushrooms-the-new-prozac

Willing, R. "Researchers Tested Pot, LSD on Army Volunteers." *USA Today.* 6 April 2007. Available http://www.usatoday.com/news/washington/2007-04-05-army-experiments_N.htm

Zickler, P. "NIDA Launches Initiative to Control Club Drugs." *NIDA Notes* 14 (2000): 1.

CHAPTER 13

Marijuana

Learning ◎bjectives

On completing this chapter you will be able to:

- ◎ Explain what marijuana is and why it remains so controversial.
- ◎ Differentiate between the effects of low and high doses of marijuana.
- ◎ List and explain the potential effects marijuana use has on the body.
- ◎ Understand and be able to explain how marijuana use can become psychologically addictive.
- ◎ Describe how tolerance and dependence affect the response to marijuana and its use.
- ◎ Explain the medical uses of marijuana.
- ◎ Explain what age groups are most likely to use marijuana.
- ◎ Explain the major characteristics of first-time marijuana users.
- ◎ Explain how the perceived danger of marijuana use has changed with regard to high school seniors and younger age groups.
- ◎ Differentiate between prior and current beliefs regarding the effects of chronic marijuana use.

Did You Know?

- ○ George Washington grew marijuana plants at Mount Vernon for medicine and rope making.
- ○ Out of 20.1 million illicit drug users in the United States, marijuana was used by approximately 15.2 million of them, or 76% of current illicit drug users.
- ○ In some states, marijuana is one of the largest cash-producing crops.
- ○ Marijuana still grows wild in many U.S. states today.
- ○ Research shows that many users have difficulty learning and remembering what they have learned when they are "high."
- ○ In a 2010 Associated Press/CNBC poll, "only 33% favor legalization while 55% oppose it. People under 30 were the only age group favoring legalization (54%), and opposition increased with age, topping out at 73% of those 65 and older. Opposition also was prevalent among women, Republicans and those in rural and suburban areas" (Risling 2010, pp 1–2).
- ○ From 1976 to the present day, between 83% and 90% of every senior middle school class have said they could get marijuana fairly easily or very easily if they wanted some (Johnston et al. 2009).
- ○ The "high" experienced by using marijuana not only varies according to expectations and the surroundings but also how the drug is taken, whether smoked, inhaled through a vaporizer, or ingested (eaten).

Drugs and Society Online is a great source for additional drugs and society information for both students and instructors. Visit **go.jblearning.com/hanson11** to find a variety of useful tools for learning, thinking, and teaching.

Introduction

First interview:

Since I was in college and tried my first hit, I have always been a connoisseur of what we used to call grass, now it's weed or even "the ganja." I first went through a period of using it a lot—it was a different way to get a buzz. Then I got married, and my wife did not like me smoking it, and we had kids, so except for a few occasional puffs from my neighbor, I just about gave it up. Then I got divorced [from my wife] and I married a woman who does not object to me smoking a little weed every now and then, even though she does not do it herself. So sometimes on weekends, I will roll a joint before going to bed and take a few puffs off of it. I know it is illegal, but big deal, who knows about it? I used to watch that program *Cops* and just found it silly when police officers would arrest someone (usually a young kid) for possession. Big bust, I would think. Isn't it silly to charge someone with possession of marijuana? I consider it to be like alcohol and cigarettes. I don't think it should be illegal anymore. I know so many people who do it and there are dozens of people who probably use this drug that I am not even aware of their using it. What happens if two-thirds of our population uses this drug? Are we going to charge and arrest all these people? The whole illegality of it is silly. *(From Venturelli's research files, male restaurant owner, age 48, residing in Reno, Nevada, June 10, 2000)*

Second interview:

My kids know that I still smoke dope, and I know they are used to me doing this since from the day they were born. I never hid this habit of mine. I am now 59, and I never even thought of quitting. You see I started back in the late 60s when I was 17 years old. My wife does not do it as much as I do. Usually a couple of times a week, late at night I go outside on the deck and take a few hits. I don't think it is much different than having a drink. Why I have always done it, so what is the big deal? I have a few friends about my age who do the same thing and we don't bother anyone, we work five and often six days a week at our full time jobs, and only do this away from work, and as I said only a few times a week. I ask again, what's the big

deal? Now society may look down on me, but at this age, I don't give a rat's ass what society thinks. I don't tell anyone about this long-time habit that brings me relief and relaxation and outside of a few friends, my wife, and kids, no one else knows that I do this. As you asked, I really don't care what the law says; I will always do it until I die. It is so natural for me to do this that I don't even think about breaking drug laws. This is a private matter between my family and me. My kids don't smoke dope, and I never thought I would have kids who would not. Especially when I grew up in the 60s everyone I knew smoked dope and I never thought it would change, but today the world is different so I keep to myself with my habits. To me, honestly professor, if marijuana is outlawed and if I wanted to say smoke oregano then they should outlaw oregano. Outlawing a naturally growing plant is just plain stupid. What threat to the world is my smoking weed? I just think this law making marijuana illegal is ridiculous, especially when smoking it is viewed as a violation of law. What a stupid law it is and how effective this law is in that I have smoked dope all my life. *(From Venturelli's research files, male, living in a Midwestern rural area, August 10, 2010)*

Third interview:

We used to have one great big bong and fill it with dope [referring to marijuana], and all of us in someone's fraternity room would each take hits from the bong. Today, it's a different life altogether. I am working three different jobs, one teaching at a junior high school, [one] working at a film production studio, and my third claim to fame is my job as a part-time waiter. . . . I feel that I wasted many nights by just "smokin'," "dopin'," and "drinkin'" back during those college days. I sometimes think that I could have accomplished a lot more if I would not have inhaled so much dope. If I had to do it over again I would not have wasted so much time. *(From Venturelli's research files, male, age 28, August 9, 1996)*

The preceding interviews illustrate contrasting views regarding marijuana usage as a subcultural phenomenon. The first and second interviews present "die-hard" users who refuse to relinquish their use of this drug. These individuals have been using marijuana for many years and they consider it an essential recreational drug. Conversely, the third interviewee expresses some regret over the time "wasted" while becoming intoxicated with marijuana when he could have been pursuing other, more career-oriented activities.

Although marijuana is potentially less addictive than other drugs, such as cocaine, crack, heroin, and barbiturates (to name a few), it remains one of the few drugs that is controversial. (As an example of the controversy that surrounds this drug, see "Here and Now: A Recent Attempt to Legalize Recreational Marijuana Use"). It is difficult to wade through the emotion, politics, and rigidity found in the writings on marijuana to tease out the objective, clinical reality. In the United States, extreme views go back to the 1930s, when the film *Reefer Madness* portrayed an after-school marijuana "club" for high school students in suits and ties who became hallucinatory, homicidal, violent, and suicidal; such symptoms were highly exaggerated. As a complete contradiction, in the same decade, the Rastafarian religion spread among Jamaican agricultural workers, who named marijuana a holy plant.

[In] *Ganja in Jamaica* (Rubin and Comitas 1975) [the book] focused its findings to refute the claim that marijuana users damaged their productive capability. The study found that most rural Jamaicans who smoked ganja (marijuana) were extraordinarily diligent peasants who invested impressive amounts of time and energy in multiple income-bearing schemes every day of the year. Starting before sunrise, they tended livestock and poultry; farmed gardens; hired out their labor for wages; exchanged goods and services in an indigenous marketing system; maintained churches, self-help associations, political parties, guilds, schools, and households; and sometimes, at night, clandestinely cleared acres of forest to cultivate marijuana. They listened to the radio, watched television, and read newspapers to perform better as citizens in a modern democracy. These active, clear-sighted economic strategist and community

Here and Now

A Recent Attempt to Legalize Recreational Marijuana Use

On November 2, 2010, a California statewide ballot, California Proposition 19, also referred to as the Regulate, Control, and Tax Cannabis Act of 2010, was defeated. Backers of the ballot ". . . said they would mount another legalization campaign in 2012" (Sanchez 2010). On January 1, 2011, the governor of California, Arnold Schwarzenegger, signed and put into effect SB 1449, which changed possession of less than an ounce of marijuana from a criminal misdemeanor to a civil infraction. This is in addition to medical marijuana being legal in California, although federal law continues to prohibit medical marijuana use. Although Proposition 19 was defeated by 53.5% of voters, 46.5% voted for the proposition. If it had passed, it ". . . would have allowed Californians 21 and older to grow up to 25 square feet of cannabis plants, and to possess up to an ounce of marijuana. The measure also would have authorized local governments to regulate commercial cannabis cultivation, as well as the sale and use of marijuana at licensed establishments" (Knickerbocker 2010, p. 2). Analysis of the vote indicates that people voted generationally in

that voters over 30 were strongly against the proposition, whereas voters under 30 were in favor.

Supporters of the defeated measure said the referendum brought unprecedented attention to their cause. [Ethan Nadelmann, executive director of the Drug Policy Alliance, emphasized that] "Prop. 19 has elevated and legitimized the discourse around marijuana policy like nothing ever before, . . . This is the first time major elected officials and labor unions and civil rights organizations have endorsed a marijuana legalization measure. The debate is less about whether to legalize marijuana and increasingly about how to legalize marijuana."

Opponents believed that Proposition 19 not only threatened public safety, but also violated federal law including laws and ordinances against drug-free workplaces. Others strongly opposed to this proposition include Mothers Against Drunk Driving (MADD) and most law enforcement officials (Sanchez 2010).

Sources: Knickerbocker, B. "Prop. 19 in California: Legalized Marijuana Goes Up in Smoke." *Christian Science Monitor.* 3 November 2010. Available at: http://www.csmonitor.com/USA/Politics/The-Vote/2010/1103/Prop.-19-in-California-legalized-marijuana-goes-up-in-smoke. Accessed February 17, 2011; and Sanchez, R. "California's Proposition 19 Rejected by Voters." ABCNews.com. 3 November 2010. Available at: http://abcnews.go.com/Politics/proposition-19-results-california-votes-reject-marijuana-measure/story?id=12037727. Accessed February 17, 2011.

builders depended on a heavy daily intake of ganja for nourishment as "brain food," and relied on it specifically to improve production. Adult Jamaican marijuana smokers consumed some six or more large "spliffs" (hand-rolled cigars) of ganja a day, or a few ounces. They also consumed it in teas, tisanes, and tonics. As employers, they preferred to pay their employees ganja rather than money and encouraged its use in the workplace. (Rubin and Comitas 1975, cited in Hamid 1998, p. 61)

Marijuana is a hemp plant, *Cannabis sativa,* that is green, brown, or a gray mixture of dried, shredded leaves, stems, seeds, and flowers. It has been cultivated for thousands of years. When smoked, the dried and crushed leaves, stems, and seeds of cannabis produce sedative and mind-altering effects, which vary according to the potency of the variety of plant used. Usage in the United States began in the 1920s, rose during the 1960s and 1970s, and fell in every year from 1978 until 1991. From 1991 on, however, usage began to climb. In this chapter, we review the history, past and current usage trends, attitudes, and controversies surrounding marijuana (including the amotivational syndrome and the current debate regarding the legalization of marijuana for medical purposes), and its physiological and behavioral effects on the user.

History and Trends in Marijuana Use

In many societies, marijuana has historically been a valued crop called hemp because the woody stems yield a fiber that can be made into cloth and rope. The term *cannabis* comes from the Greek word for hemp. Initially, the Spaniards brought cannabis to the Western Hemisphere as a source of fiber and seeds. For thousands of years, the seeds have been pressed to extract red oil used for medicinal and euphorigenic purposes (Abood and Martin 1992; Iversen 1993). The plant (both male and female) also produces a resin with active ingredients that affect the central nervous system (CNS). Marijuana contains hundreds of chemical compounds, but only a few found in the resin are responsible for producing the euphoric high.

Even the original uses of marijuana remain controversial. Botanists have never been able to trace cannabis to its origins, although some think it originated in Asia. Ancient Chinese documents contain the earliest recorded name of hemp—*ma,* mean-

ing fiber-producing plant, as well as "valuable" or "endearing." The term *ma* was still used as late as 1930. In the late 1970s, during an archeological dig in Gansu, the seat of Chinese civilization, workers uncovered cannabis seed stored in an earthen jar.

Ayurvedic documents from 600 BC describe an intoxicating resin from the plant. The fifth-century BC Greek historian Herodotus recorded that the Scythians burned the tops of the plant, producing a narcotic smoke. And a first-century Greek physician wrote that hemp was made into intoxicating cakes, perhaps the forerunners of the marijuana brownies of 1960s fame (Pollan 1998, p. 39).

Other sources report that the first known record of marijuana use is in the *Book of Drugs,* written about 2737 BC by the Chinese Emperor Shen Nung; he prescribed marijuana for treating gout, malaria, gas pains, and absentmindedness. The Chinese apparently had much respect for the plant. They obtained fiber for clothes and medicine from it for thousands of years.

Around 500 BC, another Chinese book of treatments referred to the medical use of marijuana. Nonetheless, the plant got a bad name from the moralists of the day, who claimed that youngsters became wild and disrespectful from the recreational use of *ma.* They called it the "liberator of sin" because, under its influence, the youngsters refused to listen to their elders and did other scandalous things. Although the Chinese recognized *ma*'s medical usefulness, they eventually banned it because of its unpredictable intoxicating effects. Later, because of rampant use, it was legalized again.

India also has a long and varied history of marijuana use. It was an essential part of Indian religious ceremonies for thousands of years. The well-known *Rig Veda* and other chants describe the use of *soma,* which some believe was marijuana. Early writings describe a ritual in which resin was collected from the plants. After fasting and purification, certain men ran naked through the cannabis fields. The clinging resin was scraped off their bodies, and cakes were made from it and used in feasts. For centuries, missionaries in India tried to ban the use of marijuana, but they were never successful, because its use was too heavily ingrained in the culture. From India, the use of marijuana spread throughout Asia, Africa, Europe, and the Americas—English settlers brought it to the U.S. colonies.

Assyrian records dating back to 650 BC refer to a drug called *azulla* that was used for making rope and cloth and was consumed to experience euphoria. The ancient Greeks also knew about marijuana. Galen described the general use of hemp in cakes, which, when eaten in excess, produced narcotic effects. Herodotus described the Scythian custom of burning marijuana seeds and leaves to produce a narcotic smoke in steam baths. It was believed that breathing the smoke from the burning plants would cause frenzied activity. Groups of people stood in the smoke, laughed, and danced as it took effect.

One legend about cannabis is based on the travels of Marco Polo in the 12th century. Marco Polo told of the legendary Hasan Ibn-Sabbah, who terrorized a part of Arabia in the early 1100s. His men were some of the earliest political murderers, and he ordered them to kill under the influence of hashish, a strong, unadulterated cannabis derivative. The cult was called the *hashishiyya,* from which came the word *hashish.* (The word *assassin* may be derived from the name of Sheik Hasan, who was a political leader in the 10th century.) It is unlikely, however, that using hashish can turn people into killers. Experience suggests that people tend to become sleepy and indolent rather than violent after eating or smoking hashish or another of the strong cannabis preparations available in Arabia (Abel 1989). Napoleon's troops brought hashish to France after their campaign in Egypt at the beginning of the 19th century, despite Napoleon's strict orders to the contrary. By the 1840s, the use of hashish, as well as opium, was widespread in France, and efforts to curb its spread were unsuccessful.

In North America, hemp was planted near Jamestown in 1611 for use in making rope. By 1630, half of the winter clothing at this settlement was made from hemp fibers. There is no evidence that hemp was used medicinally at this time. Hemp was also valuable as a source of fiber for clothing and rope for the Pilgrims at Plymouth. To meet the demand for fiber, a law was passed in Massachusetts in 1639 requiring every household to plant hemp seed. However, it took much manual labor to work the hemp fiber into usable form, resulting in a chronic shortage of fiber for fishnets and the like (Abel 1989).

George Washington cultivated a field of hemp at Mount Vernon, and there is some indication that it was used for medicine as well as for making rope. In his writings, Washington once mentioned that he forgot to separate the male and female plants, a process usually done because the female plant gave more resin if not pollinated.

In the early 1800s, U.S. physicians used marijuana extracts to produce a tonic intended for both medicinal and recreational purposes. This practice changed in 1937 with passage of the Marijuana Tax Act. The Marijuana Tax Act was modeled after the Harrison Act of 1914 in that marijuana was considered a narcotic and subject to the same legal controls as cocaine and the opiates (see Chapter 3). Like these opiates, marijuana distributors had to register and pay a tax to legally import, buy, or sell this drug (Musto 1999). As a result, the Marijuana Tax Act prohibited the use of this drug as an intoxicant and regulated its use as a medicine.

Most of the abuse of marijuana in the United States during the early part of the 20th century took place near the Mexican border and in the ghetto areas of major cities. Cannabis was mistakenly considered a narcotic, like opium, and legal authorities treated it as such (Abood and Martin 1992). In 1931, Harry Anslinger, who was the first appointed head of the Bureau of Narcotics and later would become responsible for the enforcement of marijuana laws, believed that the problem was slight (Musto 1999). By 1936, however, he claimed that the increase in the use of marijuana was of great national concern (Anslinger and Cooper 1937) (see **Figure 13.1**). Anslinger set up an informational program that ultimately led to the federal law that banned marijuana. The following sensationalized statement was part of Anslinger's campaign to outlaw the drug:

> What about the alleged connection between drugs and sexual pleasure? . . . What is the real relationship between drugs and sex? There isn't any question about marijuana being a sexual stimulant. It has been used throughout the ages for that: in Egypt, for instance. From what we have seen, it is an aphrodisiac, and I believe that the use in colleges today has sexual connotations. (Anslinger and Cooper 1937, p. 19)

FIGURE 13.1

This antimarijuana poster was distributed by the Federal Bureau of Narcotics in the late 1930s.

Courtesy of Federal Bureau of Narcotics.

In addition, during this time, some usually accurate magazines reported that marijuana was partly responsible for crimes of violence. In 1936, *Scientific American* reported that "marijuana produces a wide variety of symptoms in the user, including hilarity, swooning, and sexual excitement. Combined with intoxicants, it often makes the smoker vicious, with a desire to fight and kill" ("Marijuana Menaces Youth" 1936, p. 151). A famous poster of the day, called "The Assassination of Youth," was effective in molding attitudes against drug use.

Largely because of the media's influence on public opinion, Congress passed the Marijuana Tax Act in 1937. However, because of the discussions and debates before the passage of the 1970 Comprehensive Drug Abuse Prevention and Control Act, which replaced or updated all other laws concerning narcotics and dangerous drugs, the Marijuana Tax Act of 1937 was declared unconstitutional in 1969 because it classified marijuana as a narcotic. (For further historical drug law details, see Chapter 3.) Marijuana has not been classified as a narcotic since 1971.

In the early 1900s, marijuana was brought across the U.S. border by Mexican laborers who entered the United States seeking jobs. From the border areas of the United States, recreational use of marijuana spread into mainly the southwestern region of the United States. Such use reached major cities in Texas and surrounding states as well as a number of African American communities in these cities. Heavy users of marijuana included a subpopulation of jazz musicians as well as other "bohemian types" who led more of an unstructured existence in unconventional jobs and occupations (e.g., artists, entertainers, poets, criminals). Thus, before the 1960s, marijuana use was largely confined to small segments of African American urban youth, jazz musicians, and particularly artists and writers who belonged to the 1950s Beat Generation. Use rose tremendously in the 1960s, when it was closely associated with the hippie counterculture, in which marijuana was categorized as a psychedelic (consciousness-expanding) sacrament. It spread into other youth categories during the 1970s, until approximately 1978. In each year from 1978 until 1991, marijuana use fell. After 1991, researchers and prevention specialists were astounded to see a rise in usage among youth.

Marijuana still grows wild in many U.S. states today. Curiously, one reason for the survival of this supply is that, during World War II, the fiber used to make rope (sisal) was hard to import, so the government paid subsidies to farmers who grew hemp.

Much of today's crop comes from these same plants. Another reason for the spread of the plants is that, until recently, the seeds were used in birdseed. Leftover seed was discarded in the garbage and thus spread to landfill dumps, where it sprouted. Birdseed containing marijuana seeds is still available, but the seeds are sterilized so that they cannot germinate.

The Indian Hemp Drug Commission Report in the 1890s and the 1930 Panama Canal Zone Report on marijuana stressed that available evidence did not prove marijuana as dangerous as it was popularly thought; these reports were given little publicity, however, and for the most part were disregarded. In 1944, a report was issued by the LaGuardia Committee on Marijuana, which consisted of 31 qualified physicians, psychiatrists, psychologists, pharmacologists, chemists, and sociologists appointed by the New York Academy of Medicine. They stated in one key summary that marijuana was not the killer many thought it to be:

> It was found that marijuana in an effective dose impairs intellectual functioning in general. . . . Marijuana does not change the basic personality structure of the individual. It lessens inhibition and this brings out what is latent in his thoughts and emotions but it does not evoke responses that would otherwise be totally alien to him. . . . Those who have been smoking marijuana for years showed no mental or physical deterioration that may be attributed to the drug.
> (Solomon 1966, p. 37)

Much of the early research conducted did not consider the potency of marijuana. As a result, findings from various studies are often conflicting and difficult to compare. Because the quality of marijuana varies so greatly, it is impossible to know the amount of drug taken without analyzing the original material and the leftover stub, or "roach." Conditions such as type of seed, soil moisture and fertility, amount of sunlight, and temperature all have an effect on the amounts of active ingredients found in the resulting marijuana plant.

Current Use of Marijuana

The National Survey on Drug Use and Health (NSDUH) reported that among persons age 12 or older, the overall rate of past-month marijuana use in 2008 was 6.1%; this rate was similar to the rate in 2007 and to earlier years going back to 2002 (SAMHSA 2009). **Figure 13.2** shows that in 2008, out

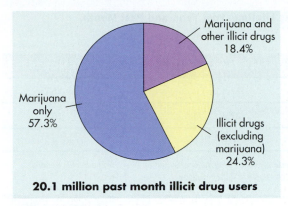

FIGURE 13.2

Types of drugs used in the past month, illicit drug users age 12 or older in 2008.

....

Source: Substance Abuse and Mental Health Services Administration (SAMHSA). *Results from the 2008 National Survey on Drug Use and Health: National Findings.* Office of Applied Studies, NSDUH Series H-36, DHHS Publication No. SMA 09-4435. Rockville, MD, 2009.

of an estimated 20.1 million Americans age 12 or older who were current users of any type of illicit drugs, the percentage of past-month marijuana users was a staggering 75.7% (57.3% + 18.4%). This leaves a minority of illicit drug users (24.3%, approximately 4.8 million)[1] who did not use marijuana. An estimated 57.3% of current illicit drug users used only marijuana, and 18.4% used marijuana and another illicit drug (SAMHSA 2009).

Other current findings regarding marijuana use are as follows (SAMHSA 2009):

- In 2008, 2.2 million persons had used marijuana for the first time within the past 12 months; this averages to approximately 6000 initiates per day! Somewhat dampening this large number of new users is the fact that this estimate was not significantly different from the number in 2007 (2.1 million) and 2002 (2.2 million) (see **Figure 13.3**).

- Most (61.8%) of the 2.2 million recent marijuana initiates were younger than age 18 when they first used the drug.

- Among youths ages 12 to 17, an estimated 5% had used marijuana for the first time within the past year, similar to the rate in 2007 (4.6%).

- In 2008, the average age at first marijuana use among recent initiates ages 12 to 49 was 17.8 years. This average increased from 17.0 years in 2002, 16.8 years in 2003, 17.1 years

---

[1]Current drug use is defined as having used an illicit drug in the month before the NSDUH surveys were conducted.

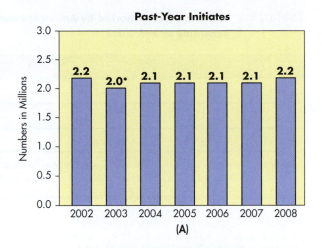

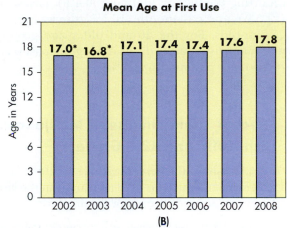

FIGURE 13.3

(**A**) Past-year marijuana initiates among persons aged 12 or older. (**B**) Mean age at first use of marijuana among past-year marijuana initiates aged 12 to 49: 2002–2008.

....

The mean age at first use estimates are for recent initiates aged 12–49.

*Difference between this estimate and the 2008 estimate is statistically significant at the 0.05 level.

Source: Substance Abuse and Mental Health Services Administration (SAMHSA). *Results from the 2008 National Survey on Drug Use and Health: National Findings.* Office of Applied Studies, NSDUH Series H-36, DHHS Publication No. SMA 09-4435. Rockville, MD, 2009.

in 2004, 17.4 in 2005 and 2006, and 17.6 in 2007 (not much throughout these years).

- In 2008, the youth marijuana initiation rate—the percentage of those ages 12 to 17 who had not used marijuana prior to the past year—(5.6%) was similar to the rate in 2007 (5.2%).

- The prevalence of past-month marijuana use among youths ages 12 to 17 decreased between 2002 (8.2%) and 2005 (6.8%), and then remained stable between 2005 and 2008 (6.7%).

As **Table 13.1** shows, the frequency of marijuana use is strongly correlated with age. The age group

Table 13.1 Marijuana Use Reported by Americans During Lifetime, Past Year, and Past Month, According to Age: 2008

AGE (YEARS)	LIFETIME (%)	PAST YEAR (%)	PAST MONTH (%)
12–17	16.5	12.5	6.7
18–25	50.4	27.5	16.5
26 or older	42.6	6.9	4.2

Source: Substance Abuse and Mental Health Services Administration (SAMHSA). *Results from the 2008 National Survey on Drug Use and Health: National Findings.* Office of Applied Studies, NSDUH Series H-36, DHHS Publication No. SMA 09-4435. Rockville, MD, 2009.

reporting the highest lifetime (50.4%), past-year (27.5%), and past-month (16.5%) use was 18- to 25-year-olds. For the 26 and older age group, marijuana use sharply drops during the past year (6.9%) and past month (4.2%).

Recent Trends in Use of Marijuana: 8th, 10th, and 12th Graders

Figure 13.4A shows the percentage of 8th-, 10th-, and 12th-grade students who used marijuana in the last 12 months. Some of the major findings are:

- Since 1960 (not shown), annual percentages of marijuana use among 12th graders peaked in 1979 at approximately 51%.
- Use declined steadily for 13 years, bottoming at 22% in 1992.
- For 8th, 10th, and 12th graders, marijuana use continued to increase after 1993, to approximately 34% for 12th graders in 2008.
- 8th- and 12th-grade students showed a very slight increase in use from 2006–2008.

Figure 13.4B shows the trends in perceived harmfulness of marijuana use for 12th graders. The figure shows the percentage that say there is a "great risk" from using marijuana. Some of the major findings are:

- Approximately 50% of all 12th graders thought that regular use of marijuana involves a great risk to the user; 50% did not.
- Approximately 24% of all 12th graders thought that occasional use of marijuana is harmful; 76% did not.
- Approximately 17% of 12th graders believed that using marijuana once or twice is harmful; 83% did not.

Figure 13.4C shows the trends in disapproval of marijuana use for 12th graders. This is the percentage saying they "disapprove" of using marijuana. Some of the major findings are:

- Approximately 79% of 12th graders disapproved of using marijuana on a regular basis; 21% did not.
- Approximately 68% of 12th graders disapproved of using marijuana on an occasional basis; 32% did not.
- Approximately 55% of 12th graders disapproved of using marijuana one or twice; 45% did not.

Figure 13.4D shows 30-day comparative trends between perceived availability, risk, and use of marijuana by 12th graders. Availability of marijuana often includes the belief that marijuana is "fairly easy" or "very easy" to get. Some of the major findings are:

- Since the study began in 1976, between 83% and 90% of every senior high school class has said they could get marijuana easily or very easily if they wanted some.
- Marijuana appears to be readily available to almost all 12th graders; in 2008, 84% reported that they think it would be very easy or easy for them to get it—nearly twice the number who reported ever having used it (43%).
- Since 1991, the perceived risk of using marijuana has been steadily decreasing, from 79% in 1991 to approximately 51% in 2008.
- Marijuana use by 12th graders (approximately 18%) is much lower than the perceived availability of marijuana (approximately 84%).

According to the national Monitoring the Future (MTF) survey, 12th graders' perceived risk of harm from regular marijuana use has declined from 58% of U.S. high school seniors in 2006 to 52% in 2008 and 2009 who thought there was great risk of

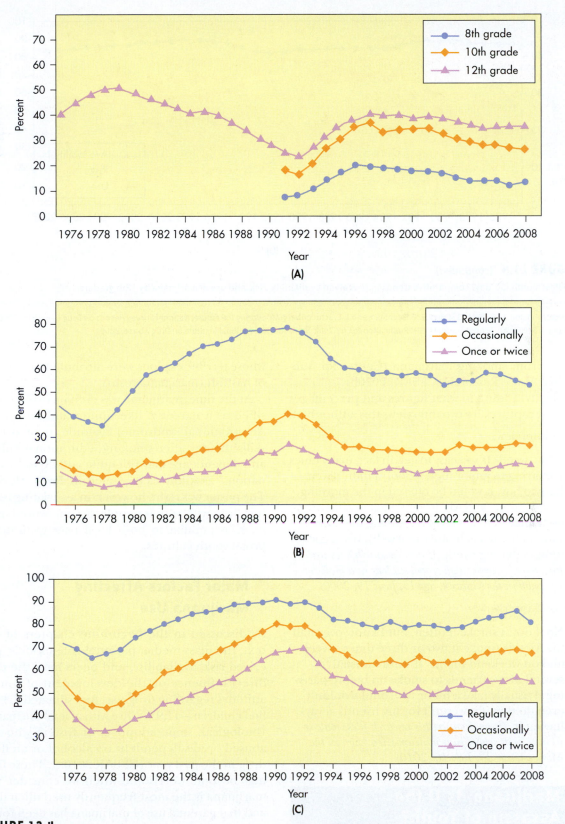

FIGURE 13.4

(**A**) Percentage of 8th, 10th, and 12th grade students using marijuana in the last 12 months. (**B**) Trends in perceived harmfulness of marijuana use for 12th graders. (**C**) Trends in disapproval of marijuana use for 12th graders.

(continues)

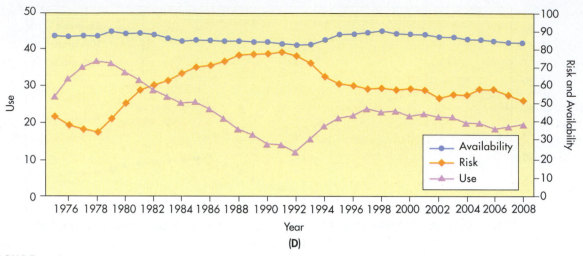

FIGURE 13.4 *(continued)*

(D) Past month (30-day) comparative trends in perceived availability, risk, and use of marijuana by 12th graders.

Source: Johnston, L. D., P. M. O'Malley, J. G. Bachman, and J. E. Schulenberg. *Monitoring the Future: National Survey Results on Drug Use, 1975–2008: Volume I, Secondary School Students.* NIH Publication No. 09-7402. Bethesda, MD: National Institute on Drug Abuse, 2009.

harm from smoking marijuana (Center for Substance Abuse Research [CESAR] 2010b).

Finally, adding to what figures and percentages cannot capture, are two interviews this author had:

First interview:

> What, weed? It's so easy to get. In fact, many times [referring to junior high school] I didn't even have to buy, it would be offered in the morning, at lunchtime, and whenever we get together, even after school it is there. Among the users (and we know each other real well), it's as common as sharing candy. *(From Venturelli's research files, male first-year high school student in a medium-size town in the Midwest, age 15, June 19, 2000)*

Second interview:

> No, I don't smoke it often, but I know over half my friends smoke it two or three times a week and on weekend nights. It's not unusual for several of my friends to smoke up before partying. I usually take a hit or two, but I wouldn't even do that if it weren't for my friends always having it. *(From Venturelli's research files, male senior in high school in a medium-sized town in the Midwest, age 17, July 16, 2010)*

Marijuana: Is It the Assassin of Youth?

In the late 1930s, the poster "Marijuana: Assassin of Youth" made a clever play on words, bringing up reminders of the Middle Eastern "*hashashin*" cult, whose terrible exploits were attributed to their use of hashish (marijuana resin).

At the time, marijuana was even incorrectly classified as a narcotic, like opium and morphine. Amotivational syndrome, lassitude, poor driving skills the day after smoking, educational failure, and dependence may not quite add up to "assassination," as wildly exaggerated in *Reefer Madness*. The poster was right, however, in associating use of this drug with young people, among whom marijuana is popular in both local peer groups and broad youth cultures.

■ Major Factors Affecting Marijuana Use

As discussed in the beginning chapters of this text, the mass media, parental role models, perceived risk, availability, and peers have the most direct influence on the development of youths' attitudes regarding drug use. An estimated 8.3 million children—11.9%—live with at least one parent (biological, step-, adoptive, or foster) who had abused or was dependent on alcohol or an illicit drug in the past year (CESAR 2010a). These findings become worrisome when we consider that marijuana is the most frequently used illicit drug and that parental use of marijuana has been found to be a significant influence on teens' use of this drug.

In a study by Kandel et al. (2001), when parents had used marijuana at some time in their lives, their teen children were 40% more likely to have used the drug in their lifetime than teens whose parents had never used marijuana. Moreover, when parents had used marijuana in the past year, their children were twice as likely to have used in the same time period as were teens whose parents had not used in the past year. This same study also found that when parents had used marijuana in the past year, their teen children were more likely to have used marijuana in the past year when compared with the children of parents who had used at some time in their life, but not in the last year. Similarly, parental use of other drugs, such as alcohol, nicotine, and cocaine, was also found to have an impact on their teen children's use of marijuana. More importantly, the perceived risk of use is the most important influence on teen marijuana use. In the Kandel et al. (2001) study, it was found to be five times more important than parental use.

As shown in Figure 13.4A, when comparisons are made among 8th, 10th, and 12th graders, marijuana use rises sharply by 12th grade. One main reason for this is because children in lower grades are less likely to have friends and access to friends who use marijuana (as well as access to other major drugs of abuse). Marijuana has been almost universally available to American high school seniors (from 83% to 90%) over at least the past 30 years (Johnston et al. 2009).

Beginning several years before age 13 (early adolescence), peers and peer groups begin to exert the most influence (Bauman and Ennett 1996; Greenblatt 1999; Heitzeg 1996; Tudor, Peterson, and Elifson 1987; Venturelli 2000). In fact, even in acquiring the drug, a relatively recent finding stated that "Marijuana distribution relies primarily on informal dealing through social networks . . ." (CESAR 2007). More than one-half (58%) of household residents who had used marijuana in the past year reported that they most recently obtained their marijuana for free, compared to 39% who reported purchasing it. Nearly all marijuana users (89%) reported getting their most recent acquisition from a friend or relative. Unlike users of more expensive drugs such as cocaine and heroin, the majority of people who used marijuana in the past year (58%) gave away or shared some of their most recent acquisition (CESAR 2007).

Research shows that it is unlikely that an individual will use drugs when his or her peers do not use them. Marijuana use, in particular, is a group-motivated behavior that is strongly affected by peer pressure and influence. In effect, habitual drug users

A common example of polydrug use (alcohol and marijuana).

are likely to belong to drug-using groups. In contrast, people who do not use drugs belong to groups in which drug use is perceived as an unacceptable and devious form of social recreation. Learning theory (see Chapter 2) explains how peers can influence one another; drug-using peer members serve as role models, legitimizing use. Peers in such groups are saying, in essence, "It's perfectly normal to use drugs"; in turn, this justifies usage.

In addition to these major factors (the mass media, parental role models, perceived risk, availability, and peer influences), six other factors must be taken into account as influencing drug use:

1. Structural factors, such as age, gender, family background, and religious beliefs.
2. Social and interactional factors, such as the type of interpersonal relationships, friendship cliques, and drug use within the peer group setting.
3. Setting, such as the type of community and neighborhood (physical location where drugs are used).
4. Attitudinal factors, such as personal beliefs and attitudes regarding drug use, and personality factors, such as self-esteem, level of security versus insecurity, and maturation level.
5. Participation in after-school activities is associated with higher levels of academic achievement and self-esteem, as well as lower levels of substance use (SAMHSA 2007b). Regardless of family income, youth ages 12 to 17 who did not participate in any activities had higher rates of past-month cigarette and illicit drug use than those who participated in four, six, seven, or more activities (SAMHSA 2007b).
6. Finally, even the amount of religious involvement affects illicit drug use (which includes marijuana use). In regard to religious involvement and substance use, adults who reported

that religious beliefs are a very important part of their lives were less likely to use illicit drugs in the past month than those who reported that religious beliefs are not a very important part of their lives (6.1% vs. 14.3%) (SAMHSA 2007a). Thus, religiosity has been identified in other research as an important protective factor against substance use (Brigham Young University 2006; Kendler, Gardner, and Prescott 1997; National Center on Addiction and Substance Abuse 2001; Wallace, Myers, and Osai 2004).

Keep in mind these factors can easily overlap; they are not separate and distinct. Sociologists have long studied "youth cultures" (Coleman 1961). In the 1970s, sociologists began to examine different subcultures of youth in terms of the behaviors that symbolically represent the group, in which participation in drug use is a ritual that marks off entrance into the group and out of childhood—a rite of passage. Typically, American high school culture includes a leading clique, often associated with team sports, whose members might be called "jocks," "collegiates," or "rah-rahs," and a marginal, deviant, or rebellious group (Eckert 1989). In some cases, the latter group is associated with marijuana use. In the mid-1960s, hippies were perceived as a group whose members were part of a counterculture committed to unconventional values, pacifism, and communalism in addition to psychedelic drugs. By 1970, this name denoted broader segments of youth who adhered merely to hippie styles of clothing and drug use (Buff 1970). By the 1980s, marijuana use was identified with subgroups of youth often called "burnouts." In many communities that were studied by sociologists, burnouts came from all social levels, but were often overrepresented in upper-middle classes, and they were marginal and/or rebellious within the educational system, if not dropouts (Eckert 1989; Gaines 1992). Membership in such marijuana-using subcultures often bonds the youth to ongoing and persistent drug use.

Is Marijuana Really a Gateway Drug?

Gateway drugs (also known as gateway theory, gateway hypothesis, and gateway effect) are drugs that serve as the gate or path that usually precedes the use of illicit drugs, such as marijuana, heroin, and LSD. Gateway drugs, or drugs of entry, serve to initiate a novice user into the drug-using world. Although the linkage is not biochemical, common gateway drugs include tobacco, inhalants, alcohol, anabolic steroids, and recently prescription pain killers (prescription opioid medications) are included (Benson 2010).

The claim that marijuana use most often leads to the use of other more serious drugs, such as heroin, remains controversial (Gardner 1992). A Rand press release reported that the gateway theory does not explain the progression to other more addictive drugs; instead, "The people who are predisposed to use drugs and have the opportunity to use drugs *are more likely* than others to use both marijuana and harder drugs. . . . Marijuana typically comes first because it is more available" (Rand Drug Policy Research Center 2002). Thus, instead of assuming that marijuana, alcohol, and other more commonly used drugs are simply gateway drugs responsible for leading to more serious drugs, it is more likely that factors such as (1) the age when teens have opportunities to use marijuana and other drugs; (2) associated opportunities; and (3) the willingness, mindset, or predisposition to use drugs may be better predictors of the progression from less addictive to more addictive and powerful types of drugs.

For example, the gateway theory cannot explain the fact that although it is true many heroin addicts began drug use with marijuana, it is also true that many, if not most, also used coffee and cigarettes. Millions of marijuana users never go beyond the gateway drugs used. "There are only a few thousand opiate addicts in Great Britain, yet there are millions who have tried cannabis" (Gossop 1987, p. 9).

Nevertheless, gateway theory may offer a plausible explanation as to why a small percentage of marijuana users progress to hard drugs such as cocaine or heroin. In many cases, it may be unlikely that the use of marijuana as well as other drugs considered to be gateway drugs would be the *principal cause* for progressing to harder and more addictive types of drugs.

As discussed in Chapter 16, youths who turn to drugs are usually slightly to seriously alienated individuals. Thus, progression from marijuana to other drugs is more likely to depend on peer group composition, family relationships, social class, and the age at which drug use begins (Indiana Prevention Resource Center 1996).

It is important to note, however, that many, if not most, young drug users do eventually leave drug-using groups and abandon their drug-using behavior, a process sometimes called maturing out. An example that often typifies maturing out is found in the following interview:

> Up until I started my full time job after graduation from college I was smoking weed and at parties using other even worse types of drugs without any hesitation. Even during my senior year in high school I was smoking weed nearly every day and graduated with a B average. But then, once I joined this company I am still working at today, they were drug testing, so I quit everything. I just did not want to risk a good paying job that I liked for drugs. Plus the embarrassment of not passing a drug test, when my dad is a CEO in the company I am working at. Now, I am even a Boy Scout leader and known as the Scout who is totally against any unnecessary drug use. What a change from those younger days! *(From Venturelli's research files, male working for a major corporation in Chicago, age 29, May 12, 2010)*

Misperceptions of Marijuana Use

In a world in which marijuana can be considered either an assassin or a sacrament, and in which it is associated with membership in prized or despised peer groups, it is not surprising that estimates of its use vary widely and inaccurately. Parents, for example, tend to underestimate their children's use of drugs. Findings from one study indicated that, "only 14% of the parents interviewed thought their children had experimented with marijuana while 38% of the teenagers said they had tried it" (Wren 1996, p. 1). In the same survey, 52% of teenagers reported having been offered drugs, whereas 34% of the parents thought their children might have been offered drugs. Other recent research indicates that parents who more carefully and consistently monitor their children and maintain more open communication are more likely to underestimate their children's risky behavior and ". . . parents of adolescents who perceived themselves as better than average in school performance and who participated in religious services were more likely to underestimate adolescents' substance use . . ." (Hongmei et al. 2006, p. 1).

Interestingly, another report by the former president of the National Center on Addiction and Substance Abuse at Columbia University stated the following with regard to baby boomer parents (parents born from the late 1940s through late 1950s):

> Almost half know someone who uses illegal drugs; a third have friends who use marijuana. Almost half expect their children to try illegal drugs, and 65 percent of those who smoked pot regularly when young believe their kids will try drugs . . . almost half of the parents don't think they can have much influence on whether their kids will use drugs. (Califano 1996, p. 19)

Even with regard to users' perceptions of other users, beliefs about marijuana remain distorted. College students tend to have exaggerated misperceptions of use, believing that their peers use marijuana much more than is true (Berkowitz 1991; Johnston et al. 2009). For example, at one campus in northern New Jersey, two-thirds of students reported never using marijuana, yet most students polled believed that the average student uses marijuana once per week. Other research also shows a widespread misperception in usage of marijuana. In 2005, in a randomly selected sample of 3639 college students, a large proportion (51%) of undergraduate students overestimated the use of marijuana among their peers on campus (McCabe 2008).

These findings of misperception in the use of marijuana are important because actual marijuana usage remains high for the time being. Recent findings show that marijuana continues to be the most commonly used illicit drug. An estimated 102 million Americans age 12 or older have tried marijuana at least once in their lifetime, representing 41% of the U.S. population in that age group. The number of past-year marijuana users in 2008 was approximately 25.8 million (10.3% of the population age 12 or older), and the number of past-month marijuana users was 15.2 million (6.1%) (SAMHSA 2009).

Characteristics of Cannabis

In 1753, Carolus Linnaeus, a Swedish botanist, classified marijuana as *Cannabis sativa* (see **Figure 13.5**). *Cannabis sativa* is a plant that grows readily in many parts of the world. Most botanists agree that there

KEY TERMS

Cannabis sativa
biological species name for the variety of hemp plant known as marijuana

FIGURE 13.5
Marijuana plant.

is only one species (*sativa*) and that all the variants (*indica, Americana,* and *Africana*) belong to that species, whereas others believe that the variants are three distinct species (Schultes 1978). *Indica* is considered to have the most potent resin, but climate, soil, and selective plant breeding all influence potency. The world's largest marijuana plant was 39 feet tall, and its woody stem was nearly 3 inches in diameter.

Cannabis is *dioecious,* meaning that there are male and female plants. After the male plant releases its pollen, it usually dies. In any case, even before the male plant dies, cultivators of marijuana often eliminate or remove the male plants before the female plant has been pollinated.

There are more than 421 different chemicals in the cannabis plant, many of which have not yet been identified. Tetrahydrocannabinol, or THC, is the primary mind-altering (psychoactive) agent in marijuana (Abood and Martin 1996; National Institute on Drug Abuse [NIDA] 2009b; Swan 1996) and appears to be important for the reinforcing properties of this substance (Kelly et al. 1994). THC is most highly concentrated in the flowering tops and upper leaves of the female plant. When crushed or

beaten, these flowering tops produce a resin in which the psychoactive ingredient THC is found.

In cultivated marijuana crops, as mentioned earlier, male plants are eradicated from the growing fields so that they cannot pollinate the female plants. The lack of pollination makes the potency of female plants increase dramatically. **Sinsemilla** (meaning "without seeds" in Spanish) is one of the most potent derivatives of the cannabis plant known in the United States, with an average THC content of 9.6%, but reaching as high as 24%. Sinsemilla is made from the buds of flowering tops of female plants (NIDA 1998). Other known types that have a much higher THC content include "hydro" (which means grown in water) and "kind bud."

In the United States, the amount of THC found in street-sold marijuana ranges broadly from 0.5% to 11%. Reports indicate that the amount of THC in marijuana has risen dramatically since the 1960s (ElSohly 2009; Kaplan and Whitmire 1995; MSNBC 2007; NIDA 1998). "More efficient agriculture—new methods of harvesting and processing marijuana plants—has made pot about 20 times more potent than the marijuana on the street in the 1960s and 1970s, drug treatment experts and law officials say" (Henneberger 1994, p. F-18). Further, the quantities of other, more potent types of marijuana such as sinsemilla as well as hydroponic types of marijuana (hydro) are more readily available in illegal drug markets. The actual potencies of the more generic types of marijuana have remained the same in the past 30 years. According to the latest data on marijuana samples analyzed, the average amount of THC in *seized* samples has reached 8.5%. This compares to an average of just under 4% reported in 1983, and represents more than a doubling in the potency of the drug since that time (Office of National Drug Control Policy [ONDCP] 2007). In addition, recently developed **drug trafficking organizations (DTOs)**—which are complex illegal organizations with highly defined command-and-control structures—produce, transport, and/or distribute large quantities of one or more illicit drugs.

Another finding is that:

> Marijuana produced in Mexico remains the most widely available in the United States. High potency marijuana has also entered the U.S. drug market from Canada. Another source for marijuana in the United States is domestically grown marijuana, which includes both indoor and outdoor operations. Groups [such as more recently identified drug trafficking organization (DTOs)] operating from Mexico employ a

KEY TERMS

sinsemilla
meaning without seeds, this marijuana is made from the buds and flowering tops of female plants and is one of the most potent types

drug trafficking organizations (DTOs)
refers to complex organizations with highly defined command-and-control structures that produce, transport, and/or distribute large quantities of one or more illicit drugs

variety of transportation and concealment methods to smuggle marijuana into the United States. Most of the marijuana smuggled into the United States is concealed in vehicles—often in false compartments—or hidden in shipments of legitimate agricultural or industrial products. Marijuana is also smuggled across the border by rail, horse, raft, and backpack. Canada is becoming a source country for indoor-grown, high potency (15% to 25% THC) marijuana destined for the United States. Such indoor-grow operations have become an enormous and lucrative illicit industry, producing a potent form of marijuana that has come to be known as "BC Bud." (ONDCP 2003)

Though the amount of THC found in marijuana samples vary depending on different seizures of this drug, we know for certain that the average potency of marijuana has been rising dramatically. One of many current reports finds that "Marijuana potency . . . [has increased] to the highest level in more than 30 years, posing greater health risks to people who may view the drug as harmless, according to a report released . . . by the White House." Another report states that "[t]he 9.6% [THC] level represents more than a doubling of marijuana potency since 1983, when it averaged just under 4%" (Yen 2008). It is probably safe to say that today the THC levels range from 8.5% to 9.6%.

Native U.S. street-variety marijuana, often referred to as domestic and sometimes referred to as "ditch weed," averages 5.62% THC; nondomestic varieties, which include Jamaican, Colombian, Mexican, and Canadian, averaged 9.57% THC. Out of 788 samples seized between 2008 and 2009, which included both domestic and nondomestic marijuana, the average was 8.52% THC (ElSohly 2009, p. 6).

Hashish (or hasheesh) is a second derivative of cannabis that contains the purest form of resin. This type of marijuana consists of the sticky resin from the female plant flowers. Domestic samples had an average of 12.14% THC, nondomestic had 7.03% THC, and all samples seized, which includes samples with much higher amounts of THC averaged, had 20.76% THC (ElSohly 2009, p. 6). Historically, hashish users have represented a somewhat small percentage of the cannabis user population in the United States, whereas in Europe use is much more prevalent. Hashish often is produced in Lebanon, Afghanistan, and Pakistan.

A third derivative of the cannabis plant is ganja, which is produced in India. This preparation consists of the dried tops of female plants. Ganja is also used as a slang term for marijuana (as are pot, herb, weed, grass, boom, Mary Jane, gangster, or chronic). There are more than 200 slang terms for marijuana.

The Behavioral Effects of Marijuana Use

This section will discuss the "high" experienced from marijuana, the subjective euphoric effects of this drug, how the use of marijuana affects driving performance and critical-thinking skills, and the amotivational syndrome that appears to be a characteristic effect of marijuana use.

■ The High

The widely held belief of the 1930s that marijuana was a destructive assassin of youth is no longer considered valid for casual or occasional users of this drug. In most individuals, low to moderate doses of cannabis produce euphoria and a pleasant state of relaxation (Goldstein 1994). What are the common effects experienced from marijuana use? After a few delayed moments of forcibly holding the smoke in the lungs, most users suddenly experience the high. In this state of euphoria, the user experiences a dry mouth, elevated heartbeat, and some loss of coordination and balance, coupled with slower reaction times and a feeling of euphoria (mild to elevated intoxication). Blood vessels in the eyes expand, which accounts for reddening of the eyes. Some people experience slightly elevated blood pressure, which can double the normal heart rate. These effects can become intensified when other drugs, such as LSD and/or psychedelic ("magic") mushrooms, are combined with the marijuana.

The state of euphoria that results from the high is usually mild and short-lived; a typical high from one joint may last from 2 to 3 hours. Subjectively, the user experiences altered perception of space and time, impaired memory of recent events, and impaired physical coordination (Abood and Martin 1992). (More of these subjective effects are discussed at length in the next section.) An occasional

KEY TERMS

hashish
sticky resin from the female plant flowers, which has an average THC level of 3.6% but can contain as much as 28%

high is not usually hazardous unless the person attempts to drive a car, operate heavy machinery, fly a plane, or function in similar ways requiring coordination, good reflexes, or quick judgment (Nahas and Latour 1992). Even low doses of marijuana alter perception, such as being able to judge the speed of an approaching vehicle or how much to slow down on an exit ramp.

> In trying to describe the high, it's not like an alcohol high. In an alcohol high, you are a lot more uncoordinated if drinking a lot. With weed, it's like reality changes—you add a lot more bass so-to-speak to what you see, hear, think, and feel. The reality is tempered with some distortion that to me and many others is pleasurable. You know how you feel after three or four very strong drinks [referring to alcoholic beverages]. Well take two more of those drinks and then look around the room you are in. Now, the difference between alcohol and weed is that you can walk to the bathroom quite well while under the influence of weed, while with alcohol you walk carefully so that no one notices that you are just about drunk. Weed is a mind high while alcohol is more of a body high. *(From Venturelli's research files, female professionally employed and residing in San Francisco, age 23, May 19, 2000)*

Three additional interviews attempted to compare the high from marijuana with the effects of alcohol.

First interview:

> The marijuana high is also not nearly as harsh on the body. Being high doesn't give you that painful hangover as alcohol does. The actual high is very functional; I tend to do some of my best work (after burning a "dubbie") in that state [of mind]. It is part of the lifestyle of marijuana. [In contrast], alcohol makes me (and most people I know) very unproductive when the "buzz" is reached. *(From Venturelli's research files, "Lectus Ferberger," male undergraduate student at a Midwestern university, age 21, August 10, 2000)*

Second interview with the same person a day later:

> There seems to be a small misconception about the effects of marijuana and alcohol. For me, anyway, in looking at the physical "buzz" you get from alcohol, it is very physically disabling.

You get drunk and stumble around, your lips loosen up, and you say things that you would not normally say. I find that marijuana has more of a calming effect. It makes you relaxed, a little more perceptive to some stimuli, and obviously less perceptive to other stimuli. It is a light feeling, but not overwhelming to the equilibrium. *(From Venturelli's research files, same student as above, August 11, 2000)*

Third interview:

> I can't drink much, because I feel the effects of alcohol more than the average person. I also don't like the effects of being high on alcohol. I feel very loopy and uncoordinated. Then, the next morning after drinking the night before is very unpleasant for me with headaches and sometimes even nausea. This is why I like to smoke weed. With weed you don't have all the impairment, the sick feelings, and you don't wake all messed up. I also have great conversations with people who are high on marijuana and find myself in a good mood while high. Also with regard to impairment, I would never drive under the influence of alcohol, but with marijuana, I have no problem driving. I even had a police officer stop me one night when my tail light was out on one side while on weed, and he never detected my marijuana high. He just wrote me a warning notice. Now, if it were alcohol, he probably would have become suspicious. Everyone is different, and this is my take on comparing these two drugs. *(From Venturelli's research files, female student at a Midwestern university, age 22, September 9, 2010)*

An acute dose of cannabis can produce adverse reactions, ranging from mild anxiety to panic and paranoia in some users. These reactions occur most frequently in individuals who are under stress or who are anxious, depressed, or borderline schizophrenic (Nahas and Latour 1992). Such effects also may be seen in normal users who accidentally take much more than they feel they can handle.

Extreme reactions can also occur because of ingesting marijuana treated (or "laced") with such things as opium, PCP, or other additives. Based on limited evidence from survey studies, mild or often adverse reactions are experienced on one or more occasions by more than one-half of regular users; they are mainly self-treated and usually go unreported (see "Signs and Symptoms: Specific Indicators of Marijuana Use").

Signs & Symptoms   Specific Indicators of Marijuana Use

A sweet odor similar to burnt rope in room, on clothes, and so on.
Roach: The small butt end of a marijuana cigarette.
Joint: Looks like a hand-rolled cigarette; usually the ends are twisted or crimped.
Roach clips: Holders for the roach could be any number of common items such as paper clips, bobby pins, or hemostats. They also could be of a store-bought variety in a number of shapes and disguises.
Seeds or leaves in pockets or possession.
Plastic baggies, either with some amount of marijuana inside the baggie or an empty baggie often found in pant or shirt pockets.
Rolling papers or pipes, usually hidden somewhere.
Eye drops: For disguising red eyes.
Excessive use of incense, room deodorizers, or breath fresheners.
Devices for storing the substance, such as film canisters, boxes, or cans.
Eating binges: An after effect for some marijuana users.
Appearance of intoxication, yet no smell of alcohol.
Excessive laughter.
Initial use (first hour): Animated behavior (loud or excessive talking).
Hours later: Fatigue or drowsiness.

■ Subjective Euphoric Effects

Subjective euphoric effects associated with marijuana use refer to the ongoing social and psychological experiences incurred while intoxicated by marijuana. These effects of intoxication include both the user's altered state of consciousness and his or her perceptions. Subjective effects in experienced users include a general sense of relaxation and tranquility, coupled with heightened sensitivity to sound, taste, and emotionality. For inexperienced users the subjective effects can vary from very similar experiences that experienced users have to some anxiety from anticipation of the effects. Often, it depends on the set (state of mind and mood) and setting (surroundings where the drug is taken, which includes the people in the immediate environment when the drug is consumed). Some users report occasional similarities to the typical hallucinogenic high, emphasizing much less intensity. How closely the marijuana high resembles a hallucinogenic high depends on the amount of THC absorbed from marijuana. For example, higher amounts of THC found in more potent plants of marijuana, like sinsemilla, hydro, and kind bud, more clearly mimic a hallucinogenic high. These effects are especially evident when considering the extent to which the senses of hearing, vision, sound, and taste are distorted by use of highly potent forms of marijuana.

Some marijuana users become very attached to these euphoric effects (in search of re-experiencing these effects). Such users often pride themselves on their extensive knowledge of this drug and maintain interest in discussing past experiences of "when I was really high" or "let me tell you about that night we smoked hydro. . . ." Devotees stay current with developments in the marijuana field by avidly

KEY TERMS

subjective euphoric effects
ongoing social and psychological experiences incurred while intoxicated with marijuana

reading monthly issues of magazines devoted to marijuana (the art of marijuana use) and frequently scan the Internet for information and conversations in chat rooms about the best varieties of marijuana, best growing techniques, announcements of hemp festivals, advice, and information regarding current laws, fines, and other information. A vivid example of such an enthusiast is recalled in the following observation:

This author recalls visiting a neighbor's one evening and noticing that one of the visitors sat very quietly with a pleasant smile while several intense conversations were occurring. I recall noticing this student in that he sat very quietly appearing somewhat distant and occasionally displaying several facial gestures in either approval or disapproval of comments and suggestions during the ongoing conversations. After approximately one hour during my visit, while others continued having multiple conversations, I directed my attention to this "quiet" individual with some introductory comments. He made minimal responses in the conversation. As others were discussing multiple topics, several of the guests began talking about drug use. Immediately, this quiet and reserved individual became very lively and began talking about the best types of marijuana on campus. Within several minutes, I literally saw a transformation in his involvement with the ongoing conversation. He was incessantly talking about marijuana and dominated the conversation with his many insights about the drug. I realized, prior to the topic of drug use and marijuana, he probably did not have much interest in the other topics. However, when we "hit" what appeared to be an interesting topic, which was a passion for marijuana use, an intensive amount of enthusiasm emerged. Clearly, this former "quiet young man" had transformed and clearly appeared to be quite a connoisseur about the varieties and the subjective euphoric effects of marijuana. By his overall conversational enthusiasm, he appeared quite content in letting us know how much he knew about this topic—and it was an extensive amount of knowledge. *(Observation from Venturelli visiting a neighbor's home in a small Midwestern town, June 9, 2010)*

KEY TERMS

differential association
process by which individuals become socialized into the perceptions and values of a group

Why is marijuana so attractive to many individuals? One quote from an interview illustrates the extensive psychological and social reinforcement experienced by marijuana users:

It's the high that I particularly like. Everything becomes mellower. Everyday tensions are released or submerged by more inner-like experiences. I can review the day and how happy or miserable I feel. Actually, when I am thinking and I am high on grass, I always feel that my thoughts are profound. You think from another perspective, one that numbs the more reality-based everyday strains. On the other hand, there are moments when this drug affects your mood and channels it [in] different ways. You have moments when you either feel sad, happy, angry (in a more contemplative way), or worried. These moods are both good and bad. If for the moment you feel good, then your mood is positive. If you feel down, your mood is negative in a particular way. If I am with friends and we are all sharing the bong or joint or pipe, we laugh a lot together. It's a type of drug that makes you more jovial, more introspective, and friendly, gregarious. . . . *(From Venturelli's research files, male personnel manager, age 40, August 20, 1996)*

As documented above, marijuana enthusiasts have a strong attachment to their passionate feelings surrounding the use of marijuana. As explained in Chapter 2, largely through the reinforcement of pleasurable feelings, psychologists believe the drug user becomes attached and habituated to the drug. If these subjective euphoric experiences were to become largely negative, attachment to and repeated use of this drug would cease. Thus, the theory of differential association applies. This theory, developed by Edwin Sutherland in 1939 and revised in 1947, attempts to explain delinquent behavior. Sociologists define the term **differential association** as the process by which individuals become socialized into the perceptions and values of a group. Differential association can apply to drug use. In using this drug, the *camaraderie,* the conversations and banter that often occur among friends, is often perceived as fun activity. It can include the perception that marijuana relieves boredom or stress, or is the perfect drug for just hanging out, partying, and getting high together. Specifically, the definition of differential association can include the behavioral satisfaction derived from friends who use marijuana. In this situation, getting high with others is the positive reward that solidifies the user to his or her friends and the drug.

Driving Performance

Evidence shows that the ability to perform complex tasks, such as driving, can be impaired while under the influence of marijuana (Couper and Logan 2004; Goldstein 1994; Mathias 1996; TheWeek.com 2010). Research indicates that "Cannabis consumption impairs motor coordination, reaction time, sensory perceptions and glare recovery" (Teen Challenge 2000, p. 1). This effect has been demonstrated in laboratory assessments of driving-related skills such as eye–hand coordination and reaction time, in driver simulator studies, in test course performance, and in actual street driving situations (Chait and Pierri 1992; Couper and Logan 2004; Mathias 1996; Teen Challenge 2000). Another study tested the effects of known amounts of marijuana, alcohol, or both on driving. The subjects drove a course rigged with various traffic problems. There was a definite deterioration in driving skills among those who had used either drug, but the greatest deterioration was observed in subjects who had taken both. In another test, 59 subjects smoked marijuana until they were intoxicated and then were given sobriety tests on the roadside by highway patrol officers. Overall, 94% of the subjects did not pass the test 90 minutes after smoking, and 60% failed at 150 minutes, even though the blood THC was much lower at this time (Hollister 1986). Other studies on driving show this same inability to drive for as long as 12 to 24 hours after marijuana use.

A more recent study detailing results from driving performance found that the short-term effects of marijuana use include problems with memory and learning, distorted perception, difficultly in thinking and problem-solving, and loss of coordination (IdeaConnection.com 2011, p. 2). Heavy users may have increased difficulty sustaining attention, shifting attention to meet the demands of changes in the environment, and in registering, processing, and using information. In general, laboratory performance studies indicate that sensory functions are not highly impaired, but perceptual functions are significantly affected. The ability to concentrate and maintain attention is decreased during marijuana use, and impairment of hand–eye coordination is dose-related over a wide range of dosages. Impairment in retention time and tracking, subjective sleepiness, distortion of time and distance, vigilance, and loss of coordination in divided attention tasks have been reported. Note, however, that subjects can often "pull themselves together" to concentrate on simple tasks for brief periods of time. However, significant performance impairments are usually observed for at least 1–2 hours following marijuana use, and residual effects have been reported for up to 24 hours (Couper and Logan 2004, p. 1).

Another, slightly less critical study of city driving

> . . . showed that drivers who drank alcohol over-estimated their performance quality [often by speeding and overconfidence] whereas those who smoked marijuana under-estimated it [slower speed and more cautious driving]. . . . Drivers under the influence of marijuana retain insight in their performance and will compensate where they can, for example, by slowing down or increasing effort. As a consequence, THC's adverse effects on driving performance appear relatively small. Still we can easily imagine situations where the influence of marijuana smoking might have an exceedingly dangerous effect; i.e., emergency situations which put high demands on the driver's information processing capacity, prolonged monotonous driving, and after THC have been taken with other drugs, especially alcohol. (U.S. Department of Transportation 1993)

In surveys, from 70% to 80% of marijuana users indicate that they sometimes drive while high. A study of drivers involved in fatal accidents in the greater Boston area showed that marijuana smokers were overrepresented in fatal highway accidents as compared with a control group of nonusers of similar age and gender. A 1998 study found that, of nearly 1800 blood samples taken from drivers arrested for driving while intoxicated, 19% tested positive for marijuana. In a large study of almost 3400 fatally injured drivers from three Australian states (Victoria, New South Wales, and Western Australia) between 1990 and 1999, drugs other than alcohol were present in 26.7% of the cases, and this included cannabis (13.5%) (NIDA 2009a).

More recent research by the Drug Enforcement Administration (DEA 2010) involving government surveys that ask young people about their drug use patterns indicate that about 600,000 high school seniors drive after smoking marijuana. Thirty-eight thousand seniors told surveyors that they had been involved in accidents while driving under the influence of marijuana. Other surveys conducted by MADD and the Liberty Mutual insurance company revealed that many teenagers (41%) were not concerned about driving after taking drugs. Medical data indicate a connection between drugged driving and accidents—a study of patients in a shock trauma unit who had been in collisions revealed that 15% of those who had been driving a car or motorcycle had been smoking marijuana, and another 17% had both THC and alcohol in their blood.

Recent research conducted by the University of Auckland, New Zealand, proves the link between marijuana use and car accidents. The research found that habitual cannabis users were 9.5 times more likely to be involved in crashes, with 5.6% of people who had crashed having taken the drug, compared to 0.5% of the control group (Blows et al. 2005).

A study published by researchers at the University of Maryland Medical Center Shock Trauma Center indicates that during a 90-day study, about half of the drivers admitted to the Maryland Shock Trauma Center tested positive for drugs other than alcohol. Additionally, one in four drivers admitted to the shock trauma unit tested positive for marijuana.

> This population-based case–control study indicates that habitual use of marijuana is strongly associated with car crash injury. The nature of the relationship between marijuana use and risk-taking is unclear and needs further research. The prevalence of marijuana use in this driving population was low, and acute use was associated with habitual marijuana use, suggesting that intervention strategies may be more effective if they are targeted towards high use groups. (Blows et al. 2005, p. 605)

One notable interview presents us with a negative experience regarding use of marijuana and driving experiences:

> One time I smoked some real strong dope at my friend's house, then had to drive back home, which was 2 miles in one direction. I remember wigging out (panicking) in trying to get home. There were moments when I did not know where I was until I would see the next marker of my neighborhood. I remember having seconds of panic because I did not know where I was; then suddenly, I would notice a neighborhood restaurant or some other marker that said I was right around my neighborhood. I took smaller streets on the way home and even took a longer way home because I was freaking out about the cops—what if one would spot me? This was bogus thinking because how the hell would anyone suddenly spot me while driving home? Well, that's an example of wigging out on weed. But, I still don't think that even that time I would be getting into an accident. I was so freaked out that I was extra careful not

to speed, pass stop signs, or violate any law for fear of being seen. If anything, I drive slower when I am really high, not more dangerously. *(From Venturelli's research files, male college student in a Midwestern town, age 20, July 19, 2000)*

In contrast to this student's beliefs, scientific research indicates that some perceptual or other performance deficits resulting from marijuana use may persist for some time after the high, and users who attempt to drive, fly, operate heavy machinery, perform surgery, and so on may not recognize their impairment because they do not feel intoxicated. States such as California have established testing procedures to detect the presence of THC in urine or blood samples from apparently intoxicated drivers.

If the use of marijuana becomes more socially acceptable (or perhaps even legal) and penalties for simple possession become more lenient, it is likely that individuals will feel less inclined to hide their drug use. Unfortunately, it follows that these individuals may also be more inclined to drive while high, endangering themselves and others.

■ Critical Thinking Skills

Marijuana has been found to have a negative impact on critical thinking skills. Recent research by NIDA shows that heavy marijuana use impairs critical skills related to attention, memory, and learning. Another study showed that even alertness, coordination, and reaction time were impaired by marijuana usage (Couper and Logan 2004; National Clearinghouse on Alcohol and Drug Information [NCADI] 1998). Impairment from marijuana continues even after discontinuing use of the drug for at least 24 hours (Brown and Massaro 1996).

In the same study, researchers compared 65 heavy users (using approximately every other day) with light users (using once or twice per week). Heavy users made more mistakes and had greater difficulty sustaining attention, shifting attention to meet demands of challenges in the environment, and registering, processing, and using information (Brown and Massaro 1996; Fuller 2008; Norton 2009) compared with the light users. In addition, heavy users had greater difficulty completing the tests, which specifically measured aspects of attention, memory, and learning, such as intellectual functioning, abstraction ability, attention span, verbal fluency, and learning and recalling abilities (Brown and Massaro 1996; Teen Challenge 2000). One researcher stated, "If you could get heavy users to learn an item, then they could remember it; the problem was getting them to learn it in the first place" (Brown and Massaro 1996, p. 3). The researchers surmised that marijuana alters brain activity because residues of the drug persist in the brain or because a withdrawal syndrome follows the euphoric effects of the marijuana. In another study, researchers tested the cognitive functioning of 65 marijuana-using college students. Residual impairments were seen the 24 hours after use in terms of sustaining attention, shifting attention, and hence in registering, organizing, and using information (Pope and Yurgulen-Todd 1996). This study, which was undertaken during the 1990s, is significant because it was carefully controlled. The unresolved question is whether these memory impairments are short term or long term. These noteworthy findings complement many other similar findings that identified protracted cognitive impairment among heavy users of marijuana (Fuller 2008; NCADI 1998; Norton 2009).

Amotivational Syndrome

The so-called **amotivational syndrome** (sometimes referred to as antimotivational syndrome) is a flashpoint of controversy about marijuana, although not as newsworthy as that regarding medical legalization. Amotivational syndrome refers to a belief that heavy use of marijuana causes a lack of motivation or "impaired desire" and reduced productivity. Specifically, users show apathy, poor short-term memory, difficulty in concentration, and a lingering disinterest in pursuing goals (Abood and Martin 1992; Wrongdiagnoses.com 2010).

In the past, this syndrome received considerable attention. People who are high, or stoned, lack the

desire to perform hard work and are not interested in doing difficult tasks. There is some evidence of this behavior in regular marijuana users (Nahas and Latour 1992). Overall, although not solely the result of cannabis use, chronic users have lower grades in school, are more likely to be absent from classes, and are likely not to complete assignments and to drop out of school (Henneberger 1994; Liska 1997). In terms of age, the earlier someone begins smoking marijuana, coupled with heavier use, the more likely the amotivational characteristics will prevail and the more difficult it will be to cease using this drug.

Although the effects of marijuana per se are somewhat responsible for creating this syndrome, other factors contribute as well. For instance, is the lack of motivation caused by the drug itself or is it that poorly motivated people begin using marijuana, which then further exacerbates their lack of motivation? Surveys show that a sizable number of marijuana users and their peer groups tend to be alienated from society and are likely to be classified as nonconformists and/or rebellious youths. They may, in fact, select to emphasize pleasure and nonconformity rather than goal-directed behavior. Another challenge to the concept of amotivational syndrome argues that the lack of motivation may simply be due to the effects of marijuana while under its influence and not any type of longer term or unique syndrome (Iverson 2005; Johns 2001).

Advocates of marijuana legalization stress data that tend to debunk research on amotivational syndrome. One institute that supports legalization, the Lindesmith Center, published a study asserting that college students who are users have higher grades than nonusers (Zimmer and Morgan 1997). How can we account for the discrepancies between this study and others, not to mention the clinical experiences of students, who often report academic repercussions of heavy use? One factor in the explanation is sociocultural:

> In the New York–New Jersey metro region, there are "druggy" schools and "drinking" schools. The "druggy" schools are more upper-middle class, liberal arts schools, artsy types, latter-day hippies, etc. The boozer campuses

Typical effects of amotivational syndrome.

are filled with blue-collar and lower-middle-class kids—sometimes big fraternity schools. Frontloading at basketball games, comas after pledge parties. . . . Not as good educational backgrounds as the artsy potheads, who went to better schools, private schools, read a lot, or heard a lot at dinner before college, so they get by with their profs. However, the potheads ratchet down into easier majors, and they get crummier grades as they get into regular use. *(Interview with Pearl Mott for a prevention newsletter, prevention specialist, Drug Prevention Programs in Higher Education, Washington, DC, October 1994)*

A second methodological factor complicating drug research among such students is simply that academic failures stay in "F" categories for only one or two semesters. Many then disappear from statistics entirely, via academic attrition.

A more serious challenge to the notion of amotivational syndrome comes from the same ethnographic research that was mentioned at the beginning of this chapter. The most well-known of these investigations was carried out by Vera Rubin and Labros Comitas, as reported in their book *Ganja in Jamaica* (1975). Follow-up studies were done in Jamaica (Dreher 1982; Hamid 1998) and Costa Rica (Carter 1980; Pollan 1998). None of these works found that chronic use impaired occupational or other functioning; in fact, the main point of the Jamaican studies was that users defined this drug as helpful and motivating for work—a "motivational syndrome." This work is often cited to counter amotivational syndrome claims. By this logic, dropping out of the rat race is a cultural posture, with marijuana being secondary to, or, at most, reinforcing the drift away from a mainstream lifestyle. The Jamaican and Costa Rican subjects, however, were not observed engaging in an academic, cognitively complex, or rapid reflex activity, nor were they found in occupations that are competitive and striving for mobility. Rather, these subjects were involved in repetitive, physical labor such as sugar-cane cutting. In such a context, marijuana drug use functions to provide a pleasant sedation that counters the monotony and physical discomfort of such labor. When studies in other cultures contradict the largely American notion of amotiva-

tional syndrome, we are left to be cautious in making a direct assumption that marijuana use leads to such a syndrome. (For related information on how marijuana affects personality, see "Case in Point: A Letter to an Editor.")

Therapeutic Uses and the Controversy over Medical Marijuana Use

Though the use of marijuana for medical purposes is far more accepted than it was 7 years ago, the controversy about the medical uses of marijuana remains. Basically, **medical marijuana** use involves using cannabis, primarily THC, as a drug to calm or to relieve symptoms of an illness. At the heart of this controversy is the use of an illicit drug for medical purposes. However, the desire to use cannabis in this fashion is nothing new. Between 1840 and 1900, European and American medical journals published more than 100 articles on the therapeutic use of the drug known then as *Cannabis indica* (or Indian hemp) and now as marijuana. It was recommended as an appetite stimulant, muscle relaxant, analgesic, hypnotic, and anticonvulsant. As late as 1913, Sir William Osler recommended it as the most satisfactory remedy for migraines (Grinspoon and Bakalar 1995).

Marijuana was used to treat a variety of human ills in folk and formal medicine for thousands of years in South Africa, Turkey, South America, and Egypt as well as such Asian countries as India, Malaysia, Myanmar, and Siam. Thus, marijuana, known as *cannabis* back then, has a 5000-year medical history that came to an abrupt end in the United States by passage of the Marijuana Tax Act of 1937. When the Marijuana Tax Act became law, marijuana was legally classified as a narcotic, and at that time medical use of this substance effectively ceased. Only in the past two decades has there been organized renewed interest in possible medical uses for cannabis. Because of potential clinical uses for marijuana, enforcement of laws prohibiting the use of this substance has been very controversial (see "Holding the Line: States Currently Allowing the Sale of Medical Marijuana Although Cannabis Buyers' Clubs Are Not Fully Legal").

Marijuana has been shown to be effective in the treatment of certain types of medical conditions. However, because medicines exist that are at least as effective and without abuse potential, none of these applications is currently approved by the

KEY TERMS

medical marijuana
use of the THC in cannabis as a drug to calm or to relieve symptoms of an illness

►Case in Point   A Letter to an Editor: No Valid Reason to Ban Marijuana ◄

An Associated Press release printed recently in the *Kentucky Enquirer* had the head of the White House Office of Drug Control Policy, Gil Kerlikowske, President Obama's Drug Czar, extolling the necessity of continuing the prohibition of marijuana. The reasons he cites for continuing the 70-year war on marijuana smokers are a clear indication that history is correct in judging marijuana prohibition as one of the greatest policy failures in the history of the federal government. The letter is as follows:

Those who support prohibition started in 1933 at the end of alcohol prohibition to shift all the bad outcomes of alcohol use to marijuana. The films and newspaper stories of the day claimed that using marijuana leads to violence, murder, and insanity. Think of the movie, "Reefer Madness." Cut to the present and the Drug Czar is reduced to claiming that marijuana causes lung cancer, and that marijuana use is the cause of a significant amount of traffic accidents. The lung cancer, marijuana connection is a myth that grows out of the fact that tobacco smoking causes lung cancer therefore marijuana smoking should too. With this in mind, the Government originally supported the work of Dr. Donald Tashkin. His study on marijuana smoking and head, neck, and lung cancer was expected to be a slam-dunk for the Government. The problem is that the results of Dr. Tashkin's and other studies is that the opposite is true. Dr. Tashkin's study showed that people who regularly use marijuana get head, neck, and lung cancer at the same rate as people who do not smoke at all. He reported that marijuana seemed to have an anti-cancer effect and acted as a cancer preventer. One would think medical researchers would be all over this like "stink on poopy" looking for a cancer cure, but the forces of prohibition continue to block research, even though compassion for one's fellow men and the saving of lives would indicate the opposite.

Mr. Kerlikowske's claim about marijuana being the cause of a significant amount of traffic accidents is a "fact" that he must have pulled out of a lower opening. There is no data to support this. Again, what studies have been done on this angle do not support his claim. Studies have found that marijuana smokers get into accidents as often as those who do not use marijuana. Think about it! I returned to Northern Kentucky in 1996. I watch local news at least once a day and read the paper every day.

In the 14 years since 1996, I have seen only one report of a marijuana caused traffic accident. If I remember right, a young man had blown through an intersection and someone was killed in the resulting accident. The local media reported that the driver had been smoking marijuana and that was the cause of the accident. A follow up report later claimed the driver was texting when he blew the intersection. You have to ask yourself that if there are so many marijuana caused accidents, where are all the marijuana accident stories, arrests, trials, and incarcerations.

Marijuana prohibition is an idea that has lived long past the point of being something that is "good" for America. Marijuana use is not as Reagan said that it's the greatest threat faced by America. The end of the federal ban on marijuana is long overdue. It has no basis in science or logic, costs billions of tax dollars, and causes more harm than good. At a time when Americans need jobs and economic growth, we are shooting ourselves in the foot by continuing to suppress the marijuana/hemp industry, an industry that could go a long way in creating jobs and economic activity worth billions of dollars.

Msgt Thomas Vance, USAF Ret., Alexandria

Questions to Consider

1. What is your initial reaction to this letter?

2. Like the firmly established link between lung cancer and smoking tobacco, do you think a similar argument can be made between smoking marijuana and lung cancer? What are the reasons for your answer?

3. Do you think the "forces of prohibition" are masking potential benefits of using marijuana, as the writer claims? Explain.

4. What is your opinion about using marijuana and driving? Do you think drivers under the influence are adversely affected by the effects of this drug? Explain.

5. How do you generally feel about marijuana drug users?

6. How much of a threat to society is marijuana use? Should marijuana be decriminalized? If yes, why? Should it remain illegal? If so, what penalties should apply and why?

Source: Cincinnati.com. Letters to the Editor: "No Valid Reason to Ban Marijuana." *The Enquirer.* 9 August 2010. Available at: http://cincinnati.com/blogs/letters/2010/08/09/no-valid-reason-to-ban-marijuana. Accessed February 17, 2011.

Holding the Line

States Currently Allowing the Sale of Medical Marijuana Although Cannabis Buyers' Clubs Are Not Fully Legal

Currently 15 states and the District of Columbia are medical marijuana states. The 15 states are Alaska, Arizona, California, Colorado, Hawaii, Maine, Michigan, Montana, Nevada, New Jersey, New Mexico, Oregon, Rhode Island, Vermont, and Washington (ProCon.org 2010). Eight states that currently have pending legislation or ballot measures to legalize medical marijuana are Illinois, Massachusetts, New York, North Carolina, Ohio, Pennsylvania, and South Dakota. Out of approximately 304 million people living in 12 of the 15 states and Washington, DC, 577,712 people are registered as medical marijuana patients (ProCon.org 2010).

Why should medically ill patients, those afflicted with AIDS and AIDS wasting, lack of appetite, nausea, arthritis, hepatitis C, migraines, multiple sclerosis, muscle spasms, chronic pain, or those suffering the deleterious effects of chemotherapy and/or radiation, glaucoma, and other illnesses not be able to legally purchase marijuana if they find relief from the effects of their illnesses? The first cannabis buyers' club began in 1996, when the voting citizens of Marin County, California, passed ". . . Proposition 215, which authorized the use of medical marijuana . . . for those who have a doctor's recommendation" (Cannabis News 2002). The main problem with this club in Marin County, and all the other cannabis buyers' clubs throughout the United States, is that although the counties have legalized such enterprises, they continue to violate federal drug laws. This conflict is between federal and state law. Usually, the clubs are ordered closed by a superior court judge, resulting in federal agents raiding the clubs, confiscating the marijuana, and arresting the owners and operators of these establishments.

To date, this cyclical pattern of raids and arrests by federal officials is repetitive and ongoing because of this rift between state and federal laws. The clubs are either for-profit or nonprofit organizations whose sole intent is to distribute marijuana for medicinal purposes when prescribed by a licensed physician. Many of the buyers (known as patients) report relief and satisfaction from their use of marijuana. For example, a man by the name of Clay Shinn, 46, was diagnosed with AIDS in 1992. He's been going to the Marin Alliance's Cannabis Buyers' Club for 5 years. "'It's made a major difference in my life,' he said. After taking his [AIDS] medication morning, afternoon, and evening, he said, 'I was always getting nauseated . . . I could set my watch by it. I hate it. God, it's awful. Now I don't barf anymore'" (Cannabis News 2002). Another interviewee, who is an arthritic, HIV-positive cabaret performer, said, "After I leave here . . . I won't feel my pain" (Goldberg 1996). Another man, the club's director, reiterated that, "'You have to be sick or dying' . . . If you are, with a doctor's note to prove that you have AIDS or cancer or another condition with symptoms that marijuana is known to alleviate, Mr. Peron [the club's director] is willing to sell some relief" (Goldberg 1996). Finally, another statement from Dennis Peron, the founder of the San Francisco Buyers' Club, noted that "We have over four hundred senior citizens that come here for arthritis, glaucoma, pain, etc. We have an old woman trapped in her wheelchair, day in and day out. Marijuana makes her feel a little bit better. I don't require a letter of diagnosis for people sixty-five or older—things wear out—or for people who are blind or deaf, as they say it helps their other senses" (Fuhrman 1995).

How would you answer the following questions?

1. What are your views regarding the prescribed use of marijuana, especially when these clubs or cooperatives provide seriously ill patients with a safe and reliable source of medical cannabis information and patient support?

2. Would you support a cannabis buyers' club or cooperative in your community?

3. What are your views regarding federal laws that prohibit such establishments while states pass laws allowing these establishments to operate legally?

4. How do you think this current problem of the illegality on the federal level should be resolved?

5. Finally, in your lifetime, how do you think this dilemma will be resolved?

Sources: Cannabis News. "Medical Pot War Rages On." *Marin Independent Journal.* 1 July 2002. Available at: http://cannabisnews.com/news/13/thread13278.shtml. Accessed February 17, 2011; Goldberg, C. "Marijuana Club Helps Those in Pain." *New York Times.* 26 February 1996. Available at: http://query.nytimes.com/gst/fullpage.html?res=9C06E6DF1139F936A15751C0A960958260&sec=&spon=&pagewanted=all. Accessed February 17, 2011; Fuhrman, R. A. *Cannabis Buyers' Club Flourishes in "Frisco."* San Francisco: Cannabis Buyers' Club, 1995; and ProCon.org. "Fourteen Legal Medical Marijuana States and DC." 2010. Available at: http://www.procon.org. Accessed February 17, 2011.

Food and Drug Administration (FDA). According to researchers (Abood and Martin 1992; Consroe and Sandyk 1992; Iversen 1993; ProCon.org 2010) and proponents for the medical uses of marijuana, the potential uses are as listed in the following sections.

Reduction in Intraocular (Eye) Pressure

Marijuana lowers glaucoma-associated intraocular pressure, even though it does not cure the condition or reverse blindness (Goldstein 1995; Green 2002; NIDA 2010). **Glaucoma** is the second leading cause of blindness, and is caused by uncontrollable eye pressure (Julian 1994; National Eye Institute 2010).

Antiasthmatic Effect

Some research indicates that short-term smoking of marijuana improves breathing for asthma patients. Marijuana smoke dilates the lungs' air passages (bronchodilation). Other findings also show, however, that the lung-irritating properties of marijuana smoke seem to offset its benefits. Adverse effects of marijuana smoke remains controversial (NIDA 2006, 2010). Regardless, marijuana may still prove useful when other drugs are not effective because of a different mode of action in causing bronchodilation.

Muscle-Relaxant Effect

Some studies indicate that muscle spasms are relieved when patients with muscle disorders, such as multiple sclerosis, use marijuana.

Antiseizure Effect

Marijuana has both convulsing and anticonvulsant properties and has been considered for use in preventing seizures associated with epilepsy. In animal

experimentation, the cannabinoids reduced or increased seizure activities, depending on how the experiments were conducted. One or more of the marijuana components may be useful in combination with other standard antiseizure medication.

Antidepressant Effect

Cannabis and the synthetic cannabinoid synhexyl have been used successfully in Great Britain as a specific euphoriant for the treatment of depression.

Analgesic Effect

Published testimonials have reported that marijuana can relieve the intense pain (Green 2002) associated with migraine and chronic headaches or inflammation (Grinspoon and Bakalar 1995). "Survey data indicates that the use of cannabis is common in chronic pain populations and several recent clinical trials indicate that inhaled marijuana can significantly alleviate neuropathic pain" (Green 2006; Cone et al. 2008, p. 532; Gardner 2010; National Organization for the Reform of Marijuana Laws [NORML] 2010). In South Africa, native women smoke cannabis to dull the pain of childbirth (Hamid 1998; Solomon 1966). The pain-relieving potency of marijuana has not been carefully studied and compared with other analgesics, such as narcotics or aspirin-type drugs.

Antinauseant

Marijuana can relieve the nausea that accompanies chemotherapy for cancer treatment (NIDA 2010; Robson 2001).

Appetite Stimulant

Marijuana appears to stimulate appetite (NIDA 2010). The stimulant effects on appetite are seen as useful for patients with HIV and some eating disorders (Sewester 1993) (see Chapter 16).

Short-Term Dangers of Smoking Marijuana

According to Brown University's health education web site (Brown University Health Education 2007), discomforts associated with smoking marijuana

In July 2000, California began to issue cards that allow the cardholders to purchase marijuana for medicinal purposes.

include dry mouth, dry eyes, increased heart rate, and visible signs of intoxication such as bloodshot eyes and puffy eyelids. Other problems during intoxication include:

- Impaired short-term memory and ability to learn (NIDA 2010).
- Difficulty thinking and problem solving (NIDA 2010).
- Anxiety attacks or feelings of paranoia.
- Impaired muscle coordination and judgment.
- Impairment of driving skills. Studies show that it impairs braking time, attention to traffic signals, and other driving behaviors.
- Cardiac problems for people with heart disease or high blood pressure because marijuana increases the heart rate (Brown University 2007; NIDA 2010).
- Psychotic episodes (NIDA 2010).

Long-Term Consequences of Smoking Marijuana

Long-term consequences, lasting longer than intoxication, and cumulative effects of chronic abuse of smoking marijuana include:

- *Respiratory problems:* Many of these are the same as for cigarette smokers. Persistent coughing, symptoms of bronchitis, and more frequent chest colds are possible symptoms from the 400-plus chemicals (some carcinogenic) in marijuana smoke. "Researchers report that marijuana cigarettes release five times as much carbon monoxide into the bloodstream and three times as much tar into the lungs of smokers as tobacco cigarettes" (MarijuanaDetox.com 2008, p. 1; NIDA 2010).
- *Memory and learning:* Regular marijuana use compromises the ability to learn and to remember information by impairing the ability to focus, sustain, and shift attention. One study also found that long-term use reduces the ability to organize and integrate complex information. Marijuana impairs short-term memory and decreases motivation to accomplish tasks, even after the high is over.
- *Fertility:* Long-term marijuana use suppresses the production of hormones that help regulate the reproductive system. For men, this can cause decreased sperm counts, and very heavy users can experience erectile dysfunction. Women may experience irregular periods from heavy marijuana use.

- *Marijuana can also be addictive:* More studies are finding that marijuana has addictive properties (NIDA 2010). Both animal and human studies show physical and psychological withdrawal symptoms from marijuana, including irritability, restlessness, insomnia, nausea, and intense dreams. Tolerance to marijuana also builds up rapidly. Heavy users need eight times higher doses to get the same effects as infrequent users. For a small percentage of people who use it, long-term marijuana use can lead to addiction (NIDA 2010). It is estimated that 10% to 14% of users will become heavily dependent. More than 120,000 people in the United States seek treatment for marijuana addiction every year (Brown University 2007). Why would abusers go to treatment centers if this drug were not addictive? Finally, ". . . marijuana addiction is also linked to a withdrawal syndrome similar to that of nicotine withdrawal, which can make it difficult to quit. People trying to quit report irritability, sleeping difficulties, craving, and anxiety" (NIDA 2010, p. 7).

All of these reasons have either been disputed or shown to be exaggerated claims by proponents who are in favor of allowing marijuana to be medically used. Proponents for medical use argue that "its illegality [marijuana] . . . imposes much anxiety and expense on suffering people, forces them to bargain with illicit drug dealers, and exposes them to the threat of criminal prosecution" (Grinspoon and Bakalar 1995, p. 1876). For a list of states currently allowing the use of marijuana for medical purposes, see the "Holding the Line" feature earlier in this chapter.

The Physiological Effects of Marijuana Use

Although the literature on marijuana use repeatedly states that "in 5,000 years of medical and nonmedical use, marijuana has not caused a single overdose death" (Grinspoon and Bakalar 1995, p. 1875), the effects of marijuana use should not be overlooked. We begin by examining the effects of marijuana on the lungs.

When marijuana smoke is inhaled into the lungs, THC, the psychoactive ingredient, leaves the blood rapidly through metabolism and efficient uptake into the tissues. THC and its metabolites tend to bind to proteins in the blood and remain stored for long periods in body fat. Five days after a single dosage of THC, 20% remains stored, whereas 20% of its metabolites remain in the blood (Indiana Prevention Resource Center 1996; Kryger 1995). Complete elimination of a single dose can take up to 30 days. Measurable levels of THC in blood from chronic users can often be detected for several days or even weeks after their last marijuana cigarette (joint).

In smokers, lung absorption and transport of THC to the brain are rapid; THC reaches the brain within as little as 14 seconds after inhalation. Marijuana is metabolized more efficiently through smoking than via intravenous injection or oral ingestion. Smoking is also three to five times more potent than these two methods (Jones 1980; Kaplan and Whitmire 1995; Kryger 1995). Other findings that compare the amounts of marijuana with tobacco conclude, "three to four joints a day is about as harmful to your lungs as smoking a pack of cigarettes a day" (Reaney 2000, p. 1).

Some effects of cannabis described in the following sections are unquestionably toxic in that they can either directly or indirectly produce adverse health effects. Other effects may be beneficial in treating some medical conditions. The use of marijuana, THC, and synthetic cannabinoids, either alone or in combination with other drugs, continues to be discussed and investigated for treating pain, inflammation, glaucoma, nausea, and muscle spasms (Iversen 1993; NIDA 2010).

Effects on the Brain

As THC enters the brain, it causes the user to feel euphoric—or high—by acting on the brain's reward system, which is made up of regions that govern the response to pleasurable things like sex and chocolate, as well as to most drugs of abuse. THC activates the reward system in the same way that nearly all drugs of abuse do: by stimulating brain cells to release the chemical dopamine (NIDA 2010). THC affects the nerve cells in the part of the brain where memories are formed. This makes it hard for the user to recall recent events (such as what happened a few minutes ago). It is hard to learn while high—a working short-term memory is required for learning and performing tasks that call for more than one or two steps (NIDA 2007, 2010).

Among a group of long-time heavy marijuana users in Costa Rica, researchers found that the peo-ple had great trouble when asked to recall a short list of words (a standard test of memory). People in that study group also found it very hard to focus their attention on the tests given to them.

As people age, they normally lose nerve cells in a region of the brain that is important for remembering events. Chronic exposure to THC may hasten the age-related loss of these nerve cells. In one study, researchers found that rats exposed to THC every day for 8 months (about one-third of their lifespan) showed a loss of brain cells comparable to rats that were twice their age. It is not known whether a similar effect occurs in humans. Researchers are still learning about the many ways that marijuana could affect the brain (NIDA 2007).

When someone smokes marijuana, THC stimulates the cannabinoid receptors (CBRs) artificially, disrupting function of the natural, or endogenous, cannabinoids. An overstimulation of these receptors in key brain areas produces the marijuana high, as well as having other effects on mental processes. Over time, this overstimulation can alter the function of CBRs, which, along with other changes in the brain, can lead to addiction and to withdrawal symptoms when drug use stops (NIDA 2010).

Effects on the Central Nervous System

The primary effects of marijuana—specifically, of THC—are on CNS functions. The precise CNS effects of consuming marijuana or administering THC can vary according to the expectations of the user, the social setting, the route of administration, and previous experiences (Abood and Martin 1992; Jaffe 1990). Smoking a marijuana cigarette can alter mood, coordination, memory, and self-perception. Usually, such exposure causes some euphoria, a sense of well-being, and relaxation. Marijuana smokers often claim heightened sensory awareness and altered perceptions (particularly a slowing of time), associated with hunger (the munchies) and a dry mouth (Hubbard, Franco, and Onaivi 1999; Swan 1994). High doses of THC or greater exposure

KEY TERMS

altered perceptions
changes in the interpretation of stimuli resulting from marijuana

munchies
hunger experienced while under the effects of marijuana

to marijuana can cause hallucinations, delusions, and paranoia (American Psychiatric Association [APA] 1994; Goldstein 1995; Hubbard et al. 1999; NIDA 2007). Some users describe anxiety after high-dose exposure. Due to the availability and widespread use of marijuana, psychiatric emergencies from marijuana overdose are becoming somewhat common. Long-term, chronic users often show decreased interest in personal appearance or goals (part of the amotivational syndrome discussed earlier in this chapter) as well as an inability to concentrate, make appropriate decisions, and recall information from short-term memory (Abood and Martin 1992; Block 1996).

The precise classification of THC is uncertain because the responses to marijuana are highly variable and appear to have elements of all three major groups of drugs of abuse. Consequently, marijuana use can cause euphoria and paranoia (like stimulants), drowsiness and sedation (like depressants), and hallucinations (like psychedelics). It is possible that THC alters several receptor or transmitter systems in the brain and this action would account for its diverse and somewhat unpredictable effects.

The dramatic discovery of a specific receptor site in the brain for THC, called the *cannabinoid* receptor (mentioned earlier), suggests that a selective endogenous marijuana system exists in the brain and is activated by THC when marijuana is consumed (Hudson 1990; NIDA 2007). Some researchers speculate that an endogenous fatty acid–like substance called *anandamide* naturally works at these marijuana sites; efforts are being made to characterize this substance, which is a neurotransmitter (Iversen 1993; NIDA 2010). It is possible that, from this discovery, a group of new therapeutic agents that can selectively interact with the marijuana receptors will be developed, resulting in medical benefits without the side effects that generally accompany marijuana use (Iversen 1993; Swan 1993).

■ Effects on the Respiratory System: Smoking Marijuana

Marijuana is often smoked like tobacco and, like tobacco, it can cause damage to the lungs (Adams and Martin 1996; Consroe and Sandyk 1992; NIDA 2010). When smoking tobacco, nearly 70% of the total suspended particles in the smoke are retained in the lungs. Because marijuana smoke is inhaled more deeply than tobacco smoke, even more tar residues may be retained with its use.

Smoke is a mixture of tiny particles suspended in gas, mostly carbon monoxide. These solid particles combine to form a residue called tar. Cannabis produces more tar (as much as 50% more) than an equivalent weight of tobacco and is smoked in a way that increases the accumulation of tar (Jones 1980).

More than 140 chemicals have been identified in marijuana smoke and tar. A few are proven carcinogens; many others have not yet been tested for carcinogenicity. The carcinogen benzopyrene, for example, is 70% more abundant in marijuana smoke than in tobacco smoke. When cannabis tar is applied to the skin of experimental animals, it causes precancerous lesions similar to those caused by tobacco tar. Similarly, whenever isolated lung tissue is exposed to these same tars, precancerous changes result (Hollister 1986; Jones 1980; Turner 1980).

Special white blood cells in living lung tissue—alveolar macrophages—play a role in removing debris from the lungs. When exposed to smoke from cannabis, these cells are less able to remove bacteria and other foreign debris.

Smoking only a few marijuana cigarettes a day for 6 to 8 weeks can significantly impair pulmonary function. Laboratory and clinical evidence often indicate that heavy use of marijuana causes cellular changes, and those heavy users have a higher incidence of such respiratory problems as laryngitis, pharyngitis, bronchitis, asthma-like conditions, cough, hoarseness, and dry throat (Goldstein 1995; Hollister 1986). Some reports emphasize the potential damage to pulmonary function that can occur from chronic marijuana use (NIDA 1991). Evidence suggests that many 20-year-old smokers of both hashish and tobacco have lung damage comparable to that found in heavy tobacco smokers older than 40 years of age. It is believed that the tar from tobacco and marijuana has damaging effects, but it is not known whether smokers who use both products suffer synergistic or additive effects (Hollister 1986; Jones 1980).

■ Effects on the Respiratory System: Vaporizing Marijuana

As presented above, the evidence shows that smoking marijuana clearly appears to be hazardous to the respiratory system, having the most negative impact on the lungs. A newer method of use, known as vaporizing marijuana, is slowly increasing among users, even though one major study of 6883 people surveyed showed that "only 152 participants (2.2%) reported vaporizing as their primary method for cannabis use" (Earleywine and Smucker Barnwell 2007, p. 3).

Cannabis smoke contains gaseous and particulate matter with the potential to create symptoms of respiratory problems. Although cannabis creates fewer problems than cigarette smoking, increasing its safety has the potential to improve quality of life. One step toward increasing the safety of cannabis involves the use of vaporizers. Vaporizers heat cannabis to temperatures that release cannabinoids in a fine mist without creating the toxins associated with combustion. Although vaporizers are not common knowledge in popular culture, a recent photograph of one appeared in the *New England Journal of Medicine,* and information about the machine is becoming more available. A vaporizer has the potential to increase the safety of cannabis use, but data from human users appear only rarely (Earleywine and Smucker Barnwell 2007, p. 2).

The results from the study quoted above "suggest that the respiratory effects of cannabis can decrease with the use of a vaporizer. The data reveal that respiratory symptoms like cough, phlegm, and tightness in the chest increase with cigarette use and cannabis use, but are less severe among users of a vaporizer" (Earleywine and Smucker Barnwell 2007, p. 3).

The cost of a vaporizer unit can usually run several hundred dollars. Using a vaporizer for marijuana use may decrease respiratory problems; however, other hazards continue to exist. Users who replace smoking marijuana with vaporizing marijuana continue to run the risk of marijuana dependence (addiction); impaired driving skills; and cognitive,

mainly short-term memory impairment. Also, users often mix smoking with vaporizing, resulting in increased usage. Thus, although pulmonary damage is likely to be minimized when using a vaporizer, other deleterious consequences from marijuana use are continued and even increased.

■ Effects on the Cardiovascular System

In human beings, cannabis causes both *vasodilation* (enlarged blood vessels) and an increase in heart rate related to the amount of THC consumed (Abood and Martin 1992; NIDA 2000, 2010). The vasodilation is responsible for the reddening of the eyes often seen in marijuana smokers. In physically healthy users, these effects, as well as slight changes in heart rhythm, are transitory and do not appear to be significant. In patients with heart disease, however, the increased oxygen requirement due to the accelerated heart rate may have serious consequences. The effect of cannabis on people with heart rhythm irregularities is not known. Because of vasodilation caused by marijuana use, abnormally low blood pressure can occur when standing. In addition, if a user stands up quickly after smoking, a feeling of lightheadedness or fainting may result. Chronic administration of large doses of THC to healthy volunteers shows that tolerance develops to the increase in heart rate and vasodilation.

People with cardiovascular problems seem to be at an increased risk when smoking marijuana (Hollister 1986; NIDA 2010). Marijuana products also bind hemoglobin, limiting the amount of oxygen that can be carried to the heart tissue. In a few cases, this deficiency could trigger heart attacks in susceptible people (Palfai and Jankiewicz 1991). The National Academy of Sciences' Institute of Medicine recommends that people with cardiovascular disease avoid marijuana use because there are still many unanswered questions about its effects on the cardiovascular system.

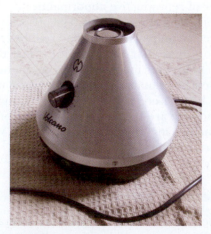

Cannabis vaporizer.

■ Effects on Sexual Performance and Reproduction

Drugs may interfere with sexual performance and reproduction in several ways (Hanson 2010). They may alter sexual behavior, affect fertility, damage the chromosomes of germ cells in the male or female, or adversely affect fetal growth and development.

The Indian Hemp Commission (Taylor 1963, 1966), which wrote the first scientific report on cannabis, commented that it had a sexually stimulating effect, like alcohol. However, the report also said that cannabis was used by Asian Indian ascetics to destroy the sexual appetite. This apparent discrepancy may be a dose-related effect. Used occasionally over the short term, marijuana may act as an **aphrodisiac** by decreasing CNS inhibitions. In addition, the altered perception of time under the influence of the drug could make the pleasurable sensations appear to last longer than they actually do.

Marijuana affects the sympathetic nervous system, increasing vasodilation in the genitals and delaying ejaculation. High doses over a period of time lead to depression of libido and impotence—possibly due to the decreased amount of testosterone, the male sex hormone. "Some research has found a relationship between long-term use of marijuana . . . [and] increased erectile dysfunction" (Silverberg 2007).

Cannabis has several effects on semen (Cadena 2007). The total number of sperm cells and the concentration of sperm per unit volume are decreased during ejaculation (Cadena 2007). Moreover, there is an increase in the proportion of sperm with abnormal appearance and reduced motility. These qualities are usually associated with lower fertility and a higher probability of producing an abnormal embryo should fertilization take place.

Despite these effects, there are no documented reports of children with birth defects in which the abnormality was linked to the father's smoking marijuana. It is possible that damaged sperm cells are incapable of fertilization (so that only normal sperm cells reach the egg) or that the abnormal sperm appearance is meaningless in terms of predicting birth defects. When marijuana use stops, the quality of sperm gradually returns to normal over several months.

"Heavy marijuana use in women has been associated with inhibiting ovulation, and marijuana use during pregnancy can have a variety of harmful developmental effects on the fetus including neurobehavioral and physical abnormalities, as well as increasing the chance of a premature birth" (Silverberg 2007). Less reliable data are available on the effects of cannabis on female libido, sexual response (ability to respond to sexual stimulation with vaginal lubrication and orgasm), and fertile reproductive (menstrual) cycles (Consroe and Sandyk 1992; Grinspoon 1987). Data from the Reproductive Biology Research Foundation show that chronic smoking of cannabis (at least three times per week for the preceding 6 months) adversely affects the female reproductive cycle. Results with women were correlated with work in rhesus monkeys; it was found that THC blocks ovulation (due to effects on female sex hormones).

Data on effects of marijuana use during pregnancy and lactation are inconclusive. Some evidence suggests that the use of this drug by pregnant women can result in intrauterine growth retardation, which is characterized by increased fetal mortality, prolonged labor, low-birth-weight babies (Foley 2007), and behavioral abnormalities in newborns (Fernandez-Ruiz et al. 1992; Nahas and Latour 1992; Roffman and George 1988). THC and other cannabinoids pass through the blood–placenta barrier and concentrate in the fetus's fatty tissue, including its brain. Ethical considerations prevent duplication of the experiment in humans.

Women who smoke marijuana during pregnancy also often use other drugs—such as alcohol, tobacco, and cocaine—that are known to have adverse effects on the developing fetus. Because multiple drugs are used, it is difficult to isolate the specific effects of marijuana during pregnancy. Like many other substances, THC is taken up by the mammary glands in lactating women and is excreted in the breast milk. Effects of marijuana in the breast milk on human infants have not been determined (Christina 1994; Murphy and Bartke 1992).

In studies on mice and rats (but not humans), the addition of THC to pregnant animals lowered litter size, increased fetal reabsorption, and increased the number of reproductive abnormalities in the surviving offspring (Dewey 1986). The offspring of the drug-treated animal mothers had reduced fertility and more testicular abnormalities. The dose of cannabinoids used in these studies was higher than that used by humans. Clearly, pregnant women should be advised against using marijuana, even though there are few direct data on its prenatal effects in humans (Dewey 1986; Foley 2007; Murphy and Bartke 1992).

KEY TERMS

aphrodisiac
a compound that is believed to be the cause of sexual arousal

■ Tolerance and Dependence

It has been known for many years that tolerance to some effects of cannabis builds rapidly in animals—

namely, the drug effect becomes less intense with repeated administration. Frequent use of high doses of marijuana or THC in humans produces similar tolerance. For example, increasingly higher doses must be given to obtain the same intensity of subjective effects and increased heart rate that occur initially with small doses (Abood and Martin 1992; NIDA 2010).

Frequent high doses of THC also can produce mild physical dependence. Healthy subjects who smoke several joints a day or who are given comparable amounts of THC orally experience irritability, sleep disturbances, weight loss, loss of appetite, sweating, and gastrointestinal upsets when drug use is stopped abruptly. However, not all subjects experience this mild form of withdrawal.

It is much easier to show psychological dependence in heavy users of marijuana (Abood and Martin 1992; Hollister 1986; NIDA 2010). Psychological dependence involves an attachment to the euphoric effects of the THC content in marijuana and may include craving for the drug. The subjective psychological effects of marijuana intoxication include a heightened sensitivity to and distortion of sight, smell, taste, and sound; mood alteration; and diminished reaction time.

Diagnosis: Cannabis Dependence

In general, outright cannabis addiction, with obsessive drug-seeking and compulsive drug-taking behavior, is relatively rare with low-THC cannabis. Contributing to this is the fact that the less potent forms of marijuana are most readily available in the United States, resulting in most chronic users in this country having little problem controlling or eliminating their cannabis habit if they so desire.

The *Diagnostic and Statistical Manual of Mental Disorders,* 4th edition, text revision (DSM-IV-TR) recognizes a diagnosis of cannabis dependence. It is characterized by compulsive use and spending hours per day acquiring and using the substance. Compulsive users persist in their use despite knowledge of physical problems (for example, chronic cough related to smoking) or psychological problems (for example, excessive sedation resulting from repeated use of high doses) (APA 2000).

■ Chronic Use

Research on chronic use of marijuana (repeated daily use of this drug) in the 1970s indicated the possibility of three types of damage: (1) chromosomal damage (Stenchever, Kunysz, and Allen 1974);

(2) cerebral atrophy (shrinking of the brain) (Campbell et al. 1971); and (3) lowered capacity of white blood cells to fight disease (Suciu-Foca, Armand, and Morishima 1974). These findings have all been contradicted or refuted by subsequent research. The only finding that appears very credible is that heavy use of this drug impairs lung capacity (Bloodworth 1987; Henneberger 1994; Kaplan and Whitmire 1995; NIDA 2010; Oliwenstein 1988; Swan 1994).

Other evidence indicates that chronic, heavy use of cannabis can lead to unforeseen calamities in some users (see "Case in Point: Chronic Marijuana Use").

We have pointed out that marijuana produces a variety of psychoactive effects. One of those effects is sedation of unwanted emotional states such as anxiety, which are inevitable given the conflicts and turmoil of living in our fast-paced society today. As with the chronic use of any psychoactive drug that produces sedating effects, normal emotional and psychosocial development can be arrested by heavy marijuana consumption. For example, a youth who is usually high at a party avoids the anxieties and embarrassments of introspective and critical interpersonal interactions but instead will be interested in thrill-seeking behavior, such as romantic and sexual involvements, experimentation with and heavy use of other drugs, and other types of more daring experiences.

From years of research with this drug, we find that heavy and chronic use of marijuana can very easily compromise cognitive functions, such as short-term memory, concentration, moderately taxing problem solving, and even spiritual growth and development. Often, the more serious costs in using this drug are that the individual acquires a poor record for development and advancement of learning, as is often expected in educational settings (schools, colleges, trade schools, and universities). Another cost that is more serious is the retardation in emotional development. Such types of development are often obscured by being high all the time. Further, in such chronic use cases, much time is wasted seeking the pleasures and sometimes the longed-for thrills derived from the habitual use of marijuana.

The amotivational syndrome, in fact, can be deconstructed into the sedation, depression, and cognitive impairment discussed throughout this chapter. The user who is experiencing a subjective euphoric effect, enjoying the presence and social reinforcement of peers, feeling no pain, and remaining cognitively unfocused finds it difficult to

►Case in Point Chronic Marijuana Use

The following comments show how marijuana use can become a disturbing habit:

I guess you could say it was peer pressure. Back in 1969, I was a sophomore in college, and everyone was smoking "dope." The Vietnam War was in progress, and most students on college campuses were heavily involved in the drug scene. I first started smoking marijuana when my closest friends did. I was taught by other students who already knew how to enjoy the effects of "pot."

I recall that one of my fellow students used to supply me with "nickel bags," and many users nicknamed him "God." How did he get such a name? Because he sold some very potent marijuana that at times caused us to hallucinate.

I used pot nearly every day for about a year and a half, and hardly an evening would pass without smoking dope and listening to music. Smoking marijuana became as common as drinking alcohol. I used it in the same manner a person has a cocktail after a long day. At first, I liked the effects of being "high," but later I became so accustomed to the stuff that life appeared boring without it.

After graduating, my college friends went their separate ways, and I stopped using marijuana for a few years. A year later, in graduate school, a neighborhood friend reintroduced me to the pleasure of smoking pot. I began to use it again but not as often. Whenever I experienced some pressure, I would use a little to relax.

After finishing my degree, I found myself employed at an institution that at times was boring. Again, I started using pot at night to relax, and somehow it got out of control. I used to smoke a little before work and sometimes during lunch. I thought all was well until one day I got fired because someone accused me of being high on the job.

Soon afterward, I came to the realization that the use of marijuana can be very insidious. It has a way of becoming psychologically addictive, and you don't even realize it. When I was high, I thought that no one knew, and that I was even more effective with others. Little did I know, I was dead wrong and fooling no one.

Source: From Venturelli's files, male, age 39, May 1990.

---

intellectually grasp the learned experiences from such developmental delays. Although many do mature out of use, this step may occur only after years of development have slipped away, never to be regained. Sometimes treatment interventions are necessary to get the subject into a drug-free state and reunited with non–drug-using peer groups.

In concluding this chapter, we note that the history of this drug indicates that usage and availability will remain widespread despite all the efforts to eradicate its existence. Despite all the prevention efforts to date, marijuana remains the most popular illicit drug, topped only by alcohol and tobacco, which are licit drugs.

Discussion Questions

1. What are the pharmacological, sociological, and psychological reasons why the very young continue to use marijuana at alarming rates despite the illegality of usage?

2. Do you believe that prosecution for marijuana possession should be more or less rigid than it currently is? Why?

3. Debate whether marijuana use adversely affects driving capabilities.

4. Either directly interview or imagine interviews of several users and nonusers of marijuana. How do you think they would answer the question of whether their critical thinking skills are adversely affected by this drug?

5. Among marijuana users, do you believe that the amotivational syndrome exists as a syndrome? Interview several users and try to either add to the characteristics of this syndrome from your interviews or modify the syndrome as discussed in this chapter.

6. In light of the information in "Holding the Line," do you believe the sale of marijuana for medical purposes will ever be completely legalized at the state and federal levels in all 50 states? Why or why not?

7. What is your reaction to legalizing marijuana as a controlled substance like alcohol and tobacco products? Give reasons either for or against legalization.

8. Do you believe consistent use of marijuana changes personality? If so, how?

9. Summarize how marijuana affects the brain, CNS, respiratory system, cardiovascular system, and sexual performance and reproduction.

10. Debate how much family upbringing and attachment to a religion affect later drug use.

11. From reading this chapter, try to explain why most heroin users have used marijuana, whereas the vast majority of marijuana users never advance to such highly addictive drugs.

12. Explain how a user of cannabis might develop psychological dependence.

13. Do you believe that use of marijuana is more or less harmful than use of tobacco products? Should they be regulated differently?

14. Why do you think such a high percentage of 12th graders do not disapprove of using marijuana? (The 2009 results were that 45% thought that using once or twice was acceptable and 32% thought that occasional use was acceptable.)

Summary

1 Marijuana consists of the dried and crushed leaves, flowers, stems, and seeds of the *Cannabis sativa* plant. THC (tetrahydrocannabinol) is the primary mind-altering (psychoactive) ingredient in marijuana.

2 Marijuana remains very controversial for the following reasons: (a) a high percentage of the U.S. population uses this drug; (b) it remains illegal; (c) 15 states and the District of Columbia have legalized the sale of marijuana for medical purposes, although the use and sale of marijuana in these states remains illegal at the federal level; (d) marijuana accounts for a large number of arrests for simple possession; (e) it is one of the least addictive-type drugs; and (f) most marijuana users do not graduate to other, more addictive illicit drugs.

3 The effects of marijuana can vary according to expectations and surroundings. At low doses, such as when smoked or ingested (eaten), marijuana often has a sedative effect. At higher doses, it can produce hallucinations and delusions.

4 As with tobacco, heavy use of marijuana can impair pulmonary function, cause chronic respiratory diseases (such as bronchitis and asthma), and promote lung cancer. Marijuana causes vasodilation and a compensatory increase in heart rate. The effects of marijuana on sexual performance and reproduction are controversial. Some studies have suggested this substance not only enhances sexual arousal, but also promotes risky sexual behavior (unprotected sex).

5 Tolerance to the CNS and cardiovascular effects of marijuana develop rapidly with repeated use. Although physical dependence and associated withdrawal are minor, psychological dependence can be significant in chronic, heavy users.

6 The active ingredient in marijuana, THC, has been used for treating a variety of seemingly unrelated medical conditions. This drug is indicated for treatment of nausea and vomiting in cancer patients receiving chemotherapy and for treatment of anorexia (lack of appetite) in AIDS patients. Other potential therapeutic uses for THC include relief of intraocular pressure associated with glaucoma, as an antiasthmatic drug, for muscle relaxation, as prevention for some types of seizures, as an antidepressant, and as an analgesic to relieve migraines and other types of pain.

7 The age groups most likely to use marijuana are the following: (a) highest lifetime use, adults between 18 and 25 years of age (50.4%); (b) highest past-year (27.5%) and past-month (16.5%) use, 18- to 25-year-olds; and (c) sharp drop in use, 26 and older age group.

8 From 1996 to 2005, annual use of marijuana slowly decreased for 12th graders; however, in 2007 through 2008 use of marijuana began to increase. In 2008, approximately 35% of 12th graders used marijuana.

9 Among 8th, 10th, and 12th graders, some of the major findings in 2008 were: (a) 50% of all 12th graders think that regular use of marijuana involves a great risk to the user, whereas 50% do not; (b) approximately 24% of 12th graders believe that using marijuana once or twice is harmful, whereas 76% do not; (c) approximately 79% of 12th graders disapprove of using marijuana on a regular basis, whereas 21% do not; (d) approximately 68% of 12th graders disapprove of using marijuana on an occasional basis, whereas 32% do not; (e) approximately 55% of 12th graders disapprove of using marijuana once or twice, whereas 45% do not; and (f) since the study began in 1975, between 83% and 90% of every senior high school class have said they could get marijuana fairly easily or very easily if they wanted some (Johnston et al. 2009).

10 Research by the Drug Enforcement Administration (DEA 2006) involving government surveys that ask young people about their drug use patterns showed that about 600,000 high school seniors drive after smoking marijuana. Thirty-eight thousand seniors told surveyors that they had been involved in accidents while driving under the influence of marijuana. Other surveys conducted by MADD and the Liberty Mutual insurance company revealed that many teenagers (41%) were not concerned about driving after taking drugs. Medical data indicate a connection between drugged driving and accidents—patients in a shock-trauma unit who had been in collisions revealed that 15% of those who had been driving a car or motorcycle had been smoking marijuana and another 17% had both THC and alcohol in their blood. Another significant and notable study revealed the link between smoking marijuana and car accidents. Habitual marijuana users (used every day) were 9.5 times more likely to be involved in crashes, with 5.6% of people who had crashed having taken the drug, compared to 0.5% of the control group. This study revealed that habitual use of marijuana is strongly associated with car crash injury.

11 Currently 15 states and the District of Columbia are medical marijuana states. The 15 states are Alaska, Arizona, California, Colorado, Hawaii, Maine, Michigan, Montana, Nevada, New Jersey, New Mexico, Oregon, Rhode Island, Vermont, and Washington (ProCon.org 2010). Eight states that currently have pending legislation or ballot measures to legalize medical marijuana are Arizona, Illinois, Massachusetts, New York, North Carolina, Ohio, Pennsylvania, and South Dakota. Out of the approximately 304 million people living in 12 of the 14 states and Washington, DC, 577,712 people are registered as medical mari-

juana patients (ProCon.org 2010). Legalization of the medical use of marijuana entails permitting physicians to prescribe marijuana for medical problems, with the idea that terminally ill as well as other types of sick patients could be given the option of smoking marijuana as opposed to taking the already-approved **Marinol** (dronabinol), an FDA-approved THC in capsule form.

References

Abel, E. L. *Marijuana: The First Twelve Thousand Years.* New York: Plenum, 1989.

Abood, M., and B. Martin. "Neurobiology of Marijuana Abuse." *Trends in Pharmacological Sciences* 13 (May 1992): 201–206.

Abood, M. E., and B. R. Martin. "Molecular Neurobiology of the Cannabinoid Receptor." *International Review of Neurobiology* 39 (May 1996): 197–219.

Adams, I. B., and B. R. Martin. "Cannabis: Pharmacology and Toxicology in Animals and Humans." *Addiction* 91 (1996): 1585–1614.

American Psychiatric Association (APA). *Diagnostic and Statistical Manual of Mental Disorders,* 4th ed. [DSM-IV]. Washington, DC: APA, 1994.

American Psychiatric Association (APA). *Diagnostic and Statistical Manual of Mental Disorders,* 4th ed., text revision [DSM-IV-TR]. Washington, DC: APA 2000.

Anslinger, H. J., and C. R. Cooper. "Marijuana: Assassin of Youth." *American Magazine* 124 (July 1937): 19–20, 150–153.

Bauman, K. E., and S. T. Ennett. "On the Importance of Peer Influence for Adolescent Drug Use: Commonly Neglected Considerations." *Addiction* 91 (February 1996): 185–198.

Benson, J. "Prescription Painkillers Now Gateway Drugs to Hard Drug Use." Natural News.com. 30 August 2010. Available http://www.naturalnews.com/029606_prescription_opioids_gateway_drugs.html

Berkowitz, A. "Following Imaginary Peers: How Norm Misperceptions Influence Student Substance Abuse." In *Project Direction,* edited by G. Lindsay and G. Rulf, 12–15 (Module No. 2). Muncie, IN: Ball State University, 1991.

Block, R. I. "Does Heavy Marijuana Use Impair Human Cognition and Brain Function?" *Journal of the American Medical Association* 275 (1996): 560–561.

Bloodworth, R. C. "Major Problems Associated with Marijuana Use." *Psychiatric Medicine* 3 (1987): 173–184.

Blows, S., R. Q. Ivers, J. Connor, S. Ameratunga, M. Woodward, and R. Norton. "Marijuana Use and Car Crash Injury." *Society for the Study of Addiction* 100 (2005): 605–611.

Brigham Young University. "News Release: National Study Finds Religiosity Curbs Teen Marijuana Use by Half." (1 October 2008). Available http://news.byu.edu/archive08-oct-religiosity.aspx

Brown, M. W., and S. Massaro. *Attention and Memory Impaired in Heavy Users of Marijuana.* Rockville, MD: NIDA, 20 February 1996.

Brown University Health Education. "Marijuana." 2007. Available http://brown.edu/Student_Services/Health_Services/Health_Education/alcohol,_tobacco,_&_other_drugs/marijuana.php

Buff, J. "Greasers, Dopers, and Hippies: Three Responses to the Adult World." In *The White Majority*, edited by L. Howe, 60–70. New York: Random House, 1970.

Cadena, C. "Marijuana Promotes Relaxation in Sexual Activity but Depresses Libido." Associated Content from Yahoo!.(13 November 2007). Available http://www.associatedcontent.com/article/443811/marijuana_promotes_relax ation_in_sexual.html

Califano, J. A. "Dangerous Indifference to Drugs." *Washington Post* (23 September 1996): A-19.

Campbell, A. G., M. Evans, J. L. Thomson, and M. J. Williams. "Cerebral Atrophy in Young Cannabis Smokers." *Lancet* 19 (1971): 1219–1225.

Carter, E. *Cannabis in Costa Rica*. Philadelphia, PA: Institute for the Study of Human Issues, 1980.

Center for Substance Abuse Research (CESAR). "Marijuana Distribution Relies Primarily on Generosity of Friends and Family." CESAR FAX 16. (19 March 2007). Available http://www.cesar.umd.edu/cesar/cesarfax/vol16/16-11.pdf

Center for Substance Abuse Research (CESAR). "More than One in Ten Children in the U.S. Live with Substance-Abusing or Substance-Dependent Parent." CESAR FAX 18. (11 May 2010a). Available http://www.cesar.umd.edu/cesar/cesarfax/vol18/18-18.pdf

Center for Substance Abuse Research (CESAR). "U.S. High School Seniors' Perception of Harm from Regular Marijuana Use Decreasing." CESAR FAX 19. (19 January 2010b). Available http://www.cesar.umd.edu/cesar/cesarfax/vol19/19-02.pdf

Chait, L., and J. Pierri. "Effect of Smoked Marijuana on Human Performance: A Critical Review." In *Marijuana/Cannabinoids, Neurobiology and Neurophysiology*, edited by L. Murphy and A. Bartke, 387–424. Boca Raton, FL: CRC Press, 1992.

Christina, D. *Marijuana: Personality and Behavior*. Tempe, AZ: Do It Now, 1994.

Cincinnati.com. Letters to the Editor: "No Valid Reason to Ban Marijuana." *Enquirer*. (9 August 2010). Available http://cincinnati.com/blogs/letters/2010/08/09/no-valid-reason-to-ban-marijuana

Coleman, J. S. *The Adolescent Society*. New York: Free Press of Glencoe, 1961.

Cone, E. J., Y. H. Caplan, D. L. Black, T. Robert, and F. Moser. "Urine Drug Testing of Chronic Pain Patients: Licit and Illicit Drug Patterns." *Journal of Analytic Toxology* 32 (2008): 532–543.

Consroe, P., and R. Sandyk. "Potential Role of Cannabinoids for Therapy of Neurological Disorders." In *Marijuana/Cannabinoids, Neurobiology and Neurophysiology*, edited by L. Murphy and A. Bartke, 459–524. Boca Raton, FL: CRC Press, 1992.

Couper, F. J., and B. K. Logan. *Cannabis/Marijuana (Δ⁹ Tetrahydro-cannabinol, THC)*. Drugs and Human Performance Fact Sheets. Washington, DC: National Highway Traffic Safety Administration, March 2004.

Drug Enforcement Administration (DEA). "DEA Position on Marijuana." (July 2010). Available http://www.justice.gov/dea/marijuana_position_july10.pdf

Dewey, W. L. "Cannabinoid Pharmacology." *Pharmacological Reviews* 38 (1986): 48–50.

Dreher, M. C. *Working Men and Ganja: Marijuana Use in Rural Jamaica*. Philadelphia, PA: Institute for the Study of Human Issues, 1982.

Earleywine M., and S. Smucker Barnwell. "Decreased Respiratory Symptoms in Cannabis Users Who Vaporize." *Harm Reduction Journal* 4 (16 April 2007): 1–6.

Eckert, P. *Jocks and Burnouts: Social Categories and Identity in the High School*. New York: Teachers College, Columbia University, 1989.

ElSohly, M. *Quarterly Report: Potency Monitoring Projected, Report 104, December 16, 2008 thru March 15, 2009*. National Institute on Drug Abuse (NIDA). Oxford, Mississippi: National Center for Natural Products Research, Research Institute of Pharmaceutical Sciences, School of Pharmacy, University of Mississippi, 2009.

Fernandez-Ruiz, J., F. Rodriguez de Fonseca, M. Navarro, and J. Ramos. "Maternal Cannabinoid Exposure and Brain Development: Changes in the Ontogeny of Dopaminergic Neurons." In *Marijuana/Cannabinoids, Neurobiology and Neurophysiology*, edited by L. Murphy and A. Bartke, 118–164. Boca Raton, FL: CRC Press, 1992.

Foley, M. R. "Drug Use During Pregnancy." *The Merck Manuals Online Edition*. Whitehouse Station, NJ: Merck & Co, 2007. Available http://www.merck.com/mmhe/sec22/ch259/ch259a.html

Fuhrman, R. A. *Cannabis Buyers' Club Flourishes in "Frisco."* San Francisco: Cannabis Buyers' Club, 1995.

Fuller, D. "Adolescent Brain Function Adversely Affected By Marijuana Use." Medical News Today. (October 2008). Available http://www.medicalnewstoday.com/articles/125443.php

Gaines, G. *Teenage Wasteland: Suburbia's Dead-End Kids*. New York: Harper Perennial, 1992.

Gardner, A. "Study: Smoking Pot May Ease Chronic Pain." CNN.com, Health Magazine. (30 August 2010). Available http://www.cnn.com/2010/HEALTH/08/30/health.pot.reduce.pain/index.html

Gardner, E. "Cannabinoid Interaction with Brain Reward Systems: The Neurobiological Basis of Cannabinoid Abuse." In *Marijuana/Cannabinoids, Neurobiology and Neurophysiology*, edited by L. Murphy and A. Bartke, 275–335. Boca Raton, FL: CRC Press, 1992.

Goldberg, C. "Marijuana Club Helps Those in Pain." *New York Times*. (25 February 1996). Available http://www.nytimes.com/1996/02/25/us/marijuana-club-helps-those-in-pain.html?ref=carey_goldberg

Goldstein, A. *Addiction from Biology to Drug Policy*. New York: Freeman, 1994.

Goldstein, F. "Pharmacological Aspects of Substance Abuse." *Remington's Pharmaceutical Sciences*, 19th ed. Easton, PA: Mack, 1995.

Gossop, M. *Living with Drugs,* 2nd ed. Aldershot, England: Wildwood House, 1987.

Green, C. A. "Gender and Use of Substance Abuse Treatment Services." *Alcohol Research and Health* 29 (2006): 55–62.

Greenblatt, J. C. *Adolescent Self-Reported Behaviors and Their Association with Marijuana Use.* Office of Applied Studies (OAS) of the Substance Abuse and Mental Health Services Administration (SAMHSA). Rockville, MD: National Clearinghouse for Alcohol and Drug Information, July 1999.

Grinspoon, L. "Marijuana." *Harvard Medical School Mental Health Letter* 4 (November 1987): 1–4.

Grinspoon, L., and J. B. Bakalar. "Commentary, Marijuana as Medicine: A Plea for Reconsideration." *Journal of the American Medical Association* 273 (1995): 1875–1876.

Hamid, A. *Drugs in America: Sociology, Economics, and Politics.* Gaithersburg, MD: Aspen, 1998.

Hanson, D. "Sex, Drugs, and . . . Sex: Pharmaceuticals and Sexual Performance." Addiction Inbox, The Science of Substance Abuse. (15 September 2010). Available http:// addiction-dirkh.blogspot.com/2010/09/sex-drugs-and-sex.html

Heitzeg, N. *Deviance: Rulemakers and Rulebreakers.* St. Paul, MN: West Publishing, 1996.

Henneberger, M. "Pot Surges Back, It's Like a Whole New World." *New York Times* (6 February 1994): C19.

Hollister, L. E. "Health Aspects of Cannabis." *Pharmacological Reviews* 38 (1986): 39–42.

Hongmei, Y., B. Stanton, L. Cottrel, L. Kaljee, J. Galbraith, et al. "Parental Awareness of Adolescent Risk Involvement: Implications of Overestimates and Underestimates." *Journal of Adolescent Health* 39 (September 2006): 353–361.

Hubbard, J. R., S. E. Franco, and E. S. Onaivi. "Marijuana: Medical Implications." *American Family Physician* 283 (1999): 231–240.

Hudson, R. "Researchers Identify Gene That Triggers Marijuana's 'High.' " *Wall Street Journal* (9 August 1990): B2.

IdeaConnection.com. "Cannabis Abuse." 2011. Available http://www.ideaconnection.com/solutions/558-Cannabis-abuse.html

Indiana Prevention Resource Center. *Factline on: Marijuana.* Bloomington, IN: Indiana Prevention Resource Center, 1996.

Iversen, L. "Medicinal Use of Marijuana." *Nature* 365 (1993): 12–13.

Iverson, L. "Long-Term Effects of Exposure to Cannabis." *Current Opinion in Pharmacology* 5 (2005): 69–72.

Jaffe, J. H. "Drug Addiction and Drug Abuse." In *The Pharmacological Basis of Therapeutics,* 8th ed., edited by A. Gilman, T. Rall, A. Nies, and P. Taylor, 522–575. New York: Pergamon, 1990.

Johns, A. "Psychiatric Effects of Cannabis." *British Journal of Psychiatry* 178 (2001): 116–122.

Johnston, L. D., P. M. O'Malley, J. G. Bachman, and J. E. Schulenberg. *Monitoring the Future: National Survey Results on Drug Use.* Bethesda, MD: National Institute on Drug Abuse, 2009.

Jones, R. T. "Human Effects: An Overview." In *Marijuana Research Findings: 1980.* NIDA Research Monograph No. 31. Washington, DC: National Institute on Drug Abuse, 1980.

Julian, B. S. "alt.hemp Cannabis/Marijuana FAQ." University of Massachusetts at Amherst. 1994. Available http://www.faqs.org/faqs/drugs/hemp-marijuana

Kandel, D. B., P. C. Griesler, G. Lee, M. Davies, and C. Shaffsan. *Parental Influences on Adolescent Marijuana Use and the Baby Boom Generation: Findings from the 1995–1996 National Household Surveys on Drug Abuse.* Rockville, MD: Substance Abuse and Mental Health Services Administration, 2001.

Kaplan, L. F., and R. Whitmire. "Pot—It's Potent, Prevalent and Preventable." *Salt Lake Tribune* 250 (21 May 1995): 9.

Kelly, T., R. Foltin, C. Enurian, and M. Fischman. "Effects of THC on Marijuana Smoking, Drug Choice and Verbal Report of Drug Liking." *Journal of Experimental Analysis of Behavior* 61 (1994): 203–211.

Kendler, K. S., C. O. Gardner, and C. A. Prescott. "Religion, Psychopathology, and Substance Use and Abuse: A Multimeasure, Genetic-Epidemiologic Study." *American Journal of Psychiatry* 154 (1997): 322–329.

Knickerbocker, B. "Prop. 19 in California: Legalized Marijuana Goes Up in Smoke." *Christian Science Monitor.* (3 November 2010). Available http://www.csmonitor.com/USA/Politics/The-Vote/2010/1103/Prop-19-in-California-legalized-marijuana-goes-up-in-smoke

Kryger, A. H. "Preventive Medicine Clinic of Monterey: Marijuana Mental Disturbances." Virtual Hospital Home Page. (24 October 1995). Available http://vh.radiology.uiowa.edu

Liska, K. *Drugs and the Human Body,* 5th ed. Upper Saddle River, NJ: Prentice Hall, 1997.

MarijuanaDetox.com. "Marijuana Detox." 2008. Available http://www.marijuana-detox.com/m-facts.htm

"Marijuana Menaces Youth." *Scientific American* 154 (1936): 151.

Mathias, R. "Marijuana Impairs Driving-Related Skills and Workplace Performance." *NIDA Notes* 11 (January/February 1996): 6.

McCabe, S. E. "Misperceptions of Nonmedical Prescription Drug Use: A Web Survey of College Students." *Addictive Behavior* 33 (May 2008): 713–724.

MSNBC.com. "Marijuana Sold in U.S. Stronger than Ever." Reuters Limited. (28 April 2007). Available http://www.msnbc.msn.com/id/18310976

Murphy, L., and A. Bartke. "Effects of THC on Pregnancy, Puberty, and the Neuroendocrine System." In *Marijuana/Cannabinoids, Neurobiology and Neurophysiology,* edited by L. Murphy and A. Bartke, 539. Boca Raton, FL: CRC Press, 1992.

Musto, D. F. *The American Disease: Origins of Narcotic Control,* 3rd ed. New York: Oxford University Press, 1999.

Nahas, G., and C. Latour. "The Human Toxicity of Marijuana." *Medical Journal of Australia* 156 (1992): 495–497.

National Center on Addiction and Substance Abuse at Columbia University. "Casa Report: Spirituality and Religion Reduce Risk of Substance Abuse." 2001. Available http://

www.casacolumbia.org/absolutenm/templates/Press Releases.aspx?articleid=115&zoneid=48

National Clearinghouse on Alcohol and Drug Information (NCADI). *Marijuana: Facts Parents Need to Know. Quick Screen, At Home Drug Test.* Rockville, MD: National Clearinghouse on Alcohol and Drug Information, November 1998.

National Eye Institute. *Facts about Glaucoma.* Bethesda, MD: U.S. Department of Health and Human Services (USDHHS) and National Institutes of Health (NIH), 2010.

National Institute on Drug Abuse (NIDA). *Drug Abuse and Drug Abuse Research.* DHHS Publication No. 91-1704. Washington, DC: U.S. Department of Health and Human Services, 1991.

National Institute on Drug Abuse (NIDA). *Marijuana: Facts Parents Need to Know.* NIH Publication No. 95-4037. Rockville, MD: National Clearinghouse on Alcohol and Drug Information, 1998. Available http://web.archive.org/web/20000307153943

National Institute on Drug Abuse (NIDA). *InfoFacts: Marijuana.* Bethesda, MD: U.S. Department of Health and Human Services, 29 March 2000. Available http://www.nida.nih.gov/infofax/marijuana.html

National Institute on Drug Abuse (NIDA). *Marijuana Smoking Is Associated with a Spectrum of Respiratory Disorders.* Bethesda, MD: National Institute on Drug Abuse (NIDA) and National Institutes of Health (NIH), 21 October 2006.

National Institute on Drug Abuse (NIDA). *Marijuana: Facts Parents Need to Know.* Bethesda, MD: National Institute on Drug Abuse (NIDA) and National Institutes of Health (NIH), August 2007.

National Institute on Drug Abuse (NIDA). *InfoFacts: Drugged Driving.* Bethesda, MD: National Institute on Drug Abuse (NIDA) and National Institutes of Health (NIH), October 2009a.

National Institute on Drug Abuse (NIDA). *InfoFacts: Marijuana.* Bethesda, MD: National Institute on Drug Abuse (NIDA) and National Institutes of Health (NIH), 2009b.

National Institute on Drug Abuse (NIDA). "Research Report Series: Marijuana Abuse." Bethesda, MD: U.S. Department of Health and Human Services (USDHHS) and National Institutes of Health (NIH), September 2010. Available http://www.drugabuse.gov/PDF/RRMarijuana.pdf

National Organization for the Reform of Marijuana Laws (NORML). "Chronic Pain." 30 January 2010. Available http://norml.org/index.cfm?Group_ID=7786

Norton, A. "Address Client Myths About Marijuana: Professionals Can Counteract Mixed Messages in Society That Impede Healing." *Addiction Professional* 4 (July/August 2009): 32–34.

Office of National Drug Control Policy (ONDCP). "Drug Facts: Marijuana." Washington, DC: ONDCP, 2003. Available http://whitehousedrugpolicy.gov/drugfact/marijuana/index.html

Office of National Drug Control Policy (ONDCP). "Marijuana Potency." White House Drug Policy. 2007. Available http://www.whitehousedrugpolicy.gov/dfc/files/marijuana_potency.pdf

Oliwenstein, L. "The Perils of Pot." *Discover* 9 (1988): 18.

Palfai, T., and H. Jankiewicz. *Drugs and Human Behavior.* Dubuque, IA: William C. Brown, 1991.

Pollan, M. "Medical Marijuana: Can It Help You? Should It Be Legal? A Report from California." *Herbs for Health* (March/April 1998): 38–50.

Pope, H. G., Jr., and D. Yurgulen-Todd. "The Residual Cognitive Effects of Heavy Marijuana Use in College Students." *Journal of the American Medical Association* 275 (1996): 521–527.

ProCon.org. "Fourteen Legal Medical Marijuana States and DC." 2010. Available http://www.procon.org

Rand Drug Policy Research Center. "Rand Releases Study on Marijuana 'Gateway Effect.'" Press Release. (26 December 2002). Available http://www.jointogether.org

Reaney, P. "Getting High May Not Be So Harmless After All." Reuters Limited. (20 March 2000).

Risling, G. "Most in the U.S. Against Legalizing Pot, Poll Shows." Associated Press. (20 April 2010). Available http://www.msnbc.msn.com/id/36650347/ns/health-health_care

Robson, P. "Therapeutic Aspects of Cannabis and Cannabinoids." *British Journal of Psychiatry* 178 (2001): 107–115.

Roffman, R. A., and W. H. George. "Cannabis Abuse." In *Assessment of Addictive Behaviors,* edited by D. M. Donovan and G. A. Marlatt, 78–86. New York: Guilford, 1988.

Rubin, V., and L. Comitas. *Ganja in Jamaica: A Medical Anthropological Study of Chronic Marijuana Use.* Paris: Mouton, 1975.

Sanchez, R. "California's Proposition 19 Rejected by Voters." ABCNews.com. (3 November 2010). Available http://abcnews.go.com/Politics/proposition-19-results-california-votes-reject-marijuana-measure/story?id=12037727

Schultes, R. E. "Ethnopharmacological Significance of Psychotropic Drugs of Vegetal Origin." *Principles of Psychopharmacology,* 2nd ed., edited by W. G. Clark and J. del Giudice. New York: Academic Press, 1978.

Sewester, S. *Drug Facts and Comparisons.* St. Louis, MO: Kluwer, 1993: 259h–259k.

Silverberg, C. "Sexuality: Sex and Marijuana." About.com. (5 July 2007). Available http://sexuality.about.com/od/sex_and_drugs/a/marijuana_sex.htm

Solomon, D., ed. *The Marihuana Papers.* New York: New American Library, 1966.

Stenchever, M. A., T. J. Kunysz, and M. A. Allen. "Chromosome Breakage in Users of Marijuana." *American Journal of Obstetrics and Gynecology* 118 (January 1974): 106–113.

Substance Abuse and Mental Health Services Administration (SAMHSA). *Results from the 2008 National Survey on Drug Use and Health (NSDUH): National Findings.* Rockville, MD: Office of Applied Studies, 2009.

Substance Abuse and Mental Health Services Administration (SAMHSA), Office of Applied Studies. "The NHSDA Report. Religious Involvement and Substance Use among Adults." 23 March 2007a. Available http://www.oas.samhsa.gov

Substance Abuse and Mental Health Services Administration (SAMHSA), Office of Applied Studies. "The NHSDA Report. Youth Activities, Substance Use, and Family

Income." 19 April 2007b. Available http://www.oas.samhsa.gov

Suciu-Foca, N., J. P. Armand, and A. Morishima. "Inhibition of Cellular Immunity in Marijuana Smokers." *Science* 183 (1974): 419–420.

Swan, N. "Researchers Make Pivotal Marijuana and Heroin Discoveries." *NIDA Notes* 8 (10 September 1993): 1.

Swan, N. "A Look at Marijuana's Harmful Effects." *NIDA Notes* 9 (February/March 1994): 3–4.

Swan, N. "Facts About Marijuana and Marijuana Abuse." *NIDA Notes* 11 (March/April 1996): 15.

Taylor, N. *Narcotics: Nature's Dangerous Gifts.* New York: Dell, 1963.

Taylor, N. "The Pleasant Assassin: The Story of Marijuana." In *The Marijuana Papers,* edited by D. Solomon. New York: Signet Books, 1966.

Teen Challenge. *Drugs: Frequently Asked Questions.* South Australia: Pragin Press, 2000.

TheWeek.com. "Do Marijuana and Driving Mix?" (7 June 2010). Available http://theweek.com/article/index/203778/do-marijuana-and-driving-mix

Tudor, C. G., D. M. Petersen, and K. W. Elifson. "An Examination of the Relationships Between Peer and Parental Influences and Adolescent Drug Use." In *Chemical Dependencies: Patterns, Costs, and Consequences,* edited by C. D. Chambers, J. A. Inciardi, D. M. Petersen, H. A. Siegal, and O. Z. White. Athens, OH: Ohio University Press, 1987.

Turner, C. E. "Chemistry and Metabolism." In *Marijuana Research Findings: 1980.* NIDA Research Monograph No. 31. Washington, DC: National Institute on Drug Abuse, 1980.

U.S. Department of Transportation. *Marijuana and Actual Driving Performance: Effects of THC on Driving Performance.* DOT HS 808 078. Washington, DC: National Highway Traffic Safety Administration (NHTSA), November 1993.

Venturelli, P. J. "Drugs in Schools: Myths and Reality." In *The Annals of the American Academy of Political and Social Science,* edited by W. Hinkle and S. Henry, 72–87. Thousand Oaks, CA: Sage Publications, January 2000.

Wallace, J. M., V. L. Myers, and E. R. Osai. *Faith Matters: Race/Ethnicity, Religion and Substance Use.* Baltimore, MD: Annie E. Casey Foundation, 2004.

Wren, C. S. "Youth Marijuana Use Rises." Themes of the Times, *New York Times* (20 February 1996): 1.

WrongDiagnoses.com. "Amotivational Syndrome." Health Grades Inc. (August 2010). Available http://www.wrongdiagnosis.com/a/amotivational_syndrome/intro.htm#whatis

Yen, H. "Study: Marijuana Potency Increases in 2007." Huffington Post. (12 June 2008). Available http://www.huffingtonpost.com/2008/06/13/study-marijuana-potency-i_n_106953.html#

Zimmer, L., and J. P. Morgan. *Marijuana Myths, Marijuana Facts: A Review of the Scientific Evidence.* New York: Lindesmith Center, 1997.

CHAPTER 14

Inhalants

Did You Know?

○ More than 1000 different commercial and household products are abused commonly in the United States.

○ Ordinary household products are misused as inhalants: glues/adhesives, nail polish remover, gasoline, paint thinner, spray paint, butane lighter fluid, propane gas, typewriter correction fluid, household cleaners, cooking sprays, deodorants, whipping cream aerosols, marking pens, and air conditioning coolants.

○ Inhalant abuse is typically a problem of adolescents and teenagers. By the time children reach 8th grade, 14.9% will have misused inhalants.

○ Each year, young people in this country die of inhalant abuse or suffer severe consequences, including permanent brain damage and damage to the heart, kidneys, and liver.

○ Inhalant abusers can die suddenly and without warning; even first-time abusers have died from sniffing inhalants.

Learning ◎bjectives

On completing this chapter you will be able to:

◎ Understand that inhalant use is not harmless and that even one-time use could lead to sudden sniffing death syndrome.

◎ List the household and commercial products that are most often abused as inhalants.

◎ Describe the principal means of using household and commercial products as inhalants.

◎ Identify signs of abuse.

◎ Examine the current patterns of abuse among various groups.

◎ List the dangers of inhalant abuse.

Drugs and Society Online is a great source for additional drugs and society information for both students and instructors. Visit **go.jblearning.com/hanson11** to find a variety of useful tools for learning, thinking, and teaching.

Introduction

Inhalants are **volatile** substances that elicit psychological or physiological changes when introduced into the body via the lungs. They are rarely administered by any other route. Most cause intoxicating and/or **euphorigenic** effects. Many of these substances were never intended to be used by humans as drugs; consequently, they are not often thought of as having abuse potential. However, abuse of inhalants is a serious public health problem; according to data obtained from the National Institute on Drug Abuse (NIDA)-sponsored *Monitoring the Future* study, 14.9% of 8th graders have misused an inhalant at least once in their lifetime. Among 10th and 12th graders, lifetime reported use was 12.3% and 9.5%, respectively (Johnston et al. 2010). This frequency of inhalant abuse among 8th graders surpasses the frequency of abuse of such highly publicized drugs as cocaine (2.6%) and amphetamines (6.0%), and approaches that of marijuana (15.7%) in this age group (Johnston et al. 2010). Noteworthy, in 2009, 813,000 persons age 12 or older used inhalants for the first time within the previous 12 months (Substance Abuse and Mental Health Service Administration [SAMHSA] 2010b).

A widespread misconception is that inhalant abuse is a harmless phase that occurs commonly during normal childhood and teenage development and as such is not worthy of significant concern because young people will grow out of it without experiencing harm. On the contrary, numerous adolescents and teenagers in the United States die or are seriously injured each year as a result of inhalant abuse. Even first-time users may die from sudden sniffing death syndrome (SSDS), a condition characterized by serious cardiac **arrhythmia** occurring during or immediately after inhaling. Accurate statistics regarding the number of inhalant-associated deaths and injuries each year are unavailable, in part because medical examiners often attribute deaths from inhalant use to suicide, suffocation, or accidents. Nevertheless, every year young people in the United States die from inhalant abuse, and many more suffer severe consequences such as damage to the brain, heart, kidneys, and liver (U.S. Consumer Product Safety Commission n.d.).

Most inhalants are household or commercial products composed of several different chemicals. These compounds can act alone or synergistically to exert toxic effects. The potential of these agents to cause harm is compounded by the high concentrations of these substances absorbed in the body by inhalation and the tendency for these often lipid-rich (oil or fat) substances to be retained in lipid-containing vital organs. Another important consideration is that the users are often developmentally immature and as such can be more susceptible to the toxic effects of inhalants. The summation of these factors makes inhalants dangerous substances of abuse.

History of Inhalants

The modern era of inhalant abuse can be traced to 1776, when British chemist Joseph Priestley synthesized nitrous oxide (Kennedy and Longnecker 1990), a colorless gas with a slightly sweet odor and no noticeable taste. Roughly 20 years later, he and Humphry Davy suggested correctly that the gas might be useful as an anesthetic, and experiments were conducted to test this possibility. Meanwhile, many people learned that inhalation of nitrous oxide produces a euphoria that lasts for minutes. Hence, during the decades between its discovery and clinical use, the inhalant was abused. Its abuse continued to be fashionable into the early 19th century because it served as a means of rapidly attaining drunkenness without consuming alcohol.

Dentists contributed greatly to the introduction of nitrous oxide as an anesthetic. At a stage show in the 1840s, Horace Wells, a dentist, noticed that one of the persons involved in the show injured himself while under the influence of nitrous oxide yet felt no pain. Wells was so impressed by this anesthetic effect that he subsequently allowed his own tooth to be extracted while under the influence of the gas. His experiment was a success; Wells felt no pain. He went on to attempt to demonstrate his discovery at Massachusetts General Hospital in Boston; unfortunately, the patient cried out during the operation and the experiment was deemed unsuccessful. Nevertheless, word of this demon-

KEY TERMS

volatile
readily evaporated at low temperatures

euphorigenic
having the ability to cause feelings of pleasure and well-being

arrhythmia
an irregular heartbeat

stration and others like it spread, ultimately leading to the use of nitrous oxide and other volatile anesthetics as legitimate medical therapy (Kennedy and Longnecker 1990).

Over the years, it was discovered that many chemicals, in addition to nitrous oxide, could be inhaled so as to alter psychological function. Such abuse of inhalants came to public attention in the 1950s when the news media reported that young people were getting high from sniffing glue. The term *glue sniffing* is still used today, but it is often used to describe inhalation of many products besides glue. In fact, more than 1000 different products are currently misused as inhalants (U.S. Consumer Product Safety Commission n.d.), some of which are listed in **Table 14.1.** These chemicals are not regulated like other drugs of abuse; hence, they are readily available to young people. This category of drugs can be classified into three major groups: volatile substances, anesthetics, and nitrites.

Types of Inhalants

Volatile Substances

Over the past 50 years, the number of products containing volatile substances has increased substantially. This category of agents includes aerosols (e.g., spray paints, hair sprays, deodorants, air fresheners), art or office supplies (e.g., correction fluids, felt-tip marker fluids), adhesives (e.g., airplane and other glues), fuels (e.g., propane, gasoline), and industrial or household solvents (e.g., nail polish remover, paint thinners, dry-cleaning fluids). Some volatile substances exist as gases (e.g., nitrous oxide, the propellant in whipping cream cans), whereas others are liquids that vaporize at room temperature (e.g., gasoline). In some cases, the abuser inhales vapors directly from their original containers (called *sniffing* or *snorting*). Still others inhale volatile solvents from plastic bags (called *bagging*) or from old rags or bandannas soaked in the solvent fluid and held over the mouth (called *huffing*).

Acute effects of the volatile chemicals that are commonly abused include initial nausea with some irritation of airways causing coughing and sneezing. Low doses often bring a brief feeling of lightheadedness, mild stimulation followed by a loss of control, lack of coordination, and disorientation accompanied by dizziness and possible hallucinations. In some instances, higher doses can produce relaxation, sleep, or even coma. If inhalation is contin-

Table 14.1 Inhalants

VOLATILE SOLVENTS
Adhesive
Airplane glue
Polyvinychloride cement
Rubber cement
Aerosols
Analgesic spray
Deodorant, air freshener
Hair spray
Spray paint
Solvents and Gases
Cigarette lighter fluid
Typing correction fluid and thinner
Fuel gas
Gasoline
Nail polish remover
Paint remover
Paint thinner
Cleaning Agents
Dry-cleaning fluid
Degreaser
Spot remover
Dessert Topping Sprays
Whipped cream, whippets
ANESTHETICS
Gas
Liquid
NITRATES
"Poppers"

Source: Adapted from National Institute on Drug Abuse (NIDA). *Research Report Series—Inhalant Abuse.* NIH Publication No. 94-3818. July 2009.

Here and Now

Chronic Solvent Abuse, Brain Abnormalities, and Cognitive Deficits

Chronic inhalant abuse has long been associated with neurological damage and cognitive abnormalities that can range from mild impairment to severe dementia. In fact, the severity of these problems can be greater than for drugs often considered by the general population as being more harmful. For example, a 2002 report published by Neil Rosenberg of the University of Colorado Health Sciences Center found that chronic solvent abusers performed worse than chronic users of other drugs (especially cocaine and alcohol) on tests of working memory and executive function. In this study, abusers inhaled primarily vapors from spray paint containing toluene, and averaged more than 10 years of abuse. More than half of the group reported near-daily inhalant intoxication.

According to Rosenberg,

the extensive neurological damage and cognitive impairments we found among chronic solvent abusers in our study could limit their ability to control their behavior and perceive problems associated with their substance abuse. . . . Some of the brain damage and cognitive deficits seen in both primary inhalant and cocaine abusers in the study could stem from the heavy use of alcohol that was common among both groups. . . . However, the diffuse white matter changes and abnormalities found in the thalamus have not been seen in alcohol abusers and are clearly from solvent abuse.

Sources: Mathias, R. "Chronic Solvent Abusers Have More Brain Abnormalities and Cognitive Impairments Than Cocaine Abusers." *NIDA Notes* 17(4). November 2002. Available at: http://archives.drugabuse.gov/NIDA_notes/NNVol17N4/Chronic.html. Accessed February 17, 2011; and Rosenberg, N. L., J. Grigsby, J. Dreisbach, D. Busenbark, and P. Grisby. "Neuropsychologic Impairment and MRI Abnormalities with Chronic Solvent Abuse." *Journal of Clinical Toxicology* 40 (2002): 21–34.

ued, dangerous **hypoxia** may occur and cause brain damage or death. In other cases, SSDS can occur. Other potential toxic consequences of inhaling such substances include hypertension and damage to the cardiac muscle, peripheral nerves, brain, and kidneys. In addition, chronic users of inhalants frequently lose their appetite, are continually tired, and experience nosebleeds. If use of inhalants persists, some of the damage may become irreversible (see "Here and Now: Chronic Solvent Abuse, Brain Abnormalities, and Cognitive Deficits").

Aerosols

Chemicals associated with aerosol sprays are popular among young inhalant abusers. They include spray paints, deodorant and hair sprays, vegetable oil sprays for cooking, and fabric protector sprays (National Institute on Drug Abuse [NIDA] 2009). Aerosol sprays are often abused not because of the effects produced by their principal ingredients but rather because of the effects of their propellant gases. Inhalation of aerosol preparations can be dangerous because these devices are capable of generating very high concentrations of the inhaled chemicals, much greater than those released more slowly from liquid products.

Toluene

Toluene is a chemical found in some glues, paints, thinners, nail polishes, and typewriter correction fluid. It is a principal ingredient in "Texas shoe shine" (a shoe spray containing toluene; NIDA 2009). Toluene is detectable in the arterial blood within 10 seconds of inhalation exposure (National Highway Traffic Safety Administration [NHTSA] 2010). Because this molecule is highly lipid-soluble the brain, heart, and liver rapidly absorb it. Accord-

KEY TERMS

hypoxia
a state of oxygen deficiency

ingly, toluene abuse can cause brain damage. Other damage can include impaired cognition and gait disturbances. Loss of coordination, equilibrium, hearing, and vision can also occur. Liver and kidney damage have also been reported (NIDA 2009). Of note, a recent study indicates that toluene activates dopaminergic activity in the brain (NIDA 2009). As discussed in Chapter 4, the dopamine system is important for the rewarding effects of nearly all drugs of abuse.

Butane and Propane

Butane and propane are found commonly in lighter fluid and hair and paint sprays. Serious burn injuries (because of flammability) and SSDS via cardiac effects have resulted from their abuse (NIDA 2009).

Gasoline

Because of its widespread availability, young people, often in rural settings, sometimes abuse gasoline. Gasoline is a mixture of volatile chemicals, including toluene, benzene, and triorthocresyl phosphate (TCP). As a mixture of chemicals, the intentional inhalation of gasoline can be especially dangerous. Benzene is an organic compound that causes impaired immunologic function, bone marrow injury, increased risk of leukemia, and reproductive system toxicity (NIDA 2009). TCP is a fuel additive that causes degeneration of motor neurons (National Inhalant Prevention Coalition [NIPC] 2010). Lead, formerly a common constituent of gasoline, can cause lead poisoning, which leads to persistent CNS damage. Furthermore, gasoline is highly flammable; as with butane and propane, fires and serious burn injuries have resulted when gasoline inhalation has been combined with smoking of marijuana, tobacco, or other drugs.

Freon

Freon and other fluorinated hydrocarbons are used in a number of products including refrigerators, air conditioners, and airbrushes. Their inhalation can cause not only serious liver damage but also SSDS (NIDA 2009). Inhaling these agents also poses other dangers; freeze injuries can occur when individuals inhaling freon lose consciousness, leaving unprotected skin in close proximity to cold. In one serious, but rare, case, a 16-year-old male attempted to get high by inhaling airbrush propellant. The patient lost consciousness. When he awoke, he discovered that his tongue and lips were frozen and that he had suffered serious burns on his larynx, vocal cords, trachea, bronchi, and esophagus (Kuspis and Krenzelok 1999).

■ Anesthetics

When used properly, other forms of inhalants with abuse potential are important therapeutic agents. Included in this category are anesthetics such as ether, chloroform, halothane, and nitrous oxide. Although all the anesthetic gases work much like the central nervous system (CNS) depressants, only nitrous oxide is available widely enough to be a significant abuse concern. Nitrous oxide is a colorless gas that is used frequently for minor outpatient procedures in offices of both physicians and dentists. It is often referred to as "laughing gas" because it can cause giggling and laughter in the patient receiving it. Nitrous oxide produces a unique profile of stimulant, hallucinogenic, and depressant effects. Because it is readily accessible, health professionals themselves or their staffs are most likely to abuse nitrous oxide.

In addition to being found in a clinical setting, nitrous oxide can also be sold in large balloons from which the gas is released and inhaled for its mind-altering effects. It is also found in small cylindrical cartridges used as charges for whipped cream dispensers. These cylinders and other plastic containers filled with nitrous oxide are referred to as "whippets." Although significant abuse problems of nitrous oxide are infrequent (Dohrn et al. 1993), there are occasional reports of severe hypoxia (i.e., a lack of oxygen) or death due to acute overdoses. Nitrous oxide can also cause loss of sensation, limb spasms, altered perception and motor coordination, blackouts resulting from blood pressure changes, and depression of heart muscle functioning (NIDA 2009). For the most part, nitrous oxide does not pose a significant abuse problem for the general public.

■ Nitrites

Nitrites are chemicals that cause vasodilation. Owing to this property, the prototype of this group, amyl nitrite, is available by prescription to treat angina. Nitrites were first abused in the 1960s when ampules of the compound were available over the counter (OTC). The ampules were popped between the fingers (hence, the name "poppers") and held to the nostrils for inhalation. According to a recent survey, only 1.1% of 12th graders reported any nitrite use (Johnston et al. 2010).

Mainly adults and older adolescents abuse nitrites. Typically, individuals who abuse nitrites are attempting to enhance sexual pleasure and function. According to NIDA (2009), abuse of nitrites in this context is associated with unsafe sexual practices

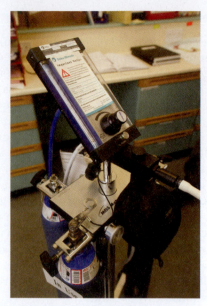

Anesthetics are an example of an inhalant.

that increase the risk of contracting and spreading infectious diseases such as HIV/AIDS and hepatitis. Further, animal research suggests that there may also be an association between the abuse of nitrites and the development and progression of tumors and infectious diseases (NIDA 2009).

Legislation

Inhalants of abuse are generally not regulated under the Controlled Substances Act; however, according to the National Conference of State Legislatures, by 2000, 38 states had adopted laws preventing the use, sale, and/or distribution to minors of various products abused commonly as inhalants. Some states have introduced fines, incarceration, or mandatory treatment for the distribution, sale, use, and/or possession of inhalable chemicals (Office of National Drug Control Policy [ONDCP] 2010).

Current Patterns and Signs of Abuse

Inhalants, particularly gases and aerosols, are often among the first drugs that young children misuse. The inhalants are popular for several reasons:

- They are legally obtained.
- They are readily available in most households and workplaces.
- They are inexpensive.

- They are easy to conceal.
- Most users are uninformed about the potential dangers.

In addition, inhalation is popular because it causes feelings of intoxication and euphoria much more rapidly than does the consumption of agents such as alcohol. Furthermore, the withdrawal (hangover) is often less severe than with alcohol.

Adolescent and Teenage Usage

Adolescents most commonly use inhalants, with usage decreasing as students grow older. For example, according to the 2009 Monitoring the Future study (Johnston et al. 2010), 3.8% of 8th graders reported using inhalants within the past month, whereas only 2.2% of 10th graders and 1.2% of high school seniors reported a similar pattern of use (see **Table 14.2**). By comparison, in 2009, past-month use among individuals ages 26–29 was 0.3%. One reason for this age difference is that older individuals often view use of inhalants with disdain and consider it unsophisticated and a kid's habit.

Inhalants were used by high percentages of 10th and 12th graders in 2009. Lifetime inhalant use among 12th graders in 2009 was 9.5%, compared with 12.3% among 10th graders. Of considerable concern are reports that inhalant abuse can begin as early as the preschool years (Spiller and Krenzelok 1997). Researchers and poison information centers have described cases of 2- to 6-year-old children inhaling gasoline vapors. Imitation of older siblings or neighbors often accounts for this initial exposure. At least one study indicates that many 7- and 8-year-olds are familiar with the psychological effects of inhaling gasoline (Kaufman 1973). Hence, education efforts should be directed at very young children as well as adolescents and their parents.

Gender, Race, Socioeconomics, and Abuse

According to the 2008 National Survey on Drug Use and Health, a greater percentage of men (1.1%) than women (0.6%) age 12 or older have used an inhalant during the past year. However, that gender difference is diminishing, as evidenced by recent findings that rates of past-year inhalant use were similar among females (4.0%) and males (3.9%) ages 12 to 17. Nearly 11.1% of American Indian

Table 14.2 Inhalant Use Among 8th, 10th, and 12th Graders

Data show the percentages of 8th, 10th, and 12th graders who used inhalants.

	8TH GRADERS			10TH GRADERS			12TH GRADERS		
	2008	2009	2010	2008	2009	2010	2008	2009	2010
Lifetime	15.7	14.9	14.5	12.8	12.3	12.0	9.9	9.5	9.0
Annual	8.9	8.1	8.1	5.9	6.1	5.7	3.8	3.4	3.6
30-day	4.1	3.8	3.6	2.1	2.2	2.0	1.4	1.2	1.4

Sources: Johnston, L D., P. M. O'Malley, J. G. Bachman, and J. E. Schulenberg. *Monitoring the Future.* "Trends in Lifetime Prevalence of Use of Various Drugs in Grades 8, 10, and 12 (Table 1)." Ann Arbor, MI: University of Michigan, 2010. Available at: http://www.monitoringthefuture.org/data/10data/pr10t1.pdf. Accessed April 22, 2011; Johnston, L D., P. M. O'Malley, J. G. Bachman, and J. E. Schulenberg. *Monitoring the Future.* "Trends in Annual Prevalence of Use of Various Drugs in Grades 8, 10, and 12 (Table 2)." Ann Arbor, MI: University of Michigan, 2010. Available at: http://www.monitoringthefuture.org/data/10data/pr10t2.pdf. Accessed April 22, 2011; and Johnston, L D., P. M. O'Malley, J. G. Bachman, and J. E. Schulenberg. *Monitoring the Future.* "Trends in 30-Day Prevalence of Use of Various Drugs in Grades 8, 10, and 12 (Table 3)." Ann Arbor, MI: University of Michigan, 2010. Available at: http://www.monitoringthefuture.org/data/10data/pr10t3.pdf. Accessed April 22, 2011.

or Alaskan Natives ages 12–17 have abused an inhalant at least once. White, non-Hispanic; Hispanic; black; and Asian individuals ages 12 to 17 abused inhalants at least once in their lifetime at rates of 8.8%, 9.5%, 9.8%, and 10.5%, respectively (SAMHSA 2010b).

Chronic inhalant users frequently have a profile like that associated with other substance abusers; that is, often they live in unhappy surroundings with severe family or school problems, have poor self-images, and sniffing gives them an accessible escape. Poverty, history of child abuse, and poor grades all are associated with inhalant abuse (NIDA 2009). The problem of inhalant abuse is not unique to the United States. According to research data reported by NIDA, inhalant abuse is of worldwide concern.

Signs of Inhalant Abuse

Individuals under the influence of inhalants are often uncoordinated and disoriented and appear drunken, as if having consumed alcohol. Red and watery eyes, slurred speech, nausea, headaches, and nosebleeds are also common. Rashes around the nose and mouth or unexplained paint on the hands and mouth can be signs of inhalant abuse. Other signs include smelling a chemical odor in the room or in unusual containers (e.g., soda cans, plastic bags), finding cans of aerosol whipped cream that will not foam, or discovering air conditioners that do not work. In addition, children who are frequent users of inhalants have the following characteristics:

- Often collect an unusual assortment of chemicals (such as glues, paints, thinners and solvents,

Signs & Symptoms Inhalants: Possible Signs of Misuse

Drunken behavior	Unexplained paint on the hands and mouth
Red and watery eyes	Room has a chemical odor
Slurred speech	Having the sniffles without other cold symptoms
Nausea	Vomiting
Headaches	Respiratory depression
Nosebleeds	Loss of consciousness
Rashes around the nose and mouth	Possible death

nail polish, liquid eraser, and cleaning fluids) in bedrooms or with belongings
- Have breath that occasionally smells of solvents
- Often have the sniffles similar to a cold but without other symptoms of the ailment
- Appear drunk for short periods of time (15 to 60 minutes) but recover quickly
- Do not do well in school and are often unkempt

Other signs of inhalant abuse can include the following:

- Sitting with a pen or marker near nose
- Constantly smelling clothing sleeves
- Hiding rags, clothes, or empty containers of the potentially abused products in closets, boxes, and other places
- Possessing chemical-soaked rags, bags, or socks
- Abusable household items missing

Dangers of Inhalant Abuse

The dangers of inhalant abuse stretch beyond simply the direct physical damage to the heart, lungs, liver, and brain. Other dangers can include death by choking on their own vomit or by fatal injury from accidents, including car crashes (NIDA 2010).

Use of inhalants by pregnant women also may put newborns at risk of developmental deficits. Although it is not yet possible to link prenatal exposure to specific inhalants with a specific birth defect, case reports have documented developmental abnormalities in offspring of mothers who chronically abuse inhalants (NIDA 2009).

According to NIDA (2009), many individuals who have abused inhalants for prolonged periods over many days report a strong need to continue inhalant use. A mild withdrawal syndrome and compulsive use can occur with long-term inhalant abuse.

A recent survey of 43,000 U.S. adults indicates that inhalant users, on average, initiate use of alcohol, cigarettes, and almost all other drugs at younger ages than those who don't abuse inhalants. Further, these individuals display a higher lifetime prevalence of substance use disorders, including prescription drug abuse, when compared with substance abusers without a history of inhalant use (NIDA 2009).

Of note, between 2006 and 2008, nearly 1 in 20 adolescents with at least one of four respiratory conditions (asthma, bronchitis, pneumonia, or sinusitis) also reported past-year use of an inhalant. This is significant because inhalant use may exacerbate existing medical conditions, including respiratory conditions. Still, adolescents with respiratory conditions are no less likely to use inhalants than those in the general population. Thus, continuing efforts are needed to educate individuals about the health risks of inhalant abuse (SAMHSA 2010a).

Treatment

From 1997 to 2007, the number of admissions to treatment in which inhalants were the primary drug of abuse decreased from 1819 in 1997 to 992 in 2007. Inhalant admissions represented 0.1% of the total drug/alcohol admissions to treatment during both 1997 and 2007. Those admitted to treatment for inhalants during 2007 were primarily male (63.9%) and white (64%). Approximately 50% of the inhalant admissions in 2007 involved clients under the age of 20 (ONDCP 2010).

Discussion Questions

1. Name the three types of inhalants and list examples of each type. List the dangerous side effects associated with the misuse of each type of inhalant.

2. Why are inhalants widely abused?

3. What is sudden sniffing death syndrome?

4. What chemical properties of inhalants make these agents particularly dangerous?

5. Who is most likely to abuse inhalants?

6. List several signs of inhalant abuse.

7. List several dangers of inhalant abuse other than the direct physical damage done by the chemical itself.

Summary

1 Inhalants are volatile substances that cause intoxicating and/or euphorigenic effects. Most were never intended to be used as drugs and are not often thought of as having abuse potential. However, inhalant abuse is a serious public health problem. Hundreds of adolescents and teenagers in the United States die or are seriously injured each year as a result of inhalant abuse. Even first-time users can die from a condition referred to as sudden sniffing death syndrome (SSDS).

2 Most inhalants are household or commercial products composed of several different fat-soluble chemicals that can act alone or synergistically to exert toxic effects. These agents can be classified into three groups: volatile substances, anesthetics, and nitrites.

3 Volatile substances include aerosols, adhesives, fuels, and household solvents. Abusers inhale vapors directly from their original containers (called sniffing or snorting), from plastic bags (called bagging), or from old rags or bandannas soaked in the solvent fluid and held over the mouth (called huffing). Abuse of these agents can cause damage to the liver, brain, kidneys, and immune system as well as SSDS.

4 Anesthetics include ether, chloroform, halothane, and nitrous oxide. When used properly, these forms of inhalants are important therapeutic agents; however, their misuse can cause severe hypoxia and death.

5 Nitrites are vasodilators abused by only a few, selective groups to enhance sexual pleasure.

6 Inhalants are popular because they are legally obtained, readily available, inexpensive, and easy to conceal.

7 Inhalant abuse is typically a problem of adolescents and teenagers.

8 Signs of inhalant abuse include a drunken appearance, watery eyes, nausea, headaches, and nosebleeds. Rashes around the nose and mouth or unexplained paint on the hands and mouth can be signs of inhalant abuse. Other signs can include smelling a chemical odor in the room or in unusual containers (e.g., soda cans, plastic bags), finding cans of aerosol whipped cream that will not foam, or discovering air conditioners that do not work.

References

Dohrn, C., J. Lichtor, A. Coalson, H. Uitvlugt, H. deWit, and J. Zachny. "Reinforcing Effects of Extended Inhalation of Nitrous Oxide in Humans." *Drugs and Alcohol Dependence* 31 (1993): 265–280.

Johnston, L. D., P. M. O'Malley, J. G. Bachman, and J. E. Schulenberg. *Monitoring the Future: National Survey Results on Drug Use, 1975–2009. Volume I: Secondary School Students.* NIH Publication No. 10-7584. Bethesda, MD: National Institute on Drug Abuse, 2010.

Kaufman, A. "Gasoline Sniffing Among Children in a Pueblo Indian Village." *Pediatrics* 51 (1973): 1060–1064.

Kennedy, S. K., and D. E. Longnecker. "History and Principles of Anesthesiology." In *The Pharmacological Basis of Therapeutics,* edited by A. G. Gilman, T. W. Rall, A. S. Nies, and P. Taylor, 269. New York: Pergamon Press, 1990.

Kuspis, D. A., and E. P. Krenzelok. "Oral Frostbite Injury from Intentional Abuse of a Fluorinated Hydrocarbon." *Journal of Toxicology and Clinical Toxicology* 37 (1999): 873–875.

Mathias, R. "Chronic Solvent Abusers Have More Brain Abnormalities and Cognitive Impairments Than Cocaine Abusers." *NIDA Notes.* (17 November 2002). Available http://archives.drugabuse.gov/NIDA_notes/NNVol17N4/Chronic.html

National Highway Traffic Safety Administration (NHTSA). "Drug and Human Performance Fact Sheets: Toluene." 2010. Available http://www.nhtsa.gov/people/injury/research/job185drugs/toluene.htm

National Inhalant Prevention Coalition (NIPC). "Commonly Abused Products and Chemical Effects." 2010. Available http://www.inhalants.org/scatter.htm

National Institute on Drug Abuse (NIDA). *Research Report, Inhalant Abuse.* NIH Publication No. 09-3818. (November 2009). Available http://www.nida.nih.gov/PDF/RRinhalants.pdf

National Institute on Drug Abuse (NIDA). "NIDA for Teens: Inhalants." 2010. Available http://teens.drugabuse.gov/facts/facts_inhale2.php

Office of National Drug Control Policy (ONDCP). "Inhalant Facts and Figures." 2010. Available http://www.whitehousedrugpolicy.gov/drugfact/inhalants/inhalants_ff.html

Rosenberg, N. L., J. Grigsby, J. Dreisbach, D. Busenbark, and P. Grigsby. "Neuropsychologic Impairment and MRI Abnormalities with Chronic Solvent Abuse." *Journal of Clinical Toxicology* 40 (2002): 21–34.

Spiller, H. A., and E. P. Krenzelok. "Epidemiology of Inhalant Abuse Reported to Two Regional Poison Centers." *Clinical Toxicology* 35 (1997): 167–173.

Substance Abuse and Mental Health Service Administration (SAMHSA). "Adolescent Inhalant Use and Selected Respiratory Conditions." 2010a. Available http://oas.samhsa.gov/2k10/175/175RespiratoryCond.htm

Substance Abuse and Mental Health Services Administration (SAMHSA). *Results from the 2009 National Survey on Drug Use and Health: Volume I. Summary of National Findings.* NSDUH Series H-38A, HHS Publication No. SMA 10-4586. Rockville, MD: Office of Applied Studies, 2010b.

U.S. Consumer Product Safety Commission. "A Parent's Guide to Preventing Inhalant Abuse." n.d. Available http://www.cpsc.gov/cpscpub/pubs/389gph.html

CHAPTER 15

Over-the-Counter, Prescription, and Herbal Drugs

Learning Objectives

On completing this chapter you will be able to:

- Outline the general differences between prescription and nonprescription drugs.
- Explain why the FDA occasionally switches prescription drugs to over-the-counter (OTC) status.
- Describe potential abuse problems with OTC, prescription, and herbal drugs.
- Identify some of the drugs that have been switched to OTC.
- Discuss the potential problems of making more effective OTC drugs available to the public for self-care.
- Describe the type of information that is included on the labels of nonprescription medicines.
- Discuss the rules for safe use of nonprescription drugs.
- Determine the difference between herbal products and OTC medications.
- Explain why the FDA has removed ephedrine and ephedra from its list of approved OTC products.
- Compare problems of abuse/addiction of illicit and prescription drugs and explain why prescription abuse has become so widespread.
- Discuss the type of information that should be communicated between doctor and patient to avoid unnecessary drug side effects.
- Explain the advantages and disadvantages of generic and proprietary drugs.
- Explain which prescription drugs are most likely to be abused and why.

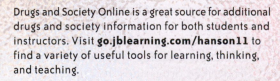

Drugs and Society Online is a great source for additional drugs and society information for both students and instructors. Visit **go.jblearning.com/hanson11** to find a variety of useful tools for learning, thinking, and teaching.

Did You Know?

- More than 700 of the current over-the-counter (OTC) drug products were available only by prescription 30 years ago.
- Pharmacists can provide useful counseling in selecting appropriate OTC products.
- Careless, excessive use of some OTC medications can cause addiction, physical dependence, tolerance, and withdrawal symptoms.
- When used together, prescription drugs or drugs of abuse can interact with OTC or herbal drugs in a dangerous and sometimes even lethal manner.
- Most herbal remedies are very popular products that, despite containing drugs, are available without a prescription and by law are excluded from routine OTC regulation by the Food and Drug Administration (FDA).
- More people die in the United States from adverse reactions to legal medications than succumb to all illegal drug use.
- Twenty percent of the people in the United States have used prescription drugs for nonmedical purposes.
- One-fifth of college students take prescription drugs to either get high or enhance their academic performance.
- Most generic drugs are as effective as, but substantially less expensive than, their proprietary counterparts.

Introduction

Drug costs approach 15% of overall health spending in the United States (Kaiser Family Foundation [KFF] 2010), and medication errors kill a person every day and injure approximately 1.3 million people annually by errors in prescribing, dispensing, or taking these products (Food and Drug Administration [FDA] 2009). Over-the-counter (OTC) and prescription drugs have been viewed differently by the public since these classifications were formally established by the Durham-Humphrey Amendment of 1951. In general, we view OTC medications as less effective, relatively free from side effects, and rarely abused; in contrast, we often consider prescription drugs as much more potent, typically used for more serious medical conditions, and frequently dangerous. However, distinctions between prescription and nonprescription drugs, which at one time appeared to be obvious, have become blurred by changes in public demand and federal policies. Because of escalating health costs and a growing interest in self-care, people today want access to effective medications, and governmental agencies such as the Food and Drug Administration (FDA) are responding to their demands. Consequently, the FDA has been involved in switching effective and relatively safe prescription medications to OTC status. In fact, more than 700 drug products sold OTC today were available only by prescription 30 years ago (Pal 2006). It is likely that in the future, other drugs will be removed from behind the pharmacist's counter and made available for public access as nonprescription medications (FDA 2010b). These changes emphasize the somewhat arbitrary nature of classifying drugs as prescription and OTC and remind us that similar care should be taken with all medications to achieve maximal benefit and minimal risk.

In this chapter, we begin by discussing OTC (nonprescription) drugs. The first topic encompasses policies regarding OTC drug regulation and is followed by a discussion of safe self-care with nonprescription drug products. Explanations of some of the most common medications in this category, including herbal remedies, conclude the section on OTC drugs. The second part of this chapter gives a general overview of prescription drugs. The consequences of misusing prescription drugs, as well as ways for you to avoid such problems, are discussed. A brief presentation of some of the most commonly prescribed drugs ends the chapter.

OTC Drugs

Each year people in the United States spend more than $18 billion on drug products that are purchased OTC, at a savings of $20 billion in healthcare costs annually. Today, more than 300,000 different OTC products are available to treat everything from age spots to halitosis; they account for 60% of the annual drug purchases in this country. An estimated three out of four people routinely self-medicate with these drug products (Pal 2006). Some of the 80 major drug classes currently approved for OTC status are shown in **Table 15.1**.

OTC remedies are nonprescription drugs that may be obtained and used without the supervision of a physician or other health professional. Nevertheless, for some people, certain OTC products can be dangerous when used alone or in combination with other drugs. Although some OTC drugs are very beneficial in the self-treatment of minor to moderate uncomplicated health problems, others are of questionable therapeutic value, and their usefulness is often misrepresented by manufacturers.

■ Abuse of OTC Drugs

A couple of high school students from Oregon became extremely ill from overdosing on multiple boxes of cold and cough OTC products that they had shoplifted while ditching school. The students were found stumbling around in an alley near their school, disoriented and lethargic. A local secondary education official implied that the practice was routine and referred to by the local kids as "popping Skittles" because the cold medicine capsules are multicolored. Although, as illustrated above, the consequences of abusing OTC drugs can be substantial, relatively speaking the occurrence rate is low; however, there are some notable exceptions such as cough medicines and decongestants (Martinez 2007).

Because these drugs are usually available on demand, perceived as being exceptionally safe, and poorly understood by the general public, their abuse patterns differ somewhat from those seen with the so-called hard-core drugs of abuse; nevertheless, they can be equally harmful. Even though the OTC products generally have a greater margin of safety than their prescription counterparts, issues of abuse need to be considered. For example, many OTC drugs, when misused, can cause physical

Table 15.1 **Some Major Drug Classes Approved by the FDA for OTC Status**

DRUG CLASS	EFFECTS
Analgesics and anti-inflammatories	Relieve pain, fever, and inflammation
Cold remedies	Relieve cold symptoms
Antihistamines and allergy products	Relieve allergy symptoms
Stimulants	Diminish fatigue and drowsiness
Sedatives and sleep aids	Promote sleep
Antacids	Relieve indigestion from rebound activity
Laxatives	Relieve self-limiting constipation
Antidiarrheals	Relieve minor, self-limiting diarrhea
Gastric secretion blockers	Relieve heartburn
Topical antimicrobials	Treat skin infections
Bronchodilators and antiasthmatics	Assist breathing
Dentifrices and dental products	Promote oral hygiene
Acne medications	Treat and prevent acne
Sunburn treatments and sunscreens	Treat and prevent skin damage from ultraviolet rays
Dandruff and athlete's foot medications	Treat and prevent specific skin conditions
Contraceptives and vaginal products	Prevent pregnancy and treat vaginal infections
Ophthalmics	Promote eye hygiene and treat eye infections
Vitamins and minerals	Provide diet supplements
Antiperspirants	Promote body hygiene
Hair growth stimulators	Promote hair growth

Source: Pal, S. "Self Care and Nonprescription Pharmacotherapy." *Handbook of Nonprescription Drugs*, 15th ed., edited by I. Bernardi, 3–14. Washington DC: American Pharmacists Association, 2006.

and psychological dependence. Nonprescription products that can be severely habit-forming include nasal and ophthalmic (eye) decongestants, laxatives, antihistamines, sleep aids, and antacids. Of particular abuse concern are OTC stimulants, such as ephedrine, that can be severely toxic by themselves or can be used as precursors to the synthesis of the extremely addicting and dangerous amphetamines. In fact, because of these concerns, the FDA ruled that ephedrine no longer can be included in OTC or herbal products, and most states require that cold products containing amphetamine precursors be safeguarded behind the counter (Leinwand 2007).

Because use of OTC products is unrestricted, the patterns of abuse are impossible to determine accurately. However, these products are more likely to be abused by members of the unsuspecting general public who inadvertently become dependent due to excessive self-medication than by hard-core drug addicts who obtain the most potent drugs of abuse by illicit means.

■ Federal Regulation of OTC Drugs

In the United States, the FDA is responsible for regulating OTC drugs. Under the direction of the FDA, the active ingredients in OTC drugs have been, and continue to be, evaluated and classified according to their effectiveness and safety (Pal 2006). At this time, the principal ingredients included in nonprescription drug products are category I (that is, they are considered safe and effective) (Bernstein and Rickert 2006).

The FDA has attempted to make even more drugs available to the general public by switching some frequently used and safe prescription medications to OTC status. This policy is in response to public demand to have access to effective drugs for self-medication and has resulted in approximately 80–90 successful switches, leading to hundreds of new OTC products (Consumer Healthcare Products Association [CHPA] 2010; FDA 2010b; Pal 2006). This policy helps to cut medical costs by eliminating the need for costly visits to healthcare providers for treatment of minor, self-limiting ailments (FDA 2010b). A few of the more notable drugs that have been switched from prescription to nonprescription status since 1985 (CHPA 2007; FDA 2010b) are naproxen (analgesic, anti-inflammatory: Aleve); ketoprofen (analgesic: Orudis); hydrocortisone (anti-inflammatory steroid: Cortaid); loperamide (antidiarrheal: Imodium); tioconazole (vaginal antifungal: Vagistat-1); epinephrine (bronchodilator: Bronkaid Mist); miconazole (antifungal: Monistat 7); cimetidine (heartburn medication: Tagamet); increased-strength minoxidil (hair growth stimulant: Rogaine); nicotine patch (smoking cessation aid: Nicotrol); cromolyn (allergy medication: Nasalcrom); triclosan (antibacterial for gum disease: Colgate Total toothpaste); loratadine (nonsedating antihistamine: Claritin); levonorgestrel (contraceptive: Plan B); orlistat (weight loss: Alli); lansoprazole (gastric acid reducer: Prevacid); cetirizine (antihistamine: Zyrtec); terbinafine (topical antifungal: Lamisil); and polyethylene glycol (laxative: Miralax).

A major concern of health professionals is that reclassification of safe prescription drugs to OTC status will result in overuse or misuse of these agents. The reclassified drugs may tempt individuals to self-medicate rather than seek medical care for potentially serious health problems or encourage the use of multiple drugs at the same time, increasing the likelihood of dangerous interactions (Stolberg 2000). Clearly, the FDA has slowed down this process. Since 2002, approximately nine ingredients have been switched, including OTC versions of Claritin and the heartburn medication Prilosec (FDA 2010b).

It is likely that effective and safe prescription drugs will continue to be made available OTC, albeit at a slower pace. In fact, the FDA is considering other groups of drugs currently available by prescription for OTC status in the next several years.

■ OTC Drugs and Self-Care

Of the approximately 3.5 billion health problems treated in the United States annually, almost 2 billion can be treated with an OTC drug. This fact demonstrates that the public frequently engages in medical self-care with OTC products. Self-care with nonprescription medications occurs because we decide that we have a health problem that can be adequately self-medicated without involving a health professional. Proper self-care assumes that the individual has made a correct diagnosis of the health problem and is informed enough to select the appropriate OTC product. If done correctly, self-care with OTC medications can provide significant relief from minor, self-limiting health problems at minimal cost. However, a lack of understanding about the nature of the OTC products—what they can and cannot do—and their potential side effects can result in harmful misuse. For this reason, it is important that those who consume OTC medications be fully aware of their proper use. This goal usually can be achieved by reading product labels carefully and asking questions of health professionals such as pharmacists and physicians.

OTC Labels

Information about proper use of OTC medications is required to be cited on the drug label and is regulated by the FDA. Required label information includes (1) approved uses of the product, (2) detailed instructions on safe and effective use, and (3) cautions or warnings to those at greatest risk when taking the medication. FDA regulations require that this information be readily intelligible to the lay public and easily read (Bernstein and Rickert 2006) (see **Figure 15.1**). Many consumers experience adverse side effects because they either choose to ignore the warnings on OTC labels or simply do not bother to read them. For example, as previously mentioned, excessive or inappropriate use of some nonprescription drugs can cause drug dependence; consequently, people who are always dropping medication in the eyes "to get the red out" or popping antacids like dessert after every meal are likely

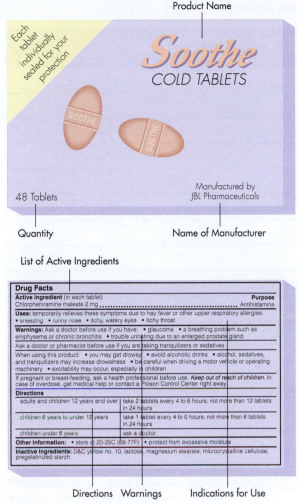

Product Name

Soothe
COLD TABLETS

Each tablet individually sealed for your protection

48 Tablets

Manufactured by JBL Pharmaceuticals

Quantity

Name of Manufacturer

List of Active Ingredients

Drug Facts

Active ingredient (in each tablet)	Purpose
Chlorpheniramine maleate 2 mg	Antihistamine

Uses: temporarily relieves these symptoms due to hay fever or other upper respiratory allergies: • sneezing • runny nose • itchy, watery eyes • itchy throat

Warnings: Ask a doctor before use if you have: • glaucoma • a breathing problem such as emphysema or chronic bronchitis • trouble urinating due to an enlarged prostate gland

Ask a doctor or pharmacist before use if you are taking tranquilizers or sedatives

When using this product: • you may get drowsy • avoid alcoholic drinks • alcohol, sedatives, and tranquilizers may increase drowsiness • be careful when driving a motor vehicle or operating machinery • excitability may occur, especially in children

If pregnant or breast-feeding, ask a health professional before use. *Keep out of reach of children.* In case of overdose, get medical help or contact a Poison Control Center right away.

Directions

adults and children 12 years and over	take 2 tablets every 4 to 6 hours; not more than 12 tablets in 24 hours
children 6 years to under 12 years	take 1 tablet every 4 to 6 hours; not more than 6 tablets in 24 hours
children under 6 years	ask a doctor

Other Information: • store at 20-25C (68-77F) • protect from excessive moisture

Inactive Ingredients: D&C yellow no. 10, lactose, magnesium stearate, microcrystalline cellulose, pregelatinized starch

Directions   Warnings   Indications for Use

FIGURE 15.1

Certain information must appear on the labels of OTC medications.

dependent. They continue to use OTC products to avoid unpleasant eye redness or stomach acidity, which are likely withdrawal consequences of excessive use of these medications.

Rules for Proper OTC Drug Use

The OTC marketplace for drugs operates differently than does its prescription counterpart. The use of OTC drugs is not restricted, and consumers are responsible for making correct decisions about these products. Thus, to a large degree, the consumer sets policy and determines use patterns.

Because there are no formal controls over the use of OTC drugs, abuse often occurs. In extreme situations, the abuse of OTC medication can be very troublesome, even causing structural damage to the body and, on rare occasions, death. Proper

education about the pharmacological features of these agents is necessary if consumers are to make intelligent and informed decisions about OTC drug use. To reduce the incidence of problems, the following rules should be observed when using nonprescription products (Center for Drug Evaluation and Research [CDER] 2002):

- Always know what you are taking. Identify the active ingredients in the product.
- Know the effects. Be sure you know both the desired and potential undesired effects of each active ingredient.
- Read and heed the warnings and cautions. The warnings are not intended to scare but to protect.
- Do not use OTC drug products for more than 1 to 2 weeks. If the problem being treated persists beyond this time, consult a health professional.
- Be particularly cautious if you are also taking prescription or herbal drugs. Serious interactions between OTC drugs and these medications frequently occur. If you have a question, be sure to find out the answer.
- If you have questions, ask a pharmacist. Pharmacists are excellent sources of information about OTC drugs. They possess up-to-date knowledge of OTC products and can assist consumers in selecting correct medications for their health needs. Ask them to help you.
- Most importantly: If you don't need it, don't use it!

■ Types of OTC Drugs

It is impossible to provide a detailed description of the hundreds of active ingredients approved by the FDA for OTC distribution; however, the following includes a brief discussion of the most common OTC drugs available in this country.

Internal Analgesics

We spend more than $2 billion on internal (taken by mouth) analgesics, the largest sales category of OTC drugs in the United States. Most of the money is for **salicylates** (aspirin products—Anacin, Bayer),

KEY TERMS

salicylates
aspirin-like drugs

Table 15.2 Compositions of OTC Internal Analgesics (dose per unit)

PRODUCT	ASPIRIN (MG)	ACETAMINOPHEN (MG)	IBUPROFEN (MG)	OTHER
Bayer Aspirin	325	—	—	—
Empirin	325	—	—	—
Alka-Seltzer, Extra Strength	325	—	—	Antacid
Ecotrin	325	—	—	Coated tablet
Tylenol, Children's	—	80	—	—
Advil	—	—	200	—
Motrin IB	—	—	200	—
Motrin, Children's	—	—	100	—
Nuprin	—	—	200	—
Aleve	—	—	—	Naproxen (220 mg)
Orudis	—	—	—	Ketoprofen (12.5 mg)

Source: Remington, T. "Headache." *Handbook of Nonprescription Drugs,* 15th ed., edited by I. Bernardi, 69–90. Washington DC: American Pharmacists Association. Updated 2011.

acetaminophen (Tylenol, Datril, Pamprin, Panadol), ibuprofen (Advil, Nuprin), and ibuprofen-like drugs such as naproxen (Aleve) and ketoprofen (Orudis). The compositions of common OTC internal analgesics are given in **Table 15.2**.

Therapeutic Considerations

The internal analgesic products are effective in treating several common ailments.

- *Analgesic action:* The OTC analgesics effectively relieve mild to moderate somatic pain associated with musculoskeletal structures such as bones, skin, teeth, joints, and ligaments. Pains

that are relieved by the use of these drugs include headaches, toothaches, earaches, and muscle strains. In contrast, these drugs are not effective in the treatment of severe pain or pain associated with internal organs, such as the heart, stomach, and intestines (*Drug Facts and Comparisons* 2007).

- *Anti-inflammatory effects:* Use of high doses (two to three times the analgesic dose) of the salicylates and ibuprofen relieves the symptoms of inflammation such as those associated with arthritis (*Drug Facts and Comparisons* 2007). In contrast, even high doses of acetaminophen have little **anti-inflammatory** action. Because of this anti-inflammatory effect, these drugs are frequently compared with a group of natural, very potent anti-inflammatory compounds, the steroids. To distinguish drugs such as the salicylates and ibuprofen from steroids, these drugs are often called **nonsteroidal anti-inflammatory drugs (NSAIDs)**.

- *Antipyretic effects:* The OTC analgesics, such as aspirin and acetaminophen, reduce fever but do not alter normal body temperature (*Drug Facts and Comparisons* 2007). Such drugs are

KEY TERMS

anti-inflammatory
relieves symptoms of inflammation

nonsteroidal anti-inflammatory drugs (NSAIDs)
anti-inflammatory drugs that do not have steroid properties

Signs & Symptoms Common Side Effects of OTC NSAIDs

DRUGS	SYSTEM AFFECTED	SIDE EFFECTS
Salicylates (aspirin-like)	Gastrointestinal	Can cause irritation, bleeding; aggravate ulcers
	Blood	Interfere with clotting; prolong bleeding
	Ears	Chronic high doses cause ringing (tinnitus) and hearing loss
	Pediatric	Can cause Reye's syndrome
Acetaminophen	Liver	High acute doses or chronic exposure can cause severe damage
Ibuprofen (includes other, newer NSAIDs)	Gastrointestinal	Similar to salicylates but less severe
	Blood	Similar to salicylates but less severe
	Kidneys	Damage in elderly or those with existing kidney disease

called **antipyretics**. The frequent use of these drugs to eliminate fevers is very controversial. Some clinicians believe that low-grade fever may be a defense mechanism that helps destroy infecting microorganisms such as bacteria and viruses; thus, interfering with fevers may hamper the body's ability to rid itself of infection-causing microorganisms. Because no serious problems are associated with fevers of 102°F or less, they are probably better left unmedicated.

- *Side effects:* When selecting an OTC analgesic drug for relief of pain, inflammation, or fever, possible side effects should be considered. Although salicylates such as aspirin are frequently used, they can cause problems for both children and adults (see "Signs & Symptoms: Common Side Effects of OTC NSAIDs"). Because of their side effects, salicylates are not recommended for (1) children, because of the potential for **Reye's syndrome**; (2) people suffering gastrointestinal problems, such as ulcers; or (3) people with bleeding problems, who are taking anticlot medication, who are scheduled for surgery, or who are near term in pregnancy, because salicylates interfere with blood clotting and prolong bleeding.

For minor aches and pains, acetaminophen substitutes adequately for salicylates, has no effect on blood clotting, and does not cause stomach irritation. In addition, acetaminophen does not influence the occurrence of Reye's syndrome, a potentially deadly complication of colds, flu, and chicken pox in children up to the age of 18 years who are using salicylates (*Drug Facts and Comparisons* 2007). However, even acetaminophen, if used in high doses, can have serious health consequences. Concern that excessive use of acetaminophen can cause permanent and even fatal liver damage has caused the FDA to put out warnings to consumers of acetaminophen-containing products to avoid the use of high doses of this drug (Heller 2011).

Caffeine and Other Additives

A number of OTC analgesic products contain caffeine. Caffeine may relieve the aversion of pain due to its stimulant effect, which may be perceived as pleasant and energizing. The combination of caffeine with OTC analgesics may enhance pain relief (*Drug Facts and Comparisons* 2007) and be especially useful in treating vascular headaches because of the vasoconstrictive properties on cerebral blood vessels caused by this stimulant. In most OTC analgesic products—for example, Anacin or Excedrin—the amount of caffeine is less than that found in one-fourth to one-half cup of coffee (about 30 milligrams/tablet). Other ingredients—such as antacids, antihistamines, and decongestants—sometimes included in OTC pain-relieving products

KEY TERMS

antipyretics
drugs that reduce fevers

Reye's syndrome
potentially fatal complication of colds, flu, or chicken pox in children

have little or no analgesic action and usually add little to the therapeutic value of the medication. A recent development for OTC analgesic products was FDA permission to advertise pain-relieving products effective in the relief of migraine headaches. Although these products have been found to provide relief from minor migraine headaches, they do not contain any new breakthrough drugs; these products contain previously available ingredients, such as aspirin, ibuprofen, and caffeine, just in higher doses (e.g., Migraine Extra Strength Excedrin).

Cold, Allergy, and Cough Remedies

More than 50% of the population routinely use OTC medicines to treat cold symptoms (OTCmedicines 2010). The incidence of the common cold varies with age. Children between 1 and 5 years are most susceptible; each child averages 6 to 12 respiratory illnesses per year, most of which are common colds. Individuals 25 to 30 years old average about six respiratory illnesses a year, and older adults average two or three. The declining incidence of colds with age is owing to the immunity that occurs after each infection with a cold virus; thus, if reinfected with the same virus, the microorganism is rapidly destroyed by the body's defense system and the full-blown symptoms of a cold do not occur (Scolaro 2006).

Most colds have similar general symptoms. In the first stage, the throat and nose are dry and scratchy; in the second stage, secretions accumulate in the air passages, nose, throat, and bronchial tubes. The second stage is marked by continuous sneezing, nasal obstruction, sore throat, coughing, and nasal discharge. There may be watering and redness of the eyes and pain in the face (particularly near the sinuses) and ears. One of the most bothersome symptoms of the common cold is the congestion of the mucous membranes of the nasal passages, due

in part to capillary dilation, which causes these blood vessels to enlarge and become more permeable. Such vascular changes allow fluids to escape, resulting in drainage and also inflammation due to fluid-swollen tissues (Scolaro 2006).

There has been a growing problem of young people abusing these OTC products. Recent surveys suggest that up to 7% of high school seniors have used cough medicine with dextromethorphan to get high (Johnston et al. 2010). This practice is sometimes referred to as "robo-tripping" or "skittling." Common side effects include confusion, dizziness, excessive sweating, stomach pain, numbness, and blurred vision (Martinez 2007).

Decongestants

The cold and allergy products we use are formulated with such drugs as decongestants (sympathomimetics), antihistamines (chlorpheniramine and pheniramine), analgesics (aspirin and acetaminophen), and an assortment of other substances (vitamin C, alcohol, caffeine, and so on). **Table 15.3** lists the ingredients found in many common OTC cold and allergy products.

Antihistamines reduce congestion caused by allergies, but their effectiveness in the treatment of virus-induced colds is controversial. In high doses, the anticholinergic action of antihistamines (see Chapter 4) also decreases mucus secretion, relieving the runny nose; however, this action is probably insignificant at the lower recommended doses of OTC preparations (Mackowiak 1999; Scolaro 2006). An anticholinergic drying action may actually be harmful because it can lead to a serious coughing response. Due to anticholinergic effects, antihistamines also may cause dizziness, drowsiness, impaired judgment, constipation, and dry mouth; they sometimes are abused because of psychedelic effects resulting from high-dose consumption. Be-

Table 15.3 Compositions of Common OTC Cold and Allergy Products (dose per tablet)

PRODUCT	SYMPATHOMIMETIC (MG)	ANTIHISTAMINE (MG)	ANALGESIC (MG)
Actifed	Pseudoephedrine (30)	Triprolidine (2.5)	—
Chlor-Trimeton Allergy	—	Chlorpheniramine (4)	—
Advil Allergy Sinus	Pseudoephedrine (30)	Chlorpheniramine (2)	Ibuprofen (200)
Sudafed Sinus	Pseudoephedrine (30)	—	—

Source: Scolaro, K. "Disorders Related to Colds and Allergies." *Handbook of Nonprescription Drugs,* 15th ed., edited by I. Bernardi, 203–228. Washington DC: American Pharmacists Association, 2006. Updated January 2011.

cause of the limited usefulness and the side effects of antihistamines for treating colds, decongestant products without such agents are usually preferred for these viral infections. In contrast, antihistamines are very useful in relieving allergy-related congestion and symptoms.

The sympathomimetic drugs used as decongestants cause nasal membranes to shrink because of their vasoconstrictive effect, which reduces the congestion caused by both colds and allergies. Such drugs can be used in the form of sprays or drops (topical decongestants) or systemically (oral decongestants) (see **Table 15.4**). FDA-approved sympathomimetics include pseudoephedrine, phenylephrine (probably the most effective topical), naphazoline, and oxymetazoline (Scolaro 2006). Another substantial problem associated with the sympathomimetic decongestant ingredients in cold medicines is that they can easily be chemically converted into methamphetamine. For this reason, state and local governments have passed laws that typically require these decongestant products to be kept behind the counter and records to be kept of those who purchase these medications (Baldauf 2006) (see "Here and Now: Fighting the 'Common Cold' Pills").

Someone using decongestant nasal sprays frequently can experience **congestion rebound** due to tissue dependence. After using a nasal spray regularly for longer than the recommended period of time, the nasal membranes adjust to the effect of the vasoconstrictor and become very congested when the drug is not present. One can become hooked and use the spray more and more with less and less relief until one's tissues no longer respond and the sinus passages become almost completely obstructed (Mackowiak 1999). Allergists frequently see new patients who are addicted to nasal decongestant sprays and are desperate for relief from

The common cold accounts for 20% of all acute illness in the United States.

congestion. This problem can be prevented by using nasal sprays sparingly and for no longer than the recommended time.

Orally ingested sympathomimetic drugs give less relief from congestion than the topical medications but are less likely to cause rebound effects. In contrast, systemic administration of these drugs is more likely to cause cardiovascular problems (that is, stimulate the heart, cause arrhythmia, increase blood pressure, and cause stroke).

Antitussives

Other drugs used to relieve the common cold are intended to treat coughing. The cough reflex helps clear the lower respiratory tract of foreign matter, particularly in the later stages of a cold. There are two types of cough: productive and nonproductive. A *productive cough* removes mucus secretions and foreign matter so that breathing becomes easier and the infection clears up. A *nonproductive, or dry, cough* causes throat irritation; this type of cough is of little cleansing value. Some types of cough suppressant (antitussive) medication are useful for treating a nonproductive cough but should not be used to suppress a productive cough (Tietze 2006).

Table 15.4 **Compositions of OTC Topical Decongestants (drug concentrations)**

PRODUCT	SYMPATHOMIMETIC
Afrin nasal spray	Oxymetazoline (0.05%)
Neo-Synephrine, 12-Hour	Oxymetazoline (0.025%)
Vicks Sinex, 12-Hour	Phenylephrine (0.5%)

Source: Scolaro, K. "Disorders Related to Colds and Allergies." *Handbook of Nonprescription Drugs*, 15th ed., edited by I. Bernardi, 203–228. Washington DC: American Pharmacists Association, 2006. Updated January 2011.

KEY TERMS

congestion rebound
withdrawal from excessive use of a decongestant, resulting in congestion

Here and Now

Fighting the "Common Cold" Pills

It is becoming harder and harder to get those pills we all buy to fight the common cold. This problem is not because drugs like Sudafed are themselves particularly addicting; rather, the concern arises because of what they can become, and this is leading to the imposition of tighter controls on these popular decongestants. Because ingredients in OTC cold medicines, such as pseudoephedrine, can easily be converted into methamphetamine, these products have been bought in large quantities to be used in makeshift meth labs across the country. As a result, law enforcement agencies and even Congress itself have pointed out these drugs' potential dangers. Besides requiring that these OTC products be kept behind the counter in pharmacies, there have been attempts to pass local and national legislation to limit purchases of these drugs to about 9 grams (roughly 300 pills) in a 30-day period. This quantity of pseudoephedrine can be turned into approximately 25 doses of methamphetamine. Such restrictions have made it difficult, although not impossible, for small neighborhood meth labs to cook their dangerous brew. However, as the local "mom-and-pop" domestic producers have been significantly curtailed, Mexican drug cartels have filled the gap with large quantities of methamphet-

amine manufactured in Mexico and smuggled across the border. The cartels are using dummy corporations and false labeling to bring ordinary cold, flu, and allergy medicines into Mexico from China, India, and Bangladesh and converting the ingredients from these common decongestants into large quantities of methamphetamine for illicit sale. Despite efforts by both the Mexican and U.S. governments, these trafficking groups are very resilient, keeping ahead of the law, and have become the primary source for illegal U.S. methamphetamine.

Source: Reuters Health. "Bill Would Restrict Cold Pills to Fight 'Meth.' " 27 January 2005; and Booth, W., and A. O'Connor. "Mexican Cartels Emerge as Top Source for U.S. Meth." *Washington Post.* 28 November 2010. Available at: http://www.washingtonpost.com/wp-dyn/content/article/2010/11/23/AR2010112303703.html?sid=ST2010112303730. Accessed March 29, 2011.

Two kinds of OTC preparations are available to treat coughing:

1. **Antitussives**—such as codeine, dextromethorphan, and diphenhydramine (an antihistamine)—that act on the central nervous system (CNS) to raise the threshold of the cough-coordinating center, thereby reducing the frequency and intensity of a cough
2. **Expectorants**—such as guaifenesin and terpin hydrate—which theoretically (but not very effectively) increase and thin the fluids of the respiratory tract in an attempt to soothe the irritated respiratory tract membranes and decrease the thickness of the accumulated secretions so that coughing becomes more productive

Table 15.5 lists commonly used OTC antitussives and their compositions. Often, the tickling sensation in the throat that triggers a cough can be eased by sucking on a cough drop or hard candy, which stimulates saliva flow to soothe the irritated membranes. Unless the cough is severe, sour hard candy often works just as well as more expensive cough lozenges.

Cough remedies, like other medications, have a psychological value. Many patients with respiratory tract infections claim they cough less after using cough remedies, even when it is objectively demonstrated that the remedies reduce neither the frequency nor the intensity of the cough. Cough remedies work in part by reducing patients' anxiety about the cough and causing them to believe

KEY TERMS

antitussives
drugs that block the coughing reflex

expectorants
substances that stimulate mucus secretion and diminish mucus viscosity

Table 15.5 Compositions of Common OTC Antitussives (dose per unit)

PRODUCT	DEXTROMETHORPHAN (MG)	EXPECTORANT	OTHER
Benylin Adult	15/5 mL	—	—
Hold DM Lozenges	5	—	—
Benylin	5/5 mL	Guaifenesin	—
Robitussin CF	10	Guaifenesin	—
Vicks NyQuil	10	—	Sympathomimetic; antihistamine; analgesic

Source: Tietze, K. "Cough." In *Handbook of Nonprescription Drugs*, 15th ed., edited by I. Bernardi, 229–242. Washington DC: American Pharmacists Association, 2006. Updated January 2011.

that their cough is lessening. If one believes in the remedy, one often can get as much relief from a simple, inexpensive product as from the most sophisticated and costly one. If a cough does not ease in a few days, one should consult a doctor (Tietze 2006).

As mentioned earlier, abuse of antitussive products by teenagers is a significant problem in some regions of this country. This abuse likely relates to the fact that the antitussive ingredient, dextromethorphan, in high doses can have a phencyclidine (PCP)–like effect (see "Here and Now: The Dextromethorphan Trip"). Up to 10% of young people use high doses of antitussives that contain dextromethorphan to get high (Leong 2010). Even though possession of cough medicines is not controlled, the National Institute on Drug Abuse advises parents to control access to cough and cold medications at home to prevent this potential problem (Mitchell 2010).

What Really Works?

With all the advances in medicine today, there is still no cure for the common cold. In most cases, the best treatment is plenty of rest, increased fluid intake to prevent dehydration and to facilitate productive coughing, humidification of the air if it is dry, gargling with diluted salt water (2 teaspoons per quart), an analgesic to relieve the accompanying headache or muscle ache, and perhaps an occasional decongestant if nasal stuffiness is unbearable. Allergy symptoms, in contrast, are best relieved by antihistamines.

Sleep Aids

In 1995, an estimated 49% of the U.S. population experienced insomnia (the inability to fall asleep or stay asleep) at least 5 nights each month (Gill 1999). About 1% of the adult population routinely self-medicate their insomnia with OTC sleep aids that are advertised as inducing a "safe and restful sleep." Described as nonbarbiturate and non-habit forming, these low-potency products are frequently misused (Shuster 1996). For example, the parents of a young child were traveling cross-country. They knew the trip would be long and the child would likely grow tired and cranky. To keep the child quiet and manageable, the parents used Benadryl, an allergy medication, that contained an antihistamine to cause sedation (personal communication to Hanson 2010). Use of these products in young children is inappropriate and can be dangerous. The drugs commonly used in OTC sleep aids are antihistamines, particularly diphenhydramine (Kirkwood and Melton 2006). Although antihistamines have been classified as OTC category I sleep aid ingredients (see Chapter 3), their usefulness in treating significant sleep disorders is highly questionable (Kirkwood and Melton 2006). At best, some people who suffer mild, temporary sleep disturbances caused by problems such as physical discomfort, short-term disruption in daily routines (such as jet lag), and extreme emotional upset might experience temporary relief. However, even for those few who initially benefit from these agents, tolerance develops within 4 days. For long-term sleep problems, OTC sleep aids are of no therapeutic value and are rarely recommended by health professionals. Actually, their placebo benefit is likely more significant than their actual pharmacological benefit. Usually counseling and psychotherapy are more effective approaches for resolving chronic insomnia than

Here and Now

The Dextromethorphan Trip

Dextromethorphan is the antitussive ingredient frequently found in nonprescription cough medicine. Because of pharmacological properties that resemble those of PCP, OTC cough medicines are sometimes abused by teenagers. One such person, who had consumed almost an entire bottle of a popular anticough product, described his experience. He related that the effects of the drug hit first with light-headedness and slight disorientation. After 1 hour, the disorientation became severe. He explained that it felt as though he were outside of himself looking in. The hallucinations were somewhat subtle with things appearing grainy and distorted. He found that breathing was sometimes constricted, as though he were wearing a tight shirt collar. Then came hot flashes, which caused him to turn on a fan to cool down. He found walking was difficult, and time became distorted. The trip lasted 1 to 2 hours for the strong effects, but it seemed to continue forever. This person was an experienced user of acid (LSD) and mushrooms, but he had never been on a trip as scary as the one with the cough medicine. Several times he thought he was going to die. He found that coming down took a while. He decided that he would never do "dex" (dextromethorphan) again. Because of such side effects, these antitussive products are not considered to be especially addicting, although in 2008 there were about 8000 visits to emergency departments in the United States due to abuse of these OTC medications, a number almost twice that reported in 2004. Despite concern for this trend, for now the FDA has decided not to restrict dextromethorphan-containing OTC antitussive products as prescription medicines. A panel of medical experts recommended against such an action because they felt that the reduced availability of these cough medicines would do more harm than good.

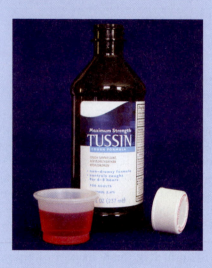

Source: Allen, J. "Over-the-Counter Cough Medicines Escape FDA Restrictions." ABC Good Morning America. 14 September 2010. Available at: http://abcnews.go.com/Health/Wellness/dextromethorphan-ingredient-robutussin-cough-medicines-escapes-fda-restrictions/story?id=11638160. Accessed March 16, 2011.

OTC or even prescription sleep aid drugs (Kirkwood and Melton 2006).

Because antihistamines are CNS depressants, in low doses they can cause sedation and antianxiety action (see Chapter 6). Although in the past, some OTC products containing antihistamines were promoted for their relaxing effects (e.g., Quietworld, Compoz), currently, no sedatives are approved for OTC marketing. The FDA decided that the earlier products relieved anxiety by causing drowsiness, so, in fact, they were not legitimate sedatives. Because of this ruling, medications that are promoted as antianxiety products are no longer available without a prescription. However, antihistamines have been added to an array of other OTC drug products marketed for the purpose of causing relaxation or promoting sleep; such products include analgesics (e.g., Excedrin PM), cold medicines (e.g., Triaminic Cold and Allergy), Midol PM, Tylenol Cold Relief Nighttime, and many others (Drugs.com 2010). The rationale for such combinations is questionable, and their therapeutic value unsubstantiated.

Melatonin

The hormone melatonin is currently being used by millions to induce sleep or to help the body's natural clock readjust after the effects of jet lag. Melatonin was referred to as the "all-natural nightcap of the 1990s." Although most users of this hormone want assistance in falling asleep, melatonin is also claimed to slow the aging process, stimulate the immune system, and enhance the sex drive. Melatonin is a naturally occurring hormone, also found in some foods. Under the 1994 Dietary Supplement and Education Act, melatonin is considered a dietary supplement and is not regulated by the FDA. Despite the popularity of melatonin products, little is known about the benefits or the potential adverse effects of this hormone; consequently, these products should be used cautiously, if at all (van den Heuval et al. 2005).

Stimulants

Some OTC drugs are promoted as stay-awake (e.g., NoDoz) or energy-promoting (e.g., Vivarin) products (Anderson and Nykamp 2006). In general, these medications contain high doses of caffeine (100–200 milligrams per tablet). (Caffeine and its pharmacological and abuse properties are discussed at length in Chapter 10.) Although it is true that CNS stimulation by ingesting significant doses of caffeine can increase the state of alertness during periods of drowsiness, the repeated use of such an approach is highly suspect.

For example, college students sometimes rely on such products to repeatedly enhance mental endurance during cramming sessions for examinations. In fact, at one western U.S. university, the back page of a quarterly class schedule, printed and distributed by the university, included a full-page advertisement for the OTC stimulant Vivarin with the caption, "Exam Survival Kit." The implications of such promotions are obvious and disturbing. Due to the objections of the faculty, the advertisement was not run again at the university.

Routine use of stay-awake or energy-promoting products to enhance performance at work or in school can lead to dependence, resulting in withdrawal when the person stops using the drug. Most health professionals agree that there are more effective and safer ways to deal with fatigue and drowsiness—for example, managing time efficiently and getting plenty of rest (Anderson and Nykamp 2006).

Sympathomimetics

Mild OTC sympathomimetics have been marketed as safe stimulants and as legal alternatives to cocaine and other illicit stimulants (Associated Press 2003). The principal ingredients found in the mild stimulants are drugs such as phenylephrine and caffeine. The same drugs are also found in OTC decongestants and diet aids (Scolaro 2006). Ephedrine, a naturally occurring stimulant (i.e., in the ephedra plant) was withdrawn from OTC use due to its potential toxicity on the cardiovascular system (FDA 2004).

Although much less potent than amphetamines, when used in high doses, the OTC stimulants can cause anxiety, restlessness, throbbing headaches, breathing problems, and tachycardia (rapid heartbeat). There have been reports of death due to heart arrhythmia, cerebral hemorrhaging, and strokes, as discussed earlier from excessive ephedrine use (see Chapter 10).

Gastrointestinal Medications

The gastrointestinal (GI) system consists principally of the esophagus, stomach, and intestines and is responsible for the absorption of nutrients and water into the body, as well as the elimination of body wastes. The function of the GI system can be altered by changes in eating habits, stress, infection, and diseases such as ulcers and cancers. Such problems may affect appetite, cause discomfort or pain, result in nausea and vomiting, and alter the formation and passage of stools from the intestines.

A variety of OTC medications are available to treat GI disorders such as indigestion (antacids), heartburn (gastric secretion blockers), constipation (laxatives), and diarrhea (antidiarrheals) (Curry and Butler 2006; Walker 2006; Zweber and Berardi 2006). However, before individuals self-medicate with nonprescription drugs, they should be certain that the cause of their GI problem is minor, is self-limiting, and does not require professional care. Because antacids are the most frequently used of the GI nonprescription drugs, they are discussed next.

More than $1 billion is spent each year on antacid products such as this in the United States.

Antacids and Antiheartburn Medication

More than $1 billion is spent annually on antacid preparations that claim to give relief from heartburn and indigestion caused by excessive eating or drinking and to provide long-term treatment of chronic peptic ulcer disease. It is estimated that as much as 50% of the population has had one or more attacks of **gastritis**, often referred to as "acid indigestion, heartburn, upset stomach, and sour or acid stomach." These attacks are often due to acid rebound, occurring 1 to 2 hours after eating; by this time, the stomach contents have passed into the small intestine, leaving the gastric acids to irritate or damage the lining of the empty stomach. Heartburn, or gastroesophageal reflux, occurs after exposure of the lower esophagus to these very irritating gastric chemicals.

Some cases of severe, chronic acid indigestion may progress to peptic ulcer disease. Peptic ulcers (open sores) most frequently affect the duodenum (first part of the intestine) and the stomach. Although this condition is serious, it can be treated effectively with antacids, which are often combined with drugs available OTC or by prescription such as cimetidine (Tagamet), ranitidine (Zantac), and famotidine (Pepcid). A person with acute, severe stomach pain; chronic gastritis; blood in the stools (common ulcer symptoms); diarrhea; or vomiting should see a physician promptly and should not attempt to self-medicate with OTC antacids (Zweber and Berardi 2006).

Most bouts of acid rebound, however, are associated with overeating or consuming irritating foods or drinks; these self-limiting cases can usually be managed safely with OTC antacids (such as sodium bicarbonate, calcium carbonate, aluminum salts, and magnesium salts). Because of their alkaline (opposite of acidic) nature, the nonprescription products neutralize gastric acids and give relief.

Generally speaking, OTC antacid preparations are safe for occasional use at low recommended doses, but excessive use can cause serious problems. In addition, all antacids can interact with other drugs; they may alter the GI absorption or renal elimination of other medications. For example, some antacids inhibit the absorption of tetracy-cline antibiotics; thus, these products should not be taken at the same time. Consequently, patients using prescription drugs should consult with their physicians before taking OTC antacids (Zweber and Berardi 2006).

Heartburn can be treated effectively with low doses of Tagamet, Zantac, or Pepcid. These drugs were switched to OTC status in the mid-1990s and help reduce gastric secretions (Zweber and Berardi 2006).

Diet Aids

In U.S. society, being slim and trim are prerequisites to being attractive. It is estimated that approximately 34% of the people in the United States are obese (body fat in excess of 20% of normal) and 50% are overweight (Crespo and Arbesman 2003; Today Health Info 2011). Being obese has been linked to cardiovascular disease, some cancers, diabetes, chronic fatigue, and an array of aches and pains, not to mention psychological disorders such as depression (Miller and Bartels 2006). Popular remedies for losing weight often include fad diets advertised in supermarket journals, expensive weight loss programs, or both prescription and OTC diet aids.

Using drugs as diet aids is highly controversial (Miller and Bartels 2006). Most experts view them as useless or even dangerous. These drugs are supposed to depress the appetite, which helps users maintain low-calorie diets. The most effective of these agents are called **anorexiants**. Potent anorexi-

Approximately 34% of the people in the United States are obese and 50% are overweight.

ants, such as amphetamine-like drugs (including the once-popular diet aid, Phen-fen), can cause dangerous side effects (see Chapter 10) and are available only by prescription. The appetite suppression effects of prescription anorexiants are usually temporary, after which tolerance often builds. Thus, even prescription diet aid drugs are usually effective for only a short period. There are no wonder drugs to help the obese lose weight permanently.

The most potent and most frequently used OTC diet aid ingredients were the sympathomimetic drugs phenylpropanolamine and ephedrine, but several years ago the FDA removed both drugs from all OTC products (UMassMemorial Health Care 2010). The current OTC diet aids are minimally effective and of no value in the treatment of significant obesity; they typically contain high doses of caffeine and sometimes natural ingredients such as "bitter orange," which contains the mild sympathomimetic, synephrine. Despite their questionable value, frequent use of high doses of the OTC diet aid products is a common practice by weight-conscious female high school and college students. As one college sophomore who routinely carried a package of Dexatrim in her purse said, "Popping two or three of these before an important date helps me to eat like a bird and appear more petite" (personal communication to Hanson). Interestingly, this same woman also occasionally induced vomiting after eating because of her fear that she was gaining weight. Such weight-management practices are extremely worrisome and may be part of strategies of young people suffering from eating disorders such as anorexia and bulimia (Life Challenges 2010).

Skin Products

Because the skin is so accessible and readily visible, most people are sensitive about its appearance. These cosmetic concerns are motivated by attempts to look good and preserve youth. Almost 5% of the population in the United States have a chronic skin problem; many others suffer from seasonal or acute skin disorders (Scott and Martin 2006). Only a few of the most commonly used products are mentioned here: acne medications, sun products, and basic first-aid products.

Acne Medications

Acne is the most common skin disorder that affects adolescents (Foster and Coffrey 2006) and typically occurs during puberty in response to the secretion of the male hormone androgen (both males and females have this hormone; Foster and Coffrey

2006). Acne is usually chronic inflammation caused by bacteria trapped in plugged sebaceous (oil) glands and hair follicles. This condition consists of whiteheads, pimples, nodules, and, in more severe cases, pustules, cysts, and abscesses. Moderate to severe acne can cause unsightly scarring on the face, back, chest, and arms and should be treated aggressively by a dermatologist with drugs such as antibiotics (tetracycline) and potent **keratolytics**, such as Retin-A (retinoic acid) or vitamin A, or Accutane (isotretinoin). Usually, minor to moderate acne does not cause scarring or permanent skin damage and often can be safely self-medicated with OTC acne medications (Foster and Coffrey 2006).

Several nonprescription approaches to treating mild acne are available, including the following:

- *Sebum removal:* Oil and fatty chemicals (sebum) can accumulate on the skin and plug the sebaceous glands and hair follicles. Use of OTC products such as alcohol wipes (e.g., Stri-Dex) can help remove such accumulations.
- *Peeling agents:* The FDA found several keratolytic agents safe and effective for treatment of minor acne: benzoyl peroxide (Oxy 5 and Oxy 10), salicylic acid (Oxy Clean Medicated Pads), resorcinol, and sulfur (Liquimat Lotion), alone or in combination. These drugs help to prevent acne eruption by causing the **keratin layer** of the skin to peel or by killing the bacteria that cause inflammation associated with acne. If multiple concentrations of a keratolytic are available (such as Oxy 5 and Oxy 10 Advanced Formula), it is better to start with a lower concentration and move up to the higher one, allowing the skin to become accustomed to the caustic action of these products. The initial exposure may worsen the appearance of acne temporarily; however, with continual use, the acne usually improves.

Sun Products

The damaging effects of sun exposure on the skin have been well publicized in recent years. It is now clear that the ultraviolet (UV) rays associated with sunlight have several adverse effects on the skin. It has been demonstrated that almost 1 million cases

KEY TERMS

keratolytics
caustic agents that cause the keratin skin layer to peel

keratin layer
outermost protective layer of the skin

of skin cancer each year occur in the United States, most of which are a direct consequence of exposure to UV rays and cause cumulative skin damage throughout our lives (Carroll and Crosby 2006). Almost 10,000 deaths occur from skin cancer each year, most of which are melanomas (American Cancer Society 2011).

The majority of cases will be cancers of skin cells called basal cell or squamous cell carcinomas (Carroll and Crosby 2006). These cancers usually are easily removed by minor surgery, and patients have a good prognosis for recovery. About 0.5% of the population will suffer a much more deadly form of skin cancer called *melanoma*. Melanomas are cancers of the pigment-forming cells of the skin, called *melanocytes,* and spread rapidly from the skin throughout the body, causing death in 20% to 25% of patients (Carroll and Crosby 2006).

Another long-term concern related to UV exposure is premature aging. Skin frequently exposed to UV rays, such as during routine tanning, experiences deterioration associated with the aging process. Elastin and collagen fibers are damaged, causing a loss of pliability and elasticity in the skin and resulting in a leathery, wrinkled appearance (Carroll and Crosby 2006).

Because of these damaging effects of sun exposure, an array of protective sunscreen products are available OTC. Most sunscreens are formulated to screen out the shorter UVB rays. These products have deliberately been designed to allow passage, in varying degrees, of the UVA rays because researchers once thought that these longer rays would help skin to tan without causing damage. Now it appears scientists were mistaken. Due to their deep penetration in the skin, UVA rays likely contribute to melanoma as well as chronic skin damage, causing skin to wrinkle, sag, and lose tone (Carroll and Crosby 2006).

The protection afforded by sunscreens is designated by an **SPF (sun protection factor) number**. This designation tells users the relative length of time they can stay in the sun before burning, and includes ratings of 2 to 11 (minimum), 12 to 30 (moderate), and greater than 30 (high) (Carroll and Crosby 2006). For example, proper application of a product with an SPF of 10 allows users to remain in the sun without burning 10 times longer than if it was not applied. It is important to remember that the SPF designation does not indicate protection against UVA rays. Although there currently is no convenient rating system to assess UVA screening, products with SPF ratings of 15 or greater usually offer some protection against the longer UV radiation. In addition, a compound called *avobenzone* appears to offer the fullest protection against UVA rays (Carroll and Crosby 2006). Because the natural pigment in the skin affords some UV protection, people with fair complexions (less skin pigmentation) require products with higher SPF numbers than do dark-skinned people.

People who want complete protection from UVB exposure can use OTC sunblockers, which prevent any tanning. Sunscreen ingredients in high concentrations essentially become sunblockers. In addition, an opaque zinc oxide ointment is a highly effective and inexpensive sun-blocking product and is available OTC.

Skin First-Aid Products

A variety of unrelated OTC drugs are available as first-aid products for the self-treatment of minor skin problems (Bowman 2006). Included in this category of agents are the following products:

- Local anesthetics, such as benzocaine (e.g., Dermoplast) to relieve the discomfort and pain of burns or trauma
- Antibiotics and antiseptics, such as bacitracin (Polysporin), neomycin (Neosporin), betadine, and tincture of iodine to treat or prevent skin infections
- Antihistamines (Benadryl) or corticosteroids (hydrocortisone [Cortaid]) to relieve itching or inflammation associated with skin rashes, allergies, or insect bites

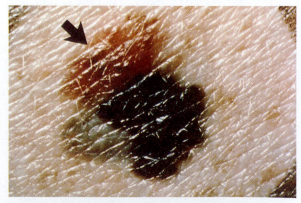

This skin cancer is melanoma and is caused by excessive exposure to ultraviolet light.

These first-aid skin products can be effective when used properly. In general, side effects to such topical products are few and minor when they occur.

■ OTC Herbal (Natural) Products

There are over 5000 brands of herbal medicines currently available in the United States and other countries with approximately 1000 active ingredients (National Library of Medicine 2010). Herbal products are a unique category of OTC remedies that account for almost $5 billion a year in U.S. sales (Nutraceuticals World 2011). They are unique because, despite the presence of active ingredients, there is little or no federal regulation due to a 1994 law, supported by the dietary supplement industry, called the Dietary Supplement Health and Education Act (National Library of Medicine 2010). This law requires the government to demonstrate that substances in the herbal products are harmful before such products can be removed from the market; the burden of proof lies with the FDA, not the manufacturer (Bernstein and Rickert 2006).

This act also (1) makes the manufacturer responsible for its product's safety; (2) explains how product literature is used for product promotion; and (3) describes what can be included on labels. Due to these regulations, manufacturers cannot use terms such as *diagnose, treat, prevent,* or *cure* to describe their herbal products. Companies can, however, make claims about affecting body function. For example, manufacturers of glucosamine cannot claim their product helps cure arthritis, but they can say products with glucosamine help the joints function better (National Library of Medicine 2010). Because of the lack of regulation, these products often are not scientifically tested, and they vary considerably in both the quantity and quality of active ingredients (National Library of Medicine 2010). Herbal products have been viewed with considerable skepticism by many experts who argue that "assertions, speculation and testimonials do not substitute for evidence" when it comes to establishing the value of a drug (McQueen and Hume 2006).

In the past few years, some changes in attitude toward herbal products have occurred. More people, including a few traditional health professionals, believe that some herbs may be useful in the treatment of minor health problems (McQueen and Hume 2006). However, physicians are typically not taught about herbal medicines in medical school and are generally perceived as ignorant about herbal products and know little about their therapeutic value or

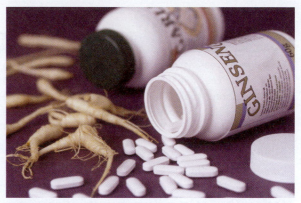

Herbal products have become very popular and are widely accepted.

their ability to interact with prescribed drugs (Medical News Today 2010). Despite greater acceptance, the fact that most people who use herbs to treat medical conditions still consider prescription drugs to be considerably more effective suggests there exists persistent skepticism regarding these products, even among consumers (*Consumer Reports* 2000).

Frequent uses of herbal products include treatment of anxiety, chronic fatigue, arthritis, and digestive problems (Hume and Strong 2006). Another common use of these natural products is to elevate mood. The most popular herbs for these purposes are St. John's wort, S-adenosylmethionine (SAM-e), and kava kava (Hume and Strong 2006; Williams et al. 2005) (see "Here and Now: Herbal Options"). It is generally thought that although these products do have some effect in the treatment of minor to moderate depression and anxiety, there is no evidence they elevate a normal, undisturbed mood or that they are particularly effective against severe mood disturbances (National Center for Complementary and Alternative Medicine [NCCAM] 2010). A major risk of self-administering these remedies for mood disorders is that some of the people self-treating their depression are severely emotionally unstable. Overall, depression leads to approximately 20,000 suicides in this country each year. Another considerable problem of self-medicating with herbal products for mood disorders is the lack of standardization for these substances. A recent survey revealed that the actual amount of active SAM-e per pill in products claiming to contain 200 mg active ingredient ranged from 80 to 250 mg. For these reasons, it is almost universally recommended that patients with serious emotional disturbances, especially depression, be diagnosed by a mental health professional even though some of these professionals may

Here and Now

Herbal Options

With the increasing popularity of herbal products, an array of choices have become available for dealing with many common, usually self-limiting health problems. The following is a list of some of the most popular of these medicinal herbs.

Echinacea

Common Claim: Stimulates immune system and helps fight infections.

Common Use: Reduce cold symptoms and help accelerate recovery.

Effectiveness: May shorten duration of cold, but does not prevent it; however, even this is controversial.

Concerns: Relatively well tolerated, but fatigue and sleepiness occasionally occur.

Garlic

Common Claim: Inhibits production of cholesterol and reduces blood sugar.

Common Use: Treat diabetes and prevent cardiovascular disease.

Effectiveness: Most studies do not find garlic effective against serious diseases.

Concerns: Mild stomach discomfort and possible interaction with blood-thinning (anticlotting) prescription drugs occur.

Ginkgo Biloba

Common Claim: Improves memory.

Common Use: Often promoted to enhance memory for patients with Alzheimer's disease.

Effectiveness: At best helps to prevent some mental decline in Alzheimer's patients but does not appear to reverse memory loss or help normal or age-related memory losses.

Concerns: Can interact with blood-thinning medications such as aspirin.

Glucosamine and Chondroitin

Common Claim: Contributes to joint strength.

Common Use: Relieve the discomfort of arthritis.

Effectiveness: Provides moderate relief from the pain of arthritis and may help to slow progress of the disease.

Concerns: May interact with blood thinners and adversely affect adult-onset diabetes.

Saw Palmetto

Common Claim: Relieves discomforts associated with prostate gland.

Common Use: Shrink enlarged prostate and facilitate urination.

Effectiveness: Provides relief for most men within a month of use.

Concerns: Well tolerated by most men.

SAM-e

Common Claim: Helps regulate brain transmitters such as dopamine.

Common Use: Relieve symptoms of depression.

Effectiveness: Some evidence that it relieves moderate depression.

Concerns: Side effects are typically mild, such as stomach upset, insomnia, and nervousness. Can be very expensive, ranging from $55 to $260 per month.

St. John's Wort

Common Claim: Elevates mood.

Common Use: To treat mild to moderate depression.

Effectiveness: Appears to relieve some cases of mild depression for the short term.

Concerns: Recent alert from the FDA warns about interactions with numerous medications, such as birth-control pills and other antidepressants.

Ginseng

Common Claim: Increases energy.

Common Use: Treat fatigue and enhance performance.

Effectiveness: There may be some mild stimulation, but there is no evidence of enhanced performance.

Concerns: Well tolerated for the most part, although there are some reports of minor addiction.

Source: Hume, A., and K. Strong. "Botanical Medicines." In *Handbook of Nonprescription Drugs*, 15th ed., edited by I. Bernardi, 1103–1136. Washington DC: American Pharmacists Association, 2006; and National Center for Complementary and Alternative Medicine (NCCAM). "Herbs at a Glance." 2010. Available at: http://nccam.nih.gov/health/herbsataglance.htm. Accessed March 29, 2011.

find use of the natural products to be acceptable for treatment of mild emotional problems.

Other concerns with herbal products include the possibility of interaction with other OTC and prescription medications, especially in the elderly population (NCCAM 2010). This is becoming more problematic as the routine use of herbs becomes common, especially because unscrupulous manufacturers may deceive customers into thinking that these products are perfectly safe and do not really contain any drugs but "only natural ingredients." Products containing herbs such as garlic, ginkgo biloba, ephedra, and ginseng have been shown to interact with some drugs (Fugh-Berman 2000). A notable example of drug interactions has been reported with St. John's wort and kava, which increase the metabolism and inactivate drugs used to treat heart failure, asthma, infections, or blood clots (Fugh-Berman 2000; Hume and Strong 2006).

Finally, lack of regulation has encouraged such a lackadaisical attitude concerning herbs that their use has been trivialized to the extent that they and their associated active drugs are now being included in foods and marketed in both health-food stores and supermarkets. Recent snacks, cereals, and beverages spiked with medicinal herbs include ginseng ginger ale, kava kava corn chips, echinacea fruit drinks, and ginkgo-biloba chocolate bars. These products, sometimes referred to as "functional foods," are typically packaged in colorful containers with cartoon figures that are likely to appeal to kids and accompanied by subtle suggestive promotions implying that they can "support emotional and mental balance." The exact quantities of herbal substances added to such food and snack products and their actual effects (if any) are difficult to monitor. Although concerned, regulatory agencies are uncertain as to how to deal with the potential problems associated with this marketing strategy (Brophy and Schardt 2010).

Herbals and Abuse

Despite the lack of governmental control, drugs found naturally in plants or herbs can have serious side effects or can be abused. In fact, some of the most powerful substances of abuse are extracted from plants, including drugs such as cocaine (*Erythroxylum coca*), marijuana (*Cannabis sativa*), peyote (*Lophophora williamsii*), and tobacco (*Nicotiana tabacum*). Because these substances are reviewed elsewhere in this book, they will not be discussed further here; they are mentioned to emphasize the point that being associated with herbs and natural products does not exclude a drug from being abused. Of concern in this section are unregulated herbal prod-

ucts and their potential for abuse and addiction. As a general rule, if a substance (including a natural product) elevates mood, causes a feeling of energy, or brings on a feeling of relaxation and relief from stress, it likely has potential for abuse. Based on these principles, the herbal products most likely to be abused include those containing ma huang, ginseng, kava kava, and ephedrine (NCCAM 2010). Of course, with addiction typically comes high-quantity use and a greater chance of serious side effects. Even though serious abuse of herbal products is possible, it does not occur frequently and, when it does occur, it is generally relatively easy to treat.

Prescription Drugs

The Durham-Humphrey Amendment of 1951 established the criteria that are still used today to determine whether a drug should be used only under the direction of a licensed health professional, such as a physician. According to this piece of legislation, drugs are controlled with prescriptions if they are (1) habit-forming, (2) not safe for self-medication, (3) intended to treat ailments that require the supervision of a health professional, or (4) new and without an established safe track record. Currently more than 10,000 prescription products are sold in the United States, representing approximately 1500 different drugs, with 20 to 50 new medications approved each year by the FDA (Borgsdorf 2007; KFF 2010). In 2009, 3.9 billion drug prescriptions were written at a cost of about $300 billion; this cost is expected to rise to $400 billion by 2014 (Bartholow 2010; KFF 2010). With statistics like these it is not surprising that the United States leads the world in prescription drug consumption on a per capita basis (Hanson 2010).

Because of their specialized training, physicians, dentists, and, under certain conditions, podiatrists, physician assistants, nurse practitioners, pharmacists, and optometrists are granted drug-prescribing privileges. The health professionals who write prescriptions are expected to accurately diagnose medical conditions requiring therapy, consider the benefits and risks of drug treatment for the patient, and identify the best drug and safest manner of administering it. The responsibility of the health professional does not conclude with the writing of a prescription; in many ways, it only just begins. Professional monitoring to ensure proper drug use and to evaluate the patient's response is crucial for successful therapy.

■ Prescription Drug Abuse

Daniel had been sober for 1 1/2 years, and his parents thought he had finally got his addiction to painkiller prescription drugs under control after multiple attempts at treatment. But for no apparent reason, his drug problems all came back and spiraled out of control. Daniel, a well-liked former hockey player, died at his best friend's house after overdosing on OxyContin and cocaine. "We heard that he had told his girlfriend that he wanted to start again and turn his life around, and that night he overdosed," said his mother (Thomas 2010).

In many places, abuse of prescription drugs is a greater problem than use of illicit drugs (Burke 2007). This is supported by the following:

- Overdoses of painkillers are causing more deaths than heroin and cocaine use combined (Thomas 2010).
- There has been a four-fold increase in admissions for treatment of persons addicted to prescription drugs in the past 10 years (Thomas 2010).
- There has been a doubling of emergency department visits for nonmedical use of prescription opioid analgesics (Quest Diagnostics 2010); specifically, in 2004, 627,000 persons went to emergency rooms due to problems with pharmaceutical drugs, compared to 1.2 million in 2009 (Goodnough 2011).
- In the past 5 years there has been an approximate 50% increase in U.S. workers and job applicants who tested positive for prescription opiates in their urine (Quest Diagnostics 2010).
- Although most people take their medicines as prescribed by their healthcare providers, it is now estimated that 20% of people in the United States have used prescription drugs for nonmedical reasons (MedlinePlus 2010).
- It is estimated that one-fifth of U.S. college students are taking prescription drugs to either get high or enhance their academic performance (Freundlich 2010).
- One in five teens has abused prescription drugs, and every day an additional 4000 teens abuse these drugs for the first time (TransWorldNews 2010).

The three classes of prescription drugs most likely to be abused, in order of their abuse frequency, are narcotic analgesics, CNS depressants, and stimulants (used to treat obesity and attention-deficit hyperactivity disorder [ADHD]). Particularly troubling is what appears to be an exploding epidemic of abusing prescription narcotic painkilling drugs such as OxyContin and Vicodin (Freundlich 2010; Johnston et al. 2010). Headlines announcing a celebrity seeking treatment for dependence on, or even death because of, these drugs are becoming disturbingly routine (Moscatello 2010; Rosen-Cohen 2010). In fact, as mentioned earlier, abuse of prescription narcotics appears to be the leading problem with prescription drugs (Preda 2011). Often young people abuse a combination of these prescribed drugs, and their sources include the medicine cabinets in their parents' or friends' homes or the Internet from "web pharmacies" that do not require legitimate prescriptions (Thomas 2010). This is a problem with youth and adults from all backgrounds (Kaus 2010). For example, Wade Juracek, mayor of the town of Gregory, personally became acquainted with the dangers of prescription drugs. While taking painkillers to treat an intestinal inflammatory disease, Wade developed an addiction to narcotic analgesics that caused him to ingest up to 100 Vicodin pills daily. His dependence led to numerous illegal activities and his conviction on three felony counts that included drug theft, misrepresentation, and prescription forgery. After getting clean and sober, Wade has shared his story with many audiences to help educate about the unexpected nature of prescription addictions. Wade tells others, "I think when people think of an addict, they think of some junkie lying in the streets or somebody shooting up. It can happen to anybody. There are lawyers, doctors, pastors, and priests that struggle (with this problem)" (Kaus 2010).

In order to deal with this escalating problem, it is important to determine why nonmedical prescription drug abuse occurs. Although there are many general and personal explanations for taking medications that were not prescribed for you, the most frequent are as follows (McCabe, Boyd, and Teter 2009):

- Thirteen percent abuse the prescription drugs for recreation, usually to get high or to try to feel better.
- Thirty-nine percent try to self-medicate a preexisting medical/emotional problem with someone else's prescription medication (e.g., use a benzodiazepine to relieve anxiety).
- Forty-eight percent have elements of both explanations 1 and 2.
- Prescription abuse is part of a bigger picture of substance abuse that includes the abuse of other drugs (both licit and illicit). One drug may be used to either embellish or relieve withdrawal

from another drug of abuse (e.g., benzo-diazepines taken to relieve the withdrawal from alcohol) (DiGravio 2010).

- Use of prescribed syringes (for insulin injections) can provide a source of fresh, clean needles for injecting drugs of abuse.

Dealing with suspected abuse of prescription medication can pose a difficult management problem for physicians and pharmacists. It has become such a major issue that some third-party payers (that is, health insurance companies) have implemented tight monitoring procedures. Those who try to fraudulently obtain controlled substances with valid and invalid prescriptions include persons from all walks of life.

In the United States, young people frequently abuse prescription drugs. A recent trend is called "pharm parties," where high school students get together and try to get high on a mixture of prescription drugs followed by a chaser of alcohol (WIXT/WSYR 2007) (see "Here and Now: Pharm Parties and Russian Roulette"). However, young people rarely obtain the drugs by theft, fraud, or doctor shopping, although occasionally unscrupulous doctors will write prescriptions without questions for money (Reavy 2007). Instead, they usually obtain their prescription drugs from peers, friends, or family members or sometimes purchase them from rogue Internet pharmacies. In some areas, the problem is so severe that high schools have implemented programs to prevent such sharing. Abusers of prescription drugs often have multiple addictions, including dependence on caffeine, alcohol, or nicotine. In addition, once a pharmacy is recognized as an easy target, word spreads and other abusers often begin to frequent the same store. Signs of patients with drug-seeking behavior include the following:

- Use of altered or forged prescriptions
- Claims that a prescription has been lost and a physician is unavailable for confirmation
- Frequent visits to emergency rooms or clinics for poorly defined health problems
- Visits made to a pharmacy late in the day, on weekends, or just before closing

Here and Now

Pharm Parties and Russian Roulette

One expression of prescription abuse is seen with high school students who bring samples of prescription drugs from home and dump them into a common bowl. The teens then grab a handful and pop them into their mouths like trail mix and swallow. The objective is to try to produce bizarre feelings and unusual highs. The mixtures often include medications such as antidepressants, stimulants, sleeping pills, antianxiety drugs, and narcotic pain relievers. One doctor described the activity as "Russian roulette," only with pills instead of bullets. The source of the drugs are often parents' or grandparents' medicine cabinets that frequently are filled with years of drug accumulation. For example, one 15-year-old said he wanted to be "cool" and told his friends that he could get some Percocets out of his stepdad's bottle. He explained that his stepdad had undergone many surgeries, so he had a lot of pills. The young man explained that the pills went down quick and the smooth buzz was free and everyone thought it was safe. Soon other friends joined the group and each would bring medicines from their own homes—a little Vicodin here, some OxyContin there, usually with some whiskey and vodka to wash it down. As word got around, other friends joined the "cool" group and more prescription drugs were pooled and the activity had escalated into a "pharm party." While at first everything seemed innocent and fun, the group soon learned that use of high quantities and mixed assortments of drugs that belong to someone else can be disastrous and even deadly.

Source: WIXT/WSYR, TV ABC 9. "Pharm Parties. Popping Prescriptions." Syracuse. 18 May 2007; and Fagan, K. "'Pharma Parties' A Troubling Trend Among Youths." *San Francisco Chronicle.* 16 March 2010. Available at: http://articles.sfgate.com/2010-03-4/news/18835066_1_parents-medicine-calls-pharma. Accessed March 29, 2011.

- Alteration of doses on a legitimate prescription
- Loud, abusive, and insulting behavior
- Use of several names
- Being particularly knowledgeable about drugs

■ Necessary Drug Information for Healthcare Providers

Many unnecessary side effects and delays in proper care are caused by poor communication between the health professional and the patient or a lack of a doctor's knowledge concerning the patient's medical history when a drug is prescribed. The smaller a drug's margin of safety (the difference between therapeutic and toxic doses), the more critical it becomes that the doctor has all relevant information regarding the patient's medical needs and vulnerabilities. The following is a brief overview of principles to help ensure that the health professional has the necessary information to properly prescribe and manage drug use for the patient.

Doctor–patient communication must be reciprocal. We tend to think that patients listen while doctors talk when it comes to deciding on the best medication for treatment. To ensure a proper diagnosis, precise and complete information from the patient is also essential. In fact, if a doctor is to select the best and safest drug for a patient, he or she needs to know everything possible about the medical problems to be treated. In addition, the patient should provide the doctor with a complete medical and drug history, particularly if there has been a problem with the patient's cardiovascular system, kidneys, liver, or mental functions. Other information that should be shared with the doctor includes previous drug reactions as well as a complete list of drugs routinely being used, including prescription, nonprescription, and herbal products. In this regard, more and more states are establishing database systems that include up-to-date information concerning prescription drug histories that allow monitoring of what has been prescribed and dispensed to individual patients. Currently more than 40 states have passed legislation authorizing, and in some cases mandating, such programs, but making these databases real-time can be extremely expensive and must adequately address issues such as patient confidentiality. However, it is expected that eventually there will be a nationwide program that allows pharmacies, doctors, and other medical personnel to contribute to and access information from the prescription drug history of their patients

To maximize benefit and minimize risk, there must be proper doctor–patient communication.

in order to avoid dangerous and unnecessary prescribing practices and to be aware of potential prescription abuse problems (Risling 2010).

The patient needs to be educated about proper drug use. If the doctor does not volunteer this information, the patient should insist on answers to the following questions:

- *What is being treated?* This question does not require a long, unintelligible scientific answer. It should include an easy-to-understand explanation of the medical problem.
- *What is the desired outcome?* The patient should know why the drug is prescribed and what the drug treatment is intended to accomplish. It is difficult for the patient to become involved in therapy if he or she is not aware of its objectives.
- *What are the possible side effects of the drug?* This answer does not necessitate an exhaustive list of every adverse reaction ever recorded in the medical literature; however, it is important to realize that adverse drug reactions to prescription drugs are very common. In the United States, more people die from adverse reactions to legal medications than succumb to all illegal drug use. It is estimated that approximately 20,000 people die while another 2.1 million are seriously injured in this country each year from reactions to legal medications (Whitney 2007). In general, if adverse reactions occur in more than 1% of users, this should be mentioned to the patient. In addition, the patient should be made aware of ways to minimize the

Here and Now

OBRA '90: The Evolving Role of Pharmacists in Drug Management

In 1990, the U.S. Congress passed section 4401 of the Omnibus Budget Reconciliation Act (commonly referred to as OBRA '90), which substantially altered the role of pharmacists in drug management. This act designated the pharmacist as the key player in improving the quality of drug care for patients in this country. Because OBRA '90 is federal legislation, it can require drug-related services for Medicare patients only; however, most states have recognized that similar services should be made available to all patients and have enacted legislation to that end. OBRA '90 requires pharmacists to conduct a drug use review (DUR) for each prescription to improve the outcome of drug therapy and reduce adverse side effects. The DUR program describes four basic professional services that a pharmacist must render whenever a drug prescription is filled:

1. Prescriptions and patients' records must be screened to avoid problems caused by drug duplications, adverse drug–drug interactions, medical complications, incorrect drug doses, and incorrect duration of drug treatment.

2. Patients should be counseled regarding the following:
   - How to safely and effectively administer the drug
   - Common adverse effects and interactions with other drugs, food, and so forth
   - How to avoid problems with the drug
   - How to monitor the progress of drug therapy
   - How to store the drug properly
   - Whether a refill is intended
   - What to do if a dose is missed

3. Patient profiles, including information on disease, a list of medications, and the pharmacist's comments relevant to drug therapy, must be maintained. This information should be stored in computer files for future reference.

4. Documentation must record if the patient refuses consultation from the pharmacist, or if a potential drug therapy problem is identified and the patient is warned.

Note: In 2011, the OBRA '90 act was still being enforced.

Source: Abood, R. "OBRA '90: Implementation and Enforcement." *NABP U.S. Pharmacists, State Boards—A Continuing Education Series.* Park Ridge, IL: National Association of Pharmacy, 1992.

---

occurrence of side effects (e.g., an irritating drug should not be taken on an empty stomach, to minimize nausea) as well as what to do if a side effect occurs (e.g., if a rash occurs, call the doctor immediately).

- *How should the drug be taken to minimize problems and maximize benefits?* This answer should include details on how much, how often, and how long the drug should be taken.

Although it is a health professional's legal and professional obligation to communicate this information, patients frequently leave the doctor's office with a prescription that gives them legal permission to use a drug but without the knowledge of how to use it properly. Because of this all-too-common problem, pharmacists have been mandated by legislation referred to as the Omnibus Budget Reconciliation Act of 1990 to provide the necessary information to patients on proper drug use (Warholak-Juarez et al. 2000; Zak 1993) (see "Here and Now: OBRA '90"). Patients should be encouraged to ask questions of those who write and fill prescriptions.

■ Drug Selection: Generic Versus Proprietary

Although it is the primary responsibility of the doctor or healthcare provider to decide which drug is most suitable for a treatment, often an inexpensive choice can be as effective and safe as a more costly option. This statement frequently is true when choosing between generic and proprietary drugs. The term **generic** refers to the common name of a drug that is not subject to trademark rights; in contrast, **proprietary** denotes medications marketed under specific brand names. For example, diazepam is the generic designation for the proprietary name Valium. Often, the most common proprietary name

KEY TERMS

generic
official, nonpatented, nonproprietary name of a drug

proprietary
brand or trademark name that is registered with the U.S. Patent Office

associated with a drug is the name given when it is initially released for marketing. Because such drugs are almost always covered by patent restrictions for several years when first sold to the public, they become identified with their first proprietary names. After the patent lapses, the same drug often is also marketed by its less-known generic designation (Stoppler and Hecht 2010).

Because the pharmaceutical companies that market the generic products usually have not invested in the discovery or development of the drug, they often charge much less for their version of the medication. This situation contrasts with that of the original drug manufacturer, which may have invested as much as $0.5–1 billion for research and development (see Chapter 3). Even though the generic product frequently is less expensive, because of FDA regulations the quality is not inferior to the related proprietary drug; thus, substitution of generic for proprietary products does not compromise therapy (Stoppler and Hecht 2010).

Because of reduced cost, generic products have become very popular. Currently, generic drugs account for approximately 75% of prescriptions dispensed (Kaiser 2010), up from 57% in 2004, and they account for $74 billion in annual sales (Bartholow 2010). Due to the great demand, all states have laws that govern the use and substitution of generic drugs; unfortunately, the laws are not all the same. Some states have positive laws that require pharmacists to substitute a generic product unless the physician gives specific instructions not to do so. Other states have negative laws that forbid substitution without the physician's permission. Some physicians use convenient prescription forms with "May" or "May Not" substitution boxes that can be checked when the prescription is filled out.

■ Common Categories of Prescription Drugs

Of the approximately 10,000 different prescription drugs available in the United States, the top 50 drugs in sales account for almost 30% of all new and refilled prescriptions (RxList 2010). As an example, a list of the 25 top-selling prescription drugs in 2009 is shown in **Table 15.6**. The following includes a brief discussion of some of the more popular prescription drug groups used in the United States. This list is not intended to be all-inclusive, but gives only a sampling of common prescription products.

Analgesics

The prescription analgesics consist mainly of narcotic and NSAID types. The narcotic analgesics most often dispensed to patients by prescription are (1) codeine and hydrocodone (e.g., Lortab, Vicodin), (2) the moderate-potency agents pentazocine (e.g., Talwin) and oxycodone (e.g., Percodan), and (3) the high-potency drug meperidine (e.g., Demerol). All narcotic analgesics are scheduled drugs because of their abuse potential and are effective against most types of pain. The narcotic analgesic products are often combined with aspirin or acetaminophen (e.g., Lortab and Vicodin are combinations of hydrocodone and acetaminophen) to enhance their pain-relieving actions. These are the most likely prescription drugs to be abused and can cause severe substance dependence. For additional information about the narcotics, see Chapter 9.

The NSAIDs constitute the other major group of analgesics available by prescription. The pharmacology of these drugs is very similar to that of the OTC compound ibuprofen, discussed earlier in this chapter. These medications are used to relieve inflammatory conditions such as arthritis and are effective in relieving minor to moderate musculoskeletal pain (pain associated with body structures such as muscles, ligaments, bones, teeth, and skin). These drugs have no abuse potential and are not scheduled; several are also available OTC (see the discussion of OTC analgesics). Their principal adverse side effects include stomach irritation, kidney damage, tinnitus (ringing in the ears), dizziness, and swelling from fluid retention. Most prescription NSAIDs have similar pharmacological and side effects. Included in the group of prescription NSAIDs are ibuprofen (e.g., Motrin), naproxen (e.g., Anaprox), indomethacin (e.g., Indocin), sulindac (e.g., Clinoril), mefenamic acid (e.g., Ponstel), tolmetin (e.g., Tolectin), piroxicam (e.g., Feldene), and ketoprofen (e.g., Orudis) (*Drug Facts and Comparisons* 2010a).

Antibiotics

Drugs referred to by the layperson as "antibiotics" are more accurately described by the term *antibacterials,* although the more common term will be used here. For the most part, antibiotics are effective in treating infections caused by microorganisms classified as bacteria. Bacterial infections can occur anywhere in the body, resulting in tissue damage, loss of function, and, if untreated, ultimately death. Even though bacterial infections continue to be the

Table 15.6 **The Top 25 Prescription Drugs by U.S. Sales: 2009**

RANK	PROPRIETARY NAME	GENERIC NAME	PRINCIPAL CLINICAL USE
1	Lipitor	Atorvastatin	Reduce cholesterol
2	Nexium	Esomeprazole	Relieve ulcers
3	Plavix	Clopidogrel	Reduce clots
4	Advair Diskus	Corticosteroid	Treat asthma
5	Seroquel	Quetiapine	Antipsychotic
6	Abilify	Aripiprazole	Antipsychotic
7	Singulair	Montelukast	Treat asthma
8	Actos	Pioglitazone	Treat diabetes
9	Enbrel	Entanercept	Treat autoimmune disorders
10	Epogen	Epoetin alfa	Treat anemia
11	Remicade	Infliximab	Treat rheumatoid arthritis
12	Crestor	Rosuvastatin	Reduce cholesterol
13	Avastin	Bevacizumab	Treat cancer
14	Neulasta	Pegfilgrastim	Reduce chance of infection in patients with cancer
15	OxyContin	Oxycodone	Relieve pain
16	Cymbalta	Duloxetine	Antianxiety
17	Effexor XR	Venlafaxine	Antidepressant
18	Lexapro	Escitalopram	Antidepressant
19	Lovenox	Enoxaparin	Prevent clots
20	Zyprexa	Olanzapine	Bipolar/schizophrenia
21	Rituxan	Rituximab	Treat cancer
22	Humira	Adalimumab	Reduces swelling
23	Prevacid	Lansoprazole	Relieve ulcers
24	Aricept	Donepezil	Treat Alzheimer's disease
25	Flomax	Tamsulosin	Treat enlarged prostate

Source: Bartholow, M. "Top 200 Prescription Drugs of 2009." *Pharmacy Times.* 11 May 2010. Available at: http://www.pharmacytimes.com/issue/pharmacy/2010/May2010/RxFocusTopDrugs-0510. Accessed March 16, 2011.

most common serious diseases in the United States and throughout the world today, the vast majority of these can be cured with antibiotic treatment.

There are currently close to 100 different antibiotic drugs, which differ from one another in (1) whether they kill bacteria (*bactericidal*) or stop their growth (*bacteriostatic*), and (2) the species of bacteria that are sensitive to their antibacterial action (*Drug Facts and Comparisons* 2010a). Antibiotics that are effective against many species of bacteria are classified as broad-spectrum types, whereas those antibiotics that are relatively selective and effective against only a few species of bacteria are considered narrow-spectrum drugs.

Although most antibiotics are well tolerated by patients, they can cause very serious side effects, especially if not used properly. For example, the penicillins have a very wide margin of safety for most patients, but 5% to 10% of the population are allergic to these drugs, and life-threatening reactions can occur in sensitized patients if penicillins are used.

The most common groups of antibiotics include penicillins (e.g., amoxicillin [Amoxil, Augmentin, and Trimox]), cephalosporins (e.g., cephalexin), fluoroquinolones (e.g., ciprofloxacin [Cipro]), tetracyclines (e.g., minocycline [Minocin]), aminoglycosides (e.g., streptomycin), sulfonamides (e.g., sulfamethoxazole [Bactrim and Septra]), and macrolides (e.g., erythromycin [E-Mycin]).

Antidepressants

Severe depression is characterized by diminished interest or pleasure in normal activities accompanied by feelings of fatigue, pessimism, and guilt as well as sleep and appetite disturbances and suicidal desires (American Psychiatric Association 2000). Major depression afflicts approximately 6% to 7% of the population at any one time, and it is estimated that about 23% of the population will become severely depressed during their life (Beck and Alford 2009). This high prevalence makes depression the most common psychiatric disorder. According to the classification of the *Diagnostic and Statistical Manual of Mental Disorders* (DSM-IV-TR)

of the American Psychiatric Association, several types of depression exist, based on their origin:

- *Endogenous major depression:* A genetic disorder that can occur spontaneously and is due to transmitter imbalances in the brain
- *Depression associated with bipolar mood disorder:* That is, manic-depressive disorder
- *Reactive depression:* The most common form of depression, which is a response to situations of grief, personal loss, illness, or other very stressful situations

Antidepressant medication is typically used to treat endogenous major depression, although on occasion these drugs are used to treat other forms of depression if they are resistant to conventional therapy (Beck and Alford 2009).

Several groups of prescription antidepressant medications are approved for use in the United States (Beck and Alford 2009; *Drug Facts and Comparisons* 2010a). The most commonly used category is the **tricyclic antidepressants**. Included in this group are drugs such as amitriptyline (e.g., Elavil), imipramine (e.g., Tofranil), and nortriptyline (e.g., Pamelor). Although usually well tolerated, the tricyclic antidepressants can cause annoying side effects due to their anticholinergic activity. These adverse reactions include drowsiness, dry mouth, blurred vision, and constipation. Tolerance to these side effects usually develops with continued use.

The second group of drugs used to treat depression is referred to as the **monoamine oxidase inhibitors (MAOIs)**. Historically, these agents have been backup drugs for the tricyclic antidepressants. Because of their annoying and sometimes dangerous side effects as well as problems interacting with other drugs or even food, the MAOIs have become less popular with clinicians. These drugs can have deadly interactions with many of the stimulants of abuse such as methamphetamine, cocaine, and Ecstasy. Drugs belonging to this group include phenelzine (Nardil) and tranylcypromine (Parnate).

Agents from a third, somewhat disparate, group of antidepressants that are safer and with fewer side effects than the tricyclic or MAOI antidepressants are very popular. They include fluoxetine (Prozac), sertraline (Zoloft), paroxetine (Paxil), fluvoxamine (Luvox), bupropion (Wellbutrin), and trazodone (Desyrel). Although side effects and the margin of safety of these groups of antidepressants may differ, in general they all appear to have similar therapeutic benefits. Of this third group of antidepressants, Prozac is the best known and used to be the most frequently prescribed antidepressant; in 2003 it was

KEY TERMS

tricyclic antidepressants
most commonly used group of drugs to treat severe depression

monoamine oxidase inhibitors (MAOIs)
drugs used to treat severe depression

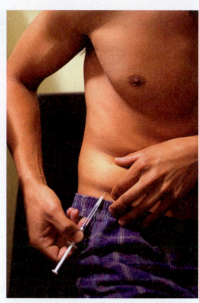

Insulin is self-administered by diabetic patients in subcutaneous injections.

the 11th most frequently prescribed drug in the United States, although by 2009 it had been replaced by other antidepressants such as Lexapro (escitalopram) (Bartholow 2010). Although most commonly used to treat depression, Prozac has also been prescribed by physicians to treat more than 30 other conditions ranging from drug addiction (although not found to be generally effective) to kleptomania. The vast majority of these uses are not proven to be effective nor are they approved by the FDA.

Antidiabetic Drugs

Diabetes mellitus is likely the leading metabolic endocrine disease in this country; it afflicts approximately 20 million people in the United States. It is the result of insufficient or ineffective activity of insulin, a hormone secreted from the pancreas (Centers for Disease Control and Prevention [CDC] 2007; Davis 2006). Due to the lack of insulin, untreated diabetics have severe problems with cellular and systemic metabolism and elevated blood sugar (called **hyperglycemia**). The two major types of diabetes are type 1 (or juvenile type) and type 2 (or adult-onset type). **Type 1 diabetes** is caused by total destruction of the insulin-producing cells in the pancreas and usually begins in juveniles, although it occasionally begins during adulthood. In contrast, **type 2 diabetes** typically occurs after age 40 and is frequently associated with obesity. Recently, however, because severe obesity is occurring more often in younger persons (about 17% of

Americans), an epidemic of type 2 diabetes has erupted in adolescents (endocrineweb 2010), making the term "adult-onset" diabetes less meaningful. In type 2 diabetes, the pancreas is able to produce insulin, but insulin receptors no longer respond normally to this hormone (Seeringer et al. 2010). In both types of diabetes mellitus, drugs are administered to restore proper insulin function.

Because of the inability to produce or release insulin in the type 1 diabetic, these patients are universally treated with subcutaneous injections of insulin one to three times per day, depending on their needs. Usually the levels of sugar (glucose) in the blood are evaluated to determine the effectiveness of treatment. Insulin products are characterized by their onset of action (either rapid or delayed onset) and duration (short to long) (*Drug Facts and Comparisons* 2010a).

The strategy for treating type 2 diabetics is somewhat different. For many of these patients, the symptoms of diabetes and problems of insufficient insulin function subside with proper diet, weight, and exercise management. If an appropriate change in lifestyle does not correct the diabetes-associated problems, drugs called **oral hypoglycemics** (meaning they are taken by mouth and lower blood sugar) are often prescribed. These drugs, which stimulate the release of additional insulin from the pancreas, include popular drugs such as rosiglitazone (Avandia). Recently, however, there have been concerns that although these drugs are effective in controlling glucose levels, some of them might increase the incidence of cardiovascular disease (FDA 2010a). If the diabetic symptoms are not adequately controlled with the oral hypoglycemic drugs, type 2 diabetics are treated with insulin injections, as are type 1

KEY TERMS

diabetes mellitus
disease caused by elevated blood sugar due to insufficient insulin

hyperglycemia
elevated blood sugar

type 1 diabetes
disease associated with complete loss of insulin-producing cells in the pancreas

type 2 diabetes
disease usually associated with obesity; does not involve a loss of insulin-producing cells

oral hypoglycemics
drugs taken by mouth to treat type 2 diabetes

patients. There has been substantial improvement in the treatment of diabetes in the past few years due to new, more selective and effective drugs that control glucose blood levels (de Beaufort et al. 2007).

Antiulcer Drugs

Peptic ulcers are sores that recur in the lining of the lower stomach (*gastric ulcer*) or most often in the upper portion of the small intestine (*duodenal ulcer*). It is apparent that secretions of gastric acids and digestive enzymes are necessary for ulcer development. Because gastric secretions are involved in developing peptic ulcers, several drug types are useful in ulcer treatment.

Antacids help to relieve acute discomfort due to ulcers by neutralizing gastric acidity. These drugs are discussed in greater detail in the OTC section of this chapter. Prescription drugs that block gastric secretion have been the mainstay of ulcer treatment. Because the endogenous chemical histamine is important in regulating gastric secretions, drugs that selectively block the activity of gastric histamine (called H_2 blockers) substantially reduce secretion of gastric acids and digestive enzymes. The very popular drugs cimetidine (Tagamet), ranitidine (Zantac), and famotidine (Pepcid) function in this manner. Because Tagamet, Zantac, and Pepcid are used so frequently, they have been switched to OTC status by the FDA—not to treat ulcers but to relieve heartburn (esophageal reflux) (FamilyDoctor 2010).

Although the exact causes of peptic ulcers are not completely understood, it is widely accepted that the bacteria *Helicobacter pylori* plays a role. Because of the involvement of these microorganisms, most clinicians treat patients with recurring ulcers with multiple antibiotics to eliminate these bacteria (National Digestive Diseases Information Clearinghouse [NDDIC] 2010).

Bronchodilators

Drugs that widen air passages (*bronchi*) facilitate breathing in patients with air passage constriction

Obesity in young children has reached epidemic status and is causing type 2 diabetes to occur at a younger age.

or obstruction. Such drugs are called **bronchodilators** and are particularly useful in relieving respiratory difficulty associated with asthma. Asthmatic patients frequently experience bouts of intense coughing, shortness of breath, tightness in the chest, and wheezing resulting in breathing difficulties. Many of the symptoms of asthma are due to an increased sensitivity of the airways to irritating substances and can result in serious asthma attacks that are life threatening if not treated promptly (Mayo Clinic 2010). Two major categories of bronchodilators are the sympathomimetics known as **β-adrenergic stimulants**—for example, isoproterenol (e.g., Isuprel) and albuterol (e.g., Proventil, Ventolin)—and xanthines (caffeine-like drugs) such as theophylline and its derivatives. These drugs relax the muscles of the air passages, cause bronchodilation, and facilitate breathing (National Heart Lung and Blood Institute [NHLBI] 2010b). In the early 1990s, some bronchial dilator medications were switched to OTC status, such as Bronkaid Mist and Primatene Mist. These contain relatively low amounts of epinephrine and are safe and effective when used for mild, intermittent disease. Typically these OTC medications should not be used by patients with cardiovascular disease (Bass 2010) and may dangerously interact with sympathomimetic stimulants of abuse such as cocaine and the amphetamines.

Cardiovascular Drugs

Cardiovascular disease has been the number one cause of death in the United States for the past several decades. Consequently, of the 25 top-selling drugs in this country, 5 are medications for diseases related to the cardiovascular system (Bartholow 2010). The following are brief discussions of the major categories of cardiovascular drugs (NHLBI 2010a).

KEY TERMS

peptic ulcers
open sores that occur in the stomach or upper segment of the small intestine

bronchodilators
drugs that widen air passages

β-adrenergic stimulants
drugs that stimulate a subtype of adrenaline and noradrenaline receptors

Antihypertensive Agents

It is estimated that about 50% of U.S. adults over the age of 60 require treatment for **hypertension** (persistent elevated high blood pressure) (Hoffman 2006). Because hypertension can result in serious damage to the heart, kidneys, and brain, this condition needs to be treated aggressively. Treatment should consist of changes in lifestyle, including exercise and diet, but usually also requires drug therapy. Two of the principal classes of antihypertensive agents are diuretics and direct vasodilators (*Drug Facts and Comparisons* 2010b; Hoffman 2006):

1. *Diuretics* lower blood pressure by eliminating sodium and excess water from the body. Included in this category is hydrochlorothiazide.
2. *Direct vasodilators* reduce blood pressure by relaxing the muscles in the walls of blood vessels that cause vasoconstriction, thereby dilating the blood vessels and decreasing their resistance to the flow of blood. Drugs included in this category are calcium-channel blockers (diltiazem [Cardizem], verapamil [Calan], nifedipine [Procardia]); inhibitors of the enzyme that synthesizes the vasoconstricting hormone, angiotensin II (enalapril [Vasotec]); and drugs that block the vasoconstricting action of the sympathetic nervous system (clonidine [Catapres] and prazosin [Minipress]).

Antianginal Agents

When the heart is deprived of sufficient blood (a condition called **ischemia**), the oxygen requirements of the cardiac muscle are not met and the breakdown of chemicals caused by the continual activity of the heart results in pain; this viselike chest pain is called **angina pectoris**. The most frequent cause of angina is obstruction of the coronary vessels (Michel 2006). Angina pectoris frequently occurs in patients with hypertension; left untreated, the underlying blockage of coronary vessels can result in heart attacks. All the drugs used to relieve or prevent angina decrease the oxygen deficit of the heart either by decreasing the amount of work required of the heart during normal functioning or by increasing the blood supply to the heart (Michel 2006). The three types of drugs prescribed for treating angina pectoris are (*Drug Facts and Comparisons* 2010b): (1) calcium-channel blockers (e.g., verapamil [Calan], diltiazem [Cardizem]); (2) nitrates and nitrites (e.g., amylnitrite [Vaporate], nitroglycerin [Transderm-Nitro]); and (3) blockers of the sympathetic nervous system, specifically classified as β-adrenergic blockers (e.g., atenolol [Tenormin], propranolol [Inderal]).

Drugs to Treat Congestive Heart Failure

When the cardiac muscle is unable to pump sufficient blood to satisfy the oxygen needs of the body, **congestive heart failure** occurs. This condition causes an enlarged heart, decreased ability to exercise, shortness of breath, and accumulation of fluid (**edema**) in the lungs and limbs (Rocco and Fang 2006). The principal treatment for congestive heart failure consists of drugs that improve the heart's efficiency, such as digoxin (Lanoxin) (*Drug Facts and Comparisons* 2010b).

Drugs that cause vasodilation are also sometimes used successfully to reduce the work required of the heart as it pumps blood through the body. Among the drugs causing vasodilation are those already discussed in conjunction with other heart conditions such as hypertension and angina pectoris (e.g., enalapril [Vasotec], captopril [Capoten]).

Cholesterol- and Lipid-Lowering Drugs

Cholesterol and some types of fatty (*lipid*) molecules can accumulate in the walls of arteries and narrow the openings of these blood vessels. Such arterial changes cause hypertension, heart attacks, strokes, and heart failure and are the leading cause of death in the United States, costing about $316 billion annually (CDC 2010; Mahley and Bersot 2006). These health problems can often be avoided by adopting a lifestyle that includes a low-fat and low-cholesterol diet combined with regular, appropriate exercise. However, sometimes lifestyle changes are insufficient; in such cases, cholesterol-lowering drugs can be used to prevent the damaging changes in blood vessel walls. The drugs most often used include

KEY TERMS

hypertension
elevated blood pressure

ischemia
tissue deprived of sufficient blood and oxygen

angina pectoris
severe chest pain usually caused by a deficiency of blood to the heart muscle

congestive heart failure
the heart is unable to pump sufficient blood for the body's needs

edema
swollen tissue due to an accumulation of fluid

lovastatin (Mevacor), cholestyramine (Questran), and niacin (vitamin B₃) (*Drug Facts and Comparisons* 2010b).

Hormone-Related Drugs

As explained in Chapter 4, hormones are released from endocrine (ductless) glands and are important in regulating metabolism, growth, tissue repair, reproduction, and other vital functions. When there is a deficiency or excess of specific hormones, body functions can be impaired, causing abnormal growth, imbalance in metabolism, disease, and often death. Hormones, or hormone-like substances, are sometimes administered as drugs to compensate for an endocrine deficiency and to restore normal function. This is the case for (1) insulin used to treat diabetes (see the earlier discussion for more details), (2) levothyroxine (Synthroid, an artificial thyroid hormone) to treat **hypothyroidism** (insufficient activity of the thyroid gland), and (3) conjugated estrogens (Premarin) to relieve the symptoms caused by estrogen deficiency during menopause.

Hormones also can be administered as drugs to alter normal body processes. Thus, drugs containing the female hormones, estrogen and progesterone (norethindrone, ethinyl estradiol [Ortho Novum]), can be used as contraceptives to alter the female reproductive cycles and prevent pregnancy. Another example involves drugs related to *corticosteroids* (hormones from the cortex of the adrenal glands), which are often prescribed because of their immune-suppressing effects. In high doses, the corticosteroid drugs (e.g., triamcinolone [Kenalog]) reduce symptoms of inflammation and are used to treat severe forms of inflammatory diseases, such as arthritis (Schimmer and Parker 2006). Finally, new hormone-linked drugs such as etanercept (Enbrel), which depress the important immune mediator, tissue necrosis factor (TNF), have also become very popular for suppressing serious inflammatory diseases such as arthritis.

Sedative-Hypnotic Agents

The sedative-hypnotics are discussed in considerable detail in Chapter 6. About 12.5% of U.S. adults use these drugs annually and 2% use them daily (Sola 2010). The most popular sleeping medications include Ambien, Lunesta, Rozerem, Sona, and Silenor (WebMD 2010). If one is not careful, these drugs can be used excessively for reducing stress and aiding sleep, leading to addictions and adverse consequences. Benzodiazepines commonly prescribed for these purposes are clonazepam (Klonopin) and lorazepam (Ativan) (Charney, Mihic, and Harris 2006).

Stimulants

One of the most common uses for prescription stimulants is the treatment of attention deficit hyperactivity disorder (ADHD). This neurobehavioral disorder is the most common mental health problem in children, affecting approximately 8% of all children ages 5 to 17 years (National Institute of Mental Health [NIMH] 2010). Of those children diagnosed with ADHD, the majority will continue to manifest associated impairment into adolescence and even adulthood (NIMH 2010). The most frequent treatment for ADHD includes stimulants such as Ritalin and Adderall (amphetamine), which have been proven to improve attention while controlling impulsivity and disruptive behaviors. Of some concern is a dramatic increase in stimulant prescriptions for ADHD treatment and whether they are the best drug choice for treating ADHD patients (Helpguide 2010; Wallis 2006). This rise in ADHD-related medication use has corresponded with a disturbing increase in the use of these stimulants without prescriptions. It has been estimated that approximately 21 million people age 12 or older in the United States annually are prescribed these stimulants, and these drugs are abused by 7.3 million persons, many of whom are not the legal recipients of the prescriptions.

Perhaps the most troubling issue is the trend for college students to abuse these short-acting stimulants to enhance performance during studying to prepare for examinations or stay awake to party well into the night (Jaffe and Chip 2006; Tuttle, Scheurich, and Ranseen 2010). Another common reason for this group to abuse these drugs is to lose weight due to their appetite-suppressing actions. It is likely that the increase of stimulant abuse by college students reflects an assumption that these agents must be safe or they would not be prescribed by physicians. Due to this growing problem, there is a major effort by scientists and drug companies to develop nonaddicting medications to treat ADHD.

Drugs to Treat HIV

Although not included in the top-25 list of prescription drugs (see Table 15.6), medications to

KEY TERMS

hypothyroidism
thyroid gland does not produce sufficient hormone

treat HIV infection are of special relevance to drug abuse because of the high prevalence of infection by this deadly virus in intravenous drug addicts. The issue of AIDS and drug abuse is discussed at length in Chapter 17; of relevance to our discussion on prescription drugs are recent advances in pharmacological management of this disease. Although no cure for HIV or immunization against this virus is available yet, some drug therapies can delay the onset or slow the progression of this infection. The first drugs to be used effectively in AIDS therapy were the transcriptase inhibitors such as AZT (zidovudine) and Zerit (stavudine), which block a unique enzyme essential for HIV replication (Flexner 2006). Another group of anti-AIDS drugs called the protease inhibitors prevent HIV maturation; they include aquinavir (Fortovase). The protease inhibitors

are particularly effective when used in combination with the transcriptase inhibitor drugs (Flexner 2006). Most current strategies for AIDS therapy include drug combinations based on issues such as viral susceptibility, drug toxicity, drug metabolism, drug interaction potential, and medical conditions of the patient. There are more than 20 approved anti-HIV drugs from 6 different mechanistic classes that can be used to design combination-drug treatments. These include drug categories such as the transcriptase inhibitors, protease inhibitors, fusion inhibitors, and CCR5 antagonists. Strategies for more effective drug treatments are continually being developed (Aidsinfo 2009). Research suggests that if done properly, antiviral treatment is more than 80% effective in suppressing the symptoms of AIDS and preventing death (Marconi et al. 2010).

Prescription for Abuse: Invitation for Prescription Abuse

Michael was polite, clean-cut, and a typical white-collar professional. To consider him a drug addict would be unthinkable. And yet, Michael would be the first to admit his drug addiction on prescription medication is as strong and debilitating as an addiction to illegal drugs such as cocaine and heroin. Michael became extremely skilled in his ability to feign back pain in a doctor's office or emergency room so he could walk away with a prescription for potent narcotic painkillers. When asked if he drove himself to the office, Michael would always say no, so he could also get an injection of the potent narcotic Demerol. If he had difficulty getting a medication from legitimate or forged prescriptions, Michael would steal pills from easy targets in the suburbs. For example, at garage sales he would ask to use the bathroom, and unsuspecting homeowners would nicely open their houses to him and leave him unsupervised. People trying to sell their house would usually invite him in as a prospective buyer, and, as he looked around unattended, he would sneak into a bathroom or bedroom and rifle through medicine cabinets and dresser drawers for drugs to satisfy his cravings. Michael tells of one experience when he went to an open house pretending to be an interested buyer. When the owner wasn't looking, Michael slipped into a bedroom and snatched a large bottle of Vicodin and an unfilled prescription next to a wheelchair and crutches. At the

peak of his addiction, Michael was consuming up to 120 narcotic painkillers a day. Michael explains that using large quantities of these prescriptions was not all that difficult. He claims that "doctors and psychiatrists would hand out drugs like candy" and people were so unsuspecting that it was easy to take unsecured prescription drugs from bathrooms and bedrooms.

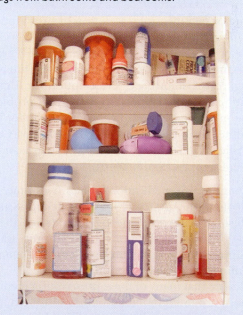

Source: Sotonoff, J. "Addiction Began with Prescription Drugs He Got from Your Homes." *Chicago Daily Herald.* 26 July 2010. Available at: http://www.dailyherald.com/story/?id=396310. Accessed March 16, 2011.

Common Principles of Drug Use

Probably the most effective way to teach people not to use drugs improperly is to help them understand how to use drugs correctly. This goal can be achieved by educating the drug-using public about prescription, OTC, and herbal drug products. If people can appreciate the difference between the benefits of therapeutic drug use and the negative consequences of drug misuse or abuse, they will be more likely to use medications in a cautious and thoughtful manner. To reach this level of understanding, patients must be able to communicate freely with health professionals. Before prescription or OTC drugs are purchased and used, patients should have all questions answered about the therapeutic objective, the most effective mode of administration, and side effects. Education about proper drug use greatly diminishes drug-related problems and unnecessary health costs.

To minimize problems, before using any drug product, the patient should be able to answer the following questions:

- Why am I using this drug?
- How should I be taking this drug?
- What are the active ingredients in this drug product?
- What are the most likely side effects of this drug?
- How long should this drug be used?

A major factor in the escalation of prescription drug misuse is that excess unused medications are not dealt with appropriately and are readily available to those who would abuse them or use them in a dangerous fashion (see "Prescription for Abuse: Invitation for Prescription Abuse"). This problem can be prevented by complying with the following guidelines from the Office of National Drug Control Policy (ONDCP) that explain how to manage these extra drugs (Smith 2010):

- Do not flush medications. The Environmental Protection Agency (EPA) has declared that flushing drugs down the toilet results in high levels of many medications in community water supplies, causing health problems for people, animals, and the environment.
- Realize that many of these prescription medications are in high demand on the Internet and street, are often sold for a considerable amount of money, and can be very tempting to young people. Consequently, teens frequently raid home medicine cabinets to use these drugs for

"pharm parties," where the pills are mixed together and shared or sold to friends and acquaintances. For these reasons, all prescription drugs should be stored in a secure (even locked) place (*Alcoholism & Drug Abuse Weekly* 2010).

- Do not dispose of your medications or their containers with labels in the trash. The bright labels of these bottles are highly visible in garbage cans and landfills and contain important personal information that can be used to steal your identity.
- The FDA recommends placing unused prescription medications into a plastic bag with moist coffee grounds or used cat litter before disposing of the pills/tablets in the garbage. The moisture from the coffee grounds or cat litter will help dissolve the capsules, pills, or tablets, making them unusable.
- Many communities have secured drop-off boxes that are attended by certified law-enforcement personnel. Medications left in these boxes are collected by authorized personnel and properly disposed of. Locations of these drop-off containers can usually be determined by checking with local police.

Discussion Questions

1. Why are some prescription drugs appropriate for switching to OTC status?

2. What should the FDA use as a standard of safety when evaluating OTC and prescription drugs?

3. What role should the pharmacist play in providing information about OTC and prescription drugs to patients?

4. What type of formal training should be required before a health professional is allowed to prescribe drugs?

5. What kinds of questions should be asked by a health professional to ensure that a patient has sufficient understanding concerning a drug to use it properly and safely?

6. What are the basic rules for using OTC drugs properly?

7. Why is abuse of prescription drugs such a common problem?

8. Why are the opioid painkillers the most frequently abused of the prescription drugs?

9. How should users of prescription drugs handle their medications to prevent their abuse by others?

10. Why are some people more likely to abuse prescription drugs than illegal substances?

11. Even though some antibiotics have a wide margin of safety, currently there is no systemic antibiotic available OTC. Why is the FDA not willing to make some of these drugs available on a nonprescription basis?

12. Should herbal remedies be required to be safe and effective by the FDA like other OTC drug products?

13. What role, if any, should the FDA have in regulating herbal products?

Summary

1 Prescription drugs are available only by recommendation of an authorized health professional, such as a physician. Nonprescription (OTC) drugs are available on request and do not require approval by a health professional. In general, OTC medications are safer than their prescription counterparts but often less effective.

2 The switching policy of the FDA is an attempt to make available more effective medications to the general public on a nonprescription basis. This policy has been implemented in response to the interest in self-treatment by the public and in an attempt to reduce healthcare costs.

3 Drugs switched by the FDA to OTC status include ulcer medications, such as Tagamet and Zantac, medications for asthma and allergies, the contraceptive levonorgestral, and the weight loss drug orlistat.

4 Potential problems that come by making more effective drugs available OTC include overuse and inappropriate use, leading to dependence and other undesirable side effects. For example, these more effective drugs could encourage self-treatment of medical problems that usually require professional care.

5 Information on OTC product labels is crucial for proper use of these drugs and thus is regulated by the FDA. Product labels must list the active ingredients and their quantities in the product. Labels must also provide instructions for safe and effective treatment with the drug as well as cautions and warnings.

6 Many herbal products contain active drugs and have become very popular. The lack of regulation makes these remedies difficult to assess for either efficacy or safety.

7 Although OTC drug products can be useful for treatment of many minor to moderate, self-limiting medical problems, when used without proper precautions, they can cause problems.

8 The principal drug groups available OTC are used in the treatment of common, minor medical problems and include analgesics, cold remedies, allergy products, mild stimulants, sleep aids, antacids, laxatives, antidiarrheals, antiasthmatics, acne medications, sunscreens, contraceptives, and nutrients.

9 For drugs to be prescribed properly, patients need to provide complete and accurate information about their medical condition and medical history to their physicians. In turn, providers need to communicate to patients what is being treated, why the drug is being used, how it should be used for maximum benefit, and what potential side effects can occur.

10 Proprietary drug names can be used legally only by the drug company that has trademark rights. Often, the original proprietary name becomes the popular name associated with the drug. Because the pharmaceutical company that develops a drug is trying to recover its investment, a newly marketed proprietary drug is expensive. Once the patent rights expire, other drug companies can also market the drug but under a different name; often, the common, generic name is used because it cannot be trademarked. The generic drugs are less expensive because the manufacturers do not need to recover any significant investment. The FDA requires the less expensive generic drug to be as effective and safe as the proprietary counterpart.

11 Of the approximately 1500 different prescription drugs currently available in the United States, the most commonly prescribed groups are analgesics, antibiotics, antidepressants, drugs used for diabetes, antiulcer drugs, antiepileptic drugs, bronchodilators, drugs used to treat cardiovascular diseases, hormone-related drugs, and sedative-hypnotics.

12 Abuse of prescription drugs is a serious problem in the United States. Some patients try to

persuade clinicians or pharmacists to make pre-scription medications available by using deceit or intimidation. Legal drugs obtained in this manner are often used to relieve drug dependence or to re-duce withdrawal symptoms from illicit substances. Those who abuse prescription drugs often abuse other substances as well such as alcohol, tobacco, or even illicit drugs.

13 To help reduce prescription abuse, those who use these drugs legitimately should make sure their medications are securely stored and that un-used prescriptions are disposed of properly.

References

Abood, R. "OBRA '90: Implementation and Enforcement." *NABP U.S. Pharmacists, State Boards—A Continuing Educa-tion Series.* Park Ridge, IL: National Association of Phar-macy, 1992.

Aidsinfo. "Guidelines for the Use of Antiretroviral Agents in HIV-1-Infected Adults and Adolescents." NIH.gov. (December 2009). Available http://aidsinfo.nih.gov/contentfiles/AdultandAdolescentGL.pdf

Alcoholism & Drug Abuse Weekly. "Only Federal Prevention Message About Prescription Drugs: Lock Up or Throw Out." (15 March 2010). Available http://onlinelibrary.wiley.com/doi/10.1002/adaw.20225/abstract

Allen, J. "Over-the-Counter Cough Medicines Escape FDA Restrictions." ABC Good Morning America. (14 Septem-ber 2010). Available http://abcnews.go.com/Health/Wellness/dextromethorphan-ingredient-robutussin-cough-medicines-escapes-fda-restrictions/story?id=11638160

American Cancer Society. "Skin Cancer Facts." 2011. Available http://www.cancer.org/Cancer/CancerCauses/Sunand UVExposure/skin-cancer-facts#skipnavigation

American Psychiatric Association (APA). *Diagnostic and Statis-tical Manual of Mental Disorders,* 4th ed., text revision (DSM-IV-TR). Washington, DC: Author, 2000.

Anderson, R., and D. Nykamp. "Drowsiness and Fatigue." In *Handbook of Nonprescription Drugs,* 15th ed., edited by I. Bernardi, 1009–1020. Washington, DC: American Phar-macists Association, 2006.

Associated Press. "FDA Warns on Sales of Street Drug Alter-natives." *Washington Post* (1 April 2003): A-9.

Baldauf, S. "Vanished Behind the Counter." *U.S. News and World Report.* (2 October 2006). Available http://health.usnews.com/usnews/health/articles/060924/2cold.htm.

Bartholow, M. "Top 200 Prescription Drugs of 2009." *Phar-macy Times.* (11 May 2010). Available http://www.pharma cytimes.com/issue/pharmacy/2010/May2010/RxFocus TopDrugs-0510

Bass, P. "Is Over-the-Counter Asthma Medication Avail-able in the United States?" About.com. (23 November 2010). Available http://asthma.about.com/od/treatment options/f/Is-Over-The-Counter-Asthma-Medication-Available-In-The-United-States.htm

Beck, A., and B. Alford. *Depression Causes and Treatment,* 2nd ed. Philadelphia: University of Pennsylvania Press, 2009.

Bernstein, I., and E. Rickert. "Legal and Regulatory Issues in Self-Care Pharmacy Practice." In *Handbook of Nonprescrip-tion Drugs,* 15th ed., edited by I. Bernardi, 51–65. Washing-ton, DC: American Pharmacists Association, 2006.

Booth, W., and A. O'Connor. "Mexican Cartels Emerge As Top Source For U.S. Meth." *Washington Post.* (28 November 2010). Available http://www.washingtonpost.com/wp-dyn/content/article/2010/11/23/AR201011 2303703.html?sid=ST2010112303730

Borgsdorf, L. "Preface." In *Drug Facts and Comparisons,* edited by L. Borgsdorf, et al., xi. St. Louis: Wolters & Kluwar, 2007.

Bowman, J. "Minor Burns and Sunburn." In *Handbook of Nonprescription Drugs,* 15th ed., edited by I. Bernardi, 853–868. Washington, DC: American Pharmacists Asso-ciation, 2006.

Brophy, B., and D. Schardt. "Functional Foods (Products Enriched with Popular Herbs Make Questionable Health Claims)." HighBeam Research. 2011. Available http://www.highbeam.com/doc/1G1-54271809.html

Burke, J. "Worldwide Prescription Drug Abuse." *Pharmacy Times.* (19 April 2007). Available http://associationdata base.com/aws/NADDI/asset_manager/get_file/2905/pharmacytimes-2007-04_worldwideprescriptiondrug abuse.pdf

Carroll, D., and K. Crosby. "Prevention of Sun-Induced Skin Disorders." In *Handbook of Nonprescription Drugs,* 15th ed., edited by I. Bernardi, 817–837. Washington, DC: Ameri-can Pharmacists Association, 2006.

Center for Drug Evaluation and Research (CDER). "Over-the-Counter Medicine: What's Right for You?" FDA. (February 2002). Available http://www.fda.gov/cder

Centers for Disease Control and Prevention (CDC). "Basics About Diabetes." Diabetes Public Health Resource. 2007. Available http://www.cdc.gov/diabetes/consumer/index.htm

Centers for Disease Control and Prevention (CDC). "Heart Disease Facts." 2010. Available http://www.cdc.gov/heart disease/facts.htm

Charney, D., S. Mihic, and R. Harris. "Hypnotics and Seda-tives." In *The Pharmacological Basis of Therapeutics,* 11th ed., edited by L. Brunton, J. Lazo, and K. Parker, 401–427. New York: McGraw-Hill, 2006.

Consumer Healthcare Products Association. "White Paper on the Benefits of OTC Medicines in the United States." 2010. Available http://www.chpainfo.org/media/resources/r_6842.pdf

Consumer Reports. "The Mainstreaming of Alternative Medi-cine." (May 2000): 17–24.

Crespo, C., and J. Arbesman. "Obesity in the United States." *The Physician and Sports Medicine* 31 (November 2003): 1.

Curry, C., and D. Butler. "Constipation." In *Handbook of Non-prescription Drugs,* 15th ed., edited by I. Bernardi, 299–326. Washington, DC: American Pharmacists Association, 2006.

Davis, S. "Insulin, Oral Hypoglycemic Agents, and the Phar-macology of the Endocrine Pancreas." In *The Pharmaco-*

logical Basis of Therapeutics, 11th ed., edited by L. Brunton, J. Lazo, and K. Parker, 1613–1645. New York: McGraw-Hill, 2006.

de Beaufort, C., P. Swift, C. Skinner, H. Aanstoot, J. Aman, F. Cameron, et al. "Continuing Stability of Center Differences in Pediatric Diabetes Care: Do Advances in Diabetes Treatment Improve Outcome?" *Diabetes Care* 30 (2007): 2245–2250.

DiGravio, G. "In a Primary Care Setting Researchers Define Traits Associated with Prescription Drug Disorders." Medical News Today. (17 May 2010). Available http://www.medicalnewstoday.com/articles/188891.php

Drug Facts and Comparisons. St. Louis, MO: Wolters Kluwer Health, 2007.

Drug Facts and Comparisons, Pocket Version. St. Louis, MO: Wolters Kluwar, 2010a.

Drug Facts and Comparisons. "Cardiovascular Agents." St. Louis, MO: Wolters Kluwar Health, 2010b: 251–390.

Drugs.com. " Excedrin PM." 2010. Available http://www.drugs.com/mtm/excedrin-pm.html

endocrineweb. "Diabetes News and Research." 2010. Available http://www.endocrineweb.com/news/diabetes

Fagan, K. " 'Pharma Parties' A Troubling Trend Among Youths." *San Francisco Chronicle.* (16 March 2010). Available http://articles.sfgate.com/2010-03-4/news/18835066_1_parents-medicine-calls-pharma/3

FamilyDoctor. "What Is Heartburn?" 2010. Available http://familydoctor.org/online/famdocen/home/common/digestive/disorders/087.html

Flexner, C. "Antiretroviral Agents and Treatment of HIV Infection." In *The Pharmacological Basis of Therapeutics,* 11th ed., edited by L. Brunton, J. Lazo, and K. Parker, 1273–1314. New York: McGraw-Hill, 2006.

Food and Drug Administration (FDA). "Final Rule Declaring Dietary Supplements Containing Ephedrine Alkaloids Adulterated Because They Present an Unreasonable Risk. Final Rule." *Federal Registrar* 69 (2004): 6787–6854.

Food and Drug Administration (FDA). "Medication Error Reports." 2009. Available http://www.fda.gov/Drugs/DrugSafety/MedicationErrors/ucm080629.htm

Food and Drug Administration (FDA). "FDA Significantly Restricts Access to the Diabetes Drug Avandia." FDA News Release. (23 September 2010a). Available http://www.fda.gov/NewsEvents/Newsroom/PressAnnouncements/ucm226975.htm

Food and Drug Administration (FDA). "Rx-to-OTC Switch List." 2010b. Available http://www.fda.gov/AboutFDA/CentersOffices/CDER/ucm106378.htm

Foster, K., and C. Coffrey. "Acne." In *Handbook of Nonprescription Drugs,* 15th ed., edited by I. Bernardi, 803–816. Washington, DC: American Pharmacists Association, 2006.

Freundlich, N. "Illicit Drugs on Campus Are Increasingly the Rx Variety." Taking Note. (13 July 2010). Available http://takingnote.tcf.org/2010/07/illicit-drugs-on-campus-are-increasingly-the-rx-variety.html

Fugh-Berman, A. "Herb–Drug Interactions." *Lancet* 355 (2000): 134–138.

Gill, M. "The Pharmacist's Role in Sleep Disorders." *Pharmacy Times* (August 1999): 103–116.

Goodnough, A. "Prescription Drug Abuse Sends More People to the Hospital." *New York Times.* (5 January 2011). Available http://www.nytimes.com/2011/01/06/health/06drugs.html

Hanson, D. "U.S. Leads World in Prescription Drug Use." Addiction Inbox. (28 July 2010). Available http://addiction-dirkh.blogspot.com/2010/07/us-leads-world-in-prescription-drug-use.html

Heller, M. "FDA Caps Acetaminophen Dosage in Painkillers to Cut Liver Damage Risk." Fairwarning. (13 January 2011). Available http://www.fairwarning.org/2011/01/fda-caps-acetaminophen-dosage-in-painkillers-to-cut-liver-damage-risk

Helpguide. "ADD/ADHD Medications." 2010. Available http://helpguide.org/mental/adhd_medications.htm

Hoffman, B. "Therapy of Hypertension." In *The Pharmacological Basis of Therapeutics,* 11th ed., edited by L. Brunton, J. Lazo, and K. Parker, 845–897. New York: McGraw-Hill, 2006.

Hume, A., and K. Strong. "Botanical Medicines." In *Handbook of Nonprescription Drugs,* 15th ed., edited by I. Bernardi, 1103–1136. Washington, DC: American Pharmacists Association, 2006.

Jaffe, H., and A. Chip. "Got Any Smart Pills?" *Washingtonian* (January 2006): 41–45. Available http://www.washingtonian.com/articles/education/1729.html

Johnston, L., P. M. O'Malley, J. G. Bachman, and J. E. Schulenberg. *Monitoring the Future. National Survey Results on Drug Use, 1975–2009. Volume II: College Students.* 2009. Available http://monitoringthefuture.org/pubs/monographs/vol2_2009.pdf

Kaiser Family Foundation. "Prescription Drug Trends." (May 2010). Available http://www.kff.org/rxdrugs/upload/3057-08.pdf

Kaus, A. "A 'Trendy and Popular' Problem." *Daily Republic.* (15 May 2010). Available https://secure.forumcomm.com/?publisher_ID=4&article_id=43079&CFID=283784732&CFTOKEN=52166350

Kirkwood, C., and S. Melton. "Insomnia." In *Handbook of Nonprescription Drugs,* 15th ed., edited by I. Bernardi, 995–1008. Washington, DC: American Pharmacists Association, 2006.

Leinwand, D. "Feds Score Against Homegrown Meth." *USA Today.* (2 July 2007). Available http://www.usatoday.com/news/nation/meth.htm

Leong, K. "The Dangers of Dextromethorphan Abuse." Associated Content. (9 March 2010). Available http://www.associatedcontent.com/article/2740915/the_dangers_of_dextromethorphan_abuse.html

Life Challenges. "Anorexia and Bulimia—Serious Consequences." 2010. Available http://www.allaboutlifechallenges.org/anorexia-bulimia.htm

Mackowiak, E. "The Common Cold: Prevention and Treatment." *Pharmacy Times* (November 1999): 95–106.

Mahley, R., and T. Bersot. "Drug Therapy for Hypercholesterolemia and Dyslipidemia." In *The Pharmacological Basis of Therapeutics,* 11th ed., edited by L. Brunton, J. Lazo, and K. Parker, 933–966. New York: McGraw-Hill, 2006.

Marconi, V., G. Grandits, A. Weintrob, H. Chun, M. Landrum, A. Ganesan, et al. "Outcomes of Highly Active Antiretroviral Therapy in the Context of Universal Access to Healthcare: The U.S. Military HIV Natural History Study." *AIDS Research and Therapy* 7 (2010): 14.

Martinez, B. "Study Shows Teens Using Prescription, OTC Drugs to Get High." Defiance Crescent News. (16 January 2007). Available http://www.crescent-news.com/news/article/1486152

Mayo Clinic. "Asthma Symptoms." (27 May 2010). Available http://www.mayoclinic.com/health/asthma/DS00021/DSECTION=symptoms

McCabe, S., C. Boyd, and C. Teter. "Subtypes of Nonmedical Prescription Drug Misuse." *Drug and Alcohol Dependence* 102 (2009): 63–70.

McQueen, C., and A. Hume. "Introduction to Botanical and Nonbotanical Natural Medicines." In *Handbook of Nonprescription Drugs,* 15th ed., edited by I. Bernardi, 1095–1101. Washington, DC: American Pharmacists Association, 2006.

Medical News Today. "Are Doctors Knowledgeable About Herbal Medicines?" Medical News Today. 2010. Available http://www.medicalnewstoday.com/articles/184716.php

MedlinePlus. "Prescription Drug Abuse." 2010. Available http://www.nlm.nih.gov/medlineplus/prescriptiondrugabuse.html

Michel, T. "Treatment of Myocardial Ischemia." In *The Pharmacological Basis of Therapeutics,* 11th ed., edited by L. Brunton, J. Lazo, and K. Parker, 823–844. New York: McGraw-Hill, 2006.

Miller, S., and C. Bartels. "Overweight and Obesity." In *Handbook of Nonprescription Drugs,* 15th ed., edited by I. Bernardi, 553–573. Washington, DC: American Pharmacists Association, 2006.

Mitchell, D. "Is Your Child Abusing Cough and Cold Medications?" EmaxHealth.com. 2010. Available http://www.emaxhealth.com/1275/your-child-abusing-cough-and-cold-medications

Moscatello, C. "Corey Haim's Death Highlights Growing Prescription Drug Abuse Trend." AOLNews.com. 11 March 2010. Available http://www.aolhealth.com/bloggers/caitlin-moscatello

National Center for Complementary and Alternative Medicine (NCCAM). "Herbs at a Glance." 2010. Available http://nccam.nih.gov/health/herbsataglance.htm

National Digestive Diseases Information Clearinghouse (NDDIC). "*H. pylori* and Peptic Ulcers." 2010. Available http://digestive.niddk.nih.gov/ddiseases/pubs/hpylori

National Heart Lung and Blood Institute (NHLBI). "Heart and Vascular Information." 2010a. Available http://www.nhlbi.nih.gov/health/public/heart/index.htm

National Heart Lung and Blood Institute (NHLBI). "What's New/Highlights." 2010b. Available http://hp2010.nhlbihin.net/as_frameset.htm

National Institute of Mental Health (NIMH). "Attention Deficit Hyperactivity Disorder (ADHD)." 2010. Available http://www.nimh.nih.gov/health/publications/attention-deficit-hyperactivity-disorder/complete-index.shtml

National Library of Medicine. "Dietary Supplements Labels Database." 2010. Available http://dietarysupplements.nlm.nih.gov/dietary

Nutraceuticals World. "Herbal Supplement Sales Increase to $5 Billion in Sales in the U.S." 2011. Available http://www.nutraceuticalsworld.com/contents/view/24313

OTCmedicines. "White Paper on the Benefits of OTC Medicines in the United States." 2010. Available http://www.chpa-info.org/media/resources/r_6842.pdf

Pal, S. "Self Care and Nonprescription Pharmacotherapy." In *Handbook of Nonprescription Drugs,* 15th ed., edited by I. Bernardi, 3–14. Washington, DC: American Pharmacists Association, 2006.

Preda, A. "Opioid Abuse." eMedicine from WebMD. (11 January 2011). Available http://emedicine.medscape.com/article/287790-overview

Quest Diagnostics. "U.S. Worker Use of Prescription Opiates Climbing, Shows Quest Diagnostics Drug Testing Index." (2 September 2010). Available http://www.questdiagnostics.com/employersolutions/dti/2010_09/dti_index.html

Reavy, P. "Murray Doctor Arrested—Called the Drug 'Candyman.' " *Deseret News* 157 (2007): A1.

Remington, T. "Headache." In *Handbook of Nonprescription Drugs,* 15th ed., edited by I. Bernardi, 69–90. Washington, DC: American Pharmacists Association, 2006.

Reuters Health. "Bill Would Restrict Cold Pills to Fight 'Meth.' " (27 January 2005). Available http://naturalsolutionsradio.com/blog/natural-solutions-radio/bill-would-restrict-cold-pills-fight-meth

Risling, G. "State Databases Blocking 'Doctor Shoppers.' " *Washington Post.* (16 May 2010). Available http://www.highbeam.com/doc/1P2-22027753.html

Rocco, T., and J. Fang. "Pharmacotherapy of Congestive Heart Failure." In *The Pharmacological Basis of Therapeutics,* 11th ed., edited by L. Brunton, J. Lazo, and K. Parker, 869–897. New York: McGraw-Hill, 2006.

Rosen-Cohen, N. "The Quiet Epidemic." *Baltimore Sun.* (21 April 2010). Available http://articles.baltimoresun.com/2010-04-21/news/bs-ed-prescription-drug-abuse-20100421_1_prescription-drugs-opiates-addictive

RxList. "Top 200 Drugs." 2010. Available http://www.rxlist.com/script/main/hp.asp

Schimmer, B., and K. Parker. "Adrenocorticotropic Steroids and Their Synthetic Analogs: Inhibitors of the Synthesis and Actions of Adrenocortical Hormones." In *The Pharmacological Basis of Therapeutics,* 11th ed., edited by L. Brunton, J. Lazo, and K. Parker, 1587–1612. New York: McGraw-Hill, 2006.

Scolaro, K. "Disorders Related to Colds and Allergies." In *Handbook of Nonprescription Drugs,* 15th ed., edited by I. Bernardi, 203–228. Washington, DC: American Pharmacists Association, 2006.

Scott, S., and R. Martin. "Atopic Dermatitis and Dry Skin." In *Handbook of Nonprescription Drugs,* 15th ed., edited by

I. Bernardi, 711–728. Washington, DC: American Pharmacists Association, 2006.

Seeringer, A., S. Parmar, A. Fischer, B. Altissimo, L. Zondler, E. Lebedeva, et al. "Genetic Variants of the Insulin Receptor Substrate-1 Are Influencing Therapeutic Efficacy of Oral Antidiabetics." *Diabetes, Obesity and Metabolism* 12 (2010): 1106–1112.

Shuster, J. "Insomnia: Understanding Its Pharmacological Treatment Options." *Pharmacy Times* 62 (August 1996): 67–76.

Smith, E. "Proper Disposal of Prescription Medication or Prescription Drugs." Suite101.com. (14 November 2010). Available http://www.suite101.com/content/proper-disposal-of-prescription-medication-or-prescription-drugs-a308788

Sola, C. "Sedative, Hypnotic, Anxiolytic Use Disorders." Emedicine from WebMD. 2010. Available http://emedicine.medscape.com/article/290585-overview

Sotonoff, J. "Addiction Began with Prescription Drugs He Got from Your Homes." *Chicago Daily Herald.* 26 July 2010. Available http://www.dailyherald.com/story/?id=396310

Stolberg, S. "FDA Considers Switching Some Prescription Drugs to Over-the-Counter Status." *New York Times* on the Web (28 June 2000): A1.

Stoppler, M., and B. Hecht. "Generic Drugs, Are They As Good As Brand Names?" MedicineNet.com. (29 December 2010). Available http://www.medicinenet.com/script/main/art.asp?articlekey=46204

Thomas, M. "Prescription Drug Abuse Is Fastest-Growing Drug Problem in Country." *Chicago Sun-Times.* (26 December 2010). Available http://www.suntimes.com/news/metro/2989811-418/drug-prescription-abuse-daniel-drugs.html

Tietze, K. "Cough." In *Handbook of Nonprescription Drugs,* 15th ed., edited by I. Bernardi, 229–242. Washington, DC: American Pharmacists Association, 2006.

Today Health Info. "Study: US Has Much Higher Obesity Rate Than Canada." 2011. Available http://todayhealth-info.info/health/study-us-has-much-higher-obesity-rate-than-canada-ap

TransWorldNews. "Who Is More Likely to Abuse Prescription Drugs?" (1 April 2010). Available http://www.transworldnews.com/NewsStory.aspx?id=295072&cat=10

Tuttle, J., N. Scheurich, and J. Ranseen. "Prevalence of ADHD Diagnosis and Nonmedical Prescription Stimulant Use in Medical Students." *Academic Psychiatry* 34 (2010 May–June). Available http://www.biomedsearch.com/nih/Prevalence-ADHD-diagnosis-nonmedical-prescription/20431104.html

UMassMemorial Health Care. "Special Health Information, Phenylpropanolamine." 2010. Available http://umass-memorial.org/systemip.cfm?xyzpdqabc=0&id=3722&action=detail&AEProductID=HW_CAM&AEArticleID=hn-1462003

van den Heuval, C., S. Ferguson, M. Macchiand, and D. Dawson. "Melatonin as a Hypnotic: Con." *Sleep Medicine Review* 9 (2005): 71–80.

Walker, P. "Diarrhea." In *Handbook of Nonprescription Drugs,* 15th ed., edited by I. Bernardi, 326–350. Washington, DC: American Pharmacists Association, 2006.

Wallis, C. "Status Report: Getting Hyper About Ritalin." *Time.* (12 February 2006). Available http://www.time.com/time/magazine/article/0,9171,1158957,00.html

Warholak-Juarez, T., M. Rupp, T. Salazar, and S. Foster. "Effect of Patient Information on the Quality of Pharmacists' Drug Use Review Decisions." *Journal of American Pharmaceutical Association* 40 (2000): 500–508.

WebMD. "Drugs to Treat Insomnia." 2010. Available http://www.webmd.com/sleep-disorders/guide/insomnia-medications

Whitney, M. "Prescription Drug Deaths Skyrocket 68 Percent over Five Years as Americans Swallow More Pills." NewsTarget.com. (14 September 2007). Available http://www.newstarget.com/z021635.html

Williams, A., C. Girard, D. Jui, A. Sabina, and D. Katz. "SAMe as Treatment for Depression: A Systemic Review." *Clinical Investigation of Medicine* 28 (2005): 132–139.

WIXT/WSYR, TV ABC 9. "Pharm Parties. Popping Prescriptions." Syracuse (18 May 2007).

Zak, J. "OBRA '90 and DUR." *American Druggist* (October 1993): 57.

Zweber, A., and R. Berardi. "Heartburn and Dyspepsia." In *Handbook of Nonprescription Drugs,* 15th ed., edited by I. Bernardi, 265–282. Washington, DC: American Pharmacists Association, 2006.

CHAPTER 16

Drug Use in Subcultures of Special Populations

Did You Know?

- ○ Athletes are much more likely than other subcultural groups to take drugs that enhance physical attributes.
- ○ In the United States, approximately 500,000 teenagers use steroids and 52,000 children (12 and younger) use anabolic steroids.
- ○ In general, compared with men, women are more likely to become addicted to tobacco.
- ○ In comparison to men, women are more reluctant to seek substance abuse treatment.
- ○ Approximately 70% of women in drug abuse treatment report histories of physical and sexual abuse, with victimization beginning before 11 years of age and occurring repeatedly.
- ○ The major reasons adolescents use drugs are to cope with boredom, unpleasant feelings, emotions, and stress or to relieve depression and reduce tension and alienation.
- ○ Prescription drugs are the drugs of choice among 12- to 13-year-olds.
- ○ Street gangs, outlaw motorcycle gangs (OMGs), and prison gangs are the primary distributors of illegal drugs on the streets of the United States.
- ○ Alcohol use is implicated in one-third to two-thirds of sexual assaults and acquaintance or date rape cases among teens and college students.
- ○ The amount and proportion of alcohol consumed by college students varies depending on where they live.
- ○ AIDS is a common killer, second only to cancer and heart disease for women. It is the third most-deadly disease for women in the United States.
- ○ An HIV-infected individual may not manifest symptoms of AIDS for as many as 10 to 12 years after the initial infection.

Learning Objectives

On completing this chapter, you will be able to:

- ◎ Know which drugs are most likely to be abused by athletes and why.
- ◎ Describe the use of drug testing in athletic competitions.
- ◎ Determine where anabolic steroids come from.
- ◎ Describe the purpose and goals of the Adolescents Training and Learning to Avoid Steroids (ATLAS) prevention program.
- ◎ Explain two major ways women's history differs from men's history with regard to drug abuse.
- ◎ Explain the major reasons why adolescents use substances of abuse.
- ◎ Explain which types of parents are more likely to raise drug-abusing adolescents.
- ◎ List which types of drugs adolescents are most likely to abuse.
- ◎ List two major findings from research regarding drug use by college student subcultures.
- ◎ Know what club drugs are and how they are used.
- ◎ Explain how drug abuse contributes to the spread of AIDS.
- ◎ Know the key statistics regarding AIDS.
- ◎ List the major strategies to prevent contracting HIV infection.
- ◎ Know how the use of alcohol and other drugs is presented in popular movies and songs.
- ◎ Understand how Internet access can lead to drug use and abuse.

 Drugs and Society Online is a great source for additional drugs and society information for both students and instructors. Visit **go.jblearning.com/hanson11** to find a variety of useful tools for learning, thinking, and teaching.

Introduction

Although similarities appear in the patterns of addiction among drug users, the development of initial use and eventual abuse varies immensely from individual to individual. When attempting to understand common patterns and causes of drug use, examining the subcultures of special populations provides a better grasp of commonalities within such groups. A **subculture** is defined as a special population or subgroup whose members share similar values, attitudes, and patterns of related behaviors that differ from those of other subcultures within the larger population. Even though many subcultures are often so broad and diverse that not all members may be consciously aware of one another, from an **outsider's perspective** (discussed in Chapter 1) they qualify as subcultures because they share similar behavior patterns. For example, racial and ethnic, gender, age, and drug subcultures are often very large across the United States, and most members of such subcultures are not aware of one another. However, in looking at them from the outside (an outsider's perspective), they have patterns of behavior that are similar. An **insider's perspective** refers to viewing the subculture from the inside, as the members of this subculture are experiencing ongoing activity within their group. For example, a group of adolescents using drugs from a particular locality in a city or town and divorced women meeting to discuss coping with separation and being single qualify as distinct subcultures. Although both insiders' and outsiders' perspectives may include similar behavior patterns, the inside and outside perspectives differ. An insider's perspective looks at the group and its behavior from the inside and an outsider's perspective is looking at the group and its behavior from the outside.

When defining a subculture, some sociologists refer to it as a "world within a world." Subcultures create and provide their members with lifestyle patterns that are observable, fairly consistent, and interwoven. For example, viewing a drug using group as a subculture offers a way to look for more generalized and distinctive patterns of drug use. In looking at this example of a subculture of drug users, we can begin examining why individuals within various subcultures might initially turn to drugs. The two types of forces that affect members of a subculture are internal and external forces, both of which affect these individuals' drug use behavior.

Internal subcultural forces include:

- Shared in-group attitudes about people who do and do not use drugs (drug users versus nonusers)
- Compatibility with other members of the peer group (often peer members share complementary personality traits)
- Shared attitudes favorable to drug use despite conventional society's view that such behavior is deviant
- Addiction to drugs or, at minimum, habitual drug usage
- A common secrecy about drug use (who you can and cannot trust in knowing about your drug usage)

External subcultural forces include:

- Preoccupation with law enforcement while procuring the drugs and while under the effects of illicit drugs
- A desire to identify other users and dealers of illicit drugs, such as verifying the dependability of the drug dealer (who best to hook up with and who has the best quality drugs)
- Constant preoccupation regarding when more difficult to acquire types of drugs are available and seizing this opportunity
- Preoccupation with being observed using or acting "high" in public, at work, at school, or at a social function where drug use would be perceived as deviant social behavior

To further understand how similar patterns of drug use and/or abuse occur, in this chapter, we look at drug use and users from both outsiders' and insiders' perspectives, from the vantage point of the members belonging to a distinct subculture and how they are perceived by society. This chapter examines drug use and potential abuse in the following seven drug-using subcultures:

1. Sports/athletics
2. Women

KEY TERMS

subculture
subgroup within the population whose members share similar values and patterns of related behaviors that differ from other subcultures and the larger population

outsider's perspective
viewing a group or subculture from outside the group and viewing the group and its members as an observer; looking "in" at the members

insider's perspective
viewing a group or subculture from inside the group; seeing members as they perceive themselves

3. Adolescents
4. College students
5. HIV and AIDS carriers
6. A certain percentage of professional actors, actresses, and entertainers who perform in movies
7. Internet users who are seeking and purchasing illicit drugs

Athletes and Drug Abuse

Drug abuse has been reported since the Greeks started the Olympics in 776 BC. It was then reported that certain substances were ingested by competitors in attempts to gain some ground against fellow competitors (Lajis 2007).

Using performance-enhancing drugs for increased athletic ability is known as **doping** (NIDA 2009). Current reports reveal that "'Doping' among world-class competitors is rampant . . . and the governing bodies of individual sports, as well as the International Olympic Committee, turn a blind eye" (Begley et al. 1999, p. 49). The reasons boil down to winning in sports, especially when millisecond differences exist between gold and silver medals. The differences between the two medals "can amount to millions in endorsement contract and appearance fees" (Begley et al. 1999, p. 49), and apparently the world of professional sports and "drugs [performance-enhancing drugs] go together like socks and sweat" (Begley et al. 1999, p. 49). Mr. Yesalis, an epidemiologist at Pennsylvania State University at University Park, stated that

> Elite athletes stay away from traditional anabolic steroids. They use testosterone creams or gels, which dramatically reduce the chance of being caught, in conjunction with insulin or insulin-like growth factor, and we don't even have a test for those. . . . The supplement industry has exploded since the passage of the Dietary Supplement Health and Education Act in 1994. . . . Anyone can buy substances like testosterone, human-growth hormone HGH, and insulin-like growth factor over the Internet. One site requires a doctor's prescription, but will sell one to any customer for $100 or someone can just walk down to the local GNC, like Mr. Jackson's teammates at Florida State. There, one can buy muscle-building steroid "precursors" like androstenedione and creatine monohydrage. "Andro" is banned by the [World Anti-Doping Agency (WADA 2009) and

the] National Collegiate Athletic Association and other sports governing bodies, but it's legal to buy. They're not as effective as older anabolic steroids, but they do provide some benefits . . . . The law allows stores to sell vitamins, herbal remedies, and other supplements over-the-counter. (Suggs 2003, p. 36)

Another finding as to why athletes want to take performance-enhancing substances lists three important reasons: (1) inadvertent (or alleged inadvertent) consumption of any pharmaceutical medicine that is protected from commercial competition either because the ingredients or manufacturing method is kept secret or is protected by trademark or copyright (also known as a **proprietary medicine**); (2) "deliberate consumption for misuse as a recreational drug; and (3) deliberate consumption to enhance performance" (Docherty 2008, p. 606). To further our understanding of why athletes are willing to risk using these drugs, it is necessary to further explore their mind-set.

To excel in athletic competition is admirable. Most high school, college, amateur, and professional athletes participate in sports for the opportunity to pit their abilities against those of their peers, and to experience the satisfaction that comes from playing to their potential. Others do so to satisfy a desire for recognition and fame. Unfortunately, that creates some athletes who are determined to win at any cost. And, they may use that determination to justify the use of anabolic steroids, despite evidence that these drugs can inflict irreversible physical harm and have significant side effects (New York State Department of Health 2010).

Young athletes receive exaggerated attention and prestige in almost every university, college, high school, and junior high school in the United States. Pressure to excel or be the best is placed on athletes by parents, peers, teachers, coaches, school administrators, the media, and the surrounding community. The importance of sports is frequently distorted and even used by some to evaluate the

KEY TERMS

doping
the use of performance-enhancing drugs to increase athletic ability

proprietary medicine
pharmaceutical medicine that is protected from commercial competition because the ingredients or manufacturing method is kept secret or because it is protected by trademark or copyright

quality of educational institutions (Lawn 1984; New York State Department of Health 2010) or the quality of living conditions in a city. Athletic success can determine the level of financial support these institutions receive from local and state governments, alumni, and other private donors; thus, winning in athletics often translates into fiscal stability and institutional prosperity.

For the athlete, success in sports means psychological rewards such as the admiration of peers, school officials, family, and the community. In addition, athletic success can mean financial rewards such as scholarships, paid living expenses in college, advertising endorsement opportunities, and, for a few, incredible salaries as professional athletes. With the rewards of winning, athletes have to deal with the added pressures of not winning: "What will people think of me if I lose?" "When I lose, I let everybody down." "Losing shows that I am not as good as everyone thinks." These pressures on young, immature athletes can result in poor coping responses. Being better than competitors, no matter the cost, becomes the driving motivation, and doing one's best is no longer sufficient. Such attitudes may lead to serious risk-taking behavior in an attempt to develop an advantage over the competition; this situation can include using drugs to improve performance.

The Canadian sprinter Ben Johnson, once known as the fastest human in history, was banned for life from competitive running in March 1993 (Begley et al. 1999; Hoberman and Yesalis 1995). Five years earlier, at the 1988 Seoul Olympics, Johnson was stripped of a world's record for the 100-meter dash and forfeited the gold medal when his urine tested positive for steroids. Because of the first incident, Johnson was suspended from competition for 2 years. However, in 1992, the 31-year-old sprinter was attempting a comeback, with speeds that approached his world record times. In January 1993, a routine urine test determined Johnson was again using steroids to enhance his athletic performance (Ferrente 1993).

Another, more recent incident involving the use of steroids that ended in shocking tragedy was the case of wrestler Chris Benoit's double murder–suicide. Evidence proved that the pro wrestler asphyxiated his son and wife before he hanged himself in a basement weight room using a cord from one of the weight machines (ESPN.com News Services 2007). "Steroids were among the prescription medications found by investigators going through . . . Benoit's house" (Donaldson-Evans 2007). "Anabolic steroids affect neurochemicals in the brain. . . . It's those neurochemical changes that cause the extreme anger. . . . Officials found many different prescription medications—including prescription anabolic steroids—inside the house . . ." (Donaldson-Evans 2007).

In another story, "eighty-three players have been suspended under baseball's controversial new steroids policy" (Anonymous, as told by Penn 2005, p. 292). "Guys did steroids because it was easy to get away with." Several other noteworthy and revealing quotes from this report are: "So many people were doing it that it didn't feel like cheating. If anything, it felt like leveling the field. . . . I juiced because I love playing more than anything else in the world, and I would have pretty much done anything to keep my career going" (Anonymous, as told by Penn 2005, p. 297). Widely publicized incidents such as these concerning illicit use of so-called **ergogenic** (performance-enhancing) drugs by professional and amateur athletes have created intense interest in the problems of drug abuse in sports (Begley et al. 1999; Merchant 1992) (see "Point/Counterpoint: How the 'Juice' Is Flowing in Baseball").

A more recent case of steroid use in professional sports involves Alexander Emmanuel "Alex" Rodriguez. Rodriguez (born in 1975) is currently an American major league baseball player for the New York Yankees. He is considered one of the youngest best players in baseball history, and in 2007, he signed a 10-year, $252 million contract (Britannica.com 2010). "The Slugger [Rodriguez] who might someday become baseball's all-time home run king remembered more details about performance-enhancing drugs Tuesday, saying his cousin repeatedly injected him from 2001–03 with a mysterious substance from the Dominican Republic. 'I didn't think they were steroids' the New York Yankees star said. Later, he admitted, 'I knew we weren't taking Tic Tacs' " (Blum 2009, p. A11). It was at this press conference that Rodriguez made ". . . his second public attempt to explain a 2003 positive drug test while with Texas . . . while his cousin persuaded him to use 'boli'—a substance he said the cousin obtained without a prescription and without consulting doctors or trainers" (Blum 2009, p. A11).

KEY TERMS

ergogenic
drugs that enhance athletic performance

Point/Counterpoint

How the "Juice" Is Flowing in Baseball

We embrace instant gratification in the United States. We are a society that embraces "bigger, faster, stronger" and winning at all costs (Dvorchak 2005). This concept now applies to professional sports with a devious outcome. A sampling from news sources reveals the following:

- Jose Canseco, a Major League Baseball player for the Oakland Athletics and Texas Rangers (among other teams), wrote a tell-all book titled *Juiced*, in which he exposed "not only the rampant use of performance-enhancing substances in baseball. . . . A steroid devotee since the age of 20, Conseco goes beyond admitting his own usage . . . [to claiming that] he often injected [Mark] McGwire while they were teammates. . . . According to Canseco, steroids and human growth hormone gave McGwire and Sammy Sosa (whose own usage was 'so obvious, it was a joke') the strength, stamina, regenerative ability, and confidence they needed for [the] record setting home run duels often credited with restoring baseball's popularity after the 1994 strike" (Amazon.com 2005).

- "[S]everal star athletes, including New York Yankees slugger Jason Giambi, have reportedly told a federal grand jury investigating the [Balco] lab that they used illegal steroids, prompting Congress to hold hearings on the testing policies of all the major sports leagues" (Coile 2005).

- "Seattle Mariners minor-league outfielder Jamal Strong was suspended for 10 days . . . making him the fourth player to test positive under Major League Baseball's new policy on performance-enhancing drugs" (Associated Press 2005).

- "Washington—How lawmakers introduced a bill . . . that would create a national standard for steroids testing for all professional sports and require a two-year suspension for the first positive test and a lifetime ban for a second offense" (Coile 2005).

- "The same anti-steroid rules that apply to badminton, billiards and bridge ought to apply to baseball, basketball and football, according to U.S. lawmakers who introduced a bill on Tuesday requiring American professional sports to adopt international drug testing standards" (Health Reuters and Yahoo! News 2005).

- "MLB's [Major League Baseball's] drug policy was denounced as laced with loopholes and lawmakers threatened to draft legislation calling for a national testing standard" (Health Reuters and Yahoo! News 2005).

- "McGwire's shameful refusal to answer questions about his alleged steroid use before a congressional committee and Bonds' unbelievable claim that he did not know that substances rubbed into his body were steroids clearly suggest deceit and dishonesty" (Eilek 2005).

- "Robert Eilek is a teacher at Temecula Middle School. He recently removed dozens of pieces of Mark McGwire memorabilia from his classroom in protest of McGwire's refusal to answer questions at a congressional inquiry on steroid use" (Eilek 2005).

Questions to Consider

1. Are professional sports players entitled to claim records set if they were on drugs during their successful career? If they are entitled to their accomplishments regardless of their drug usage, how would it affect non–drug-using players? Is it fair to the sport and to the fans supporting the players? If they are not entitled to their accomplishments under drugged conditions, what should the penalty be?

2. Should all players in professional sports be continuously tested for drugs? Should this policy extend to both high school and college sport players? If so, what should the penalties for such drug violations be? If high school and college sports players should not be tested for drugs, why not?

3. What if we find clear evidence that some currently admired major sports figures who scored big-time records in the past were using steroids or other performance-enhancing drugs while setting new and impressive records? Should anything be done about such evidence? If so, what penalties should the athletes receive? If not, why should we let them remain unblemished?

4. Are the real victims of this tragedy America's youth? Have athletes such as McGwire and Bonds betrayed the young who admire and emulate them? Do you think America's youth are affected by drug use in professional sports?

(continued)

How the "Juice" Is Flowing in Baseball (continued)

5. Does this scandal about professional sports and drug use suggest anything about the findings by the Centers for Disease Control and Prevention that steroid use among high school students more than doubled from 1991 to 2003?

6. As a middle school teacher, is Robert Eilek being overly severe regarding his treatment of McGwire's refusal to answer questions on steroid use at a congressional inquiry on steroid use?

Sources: Amazon.com. "Editorial Reviews." Available at: http://www.amazon.com/exec/obidos/asin/0060746408/ref=bxgy. Accessed February 17, 2011; Associated Press. "Strong Suspended for Performance-Enhancing Drugs." Sports ESPN. (26 April 2005). Available at: http://sports.espn.go.com/ mlb/news/story?id=2046762. Accessed April 18, 2011; Coile, Z. "House Bill Seeks to Toughen Steroid Rules: Athletes in All Leagues Would Be Held to the Strict Standards Used in Olympics." *San Francisco Chronicle,* Washington Bureau. (27 April 2005): 1–2; Dvorchak, R. "Former Steeler Courson Outlines Solutions for Steroid Use." Post-Gazette.com. (27 April 2005). Available at: http://www.post-gazette.com/pg/05117/494862.stm. Accessed February 17, 2011; Eilek, R. "Pro Sports Keep Heads in Sand on Steroids." *North County Times* (North San Diego and Southwest Riverside County). (23 April 2005). Available at: http://www.nctimes.com/articles/2005/04/24/opinion/commentary/19_31_454_23 _05.txt. Accessed February 17, 2011; and Health Reuters and Yahoo! News. "Anti-steroid Rules Proposed for U.S. Pro Sports." (27 April 2005).

■ Laws Intended to Stop the Use of Performance-Enhancing Drugs in Professional Sports

In 2003, the **World Anti-Doping Code** was approved and remained in effect from January 1, 2004, to December 31, 2008. (This code is the core document that provides the framework for harmonized anti-doping policies, rules, and regulations within sport organizations and among public authorities.)

The code consultation process, which was revised in April 2006, was similar to that used in the original drafting of the document between 2001 and 2003. The process included three stages of consultation, and culminated at the Third World Conference on Doping in Sport, which was held in November 2007. The revised code was endorsed by delegates at the World Conference on November 17, 2007, and unanimously adopted by the World Anti-Doping Agency's (WADA's) Foundation Board (WADA 2009).

This code has proven to be a very powerful and effective tool in the harmonization of anti-doping efforts worldwide since it came into force on January 1, 2004 (WADA 2009). In January 2009, the code's key principles and elements, along with several changes, were reapproved by WADA's Foundation Board for implementation. In addition, governments and sports leagues have shown overwhelming support in adopting the code and have supported the growing body of jurisprudence from the Court of Arbitration for Sport (CAS) that furthers the code's tenets.

The major changes in the 2009 code include ". . . firmness and fairness" (WADA 2009) so that what is already in place strengthens the prevention of doping in sport. There also are provisions for increased sanctions, greater flexibility (the accused athlete has the option to provide evidence that the substance used was not intended to enhance performance), clear listing and definition of specified substances violating the rules, incentives to come forward and report personal usage or use by other athletes of performance-enhancing drugs, financial sanctions (including clearly specified periods of ineligibility), and WADA's right to appeal to a Court of Sport Arbitration (WADA 2009).

■ Drugs Used by Athletes

A very memorable interview:

Yes, the steroids I used certainly made me get bigger. I was going out for football and I had just made the team, so I kept using them and the results were phenomenal. Now, 2 years later, I won't be graduating. Several months ago, they removed a tumor on my liver, but they didn't get all the cancer. I am going home at the end of this semester. My parents want me to stay with them for the time I have left. When I go, I only have one wish—I want to die big and always be known as big Jim. *(From Venturelli's research files, male, age 20, December 13, 1996)*

Studies have shown that athletes are less likely than nonathletes to use other drugs of abuse such

KEY TERMS

World Anti-Doping Code
the core document providing a framework for harmonized anti-doping policies, rules, and regulations within sport organizations and among public authorities

as marijuana, alcohol, barbiturates, cocaine, and hallucinogens (Hoberman and Yesalis 1995; Substance Abuse and Mental Health Services Administration [SAMHSA] 2007). However, athletes are much more likely than other populations to take drugs that enhance (physically or psychologically) or are thought to enhance competitive performance; these drugs include stimulants such as amphetamines and cocaine and an array of drugs with presumed ergogenic effects, such as anabolic steroids (Bell 1987; National Institute on Drug Abuse [NIDA] 2006b). Some of the major drugs abused by athletes are listed in **Table 16.1**, along with their desired effects. The sections that follow discuss the drugs that are most frequently self-

Table 16.1 Partial List of Ergogenic Substances and Expected Effects

Ergogenic drugs are substances that are used to enhance athletic performance.

DRUGS	EXPECTED RESULTS
Amino acids	Stimulate natural production of growth hormone
Amphetamines and cocaine	Increase strength, alertness, and endurance
Anabolic steroids	Increase muscle mass and strength
Asthma medication	Improve breathing
B-complex vitamins	Enhance body metabolism and increase energy
Beta-blockers	Reduce hand tremor and stimulate growth hormone
Caffeine	Reduce fatigue
Chromium	Enhance carbohydrate metabolism
Ephedrine	Improve breathing
Furosemide	Mask steroid use and enable rapid weight loss
Methylphenidate	Enhance alertness and endurance
Over-the-counter decongestants	Increase endurance
Thyroid hormone and energy	Enhance metabolism

Source: Harlan, R., and M. Garcia. "Neurobiology of Androgen Abuse." *Drugs of Abuse and Neurobiology,* edited by R. Watson, 185–201. Boca Raton, FL: CRC Press, 1992. Reprinted with permission. Copyright CRC Press.

administered by athletes in an effort to improve their competitive performance.

Anabolic Steroids

Anabolic steroids consist of a group of natural and synthetic drugs that are chemically similar to cholesterol and related to the male hormone testosterone (Guide4living.com 2005; Lukas 1993) and its artificial derivatives. Steroids are used for treatment of certain diseases such as specific types of anemia, some breast cancers, and testosterone deficiency. Although illegal when taken for nonmedical purposes, steroids have been illegally used by both athletes and nonathletes since the late 1950s to improve athletic ability and physical appearance because steroids have performance-enhancing and bodybuilding properties. Steroids are taken orally or injected into the muscles. Although males and females use steroids, males have higher rates of use (NIDA 2009; SAMHSA 1999b).

Naturally occurring male hormones, or androgens, are produced by the testes in males. These hormones are essential for normal growth and development of male sex organs as well as secondary sex characteristics such as muscular development, male hair patterns, voice changes, and fat distribution. The androgens are also necessary for appropriate growth spurts during adolescence (*Drug Facts and Comparisons* 1994). The principal accepted therapeutic use for androgens is for hormone replacement in males with abnormally functioning testes. In such cases, the androgens are administered before puberty and for prolonged periods during puberty to stimulate proper male development (*Drug Facts and Comparisons* 1994).

The Major Reasons for the Abuse of Anabolic Steroids

Under some conditions, androgen-like drugs can increase muscle mass and strength; for this reason, they are referred to as anabolic (able to stimulate the conversion of nutrients into tissue) steroids (because chemically, they are similar to the steroids produced in the adrenal glands). They are used by many athletes to improve performance (Burke and Davis 1992; NIDA 2006b).

One of the major reasons athletes give for abusing steroids is to improve their athletic performance. Another reason for taking steroids is to increase their muscle size or to reduce their body fat (NIDA 2006b). Others who abuse steroids in order

KEY TERMS

anabolic steroids
androgen-like drugs that can increase muscle mass and strength

to boost their muscle size have experienced physical or sexual abuse. In one series of interviews with male weightlifters, 25% who abused steroids reported memories of childhood physical or sexual abuse. Similarly, female weightlifters who had been raped were found to be twice as likely to report use of anabolic steroids or another purported muscle-building drug, compared with those women who had not been raped. Moreover, almost all of those who had been raped reported that they markedly increased their bodybuilding activities after the attack (NIDA 2006b). Finally, regarding adolescent steroid abuse, it is part of a pattern of high-risk behaviors. Such steroid-abusing adolescents have been found to take risks such as drinking and driving, carrying a gun, driving a motorcycle without a helmet, and abusing other illicit drugs. In conclusion, conditions such as **muscle dysmorphia** (a behavioral syndrome that causes individuals to have a distorted image of their bodies, perceiving themselves as looking small and weak, even when they may be large and muscular), a history of physical or sexual abuse, or a history of engaging in high-risk behaviors have all been associated with an increased risk of initiating or continuing steroid abuse.

It is estimated that as many as 1 million Americans have used or are currently using these drugs to achieve a competitive edge or for other purposes (Welder and Melchert 1993) (see **Figure 16.1**). The most commonly abused steroids are in two categories: oral and injectable steroids. Oral steroids include:

- Anadrol (oxymetholone)
- Oxandrin (oxandrolone)
- Dianabol (methandrostenolone)
- Winstrol (stanozolol)

Injectable steroids include:

- Deca-Durabolin (nandrolone decanoate)
- Durabolin (nandrolone phenylpropionate)
- Depo-Testosterone (testosterone cypionate)
- Equipoise (boldenone undecylenate)
- Tetrahydrogestrinone (THG)

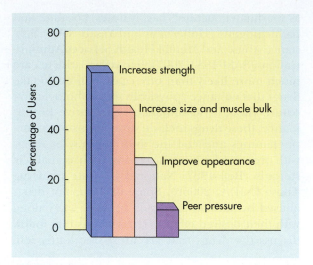

FIGURE 16.1

Reasons for nonmedical steroid use by college students.

Source: Harlan, R., and M. Garcia. "Neurobiology of Androgen Abuse." In *Drugs of Abuse and Neurobiology*, edited by R. Watson, 186. Boca Raton, FL: CRC Press, 1992. Reprinted with permission. Copyright CRC Press.

Studies suggest that approximately 2% of college-age men and 6.7% of male high school students use anabolic steroids (Harlan and Garcia 1992). More recent findings from a 2009 study funded by the National Institute on Drug Abuse (NIDA) found that only 1.3% of 8th and 10th graders and 2.2% of 12th graders had used steroids at least once in their lifetimes (NIDA 2010). "A 2001 NCAA survey found that usage of stimulants, including ephedrine and amphetamines, and anabolic steroids had risen slightly since 1997. Between 3% and 4% of athletes surveyed admitted using stimulants, and 1.4% admitted using steroids" (Suggs 2003). Also realize that these percentages are much lower than what the survey revealed because athletes are inclined to hide drug usage for fear of jeopardizing their eligibility to play sports as well as other more personal reasons having to do with image in the eyes of others. Further, in the United States, approximately 500,000 adolescents use steroids, and 52,000 children use anabolic steroids; "a study in the journal *Pediatrics* . . . found that 2.7% of Massachusetts middle-school athletes were using steroids" (Begley et al. 1999, p. 54). Another source indicates that males are more likely to use and abuse steroids than females (Johnston et al. 2006a). In a much larger nationwide study, in 2005, annual use rates were 1.2%, 1.8%, and 2.6% for boys in grades 8, 10, and 12, compared with 0.9%, 0.7%, and 0.4% for girls in those grades (Johnston et al. 2006a). Encourag-

KEY TERMS

muscle dysmorphia
behavioral syndrome that causes men to have a distorted image of their bodies, perceiving themselves as looking small and weak, even when they may be large and muscular; women with this condition think they look fat and flabby, even though they may actually be lean and muscular

ing results indicate that steroid use among adolescents in 8th, 10th, and 12th grade is significantly lower than in previous years (Johnston et al. 2006a). Competition for scholarships and entry into professional sports are major factors that influence young athletes to use steroids (Scott, Wagner, and Barlow 1996).

Although the vast majority of anabolic steroid users are male, women involved in bodybuilding and strength and endurance sports also abuse these drugs. Among seniors in high school, 3.2% of the males reported steroid use in the past year compared with 1.1% of the females. These statistics are much lower among 19- to 32-year-olds—0.4%—with males accounting for all steroid use (Johnston et al. 2004).

The first report of use of anabolic steroids to improve athletic performance was in 1954 by the Russian weightlifting team. These drugs' performance-enhancing advantages were quickly recognized by other athletes, and it has been estimated that as many as 90% of the competitors in the 1960 Olympic Games used some form of steroid (Toronto 1992). Because of the widespread misuse and associated problems with the use of these drugs, anabolic steroids were classified as Schedule III controlled drugs in 1991 (see Chapter 3 for drug schedules) (Merchant 1992).

Due to federal regulations, individuals convicted of a first offense of trafficking with anabolic steroids can be sentenced to a maximum prison term of 5 years and a $250,000 fine. For a second offense, the prison term can increase to 10 years with a $500,000 fine. Even possession of illicitly obtained anabolic steroids can result in a 1-year term with at least a $1000 fine (U.S. Department of Justice 1991–1992).

Besides risking their health, athletes who choose to dope should remember that they are role models. Seventy-three percent of youth want to be like a famous athlete; 53% of youth say it is common for famous athletes to use banned substances to get ahead.

Patterns of Abuse

Geographical factors appear to have little to do with the use of anabolic steroids among athletes. In both innercity and suburban schools, all are equally attracted to these drugs. However, some athletes are more inclined to abuse anabolic steroids than others. For example, football players have the highest rate of abuse; in a survey conducted by the National Collegiate Athletic Association (NCAA) of 11 NCAA colleges and universities, 9% of football players self-reported, whereas track and field athletes have the lowest rate of abuse (4% reported) (National Institutes of Health [NIH] and NIDA 1998). Another study using a more indirect method of interviewing found rates three times higher than the percentages just reported. In addition, the likelihood of abusing these drugs increases as the level of competition increases. Usage rates were approximately 14% in NCAA Division I athletes and 30% to 75% in professional athletes (Lukas 1993). In general, usage patterns for anabolic steroids vary considerably according to athletes' motivation, the level of competition, the type of sport, and the pressure for winning.

The pattern usually consists of self-administering doses that are 10 to 200 times greater than dosages used for legitimate medical conditions (Welder and Melchert 1993). Users take nonmedical anabolic-androgenic steroids in cycles, periods of use lasting 6 to 12 weeks or longer. **Stacking** these drugs means taking more than one at a time, which is common. The use of different steroids taken singly but in sequence is called **cycling**. To avoid developing tolerance to a particular steroid (**plateauing**), athletes often stagger the various drugs, sometimes taking them in overlapping patterns or alternately. Users often move from a low daily dose at the beginning of a cycle to a higher dose, then reduce their use toward the end of the cycle (**pyramiding**). To combat the unwanted side effects of steroids, such as

KEY TERMS

stacking
use of several types of steroids at the same time

cycling
use of different types of steroids singly but in sequence

plateauing
developing tolerance to the effects of anabolic steroids

pyramiding
moving from a low daily dose at the beginning of the cycle to a higher dose, then reducing use toward the end of the cycle

severe skin rashes and development of irreversible masculine traits in women, as well as sudden anger and explosive physical aggressiveness (known as "roid rage" in men), other drugs such as diuretics, antiestrogens, human chorionic gonadotropin, and antiacne medication are often taken concurrently. This pattern of use is referred to by users as an **array**. In general, power athletes prefer stacking, whereas bodybuilders prefer cycling. (See **Table 16.2**, which lists the class of performance-enhancing substances, examples, what these drugs do, who is likely to use such drugs, status regarding whether the drug is illicit or licit, and where athletes are likely to secure the drug.)

Because steroid use has been prohibited by all legitimate sporting organizations, urine testing just before the athletic event has become commonplace (Lukas 1993). Steroid-using athletes attempt to avoid detection by trying to fool the tests. These highly questionable strategies include the following (Lukas 1993; Merchant 1992):

- Using the steroid only during training for the athletic events, but discontinuing its use several weeks before the competition to allow the drug to disappear from the body. Because oral steroids are cleared from the body faster than the injectable types, they are usually discontinued 2 to 4 weeks prior to competition, and the injection steroids are stopped 3 to 6 weeks before competition.
- Taking drugs, such as probenecid, that block the excretion of steroids in the urine. Probenecid inhibits the substance from reaching the urine. Urine tests are all that the International Olympic Committee (IOC) requires (Begley et al. 1999).
- Using diuretics and drinking large quantities of water to increase the urine output and dilute the steroid so it cannot be detected by the test.
- Adding adulterant chemicals to the urine, such as Drano, Clorox, ammonia, or eye drops to invalidate the tests.

Recent Developments in Evading Detection

One serious problem today, according to Prince Alexandre de Merode, who has been in charge of

the IOC's Medical Commission for 31 years, is that:

> the newest doping agents pose the risk of serious health problems, and even death. But a larger reason is that it is ridiculously easy to dope and not be caught. Doping and detection are like an arms race. First trainers discover a performance-enhancing drug. Then, sports officials develop a test for it. Trainers retaliate by inventing a way to elude the detectors. So far, doping has stayed a lap ahead.

Other comments from the same source:

> "Undetectable drugs are 90 percent of estimated doping cases," said Hein Verbruggen, head of [the] International Cycling Union. (Begley et al. 1999, p. 50)

Chemists constantly use the 72 banned steroids to change the testosterone molecule. "All you have to do is take a steroid not on the list. Or, simply by going cold turkey a few weeks before competition, an athlete can get the muscle-bulking effects without getting caught" (Begley et al. 1999, p. 51).

Some of the most recent types of drugs that athletes use, even though they are all banned by WADA, are listed in **Table 16.3**. This table summarizes the 2010 list of prohibited performance-enhancing substances banned by the World Anti-Doping Code—International Standard.

Effects of Anabolic Steroids

Low to moderate doses of anabolic steroids have little effect on the strength or athletic skills of the average adult. However, when high doses are used by athletes during intense training programs, these drugs cause significant gains in lean body mass (i.e., muscle) and strength while decreasing fat (Lukas 1993). Because most of these effects are transient and will disappear when steroid use is stopped, athletes feel compelled to continue using them and become psychologically hooked (Toronto 1992). The drugs are most likely to benefit athletes in contact and strength sports in which increased muscle mass provides an advantage, such as weightlifting and football; anabolic steroids are less likely to benefit athletes involved in sports requiring dexterity and agility, such as baseball or tennis.

The risks associated with anabolic steroids are not completely understood. Most certainly, the higher the doses and the longer the use, the greater the potential damage these drugs can do to the body. Some of the adverse effects thought to occur with

KEY TERMS

array
use of other drugs while taking anabolic steroids to avoid possible side effects

Table 16.2 Performance-Enhancing Substances Banned by the NCAA

The following are among the substances many athletes use even though these are banned by the National Collegiate Athletic Association (NCAA) and even though some are illegal under federal and state laws.

CLASS	EXAMPLES	WHAT DOES IT DO	WHO USES IT?	IS IT LEGAL?	WHERE DO ATHLETES GET IT
Steroids	Nandrolone, stanozol	Increases testosterone levels, thus building muscle	Any athlete in a sport that requires strength and doesn't penalize muscle bulk can benefit; in an NCAA survey, football, baseball, rifle, and water-polo athletes admitted using steroids	Not without a prescription	Over the Internet or from a complicit doctor
Steroids precursors	Androstenedione, 19-norandro-stenediol	Can be converted into testosterone in the body	Same as above	Yes, under the Dietary Supplement and Health Education Act of 1994	In drug stores, gyms, nutritional supplement stores, and some grocery stores
Hormones	Human growth hormone (HGH), erythropoietin (EPO)	HGH promotes growth in children and muscle development in adults; EPO increases production of red blood cells	HGH is used by the same kinds of athletes who use steroids; endurance athletes benefit from EPO	Not without a prescription	Over the Internet
Stimulants	Ephedrine, caffeine (in excessive amounts)	Raises metabolic rate, giving a burst of energy	Virtually all types of athletes; not only do strength-orientated athletes like football players get pumped up for workouts but athletes like gymnasts use them to try to lose weight	Yes; the FDA has banned ephedrine and caffeine (if the concentration in urine exceeds 15 mg/mL) as of 2001	Generally available in drug stores and specialty stores

Source: Suggs, W. "Deadly Fuel: As Supplements and Steroids Tempt and Endanger More Athletes, What Are Colleges Doing?" *The Chronicle of Higher Education* XLIX (14 March 2003): A37. Copyright 2003, The Chronicle of Higher Education. Reprinted with permission.

heavy steroid use (10 to 30 times the doses used therapeutically) include the following:

- Increased bad blood cholesterol levels, which could eventually clog arteries and cause heart attacks and strokes (National Clearinghouse for Alcohol and Drug Information [NCADI] 1999)
- Increased risk of liver disorders, such as jaundice and tumors (Lukas 1993)

- Psychological side effects, including irritability, outbursts of anger, mania, psychosis, and major depression
- Possible psychological and physical dependence with continual use of high doses, resulting in withdrawal symptoms, such as steroid craving (52%), fatigue (43%), depression (41%), restlessness (29%), loss of appetite (24%), insomnia (20%), diminished sex drive (20%), and headaches (20%) (Lukas 1993)

Table 16.3   **Extract from WADA's 2011 List of Prohibited Substances and Methods***

ANABOLIC AGENTS
Anabolic androgenic steroids (AASs)
Endogenous steroids (e.g., androstenediol, androstenedione, testosterone)
Other Anabolic Agents
Other steroids (e.g., clenbuterol, selective androgen receptor modulators [SARMs], tibolone, zeranol, zilpaterol)
Peptide hormones and growth factors and related substances (e.g., erythropoisis)
Stimulating agents (e.g., erythropoietin A [EPO]), darbepoetin (dEPO), and hematide
Chorionic gonadotropin (CG) and luteinizing hormone (LH) in males
Insulins
Corticotropins
Human growth hormone (HGH), insulin-like growth factor-1 (IGF-1), mechano growth factors (MGFs) (e.g., platelet-derived growth factor [PDGF], fibroblast growth factors [FGFs])
Platelet-derived preparations (e.g., platelet-rich plasma, "blood spinning") administered by intramuscular; use requires declaration in accordance with the International Standards for Therapeutic Use Exemptions
β-2 AGONISTS
Hormone Antagonist and Modulators
Aromatase inhibitors (e.g., aminoglutethimide, anastrozole, exemestane, formestane, letrozole)
Selective estrogen receptor modulators (SERMs) (e.g., raloxifene, tamoxifen, toremifene)
Other anti-estrogenic substances (e.g., clomiphene, cyclofenil, fulvestrant)
Agents modifying myostatin functions(s) (e.g., myostatin inhibitors)
Diuretics and Other Masking Agents
Diuretics (e.g., acetazolamide, bumetanide, canrenone, furosemide, thiazides)
Masking agents (e.g., probenecid, plasma expanders [glycerol], intravenous administration [of albumin, dextran, hydroxyethyl starch, and mannitol]) and other substances with similar biological effects
SUBSTANCES AND METHODS PROHIBITED IN COMPETITION
Stimulants
Nonspecified stimulants (e.g., adrafinil, amphetamine, cocaine, crotetamide, fencamine, others not specified)
Specified stimulants (e.g., adrenaline, cathine, ephedrine, heptaminol, pemoline, strychnine, others with similar chemical structure and similar biological effects)
Narcotics
Narcotics (e.g., buprenorphine, dextromoramide, diamorphine [heroin], fetanyl [and its derivatives], hydromorphone, methadone, k, morphine, oxycodone, oxymorphone, pentazocine, pethidine)

Table 16.3 (*continued*)

SUBSTANCES AND METHODS PROHIBITED IN COMPETITION
Cannabinoids
Natural or synthetic THC and THC-like cannabinoids (e.g., hashish, marijuana, HU-210)
Glucocorticosteroids
All (when administered orally, intravenously, intramuscularly, or rectally)
SUBSTANCES PROHIBITED DURING COMPETITION
Alcohol (detection will be conducted by analysis of breath and/or blood; the doping violation threshold is 0.10 g/L)
β-blockers (e.g., acebutolol, alprenolol, bunolol, labetalol, nadolol, pindolol, sotalol, timolol)

*The List of Prohibited Substances and Methods is the World Anti-Doping Agency's (WADA) International Standard identifying substances and methods prohibited in-competition, out-of-competition, and in particular sports. The complete and current List can be found on WADA's website at http://www.wada-ama.org/prohibitedlist. Please be advised that the official text of the List shall be maintained by WADA and, in the event of any discrepancy between this extract and the List, the official WADA List shall prevail.

Source: World Anti-Doping Agency (WADA). www.wada-ama.org. Printed with permission. May 2011.

- Alterations in reproductive systems and sex hormones, causing changes in gender-related characteristics (Burke and Davis 1992): breast enlargement in males, breast reduction and bodily hair growth in females, infertility in both genders, and changes in genitalia—atrophy (shrinkage) of the penis and testicles in males and enlargement of external genitalia in females (Street, Antonio, and Cudlipp 1996)
- Changes in skin and hair in both genders: increased incidence and severity of acne, male pattern baldness, and increased body hair (Burke and Davis 1992)
- Persistent unpleasant breath odor (NCADI 1999)
- Swelling of the feet or lower limbs (NCADI 1999)
- Other changes, including stunted growth in adolescents, deepening of voice in females, and water retention, causing bloating (Burke and Davis 1992; Street et al. 1996)

Sources of Steroids

Where do the anabolic steroids come from? About 50% of the anabolic steroids used in the United States are prescribed by doctors; the other 50% are obtained from the black market. Black market sources of steroids include drugs diverted from legitimate channels, smuggled from foreign countries— including Brazil, Italy, Mexico, Great Britain, Portugal, France, and Peru (NIDA 1996)—that are designated for veterinarian use, or inactive counterfeits (U.S. Department of Justice 1991–1992). A primary source for steroids in the United States is the Baja, California, area of Mexico (Yesalis and Cowart 1998). The steroids are manufactured in Mexico City and shipped to pharmacies in the Baja region. Some health food stores and mail-order firms also offer products with names similar to the prescription anabolic steroids, such as Dynabdin, Metrobolin, and Diostero. These sham steroids contain only vitamins, amino acids, or micronutrients (Merchant 1992; NIDA 2006).

Most steroids used for nonmedical purposes are obtained illegally. A major federal report indicates that sources of illicit steroids fall into three rough categories: (1) smuggled steroids manufactured licitly or illicitly abroad, (2) drugs legally manufactured in this country and diverted to illicit sales at various places in the distribution chain, and (3) drugs clandestinely produced domestically. Small minorities of users obtain their drugs by prescription. Actual doses are often difficult to estimate because the product may have been produced in an uncontrolled laboratory with unknown quality control, may have been intended for veterinary use with its human equivalent doses not known, or may be counterfeit (NIH and NIDA 1998). Another source noted that the majority of young people report that steroids are easily available through their friends and coaches (McCaffrey 1999).

Stimulant Use Among Athletes

There are often reports in the media of football, basketball, or baseball players who have tested positive in a drug-screening evaluation or who have been suspended from competition due to drug abuse. In 1986, reports of cocaine-related deaths of sports figures included basketball star Len Bias and professional football player Don Rogers. Perhaps such sports tragedies helped convince some U.S. youth of the dangers of stimulant abuse and contributed to the decline in drug abuse in the late 1980s (Johnston et al. 1993). Clearly, no one—not even an athlete—is immune from the risks of these drugs.

Amphetamines and cocaine are abused to improve athletic skills (McDonald 1995). However, it is not clear if stimulants actually enhance athletic performance or merely the athlete's perception of performance. Many athletes believe these drugs promote quickness, enhance endurance, delay fatigue, increase self-confidence and aggression, and

mask pain (Hoberman and Yesalis 1995). In fact, some studies have shown that stimulants can improve some aspects of athletic performance, especially in the presence of fatigue (NIDA 1996). However, the risk of using stimulants in sports is substantial because these drugs mask extreme fatigue, increase the risk of heat exhaustion, and can have severe cardiovascular consequences, such as heart attacks and strokes (Bell 1987) (see "Case in Point: When Drugs Enter the Boxing Ring").

Although some athletes would never consider using the hard stimulants, such as cocaine and amphetamines, milder stimulants that are legal and available over-the-counter (OTC) may be thought to be acceptable. Such stimulants include caffeine and OTC decongestants (for example, phenylpropanolamine and phenylephrine). These drugs can be a double-edged sword for the athlete. Their use can reduce fatigue, give a sense of energy, and even mask pain. Nevertheless, in high doses, especially when combined, they can cause nervousness, tremors, and restlessness; impair concentration; accelerate dehydration; and interfere with sleep ("OTC Drugs and Athletes" 1992). Some athletic competitions limit permissible blood levels of caf-

---

►Case in Point   When Drugs Enter the Boxing Ring◄

When Oliver McCall entered the boxing ring to fight for the heavyweight championship on February 7, 1997, he was not alone. With him came the specter of years of drug abuse. Just 7 weeks before, McCall had been arrested for swinging a Christmas tree around a hotel lobby while in a drug-induced haze. A few years earlier, he was found in a crack house after having been mugged by a fellow addict, to whom he lost the $1.5 million check he had carried with him in a sock to buy drugs. These events were just two of many drug-related occurrences on his record. His most recent arrest, however, had been followed by a drug treatment program, which he attended daily.

But something went wrong the night of February 7. After having announced to a friend, "I want my title. I'm fighting for my life," McCall seemed to want to get knocked out. In the third round, in the middle of the ring, in front of a packed audience, he listlessly walked around as his opponent, Lennox Lewis, threw punches

at him. McCall dodged and bobbed his head, yet refused to fight back. After the fourth round, McCall stood alone, away from his corner, sobbing uncontrollably, seemingly having a nervous breakdown in front of a worldwide cable television audience. Fifty-five seconds into the fifth round, referee Mills Lane stopped the fight. Lewis was the winner. McCall, in more ways than one, was not.

Although drugs have been an unwelcome part of sports in recent years, there are few cases where the consequences became more publicly evident. Here was a great contradiction for the world to see: Lennox Lewis, the athlete who had never been knocked down, and Oliver McCall, the man floored by the pain and drugs in his life. McCall's trainer, George Benton, said, "It was hard to watch, but it could be the best thing that ever happened to the human race. Now a father can tell his kids, 'You see what you saw on T.V.? You see what happens on drugs?' It was a hell of a lesson."

Source: Eskenazi, G. "McCall Tries to Explain Bizarre Action." *New York Times.* (9 February 1997). Available at: http://www.nytimes.com/1997/02/09/sports/mccall-tries-to-explain-bizarre-actions.html?scp=4&sq=oliver%20mccall&st=cse. Accessed April 18, 2011.

feine and do not allow the use of OTC stimulants such as decongestant drugs.

Miscellaneous Ergogenic Drugs

Most athletic organizations have banned the use of anabolic steroids and stimulants and are using more effective screening procedures to detect offenders. A result of this clampdown has been the search for alternative performance-enhancing drugs by athletes who feel a need for such pharmacological assistance. The following are brief discussions of a few of these substitute ergogenic substances.

Clenbuterol

At the 1992 Olympic Games in Barcelona, Spain, at least four athletes, including German world sprint champion Katrina Krabbe, were disqualified from competition for using the drug clenbuterol to enhance their athletic performance (Merchant 1992). Not legally available in the United States, this drug is known as "Doper's Delight" and is supposed to improve breathing and increase strength. Currently, most athletic urine examinations test for it.

Erythropoietin

Clinically, erythropoietin is a drug used to treat patients with anemia (Kennedy 2000). Because it stimulates the production of red blood cells (the oxygen-carrying cells in the blood), it is thought that this drug enhances oxygen use and produces additional energy. Erythropoietin is being used as a substitute for blood doping. *Blood doping* is when athletes attempt to increase their number of red blood cells by reinfusing some of their own blood (which has been stored) before an athletic event.

Currently tests for presence of Erythropoietin is detectable and has been reported to be used by athletes engaged in endurance activities such as long-distance cycling. The use of erythropoietin by athletes is extremely dangerous and is thought to be responsible for several deaths. It is also very expensive, which likely has helped to limit its abuse (Merchant 1992).

Human Growth Factor and Human Growth Hormone

Athletes sometimes abuse two types of steroids: **human growth factor (HGF)** and its designer drug synthetic version, **human growth hormone (HGH)**. HGH also is referred to simply as GH (growth hormone). HGF, also known as *somatotropin,* is a hormone nat-

urally secreted by the pituitary gland at the base of the brain that helps to achieve normal growth potential of muscles, bones, and internal organs. Some athletes claim that release of natural HGF can be simulated by using drugs such as levodopa (used to treat Parkinson's disease), clonidine (used to treat hypertension), and amino acids. Athletes use commercially prepared HGH because it cannot be distinguished from naturally occurring HGF (Kennedy 2000).

Use of this hormone by athletes is limited, however, by its high cost. The benefits of HGF to athletic performance are very controversial, although the potential side effects are substantial, including abnormal growth patterns (called acromegaly), diabetes, thyroid gland problems, heart disease, and loss of sex drive (Merchant 1992).

The synthetic HGH is available in the form of a structured steroid-type analog sold in vials; this product is used to build muscle tissue, with corresponding decreases in body fat, without exercise (McDonald 1995). HGH is probably the most potent anabolic agent ever discovered, but it is also one of the most expensive. In fact, HGH is so expensive that until the mid-1990s, "its use in the United States was confined to pediatric endocrinologists who used it to treat undersized children" (McDonald 1995, p. C1). To date, tests are capable of detecting HGH in the blood (WebMD.com 2008). In addition, the side effects of this drug remain largely unknown. As a result, this drug is highly vulnerable to abuse.

Beta (β)-Adrenergic Blockers

The β-adrenergic blockers are drugs that affect the cardiovascular system and are frequently used to treat hypertension. They have been used in sports because they reduce heart rate and signs of nervousness, which in turn quiets hand tremors. Consequently, these drugs are most likely to be used by individuals participating in sports that require steady hands, such as competitive shooting. The use of these drugs is prohibited by most athletic organizations (Kennedy 2000; Merchant 1992).

KEY TERMS

human growth factor (HGF)
a hormone that stimulates normal growth

human growth hormone (HGH)
a designer drug synthetic version of HGF; also referred to as simply GH (growth hormone)

Gamma-Hydroxybutyrate

The substance gamma-hydroxybutyrate (GHB) is found naturally in the brain and has been used in England to treat insomnia. Athletes and bodybuilders have used GHB to increase muscle mass and strength (Kennedy 2000). Although the actual effects of the compound are not known, it has been reported to cause euphoria and increase the release of growth hormone. Acute poisoning with GHB has occurred, causing hospitalization; other adverse effects can include headaches, nausea, vomiting, muscle jerking, and even short-term coma, though full recovery has been universal ("Bodybuilding Drug" 1992; "Multistate Outbreak" 1994). Prolonged use may cause withdrawal (insomnia, anxiety, and tremor). GHB is especially dangerous when combined with central nervous system (CNS) stimulants such as amphetamines and cocaine.

■ Prevention and Treatment

If the problem of drug abuse among athletes is to be dealt with effectively, sports programs must be designed to discourage inappropriate drug use and assist athletes who have developed drug abuse problems. Coaches and administrators should make it clear to sports participants that substance abuse will never give an athlete a competitive advantage in their programs and will not be tolerated. The **Adolescents Training and Learning to Avoid Steroids (ATLAS) program**, which was developed by Dr. Linn Goldberg of Oregon Health Sciences at the University of Portland, is one of the most successful prevention programs for steroid abuse.

> The Adolescent[s] Training and Learning to Avoid Steroids Program (ATLAS) was designed to lower the use of anabolic steroids among high school athletes. The program combined classroom and weight-training sessions, to teach students about strength training, nutrition, and risk factors for steroid use. Overall, the ATLAS program was found to reduce the use of steroids. (Child Trends 2009)

Athletes, coaches, and team leaders are trained to educate team members about the effects of anabolic steroid abuse. Because adolescents already know that anabolic steroids build muscles and can increase athletic abilities, both desirable and adverse effects of steroid use are taught. Research has shown that information about anabolic steroids that fails to acknowledge potential benefits creates a credibility gap that can make youths distrustful of the prevention program. The program consists of three components: classroom, weight training, and parent information components to "give the student athletes the knowledge and skills to resist steroid use and achieve their athletic goals in more effective, healthier ways" (Goldberg et al. 1996, p. 1555):

1. The classroom component consists of football coaches and student leaders conducting highly interactive sessions that explore the effects of steroids, the elements of sports nutrition, and strength training alternatives to steroid use. In this setting, while the coaches introduce topics and act as leaders, the students are exploring and learning from one another (Goldberg et al. 1996).
2. In the weight-training component, research staff members conduct seven hands-on sessions that teach the students proper weight-training techniques (Goldberg et al. 1996).
3. The parent information component consists of discussions and information sessions with parents. The staff provides nutrition guidelines and seeks compliance while stressing the very best nutrition for the athletes and their families. Parents become more vigilant against steroid use and learn to enjoy well-balanced, nutritious meals (Goldberg et al. 1996).

Briefly summarized, results indicate that the students who participated in this program in comparison with the control group (a group of students not participating in the program) showed they (1) knew more about proper exercise, (2) had a clear understanding of the dangers of using steroids and had become much more sensitized to the harmful effects of such drugs, (3) held more unfavorable views of others' use of anabolic steroids, and (4) were more likely to avoid unhealthy eating (such as frequenting fast-food restaurants) (Child Trends 2009; Goldberg et al. 1996).

KEY TERMS

Adolescents Training and Learning to Avoid Steroids (ATLAS) program
an anabolic abuse prevention educational program that empowers student athletes to make the right choices about steroid use

Drug Use Among Women

Until recently, little was known about the patterns of female drug abuse. In general, most clinical drug abuse research, including treatment and rehabilitation outcomes, was either conducted in male populations and the results were extrapolated to women or the research was done in general populations with little regard to gender influences (About.com 2007b; Dicker and Leighton 1994; Klee and Jackson 2002; Lin 1994; NIDA 2006a; U.S. Department of Health and Human Services (USDHHS) and NIDA 1999). Most researchers considered drug abuse to be a male problem. Today, the research focusing on women and drug use is better, but a greater amount of study is still needed. Even today, scientists performing even basic research with animals generally prefer male animal models to avoid the hormonal complexities of female animals. However, a growing concern for the importance of unique emotional, social, biochemical, and hormonal features in females has caused researchers to acknowledge the importance of gender differences.

■ Women More Concerned About Drug Use than Men

Women are expressing greater initial concerns about drug use than men. While "most recent studies suggest that gender either has no effect on treatment initiation, or, if it has an effect, women are more likely than men to initiate treatment" (Green 2006, p. 6). When asked whether drug abuse is a greater problem now than 5 years earlier, 51% of women and 42% of men answered "yes" (Drug Strategies 1998). When asked whether drug use is a big concern among youth, 58% of women and 48% of men answered "yes" (Drug Strategies 1998). Further, 58% of women and 50% of men thought it was wrong to reduce prevention funds while increasing prison funds (Drug Strategies 1998). One reason for this discrepancy may be that women traditionally have been primary caregivers; therefore, they feel more responsible about issues that can plague their communities and their families and often feel the need to be more vocal and be in positions that maintain harmony within the family setting (Green 2006). Women also generally express more concerns about safety issues than men because they are more likely to be victims of violent crimes, such as muggings or sexual assaults.

■ Patterns of Drug Use: Comparing Females with Males

Recent surveys comparing male and female drug use patterns confirm that differences exist among the licit and illicit drug-using populations. **Table 16.4** compares annual female and male drug use among respondents ages 19 to 30. The research findings in this table indicate the following gender-related differences in drug use (Johnston et al. 2009b):

- Overall, females consistently use fewer licit and illicit drugs (30% of females versus 37% of males use illicit drugs).
- Most types of abused drugs (in descending order) for females were: alcohol (84.3%), flavored alcoholic beverages (62.4%), cigarettes (31.8%), binge drinking (five or more drinks in a row in last 2 weeks; 30.5%), any illicit drug (30.3%), marijuana (24.3%), and any illicit drug other than marijuana (16.9%).
- Males have higher annual prevalence rates for nearly all of the specific illicit drugs, with ratios of two or greater for inhalants, LSD, hallucinogens other than LSD, PCP, heroin (with and without using a needle), GHB, ketamine, and steroids. For example, among 19- to 30-year-olds, LSD was used by 1.8% of males versus 0.9% of females during the prior 12 months (see Table 16.4).
- Females (62.4%) have a much greater tendency to drink flavored alcoholic beverages than males (47.5%), and females are slightly more likely to use methamphetamine (1.1%) than males (0.6%) and smoke crack (1%) than males (0.8).
- All three measures of cocaine (cocaine, other cocaine, and crack) showed higher rates of use by males than females (19- to 30-year-olds).
- Other, greater gender differences among 19- to 30-year-olds are found in marijuana use (32.5% for males versus 24.3% for females), daily alcohol use (7.5% versus 3.7%; not shown in table), and occasions of drinking five or more drinks in a row in the prior 2 weeks (46.5% versus 30.5%). This gender difference in occasions of heavy drinking is even greater among young adults than among 12th graders, which is 28% for males versus 21% for females.
- MDMA (Ecstasy) use is only modestly higher among males than among females in the young adult sample overall (annual prevalence 3.8% versus 2.6%, respectively).
- The use of narcotics other than heroin outside of medical supervision is at 10.3% annual prevalence for males versus 7.7% for females. Use of Vicodin (not shown in table), one of the most widely used drugs, differs a bit more (11.1% versus 7.7%). There is also a gender contrast for

Table 16.4 **Annual Use of Various Types of Drugs by Gender Among Respondents of Modal, Age 19–30 (percentage of total population)**

	FEMALES	MALES	TOTAL
Alcohol	84.3	84.3	84.3
Flavored alcoholic beverages	62.4	48.5	56.9
Cigarettes	31.8	38.2	34.4
Five or more drinks in a row in last 2 weeks	30.5	46.5	37.0
Any illicit drug	30.3	36.8	32.9
Marijuana	24.3	32.5	27.6
Any illicit drug other than marijuana	16.9	21.0	18.5
Narcotics other than heroin*	7.7	10.3	8.8
Tranquilizers*	6.2	7.6	6.7
Cocaine	4.4	8.0	5.8
Amphetamines, adjusted*	4.4	5.5	4.9
Other cocaine	4.1	7.4	5.4
Sedatives (barbiturates)*	4.1	4.8	4.4
MDMA (Ecstasy)	2.6	3.8	3.1
Hallucinogens	2.4	5.6	3.7
Hallucinogens other than LSD	2.0	5.1	3.2
Methamphetamines	1.1	0.6	0.9
LSD	0.9	1.8	1.3
Crack	0.8	1.0	0.9
Inhalants	0.8	1.9	1.3
Crystal methamphetamine (ice)	0.7	0.7	0.7
Heroin	0.4	0.6	0.5
Steroids	0.2	0.7	0.4
PCP	0.2	0.5	0.3
Heroin (with a needle)	0.1	0.2	0.1
Heroin (without a needle)	0.1	0.7	0.4

*Nonprescription use.

Source: Johnson, L. D., P. M. O'Malley, J. G Bachman, and J. E Schulenberg. *Monitoring the Future: National Survey Results on Drug Use, 1975–2008. Volume II: College Students and Adults.* NIH Publication No. 09-7430. Bethesda, MD: National Institute on Drug Abuse, 2009.

OxyContin (also not shown in the table; annual prevalence of 4.9% for males versus 2.7% for females).

- The use of amphetamines, which is now about equivalent among males and females in high school, is also fairly similar for both genders in this post–high school period (annual prevalence of 5.5% vs. 4.4%, respectively).
- Males are also more likely to smoke cigarettes than females (38.2% for males versus 31.8% for females).
- Steroid use among young adults (19- to 30-year-olds) is much more prevalent among males than females, as is true for 12th graders. Among 12th graders, 2.5% of males reported steroid use in the past year versus 0.4% of females.

One finding that is often hidden by current drug use statistics is that nationwide surveys confirm that drug use is increasing among women, often more rapidly than among men (Drug Strategies 1998; National Survey on Drug Use and Health [NSDUH] 2007). From 1990 through 1996, the number of women seeking emergency drug treatment rose more rapidly than the number of men seeking such emergency treatment. Hospital records indicate that there were more women seeking emergency drug treatment for heroin and marijuana (Drug Strategies 1998). Other gender differences are that older women (over 60) tend to abuse tranquilizers, sedatives, and antidepressants (Drug Strategies 1998) and, in some cases, girls in junior high and high school are now surpassing boys with regard to alcohol and tobacco use. Drinking rates are increasing more rapidly for girls than for boys (Drug Strategies 1998), and women in general are more likely than men to become addicted to tobacco. Two factors that make smoking attractive to women (and girls) are that they believe it reduces stress and controls weight (Drug Strategies 1998).

Although some similarities appear between genders in drug usage rates for specific types of drugs, the general differences in the prevalence rates for females and males compel researchers to look for explanations so that we can better understand and deal with gender-related drug abuse problems.

■ Female Roles, Seeking Treatment, and Drug Addiction

Women are expected to take on more responsibilities than in my mother's day. Not only are we expected to work like men, but we also take care of the house, worry about the children, and get dinner on the table. If the house needs cleaning, everyone looks at the woman of the house. Men still have these expectations. I know things are changing with more equality between the sexes, but real equality of responsibilities has yet to occur. After everyone gets to bed on weekdays, I have a few drinks in order to calm me down before I go to bed. *(From Venturelli's research files, female employed full-time, age 43, June 30, 1996)*

Another interview revealed the following:

My boyfriend does vacuum when I ask, but not much else. Of course, if his boss is coming to visit, then he appears concerned about cleaning the house. How many times is he fast asleep and I am having some hard liquor and a few puffs from a joint after cleaning everything before we get up the next morning. I used to complain but he does not really care about the housework, so I compensate by getting buzzed before going to sleep. *(From Venturelli's research files, female employed part-time, age 29, 1997)*

Recent research indicates that most people who have a substance use problem do not receive treatment. In comparing men with women, women are at a greater disadvantage for receiving substance abuse treatment.

In 2006, 7.4 million women aged 18 or older needed treatment for a substance abuse disorder involving alcohol or illicit drugs, but only 822,000 (11.2%) received treatment. . . . Of the women aged 18 to 49 who needed substance abuse treatment in the past year, 5.5% felt they needed treatment but did not receive it, and 84.2% neither received treatment nor perceived a need for it. (NSDUH 2007)

The reasons why and percentage of women ages 18 to 49 who needed treatment and did not receive it were:

- Not ready to stop using (36%)
- Cost/insurance barriers (34%)
- Social stigma (29%)
- Did not feel need for treatment/could handle the problem without treatment (15.5%)
- Did not know where to go for treatment (13.2%)
- Did not have the time (4.7%)
- Treatment would not help (2.7%)
- Other access barriers (15.7%) (NSDUH 2007; SAMHSA 2010)

To appreciate the impact of drug abuse on women and the reasons why they are more reluctant to seek substance abuse treatment, it is necessary to understand the uniqueness of female roles in our society. Relative to drug abuse problems, women today are often judged by a double standard. Women suffering from drug addictions are often perceived less tolerantly than comparably addicted men (Erickson and Murray 1989). Because of these social biases, women are afraid of being condemned and are less likely to seek professional help for their own personal drug abuse problems. In addition, family, friends, and associates are less inclined to provide drug-dependent women with important emotional support (Klee and Jackson 2002; NSDUH 2007; USDHHS and NIDA 1999).

The image of the alcoholic woman has always been that of one who is boisterous, flirtatious, effusive, and, sometimes, loudmouthed. This may be the person she might become on occasion, but more often she is secluded in the privacy of her apartment or home after getting the kids off to school or having just come home from the office, classroom, or business. She is shy, reclusive to a point, alienated, retrospective, and lacking in self-esteem. Later in her drinking, she may become self-pitying, resentful, and even childishly cruel because of alcohol usage (Kirkpatrick 1999; Verhaak et al. 2010).

Due to their unique socioeconomic and family roles, women are especially vulnerable to emotional disruptions resulting from divorce, loneliness, and professional failures. Studies suggest that such stresses aggravate tendencies for women to abuse alcohol and other substances (Kirkpatrick 1999; Korolenko and Donskih 1990). More specifically, "women drink from a feeling of inadequacy and from a need for love, the kind of love not found within a sexual relationship but, rather, a love that is deeper and more primal" (Kirkpatrick 1999, p. 1; Verhaak et al. 2010).

In addition, drug addiction can occur in some women as a result of domestic adversities. Consequently, there is a high prevalence of drug dependence in women who are victims of sexual and/or physical abuse (Ladwig and Anderson 1989). "Approximately 70% of women in drug abuse treatment report histories of physical and sexual abuse, with victimization beginning before 11 years of age and occurring repeatedly" (SAMHSA 1999a, p. 1). These physical and emotional traumas result in, or

are precursors to, factors leading to drug abuse, such as low self-esteem, self-condemnation, anxiety and personal conflicts, dysfunctional dependencies, and overwhelming feelings of guilt (Kirkpatrick 1999; Verhaak et al. 2010). In addition, because of the crucial nurturing roles women hold, drug abuse problems can be particularly damaging to family stability.

Another unique role for women in drug abuse situations is that of a spouse, significant other, or mother to a drug addict. Often, in both traditional and nontraditional family relationships, women are expected to be nurturing, understanding, and willing to sacrifice to preserve the family integrity. If a family member becomes afflicted by drug dependence, the wife or mother is viewed as a failure. In other words, if the woman had maintained a good home and conducted her domestic chores properly, the family member would not have been driven to drugs (Klee and Jackson 2002; USDHHS and NIDA 1999).

Despite the disruption and considerable stress caused by drug addiction in the home, women continue to bear the burden of raising children, performing domestic chores, and keeping the family together. In addition, women in such circumstances are frequently put at great physical risk. The risk is from an addicted spouse who becomes abusive to his partner or from exposure to sexually transmitted infections, such as HIV or hepatitis, transmitted by a careless infected partner. The anxiety and frustrations resulting from these stressful circumstances can encourage women themselves to become dependent as they seek emotional relief by using drugs.

■ Women's Response to Drugs

Research continues to lag regarding how women respond to substances of abuse. Although matters are slowly changing, the trend in drug abuse studies is still to avoid female populations; the effects of the drugs in men are still extrapolated to women. Even when drug abuse research is conducted on women, frequently the woman's response is not of primary concern; the objective is to determine the effects on a fetus during pregnancy or an infant during nursing (Klee and Jackson 2002; NSDUH 2007; USDHHS and NIDA 1999).

Although it generally can be assumed that the physiological and drug responses of men and women are similar, some distinctions should be recognized. For example, one study compared the risk for lung cancer in men and women after a lifetime of cigarette smoking. It was found that female smokers were twice as likely to get lung cancer as males who had smoked an identical number of cigarettes in their lifetimes ("Women Smokers" 1994). Another study indicated that women are *three* times more likely to contract lung cancer than men when smoking the same amount of cigarettes (Kirkpatrick 1999). These differences clearly indicate that cigarette smoking is far more dangerous for women than for men. Finally, women's unique response to drugs includes a finding discovered by researchers at the University of California at San Francisco that women respond to a class of painkillers called kappa-opioids, which are ineffective in men (*Science Daily* 2000).

Drug Abuse and Reproduction

A very important physiological distinction that sets women apart from men about taking drugs is their ability to bear children. Because of this unique function, men and women have different endocrine (hormone) systems, organs, and structures, and women have varied drug responses according to their reproductive state. The unique features of women have a substantial impact on the response to drug abuse in the presence and absence of pregnancy.

Drug abuse patterns can influence the outcome of pregnancy even if they occur before a woman becomes pregnant. For example, women who are addicted to heroin are more likely to have poor health, including chronic infections, poor nutrition, and sexually transmitted infections such as HIV, which can damage the offspring if pregnancy occurs. If substances are abused during pregnancy, they may directly affect the fetus and adversely alter its growth and development. The incidence of substance abuse during pregnancy is not known precisely, but undoubtedly hundreds of thousands of children have been exposed to drugs in utero. The effects of individual drugs of abuse taken during pregnancy are discussed in detail in the corresponding chapters, but several specific observations merit reiteration here:

- Cocaine is a substantial threat for both the pregnant woman and the fetus. Although a number of specific claims for the fetal effects of cocaine are controversial (see Chapter 10), several observations appear legitimate: Cocaine use increases the likelihood of miscarriage when used during pregnancy; cocaine use in the late stages of pregnancy can cause cardiovascular or CNS complications in the baby at birth and immediately thereafter; and due to its vasoconstrictor effects, cocaine may deprive the fetal brain of oxygen, resulting in strokes and permanent physical and mental damage to the child.

- The impact of alcohol consumption during pregnancy has been well documented and publicized (Mathias 1995). When alcohol is consumed by the mother, it crosses the placenta, but the effect of this drug on the fetus is highly variable and depends on the quantity of alcohol consumed, timing of exposure, maternal drug metabolism, maternal state of health, and presence of other drugs. A particularly alarming consequence of high alcohol intake during pregnancy is an aggregate of physical and mental defects called fetal alcohol syndrome (FAS). Characteristics of this syndrome include low birth weight, abnormal facial features, mental retardation, and retarded sensorimotor development. For additional details, see Chapters 7 and 8. In addition to its direct effects on the fetus, alcohol has played a major role in many unwanted pregnancies or has resulted in women's exposure to sexually transmitted infections. As a CNS depressant, alcohol impairs judgment and reason and, in turn, encourages sexual risk taking that normally would not occur. The results are all too frequently tragic for women (SAMHSA 1999a).

- Tobacco use during pregnancy is particularly rampant in the United States. Specifically, 20% of the smoking female adult population is pregnant. Some experts suggest smoking cigarettes during pregnancy may pose a greater risk to the fetus than taking cocaine. Tobacco use by pregnant women may interfere with blood flow to the fetus, deprive it of oxygen and nutrition, and disrupt development of its organs—particularly the brain. Also of significant concern is the possibility that exposure of nonsmoking pregnant women to secondhand tobacco smoke may be damaging to the fetus.

- Other drugs of abuse that have been associated with abnormal fetal development when used during pregnancy include barbiturates, benzodiazepines, amphetamines, marijuana, lysergic acid diethylamide (LSD), and even caffeine when consumed in high doses.

Clearly, women should be strongly urged to avoid all substances of abuse, especially during pregnancy.

Women and Alcohol

Alcohol is the drug most widely used and abused by women in the United States. According to the 2005 *National Household Survey on Drug Abuse,* among women age 12 or older, 45.9% used alcohol in the past month and 15.2% reported binge drinking (SAMHSA 2007). Alcohol abuse is also a major problem for women on college campuses, even though male college students are more likely than their female counterparts to use alcohol on a daily basis.

As a rule, women are less likely than men to develop severe alcohol dependence; thus, only 25% of the alcoholics in the United States are female. Women are also likely to initiate their drinking patterns later in life than men (Klee and Jackson 2002; USDHHS and NIDA 1999). Interesting ethnic patterns of alcohol consumption have been reported in females, with black and white women manifesting similar drinking patterns. Although the proportions are similar, black women are more likely to completely abstain from alcohol than white women are.

Women who are dependent on alcohol are usually judged more harshly than men with similar difficulties. Alcoholic males are more likely to be excused because their drinking problems are often perceived as being caused by frustrating work conditions, family demands, economic pressures, or so-called nagging wives and children. In contrast, women with drinking problems are often perceived as spoiled or pampered, weak, deviant, or immoral. Such stigmas, referred to as labels in Chapter 2 (see labeling theory), cause women to experience more guilt and anxiety about their alcohol dependence and discourage them from admitting their drug problems and seeking professional help (Kirkpatrick 1999).

The principal reasons for excessive alcohol consumption in women range from loneliness, boredom, and domestic stress in the housewife drinker to financial problems, sexual harassment, lack of challenge, discrimination, and powerlessness in the career woman. Depression is often associated with alcohol problems in women, although it is not clear whether this condition is a cause or an effect of the excessive use.

Women's Physiological Responses to Alcohol

Health consequences for excessive alcohol consumption appear to be more severe for women than for men. For example, alcoholic women are more likely to suffer premature death than alcoholic men. In addition, liver disease is more common and occurs at a younger age in female drinkers than in male alcoholics. In general, higher morbidity rates are experienced by alcoholic women than their male counterparts.

Several explanations have been suggested for the higher rate of adverse effects seen in female alcoholics. Their higher blood alcohol concentrations may be due to a smaller blood volume and more rapid absorption into the bloodstream after drinking. Alternatively, slower alcohol metabolism in the stomach and liver might cause more alcohol to reach the brain and other organs as well as prolong exposure to the drug following consumption (Goldstein 1995). Studies have shown that for a woman of average size, one alcoholic drink has effects equivalent to two drinks in an average-size man (see Chapter 7).

Dealing with Women's Alcohol Problems

Alcoholic consumption varies considerably in women, ranging from total abstinence or an occasional drink to daily intake of large amounts of alcohol. Clearly, much is yet to be learned about the cause of some women's excessive drinking and dependence on alcohol. The role of genetic factors in predisposing women to alcohol-related problems is still unclear. The environment is certainly a major factor contributing to excessive alcohol consumption in women. It is well established that depression, stress, and trauma encourage alcohol consumption because of the antianxiety and amnesic properties of this drug. Because of unreasonable societal expectations and numerous socioeconomic disadvantages, women are especially vulnerable to the emotional upheavals that encourage excessive alcohol consumption.

As with all drug dependence problems, prevention is the preferred solution to alcohol abuse by women. Alcohol usually becomes problematic when it is no longer used occasionally to enhance social events but used daily to deal with personal problems. Such alcohol dependence can best be avoided by using constructive techniques to manage stress and frustrations. Because of unique female roles and society's expectations, women especially need to learn to be assertive with family members, associates in the workplace (including bosses), and other contacts in their daily routines. By expecting and demanding equitable treatment and consideration in personal and professional activities, stress and anxiety can often be reduced. Education, career training, and development of communication abilities can be particularly important in establishing a sense of self-worth (see also Chapter 17). With these skills and confidence, women are better able to manage problems associated with their lives and less likely to resort to drugs for an escape.

Women and Prescription Drugs

Women are more likely than men to suffer depression, anxiety, and panic attacks (About.com 2006); be unable to express anger; be victims of physical and sexual abuse; and be subject to overwhelming guilt feelings (Kirkpatrick 1999). Consequently, they are also more likely to take and become addicted to the prescription drugs used in treating these disorders. Because these drugs are used as part of psychiatric therapy and under the supervision of a physician, drug dependence frequently is not recognized and may be ignored for months or even years. This type of legitimate drug abuse occurs most often in elderly women and includes the use of sedatives, antidepressants, and antianxiety medications. A recent study found that one in four women older than age 60 takes at least one of these drugs daily and that some of them develop serious drug problems (Drug Strategies 1998). Excessive use of these drugs by older women results in side effects such as insomnia, mood fluctuations, and disruption of cognitive and motor functions that can substantially compromise the quality of life.

■ Treatment of Drug Dependency in Women

As previously discussed, women are less likely than men to seek treatment for, and rehabilitation from, drug dependence (Kirkpatrick 1999; SAMHSA 2010). Possible reasons for their reluctance are as follows:

- In more traditional families, women have unique roles with high expectations. They are expected to assume demanding and ongoing responsibilities, such as motherhood, child rearing, and family maintenance, that cannot be postponed and often cannot be delegated, even temporarily, to others. Consequently, many women feel that they are too essential for the well-being of other family members to leave the home and seek time-consuming treatment for drug abuse problems.
- Drug treatment centers often are not designed to handle the unique health requirements of females—thus, women face more obstacles. These obstacles involve barriers to treatment entry, treatment engagement, and long-term recovery (About.com 2007a; NIDA 1999). Women have been shown to have greater health needs than men due to more frequent respiratory, genitourinary (associated with the sex and urinary organs), and circulatory problems. If drug treatment centers are not capable of providing the necessary physical care, women are less likely to participate in associated drug abuse programs.
- Drug-dependent women are more inclined to be unemployed than their male counterparts and more likely to be receiving public support. The implications of this difference are twofold. First, because concerns about one's job often motivate drug-dependent workers to seek treatment, this issue is less likely to be a factor in unemployed women. Second, without the financial security of a job, unemployed women may feel that good treatment for their drug problems is unaffordable. (For more on treatment, see Chapter 18.)

The unique female requirements must be recognized and considered if women are to receive adequate treatment for drug dependence. Some considerations on how to achieve this objective include the following: (1) availability of female-sensitive services; (2) nonpunitive and noncoercive treatment that incorporates supportive behavior change approaches; and (3) treatment for a wide range of medical problems, mental disorders, and psychosocial problems (NIDA 1999). The role of motherhood needs to be used in a positive manner in drug treatment strategies. For most women, motherhood is viewed with high regard and linked to self-esteem. Approximately 90% of female drug abusers are in their childbearing years, and many have family responsibilities. Consequently, treatment approaches need to be tailored to allow women to fulfill their domestic responsibilities and satisfy their maternal obligations.

Women dependent on drugs often lack important coping skills. Because many women lead restricted, almost isolated lives that focus entirely on domestic responsibilities, they face limited alternatives for dealing with stressful situations. Under these restrictive circumstances, the use of drugs to cope with anxieties and frustrations is very appealing. To enhance their ability to cope, drug-dependent women need to develop communication and assertiveness skills. Further, they need to be encouraged to control situations rather than allowing themselves to be controlled by the situation. Specific techniques that have proven useful in coping management are exercise (particularly relaxation types), relaxing visual imagery, personal hobbies, and outside interests that require active participation. Many drug-dependent women require experiences that divert their attention from the source of their frustrations while affording them an opportunity to succeed and develop a sense of self-worth.

Finally, one research study found that the most effective treatment for women included a mutually supportive therapeutic environment that addressed the following issues: psychopathology (such as depression), a woman's role as mother, interpersonal relationships, and the need for parenting education. Another study found that cocaine-using women whose children were living with them during residential treatment remained in the treatment programs significantly longer than women whose children were not living with them at the facility. Thus, having the children in the treatment facility provides opportunities to assess and meet women's needs, which in turn affects the women's prognosis (About.com 2007a; NIDA 1999).

Prevention of Drug Dependence in Women

The best treatment for drug addiction is prevention. To help prevent drug problems in women as opposed to men, socioeconomic disadvantages need to be recognized as factors that make women more vulnerable to drug dependence, especially from prescription medication. Women need to learn that nondrug approaches are often more desirable for dealing with situational problems than prescribed medications. For example, for older women suffering loneliness, isolation, or depression, it is better to encourage participation in outside interests, such as hobbies and service activities. In addition, social support and concern should be encouraged from family, friends, and neighbors. Such nonmedicinal approaches are preferred over prescribing sedatives and hypnotics to cope with emotional distresses. Similarly, medical conditions such as obesity, constipation, or insomnia should be treated by changing lifestyle, eating, and exercise habits rather than using drug "bandage therapy."

When women are prescribed drugs, they should ask about the associated risks, especially as they relate to drug abuse potential. Frequently, drug dependency develops insidiously and is not recognized by either the patient or attending physician until it is already firmly established. If a woman taking medication is aware of the potential for becoming dependent and is instructed on how to avoid its occurrence, the problems of dependence and abuse can frequently be averted. (See Chapter 17 for more on prevention and education.)

Drug Use in Adolescent Subcultures

I love waking up in the morning and smoking a nice fat joint. I live above the garage now, and my mom lives across the yard from the garage. This is a great living arrangement! I go to my room a few hours before crashing on many school nights, get high, drink some vodka that my older brother buys for me, then finally crash. In the morning, I always wake myself up so my mom stays away from my room, and my hideaway stash box is always locked. I roll me a joint and get a little high before I greet mom in the morning for a quick breakfast. I think she gets high too, but if I ask her and she says "no," what if she then asks me and gets all suspicious and shit? Besides, my Uncle Prentice always gets high with me, so I still think my mom really does not care about smoking weed. In fact, I know she is more worried about me drinking and driving than my friend "Mary Jane" [nickname for marijuana]. That's just my private life and no one needs to know. *(From Venturelli's research files, male residing in Chicago, age 18, July 10, 2000)*

From ages 13 through 18, adolescents are more likely to experience heightened psychological, social, and biological changes (Office of the Surgeon General 2007). Often, such internal and external changes are manifested by emotional outbursts. Why do such changes and urges arise? The adolescent's body is stretching, growing, and sometimes appearing out of control due to the hormonal changes of puberty.

Adolescents are uncertain and confused about not knowing who or what they are becoming. They often are confused as to their worth to family, peers, society, and even to themselves (Kantrowitz and Wingert 1999). Adding to the frustration of growing up, the cultural status of adolescents is poorly defined. They find themselves trapped in a "no-man's land" between the acceptance, simplicity, and security of childhood, and the stress, complexities, expectations, independence, and responsibilities of adulthood. Not only do adolescents have difficulty deciding who and what they are, but adults are equally unsure as to how to deal with these transitional human beings. Although the grown-up world tries to push adolescents out of the secure nest of childhood, it is not willing to bestow the full membership and rights of adulthood upon them (Johnson et al. 1996; Kantrowitz and Wingert 1999).

Because of their uniquely rapid development, several developmental issues are particularly important to evolving adolescents (Elmen and Offer 1993; Johnson et al. 1996; Kantrowitz and Wingert 1999; Office of the Surgeon General 2007; Von Der Haar 2005):

- Discovering and understanding their distinctive identities
- "Feeling awkward or strange about one's self and one's body" (American Academy of Child and Adolescent Psychiatry 2006)
- Forming more intimate and caring relationships with others
- Conflicts with parents over the need for independence
- Increased interest in sexuality and concern with heterosexual versus homosexual identities
- "Experimentation with sex and drugs (cigarettes, alcohol, and marijuana)" (American Academy of Child and Adolescent Psychiatry 2006)
- Establishing a sense of autonomy
- Coming to terms with the hormone-related feelings of puberty and expressing their sexuality
- Learning to become productive contributors to society
- Feeling alone and alienated

Due to all this developmental confusion, "normal" behavior for the adolescent is difficult to define precisely. Experts generally agree that persistent low self-esteem, depression, feelings of alienation, and other emotional disturbances can be troublesome for teenagers (Von Der Haar 2005). Most adolescents are relatively well adjusted and are able to cope with **sociobiological changes**. Emotionally stable adolescents relate well to family and peers and function productively within their schools, neighborhoods, and communities. The majority of adolescents experience transient problems, which they are able to resolve, but some become deeply disturbed and are unable to grow out of their problems without counseling and therapy (see also Jayson 2007). Those adolescents who are unable or unwilling to ask for assistance often turn to destructive devices, such as drugs or violence

(Kantrowitz and Wingert 1999), for relief from their emotional dilemmas.

Consequences of Underage Drug Use

Some of the well-known consequences of underage drug use by adolescents are (Office of the Surgeon General 2007):

- Even more than marijuana, alcohol poses a greater risk to the largest number of teens than does any other drug, largely because of the availability of this drug.
- Underage alcohol use is the major cause of death from injuries among young people. Each year approximately 5000 people under the age of 21 die as a result of underage drinking; this includes about 1900 deaths from motor vehicle crashes, 1600 as a result of homicides, and 300 from suicide as well as hundreds from other injuries such as falls, burns, and drowning.
- Alcohol use increases the risk of carrying out, or being a victim of, a physical or sexual assault.
- Underage alcohol use can affect the body in many ways. The effects of alcohol and other drug use ranges from hangovers to death from alcohol and/or other drug abuse.
- Alcohol and other drugs can lead to other problems such as bad grades in school and run-ins with the law.
- Alcohol and other drugs affect how well a young person judges risk and makes sound decisions, such as driving while under the influence and riding with a driver under the influence.
- Alcohol and other drugs play a role in risky sexual activity, which can increase the chance of teen pregnancy and sexually transmitted infections (STIs), including HIV.
- Alcohol can harm the growing brain. (Current research clearly shows that the brain continually develops from birth through the teen years into the mid-20s.)

Why Adolescents Use Drugs

Although there is no such thing as a typical substance-abusing adolescent, certain physiological, psychological, and sociological factors are often

KEY TERMS

sociobiological changes
the belief that biological forces (largely genes) have a direct influence on the root causes of social psychological behavior

associated with drug problems in this subculture (Johnson et al. 1996; Johnston et al. 2009a). In looking at an array of explanations regarding why adolescents use drugs, one study by Columbia University's National Center on Addiction and Substance Abuse found that children ages 12 to 17 who are frequently bored are 50% more likely to smoke, drink, get drunk, and use illegal drugs. In addition, kids with $25 or more a week in spending money are nearly twice as likely to smoke, drink, or use drugs as children with less money. Anxiety is another risk factor. The study found that youngsters who said they're highly stressed are twice as likely as low-stress kids to smoke, drink, or use drugs (Associated Press 2003).

It is important to remember that not all drug use by adolescents means therapy is necessary or even desirable. More traditional proven and accepted explanations stress that most excessive drug use that often leads to abuse by adolescents results from the desire to experience new behaviors and sensations, a passing fancy of maturation, an attempt to relieve peer pressure, feelings of alienation, or an inclination to enhance a social setting with chemistry (Jayson 2007; Kantrowitz and Wingert 1999). Most of these adolescent users will not go on to develop problematic dependence on drugs and, for the most part, should be watched but not aggressively confronted or treated. The adolescents who usually have significant difficulty with drug use are those who turn to drugs for extended support as coping devices and become drug reliant because they are unable to find alternative, less destructive solutions to their problems. Several major factors can contribute to serious drug dependence in adolescents (Archambault 1992; Johnson et al. 1996; Walsh and Scheinkman 1992).

Research indicates that the most important factor influencing drug use among adolescents is peer drug use (Bahr, Marcos, and Maughan 1995; Focus Adolescent Services 2008; Jayson 2007; Kandel 1980; NIDA 1999; Swadi 1992; Winters 1997). Other primary factors that can either increase or decrease drug use include how teens perceive the risk in the use of drugs, perceived social approval, and perceived availability of drugs (Adolescent Substance Abuse Knowledge Base 2007).

Consequently, eventual transition to heavier substance use also directly correlates with peer use (Steinberg, Fletcher, and Darling 1994). Conversely, individuals whose peer groups do not use or abuse drugs are less likely to use drugs themselves (Venturelli 2000). Research has identified a correlation between strong family bonds and non–drug-using peer groups (NIDA 1999). "Adolescents with higher [stronger] family bonds are less likely than adolescents with lower [weaker] bonds to have close friends who use drugs" (Bahr et al. 1995, p. 466). In addition, family bonding is highly correlated with educational commitment. In essence, family bonding influences choice of friends and educational goals and aspirations (Bahr et al. 1995). Three noteworthy differences exist between male and female adolescents: (1) males demonstrate a stronger association between educational achievement and family bonds; (2) among females, peer drug use is negatively associated with family bonds, so peer drug use and family bonds are not likely to influence the use of licit and illicit drugs by females; and (3) the impact of age on peer drug use (the younger the age, the more vulnerable to peer pressure) and on the amount of alcohol consumed can be predicted with slightly greater accuracy for males than females (Teen Challenge 2000).

Many adolescents use drugs to help cope with boredom, unpleasant feelings, emotions, and stress or to relieve depression, reduce tension, and reduce alienation (Teen Challenge 2000). Psychological differences among adolescents who are frequent drug users, experimenters, and abstainers often can be traced to early childhood, the quality of parenting in their homes, and their home environment. It has been suggested that certain types of parents are more likely to raise children at high risk for substance abuse (Archambault 1992). For example, an alcoholic adolescent usually has at least one parent of the following types:

- *Alcoholic:* This parent serves as a negative role model for the adolescent. The child sees the parent dealing with problems by consuming drugs. Even though drinking alcohol is not illegal for adults, it sends the message that drugs can solve problems. The guilt-ridden alcoholic parent is unable to provide the child with a loving, supportive relationship. In addition, the presence of the alcoholic parent is often disruptive or abusive to the family and creates fear or embarrassment in the child.

- *Nonconsuming and condemning:* This type of parent not only chooses to abstain from drinking, but also is very judgmental about drinkers and condemns them for their behavior. Such persons, who are often referred to as teetotalers, have a rigid, moralistic approach to life. Their black-and-white attitudes frequently prove inadequate and unforgiving in an imperfect, gray world. Children in these families can feel inferior and guilty when they are unable to live up to parental expectations, and they may resort to drugs to cope with their frustrations.

- *Overly demanding:* This type of parent forces unrealistic expectations on his or her children. These parents often live vicariously through their children and require sons and daughters to pursue endeavors in which the parents were unable to succeed. Particular emphasis may be placed on achievements in athletics, academics, or career selections. Even though the parents' efforts may be well intended, the children get the message that their parents are more concerned about what they are than who they are. These parents frequently encourage sibling rivalries to enhance performance, but such competitions always yield a loser.

- *Overly protective:* These types of parents do not give their children a chance to develop a sense of self-worth and independence. Because the parents deprive their children of the opportunities to learn how to master their abilities within their surroundings, the children are not able to develop confidence and a positive self-image. Such children are frequently unsure about who they are and what they are capable of achieving. Parents who use children to satisfy their own ego needs or who are trying to convince themselves that they really do like their children tend to be overly protective.

The principal influence for learned behavior is usually the home; therefore, several other family-related variables can significantly affect adolescents' decision to start, maintain, or cease a drug habit (Kinney 2000; Lawson and Lawson 1992). For example, adolescents usually learn their attitudes about drug use from family models. In other words, what are the drug-consuming patterns of parents and siblings? Adolescents are more likely to develop drug problems if other members of the family (1) are excessive in their drug (legal or illegal) consumption, (2) approve of the use of illicit drugs, or (3) use drugs as a problem-solving strategy.

Sociological factors that damage self-image can also encourage adolescent drug use. Feelings of rejection may cause poor relationships with family members, peers, school personnel, or coworkers. Ethnic differences sometimes contribute to a poor self-image because people of minority races or cultures are frequently socially excluded and are sometimes viewed as being inferior and undesirable by the majority population. This type of negative message is very difficult for adolescents to deal with. Sometimes, to ensure acceptance, adolescents adopt the attitudes and behaviors of their affiliated groups. If a peer group, or a gang, views drug use as cool, desirable, or even necessary, members (or those desiring membership) feel compelled to conform and become involved in drugs.

■ Patterns of Drug Use in Adolescents

Growing minorities of younger teenagers are exposed to drug use within their own families. One study reported that "20% of . . . 600 teens in drug treatment in New York, Texas, Florida and California said they have shared drugs other than alcohol with their parents, and that about 5% of the teens actually were introduced to drugs—usually marijuana—by their moms and dads" (Leinwand 2000, p. 1). In 1999, Partnership for a Drug-Free America reported similar shocking findings (Leinwand 2000).

Jason, 17, a recovering addict from an upper-middle-class family in Simi Valley, California, says he wishes his father had been more of a parent and less of a buddy when it came to marijuana. "[Jason] made his drug purchase: a $5 bag of pot. Jason says his father walked by his room's open door as he was stashing it in a dresser drawer. [His father then] '. . . told about his marijuana use,' Jason says. 'We went into his [dad's] office, and he had a (water pipe) and we got high together.' [Jason reports that at the time, he] '. . . thought it was sooo cool' " (Leinwand 2000, p. 2).

In another example, La'kiesha, 15, of southern California, is the third generation of a family in which members have become addicted to drugs. La'kiesha said her grandmother smoked pot regularly and gave her a few puffs when she was 5 years old to settle her down before bedtime (Leinwand 2000).

A more recent phenomenon, especially in middle- and upper-middle-class families, is that teenagers are being introduced to drugs or using drugs with parents. Years ago, alcohol may have been shared between parents and their children in a low percentage of cases; however, today there are parents who either have been or are currently using illicit drugs and they appear to be influencing their children in the use of these drugs. Currently, this occurs in a small minority of families; nevertheless, it remains shocking.

Recent surveys regarding drug use patterns found that by 12th grade (seniors in high school), approximately 72.3% of the teens had used alcohol, approximately 44% had used cigarettes, 42% had used marijuana, and 9.5% had used inhalants in 2009. (See **Table 16.5**, which details 8th, 10th, and 12th graders' use of other drugs from 2006 through 2009.)

■ Current Changes in Teen Drug Use Cause Concern

There are now more new users (age 12 or older) of prescription drugs than any other illegal drug—even marijuana. Teens are turning away from street drugs and the stigma that goes along with using them, and abusing prescription drugs to get the same type of high. Many young people are under the false notion that prescription and OTC drugs are medically safer, when in fact, they can be just as dangerous and addictive as street drugs (National Youth Anti-Drug Media Campaign 2007).

In a press conference, White House drug czar John Walters stated "The drug dealer is us . . ." (*USA Today* 2007). What the national drug policy director was alluding to was that ". . . many teenagers are obtaining drugs over the Internet, getting them free from their family members, friends, or taking them from other people's medicine cabinet . . ." and that ". . . 2.1 million teenagers abused prescription drugs in 2005" (*USA Today* 2007).

The three most common sources for obtaining prescription drugs were: "given for free by a friend or relative," which was stated by approximately 51% of adolescents; "bought from a friend or relative," which was stated by approximately 35% of adolescents; and "taking the drug from a friend or relative without asking," which was reported by approximately 12% of adolescents. Surprisingly, only 2% of adolescents "bought prescription drugs on the Internet" (Johnston et al. 2009a). Clearly, the informal network of family and friends is a major source of these drugs for adolescents.

Another source indicates that although teen marijuana use declined from 30.1% to 25.8% from 2002 to 2006, use of OxyContin rose among 12th graders (Johnston et al. 2006a). Between 2002 and 2005, annual prevalence increased almost 40% among 12th graders, to 5.5%. Considering the addictive poten-

tial of this drug, this rate seems quite high for them to have attained. Another, more recent finding is that ". . . a significant proportion of 12th graders have used one or more of these drugs [referring to prescription drugs like amphetamines, sedatives (barbiturates), and tranquilizers] . . . without a doctor's order—21.5%, 15.4%, and 7.2% for lifetime, annual, and 30-day prevalence, respectively, in 2008. Rates have fallen somewhat in recent years, but significant numbers of teens are still misusing prescription drugs" (Johnston et al. 2009a). Finally, "Teens are also abusing stimulants like Adderall and anti-anxiety drugs like Xanax because they are readily available and perceived as safer than street drugs," says White House drug czar Walters (*USA Today* 2007). The extent of naiveté is best illustrated by the interview of one female in Indiana, as stated in the *Daily News,* Muncie, on November 6, 2006: "It's not like I'm taking cocaine or crack—it's OK, these are pharmaceutical drugs made by professionals who know what they are doing" (National Youth Anti-Drug Media Campaign 2007).

The use of prescription-type drugs by high numbers of young people is of special concern. In looking at past-year initiates (new users), the following findings are noteworthy regarding teen prescription drug abuse (Office of National Drug Control Policy [ONDCP] 2008):

- In 2006, more than 2.1 million teens abused prescription drugs.
- Every day, 2500 youth (12–17 years old) abuse a prescription pain reliever for the very first time.
- One-third of all new abusers of prescription drugs in 2006 were 12- to 17-year-olds.
- Three percent of teens (12–17 years old) reported current abuse of prescription drugs in 2006, following only marijuana (7%) and well ahead of cocaine (0.4%), Ecstasy (0.3%), meth (0.2%), and heroin (0.1%).
- Prescription drugs are the drug of choice among 12- to 13-year-olds.
- Among teens, 13 is the mean age of first nonprescribed use of sedatives and stimulants. Sixty percent of teens (12–17 years old) who have abused prescription painkillers first tried them before age 15 (Wu, Pilowsky, and Patkar 2007).
- Among teens who have abused painkillers, nearly one-fifth (18%) used them at least weekly in the past year (Wu et al. 2007).
- The prescription drugs most commonly abused by teens are painkillers; powerful narcotics prescribed to treat pain; depressants, such as sleep-

Table 16.5 **Drug Use Among 8th, 10th, and 12th Graders**

	8TH GRADERS				10TH GRADERS				12TH GRADERS			
	2006	2007	2008	2009	2006	2007	2008	2009	2006	2007	2008	2009
Any illicit drug												
Lifetime	20.9	19.0	19.6	19.9	36.1	35.6	34.1	36.0	48.2	46.8	47.4	46.7
Annual	14.8	13.2	14.1	14.5	28.7	28.1	26.9	29.4	36.5	35.9	36.6	36.5
30-day	8.1	7.4	7.6	8.1	16.8	16.9	15.8	17.8	21.5	21.9	22.3	23.3
Alcohol												
Lifetime	40.5	38.9	38.9	36.6	61.5	61.7	58.3	59.1	72.7	72.2	71.9	72.3
Annual	33.6	31.8	32.1	30.3	55.8	56.3	52.5	52.8	66.5	66.4	65.5	66.2
30-day	17.2	15.9	15.9	14.9	33.8	33.4	28.8	30.4	45.3	44.4	43.1	43.5
Cigarettes (any use)												
Lifetime	24.6	22.1	20.5	20.1	36.1	34.6	31.7	32.7	47.1	46.2	44.7	43.6
Annual*	—	—	—	—	—	—	—	—	—	—	—	—
30-day	8.7	71	6.8	6.5	14.5	14.0	12.3	13.1	21.6	21.6	20.4	20.1
Marijuana/hashish												
Lifetime	15.7	14.2	14.6	15.7	31.8	31.0	29.9	32.3	42.3	41.8	42.6	42.0
Annual	11.7	10.3	10.9	11.8	25.2	24.6	23.9	26.7	31.5	31.7	32.4	32.8
30-day	6.5	5.7	5.8	6.5	14.2	14.2	13.8	15.9	18.3	18.8	19.4	20.6
Inhalants												
Lifetime	16.1	15.6	15.7	14.9	13.3	13.6	12.8	12.3	11.1	10.5	9.9	9.5
Annual	9.1	8.3	8.9	8.1	6.5	6.6	5.9	6.1	4.5	3.7	3.8	3.4
30-day	4.1	3.9	4.1	3.8	2.3	2.5	2.1	2.2	1.5	1.2	1.4	1.2
Amphetamines												
Lifetime	7.3	6.5	6.8	6.0	11.2	11.1	9.0	10.3	12.4	11.4	10.5	9.9
Annual	4.7	4.2	4.5	4.1	7.9	8.0	6.4	7.1	8.1	7.5	6.8	6.6
30-day	2.1	2.0	2.2	1.9	3.5	4.0	2.8	3.3	3.7	3.7	2.9	3.0
Hallucinogens												
Lifetime	3.4	3.1	3.3	3.0	6.1	6.4	5.5	6.1	8.3	8.4	8.7	7.4
Annual	2.1	1.9	2.1	1.9	4.1	4.4	3.9	4.1	4.9	5.4	5.9	4.7
30-day	0.9	1.0	0.9	0.9	1.5	1.7	1.3	1.4	1.5	1.7	2.2	1.6

(continued)

Table 16.5 (*continued*)

	8TH GRADERS				10TH GRADERS				12TH GRADERS			
	2006	2007	2008	2009	2006	2007	2008	2009	2006	2007	2008	2009
Cocaine												
Lifetime	3.4	3.1	3.0	2.6	4.8	5.3	4.5	4.6	8.5	7.8	7.2	6.0
Annual	2.0	2.0	1.8	1.6	3.2	3.4	3.0	2.7	5.7	5.2	4.4	3.4
30-day	1.0	0.9	0.8	0.8	1.5	1.3	1.2	0.9	2.5	2.0	1.9	1.3
Crack												
Lifetime	2.3	2.1	2.0	1.7	2.2	2.3	2.0	2.1	3.5	3.2	2.8	2.4
Annual	1.3	1.3	1.1	1.1	1.3	1.3	1.3	1.2	2.1	1.9	1.6	1.3
30-day	0.6	0.6	0.5	0.5	0.7	0.5	0.5	0.4	0.9	0.9	0.8	0.6
Steroids												
Lifetime	1.6	1.5	1.4	1.3	1.8	1.8	1.4	1.3	2.7	2.2	2.2	2.2
Annual	0.9	0.8	0.9	0.8	1.2	1.1	0.9	0.8	1.8	1.4	1.5	1.5
30-day	0.5	0.4	0.5	0.4	0.6	0.5	0.5	0.5	1.1	1.0	1.0	1.0
Heroin												
Lifetime	1.4	1.3	1.4	1.3	1.4	1.5	1.2	1.5	1.4	1.5	1.3	1.2
Annual	0.8	0.8	0.9	0.7	0.9	0.8	0.8	0.9	0.8	0.9	0.7	0.7
30-day	0.3	0.4	0.4	0.4	0.5	0.4	0.4	0.4	0.4	0.4	0.4	0.4

*Not available at time of printing.

Source: Johnson, L. D., P. M. O'Malley, J. G. Bachman, and J. E. Schulenberg. *Monitoring the Future: National Results on Adolescent Drug Use. Overview of Key Findings, 2009.* NIH Publication No. 10-7583. Bethesda, MD: National Institute on Drug Abuse, 2010.

ing pills or anti-anxiety drugs; and stimulants, mainly prescribed to treat attention deficit hyperactivity disorder (ADHD).

- Pain relievers like Vicodin and OxyContin are the prescription drugs most commonly abused by teens.
- Among 12th graders, past-year abuse of Oxy-Contin increased 30 percent between 2002 and 2007.
- Past-year abuse of Vicodin is particularly high among 8th, 10th, and 12th graders, with nearly 1 in 10 high school seniors reporting taking it in the past year without a doctor's approval.

Teens also are abusing some over-the-counter (OTC) drugs, primarily cough and cold remedies that contain dextromethorphan (DXM), a cough suppressant, to get high. Products with DXM include NyQuil, Coricidin, and Robitussin, among others. This type of drug abuse is a particular concern, given the easy access teens have to these products. Teens who abuse prescription or OTC drugs may be abusing other substances as well. Sometimes they abuse prescription and OTC drugs together with alcohol or other drugs, which can lead to dangerous consequences, including death. Teens are abusing prescription drugs because they are widely available, free or inexpensive, and they believe they are not as risky as street drugs. The majority of teens who abuse these products say they get them for free, usually from friends and relatives, and often without their knowledge. Because these drugs are so readily available, teens who otherwise would not touch street drugs might abuse prescription drugs (ONDCP 2008).

Two licit drugs plaguing early and mid-teens are cigarettes and alcohol. Alcohol use is more widespread than use of any of the illicit drugs. Almost three out of every four 12th-grade students (72%) have at least tried alcohol, and over two-fifths (43%) are current drinkers. Even among 8th graders, the proportion of students who reported some alcohol use in their lifetime is nearly two-fifths (39%), and a sixth (16%) are current (past–30-day) drinkers. Of greater concern than just any use of alcohol is its use to the point of inebriation: 18% of 8th graders, 37% of 10th graders, and 55% of 12th graders said they have been drunk at least once in their lifetime. Use of cigarettes, or alcohol, is generally more widespread than use of any of the illicit drugs. Almost half (45%) of 12th graders reported having tried cigarettes at some time, and one-fifth (20%) smoked at least some in the prior 30 days. Daily use of cigarettes in the prior 30 days of having been surveyed is considerably higher for cigarettes than for marijuana or alcohol (Johnston et al. 2009a).

Adolescent Versus Adult Drug Abuse

Adolescent patterns of drug abuse are very different from drug use patterns in adults (Moss et al. 1994). The uniqueness of adolescent drug abuse means that drug-dependent teenagers usually are not successfully treated with adult-directed therapy. For example, compared with adults who abuse drugs, drug-using adolescents are (1) more likely to be involved in criminal activity and at earlier ages; (2) more likely to have other members of the family who abuse drugs; (3) more likely to be associated with a dysfunctional family that engages in emotional and/or physical abuse of its members; and (4) more likely to begin drug use because of curiosity or peer pressure (Bahr et al. 1995; Daily 1992b; Hoshino 1992; Steinberg et al. 1994; Teen Challenge 2000). Such differences need to be considered when developing adolescent-targeted treatment programs.

Consequences and Coincidental Problems

Researchers have concluded that the problem of adolescent drug use is a symptom and not a cause of personal social maladjustment. Even so, because of the pharmacological actions of drugs, routine use can contribute to school and social failures, unintended injuries (usually automobile-related), criminal and violent behavior, sexual risk taking, depression, and suicide (Curry and Spergel 1997).

It is important to realize that, because serious drug abuse is usually the result of emotional instability, consequences of the underlying disorders may be expressed with chemical dependence, making diagnosis and treatment more difficult. The undesirable coincidental problems may include self-destruction, risk taking, abuse, or negative group behaviors. Some of these adolescent problems and their relationship to drug abuse are discussed in the following sections.

Adolescent Suicide

Current research shows that although no cause-and-effect relationship exists between use of alcohol and/or other drugs and suicide, such drugs are often contributing factors (About.com 2005; Minnesota Institute of Public Health 1995). Adolescents are particularly vulnerable to suicide actions; in fact, white males between 14 and 20 years old are the most likely to commit suicide in the United States (Daily 1992b). Further, the teenage suicide rate has doubled since 1980 (Siegel and Senna 1997; Siegel and Welsh 2009). "Suicides among young people continue to be a serious problem. Each year in the U.S., thousands of teenagers commit suicide. Suicide is the third leading cause of death for 15-to-24-year-olds, and the sixth leading cause of death for 5-to-14-year-olds" (American Academy of Child and Adolescent Psychiatry 2004). Twenty percent to 36% of suicide victims have a history of alcohol abuse or were drinking shortly before their suicide. Some experts have described severe chemical dependence as a form of slow, drug-related suicide. For clinicians, every case of serious drug addiction conceals a suicidal individual because all drug abuse inevitably constitutes a game of life and death very similar to "Russian roulette," which comes back into fashion at certain times and under certain circumstances (Bergeret 1981).

Clearly, many teenagers who abuse alcohol and other drugs possess a self-destructive attitude (About.com 2005), as this quote from an online chat with Dr. David Shaffer, a teen suicide expert, demonstrates: "[T]wo-thirds of all suicides amongst boys occur in boys who are abusing alcohol or other drugs; so the link between suicide and alcohol and certain drugs, like cocaine and Ecstasy and other stimulant drugs, is a very close one" (Schaefer et al. 1993, p. 39). According to Shaffer, adolescents who attempt suicide are more likely to (1) have disciplinary problems, then abuse alcohol and feel even more depressed; (2) be very anxious and not display any bad behavior problems; or (3) have a perfectionist attitude and never be satisfied with their outcomes. Nearly all suffer from depression before their suicide attempts. Females generally differ from males in that they are prone to even greater amounts of depression with fewer cases of alcohol or other drug abuse (Merrill 2009).

Besides posing a direct health threat because of their physiological effects, drugs of abuse can precipitate suicide attempts due to their pharmacological impact. A number of studies have found a very high correlation between acute suicidal behavior and drug use (About.com 2005; Buckstein et al. 1993). One report noted that adolescent alcoholics have a suicide rate 58 times greater than the national average. In another study, 30% of adolescent alcoholics had made suicide attempts, although 92% admitted to a history of having suicidal thoughts (Daily 1992b). It has been speculated that the incidence of suicide in drug-consuming adolescents is high because both types of behavior are the consequence of an inability to develop fundamental adult attributes of confidence, self-esteem, and independence. When drug use does not make up for their need for these characteristics, the resulting frustrations are intensified and ultimately played out in the suicide act.

Most adolescents experiment with drugs for reasons not related to antisocial or deviant behavior but rather due to curiosity, desire for recreation, boredom, peer pressure, desire to gain new insights and experiences, or urge to heighten social interactions. These adolescents are not likely to engage in self-destructive behavior. In addition, adolescents from "healthy" family environments are not likely to attempt suicide. Specifically, Daily (1992b) stated that the families least likely to have suicidal members are those that:

- Express love and show mutual concern
- Are tolerant of differences and overlook failings
- Encourage the development of self-confidence and self-expression
- Have parents who assume strong leadership roles but are not autocratic
- Have interaction characterized by humor and good-natured teasing
- Are able to serve as a source of joy and happiness to their members

Suicide is more likely to be attempted by those adolescents who turn to alcohol and other drugs to help them cope with serious emotional and personality conflicts and frustrations. These susceptible teenagers represent approximately 5% of the adolescent population (Beschner and Friedman 1985; Siegel and Senna 1997; Siegel and Welsh 2009). Wright (1985) found that four features significantly contribute to the likelihood of suicidal thought in high school students:

1. Parents with interpersonal conflicts who often use an adolescent child with drug problems as the scapegoat for family problems
2. Fathers who have poor, and often confrontational, relationships with their children
3. Parents who are viewed by their adolescent children as being emotionally unstable, usually suffering from perpetual anger and depression
4. A sense of frustration, desperation, and inability to resolve personal and emotional difficulties through traditional means

Clearly, it is important to identify those adolescents who are at risk for suicide and to provide immediate care and appropriate emotional support.

Sexual Violence and Drugs

Alcohol use has been closely associated with almost every type of sexual abuse in which the adolescent is victimized. "For the perpetrator, being under the influence may remove both physical and psychological inhibitors which keep people from acting out violently. They may also use alcohol or drugs as an excuse for criminal behavior" (Wisconsin Coalition Against Sexual Assault [WCASA] 1997, p. 13). For example, alcohol is by far the most significant factor in date, acquaintance, and gang rapes involving teenagers (Office of the Surgeon General 2007; Parrot 1988; Prendergast 1994). The evidence for alcohol involvement in incest is particularly overwhelming. Approximately 4 million children in the United States live in incestuous homes with alcoholic parents. In addition, 42% of drug-abusing female adolescents have been victims of sexual abuse (Daily 1992a). It is estimated that almost half of the offenders consume alcohol before molesting a child and at least one-third of the perpetrators are chronic alcoholics (Baltieri and de Andrad 2008, p. 77). Finally, 85% of child molesters were sexually abused themselves as children, usually at the same age as their victims, and the vast majority of these molesters abused drugs as adolescents (Daily 1992a).

These very disturbing associations illustrate the relationship between drugs and violent sexual behavior both in terms of initiating the act and because of the act. The effects of such sexual violence are devastating and far-reaching. Thus, incest victims are more likely than the general population to abuse drugs as adolescents and to engage in antisocial delinquency, prostitution, depression, and suicide (Daily 1992a).

Gangs and Drugs

The very disturbing involvement of adolescents in gangs and gang-related activities and violence is a social phenomenon that first became widely recognized in the 1950s and 1960s. Hollywood, for example, introduced America to the problems of adolescent gangs in the classic movies *Blackboard Jungle* and *West Side Story*. Although the basis for gang involvement has not changed over the years, the levels of violence and public concern have increased dramatically. Many communities consider gang-related problems to be their number one social issue. Access to sophisticated weaponry and greater mobility has drawn unsuspecting neighborhoods and innocent bystanders into the often-violent clashes of **intragang** and **intergang** warfare. Individuals and communities have been reacting angrily to this growing menace. To deal effectively with the threats of gang-initiated violence and crime, however, it is important to understand why gangs form, what their objectives are, how they are structured, and how to discourage adolescent involvement.

Children often join gangs because they are neglected by their parents, lack positive role models, and fail to receive adequate adult supervision. Other motivations for joining a gang include peer pressures, low self-esteem, and the perceived easy acquisition of money from gang-related drug dealing and other criminal activities.

In comparison to traditional, formal youth organizations, juvenile gangs may appear disorganized. Research shows, however, that verbal rules, policies, customs, and hierarchies of command are rigidly observed within the gang. Thus, common values and attitudes exist:

- Gang membership is usually defined in socioeconomic, racial, and ethnic terms, and adolescents involved have similar backgrounds.
- Gang members are distinguished by a distinctive and well-defined dress code. Violation of this code by members, or mimicking of the dress code by non–gang members, can result in ostracism, ridicule, physical abuse, and violence.
- Leadership and seniority within the gang are defined by vested time in belonging to the gang, age, loyalty, and demonstrated delinquent cleverness (often related to drug dealing and other crimes).
- Gang members use gang slang to ensure camaraderie and group loyalty.

Although a stable home life does not ensure that an adolescent will not become involved with gang-related activity, a strong family environment and guidance from respected parents and guardians are clearly deterrents (Lale 1992). Many gang members are children from dysfunctional, broken, or single-parent homes. Many parents are aware of their children's gang involvement but they lack the skill, confidence, and authority to deter the gang or curtail drug involvement of their teenagers. To make matters worse, ineffective parents often discourage or even interfere with involvement by outside authorities due to misdirected loyalty to their children and/or to avoid embarrassment to their family and community.

Because troubled adolescents are often estranged from their families, they are particularly influenced by their peer groups. These teenagers are most likely to associate with groups whose members have similar backgrounds and problems and who make them feel accepted. Because of this vulnerability, adolescents may become involved with local gangs. In summary, gangs offer the following:

- Fellowship and camaraderie
- Identity and recognition
- Membership and belonging
- Family substitution and role models
- Security and protection
- Diversion and excitement
- Friendships and structure
- Money and financial gain for relatively little effort
- Ability to live the crazy life (*vida loca*) (Sanders 1994; Shelden et al. 2001) or *locura* (craziness) (Shelden et al. 2004)

In the United States, estimates of the total number of existing gangs vary widely. There are at least 21,500 gangs and more than 731,000 active gang

KEY TERMS

intragang
between members of the same gang

intergang
between members of different gangs

members in the United States. Gangs conduct criminal activity in all 50 states and U.S. territories. Although most gang activity is concentrated in major urban areas, gangs also are proliferating in rural and suburban areas of the country as gang members flee increasing law enforcement pressure in urban areas or seek more lucrative drug markets. This proliferation in nonurban areas increasingly is accompanied by violence and is threatening society in general (National Drug Intelligence Center [NDIC] 2009).

For example, in Chicago, estimates range from 12,000 to 120,000 gang members. Spergel (1990) provided the following percentages of those who are reportedly in gangs within a particular school population in the Chicago area: ". . . 5% of the elementary school youths, 10% of all high school youths, 20% of those in special school programs, and, more alarmingly perhaps, 35% of those between 16 and 19 years of age who have dropped out of school" (Shelden et al. 2004, p. 29). Keep in mind that these data are for just one city.

Street gangs, outlaw motorcycle gangs (OMGs), and prison gangs are the primary distributors of illegal drugs on the streets of the United States. Gangs also smuggle drugs into the United States and produce and transport drugs within the country.

Street gang members convert powdered cocaine into crack cocaine and produce most of the phencyclidine (PCP) available in the United States. Gangs, primarily OMGs, also produce marijuana and methamphetamine. In addition, gangs increasingly are involved in smuggling large quantities of cocaine and marijuana and lesser quantities of heroin, methamphetamine, and MDMA (also known as Ecstasy) into the United States from foreign sources of supply. Gangs primarily transport and distribute powdered cocaine, crack cocaine, heroin, marijuana, methamphetamine, MDMA, and PCP in the United States.

Located throughout the country, street gangs vary in size, composition, and structure. Large, nationally affiliated street gangs pose the greatest threat because they smuggle, produce, transport, and distribute large quantities of illicit drugs throughout the country and are extremely violent. Local street gangs in rural, suburban, and urban areas pose a growing threat (NDIC 2009).

Another recent survey claims that 27% of public school students ages 12 to 17 attend schools that are both gang and drug-infected. That means 5.7 million students attend schools that are both gang and drug dominated. Nearly 50% of all public school students report drug use or sales on school grounds (Funk 2010). Research shows that teenage gangs are becoming major players in the drug trade (Siegel and Senna 1997; Siegel and Welsh 2009). Two of the largest gangs in Los Angeles, the Bloods and the Crips, are examples of this trend. Estimated membership in these two gangs exceeds 20,000. In the past, organized crime families maintained a monopoly on the Asian heroin market. Today, youth gangs have entered this trade, for two reasons: (1) Recent efforts and successes in prosecuting top mob bosses by criminal justice officials have created opportunities for new players, and (2) demand has grown for cocaine and synthetic drugs that are produced locally in many U.S. cities. In Los Angeles and most major larger cities, drug-dealing gangs maintain "rock houses" or "stash houses" (where crack cocaine is used and sold) that serve as selling and distribution centers for hard drugs. The crack cocaine found in these "rock houses" is often supplied or run by gang members (Siegel and Senna 1997; Siegel and Welsh 2009).

To a lesser extent, other, less violent gangs with smaller memberships are also involved in drug dealing. Recent research shows that the media may exaggerate the percentage of gangs involved in drug dealing. Citywide drug dealing by tightly organized "super" gangs appears to be on the decline and is being superseded by the activities of loosely organized, neighborhood-based groups (Siegel and Senna 1997). The main reason for this shift is that federal and state law enforcement of drug laws have forced drug dealers to become "flexible, informal organizations [rather] than rigid vertically organized gangs with . . . [leaders] . . . who are far removed from day-to-day action [on the street]" (Siegel and Senna 1997, p. 409).

Drug use and gang-related activities are often linked, but the relationship is highly variable (Curry and Spergel 1997; Fagan 1990). Clearly, problems with drugs exist without gangs, and gang-related activities can occur despite the absence of drugs; however, because they have common etiologies, their occurrences are often intertwined. Most adolescents who are associated with gangs are knowledgeable about drugs. Many gang members have experimented with drugs, much like other adolescents their age. However, the hard-core gang members are more likely to be engaged not only in drug use but also in drug dealing as a source of revenue to support the gang-related activities (Lale 1992; Siegel and Senna 1997). The types of drugs used and their significance and functions vary from gang to gang (Fagan 1990; Siegel and Senna 1997). For example, many Latino gangs do not profit from drug trafficking but are primarily interested in using hard-core drugs such as heroin and PCP. In contrast, African American gangs tend to be more interested in the illicit commercial value of drugs and often engage in dealing crack and other cocaine forms.

Prevention, Intervention, and Treatment of Adolescent Drug Problems

The most effective way to prevent adolescent gang involvement is to identify, at an early age, those children at risk and provide them with lifestyle alternatives. Important components of such strategies are as follows:

- Encourage parental awareness of gangs and teach parents how to address problems in their own families that may encourage gang involvement.
- Provide teenagers with alternative participation in organizations or groups that satisfy their needs for camaraderie, participation, and emotional security in a constructive way. These groups can be organized around athletics, school activities, career development, or service rendering.
- Help children to develop coping skills that will enable them to deal with the frustration and stress in their personal lives.
- Educate children about gang-related problems and help them understand that, like drugs, young people who join gangs create more problems for themselves, and gang membership is not a solution to their personal or family problems.

As with most health problems, the sooner drug abuse is identified in the adolescent, the greater the likelihood that the problem can be resolved. It can be difficult to recognize signs of drug abuse in teenagers because their behavior can be erratic and unpredictable even under the best of circumstances. In fact, many of the behavioral patterns that occur coincidentally with drug problems are also present when drugs are not a problem. However, frequent occurrence or clustering of these behaviors may indicate the presence of substance abuse. The behaviors that can be warning signs include the following (Archambault 1992):

- Abruptly changing the circle of friends
- Experiencing major mood swings
- Continually challenging rules and regulations
- Overreacting to frustrations
- Being particularly submissive to peer pressures
- Sleeping excessively
- Keeping very late hours
- Withdrawing from family involvement
- Letting personal hygiene deteriorate
- Becoming isolated
- Engaging in unusual selling of possessions
- Manipulating family members
- Becoming abusive toward other members of the family
- Frequently coming home at night high

Prevention of Adolescent Drug Abuse

Logically, the best treatment for drug abuse is to prevent the problem from starting. This approach, referred to as **primary prevention**, typically has been viewed as total abstinence from drug use (see Chapter 17). Informational scare tactics are frequently used as a component of primary prevention strategies. These messages often focus on a dangerous (although in some cases rare) potential side effect and present the warning against drug use in a graphic and frightening fashion. Although this approach may scare naive adolescents away from drugs, many adolescents today, especially if they are experienced, question the validity of the scare tactics and ignore the message.

Another form of primary prevention is to encourage adolescents to become involved in formal groups, such as structured clubs or organizations, in an effort to reduce the likelihood of substance abuse (Howard 1992). Group memberships can help adolescents develop a sense of belonging and contributing to a productive, desirable objective. This involvement can also provide the adolescent with the strength to resist undesirable peer pressures. In contrast, belonging to informal groups such as gangs—groups with loose structures and ill-defined, often antisocial objectives—can lead to participation in poorly chaperoned parties, excessive sexual involvement, and nonproductive activi-

KEY TERMS

primary prevention
prevention of any drug use

ties. Adolescent members of such poorly defined organizations tend to drink alcohol at an earlier age and are more likely to use other substances of abuse.

Some experts claim that primary prevention against drug use is unrealistic for many adolescents. They believe that no strategy is likely to stop adolescents from experimenting with alcohol or other drugs of abuse, especially if these substances are part of their home environment (e.g., if alcohol or tobacco is routinely used) and are viewed as normal, acceptable, and even expected behaviors (Howard 1992). For these adolescents, it is important to recognize when drug use moves from experimentation or a social exercise to early stages of a problem and to prevent serious dependence from developing. This approach, referred to as **secondary prevention**, consists of (1) teaching adolescents about the early signs of abuse, (2) teaching adolescents how to assist peers and family members with drug problems, and (3) teaching adolescents how and where help is available for people with drug problems (Archambault 1992). Regardless of the prevention approach used, adolescents need to understand that drugs are never the solution for emotional difficulties, nor are they useful for long-term coping.

Treatment of Adolescent Drug Abuse

To provide appropriate treatment for adolescent drug abuse, the severity of the problem must be ascertained. The criteria for such assessments include the following:

- Differentiating between abuse and normal adolescent experimentation with drugs
- Distinguishing between minor abuse and severe dependency on drugs
- Distinguishing among behavioral problems resulting from (1) general behavioral disorders, such as juvenile delinquency; (2) mental retardation; and (3) drugs of abuse

There is no single best approach for treating adolescent substance abuse. Occasionally, the troubled adolescent is admitted to a clinic and treated on an inpatient basis. The inpatient approach is very expensive and creates a temporary artificial environment that may be of limited value in preparing adolescents for the problems to be faced in their real homes and neighborhoods. However, the advantage of an inpatient approach is that adolescents can be managed better and their behavior can be more tightly monitored and controlled (Hoshino 1992). A more practical and routine treatment approach is to allow adolescents to remain in their natural environment and to provide the necessary life skills to be successful at home, in school, and in the community. For example, adolescents being treated for drug dependence should be helped with:

- Schoolwork, so that appropriate progress toward high school graduation occurs
- Career skills, so that adolescents can become self-reliant and learn to care for themselves and others
- Family problems and learning to communicate and resolve conflicts

If therapy is to be successful, it is important to improve the environment of the drug-abusing adolescent. This aspect of treatment includes disassociation of the adolescent from groups (such as gangs) or surroundings that encourage drug use and promoting association with healthy and supportive groups (such as a nurturing family) and experiences (such as athletics and school activities). Although desirable, such separation is not always possible, especially if the family and home environment are factors that encourage abuse; the likelihood of therapeutic success is substantially diminished under these circumstances.

Often, therapeutic objectives are facilitated by positive reinforcement that encourages life changes that eliminate access to and use of drugs. This goal frequently can be achieved by association with peers who have similar drug and social problems but are motivated to make positive changes in their life. Group sessions with such peers are held under the supervision of a trained therapist and consist of members sharing problems and solutions (Hoshino 1992). Some other recent options include holistic therapies such as acupuncture, homeotherapy, massage therapy, aromatherapy, yoga, nutrition therapy, and many more options that were once marginalized by the medical profession (Apostolides 1996).

Another useful approach is to discourage use of drugs by reducing their reinforcing effects. This result can sometimes be achieved by substituting a stronger positive or negative reinforcer. For example, if adolescents use drugs because they believe these substances cause good feelings and help them cope with emotional problems, it may be necessary to replace the drug-taking behavior with other activities that make the adolescent feel good without the drug (such as participation in sports or recreational activities). Negative reinforcers, such as parental discovery and punishment or police apprehension, may discourage drug use by teenagers who are willing to conform and respect authorities; however, negative approaches are ineffective deterrents for nonconforming, rebellious adolescents. Negative reinforcers also do not tend to discourage adolescent use of substances that are more socially acceptable, such as alcohol, tobacco, and even marijuana (Howard 1992).

Regardless of the treatment approach, adolescents must meet several basic objectives if therapy for their drug dependence is to be successful (Daily 1992b):

- Realize that drugs do not solve problems—they only make the problems worse.
- Understand why they turned to drugs in the first place.
- Be convinced that abandoning drugs grants them greater independence and control over their own lives.
- Understand that drug abuse is a symptom of underlying problems that need to be resolved.

Summary of Adolescent Drug Abuse

Drug abuse by adolescents is particularly problematic in the United States. The teenage years are filled with experimentation, searching, confusion, rebellion, poor self-image, and insecurity. These attributes, if not managed properly, can cause inappropriate coping and lead to problems such as drug dependence, gang involvement, violence, criminal behavior, and suicide. Clearly, early detection of severe underlying emotional problems and application of effective early preventive therapy are important for proper management. Approaches to treatment of drug abuse problems must be individualized because each adolescent is a unique product of physiological, psychological, and environmental factors.

Almost as important as early intervention for adolescent drug abuse problems is recognizing when treatment is unnecessary. We should not be too quick to label all young drug users as antisocial and emotionally unstable. In most cases, teenagers who have used drugs are merely experimenting with new emotions or exercising their newfound freedom. In such situations, nonintervention is usu-

ally better than therapeutic meddling. For the most part, if adolescents are given the opportunity, they will work through their own feelings, conflicts, and attitudes about substance abuse, and they will develop a responsible philosophy concerning the use of these drugs.

Drug Use in College Student Subcultures

Chapter 8 includes a lengthy discussion of alcohol use and abuse by college students. This section focuses on college undergraduate use of alcohol not discussed in that chapter, with additional emphasis on the use and abuse of illicit drugs by college students currently attending institutions of higher education.

Table 16.6 compares trends in the annual use of various types of licit and illicit drugs by full-time college students with others who are the same age (1 to 4 years beyond high school) but are not attending college. Overall, Table 16.6 shows the following noteworthy prevalence trends (Johnston et al. 2009b):

- Full-time college students were slightly less likely to use any illicit drugs in 2008 than others (35% versus 37%). A slightly larger proportional difference exists for the annual prevalence of any illicit drug other than marijuana (15% versus 23%).
- Annual marijuana use is very similar among college students and high school graduates of the same age that are not in college (32.3% versus 33.1%). However, the rate of current daily marijuana use (not shown in this table) is lower among college students than among their out-of-school counterparts (15% versus 23%).
- Annual prevalence for inhalants, cocaine, crack cocaine, other cocaine, heroin, heroin with a needle, heroin without a needle, methamphetamine, crystal methamphetamine (ice), sedatives (barbiturates), other narcotics including Oxycontin and Vicodin, and steroids is two or more times higher for noncollege respondents than for college students. It is clear that use of a number of the illicit drugs other than marijuana tends to be distinctly higher among those not in colleges.
- Ritalin, a drug in the amphetamine class, shows a reversed pattern in that there is higher use among college students (3%) versus 2% in the non–college-age peers reporting past-year usage. (Quite possibly these differences could

Table 16.6 **Annual Prevalence of Use of Drugs, 2008: Full-Time College Students Versus Others, 1 to 4 Years Beyond High School**

	FULL-TIME COLLEGE STUDENTS	OTHERS
Any illicit drug*	35.2	37.1
Any illicit drug* other than marijuana	15.3	22.5
Alcohol	82.1	77.0
Cigarettes	30.0	41.9
Marijuana	32.3	33.1
Other narcotics+	6.5	11.7
OxyContin	3.6	6.5
Vicodin	6.7	13.0
Hallucinogens	5.1	5.7
LSD	2.6	1.9
Amphetamines+	5.7	7.1
Ritalin	3.2	2.1
Methamphetamine	0.5	1.2
Ice	0.1	1.1
Tranquilizers	5.0	9.4
Cocaine	4.4	9.0
Crack	0.5	2.0
MDMA (Ecstasy)	3.7	6.3
Sedatives+ (barbiturates)	3.7	7.4
Inhalants	1.1	2.5
Ketamine	0.4	0.3
Rohypnol	0.3	0.1
Heroin	0.3	1.5
GHBs	0.2	0.2

Note: All full-time college entries, except for the first two percentage entries, are from highest to lowest.

*Use of any illicit drug includes use of marijuana, hallucinogens, cocaine, or heroin or any use of other narcotics, amphetamines, sedatives (barbiturates), or tranquilizers not under a doctor's orders.

+Drug use not under a doctor's orders.

Source: Johnson, L. D., P. M. O'Malley, J. G. Bachman, and J. E Schulenberg. *Monitoring the Future: National Survey Results on Drug Use, 1975–2008. Volume II: College Students and Adults.* NIH Publication No. 09-7430. Bethesda, MD: National Institute on Drug Abuse, 2009.

be explained by college students using Ritalin to stay awake late at night to finish assignments or study for tests.)

- In 2008, college students were modestly higher in lifetime, annual, and 30-day use of alcohol than the non-college group, with the difference being largest in the 30-day rate (69% vs. 55%, not shown in Table 16.6).
- College students also had a significantly higher prevalence of occasions of heavy drinking (five or more drinks in a row in the past 2 weeks)— 40% versus 30% among their age peers—but their rates of daily drinking were not significantly different from rates of their age peers (4% versus 3.7%).
- In 2008, nearly two-thirds (65%) of college students reported using flavored alcoholic beverages (not shown in this table) in the prior years compared to a lower rate for the noncollege group (51%).

In summary, the noncollege segment is generally more drug-involved than the college student segment. This pattern is a continuation of the high school scenario in which those without college plans are more likely to use drugs. The only substance that college students are significantly and substantially more likely to be users of is alcohol (particularly getting drunk and binge drinking), and this difference emerges primarily after high school.

Table 16.7 shows yearly trends in drug use among U.S. college students from 2005 through 2008 (Johnston et al. 2009b). This table details the percentages of college students who used drugs in the past 12 months before the surveys were administered. The main finding is that the overall use of any illicit drugs remained fairly constant from 2005 to 2008—approximately 35%, when averaging the 4 years of surveying. From 2005 to 2008, some slight increases and decreases (depending on the drug) in the overall use of illicit drugs, including marijuana, MDMA, and opioids, were noted. The following show those drugs with modest increases, decreases, and not much change.

Modest percentage of *increased usage* from 2005 to 2008 (unless noted otherwise):

- LSD
- OxyContin

Modest percentage of *decreased usage* from 2005 to 2008:

- Any illicit drug other than marijuana
- Cigarettes
- Hallucinogens
- MDMA (Ecstasy)

Table 16.7 **Trends in Annual Use of Drugs Among College Students 1 to 4 Years Beyond High School**

	2005	2006	2007	2008
Any illicit drug*	36.6	33.9	35.0	35.2
Any illicit drug other than marijuana*	18.5	18.1	17.3	15.3
Alcohol	83.0	82.1	80.9	82.1
Cigarettes	36.0	30.9	30.7	30.0
Marijuana	33.3	30.2	31.8	32.3
Hallucinogens	5.0	5.4	4.7	4.4
LSD	0.7	1.4	1.3	2.6
MDMA (Ecstasy)	2.9	2.6	2.2	3.7
Amphetamines+	6.7	6.0	6.9	5.7
Ritalin	4.2	3.9	3.7	3.2
Methamphetamine	1.7	1.2	0.4	0.5
Ice	1.4	0.6	0.7	0.1
Cocaine	5.7	5.1	5.4	4.4
Crack	0.8	1.0	0.6	0.5
Other narcotics+	8.4	8.8	7.7	6.5
OxyContin	2.1	3.0	2.8	3.6
Vicodin	9.6	7.6	6.7	6.7
Tranquilizers	6.4	5.8	5.5	5.0
Sedatives (barbiturates)+	3.9	3.4	3.6	3.7
Inhalants	1.8	1.5	1.5	1.1
Heroin	0.3	0.3	0.2	0.3
Rohypnol	0.1	0.2	0.1	0.3
GHB	0.4	0.1	0.1	0.2
Ketamine	0.5	0.9	0.2	0.4

Note: Includes percentage of students who used in the past 12 months, except where noted.

*Use of any illicit drug includes use of marijuana, hallucinogens, cocaine, or heroin or any use of other narcotics, amphetamines, sedatives (barbiturates), or tranquilizers not under a doctor's orders.

+Drug use not under a doctor's orders.

Source: Johnson, L. D., P. M. O'Malley, J. G. Bachman, and J. E Schulenberg. *Monitoring the Future: National Survey Results on Drug Use, 1975–2009. Volume II: College Students and Adults.* NIH Publication No. 09-7430. Bethesda, MD: National Institute on Drug Abuse, 2010.

- Ritalin
- Methamphetamine
- Crystal methamphetamine (ice)
- Crack
- Other narcotics
- Vicodin

Not much change (fairly stable percentages) in usage from 2005 to 2008:

- Any illicit drug
- Alcohol
- Marijuana
- Amphetamines
- Cocaine
- Tranquilizers
- Sedatives (barbiturates)
- Inhalants
- Heroin
- Rohypnol
- GHB
- Ketamine

■ Reasons for College Students' Drug Use

Figure 16.2 shows the primary reasons why a sample survey of 776 male and female college students used alcohol and other drugs (48.9% were male and 51.1% were female). The major reasons cited in this sample survey were (1) breaks the ice (74.3%), (2) enhances social activity (73.8%), (3) gives people something to do (72.6%), (4) gives people something to talk about (66.8%), (5) allows people to have more fun (62.2%), (6) facilitates contact with peers (61.1%), (7) facilitates sexual opportunities (53.7%), and (8) facilitates male bonding (63.2%). Though not shown in this figure, this same survey revealed that 30.7% consumed 1 to 4 drinks in a week, 18.1% consumed 5 to 10 drinks, and 11.5% consumed 11 or more drinks in a week. Further, 56.5% did not binge drink, 12.8% binged once, 11.4% binged twice, and 13.8% binged three to five times. In addition, 4.7% used marijuana six times per year and 11.1% used marijuana once per year from the time they began their college career to the date of this survey. Approximately 65.5% taking this survey were white, 13.2% Hispanic, 6.6% black, 11.1% Asian/Pacific Islander, 0.1% American Indian/Alaska Native, and 3.4% were classified as other ethnicity (GatorWell Health Promotion Services 2010). This survey may indicate that the use of alcohol and other drugs on a fairly typical larger state campus continues to be readily prevalent.

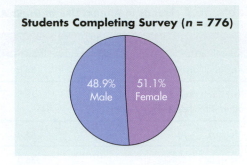

Students Completing Survey (*n* = 776)

48.9% Male
51.1% Female

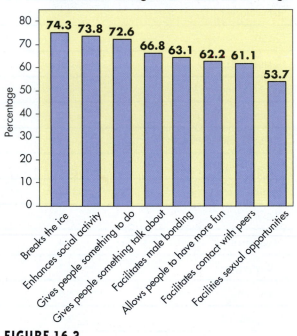

Reasons for Using Alcohol and Other Drugs

74.3 73.8 72.6 66.8 63.1 62.2 61.1 53.7

Breaks the ice
Enhances social activity
Gives people something to do
Gives people something talk about
Facilitates male bonding
Allows people to have more fun
Facilitates contact with peers
Facilities sexual opportunities

FIGURE 16.2

Sample of reasons for using alcohol and other drugs.

Source: GatorWell Health Promotion Services, Division of Student Affairs. "Core Alcohol and Drug Survey, Long Form" Fall 2009. Gainesville, FL: University of Florida, 2010.

■ Additional Noteworthy Findings Regarding Drug Use by College Students

The following sections describe the most recent significant studies and findings regarding the use of drugs by college students.

Patterns of Alcohol and Other Drug Use

Literature reviews of undergraduates' substance use and abuse and the prevalence patterns of alcohol and other drug use found that the most popular substance used by undergraduates is alcohol, which was used by about 90% of students at least once a year. Heavy alcohol use, which includes binge drinking, ranged from 20% to 40% in this group, "while binge drinking decreased by 6% among dormitory residents between 1993 and 1999, it increased by about the same amount among those living off campus. Nearly 80% of binge drinkers live in a fraternity or sorority house, often off campus" (Marklein 2000, p. 1). Other results showed that alcohol use was associated with serious and acute problems such as alcoholism, poor academic performance, drinking and driving, and criminalistic behavior (e.g., driving while intoxicated, vandalism, violence). From 1997 to 1998, alcohol arrests in the nation's colleges increased by 24.3%; this is reported as the largest increase in 7 years. In comparing the same 2 years, drug law violations on U.S. campuses increased by 11.1% (Nicklin 2000).

Other research findings regarding college student drinkers include:

- Male college students tend to drink more than female college students.
- White college students tend to drink more than their African American and Hispanic peers.
- Members of fraternities and sororities tend to drink more than students who do not participate in the Greek system.
- College athletes tend to drink more than peers who are not involved with campus-based sports.
- As a group, college students are less likely to use drugs than their noncollege peers.

College students vary greatly in their use of alcohol and their beliefs about its positive and negative effects. Studies show that two major drinking patterns appear dominant among college students: (1) drinking related to impulsivity, disinhibition, and sensation-seeking and (2) drinking to manage negative emotional states, such as depression (National Institute on Alcohol and Alcoholism [NIAAA] 2005a).

Summarized in the following list are other significant findings regarding alcohol and other drug use:

- *High risk drinking:* Studies show that about 43% of all students report drinking in a high-risk manner at some point in their college career. Twenty percent of students report drinking in a high-risk manner often.
- *Poor grades:* College students who received grades of D or below were more likely than those with higher grades to have used cigarettes, alcohol, or illicit drugs during the past month.

- *Death:* Each year, 1825 college students between the ages of 18 and 24 die from alcohol-related unintentional injuries, including motor vehicle crashes (NIAAA 2005a; Hingson, Zha, and Weitzman 2009).
- *Injury:* Each year, 599,000 students between the ages of 18 and 24 are unintentionally injured under the influence of alcohol (NIAAA 2005a; Hingson et al. 2009).
- *Assault:* Each year, 696,000 students between the ages of 18 and 24 are assaulted by another student who has been drinking (NIAAA 2005b; Hingson et al. 2009).
- *Sexual abuse:* Each year, 97,000 students between the ages of 18 and 24 are victims of alcohol-related sexual assault or date rape (NIAAA 2005b; Hingson et al. 2009). Researchers estimate that alcohol use is implicated in one-third to two-thirds of sexual assault and acquaintance or date rape cases among teens and college students.
- *Unsafe sex:* Each year, 400,000 students between the ages of 18 and 24 have unprotected sex, and more than 100,000 students between the ages of 18 and 24 report having been too intoxicated to know if they consented to having sex (NIAAA 2005a).
- *Academic problems:* About 25% of college students report academic consequences of their drinking including missing class, falling behind, doing poorly on exams or papers, and receiving lower grades overall (NIAAA 2005a).
- *Health problems/suicide attempts:* More than 150,000 students develop an alcohol-related health problem each year (Hingson et al. 2009), and between 1.2% and 1.5% of students indicate that they tried to commit suicide within the past year due to drinking or drug use (NIAAA 2005a).
- *Drunk driving:* Each year, 3,360,000 students between the ages of 18 and 24 drive under the influence of alcohol (NIAAA 2005a; Hingson et al. 2009).
- *Vandalism:* About 11% of college student drinkers report that they have damaged property while under the influence of alcohol.
- *Property damage:* More than 25% of administrators from schools with relatively low drinking levels and over 50% from schools with high drinking levels say their campuses have a "moderate" or "major" problem with alcohol-related property damage.
- *Police involvement:* About 5% of 4-year college students are involved with the police or campus

security as a result of their drinking (Wechsler et al. 2002), and 110,000 students between the ages of 18 and 24 are arrested each year for an alcohol-related violation such as public drunkenness or driving under the influence.

- *Alcohol abuse and dependence:* In the past 12 months, 31% of college students met criteria for a diagnosis of alcohol abuse and 6% for a diagnosis of alcohol dependence, according to questionnaire-based self-reports about their drinking (NIAAA 2005a).
- *Binge drinking:* Young adults ages 18 to 25 are most likely to binge or drink heavily; 54% of the drinkers in this age group binge and about one in four are heavy drinkers.
- *Victimization:* Almost half of college students who were victims of campus crimes said they were drinking or using other drugs when they were victimized.
- The amount and proportion of alcohol consumed by college students varies depending on where they live. Drinking rates are highest in fraternities and sororities, followed by on-campus housing (e.g., dormitories, residence halls). Students who live independently off-site (e.g., in apartments) drink less, and commuting students who live with their families drink the least (NIAAA 2005b).

Predicting Drug Use for First-Year College Students

One of the best predictors of drug use for first-year college students was drug use during a typical month in the senior year of high school. Overall, college students responding to a questionnaire were found to use marijuana less frequently than they did in high school. Further, alcohol use increased early in the college years. Although the frequency of alcohol use increased, the number of times that college students got drunk did not rise. Most of these students found new friends in college with whom they got drunk. Alcohol and drug use depended on the choice of new college friends (Leibsohn 1994).

Another more recent finding includes personality dispositions to risky behavior as a predictor of first-year college drinking. Research findings from 418 first-year U.S. college students at the University of Kentucky reveal that students with a preponderance of sensation-seeking predispositions (risk taking) are more likely to drink more frequently, consume greater quantities of alcohol, and experience negative outcomes from drinking than students scoring significantly lower on the UPPS-R Impulsive Behavior Scale, the positive urgency

measure (PUM), and the Drinking Styles Questionnaire (DSQ). Sensation-seeking students experience more lack of control (dyscontrol) stemming from extreme positive mood swings and it is during these times that alcohol consumption rapidly increases (Cyders et al. 2009).

Dormitories for Non–Drug-Using Students

In 1988, Rutgers University was one of the first universities to create a dormitory for students who are recuperating addicts and who want to stay away from the alcohol-charged atmosphere of conventional dormitories. The dormitory at Rutgers maintains strict rules and careful management (Witham 1995). Other universities offer similar variations for on-campus living. In 1989, the University of Michigan opened a substance-free housing facility and set aside 500 dormitory spaces; 1200 students applied for these spaces (Belsie 1995). More recent findings indicate that "[N]ow that substance-free housing is commonplace, a handful of campuses, including Rutgers, have gone [even] further, offering 'recovery' housing for students who have been in treatment for addiction" (Lewin 2005). Today, substance-free housing has become a nationwide choice. This type of housing is found ". . . at dozens of campuses nationwide, from huge state universities like the University of Michigan to Ivy League schools like Dartmouth and small liberal arts colleges like Vassar" (Lewin 2005). For example,

> . . . a junior at Earlham College who asked that his name not be used . . . [said] "When I got to college, I didn't want to have to worry about having all that stuff in my face [in reference to having to live with drunk and drugged students in the dorm]. I've been in wellness housing my whole time here. I could handle normal housing now, but I like the people I live with, and there's a very good atmosphere." (Lewin 2005)

Further, on some campuses, large numbers of entering freshmen prefer substance-free living accommodations, mainly dormitories as well as other types of housing. "At Dartmouth, for example, about 400 of the 1075 incoming freshmen requested it, compared with only about 200 of the 2200 sophomores, juniors and seniors who live on campus" (Lewin 2005).

Remaining Popularity of Certain Types of "Softer" Drugs

Marijuana and psilocybin mushrooms are two types of illicit recreational drugs whose popularity appeared to grow in the 1990s and to date remain popular on most college campuses. Referred to as "soft drugs," these substances are commonly used on most college campuses (Ravid 1995).

> Weed and coke are great, but when the "shrooms" [referring to psilocybin mushrooms] are in town, it is a special treat. Friends on other campuses, the big state university campuses, are lucky to have more different types of drugs available. At our university, both "shrooms" and real hydroponic weed happen about one or two times a semester. *(From Venturelli's research files, male attending a smaller comprehensive university in the Midwest, age 21, June 12, 2003)*

Nationwide surveys studying yearly drug use averages from 1984 through 1999 showed a steady, progressive increase in the use of hallucinogens, which includes psilocybin mushrooms, Ecstasy, and LSD. In 1984 (the first year of the survey), 3.7% of college students used LSD; in 1999, 5.4% used this same drug. Similarly, in 1984, 6.2% used hallucinogens (excluding LSD) and in 1999, 7.8% used these same hallucinogenic-type drugs (Johnston et al. 2000a, 2000b). Updated findings show hallucinogen use has been dropping from 7.4% in 2003 to 5.1% in 2008. One noteworthy finding is that the use of LSD slightly increased from 2007 (1.3%) to 2008 (2.6%) (a 1.3% increase over a 2-year period) (Johnston et al. 2009b). Concerning college students' use of MDMA (Ecstasy), the annual use was 9.1% in 2000, 4.4% in 2003, dropping to 2.2% in 2007, then rising to 3.7% in 2008 (an increase of 1.6% over a 2-year period) (Johnston et al. 2009b).

Rohypnol and Date Rape

Rohypnol, also known as the "date-rape drug," is one of six drugs referred to as *club drugs*. The other club drugs are MDMA (Ecstasy), gamma-hydroxybutyrate (GHB), ketamine, methamphetamine, and LSD. Club drugs are used by individuals at all-night dance parties such as raves or trances, dance clubs, and bars. All of these drugs are colorless, tasteless, and odorless. They can be added unobtrusively to beverages by individuals who may want to intoxicate or sedate others (NIDA 2000). In cases of sexual assault or rape, the small white Rohypnol pills are slipped into a person's drink, causing the person to black out and have no memories of events that occurred while he or she was under the influence of the drug. A minority of undergraduates also use the drug to intensify the effects of marijuana and alcohol. One problem with identifying whether this drug has been given to an unwilling recipient is that Rohypnol can be detected only for 60 hours after ingestion (Lively 1996).

Rohypnol (flunitrazepam) belongs to a class of drugs known as benzodiazepines (such as Valium and Xanax). Although this drug is not approved for prescription use in the United States, it is approved and used in more than 60 countries as a treatment for insomnia, as a sedative, and as a presurgery anesthetic (NIDA 2000).

Recommendations for Reducing Drug Use and Abuse on College Campuses

There is an elevated risk of increased drug use and abuse when students move to a college campus. Approaches to minimize increased drug use include the following:

- *Alcohol-free options:* ". . . offer and promote social, recreational, extracurricular, and public service options that do not include alcohol and other drugs" (Ross and Dejong 2008, p. 3).
- *Normative environment:* ". . . create a social, academic, and residential environment that supports health-promoting norms" (Ross and Dejong 2008, p. 3).
- *Alcohol availability:* ". . . limit alcohol availability both on and off campus" (Ross and Dejong 2008, p. 3).
- *Alcohol marketing and promotion:* ". . . restrict marketing and promotion of alcohol beverages both on and off campus" (Ross and Dejong 2008, p. 3)
- *Policy development and enforcement:* ". . . develop and enforce campus policies and enforce local, state, and federal laws, and make sure everyone knows what the policies are" (Ross and Dejong 2008, p. 3).

HIV and AIDS

AIDS came to the attention of medical authorities in the United States on June 4, 1981, in a newsletter from the Centers for Disease Control and Prevention (CDC) in Atlanta, Georgia (Zuger 2000). HIV, the virus that causes AIDS, was not discovered until 1983. Estimates are "that [worldwide] there were 33.3 million people living with HIV at the end of

KEY TERMS

Rohypnol
the "date-rape drug," used on many college campuses

2009 compared with 26.2 million in 1999—a 27% increase" (UNAIDS 2010, p. 23; Centers for Disease Control and Prevention [CDC] 2010). In the United States, "an estimated 1.1 million Americans have HIV, and about 20% of them don't know it. About 55,000 new infections occur each year in the U.S., a number that has held steady for a decade" (*USA Today* 2010). The CDC also estimates that more than one million people are living with HIV in the United States. One in five (21%) of those living with HIV is unaware of the infection (CDC 2010d).

During 2005, 74% of those diagnosed with HIV/AIDS were male and 26% were female. Forty-nine percent were black, 31% white, 18% Hispanic, 1% Asian/Pacific Islander, and less than 1% American Indian/Alaska Native. The noteworthy finding is that in 2008, blacks (including African Americans), who make up approximately 13% of the U.S. population, accounted for almost half (47%) of the estimated number of HIV/AIDS cases diagnosed (CDC 2006; Gupta 2008). From 1981 through 2005, the CDC estimates that 952,629 cases of AIDS were diagnosed; of these, 530,756 died with AIDS as a major cause of death, and as of 2005, 421,873 people were living with AIDS (CDC 2006).

In comparing years 2001 and 2009 regarding HIV and AIDS statistics in major regions of the world, the regional figures and percentages of adults and children newly infected and living with HIV and AIDS-related deaths the most significant are (UNAIDS 2010, pp. 20–21):

- The Middle East and North Africa had a significant increase (155.6%) in the percentage of adults and children living with HIV.
- Oceania had a very significant increase (857.4%) in the number of adults and children newly infected with HIV.
- Eastern Europe and Central Asia had a very significant increase (322.2%) in the number of AIDS-related deaths among adults and children

At the end of 2009, regarding regional statistics for HIV and AIDS (from highest to lowest adults and children living with HIV/AIDS) shows that (Avert 2011b, p. 2; UNAIDS 2010):

- Sub-Saharan Africa had 22.5 million adults and children living with HIV/AIDS and had 1.3 million AIDS-related deaths in adults and children.
- South and South-East Asia had 4.1 million adults and children living with HIV/AIDS and had 260,000 AIDS-related deaths in adults and children.

- North America had 1.5 million adults and children living with HIV/AIDS and 26,000 AIDS-related deaths in adults and children.
- Eastern Europe and Central Asia had 1.4 million adults and children living with HIV/AIDS and 76,000 AIDS-related deaths in adults and children.
- Central & South America had 1.4 million adults and children living with HIV/AIDS and 58,000 AIDS-related deaths in adults and children.
- Western and Central Europe had 820,000 adults and children living with HIV/AIDS and 8500 AIDS-related deaths in adults and children.
- East Asia had 770,000 adults and children living with HIV/AIDS and 36,000 AIDS-related deaths in adults and children.
- North Africa and Middle East had 460,000 adults and children living with HIV/AIDS and 26,000 AIDS-related deaths in adults and children.
- Caribbean had 240,000 adults and children living with HIV/AIDS and 12,000 AIDS-related deaths in adults and children.
- Oceania had 57,000 adults and children living with HIV/AIDS and 1,400 AIDS-related deaths in adults and children.

UNAIDS reports the following regarding worldwide totals of adults and children with HIV/AIDS in 2009, (UNAIDS 2010, pp. 20–21):

- The total worldwide figure shows that there was an *increase* in adults and children living with HIV from 28.6 million in 2001 to 33.3 million in 2009.
- The total number of adults and children newly infected with HIV *decreased* from 3.1 million in 2001 to 2.6 million in 2009 (good news).
- The percentage of total HIV adult prevalence for those ages 15–49 years *remained the same* throughout the world in 2001 (0.8%) and 2009 (0.8%).
- The total number of AIDS-related deaths among adults and children in 2001 (1.8 million) *remained the same* in 2009 (1.8 million).

Finally, UNAIDS also reports that:

[T]he number of annual AIDS-related deaths worldwide is steadily decreasing from the peak of 2.1 million in 2004 to an estimated 1.8 million in 2009. The decline reflects the increased availability of antiretroviral therapy, as well as care and support, to people living with HIV, particularly in middle- and low-income countries; it is also a result of decreasing incidence starting in the late 1990s. (UNAIDS 2010, p. 19)

Major U.S. Statistics and Trends in Specific Populations Living with HIV/AIDS

In the United States, the following are major significant findings regarding this disease:

- More than 1 million people are living with HIV in the United States (an estimated 1,106,400 adults and adolescents), and approximately one in five of those (21%) are unaware of their infections.

- Despite increases in the total number of people living with HIV in the United States in recent years, the annual number of new infections has remained relatively stable.

- However, HIV infections continue at far too high a level, with an estimated 56,300 Americans becoming newly infected with HIV each year. On average, that's one new infection every 9½ minutes.

- More than 14,000 people with AIDS still die each year in the United States.

- Men account for roughly three-quarters of individuals living with and newly infected with HIV.

- HIV has a severe impact on all regions of the country. Areas hardest hit include Miami; New Orleans and Baton Rouge, Louisiana; Washington, DC; Baltimore; New York City; San Francisco; and Jackson, Mississippi (CDC 2009).

Heterosexuals and injection drug users continue to be affected by HIV:

- Individuals infected through heterosexual contact account for 31% of annual new HIV infections and 28% of people living with HIV.

- As a group, women account for 27% of annual new HIV infections and 25% of those living with HIV.

- Injection drug users represent 12% of annual new HIV infections and 19% of those living with HIV.

With regard to women and HIV/AIDS, the following are noteworthy:

- Women of color (especially African American women) are the hardest hit. "HIV is the lead-ing cause of death among young African American women between the ages of 25–34 years" (McComsey 2001).

- Younger women are more likely than older women to get HIV. "The majority of new HIV cases amongst young women are contracted through unprotected heterosexual sex" (McComsey 2009).

- AIDS is a common killer, second only to cancer and heart disease for women. It is the third most-deadly disease for women in the United States.

- "More than 25% of new cases diagnosed every year are in women" (McComsey 2011).

- The most common ways women get HIV (in order) are having sex with a man who has HIV and sharing injection drug works (e.g., needles, syringes) used by someone with HIV (CDC 2010a).

The following provides information about HIV/AIDS by race and ethnicity:

African Americans:

- Among racial/ethnic groups, African Americans face the most severe burden of HIV and AIDS in the nation.

- Although blacks represent approximately 12% of the U.S. population, they account for almost half (46%) of people living with HIV in the United States, as well as nearly half (45%) of new infections each year. HIV infections among blacks overall have been roughly stable since the early 1990s.

- At some point in their life, approximately 1 in 16 black men will be diagnosed with HIV, as will 1 in 30 black women.

- The rate of new HIV infections for black men is about six times as high as that of white men, nearly three times that of Hispanic/Latino men, and more than twice that of black women.

- The HIV incidence rate for black women is nearly 15 times as high as that of white women, and nearly 4 times that of Hispanic/Latino women.

Hispanics/Latinos:

- Hispanics/Latinos are also disproportionately impacted by HIV/AIDS. Hispanics/Latinos represent 15% of the population but account for an estimated 17% of people living with HIV and 17% of new infections. HIV infections among Hispanics/Latinos overall have been roughly stable since the early 1990s.

- The rate of new HIV infections among Hispanic/Latino men is more than double that of white men, and the rate among Hispanic/Latino women is nearly four times that of white women (CDC 2009).

Nature of HIV Infection and Related Symptoms

AIDS (acquired immunodeficiency syndrome) is caused by the human immunodeficiency virus (HIV). AIDS is a disease in which the body's immune system breaks down and is unable to fight off certain infections, known as "opportunistic infections," and other illnesses that take advantage of a weakened immune system.

When a person is infected with HIV, the virus enters the body and lives and multiplies primarily in the white blood cells (see **Figure 16.3**). These immune cells normally protect us from disease. The hallmark of HIV infection is the progressive loss of a specific type of immune cells called T-helper or CD4+ cells.

As the virus grows, it damages or kills CD4+ and other cells, weakening the immune system and leaving the individual vulnerable to numerous opportunistic infections and other illnesses, ranging from pneumonia to cancer. The CDC defines someone as having a clinical diagnosis of AIDS if he or she has tested positive for HIV and has one or both of these conditions:

- The person has experienced one or more AIDS-related infections or illnesses.
- The number of CD4+ cells has reached or fallen below 200 per cubic millimeter of blood (a measurement known as a T-cell count) (Schernoff and Smith 2001).

As mentioned previously, the immune systems of HIV-positive individuals become severely compromised as important immune cells called CD4+ helper T lymphocytes and macrophages are destroyed. Because these immune cells are crucial in identifying and eliminating infection-causing microorganisms such as bacteria, fungi, and viruses, their deficiency substantially increases the likelihood and severity of infectious diseases. Progression of the disease brings weight loss, infections in the throat ("thrush") and skin (shingles), and other opportunistic infections and/or cancer (e.g., Kaposi's sarcoma). Infections become increasingly difficult to control with medication, and consequently severe opportunistic infections, such as pneumonia, meningitis, hepatitis, and tuberculosis, occur and eventually lead to death. The likelihood of introducing these opportunistic infections into the body increases in patients who are injection drug users because they often share injection equipment, such as needles and syringes that are contaminated with disease-causing microorganisms.

An HIV-infected individual may not manifest symptoms of AIDS for as many as 10 to 12 years after the initial infection. Although the HIV-infected individual may experience no symptoms, he or she is highly contagious.

After an individual has become infected, he or she may have a brief flu-like illness, usually within 6 to 12 weeks. It is not known what determines the length of the latency period, when symptoms are not present. The asymptomatic period eventually ends, however, and signs of immune disorder appear. Initial symptoms of this disease include night sweats, swollen lymph glands, fever, and/or headaches.

Diagnosis and Treatment

It is crucial that HIV-infected people be aware of their condition to avoid activities that might transmit the infection to others. Testing for the presence of infection has been available since 1985 and is done by determining whether the body is producing antibodies against HIV. Further, since 1996, newspapers, magazines, radio, and television have been advertising a take-at-home HIV antibody test (even though such advertisements are not as widely publicized today but can readily be found on the Internet). The presence of these specific antibodies indicates HIV infection. If an individual is infected, it takes 6 to 12 weeks after the HIV exposure before the body produces enough antibodies to be detected in currently available tests. If the antibody is not present within 6 months after HIV exposure, it is likely that infection did not occur (Pietroski 1993).

Although the tests for HIV infection are reliable, false negatives (i.e., the test says no HIV is present even though the individual is infected) and false positives (i.e., the test says the individual is infected even though no HIV is present) occur in 1 out of 30,000 tests. Because testing positive for HIV is currently perceived as eventually life-threatening and is a highly emotional diagnosis, great effort is made to ensure confidentiality of the test results. The blood

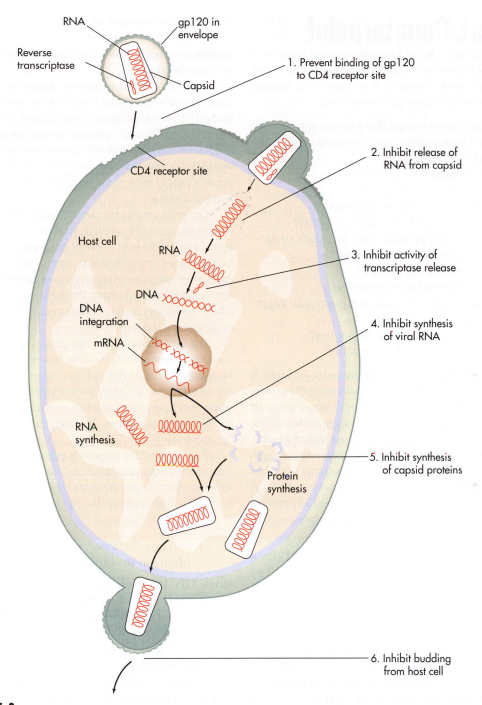

RNA

gp120 in envelope

Reverse transcriptase

Capsid

1. Prevent binding of gp120 to CD4 receptor site

CD4 receptor site

Host cell

2. Inhibit release of RNA from capsid

RNA

3. Inhibit activity of transcriptase release

DNA

DNA integration

4. Inhibit synthesis of viral RNA

mRNA

RNA synthesis

5. Inhibit synthesis of capsid proteins

Protein synthesis

6. Inhibit budding from host cell

FIGURE 16.3

Disrupting the assembly line, HIV survives by invading white blood cells and turning them into virus factories. There are six possible approaches for developing anti-HIV therapies by interfering with the replication of HIV.

specimens to be tested are coded, and the personnel conducting the tests are not allowed to divulge the results to anyone but the individual who was tested. The issue of confidentiality is very controversial, however. It often is difficult to decide who has the right to know when HIV has been detected

(see "Point/Counterpoint: Who Should Know the Results of Your HIV Test If You Test Positive?").

After a positive HIV diagnosis, the best way to lengthen one's life is to immediately begin drug treatments. The first prescription drug treatment for AIDS, AZT, was introduced in 1987. In 1996,

cient in controlling HIV (Chong 2006). "Integrase inhibitors prevent HIV, or human immunodeficiency virus, from replicating by blocking its ability to patch its DNA onto cells" (Chong 2006, p. A9). When combined with two other drugs, tenoflovir and lamivudine, it appears promising. Used as part of a drug cocktail, "the amount of HIV in 90% of patients . . . [was reduced to] . . . undetectable levels in 24 weeks" (Chong 2006, p. A9). Unfortunately, many health insurance companies continue to actively issue restrictive amendments on their policies that cap reimbursement for such expensive drug therapies. As a result, infected individuals with extensive debt obligations and patients without health insurance are often unable to afford the latest drug therapy.

Some HIV-infected persons taking the current treatment regimens suffer side effects that are so severe they choose to stop taking some of the drugs necessary to hold off the development of AIDS. Side effects can include diarrhea, bone-marrow suppression, an inability to tolerate the drugs, and tumor-like growths on the neck and other parts of the body. However, the overall success in treating HIV-positive patients resulted in a 23% drop in HIV-related deaths in 1996 and a 40% drop in such deaths in 1997. Because the drugs halt the progression of HIV to AIDS, the rates of new AIDS cases fell 25% by 1998 (Zuger 2000). Today, there is approximately 70% survival rate for those on daily medication (CDC 2010c).

A successful prognosis for HIV infection and AIDS relies on three factors: (1) initiation of a drug regimen as soon as possible after an HIV-positive diagnosis, (2) strict adherence to medical advice and treatment, and (3) maintenance of a healthy diet without drug use or abuse in order to avoid taxing the immune system.

Scientists are optimistic that eventually there will be a vaccine against HIV/AIDS. Although approximately 30 types of vaccines are being studied, the development of such a vaccine after clinical trials can take more than a decade (Fischer 2000). The key is to invent "killer" T cells to shut down or destroy HIV-infected cells (Fischer 2000).

■ Who Is at Risk for AIDS?

Although anyone can become infected with HIV, its routes of transmission are limited to blood, semen, vaginal fluid, and possibly some other body fluids (Grinspoon 1994). Before the advent of AZT, mothers were more likely to pass the virus to

their children prenatally or through breast milk. HIV is a virus that is not likely to survive outside of the body. Consequently, it is not spread by casual contact, such as by shaking hands, touching, hugging, or kissing (although "deep" kissing with an infected person is not recommended). In addition, it is not spread through food or water, by sharing cups or glasses, by coughing and sneezing, or by using common toilets. It is not spread by mosquitoes or other insects.

The following populations are at greatest risk for contracting AIDS:

- Men with a history of having had multiple homosexual or bisexual partners. Men who have sex with men (MSM) account for more than half of all new HIV infections in the United States each year (53%), as well as nearly half of people living with HIV (48%) (CDC 2010b). Although new HIV infections have declined among both heterosexuals and injection drug users, infections among MSM have been steadily increasing since the early 1990s (CDC 2010b).
- Injecting drug users and their sexual partners.
- Heterosexuals with multiple partners.
- Infants born to HIV-infected women (approximately 10% of all HIV-positive mothers have HIV-positive babies).
- People who receive contaminated blood products, such as for transfusions or treatment of blood disorders. (Blood banks have improved the screening of their blood supplies in the last decade.)

See **Figure 16.4** and **Figure 16.5** for a detailed breakdown of categories of U.S. AIDS cases by type of HIV exposure.

Figure 16.4 shows that approximately 60% of all adult/adolescent men with AIDS report sex with men, and another approximately 21% report injection drug use. An estimated 9% of cases are attributed to male-to-male sexual contact and injection drug use, 8% of male cases are attributed to heterosexual contact, and other risk exposures account for the remaining 2% of cases. Figure 16.5 shows that 57% of women with AIDS attribute their exposure to heterosexual contact and 40% attribute their exposure to injection drug use.

■ AIDS and Drugs of Abuse

The AIDS epidemic is closely associated with drug abuse problems. As mentioned earlier, individuals addicted to illicit drugs are currently the second

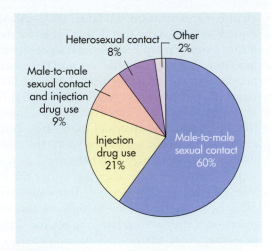

FIGURE 16.4

Approximate percentage of AIDS cases in adult/adolescent men by risk exposure, United States: 2005–2008.

....

Source: Centers for Disease Control and Prevention (CDC). *HIV/AIDS Statistics and Surveillance Report.* Atlanta, GA: U.S. Department of Health and Human Services, 2008.

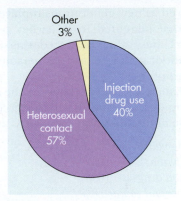

FIGURE 16.5

Approximate percentage of AIDS cases in adult/adolescent women by risk exposure, United States: 2005–2008.

....

Source: Centers for Disease Control and Prevention (CDC). *HIV/AIDS Statistics and Surveillance Report.* Atlanta, GA: U.S. Department of Health and Human Services, 2008.

largest risk group for contracting AIDS. AIDS in women is particularly linked to drug abuse. Nearly 70% of female AIDS patients are infected because of their own or their sexual partner's injection drug use (Glave 1994). Several reasons account for the high incidence of this deadly infection in the drug-abusing population.

Intravenous Drugs

Intravenous drug use has become the most important factor in the spread of AIDS in the United States. Of the AIDS cases diagnosed around the turn of the 21st century, 29% resulted from injection drug use (CDC 2000), with heroin, cocaine, or both being the primary drugs injected. Among severely addicted populations, intravenous drug use is often undertaken with little regard to hygiene, and injection paraphernalia such as needles, syringes, and cotton are frequently shared with other drug addicts (Millstein 1993). Sharing HIV-contaminated injection equipment can easily result in the transmission of this virus. The likelihood of an intravenous drug user contracting AIDS is directly correlated with (1) the frequency of drug injections, (2) the number of partners with whom injection equipment is shared, (3) the frequency of needle sharing, and (4) the frequency of injections in locations where there are high AIDS infection rates, such as in shooting galleries or crack houses (Booth, Watters, and Chitwood 1993).

Crack

Use of drugs such as crack (Ciba Foundation 1992) and alcohol (Colthurst 1993) tends to compromise judgment and encourage high-risk activities such as injection drug use or sexual risk taking (Beard and Kunsman 1993; Inciardi, Lockwood, and Pottieger 1993). In particular, the use of crack has been associated with high rates of HIV infection (Campsmith, Nakashima, and Jones 2000). Further, another study found that "In poor, inner-city communities young smokers of crack cocaine, particularly women who have sex in exchange for money or drugs, are at a high risk for HIV infection. Crack use promotes the heterosexual transmission of HIV" (Edlin et al. 1994). Crack addicts often exchange sex for drugs or money to purchase drugs (Inciardi et al. 1993; Mathias 1993). These dangerous activities frequently occur in populations with an already high rate of HIV infection. Once infected, almost half of crack users continue to use sex to obtain their drugs and become a source of HIV infection for others (Diaz and Chu 1993).

■ Youth and AIDS

The Centers for Disease Control and Prevention (2008) reports that young people in the United States are at persistent risk for HIV infection. This risk is especially notable for youth of minority races and ethnicities. Continual HIV prevention outreach and education efforts, including programs on abstinence and on delaying the initiation of sex, are required as new generations replace the generations that benefited from earlier prevention strategies. Unless otherwise noted, this section defines youth, or young people, as persons who are 13–24 years of age.

In 2002, male adolescents between the ages of 13 and 19 who were diagnosed with AIDS contracted the disease in the following ways (CDC 2004b):

- *Male-to-male sexual contact:* 41%
- *Hemophilia:* 27%
- *Injection drug use:* 10%
- *Heterosexual contact:* 8%
- *Male-to-male sexual contact and injection drug use:* 6%
- *Other/not identified:* 6%
- *Transfusion recipient:* 4%

Other recent important findings include the following (CDC 2010a):

- An estimated 4883 young people received a diagnosis of HIV infection or AIDS, representing about 13% of the persons given a diagnosis during that year.
- HIV infection progressed to AIDS more slowly among young people than among all other persons with a diagnosis of HIV infection. The following are the proportions of persons in whom HIV infection did not progress to AIDS within 12 months after diagnosis of HIV infection:
  - 81% of persons ages 15–24
  - 70% of persons ages 13–14
  - 61% of all persons
- African Americans were disproportionately affected by HIV infection, accounting for 55% of all HIV infections reported among all other persons ages 13–24.
- Young men who have sex with men (MSM), especially those of minority races or ethnicities, were at high risk for HIV infection. In the seven cities that participated in the CDC's Young Men's Survey during 1994–1998, 14% of African American MSM and 7% of Hispanic MSM ages 15–22 were infected with HIV.
- During 2001–2004, in the 33 states with long-term, confidential name-based HIV reporting, 62% of the 17,824 persons 13–24 years of age given a diagnosis of HIV/AIDS were males, and 38% were females.
- "It is estimated that 50% of all new HIV infections are among young people (about 7,000 young people become infected every day), and that 30% of the 40 million people living with HIV/AIDS are in the 15–24 age group" (World Health Organization [WHO] 2000–2004). Equally serious is the fact that "[T]he vast majority of young people who are HIV positive do not know that they are infected, and few young people who are engaging in sex know the HIV status of their partners" (WHO 2000–2004).

- Young people in the United States use alcohol, tobacco, and other drugs at high rates. Both casual and chronic substance users are more likely to engage in high-risk behaviors, such as unprotected sex, when they are under the influence of drugs or alcohol. Runaways and other homeless people are at high risk for HIV infection if they are exchanging sex for drugs or money (CDC 2007).
- Approximately two-thirds of AIDS cases among adolescent and young adult women were attributed to heterosexual contact as the mode of exposure to HIV. Cases among 13- to 19-year-old women were less likely to be attributed to injection drug use (19%) than were cases among 20- to 24-year-old women (29%).
- Most 13- to 19-year-old females reported contracting HIV followed by AIDS through heterosexual contact (66%), injection drug use (19%), and other/not identified causes (15%) (CDC 2004a).
- A recent United Nations AIDS (UNAIDS) report estimated that throughout the world, "one-third of those living with AIDS are aged 15–24" (MSNBC 2004). Further, most of these individuals who contract HIV do not even know they have the disease.
- HIV infection is spreading rapidly among younger urban gay men who are too young to recall the beginning of the AIDS epidemic two decades ago.
- Nearly half of the roughly 40,000 Americans who become newly infected with HIV each year are younger than the age of 25. Approximately 25% of the people now living with HIV in this country became infected when they were teenagers. More importantly, many young people also use drugs and alcohol, which can increase the likelihood that they will engage in high-risk sexual behavior.
- Adolescents who are most vulnerable to HIV infection include those who are homeless or runaways, juvenile offenders, and school dropouts.
- Worldwide, sexual intercourse is by far the most common mode of HIV transmission. In the United States, however, as many as half of all new HIV infections are associated either directly or indirectly with injection drug use

(i.e., using HIV-contaminated needles to inject drugs or having sexual contact with an HIV-infected drug user) (amFAR 2006).

Three of the principal ways adolescents become infected with HIV are as follows: (1) high-risk sexual activity (unprotected sexual intercourse is reported by more than half of adolescents by the age of 17 years); (2) injection of substances of abuse; and (3) sex with multiple partners (CDC 2004b, 2004c, 2010a; Schaefer et al. 1993). Clearly, young people must be better educated about HIV, its transmission, and potential consequences before this epidemic becomes even more disastrous in adolescents.

■ What to Do About HIV and AIDS

What can I do about being HIV-positive? I was diagnosed 3 years ago, and so far, I am basically okay. I have started taking medication to slow down the rate of infection, but one never knows when the first symptoms will suddenly pop up. My lover is clear of the infection and we are careful—usually. I am worried about my condition, but nothing can be done about it. Life is full of good luck and bad luck; so far I have been spared. Regarding tomorrow, who knows. *(From Venturelli's research files, male hospital administrator, age 32, October 10, 1996)*

To date, the combination of various types of protease inhibitors and antiretroviral therapy medications is the most promising treatment for remaining relatively healthy with HIV. Although protease inhibitors do not completely rid the body of HIV antibodies, this category of drugs is usually successful in holding the virus at low levels in the bloodstream. The current lack of a permanent cure makes prevention the most important element in dealing with the AIDS problem. There are two main strategies for preventing HIV:

- People should be encouraged to adopt safer sexual behavior. Some of the steps to help achieve this include (1) avoiding multiple sex partners, especially if they are strangers or only casual acquaintances; (2) avoiding risk-taking sexual behavior that may allow HIV transmission, such as unprotected vaginal, oral, and anal intercourse; and (3) encouraging individuals who choose to continue high-risk sexual behaviors to use condoms or insist that their sexual partner use a condom.
- Drug abusers should be educated about their risk of contracting AIDS. They should be encouraged to reduce their risk by (1) abstaining from injecting drugs; (2) not sharing injection paraphernalia or always using clean needles (if available through needle exchange programs); (3) not sharing drugs with groups with high rates of HIV infection such as those in shooting galleries or crack houses; and (4) disinfecting the equipment (cleaning and boiling equipment for at least 15 minutes) between uses if they continue to share injection equipment.

One of the major difficulties in controlling the AIDS epidemic is identifying where preventive efforts should be focused. Because of limited resources, it is impossible to personally educate everyone in this country about HIV and AIDS. Consequently, our most intense efforts must be targeted at populations and neighborhoods with particularly high HIV infection rates. The National Research Council has declared that, although anyone can acquire AIDS, a handful of neighborhoods have been devastated by this infection, whereas most of the nation remains relatively unscathed (Kolata 1993). It has been speculated that some 35 to 45 large neighborhoods in the United States fuel the AIDS epidemic throughout the country; if HIV infection could be controlled in these areas, the national epidemic would diminish significantly. Because of this hypothesis, it has been proposed that AIDS prevention efforts particularly be focused on younger gay men and injection drug users who have multiple sex partners in the high-density AIDS neighborhoods found in many large metropolitan cities throughout the United States. Even with this focused approach, no one should be fooled into thinking that the HIV/AIDS problem will be eliminated. Everyone should approach potential sexual partners with some degree of caution, especially because the carrier of HIV may be unaware of infection or be reluctant to admit being a carrier for fear of abandonment. One thing is evident: If any doubt exists, we strongly recommend both partners being tested several times in a row before engaging in potentially life-threatening sexual contact.

The Entertainment Industry and Drug Use

Musicians sing about guzzling liquor and movie stars puff cigarettes and take drugs on the big screen. However, federal officials ask: Where is the unglamorous side of substance use—like hangovers, slurred speech, or trouble with the law (*News Tribune* 1999)? Drug use has a tendency to be displayed or fueled (depending on your perspective) by popular culture. In this section, we discuss three important genres of popular culture—movies, music, and the Internet—as one electronic subculture that depicts and promotes drug use.

At the Lollapalooza music festival held in July 1997 in an amphitheater in Massachusetts, the mostly white, suburban teen crowd cheered wildly when rap group Cypress Hill pushed a 6-foot-tall bong, or water pipe, onstage. The group sold 5 million copies of its first two albums, one of which included songs titled "Legalize It," "Hits from the Bong," and "I Wanna Get High" (Winters 1997).

In a research study for Columbia's Center on Addiction and Substance Abuse, 76% of 12- to 17-year-olds indicated that the entertainment industry encourages illegal drug use. One 16-year-old daily marijuana user said, "All I know is that almost every song you listen to says something about [drug use]. It puts it into your mind constantly. . . . When you see the celebrities doing it, it makes it seem okay" (Winters 1997, p. 41).

Nearly 20 years ago, the rock and rap music industries experienced a heroin epidemic. Although many other rock stars before Kurt Cobain used and abused drugs, Cobain's struggle with heroin and his 1994 suicide appear to have glamorized the use of this drug. "The number of top alternative bands that have been linked to heroin through a member's overdose, arrest, admitted use, or recovery is staggering: Nirvana, Hole, Smashing Pumpkins, Everclear, Blind Melon, Skinny Puppy, 7 Year Bitch, Red Hot Chili Peppers, Stone Temple Pilots, Breeders, Alice in Chains, Sublime, Sex Pistols, Porno for Pyros, and Depeche Mode" (Schoemer 1996, p. 50).

Together these bands have sold more than 60 million albums—"that's a heck of a lot of white, middle-class kids in the heartland" (Schoemer 1996, p. 50). Despite some factions in the music industry attempting to curtail heroin use by rock stars, many claim that the music industry still glamorizes heroin and other drug use.

How pervasive is drug use in today's popular movies and music? Research indicates that there is much substance abuse in popular movies and music. Studies revealed that 98% of movies reviewed depicted illicit drugs, alcohol, tobacco, or OTC and prescription medicines. Alcohol and tobacco appeared in more than 90% of movies, and illicit drugs appeared in 22%. About one-fourth (26%) of the movies that depicted illicit drugs contained explicit, graphic portrayals of their preparation and/

Mel Gibson consuming a drug. Do such pictures have any effect on viewers?

or ingestion. Substance use was almost never a central theme, and very few movies ever specified motivations for use. Less than one-half (49%) of the movies portrayed short-term consequences of substance use, and about 12% depicted long-term consequences. Of the 669 adult major characters featured in the 200 movies studied, 5% used illicit drugs, 25% smoked tobacco, and 65% consumed alcohol. At least two major characters used illicit drugs in 12% of the movies, tobacco in 44%, and alcohol in 85% (ONDCP 1999).

In summarizing main findings from a study conducted by the Office of National Drug Control Policy (1999) regarding substance use in both movies and songs, the following results were found:

- Alcohol appeared in 93% of the movies and 17% of the songs; tobacco appeared in 89% of the movies but only 3% of the songs.
- "About one-third of hit songs—including three-quarters of rap songs—have some form of explicit reference to drug, alcohol or tobacco use . . ." (Yahoo! News 2008).
- Alcohol use was associated with wealth or luxury in 34% of the movies in which it appeared, with sexual activity in 19%, and with crime or violence in 37%.
- Alcohol use was associated with wealth or luxury in 24% of the songs in which it was referenced, with sexual activity in 3%, and with crime or violence in 13%.
- In movies depicting illicit drugs, marijuana appeared most frequently (51%), followed by powder cocaine (33%); hallucinogens, heroin or other opiates, and miscellaneous others (each 12%); and crack cocaine (2%).

- In songs referring to illicit drugs, marijuana appeared most frequently (63%), followed by crack cocaine (15%); powder cocaine (10%); and hallucinogens, heroin or other opiates, and miscellaneous others (4% each).

These findings clearly indicate that both movies and songs continue to reflect widespread use of alcohol and other drugs in our culture. Furthermore, their influence on the public viewing audiences continues to have an impact on values and attitudes about the use and/or abuse of drugs. One executive director of a Washington, DC, area youth group, said, "It's becoming increasingly difficult to administer our preventive drug programs because the youth culture has changed in a manner that a lot more of popular music idolizes the use of marijuana and hallucinogens and that has a profound effect on young people" (Haywood 1996, p. 14).

Another top administrator at the Center for Substance Abuse Prevention of the Substance Abuse and Mental Health Services Administration agreed, "Our pop culture is sending a lot of pro-drug messages" (Haywood 1996). In addition to these observations, the major findings noted earlier with regard to substance use in movies and songs support the amount of alcohol and other drugs used in these two major types of electronic and audio mediums.

More Recent Promoter of Drug Use: The Internet

According to the UCLA Center for Communication Policy, for those who use online technology, the Internet is considered the most important source for information—more important than TV or radio. "Some 55% of Internet users said 'most' or 'all' information in cyberspace is reliable and accurate, while only a third of non-users agreed" (Reuters and CNN.com 2000b). A survey of 55,000 Internet users performed by a market research firm called Media Matrix discovered that low-income World Wide Web users are now the fastest-growing U.S. market (Reuters and CNN.com 2000a).

There is no question that pro-drug messages and detailed information are readily available over the Internet. The Internet maintains a unique subculture of drug enthusiasts. Drug use information found online includes how to roll super-joints, bake marijuana-laced brownies, grow "magic" psilocybin mushrooms, and create formulas for making amphetamine-like drugs; where to purchase the latest equipment for indoor growing of marijuana; and where to obtain catalogs that offer drug paraphernalia for sale. Similarly, magazines such as *High Times* and *Hemp Times* claim growing numbers of subscribers. These magazines devote most of their articles, features, advice columns, hemp festival information, and advertisements to the pleasures of drug consumption. Further, chat rooms devoted to finding, growing, purchasing, and making drug substances are growing in popularity. Those who don't use illicit drugs are often oblivious to the chat rooms and exchange of information found on the Internet.

A more recent and alarming occurrence is the boom in illicit drug sales online. Prescription drugs are being sold without a prescription over the Internet. Often solicitations are in the form of spam (unsolicited emails), including multiple offers each day. The International Narcotics Control Board (INCB) reported recently, "90% of online drug sales take place without a medical prescription" (Join Together Online and BBC News 2005). The INCB said, "The illicit trade over the Internet has been identified as one of the major sources for prescription medicines abused by children and adolescents in certain countries such as the United States."

> Billions of [doses of] controlled substances—some of them highly potent drugs such as oxycodone, equivalent to morphine, and fentanyl, which is many times stronger than morphine, [including Viagra, Xanex and OxyContin (to name a few)]—are being sold by unlicensed Internet pharmacies. (Join Together Online and BBC News 2005)

Another report indicated that

> Despite new efforts to regulated Internet pharmacies, 85% of sites selling controlled drugs do not require a prescription. Most orders filled by the 365 Internet pharmacies examined were for controlled substances, especially benzodiazepines like Xanax and Valium, according to the report by the National Center on Addiction and Substance Abuse at Columbia University in New York. (Seetharaman 2008)

Recently, *USA Today* reported that ". . . more than 10 million online messages written by teens in the past year shows they regularly chat about drinking alcohol, smoking pot, partying and hooking up" (Leinwand 2007). "Many of the teens who posted messages about drugs or alcohol often traded information about using illicit substances without getting hurt or caught. Some teens debated drug legalization and the drinking age. Other teens recounted their partying experiences, including sexual liaisons while drunk or high" (Leinwand 2007).

Clearly, the Internet is becoming a source of illicit drugs for anyone having access to computers, and this audience includes younger teens and adults. Legal suppliers appear to be fueling the trade by providing their products to unlicensed Internet pharmacies that then sell these legally restricted types of drugs (Join Together Online and BBC News 2005). The potential impact of acquiring illicit drugs from Internet sites was emphasized by a journalist warning that we should "Forget the drug dealer on the corner, teens are increasingly turning to the Internet to get high" (Fiore 2008).

Although the Internet serves as an immensely valuable medium for learning, conducting business, communicating, and making information available, it is also used by a growing number of drug users as a forum for exchanging and learning about the latest information and techniques of drug consumption. Individuals who use the Internet for this type of information should be particularly wary because it is difficult, if not impossible, for harmful myths and fallacies posted on the web to be regulated.

Discussion Questions

1. What are two strengths and two weaknesses of studying subcultures from (a) an insider's perspective and (b) an outsider's perspective?

2. What are the principal drugs abused by athletes?

3. What are the principal effects and side effects of steroids?

4. What factors encourage drug use by athletes?

5. From the world of steroid abusers, define and give an example of the following terms: *stacking, cycling, plateauing, pyramiding,* and *array.*

6. Argue both for and against drug testing in sports.

7. What type of penalties do you think should be used against athletes who abuse drugs?

8. Review the ATLAS steroid prevention program. Can you improve its methods for lessening steroid use among adolescents? How effective do you think this program would be at your college or university?

9. List the reasons why women are more concerned about drug use and abuse than men.

Can you add several reasons not mentioned in this chapter?

10. Do you believe that drug prevention programs should be created uniquely for males and females? Support your answer.

11. What factors in the unique female roles encourage the use of substances of abuse?

12. Should childbearing women who abuse drugs be punished? Why or why not?

13. Why are women who have been or are sexually abused more likely to become addicted to drugs?

14. Why are adolescents especially vulnerable to drug abuse problems?

15. List and explain three reasons why you think adolescents from upper-middle-class socioeconomic backgrounds become drug abusers.

16. What types of parents are most likely to have children who develop drug abuse problems?

17. How do adolescent drug abuse patterns differ from those in adults?

18. In what way are drugs of abuse associated with juvenile gang activity?

19. Should all adolescents who use drugs of abuse be treated for drug dependence? Explain your answer.

20. Do you think that it is realistic to expect drug abusers to change their habits to prevent the spread of AIDS? Why or why not?

21. Should prisoners who test positive for HIV be segregated from the non–HIV-positive populations? Should prisoners be given free access to condoms in prisons? Why or why not?

22. John was caught by city police growing psilocybin (hallucinogenic) mushrooms in his off-campus college apartment. Should John be punished by his college or university in addition to the punishment that will be meted out by the criminal justice system? Why or why not?

23. What if you discover that your roommate is HIV positive? How would you handle this situation?

24. Do you think that the excessive use of alcohol and other drugs in movies influences viewers? Further, are people who enjoy rap or rock music affected by the lyrics that refer to drug use and/or abuse? Why or why not?

25. Do you believe that drug information over the Internet, such as chat rooms devoted to the use of certain drugs (e.g., where to purchase equipment for growing marijuana, OTC stimulant pills, and the spores of psilocybin mushrooms), promotes drug use? Why or why not?

Summary

1 The most common drugs abused by athletes are the ergogenic (performance-enhancing) substances. They include the anabolic steroids, for building muscle mass and strength, and the CNS stimulants, to achieve energy, quickness, and endurance.

2 Drug testing is conducted for most professional athletic competitions and usually includes screens for steroids and stimulants. Unlike years ago, nearly all performance-enhancing drugs are now detectable. Even though athletes often go to great lengths to avoid detection, it is virtually impossible to mask usage drug tests.

3 About 50% of the anabolic steroids used in the United States are prescribed by doctors; the other 50% are obtained from the black market. Black market steroids include drugs diverted from legitimate channels smuggled from foreign countries—for example, Brazil, Italy, Mexico, Great Britain, Portugal, France, and Peru—designated for veterinarian use, or inactive counterfeits.

4 The ATLAS prevention program uses athletes, coaches, and team leaders who are trained to educate team members about the effects of anabolic steroid abuse. They emphasize both desirable and adverse effects of steroid use. Presenting a balanced perspective is stressed because adolescents know very well how anabolic steroids build muscles and can increase athletic abilities.

5 In general, women are more likely than men to (a) be concerned about drugs and drug use; (b) believe in drug prevention programs, such as needle exchange and testing reckless drivers for drug use; and (c) speak with their children about drug use (Drug Strategies 1998).

6 There is a high prevalence of drug dependence in women who are victims of sexual and/or physical abuse. Approximately 70% of women in drug abuse treatment report histories of physical abuse, with victimization beginning at 11 years of age and occurring repeatedly. Further, women and men have different endocrine (hormone) systems, organs, and structures, and women's responses to drugs vary according to their reproductive states.

7 For women to receive adequate treatment for drug dependence, certain considerations must be met: (a) availability of female-sensitive services, (b) nonpunitive and noncoercive treatment that incorporates supportive behavior change approaches, and (c) treatment for a wide range of medical problems, mental disorders, and psychosocial problems.

8 Most adolescents who use substances of abuse are going through normal psychosocial development and will not develop problematic dependence on these drugs. The adolescent users who have difficulty with drugs often lack coping skills to deal with their problems, have dysfunctional families, possess poor self-images, and/or feel socially and emotionally insecure.

9 Parents who are most likely to raise drug-abusing adolescents are (a) drug abusers, (b) non–drug-using coupled with being constantly condemning, (c) overly demanding, (d) overly protective, or (e) unable to communicate effectively with their children.

10 The substances adolescents are most likely to abuse are alcohol, cigarettes, inhalants, marijuana, LSD, Ecstasy, and prescription stimulants. High-frequency use is most likely to occur with cigarettes, alcohol, and marijuana.

11 Research continues to show that the most important factor influencing drug use among adolescents is peer drug use.

12 People who become gang members were often neglected by their parents, lacked positive role models, and failed to receive adequate adult supervision. Other motivations for joining a gang include peer pressure, low self-esteem, and perceived easy acquisition of money from gang-related drug dealing and other criminal activities.

13 The major reasons cited by college students for their use of drugs were: (a) breaks the ice, (b) enhances social activity, (c) gives people something to do, (d) gives people something to talk about, (e) allows people to have more fun, (f) facilitates contact with peers, (g) facilitates sexual opportunities, and (h) facilitates male bonding.

14 Two interesting findings from research regarding drug use by college student subcultures are that (a) the best predictor of drug use for first-year college students is drug use during a typical month in the senior year of high school, and (b) usually recreational drug use does not begin in college but has already been established in high school. Another more recent finding includes personality dispositions to risky behavior as a predictor of first-year college drinking (mainly impulsivity and sensation-seeking types of students).

15 Club drugs include MDMA (Ecstasy), GHB, Rohypnol, ketamine, methamphetamine, and LSD. The phrase "club drug" is derived from the use of these drugs at all-night dance parties such as raves or trances, dance clubs, and bars. All these drugs are colorless, tasteless, and odorless. Individuals who want to intoxicate, sedate, and later sexually take advantage of others can add them unobtrusively to beverages.

16 After homosexual men, individuals who are addicted to illicit drugs are the second largest group at risk for contracting AIDS. This risk results from sharing of blood-contaminated needles and syringes and increased involvement in sexual risk taking because of the effects of drugs or in securing payment for drugs.

17 "An estimated 1.1 million Americans have HIV, and about 20% of them don't know it. About 55,000 new infections occur each year in the United States, a number that has held steady for a decade" (USA Today 2010). For the United States, the latest numbers indicate that by 2004, 1 million Americans were living with HIV—and one in five of them did not know it (CDC 2010c). Another source indicates that at the end of 2003, an estimated 1,039,000 to 1,185,000 persons in the United States were living with HIV/AIDS (Glynn and Rhodes 2007). During 2005, 74% of those diagnosed with HIV/AIDS were male and 26% were female. Forty-nine percent were black, 31% white, 18% Hispanic, 1% Asian/Pacific Islander, and less than 1% American Indian/Alaska Native. The noteworthy finding is that in 2008, blacks (including African Americans), who make up approximately 13% of the U.S. population, accounted for almost half (47%) of the estimated number of HIV/AIDS cases diagnosed (CDC 2006; Gupta 2008). From 1981 through 2005, the CDC estimates that 952,629 cases of AIDS were diagnosed; of these, 530,756 died with AIDS as a major cause of death, and as of 2005, 421,873 people were living with AIDS (CDC 2006).

18 Major ways to prevent contracting HIV include (a) engaging in safe (protected) sexual behavior, (b) avoiding use of contaminated drug paraphernalia and especially use of intravenous drugs, (c) avoiding use of drugs in groups with high rates of HIV infection, and (d) frankly discussing past sexual histories with potential sexual partners and, if in any doubt, having potential partners be tested for HIV several times in a row.

19 The extent of alcohol and drug use in movies and songs is startling. Overall, findings of one study revealed that 98% of movies reviewed depicted illicit drugs, alcohol, and tobacco or OTC/prescription medicines. In this same detailed study, alcohol appeared in 93% of the movies and in 17% of the songs; tobacco appeared in 89% of movies but only 3% of songs. The lyrics of 63% of rap songs versus about 10% of the lyrics in other categories had substance references.

20 The music industry has been setting up drug-using celebrities as teen role models. The message conveyed by much of the music and by many bands is that drug use is acceptable.

21 New media influences contribute to drug use. The Internet is considered to be the latest source of information where knowledge about use of illicit drugs is burgeoning.

References

About.com. "Alcoholism: Sex, Drug Use Increase Teen Depression, Suicide." New York Times Company. (9 April 2005). Available http://alcoholism.about.com/od/tips forparents/a/blnida050408.htm

About.com. "Alcohol and Hormones." Alcohol Alerts from the National Institute on Alcohol Abuse and Alcoholism (NIAAA). 2006. Available http://alcoholism.about.com/cs/alerts/1/binaa26.htm

About.com. "Alcoholism and Substance Abuse." Alcohol Alerts from the National Institute on Alcohol Abuse and Alcoholism (NIAAA). June 2007a. Available http://alcoholism.about.com/cs/alerts/1/blnaa10.htm

About.com. "Alcohol and Women." Alcohol Alerts from the National Institute on Alcohol Abuse and Alcoholism (NIAAA). June 2007b. Available http://alcoholism.about.com/cs/alerts/1/binaa10.htm

Adolescent Substance Abuse Knowledge Base. "Factors of Teen Drug Use." CRC Health Group. 2007. Available http://www.adolescent-substance-abuse.com

American Academy of Child and Adolescent Psychiatry. *Facts for Families: Teen Suicide.* Washington, DC: American Academy of Child Adolescent Psychiatry, 2004. Available http://www.aacap.org/cs/root/facts_for_families/teen_suicide

American Academy of Child and Adolescent Psychiatry. *Facts for Families: Normal Adolescent Development.* Number 57.

Washington, DC: American Academy of Child and Adolescent Psychiatry, 2006.

American Foundation for AIDS Research (amfAR). *Facts About HIV/AIDS, 2001.* New York: Body Health Resources Corporation, 2001.

American Foundation for AIDS Research (amfAR). "Facts for Life: What You and the People You Care About Need to Know About HIV/AIDS." 2006. Available http://www.amfar.org/community/article.aspx?id=3710&terms="Facts+for+Life%3a+What+You+and+the+People+You+Care+About+Need+to+Know+About+HIV%2fAIDS."

Anonymous, as told by Penn, N. "Confession: Why I Juiced." *Gentleman's Quarterly* (September 2005): 292–297.

Apostolides, M. "How to Quit the Holistic Way." *Psychology Today* 29 (September/October 1996): 30–43, 75–76.

Archambault, D. "Adolescence, a Physiological, Cultural and Psychological No Man's Land." In *Adolescent Substance Abuse, Etiology, Treatment and Prevention,* edited by G. Lawson and A. Lawson, 11–28. Gaithersburg, MD: Aspen, 1992.

Associated Press. "Boredom, Stress, Money Linked to Drug Abuse." *Chesterton/Valparaiso Post Tribune* (20 August 2003): A1, A8.

Associated Press. "Surviving with AIDS Carries Big Price Tag." *Post Tribune* (11 November 2006): 7.

AVERT.org. "AIDS, Drug Prices and Generic Drugs." 2011a. Available http://www.avert.org/generic.htm

AVERT.org. "Worldwide HIV and AIDS Statistics." 2011b. Available http://www.avert.org/worldstats.htm

Bahr, S. J., A. C. Marcos, and S. L. Maughan. "Family, Educational and Peer Influences on Alcohol Use of Female and Male Adolescents." *Journal of Studies on Alcohol* 56 (1995): 457–469.

Baltieri, D. A., and A. G. de Andrad. "Alcohol and Drug Consumption and Sexual Impulsivity Among Sexual Offenders." In *Sexual Offenders: Management, Treatment and Bibliography,* edited by J. V. Fenner, 73–96. New York: Nova Science, 2008.

Beard, B., and V. Kunsman. "A Cause for Concern: Alcohol-Induced Risky Sex on College Campuses." *Prevention Pipeline* 6 (September–October 1993): 24.

Begley, S., and M. Brant with C. Dickey, K. Helmstaedt, R. Nordland, and T. Hayden. "The Real Scandal." *Newsweek* 133 (15 February 1999): 48–54.

Bell, J. "Athletes' Use and Abuse of Drugs." *The Physician and Sports Medicine* 15 (March 1987): 99–108.

Belsie, L. "Temperance Movement Hits College Dorms." *Christian Science Monitor* 87 (30 August 1995): 1, 2.

Bergeret, J. *Young People, Drugs . . . and Others.* Rockville, MD: United Nations Office for Drug Control Office for Drug Control and Crime Prevention (UN/ODCCP), 1 January 1981.

Beschner, G., and A. Friedman. "Treatment of Adolescent Drug Abusers." *International Journal of the Addictions* 20 (1985): 977–993.

Blum, R. "Rodriguez: 'Amateur Hour.' " *Post-Tribune,* Nation/World (18 February 2009): A11.

"Bodybuilding Drug Yields 'High.' " *Pharmacy Times* (June 1992): 14.

Booth, R., J. Watters, and D. Chitwood. "HIV Risk-Related Sex Behaviors Among Injection Drug Users, Crack Smokers, and Injection Drug Users Who Smoke Crack." *American Journal of Public Health* 83 (1993): 1144–1148.

Britannica.com. Alex Rodriguez. "Encyclopaedia Britannica Online." (31 October 2010). Available http://www.britannica.com/EBchecked/topic/914723/Alex-Rodriguez

Buckstein, D., D. Brent, J. Perper, G. Moritz, M. Baugher, J. Schweers, et al. "Risk Factors for Completed Suicide Among Adolescents with a Lifetime History of Substance Abuse: A Case-Control Study." *Acta Psychiatrica Scandinavia* 88 (1993): 403–408.

Burke, C., and S. Davis. "Anabolic Steroid Abuse." *Pharmacy Times* (June 1992): 35–40.

Campsmith, M. L., A. K. Nakashima, and J. L. Jones. "Association Between Crack Cocaine Use and High-Risk Sexual Behaviors After HIV Diagnosis." *Journal of Acquired Immune Deficiency Syndrome (JAIDS)* 25 (1 October 2000): 192–198.

Campus Alcohol and Drug Resource Center at the University of Florida. "Core Alcohol and Drug Survey Long Form: Key Findings 2006." Gainesville, FL: Division of Student Affairs, 2006.

Centers for Disease Control and Prevention (CDC). "Adult/Adolescent AIDS Cases by Exposure Category and Year of Diagnosis, 1985–June 1999, United States. HIV/AIDS Surveillance," General Epidemiology 178 Slide Series Through 1999, Slide 8 of 24. Atlanta, GA: National Center for HIV, STD, and TB Prevention, January 2000.

Centers for Disease Control and Prevention (CDC). *Estimated AIDS Cases Among Female Adolescents and Young Adults by Exposure Category, Diagnosed through 2002, United States.* Washington, DC: CDC, National Center for HIV, STD, and TB Prevention, Divisions of HIV/AIDS Prevention Surveillance Branch, 2004a.

Centers for Disease Control and Prevention (CDC). *Estimated AIDS Cases Among Male Adolescents and Young Adults by Exposure Category, Diagnosed Through 2002, United States.* Washington, DC: CDC, National Center for HIV, STD, and TB Prevention, Divisions of HIV/AIDS Prevention Surveillance Branch, 2004b.

Centers for Disease Control and Prevention (CDC). *HIV/AIDS Surveillance Report, 2003,* Vol. 15. Atlanta, GA: U.S. Department of Health and Human Services, CDC, 2004c.

Centers for Disease Control and Prevention (CDC). "HIV/AIDS Among Youth." The Body Health Resources Corporation. 2007. Available http://www.thebody.com/content/art17110.html

Centers for Disease Control and Prevention (CDC). *HIV/AIDS Among Youth.* Atlanta, GA: Division of HIV/AIDS Prevention, National Center for HIV/AIDS, Viral Hepatitis, STD, and TB Prevention, 2008.

Centers for Disease Control and Prevention (CDC). *HIV and AIDS in America: A Snapshot.* Atlanta, GA: Division of HIV/AIDS Prevention, National Center for HIV/AIDS, Viral Hepatitis, STD, and TB Prevention, 2009.

Centers for Disease Control and Prevention (CDC). *HIV and AIDS in America: A Snapshot.* Atlanta, GA: Division of HIV/AIDS Prevention, National Center for HIV/AIDS, Viral Hepatitis, STD, and TB Prevention, 2010a.

Centers for Disease Control and Prevention (CDC). *HIV/AIDS and Women.* Atlanta, GA: Division of HIV/AIDS Prevention, National Center for HIV/AIDS, Viral Hepatitis, STD, and TB Prevention, 2010b.

Centers for Disease Control and Prevention (CDC). *Questions and Answers on the Use of HIV Medications to Help Prevent the Transmission of HIV.* Atlanta, GA: Division of HIV/AIDS Prevention, National Center for HIV/AIDS, Viral Hepatitis, STD, and TB Prevention, 2010c.

Centers for Disease Control and Prevention (CDC). *HIV in the United States.* Atlanta, GA: Divisions of HIV/AIDS Prevention, National Center for HIV/AIDS, Viral Hepatitis, STD, and TB Prevention, 2010d.

Child Trends. "Adolescents Training and Learning to Avoid Steroids Program (ATLAS)." 2009. Available http://www.childtrends.org/lifecourse/programs/Avoid Steroids.htm

Chong, J-R. "Study Casts Positive Light on AIDS Drug." *Los Angeles Times,* reported in *Post Tribune,* Merrillville, IN (13 August 2006): A9.

Ciba Foundation. "AIDS and HIV Infection in Cocaine Users." In *Cocaine: Scientific and Social Dimensions,* edited by G. Block and J. Whelan, 181–194. New York: Wiley, 1992.

Clark, E. "HIV Progress and Prevention." Boston, MA: Science in the News (SITN), Harvard Graduate School of Arts and Sciences, 2010.

Colthurst, T. "HIV and Alcohol Impairment: Reducing Risks." *Prevention Pipeline* 6 (July–August 1993): 24.

Crowley, G. "Targeting a Deadly Scrap of Genetic Code." *Newsweek* (2 December 1996): 68–69.

Curry, D. G., and I. A. Spergel. "Gang Homicide, Delinquency, and Community." In *Gangs and Gang Behavior,* edited by G. Larry Mays, 314–336. Chicago, IL: Nelson-Hall, 1997.

Cyders, M. A., K. Flory, S. Rainer, and G. T. Smith. "The Role of Personality Dispositions to Risky Behavior in Predicting First-Year College Drinking." *Addiction* 104 (2009): 193–202.

Daily, S. "Alcohol, Incest, and Adolescence." In *Adolescent Substance Abuse, Etiology, Treatment and Prevention,* edited by G. Lawson and A. Lawson, 251–266. Gaithersburg, MD: Aspen, 1992a.

Daily, S. "Suicide Solution: The Relationship of Alcohol and Drug Abuse to Adolescent Suicide." In *Adolescent Substance Abuse, Etiology, Treatment and Prevention,* edited by G. Lawson and A. Lawson, 233–250. Gaithersburg, MD: Aspen, 1992b.

Diaz, T., and S. Chu. "Crack Cocaine Use and Sexual Behavior Among People with AIDS." *Journal of the American Medical Association* 269 (1993): 2845–2846.

Dicker, M., and E. A. Leighton. "Trends in the U.S. Prevalence of Drug-Using Parturient Women and Drug-Affected Newborns, 1979 Through 1990." *American Journal of Public Health* 84 (September 1994): 1433.

Docherty, J. R. "Pharmacology of Stimulants Prohibited by the World Anti-Doping Agency (WADA)." *British Journal of Pharmacology* 154 (June 2008): 606–622.

Donaldson-Evans, C. "Wrestler Chris Benoit Double Murder-Suicide: Was It 'Roid Rage'?" FoxNews.com. (27 June 2007). Available http://www.foxnews.com/printer_friendly_story/0,3566,286834,00.html

Drug Facts and Comparisons. St. Louis, MO: Kluwer, 1994, 109–109c.

Drug Strategies. "Keeping Score, 1998: Drug Use and Attitudes." 1998. Available http://www.drugstrategies.org/ks1998/use.html

EBSCO. "Reverse Transcriptase Inhibitors." EBSCO CAM Review Board. 2009. Available https://healthlibrary.epnet.com/GetContent.aspx?token=e0498803-7f62-4563-8d47-5fe33da65dd4&chunkiid=111797

Edlin, B. R., K. L. Irwin, S. Faruque, C. B. McCoy, C. Word, Y. Serrano, et al. "Intersecting Epidemics—Crack Cocaine Use and HIV Infection among Inner-City Young Adults. Multicenter Crack Cocaine and HIV Infection Study Team." *New England Journal of Medicine* 331 (24 November 1994): 1422–1427.

Elmen, J., and D. Offer. "Normality, Turmoil and Adolescence." In *Handbook of Clinical Research and Practice with Adolescents,* edited by P. Tolan and B. Cohler, 5–19. New York: Wiley, 1993.

ESPN.com. "Steroids Discovered in Probe Slayings, Suicide." (27 July 2007). Available http://sports.espn.go.com/espn/news/story?id=2917133

Erickson, P. G., and G. F. Murray. "Sex Differences in Cocaine Use and Experiences: A Double Standard Revived?" *American Journal of Drug and Alcohol Abuse* 15 (1989): 135–152.

Fagan, J. "Social Processes of Delinquency and Drug Use Among Urban Gangs." In *Gangs in America,* edited by C. R. Huff, 183–213. Newbury Park, CA: Sage, 1990.

Ferrente, R. "Ben Johnson Retires from Running After Positive Test." Morning Edition on National Public Radio (8 March 1993).

Fiore, M. "Using the Internet to Get High." FoxNews.com. (9 September 2008). Available http://www.foxnews.com/story/0,2933,419582,00.html

Fischer, J. S. "Searching for That Ounce of Prevention: Promising Strategies for an AIDS Vaccine." *U.S. News and World Report* (17 July 2000).

Focus Adolescent Services. "Your Teen's Friends: Peer Influence and Peer Relationships" *InFocus Newsletter,* Salisbury, MD: Focusas.com, 2008. Available http://www.focusas.com/PeerInfluence.html#Negative_Peer_Pressure

Funk, L. "Shocking School Drug and Gang Survey." MyFoxNY.com. (19 August 2010). Available http://www.myfoxny.com/dpp/news/education/shocking-school-drug-and-gang-survey-20100819-lgf

GatorWell Health Promotion Services. *Healthy Gators Student Survey Report 2010.* Gainesville, FL: University of Florida, GatorWell Health Promotion Services, Division of Student Affairs, Healthy Gators Coalition, 2010. Available http://gatorwell.ufsa.ufl.edu/Health-Data.aspx

Glave, J. "Betty Ford Got Help, But Addiction Stalks Thousands of Women." *Salt Lake Tribune* 248 (3 June 1994): A-1.

Glynn, M., and P. Rhodes. "A Glance at the HIV/AIDS Epidemic." CDC/HIV Fact Sheet National HIV Prevention Conference. Revised June 2007. Available http://www.cdc.gov/hiv/resources/factsheets/at-a-glance.pdf

Goldberg, L., D. Elliot, G. N. Clarke, D. P. MacKinnon, E. Moe, L. Zoref, et al. "Effects of a Multidimensional Anabolic Steroid Prevention Intervention: The Adolescents Training and Learning to Avoid Steroids (ATLAS) Program." *Journal of the American Medical Association* 276 (1996): 1555–1562.

Goldstein, F. "Pharmacological Aspects of Substance Abuse." In *Remington's Pharmaceutical Sciences*, 19th ed., edited by the American Journal of Pharmaceutical Education. Easton, PA: Mack, 1995.

Green, C. A. "Gender and Use of Substance Abuse Treatment Services." Bethesda, MD: NIAAA, 2006: 1–12.

Grinspoon, L. "AIDS and Mental Health—Part 1." *Harvard Mental Health Letter* 10 (January 1994): 1–4.

Guide4Living.com. "Steroid Abuse and Addiction." 2005. Available http://www.guide4living.com/drugabuse/steroids.htm

Gupta, S. "Paging Dr. Gupta: AIDS in the US." CNN.com. (30 July 2008). Available http://pagingdrgupta.blogs.cnn.com/2008/07/30/aids-in-the-us

Harlan, R., and M. Garcia. "Neurobiology of Androgen Abuse." In *Drugs of Abuse*, edited by R. Watson, 185–201. Boca Raton, FL: CRC Press, 1992.

Haywood, R. L. "Why More Young People Are Using Drugs." *Jet* 90 (9 September 1996).

Hingson, R. W., W. Zha, and E. R. Weitzman. "Magnitude of and Trends in Alcohol-Related Mortality and Morbidity Among U.S. College Students Ages 18–24, 1998–2005." *Journal of Studies on Alcohol and Drugs*, Suppl. No. 16 (2009): 12–20.

Hoberman, J. M., and C. E. Yesalis. "The History of Synthetic Testosterone." *Scientific American* (February 1995).

Hoshino, J. "Assessment of Adolescent Substance Abuse." In *Adolescent Substance Abuse, Etiology, Treatment and Prevention*, edited by G. Lawson and A. Lawson, 87–104. Gaithersburg, MD: Aspen, 1992.

Howard, M. "Adolescent Substance Abuse: A Social Learning Theory Perspective." In *Adolescent Substance Abuse, Etiology, Treatment and Prevention*, edited by G. Lawson and A. Lawson, 29–40. Gaithersburg, MD: Aspen, 1992.

Inciardi, J. A., D. Lockwood, and A. E. Pottieger. *Women and Crack-Cocaine*. New York: Macmillan, 1993.

Jayson, S. "Expert: Risky Teen Behavior Is All in the Brain." USAToday.com. (5 April 2007). Available http://www.usatoday.com/news/health/2007-04-04-teen-brain_N.htm

Johnson, R. A., J. P. Hoffmann, and D. R. Gerstein. *The Relationship Between Family Structure and Adolescent Substance Use*. Rockville, MD: SAMHSA, Office of Applied Studies, July 1996.

Johnston, L. D., P. M. O'Malley, and J. G. Bachman. *National Survey Results from the Monitoring the Future Study, 1975–1992*. Rockville, MD: National Institute on Drug Abuse, 1993.

Johnston, L. D., P. M. O'Malley, and J. G. Bachman. *National Survey Results from the Monitoring the Future Study, 1975–1994*. Rockville, MD: National Institute on Drug Abuse, 1996.

Johnston, L. D., P. O'Malley, and J. G. Bachman. *The Monitoring the Future National Results on Adolescent Drug Use: Overview of Key Findings, 1999*. Ann Arbor, MI: The University of Michigan Institute for Social Research and Bethesda, MD: National Institute on Drug Abuse, U.S. Department of Human Services, National Institutes of Health, 2000a.

Johnston, L. D., P. O'Malley, and J. G. Bachman. *National Survey Results on Drug Use from the Monitoring the Future Study, 1975–1999. Vol. 2, College Students and Young Adults*. U.S. Department of Health and Human Services (USDHHS), National Institute on Drug Abuse (NIDA). Washington, DC: U.S. Government Printing Office, 2000b.

Johnston, L. D., P. M. O'Malley, J. G. Bachman, and J. E. Schulenberg. *Monitoring the Future: National Survey Results on Drug Use, 1975–2003. Volume I: Secondary School Students*. Bethesda, MD: National Institute on Drug Abuse, 2004.

Johnston, L. D., P. M. O'Malley, J. G. Bachman, and J. E. Schulenberg. *Monitoring the Future: National Results on Adolescent Drug Use*. Bethesda, MD: National Institute on Drug Abuse, 2006a.

Johnston, L. D., P. M. O'Malley, J. G. Bachman, and J. E. Schulenberg. *Monitoring the Future: National Results on Adolescent Drug Use 1975–2005, Volume II: College Students and Adults 19–45*. Bethesda, MD: National Institute on Drug Abuse, 2006b.

Johnston, L. D., P. M. O'Malley, J. G. Bachman, and J. E. Schulenberg. *Monitoring the Future: National Results on Adolescent Drug Use 1975–2008. Volume I: Secondary School Students 2008*. Bethesda, MD: National Institute on Drug Abuse, 2009a.

Johnston, L. D., P. M. O'Malley, J. G. Bachman, and J. E. Schulenberg. *Monitoring the Future: National Results on Adolescent Drug Use 1975–2008. Volume II: College Students and Adults 19–50*. Bethesda, MD: National Institute on Drug Abuse, 2009b.

Join Together Online and BBC (British Broadcasting Company) News. *Illicit Drug Sales Booming Online*. Boston, MA: Boston University School of Public Health, 2005.

Kandel, D. B. "Drug and Drinking Behavior Among Youth." *Annual Review of Sociology* 6 (1980): 235–285.

Kantrowitz, B., and P. Wingert. "Beyond Littleton: How Well Do You Know Your Kid?" *Newsweek* (10 May 1999).

Kennedy, M. C. "Newer Drugs Used to Enhance Sporting Performance." *Medical Journal of Australia* 273 (2000): 314–317.

Kinney, J. *Loosening the Grip*, 6th ed. Boston: McGraw-Hill, 2000.

Kirkpatrick, J. *The Woman Alcoholic*. Quakertown, PA: Women for Sobriety, 1999.

Klee, H., and M. Jackson. *Drug Misuse and Motherhood*. New York: Routledge, 2002.

Kolata, G. "Targeting Urged in Attack on AIDS." *New York Times* 142 (7 March 1993): 1.

Korolenko, C. P., and T. A. Donskih. "Addictive Behavior in Women: A Theoretical Perspective." *Drugs and Society* 4 (1990): 39–65.

Ladwig, G. B., and M. D. Anderson. "Substance Abuse in Women: Relationship Between Chemical Dependency of Women and Past Reports of Physical and/or Sexual Abuse." *International Journal of the Addictions* 24 (1989): 739–754.

Lajis, R. H. "Steroids: The Next Drug Problem." Malaysian Drug and Poison Net, PRN 8099. Malaysia: Professional Bulletin of the National Poison Center, 2007. Available http://www.cedu.niu.edu/~shumow/itt/doc/Steroid Abuse.pdf

Lale, T. "Gangs and Drugs." In *Adolescent Substance Abuse, Etiology, Treatment and Prevention,* edited by G. Lawson and A. Lawson, 267–281. Gaithersburg, MD: Aspen, 1992.

Lawn, J. *Team Up for Drug Prevention with America's Young Athletes.* Washington, DC: Drug Enforcement Administration, U.S. Department of Justice, 1984.

Lawson, G., and A. Lawson, "Etiology." In *Adolescent Substance Abuse, Etiology, Treatment and Prevention,* edited by G. Lawson and A. Lawson, 1–10. Gaithersburg, MD: Aspen, 1992.

Leibsohn, J. "The Relationship Between Drug and Alcohol Use and Peer Group Associations of College Freshmen as They Transition from High School." *Journal of Drug Education* 24 (1994): 177–192.

Leinwand, D. "20% Say They Used Drugs with Their Mom or Dad. Among Reasons: Boomer Culture and Misguided Attempts to Bond." *USA Today.* (27 August 2000).

Leinwand, D. "Study: Drug Chat Pervasive Online—Teens Use Internet to Share Stories, Get How-To Advice." *USA Today.* 2007. Available http://www.usatoday.com/print edition/news/20070619/a_online19.art.htm

Lewin, T. "Does it Work? Substance-Free Dorms—Clean Living on Campus." *The New York Times.* (6 November 2005). Available http://www.nytimes.com/2005/11/06/education/edlife/work.html

Lin, A. Y. F. "Should Women Be Included in Clinical Trials?" *Pharmacy Times* 10 (November 1994): 27.

Lively, K. "The 'Date-Rape Drug': Colleges Worry about Reports of Growing Use of Rohypnol, a Sedative." *Chronicle of Higher Education* 42 (28 June 1996): A-29.

Lukas, S. "Urine Testing for Anabolic-Androgenic Steroids." *Trends in Pharmacological Sciences* 14 (1993): 61–68.

Marklein, M. B. "College Binge Drinking Heads Off Campus." *USA Today.* (14 March 2000).

Mathias, R. "Sex-for-Crack Phenomenon Poses Risk for Spread of AIDS in Heterosexuals." *NIDA Notes* 8 (May/June 1993): 8–11.

Mathias, R. "NIDA Survey Provides First National Data on Drug Use During Pregnancy." *NIDA Notes* 10 (January/February 1995): 6–7.

McCaffrey, B. R. "McCaffrey Announces Strategy to Fight Drug Use in Sports." *Daily Washington File* (21 October 1999).

McComsey, G. A. *HIV and AIDS.* Cincinnati, OH: Net Wellness Consumer Health Information, University of Cincinnati, 3 January 2011.

McDonald, M. "Fast, Strong, Dead?" *Salt Lake Tribune* 250 (22 June 1995): C1, C8.

Merchant, W. "Medications and Athletes." *American Druggist* (October 1992): 6–14.

Merrill G. "Depression Affects Women More than Men for a Number of Reasons." ArticleInput.com. 2009. Available http://www.articleinput.com/e/a/title/Depression-affects-women-more-than-men-for-a-number-of-reasons

Millstein, R. *Community Alert Bulletin.* Rockville, MD: National Institute on Drug Abuse, U.S. Department of Health and Human Services, 25 March 1993.

Minnesota Institute of Public Health. *Alcohol and Other Drugs and Suicide.* Mounds View, MN: Chemical Health Division, Minnesota Department of Human Services, Spring 1995.

Moss, H., L. Kirisci, H. Gordon, and R. Tarter. "A Neuropsychological Profile of Adolescent Alcoholics." *Alcoholism: Clinical and Experimental Research* 18 (1994): 159–163.

MSNBC. "AIDS Outruns Efforts to Combat It, Says U.N. Report: New HIV Infections Hit Record High Last Year." Health News. 2004. Available http://www.msnbc.msn.com/ID/5377027

"Multistate Outbreak of Poisonings Associated with Illicit Use of GHB." *Prevention Pipeline* 7 (May–June 1994): 95, 96.

MyDNA.com. "News Center: HAART Therapy Slows Progression to AIDS." Washington, DC: American Medical Association, 2005.

National Clearinghouse for Alcohol and Drug Information (NCADI). *Drugs of Abuse.* Rockville, MD: Substance Abuse and Mental Health Services Administration, 1999.

National Drug Intelligence Center (NDIC). *Drugs and Gangs: Fast Facts, Questions and Answers.* Washington, DC: National Drug Intelligence Center, 2009.

National Institute on Alcohol and Alcoholism (NIAAA). "High-Risk Drinking in College: What We Know and What We Need to Learn." College Drinking—Changing the Culture. 2005a. Available http://www.collegedrinking prevention.gov/niaaacollegematerials/panel01/exec sum_01.aspx

National Institute on Alcohol and Alcoholism (NIAAA). "Living Arrangements." College Drinking—Changing the Culture. 2005b. Available http://www.collegedrinking prevention.gov/NIAAACollegeMaterials/TaskForce/Factors_01.aspx

National Institute on Alcohol and Alcoholism (NIAAA). "A Snapshot of Annual High-Risk College Drinking Consequences." College Drinking—Changing the Culture. 2010. Available http://www.collegedrinkingprevention.gov/StatsSummaries/snapshot.aspx

National Institute on Drug Abuse (NIDA). *Anabolic Steroid Abuse.* Capsule 43. Rockville, MD: NIDA, 1996.

National Institute on Drug Abuse (NIDA). *Drug Abuse and Addiction Research: The Sixth Triennial Report to Congress.* Rockville, MD: U.S. Department of Health and Human Services, 1999.

National Institute on Drug Abuse (NIDA). "Club Drugs: Community Alert Bulletin." *NIDA Notes* 14 (30 March 2000).

National Institute on Drug Abuse (NIDA). *NewsScan for October 13, 2006—Women and Substance Abuse Issue.* Bethesda, MD: NIDA and the National Institutes of Health (NIH), 2006a.

National Institute on Drug Abuse (NIDA). *Research Report Series—Anabolic Steroid Abuse.* Bethesda, MD: U.S. Government Printing Office, 2006b.

National Institute on Drug Abuse (NIDA). *Drugs and HIV.* U.S. Department of Health and Human Services (UDHHS). Bethesda, MD: U.S. Government Printing Office, 2007.

National Institute on Drug Abuse (NIDA). *NIDA InfoFacts: Steroids (Anabolic-Androgenic).* Bethesda, MD: NIDA and National Institutes of Health (NIH), 2009.

National Institute on Drug Abuse (NIDA). "Monitoring the Future: Data Tables and Figures." Bethesda, MD: NIDA, National Institutes of Health (NIH), and Department of Health and Human Services (DHHS). December 2010. Available http://monitoringthefuture.org/data/09data/pr09t1.pdf

National Institutes of Health (NIH) and National Institute on Drug Abuse (NIDA). *Drug Abuse and Drug Abuse Research: Executive Summary.* Rockville, MD: Substance Abuse and Mental Health Services Administration, 1998.

National Survey on Drug Use and Health (NSDUH). *The NSDUH Report: Substance Use Treatment among Women of Childbearing Age.* Research Triangle Park, NC: Office of Applied Studies (OAS), Substance Abuse and Mental Health Services Administration (SAMHSA) and RTI International, 4 October 2007

National Youth Anti-Drug Media Campaign. "The 411 on Rx Drugs." 2007. Available http://www.theantidrug.com/drug_info/prescription_411.asp

News Tribune. "Alcohol, Tobacco or Drugs Used in 98% of Popular Movies." (29 April 1999): 7–8, 14.

New York State Department of Health. "Anabolic Steroids and Sports: Winning at Any Cost." 2010. Available http://www.health.state.ny.us/publications/1210

Nicklin, J. L. "Arrests at Colleges Surge for Alcohol and Drug Violations." *Chronicle of Higher Education* (9 June 2000).

Office of National Drug Control Policy (ONDCP). *Substance Use in Popular Movies and Music. Media Campaign, Campaign Publications.* Rockville, MD: ONDCP Drugs and Crime Clearinghouse, 1999.

Office of National Drug Control Policy (ONDCP). *Prescription for Danger.* Rockville, MD: ONDCP, January 2008.

Office of the Surgeon General. "Surgeon General's Call to Action to Prevent and Reduce Underage Drinking." Washington, DC: U.S. Department of Health and Human Services (DHHS), 2007. Available http://www.surgeongeneral.gov/topics/underagedrinking/family guide.pdf

"OTC Drugs and Athletes." *Pharmacy Times* (June 1992): 16.

Parrot, A. *Date Rape and Acquaintance Rape.* New York: Rosen, 1988.

Pietroski, N. "Counseling HIV/AIDS Patients." *American Druggist* (August 1993): 50–56.

positivelyaware.com. "12th Annual HIV Drug Guide." Test Positive Network. January/February 2008. Available http://positivelyaware.com/2008/08_01/drug_guide.html

Prendergast, M. L. "Substance Use and Abuse Among College Students: A Review of Recent Literature." *Journal of American College Health* 43 (1994): 99–113.

Ravid, J. "The Hard-Core Curriculum." *Rolling Stone* 719 (19 October 1995): 99.

Reuters and CNN.com. "Study: Lower-Income Web Users Now Fastest-Growing U.S. Market." Reuters (22 August 2000a): 9.

Reuters and CNN.com. "Users See Internet as Key Information Source." Reuters (16 August 2000b): 2–3.

Ross, V., and W. Dejong. *Alcohol and Other Drug Abuse Among First-Year College Students.* Newton, MA: The Higher Education Center for Alcohol and Other Drug Abuse and Violence Prevention, March 2008: 1–8.

Sanders, W. B. *Gangbangs and Drive-bys.* New York: Aldine De Gruyter, 1994.

Schaefer, M. A., J. F. Hilton, M. Ekstrand, and J. Keogh. "Relationship Between Drug Use and Sexual Behaviors and the Occurrence of Sexually Transmitted Diseases Among High-Risk Male Youth." *Sexually Transmitted Diseases* 20 (November–December 1993): 39–47.

Schernoff, M., and R. A. Smith. "HIV Treatments: A History of Scientific Advance." *Body Positive* XIV (July 2001): 1–7.

Schoemer, K. "Rockers, Models and the New Allure of Heroin." *Newsweek* (26 August 1996): 24–36.

Science Daily. "Pain Drug Reveals What Most Already Know—Men's and Women's Brains Are Simply Different." 15 March 2000. Available http://www.sciencedaily.com/releases/2000/03/000315075845.htm

Scott, D. M., J. C. Wagner, and T. W. Barlow. "Anabolic Steroids Use Among Adolescents in Nebraska Schools." *American Journal of Health-System Pharmacy* 53 (1996): 2068–2072.

Scripps Howard News Service. "AIDS Fear: Complacency: Infection Rate Is on Rise for First Time Since 1994." *Post-Tribune* (21 August 2003): A-10.

Seetharaman, D. "Prescription Drugs Easily Purchased Online: Study." Thomson Reuters. (9 July 2008). Available http://www.usatoday.com/news/health/2008-07-09-online-pharmacies_N.htm

Shelden, R. G., S. Tracy, and W. Brown. *Youth Gangs in American Society.* Belmont, CA: Wadsworth/Thomson Learning, 2001.

Shelden, R. G., S. K. Tracy, and W. B. Brown. *Youth Gangs in American Society,* 3rd ed. Belmont, CA: Wadsworth/Thomson Learning, 2004.

Siegel, L., and J. Senna. *Juvenile Delinquency,* 6th ed. St. Paul, MN: West, 1997.

Siegel, L. J., and B. C. Welsh. *Juvenile Delinquency: Theory, Practice, and Law,* 10th ed. Belmont, CA: Wadsworth, Cengage Learning, 2009.

Spergel, I. A. *Youth Gangs: Problem and Response.* Chicago, IL: University of Chicago, School of Social Service Administration, 1990.

Steinberg, L., A. Fletcher, and N. Darling. "Parental Monitoring and Peer Influences on Adolescent Substance Use." *Pediatrics* 93 (1994): 1060–1064.

Street, C., J. Antonio, and D. Cudlipp. "Androgen Use by Athletes: A Reevaluation of the Health Risks." *Canadian Journal of Applied Physiology* 2 (1996): 421–440.

Substance Abuse and Mental Health Services Administration (SAMHSA). *Making the Connection Between Substance Abuse and HIV/AIDS Prevention for Women of Color and Youth.* Rockville, MD: U.S. Department of Health and Human Services, 1999a.

Substance Abuse and Mental Health Services Administration (SAMHSA). *Tips for Teens: About Steroids. Center for Substance Abuse Prevention.* Rockville, MD: U.S. Department of Health and Human Services, 1999b.

Substance Abuse and Mental Health Services Administration (SAMHSA), Office of Applied Studies. *National Household Survey on Drug Abuse, The NHSDA Report. Team Sports Participation and Substance Use Among Youths.* Rockville, MD: SAMHSA, 17 March 2007.

Substance Abuse and Mental Health Services Administration (SAMHSA), Office of Applied Studies (OAS). *The TEDS (Treatment Episode Data Set) Report: Trends in Adult Female Substance Abuse Treatment Admissions Reporting Primary Alcohol Abuse: 1992 to 2007.* Rockville, MD, U.S. Department of Health and Human Services, 7 January 2010.

Suggs, W. "Deadly Fuel: As Supplements and Steroids Tempt and Endanger More Athletes, What Are Colleges Doing?" *Chronicle of Higher Education* 49 (14 March 2003): A36–A38.

Swadi, H. "Relative Risk Factors in Detecting Adolescent Drug Abuse." *Drug and Alcohol Dependence* 29 (1992): 253–254.

Teen Challenge. *Drugs: Frequently Asked Questions.* South Australia: Pragin Press, 2000.

Toronto, R. "Young Athletes Who Use 'Enhancing' Steroids Risk Severe Physical Consequences." *Salt Lake Tribune* 244 (6 July 1992): C-5.

UNAIDS. *Global Report: UNAIDS Report on the Global Aids Epidemic 2010.* Geneva, Switzerland: Joint United Nations Programme on HIV/AIDS (UNAIDS), 2010: 20–21.

U.S. Department of Health and Human Services (USDHHS), National Institute on Drug Abuse (NIDA). *Drug Abuse and Addiction Research: The Sixth Triennial Report to Congress. NIDA Research Priorities and Highlights, Role of Research: Women's Health and Gender Differences.* Washington, DC: U.S. Government Printing Office, 1999.

U.S. Department of Justice. *Anabolic Steroids and You.* Washington, DC: Demand Reduction Section, Drug Enforcement Administration, 1991–1992.

USA Today. "AIDS Likely to Devastate Teen Population." Health (28 August 2000): 1.

USA Today. "Teen Prescription Drug Abuse Reportedly Holding Steady." Associated Press. (14 February 2007). Available http://www.usatoday.com/news/health/2007-02-14-teens-rxdrugs_x.htm?csp=34

USA Today. "Treating HIV Also Prevent Its Spread, Study Finds." Associated Press, Health. 18 July 2010. Available http://www.usatoday.com/news/health/2010-07-18-hiv-spread-study_N.htm

Venturelli, P. J. "Drugs in Schools: Myths and Reality." In *The Annals of the American Academy of Political and Social Science,* edited by W. H. Hinkle and S. Henry, (567) 72–87. Thousand Oaks, CA: Sage, January 2000.

Verhaak, C. M., A. M. E. Lintsen, A. W. M. Evers, and D. D. M. Braat. "Who Is at Risk of Emotional Problems and How Do You Know? Screening of Women Going for IVF Treatment." *Human Reproduction* 25 (2010): 1234–1240.

Von Der Haar, C. M. *Social Psychology: A Sociological Perspective.* Upper Saddle River, NJ: Pearson Education, 2005.

Walsh, F., and M. Sheinkman. "Family Context of Adolescence." In *Adolescent Substance Abuse, Etiology, Treatment and Prevention,* edited by G. Lawson and A. Lawson, 149–171. Gaithersburg, MD: Aspen, 1992.

WebMD.com. "Information and Resources: Growth Hormone." Healthwise, Inc. (14 August 2008). Available http://www.webmd.com/a-to-z-guides/growth-hormone

Wechsler, H., J. E. Lee, M. Kuo, M. Seibring, T. F. Nelson, H. P. Lee. "Trends in College Binge Drinking During a Period of Increased Prevention Efforts: Findings From Four Harvard School of Public Health Study Surveys, 1993–2001." *Journal of American College Health* 50 (2002): 203–217.

Welder, A., and R. Melchert. "Cardiotoxic Effects of Cocaine and Anabolic-Androgenic Steroids in the Athlete." *Journal of Pharmacological and Toxicological Methods* 29 (1993): 61–68.

Winters, P. A. *Teen Addiction.* San Diego, CA: Greenhaven Press, 1997.

Wisconsin Coalition Against Sexual Assault (WCASA). *Sexual Violence and Sexual Abuse.* Madison, WI: WCASA, 1997.

Witham, D. "Recovery in the Dorm: Rutgers University's Special Housing for Addicted Students." *Chronicle of Higher Education* 42 (10 November 1995): A-33.

"Women Smokers Run High Risk for Lung Cancer." *Prevention Pipeline* 7 (May–June 1994): 7.

World Anti-Doping Agency (WADA). *Questions and Answers on 2009 World Anti-Doping Code.* Montreal (Quebec), Canada: World Anti-Doping Agency, 2009. Available http://www.wada-ama.org/en/Resources/Q-and-A/Why-is-it-important-to-combat-doping-in-sport

World Health Organization (WHO). "HIV/AIDS: HIV/AIDS and Adolescents." 2000–2004. Geneva, Switzerland: World Health Organization, 2005.

Wright, L. "Suicidal Thoughts and Their Relationship to Family Stress and Personal Problems Among High School Seniors and College Undergraduates." *Adolescence* 20 (1985): 575–580.

Wu, L. T., D. J. Pilowsky, and A. A. Patkar, "Non-Prescribed Use of Pain Relievers among Adolescents in the United States." *Drug Alcohol Dependency* 94 (April 1, 2008): 1–11. Epub ahead of print December 3, 2007.

Yahoo! News. "1 in 3 Hit Songs Mentions Substance Abuse, Smoking." *HealthDay.* (4 February 2008).

Yesalis, C. E., and J. S. Cowart. *The Steroids Game.* Champaign, IL: Human Kinetics, 1998.

Zuger, A. M. D. "Epidemic: An Overview." *New York Times.* (8 August 2000). Available http://www.nytimes.com/library/national/science/aids/aids-overview.html

Learning ⦿bjectives

On completing this chapter, you will be able to:

◎ List the 10 most prominent factors influencing alcohol and other drug use surrounding the individual.

◎ List and briefly explain the three major types of drug prevention programs.

◎ List the five types of drug users that have to be considered before implementing a drug prevention program.

◎ List the four levels of comprehensive prevention programs for drug use and abuse.

◎ List the three family factors that can prevent initiation to drugs or extensive drug use.

◎ List four existing prevention programs largely found in higher education.

◎ Understand the main goals of the following large-scale drug prevention programs: the BACCHUS Network, D.A.R.E., and drug courts.

◎ Describe two alternatives to drug use.

Did You Know?

○ Comprehensive prevention programs involving the community, school, and family are more effective than single-unit programs.

○ The harm reduction drug prevention model that is practiced in the Netherlands is a preventive model that meets drug users on their own turf in dealing with drug use and/or abuse.

○ Drug prevention programs must distinguish among early experimenters, nonproblem drug users, undetected committed or secret users, problem users, and former users.

○ Students in drug prevention programs who do not know how to say "no" need refusal skills training or peer resistance training.

○ Drug education actually began in the 1830s with the temperance movement.

○ Drug courts are a newer form of drug prevention in which drug defendants are more likely to undergo treatment (rehabilitation) than incarceration (punishment).

○ Other strategies for dealing with drug use include the alternatives approach and meditation.

Drugs and Society Online is a great source for additional drugs and society information for both students and instructors. Visit **go.jblearning.com/hanson11** to find a variety of useful tools for learning, thinking, and teaching.

Introduction

When someone tells another person "Just don't do drugs" and, if that person is addicted to, say, cocaine like I was, that comes across as an ignorant answer. You cannot just quit when you are addicted because even the idea of addiction continually blocks the possibility of casually deciding to stop using the drug. A lot has to go into the day you actually stop using the drug. First of all, the craving for the drug continually reminds you to do it maybe just a few more times. Then, your life appears to be less engaging because your body is missing the chemical properties of the drug that it became accustomed to and this affects your level of depression. So you have to sort of go through that slow abstinence period—you are without the drug and sometimes you can only deal with abstaining 1 hour at a time for the first week or so. Then slowly, ever so slowly, for me at least, the addict has to rebuild her or his daily living without the drug. It's just not easy. If it were, most people addicted to drugs would probably quit on their own. Especially when you realize that you are not controlling the drug, the drug is controlling you. Just remember, most addicts continually deceive [lie to] themselves and others that they are not "really" addicted. Do you know how hard it is to become aware that these lies are part of the addiction? Before the extended therapy I had, no one could convince me that the daily cocaine I was snorting and smoking was bad. *(From Venturelli's research files, female academic administrator in higher education who has been drug free for 3 years, age 37, June 21, 2000)*

A second interview revealed the following:

I started doing cocaine at age 52. One night, I was having a few beers with a friend of mine and another friend of his over at his apartment. I know I was older than both of them were since they were in their early thirties. After the first few beers, this friend of mine went into his bedroom and came out into the living room with a bag of coke. Soon as he en-

tered the room, he threw the bag into my lap and said, "Do you want to try some of this?" I told them I never did this drug and said, "Okay I will try it once." All I remember that night is that I kept doing lines and often said, "Boy, this stuff is so easy to do—nothing to it." When the night was over, I got back into my car and went home. After that night, I started buying the coke each week and for over 2 years had spent thousands of dollars. It became a nightly thing to do. One day, I decided to stop buying coke since I was very worried about all the money I had been charging to my credit card as cash advances. For the first few nights it was difficult to not go out and pick up coke from a dealer I had gotten to know quite well. This dealer kept calling asking who I was buying from since he hadn't seen me in over a week. I repeatedly tried telling him that I was quitting and had no other dealer but he would not believe me. This added to the difficulty in giving up the drug but I did it. It was "cold turkey" and I had succeeded since now it has been 5 years and I never bought my supply again since that one night when I decided to quit. It is so easy to do this drug and become attached to it. I don't think I was really addicted when I was doing it, but I sure did it often. My problem was more of a mental attachment to the drug. I think I was certainly close to a serious addiction but the cost of the drug, using money I did not have, forced me to quit. In my case, the best prevention is to never start doing this drug or any other drug that is easy to do and makes you feel so good when you are doing it. I have several friends who continue to use this drug mostly on weekends. I am glad I am not in their shoes anymore. *(From Venturelli's research files, male mechanical engineer, age 59, November 5, 2010)*

This chapter explores and provides information on doing *something* about drug use and abuse. With so many potential causes for the unnecessary and nonmedical use of psychoactive substances, it becomes increasingly important to discuss methods, programs, and strategies that prevent, delay, or at the very least, moderate the habitual use of drugs. **Figure 17.1** shows many of the potential environmental factors involved in what influences alcohol and other drug use (**AOD**). The core in this figure starts with the individual, and each concentric zone represents clusters of factors that influence an individual's views, attitudes, and behaviors toward drug use. With so many factors, each having an indepen-

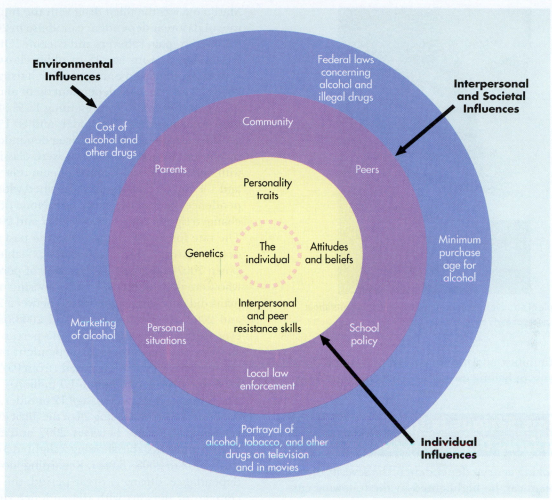

FIGURE 17.1

Potential factors that influence alcohol and other drug use.

Source: U.S. Department of Health and Human Services, Office of Substance Abuse Prevention. "Factors that Influence Alcohol and Other Drug Use." In *Prevention Plus II: Tools for Creating and Sustaining Drug-Free Communities* (Figure 2.1, p. 19). DHHS Publication No. 89-1649. Rockville, MD: Author, 1989. Distributed by the National Clearinghouse for Alcohol and Drug Information.

dent potential effect on the individual, you can see why comprehensive prevention programs involving the community, school, and family are more effective than single-unit programs, such as having a mandatory drug education program in elementary grades without other complementary and overlapping drug programs in the community and the family. Prevention research clearly shows that "we must attend to all factors; prevention that focuses on only one or two factors and ignores or discounts the rest is likely to fail to have a long-term, permanent impact" (Tinzmann and Hixson 1992, p. 3).

Through comprehensive prevention programs that are multifaceted and complementary, we are able to more effectively tease out which factors are most influential. The televised commercial in the early 1990s that showed two eggs frying in a pan: "This is your brain . . . this is your brain on drugs," sponsored by the Partnership for a Drug-Free America, was an early attempt at prevention through a disturbing analogy. Although its effect was poor on drug users, who had never felt their brains frying, it was an initial step toward innovative prevention efforts. Was it worth the airtime? Can the success of these programs be adequately measured?

In 1997, 15 states thought prevention of alcohol and other drug abuse was important enough to maintain certified prevention specialist credentialing. Today, a bewildering variety of programs exist from coast to coast in school districts, churches, and other

Example of an advertisement aimed at alerting parents about the dangers of early drug use.

communities, all with the goal of preventing initial drug use or halting use before it becomes a problem.

How Serious Is the Problem of Drug Dependence?

In looking at drug dependence, the severity of this problem can be highlighted by the following current trends (SAMHSA 2009).

Substance dependence or abuse:

- In 2008, an 22.2 million persons age 12 or older were classified with substance dependence or abuse in the past year (8.9% of the population age 12 or older). Of these, 3.1 million were classified with dependence on or abuse of both alcohol and illicit drugs, 3.9 million were dependent on or abused illicit drugs but not alcohol, and 15.2 million were dependent on or abused alcohol but not illicit drugs.

- The number of persons with substance dependence or abuse was relatively stable, ranging from a low of 21.6 million in 2003 to a high of 22.6 million in 2006. In 2007 and 2008, approximately 22.2 million people had experienced substance dependence.

- In 2008, 18.3 million persons age 12 or older were classified with dependence on or abuse of alcohol. This represents 7.3% of the population. The number and percentage have remained similar since 2002.

- Marijuana was the illicit drug with the highest rate of past-year dependence or abuse in 2008, followed by pain relievers and cocaine. Of the 7.0 million persons age 12 or older classified with dependence on or abuse of illicit drugs in 2008, 4.2 million were dependent on or abused marijuana or hashish (representing 1.7% of the total population age 12 or older, and 60.1% of all those classified with illicit drug dependence or abuse), 1.7 million persons were classified with dependence on or abuse of pain relievers, and 1.4 million persons were classified with dependence on or abuse of cocaine. None of this changed significantly between 2007 and 2008.

- The rate for use of marijuana in the past year decreased from 2002 to 2008 but was stable between 2007 and 2008. The number of persons who were dependent on or were abusing marijuana did not change significantly between 2002 and 2008 and between 2007 and 2008. However, between 2004 and 2008, the percentage and the number of persons dependent on or abusing pain relievers increased (from 0.6% to 0.7% and from 1.4 million to 1.7 million).

- The percentage of persons age 12 or older with dependence on or abusing all of the illicit drugs remained the same between 2007 and 2008 (2.8%) and was stable showing a slight increase from 2002 to 2008 (3.0%). Regarding alcohol dependence, during a 7-year period, the percentage of persons with dependence on or abusing alcohol remained stable as well (7.7% in 2002, 7.5% in 2007, and 7.3% in 2008).

- In 2008, among adults age 18 or older, age at first use of marijuana was associated with dependence on or abuse of marijuana. Among those who first tried marijuana at age 14 or younger, 13.5% were classified with illicit drug dependence or abuse, higher than the 2.2% of adults who had first used marijuana at age 18 or older.

- Among adults, age at first use of alcohol was associated with dependence on or abuse of alcohol. Among adults age 18 or older who first tried alcohol at age 14 or younger, 16.5% were classified with alcohol dependence or abuse compared with only 3.9% of adults who had first used alcohol at age 18 or older. Adults age 21 or older who had first used alcohol before age 21 were more likely than adults who had their first drink at age 21 or older to be classified with alcohol dependence or abuse (15.1%, 9.3%, and 4.7% for adults who first used alcohol at age 14 or younger, ages 15 to 17, and ages 18 to 20, respectively, vs. 2.6% for first use at age 21 or older).

- Rates of substance dependence or abuse were associated with age. In 2008, the rate of substance dependence or abuse among adults ages 18 to 25 (20.8%) was higher than that among youths ages 12 to 17 (7.6%) and among adults age 26 or older (7.0%). None of these rates changed significantly between 2007 and 2008. For youths ages 12 to 17, the rate decreased from 8.9% in 2002 to 7.6% in 2008. For young adults ages 18 to 25 and adults age 26 or older, these rates remained stable from 2002 to 2008.

- In 2008, among persons with substance dependence or abuse, the proportion with dependence on or abuse of illicit drugs also was associated with age: 60.6% of youths ages 12 to 17 were dependent on or abused illicit drugs compared with 37.4% of young adults ages 18 to 25 and 24.3% of adults age 26 or older.

- The rate of alcohol dependence or abuse among youths ages 12 to 17 was 4.9% in 2008, which was down from 5.4% in 2007 and from 5.9% in 2002. Among adults age 26 or older, the rate remained stable between 2007 (6.2%) and 2008 (6.0%) and between 2002 (6.2%) and 2008. Among young adults ages 18 to 25, the rate of alcohol dependence or abuse remained similar between 2007 (16.8%) and 2008 (17.2%) and between 2002 (17.7%) and 2008.

Gender:

- As was the case from 2002 through 2007, the rate of substance dependence or abuse for males age 12 or older in 2008 was about twice as high as the rate for females. For males in 2008, the rate was 11.5%, which was down from 12.5% in 2007; for females, it was 6.4%, which was higher than the 5.7% in 2007.

- In contrast, among youths ages 12 to 17, the rate of substance dependence or abuse among males was lower than the rate among females in 2008 (7.0% vs. 8.2%).

Race/ethnicity:

- In 2008, among persons age 12 or older, the rate of substance dependence or abuse was the lowest among Asians (4.2%).

- Racial/ethnic groups with similar rates included American Indians or Alaska Natives (11.1%), persons reporting two or more races (9.8%), whites (9.0%), blacks (8.8%), and Hispanics

(9.5%). These rates in 2008 were similar to the rates in 2002 through 2007.

Education/employment:

- Rates of substance dependence or abuse were associated with level of education in 2008. Among adults age 18 or older, those who graduated from a college or university had a lower rate of dependence or abuse (7.0%) than those who graduated from high school (9.4%), those who did not graduate from high school (9.5%), and those with some college (10.5%).

- Rates of substance dependence or abuse were associated with current employment status in 2008. A higher percentage of unemployed adults age 18 or older were classified with dependence or abuse (19.0%) than were full-time employed adults (10.2%) or part-time employed adults (11.0%).

- Most adults age 18 or older with substance dependence or abuse were employed full time in 2008. Of the 20.3 million adults classified with dependence or abuse, 12.5 million (61.5%) were employed full time.

Criminal justice populations:

- In 2008, adults age 18 or older who were on parole or a supervised release from jail during the past year had higher rates of dependence on or abuse of a substance (27.8%) than their counterparts who were not on parole or supervised release during the past year (8.9%).

- In 2008, probation status was associated with substance dependence or abuse. The rate of substance dependence or abuse was 34.0% among adults who were on probation during the past year, which was significantly higher than the rate among adults who were not on probation during the past year (8.4%).

Geographic areas:

- In 2008, rates of substance dependence or abuse for persons age 12 or older showed evidence of differences by region, with the West (9.6%) having a higher rate than the South (8.2%), but a similar rate to the Midwest (9.4%) and the Northeast (8.9%).

- Rates for substance dependence or abuse among persons age 12 or older in 2008 also varied by county type, with large metropolitan counties (9.3%) having a significantly higher rate than nonmetropolitan counties (8.0%), but a similar rate when compared with small metropolitan counties (8.6%).

After reviewing such significant findings in terms of numbers and percentages of substance-dependent or abusing populations, we can now understand the need for discussing drug prevention in this chapter and drug treatment in the next chapter.

Drug Prevention

"In the broadest sense, prevention is organized activity designed to avoid or decrease health problems" (Wilson and Kolander 2011, p. 7). In addition to this definition of prevention, we add that in this chapter, **drug prevention** is aimed at preventing and/or decreasing not only health problems, but also social and personal problems. In previous chapters, we learned that when both licit and illicit types of drugs are used and/or abused for nonmedical purposes, they compromise psychological, social, and biological behavior. In the remaining sections of this chapter, we will review what drug prevention entails.

Risk Factors and Protective Factors

From a broad perspective, when considering any drug prevention program, both **protective factors** and **risk factors** have to be considered. "Protective factors are those associated with reduced potential for drug use and risk factors are those that make drug use more likely" (National Institute on Drug Abuse [NIDA] 2002). The following are the main

principles that have to be considered when planning effective drug prevention programs:

- Drug prevention programs should enhance protective factors and reverse or reduce risk factors. Protective factors include:
  - Strong and positive family bonds
  - Parental monitoring of children's activities and peers
  - Clear rules of conduct consistently enforced within the family
  - Involvement of parents in the lives of their children
  - Success in school performance
  - Strong bonds in institutions, such as school and religious organizations
  - Adoption of conventional norms about drug use
- Risk factors include:
  - Chaotic home environment, particularly in homes where parents abuse substances or suffer from mental illnesses
  - Ineffective parenting, especially with children with difficult temperaments or conduct disorders
  - Lack of parent–child attachments and nurturing
  - Inappropriately shy or aggressive behavior in the classroom
  - Failure in school performance
  - Poor social coping skills
  - Affiliations with peers displaying deviant behaviors
  - Perceptions of approval of drug-using behaviors in family, work, school, peer, and community environments (NIDA 2002)
- The risk of becoming a drug abuser involves the relationship among the number and type of risk factors (e.g., deviant attitudes and behaviors) and protective factors (e.g., parental support).
- The potential impact of specific risk and protective factors changes with age. For example, risk factors within the family have greater impact on a younger child whereas association with drug-abusing peers may be a more significant risk factor for an adolescent.
- Early intervention with risk factors (e.g., aggressive behavior and poor self-control) often has a greater impact than later intervention by changing a child's life path (trajectory) away from problems and toward positive behaviors.
- Although risk and protective factors can affect people of all groups, these factors can have a

KEY TERMS

drug prevention
aimed at preventing or decreasing health problems, including social and personal problems, caused by drug dependency

protective factors
factors associated with preventing the potential for drug abuse such as self-control, parental monitoring, academic competence, anti–drug use policies, and strong neighborhood attachment

risk factors
drug prevention is aimed at reducing risk factors, such as early aggressive behavior, lack of parental supervision, the lure of gang membership, drug availability, and poverty

different effect depending on a person's age, gender, ethnicity, culture, and neighborhood environment.

- Prevention programs should address all forms of drug abuse, alone or in combination, including the underage use of legal drugs (e.g., tobacco, alcohol), the use of illegal drugs (e.g., marijuana, heroin), and the inappropriate use of legally obtained substances (e.g., inhalants), prescription medications, or over-the-counter drugs.
- Prevention programs should address the type of drug abuse problem in the local community, target modifiable risk factors, and strengthen identified protective factors.
- Prevention programs should be tailored to address risks specific to population or audience characteristics, such as age, gender, and ethnicity, to improve program effectiveness (quoted extensively from Robertson et al. and NIDA 2003, p. 7).

There are three levels of drug prevention programs, each suited to different types of drug users. **Primary drug prevention programs** are aimed at either nonusers who need to be "inoculated" against potential drug use or helping at-risk individuals avoid the development of addictive behaviors. For example, primary prevention often targets at-risk youth who may live in areas where licit and illicit types of drugs are rampant, youth who may come from problem families, or youth who are surrounded by drug-abusing peers.

The other two major types of drug prevention programs are (1) **secondary drug prevention programs**, which consist of uncovering potentially harmful substance use prior to the onset of overt symptoms or problems and/or targeting newer drug users with a limited or early history of drug use, and (2) **tertiary drug prevention programs**, which focus directly on intervention and target chemically dependent individuals who need treatment. Tertiary prevention involves treating the medical consequences of drug abuse and facilitating entry into treatment so further disability is minimized.

Usually primary, secondary, and tertiary programs are used in combination because, in most settings, all three types of drug users constitute the targeted population. **Table 17.1** further illustrates these levels of drug prevention and corresponding suggested activities; what can be accomplished is listed under each of the three types of prevention (primary, secondary, and tertiary).

Considering the Audience and Approach

It is important to be aware that drug users vary in their exposure and past histories of substance use and/or abuse. The audience for drug prevention comprises both users and nonusers. In analyzing the population of users, categories include the following:

- Nonusers
- Early experimenters
- Nonproblem drug users—those who abuse drugs on occasion, mostly for recreational purposes
- Undetected, committed, or secret users—those who abuse drugs and have no interest in stopping their drug use
- Problem users who are often drug dependent and/or addicted to drugs
- Former users

It is important that role models, counselors, teachers, and anyone else involved in drug prevention programs take into consideration that there are different types of substance users/abusers. Therefore, drug prevention programs must cater to the specific needs of these groups. For nonproblem users, drug education programs should examine the abuse of drugs and reinforce the message that uncontrolled use leads to abuse. For committed users, drug education should aim to prevent or delay

KEY TERMS

primary drug prevention programs
drug prevention programs with a very broad range of activities aimed at reducing the risk of drug use among nonusers and ensuring continued nonuse and helping at-risk individuals avoid the development of addictive behaviors

secondary drug prevention programs
programs that consist of uncovering potentially harmful substance use prior to the onset of overt symptoms or problems and/or targeting newer drug users with a limited history of use; the main goal is to target at-risk groups, experimenters, and early-abuse populations

tertiary drug prevention programs
drug prevention programs focusing on intervention and targeting chemically dependent individuals who need treatment; tertiary prevention involves treating the medical consequences of drug abuse and facilitating entry into treatment so further disability is minimized (basically the same as drug abuse treatment)

Table 17.1 **Levels of Drug Prevention and Suggested Activities**

PRIMARY PREVENTION (RISK REDUCTION BEFORE ABUSE)	
Intrapersonal factors	Affective education (emotional literacy)
	Resilience training
	Values clarification
	Personal and social skills development
	Assertiveness skills training
	Refusal skills
	Drug information and education
Small group factors	Peer mentoring, counseling, outreach, modeling
	Conflict resolution
	Curriculum infusion
	Activities demonstrating misperception of peer norms
	Alternatives to use: recreational, cultural, athletic
	Strengthening families
Systems level	Strengthening school–family links
	Strengthening school–community group links
	Strengthening community support systems
	Media advocacy efforts, reducing alcohol marketing
SECONDARY PREVENTION (INTERVENING IN EARLY ABUSE)	
	Assessment strategies: identification of abuse subgroups and individual diagnoses
	Early intervention coupled with sanctions
	Teacher–counselor–parent team approach
	Developing healthy alternative youth culture
	Recovering role models
TERTIARY PREVENTION (INTERVENING IN ADVANCED ABUSE)	
	Assessment and diagnosis
	Referral into treatment
	Case management
	Reentry

drug abuse. Former users should be given information that will reinforce their decision to stop abusing drugs.

A number of questions should be considered by a professional planning a prevention program. To what type of audience should the drug information be targeted? Youths or adults? Peers or parents? Should information focus on knowledge, attitudes, or behavior?

Should the program emphasize and recommend abstinence or responsible use? In most cases, it is appropriate for drug prevention to focus on knowledge, attitudes, and behavior; the three are clearly related. For instance, if the goal is to increase knowledge, should we assume that attitudes and behavior would change accordingly, or should knowledge about the harmful effects of drugs be kept separate from attitudes and behavior? For example, if you learn that smoking marijuana is a health hazard, equal to or more destructive than smoking cigarettes, does this knowledge limit the satisfaction you derive from smoking marijuana with friends? Some would say yes. Unfortunately, many would say no. In fact, knowledge about the harmful effects of certain types of drugs has very little effect on the personal attitudes and habits of most people. Most cigarette smokers are aware of the health hazards before they start smoking, but this does not always stop them from starting or becoming addicted.

Drug education programs have to direct their attention to a small range of behavioral objectives. They will not be effective if they address too many issues. Drug prevention programs also must decide whether they will stress total abstinence or responsible use. Abstinence is radically different from responsible use. A program cannot advocate both. Information and scare tactics alone have no effect on drug use. Educational prevention models have been modified lately to achieve the following goals:

- Convey the message that society is inconsistent concerning drug use. For example, certain drugs that cause serious harm to a large percentage of the population are legal, whereas other drugs that have less impact are illegal.
- Convey that the reasons for drug use are complex and that drug users vary.
- Demonstrate to youth that young and old alike are affected by role models, in that attitudes regarding drug use are often patterned from family members who are role models.
- Acknowledge that other influential role models in music, sports, art, drama, business, and education who use and abuse drugs can affect attitudes toward drug use (see Chapter 16).

Prevention Research: Key Findings

"Each year, drug abuse and addiction cost taxpayers nearly $534 billion in preventable health care, law enforcement, crime, and other costs" (NIDA 2007). Three major outcomes regarding drug abuse prevention are listed as key findings from the National Institute on Drug Abuse (NIDA 2007).

- *Addiction is a complex disease.* No single factor can predict who will become addicted to drugs. Addiction is influenced by a tangle of factors involving genes, environment, and age of first use. Recent advances in genetic research have enabled researchers to begin to uncover which genes make people more vulnerable, which protect a person against addiction, and how genes and environment interact.
- *Addiction is a developmental disease.* It usually begins in adolescence or even childhood when the brain continues to undergo changes. The prefrontal cortex—located just behind the forehead—governs judgment and decision-making functions and is the last part of the brain to develop. This may help explain why

teens are prone to risk-taking, why they are particularly vulnerable to drug abuse, and why exposure to drugs at this critical time may affect the possibility of future addiction.
- *Prevention and early intervention work best.* The developmental years might also present opportunities for resiliency and for receptivity to intervention that can alter the course of addiction. We already know many of the risk factors that lead to drug abuse and addiction—mental illness, physical or sexual abuse, aggressive behavior, academic problems, poor social skills, and poor parent–child relations. This knowledge, combined with better understanding of the motivational processes at work in the young brain, can be applied to prevent drug abuse from starting or to intervene early to stop it when warning signs emerge.

■ An Example of Drug Prevention at Central High in Elmtown

This section describes how a school-based prevention program is implemented and demonstrates that programs must be comprehensive and multifaceted to be successful.

Let us stand in the shoes of a parent and teacher committee trying to design a primary prevention program for students at Central High in Elmtown. The group has some prevention research materials that it received from the National Clearinghouse for Alcohol and Drug Information. After some thought, most members of the committee decide not to address individual, personal risk factors (discussed in Chapters 2 and 18) that may generate anxieties, conflicts, or painful or threatening feelings. They have spoken with some students and ascertained that most of the 9th and 10th graders—even those who tend toward rebelliousness and avant-garde styles—are against taking drugs. Although many students feel this way, there are trends in the school that worry the committee members. Some popular 11th- and 12th-grade peer group leaders are drug users, and drug sales have been occurring on school grounds. The presence and availability of drugs and the beginning of a drug-using atmosphere make it more likely that some of the younger students will initiate use.

In brainstorming sessions, different committee members suggest ways to help these students avert initiation of drug use. Depending on their thinking, theoretical perspective, and exposure to prevention models, members come up with the following ideas:

- Students need to be grounded in good, solid knowledge about the negative effects and dangers of drugs (1) as provided in a drug education course or (2) more subtly, in a curriculum concerning drug effects and drug-using behaviors (also covered later in this chapter in the section on higher education).

- Students with low self-esteem will feel uncomfortable asserting individual choices or points of view that deviate from those held by peers or peer leaders. Bolstering a positive self-image would allow such students to refuse drugs.

- Students who have low expectations regarding their ability to refuse drugs will be least likely to actually refuse. The school might try to increase their *self-efficacy*—that is, their belief that their behaviors are powerful and will have results.

- Students just do not know how to say "no" and need refusal skills training or peer-resistance training.

- Although a clique leadership may set a pro-use tone, it is probable that the quiet antidrug students represent a silent majority. They may misperceive the amount of drug use that occurs in their school. If the antidrug students are shown that their own attitudes and beliefs are actually in the majority, they will see that the "emperor has no clothes."

- A more confrontational approach involves removing drugs from the school environment by infiltrating the student body or using informants to gather information about who is distributing drugs. Dealers and users can then be identified or counseled and their parents notified. The school could make the decision to go as far as having the student arrested or expelling him or her.

With so many options put forth, some of the committee members become frustrated and fear that a sufficient program will never be created. Some of them have experienced alcoholism in their families and fear that many of these approaches are too ineffective for helping the students who are already experimenting.

Seeing a disaster brewing, the committee chair makes a call to the Division of Substance Abuse Services in the state Department of Health to inquire about drug prevention programs. The operator refers the call to the prevention specialists at the agency, who are linked to the National Prevention Network, which is part of the National Association of State Alcohol and Drug Abuse Directors. The specialist schedules a meeting with the committee, in which she makes the following points:

- A prevention needs assessment is helpful, and necessitates using validated survey instruments to determine the patterns of behavior and attitudes regarding drug use among the student body.

- A combination of primary and secondary prevention would be good for the majority of the student body, and group treatment for substance abuse should be made available at an adolescent outpatient clinic. The outpatient clinic will assess some students who are well on their way to addiction and refer them into inpatient treatment. Because this intervention occurs when the student is at an advanced abuse state, this is considered tertiary prevention.

Notice how all three types of approaches (primary, secondary, and tertiary) are necessary to implement a comprehensive prevention strategy.

The specialist brought along a staff member of the Local Council on Alcoholism and Drug Dependence, an affiliate of the National Council on Alcoholism and Drug Dependence (NCADD) branch serving a three-county region of the state. Thousands of branches of NCADD exist in the United States, and their goal is to help local groups design and implement prevention programs. Many branches have developed specialized programs for teens, children, women, and the elderly. The staff member conducts preliminary sessions with the prevention committee and arranges to sign an affiliation agreement with the school administration, whereby NCADD will act as consultants to the school, aiding it in designing a prevention program to fit its particular needs. It will design a project, which will be based on a needs assessment that incorporates a survey of chemical attitudes and use and interviews with parents, teachers, and students. The project design will include the program objectives, a method and management plan, a timeline, and an evaluation component.

To help those members bewildered by the many possible factors identified by the committee in its brainstorming session (such as self-esteem, self-efficacy, and refusal skills), the staff member invites the committee to sample a number of available, attractive packages of user-friendly activities, such as the following:

- Broad-brush packages, which cover a variety of personal choice and primary prevention areas (Holstein, Cohen, and Steinbroner 1995)
- More targeted strategies, which might include a training package to be implemented by a consultant hired by the school district to address issues such as assertiveness training

Assertiveness training skills, which include a variety of personal and social skills, enable people to communicate their needs and feelings in an open, direct, and appropriate manner, while still recognizing the needs and feelings of others. They make people feel more powerful and better about themselves (less like doormats), and they offer strategies for saying "no" without hurting, provoking, or manipulating others (Alberti and Emmons 1988). Assertive behavior contrasts with hostile or belligerent behavior, passive and helpless behavior, and passive-aggressive or indirect manipulation. The exercises included in assertiveness training are nonthreatening, concrete, direct, and enjoyable.

Many intrapersonal prevention concepts, or personal and social skills development concepts, have come and gone, with a trendy buzzword accompanying each in the year it was introduced. Many of these concepts overlap, such as life skills training, self-esteem, self-efficacy, resilience training, and assertiveness training (McIntyre, White, and Yoast 1990; Norman 1994). The danger lies in employing them as gimmicks or slogans that accomplish little. Nevertheless, as Botvin and others have shown, personal and skills training that is carefully based on known cognitive and behavioral change factors, if carefully put into place, can indeed make a difference (Botvin and Griffin 2005; Botvin and Wills 1985; Shiffman and Wills 1987). It also is true that almost any positive lifestyle activity is likely to act as an alternative to participating in a drug-using subculture.

Comprehensive Prevention Programs for Drug Use and Abuse

Harm Reduction Model

The **harm reduction model** is a very broad and comprehensive model that involves society-wide prevention. As an approach to drug use and addiction, this model is practiced in some cities in the Netherlands and the United Kingdom. It is described by Westermeyer as an addiction model that connects "with the addicted community, by having an 'open door policy' that welcomes addicts to take part in services, regardless of level of motivation for change, goals or personal ideology" (Westermeyer n.d.). In a sense, it is a model that meets addicts on their own level.

Westermeyer (n.d.) identifies three central beliefs of the harm reduction model:

1. Excessive behaviors occur along a continuum of risk ranging from minimal to extreme. Addictive behaviors are not all-or-nothing phenomena. Although a drug or alcohol abstainer has a lower risk of harm than a drug or alcohol user, a moderate drinker is causing less harm than a binge drinker is; a crystal methamphetamine smoker or sniffer is causing less harm than a crystal injector.

2. Changing addictive behavior is a stepwise process, with complete abstinence being the final step. Those who embrace the harm reduction model believe that any movement in the direction of reduced harm—no matter how small—is positive in and of itself.

3. Sobriety simply is not for everybody. This statement requires the acceptance that many people live in horrible circumstances. Some are able to cope without the use of drugs; others use drugs as a primary means of coping. Until we are in a position to offer an alternative means of survival to these individuals, we are in no position to cast moral judgment. The health and well-being of the individual are of primary concern; if individuals are unwilling or unable to change addictive behavior at this time, they should not be denied services. *Attempts should be made to reduce the harm of their habits as much as possible.*

According to Westermeyer, the Dutch (who created this approach to prevention of drug use and abuse) have "an 80% connection rate with the addicted population," whereas in the United States we are 80% disconnected from our addicted populations. In fact, through our punitive model in

KEY TERMS

harm reduction model
a society-wide approach to drug use and/or abuse that focuses on reducing the harm experienced by the drug user and/or abuser as well as the harm to society

dealing with drug users, the strongest connection we have with the addicted population in the United States comes when they are arrested and jailed.

"Harm reduction strategies meet drug users 'where they're at,' addressing conditions of use along with the use itself. . . . [the Harm Reduction Coalition] HRC considers the following principles central to harm reduction practice" (Harm Reduction Coalition [HRC] 2011). The HRC:

- Accepts, for better and for worse, that licit and illicit drug use is part of our world and chooses to work to minimize its harmful effects rather than simply ignore or condemn them.
- Understands drug use as a complex, multifaceted phenomenon that encompasses a continuum of behaviors from severe abuse to total abstinence, and acknowledges that some ways of using drugs are clearly safer than others.
- Establishes quality of individual and community life and well-being—not necessarily cessation of all drug use—as the criteria for successful interventions and policies.
- Calls for the nonjudgmental, noncoercive provision of services and resources to people who use drugs and the communities in which they live in order to assist them in reducing attendant harm.
- Ensures that drug users and those with a history of drug use routinely have a real voice in the creation of programs and policies designed to serve them.
- Affirms drugs users themselves as the primary agents of reducing the harms of their drug use, and seeks to empower users to share information and support each other in strategies which meet their actual conditions of use.
- Recognizes that the realities of poverty, class, racism, social isolation, past trauma, sex-based discrimination and other social inequalities affect both people's vulnerability to and capacity for effectively dealing with drug-related harm.
- Does not attempt to minimize or ignore the real and tragic harm and danger associated with licit and illicit drug use.

■ Community-Based Drug Prevention

Community-based programs are very broad and take into account the community's youth, parents, businesses, media, schools, law enforcement, religious or fraternal groups, civic or volunteer groups, health-care professionals, and government agencies with expertise in the field of substance abuse. The primary goal of community-based prevention is to provide coordinated programs among the numerous agencies and organizations involved in prevention.

Prevention requires communities to conduct a structured review of current prevention programs to determine (1) whether the programs in place were examined and tested according to rigorous scientific standards during their development and (2) whether these programs incorporate the basic principles of prevention that have been identified in research. Usually, prevention programs at the community level ask the following questions (Robertson et al. and NIDA 2003; Sloboda and David 1999):

- Does the program have components for the individual, the family, the school, the media, community organizations, and healthcare providers? Are the program components well integrated in theme and content so that they reinforce rather than duplicate one another?
- Does the prevention program use media and community education strategies to increase public awareness, attracting community support, reinforcing the school-based curriculum for students and parents, and keeping the public informed of the program's progress?
- Are interventions carefully designed to reach different at-risk populations, and are they of sufficient duration to make an impact?
- Does the program follow a structured organizational plan that progresses from needs assessment through planning, implementation, and review to refinement, with feedback to and from the community at all stages?
- Are the objectives and activities specific, time-limited, feasible (in terms of available resources), and integrated so that they work together across program components and can be used to evaluate program progress and outcomes?

Often, these programs set up prevention policy boards to oversee planning and implementation. Boards should include representatives from law enforcement, juvenile justice, education, recreation, social services, private industry, health and mental health agencies, churches, civic organizations, and other community agencies that serve youth and families. They should also include one or several youth members. "The community can be a target group, especially when there is extensive community denial or lack of awareness, lack of clear policies, poor law enforcement, and so on. Public awareness campaigns, political action, and similar efforts are appropriate at this level of prevention" (Tinzmann and Hixson 1992, pp. 2, 3).

Community prevention programs can also direct their attention to changing the legal and social environment regarding alcohol, tobacco, and other drug (**ATOD**) supplies and toward youth (Center for Prevention Research and Development [CPRD] 2000). This effort also includes individual and environmental strategies. For example, an environmental approach to reducing underage drinking might involve training clerks to insist on proper age identification when selling alcoholic beverages. An individual approach might involve education efforts, such as a media campaign, aimed at discouraging young people from drinking (Silver Gate Group and Robert Wood Johnson Foundation 2001).

Other community-based strategies include the following:

- Strengthening the enforcement of existing legal regulations of ATOD sales and use
- Educating merchants and servers about alcohol and tobacco sales laws
- Regulating legislation regarding the sale of alcohol and tobacco to minors
- Implementing use and lose laws, which allow for the suspension of the driver's license of a person younger than 21 years of age following a conviction for any alcohol or drug violation (e.g., use, possession, or attempt to purchase with or without false identification)
- Imposing regulations on location and density of retail outlets—that is, monitoring the number of unsupervised vending machines dispensing cigarettes to minors in a given community and monitoring the number of retail establishments selling alcohol and tobacco near schools

Community-based prevention programs recently have been endorsed, supported as not only viable but also as cost-effective:

Drug use prevention programmes are effective when they respond to the needs of a community, involve all the relevant sectors, and are based on evidence; effective programmes should also incorporate strong monitoring and evaluation components. Such programmes are also cost effective. . . . If other costs to society were to be counted, such as the costs resulting from crime, unemployment, and ill health, the cost effectiveness of good drug use prevention

programmes is likely to be even greater. (United Nations Office on Drugs and Crime [UNDOC] 2011)

A community-based organization that has to be mentioned is Community Anti-Drug Coalitions of America (CADCA), which was organized in 1992. This organization

. . . has been training local grassroots groups, known as community anti-drug coalitions, in effective problem-solving strategies, teaching them how to assess their local substance abuse-related problems, identify root causes and local conditions and develop comprehensive plans to address them. Today, CADCA is the nation's leading national substance abuse prevention organization, representing the interests of thousands of community coalitions in the United States and around the world. (Community Anti-Drug Coalitions of America [CADCA] 2010)

CADCA's reach includes more than 5000 community coalitions and their affiliates across the United States, and a growing number of community groups around the world. It has 2000 dues-paying members and 17,000 subscribers to its e-newsletter; trains thousands of leaders, members, and volunteers; and even airs a televised program (CADCA TV) that reaches approximately 2.6 million households (CADCA 2010).

The core services that CADCA provides include:

- Training and technical assistance
- Dissemination and coalition relations
- Research and evaluation
- Public policy and advocacy
- Membership and communicating
- Special events and conferences
- International programs (CADCA 2010)

In conclusion, community prevention emphasizes comprehensive drug abuse prevention programs that include multiple components, such as the use of media, drug education in schools, parent education, community organizations, and formulation of drug-related health policy. In essence, community drug prevention seeks to reduce drug abuse by informing, coordinating, and decreasing the level of drug use at the community level.

KEY TERMS

ATOD
alcohol, tobacco, and other drugs

■ School-Based Drug Prevention

Education has been used extensively in the past to control the use and abuse of drugs, especially alcohol and tobacco. Drug education actually began in the late 1800s, when most states required that the harmful effects of certain drugs be taught. An example of an early educational attempt to curb or stop drug abuse is the temperance movement in the late 19th century. The Women's Christian Temperance Union (WCTU) and the Anti-Saloon League taught that alcohol consumption was harmful and contrary to Christian morality.

Years ago, when drug prevention was first attempted, most substance abuse experts thought that schools should be responsible for educating the public about the dangerous use and eventual abuse of drugs because education is school's main objective. Schools began teaching about drug use, but in the beginning, drug prevention focused on individual factors, such as the dangers of particular types of drugs, the dangers of trusting individuals who sell drugs, and other scare tactics. One problem with this approach was that students varied enormously with regard to their drug experiences. Often, the students had already tried the dangerous drugs and had experienced only pleasurable effects with few negative consequences. Their experiences occurred before their exposure to drug prevention programs that relied on negative information, which is generally known as the **scare tactic approach**. Many self-reported use surveys revealed that these programs were not successful. With such audiences of drug users, the warnings are short lived, not believed, or perceived as exaggerations. Today the use of evidence-based drug education is ". . . based on life skills that offer personal, social, resistance and communication skills, as well as information about the short-term effects of drugs through a series of sessions offered by trained teachers" (UNDOC 2011).

Table 17.2 summarizes the most popular, common, school-based drug prevention programs by including the premise, strategies, and effectiveness of the following approaches: (1) cognitive, (2) affec-

tive, (3) combined cognitive and affective, (4) social learning/cognitive-behavioral, and (5) normative education. Table 17.2 also details the strengths (if any) and weaknesses of each approach.

Finally, two recent very successful school drug prevention programs that "speak" to their audiences are the Athletes Training and Learning to Avoid Steroids (ATLAS) for males and Athletes Targeting Healthy Exercise and Nutrition Alternatives (ATHENA) for females. These two programs target teenage athletes and specifically focus on addressing steroid abuse and other unhealthy behaviors (e.g., drinking and driving). These two programs leverage the influence of coaches and peer groups to highlight proper sports nutrition, strength training, and other positive alternatives to using drugs to improve performance and build confidence. ATLAS and ATHENA have now been adopted by schools in 29 states and Puerto Rico, and have been endorsed by Congress as exemplary prevention programs (NIDA 2007).

Curriculum-Based Drug Education Objectives

In an effort to educate students about the dangers of drug use, school-based drug education programs and objectives have been implemented in most U.S. school curriculums. Specific educational topics have been established for elementary, junior high, and senior high and college levels.

Elementary level:

- Drugs versus poisons
- Effects of alcohol, tobacco, and marijuana on the body
- Differences between candy and drugs
- Drug overdoses
- Dangers of experimentation
- How to say "no" to peers offering drugs
- Reasons for taking drugs: curing illness, pleasure, escape, parental use, and ceremony

Junior high level:

- How peer pressure works
- How to say "no" to peer pressure
- How drugs affect the body, physiologically and psychologically
- Where to seek help when needed
- Attitudes toward drug use
- How to have fun without drugs
- Harmful effects of tobacco, alcohol, and marijuana on the body
- Stress management and building positive self-esteem

KEY TERMS

scare tactic approach
drug prevention information based on emphasizing the extreme negative effects of drug use—scaring the audience of potential and current drug users/abusers into not using drugs

Table 17.2 **Summary of Common School-Based Drug Prevention Approaches**

APPROACH	PREMISE	STRATEGIES	EFFECTIVENESS
Cognitive	If youths understand the dangers of AOD, they will not use them.	Teach pharmacology of alcohol and other drugs, how they are used, long-range consequences of use—usually through scare tactics.	Seldom effective; sometimes detrimental—arouses curiosity and encourages experimentation. Dire facts are not credible; knowledge alone does not counteract peer pressure. Knowledge is necessary, but not sufficient; focus on more immediate physical/social consequences may work.
Affective	High self-esteem, values consistent with nonuse, and good problem-solving and decision-making skills help youth avoid AOD.	Raise self-esteem. Teach values and life skills. Typically, do not include AOD information.	Do not decrease rate of use. Some community members and parents protest teaching values and decision making. Need to include AOD information.
Combined cognitive and affective	Students need both information and life skills to avoid AOD use.	Teach problem-solving, decision-making, peer pressure resistance skills; and provide explicit information about AOD to connect life skills and AOD use and consequences.	Little consistent effect on reducing AOD use, although some successes have been reported.
Social learning/ cognitive-behavioral approach	AOD use usually begins in a social setting between grades 5 and 9, usually with peers, but sometimes adults; youth need skills for resisting these pressures. (Based on Bandura's social learning theory.)	Teach how to identify pressures from peers, media, advertising, families. Teach resistance skills, model counterarguments. Students role play pressure situations and actively practice resisting.	Sometimes effective, especially if peers are involved in instruction and when students already have other fairly well-developed social skills. Little evidence that effects last.
Normative education approach	Youth overestimate the extent of AOD use among peers and thus may use AOD to feel part of the group.	Correct misconceptions, demonstrate actual norms through discussion, develop nonuse norms.	Success with some drugs; not very effective with alcohol. Some youngsters may believe that fewer peers use AOD than actually do, and may come to feel AOD use is more acceptable than they did before entering the program.

AOD, alcohol and other drugs.

Source: U.S. Department of Health and Human Services, Office of Substance Abuse Prevention. "Factors that Influence Alcohol and Other Drug Use." In *Prevention Plus II: Tools for Creating and Sustaining Drug-Free Communities* (Figure 2.1, p. 19). DHHS Publication No. 89-1649. Rockville, MD: Author, 1989. Distributed by the National Clearinghouse for Alcohol and Drug Information.

- How advertisers push drugs
- Consequences of breaking drug laws
- Differences between wine, beer, and distilled spirits
- Family drug use
- Family drinking problems and family members who may have drug addiction problems
- Images of violence and drug use in rock and rap music
- Teenage drug abuse and associated problems

Senior high and college level:

- Responsible use of medications
- How drugs affect the body and the mind
- Legal versus illegal drugs
- Drinking and driving
- Drug effects on the fetus
- Recreational drug use
- Ways of coping with problems: anger and stress management
- How to detect problem drug users
- Drug education, prevention, and treatment
- Positive and negative role models
- How to build positive self-esteem
- Criminal sanctions for various types of drug use
- Binge drinking
- Drugs and driving
- Date rape
- Addiction to drugs and alcoholism

Principal Questions for School-Based Programs

The following questions should be asked to improve the outcomes of drug education programs:

- Do the school-based programs reach children from kindergarten through high school? If not, do they at least reach children during the critical middle school or junior high years?
- Do the programs contain multiple years of intervention (all through the middle school or junior high years)?
- Do the programs use a well-tested, standardized intervention with detailed lesson plans and student materials?
- Do the programs use age-appropriate interactive teaching methods (modeling, role-playing, discussion, group feedback, reinforcement, extended practice)?
- Do the programs foster social bonding to the school and community?
- Do the programs teach social competence (communication, self-efficacy, assertiveness) and drug resistance skills that are culturally and developmentally appropriate?

- Do the programs promote positive peer influence?
- Do the programs promote antidrug social norms?
- Do the programs emphasize skills-training teaching methods?
- Do the programs include an adequate "dosage" (10–15 sessions in year 1 and another 10–15 booster sessions)?
- Is there periodic evaluation to determine whether the programs are effective?

■ Family-Based Prevention Programs

Primary family risk factors that predispose youth to find drugs attractive include the following:

- Chaotic home environments, particularly in which parents abuse substances or suffer from mental illnesses
- Ineffective parenting, especially with children with difficult temperaments and conduct disorders
- Lack of mutual attachments and nurturing

"Results from longitudinal studies of children, particularly those children most at risk for problems, indicate that families can protect children and youth against drug use and abuse through effective family management practices that impart skills young people can use in resisting social pressures to use drugs" (National Institutes of Health [NIH] and NIDA 1998, p. 49).

If the just-listed risk factors are the primary risk factors, *protective factors*—the factors that can insulate against drug use—include the following:

- Strong parent–child bonds
- Parental monitoring with clear rules of conduct within the family unit and involvement of parents in the lives of their children
- Open communication of values within the family
- High levels of supervision and monitoring
- No inconsistent disciplining from lackadaisical to extreme enforcement of rules and no saying one thing and then doing another
- Consistent high levels of parental warmth, affection, and emotional support

In addition, research shows that protective family factors can moderate the effects of risk factors. The risk of associating with peers who use drugs can be offset by protective family factors, such as parent conventionality, maternal adjustment, and strong parent–child attachment.

Prevention at the family level needs to stress parent–child interaction strategies, communication skills, child management practices, and family management skills. Research has also shown that parents need to take a more active role in their children's lives. This includes talking to their children about drugs, monitoring their activities, getting to know their friends, and understanding their problems and personal concerns (NIH and NIDA 1998).

Prevention Principles for Family-Based Programs

In conclusion, family-based prevention programs need to do the following:

- Reach families of children at each stage of development.
- Train parents in behavioral skills to:
  - Reduce conduct problems in children.
  - Improve parent–child relations, including positive reinforcement, listening and communication skills, and problem solving.
  - Provide consistent discipline and rule making.
  - Monitor children's activities during adolescence.
- Include an educational component for parents with drug information for them and their children.
- Focus on families whose children are in kindergarten through 12th grade to enhance protective factors.
- Provide access to counseling services for families at risk.

Drug Prevention Programs in Higher Education

The seriousness of alcohol and other drug use on college campuses is underscored by the following findings (Phoenix House 2000):

- According to the Core Institute, an organization that surveys college drinking practices, 300,000 of today's college students will eventually die of alcohol-related causes, such as drunken driving accidents, cirrhosis of the liver, various cancers, and heart disease.
- Of today's first-year college students, 159,000 will drop out of school next year because of alcohol or other drug-related reasons.

- Almost one third of college students admit to having missed at least one class because of their alcohol or drug use.
- One night of heavy drinking can impair a person's ability to think abstractly for up to 30 days, limiting the ability to relate textbook reading to classroom discussions or to think through processes such as football plays.

As we can see, the use of alcohol and other drugs is a serious problem within the college or university environment. Major problems on college campuses resulting from such drug abuse include property damage, poor academic performance, damaged relationships, unprotected sexual activity, physical injuries, date rape, and suicide (Perkins 1997).

It is obvious that with all these negative findings regarding alcohol and other drug use on college campuses, prevention programs are vital. Next, we review the major prevention programs that currently exist in higher education.

■ Overview and Critique of Existing Prevention Programs

Information-Only or Awareness Model

One of the earliest preventive interventions, this model is based on the belief that if people are given extensive information about the harmful effects of drugs, it will change their attitudes about use and abuse. This model assumes that people are rational enough to seriously curtail or stop drug use based on information. Obviously, today we know that, at most, the majority of drug users exposed to the **information-only or awareness model** become more knowledgeable about the effects of drugs, but this approach has very little influence on the use of habitual or addictive-type drugs.

Attitude Change or Affective Education Model

The **attitude change or affective education model** assumes that people use drugs because they have poor self-esteem (Gonzalez and Clement 1994). As a result, prevention focuses on strengthening self-image, building up positive self-esteem, and boosting self-confidence. A problem with this model is that attitudes often are resistant to change and fluctuate depending on such environmental influences as peer and party settings. Attitudes that were formed in an educational setting (drug and alcohol classes) are abandoned in substance use settings.

Social Influences Model

The **social influences model** assumes that substance abuse results from multiple influences. Although outside influences are perceived as major influences, inner influences, such as prior socialization, a vulnerability to pleasing others, and a need to be accepted by friends and peers, are likewise taken into account. This prevention strategy emphasizes peer resistance and inoculation techniques. Techniques primarily include the following (Gonzalez and Clement 1994):

- Offering factual information about the consequences of drug use
- Guiding development of skills to recognize outer and inner pressures to use drugs, and methods and techniques to resist usage
- Communicating correct information about the extent of drug use by students of similar ages
- Modeling, rehearsing, and reinforcing skills for resisting drugs when friends or peers expect compliance
- Persuading students to try these resistance approaches and techniques in classroom or group settings and in peer group settings away from the classroom

By far, this method has been more successful than the information-only and attitude change models. Although it works best when it begins at the junior high school level, refresher courses should be administered at least every 2 years. Some research findings indicate that although this method is least effective with alcohol consumption, it is effective

with marijuana and cigarette smoking (Gonzalez and Clement 1994).

Ecological or Person-in-Environment Model

This model is one of the newest types of prevention programs. "Interventions based on this model have multiple components and are designed to address individuals and the policies, practices, and social norms that affect students on campuses or in the community" (Gonzalez and Clement 1994, p. 3). Developed from human ecology, the **ecological or person-in-environment model** stresses that change(s) in the environment change people. Although the ecological or person-in-environment model does not ignore substance use from individual causes, such as personal beliefs and perception of risk, it does primarily focus on the causes from the social environment (Hansen 1997, p. 6). "The central tenet [belief] of social ecology is that individual behavior is mainly the result of socialization; to change the behavior, we must change the social institutions that shape it" (Hansen 1997, p. 6). Hansen also stated "the strongest predictors of alcohol and drug abuse among young people are social" (p. 6).

This perspective emphasizes that it is important to take into account all of the environments that may have an impact on drug use. Friends, acquaintances, roommates, and classmates in dorms, sororities, and fraternities, at parties, cafes, and nightspots can influence students (U.S. Department of Education 1994).

As a result, this model advocates the following drug prevention strategies (Gonzalez and Clement 1994):

- Dissemination of drug information
- Cognitive and behavioral skills training for youth, parents, and professionals
- Mass media programming
- Development of grassroots citizen interest groups
- Leadership training for key organization and community officials
- Policy analysis and reformulation

In applying this model to the college campus, we find that college campuses have long served as an environment for initiating and perpetuating drug use and abuse. Fraternity drunkenness, for example, was decried as early as 1840 (Horowitz 1987). In 1988, an 18-year-old student attending Rutgers

KEY TERMS

social influences model
assumes that drug users lack resistance skills

ecological or person-in-environment model
stresses that changes in the environment change people's attitudes about drugs

University died of alcohol poisoning at a fraternity party. In a television interview following the incident, then-Chancellor Edward Bloustein described fraternities as "organized conspiracies dedicated to the consumption of alcohol" (Hansen 1997, p. 5).

Using the ecological or person-in-environment model as a preventative measure can alleviate drug use and abuse on college campuses, lessening the vast majority of vandalism, fights, accidents, sexually transmitted infections, unplanned pregnancies, racial bias incidents, date rape, and at least one-third of academic attrition often caused by drug use and abuse (Koss, Gidycz, and Wisniewski 1987). Although campus prevention programs and research date back several decades, such efforts remained isolated and sporadic until the late 1970s. All campuses now have medium to extensive alcohol and other drug prevention programs in effect. Tailoring this type of prevention on college environments is certainly worthy of consideration.

Examples of Large-Scale Drug Prevention Programs

BACCHUS Peer Education Network

In 1975, an organization known as Boosting Alcohol Consciousness Concerning the Health of University Students (BACCHUS) was developed as a national student organization. Soon BACCHUS realized that many of its affiliates were members of sororities and fraternities; therefore, it renamed the organization, then known as BACCHUS and GAMMA (Greeks Advocating Mature Management of Alcohol), to the **BACCHUS Network** effective July 1, 2005. Today there are "more than 32,000 student leaders and advisors who work with over eight million peers on more than 900 campuses throughout the world . . . The BACCHUS Network is a university and community-based network focusing on comprehensive health and safety initiatives" (BACCHUS Network 2007, 2011).

The original goal of this program was to prevent alcohol abuse. Today, the program has broadened its goals to include other student health and safety issues, such as sexual responsibility, tobacco use, marijuana use, and sexual assault. The organization devotes a substantial portion of its resources and activities to the following goals on university-affiliated campuses:

- Create and foster a thriving network of institutions and young adult–led peer education groups supporting health and safety initiatives
- Empower students and administrators to voice their opinions and needs to create healthier and safer campus communities
- Develop and promote cutting edge resources and health promotion campaigns that support peer education, campus leadership, and activism on health and safety issues
- Provide exceptional conferencing and training opportunities for students, young adults, and professionals to support health and safety strategies
- Encourage national forums on young adult health and safety concerns
- Promote and disseminate research and effective strategies that better help campuses and communities address health and safety issues
- Advocate for effective and sensible policies and practices for campus and community health and safety issues (BACCHUS Network 2007, 2011)

The BACCHUS philosophy is that students can play a uniquely effective role—unmatched by professional educators—in encouraging their peers to consider, talk honestly about, and develop responsible habits and attitudes toward high-risk health and safety issues. The organization now hosts four web sites to assist students in their prevention efforts. Bacchusnetwork.org contains information about the organization's activities, services, conferences, campaigns, and resource materials. Smartersex.org addresses sexual health, features an "Ask the Sexpert" area, and offers complete information on sexually transmitted infections, HIV, abstinence, and birth control. TobaccofreeU.org contains complete information on tobacco control, prevention, and cessation. Friendsdrivesober.org is the newest addition to the network, and focuses primarily on highway safety and preventing impaired driving (BACCHUS Network 2007). The network:

. . . is a university- and community-based network focusing on comprehensive health and

KEY TERMS

BACCHUS Network
a national and international association of college and university peer education programs focused on alcohol abuse prevention and other related student health and safety issues

safety initiatives. It is the mission of this . . . nonprofit organization to actively promote student- and young adult-based, campus- and community-wide leadership on healthy and safe lifestyle decisions concerning alcohol abuse, tobacco use, illegal drug use, unhealthy sexual practices, and other high-risk behaviors. (BACCHUS Network 2007, p. 1)

Fund for the Improvement of Postsecondary Education Drug Prevention Programs

In 1987, a huge explosion of campus drug prevention programs began. It was sparked by a $14 billion annual budget for college drug prevention placed in the Drug-Free Schools and Communities Act of 1986 (now titled the Safe and Free Schools and Communities Act). The funding was parceled out by the Department of Education, Fund for the Improvement of Postsecondary Education (FIPSE). FIPSE Drug Prevention Programs awarded about 100 grants per year from 1987 until 1996 via a grant competition that called for colleges to mount institution-wide programs. The guiding philosophy included the following points:

- A small, isolated program was seen as making little difference, but a comprehensive program reaching into several areas of the institution could send many consistent anti-use messages that would eventually reach critical mass and change the campus environment.
- There should be well-known, top-down administrative support for prevention programming.
- There should be well-written and carefully implemented policies about chemical use on campus.

The hundreds of new programs, whose administrators met and interacted in annual grantee conferences, generated the sense that there was a national prevention movement in higher education. The Network of Colleges and Universities Dedicated to Prevention of Alcohol and Other Drug Abuse was founded, incorporating 900 institutions. The network is supported by the Higher Education Center for Alcohol and Other Drug Prevention funded by the U.S. Department of Education, which provides a range of materials and newsletters (Ryan, Colthurst, and Segars 1995).

In 1989, FIPSE initiated a grant program for regional campus prevention consortia. By joining a consortium, colleges and universities could pool scarce resources, create support networks, and train new workers. In 1994, more than 100 regional consortia were listed on a database maintained by the Higher Education Center. In 1999, more than two-thirds of all 3300 institutions of higher education were affiliates of the network, belonged to a regional consortium, or had started other programs under the aegis of FIPSE.

From more than a decade of experience, several exemplary approaches emerged. These strategies might be the predominant focus of a program or one of a number of complementary components of a comprehensive effort. The strategies are addressed next.

Peer-Based Efforts

Student peers can be involved in a number of ways: as educators, mentors, counselors, or facilitators of prevention and outreach work. Such an approach multiplies manpower tremendously, reaches the students who are apt to become lost in the flow, is not perceived as an outside or authoritarian intrusion, speaks the language of students, and works to change the predominant cultural tone on campus. Peers can conduct classroom presentations, work informational tables or drop-in centers, create prevention newsletters, and establish links to community groups. It is important to carefully train and supervise peer facilitators. Many peer programs are residence hall based, taking advantage of the training of residence hall assistants and peer facilitators (BACCHUS and GAMMA 1994).

Curriculum Infusion

Infusion of a skill or topic across the curriculum has been used in conjunction with classes on writing skills, gender issues, and other areas. Curriculum infusion can be undertaken at individual institutions or as a consortium project. The advantage of curriculum infusion is that it involves faculty members, achieves open discussion of drug issues in the classroom as part of the normal educational process, and stimulates critical thinking about drug issues.

Improvisational Theater Groups

Improvisational theater groups that tackle health and wellness issues can be lively, stimulating, and provocative, often breaking through peer and institutional denial and bringing issues home to students with a dramatic emotional impact. Improvisational topics can include date rape, sexually transmitted disease, children of alcoholics on campus, and denial of chemical dependency.

Strategies to Change Misperceptions of Use

Social psychologists Alan Berkowitz and Wesley Perkins, both of Hobart and William Smith Colleges, have conducted influential research illustrating that students often have incorrect estimates (exaggerated misperceptions) of drug use by their peers (Perkins 1991, 1997; Perkins and Berkowitz 1986). Thus, they misperceive the peer norms governing drug use, which may lead them to follow imaginary peers. This idea is a modification of the traditional understanding that peers influence peers. It follows logically that activities demonstrating the accurate use pattern to students and correcting misperceptions will indirectly affect overall use patterns. These efforts have included simply publicizing the results of alcohol and drug use surveys and awarding prizes for coming up with correct estimates.

Alternative Events

Alternative events, such as alcohol-free cocktail parties ("mocktail" parties), alcohol-free discos, and indoor rock climbing, especially as alternatives to presporting events and holiday parties, help avoid some events that are traditionally associated with chemical abuse.

Programs That Change Marketing of Alcohol on and Near Campuses

Institutions of higher education are a major focus of alcohol marketing. Alcoholic beverage producers sponsor many campus events, and these companies buy considerable newspaper advertising. One report indicates,

> Alcohol advertising is pervasive in college sporting events. According to a recent report in *USA Today*, "NCAA tournament games led all other sports events in alcohol-related TV advertising in 2002, with 939 ads costing $28 million. That compares with a combined 925 ads aired during the Super Bowl, World Series, college bowl games and the NFL's Monday Night Football." (StateUniversity.com 2011, p. 1).

Finally, it is better to embed prevention messages within an overall wellness perspective. Students are concerned about health and wellness issues, not programs that come off as dogmatic or preachy, moralizing, exaggerating, and nagging—perhaps reminding them of life at home.

■ Drug Abuse Resistance Education (D.A.R.E.)

One major drug prevention program that had high hopes for success was the school-based drug education programs incorporated into our nation's school districts—**Drug Abuse Resistance Education (D.A.R.E.)**.

Established in 1983, D.A.R.E. operates in about 80 percent of all school districts across the United States and in numerous foreign countries. In addition to the D.A.R.E. elementary school curriculum, the D.A.R.E. program includes middle school and high school curricula that reinforce lessons taught at the elementary school level. "In fiscal year 2000, the Department of Justice's Bureau of Justice Assistance, which supports various substance abuse prevention programs for youth, provided about $2 million for D.A.R.E. regional training centers to support the training of new police officers that help deliver the D.A.R.E. program lessons" (quoted from U.S. Government Accountability Office (GAO) in Common Sense for Drug Policy 2009).

D.A.R.E. reports that the program "has proven so successful that it is now being implemented in 75 percent [currently it is 80%] of our nation's school districts and in more than 43 countries around the world" (D.A.R.E. America 1996). Recent evaluations of this program show that, on a short-term basis, D.A.R.E. improved students' views of themselves and increased their sense of personal responsibility. However, the program has *not* yielded a measurable, significant change in drug use (Rosenbaum and Hanson 1998; Vogt 2003, p. 1). Moreover, this drug education program showed a strong inconsistency between students' self-reported attitudes about use and actual drug use (Clayton et al. 1991; Ennett et al. 1994; Vogt 2003). See "Holding the Line: Frustrating and Dubious Results from National Drug Prevention Campaigns and Programs" for more information on D.A.R.E. and several other programs that attempt to prevent drug use.

One major problem is that "over the past decade, a flurry of studies—by the U.S. surgeon general and the General Accounting Office, among others—found no significant difference in

KEY TERMS

Drug Abuse Resistance Education (D.A.R.E.)
drug education program presented in elementary and junior high schools nationwide by police officers

Holding the Line

Frustrating and Dubious Results from National Drug Prevention Campaigns and Programs

In 1995, a disturbing study published by a group of researchers at the University of Michigan and backed by the U.S. Department of Health and Human Services (DHHS) and the National Institute on Drug Abuse (NIDA) showed that the use of illicit drugs by young people had been rising steadily since 1992. The results of this study were even more perplexing because overall drug use had been declining over the same period. The increase was happening despite several seemingly successful efforts to combat drug abuse with high-powered prevention programs.

Since the 1980s, most funds allocated for drug prevention have been spent in three areas: criminal justice, major advertising campaigns, and D.A.R.E. Law enforcement professionals who work with hard-core addicts, especially in poor urban neighborhoods, have favored compulsory preventive programs. According to William N. Brownsberger, former Assistant State Attorney General in the Massachusetts Narcotics and Special Investigations Division, addicts who are forced against their will to enter and remain in therapy can overcome their addiction. Roughly 90% of all addicts are arrested at least once every year, giving the criminal justice system plenty of opportunities to help them kick their habits.

One highly visible persuasive effort to end drug abuse has been the advertising campaign created by the Partnership for a Drug-Free America. The nation's advertising industry developed the partnership and funded it by collaborating with advertisers and a variety of health and educational agencies. The goal was to promote images designed to make drug use look "uncool," especially to younger people. In addition to the creative services donated by advertising agencies, media organizations donated more than $2 billion of public service and advertising space to the partnership between the late 1980s and 1990s.

In the early 1990s, the partnership commissioned surveys to measure the effect of its media campaign on students in the Los Angeles and New York City school systems. On both coasts, increased exposure to the partnership's messages appeared to dramatically change students' attitudes toward drugs. At the same time, however, the number of students who admitted using drugs actually increased.

Another high-visibility persuasive effort has been the nationwide D.A.R.E. program, which was launched in Los Angeles in 1983. "D.A.R.E.'s curriculum reflects mainstream theories about the best way to reduce drinking, smoking, and drug use by children. . . . The program began as collaboration between the Los Angeles Police Department and the city's school district" (Miller 2001, p. A14). Using role-playing techniques and resistance training, uniformed police officers become social workers, talking with students in their classrooms, educating them about the dangers of drugs, and giving them the tools to resist temptation or peer pressure. They generally teach 17 classroom sessions.

Today most school-based prevention programs, including D.A.R.E., assume that adolescents need grown-ups' help in resisting social pressures to use [drugs]. Therefore, they try to correct children's exaggerated beliefs about the prevalence of drug use among their peers. They offer them information about the physical and social effects of using and they try to impart "resistance skills" for making and acting on thoughtful decisions. (Miller 2001, p. A14)

Although D.A.R.E. is the most popular drug education program ever developed for children, increasing numbers of critics claim that its benefits, if any, are short lasting. Most D.A.R.E. training begins in the fifth grade. At this age, students accept most of what they hear. By middle school, however, the effectiveness of D.A.R.E. begins to erode. By high school, many students resist participation in the program. According to a researcher from the Research Triangle Institute in Durham, North Carolina, which conducted a $300,000 study on the impact of D.A.R.E., "Unless there's some sort of booster session that reinforces the original curriculum, the effects of most drug use prevention programs decay rather than increase over time." The findings of numerous research studies conducted on D.A.R.E.'s effectiveness suggest that D.A.R.E. students were no less likely to use drugs than students who had not gone through the program (Ennett et al. 1994; Vogt 2003, p. 3). Some have even claimed that the D.A.R.E. program teaches kids to become curious about illicit drug use or actually motivates them to do drugs (Vogt 2003, p. 3).

Another major negative finding came from the U.S. Government Accountability Office (GAO), which released a review of current research findings regarding alcohol and other drug abuse prevention programs, particularly D.A.R.E., in 2003. In brief, the six long-term evaluations of the D.A.R.E. elementary school curriculum that we reviewed found no significant differences in illicit drug use between students who received D.A.R.E. in the fifth or sixth grade (the intervention group) and students who did not (the control group).

**Frustrating and Dubious Results from National
Drug Prevention Campaigns and Programs (*continued*)**

Three of the evaluations reported that the control groups of students were provided other drug use prevention education. All of the evaluations suggested that D.A.R.E. had no statistically significant long-term effect on preventing youth illicit drug use. Of the six evaluations we reviewed, five also reported on students' attitudes toward illicit drug use and resistance to peer pressure and found no significant differences between the intervention and control groups over the long term. Two of these evaluations found that the D.A.R.E. students showed stronger negative attitudes about illicit drug use and improved social skills about illicit drug use about 1 year after receiving the program. These positive effects diminished over time (U.S. Government Accountability Office [GAO] 2003, p. 2).

In this same report, seven school districts using the D.A.R.E. program were intensely analyzed. The findings indicated that "No statistically significant differences were observed between the intervention and control schools on students' past year marijuana use 2 years after the intervention" (GAO 2003, p. 5).

Further, "[a]s D.A.R.E. America celebrated its 20th anniversary, the nation's most widely used school-based drug prevention program was struggling with a credibility crisis that has devastated the organization financially and threatens its survival" (Vogt 2003). Reports indicate that a number of school districts throughout the country have abandoned the program, finding D.A.R.E. to be ineffective in curbing both licit and illicit drug use.

In light of the diminishing returns from various drug prevention programs, in late 1996 the former Clinton administration proposed a compulsory drug test for teenagers who are applying for their driver's licenses. Like everything else, the proposal had both supporters and critics. Although this tactic may be part of the answer, prevention programs that have measurable, long-lasting effects remain difficult to find.

Sources: Brownsberger, W. N. "Just Say 'Criminal Justice.' " *Boston Globe* (20 October 1996); Ennett, S. T., N. S. Tobler, C. L. Ringwalt, and R. L. Flewelling. "How Effective Is Drug Abuse Resistance Education? A Metaanalysis of Project D.A.R.E. Outcome Evaluations." *American Journal of Public Health* 84 (1994): 1394–1401; Gordon, P. "The Truth About D.A.R.E." *Buzz Magazine* (July 1996); Gordon, P. "Can Madison Avenue Really Save America by Making Illegal Drugs Totally Uncool?" *Buzz Magazine* (August 1996); Miller, D. W. "D.A.R.E. Reinvents Itself—With Help from Its Social-Scientist Critics." *Chronicle of Higher Education* 48 (19 October 2001): A12–A14; U.S. Government Accountability Office (GAO). *Youth Illicit Drug Use Prevention: D.A.R.E. Long-Term Evaluation and Federal Efforts to Identify Effective Programs.* GAO-03-172R. Washington, DC: U.S. Government Accountability Office (GAO), 15 January 2003; and Vogt, A. "Now Many 'Just Say No' to D.A.R.E." *Chicago Tribune* (26 January 2003): 1, 3.

drug use between D.A.R.E. graduates and students never exposed to the curriculum" (Vogt 2003, p. 1). Further, regarding graduates of the D.A.R.E. program, one official said, "I can't tell you how many kids told me D.A.R.E. introduced them to drugs. The problem with D.A.R.E., other than that it's a multimillion dollar conglomerate in the business of selling T-shirts, is that it takes the burden off parents to raise their kids [drug free]" (Vogt 2003, p. 3).

Another major problem that has been identified is that the D.A.R.E. drug education program is presented in the classroom by fully uniformed police officers. Although the officers are well intentioned and their efforts are commendable, they are hardly a mechanism for transmitting new norms that would find converts among students, except perhaps those already successfully socialized (Gopelrud 1991). More importantly, uniformed police officers used as teachers "sends the wrong message that drugs are a law enforcement issue, rather than a public health issue" (Zeese and Lewin 1998, p. 1).

Drug Courts

Although these courts of law vary in organization, in scope, and at what point intervention occurs, the underlying premise is that drug possession and use is not only a law enforcement/criminal justice problem, but also a public health problem (Sherin and Mahoney 1996). In *drug court programs,* criminal justice agencies collaborate closely with the substance abuse treatment community and other societal institutions to design and operate the program. Thus, the key goal is to divert substance abusers into supervised community treatment centers in an attempt to eliminate the destructive behavior. A committee usually composed of a judge, the district attorney, a public defender, the probation department, and treatment center officials determines whether treatment is needed and the type and length of treatment. A recent review of drug courts emphasizes that today such courts use a multidisciplinary team approach "The most effective Drug Courts require regular attendance by the judge, defense counsel, prosecutor, treatment providers and law enforcement officers at staff meetings and status hearings" (Marlowe 2010, p. 4, quoting Cary et al. 2008).

At the first National Drug Court Conference, one researcher reported, "These courts rely on strong collaboration among judges, prosecutors, defense lawyers, and related supporting agencies (such as case management, corrections, pretrial services, probation), on the one hand, and a partnership with treatment agencies (or providers) and other community organizations and representatives on the other" (Goldkamp 1993, p. 33). The treatment phase generally consists of: (1) detoxification (removal of physical dependence on drugs from the body), (2) stabilization (treating the psychological craving for the drug), and (3) after-care (helping the defendant obtain education or job training, find a job, and remain drug free) (Office of Justice Programs [OJP] 2000).

Currently, there are 2559 drug courts in the United States, serving over 120,000 people, including 482 juvenile, 272 family, and 24 combined (juvenile and family) drug courts and 83 fully operational tribal drug courts, with 35 tribal drug courts that were in planning stages, as of June 2009 (National Criminal Justice Reference Service [NCJRS] 2010). "Drug courts exist at numerous entry points throughout the justice system" (National Association of Drug Court Professionals [NADCP] 2011b). The following drug court models are currently in existence:

- Adult drug court
- Veterans treatment court
- Driving while under the influence court
- Family dependency treatment court (family drug court)
- Federal district drug court (federal reentry court)
- Juvenile drug court
- Reentry drug court
- Tribal healing to wellness court
- Back on TRAC: treatment, responsibility, accountability on campus

Eligible drug addicts can be sent to drug court instead of moving through the traditional justice system. Drug courts put individuals in treatment and closely supervise them throughout the process. For a minimum term of one year, participants are (NADCP 2011c):

- Provided with intensive treatment and other services they require to get and stay clean and sober;
- Held accountable by the Drug Court judge for meeting their obligations to the court, society, themselves and their families;
- Regularly and randomly tested for drug use;
- Required to appear in court frequently so that the judge may review their progress; and
- Rewarded for doing well or sanctioned when they do not live up to their obligations.

What is the target population of drug court participants?

> Drug courts are expected to have the greatest effects for high-risk offenders who have more severe antisocial backgrounds or poorer prognoses for success in standard treatments. Such high-risk individuals ordinarily require a combined regimen of intensive supervision, behavioral accountability, and evidence-based treatment services, which drug courts are specifically structured to provide. Consistent with the predictions of the Risk Principle, drug courts have been shown to have the greatest effects for high-risk participants who were relatively younger, had more prior felony convictions, were diagnosed with antisocial personality disorder, or had previously failed in less intensive dispositions. (Marlowe 2010, p. 3)

A report stated that,

> A recent survey of more than 120 evaluations of drug court programs showed that they outperformed virtually all other strategies that have been attempted for drug offenders within the 1 to 2 years that courts typically monitor offenders. Offenders who graduated from drug courts had significant reductions in rearrest rates and in charges for serious crimes. Data show that within the first year of release, 43.5% of drug offenders are rearrested, whereas only 16.4% of drug court graduates are rearrested. (Office of National Drug Control Policy [ONDCP] 2007, p. 25)

"Since the first drug court was established in 1989, drug court programs have been quickly adopted by communities and states across the country" (Franco

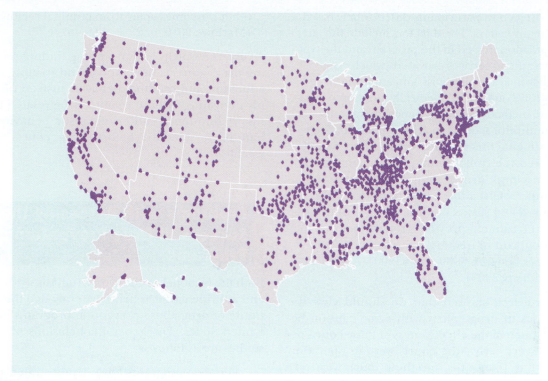

FIGURE 17.2

Drug court locations in the United States.

Source: National Institute of Justice. *Drug Court Locations in the United States as of July 2009.* Washington, DC: U.S. Department of Justice, Office of Justice Programs, 2010.

2010, p. i). Today, we are at the point where each state has multiple drug courts. **Figure 17.2** shows the current locations of drug courts in the United States in each state as of July 2009.

Overall, defendants participating in drug court sentencing have had lower rearrest rates, and there were statistically significant differences in disposition between those assigned to drug court and the comparison groups. Seventy-five percent of drug court graduates are arrest-free two years after leaving the court, and drug courts reduce crime 35% more than other court options (NADCP 2011a). "Rigorous studies examining long-term outcomes of individual Drug Courts have found that reductions in crime last at least 3 years and can endure for over 14 years" (NADCP 2011a).

Those assigned to drug court were more likely not to face further prosecution and less likely to serve probation or short jail terms. Finally, using a drug court and its system of administering treatment within a legal atmosphere is more cost-effective than criminal courts—between $1200 and $3500 per participant compared with approximately $5000 to in-

carcerate the same defendant (OJP Drug Court Clearinghouse and Technical Assistance Project [DCCTAP] 1999). In addition, more recent findings regarding cost savings include:

- Nationwide, for every $1 invested in Drug Court, taxpayers save as much as $3.36 in avoided criminal justice costs alone.
- When considering other cost offsets such as savings from reduced victimization and health-care service utilization, studies have shown benefits range up to $12 for every $1 invested.
- Drug Courts produce cost savings ranging from $4000 to $12,000 per client. These cost savings reflect reduced prison costs, reduced revolving-door arrests and trials, and reduced victimization.
- In 2007, for every Federal dollar invested in Drug Court, $9 was leveraged in state funding. (NADCP 2011a)

One other finding stated that:

Surveys completed by treatment providers indicate that the annual cost of treatment services for drug court participants differs widely based on many factors. These factors include the target population treated in the program and the type of treatment services provided (which range widely in availability, cost, and application; i.e., intensive outpatient, medically monitored inpatient, methadone maintenance, therapeutic communities, etc.). In addition, annualized treatment costs may include ancillary services offered (i.e., job training, anger management counseling), drug testing, and case management. . . . Given these variations in services offered and services delivered, 61% of drug court treatment providers report that the annual cost of treatment services per client ranges between $900 and $3500. (American University 2003)

Past research showed that we should view the successes of drug courts with some caution because much of the effectiveness of these courts occurred very early—the courts were in operation fewer than 10 months, and these courts were very selective regarding the defendants allowed to participate—the criticism being that the courts tended to select violators who would have a better chance for rehabilitation. Today, however, evidence exists that past criticisms are no longer valid: "By 2006, the scientific community had concluded beyond a reasonable doubt from advanced statistical procedures called meta-analyses that Drug Courts reduce criminal recidivism, typically measured by fewer re-arrests for new offenses and technical violations" (Marlowe 2010, p. 1).

Further, at a 2009 Annual Conference of the American Society of Criminology, research showed that,

> In addition to significantly less involvement in criminal activity, the Drug Court participants also reported significantly less use of illegal drugs and heavy use of alcohol. These self-report findings were confirmed by saliva drug tests, which revealed significantly fewer positive results for the Drug Court participants at the 18-month assessment (29% vs. 46%, p < .01). The Drug Court participants also reported significantly better improvements in their family relationships, and non-significant trends favoring higher employment rates and higher annual incomes. These findings confirm that Drug Courts elicit substantial improvements in

other outcomes apart from criminal recidivism. (Marlowe 2010, p. 2)

A very noteworthy and promising finding regarding drug courts is the emphasis on treating drug addiction and criminal behavior instead of simply punishing without treating drug-related juvenile delinquency and criminalistic behavior, as had been standard before drug courts were established.

Problems with Assessing the Success of Drug Prevention Programs

Both the National Institute on Drug Abuse (NIDA) and individual researchers have evaluated the multitude of drug abuse prevention programs in the United States. The general conclusions of these studies are as follows:

- Very few programs have demonstrated clear success or have adequately evaluated themselves.
- The relationships among information about drugs, attitudes toward use, and actual use are unclear in these programs.

Some key factors that are crucial to developing successful programs include the following:

- Prevention must be coordinated at different levels. Successful programs involve families, schools, and communities. In some cases, these efforts are not coordinated.
- The program must be integrated into the ongoing activities of schools, families, and community organizations. Superficial introduction of drug prevention strategies has limited effects. For instance, distributing literature door-to-door, making in-class presentations regarding the harmful effects of drugs, and posting banners and slogans warning of the consequences of drug abuse in communities are not successful methods. Instead, programs that are comprehensive and community-wide, integrated into neighborhood clubs, organizations, and church activities, are more likely to have a long-term impact on preventing drug use. A clear example is the yearly Great American Smokeout launched against tobacco use.

- Personal autobiographical and social experience accounts of former drug abusers should be included in drug information that is distributed. Recipients of drug prevention information should be given real-life accounts of use, abuse, despair, and successful drug rehabilitation. Just receiving drug information alone has little impact, either initially or over the long term.

Other Viable Alternatives to Drug Use

It has been suggested that people have an innate need to alter their conscious state. This belief is based on the observation that, as part of their normal play, preschoolers deliberately whirl themselves dizzy and even momentarily choke each other to lose consciousness (Wilson and Wilson 1975). Some young children progress to discovering and using chemicals (such as sniffing shoe polish or gasoline) to alter consciousness and learn to be very secretive about this behavior. They learn to be circumspect or come to feel guilty and repress the desire to alter consciousness when adults catch them in these activities.

If this desire to alter the state of consciousness is inherent in human beings, then the use of psychoactive drugs, legal or illegal, in adulthood is natural. Drug abuse is, therefore, a logical continuation of a developmental sequence that goes back to early childhood (Carroll 1977; Weil 1972).

One question in response to this is why, even if there is an innate desire to alter consciousness, only some people progress to abusing chemical substances. It appears that people who do not abuse psychoactive drugs have found positive alternatives to altering consciousness; they feel no need to take chemical substances for this purpose. Involvement in activities such as Boy Scouts and Girl Scouts, youth sports teams, music groups, the YMCA and YWCA, drug-free video game centers, drug-free dances, environmental and historical preservation projects, and social and service projects are viable alternatives to drug use. The rationale for these programs is that youth will find these activities engaging enough to forgo alcohol and drug use (Forman and Linney 1988).

This strategy is known as the **alternatives approach**. Workers in the drug abuse field tend to agree on its effectiveness. They note that young ex-abusers of common illicit drugs are more likely to stop when they gain satisfaction from exploring positive alternatives rather than from a fear of consequent harm. The alternatives approach assumes the following (Cohen 1971):

- People abuse drugs voluntarily to fill a need or basic drive.
- Most people abuse drugs for negative reasons. They may be dealing with negative feelings or situations, such as relieving boredom, anxiety, depression, tension, or other unpleasant emotional and psychological states. They may be rebelling against authority, trying to escape feelings of loneliness or inadequacy, or trying to be accepted by peers. Peer pressure is extremely important as an inducing force.
- Some people who abuse drugs believe the experience is positive. They may feel that their sensual experiences or music enjoyment is enhanced, or that they have achieved altered states of consciousness, or they may simply experience a sense of adventure. Some people may want to explore their own consciousness and reasons for the attraction to drug use.

Whether the reasons for drug use are positive or negative, the effects sought can be achieved through alternative, nondrug means. Such means are preferable to drug use and more constructive because the person is not relying on a psychoactive substance for satisfaction; rather, he or she is finding satisfaction based on personal achievements. Ideally, this approach should lead to a lifetime of self-satisfaction.

Table 17.3 lists various types of experiences, the motives for such experiences, the probable drugs of abuse with which they are associated, and alternatives to these drugs. As shown in the table, any constructive activity can be considered an alternative to drug abuse. For example, a young person who needs an outlet for increased physical energy might respond better to dance and movement training or a project in preventive medicine than working on ecological projects. In a large alternatives

KEY TERMS

alternatives approach
an approach emphasizing the exploration of positive alternatives to drug abuse, based on replacing the pleasurable feelings gained from drug abuse with involvement in social and educational activities

Table 17.3 Experiences, Motives, and Possible Alternatives for a Drug Abuser

EXPERIENCE	CORRESPONDING MOTIVES	DRUGS ABUSED	POSSIBLE ALTERNATIVES
Physical	Desire for physical well-being: physical relaxation, relief from sickness, desire for more energy	Alcohol, sedative-hypnotics, stimulants, marijuana	Athletics, dance, exercise, hiking, diet, carpentry, outdoor work, swimming, hatha yoga
Sensory	Desire to magnify sensorium: sound, touch, taste, need for sensual/sexual stimulation	Hallucinogens, marijuana, alcohol	Sensory awareness training, sky diving, experiencing sensory beauty of nature, scuba diving
Emotional	Relief from psychological pain: attempt to resolve personal problems, relief from bad mood, escape from anxiety, desire for emotional insight, liberation of feeling and emotional relaxation	Narcotics, alcohol, barbiturates, sedative-hypnotics	Competent individual counseling, well-run group therapy, instruction in psychology of personal development
Interpersonal	Desire to gain peer acceptance, break through interpersonal barriers, "communicate"; defiance of authority figures	Any, especially alcohol, marijuana	Expertly managed sensitivity and encounter groups, well-run group therapy, instruction in social customs, confidence training, emphasis on assisting others (e.g., YMCA or YWCA volunteers)
Social	Desire to promote social change, find identifiable subculture, tune out intolerable environmental conditions (e.g., poverty)	Marijuana, psychedelics	Social service community action in positive social change; helping the poor, aged, infirm, or young; tutoring handicapped individuals; ecology action; YMCA or YWCA Big Brother/Sister programs
Political	Desire to promote political change (out of desperation with the social-political order) and to identify with antiestablishment subgroup	Marijuana, psychedelics	Political service, lobbying for nonpartisan projects (e.g., Common Cause); field work with politicians and public officials
Intellectual	Desire to escape boredom, out of intellectual curiosity, to solve cognitive problems, gain new understanding in the world of ideas, research one's own awareness	Stimulants, sometimes psychedelics	Intellectual excitement through reading, debate, and discussion; creative games and puzzles; self-hypnosis; training in concentration
Creative-aesthetic	Desire to improve creative performance, enhance enjoyment of art already produced (e.g., music); enjoy imaginative mental productions	Marijuana, stimulants, psychedelics	Nongraded instruction in producing and/or appreciating art, music, drama, and creative hobbies
Philosophical	Desire to discover meaningful values, find meaning in life, help establish personal identity, organize a belief structure	Psychedelics, marijuana, stimulants	Discussions, seminars, courses on ethics, the nature of reality, relevant philosophical literature; explorations of value systems
Spiritual-mystical	Desire to transcend orthodox religion, develop spiritual insights, reach higher levels of consciousness, augment yogic practices, take a spiritual shortcut	Psychedelics, marijuana	Exposure to nonchemical methods of spiritual development; study of world religions, mysticism, meditation, yogic techniques

Source: U.S. Department of Health and Human Services, Office of Substance Abuse Prevention. "Factors that Influence Alcohol and Other Drug Use." In *Prevention Plus II: Tools for Creating and Sustaining Drug-Free Communities* (Figure 2.1, p. 19). DHHS Publication No. 89-1649. Rockville, MD: Author, 1989. Distributed by the National Clearinghouse for Alcohol and Drug Information.

program established in Idaho, the following activities were planned during a month: arts and crafts, karate, reforestation, backpacking, Humane Society dog show, horseback riding, creating artwork for posters for various programs, astronomy, camping, and volunteering in a local hospital.

■ Meditation

Some of the most intriguing research about the brain is being done on the state of the mind during **meditation**. In certain countries, such as India, people have long histories of being able to achieve certain goals through meditation. The word *yoga* is derived from the Sanskrit word for union, or yoking, meaning the process of discipline by which a person attains union with the absolute. In a sense, it refers to the use of the mind to control itself and the body.

Meditation involves brain wave activity centered on ponderous, contemplative, and reflective thought. An individual who meditates is able to decrease oxygen consumption within a matter of minutes by as much as 20%, a level usually reached only after 4 to 5 hours of sleep. However, meditation is physiologically different from sleep, based on the electroencephalograph (EEG) pattern and rate of decline of oxygen consumption. Along with the decreased metabolic rate and changes in EEG, there also is a marked decrease in blood lactate. Lactate is produced by metabolism of skeletal muscle, and the decrease is probably due to the reduced activity of the sympathetic nervous system during meditation. Heart rate and respiration also are slowed.

■ The Natural Mind Approach

Some people who take drugs eventually look for other methods of maintaining the valuable parts of the drug experience. These people may learn to value the meditation high and abandon drugs. In looking at Table 17.3, we can see how the use of different types of drugs can be replaced with possible alternatives by a drug abuser. Long-term drug users sometimes credit their drug experiences with having given them a taste of their potential, even though continued use has diminished the novelty of drug use. After these individuals become established in careers, they claim to have grown out of chemically induced altered states of consciousness.

As Andrew Weil (1972, p. 67) put it, "One does not see any long-time meditators give up meditation to become acid heads."

Although chemical highs are effective means of altering the state of consciousness, they interfere with the most worthwhile states of altered consciousness because they reinforce the illusion that highs come from external, material agents rather than from within your own nervous system.

Some people have difficulty using meditation as an alternative to drugs because, to be effective, meditation takes practice and concentration; in contrast, the effects of drugs are immediate. Nevertheless, it is within everyone's potential to meditate.

Discussion Questions

1. Figure 17.1 lists many factors that can influence drug use. Design a drug prevention program by selecting any one of the concentric circles; include all factors within that circle.

2. Look at all of the findings in the section of this chapter entitled "How Serious Is the Problem of Drug Dependence?" Which two findings regarding dependence were the most interesting, and why were they the most interesting?

3. Comment on the harm reduction model as presented here and in other literature you may have. What are the major strengths and weaknesses of this model in comparison to the way the United States views drug users and/or abusers? Why do you think the U.S. government remains opposed to this approach? Speculate on how the United States would change if it were to adopt the harm reduction model.

4. What would you emphasize in a primary prevention program for junior high school or middle school students? High school students? College students?

5. How would you design a drug prevention program for undetected committed or secret users? What would you emphasize? Similarly,

KEY TERMS

meditation
a state of consciousness in which there is a constant level of awareness focusing on one object; for example, yoga and Zen Buddhism

how would you design a drug prevention program for addicted drug users? What would you emphasize?

6. What do you think is more likely to work today in drug prevention programs for America's youth: teaching moderate use or total abstinence? Why?

7. Your boss says, "We received a much smaller amount of money than expected from the federal government to create a drug prevention program. I want you to focus on a community-based approach, school-based approach, or family-based prevention program." Which would you select and why?

8. How effective has the BACCHUS Network been on your campus? Can you give examples?

9. List and explain three major strengths of drug courts in comparison with traditional criminal courts in the United States. Do you perceive any weaknesses?

10. From everything you read in this chapter about the D.A.R.E. drug prevention program, what do you think are the major problems with this comprehensive drug prevention program? How would you improve it?

11. What is your assessment of using the alternatives approach and meditation for preventing drug use? Do you think it would be effective for alleviating drug use? Why or why not?

Summary

1 The 10 most prominent factors affecting an individual's use of drugs are as follows: (a) genetics, (b) personality traits, (c) attitudes and beliefs, (d) interpersonal and peer resistance skills, (e) community, (f) peers, (g) school policy, (h) local law enforcement, (i) personal situations, and (j) parents.

2 The seriousness of the problem with regard to drug dependence is highlighted by the fact that in 2008, an estimated 22.2 million persons age 12 or older were classified with substance dependence or abuse in the past year; this is 8.9% of the population. Of these, 3.1 million were classified with dependence on or abuse of both alcohol and illicit drugs, 3.9 million were dependent on or abused illicit drugs but not alcohol, and 15.2 million were dependent on or abused alcohol but not illicit

drugs (SAMHSA 2009). Further, the specific illicit drugs that had the highest levels of past-year dependence or abuse in 2008 were marijuana, followed by cocaine and pain relievers.

3 Three major types of prevention programs are primary, secondary, and tertiary prevention.

4 Five major types of drug users that drug prevention programs have to recognize before assembling a program are (a) early experimenters, (b) non-problem drug users/recreational users, (c) undetected committed or secret users, (d) problem users, and (e) former users.

5 The four levels of comprehensive prevention programs for drug use and abuse are (a) the harm reduction model, (b) community-based prevention, (c) school-based prevention, and (d) family-based prevention.

6 Proactive family factors can moderate the effects of drug risk factors. The risk of associating with peers who use drugs can be offset by protective family factors, such as parent conventionality, maternal adjustment, and strong parent–child attachment.

7 Four primary prevention programs that exist in higher education are the (a) information-only or awareness model, (b) attitude change model or affective education model, (c) social influences model, and (d) ecological or person-in-environment model.

8 Three of today's large-scale prevention programs are (a) the BACCHUS Network, a national and international association of college and university peer-education programs focused on alcohol abuse prevention and other related student health and safety issues; (b) D.A.R.E., a popular nationwide drug prevention program presented in middle and junior high schools by police officers that has been showing severe shortcomings; and (c) drug courts, a promising and increasingly popular nationwide approach to prevention in which the primary purpose is to focus on treatment programs and options instead of only punishment for drug offenses.

9 Two additional possibilities for lessening or eliminating drug use are the alternatives approach and meditation. Alternatives to drug abuse are based on replacing the euphoria and pleasure gained by being high with involvement in social, recreational, and educational activities. Meditation is producing a state of consciousness in which there is a constant level of very satisfying awareness that is rewarding in itself without artificial inducements (drugs). Yoga and Zen Buddhism are examples.

References

Alberti, R. E., and M. L. Emmons. *Your Perfect Right.* San Luis Obispo, CA: Impact Publishers, 1988.

BACCHUS and GAMMA. *Community College Guide to Peer Education.* Denver, CO: The BACCHUS and GAMMA Peer Education Network, 1994.

The BACCHUS Network. "Mission Statement." 2007. Available http://www.bacchusgamma.org/mission.asp

The BACCHUS Network. Mission Statement. 2011. Available http://www.bacchusgamma.org/mission.asp

Botvin, G. J., and K. W. Griffin. "School Based Programs." In *Substance Abuse: A Comprehensive Textbook,* 4th ed., edited by J. H. Lowinson, P. Ruiz, R. B. Millman, and J. G. Langrod, 1211–1228. Philadelphia, PA: Lippincott Williams and Wilkins, 2005.

Botvin, G. J., and T. A. Wills. "Personal and Social Skills Training: Cognitive-Behavioral Approaches to Substance Abuse Prevention." In *Prevention Research: Deterring Drug Abuse Among Children and Adolescents.* NIDA Research Monograph No. 64. Rockville, MD: National Institute on Drug Abuse, 1985.

Carey, S. M., M. W. Finigan, and K. Pukstas. *Exploring the Key Components of Drug Courts: A Comparative Study of 18 Adult Drug Courts on Practices, Outcomes and Costs.* Portland, OR: NPC Research, 2008.

Carroll, E. "Notes on the Epidemiology of Inhalants." In *Review of Inhalants,* edited by C. W. Sharp and M. L. Brehm. NIDA Research Monograph No. 15. Washington, DC: National Institute on Drug Abuse, 1977.

Center for Prevention Research and Development (CPRD). *Research Based Approaches in the Community Domain.* Champaign, IL: University of Illinois Urbana Champaign, 2000.

Clayton, R. R., R. Cattarello, L. E. Cay, and K. P. Walden. "Persuasive Communication and Drug Prevention: An Evaluation of the D.A.R.E. Program." In *Persuasive Communication and Drug Abuse Prevention,* edited by L. Donohew, H. Sypepher, and W. Bukowski, 83–107. Hillsdale, NJ: Erlbaum, 1991.

Cohen, A. Y. "The Journey Beyond Trips: Alternatives to Drugs." *Journal of Psychedelic Drugs* 3 (Spring 1971): 7–14.

Common Sense for Drug Policy. "D.A.R.E. Admits Failure." (9 July 2009). Available http://www.csdp.org/news/news/darerevised.htm

Community Anti-Drug Coalition of America (CADCA). *Drug Free Communities Support Program Grantee Roadmap to Success: Training and Technical Assistance Support System.* Alexandria, VA: CADCA National Coalition Institute, 2010.

D.A.R.E. America (Drug Abuse Resistance Education). "About D.A.R.E." 1996. Available http://www.dare.com/home/about_dare.asp

Ennett, S. T., N. S. Tobler, C. L. Ringwalt, and R. L. Flewelling. "How Effective Is Drug Abuse Resistance Education? A Meta-analysis of Project D.A.R.E. Outcome Evaluations." *American Journal of Public Health* 84 (1994): 1394–1401.

Forman, S. G., and J. A. Linney. "School-Based Prevention of Adolescent Substance Abuse: Programs, Implementation and Future Direction." *School Psychology Review* 17 (1988): 550–558.

Franco, C. "Drug Courts: Background, Effectiveness, and Policy Issues for Congress." Comgressional Research Service, Washington, DC: Government Printing Office, (12 October 2010). Available http://www.fas.org/sgp/crs/misc/R41448.pdf

Goldkamp, J. *Justice and Treatment Innovation: The Drug Court Movement.* Washington, DC: National Institute of Justice and the State Justice Institute, 1993.

Gonzalez, G. M., and V. V. Clement, eds. *Preventing Substance Abuse.* U.S. Department of Education. Washington, DC: U.S. Government Printing Office, 1994.

Gopelrud, E. N., ed. *Preventing Adolescent Drug Use: From Theory to Practice.* OSAP Monograph No. 8, DHHS Publication No. (ADM) 91–1725. Rockville, MD: Office of Substance Abuse Prevention, 1991.

Hansen, W. B. "A Social Ecology Theory of Alcohol and Drug Use Prevention Among College and University Students." In *Designing Alcohol and Other Drug Prevention Programs in Higher Education.* Newton, MA: Higher Education Center for Alcohol and Other Drug Prevention, U.S. Department of Education, 1997.

Harm Reduction Coalition. "Principles of Harm Reduction." 2011. Available http://www.harmreduction.org/section.php?id=62

Holstein, M. E., W. E. Cohen, and P. Steinbroner. *A Matter of Balance: Personal Strategies for Alcohol and Other Drugs.* Ashland, OR: CNS Productions, 1995.

Horowitz, H. L. *Campus Life.* New York: Knopf, 1987.

Koss, M. P., C. A. Gidycz, and R. Wisniewski. "The Scope of Rape: Incidence and Prevalence of Sexual Aggression and Victimization in a National Sample of Higher Education Students." *Journal of Consulting and Clinical Psychology* 34 (1987): 186–196.

Marlowe, D. B. *Research Update on Adult Drug Courts.* Alexandria, VA: National Association of Drug Court Professionals (NADCP) and www.allrise.org, December 2010: 1–7. Available http://www1.spa.american.edu/justice/documents/3067.pdf

McIntyre, K., D. White, and R. Yoast. *Resilience Among High-Risk Youth.* Madison, WI: University of Wisconsin, 1990.

Miller, D. W. "D.A.R.E. Reinvents Itself—With Help from Its Social-Scientist Critics." *Chronicle of Higher Education* 48 (19 October 2001): A12–A14.

National Association of Drug Court Professionals (NADCP). "Drug Courts Work." 2011a. Available http://www.nadcp.org/learn/drug-courts-work

National Association of Drug Court Professionals (NADCP). "Types of Drug Courts." 2011b. Available http://www.nadcp.org/learn/what-are-drug-courts/models

National Association of Drug Court Professionals (NADCP). "What Are Drug Courts?" 2011c. Available http://www.nadcp.org/learn/what-are-drug-courts

National Criminal Justice Reference Service. *In the Spotlight: Drug Courts—Facts and Figures.* Washington, DC: Office of Justice Programs, U.S. Department of Justice, 2010.

Treatment of Addiction

Individuals who are addicted to drugs come from all walks of life. Many suffer from occupational, social, psychiatric, or other medical problems that can make their addictions difficult to treat. Even in the absence of such complicating issues, the severity of addictions varies widely. It is essential to match treatment with the needs of the client. Further, it is valuable to intervene at the earliest possible stage of addiction with the least restrictive form of appropriate treatment. To accomplish this, it is important that treatment providers determine the severity of addiction as well as the readiness of an individual to change his or her behavior.

Assessing Addiction Severity and Readiness to Change

Addiction severity can be determined in many ways, including the administration of standardized questionnaires. Of these, the Addiction Severity Index (ASI) is among the most widely used assessment instruments in the field of addiction (McLellan et al. 1980, 1985, 1992). The ASI is one of the most reliable and valid measurements of the magnitude and characteristics of client problems. It focuses on possible problems in six areas: medical status, employment and support, alcohol and drug use, legal status, family and social relationships, and psychiatric status. The ASI provides information that can be used to identify and prioritize which problem areas are most significant and require prompt attention.

Treatment facilities provide a variety of services to people dealing with substance abuse.

When assessing and prioritizing problems, one model of individual development that is often considered is Maslow's hierarchy of needs. This theory postulates that individuals are motivated by unsatisfied needs, and that lower fundamental needs must be satisfied before higher needs can be satisfied. These primary needs include food, drink, warmth, sleep, and shelter. These can be extended in the case of substance abusers to problems such as (1) unidentified or inappropriately managed health problems, (2) medication adherence issues (particularly in the presence of co-occurring mental or physical health disorders), and (3) physical alterations due to drug and/or alcohol dependence (Stilen et al. 2007). Once these fundamental needs are addressed, a second level of needs involving security and safety can be addressed. Simplistically, these include such issues as stability, order, law, and limits. Examples of common problem areas reflecting this level include inability for self-care, management of mental health issues, personal/public safety issues, and legal issues. If these needs are not met, individuals receiving substance abuse treatment cannot move to higher levels wherein love and belonging, self-esteem, and self-actualization (i.e., fulfilling personal potential) can be attained (Stilen et al. 2007).

As important as assessing addiction severity and prioritizing problem areas on which to focus is consideration of a person's readiness to change his or her abuse behavior. Pioneering work by DiClemente and Prochaska (1998) revealed that behavioral change is a many-stage process, rather than a singular event. The stages described by DiClemente and Prochaska include:

- *Precontemplation:* An individual does not want to change or is not considering changing his or her behavior. The latter may be because he or she does not see a need for change.
- *Contemplation:* A person is considering changing his or her behavior.
- *Preparation:* A person is committed to a strategy for change.
- *Action:* A person is actively attempting to change.
- *Maintenance:* A person has changed his or her behavior. In order to complete the process of change, this behavior must become a part of his or her lifestyle.

Determining the state of change at which an individual finds him- or herself can help providers select the best treatment plan to address a client's needs. This may help prevent the individual from refusing to accept all or parts of the treatment plan.

Principles of Treatment

A variety of approaches to drug addiction treatment exist. Some include behavioral therapy, such as counseling, psychotherapy, or cognitive therapy. Others include medications ranging from treatment medications (e.g., methadone, buprenorphine, nicotine patches, nicotine gum) to those intended to treat co-occurring mental disorders (e.g., antidepressants, mood stabilizers). The most successful drug abuse treatment programs typically provide a combination of therapies and other services to meet the needs of the individual abuser. They incorporate adequate assessment of treatment needs required not only as a direct consequence of the physiological and psychological effects of the drug but also due to indirect problems, such as the need for housing, legal, and financial services; educational and vocational assistance; and family/child-care services. Such needs often are shaped by the gender, age, race, culture, and sexual orientation of the abuser.

Because drug addiction is generally a chronic disorder characterized by occasional relapses, a one-time, short-term treatment is often inadequate. Further, many individuals who enter treatment drop out before receiving all of its benefits; hence, and again, successful treatment often requires more than one treatment exposure. Of note, relapse rates for addiction resemble those of other chronic diseases such as diabetes, hypertension, and asthma (National Institute on Drug Abuse [NIDA] 2009b).

Research has shown that good outcomes are contingent on adequate duration of treatment. Generally, for residential or outpatient treatment, participation for fewer than 90 days is of limited or no effectiveness; treatments lasting significantly longer are needed (NIDA 2009b). For methadone maintenance, 12 months of treatment often is the minimum needed, and some individuals who are addicted to opiates require extended treatment lasting several years (NIDA 2009b).

To best target treatment for an individual, the type and goals of treatment must be determined. Consideration must be given to the fact that both the type and the goals of treatment largely depend on the view one holds of addiction. For example, if the disease model is applied to addiction, total abstinence is required because this model views drug abuse as a biological condition that is largely uncontrollable. The user is perceived as ill and thus irrational about continued drug use. On the other hand, if responsible drug use is the goal, then occasional and moderate drug use can be the intended end result.

Effective treatment allows addicts to stop abusing drugs, returns them to a drug-free state of existence, and transforms them into employable and productive members of society. Measures of effectiveness typically include assessing levels of family functioning, employability, criminal behavior, and medical condition.

NIDA has delineated the following 13 overarching principles that characterize effective addiction treatment (NIDA 2009b):

1. *Addiction is a complex but treatable disease that affects brain function and behavior.* Drugs of abuse can alter brain structure and function, resulting in changes that persist long after drug use has ceased. This may explain why drug abusers are at risk for relapse even after long periods of abstinence and despite the potentially devastating consequences.

2. *No single treatment is appropriate for all individuals.* Treatment settings, interventions, and services must be matched to each individual's particular problems and needs.

3. *Treatment needs to be readily available.* Individuals who are addicted to drugs are often uncertain about whether to seek treatment. Hence, it is crucial that services be available as soon as an individual makes the decision to seek help for his or her addiction. Opportunities for treatment can be lost if it is not immediately available or is not readily accessible.

4. *Effective treatment attends to multiple needs of the individual, not just his or her drug use.* To be effective, treatment must address the individual's drug use and any associated medical, psychological, social, vocational, and legal problems. It is also important that treatment be appropriate with respect to an individual's age, ethnicity, gender, and culture.

5. *Remaining in treatment for an adequate period is critical for treatment effectiveness.* The appropriate duration for an individual depends on his or her problems and needs. As noted earlier, research indicates that for most patients, the threshold of significant improvement is reached at about 3 months in treatment.

6. *Counseling—individual and/or group—and other behavioral therapies are the most commonly used forms of drug abuse treatment.* The focus of behavioral therapies varies and may involve addressing an individual's motivation to change, improving problem-solving skills, building skills to resist drug use, providing incentives for absti-

nence, replacing drug-using activities with con-struc-tive activities, and/or facilitating better interpersonal relationships.

7. *Medications are an important element of treatment for many patients, especially when combined with coun-seling and other behavioral therapies.* Specific phar-macological therapies for treating substance abusers are discussed later in this chapter.

8. *An individual's treatment and services plan must be assessed continually and modified as necessary to en-sure it meets his or her changing needs.* An individ-ual may require varying combinations of services during the course of treatment and recovery. For example, in addition to counseling, a pa-tient may require medication, medical services, family therapy, parenting instruction, vocational rehabilitation, and/or social and legal services depending upon his or her changing needs.

9. *Many drug-addicted individuals also have other mental disorders.* Because drug abuse and ad-diction often co-occur with other mental ill-nesses (see the discussion of comorbidity later in this chapter), patients presenting with one condition should be assessed for the other(s). When these problems co-occur, treatment should address both (or all), including the use of medications as appropriate.

10. *Medical detoxification is only the first stage of addic-tion treatment and, by itself, does little to change long-term drug use.* Medical detoxification (that is, the process of safely managing the acute phys-ical symptoms of withdrawal associated with stopping drug use) can be an important first step toward abstinence. However, detoxifica-tion alone is rarely sufficient to help addicts achieve long-term abstinence.

11. *Treatment does not need to be voluntary to be effec-tive.* Strong motivation can facilitate the treat-ment process. Sanctions or enticements in the family, criminal justice system, or employment setting can facilitate treatment entry and in-crease both retention rates and success of drug treatment interventions.

12. *Drug use during treatment must be monitored con-tinuously because lapses during treatment do occur.* The knowledge that one's drug use is being monitored can be a powerful incentive to help individuals to withstand urges to use drugs. Monitoring also provides an early indication of a return to drug use, signaling a possible need to adjust an individual's treatment plan to bet-ter meet his or her needs.

13. *Treatment programs should assess patients for the presence of HIV/AIDS, hepatitis B and C, tuberculo-sis, and other infectious diseases as well as provide targeted risk-reduction counseling to help patients modify or change behaviors that place them at risk of contracting or spreading infectious diseases.*

Many treatment programs apply one or more of these listed principles as part of their therapeutic strategy.

Of note, the age of the substance abuser is an im-portant consideration when designing treatment. This includes both the age of exposure to drugs and the age at which treatment is initiated. Re-search indicates that from birth through early adulthood, the brain undergoes a prolonged process of development during which a behavioral shift occurs such that actions go from being more impulsive to more reflective and reasoned. Fur-ther, the brain areas most closely associated with judgment, decision making, and self-control un-dergo a period of rapid development during ado-lescence (NIDA 2009b). Thus, adolescent drug abusers have unique needs that must be consid-ered in developing a treatment approach to their addictions.

Gender-related considerations in the treatment of substance abuse are also of importance. Treat-ment should attend not only to biological distinc-tions between genders but also to the social and environmental factors that can differentially influ-ence motivations for drug use, treatments that are most effective, reasons for seeking treatment, types of environments where treatment is obtained, and consequences of not receiving treatment. For ex-ample, many life circumstances predominate in women as a group, which may require specialized treatment approaches. These can include physical and sexual trauma followed by posttraumatic stress disorder; research indicates that these are more common in drug-abusing women than in men seek-ing treatment (NIDA 2009b). Other factors that can be unique to women and can influence the treat-ment process include issues involving financial in-dependence, pregnancy, and child care. Each must be considered in developing a treatment plan.

Criminal justice–involved substance abusers are another population that often benefits from spe-cialized treatment approaches. Of note, research indicates that treatment for drug-addicted offend-ers during and after incarceration can have a signif-icant effect on future drug use, criminal behavior, and social functioning. Combining prison- and community-based treatment for addicted offenders reduces the risk of both relapse to drug use and re-cidivism to drug-related criminal behavior. As an ex-ample, according to NIDA (2009b), one study found that prisoners who participated in a therapeutic treatment program in the Delaware State prison system and continued to receive treatment in a work-release program after prison were 70% less likely than nonparticipants to return to drug use and incur re-arrest. Unfortunately, effective treatment for criminal justice–involved individuals is often unavailable. For example, as reported in a survey summarized by NIDA (2009c), fewer than 10% of adults and approximately 20% of adolescents with substance abuse problems in the nation's prisons, jails, and probation programs can receive treatment on a given day. This survey also disclosed that only 40% of adult facilities and 29% of juvenile facilities reported having full-time personnel to provide drug abuse therapy (NIDA 2009c).

Many workplaces sponsor employee assistance programs that offer short-term assistance and/or counseling so as to link employees with substance abuse problems to local treatment resources. In addition, therapeutic work environments that provide employment for abstinent drug-abusing individuals both improve life skills and promote a continued drug-free lifestyle.

Several factors influence retention in treatment programs, including individual motivation to change drug-using behavior and degree of support from family and friends. Pressure from employers, the criminal justice system, and/or extensions of the court (i.e., child protective services) also can be important. Because individual problems such as mental illness or criminal involvement decrease the likelihood of retaining patients in treatment, broad-ranging programs (i.e., with medical and legal services) are important. It also is important for treatment providers to ensure a transition to continuing care or aftercare following a patient's completion of formal treatment (NIDA 2009b).

Comorbidity

Drug addiction is a complicated condition that often involves changes in the structure and function of specific parts of the brain. Changes in the structure and function of regions of the brain affected by drug addiction can also occur in other mental illnesses such as anxiety, psychosis, and depression. Noteworthy, overlapping factors including genetic vulnerabilities, trauma, stress, and/or underlying brain abnormalities can contribute to both substance abuse disorders and other mental illnesses.

Comorbidity is a condition in which two or more illnesses occur in the same person, simultaneously or sequentially. This term also suggests interactions between the illnesses that affect the course and prognosis of both (NIDA 2008). Comorbidity between drug addiction and mental illnesses is common (NIDA 2009a). For example, individuals diagnosed with anxiety or mood disorders are approximately twice as likely to suffer also from drug abuse or dependence. This has also been demonstrated for individuals diagnosed with conduct

Here and Now

Schizophrenia and Cigarette Smoking: Self-Medication or Shared Brain Circuitry?

Schizophrenic patients are more likely to abuse tobacco than the rest of the population. Various self-medication hypotheses have been proposed to explain this association. For example, it has been suggested that the nicotine found in tobacco may help compensate for some of the cognitive deficits experienced by schizophrenic individuals. Further, it may alleviate unpleasant side effects of antipsychotic medications and/or help deal with the anxiety that can be associated with the illness. According to NIDA (2008), research suggests the possibility of the presence of abnormalities in particular circuits of the brain that may predispose individuals to schizophrenia, increase the rewarding effects of drugs like nicotine, or reduce an individual's ability to quit smoking. The existence of common mechanisms is consistent with the observation that both nicotine and the medication clozapine (which also acts at nicotine receptors) can improve working memory and attention in an animal model of schizophrenia. Further, clozapine is effective in treating individuals with schizophrenia, and it also reduces their smoking levels. Thus, understanding how and why patients with schizophrenia use nicotine may assist in developing new treatments for both schizophrenia and nicotine dependence.

Source: National Institute on Drug Abuse (NIDA). "Comorbidity: Addiction and Other Mental Illnesses." NIH Publication No. 08-5771. 2008. Available at: http://drugabuse.gov/researchreports/comorbidity. Accessed April 22, 2011.

disorder or antisocial personality. (See "Here and Now: Schizophrenia and Cigarette Smoking" for more on tobacco use among schizophrenic patients.) Similarly, individuals diagnosed with substance disorders are approximately twice as likely to also suffer from anxiety and mood disorders (NIDA 2008).

In studies that included 1956 adults and 4930 adolescents, two-thirds of patients entering substance abuse treatment programs reported at least one co-occurring mental health problem during the previous year. Conduct and attention deficit disorders were most common in young patients, whereas depression and anxiety were most common in older patients (see Chan, Dennis, and Funk 2008 and references therein).

Mental illnesses can sometimes lead to substance abuse and addiction in that individuals sometimes abuse drugs in order to self-medicate an underlying medical condition. However, the high incidence of comorbidity between substance abuse disorders and other mental illnesses does not mean that one necessarily caused the other. In fact, a causal relationship is difficult to establish for multiple reasons, including the fact that drugs of abuse can cause abusers to display one or more symptoms of, without actually having, another mental illness. Further, some symptoms of either a substance abuse disorder or another mental illness may not be recognized until the disease has progressed considerably, and by then, it often is difficult to retrospectively determine the precise onset of these disorders (NIDA 2008).

Effective treatment of individuals with comorbid substance abuse and mental illnesses requires accurate diagnosis of both conditions. Individuals beginning treatment for substance abuse and/or addiction need to be screened for mental illnesses, and vice versa. Accurate diagnosis may require monitoring after a period of abstinence in order to distinguish the effects of substance intoxication or withdrawal from the symptoms of comorbid mental disorders. According to NIDA (2008), several fundamental barriers impede treatment of comorbid disorders. Among these, psychiatrists and physicians are the most common treatment providers for mental illness, whereas a mix of professionals with varying backgrounds and credentials provides substance abuse treatment. Often, neither background is broad enough to address the full range of problems presented by patients. In addition, a bias exists in some substance abuse treatment facilities against using any pharmacological intervention, including those necessary to treat serious mental illnesses such as depression. Many substance abuse treatment programs do not employ professionals qualified to prescribe, dispense, and monitor medications. Finally, many individuals needing treatment are in the criminal justice system, and adequate treatment services for both mental illness and drug use disorders can be largely lacking in these settings.

Drug Addiction Treatment in the United States

Research has demonstrated that treatment is less expensive than simply incarcerating addicts. For example, the average cost for 1 full year of methadone maintenance treatment is approximately $4700 per patient, whereas 1 full year of imprisonment costs approximately $24,000 per person (NIDA 2009b). Treatment has other economic benefits to society. For example, it has been estimated that every $1 invested in addiction treatment programs yields a return of between $4 and $7 in reduced drug-related crime, theft, and criminal justice costs (NIDA 2009b). With healthcare savings included, total savings can exceed costs by a ratio of 12:1 (NIDA 2009b). Further, substantial and important savings to the individual and society also come from fewer interpersonal conflicts, improvements in workplace productivity, and reductions in drug-related incidents among individuals who are treated successfully for substance abuse (NIDA 2009b).

There is a wide array of general therapeutic strategies for treatment. Some involve pharmacological interventions, such as methadone maintenance or narcotic antagonist treatment. Other programs apply a drug-free approach. Programs can be short or long term and can be individualized or involve group participation. The following is an overview of various treatment approaches. It is important to realize that many treatment programs blend one or more of these approaches as part of their therapeutic strategy.

■ Historical Approaches

Considerable effort has been expended to find treatments for substance abuse. Several approaches, or at least components of them, continue to be utilized today. These include those discussed in the following sections.

Alcoholics Anonymous

Founded in the mid-1930s, Alcoholics Anonymous (AA) is now an international organization. The desire to stop drinking is the sole criterion required to join. The original founders of AA were strongly influenced by a religious movement known as the Oxford Group. AA outlines 12 successive measures, referred to as *steps,* that alcoholics should accomplish during the recovery process. These steps include admitting that the person addicted to alcohol has no power over the drug. He or she must also believe in a greater power that can help him or her overcome shortcomings. Individuals must make initial and ongoing assessments of their life, and admit to others the character of their wrongs. In addition, individuals must make amends to those whom they have adversely affected, except in situations where such actions could harm others (Alcoholics Anonymous 2007).

AA has two types of meetings: open and closed. **Open meetings** are open to anyone who has an interest in attending and witnessing these meetings, and they last approximately 45 minutes to 1 hour. **Closed meetings** are for alcoholics who have a serious desire to completely stop drinking. These meetings are not open to viewers or "shoppers." At closed meetings, recovering alcoholics address, through testimonials, how alcohol has diminished their quality of life.

Some outgrowths of AA include Al-Anon, Adult Children of Alcoholics, and Alateen. These are parallel organizations supporting AA. Al-Anon is for spouses and other close relatives of alcoholics, and Alateen is exclusively for teenagers whose lives have been affected by someone else's alcoholism. Both relatives and teen members of alcoholic families learn means and methods for coping with destructive behaviors exhibited by alcoholic members.

Common alcohol abuse–related problems are shared at AA meetings.

Rehabilitation Programs

The first rehabilitation programs grew out of the work that AA members did with other active alcoholics. The "twelfth stepping" program involves reaching out to others in need and attempting to draw them in. The movement began in the early days of AA when the organization's founder, Bill W., had alcoholics trying to stop drinking or "dry out" living at his house in Brooklyn. At that time, "[his] home was stuffed, from cellar to attic, with alcoholics in all stages of recovery" (Al-Anon 1970). It was a natural transition to opening up "drying out houses" in the 1940s and 1950s.

Also during the 1950s, the **Minnesota model**, an inpatient rehabilitation model, was developed. It combined the AA philosophy with a multidisciplinary treatment team. A treatment plan was used, based on assessment of the individual and prioritization of goals. This model, which borrows from social work practice, is still used in treatment programs. Due to the vagaries of insurance reimbursement in Minnesota, the program lasted 28 days because that was the length covered by insurance; therefore, alcoholism programs traditionally were roughly 1 month long.

◼ General Therapeutic Strategies

In addition to the approaches mentioned previously, there are numerous strategies to drug addiction treatment. Although not all treatment programs fit perfectly into any one of these categories, the following provides an overview of the general types of services available (NIDA 1999, 2009b).

Medical Detoxification

Medical detoxification is a process whereby individuals are systematically withdrawn from drugs,

KEY TERMS

open meetings
meetings to which anyone having an interest in attending and witnessing is invited

closed meetings
meetings to which only alcoholics having a serious desire to completely stop drinking are invited

Minnesota model
a major model in the treatment of alcohol and drug abuse, involving a month-long stay in an inpatient rehabilitation facility, a multidisciplinary treatment team, systematic assessment, and a formal treatment plan with long- and short-term goals

typically under the care of a physician. Medications are available for detoxification from benzodiazepines, alcohol, barbiturates, opiates, nicotine, and other sedatives. Detoxification can be medically necessary because untreated withdrawal from some agents (that is, alcohol and barbiturates) can be fatal. Although detoxification is sometimes referred to as a distinct treatment modality, it is more appropriately considered a precursor to treatment because it is designed to treat the acute physiological effects of stopping drug use. It is not designed to address the psychological, social, and behavioral problems associated with addiction and, therefore, does not typically produce lasting behavioral changes. Detoxification is most useful when it incorporates formal processes of assessment and referral to subsequent drug addiction treatment.

Motivational Enhancement Therapy

Motivational enhancement therapy (MET) is a patient-centered counseling approach for promoting behavior change by assisting patients in resolving ambivalence about engaging in treatment and discontinuing drug use. MET employs strategies to evoke rapid and internally motivated change in the patient instead of guiding him or her through the recovery process. Treatment consists of an initial assessment battery session. This evaluation is followed by two to four individual treatment sessions. The patient is provided feedback generated from the initial assessment battery so as to stimulate conversation about personal substance abuse and to elicit self-motivational statements. Coping strategies for high-risk situations are discussed. Subsequently, the therapist monitors change, reviews the coping and cessation strategies being utilized, and continues to encourage commitment to change and/or persistent abstinence (NIDA 1999).

Outpatient Treatment Programs

The outpatient strategy varies in the intensity and forms of services offered. Such treatment often is more suitable for individuals who are employed or who have extensive family and/or community support. Low-intensity programs may offer little more than drug education, warnings, and advice. Other outpatient models, such as intensive day treatment, can be comparable to residential programs in effectiveness and services. Group counseling often is emphasized (NIDA 2009b).

Short-Term Residential Treatment

Short-term residential programs provide relatively brief treatment based on a modified 12-step approach. These programs were originally designed to treat alcoholism, but have been used to treat other forms of addiction. The original residential treatment model consisted of a 3- to 6-week hospital-based, inpatient treatment phase, followed by extended outpatient therapy and participation in a self-help group, such as AA. The latter is important to reduce the risk of relapse once a patient leaves the residential setting.

Long-Term Residential Treatment Programs

Long-term residential treatment provides care 24 hours a day, generally in nonhospital settings. The **therapeutic community (TC)** is the best-known residential treatment model. TCs focus on the "resocialization" of the individual and use the program's entire community (e.g., staff, other residents) as important treatment components. Treatment focuses on developing personal accountability and responsibility. Treatment is highly structured. It can be confrontational at times, with activities designed to assist residents in examining damaging self-concepts and beliefs, and destructive patterns of behavior. A key focus is to assume new, more constructive ways to interact with others. Planned lengths of stay in TCs are often between 6 and 12 months. TCs often offer comprehensive services, which can include employment training on site. Research shows that TCs can be modified to treat individuals with special needs, including women, adolescents, homeless individuals, people with severe mental disorders, and individuals in the criminal justice system (NIDA 2009b).

Individualized Drug Counseling

Individualized drug counseling not only focuses on stopping or reducing illicit substance abuse, but also addresses related areas of impaired functioning such as employment status, criminal activity, and family/social relationships. Such counseling assists the patient in developing coping strategies to abstain from drug use and maintain abstinence through an emphasis on short-term behavioral goals. Counselors often make referrals for needed supplemental medical, psychiatric, employment, and other services (NIDA 2009b).

KEY TERMS

therapeutic community (TC)
inpatient treatment that focuses on the "resocialization" of the individual and uses the program's entire community as important treatment components

A patient receives individual counseling in an alcoholism treatment center.

Pharmacological Strategies

Some treatment strategies employ pharmacological approaches to help patients with their addiction(s). These strategies are based on the properties of the drug to which they are addicted. Examples of these strategies are discussed in the following sections.

Methadone

Treatment for opiate addicts is often conducted in specialized outpatient settings (e.g., methadone maintenance clinics) using methadone. Methadone is an opioid agonist (that is, a drug that activates opioid receptors). It is a long-acting synthetic opiate medication administered orally for a sustained period at a dosage sufficient to prevent opiate withdrawal and decrease craving. Patients stabilized on adequate, sustained dosages of methadone can function normally. They can hold jobs, avoid the crime and violence of the street culture, and reduce their exposure to HIV by stopping or decreasing injection drug use and drug-related, high-risk sexual behavior.

Patients stabilized on opiate agonists can engage more readily in counseling and other behavioral interventions essential to recovery and rehabilitation. According to NIDA (2009b), the best, most effective opiate agonist maintenance programs include individual and/or group counseling as well as provision of or referral to other needed medical, psychological, and social services.

Naloxone and Naltrexone

As discussed earlier in this book, an antagonist is a compound that suppresses the actions of a drug. Narcotic antagonists have properties that make them important tools in the clinical treatment of narcotic drug dependence (see "Holding the Line: Expanded Options for Treatment of Heroin Addiction"). For instance, the short-acting opioid antagonist, naloxone (Narcan), is often used in the emergency treatment of opioid overdoses.

Naltrexone is a long-acting synthetic opioid antagonist used as a treatment for opioid addiction. It is usually prescribed in outpatient medical settings, although treatment initiation often begins after medical detoxification in a residential setting. Individuals must be opioid-free for several days before taking naltrexone in order to avoid withdrawal symptoms. Naltrexone is taken orally either daily or three times a week for a sustained period, and thus prevents all the effects of self-administered opioids. Naltrexone *per se* has neither subjective effects nor potential for abuse; however, patient noncompliance is a frequent problem, and thus, many treatment providers have found naltrexone to be most appropriate for highly motivated, recently detoxified patients such as professionals, parolees, and probationers, who desire total abstinence because of external circumstances.

Buprenorphine

In 2000, Congress passed the Drug Addiction Treatment Act (DATA). This legislation allowed qualified physicians to prescribe Schedule III, IV, and V medications for the treatment of opioid addiction in general medical settings (e.g., primary care offices). Such office-based treatment of opioid addiction is a cost-effective approach that increases the span of treatment and the options available to patients.

Buprenorphine is a **partial agonist** (that is, a drug that has both agonist and antagonist properties) at opioid receptors that was the first medication to be approved under DATA. It reduces or eliminates withdrawal symptoms associated with opioid dependence but generally does not produce the euphoria and sedation caused by other opioids. It is available in two formulations—Subutex, which contains

KEY TERMS

partial agonist
a drug that has both agonist and antagonist properties

Holding the Line Expanded Options for Treatment of Heroin Addiction

Until 2000, opiate dependence treatments such as methadone could be dispensed only in a very limited number of clinics that specialize in addiction treatment. As a consequence of the Drug Addiction Treatment Act of 2000 (see Chapter 3), the FDA announced approval of Subutex and Suboxone tablets for the treatment of opiate dependence by specially trained physicians. Accordingly, the drugs can be prescribed in an office setting and, therefore, can provide greater access to patients needing treatment.

Subutex and Suboxone treat opiate addiction by preventing symptoms of withdrawal from heroin and other opiates. Subutex contains only buprenorphine (a partial opioid agonist) and is intended for use at the beginning of treatment for opioid abuse once the individual has undergone detoxification. Suboxone contains both buprenorphine and the opiate antagonist naloxone and is intended to be used in maintenance treatment of opiate addiction. Naloxone has limited effects if administered sublingually, but is effective as an antagonist if administered intravenously. It has been added to Suboxone to guard against intravenous abuse of buprenorphine by individuals who are physically dependent on opiates.

only buprenorphine, and Suboxone, which contains both buprenorphine and naloxone. Naloxone is present in Suboxone so as to lessen its abuse potential, because it produces severe withdrawal symptoms if injected for abuse purposes.

Nicotine Replacement Therapy

Nicotine was the first pharmacological agent approved by the FDA for use in smoking cessation therapy. As discussed in Chapter 11, nicotine replacement therapies, such as nicotine gum, transdermal patches, nasal sprays, and inhalers, are used to relieve withdrawal symptoms. An added benefit is that these forms of nicotine have little abuse potential because they do not produce the pleasurable effects of tobacco products.

Other Pharmacological Therapies

Clonidine is useful in the treatment of opiate-dependent people during the difficult withdrawal stages (Substance Abuse and Mental Health Services Administration [SAMHSA] 2006). Clonidine is not addictive and does not cause euphoria, but it does block cravings for drugs. In contrast to some treatments, no special licensing is required to dispense this medication.

Antabuse, whose generic name is disulfiram, is a drug used for treating alcoholics. This drug causes nausea, vomiting, flushing, and anxiety if an individual consumes alcohol while taking the drug (SAMHSA 2007). Thus, this drug is perceived as a deterrent drug. Acamprosate (Campral) is a drug demonstrated to help dependent alcoholics maintain abstinence for several weeks to months, and it may be more effective in patients with severe dependence. The drug acts on both the gamma-aminobutyric acid (GABA; an inhibitory neurotransmitter) and glutamate (an excitatory neurotransmitter) systems and purportedly reduces symptoms of protracted withdrawal, such as insomnia, anxiety, restlessness, and dysphoria (NIDA 2009b).

Discussion Questions

1. Discuss the need to assess addiction severity and readiness to change.

2. List several principles that characterize effective addiction treatment.

3. Discuss the role of comorbidity in substance abuse and its treatment.

4. Describe Alcoholics Anonymous and its approach to assisting individuals addicted to alcohol.

5. Describe several therapeutic strategies to treat addiction.

6. Describe the therapeutic community approach to treating substance abuse.

7. Describe three pharmacological strategies to treat opioid dependence.

Summary

1 Individuals who are addicted to drugs come from all walks of life. It is important that treatment providers determine the severity of their addiction as well as the readiness of an individual to change his or her behavior.

2 The process of determining addiction severity can be accomplished in many ways, including the administration of standardized questionnaires such as the Addiction Severity Index (ASI). The ASI provides information that can be used to identify and prioritize which problem domains are the most critical and require immediate attention.

3 It is important to assess a person's readiness to change his or her abuse behavior because this can help providers select the best treatment plan to address a client's needs. This may help prevent the individual who is receiving treatment from rejecting all or parts of the treatment plan.

4 Comorbidity is a condition in which two or more illnesses occur in the same person, simultaneously or sequentially. This term also suggests interactions between the illnesses that affect the course and prognosis of both.

5 Changes in the structure and function in regions of the brain affected by drug addiction can also occur in mental illnesses such as anxiety, psychosis, and depression. Overlapping factors including genetic vulnerabilities, trauma, stress, and/or underlying brain abnormalities can contribute to both substance abuse disorders and mental illnesses.

6 Effective treatment of individuals with comorbid substance abuse and mental illnesses requires accurate diagnosis of both conditions. However, several fundamental barriers stand in the way of treating comorbid disorders.

7 One of the earliest real alcoholism recovery efforts was Alcoholics Anonymous (AA). Programs modeled on AA, known as 12-step fellowships, are major routes to recovery.

8 There are numerous approaches to drug addiction treatment, including outpatient and residential treatment. Medical detoxification is not a treatment *per se*, but rather a precursor to treatment.

9 Motivational enhancement therapy is a client-centered counseling approach for initiating behavior change by helping clients to resolve ambivalence about engaging in treatment and discontinuing drug use.

10 A major approach to heroin and other opiate addiction has involved the provision of methadone, a synthetic opiate.

References

Al-Anon. *Al-Anon's Favorite Forum Editorials.* New York: Al-Anon Family Group Headquarters, 1970.

Alcoholics Anonymous. "The Twelve Steps of Alcoholics Anonymous." 2007. Available http://www.aa.org/en_services_for_members.cfm?PageID=98&SubPage=117

Chan, Y. F., M. L. Dennis, and R. L. Funk. "Prevalence and Comorbidity of Major Internalizing and Externalizing Problems among Adolescents and Adults Presenting to Substance Abuse Treatment." *Journal of Substance Abuse Treatment* 34(1) (2008):14–24.

DiClemente, C. C., and J. O. Prochaska. "Toward a Comprehensive, Transtheoretical Model of Change." In *Treating Addictive Behaviors: Processes of Change,* edited by W. R. Miller and N. Heather. New York: Plenum Press, 1998.

McLellan, A. T., H. Kushner, D. Metzger, R. Peters, I. Smith, G. Grissom, et al. "The Fifth Edition of the Addiction Severity Index." *Journal of Substance Abuse Treatment* 9 (1992): 199–213.

McLellan, A. T., L. Luborsky, J. Cacciola, J. Griffith, F. Evans, H. L. Barr, et al. "New Data from the Addiction Severity Index. Reliability and Validity in Three Centers." *Journal of Nervous and Mental Disease* 173 (1985), 412–423.

McLellan, A. T., L. Luborsky, G. E. Woody, and C. P. O'Brien. "An Improved Diagnostic Evaluation Instrument for Substance Abuse Patients. The Addiction Severity Index." *Journal of Nervous and Mental Disease* 168 (1980): 26–33.

National Institute on Drug Abuse (NIDA). *Principles of Drug Addiction Treatment.* Publication No. 99-4180. Washington, DC: National Institutes of Health, October 1999.

National Institute on Drug Abuse (NIDA). "Comorbidity: Addiction and Other Mental Illnesses." NIH Publication N. 08-5771. 2008. Available http://drugabuse.gov/researchreports/comorbidity

National Institute on Drug Abuse. "Most People Entering Treatment Have Additional Mental Health Problems." *NIDA Notes* 22(5) (2009a). NIH Publication 09-6460. Available http://www.drugabuse.gov/NIDA_notes/NNvol22N5/Numbers.html

National Institute on Drug Abuse (NIDA). *Principles of Drug Addiction Treatment.* Publication No. 09-4180. Washington, DC: National Institutes of Health, April 2009b.

National Institute on Drug Abuse (NIDA). "Research Addresses Needs of Criminal Justice Staff and Offenders." *NIDA Notes* 3 (April 2009c). Available http://www.drugabuse.gov/NIDA_notes/NNvol22N3/nidaatwork.html#insert

Substance Abuse and Mental Health Services Administration (SAMHSA). *Quick Click for Clinicians, Detoxification and Substance Abuse Treatment.* DHHS Publication No. (SMA) 06-4225. 2006.

Substance Abuse and Mental Health Services Administration (SAMHSA). *What Is Substance Abuse Treatment?* DHHS Publication No. (SMA) 07-4126. 2007.

Stilen, P., D. Carise, N. Roget, and A. Wendler. *Treatment Planning M.A.T.R.S. Utilizing the Addiction Severity Index (ASI) to Make Required Data Collection Useful.* Kansas City, MO: Mid-America Addiction Technology Transfer Center in Residence at the University of Missouri–Kansas City, 2007.

APPENDIX A

Federal Agencies with Drug Abuse Missions

Drug Enforcement Administration

Because of the unique problems of drug abuse in 1930, Congress authorized the establishment of the Bureau of Narcotics in the Treasury Department to administer the relevant laws. This agency remained in the Treasury Department until 1968, when it became part of a new group in the Justice Department, the Bureau of Narcotics and Dangerous Drugs. Harry Anslinger served as head of the bureau for over 30 years, from its creation until his retirement in 1962. Anslinger was an agent during Prohibition, and later, as head of the bureau, he played an important role in getting marijuana outlawed by the federal government.

In 1973, the Bureau of Narcotics and Dangerous Drugs became the Drug Enforcement Administration (DEA) with the mission to enforce the laws of the United States that control and regulate drugs and substances with significant abuse potential. Today, the DEA has the responsibility of infiltrating and breaking up illegal drug traffic in the United States, as well as controlling the use of scheduled substances. It attempts to achieve its mission by investigating and prosecuting violators of drug laws at both the interstate and international levels. In order to achieve these objectives, the DEA and its agents identify and infiltrate drug gangs, manage national drug intelligence programs, and seize assets derived from illegal drug trade. In 2010, the DEA employed 5235 special agents with 87 foreign offices in 63 countries. It had an annual budget of $2.3 billion to deal with illegal drug activity—this budget dwarfs the initial budget of $73 million in 1974 (Joyce 2010).

The Substance Abuse and Mental Health Services Administration

With passage of the Alcohol, Drug Abuse, and Mental Health Administration (ADAMHA) Reorganization Act of 1992, the services programs of the National Institute on Drug Abuse (NIDA), National Institute on Alcohol Abuse and Alcoholism (NIAAA), and National Institute of Mental Health (NIMH) were incorporated into the newly created Substance Abuse and Mental Health Services Administration (SAMHSA). This agency was given the lead responsibility for the prevention and treatment of addictive and mental health problems and disorders. Its overall mission is to reduce the incidence and prevalence of substance abuse and mental disorders by ensuring the best therapeutic use of scientific knowledge and improving access to high-quality, effective programs (Bush 1992).

State Regulations

There have always been questions regarding the relative responsibilities of state versus federal laws and their respective regulatory agencies. In general, the U.S. form of government has allowed local control to take precedence over national control. Because of this historic attitude, states were the first to pass laws to regulate the abuse or misuse of drugs. Federal laws developed later, after the federal government gained greater jurisdiction over the well-being and lives of the citizens, and it became apparent that, due to interstate trafficking, national drug abuse problems could not be dealt with effectively on a state-by-state basis. Some early state laws banned the use of smoking opium, regulated the sale of various psychoactive drug substances, and, in a few instances, set up treatment programs. However, these early legislative actions made no effort to *prevent* drug abuse. Drug abuse was controlled to a great extent by social pressure rather than by law. It was considered morally wrong to be an alcoholic or an addict to opium or some other drug.

The drug laws varied considerably from state to state in 1932, so the National Conference of Commissioners on Uniform State Laws set up the Uniform Narcotic Drug Act (UNDA), which was later adopted by nearly all states. The UNDA provided for the control of possession, use, and distribution of opiates and cocaine. In 1942, marijuana was included under this act because it was classified as a narcotic.

In 1967, the Food and Drug Administration proposed the Model Drug Abuse Control Act and urged the states to adopt it on a uniform basis. This law extended controls over depressant, stimulant, and hallucinogenic drugs, similar to the 1965 federal law. Many states set up laws based on this model.

The federal Controlled Substances Act of 1970 stimulated the National Conference of Commissioners to propose a new Uniform Controlled Substances Act (UCSA). The UCSA permits enactment of a single state law regulating the illicit possession, use, manufacture, and dispensing of controlled psychoactive substances. At this time, most states have enacted the UCSA or modifications of it. For an example of a UCSA, see the 2010 Wisconsin Code (http://law.justia.com/wisconsin/codes/2010/961/961.html).

Today, state law enforcement of drug statutes does not always reflect federal regulations, although for the most part, the two statutory levels are harmonious. An example of where the two differ is marijuana, which has been approved for medicinal use in Alaska, Arizona, California, Hawaii, Maine, Michigan, Montana, Nevada, New Jersey, New Mexico, Oregon, Rhode Island, Vermont, Washington, and Washington, DC. Despite these state actions, marijuana is still considered a Schedule I substance by federal regulatory agencies (ProCon.org 2010).

References

Bush, G. "Statement on Signing the ADAMHA Reorganization Act." 1992. Available http://www.presidency.ucsb.edu/ws/index.php?pid=21218

Joyce, S. "Drug Enforcement Administration History." eHow. (11 October 2010). Available http://www.ehow.com/facts_7316838_drug-enforcement-administration-history.html

ProCon.org. "15 Legal Medical Marijuana States and DC." 2010. Available http://medicalmarijuana.procon.org/view.resource.php?resourceID=000881

APPENDIX B

Drugs of Use and Abuse

The table that follows provides detailed information about the drugs listed. Note that the heading *CSA Schedules* refers to categorization under the Controlled Substances Act (CSA). The roman numeral(s) to the right of each drug name specifies each as a Schedule I, II, III, IV, or V drug. The headings indicated in the first row describe the properties of the drugs listed in the first column. See Chapter 3 for more information on scheduling.

DRUGS	CSA SCHEDULES	TRADE OR OTHER NAMES	MEDICAL USES	DEPENDENCE PHYSICAL	PSYCHOLOGICAL
Narcotics					
Heroin	Substance I	Diamorphine, horse, smack, black tar, chiva, negra, H. stuff, junk, Al Capone, antifreeze, brown sugar, hard candy	None in U.S., analgesic, antitussive	High	High
Morphine	Substance II	MS-Contin, Roxanol, Oramorph SR, MSIR, God's drug, Mister Blue, morpho, unkie	Analgesic	High	High
Hydrocodone	Substance II, Product III, V	Hydrocodone w/ acetaminophen, Vicodin, Vicoprofen, Tussionex, Lortab	Analgesic, antitussive	High	High
Hydromorphone	Substance II	Dilaudid, little D, lords	Analgesic	High	High
Oxycodone	Substance II	Roxicet, oxycodone w/acetaminophen, OxyContin, Endocet, Percocet, Percodan	Analgesic	High	High
Codeine	Substance II, Product III, V	Acetaminophen, guaifenesin, or promethazine w/ codeine; Fiorinal, Fioricet, or Tylenol with codeine, coties, school boy	Analgesic, antitussive	Moderate	Moderate
Other narcotics	Substance II, III, IV	Fentanyl, Demerol, methadone, Darvon, Stadol, Talwin, Paregoric, Buprenex, T. and Blue's, designer drugs (fentanyl derivatives), China white, gravy	Analgesic, antidiarrheal, antitussive	High-low	High-low
Depressants					
Gamma hydroxybutyric acid	Substance I, Product III	GHB, liquid Ecstasy, liquid X, sodium oxybate, Xytem	None in U.S., anesthetic	Moderate	Moderate

TOLERANCE	DURATION (HOURS)	USUAL METHOD	POSSIBLE EFFECTS	EFFECTS OF OVERDOSE	WITHDRAWAL SYNDROME
Yes	3–4	Injected, snorted, smoked	Euphoria, drowsiness, respiratory depression, constricted pupils, nausea	Slow and shallow breathing, clammy skin, convulsions, coma, possible death	Watery eyes, runny nose, yawning, loss of appetite, irritability, tremors, panic, cramps, nausea, chills, sweating
Yes	3–12	Oral, injected			
Yes	3–6	Oral			
Yes	3–4	Oral, injected			
Yes	3–12	Oral			
Yes	3–4	Oral, injected			
Yes	Variable	Oral, injected, snorted, smoked			
Yes	3–6	Oral	Slurred speech, disorientation, drunken behavior without odor of alcohol, impaired memory of events, interacts with alcohol	Shallow respiration, clammy skin, dilated pupils, weak and rapid pulse, coma, possible death	Anxiety, insomnia, tremors, delirium, convulsions, possible death

(continued)

DRUGS	CSA SCHEDULES	TRADE OR OTHER NAMES	MEDICAL USES	DEPENDENCE PHYSICAL	PSYCHOLOGICAL
Depressants (continued)					
Benzodiazepines	Substance IV	Valium, Xanax, Halcion, Ativan, Restoril, Rohypnol, (roofies, R-2), Klonopin, downers, goof balls, sleeping pills, candy	Antianxiety, sedative, anticonvulsant, hypnotic, muscle relaxant	Moderate	Moderate
Other depressants	Substance I, II, III, IV	Ambien, Sonata, Meprobamate, chloral hydrate, barbiturates, methaqualone (Quaalude), tranquilizers, muscle relaxants, sleeping pills	Antianxiety, sedative, hypnotic	Moderate	Moderate
Stimulants					
Cocaine	Substance II	Coke, flake, snow, crack, coca, blanca, perico, nieve, soda, bump, toot, C, candy, nose candy	Local anesthetic	Possible	High
Amphetamine/ methamphetamine	Substance II	Crank, ice, cristal, krystal meth, speed, Adderall, Dexedrine, Desoxyn, pep pills, bennies, uppers, truck drivers, dexies, black beauties, sparklers, beens	Attention deficit hyperactivity disorder, narcolepsy, weight control	Possible	High
Methylphenidate	Substance II	Ritalin (illy's), Concerta, Focalin, Metadate, speed, meth, crystal, crank, go fast	Attention deficit hyperactivity disorder	Possible	High
Other stimulants	Substance III, IV	Adipex P, Ionamin, Prelu-2, Didrex, Provigil	Vasoconstriction	Possible	Moderate
Hallucinogens					
MDMA and analogs	Substance I	Ecstasy, XTC, Adam, MDA (love drug), MDEA (Eve), MBDB	None	None	Moderate
LSD	Substance I	Acid, microdot, sunshine, boomers, blue chairs, Loony Toons, pane, cubes	None	None	Unknown

TOLERANCE	DURATION (HOURS)	USUAL METHOD	POSSIBLE EFFECTS	EFFECTS OF OVERDOSE	WITHDRAWAL SYNDROME
Yes	1–8	Oral, injected			
Yes	2–6	Oral			
Yes	1–2	Snorted, smoked injected	Increased alertness, excitation, euphoria. increased pulse rate and blood pressure, insomnia, loss of appetite	Agitation, increased body temperature, hallucinations, convulsions, possible death	Apathy, long periods of sleep, irritability, depression, disorientation
Yes	2–4	Oral, injected, smoked			
Yes	2–4	Oral, injected, snorted, smoked			
Yes	2–4	Oral			
Yes	4–6	Oral snorted smoked	Heightened senses, teeth grinding, dehydration	Increased body temperature, electrolyte imbalance, cardiac arrest	Muscle aches, drowsiness, depression, acne
Yes	8–12	Oral	Illusions and hallucinations, altered perception of time and distance	(LSD) Longer, more intense trip episodes	None

(continued)

DRUGS	CSA SCHEDULES	TRADE OR OTHER NAMES	MEDICAL USES	DEPENDENCE	
				PHYSICAL	PSYCHOLOGICAL
Hallucinogens (continued)					
Phencyclidine and analogs	Substance I, II, III	PCP, angel dust, hog, loveboat, ketamine (special K), PCE, PCPy, TCP, peace pill	Anesthetic (ketamine)	Possible	High
Other hallucinogens	Substance I	Psilocybimushrooms, mescaline, peyote cactus, ayahausca, DMT, dextromethorphan (DXM), sacred mushrooms, magic mushrooms, mushrooms, ying yang, strawberry fields	None	None	None
Cannabis					
Marijuana	Substance I	Pot, grass, sinsemilla, blunts, mota, yerba, grifa, 420, airhead (marijuana user), bud, catnip, reefer, roach, joint, weed, loco weed, Mary Jane	None	Unknown	Moderate
Tetrahydro-cannabinol	Substance I, Product III	THC, Marinol	Antinauseant, appetite stimulant	Yes	Moderate
Hashish and hashish oil	Substance I	Hash, hash oil	None	Unknown	Moderate
Anabolic Steroids					
Testosterone	Substance III	Depo Testosterone, Sustanon, sten, cypt	Hypogonadism	Unknown	Unknown
Other anabolic steroids	Substance III	Parabolan, Winstrol, Equipose, Anadrol, Dianabol, Primabolin-Depo, D-Ball	Anemia, breast cancer	Unknown	Yes
Inhalants					
Amyl and butyl nitrate		Pearls, poppers, rush locker room	Angina (amyl)	Unknown	Unknown

TOLERANCE	DURATION (HOURS)	USUAL METHOD	POSSIBLE EFFECTS	EFFECTS OF OVERDOSE	WITHDRAWAL SYNDROME
Yes	1–12	Smoked, oral, injected, snorted		Unable to direct movement, feel pain, or remember	Drug-seeking behavior; DXM is not designated as a narcotic under CSA
Possible	4–8	Oral			
Yes	2–4	Smoked, oral	Euphoria, relaxed inhibitions, increased appetite, disorientation	Fatigue, paranoia, possible psychosis	Occasional reports of insomnia, hyperactivity, decreased appetite
Yes	2–4	Smoked, oral			
Yes	2–4	Smoked oral			
Unknown	14–28 days	Injected	Virilization, edema, testicular atrophy, gynecomastia, acne, aggressive behavior	Unknown	Possible depression
Unknown	Variable	Oral, injected			
No	1	Inhaled	Flushing, hypo-tension, headache	Methemoglobinemia	Agitation

(continued)

DRUGS	CSA SCHEDULES	TRADE OR OTHER NAMES	MEDICAL USES	DEPENDENCE	
				PHYSICAL	PSYCHOLOGICAL
Inhalants (continued)					
Nitrous oxide		Laughing gas, balloons, whippets	Anesthetic	Unknown	Low
Other inhalants		Adhesives, spray paint, hair spray, dry cleaning fluid, spot remover, lighter fluid, air blast, moon gas, sniffing, glue sniffing	None	Unknown	High
Alcohol		Beer, wine, liquor	None	High	High

Source: Adapted from Drug Enforcement Administration (DEA), U.S. Department of Justice (DOJ). "Drugs of Abuse." 2004. Available at: http://www.justice.gov/dea/pubs/abuse. Accessed March 16, 2011.

TOLERANCE	DURATION (HOURS)	USUAL METHOD	POSSIBLE EFFECTS	EFFECTS OF OVERDOSE	WITHDRAWAL SYNDROME
No	0.5	Inhaled	Impaired memory, slurred speech, drunken behavior, slow onset vitamin deficiency, organ damage	Vomiting, respiratory depression, loss of consciousness, possible death	Trembling, anxiety, insomnia, vitamin deficiency, confusion, hallucinations, convulsions
No	0.5–2	Inhaled			
Yes	1–3	Oral			

GLOSSARY

acquaintance and date rape
unplanned and unwanted forced sexual attack from a friend or a date partner

acute
immediate or short-term effects after taking a single drug dose

acute alcohol withdrawal syndrome
symptoms that occur when an individual who is addicted to alcohol does not maintain his or her usual blood alcohol level

addiction
generally refers to the psychological attachment to a drug(s); addiction to "harder" drugs such as heroin results in both psychological and physical attachment to the chemical properties of the drug, with the resulting satisfaction (reward) derived from using the drug in question

addiction to pleasure theory
a theory assuming that it is biologically normal to continue a pleasure stimulus once begun

additive interactions
effects created when drugs are similar and actions are added together

Adolescents Training and Learning to Avoid Steroids (ATLAS) program
an anabolic abuse prevention educational program that empowers student athletes to make the right choices about steroid use

adulterated
contaminating substances are mixed in to dilute the drugs

agonistic
a type of substance that activates a receptor

alcohol abuse
uncontrollable drinking that leads to alcohol craving, loss of control, and physical dependence but with less prominent characteristics than found in alcoholism

alcohol dehydrogenase
principal enzyme that metabolizes ethanol

alcoholic cardiomyopathy
congestive heart failure due to the replacement of heart muscle with fat and fiber

alcoholic hepatitis
the second stage of alcohol-induced liver disease in which chronic inflammation occurs; reversible if alcoholic consumption ceases

alcoholism
a state of physical and psychological addiction to ethanol, a psychoactive substance

altered perceptions
changes in the interpretation of stimuli resulting from marijuana

alternatives approach
an approach emphasizing the exploration of positive alternatives to drug abuse, based on replacing the pleasurable feelings gained from drug abuse with involvement in social and educational activities

amnesiac
causing the loss of memory

amotivational syndrome
a controversial syndrome claiming that heavy use of marijuana causes a lack of motivation and reduced productivity

anabolic steroids
androgen-like drugs that can increase muscle mass and strength

analgesics
drugs that relieve pain without affecting consciousness

analogs
drugs with similar structures

anandamide
a naturally occurring fatty acid neurotransmitter that selectively activates cannabinoid receptors

androgens
male sex hormones

anesthesia
a state characterized by loss of sensation or consciousness

anesthetic
a drug that blocks sensitivity to pain

angina pectoris
severe chest pain usually caused by a deficiency of blood to the heart muscle

anorexiants
drugs that suppress the activity of the brain's appetite center, causing reduced food intake

antagonistic
a type of substance that blocks a receptor

antagonistic interactions
effects created when drugs cancel one another

anticholinergic
agents that antagonize the effects of acetylcholine

antihistamines
drugs that often cause CNS depression, are used to treat allergies, and are often included in over-the-counter (OTC) sleep aids

anti-inflammatory
relieves symptoms of inflammation

antipyretics
drugs that reduce fevers

antitussives
drugs that block the coughing reflex

anxiolytic
drug that relieves anxiety

AOD
alcohol and other drugs

aphrodisiac
a compound that is believed to be the cause of sexual arousal

array
use of other drugs while taking anabolic steroids to avoid possible side effects

arrhythmia
an irregular heartbeat

ATOD
alcohol, tobacco, and other drugs

attitude change or affective education model
assumes that people use drugs because of lack of self-esteem

autonomic nervous system (ANS)
controls the unconscious functions of the body

axons
an extension of the neuronal cell body along which electrochemical signals travel

β-adrenergic stimulants
drugs that stimulate a subtype of adrenaline and noradrenaline receptors

BACCHUS Network
a national and international association of college and university peer education programs focused on alcohol abuse prevention and other related student health and safety issues

barbiturates
potent CNS depressants, usually not preferred because of their narrow margin of safety

behavioral stereotypy
meaningless repetition of a single activity

behavioral tolerance
compensation for motor impairments through behavioral pattern modification by chronic alcohol users

benzodiazepines
the most popular and safest CNS depressants in use today

binge
similar to a run, but usually of shorter duration

binge use (binge drinking)
a pattern of drinking five or more drinks for men and four or more drinks for women on a single occasion, such as the same time or within two hours of each other, on at least 1 day in the past 30 days; includes heavy use

biotransformation
process of changing the chemical properties of a drug, usually by metabolism

blood alcohol concentration (BAC)
concentration of alcohol found in the blood, often expressed as a percentage

blood–brain barrier
selective filtering between the cerebral blood vessels and the brain

bootlegging
making, distributing, and selling alcoholic beverages during the Prohibition era

bronchodilators
drugs that widen air passages

caffeinism
symptoms caused by taking high chronic doses of caffeine

cannabinoid system
biological target of tetrahydrocannabinol in marijuana

Cannabis sativa
biological species name for the variety of hemp plant known as marijuana

catatonia
a condition of physical rigidity, excitement, and stupor

catecholamines
a class of biochemical compounds including the transmitters norepinephrine, epinephrine, and dopamine

central nervous system (CNS)
one of the major divisions of the nervous system, composed of the brain and the spinal cord

characterological or personality predisposition model
the view of chemical dependency as a symptom of problems in the development or operation of the system of needs, motives, and attitudes within the individual

chewing tobacco
tobacco leaves shredded and twisted into strands for chewing purposes

chronic
long-term effects, usually after taking multiple drug doses

cirrhosis
scarring of the liver and formation of fibrous tissues; results from alcohol abuse; irreversible

closed meetings
meetings to which only alcoholics having a serious desire to completely stop drinking are invited

club drug
drug used at all-night raves, parties, dance clubs, and bars to enhance sensory experiences

cocaine babies
infants born to women who used cocaine during their pregnancy

codependency
behavior displayed by either addicted or nonaddicted family members (codependents) who identify with the alcohol addict and cover up the excessive drinking behavior, allowing it to continue and letting it affect the codependent's life

comorbidity
two or more disorders or illnesses occurring in the same person; they can occur either simultaneously or one after the other; also implies interactions between the illnesses that can worsen the course of both

compulsive users
second category of drug users, typified by an insatiable attraction followed by a psychological dependence on drugs

congestion rebound
withdrawal from excessive use of a decongestant, resulting in congestion

congestive heart failure
the heart is unable to pump sufficient blood for the body's needs

control theory
theory that emphasizes when people are left without bonds to other groups (peers, family, social groups), they generally have a tendency to deviate from upheld values and attitudes

conventional behavior
behavior largely dictated by custom and tradition, which is often disrupted by the forces of rapid technological change

crack
already processed and inexpensive "freebased" cocaine, ready for smoking

cross-dependence
dependence on a drug can be relieved by other similar drugs

cross-tolerance
development of tolerance to one drug causes tolerance to related drugs

cumulative effect
buildup of a drug in the body after multiple doses taken at short intervals

current alcohol use (current drinkers)
at least one drink in the past 30 days; can include binge and heavy use

cycling
use of different types of steroids singly but in sequence

delirium tremens (DTs)
the most severe, even life-threatening form of alcohol withdrawal, involving hallucinations, delirium, and fever

demand reduction
attempts to decrease individuals' tendencies to use drugs, often aimed at youth, with emphasis on reformulating values and behaviors

dendrites
short branches of neurons that receive transmitter signals

dependence
physiological and psychological changes or adaptations that occur in response to the frequent administration of a drug

dependency phase
synonym for addiction

designer drugs/synthetic drugs or synthetic opioids
new drugs that are developed by people intending to circumvent the illegality of a drug by modifying a drug into a new compound; Ecstasy is an example

detoxification
elimination of a toxic substance, such as a drug, and its effects from the body

diabetes mellitus
disease caused by elevated blood sugar due to insufficient insulin

differential association
process by which individuals become socialized into the perceptions and values of a group

differential reinforcement
ratio between reinforcers, both favorable and disfavorable, for sustaining drug use behavior

disease model
the belief that people abuse alcohol because of some biologically caused condition

disinhibition
loss of conditioned reflexes due to depression of inhibitory centers of the brain

disinhibitor
a psychoactive chemical that depresses thought and judgment functions in the cerebral cortex, which has the effect of allowing relatively unrestrained behavior (as in alcohol inebriation)

distillation

heating fermented mixtures of cereal grains or fruits in a still to evaporate and be trapped as purified alcohol

diuretic

a drug or substance that increases the production of urine

dopamine

a neurotransmitter present in regions of the brain that regulates movement, emotion, cognition, motivation, and feelings of pleasure; it mediates the rewarding aspects of most drugs of abuse

doping

the use of performance-enhancing drugs to increase athletic ability

dose–response

correlation between the amount of a drug given and its effects

"double wall" of encapsulation

an adaptation to pain and avoidance of reality, in which the individual withdraws emotionally and further anesthetizes himself or herself by chemical means

drug

any substance that modifies (either by enhancing, inhibiting, or distorting) mind and/or body functioning

Drug Abuse Resistance Education (D.A.R.E.)

drug education program presented in elementary and junior high schools nationwide by police officers

drug cartels

large, highly sophisticated organizations composed of multiple drug trafficking organizations (DTOs) and cells with specific assignments such as drug transportation, security/enforcement, or money laundering

drug cells

similar to a terrorist cells, consisting of three to five members and ensuring operational security; members of adjacent drug cells usually do not know each other or the identity of their leadership

drug courts

a process that integrates substance abuse treatment, incentives, and sanctions and places nonviolent, drug-involved defendants in judicially supervised rehabilitation programs

Drug Enforcement Administration (DEA)

the principle federal agency responsible for enforcing U.S. drug laws

drug interaction

presence of one drug alters the action of another drug

drug prevention

aimed at preventing or decreasing health problems, including social and personal problems, caused by drug dependency

drug testing

urine, blood screening, or hair analysis used to identify those who may be using drugs

drug trafficking organizations (DTOs)

refers to complex organizations with highly defined command-and-control structures that produce, transport, and/or distribute large quantities of one or more illicit drugs

drunken comportment

behavior exhibited while under the direct influence of alcohol; determined by the norms and expectations of a particular culture

dysphoric

characterized by unpleasant mental effects; the opposite of euphoric

ecological or person-in-environment model

stresses that changes in the environment change people's attitudes about drugs

edema

swollen tissue due to an accumulation of fluid

employee assistance programs (EAPs)

drug assistance programs for drug-dependent employees

enablers

those close to the alcohol addict who deny or make excuses for enabling his or her excessive drinking

endocrine system

relating to hormones, their functions, and sources

endorphins

neurotransmitters that have narcotic-like effects

entactogens

drugs that enhance the sensation and pleasure of touching

environmental tobacco smoke (ETS)

a term referring to secondhand smoke

ergotism

poisoning by toxic substances from the ergot fungus *Claviceps purpurea*

equal-opportunity affliction

refers to the use of drugs, stressing that drug use cuts across all members of society regardless of income, education, occupation, social class, and age

ergogenic

drugs that enhance athletic performance

ethanol

the pharmacological term for alcohol; a consumable type of alcohol that is the psychoactive ingredient in alcoholic beverages; often called grain alcohol

ethylene glycol

alcohol used as antifreeze

euphorigenic

having the ability to cause feelings of pleasure and well-being

expectorants

substances that stimulate mucus secretion and diminish mucus viscosity

experimenters

first category of drug users, typified as being in the initial stages of drug use; these people often use drugs for recreational purposes

fermentation

biochemical process through which yeast converts sugar to alcohol

fetal alcohol syndrome (FAS)

a condition affecting children born to alcohol-consuming mothers that is characterized by facial deformities, growth deficiency, and mental retardation

flashbacks

recurrences of earlier drug-induced sensory experiences in the absence of the drug

floaters or chippers

third category of drug users; these users vacillate between the need for pleasure seeking and the desire to relieve moderate to serious psychological problems; this category of drug user has two major characteristics: (1) a general focus mostly on using other people's drugs (often without maintaining a personal supply of the drug) and (2) vacillation between the characteristics of chronic drug users and experimenter types

freebasing

conversion of cocaine into its alkaline form for smoking

frontal cortex

cortical region essential for information processing and decision making

gastritis

inflammation or irritation of the gut

gateway drugs

alcohol, tobacco, and marijuana—types of drugs that when used excessively may lead to using other and more addictive drugs such as cocaine, heroin, or "crack"

generic

official, nonpatented, nonproprietary name of a drug

genetic and biophysiological theories

explanations of addiction in terms of genetic brain dysfunction and biochemical patterns

genetics

study of cellular DNA and its functions

genogram

a family therapy technique that records information about behavior and relationships on a type of family tree to elucidate persistent patterns of dysfunctional behavior

glaucoma

potentially blinding eye disease causing continual and increasing intraocular pressure

glia

supporting cells that are critical for protecting and providing sustenance to the neurons

habituation

repeating certain patterns of behavior until they become established or habitual

half-life

time required for the body to eliminate and/or metabolize half of a drug dose

hallucinogens

substances that alter sensory processing in the brain, causing perceptual disturbances, changes in thought processing, and depersonalization

harm reduction model

a society-wide approach to drug use and/or abuse that focuses on reducing the harm experienced by the drug user and/or abuser as well as the harm to society

Harrison Act of 1914

the first legitimate effort by the U.S. government to regulate addicting substances

hashish

sticky resin from the female plant flowers, which has an average THC level of 3.6% but can contain as much as 28%

heavy use (heavy drinkers)

five or more drinks on the same occasion on each of 5 or more days in the past 30 days

hepatotoxic effect

a situation in which liver cells increase the production of fat, resulting in an enlarged liver

high

4 to 16 hours after drug use; includes feelings of energy and power

highly active antiretroviral therapy (HAART)

more recent types of medications used to treat HIV/AIDS-infected individuals

high-risk drug choices

developing values and attitudes that lead to using drugs both habitually and addictively

holistic self-awareness approach

emphasizes that nonmedical and often recreational drug use interferes with the healthy balance among the mind, the body, and the spirit

homeostasis

maintenance of internal stability; often biochemical in nature

hormones

chemical messengers released into the blood by glands

human growth factor (HGF)

a hormone that stimulates normal growth

human growth hormone (HGH)

a designer drug synthetic version of HGF; also referred to as simply GH (growth hormone)

hyperglycemia

elevated blood sugar

hyperpyrexia

elevated body temperature

hypertension

elevated blood pressure

hypnotics

CNS depressants used to induce drowsiness and encourage sleep

hypothyroidism

thyroid gland does not produce sufficient hormone

hypoxia

a state of oxygen deficiency

ice

a smokable form of methamphetamine

illicit drugs

illegal drugs such as marijuana, cocaine, and LSD

increased use phase

taking increasing quantities of the drug

information-only or awareness model

assumes that teaching about the harmful effects of drugs will change attitudes about use and abuse

inoculation

a method of abuse prevention that protects drug users by teaching them responsibility

insiders

people on the inside; those who approve of and/or use drugs

insider's perspective

viewing a group or subculture from inside the group; seeing members as they perceive themselves

interdiction

the policy of cutting off or destroying supplies of illicit drugs

intergang

between members of different gangs

intragang

between members of the same gang

intramuscular (IM)

drug injection into a muscle

intravenous (IV)

drug injection into a vein

ischemia

tissue deprived of sufficient blood and oxygen

isopropyl alcohol

rubbing alcohol, sometimes used as an antiseptic

jimsonweed

a potent hallucinogenic plant

keratin layer

outermost protective layer of the skin

keratolytics

caustic agents that cause the keratin skin layer to peel

labeling theory

the theory emphasizing that other people's perceptions directly influence one's self-image

licit drugs

legalized drugs such as coffee, alcohol, and tobacco

low-risk drug choices

developing values and attitudes that lead to controlling the use of alcohol and drugs

mainline

to inject a drug of abuse intravenously

margin of safety

range in dose between the amount of drug necessary to cause a therapeutic effect and that needed to create a toxic effect

Marinol

FDA-approved synthesized THC in capsule form (dronabinol); primarily used to treat nausea and vomiting, prescribed to people diagnosed with acquired immunodeficiency syndrome (AIDS)

master status

major status position in the eyes of others that clearly identifies an individual; for example, doctor, professor, alcoholic, heroin addict

MDMA

a type of illicit drug known as "Ecstasy" or "Adam" and having stimulant and hallucinogenic properties

mead

fermented honey often made into an alcoholic beverage

medical marijuana

use of the THC in cannabis as a drug to calm or to relieve symptoms of an illness

meditation

a state of consciousness in which there is a constant level of awareness focusing on one object; for example, yoga and Zen Buddhism

mental set

the collection of psychological and environmental factors that influence an individual's response to drugs

metabolism

chemical alteration of drugs by body processes

metabolites

chemical products of metabolism

methyl alcohol
wood alcohol

Minnesota model
a major model in the treatment of alcohol and drug abuse, involving a month-long stay in an inpatient rehabilitation facility, a multidisciplinary treatment team, systematic assessment, and a formal treatment plan with long- and short-term goals

molecular biology
study of cellular functions and their regulation

monoamine oxidase inhibitors (MAOIs)
drugs used to treat severe depression

moral model
the belief that people abuse alcohol because they choose to do so

munchies
hunger experienced while under the effects of marijuana

muscarinic
a receptor type activated by ACh; usually inhibitory

muscle dysmorphia
behavioral syndrome that causes men to have a distorted image of their bodies, perceiving themselves as looking small and weak, even when they may be large and muscular; women with this condition think they look fat and flabby, even though they may actually be lean and muscular

mydriasis
pupil dilation

narcolepsy
a condition causing spontaneous and uncontrolled sleeping episodes

National Institute on Drug Abuse (NIDA)
the principle federal agency responsible for directing drug use- and abuse-related research

needle-exchange programs
publically funded programs that distribute new, uncontaminated needles to drug addicts in exchange for used injection needles in order to prevent the spread of HIV and hepatitis B and C

nervous system
relating to the brain, spinal cord, neurons and their associated elements

neurons
specialized nerve cells that make up the nervous system and release neurotransmitters

neurotransmitters
the chemical messengers released by nervous (nerve) cells for communication with other cells

nicotine
a colorless, highly volatile liquid alkaloid

nicotinic
a receptor type activated by ACh; usually excitatory

nonsteroidal anti-inflammatory drugs (NSAIDs)
anti-inflammatory drugs that do not have steroid properties

nucleus accumbens
part of the CNS limbic system and a critical brain region for reward systems

open meetings
meetings to which anyone having an interest in attending and witnessing is invited

opiate receptors
receptors activated by opioid narcotic drugs such as heroin and morphine

opioid
relating to the drugs that are derived from opium

opioids
drugs derived from opium

oral hypoglycemics
drugs taken by mouth to treat type 2 diabetes

outsiders
people on the outside; those who do not approve of and/or use drugs

outsider's perspective
viewing a group or subculture from outside the group and viewing the group and its members as an observer; looking "in" at the members

over-the-counter (OTC)
drugs sold without a prescription

paradoxical effects
unexpected effects

partial agonist
a drug that has both agonist and antagonist properties

patent medicines
the ingredients in these uncontrolled "medicines" were secret, often consisting of large amounts of colored water, alcohol, cocaine, or opiates

peptic ulcers
open sores that occur in the stomach or upper segment of the small intestine

performance enhancers
drugs taken to increase physical or mental endurance to embellish one's performance

peripheral nervous system (PNS)
includes the neurons outside the CNS

personality disorders
a broad category of psychiatric disorders, formerly called "character disorders," that includes the antisocial personality disorder, borderline personality disorder, schizoid personality disorder, and others; these serious, ongoing impairments are difficult to treat

pharmacokinetics
the study of factors that influence the distribution and concentration of drugs in the body

phocomelia
a birth defect; impaired development of the arms, legs, or both

placebo effects
effects caused by suggestion and psychological factors independent of the pharmacological activity of a drug

plateau effect
maximum drug effect, regardless of dose

plateauing
developing tolerance to the effects of anabolic steroids

polydrug use
the concurrent use of multiple drugs

posttraumatic stress disorder
a psychiatric syndrome in which an individual who has been exposed to a traumatic event or situation experiences persistent psychological stress that may manifest itself in a wide range of symptoms, including re-experiencing the trauma, numbing of general responsiveness, and hyperarousal

potency
amount of drug necessary to cause an effect

precursor chemicals
chemicals used to produce a drug

preoccupation phase
constant concern with the supply of the drug

primary deviance
any type of initial deviant behavior in which the perpetrator does not identify with the deviance

primary drug prevention programs
drug prevention programs with a very broad range of activities aimed at reducing the risk of drug use among nonusers and ensuring continued nonuse and helping at-risk individuals avoid the development of addictive behaviors

primary prevention
prevention of any drug use

proprietary
brand or trademark name that is registered with the U.S. Patent Office

proprietary medicine
pharmaceutical medicine that is protected from commercial competition because the ingredients or manufacturing method is kept secret or because it is protected by trademark or copyright

protease inhibitors
a major breakthrough class of drugs used to treat HIV-infected individuals

protective factors
factors associated with preventing the potential for drug abuse such as self-control, parental monitoring, academic competence, anti–drug use policies, and strong neighborhood attachment

pseudointoxicated
acting drunk even before alcohol has had a chance to cause its effects

psychedelics
substances that expand or heighten perception and consciousness

psychoactive drugs (substances)
drug compounds (substances) that affect the central nervous system and alter consciousness and/or perceptions

psychoactive effects
how drug substances alter and affect the brain's mental functions

psychoanalysis
a theory of personality and method of psychotherapy originated by Sigmund Freud, focused on unconscious forces and conflicts and a series of psychosexual stages

psychodrama
a family therapy system developed by Jacques Moreno in which significant interpersonal and intrapersonal issues are enacted in a focused setting using dramatic techniques

psychological dependence
dependence that results because a drug produces pleasant mental effects

psychotogenics
substances that initiate psychotic behavior

psychotomimetics
substances that cause psychosis-like symptoms

pyramiding
moving from a low daily dose at the beginning of the cycle to a higher dose, then reducing use toward the end of the cycle

rebound effect
form of withdrawal; paradoxical effects that occur when a drug has been eliminated from the body

receptors
special proteins in a membrane that are activated by natural substances or drugs to alter cell function

relapsing syndrome
returning to the use of alcohol after quitting

relief phase
satisfaction derived from escaping negative feelings in using the drug

REM sleep
the restive phase of sleep associated with dreaming

retrospective interpretation

social psychological process of redefining a person in light of a major status position; for example, homosexual, physician, professor, alcoholic, convicted felon, or mental patient

reverse tolerance

enhanced response to a given drug dose; opposite of tolerance

Reye's syndrome

potentially fatal complication of colds, flu, or chicken pox in children

risk factors

drug prevention is aimed at reducing risk factors, such as early aggressive behavior, lack of parental supervision, the lure of gang membership, drug availability, and poverty

Rohypnol

the "date-rape drug," used on many college campuses

role playing

a therapeutic technique in which group members play assigned parts to elicit emotional reactions

run

intense use of a stimulant, consisting of multiple administrations over a period of days

rush

initial pleasure after amphetamine use that includes racing heartbeat and elevated blood pressure

salicylates

aspirin-like drugs

scare tactic approach

drug prevention information based on emphasizing the extreme negative effects of drug use—scaring the audience of potential and current drug users/abusers into not using drugs

secondary deviance

any type of deviant behavior in which the perpetrator identifies with the deviance

secondary drug prevention programs

programs that consist of uncovering potentially harmful substance use prior to the onset of overt symptoms or problems and/or targeting newer drug users with a limited history of use; the main goal is to target at-risk groups, experimenters, and early-abuse populations

secondary prevention

preventing drug use from either casual or recreational to drug dependence

secondhand smoke

smoke released into the air from a lighted cigarette, cigar, or pipe tip and exhaled mainstream smoke

sedatives

CNS depressants used to relieve anxiety, fear, and apprehension

sensation-seeking individuals

types of people who characteristically are continually seeking new or novel thrills in their experiences

set and setting

set refers to the individual's expectation of what a drug will do to his or her personality; setting is the physical and social environments where the drug is consumed

side effects

unintended drug responses

sinsemilla

meaning without seeds, this marijuana is made from the buds and flowering tops of female plants and is one of the most potent types

snuff

finely ground smokeless tobacco that can be moist or dry

snuff dipping

placing a pinch of tobacco between the gums and the cheek

social influences model

assumes that drug users lack resistance skills

social influence theories

sociological theories that view a person's day-to-day social relations as a primary cause for drug use

socialization

the growth and development process responsible for learning how to become a responsible, functioning human being

social learning theory

a theory that places emphasis on how an individual learns patterns of behavior from the attitudes of others, society, and peers

social lubricant

belief that drinking (misconceived as safe) represses inhibitions, strengthens extroversion, and leads to increased sociability

sociobiological changes

the belief that biological forces (largely genes) have a direct influence on the root causes of social psychological behavior

speakeasies

places where alcoholic beverages were illegally consumed and sold during the Prohibition era from 1920–1933 (in some states, Prohibition was longer than this period of time)

speed

an injectable methamphetamine used by drug addicts

speedballing

combining heroin and cocaine

speedballs

combinations of amphetamine or cocaine with an opioid narcotic, often heroin

SPF (sun protection factor) number

designation to indicate a product's ability to screen ultraviolet rays

stacking

use of several types of steroids at the same time

steroids

hormones related to the corticosteroids released from the adrenal cortex

structural analogs

a new molecular species created by modifying the basic molecular skeleton of a compound; structural analogs are structurally related to the parent compound

structural influence theories

theories that view the structural organization of a society, peer group, or subculture as directly responsible for drug use

subculture

subgroup within the population whose members share similar values and patterns of related behaviors that differ from other subcultures and the larger population

subculture theory

explains drug use as a peer-generated activity

subcutaneous (SC)

drug injection beneath the skin

subjective euphoric effects

ongoing social and psychological experiences incurred while intoxicated with marijuana

supply reduction

a drug reduction policy aimed at reducing the supply of illegal drugs and controlling other therapeutic drugs

switching policy

an FDA policy allowing the change of suitable prescription drugs to over-the-counter status

sympathomimetic

agents that mimic the effects of norepinephrine or epinephrine

synapse

site of communication between a message-sending neuron and its message-receiving target cell

synaptic cleft

a minute gap between the neuron and target cell, across which neurotransmitters travel

synergism

ability of one drug to enhance the effect of another; also called potentiation

synesthesia

a subjective sensation or image of a sense other than the one being stimulated, such as an auditory sensation caused by a visual stimulus

teetotalers

individuals who drink no alcoholic beverages whatsoever; a term in common usage in decades past

teratogenic

something that causes physical defects in a fetus

tertiary drug prevention programs

drug prevention programs focusing on intervention and targeting chemically dependent individuals who need treatment; tertiary prevention involves treating the medical consequences of drug abuse and facilitating entry into treatment so further disability is minimized (basically the same as drug abuse treatment)

thalidomide

a sedative drug that, when used during pregnancy, can cause severe developmental damage to a fetus

therapeutic community (TC)

inpatient treatment that focuses on the "resocialization" of the individual and uses the program's entire community as important treatment components

threshold dose

minimum drug dose necessary to cause an effect

tobacco chewing

the absorption of nicotine through the mucous lining of the mouth

tolerance

changes in the body that decrease response to a drug even though the dose remains the same

toxicity

capacity of one drug to damage or cause adverse effects in the body

tricyclic antidepressants

most commonly used group of drugs to treat severe depression

tweaking

repeated administration of methamphetamine to maintain the high

type 1 diabetes

disease associated with complete loss of insulin-producing cells in the pancreas

type 2 diabetes

disease usually associated with obesity; does not involve a loss of insulin-producing cells

uppers

CNS stimulants

volatile

readily evaporated at low temperatures

Wernicke-Korsakoff's syndrome

psychotic condition connected with heavy alcohol use and associated vitamin deficiencies

withdrawal

unpleasant effects that occur when use of a drug is stopped

withdrawal phase

physical and/or psychological effects derived from not using the drug

withdrawal symptoms
psychological and physical symptoms that result when a drug is absent from the body; physical symptoms are generally present in cases of drug dependence to more addictive drugs such as heroin; physical and psychological symptoms of withdrawal include perspiration, nausea, boredom, anxiety, and muscle spasms

World Anti-Doping Code
the core document providing a framework for harmonized anti-doping policies, rules, and regulations within sport organizations and among public authorities

xanthines
the family of drugs that includes caffeine

INDEX

Figures and tables are indicated by f and t following the page number.

PHOTO CREDITS

Chapter 1

Opener © LiquidLibrary; **page 5 (right)** © Comstock Images/Getty Images; **page 12** Courtesy of DEA; **page 13 (left)** © Michael Newman/PhotoEdit, Inc.; **page 13 (right)** Courtesy of DEA; **page 14** © LiquidLibrary; **page 21** © Art-Line Productions/Brand X Pictures/Alamy Images; **page 34** Courtesy of the Advertising Council

Chapter 2

Opener © Photodisc/Creatas; **page 62** © MaxFX/ShutterStock, Inc.; **page 82** © Photos.com

Chapter 3

Opener © Davide Karp/AP Photos; **page 96** © Science Source/Photo Researchers, Inc.; **page 109** © Tony Freeman/PhotoEdit, Inc.; **page 110** © Creatas

Chapter 4

Opener © AbleStock; **page 119** Courtesy of Lisa G. Shaffer, Signature Genomic Laboratories; **page 122** Courtesy of DEA; **page 132 (top)** © Michael Albright/Dreamstime.com; **page 132 (bottom)** © ohnisko/Fotolia.com

Chapter 5

Opener © Medioimages/age fotostock; **page 142** © Monkey Business/Fotolia.com; **page 143** © Dan Steinberg/AP Photos; **page 145** © NADKI/ShutterStock, Inc.; **page 149** © Jack Sullivan/Alamy Images; **page 151** © Val Handumon/EPA/Landov

Chapter 6

Opener © LiquidLibrary; **page 162** © Evan Agostini/AP Photos; **page 165** © auremar/ShutterStock, Inc.; **page 169** Courtesy of Orange County Police Department, Florida; **page 173** © MAErtek/ShutterStock, Inc.; **page 174** © Danny Moloshok/AP Photos; **page 175** Courtesy of Orange County Police Department, Florida; **page 176** © Brian Snyder/Reuters/Landov; **page 178** © Mary Kate Denny/PhotoEdit, Inc.

Chapter 7

Opener © Bill Fritsch/Brand X Pictures/Alamy Images; **page 184** © Rebecca Erol/Alamy Images; **page 188** © Anita Patterson Peppers/ShutterStock, Inc.; **page 189** © Viorel Dudau/Dreamstime.com; **page 197** © Eric Gay/AP Photos; **page 198 (top)** © Morris Huberland/Science Source/Photo Researchers, Inc.; **page 198 (bottom)** © Biophoto Associates/Science Source/Photo Researchers, Inc.; **page 200** © Richard Pipes/Albuquerque Journal/AP Photos

Chapter 8

Opener © Ryan McVay/Photodisc; **page 220** Courtesy of NHTSA; **page 222** © AP Photos; **page 227** © Steve Lovegrove/ShutterStock, Inc.; **page 234** © Nice One Productions/age fotostock; **page 235** © Yuri Arcurs/Dreamstime.com

Chapter 9

Opener © AbleStock; **page 254 (left)** Courtesy of Library of Congress, Prints & Photographs Division, [LC-B811-2531]; **page 254 (right)** © National Library of Medicine; **page 255** © Baris Atayman/Thomson Reuters; **page 261** © STR/Reuters/Landov; **page 262** Courtesy of DEA; **page 263** © Feng Yu/Dreamstime.com; **page 266** © Oscar Knott/FogStock/Alamy Images; **page 269** © Aaron Settipane/Dreamstime.com; **page 272** Courtesy of DEA; **page 277** © Philip Scalia/Alamy Images

Chapter 10

Opener © Andrew Burns/ShutterStock, Inc.; **page 290** © Brandon_Parry/ShutterStock, Inc.; **page 291** © Karie Hamilton/AP Photos; **page 292** © Kyle Carter/The Meridian Star/AP Photos; **page 295** Courtesy of the American Dental Association; **page 296** © CREATISTA/ShutterStock, Inc.; **page 298** Courtesy of Orange County Police Department, Florida; **page 299** © Gregor Kervina/ShutterStock, Inc.; **page 301** © Photos.com; **page 302** © David Mercado/Reuters/Landov; **page 303 (left)** Courtesy of the Drug Enforcement Administration, Washington, DC; **page 303 (right)** Library of Congress, Prints & Photographs Division, [reproduction number LOT 11831-B]; **page 305** © Alexandre Meneghini/AP Photos; **page 306** Courtesy of Orange County Police Department, Florida; **page 307** © David Hoffman Photo Library/Alamy Images; **page 312** © Jim Powell/Alamy Images; **page 319** © Jerry Wachter/Sports Imagery/Landov; **page 320** © Andrea Brizzi/UN Photo

Chapter 11

Opener © AbleStock; **page 330** © BananaStock/age fotostock; **page 333** © Kevin Largent/Fotolia.com; **page 339** © Bonnie Kamin/PhotoEdit, Inc.; **page 341** © Biophoto Associates/Science Source/Photo Researchers, Inc.

Chapter 12

Opener © Dave Duprey/AP Photos; **page 350** © Neal Ulevich/AP Photos; **page 351** © Joyce Marshall/Fort Worth StarTelegram/AP Photos; **pages 352, 356** Courtesy of Philip Bailey; **page 358** Courtesy of Orange County Police Department, Florida; **page 361** © Martyn Vickery/Alamy Images; **page 636** © Vaughan Fleming/Science Photo Library/Photo Researchers, Inc.; **page 366** © Maxim Blinkov/Dreamstime.com; **page 368** © Geoff Bryant/Photo Researchers, Inc.; **page 371** Courtesy of Orange County Police Department, Florida; **page 372** © Dana Rothstein/Dreamstime.com; **page 374** © Aaron Settipane/Dreamstime.com

Chapter 13

Opener © Tiburon Studios/ShutterStock, Inc.; **page 391** © Janine Wiedel/Photolibrary/Alamy Images; **13.5** © Mitchell Brothers 21st Century Film Group/ShutterStock, Inc.; **page 401** © Sanjmur/Dreamstime.com; **page 405** © Jeff Chiu/AP Photos; **page 409** Courtesy of Anonymous

Chapter 14

Opener, page 422 © AbleStock; **page 424** © Photofusion Picture Library/Alamy Images

Chapter 15

Opener © image100/Alamy Images; **page 437** © LeahAnne Thompson/ShutterStock, Inc.; **page 438** © Reuters/ STR/Landov; **page 442** © Wendy Nero/ShutterStock, Inc.; **page 444** Courtesy of National Cancer Institute; **page 445** © Photos.com; **page 449** © Dmitriy Shironosov/ShutterStock, Inc.; **page 450** © LiquidLibrary; **page 455** © Photodisc; **page 456** © fotoluminate/ShutterStock, Inc.; **page 459** © Jamie Otto-coenen/Dreamstime.com

Chapter 16

Opener Courtesy of Danny Meyer/U.S. Air Force; **page 475** © Nicholas Piccillo/Dreamstime.com; **page 520** © Jens Kalaene/dpa/Landov

Chapter 17

Opener © Jeff Greenberg/PhotoEdit, Inc.; **page 534** Courtesy of the Office of National Drug Control Policy/Partnership for a Drug-Free America

Chapter 18

Opener © Tom McCarthy/PhotoEdit, Inc.; **page 564** © Jeff Greenberg/PhotoEdit, Inc.; **page 569** © John Boykin/PhotoEdit, Inc.; **page 571** © Michael Newman/PhotoEdit, Inc.

Unless otherwise indicated, all photographs and illustrations are under copyright of Jones & Bartlett Learning, or have been provided by the authors.